Lecture Notes in Artificial Intelligence 11173

Subseries of Lecture Notes in Computer Science

More information about this series at http://www.springer.com/series/1244

Jia-Fei Hong · Qi Su
Jiun-Shiung Wu (Eds.)

Chinese Lexical Semantics

19th Workshop, CLSW 2018
Chiayi, Taiwan, May 26–28, 2018
Revised Selected Papers

Springer

Editors
Jia-Fei Hong
National Taiwan Normal University
Taipei, Taiwan

Jiun-Shiung Wu
National Chung Cheng University
Chiayi, Taiwan

Qi Su
Peking University
Beijing, China

ISSN 0302-9743 ISSN 1611-3349 (electronic)
Lecture Notes in Artificial Intelligence
ISBN 978-3-030-04014-7 ISBN 978-3-030-04015-4 (eBook)
https://doi.org/10.1007/978-3-030-04015-4

Library of Congress Control Number: 2018960678

LNCS Sublibrary: SL7 – Artificial Intelligence

This Springer imprint is published by the registered company Springer Nature Switzerland AG
The registered company address is: Gewerbestrasse 11, 6330 Cham, Switzerland

Preface

The 2018 Chinese Lexical Semantics Workshop (CLSW 2018) was the 19th event in the series established in 2000. CLSW has been held in different Asian cities, including Hong Kong, Beijing, Taipei, Singapore, Xiamen, Hsin Chu, Yantai, Suzhou, Wuhan, Zhengzhou, Macao, Leshan, and Chia-Yi. Over the years, CLSW has become one of the most important venues for scholars to report and discuss the latest progress in Chinese lexical semantics and related fields, including theoretical linguistics, applied linguistics, computational linguistics, information processing, and computational lexicography. CLSW has significantly impacted and promoted academic research and application development in the fields, and acted as one of the most important meetings in Asia for the Chinese lexical semantics community.

CLSW 2018 was hosted by the National Chung Cheng University, Taiwan. This year 150 papers were submitted to the conference. All submissions went through a double-blind review process. Of these, 51 submissions (34%) were accepted as oral papers and 43 (29%) as poster papers. They were organized in topical sections covering all major topics of lexical semantics, semantic resources, corpus linguistics, and natural language processing.

On behalf of the Program Committee, we are most grateful to Shiwen Yu (Peking University), Chu-Ren Huang (Hong Kong Polytechnic University), Xinchun Su (Xiamen University), and the Advisory Committee for their guidance in promoting the conference. We sincerely appreciate the invited speakers: Jane Tsay (National Chung Cheng University), Jie Xu (Macau University), Barbara Meisterernst (Humboldt University at Berlin), Yangsen Zhang (Beijing University of Science and Technology), and Zhu Jing-Schmidt (University of Oregon), for their outstanding keynote talks. Also, we would like to acknowledge the chairs of the Organizing Committee, Jiun-Shiung Wu (National Chung Cheng University) and Peng Jin (Leshan Normal University), for their tremendous contribution to this event.

Our gratitude goes to all the Program Committee members and reviewers for their time and effort with the reviews. We are pleased that the accepted English papers are published by Springer as part of their *Lecture Notes in Artificial Intelligence* (LNAI) series and are indexed by EI and SCOPUS.

Last but not the least, we thank all the authors and attendees for their scientific contribution and participation, which made CLSW 2018 a successful event.

September 2018

Jia-Fei Hong
Baobao Chang
Nianwen Xue

Organization

Program Chairs

Jia-Fei Hong	National Taiwan Normal University, Taiwan
Baobao Chang	Peking University, China
Nianwen Xue	Brandeis University, USA

Program Committee

Ahrens Kathleen	Hong Kong Polytechnic University, SAR China
Xiaojing Bai	Tsinghua University, China
Shuping Gong	National Chiayi University, Taiwan
Kam Fai Wong	Chinese University of Hong Kong, SAR China
Donghong Ji	Wuhan University, China
Peng Jin	Leshan Normal University, China
Huei-Ling Lai	National Chengchi University, Taiwan
Shimin Li	Academy for Educational Research, Taiwan
Yao Liu	Institute of Scientific and Technical Information of China
Maofu Liu	Wuhan Technological University, China
Pengyuan Liu	Beijing Language and Culture University, China
Chiarung Lu	National Taiwan University, Taiwan
Liqung Qiu	Ludong University, China
Weiguan Qu	Nanjing Normal University, China
Xiaodong Shi	Xiamen University, China
Zuoyan Song	Beijing Normal University, China
Xinchun Su	Xiamen University, China
Le Sun	Institute of Software, Chinese Academy of Sciences, China
Shu-Kai Hsieh	National Taiwan University, Taiwan
Jiajuan Xiong	Southwestern University of Finance and Economics, China
JIe Xu	Macau University, SAR China
Ruifeng Xu	Harbin Institute of Technology, China
Weidong Zhan	Peking University, China
Lei Zhang	Northeastern Normal University, China
Yangsen Zhang	Beijing Information Science and Technology University, China
Zezhi Zheng	Xiamen University, China
Jingxia Lin	Nanyang Technological University, Singapore
Hong Gao	Nanyang Technological University, Singapore
Yunfang Wu	Peking University, China
Siaw-fong Chung	National Cheng Chi University, Taiwan

Contents

Lexical Semantics

Applications of Natural Language Processing

Corpus Linguistics

Lexical Semantics

Noun-Verb Pairs in Taiwan Sign Language

Jane S. Tsay(✉)

Institute of Linguistics and Taiwan Center for Sign Linguistics, National Chung Cheng University, Chiayi, Taiwan
Lngtsay15@gmail.com

Abstract. Nouns and verbs that are semantically and formationally related are called noun-verb pairs. Noun-verb pairs are found both in spoken and signed languages. A debate has been raised as to whether the noun and the verb in the pairs are distinguished by syntactic environments or they have a morphological (derivational) relation. Based on the Taiwan Sign Language data we have collected, it was found that nouns and verbs are distinguished more systematically by syntactic environments. Modality effects and non-effects in word formation in spoken versus signed languages are also discussed with a special focus on the role of iconicity.

Keywords: Noun-Verb pairs · Cross-modality · Taiwan sign language American sign language

1 Introduction

Compared with spoken languages, the history of research on signed languages is much shorter. Since the pioneering works of [1, 2], and many later works, e.g., [3], it has been demonstrated that human language can be produced in two modalities, i.e., the vocal-auditory modality for spoken languages and the gestural-visual modality for signed languages. It is expected that there will be differences (as modality effects) as well as similarities or parallels (as modality non-effects) between spoken and signed languages in all linguistic components. Thus signed languages are worth exploration and examination, especially with linguistic theories developed mainly on spoken languages.

Word classes are a major domain in the area of lexical semantics. Among the major word classes, nouns and verbs are the most fundamental natural word classes in human language. As has already been claimed more than half a century ago [4], nouns and verbs can be regarded as universal categories based on evidence in the formal analysis of language structures.

Although nouns and verbs can be formed independently of each other, some nouns and verbs are related both in form and meaning. For example, *water* in English could be a noun or a verb. These paired words that are related in form and meaning are called noun-verb pairs.

While noun-verb pairs in spoken language have been analyzed quite thoroughly, not much attention has been paid to the noun-verb pairs in signed languages. Therefore, this paper analyzes noun-verb pairs in Taiwan Sign Language (TSL), with reference to other sign languages including American Sign Language (ASL). Furthermore, by

J.-F. Hong et al. (Eds.): CLSW 2018, LNAI 11173, pp. 3–22, 2018.
https://doi.org/10.1007/978-3-030-04015-4_1

comparing noun-verb pairs in spoken versus signed languages, the modality issue is also addressed, especially the role of iconicity in word formation.

1.1 Nouns and Verbs are Universal

Nouns and verbs are natural word classes in spoken (e.g., [4–6]) and sign languages [2, 7, 8].[1] Since nouns and verbs are so fundamental in human language, they have been the focus of linguistic analysis in almost all components, especially in morphology, semantics, and syntax.

The relation and contrast between nouns and verbs have also raised important issues in psycholinguistics and neurolinguistics. For example, there has long been a debate about whether children acquire nouns before verbs, or vice versa, i.e., noun-bias (noun-first) versus no-noun-bias (verb-first) in young children's lexical development. Arguments have been drawn from grammatical structure (e.g., null subject), object and action contrast, entity vs. event, degree of concreteness, and imageability of the lexical items (e.g., [12–18]).

Nouns and verbs are also the major word classes to be dealt with in lexicography and computational linguistics, especially when nouns and verbs are identical in form as in noun-verb pairs and may cause problems in automatic language processing (e.g., [19–23]).

1.2 Noun-Verb Pairs

Nouns and verbs can be formed independently, especially with the arbitrariness in form-meaning mapping in spoken languages. For example, *chair* and *sit* in English are semantically related but do not share any formational characteristics. However, there are certain nouns and verbs that are related not only semantically, but also formationally. They are called noun-verb pairs. For example, in English *water* could be a noun that refers to the liquid substance composed of hydrogen and oxygen or a verb that refers to the action of putting water on plants. The word *hùa* 畫 in Mandarin is both a verb meaning "to draw" and a noun meaning "drawing" as the output of the action "to draw".

Noun-verb pairs have also been reported in many signed languages around the world (e.g., [2, 24, 26–28]). A noun-verb pair in ASL is defined with two criteria [24]. First, the verb expresses the activity performed with or on the object named by the noun. For example, SIT in ASL expresses the activity performed on the object CHAIR.[2] Second, the noun and verb share formational characteristics. For example, CHAIR and SIT share formational characteristics in handshape, orientation, place of articulation, and movement. (The formational characteristics of words/signs in signed languages will be presented in more details in Sect. 2.)

[1] The universality of nouns and verbs has been challenged in some languages, e.g., [9–11].

[2] Following the convention in sign language linguistics, English glosses or equivalents of the lexemes in signed languages are given in capital letters.

1.3 Cross-Modality Study

There are two modalities in human language, the vocal-auditory modality for spoken languages and the gestural-visual modality for signed languages. The similarities and parallels between spoken and signed languages are called modality non-effects, while differences between spoken and signed languages are called modality effects [29].

Based on the design features proposed by [5] for distinguishing human language from the communication systems of other animals, [29] proposes several design features as the shared properties of signed and spoken language, including conventional vocabularies, duality of patterning, productivity in vocabulary, syntactic structure, time course of child language acquisition, and brain lateralization, and claims that these are non-effects of modality (see Table 1)[3].

Table 1. Non-effects of Modality: Some shared properties between signed and spoken languages (Meier 2002:2, [29])

- Conventional vocabularies: learned pairings of form and meaning.
- Duality of patterning: meaningful units built of meaningless sublexical units, whether units of sound or of gesture:
  - Slips of the tongue/Slips of the hand demonstrate the importance of sublexical units in adult processing.
- Productivity: new vocabulary may be added to signed and spoken languages:
  - Derivational morphology;
  - Compounding;
  - Borrowing.
- Syntactic Structure:
  - Same parts of speech: nouns, verbs, and adjectives;
  - Embedding to form relative and complement clauses;
  - Trade-offs between word order and verb agreement in how grammatical relations are marked: rich agreement licenses null arguments and freedom in word order.
- Acquisition: similar timetables for acquisition.
- Lateralization: aphasia data point to crucial role for left hemisphere.

Regarding conventional vocabularies, like spoken languages, signed languages can expand their vocabularies through derivational processes, compounding, and borrowing (e.g., [3, 24, 30]).

On the other hand, there are also modality effects resulting in the structural differences between signed and spoken languages in the lexicon, phonology, morphology,

[3] Before [1], human language was thought to be only possible in the oral-aural modality [32, 33].

semantics, and syntax. While sound symbolism is rare in spoken languages [31], iconicity in sign language is overwhelmingly common and is a crucial word formation motivation. In this paper, we will address the issue of iconic motivation in word formation in spoken versus signed languages, as will be illustrated in the relation between nouns and verbs.

2 Some Background for Signed Languages

2.1 Formational Characteristics of Signs

Signs (words) in signed languages can be described in terms of phonemic contrasts in manual features (i.e., handshape, location, movement, hand orientation) and non-manual features (e.g., [2, 34] for ASL; [35] for TSL). These features are the constructing elements of signs in signed languages. Considering the scope and the relevance to the theme of this paper, only manual features are introduced in this section. TSL minimal pairs that contrast in the manual features are given as examples [35]).[4]

TOMORROW and DOCTOR (PhD) form a minimal pair of signs that contrast only in handshape. Handshape 1 is used in TOMORROW, while handshape Curved-Middle is used in DOCTOR (PhD) with the rest of the features (location, movement, and hand orientation) being the same. (See [36] for a complete list of handshapes in TSL) (Fig. 1).

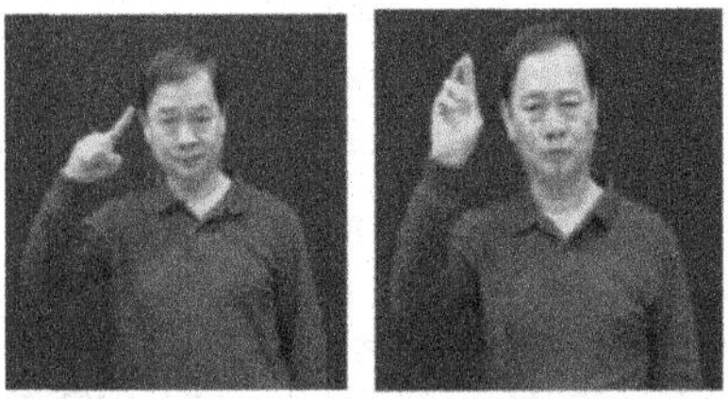

TOMORROW DOCTOR (PhD)

Fig. 1. Phonemic contrast in handshape (1 vs. Curved-Middle)

PLEASE and YES (confirmation) is a pair of signs that contrast only in location. They both use the handshape B and have the same hand orientation, except that the hand in PLEASE makes contact on the forehead, while the hand in YES touches the chin (Fig. 2).

The signs POISON and MEDICINE contrast only in movement. Both signs use the same handshape Open-8. In POISON, the middle finger touches the palm of the other hand, while in MEDICINE the middle finger makes small circles in the palm of the other hand (Fig. 3).

[4] The use of all the pictures in TSL in this paper has received the approval from the signers.

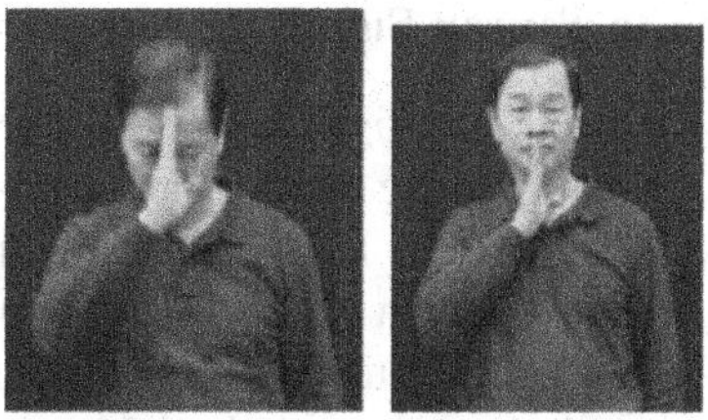

PLEASE YES

Fig. 2. Phonemic contrast in location (Forehead vs. Chin)

POISON MEDICINE

Fig. 3. Phonemic contrast in movement (Touch vs. Circle)

The signs NOW and CALM-DOWN contrast only in hand orientation. They both use handshape Open-B with downward movement. They only differ in the direction that the fingertips are pointing to. That is, while the fingertips in NOW are pointing forward, they are pointing towards each other in CALM-DOWN (Fig. 4).

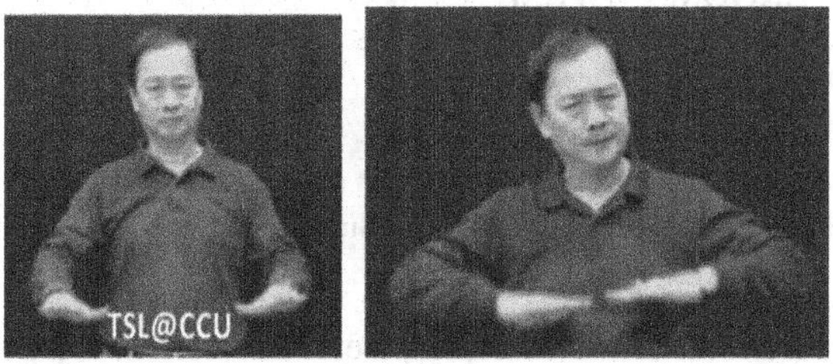

NOW CALM-DOWN

Fig. 4. Phonemic contrast in orientation (Pointing forward vs. Pointing to each other)

2.2 A Brief Introduction to Taiwan Sign Language

Compared to ASL which has been investigated since [1], linguistic research on TSL has a much shorter history, with [37] being the first linguistic study on TSL. TSL is the native language of the deaf in Taiwan. It is historically related to Japanese Sign Language (JSL) and is considered a branch of JSL [36, 38–40]. The history of TSL can be dated back to when the first school for the deaf was established in 1915 in southern Taiwan by Japanese educators during the period of Japanese occupation of Taiwan (1895–1945). Therefore, TSL is based on JSL with a mixed lexicon of JSL words and locally developed vocabulary. TSL vocabulary was also influenced through language contact with Chinese Sign Language (CSL) after 1949 when some deaf teachers from Nanjing and Shanghai came to Taiwan. Hence there are also borrowing words from CSL.

In this paper, we report TSL data of noun-verb pairs collected for comparison with other signed languages, in particular, ASL.

2.3 Noun Verb Pairs in Signed Languages

Noun-verb pairs are more common in signed languages than in spoken languages ([24] on ASL; [26] on Australian Sign Language; [27] on Austrian Sign Language; [41] on German Sign Language (DGS) and Sign Language of the Netherlands (NGT)).

In sign languages, noun-verb pairs are mostly concrete object nouns and their related action verbs, such as CHAIR (noun) and SIT (verb). Examples of noun-verb pairs are abundant. In Fig. 5 are some from the 100 pairs listed in [24] for ASL.

AIRPLANE – GO-BY-AIRPLANE (i.e., FLY)
MATCH – STRIKE-MATCH
CIGARETTE – SMOKE
TOOTHBRUSH – BRUSH-TEETH
CLIP – CLIP-FINGERNAIL
BROOM – SWEEP
STAPLER – STAPLE
HAMMER – HAMMER
COMB – COMB

Fig. 5. Some noun-verb pairs listed in Supalla and Newport (1978) [24]

As can be seen from the above examples, these are concrete objects nouns and their related action verbs. These semantically related noun-verb pairs have been reported to share formational characteristics in phonemic features such as handshape, location, and movement.

2.4 A Debate About Noun-Verb Pairs in ASL

It is claimed that noun and verb in noun-verb pairs in ASL are identical in form. That is, they have the same handshape, location, and movement [2]. They can only be distinguished by context or syntactic environments. For example, both CHAIR and SIT are signed by putting two bent fingers (index and middle, i.e., handshape Curved-V) on the index and middle fingers of the other hand. They cannot be distinguished in isolation unless they are in context. That is, the word in phrase “two ___” refers to CHAIR because only nouns can be modified by a quantifier.

However, they argue that the noun and the verb in a noun-verb pair are structurally distinct and that there is a derivational relation between the noun and the verb in the noun-verb pairs [24]. In the CHAIR—SIT pair, both signs use handshape Curved-V and have the same location. But they differ in the movement. In SIT, the movement is larger, while in CHAIR the movement is smaller (restrained) and, more importantly, repeated. See Fig. 6 for the illustration of CHAIR—SIT in ASL.

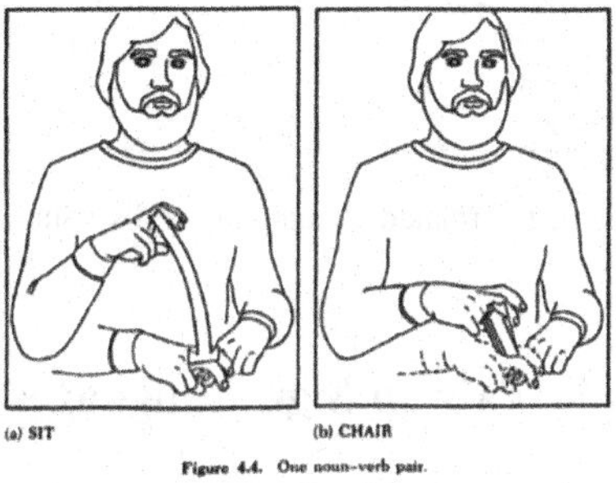

Fig. 6. SIT and CHAIR in ASL (Supalla and Newport 1978:102 [24])

A formal model was proposed to derive the noun-verb pairs from an underlying base form [24]. They argue that noun and verb in the noun-verb pairs are structurally distinct in manner of movement. Although the location, handshape, and orientation of the noun and the verb are basically the same, there is a difference in the manner of movement. They analyze movement in more detailed features such as continuous, hold, restrained (the muscles are tightened, movement is small, quick, and stiff), and frequency ([±repeated]).

The derivational relation for related nouns and verbs is illustrated in Fig. 7. Both the noun form and the verb form are derived from an underlying base form. Regarding the CHAIR—SIT pair, specifically, the manner and frequency in SIT are [continuous] and [−repeated], while in CHAIR they are [restrained] and [+repeated].

It was further claimed that, while most verbs are formed with a single movement, referring to single punctual or perfective actions, all the nouns have “restrained” manner of movement and the movement is always repeated [24]. In the following section, we test this claim with noun-verb pairs in TSL.

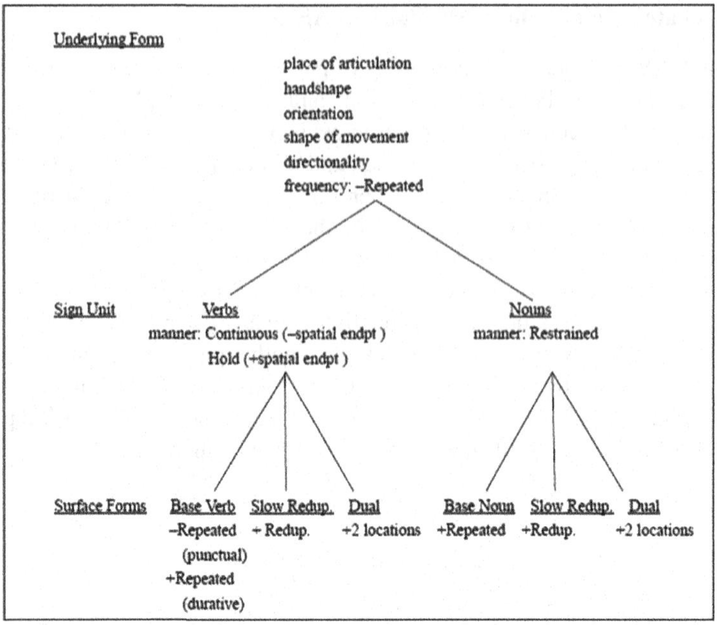

Fig. 7. The derivational system for related nouns and verbs (Supalla and Newport 1978: 119 [24])

3 Noun-Verb Pairs in Taiwan Sign Languages

3.1 TSL Noun-Verb Pairs in Citation Form

Noun-verb pairs in TSL have been studied by [25], focusing on the iconic strategies in word formation. It was found that manipulation property was the most frequently used, followed by action property, position property, and appearance property. It was also found that the noun and the verb in a noun-verb pair are identical in form and can only be distinguished by their syntactic position in context [25].

Since the goals of [25] were different from our current study, TSL noun-verb pairs were collected with more elaborated methods. TSL data discussed in this paper are part of the database, in which 73 pictures of objects and 73 pictures of actions corresponding to 73 noun-verb pairs were used to elicit data from three male deaf signers aged 72 (YS), 60 (JM), and 22 (MJ), respectively.[5] Some pairs also appeared in sentences to verify their forms in syntactic environments. Nouns and verbs were videotaped separately. Unrelated pictures were used as foils. The following two figures are pictures for eliciting CHAIR—SIT and TOOTHBRUSH-BRUSH-TEETH in citation form.[6]

[5] This list of 73 noun-verb pairs was adapted from [25] with reference to [24].

[6] To avoid copyright and portrait right issues, some pictures for actions that involve people were hand-drawn by our research assistants.

The generalizations proposed in [24], in particular, a derivational relation between the noun and the verb in a noun-verb pair, are not fully supported based on the TSL data we have collected. Instead, our data are more in support of [2] in that the noun and the verb in noun-verb pairs tend to be identical in form and are mainly distinguished by syntactic environments (Figs. 8 and 9).

Fig. 8. Pictures for eliciting CHAIR and SIT

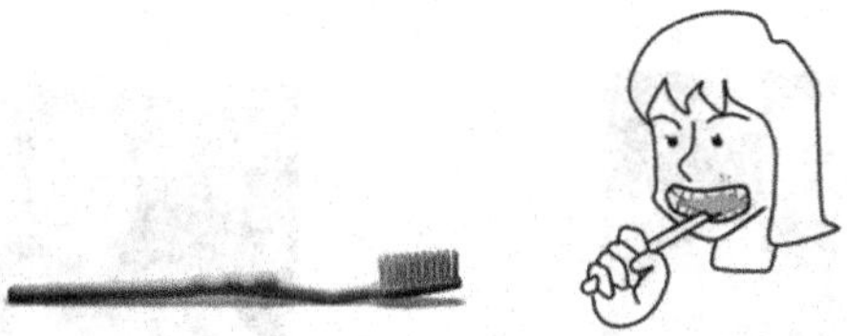

Fig. 9. Pictures for eliciting TOOTHBRUSH and BRUSH-TEETH

Five TSL noun-verb pairs in citation form by the three deaf signers are given in Table 2 below.

In the five pairs presented, only CHAIR—SIT shows a contrast between the noun and the verb. It is also the only pair that shows discrepancies among the signers.

Table 2. TSL noun-verb pairs in citation form

N-V pair	Not Identical (Supalla and Newport 1978)		Identical (Stokoe et al. 1965)
	Nouns [+repeated]	Verbs [−repeated]	
CHAIR-SIT	✓(YS)		✓ (JM)
AIRPLANE-GO-BY-AIRPLANE			✓
MATCH-STRIKE-MATCH			✓
CIGARETTE-SMOKE			✓
TOOTHBRUSH-BRUSH-TEETH			✓

Signer YS has a contrast of CHAIR [+repeated] vs. SIT [−repeated], consistent with [24], while signer JM has an identical form for both CHAIR and SIT, both being [+repeated], consistent with [2] argument, as shown in Figs. 10 and 11, respectively.

CHAIR ([+repeated]) SIT ([-repeated])

Fig. 10. CHAIR-SIT pair by YS

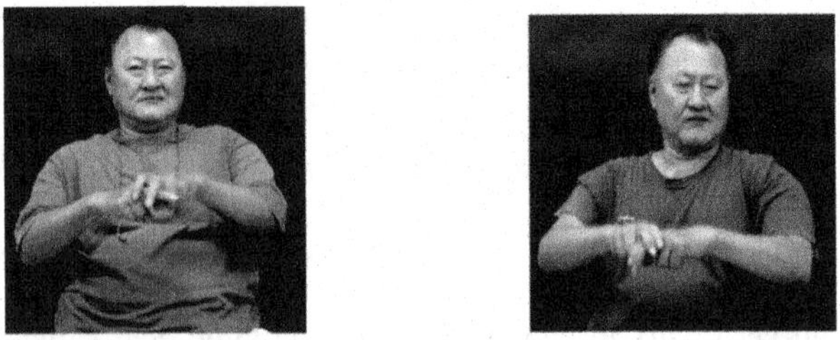

CHAIR ([+repeated]) SIT ([+repeated])

Fig. 11. CHAIR-SIT pair by JM

The other four pairs showed identical forms between the noun and the verb in the pair consistently among the three signers. Demonstrations of the pair MATCH—STRIKE-MATCH by the three signers are given in Figs. 12, 13 and 14.

If the claim in [24] was correct, as parallel to the CHAIR-SIT pair, we would expect the noun MATCH to be signed with restrained and [+repeated] movement and the verb

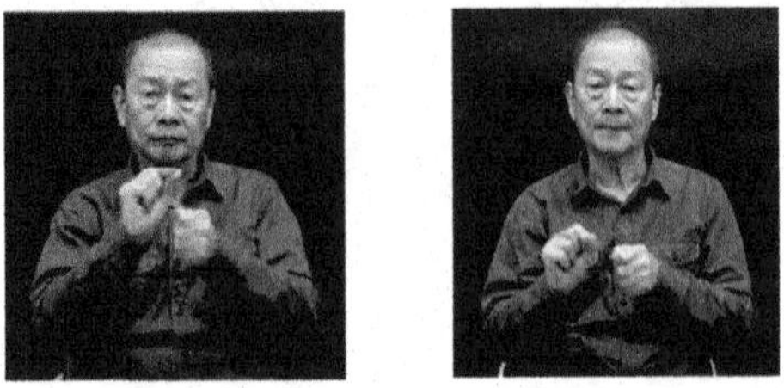

MATCH STRIKE-MATCH

Fig. 12. MATCH—STRIKE-MATCH by YS

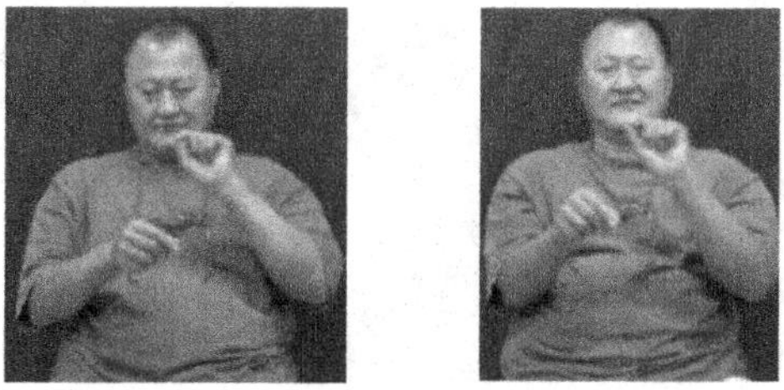

MATCH STRIKE-MATCH

Fig. 13. MATCH—STRIKE-MATCH by JM

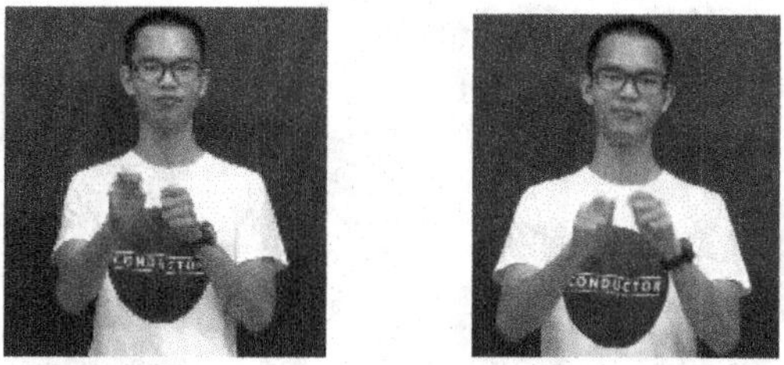

MATCH STRIKE-MATCH

Fig. 14. MATCH—STRIKE-MATCH by MJ

STRIKE-MATCH with larger and [−repeated] movement. However, all three signers signed the noun MATCH and the verb STRIKE-MATCH identically with restrained and [+repeated] movement. Therefore, the results do not support the hypothesis proposed in [24].

3.2 TSL Noun-Verb Pairs in Context

We further examined the noun-verb pairs in sentences. The pair TOOTHBRUSH-BRUSH-TEETH in citation were signed with identical form with [+repeated] movement by all three signers, as shown in Figs. 15 and 16.

TOOTHBRUSH (YS) TOOTHBRUSH (JM) TOOTHBRUSH (MJ)

Fig. 15. TOOTHBRUSH

BRUSH-TEETH (YS) BRUSH-TEETH (JM) BRUSH-TEETH (MJ)

Fig. 16. BRUSH-TEETH

TOOTHBRUSH THREE HAVE

Fig. 17. TSL "I have three toothbrushes"

When appearing in sentences, both TOOTHBRUSH and BRUSH-TEETH were still signed identically. The only difference is in the syntactic environments they appeared. TOOTHBRUSH, as a noun, was modified by a quantifier "three" in "I have three toothbrushes" (Fig. 17), while BRUSH-TEETH, as a verb, was modified by a modal "should/need" in "One should brush the teeth after meals" (Fig. 18).

EAT FINISH BRUSH-TEETH NEED

Fig. 18. TSL "One should brush the teeth after meals"

4 Discussion

4.1 Noun-Verb Pairs in Other Sign Languages

It was reported in [41] that the ASL pattern described in [24] cannot be established in German Sign Language (DGS) and Sign Language of the Netherlands (NGT).

> "In NGT, for instance, a comparable systematic relation between nouns and verbs cannot be established. The manual part of the signs for SIT and CHAIR, which are both signed with a f < -handshape, thus looks identical in some signers. Others perform CHAIR with a turn of the wrist which is not found in SIT. The two-handed noun BICYCLE is usually signed with a single alternating circular movement while the related verb CYCLE has multiple repetitions - exactly the opposite of the ASL pattern described above."
> (Baker, et al. 2016:101 [41])

Interestingly, [28] investigated two young sign languages, Israeli Sign Language (ISL) and Al-Sayyid Bedouin Sign Language (ABSL), to determine whether they have developed a distinction in the formation of noun-verb pairs. They found reliable formational distinctions between nouns and related verbs in ISL, but not in ABSL. They suggested that a formal distinction in noun-verb pairs in sign languages is not necessarily present from the beginning, but may develop gradually. More studies on noun-verb pairs in signed languages might shed light on how human language has evolved.

4.2 Noun-Verb Pairs in Spoken Languages

Words that can function as both nouns and verbs are very common in spoken languages. In addition to English and Mandarin, more than 60 languages are discussed as having this phenomenon [6], including Paiute, Chukchee, Ponapean, Nahuatl, Mende, Turkish, French, Indonesian, Malay, Hungarian, Bemba, Spanish, German, Hausa, Portuguese, Finnish, Akan, Yoruba, Igbo, Hindi, Russian, Maori, Tamil, Palestinian, Arabic, Zulu, Rukai, Nootkan, and Salishan.

In English, the substance "water" (noun) is converted to the action verb as in "water the garden" and the tool "hammer" (noun) is converted to the action of using the tool upon something as in "hammer a nail". This process is called denominalization or verbalization in the literature. On the other hand, nominalization is also a common word formation mechanism in spoken languages and is much more productive than verbalization, known as an asymmetry in the literature (e.g., [6, 42]).

Hopper and Thompson (1984:745) state that "…a nominalization names an event taken as an entity; however, a 'verbalization' does not name an 'entity taken as an event', but simply names an event associated with some entity [6:745]."

Since this has been a well-known and well-studied topic in spoken languages with a long list in the literature, in consideration of space limitation and the focus of this paper we will not discuss it further. Detailed discussions on related issues, e.g., zero derivation, regarding the derivational relation in the noun-verb pairs in spoken languages can be found in the literature (e.g., [42–44]). The so-called Chinese multi-class words hànyǔ jiānlèi (漢語兼類) phenomenon has been discussed widely since [45] and followed by many others (e.g., [46–51]).

Syntactic functions and distribution are crucial in distinguishing nouns and verbs in these pairs. If the word is located in a subject or an object position, it is a noun, as in Fig. 19(a). It is a verb if located in a predicate structure, as in Fig. 19(b).

(a) The plants in the garden need *water*.
(b) I will *water* the plants.

Fig. 19. An English noun-verb pair in syntactic contexts

Derivational morphology is also a common mechanism used in English noun-verb pairs. For example, suffixes such as -er, -al, are added to a verb to make a semantically related noun, as in the following noun-verb pairs *write* (v.) – *writer* (n.) and *propose* (v.) – *proposal* (n.).

Syntactic functions and distribution for noun-verb pairs are similar in Mandarin, as shown in Fig. 20, where the cross-class word *hùa* 畫 "draw/drawing" appears in the same sentence as both a verb ("draw") and a noun ("drawing"). In addition to syntactic environments, nouns in Mandarin can also be identified by modifiers such as number (*sān* "three") and classifiers (*fú* CLS), and verbs by aspect markers (*le* ASP).[7]

(a) 他 昨天 畫 畫 了.
tā zuótiān huà huà le
he yesterday draw drawing Asp.
"He drew drawings yesterday."

(b) 他 昨天 畫 了 三 幅 畫.
tā zuótiān huà le sān fú huà
he yesterday draw Asp. three CLS. drawings
"He drew three drawings yesterday."

Fig. 20. A Mandarin noun-verb pair in syntactic contexts

Thus in English and Mandarin, the syntactic environments are most crucial for distinguishing the noun and the verb in noun-verb pairs.

4.3 The Role of Iconicity in Lexical Semantics

Conventional vocabularies are listed as the first of the shared properties (i.e., non-effects of modality) between signed and spoken languages [29] (see Table 1 above in

[7] Diminutive affixes such as –zi 子 and –er 兒 to the end of the word is also an identification nouns. The noun form of *hùa* 畫 in the above example can hence appear as *hùa-er* 畫兒 and makes the distinction between this noun-verb pair more clearly.

Sect. 1.3). However, there is a difference in the role of iconicity in word formation in spoken versus signed languages.

Words are conventional pairings of form (be it sound or sign) and meaning. As pointed out by [52:287]: "Although conventionality of pairing between form and meaning holds true to both modalities, iconic motivations are much more pervasive in signed languages at both lexical and syntactic levels. In contrast, arbitrary association is the general rule for spoken languages, although iconicity in syntax [53, 54], and onomatopoeia and sound symbolism in phonology have been documented for spoken languages [31]."

Noun-verb pairs in signed languages can be formed with concrete object nouns and their related action verbs. Concrete objects have shapes, sizes, and materials that can be visual motivations for naming the objects. On the other hand, actions can also be a visual motivation for nouns. Signed languages as visual languages thus can maximize the advantages of the visual modality.

Therefore, an object can be named with reference to its entity or to an action or event that this object is acted upon. For example, in the noun-verb pair WATER-MELON– EAT-WATERMELON in TSL, the object WATERMELON is named by the way that watermelons are eaten and hence is identical in form to the verb EAT-WATERMELON. The pictures used for eliciting WATERMELON—EAT-WATERMELON are given in Fig. 21.

WATERMELON 西瓜		EAT-WATERMELON 吃西瓜	

Fig. 21. Pictures for eliciting WATERMELON-EAT-WATERMELON

WATER and WATERMELON by three signers are shown in Figs. 22 and 23.

WATERMELON (YS) WATERMELON (JM) WATERMELON (MJ)

Fig. 22. WATERMELON

EAT-WATERMELON (YS) EAT-WATERMELON (JM) EAT-WATERMELON (MJ)

Fig. 23. EAT-WATERMELON

Although iconicity plays a more important role in word formation in signed languages than in spoken languages due to the visual modality effect, it is not necessarily true that iconicity leads to uniformity in word forms. Abstractness and arbitrariness in form-meaning coupling also exist as a general property of human language. That is, signing is not equal to gesture and iconicity is not equal to uniformity.

For example, HORSE is signed differently in different signed languages, although it a concrete object name with clear visual properties (Fig. 24). While TSL focuses on the action of riding a horse, ASL, CSL, and JSL all highlight the ears of the horse. Sources of the pictures in Fig. 24 are: [55] for TSL, [56] for ASL, [57] for CSL, and [58] for JSL.

Another concrete object name CHAIR also shows varieties among different signed languages (Fig. 25). Pictures in Fig. 25 are from [59].

HORSE (TSL) HORSE (ASL) HORSE (CSL) HORSE (JSL)

Fig. 24. HORSE in TSL, ASL, CSL, and JSL

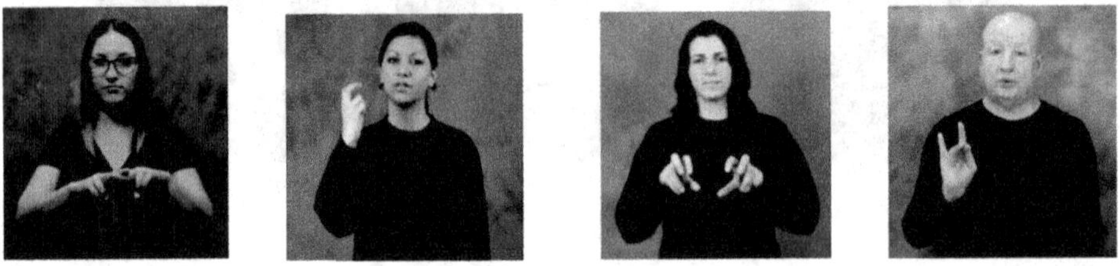

CHAIR (Spanish SL) CHAIR (German SL) CHAIR (Turkish SL) CHAIR (Russian SL)

Fig. 25. CHAIR in Spanish SL, German SL, Turkish SL, and Russian SL

5 Conclusion

Based on the TSL noun-verb pairs that we have collected, it was found that the nouns and verbs in noun-verb pairs are mainly identical in form, consistent to the pattern found in [2, 41]. Syntactic environments are crucial in distinguishing the nouns and the verbs in the noun-verb pairs. Morphological (derivational) mechanism does not play as an important role as claimed in [24]. These findings are similar to spoken languages and can be considered non-effects of modality.

Differences are found in the role of iconicity in word formation. In spoken languages, form-meaning patterning is more arbitrary, while in signed language form-meaning patterning shows higher iconic motivations. With the advantages of the gestural-visual modality, noun-verb pairs in sign languages are very often concrete object nouns and their related action verbs, although it is also common for nouns to be named by actions in word formation.

The role of iconicity in sign languages, especially the iconic motivations in word formation, is worth further exploration ([60–62] for TSL). These iconic word formation strategies have significant implications on sign language typology and child language acquisition of sign languages.

Another line for further research is the non-manual features in sign languages. It has been pointed out that in NGT there is a frequent use of mouthings that accompany the two manually identical signs to be distinguished [41].

Acknowledgments. This study was supported by the Taiwan Center for Sign Linguistics, National Chung Cheng University, Taiwan. We thank deaf signers Yu-shan Gu, Jun-ming Yu, and Meng-jun Yu for serving as informants of the TSL data reported in this paper. Research assistants Shih-kai Liu, Yu-shan Yen, and Hsiao-yin Pan helped with data collection. Special thanks go to Prof. James Tai for discussions on various aspects of this study. Comments from the audience of CLSW 2018 and the reviewers are also acknowledged. All the data and analyses are of course my sole responsibility.

References

1. Stokoe, W.C. (ed.): Sign language structure: an outline of the communication systems of the American deaf. In: Studies in Linguistics, Occasional Papers 8. Linstok Press, Silver Spring, MD (1960)
2. Stokoe, W.C., Casterline, C.G., Croneberg, C.G. (eds.): A Dictionary of American Sign Language on Linguistic Principles. Gallaudet U. Press, United States Washington, D.C (1965)
3. Klima, E.S., Bellugi, U. (eds.): The Signs of Language. Harvard University Press, Cambridge (1979)
4. Robins, R.H.: Noun and verb in universal grammar. Language **28**(3), 289–298 (1952)
5. Hockett, C.F.: The problem of universals in language. In: Greenberg, J. (ed.) Universals of Language, vol. 2, pp. 1–29 (1963)
6. Hopper, P.J., Thompson, S.A.: The discourse basis for lexical categories in universal grammar. Language **60**(4), 703–752 (1984)

7. Valli, C., Lucas, C. (eds.): Linguistics of American Sign Language: An Introduction. Gallaudet University Press, Washington, DC (1995)
8. Padden, C.A. (ed.): Interaction of Morphology and Syntax in American Sign Language. Routledge, United Kingdom Abingdon-on-Thames (2016)
9. Swadesh, M.: Nootka internal syntax. Int. J. Am. Linguist. **9**(2/4), 77–102 (1938)
10. Jacobsen, W.: Noun and verb in Nootkan. In: The Victoria Conference on Northwestern Languages. British Columbia Provincial Museum Victoria, BC (1979)
11. Kinkade, M.D.: Salish evidence against the universality of 'noun' and 'verb'. Lingua **60**(1), 25–39 (1983)
12. Brown, R. (ed.): Words and Things. Free Press, New York (1958)
13. Gentner, D. (ed.): Why Nouns Are Learned Before Verbs: Linguistic Relativity Versus Natural Partitioning. Center for the Study of Reading Technical Report, no. 257 (1982)
14. Tardif, T.: nouns are not always learned before verbs: evidence from Mandarin speakers' early vocabularies. Dev. Psychol. **32**(3), 492–504 (1996)
15. Chen, S., Bates, E.: The dissociation between nouns and verbs in Broca's and Wernicke's Aphasia: findings from Chinese. Aphasiology **12**(1), 5–36 (1998)
16. Li, P., Jin, Z., Tan, L.H.: Neural representations of nouns and verbs in Chinese: an fMRI study. Neuroimage **21**(4), 1533–1541 (2004)
17. Tsai, P.-S., Yu, B.H.-Y., Lee, C.-Y., Tzeng, O.J.-L., Hung, D.L., Wu, D.H.: An event-related potential study of the concreteness effect between Chinese nouns and verbs. Brain Res. **1253**, 149–160 (2009)
18. Moseley, R.L., Pulvermüller, F.: Nouns, verbs, objects, actions, and abstractions: local fMRI activity indexes semantics, not lexical categories. Brain Lang. **132**, 28–42 (2014)
19. Miller, G.A., Beckwith, R., Fellbaum, C., Gross, D., Miller, K.J.: Introduction to WordNet: an on-line lexical database. Int. J. Lexicography **3**(4), 235–244 (1990)
20. Miller, G.A.: WordNet: a lexical database for English. Commun. ACM **38**(11), 39–41 (1995)
21. Yu, S.-W., Zhu, X.-F., Wang, H., Zhang, Y.-Y.: The specification of the semantic knowledge-base of contemporary Chinese. J. Chin. Inf. Process. **10**(2), 1–22 (1996). 俞士汶, 朱学锋, 王惠, 张芸芸. 现代汉语语法信息词典规格说明书.《中文信息学报》**10**(2), 1–22 (1996)
22. Huang, C.-R., Nicoletta, C., Aldo, G. (eds.): Ontology and the Lexicon: A Natural Language Processing Perspective. Cambridge University Press, United Kingdom Cambridge (2010)
23. Huang, C.-R., Xie, S.-K., Hong, J.-F., Chen, Y.-Z., Su, Y.-L., Chen, Y.-X., Huang, S.-W.: Chinese Wordnet: design, implementation, and application of an infrastructure for cross-lingual knowledge processing. J. Chin. Inf. Process. **24**(2), 14–23 (2010b). 黃居仁, 謝舒凱, 洪嘉馡, 陳韻竹, 蘇依莉, 陳永祥,黃勝偉. 中文詞彙網絡:跨語言知識處理基礎架構的設計理念與實踐. 《中文信息学报》, **24**(2), 14–23 (2001)
24. Supalla, T., Newport, E.: How many seats in a chair? the derivation of nouns and verbs in American sign language. In: Siple, P. (ed.) Understanding Language Through Sign Language Research, pp. 97–132. Academic Press, New York (1978)
25. Wu, P.-L. (ed.): The Formation of Noun-Verb Pairs in Taiwan Sign Language. MA thesis, National Chung Cheng University, Chiayi, Taiwan (2007) 吳佩蘭. 《台灣手語名動同形詞構詞策略之探討 》. 嘉義, 國立中正大學碩士論文 (2007)
26. Johnston, T.: Nouns and verbs in Australian sign language: an open and shut case? J. Deaf Stud. Deaf Educ. **6**(4), 235–257 (2001)
27. Hunger, B.: Noun/Verb pairs in Austrian sign language (ÖGS). Sign Lang. Linguist. **9**(1), 71–94 (2006)
28. Tkachman, O., Sandler, W.: The noun-verb distinction in two young sign languages. Gesture **13**(3), 253–286 (2013)

29. Meier, R.P.: Why different, why the same? Explaining effects and non-effects of modality upon linguistic structure in sign and speech. In: Meier, R.P., Cormier, K., Quinto-Pozos, D. (eds.): Modality and Structure in Signed and Spoken Languages, pp. 1–25. Cambridge University Press, Cambridge (2002)
30. Newport, E.L., Bellugi, U.: Linguistic expression of category levels in a visual-gestural language: a flower is a flower is a flower. In: Rosch, E., Lloyd, B. (eds.) Cognition and Categorization, pp. 49–77. Lawrence Erlbaum, Hillsdale (1978)
31. Hinton, L., Nichols, J., Ohala, J.J. (eds.): Sound Symbolism. Cambridge University Press, Cambridge (1994)
32. Bloomfield, L. (ed.): Language. Holt, Rinehart and Winston, New York (1993)
33. Hockett, C.F.: The origin of speech. Sci. Am. **203**, 88–96 (1960)
34. Liddell, S.K., Johnson, R.E.: American sign language: the phonological base. Sign Lang. Stud. **64**(1), 195–277 (1989)
35. Tsay, J., Myers, J.: The morphology and phonology of Taiwan sign language. In: Tai, J.H.-Y., Tsay, J. (eds.) Taiwan Sign Language and Beyond, pp. 83–129. National Chung Cheng University, The Taiwan Institute for the Humanities (2009)
36. Tai, J.H.-Y., Tsay, J.: Taiwan sign language: history, structure, and adaptation. In: Wang, W. S.-Y., Sun, C. (eds.) Oxford Handbook of Chinese Linguistics, pp. 729–750. Oxford University Press, Oxford (2015)
37. Smith, W.H. (ed.): The Morphological Characteristics of Verbs in Taiwan Sign Language. Ph.D. Dissertation, Indiana University, Bloomington (1989)
38. Smith, W.H.: Taiwan sign language research: an historical overview. Lang. Linguist. **6**(2), 187–215 (2005)
39. Tai, J.H.-Y., Tsay, J.: Taiwan sign language. In: Jepsen, J.B., Clerck, G.D., Kiingi, S.L., McGregor, W.B. (eds.) Sign Languages of the World, pp. 771–809. De Gruyter Mouton, Germany (2015)
40. Tai, J.H.-Y., Tsay, J.: Sign languages: Taiwan. In: Behr, S., Handel, G., Huang, C.-T., Myers, J. (eds.) Encyclopedia of Chinese Language and Linguistics, Volume IV, pp. 92–99. Brill Academic Publishers, Leiden & Boston (2017)
41. Baker, A., van den Bogaerde, B., Pfau, R., Schermer, T. (eds.): The Linguistics of Sign Languages: An Introduction. John Benjamins Publishing Company, Amsterdam (2016)
42. Morphology and Lexicon, Symposium Series of the Institute of History and Philology
43. Clark, E., Clark, H.: When nouns surface as verbs. Language **55**, 767–811 (1979)
44. Sanders, G.A.: Zero derivation and the overt analogue criterion. In: Theoretical Morphology, pp. 155–175 (1988)
45. Chao, Y.R. (ed.): A Grammar of Spoken Chinese. University of California Press, Berkeley (1968)
46. Li, C., Thompson, S. (eds.): Mandarin Chinese: A Functional Reference Grammar. University of California Press, Berkeley (1981)
47. Zhu, D.-X. (ed.): Yǔfǎ jiǎngyì [Grammar Lecture]. The Commercial Press, Beijing (1982). 朱德熙: 《語法講義》 北京:商務印書館 (1982)
48. Tang, T.-C. (ed.): Studies on Chinese Morphology and Syntax 2. Student Book Co., Ltd, Taipei (1989)
49. Tsao, F.-F. (ed.): Sentence and Clause Structure in Chinese: A Functional Perspective. Student Book Co. Ltd., Taipei (1990)
50. McCawley, J.D.: Justifying part-of-speech assignments in Mandarin Chinese. J. Chin. Linguist. **20**(2), 211–246 (1992)
51. Lu, J.-M.: Guānyú cí de jiānlèi wèntí [About Grammatical Category Ambiguity]. Chin. Lang. Lit. J. **1**, 28–34 (1994). 陸儉明: 關於詞的兼類問題 《中國語文》 **1**, 28–34 (1994)

52. Tai, J.H.-Y.: On modality effects and relative uniformity of sign languages. In: Gang, P., Feng, S. (eds.): Eastward Flows the Great Rivers: Festschrift in Honor of Professor William S.-Y. Wang on his 80th Birthday, pp. 283–300. City University of Hong Kong Press, Hong Kong (2013)
53. Haiman, J.: The iconicity of grammar: isomorphism and motivation. Language **56**, 515–540 (1980)
54. Haiman, J. (ed.): Iconicity in Syntax. Typological Studies in Language, vol. 6. John Benjamins, Amsterdam (1985)
55. Tsay, J., Tai, J.H.-Y., Chen, Y.-J.: Taiwan Sign Language Online Dictionary, 3rd Edn. Institute of Linguistics, National Chung Cheng University, Taiwan (2015). http://tsl.ccu.edu.tw
56. Vicars,W.: American Sign Language University (1997). http://www.lifeprint.com/
57. China Association of the Deaf and Hard of Hearing. (eds.): Chinese Sign Language. Huaxia Press, Beijing (1990)
58. Yonekawa, A. (ed.): Japanese Sign Language Dictionary. Japan Institute for Sign Language Studies, Japan (1997)
59. Ilzensauer, M., Krammer, K.: A Multilingual Dictionary for Sign Languages: Spread the Sign (2015). https://www.spreadthesign.com/us/aboutus/
60. Tai, J.H.-Y.: Modality effects: iconicity in Taiwan sign language. In: Ho, D.-A., Tzeng, O.J. L. (eds.): POLA FOREVER: Festschrift in Honor of Professor William S-Y. Wang on his 70th Birthday, pp. 19–36. Institute of Linguistics, Academia Sinica, Taipei (2005)
61. Chang, J.-H. (ed.): cognitive strategies in word formation in Taiwan sign language and american sign language. Crane Publishing, Taipei (2014) 張榮興: 《台灣手語與美國手語造詞認知策略比較》. 台北,文鶴出版社 (2014)
62. Chang, J.-H. (ed.): Cognitive Structure in Word Formation Across Sign Languages. Crane Publishing, Taipei (2015). 張榮興: 《跨時空手語詞彙認知結構比較》. 台北, 文鶴出版社 (2015)

A Semantic Analysis of Sense Organs in Chinese Compound Words: Based on Embodied Cognition and Generative Lexicon Theory

Yin Zhong[1](✉) and Chu-Ren Huang[2]

[1] Faculty of Humanities, The Hong Kong Polytechnic University, Hung Hom, Hong Kong
beth.zhong@connect.polyu.hk
[2] Department of Chinese and Bilingual Studies, The Hong Kong Polytechnic University, Hung Hom, Hong Kong
churen.huang@polyu.edu.hk

Abstract. This article aims to analyse the four major sense organs of human beings, viz., 眼 (yǎn, eyes), 耳 (ěr, ears), 口/嘴 (kǒu/zuǐ, mouth) and 鼻 (bí, nose), in Chinese compound words with the combination of Generative Lexicon Theory and Embodied Cognition. It was shown that Embodied Cognition gives us an idea of the locus of the source domain in figurative use of organ-related words. Meanwhile, qualia structure in Generative Lexicon Theory, in particular, can be used to examine which sense of the word is activated when combining with other morphemes in a compound word. Moreover, the study found that the involved qualia roles vary in different syntactic structures and metaphorization of the compound words, which further demonstrates different lexical compositionality and productivity of the four basic sense organ words.

Keywords: Sense organs · Metaphor · Metonymy · Embodied cognition Qualia roles

1 Introduction

Human beings are known to use their eyes to see, ears to listen, mouth to eat and speak, and nose to smell. These four sense organs are the locus of our basic human senses, i.e., visual, auditory, gustatory and olfactory senses. They seemingly own their respective functions and interrelate with one another when we perceive and experience the outside world. However, senses are not equal. Various sensory-related studies have shown that different sensory modalities are linguistically represented to varying degrees, with a rich vocabulary in visual perception but a lack of expressions related to smell in English and other Indo-European languages [1, 2]. By examining the number of word senses for each of the above four organs in *Chinese WordNet* [3][1] and 7th edition of *Xiandai Hanyu Cidian (Contemporary Chinese Dictionary)* [4], 8 major literal and

[1] http://cwn.ling.sinica.edu.tw/.

J.-F. Hong et al. (Eds.): CLSW 2018, LNAI 11173, pp. 23–33, 2018.
https://doi.org/10.1007/978-3-030-04015-4_2

extended senses were found for 眼 (yǎn, eyes), 3 for 耳 (ěr, ears), 13 and 6 for 口 and 嘴[2] (kǒu and zuǐ, mouth) and 3 for 鼻 (bí, nose). In view of the multiple word meanings each sense organ carries, both literal and metaphorical, it is interesting to figure out what makes it possible to distinguish among various meanings and which one of the specific meanings is activated in similar and different constructions. For example, in the construction of [adjective + 眼 (yǎn, eyes)], how the meaning(s) of the same word 眼 (yǎn, eyes) vary in the compound words碧眼 (bìyǎn, blue eyes), 白眼 (báiyǎn, supercilious look), and 冷眼 (lěngyǎn, cold shoulder)? Meanwhile, given senses are not equal as mentioned earlier, how each sense organ differs from others in the lexicalization is also one of the concerns of this study.

2 Previous Related Studies

Body parts studies have been conducted largely since 'embodiment' was introduced to cognitive linguistics in 1975 [5]. Different body parts in Mandarin Chinese were investigated by Yu [6–9], including eyes, speech organs, head, heart, gallbladder, and so forth. He mainly adopted the decompositional approach by summarizing basic metaphorical mappings and listing words and expressions related, for instance, EYE FOR SEEING, EYE FOR MIND, and SPEECH ORGAN FOR SPEAKING. Although these conceptual metaphor mappings are familiar to us, the specific lexicalization method applied in the figurative uses of linguistic expressions containing different body parts are still under research. Moreover, with the 'quantitative turn' in cognitive linguistics since 2008 [10], it will be more objective and convincing if quantitative data, such as corpus, can be utilized in the metaphorical research of body parts.

With regard to Pustejovsky [11]'s qualia structure, Nissen [12] is considered the pioneer who incorporated Generative Lexicon Theory in Embodied Cognition when examining figurative meanings of 'mouth' in Danish, English, and Spanish. The study showed that mappings of mind and body are closely related to constitution, shape, and function(s) of 'mouth' and cultural differences may play a role in the metonymization and metaphorization processes.

Duann and Huang [13] also combined the two theories and studied four body parts in Mandarin Chinese, namely, blood, flesh, bone and meridian. It was suggested that metaphorization of the above four words is mainly realized when collocated with two visual verbs, 看 (kàn, to see) and 見 (jiàn, to see). Their telic role(s), that is, the function(s) of these body parts also help to explain the metaphorization.

In general, previous studies have given us an idea of metaphorical mappings related to major body parts in Mandarin Chinese and other languages. However, it has not been well researched what factor(s) motivates the lexicalization and metaphorization of the typical sense organs and body parts. It is also worthwhile to integrate quantitative method into semantic and metaphorical analysis to examine the language patterns and structures more objectively.

[2] Two words are chosen because both of them carry the meaning of 'mouth' in Mandarin Chinese.

3 Theoretical Background and Research Questions

3.1 Embodied Cognition

Challenging a long-standing view of mind-body dualism in Western cultures, cognitive scientists and philosophers have now suggested that our bodies cannot be isolated from the ways we think and speak. The subjective feelings of the body provide at least part of the fundamental grounding for the language we use and the thought we have in our mind [14, 15]. As Lakoff and Johnson [15, 16] proposed in the leading theory in cognitive linguistics - Conceptual Metaphor Theory (CMT), human beings' conceptual system is fundamentally metaphorical in nature and is reflected in linguistic expressions. The tenet of CMT is that abstract terms are understood by more concrete concepts, hence, our bodily experience can be a primary source for this mapping. Kövecses [17] holds a similar view by claiming that the human body is an ideal source domain for metaphors and plays a key role in the emergence of metaphorical meaning not only in English and other Western languages and cultures, but also in other languages and cultures around the world. Likewise, Gibbs et al. [18] suggested that many of the source domains of conceptual metaphors can reflect significant patterns of bodily experience.

In the light of the recognition that metaphor and metonymy are powerful tools for generating figurative expressions and these expressions are motivated by our bodily experiences, we can understand and identify the locus of the source domain in a metaphorical expression. However, how these expressions contribute to understanding of the conceptualization of body-part words seems hard to explain by Embodied Cognition.

3.2 Generative Lexicon Theory

Generative Lexicon Theory (GLT) was proposed by Pustejovsky in the 1990s to deal with the 'multiplicity of word meaning'. As all of the body-part related words are nouns, including the four sense organs we are examining in this study, only qualia structure in GLT is discussed here. Qualia structure was inspired by Aristotle's 'four causes' of explaining the emergence and development of the entity in the world, that is, material cause, formal cause, efficient or moving cause, and final cause [19, 20]. It depicts what X is made of, what X is, the function of X, and how X comes into being, which correspond to constitutive role, formal role, telic role and agentive role of an entity [11, 21].

Constitutive role describes the relation between an entity and its constitutive parts, as well as the relation between the parts and the entire entity. For example, with respect to eyes, they are a part of sense organs, the whole face and also the entire body. Meanwhile, the eye consists of the eyelid, orbit, pupil, sclera, etc. Formal role focuses on how the specific entity is distinguished from other objects within a larger domain in terms of its position, magnitude, shape, colour, and so forth. For instance, eyes and mouth are known to open and close voluntarily but ears and nose must keep 'open' all the time. Telic role deals with the purpose and function of the entity - the first sentence in this article has already summarized the respective functions of the four sense organs commonly agreed to by all human beings. Last but not least, agentive role discusses factors involved in the entity's origin, like the entity is a natural type, an artefact object or a complex type [22]. As for the four sense organs, they are natural kinds in most cases. However, in some compound words they can be artificial, such as 假眼 (jiǎyǎn, artificial eyes) and 隆鼻 (lóngbí, rhinoplasty).

Recent GLT studies in Mandarin Chinese found that the most active role in metaphorical noun-noun compounds is formal role, while agentive role has the least effect in this type of compounds [23]. However, in adjective-noun compounds, formal role is used the most for nouns, and telic role is considered second [24]. In verb-object compounds, if a noun cannot satisfy the consistent meaning of the verb, the verb will 'coerce' the noun into its metonymy meaning [25].

3.3 Research Questions

By combining the two theories mentioned above, on the one hand we can figure out the relationship between the meanings of the word and other words it collocates with, and on the other hand, we can locate the source it arises from when interpreting its extended meanings.

Drawing upon this perspective, this study attempts to take the four basic sense organs as a start, firstly to compile a list of compound words in Mandarin Chinese containing 眼 (yǎn, eyes), 耳 (ěr, ears), 口/嘴 (kǒu/zuǐ, mouth) and 鼻 (bí, nose), secondly to examine their respective qualia roles in the overall representations, including both literal and metaphorical meanings, and lastly, to explore the activation of different roles in metaphorical uses of the four words.

Two research questions are hereby raised:

(a) Which qualia role(s) is/are prominent in the various syntactic constructions of the four words?
(b) Which qualia role(s) is/are prominent in the metaphorical and metonymic meanings of the four words?

4 Data and Method

The data investigated in this study was collected from 7th edition of *Xiandai Hanyu Cidian (Contemporary Chinese Dictionary)* [4] and *Chinese GigaWord Corpus (Mainland)* in the *Sketch Engine* [26][3]. The source data in *Chinese GigaWord Corpus (Mainland)* mainly contains news articles from *Xinhua News Agency, Beijing,* from 1991 and 2002 with a quantity of more than 200 million words. The function of 'Word List' in the corpus was used to generate a list containing the four words. With this function, it is believed that the collected data is comprehensive and currently in use with the frequencies denoted.

[3] https://the.sketchengine.co.uk.

Only disyllabic and trisyllabic compounding expressions were chosen for further analysis because this study emphasizes on the productivity and compositionality of the word. Thus, conventional idioms were excluded, e.g. 眼疾手快 (yǎn-jí-shǒu-kuài, doing something at top speed), 眼不見爲淨 (yǎn-bù-jiàn-wéi-jìng, out of sight, out of mind), etc. In trisyllabic compound words, those with similar meanings as in disyllabic words were also not considered, for instance, the senses of 眼 (yǎn, eyes) in 眼鏡店 (yǎnjìng diàn, optical shop) and in眼鏡 (yǎnjìng, spectacles) are the same, so only the disyllabic word 眼鏡 (yǎnjìng, spectacles) was retained. Based on this criterion, 149 compound words for 眼 (yǎn, eyes), 72 for 耳 (ěr, ears), 215 for 口 (kǒu, mouth), 53 for 嘴 (zuǐ, mouth) and 36 for 鼻 (bí, nose) were compiled.

After the word list was generated, we adopted Song et al. [27] and Zhao and Song [23]'s annotation method for Chinese compound words, including lexical categories for each morpheme and the whole word, syntactic structure of the word, lexical meanings for each morpheme and the whole word, qualia roles of the word and extensions of the lexical meanings (metaphor and/or metonymy, if any).

It is hard to determine the involved qualia roles in some compound words because the meaning has become less transparent in the process of lexicalization, like 口 (kǒu, mouth) in the word 心口 (xīnkǒu, precordium/heart). As Song et al. [27] suggested, this annotation framework is only applicable to those words with high semantic transparency and strong semantic compositionality, and so these words were removed.

Those words with metonymical and metaphorical meanings were sorted separately after annotation was completed. For instance, 口徑 (kǒujìng) has two meanings; in its first meaning, 口 (kǒu, mouth) is a metaphor and the formal role (shape of the mouth) plays a part in the metaphorization; while口徑 (kǒujìng) turns out to be a metonymy in the second meaning, and the telic role – use mouth to speak is activated here. Thus, these kinds of words were recorded as two or three lexical items according to their varying extended meanings.

5 Results and Discussion

5.1 眼 (Yǎn, Eyes)

In the general pattern of the compound words containing 眼 (yǎn, eyes) as shown in Table 1, modifier-head structure tops in the syntactic constructions, with 眼 (yǎn, eyes) as the modified morpheme and other morphemes are used to modify it. Formal role and telic role are evenly used in this construction and constitutive role also plays a considerable part in this structure. Verb-object structure ranks second and telic role is used the most in this structure, such as in the words 瞪眼 (dèngyǎn, to stare) and 睜眼 (zhēngyǎn, to open one's eyes).

Table 2 presents the metaphorical and metonymical uses of 眼 (yǎn, eyes). The result generally accords with the findings in the distributions above – telic role mainly motivates the metaphorization, telic role and formal role both activate the metonymization. It further suggests that formal and telic roles are important for eyes - due to the shape of our eyes, and that the meaning has been extended metaphorically, like in the words 貓眼 (māoyǎn, peep hole), 孔眼 (kǒngyǎn, hole), and 鎖眼 (suǒyǎn, key hole). We can also get an abstract meaning based on the function of eyes, as in the word 眼福 (yǎnfú, feast one's eyes on something) and 冷眼 (lěngyǎn, cold-shoulder).

Table 1. Distributions of qualia roles in syntactic constructions of 眼 (yǎn, eyes)

Qualia Roles / Syntactic Construction	Constitutive	Formal	Telic	Agentive
Coordination (4)	4 (100%)	0 (0%)	0 (0%)	0 (0%)
Modifier-head (108)	25 (23%)	39 (36%)	32 (30%)	12 (11%)
Subject-predicate (5)	0 (0%)	4 (80%)	1 (20%)	0 (0%)
Verb-object (32)	0 (0%)	12 (38%)	19 (59%)	1 (3%)
Total	149			

Table 2. Distributions of qualia roles in metaphorical uses of 眼 (yǎn, eyes)

Qualia Roles / Metaphor/Metonymy	Constitutive	Formal	Telic	Agentive
Metaphor (67)	2 (3%)	27 (40%)	38 (57%)	0 (0%)
Metonymy (21)	5 (24%)	8 (38%)	8 (38%)	0 (0%)
Total	88			

5.2 耳 (ěr, Ears)

Although ears are seen as important as eyes for human beings, the number of compound words is much less than 眼 (yǎn, eyes). This is partly due to the formal role of 耳 (ěr, ears) - ears cannot voluntarily open or close, the shape and size also do not vary too much. In addition, the most critical function and constitution of ears are more invisible than those of eyes. These features of ears are reflected in the percentage of the formal and telic roles in the syntactic constructions of 耳 (ěr, ears) as shown in Table 3.

Table 3. Distributions of qualia roles in syntactic constructions of 耳 (ěr, ears)

Qualia Roles / Syntactic Construction	Constitutive	Formal	Telic	Agentive
Coordination (4)	1 (25%)	3 (75%)	0 (0%)	0 (0%)
Modifier-head (50)	29 (58%)	2 (4%)	8 (16%)	11 (22%)
Subject-predicate (5)	0 (0%)	1 (20%)	4 (80%)	0 (0%)
Verb-object (13)	3 (23%)	0 (0%)	9 (69%)	1 (8%)
Total	72			

Constitutive role is more important in the modifier-head construction, with agentive role following in second place. While in other constructions, telic role is more prominent than other roles although only a few instances are found. Formal role has very little influence in the lexicalization of the compound words containing 耳 (ĕr, ears) and agentive role, no doubt, has the least impact.

As in the metaphorical and metonymical uses of 耳 (ĕr, ears) presented in Table 4, the results look quite consistent with眼 (yăn, eyes), with telic role being the main role in metaphorization.

Table 4. Distributions of qualia roles in metaphorical uses of 耳 (ĕr, ears)

Qualia Roles Metaphor/Metonymy	Constitutive	Formal	Telic	Agentive
Metaphor (19)	0 (%)	4 (21%)	15 (79%)	0 (0%)
Metonymy (3)	0 (0%)	1 (33%)	2 (67%)	0 (0%)
Total	22			

5.3 口/嘴 (Kŏu/Zuĭ, Mouth)

The amount of compound words containing口 (kŏu, mouth) is the most compared to other sense organs because most of the compound words are formed based on the shape and characteristics of the mouth – it can open and things can go in and out from it, and this is considered 'formal role' in the qualia structure such as in the words 窗口 (chuāngkŏu, window) and門口 (ménkŏu, doorway). Therefore, formal role is the most important role in the lexicalization as presented in Table 5.

Table 5. Distributions of qualia roles in syntactic constructions of 口 (kŏu, mouth)

Qualia Roles Syntactic Construction	Constitutive	Formal	Telic	Agentive
Coordination (10)	0 (0%)	5 (50%)	1 (10%)	4 (40%)
Modifier-head (156)	5 (3%)	107 (69%)	40 (26%)	2 (1%)
Subject-predicate (12)	0 (0%)	0 (0%)	12 (100%)	0 (0%)
Verb-object (37)	0 (0%)	8 (22%)	27 (73%)	0 (0%)
Total	215			

There are relatively much fewer words for 嘴 (zuĭ, mouth) because formal role is lost in the compound words containing嘴 (zuĭ, mouth). Formal role is only found in words like 奶嘴 (năizuĭ, nipple of a feeding bottle) and 壺嘴 (húzuĭ, spout) though it is not about the shape of the mouth, but rather the object functions like the month when pouting. Nevertheless, telic role is seen as the most prominent role, as shown in Table 6.

Table 6. Distributions of qualia roles in syntactic constructions of 嘴 (zuǐ, mouth)

Qualia Roles / Syntactic Construction	Constitutive	Formal	Telic	Agentive
Coordination (2)	2 (100%)	0 (0%)	0 (0%)	0 (0%)
Modifier-head (35)	3 (9%)	13 (37%)	19 (54%)	0 (0%)
Subject-predicate (2)	0 (0%)	0 (0%)	2 (100%)	0 (0%)
Verb-object (14)	0 (0%)	4 (29%)	10 (71%)	0 (0%)
Total	53			

In relation to the metaphorical and metonymical meanings of mouth, formal role is much more prominent than other roles as for 口 (kǒu, mouth) while telic role is the most important for the metaphorization of 嘴 (zuǐ, mouth). Mouth is seen as the most 'useful' among the four organs due to its two functions – to eat and to speak. Between the two functions, the speaking function is deemed more pronounced. Even in words related to senses of taste and smell, like 口氣 (kǒuqì, literal meaning: bad breath; metaphorical meaning: tone of voice) and 嘴甜 (zuǐtián, honey-mouthed), telic role of speaking is activated in most cases (Tables 7 and 8).

Table 7. Distributions of qualia roles in metaphorical uses of 口 (kǒu, mouth)

Qualia Roles / Metaphor/Metonymy	Constitutive	Formal	Telic	Agentive
Metaphor (167)	0 (%)	110 (66%)	57 (34%)	0 (0%)
Metonymy (15)	0 (0%)	2 (13%)	13 (87%)	0 (0%)
Total	182			

Table 8. Distributions of qualia roles in metaphorical uses of 嘴 (zuǐ, mouth)

Qualia Roles / Metaphor/Metonymy	Constitutive	Formal	Telic	Agentive
Metaphor (37)	0 (%)	10 (27%)	27 (73%)	0 (0%)
Metonymy (4)	1 (25%)	0 (0%)	3 (75%)	0 (0%)
Total	41			

5.4 鼻 (Bí, Nose)

Olfactory sense is a relatively 'lower' sense in the sensory system and is described as the most 'ineffable' sense [2]. This peculiarity is also reflected in the number of lexical items of compound words containing 鼻 (bí, nose). Quite similar to other senses, telic role is seen as the most significant role which motivates lexicalization and metaphorization using its unitary function of smelling. Formal role has much less influence in this case than in other sense organs (Tables 9 and 10).

Table 9. Distributions of qualia roles in syntactic constructions of 鼻 (bí, nose)

Qualia Roles / Syntactic Construction	Constitutive	Formal	Telic	Agentive
Coordination (4)	2 (50%)	2 (50%)	0 (0%)	0 (0%)
Modifier-head (20)	10 (50%)	2 (10%)	1 (5%)	7 (35%)
Subject-predicate (5)	0 (0%)	0 (0%)	5 (100%)	0 (0%)
Verb-object (7)	0 (0%)	0 (0%)	6 (86%)	1 (14%)
Total	36			

Table 10. Distributions of qualia roles in metaphorical uses of 鼻 (bí, nose)

Qualia Roles / Metaphor/Metonymy	Constitutive	Formal	Telic	Agentive
Metaphor (7)	1	0 (0%)	6	0 (0%)
Metonymy (2)	1	0 (0%)	0 (0%)	0 (0%)
Total	9			

6 Conclusion

By analysing different qualia roles in the Chinese compound words containing眼 (yǎn, eyes), 耳 (ěr, ears), 口/嘴 (kǒu/zuǐ, mouth) and鼻 (bí, nose) during their lexicalization and metaphorization/metonymization, firstly we have identified that the most distinct syntactic construction among the four words is the modifier-head structure, with each sense organ being modified as the head word.

In the overall representations, including their literal and metaphorical meanings, all four qualia roles manifest in the lexicalization process but with asymmetrical distribution. Telic role is seen as the most prominent in the verb-object structure among the four roles. In other structures, all the four roles contribute to the constructions, especially formal role and constitutive role. Agentive role is seen as the least useful as all the sense organs are natural kinds.

While in the activation of different qualia roles in metaphorical uses of the four sense organs, we have found that constitutive role and agentive role lost their places while formal role and telic role are still relevant to the metaphorization and metonymization processes, with telic role being the most prominent.

This study further confirms that although we use our physical senses and experiences to generate abstract notions, senses are not in symmetrical distributions. They are reflected in the number of extended meanings and compound words as we have demonstrated in this study. It can also be explained by the qualia roles examined here. Constitutive role allows us to form new words with different parts of a sense organ and closely related sense organs; those with more distinct features, in terms of shapes and sizes, are more likely to have stronger lexical productivity than other organs. Moreover, organs with more than one function are also proved to be more productive in yielding metaphors.

The concept of embodied cognition and qualia roles in GLT allows us to study body parts in a more comprehensive way. In addition to locating the abstract notions with our embodied experiences, we can also understand the reason for such locus and identify the patterns of lexicalization and metaphorization.

References

1. Buck, C.D.: A Dictionary of Selected Synonyms in the Principal Indo-European Languages: A Contribution to the History of Ideas. University of Chicago Press, Chicago (1949)
2. Levinson, S.C., Majid, A.: Differential ineffability and the senses. Mind Lang. **29**, 407–427 (2014)
3. Huang, C.-R., et al.: Chinese WordNet: design, implementation, and application of an infrastructure for cross-lingual knowledge processing. J. Chin. Inf. Process. **24**(2), 14–23 (2010)
4. Xiandai Hanyu Cidian: Contemporary Chinese Dictionary, 7th edn. The Commercial Press, Beijing (2016)
5. Lakoff, G.: Explaining embodied cognition results. Top. Cogn. Sci. **4**(4), 773–785 (2012)
6. Yu, N.: The eyes for sight and mind. J. Pragmat. **36**(4), 663–686 (2004)
7. Yu, N.: From Body to Meaning in Culture: Papers on Cognitive Semantic Studies of Chinese. John Benjamins Pub, Amsterdam (2009)
8. Yu, N.: Speech organs and linguistic activity/function in Chinese. In: Maalej, Z., Yu, N. (eds.) Embodiment via Body Parts: Studies from Various Languages and Cultures, pp. 117–148. John Benjamins Pub, Amsterdam/Philadelphia (2011)
9. Yu, N.: The body in anatomy: looking at "head" for the mind-body link in Chinese. In: Caballero, R., Díaz Vera, J. (eds.) Sensuous Cognition: Explorations into Human Sentience: Imagination, (E)motion and Perception, pp. 53–73. De Gruyter Mouton, Berlin, Boston (2013)
10. Janda, L.A. (ed.): Cognitive Linguistics - The Quantitative Turn: The Essential Reader. De Gruyter Mouton, Berlin (2013)
11. Pustejovky, J.: The Generative Lexicon. MIT Press, Cambridge (1995)
12. Nissen, U.K.: Contrasting body parts: metaphors and metonymies of MOUTH in Danish, English and Spanish. In: Maalej, Z.A., Yu, N. (eds.) Embodiment via Body Parts: Studies from Various Languages and Cultures, pp. 71–92. John Benjamins Publishing Company, Amsterdam/Philadelphia (2011)
13. Duann, R.-F., Huang, C.-R.: When embodiment meets generative lexicon: the human body part metaphors in Sinica Corpus. In: Proceedings of the 29th Pacific Asia Conference on Language, Information and Computation, Shanghai, China (2015)
14. Lakoff, G.: Women, Fire, and Dangerous Things: What Categories Reveal About the Mind. University of Chicago Press, Chicago (1987)
15. Lakoff, G., Johnson, M.: Metaphors We Live by. University of Chicago Press, Chicago (1980)
16. Lakoff, G., Johnson, M.: Philosophy in the Flesh: The Embodied Mind and its Challenge to Western Thought. University of Chicago Press, Chicago (1999)
17. Kövecses, Z.: Metaphor: A Practical Introduction. Oxford University Press, Oxford (2002)
18. Gibbs, R.W., Lenz Costa Lima, P., Francozo, E.: Metaphor is grounded in embodied experience. J. Pragmat. **36**, 1189–1210 (2004)

19. Chou, Y.-M., Huang, C.-R.: Hantology: conceptual system discovery based on orthographic convention. In: Huang, C.-R., Calzolari, N., Gangemi, A., Lenci, A., Oltramari, A., Prévot, L., Ontology and the Lexicon: A Natural Language Processing Perspective, 2nd eds., pp. 122–143. Peking University Press, Beijing (2014)
20. Yuan, Y.L.: On a descriptive system of qualia structure of Chinese nouns and its application in parsing complex Chinese grammatical phenomena (in Chinese). Contemp. Linguist. **16** (1), 31–48 (2014)
21. Pustejovky, J.: The generative lexicon. Contemp. Linguist. **17**(4), 409–441 (1991)
22. Pustejovky, J., Jezek, E.: Semantic coercion in language: beyond distributional analysis. Ital. J. Linguist. **20**(1), 181–214 (2008)
23. Zhao, Q.Q., Song, Z.Y.: A study on disyllabic metaphorical noun-noun compounds in Mandarin Chinese: a Generative Lexicon Theory based approach (in Chinese). J. Chin. Inf. Process. **31**(2), 11–17 (2017)
24. Zhang, N.Q., Song, Z.Y.: Semantic construction of Adjective-Noun compounds in Mandarin: based on qualia structure and Conceptual Blending Theory (in Chinese). J. Chin. Inf. Process. **29**(6), 38–45 (2015)
25. Li, Q.: Verb-object structure and its semantic metonymy in Chinese from Generative Lexicon Theory (in Chinese). Lang. Teach. Linguist. Stud. **6**, 72–81 (2017)
26. Kilgarriff, A., et al.: The sketch engine: ten years on. Lexicography **1**(1), 7–36 (2014)
27. Song, Z.Y., Zhao, Q.Q., Kang, S.Y.: A lexicon of Chinese compound nouns with semantic annotation: generative lexicon theory approach (in Chinese). J. Chin. Inf. Process. **29**(3), 27–43 (2015)

The Functions of 了*liǎo* in Singapore Mandarin

Yong Kang Khoo(✉)

Nanyang Technological University,
50 Nanyang Avenue, Singapore 639798, Singapore
yongkang001@e.ntu.edu.sg

Abstract. This paper provides an account of the functions of 了 *liǎo* in Singapore Mandarin using spoken data. It is found that while *liǎo* can perform the grammatical roles of *le*, it presents its own constraints, particularly when used as a perfective aspect marker. Specifically, it occurs with verbal compounds in clause-final positions – an unacceptable construction in Mainland China Mandarin. Additionally, it is also observed that it co-occurs with 了 *le* at the sentence-final position, resulting in a rather peculiar 'double-了' construction. Some explanations are given for these occurrences of *liǎo* in Singapore Mandarin; most notably, it is hypothesized that Singapore Mandarin has retained the older construction of *liao* and the retention might have been brought on by the language contact with non-Mandarin dialects like Minnanese. The implication of this study is two-fold: (a) it can first shed light on a linguistic variation found in Singapore Mandarin and (b) it can also potentially serve as a reference study for future research conducted on 了 in general.

Keywords: Singapore mandarin · Perfective aspect · Corpus-based Particle 了 *le/liǎo* · Language contact

1 Introduction

In Mainland China Mandarin (MCM), 了 bears several functions; these functions can usually be differentiated phonetically. As a verb or a complement, 了 is pronounced as *liǎo*. When used as a verb, it expresses the meaning 'to finish; to end', as in 这件事总算了啦 *zhèjiànshì zǒngsuàn liǎo la* 'This issue is finally over' [1]. In potential verb compounds, *liǎo* functions as a complement to express the possibility of the action, as in 受得/不了 *shòu dé/bùliǎo* 'can/cannot take it' [1]. 了 can also be used as a grammatical particle with various interpretations, depending on its syntactic position, i.e., the verb-final and the sentence-final position. In the verb-final position, it is interpreted as a perfective aspect marker while in the sentence-final position, it is often more generally known as a sentence-final particle that expresses a myriad of meanings. Most notably, however, when performing its role as a grammatical particle, 了 is read as *le*, a phonetically-reduced version of *liǎo* after undergoing grammaticalization [2]. Interestingly, as noted by Chen [3], Chew and Zhou [4] and Lua [5], in Singapore Mandarin (SM), 了 can also be read as *liǎo* even when used as a grammatical particle. These scholars suggest that a free variation exists between these two pronunciations, thereby proposing the interchangeability of *liǎo* and *le* in SM. However, based on a corpus-based investigation, Khoo et al. [6] find that *liǎo* seems to exhibit a slightly different

J.-F. Hong et al. (Eds.): CLSW 2018, LNAI 11173, pp. 34–43, 2018.
https://doi.org/10.1007/978-3-030-04015-4_3

behavior from *le* and therefore refute the interchangeability account. This paper seeks to further this notion by closely examining the functions, constraints, and origins of grammatical particle *liǎo* in SM. The rest of this paper consists of the following: Sect. 2 first reviews current studies about the functions of MCM le and SM *liǎo*. Section 3 discusses the findings of the corpus-based investigation and Sect. 4 provides an analysis of the notable variations in SM *liǎo*. Section 5 concludes this paper.

2 Literature Review

Prior to examining the functions of *liǎo* in SM, it is essential to first understand the meanings and constraints behind the more typical variant, *le* – in particular, the MCM variant. This will be discussed in Sect. 2.1. After which, it is then necessary to review the current research done on SM *liǎo* and identify possible gaps and issues with the current findings and arguments about the particle; this will be done in Sect. 2.2.

2.1 Mainland China Mandarin *liǎo* and *le*

The verb-final *le* is analyzed as the perfective aspect marker by most previous studies (e.g., [1, 7–11]). It expresses temporal, spatial or conceptual boundedness as a consequence of its perfectivity [9], and in most cases, the perfective *le* (le_{PFV}) denotes termination of an action. When interacting with telic events, le_{PFV} also denotes the completion of the event [11]. While the syntactic position for le_{PFV} seems to suggest that the marker only occurs after verbs, it can collocate with adjectival predicative such as 大 *dà* 'big' and 亮 *liàng* 'bright'. However, not all verbs and adjectival predicative can collocate with le_{PFV} – the aspect marker cannot occur with semantically stative verbs like 认识 *rènshì* 'be acquainted with' as these verbs do not present a possibility of termination or completion [1, 12].

The le_{PFV} can be clearly identified when a post-verbal constituent (the object) that is referential and not generic intervenes between the verb and the end of the clause; these constituents are usually realized by classifier constituents, attributive or adjectival modifications, anaphoric pronouns and proper nouns [12]. An example is given in (1). If not, the clause containing le_{PFV} has to be followed by a clause expressing a subsequent action (2) or by a sentence-final particle (3), as le_{PFV} has to take an internal (or intra-sentence) temporal reference point for its expression of perfectivity [13]. For instance, in (2), 睡觉 *shuìjiào* 'sleep' provides for a reference point within the sentence to denote that the action of 喝酒 *hējiǔ* 'drinking alcohol' is terminated before the subsequent action (that is 睡觉 *shuìjiào* 'sleep').

1. 可是他忘了他的帽子。
   kěshì tā wàng-le tā de màozi
   'But he forgot his hat.' [12]

2. 爷爷喝了酒就睡觉。
   yéyé hē-le jiǔ jiù shuìjiào
   'Grandpa drank some wine, then fell asleep.' [12]

3. 我们吃了饭了。
   wǒmen chī-le fàn le
   'We have already eaten.' [13]

On the other hand, at the sentence-final position, *le* can express a change-of-state [11], a change-of-state *cum* a new situation [1, 7, 14], or a currently-relevant-state [9]. Among these analyses, Li and Thompson's analysis [9] is arguably the most comprehensive as their analysis covers all the various sub-functions that the sentence-final *le* can perform. These sub-functions include: (a) change of state, (b) correcting a wrong assumption, (c) reporting the progress of an action, (d) expressing what happens next and (e) closing a sentence (marker of finality), and in any given context, this sentence-final *le*, also known as the currently-relevant-state *le* (le_{CRS}), can express more than one of these subfunctions at once [9]. As Li et al. [15] point out, le_{CRS} denotes that "a state of affairs has special current relevance to some particular Reference Time", where current is with reference to "the conversational setting in which the speaker and hearer are participating as interlocutors".

Syntactically, le_{CRS} is permitted to occur in places that are considered ungrammatical for le_{PFV}, such as in clauses containing modal verbs and collocates with semantically stative verbs, negation and non-actualized events [12]. However, as opposed to le_{PFV}, le_{CRS} takes its temporal reference from its conversational setting, that is, an external time reference, it cannot occur in a clause that takes a second clause that provides an internal time reference [13]. For instance, while (2) permits the use of le_{PFV} due to the presence of an internal time reference of 睡觉 *shuìjiào* 'sleep', when re-written as (4), the internal time reference causes ungrammaticality. The sentence can only be grammatical after removing the second clause and ending immediately with le_{CRS}.

4. 爷爷喝酒了(*就睡觉)。
   *yéyé hējiǔ le (*jiù shuìjiào)*
   (intended) 'Grandad drank some wine, then fell asleep.'

The le_{CRS} can only occur at the clause-final position should it be concomitantly interpreted with the perfective aspect, as in the first *le* in (5) (marked by the underline), where it occurs at both the verb- and sentence-final positions.

5. 我已经吃<u>了</u>, 别给我做饭了。
   *wǒ yǐjīng chī-**le**, bié gěi wǒ zuò fàn le*
   'I have already eaten, so don't prepare my meal.' [1]

2.2 Singapore Mandarin *liǎo*

According to previous studies, SM *liǎo* differs from MCM *liǎo* in two major ways. First, SM *liǎo* can occur in positions that are ungrammatical for MCM *liǎo*, e.g. in the sentence-final position denoting currently-relevant-state (6). In MCM, 了 must be read as *le* in this position while performing the function of a currently-relevant-state marker (as mentioned in Sect. 2.1).

6. 现在不行了。
   xiànzài bùxíng liǎo
   'It cannot work anymore now.' [3]

Second, SM *liǎo* can occur consecutively with SM *le*, as in (7) and (8), which is only possible in MCM only when used as a verb. This, in particular, points towards the subtle differences that may exist between *liǎo* and *le* in SM due to the acceptability of the co-occurrence.

7. 我问他了了。
   wǒ wèn tā liǎo le
   'I have asked him already.' [3]

8. 还好有 mother 的 license 给我们扣，要不然我的 license 早就 gantung 了了。
   háihǎo yǒu mother *de* license *gěi wǒmen kòu, yàobùrán wǒ de* license *zǎo jiù gantung liǎo le*
   'Thankfully, we have mother's license for the demerit points, if not, mine would have been revoked already.' [5]

Various explanations for this peculiar 'double-了' usage have been given in the literature. On the one hand, Chen [3] argues that the *liǎo* in (7) is a complement expressing the completion of a change of state and is therefore compatible with the sentence-final *le* in the sentence; in her paper, she even rejects the equivalency of *liǎo* to le_{PFV} in these instances. On the other hand, Lua [5] analyzes *liǎo* as a perfective aspect marker as the *liǎo* found in her corpus-based investigation occurs verb-finally; the *le*'s in the sentences are analyzed as le_{CRS} and are therefore compatible with verb-final *liǎo*.

While both explanations seem plausible, neither can fully and clearly account for such occurrences and even present conflicting opinions yet to be resolved. If SM *liǎo* is indeed a complement expressing completion of a change, as Chen [3] puts it, then the difference between complement *liǎo* and le_{PFV} is unclear, since a typical le_{PFV} can also express the completion of a change of state, as in 大了很多 *dà-le hěnduō* 'grew in size by quite a margin'. If SM *liǎo* is indeed a perfective aspect marker, as Lua [5] argues, then it is unclear as to why SM *liǎo* has to co-occur with le_{CRS} when a single sentence-final *le* can take on both the perfective and currently-relevant-state readings. Furthermore, this also contradicts Lua's [5] support of the interchangeability account of *liǎo* and *le*, as *liǎo* can then also take on the roles of $le_{\text{PFV+CRS}}$ in the position in (8) if it were truly interchangeable with *le*. Khoo et al. [6] attempt to resolve these issues by proposing that SM *liǎo* has a third function, which they termed as le_3; their attempt is a parallel of the le_3 account proposed by Shi [16] for the realization aspect marker of *liau* in Southern Min dialects. This proposed le_3 takes a clause as its scope of modification and denotes the termination/completion of the entire event expressed in the clause. Again, this analysis also cannot account accurately for the use of SM *liǎo* as it does not clearly demonstrate the differences between le_3 and the existing analysis of *le* in Mandarin. It is, therefore, necessary to examine SM *liǎo* more closely to identify its functions and constraints.

3 Distributions of SM *liăo*

The distribution patterns of SM *liăo* will be examined in this section using a Spoken Corpus of Singapore Mandarin Variety Shows. This corpus comprises of five Singaporean variety shows aired between 2014 and 2015 and were either talk shows or game shows where the participants engaged in mostly unscripted dialogues. The corpus contains about 0.54 million words. On top of this spoken corpus, a smaller corpus comprising of three interview segments from the Oral History Interviews recorded by National Archives of Singapore was also used in order to capture the speech patterns of an older demographic. The interviewees talked about their personal experiences relating to life in pre-independence Singapore.

4385 instances containing *liăo* and *le* as grammatical particles were identified; of these instances, 449 (10.2%) contained *liăo* and the rest contained *le*. A breakdown is given in Table 1. As seen in Table 1, it is clear that SM *liăo* is used overwhelmingly in the sentence-final position and that a negligible proportion was found to occur in the verb-final position (2.5%). While SM *le* also seems to prefer the sentence-final position (62.1%), the verb-final *le* still occurred at least one-quarter of the time (25.6%), which is a rather sizeable difference from that of verb-final *liăo*.

Table 1. Distributions of liăo and le

Particle	Position	Frequency
le	Verb-final	1014 (25.6%)
	Clause-final	491 (12.2%)
	Sentence-final	2431 (62.1%)
Sub-total		3936 (100%)
liăo	Verb-final	11 (2.5%)
	Clause-final	47 (10.5%)
	Sentence-final	391 (87.0%)
Sub-total		449 (100%)
Total		4,385

In terms of the collocation patterns, it is noted that verb-final *liăo* has only occurred with verbs – a behavior distinct from that of *le* in both MCM and SM, which can occur with both verbs, verb-complement compounds and even adjectives. The clause- and sentence-final *liăo* are relatively less restricted, just like sentence-final *le* in the two varieties of Mandarin in comparison. However, at the clause-final position, SM *liăo* occurs after a verb-object compound and takes a subsequent event in a following clause; this is ungrammatical for MCM *le*, as seen in (4). This suggests a slightly different set of constraints for the use of SM *liăo*, which will be explored in Sect. 4. Another noteworthy observation is that when *liăo* and *le* occur consecutively, *liăo* always precedes *le* – this further shows that there are some inherent distinctions between the two particles that require deeper analysis.

4 Functions and Constraints of SM *liǎo*

Upon examination of the distribution patterns of SM *liǎo* with respect to SM *le*, it seems that SM *liǎo* can perform both of the functions of *le*, that is, it can function as the perfective aspect marker (*liǎo*$_{\mathrm{PFV}}$) and the currently-relevant-state marker (*liǎo*$_{\mathrm{CRS}}$). Due to space constraints, this paper will only briefly discuss *liǎo*$_{\mathrm{CRS}}$ and focus more on the constraints of *liǎo*$_{\mathrm{PFV}}$ as therein lies the most notable differences between *le*$_{\mathrm{PFV}}$ and *liǎo*$_{\mathrm{PFV}}$.

4.1 Currently Relevant State *liǎo*

As the currently-relevant state marker, *liǎo*$_{\mathrm{CRS}}$ is found to occur at the clause- and sentence-final positions, as in (9), and share the constraints of *le*$_{\mathrm{CRS}}$, that is, *liǎo*$_{\mathrm{CRS}}$ cannot occur at the clause-final position unless it is verb-final and interpreted with the perfective aspect, as in (10).

9. 二十四年多了
èrshísì nián duō liǎo
'(It's been) over twenty-four years' [17]

10. 它转了, 然后停了你才搅
tā zhuǎn liǎo, ránhòu tíng-le nǐ cái jiǎo
'You only stir after it has spun and stopped' [17]

Some studies have attempted to explain the differences between the sentence-final *le* and *liǎo*; for instance, Lee and Cheong [18] suggest that the difference is pragmatic, where *liǎo* carries the emotive weight of the speaker (in particular, of the speaker's negativity) while *le* is more neutral. Lim [19], on the other hand, suggests that sentence-final *liǎo* simply emphasizes the emotions of the speaker. However, in this particular study, no such differences were found when examining the occurrences of *liǎo* in SM.

4.2 Perfective *liǎo*

As a perfective aspect marker, SM *liǎo*$_{\mathrm{PFV}}$ can be found in the sentence-medial position and occurs verb-finally, as in (11). It shares the constraints of *le*$_{\mathrm{PFV}}$, that is, there must be a constituent that intervenes between the verb-*liǎo* compound and the end of the clause.

11. 他们走了之后, 我们会从新再check过
tāmen zǒu-liǎo zhīhòu, wǒmen huì cóngxīn zài check *guò*
'We will check again after they have left.' [17]

However, this is a relatively rare occurrence in SM, occurring only 5 out of 449 instances (1.11%). Even in double-*le* sentences, such as (12), the verb-final 了 is never read as *liǎo* but as *le*.

12. 等了五六下了，还等一下
*děng le/*liǎo wǔ liù xià le/liǎo, hái děng yīxià*
'(I've) waited for a long time, (you still want me) to wait a while more?'

Instead, it is observed that *liǎo*$_{\text{PFV}}$ occurs more often in the clause-final position, following verbs, adjectival predicatives and verbal compounds – the most distinct features of this peculiar use of clause-final *liǎo* (hereafter as 'SM clause-final *liǎo*'). This case can be the most clearly illustrated using examples where SM clause-final *liǎo* occurs after a verb-object compound at the end of the first clause (13).

13. 洗脚了才穿
*xǐ jiǎo *le/liǎo cái chuān*
'Wear (shoes) only after washing legs.' [20]

Analysing SM clause-final *liǎo* as a perfective aspect maker can also resolve the case of consecutive 了's in SM. As seen in (14), if we were to re-write it as (15), there is no observable difference in the meaning conveyed in both sentences – the water has still flowed from the inside to the outside and this event is terminated.

14. 刚才那个水流出去了了
gāngcái nàgè shuǐliú chūqù liǎo le
'The water has flowed out just now.' [17]

15. 刚才那个水流了出去了
gāngcái nàgè shuǐliú-le chūqù le
'The water has flowed out just now.'

At this point, it is essential to first explain why this analysis for SM clause-final *liǎo* is made. First, looking at the distributions, collocations, and behaviors of SM clause-final *liǎo*, it is clear that this particle differs from *le*$_{\text{CRS}}$ both syntactically and functionally. In all instances of SM clause-final *liǎo*, it is not found to occur with semantically stative verbs and negation and it takes an internal time reference, such as that in (13). Second, like *le*$_{\text{PFV}}$, SM clause-final *liǎo* presents the event as a whole that is temporally-bounded, that is, the events must contain a possibility of termination or completion. Third, like *le*$_{\text{PFV}}$, it cannot exist in an independent clause unless interpreted as *liǎo*$_{\text{PFV+CRS}}$, as in (16).

16. 洗脚了
*xǐ jiǎo *liǎo*$_{PFV}$*/liǎo*$_{PFV+CRS}$
'I have washed (my legs) already.'

Fourth, the perfective aspect interpretation of SM clause-final *liǎo* has historic roots. As Mei [19] notes in the Bianwen texts from the 8th to the 10th Century, the construction verb-object-*liǎo*, as in (17), was a very common construction. The construction is also very similar to that presented in (13).

17. 领吾言了便须行
LING WU YAN LIAO BIAN XU XING
'(You) have to practice after (you) understood what I said.' [21]

The Bianwen *liǎo* expresses a meaning similar to le_{PFV} and is typically used in the first clause of a sentence; it is also never used in the sentence-medial, verb-final position [19]. Given the similarities between Bianwen *liǎo* and SM *liǎo*, this paper has reason to believe that the SM *liǎo* is historically linked to the pre-phonetically eroded form of 了. The retention of this syntactic distribution remains to be explored though – it may be a result of language contact with local dialects such as Hokkien and Hakka, where a cognate of *liǎo* is used to mark the perfective aspect (see [22, 23] for Hokkien and [24] for Singapore Hakka). The analysis of SM clause-final *liǎo* as a perfective aspect marker with roots in historical developments of Mandarin is more comprehensive than [3, 5, 6] – not only does the analysis provide a clearer set of criteria for identifying its function, but it can also account for more of the unique uses of SM *liǎo*, particularly in its co-occurrence with the sentence-final le_{CRS}, as in (18).

18. 对，就是它了了
duì, jiùshì tā liǎo le
'Yes, that is the thing (that we are going to select)' [17]

According to Chen [3], *liǎo* in (15) will be considered a complement signaling the completion of the change of state. While it does signal completion of the change from not selecting the thing to selecting it, *liǎo*, in this case, cannot be analyzed as a complement – the immediate word preceding it is a noun, a word class that does not take complements. This implies while in more typical situations where *liǎo* follows a verb or verbal compound, a complement analysis is feasible, such an analysis is insufficient for all instances; the aspectual analysis as provided in this paper can be a possible resolution to this problem. While Lua [5] has also analyzed the *liǎo* co-occurring with *le* as a perfective aspect marker, it was applied only to those occurring with verbs and would not be able to determine the functions of *liǎo* in instances like in (15). Finally, in Khoo et al. [6], the SM clause-final *liǎo* and the *liǎo* co-occurring with *le* were given separate treatments and while the latter was analyzed as a perfective aspect marker, no explanations were given to why this could have been the case. The combined treatment of the SM clause-final *liǎo* and the *liǎo* co-occurring with *le* provides both a clearer determination of *liǎo*'s functions and a possible explanation for the co-occurrence with le_{CRS}.

The last issue with this analysis is that if, as given in Sect. 4.1, *liǎo* can perform the roles of both le_{CRS} and $le_{PFV+CRS}$, then the co-occurring 了's seems to be redundant. This paper follows from Khoo et al.'s [6] postulation that such a use arose as a result of a failure in combining the two 了's due to the difference in pronunciation. In MCM, when both le_{PFV} and le_{CRS} are used, the two are combined into one due to their identical pronunciations [7]. However, in the case of SM, the two 了's are read differently and therefore fail to combine. This is a less preferred usage, as can be seen from the corpus data – when both the perfective and currently-relevant readings have to be expressed, 158 of 449 instances (35.2%) shows that only a single *liǎo* is used, as opposed to the 10 out of 449 (2.2%) for the co-occurring 了's.

5 Conclusion

In sum, this paper has presented the two functions of SM *liǎo* that is not permitted in MCM, with a more comprehensive account of its distributions, constraints and possible origins. The previously unaccounted phenomenon has been addressed, and cloudy analysis tidied up, providing for a clearer picture of the usage of SM *liǎo*. This paper has shown that the le_{CRS} is quite likely to have developed out of *liǎo*, given the very similar pathways of development (c.f. [2] and other scholars who claim that the lexical source for le_{CRS} is 来 'to come', another common source for inchoatives and perfects), though nothing is conclusive at the moment. Further studies can be conducted to investigate why the pronunciation for *liǎo* is maintained, despite the pressure from the pronunciation of *le* that co-exists in SM. Chinese dialects, such as Min, Hakka, and Cantonese, can be explored as possible sources for the existence of *liǎo* in SM. A more in-depth analysis of sentence-final *le* and *liǎo* can also be conducted to investigate the differences between the two. Not only can this answer the question of why these two variants co-exist in SM, it can also shed light on why only the order of *liǎo le* and not *le liǎo* is possible.

References

1. Lü, S.: Eight Hundred Words in Modern Chinese (Reprinted) (in Chinese). Commercial Press, Beijing (2015)
2. Wang, L.: A History of Chinese Language (Reprinted) (in Chinese). Zhonghua Book Company, Beijing (2004)
3. Chen, C.: Grammatical features of Singapore Chinese (in Chinese). Stud. Lang. Linguist. **1**, 138–152 (1986)
4. Chew, C., Zhou, C.: Minnanese and Chinese in Singapore (in Chinese). http://www.huayuqiao.org/articles/zhouqinghai/zhouqh04.htm. Accessed 25 Dec 2017
5. Lua, Y.W.: The le-particle in Singapore Mandarin (in Chinese). B.A. thesis, Nanyang Technological University (2014)
6. Khoo, Y.K., Lin, J., Luke, K.K.: A spoken-corpus-based study of 了*le/liǎo* in Singapore Mandarin Chinese. In: International Symposium on Chinese in the Maritime Silk Road, Hong Kong (2017)
7. Zhu, D.: Lectures on Grammar (in Chinese). Commercial Press, Beijing (1982)
8. Chao, Y.: A Grammar of Spoken Chinese. University of California Press, Berkeley (1968)
9. Li, C.N., Thompson, S.A.: Mandarin Chinese. University of California Press, Berkeley (1981)
10. Chappell, H.: Towards a typology of aspect in Sinitic languages. In: Chinese Languages and Linguistics: Chinese Dialects, pp. 66–106. Academia Sinica, Taipei (1992)
11. Xiao, R., McEnery, T.: Aspect in Mandarin Chinese: A Corpus-Based Study. John Benjamins, Amsterdam (2004)
12. Chappell, H.: Aspectually-bounded structures in the Chinese Pear stories: the two le's in Chinese: a case of homonymy, polysemy or neither? In: Burridge, K., McGregor, W. (eds.) La Trobe Working Papers in Linguistics, pp. 107–134. La Trobe University, Melbourne (1988)
13. Guo, R.: Time reference and its syntactic effects in Mandarin Chinese (in Chinese). Chin. Teach. World **29**(4), 434–449 (2015)

14. Yue, A.O.: Chinese dialects: grammar. In: Thurgood, G., LaPolla, R.J. (eds.) The Sino-Tibetan Languages, pp. 84–125. Routledge, London (2003)
15. Li, C.N., Thompson, S.A., Thompson, R.M.: The discourse motivation for the perfect aspect: the Mandarin particle LE. In: Hopper, P.J. (ed.) Tense-Aspect: Between Semantics & Pragmatics, pp. 19–44. John Benjamins, Amsterdam (1982)
16. Shi, Q.: Liao (了) in Minnan dialect that expressing the realization aspect (in Chinese). Linguist. Sci. **13**(3), 252–267 (2014)
17. Spoken Corpus of Singapore Mandarin Variety Shows (2016)
18. Lee, C.L., Cheong, Z.A.: Pragmatics of liao in Singapore Mandarin. In: 17th Annual Meeting of the International Association of Chinese Linguistics, Paris (2009)
19. Lim, W.Y.: "le" and "liao" in Singapore Mandarin (in Chinese). B.A. thesis, National University of Singapore (2016)
20. National Archives of Singapore: Oral History Interviews (2018)
21. Mei, T.-L.: The origins of the modern Chinese perfective construction and the suffix le (in Chinese). Stud. Lang. Linguist. **1**, 65–77 (1981)
22. Li, R.: Structural particles in Southern Min dialects (in Chinese). Stud. Lang. Linguist. **2**, 48–56 (2001)
23. Ng, L.S.: A study on replacing le with liǎo in Malaysia Mandarin (in Chinese). J. Yangtze Univ. (Soc. Sci.) **36**(7), 99–100 (2013)
24. Chin, S.Y.: A study of Hakka dialect in Singapore and Johor Bahru. M.A. thesis, Nanyang Technological University (2001)

The Conventional Implicature of $Dōu_b(Dōu_2, Dōu_3)$: On Semantics of $Dōu_b$ from the Perspective of Discourse Analysis

Hua Zhong(✉)

Overseas Education College of Fujian Normal University, Fuzhou, China
jtingshan@163.com

Abstract. In existing studies *dōu*$_b$ *(dōu*$_2$, *dōu*$_3$*)* is a polarity-marker and a universal quantifier which sometimes expresses having done or been and has an emphatic function. This paper argues that marking-a-polarity, universal quantification and expressing having done or been are all conversational implicatures or context meanings of *dōu*$_b$ sentences. And as a kind of generalized conversational implicature the emphatic function which belongs to *dōu*$_b$ construction is drawing from a plausible inference. But it is not the conventional meaning of *dōu*$_b$. The conventional implicature of *dōu*$_b$ indicates that the speaker has made a judgment on the state of affairs described by a proposition, and he/she believes that the possibility of the state of affairs is inferior-to-expectation (or normal). As a kind of rule meaning it is a non-truth conditional, procedural and pragmatic meaning. But it is different from an ordinary rule meaning that is an explicit, literal, objective and truth conditional meaning because it is subjective, non-truth conditional and implicit. And it is different from a conversational implicature because it is non-cancellable.

Keywords: *Dōu*$_b$ · Conventional implicature · Subjective
Non-truth conditional · Implicit

1 Introduction: About the Semantic Classification of the Adverb *Dōu*

About *dōu*'s semantics, the current representative Chinese grammar works, for example that written by Ding [1], Lü [2], mostly think *dōu* has three kinds of meanings and usages (hereafter called *Trichotomy*):*dōu*$_1$ (indicates totality), *dōu*$_2$ [equivalently *shenzhi* (even)], and *dōu*$_3$ [equivalently *yijing* (already)], for example:

(1) Yitian gongfu ba zhexie shi dou banwanle
One-day time let these things all finish-Asp
All of these things were done in one day. (*dōu*$_1$)

(2) Lian ge renying'er dou kanbujian
Including one-Cl figure even unseen
Even a single one cannot be found. (*dōu*$_2$)

(3) Fan dou liang le, kuai chi ba!
Dinner already cold-Asp, hurry eat-Asp
The dinner already got cold, just have it! (*dōu*$_3$)

J.-F. Hong et al. (Eds.): CLSW 2018, LNAI 11173, pp. 44–60, 2018.
https://doi.org/10.1007/978-3-030-04015-4_4

Nonetheless, there also were many scholars having different opinions on this.

Some scholars thought, the adverb *dōu* has only one meaning and usage, i.e. *totalizing* (or *a Universal Quantifier*) (hereafter called *univocal*), such as Chieko Nakagawa [3], Lee [4], Gao [5, 6], Chiu [7, 8], Lin [9], Cheng [10], Ren [11], Lin [12], Jiang [13, 14], Wu [15], Dong [16], Pan [17], Yuan [18], Jiang and Pan [19] and etc.

Recently, more and more scholars, including me, have advocated the dichotomy of the adverb *dōu* (hereafter called *Dichotomy*), i.e. *Dōu*$_a$(*dōu*$_1$) and *dōu*$_b$ (*dōu*$_2$, *dōu*$_3$) (For the convenience of discussion, hereafter *dōu*$_1$ is referred to as *dōu*$_a$, *dōu*$_2$ and *dōu*$_3$ are *dōu*$_b$), such as Wang [20–22], Jiang [23], Xiao [24], Xu andYang [25], Zhang [26], Zhang [27], Xu [28] etc.

A major reason for divergences of the classifications of the adverb *dōu* is these different understandings of the semantic function of *dōu*$_b$. *Trichotomy* describes *dōu*$_2$ as *shenzhi* (even), and *dōu*$_3$ as *yijing* (already). This Chinese analytical description of synonyms is simple, convenient and intuitive, but also relatively vague. There is no problem using *totalizing* to indicate diachronic link between *dōu*$_a$ and *dōu*$_b$, but using *univocal* to define synchronic relation between them is inattentive.

And the established *Dichotomy*, on the one hand, describes the basic semantic function of *dōu*$_b$ in almost the same way as *Univocal*: *dōu*$_b$ (*dōu*$_2$, *dōu*$_3$) uses the means of *biaoju jiduan* (marking a polarity) *jianjie biao quanliang* (to indicates totality indirectly), such as Jiang [23], Zhang [27] etc. On the other hand, the explanation of *dōu*$_b$'s emphatic sense is also not clear, accurate, and uniform enough. For example, Wang [22] thought *dōu*$_2$, *dōu*$_3$ were emphatic modal particles, whose role in a sentence was to emphasize an unusual situation. Jiang [23] thought *dōu*$_2$, *dōu*$_3$ indicated totality through marking a polarity, and also reflected a mood of speaker, which was a modal adverb. Zhang [26] claimed that *dōu*$_2$ was a modal adverb to emphasize a subjective modality, and actually so-called *dōu*$_3$ was a special usage of the modal adverb *dōu*$_2$. And Zhang [27] thought that it was emphasizing a polarity, and etc. So the established *Dichotomy* is not successful, which still needs a further *Dichotomy*. And its primary task is just to clarify semantic and pragmatic functions of *dōu*$_b$.

The objective reason for divergences of understandings of *dōu*$_b$'s semantic function is that *dōu*$_b$ doesn't have a truth-value of semantics, but has a non-truth-value procedural pragmatic meaning. So it is unrealistic and intangible, and hard to define. The subjective reason mainly lies in that most existing literature were written in term of truth-value semantics, constrained by describing the ideational function of *dōu*$_b$. For example, *dōu*$_b$ was still described as *zongkuo* (totalizing) and *dōu*$_3$ as *yijing* (already) etc., which ignored the examination of its interpersonal function and textual function. And most of them were limited to investigate a sentence statically and independently at the syntactic and semantic level, which ignored the analysis of dynamic discourses at the pragmatic-cognitive level. And the previous studies were mainly stuck to the Componential Modal (see also Liu [29]), which easily led to confusions of the semantic and pragmatic functions of the construction or other ingredients in the construction with *dōu*$_b$, as well as inaccurate and incomplete reviews on the semantic and pragmatic functions of *dōu*$_b$.

Therefore, on the basis of investigating a large number of real corpora, referring to the discourse marker theory (see Blakemore [30], Schiffrin [31], and others), the three meta-functions theory of functional linguistics(see Halliday [32, 33]), and the construction grammar theory, this article tries to have a dynamic discourse analysis of semantic function of *dōu*$_b$ from the pragmatic and cognitive level, and to review the various views on the semantic function of *dōu*$_b$ in the existing literature, and to re-examine the semantic function of *dōu*$_b$. It is hoped that the semantic features of *dōu*$_b$ (*dōu*$_2$, *dōu*$_3$) and its construction are explained in a unified and intuitive way.

2 To Review the Various Views on the Semantic Function of *Dōu*$_b$ in the Existing Literature

2.1 As for the Semantic Function of *Dōu*$_b$, There Are Three Main Viewpoints in the Existing Literature

First, some scholars thought, *dōu*$_b$ meant *totalizing*. The descriptions on *dōu*$_b$ semantic function from *Univocal* and *Dichotomy* are basically the same. *Dōu*$_b$ (*dōu*$_2$, *dōu*$_3$) uses the means of *biaoju jiduan* (marking polarity) to indirectly indicate totality, such as Jiang [13, 14], Jiang [23], Zhang [27] etc.

Second, although there are great differences in understanding the semantic function of *dōu*$_b$, and the definitions of *dōu*$_b$'s emphatic sense are not consistent, all scholars think that *dōu*$_b$ has an emphatic sense, such as Lü [2], Jiang [13], Wang [20–22], Jiang [23], Xu and Yang [25], Zhang [26], Zhang [27] etc.

Third, many scholars also believe that *dōu*$_b$ (*dōu*$_3$) is a temporal adverb which expresses having done or been, such as Lü [2], Xing [34], Ma [35], and *the Contemporary Chinese Dictionary* (7th Edition, 2016:315). And some scholars thought, *dōu*$_b$ (*dōu*$_3$) expresses both the two grammatical meanings of time and mood, such as Guo [36], Xu and Yang [25] etc.

Therefore, before defining the semantic function of *dōu*$_b$, we must first discuss whether *dōu*$_b$ is a polarity-marker and a universal quantifier, and whether *dōu*$_b$ expresses having done or been and has an emphatic function.

2.2 Whether *Dōu*$_b$ Is a Polarity-Marker and a Universal Quantifier

Many of *dōu*$_b$ sentences really describe a polarity, for example:

(4) Zhongguoren lian si dou bu pa, hai pa kunnan ma?
Chinese including death DOU don't afraid still afraid difficulty Q
The Chinese even are not afraid of death. Are they afraid of difficulties?

(5) Meitian cihou ni, yiju haohua dou debudao
Everyday serve you, one-sentence words-of-praise even can't-get
I can't get any words of praise from you, although I serve you every day.

(6) Jiujiu shi zhongguotong, bi shangdi dou geng liaojie zhongguoren.
Uncle is china-hand, than God even more know Chinese people
My uncle is a China hand, who understands Chinese better than God.

(7) Ayi, dou baitian le, zenme hai you yueliang ya?
Aunt already daylight LE, why still there-is moon Q
My aunt, it has been already daylight. Why is there the moon still?

Sentence (4) says that Chinese are not afraid of anything, including the most feared death. Sentence (5) says that he had not gotten words of praise, even one word. Sentence (6) says that his uncle is the best who understands Chinese, even better than God. In sentence (7) the speaker expressed his confusion on the appearance of the moon during the day when it was least likely to appear. And that is probably why there are so many scholars in the literature, who thought that $dōu_b$ used the means of *biaoju jiduan* (marking a polarity) to indicate totality indirectly.

But we also find that a lot of $dōu_b$ sentences do not necessarily describe a polarity, for example:

(8) Buyao shuo bieren le, jiu lian yixie qinqi ye dou shi lengmo
Don't say others LE, only including some relatives also DOU are indifferent
rushuang.
like-frost
Don't say others, even some relatives are indifferent like frost.

(9) Zhong Wan yidu lian ta dadianhua dou bujie, shenzhi youshi
Zhong Wan once including he telephone even not answer, even sometime
zudang ta jin jihua-ke.
block him enter planning-department
Zhong Wan once didn't answer his telephone, and even sometimes blocked him from entering the office of the planning department.

(10) Zhexie hua zhiguan fengzhang, jiushi bu jian kaihua. Qiao, ta zhang de bi
These flower simply overgrow, but not see to flower. Look, it grow DE than
ren dou gao le.
person even high LE.
These flowers are just overgrowing, but not flowering. Look, it's taller than one person.

(11) Zhe zhang xiao bandeng xianzai hai mei sanjia, dou ershi duo nian le.
This CL small bench now still not fall-apart, DOU twenty more year LE
This small bench hasn't been broken yet, for more than twenty years.

In sentence (8) we can see that on the pragmatic scale of the impossibility of being indifferent like frost, some relatives are not the extreme compared with the family members. It can also be said that some relatives and even the family members are indifferent like frost. Sentence (9) also tells us that it was extremer that Zhong Wan blocked him from entering the office of the planning department, although he once didn't answer his telephone. In sentence (10–11) *being taller than one person* and *twenty years* are not necessarily polar components. And subjectively, speakers do not necessarily think that they are extreme. For example, in the speaker's mind it is very clear that the little bench might have lasted longer.

In addition, some scholars argued that *Lian* sentence in Mandarin Chinese does not necessarily have the semantic function of marking a polarity[1], such as Zhang [37], Liu [29], Jiang [14]. This is also a support for the idea that $dōu_b$ does not mark a polarity.

[1] I think this view is about the same thing with my idea that $dōu_b$ sentences do not necessarily mark a polarity. Limited to space, no expansion.

Furthermore, in Mandarin Chinese *shenzhi* has the semantic function of marking a polarity (see also Hou [38]). For example:

(12) Ta shifen jusang, wanfen de jusang, shenzhi youxie qingshi ziji.
He very depressed, very-much DE depressed, even somewhat despise himself
He is very depressed, very much depressed, even somewhat despises himself.

The corpora show that the use of *shenzhi* with $d\bar{o}u_b$ is very common. Such as:

(13) Ta yi buneng lengjing zhunque heli de jinxing siwei, ta shenzhi
He already cannot calmly accurately reasonably DE proceed think, he even
dou mei longqing jiujing chu le shenme shi
DOU not make-clear on-earth happen LE what event
He was unable to think calmly, accurately, reasonably, he didn't even know what had happened.

(14) Jinguan wo liu de hanshui bi lianzhang Liang Sanxi, shenzhi
In-spite-of I flow DE sweat than company-commander Liang Sanxi, even
bi zhanshi Duan Yuguo dou yao shao de duo, dan wode
than soldier Duan Yuguo DOU likely less DE very-much, but my
junzhuang ye shi tiantian shilulu mei gan guo.
military-uniform also be everyday wet not dry GUO
Although I sweat less than the company commander Liang Sanxi very much, even less than the soldier Duan Yuguo, but my military uniform was wet every day.

In these sentences if $d\bar{o}u_b$ marked a polarity, then it was bound to cause a semantic duplication. But these sentences have no sense of semantic duplication. There are some extreme situations in specific contexts indeed, but not all. This also seems to prove that $d\bar{o}u_b$ does not mark a polarity.

Since $d\bar{o}u_b$ does not have the semantic function of marking a polarity, then from a certain scale in the middle of a pragmatic scale, naturally it is impossible to derive an implicit set of universal quantities, nor to provide a quantified object for an all-inclusive total quantification. So $d\bar{o}u_b$ has not the semantic function of a universal quantification.

Moreover, although $dōu_b$ sentences do have some cases in which an implicit total-set can be derived by a pragmatic inference, for example:

(15) Pingri Yuqing sao shi lian yige haozi dou shebude
Ordinary-days Yuqing sister-in-law is including one-CL penny DOU grudge
yong de.
use DE
In ordinary days the sister-in-law Yuqing is even reluctant to use a penny.

(16) Fanzheng ni dui sheide hua dou ting, youqi Zhao xinmei de hua bi
Anyhow you to whose words all listen, specially Zhao xinmei DE words than
shengzhi dou ling, jiushi wode hua bu ting
imperial-edict DOU effective just my words not listen
Anyway, you listen to anyone, especially Zhao Xinmei whose words are more effective than an imperial edict. But you just don't listen to me.

(17) Ji jie-le-men'r, you zheng le qian, zhe haoshi wo xiang dou xiang
Both divert-oneself, and make LE money, this good-thing I think DOU think
bu lai ne!
not come NE
Not only to divert oneself (from boredom), but also to make money. AlthoughI am looking forward to this kind of good thing, I can't get it.

Sentence (15) says that in ordinary days the sister-in-law Yuqing is even reluctant to use any money including a penny. Sentence (16) says that the words of Zhao Xinmei are more effective than anyone's including an imperial edict. Sentence (17) says that I can't get this kind of good thing in any way including looking forward to. But $dōu_b$ sentences also have many cases in which there is an incomplete set, for example:

(18) Lian yeye dou qu le, ni hai bu qu.
Including grandpa DOU go LE, ni still not go
Even grandpa has gone, you don't go yet.

(19) Xianzai wo lai le, lian Cao daren Feng daren dou lai le,
Now I come LE, including Cao Lord Feng Lord DOU come LE,
ta Diao Guangdou weisha hai bu loumian.
He Diao Guangdou why still not appear
Now I have come, even Lord Cao and Lord Feng have come, why does not Diao Guangdou he appear yet.

(20) Jinguan lian bairen dou bu gan chengren huo xinfeng zhe yi
Though including the-white-race DOU not dare admit or believe-in this one
sixiang, ta que ganyu tichang.
idea, he but dare-to advocate
Although even the whites did not dare to admit or believe in this idea, but he dared to advocate it.

In these sentences, the total set implied in the clause *Lian X Dou Y* has been eliminated by the following clause. Obviously, the total set implied in the clause *Lian X Dou Y* can be eliminated in a certain context. Hence some implicit total sets and universal quantifications in *dōu*$_b$ sentences are just the conversational implicature and the context meaning of these *dōu*$_b$ sentences, rather than the conventional implicature and the context-free meaning of *dōu*$_b$.

And syntactically, *dōu*$_b$ can't be used in conjunction with words corresponding to the meaning of total quantity like *dōu*$_a$. Such as *dōu*$_a$ can be used in conjunction with an universal or total constituent in a sentence, for instance, *suoyou*(all) + NP, *quan* (whole) + NP, *mei*(every) + NP, *yiqie*(all), *dajia*(everyone), *daochu*(allover), *chuchu* (everywhere), *renren*(everybody), *jiajia* (every family) …… and so on. Before *dōu*$_a$ *quan*(whole), *yiban*(generally), *dabufen*(most), *yizhi* (at all times), *conglai*(all long), *xianglai*(all the time) and so on can respectively be used as a modifier. But these can't be used before *dōu*$_b$. For example:

(21) Suoyou de ren dōu$_a$ shi duanxiu baoshan, weidu Yuanjian shi quanfu
All DE person all are short-sleeve thin-shirt, only Yuanjian is full
junzhuang.
military-uniform
Everyone was dressed in short sleeves and thin shirts. Only Yuanjian was in a full military uniform.
→*(Lian) Suoyou de ren dōu$_b$ shi duanxiu baoshan,
(including) all DE person dōu$_b$ are short-sleeve thin-shirt
*Everyone *dōu*$_b$ was dressed in short sleeves and thin shirts.

(22) Quanjiaren dōu$_a$ huainian ta zunjing ta zhuidao ta
Whole-family all miss her respect her mourn-for her
The whole family missed her, respected her, and mourned for her
→*(Lian) Quanjiaren dōu$_b$ huainian ta zunjing ta zhuidao ta
(including)Whole-family dōu$_b$ miss her respect her mourn-for her
*The whole family *dōu*$_b$ missed her, respected her, and mourned for her

(23) Mei zhou dōu$_a$ you liangfeng xin yueguo Changjiang he Hanshui,
Every week all have two-CL letter cross Yangtze and Hanshui,
Every week, there are two letters crossing the Yangtze River and Hanshui River.
→*(Lian) Mei zhou dōu$_b$ you liangfeng xin yueguo Changjiang he Hanshui
(including)Every week dōu$_b$ have two-CL letter cross Yangtze and Hanshui,
*Every week, there dōu$_b$ are two letters crossing the Yangtze River and Hanshui River.

(24) Yiqie dōu$_a$ turan biande wutouwuxu, wuyiwukao, shiren gandao
Everything all suddenly become disorder, helpless, make-one feel
wangranshicuo.
panic-and-don't-know-how-to-deal-with-it
Everything suddenly became disorder and helpless, and this made us feel panic and don't know how to deal with it
→*(Lian) Yiqie dōu$_b$ turan biande wutouwuxu,
(including) Everything dōu$_b$ suddenly become disorder,
*Everything *dōu*$_b$ suddenly become disorder,

(25) Dajia dōu$_a$ guli ta,
Everyone all encourage her.
Everyone encouraged her.
→*(Lian) Dajia dōu$_b$ guli ta,
(including) Everyone dōu$_b$ encourage her.
*Everyone *dōu*$_b$ encouraged her.

(26) Huxiang guli de shengyin daochu dōu$_a$ keyi tingjian.
Mutual encourage DE voice everywhere all can hear
The voice of mutual encouragement can be heard everywhere.
→*(Lian) Huxiang guli de shengyin daochu dōu$_b$ keyi tingjian.
(including) mutual encourage DE voice everywhere dōu$_b$ can hear
*The voice of mutual encouragement *dōu*$_b$ can be heard everywhere.

(27) Zhege daoli bu shi renren dōu$_a$ nenggou zhenzheng de dongde de.
This-CL truth not is everyone all can truly DE understand DE
This truth is not something anyone can truly understand.
→* (Lian) renren dōu$_b$ nenggou zhenzheng de dongde de.
(including) everyone dōu$_b$ can truly DE understand DE
*Everyone *dōu*$_b$ can truly understand it.

(28) Jiajia dōu$_a$ wei tamen fuqi dakailüdeng
Every-family all for them couple give-a-green-light
Every family gave a green light for the couple.
→* (Lian) Jiajia dōu$_b$ wei tamen fuqi dakailüdeng
(including) Every-family dōu$_b$ for them couple give-a-green-light.
*Every family *dōu*$_b$ gave a green light for the couple

(29) Gangcai nagu qi, yixiazijiu quan dōu$_a$ (*dōu$_b$) xiao le.
Just-now that-CL anger, atonce completely all (*dōu$_b$) disappear LE
The anger just now disappeared all (**dōu*$_b$) at once.

(30) Yiban dōu$_a$ (*dōu$_b$) shi zuo zhangfu de qinzi chuma.
Usually all (*dōu$_b$) is as husband DE personally confront-the-enemy
It's usually (**dōu*$_b$) done by the husband himself.

(31) Yewan, cun li ren dabufen dōu$_a$ (*dōu$_b$) shuijiao le.
Night, village inside people most all (*dōu$_b$) sleep LE
At night, most of the villagers (**dōu*$_b$) went to bed.

(32) Ta yizhi dōu$_a$zai nuli
He at-all-times all (*dōu$_b$) in-effort
He is always (**dōu*$_b$) working hard.

(33) Xinghao zhe zhong shi conglai dōu$_a$ (*dōu$_b$) meiyou fasheng guo.
Fortunately, this kind thing all-long all (*dōu$_b$) not happen GUO
Fortunately, this kind of thing never (**dōu*$_b$) happened.

And $dōu_a$ sentences can answer some questions, but $dōu_b$ sentences can't answer them. For instance:

(34) Zhe ge ren xianglai $dōu_a$ zheme yu.
This CL person all-the-time all (*$dōu_b$) so pedantic
This man has always (*$dōu_b$) been so pedantic.

(35) Q: a. Tamen ban you-duo-shao tongxue kaoshang le yanjiusheng?
Their class how-many classmate be-enrolled LE postgraduate
How many students in their class have been enrolled in postgraduate students?

A: b. Quanban $dōu_a$ kaoshang le.
The-whole-class all be-enrolled LE
The whole class have been enrolled in.

A: *c.(Lian) Chengji zuicha de Li Ming $dōu_b$ kaoshang le,
(including) grade worst DE Li Ming $dōu_b$ be-enrolled LE
Even Li Ming, who has the worst grades, has been enrolled in.

→c_1. (Lian) Chengji zuicha de Li Ming $dōu_b$ kaoshang le,
(including) grade worst DE Li Ming $dōu_b$ be-enrolled LE
quanban $dōu_a$ kaoshang le.
the-whole-class all be-enrolled LE
Even Li Ming, who has the worst grades, has been enrolled in a postgraduate student, and the whole class have been enrolled in.

→? *c_2. (Lian) Chengji zuicha de Li Ming$dōu_b$ kaoshang le, keshi haiyou
(including) grade worst DE Li Ming$dōu_b$be-enrolled LE, but also
ji wei xuexi jiaohao de mei kaoshang
sveral CL study better DE not be-enrolled
Even Li Ming, who has the worst grades, has been enrolled in a post-graduate student. However, there were several other students, who had better grades, have failed be enrolled in.

In example (35) sentence *a* can be answered with sentence *b*, but cannot be answered with sentence *c*. The reason is that in addition to sentence *c* itself is difficult to form a sentence, the situation of sentence *c* into a sentence is not certain, there may be sentence c_1, c_2 and so on. Although sentence c_1 can be used to answer sentence *a*, but the real answer to sentence *a* is still the clause *the whole class have been enrolled in*. And sentence *a* cannot be answered with sentence c_2.

The above facts also show intuitively that $dōu_b$ has not the semantic function of a universal quantification.

2.3 Whether *$Dōu_b$($Dōu_3$)* Expresses *Having Done or Been*

The *Trichotomy* describes $dōu_3$ as *yijing*(Already). This view still has a great influence, and is generally used in the current grammar works and dictionaries, such as *the Contemporary Chinese Dictionary* (7th Edition, 2016:315). Many scholars also believe that $dōu_b$($dōu_3$) is a temporal adverb which expresses *having done or been*, such as Ma [35].

And some scholars thought, *dōu*$_b$(*dōu*$_3$) expressed both the two grammatical meanings of time and mood, such as Guo [36], Xu & Yang [25] etc.

Then, whether *dōu*$_b$(*dōu*$_3$) expresses *having done or been*? About this question, Zhang [26] has already argued and pointed out clearly that *dōu* is a modal adverb emphasizing the subjective modality, not a time adverb expressing a tense and an aspect, and the meaning of *having done or been* is mainly expressed by the tense auxiliary *le* in *dōu* XP *le* structure. The view of Li [39] is similar to this. We basically agree with the view of them. But we have found that although the eventuality in most of *dōu* XP *le* sentences is already so, the eventuality in some *dōu* XP *le* sentences is before it happens. For example:

(36) Mingtian zenme cheng, mingtian wo dou dao Shanghai le.
Tomorrow how be-able, tomorrow I DOU arrive Shanghai LE
How can I do tomorrow? I will have already arrived in Shanghai tomorrow.

Therefore, the meaning of *having done or been* in most of *dōu* XP *le* sentences is just a temporary, concomitant pragmatic function with a higher pragmatic frequency. And this is a conversational implicature and a context meaning, but not the conventional implicature of *dōu*$_b$.

2.4 Whether *Dōu*$_b$ Has an Emphatic Sense

In the existing literature, it is a consensus that *dōu*$_b$ has an emphatic sense. And indeed all *dōu*$_b$ sentences have a certain emphatic sense. For example:

(37) Zhe yi ma, bian ma chu weiguanzhe de buping lai le,
This one abuse, then abuse out onlooker DE discontent come LE
Lian xiaoxuesheng dou juede bugongping.
including pupil DOU feel unfair
Onlookers were discontent against this abuse, even pupils felt unfair.

(38) Wo chouyan de lishi bi ni nianling dou chang,
I smoke DE history than your age DOU long
nahuier tiantian kaihui tiantian xun, jiu hui le.
that time everyday attend-conferences everyday scent-smoking, then learn LE
My smoking history is longer than your age. During that period of time I attended conferences and scented smoking every day, then learned to smoke.

(39) Zhe zhang xiao bandeng xianzai hai mei sanjia, dou ershi duo nian le.
This CL small bench now still not fall-apart, DOU twenty more year LE
This small bench hasn't been broken yet, for more than twenty years.

Sentences (37–39) respectively emphasize something: it is very obvious that this abuse was unfair, it is a long history that I have been smoking, and the small bench is very strong. But we think that this kind of emphatic sense is still a conversational implicature and a context meaning, but not the conventional implicature of *dōu*$_b$. The reasons are as follows. In sentences (37–39) there are two layers of directly expressed semantics. One is an explicit expression about a kind of eventuality, for instance (37), pupils felt this abuse was unfair. Two is an implicit expression of a judgment which considers that occurrence or existence possibility of the eventuality described by the proposition is inferior-to-expectation (or normal), for instance (37), the expected age to be able to make a right judgment is usually after 18 years old. And the emphatic sense is indirectly expressed by the statement that the inferior-to-expectation (or normal) eventuality has occurred or existed. More precisely, the listener obtains it through a plausible inference (see also Xu [40], Levinson [41]). Roughly as follows:

If (p) the speaker, or the listener, or the specific speech community including the speaker and the listener, holds the expectation (or normal) for the possibility of occurrence and existence of an eventuality in a certain context. And the eventuality whose possibility is lower than the expectation (or normal) has already occurred or existed. Then (q) the degree of the situation is serious.

(p) The eventuality whose possibility is lower than the expectation (or normal) has already occurred or existed.
(q)Then the degree of the situation is serious. [i.e. the emphatic sense]
Or: $((p \rightarrow q) \wedge p) \rightarrow q$

Levinson [42] took the calculability as a criterion for distinguishing between a conventional implicature and a conversational implicature. That is, a conversational implicature is derived from an inference, and a conventional implicature as part of rule meaning is certain. So the emphatic sense derived from an inference is still a conversational implicature, more precisely, it is a generalized conversational implicature which is predictable and context-free (See also Crystal [43], Shen [44]), but not the particularized conversational implicature of Levinson [45].

The plausible inference of non-monotonic logic is a kind of default reasoning, which is a kind of inference that jumps to a conclusion, and that is cancellable. Therefore, although a generalized conversational implicature is general, it is not yet the *inherent* conventional implicature of words, and it may still be canceled in a specific context. For example:

(40) Zhe zhong shi xiang dou bu gan xiang, ke ta jingran xiang le zuo le.
This kind thing think DOU not dare think, but he unexpectedly think LE do LE
All of these people even dare not think about it, but unexpectedly he had thought about and done it.

(41) Lian ren de shengcun dou kunnan, nimen que neng fazhan
Including people DE survive DOU difficult, you but can develop
xumuye, shizai shi qiji!
Stock-farming, indeed is miracle!
Even though the survival of a person is difficult, but you can develop stock-farming, it is a miracle!

Sentence (40) emphasizes that all of these people even dared not think about this kind of thing, but he had thought about and done it. Sentence (41) emphasizes that even though the survival of a person is difficult, but you can develop stock-farming.

Therefore, the emphatic sense is the pragmatic inference and the conversational implicature of the whole $d\bar{o}u_b$ construction, and still not the conventional implicature of $d\bar{o}u_b$. So, some scholars regarded the emphasis as the semantic of $d\bar{o}u_b$, it has mistakenly added the meaning of $d\bar{o}u_b$ construction to $d\bar{o}u_b$.

3 The Conventional Implicature of $D\bar{o}u_b$ and It's Semantic Features

3.1 Definition of the Semantic Function of $D\bar{o}u_b$

For ease of expression, here are those constructions that contain $d\bar{o}u_b$ roughly formatted as "(X) + $d\bar{o}u_b$ + Y, (Z)". Thus we can roughly say that the construction of $d\bar{o}u_b$ contains two components, one: (X) Y, (Z) explicit expression of propositional meaning, i.e. the occurrence or existence of an eventuality, two: **implicit expression of $d\bar{o}u_b$ as a judgment of the eventuality, which considers that the occurrence or existence possibility of the eventuality described by the proposition is inferior-to-expectation (or normal).**

3.2 The Features of the Conventional Implicature of $D\bar{o}u_b$

From the perspective of three metafunctions of functional linguistics (see Halliday [32, 33]) in the constructions of $d\bar{o}u_b$, the component one is "(X) Y, (Z)", what it undertakesis that experiential function, which describes things and their corresponding processes in the subjective and objective world and expresses the truth-value meaning and propositional meaning, and the component two is $d\bar{o}u_b$, what it mainly undertakes is the interpersonal function and textual function, which expresses the non-propositional meaning and procedural meaning (see also Zhong [46]). $D\bar{o}u_b$ can be regarded as a conventional implicature trigger (see also Barbara [47]). The conventional implicature which $d\bar{o}u_b$ triggers is the speaker's subjective identification and evaluation of the relationship between the propositional content and the expectation (or normal), and is the speaker's subjective cognition (The listener may not have the same cognition at all). It has a strong speaker-orientation and subjectivity (see also Feng [48, 49]).

From the point of discourse comprehension, its main function is to declare the attitude and commentary of a speaker or both of speaker and listener or a speech community on propositional contents of a discourse, which imposes the pragmatic restriction and limitation on understanding propositional meaning to an addressee and leads the addressee to comprehend pragmatic information of the discourse validly, in order to make the addressee obtain the most relevant information of the speaker's intention. In other word, the meaning of $d\bar{o}u_b$ is already not the truth-value conditional meaning from the point of traditional semantics but the pragmatic meaning for leading or guiding to understand discourse (see Blakemore [30, 50, 51], Sperber & Wilson [52], Roulet [53]), for example:

(42) a. Shubao li de dongxi linshi le.
Schoolbag inside DE things splashed-wet LE
The contents of the schoolbag were splashed wet.
b. Lian shubao li de dongxi dou linshi le.
Including schoolbag inside DE things DOU splashed-wet LE
Even the contents of the schoolbag were splashed wet.

(43) a. Ba ta chaoxing le.
BA him wake up LE
Woke him up.
b. Ba ta dou chaoxing le.
BA him DOU wake up LE
Even woke him up.

(44) a. Shi'er dian le.
Twelve o'clock LE
It's twelve o'clock
b. Dou shi'er dian le.
DOU twelve o'clock LE
It's even twelve o'clock.

What expressed by (42–44) sentences *a* is the truth-value conditional meaning, under the situation of an unspecific context, they can be given diversified pragmatic comprehensions. For example, sentence (43a) *Ba ta chao xing le* (Woke him up), which can be understood as *Chaonao sheng da le* (The noises were loud), and also can be understood as *Chaonao sheng hen xiao, Ta shuijiao hen jingxing* (The noises were lowish, he was easy to be woken up) etc. If the sentence (43b) is added with $d\bar{o}u_b$, then the pragmatic comprehension of propositional meaning by a addressee shall be constrained and limited, for example, sentence (43b) *Bata dou chao xing le* (Even woke him up),normally can only be understood as *Chaonao sheng tai dale* (The noises were too loud).

By comparison with sentence *a* and sentence *b* in (42–44) sentences, it is found that both of their truth-value conditional meanings are exactly the same. Deletion of *(Lian)* ...$D\bar{o}u_b$ doesn't change the proposition meaning of a sentence, we can see that the conventional implicature of $d\bar{o}u_b$ is also non-truth conditional meaning just as a conversational implicature (see Karttunen and Peters [54], Vivien [55]). Along with the implicature of its expression, therefore the conventional implicity of $d\bar{o}u_b$ is a kind of conventional meaning but it also differs from a generalized conventional meaning which is normally an explicit and literal truth conditional meaning. And it cannot be canceled, so the conventional implicature of $d\bar{o}u_b$ that is implicit. But the conversational implicature that also can be canceled, are not definitely the same thing. For example, in sentence (45) *the possibility of waking him up is less*, which is lower than the expectation (or normal), cannot be canceled:

(45) *Ba ta dou chao xing le, keshi chao xing ta de kenengxing shi
BA him DOU wake-up LE, but wake-up him DE possibility is
hen dade.
very large DE
*Even woke him up, and the possibility of waking him up was very large.

After combining the two components of *dōu*$_b$ construction, in addition to the meaning of the above two components, *dōu*$_b$ construction has one more meaning which emphasizes on the severity of the situation. It can be seen that the generalized conversational implicature of *dōu*$_b$ construction is derived from a pragmatic inference, which makes its overall meaning more than the sum of its components meanings.

4 Conclusion

In summary, the semantic function of marking a polarity, or a universal quantification, or having done or been is the conversational implicature of a sentence which contains *dōu*$_b$, and the emphatic sense as a kind of generalized conversational implicature which belongs to *dōu*$_b$ construction is drawing from a plausible inference. But these semantic functions are not conventional meanings of *dōu*$_b$. *Dōu*$_b$ is a conventional implicature trigger, and the conventional implicature which *dōu*$_b$ triggers is the judgments of the speaker for the eventuality declared by the proposition who believes that the occurrence or existence possibility of the eventuality is inferior-to-expectation (or normal). This is the speaker's subjective cognition, and the listener may not have the same cognition at all. It has a strong speaker-orientation and subjectivity. The deletion of *(Lian)...Dōu*$_b$ in a *dōu*$_b$ construction doesn't change the proposition meaning of a sentence, and we can see that the conventional implicature of *dōu*$_b$ is also a non-truth conditional meaning just as a conversational implicature. This is no longer the true conditional meaning in the perspective of traditional semantics, but it's a non-truth procedural pragmatic meaning which leads to or guides the listener's discourse understanding.

Along with the subjectivity and the non-truth value of *dōu*$_b$'s conventional meaning, and the implicature of its expression, as a kind of rule meaning the conventional meaning of *dōu*$_b$ is a kind of rule meaning, but it also differs from a generalized conventional meaning, which is normally an explicit and literal truth-value conditional meaning. And it cannot be canceled, so the conventional implicature of *dōu*$_b$ is implicit, and is not definitely the same thing with the conversational implicature that can be canceled.

References

1. Ding, S., et al: Lectures on Modern Chinese Grammar. The commercial press, Beijing (1980 [1961]). [In Chinese]
2. Lü, S., et al: Modern Chinese Eight Hundred Words. The commercial press, Beijing (2002 [1980]). [In Chinese]
3. Nakagawa, C.: Contextual analysis and analysis of tone of Chinese Adverbs Dou(都). Chin. Transl. Jpn. Res. Pap. Anthol. Mod. Chin. (1993[1985]). [In Chinese] Translated by Xun Chunsheng, Yusunori Ohkochi, Shi Guangheng. Beijing, Beijing Languages College Press, pp. 309–322
4. Lee, T.H.: Studies on quantification in Chinese. Ph.D. diss., University of California, Los Angeles (1986)
5. Gao, M.C.F.: LF representations of quantifier scope interpretations. Ph.D. diss. Essex University (1989)
6. Gao, M.C.F.: Dou as a wide scope universal quantifier. Aust. J. Linguist. **14**, 39–62 (1994)
7. Chiu, H.-C.B.: A case of quantifier floating in Mandarin Chinese. In: The Second North America Conference on Chinese Linguistics. University of Pennsylvania, Philadelphia (1990)
8. Chiu, H.-C.B.: The inflectional structure of Mandarin Chinese. Ph.D. diss., University of California, Los Angeles (1993)
9. Lin, S.: Determination principles of range adverbs. J. Shanghai Norm. Univ. **1**, 125–126 (1993). [In Chinese]
10. Cheng, L.-S.: Lisa: on dou-quantification. J. East Asian Linguist. **4**, 197–234 (1995)
11. Ren, H.: Semantic function and ambiguity of Dou(都). J. Zhejiang Univ. **2**, 101–106 (1995). [In Chinese]
12. Lin, J.-W.: Distributivity in Chinese and its implication. Nat. Lang. Semanics **6**, 201–243 (1998)
13. Jiang, Y.: Pragmatic reasoning and syntactic/semantic characterization of Dou(都). Mod. Foreign Lang. **1**, 11–24 (1998). [In Chinese]
14. Jiang Yan: *Scalar Model and Semantic Features of Dou*(都), Conference Articles of The First International Symposium on Chinese Form and Function (2006).[In Chinese]
15. Wu, J.: Syntax and semantics of quantification in Chinese. Ph.D. diss., University of Maryland at College Park (1999)
16. Dong, X.: Definite objects and relevant questions of Dou(都). Chin. Lang. **6**, 495–507 (2002). [In Chinese]
17. Pan, H.: Focus Point and Trisection Structure and Semantic Interpretation of Chinese Dou (都), Grammar Study and Exploration (XIII). The commercial press, Beijing (2006). [In Chinese]
18. Yuan, Y.: The Information Structure of the Lian (连) construction in Mandarin. Linguist. Sci. **2**, 14–28 (2006). [In Chinese]
19. Jiang, J.Z., Haihua, P.: Semantic divides and rules of interpretation. Chin. Lang. **1**, 38–50 (2013). [In Chinese]
20. Wang, H.: Analysis of grammar meaning of adverb Dou(都). Chin. Learn. **6**, 55–60 (1999). [In Chinese]
21. Wang, H.: Syntactic, semantic and pragmatic analysis of adverb Dou(都). Jinan University, Master's Thesis (2000). [In Chinese]
22. Wang, H.: Semantic and pragmatic analysis of modal adverb Dou(都). J. Jinan Univ. Coll.E Lib. Arts **6**, 41–45 (2001). [In Chinese]

23. Jiang, J.: Evolution and classification of totalizing. Chin. Learn. **4**, 72–76 (2003). [In Chinese]
24. Xiao, S.R.: Item of total quantity and meaning of implicit comparison of Dou(都). J. Hunan Inst. Hum. Sci. Technol. **6**, 98–104 (2005). [In Chinese]
25. Xu, Y.Z., Yiming Y.: Subjectivity, objectivity, and pragmatic ambiguity of adverb Dou (都). Lang. Res. **3**, 24–29 (2005). [In Chinese]
26. Zhang, Y.S.: Grammaticalization and subjectivization of adverbs Dou(都). J. Xuzhou Norm. Univ. **3**, 56–62 (2005). [In Chinese]
27. Zhang, Y.J.: Semantic recognition strategies and discourse understanding of adverbs Dou (都) in authentic texts. J. Yangzhou Univ. **2**, 87–91 (2007). [In Chinese]
28. Liejiong, X.: Similarities and differences of Shanghai Dialect Chai(侪) and Mandarin Dou (都). Dialects **2**, 97–102 (2007). [In Chinese]
29. Liu, D.Q.: Atypical Lian(连) sentence as typical mode of sentence. Lang. Teach. Linguist. Stud. **4**, 1–12 (2005). [In Chinese]
30. Blakemore, D.: Semantic Constraints on Relevance. Basil Blackwell, Oxford (1987)
31. Schiffrin, D.: Discourse Markers. Cambridge University Press, Cambridge (1987)
32. Halliday, M.A.K.: An Introduction to Functional Grammar. Edward Arnold, London (1994)
33. Halliday, M.A.K.: An Introduction to Functional Grammar, pp. 79–81. Edward Arnold, London (2004)
34. Xing, F.Y.: On the structure of NP + Le(了). Linguist. Res. **3**, 21–26 (1984). [In Chinese]
35. Ma, Zhen.: The Methodology of Research on Function Words in Mandarin Chinese. The commercial press, Beijing (2004). [In Chinese]
36. Guo, C.G.: Similarities and differences of adverbs of time Yi Jing(已经) and Dou(都). Chin. Teach. World **2**, 35–41 (1997). [In Chinese]
37. Zhang, Y.J.: Limiting and Descriptive Functions of Adverbs. Anhui Education Publishing House, Hefei (2002). [In Chinese]
38. Hou, X.: The Dictionary of function words in Mandarin Chinese. Peking University Press, Beijing (1998). [In Chinese]
39. Li, W.H.: Forming and Mechanism of Dou(都) XP as Construction. Lang. Teach. Linguist. Stud. **5**, 57–63 (2010). [In Chinese]
40. Xu, S.H.: Pragmatic inference and plausible reasoning. Foreign Lang. Teach. Res. **3**, 163–169 (2005). [In Chinese]
41. Levinson, S.C.: Presumptive Meanings: The Theory of Generalized Conversational Implicature. MIT Press, Cambridge (2000)
42. Levinson, S.C.: Pragmatics. Cambridge University Press, Cambridge (1983)
43. Crystal, D.: A Dictionary of Linguistics and Phonetics. Blackwell Publishers Ltd., Oxford (1997)
44. Shen, J.X.: Pragmatic principles, pragmatic inference, semantic change. Foreign Lang. Teach. Res. **4**, 243–251 (2004). [In Chinese]
45. Levinson, S.C.: Three levels of meaning. In: Palmer, F.R. (ed.) Grammar and Meaning, pp. 90–105. Cambridge University Press, Cambridge (1995)
46. Zhong, H.: 都$_b$[Dou$_b$(Dou$_2$, Dou$_3$)] as A counter-expectation discourse-marker: on the pragmatic functions of Dou$_b$ from the perspective of discourse analysis. Chinese Lexical Semantics. LNCS (LNAI), vol. 9332, pp. 392–407. Springer, Cham (2015). https://doi.org/10.1007/978-3-319-27194-1_39
47. Barbara, A.: Where have some of the presuppositions gone? In: Birner, B., Ward, G. (eds.) Drawing the Boundaries of Meaning: Neo-Gricean Studies in Pragmatics and Semantics in Honor of Laurence R, pp. 1–20. John Benjamins, Horn, Philadelphia (2006)
48. Feng, G.: Exploration on Conventional Implicature of Natural Language, Foreign Languages Research, III, pp. 1–6 (2008). [In Chinese]

49. Feng, G.: A theory of conventional implicature and pragmatic markers in Chinese. Emerald Group Publishing Limited (2010)
50. Blakemore, D.: Understanding Utterances. Basil Blackwell, Oxford (1992)
51. Blakemore, D.: Relevance and Linguistic Meaning: The Semantics and Pragmatics of Discourse Markers. University Press, Cambridge (2002)
52. Sperber, D., Wilson, D.: Relevance: Communication & Cognition, vol. 2. Blackwell, Oxford (1995)
53. Roulet, E.: The description of text relation markers in the Geneva model of discourse organization. In: Fischer, K. (ed.) Approaches to Discourse Particles, pp. 115–132. Elsevier Ltd., Amsterdam (2006)
54. Karttunen, L., Peters, S.: Conventional implicature. In: Oh, C.K., Dinneen, D.A. (eds.). Syntax and Semantics II: Presupposition, pp. 1–56. New York Academic Press (1979)
55. Vivien, L.S.L.: A relevance-theoretic approach to discourse particles in Singapore English. In: Fischer, K. (ed.) Approaches to Discourse Particles, pp. 149–165. Elsevier Ltd., Amsterdam (2006)

External Causation and Agentivity in Mandarin Chinese

Shiao Wei Tham(✉)

Department of Chinese Studies, Faculty of Arts and Social Sciences,
National University of Singapore, AS8 #05-31, 10 Kent Ridge Crescent,
Singapore 119260, Singapore
chstsw@nus.edu.sg

Abstract. This work addresses a contrast in the encoding pattern of two kinds of events of caused change in Mandarin Chinese. Caused change of state events are typically expressed with a resultative verb compound, while caused change of location and caused motion events may be expressed with a monomorphemic verb. I argue that this asymmetry arises from two factors. One is a requirement in Mandarin that monomorphemic verbs of causation be agentive, which reflects a prototypical association between causers and volitional agents. The second is an ontological distinction between change of state and change of location. Changes of state may arise spontaneously without an external cause for any kind of individual. In contrast, change of location for one kind of entity – inanimates – requires the mediation of an external agent.

Keywords: Caused change · Change of state · Change of location
Prototypical causer

1 Introduction

This paper considers the contrasting encoding patterns found in two kinds of expressions involving events of caused change in Mandarin Chinese. Events of caused change of state (COS) are predominantly expressed bimorphemically using resultative verb compounds (RVCs) (1) [5], while events of caused change of location (2) and caused motion (CLM) are naturally expressed monomorphemically with a single verb[1].

(1)	三毛	打破了	杯子。				
	Sanmao	**da-po**-le	beizi				
	Sanmao	hit-break-PERF	cup				
	Sanmao broke the cup.						
(2)	三毛	在	盒子里	放了	一	支	笔。
	Sanmao	zai	hezi-li	**fang**-le	yi	zhi	bi
	Sanmao	be.at	box-interior	put-PERF	one	CL	pen
	Sanmao put a pen in the box.						

[1] Abbreviations used: 1, 3 = 1st, 3rd person; ACC = accusative; CL = classifier; PAST.PART = past participle; PERF = perfective; PL = plural; PROG = progressive; REFL = reflexive.

J.-F. Hong et al. (Eds.): CLSW 2018, LNAI 11173, pp. 61–69, 2018.
https://doi.org/10.1007/978-3-030-04015-4_5

Two questions arise from this contrast: first, why are there two lexicalization patterns for events of caused change, and second, why do the patterns fall in this particular distribution – given as type A in Table 1 – and not the other way around, e.g. as in the putative but unattested type B in Table 1?

Table 1. Attested and unattested lexicalization patterns for caused COS and caused CLM events.

Event type	Caused COS	Caused CLM
A. Major lexicalization pattern (observed)	Bimorphemic (RVC)	Monomorphemic
B. Major lexicalization pattern (putative, not observed)	Monomorphemic	Bimorphemic (RVC)

I propose that lexicalization pattern A arises from two factors. The first is a prototypical association between causers and agents [1], manifested in Mandarin as the following principle:

(3) Monomorphemic verbs of causation must specify a volitional agent.

The second is an ontological contrast between caused COS and caused CLM events, which may be characterized as follows:

(4) COS for any entity may arise spontaneously, but CLM for inanimate entities must have an external cause.

1.1 Caused COS Is Expressed Bimorphemically

This subsection briefly illustrates the distinct lexicalization patterns for events of caused change of state (COS). As the examples below show, an intransitive COS verb such as 破 *po* 'break' (5) cannot be used transitively with a meaning of causation (6). An event of breaking in which a causer is overtly specified must be encoded as in (1) above, using a resultative verb compound (RVC).

(5) 杯子 破了。
beizi po-le
cup break-PERF
The cup broke.

(6) *三毛 破了 杯子。
*Sanmao po-le beizi
Sanmao break-PERF cup
Intended: as in (1)

The encoding of caused COS events forms a contrast with that of caused CLM events, discussed below.

1.2 Caused CLM is Expressed Monomorphemically

As seen in (2) above, an event of caused change of location, i.e., one of putting, is encoded by a monomorphemic verb 放 *fang* 'put'. It might be argued that the result location is separately encoded by another predicate, here the prepositional phrase (PP) 在盒子里 *zai hezi-li* 'in the box, *lit.* be at box-interior'. But the PP is an argument selected by the verb, as shown by its ability to (i) take on a result location reading in pre-verbal position, as in (2), and (ii) to occur after both the verb and the theme object (2'). Neither of these properties is available to verbs such as 推 *tui* 'push' that do not themselves select for a result location (7)–(8). Therefore, it may be maintained that the verb 放 *fang* 'put' itself lexically specifies the change of location.

(2')	三毛	**放了**	一	支	笔	**在**	**盒子里。**
	Sanmao	**fang**-le	yi	zhi	bi	**zai**	**hezi-li**
	Sanmao	put-PERF	one	CL	pen	be.at	box-interior

Sanmao put a pen in the box.

(7)	三毛	**在**	**房里**	**推了**	一	张	椅子。
	Sanmao	**zai**	**fang-li**	**tui-le**	yi	zhang	yizi
	Sanmao	be.at	room-interior	push-PERF	one	CL	chair

Only: Sanmao was in the room pushing a chair; NOT Sanmao pushed a chair into the room.

(8)	*三毛	**推了**	一	张	椅子	**在**	**房里。**
	*Sanmao	**tui-le**	yi	zhang	yizi	**zai**	**fang-li**
	Sanmao	push-PERF	one	CL	chair	be.at	room-interior

Intended: Sanmao pushed a chair into the room.

Verbs of caused motion such as 扔 *reng* 'throw' behave similarly to 放 *fang* 'put', in that a locative PP may occur pre-verbally with a result location interpretation (9), and it may also occur felicitously after the verb and theme object.

(9)	三毛	**在**	**井里**	**扔了**	一	枚	硬币。
	Sanmao	**zai**	**jing-li**	**reng**-le	yi	mei	bi
	Sanmao	be.at	well-interior	throw-PERF	one	CL	coin

Sanmao threw a coin into the well.

(10)	三毛	**扔了**	一	枚	硬币	**在**	**井里。**
	Sanmao	**reng**-le	yi	mei	bi	**zai**	**jing-li**
	Sanmao	throw-PERF	one	CL	coin	be.at	well-interior

Sanmao threw a coin into the well.

Examples such as (9)–(10) suggest that caused motion events, like caused change of location events, may be encoded monomorphemically, in contrast to caused COS events.

In the next section, I discuss the encoding patterns of Mandarin verbs of caused COS and caused CLM in greater detail, placing them in crosslinguistic perspective. Section 3 provides data to support the claim in (3) that monomorphemic verbs of causation in Mandarin require a volitional agent. Section 4 discusses how the asymmetry between caused COS and caused CLM event encoding arises from the factors noted in (3)–(4). Section 5 concludes.

2 The Crosslinguistic Encoding of Events of Caused Change

This section sets the Mandarin data against a larger crosslinguistic backdrop, arguing that, while caused COS verbs across languages bear some kind of regular morphological relationship to their intransitive counterparts, any derivational relationship between caused CLM verbs and an intransitive counterpart is less clear.

2.1 Two Kinds of Encoding for Caused COS Events

Across languages, two kinds of morphological relationships may be observed between caused COS and their stative and intransitive COS counterparts [3]. In one paradigm, the stative word is basic. The form of the corresponding intransitive COS and transitive caused COS verbs are derived by adding morphology to the stative word. An example is found in O'odham (10) [2].

(10)	**State**	**COS**	**Caused COS**
	a. (s-)moik	b. moik-a	c. moik-a-(ji)d
	'be soft'	'become soft'	'cause to become soft'

Some parallel to this pattern may be found in Mandarin. Adjectives such as 软 *ruan* 'soft' in (11) may alternate with a COS verb (12), and may combine with an activity verb such as 泡 *pao* 'soak' to form an RVC (13), yielding a caused COS description.

(11) 香菇 很 软。
xianggu hen ruan
mushroom very soft
The mushrooms are very soft. (State)

(12) 香菇 软了。
xianggu ruan-le
mushroom soft-PERF
The mushrooms have become soft. (COS)

(13) 我们 泡软了 香菇。
women pao-ruan-le xianggu
1PL soak-soft-PERF mushroom
We soaked the mushrooms soft. (Caused COS, RVC)

In the second paradigm, the causative verb constitutes the base from which the related intransitive COS and stative predicates are derived, as exemplified in Cuzco Quechua (14–16) [3].

(14) tela-ta qhasu-sha-n
cloth-ACC tear-PROG-3
(S)he tore the shirt/is tearing the cloth. (Basic caused COS verb)

(15) tela-ta qhasu-ku-n
cloth-ACC tear-REFL-3
The cloth got/became torn. (Derived intransitive COS word)

(16) tela-ta qhasu-sqa ka-sha-n
cloth-ACC tear-PAST.PART be-PROG-3
The cloth is torn. (Derived stative word)

This paradigm has no direct parallel in Mandarin. (17–19) show that Mandarin underived intransitive COS verbs such as 裂 *lie* 'crack' in (18) may form an RVC that encodes caused COS (17), but have no corresponding stative word (19).

(17) 三毛 碰裂了 镜子。
Sanmao peng-lie-le jingzi
Sanmao bump-crack-PERF mirror
Sanmao cracked the mirror by bumping into it. (Caused COS, RVC)

(18) 镜子 裂了。
jingzi lie-le
mirror crack-PERF
The mirror cracked (Basic COS verb)

(19) *镜子 很 裂
jingzi hen lie
mirror very crack
Intended: The mirror is badly cracked (No stative counterpart)

A crucial point to note here is that, in Mandarin, regardless of whether the stative or COS word is basic, the expression of caused COS takes the form of an RVC, as indicated by the examples in (13) and (17) (although see Sect. 3.2).

2.2 Verbs of Caused Change of Location and Caused Motion in RVCs

As we saw above, events of caused change of location and caused motion (CLM) may be expressed monomorphemically. Verbs of caused CLM may also participate in RVC formation, but always as the first member of the compound, unlike COS verbs, which are always the second member. For instance, the verb of caused motion 扔 *reng* 'throw' may form 扔进 *reng-jin* 'throw-enter, i.e. throw into', but not *撞扔 **zhuang-reng* 'collide-throw' (intended as: 'collide into and cause to be thrown'). Similarly, verbs of caused change of location such as 塞 *sai* 'stuff' and 放 *fang* 'put' may form 塞进 *sai-jin* 'stuff into', 放下 *fang-xia* 'put down' etc. but not say, *挤塞 **ji-sai* 'squeeze-stuff' (intended as: 'to stuff (something) somewhere by squeezing), or *推放 'push-put' (intended as: to put (something) somewhere by pushing).

2.3 An Analogy with Caused COS and Caused CLM Encoding in English

The facts discussed here regarding caused COS and caused CLM encoding in Mandarin find an analogy in English, although the surface patterns shown in each language are distinct. Unlike Mandarin COS verbs, which show no transitivity alternation, English COS verbs such as *break* show a regular alternation between intransitive and transitive causative uses. In contrast to *break*-type verbs, English verbs of spatial configuration such as *sit*, *stand*, *lie*, *hang*, etc. have been argued not to participate in a regular causative alternation, even though such verbs may show both transitive and intransitive uses [4].

That is, across languages, caused COS verbs can be said to show a regular morphological relationship with their intransitive COS counterparts, but the same cannot be said for caused CLM verbs. In particular, caused CLM verbs cannot be said to be derived from their intransitive counterparts, unlike the case for caused COS verbs in certain cases, as discussed in Sect. 2.1 above.

3 Monomorphemic Verbs of Causation in Mandarin are Agentive

In this section, I begin to address the reasons behind the dichotomy in caused COS and caused CLM encoding in Mandarin. I argue that one factor for this asymmetry arises from a prototypical association between causers and volitional agents [1]. I show this association is manifested in Mandarin as a requirement that monomorphemic verbs of causation must be agentive, i.e. they select for a volitional agent.

3.1 Monomorphemic Caused CLM Verbs are Agentive

As shown above, caused CLM events may be expressed monomorphemically. Below, I show that such verbs require the causer subject to be a volitional agent. The following examples show that non-volitional agents such as weather conditions (20) and abstract agents (21)–(22) are not felicitous subjects for caused CLM verbs.

(20)	#大	风	在	河里	扔了	许多	落叶。
	#da	feng	zai	he-li	reng-le	xuduo	luo-ye
	big	wind	be.at	river-interior	throw-PERF	many	fall-leaf

Intended: The strong wind threw/tossed many fallen leaves into the river.

(21)	#命运	向	他们	扔了	许多	挑战。
	#mingyun	xiang	tamen	reng-le	xuduo	tiaozhan
	fate	towards	3PL	throw-PERF	many	challenge

Intended: Fate threw/tossed many challenges at them.

(22)	#这	事	会	把	他们	放	在	尴尬	的	处境。
	#zhe	shi	hui	ba	tamen	fang	zai	ganga	de	chujing
	this	matter	will	BA	3PL	put	be.at	awkward	de	situation

Intended: This matter will put them in an awkward situation.

In contrast, note that the felicitous uses of 扔 reng 'throw' (10) and 放 fang 'put' (2) above both involve volitional agents. These observations support the generalization that monomorphemic caused CLM verbs require a volitional agent.

3.2 Monomorphemic Caused COS Verbs are Agentive

It was argued above that caused COS events are predominantly encoded by RVCs in Mandarin. Still, monomorphemic caused COS verbs do exist, although these verbs are rare. The few that do exist, however, behave consistently with the generalization proposed here. That is, they also require a volitional agent. (23) shows a monomorphemic caused COS verb 热 *re* 'hot/heat' with a volitional agent. Weather elements such as the sun are not felicitous as a subject referent for this verb (24).

(23)	三毛	热了	剩菜。
	Sanmao	re-le	shengcai
	Sanmao	hot-PERF	leftovers
	Sanmao heated the leftovers.		
(24)	#太阳	热了	土地。
	#taiyang	re-le	tudi
	sun	hot-PERF	earth
	Intended: The sun heated the earth.		

(25) shows the verb 开 *kai* 'open', which may also show a causative use. Again, the subject here corresponds to a volitional agent. (26) below shows that the subject nominal of 开 *kai* 'open' cannot describe an instrument such as a key.

(25)	三毛	开了	门。
	Sanmao	kai-le	men
	Sanmao	open-PERF	door
	Sanmao opened the door.		
(26)	#钥匙	开了	门。
	#yaoshi	kai-le	men
	key	open-PERF	door
	Intended: The key opened the door.		

While monomorphemic caused COS verbs such as these are infrequently encountered, they too require a volitional agent, in keeping with the current proposal.

3.3 Complex Verbs of Causation Need not be Agentive

This subsection rounds out the picture of the encoding of verbs of caused change. I show that complex verbs of causation comprising more than one morpheme need not be agentive. All the examples in this subsection contain bimorphemic verbs of caused change, although not all are obviously obtained through resultative compounding, such as the verbs in (29)–(30) below.

(27)–(28) show that weather elements are felicitous as causers for the events described.

(27)	太阳	照热了	整个	城市。
	taiyang	zhao-re-le	zhengge	chengshi
	sun	shine-hot-PERF	whole	city
	The sun shone the whole city hot.			
(28)	寒风	吹冻了	大地。	
	han-feng	chui-dong-le	dadi	
	cold-wind	blow-freeze-PERF	earth	
	Cold winds blew the earth frozen.			

The complex verbs in (29)–(30) are not straightforwardly understood as RVCs, but they nonetheless consist of more than one morpheme.[2] As with the compounds in (27)–(28), they also allow non-agentive causer subjects.

(29)	这	次	会议	化解了	他们	的	矛盾。
	zhe	ci	huiyi	huajie-le	tamen	de	maodun
	this	time	meeting	resolve-PERF	3PL	DE	conflict
	This meeting resolved their conflict.						

(30)	环境	污染	破坏了	生态	平衡。
	huanjing	wuran	pohuai-le	shengtai	pingheng
	environment	pollution	destroy-PERF	ecology	balance
	Environmental pollution destroyed the ecological balance.				

To sum up, compound verbs of causation in Mandarin do allow non-agentive causers. That is, the restriction to volitional agents is restricted to monomorphemic verbs of caused change.

4 Discussion

With the preceding generalizations in mind, I now return to the question of why the encoding of caused COS verbs and caused CLM verbs show asymmetrical complexity: The former tend to be encoded using complex verbs, i.e. RVCs, while the latter tend to be encoded with a monomorphemic verb.

I propose this asymmetry arises from an ontological distinction between the two kinds of events of change involved. Many kinds of COS of an individual, whether animate or inanimate, may arise spontaneously without the intervention of an external agent. Although an external agent is possible, even probable, it is not necessary, and may thus be left unspecified by the verb as an argument [4]. In contrast, change of

[2] These compound verbs are formed from two COS verbs, unlike typical RVCs, which contain an activity verb describing the causing event and a COS (or potentially stative) predicate, which describes the result.

location and motion for one set of entities – inanimates – is necessarily mediated by an external agent (or at least by external forces or conditions such as a slope).

By hypothesis, Mandarin requires its monomorphemic verbs of causation to be agentive. Given this requirement, it is more likely that caused CLM verbs are expressed monomorphemically, since at least a subset of the events they describe predictably require an external cause. In contrast, describing a caused COS event with a monomorphemic (i.e., obligatorily agentive) verb would restrict the verb to describing externally-caused change, and indeed, to describing change caused by a volitional agent. Such a lexicalization strategy would be less effective in reflecting the more unpredictable nature of how COS events arise.

5 Concluding Remarks

This work links a hitherto undiscussed asymmetry in the encoding of events of caused change in Mandarin to a cross-linguistically relevant prototypical property of causers to correspond to volitional agents. In Mandarin, this property manifests itself as an obligatory requirement on monomorphemic verbs of causation to be agentive, although complex verbs consisting of more than one morpheme do not share the same restriction. The asymmetry between caused COS and caused CLM event encoding finds an indirect parallel in English, where the causative alternation is shown by COS verbs but not by verbs of spatial configuration. These patterns suggest that the nature of external causation, and the prototypical characteristics of causers, may yet provide fertile ground for exploring causative event descriptions across languages.

Acknowledgments. This work was based in part on work supported by grant no. GS031-A-15 from the Chiang Ching-kuo Foundation for International Scholarly Exchange, and on work supported by a grant (WBS no. R-102-000-113-133) from the National University of Singapore. I thank Liu Mei-chun, Lin Jingxia, and two anonymous reviewers, as well as other participants of CLSW 2018 for helpful comments, not all of which I have been able to address. Thanks also go to Ng Xinyi for help with proofreading. All errors and misinterpretations are my responsibility.

References

1. Delancey, S.: Notes on agentivity and causation. Stud. Lang. **8**(2), 181–213 (1984)
2. Hale, K., Keyser, J.: The basic elements of argument structure. MIT Working Papers in Linguistics, vol. 3, pp. 273–118 (1998)
3. Koontz-Garboden, A.: On the typology of state/change of state alternations. In: Geert, B., Maarle, J. (eds.) The Yearbook of Morphology, pp. 83–117 (2005)
4. Levin, B., Rappaport Hovav, M.: Unaccusativity: At the Syntax-Lexical Semantics Interface. MIT Press, Cambridge, MA (1995)
5. Li, C.N., Thompson, S.A.: Mandarin Chinese: A Functional Reference Grammar. University of California Press, Berkeley (1981)

Somewhere in COLDNESS Lies Nibbāna: Lexical Manifestations of COLDNESS

Jiajuan Xiong[1(✉)] and Chu-Ren Huang[2]

[1] School of Foreign Languages for Business, Southwestern University of Finance and Ecomomics, Chengdu, China
jiajuanx@163.com

[2] Department of Chinese and Bilingual Studies, The Hong Kong Polytechnic University, Hung Hom, Hong Kong
churen.huang@polyu.edu.cn

Abstract. This paper starts with an investigation of three coldness-related tactile words, viz. 寒 han2 'cold', 冷 leng3 'cold' and 涼 liang2 'cool', in their synaesthetic and metaphorical uses in Modern Chinese. It is found that 冷 leng3 'cold' is most versatile whereas 涼 liang2 'cool' is most inert with regard to their synaesthetic and metaphorical mappings, with 寒 han2 'cold' standing in the middle. Moreover, 寒 han2 'cold' tends to be object-oriented, while 涼 liang2 'cool' is likely to be subject-oriented, with 冷 leng3 'cold' allowing both subject- and object-oriented readings. We further conduct a study on the uses of these three tactile words in Buddhist texts of Āgamas, finding that 涼 liang2 'cool' was consistently employed to refer the nibbānic status. Apart from it, two counts of 冷 leng3 'cold' exhibit the nibbānic meaning. However, 寒 han2 'cold' is never attested in this philosophical meaning. It is interesting to note that a kind of tactile feeling is associated with nibbāna, even though nibbānic experience is supposed to transcend sensory experience. This finding, together with some other findings with regard to the relation between sensory expressions and nibbāna, can shed light on the linguistc expressions of the inexpressible nibbāna.

Keywords: COLDNESS · 寒 *han2* 'cold' · 冷 *leng3* 'cold' · 涼 *liang2* 'cool' Nibbāna

1 Introduction

The concept of COLDNESS embodies human beings' perception of temperatures and thus falls into the tactile domain, which parallels with other human sensory domains, such as visual domain, auditory domain, olfactory domain, gustatory domain and even mental domain. These sensory domains help to classify sensory data into different categories, which have their equivalent sense organs, viz., eye, ear, nose, tongue, and mind. Although the sensory classification is well-established, sensory data can transcend the meaning of one sensory category to express meanings in some other sensory domains. This phenomenon has been investigated in the linguistic field as synaesthesia (e.g. Ullmann [29]; Williams [31]). Synaesthesia, as a linguistic mechanism, is defined as the expression of a particular sense by means of using terms from another sense

J.-F. Hong et al. (Eds.): CLSW 2018, LNAI 11173, pp. 70–81, 2018.
https://doi.org/10.1007/978-3-030-04015-4_6

domain (Huang and Xiong [10]), such as *sweet voice* in English and 高音 *gao1yin1* 'high pitch' in Chinese. In the literautre, these expressions are also treated as a special type of metaphor (Cacciari [1]; Geeraerts [4]) and are thus accounted for under the embodiment theory (e.g. Popova [17]; Shen [23]). In this paper, we treat synaesthesia and metaphor separately, with the former being confined to the six sensory domains while the latter transcending sensory domains.

In Sect. 2, we investigate three COLDNESS-encoding Chinese characters, viz. 寒 *han2* 'cold' 冷 *leng3* 'cold' and 涼 *liang2* 'cool' in Modern Chinese, especially with regard to their non-tactile sensory meanings, i.e., synaesthetic meanings. Moreover, their non-sensory metaphorical meanings are discussed. In Sect. 3, we move to the study of the COLDNESS-encoding characters in Āgamas, an early Buddhist texts, and figure out that COLDNESS in general, and 涼 liang2 'cool' in particular, can be associated with the philosophical meaning of nibbāna, i.e., the emancipation of the mind from all defilements as the ultimate goal of Buddhist practice (Ñāṇananda [16]).

2 COLDNESS-Related Tactile Words in Modern Chinese

We collect the data of 寒 *han2* 'cold' 冷 *leng3* 'cold' and 涼 *liang2* 'cool' in Modern Chinese from *zdic.net*. Specifically, we note down those lexical collocations which transcend their tactile meanings to extend to other sensory meanings. As shown in (1), 寒 *han2* 'cold' can modify visual nouns, such as 光 *guang1* 'light' and 色 *se4* 'color'. Also, it can collocate with another visual adjective, such as 碜 *chen0* 'ugly', to intensify the degree of ugliness. Note also that this visual meaning of 'ugly' can be further extended to auditory domain to indicate the action of "rediculing" or "deriding", which involves a secondary VISUAL-TO-AUDITORY synaesthetic transfer (Huang and Xiong, [10]). The whole process is noted down as TACTILE-TO-VISUAL-TO-AUDITORY transfer.

(1) TACTILE-TO-VISUAL expressions of 寒 han2 'cold':

a. 寒光

han2guang1
cold light
'moon light; the light of the knives and sword; winter sight'

b. 寒色

han2se4
cold color
'stern look; winter sight'

c. 寒碜

han2chen0
cold ugly
'ugly, disgraceful' or 'ridicule, deride'

Moreover, the tactile word 寒 *han2* 'cold' can modify a gustatory word, such as 酸 *suan1* 'sour'. Intrestingly, the meanng of 寒酸 han2suan1 is neither tactile nor gustatory. Rather, it refers to a visual meaning of 'shabby' or 'poor', with regard to one's look or behavior. Quite on a par with (1c), (2) is also analyzed to involve a secondary transfer. The whole process is TACTILE-TO-GUSTATORY-TO-VISUAL transfer. Unlike (1c), (2) can never express any gustuatory meaning but necessarily undergoes the secondary synaesthetic transfer.

(2) TACTILE-TO-GUSTATORY expression of 寒 han2 'cold':

寒酸
han2suan1
cold sour
'poor; shabby'

寒 *han2* 'cold' modifies mental word 心 *xin1* 'heart' to express one's mental feeling of "disheartened".

(3) TACTILE-TO-MENTAL expression of 寒 han2 'cold':

a. 寒心

han2xin1
cold heart
'disheartened'

The data of 冷 *leng3* 'cold' are presented in (4) and (5). Like 寒 *han2* 'cold', 冷 *leng3* 'cold' is amenable to TACTILE-TO-VISUAL transfer, as shown in (4). Notice that 冷 *leng3* 'cold' can collocate with sensory organs, such as 眼 *yan3* 'eye', which must trigger a secondary synaesthetic transfer (Huang and Xiong [10]). Thus, (4c) indicates a person's indifferent attitude.

(4) TACTILE-TO-VISUAL expressions of 冷 leng3 'cold':

a. 冷色

leng3se4
cold color
'cold color'

b. 冷光

leng3guang1
cold light
'cold color'

c. 冷眉冷眼

leng3mei2 leng3yan3
cold eyebrow cold eye
'indifferently; cold-shoulder'

Unlike 寒 *han2* 'cold', 冷 *leng3* 'cold' can modify an auditory verb, an adjective and a noun, as shown in (5a)-(5c), in that order.

(5) TACTILE-TO-AUDITORY expressions of 冷 leng3 'cold':

a. 冷笑

leng3xiao4
cold laugh
'sneer; laugh with dissatisfaction'

b. 冷靜

leng3jing4
cold quiet
'calm'

c. 冷言冷語

leng3yan2 leng3 yu3
cold speech cold language
'mock; ironic words'

冷 *leng3* 'cold' can be gustatory, as exemplified in (6).

(6) TACTILE-TO-GUSTATORY expression of 冷 leng3 'cold':

冷盘
leng3pan2
cold dish
'cold dish'

Crucially, it seems that 凉 *liang2* 'cool' can hardly be extended to other sensory domains under the synaesthetic mechanisms. 清凉 *qing1liang3* 'purely-cool; cool' is a case to illustrate the VISUAL-TO-TACTILE synaesthetic transfer. Differing from the foregoing examples, tactile domain is the target domain in this case.

For the sake of clarity, all the above data are presented in Table 1 below:

This table can lead to the following generalizations. First, among the three COLDNESS-related tactile words, 冷 *leng3* 'cold' seems to be most versatile in synaesthetic mappings, as it can be transferred to the visual, auditory, gustatory and mental domains. Furthermore, the collocation between 冷 *leng3* 'cold' and a sensory organ, such as 冷眉冷眼 *leng3mei2leng3yan3* 'indifferently', is attested. Huang and Xiong [10] figure out the rarity of collocation between sensory epithets and sensory organs. If such a collocation occurs, it must transcend its sensory meaning and gives rise to a metaphorical meaning. This is corroborated by 冷眉冷眼 *leng3mei2-leng3yan3,* which refers to a person's indifferent attitude, something equivalent to *cold-shoulder* in English.

Second, the three COLDNESS-related tactile words differ in their degrees of inclination towards either perceivers or sensory objects. In actuality, perception depends on the interactions between sensory stimuli and sense organs, with the

Table 1. Synaesthetic Uses of 寒 *han2* 'cold', 冷 *leng3* 'cold' and 涼 *liang2* 'cool'

synaesthesia / sense domain	tactil	tactile	tactile
visual	寒	冷	涼
	寒光 *han2guang1*	冷艳 *leng3yan4*	清凉 *qing1liang3*
	寒色 *han2se4*	冷色 *leng3se4*	
	寒碜 *han2chen0*	冷眉冷眼 *leng3mei2leng3yan3*	
auditory	N/A	冷笑 *leng3xiao4*	N/A
		冷靜 *leng3jing4*	
		冷言冷语 *leng3yan2leng3yu3*	
gustatory	寒酸 *han2suan1*	冷盘 leng3pan2	N/A
olfactory	N/A	N/A	N/A
mental	寒心 *han2xin1*	心灰意冷 *xin1hui1yi4leng3*	心涼 *xin1liang2*

assistance of one's mind. Consequently, sensory perception cannot be purely object-oriented, nor can it be purely subject-oriented. However, in actual language uses, sensory words might not always give due recognition to both sides. Some sensory words tend to be ascribed to objects as their epithets, such as colors, shapes and tastes. For example, the color term 綠 *lv4* 'green' is considered as an inalienable feature of an object, as evidenced by 綠葉 *lv4ye4* 'green leaves'. On the other hand, the tactile word 痛 *tong4* 'painful' seems to be restricted to (the feeling of) a perceiver. We seldom ascribe to an object, or a pain-trigger, the property of 痛 *tong4* "painful". There are, however, a group of sensory words that can be associated with both sensory objects and perceivers. 苦 *ku3* 'bitter' is such a case in point. It can describe the taste of an object, such as 苦茶 *ku3cha2* 'bitter tea'. Simultaneously, it can modify a person's gustatory or mental perception, such as 覺得苦 *jue2de2ku3* 'feel bitter'. In the same vein, we may distinguish the tactile words along the line of temperature. 寒 *han2* 'chilly, winter', compared with 冷 *leng3* 'cold', is more object-oriented. The words containing 寒 *han2* 'chilly, winter', such as 寒光 *han2guang1* 'moon light; the light of the knives and sword; winter sight' and 寒碜 *han2chen0* 'ugly, disgraceful; ridicule', are basically properties of objects. By contrast, 冷 *leng3* 'cold' can be both objective and subjective. 冷光 *leng3guang1* 'cold light' and 冷菜 *leng3cai4* 'cold dishes' are more on the objective side. However, 冷笑 *leng3xiao4* 'sneer',冷言冷語 *leng3yan2leng3yu3* 'mock, speak ironic words',冷眼 *leng3yan3* 'indifferently' are clearly subject-oriented, as it either modifies human behaviors, such as 笑 *xiao4* 'laugh' and 言语 *yan2yu3* 'speak', or collocates with the human sensory organ 眼 *yan3* 'eye'. 涼 *liang2* 'cool' seems to be situated between 寒 *han2* 'chilly; winter' and 冷 *leng3* 'cold' in this regard. We argue that 涼 *liang2* 'cool' is more inclined to the subject than to the object, on the grounds that some objects modified by 涼 *liang2* 'cool', such as 涼鞋 *liang2xie2* 'sandal', 涼被 *liang2bei4* 'summer quilt' and 涼亭 *liang2ting2* 'summerhouse', may not be cool in temperature *per se*. Rather, these objects modified by 涼 *liang2* 'cool' are thus-called because they can bring cool comfort to people in the summer.

Apart from synaesthetic expressions, coldness-related tactile words are subject to metaphorical extensions, without the assistance of any synaesthetic mappings. Interestingly, both 寒 *han2* 'cold' and 冷 *leng3* 'cold' can collocate with 門 men 'door', as illustrated by 寒門 *han2men2* 'poverty' and 冷門 *leng3men2* 'unpopularity; unexpectedness'. These examples can be schematized as COLDNESS IS POVERTY, COLDNESS IS UNPOPULARITY and COLDNESS IS UNEXPECTEDNESS, which we argue are in an ascending order in terms of their degrees of subjectivity. The concepts of POVERTY and UNPOPULARITY are emotionally undesirable, whereas the concept of UNEXPECTEDNESS might be neutral in emotion. This also echoes our finding that 寒 *han2* 'cold' is more object-inclined and repulsive whereas 冷 *leng3* 'cold' is more subject-oriented and neutral.

3 COLDNESS-Related Tactile Words in *Āgamas*

In this section, we present the data of the three COLDNESS-related tactile words 寒 *han2* 'cold' 冷 *leng3* 'cold' and 涼 *liang2* 'cool' in the Buddhist texts of *Āgamas*.

In the *Āgamas*, 寒 *han2* 'cold' seems to be negative in meaning. For example, it indicates a type of illness in (7) and a kind of hell in (8). Also, lack of requisites is described as 寒乞 *han2qi3* 'lack of requisites', as exemplified in (9).

(7) 時，人當有九種病，一者寒，二者熱，三者飢，四者渴，五者大便，六者小便，七者欲，八者饕餮，九者老。(佛說長阿含經卷第一;後秦弘始年佛陀耶舍共竺佛念譯:第一分初大本經第一)

Shi, ren dang you jiu zhong bing, yizhe **han**, erzhe re,
then human supposedly have nine kind illness first coldness second hotness
sanzhe ji, sizhe ke, wuzhe dabian, liuzhe xiaobian, qizhe yu,
third hunger fourth thirsty fifth defecation sixth urination seventh desire
bazhe taotie, jiuzhe lao.
eighth voraciousness ninth aging
'At that time, human beings are supposed to have nine types of shortcomings. They are coldness, hotness, hunger, thirsty, defecation, urination, desire, voraciousness and aging.'

(8) 地獄有十六小獄，... 十六名寒氷。佛說長阿含經卷第十九;後秦弘始年佛陀耶舍共竺佛念譯:第四分世記經地獄品第四)

Diyu you shiliu xiao yu… shiliu ming **han** bing.
hell have sixteen small hell sixteenth name cold ice
'There are sixteen sub-types of hells … The sixteenth is icy-cold hell.'

(9) 若聖弟子成就四不壞淨者，… 不寒乞，自然富足。(雜阿含經卷第三十;宋天竺三藏求那跋陀羅譯:八三四)

Ruo shengdizi chengjiu sibu huai jing zhe, … bu **han** qi, ziran fuzu.
if saint disciple attain stream-entry person NEG cold beg naturally rich
'If a disciple attains stream-entry… he will never end with insufficient requisites. Rather, he will have abundant requisites.'

By contrast, 冷 *leng3* 'cold' is moderately cold and thus neutral, as shown in its examples in the Āgamas.

(10) 阿難白言：「今拘孫河去此不遠，清冷可飲，亦可澡浴。」(佛說長阿含經卷第三;後秦弘始年佛陀耶舍共竺佛念譯:遊行經第二中)

A nan baiyan: jin jusun he qu ci bu yuan, qing **leng** ke yin,
Ānanda say now JUSUN river from here not far clear cold can drink
yi ke zaoyu.
also can bath
'Venerable Ānanda said: Jusun River is not far away from here. The water in the river is clean and cool so that we can fetch water there for both drinking and showering.'

The most interesting finding of this study is that COLDNESS is employed to refer to mental tranquility, an instance of TACTILE-TO-MENTAL synaesthetic transfer. For example, in the *Āgamas*, 冷 *leng3* 'cold' is employed to modify the *Tathāgata,* the enlightened one. These two examples are presented in (11) and (12).

(11) 如來是梵，如來是冷，如來不煩熱，如來是不異。(中阿含經卷第五十四;東晉罽賓三藏瞿曇僧伽提婆譯大品:阿梨吒經第九)

Rulai shi fan, rulai shi **leng**, rulai shi bu fan re,
Tathāgata be Brahma Tathāgata be cold Tathāgata be not upset hot
rulai shi bu yi.
Tathāgata be not change
'Tathāgata is the Brahma, Tathāgata is cold, Tathāgata is free from the upsetting fever and Tathāgata is not changing.'

(12) 身壞後，既由命盡，正於此處一切受不歡喜，當了知清冷。(增支部經典第四卷 0324a11)

Shen huai hou, ji you ming jin, zheng chu yu cichu yiqie shou bu
body break_up after then for life end exactly exist at here all feeling not
huanxi, dang lezhi qing **leng**.
delight_in should understand clean cold

'With the breakup of the body, following the exhaustion of life, all that is felt, not being delighted in, will become **cool** right here.'

Other than the examples of 冷 *leng3* 'cold' with the indication of nibbāna, the tactile word 涼 *liang2* 'cool' is much more frequently employed to refer to nibbāna, as exemplified in (13) and (14) below.

(13)「...又有一類人，不使自苦，不專修自苦之行；亦不使他苦，不專修使他苦之行；彼不使自苦，不使他苦者，於現法（現在世）、無貪欲、達涅槃、清**涼**、感受樂，依自己成為最高者（世尊）而住之。...」

You you yi lei ren, bu shi zi ku, bu zhuan xiu zi ku

Again have one type person not make oneself suffer not exclusively practice self suffer zhi xing; yi bu shi ta ku, bu zhuan xiu shi ta ku zhi

DE practice again not make others suffer not exclusively practice make others suffer DE

xing, bi bu shi zi ku, bu shi ta ku zhe, yu xianfa,

practice others not make oneself suffer not make others suffer person at here_and_now

wu tanyu da niepan, qing **liang**, ganshou le, yi ziji

not_have desire attain nibbāna clean cool feel pleasure depend_on oneself

chengwei zui gao zhe er zhu zhi.

become most high person then abide_in it

'... Here a certain kind of person does not torment himself or pursue the practice of torturing himself, and he does not torment others and pursue the practice of torturing others. Since he torments neither himself nor others, he is here and now hungerless, extinguished, and **cooled**, and he abides experiencing bliss, having himself become holy....'

(14) 一切時樂寐，圓寂婆羅門；

不為諸欲染，清**涼**無依止；

三漏總斷已，止息苦痛心；

寂靜而樂寐，心得安靜故。

Yiqie shi le mei, yuanji poluomen

all time happy sleep nibbāna Brahmin

Bu wei zhu yu ran, qing **liang** wu yizhi

not for all desire taint clear cool not dependence

San lou zong duan yi, zhixi ku tong xin

three defilement all cut_off finish end bitterness pain heart

Jijing er le mei, xin de anjing gu.

silent and happily sleep heart attain peace reason

'He always sleeps well, the Brahmin who has attained nibbāna, **cooled off**, without acquisition, not tainted by sensual pleasures. Having cut off all attachments, having removed anguish in the heart, the peaceful one sleeps well, having attained peace of mind.'

The above examples show that COLDNESS IS MENTAL TRANSQUILTY is attested in the Buddhist texts. Such usages, however, are not attested in Modern Chinese. Morever, mental tranquility is considered as the supreme bliss, which transends the ordinary sensory perceptions (Ñāṇananda [16]). Given this, the meaning is positive, with special regard to its evaluative emotional polarity (Xiong and Huang [32]). By constrast, the mental meanings of COLDNESS in Modern Chinese, such as 寒心 *han2xin1* 'disheartened' and 心冷 *xin1leng3* 'disppointed' are of negative emotion.

4 Conclusions and Implications

It seems that nibbāna lies in the tactile feeling of COLDNESS, mostly in 涼 *liang2* 'cool' and occasionally in 冷 *leng3* 'cold'. According to the COLDNESS-encoding usages in Modern Chinese, 涼 *liang2* 'cool' is most inert in the sense that it is almost unlikely to undergo any synaesthetic transfers to express non-tactile meanings. By contrast, 冷 *leng3* 'cold' and 寒 *han2* 'cold' are relatively more versatile in their synaesthetic uses.

Nibbāna, which literally means "extinguishment of fire", refers to mental emancipation in Buddhist philosophy. In consideration of its literal meaning, it is not unexpected that COLDNESS, but not HOTNESS, is associated with nibbāna. Moreover, among the different types of COLDNESS, it is the moderate one with positive emotion (e.g., comfortable), viz. 涼 *liang2* 'cool', is selected as the most appropriate one for the expression of nibbāna. This is probably because 涼 *liang2* 'cool' can best represent the non-extreme sensory feelings.

Furthermore, it is particularly interesting to note that nibbāna, which transcends sensory perception, is however expressed by sensory words. Our preliminary study shows that a small group of sensory words, out of a rich repertoire of sensory vocabulary, has been selected to express the highest goal of Buddhist practice, i.e., nibbāna. The attested sensory words are listed in in Table 2 below.

Table 2. The Sensory Expressions of Nibbāna

	visual	auditory	gustatory	tactile
nibbāna	明 *ming2* 'lustrous' 圓寂 *yuan2ji4* 'round-silence'	寂靜 *ji4jing4* 'silent'	無味 *wu2wei4* 'without taste'	清涼 *qing1liang2* 'cool'

In the future study, we are keen on investigating how these sensory words are able to encode nibbāna and in what way they are related to one another. Put differently, what features group those sensory words together under the category of mental tranquility?

References

1. Cacciari, C.: Crossing the senses in metaphorical language. In: Raymond, G. (ed.) The Cambridge Handbook of Metaphor and Thought, pp. 425–443. Cambridge University Press, New York (2008)
2. Cytowic, R.E.: Synaesthesia: A Union of the Senses. MIT Press, Cambridge (2002)
3. Cytowic, R.E.: The Man Who Tasted Shapes: A Bizarre Medical Mystery Offers Revolutionary Insights into Reasoning, Emotion, and Consciousness. Putman, New York (1993)
4. Geeraerts, D.: Theories of Lexical Semantics. Oxford University Press, New York (2010)
5. Hong, J.-F., Huang, C.-R.: A study of Chinese sensation verbs used in linguistic synaesthesia. Chinese Lexical Semantics. LNCS (LNAI), vol. 9332, pp. 62–73. Springer, Cham (2015). https://doi.org/10.1007/978-3-319-27194-1_7
6. Hong, J.-F., Huang, C.-R.: 洪嘉馡，黃居仁. The near synonym pair Sheng and Yin: A study of the relation between sense and concept 「聲」與「音」的近義辨析：詞義與概念的關係. Paper presented at the Chinese lexical semantic workshop: current and trends in chinese lexical semantic research *漢語詞彙語意研究的現狀與發展趨勢國際學術研討會*. Peking University, Beijing (2004)
7. Hong, J.-F., Huang,C.-R.: 洪嘉馡，黃居仁. The near synonym pair Sheng and Yin: a study of the relation between sense and cognitive concept 「聲」與「音」的近義辨析：詞義與認知概 念的關係。 In: 何大安、姚玉敏、陳忠敏、孫景濤、張洪年編輯。《漢語與漢藏語前沿研究—— 丁邦新先生八秩壽慶論文集》.Beijing:社會科學文獻出版社（北京） (2018)
8. Huang, C.-R.: 黃居仁. Synaesthesia: Language, thought, cognition and culture 思考と言語. IEICE Technical report *信学技報*, vol. 116, no. 368 pp. 111–113 (2016)
9. Huang, C.-R., Hsieh, S.-K.: Chinese lexical semantics: from radicals to event structure. In: Wang, W.S.-Y., Sun, C.-F. (eds.) The Oxford handbook of Chinese Linguistics, pp. 290–305. Oxford University Press, New York (2015)
10. Huang, C.-R., Xiong, J.: Linguistic synaesthesia in Chinese. In: Huang, C.-R., Zhuo, J.-S., Meisterernst, B. (eds.) Routledge Handbook of Chinese Applied Linguistics. Routledge (to appear)
11. Karunadasa, Y.: The Buddhist Analysis of Matter. The University of Hong Kong, Hong Kong, Hong Kong (2015)
12. Lakoff, G., Johnson, M.: Philosophy in the Flesh: The Embodied Mind and Its Challenge to Western Thought. Basic Books, New York (1999)
13. Lakoff, G., Johnson, M.: Metaphors We Live By. University of Chicago Press, Chicago (1980)
14. Lynott, D., Connell, L.: Modality exclusivity norms for 423 object properties. Behav. Res. Methods **41**(2), 558–564 (2009)
15. Ñāṇananda, K.: The End of the World in Buddhist Perspective. Pothgulgala Dharmagrantha Dharmasravana Mādhya Bhāraya (2014)

16. Ñāṇananda, K.: Nibbāna - The Mind Stilled, Library edn. Pothgulgala Dharmagrantha Dharmasravana Mādhya Bhāraya, Colombo (2015)
17. Popova, Y.: Image schemas and verbal synaesthesia. In: Beate, H. (ed.) Perception to Meaning: Image Schemas in Cognitive Linguistics, pp. 395–420. de Gruyter, Berlin (2005)
18. Rakova, M.: The Extent of the Literal: Metaphor, Polysemy and the Theories of Concepts. Palgrave Macmillan, Hampshire (2003)
19. Ramachandran, V.S., Hubbard, E.M.: The emergence of the human mind: some clues from synaesthesia. In: Lynn, C.R., Sagiv, N. (eds.) Synaesthesia: Perspectives from Cognitive Neuroscience, pp. 147–192. Oxford University Press, New York (2005)
20. Ramachandran, V.S., Hubbard, E.M.: The phenomenology of synesthesia. J. Conscious. Stud. **10**(8), 49–57 (2003)
21. Ramachandran, V.S., Hubbard, E.M.: Psychophysical investigations into the neural basis of synaesthesia. Proc. R. Soc. Lond. B Biol. Sci. **268**(1470), 979–983 (2001)
22. Ramachandran, V.S., Hubbard, E.M.: Synaesthesia — a window into perception, thought and language. J. Conscious. Stud. **8**(12), 3–34 (2001)
23. Shen, Y.: Cognitive constraints on poetic figures. Cognit. Linguist. (includes Cognitive Linguistic Bibliography) **8**(1), 33–71 (1997)
24. Lievers, F.S., Huang, C.-R.: A lexicon of perception for the identification of synaesthetic metaphors in corpora. In: Calzolari, N., et al. (eds.) Proceedings of the 10th Language Resources and Evaluation Conference (LREC 2016), pp. 4032–4036. ELRA, Paris (2016)
25. Strik Lievers, F.: Synesthésies: Croisements des sens entre langage et perception. L'Information Grammaticale **146**, 25–31 (2015)
26. Strik Lievers, F.: Synaesthesia: a corpus-based study of cross-modal directionality. Funct. Lang. **22**(1), 69–94 (2015)
27. Lievers, F.S., Winter, B.: Sensory language across lexical categories. Lingua (2018). https://doi.org/10.1016/j.lingua.2017.11.002
28. Ullmann, S.: Semantic Universals. In: Universals of Language, 2nd edn., pp. 217–262. The MIT Press, Cambridge, London (1966 [1963])
29. Ullmann, S.: Romanticism and synaesthesia: a comparative study of sense transfer in Keats and Byron. Publ. Mod. Lang. Assoc. Am. **60**(3), 811–827 (1945)
30. Yu, N.: Synesthetic metaphor: a cognitive perspective. J. Lit. Semant. **32**(1), 19–34 (2003)
31. Williams, J.M.: Synaesthetic adjectives: a possible law of semantic change. Language **52**(2), 461–478 (1976)
32. Xiong, Jiajuan, Huang, Chu-Ren: Being assiduous: do we have BITTERNESS or PAIN? Chinese Lexical Semantics. LNCS (LNAI), vol. 9332, pp. 15–23. Springer, Cham (2015). https://doi.org/10.1007/978-3-319-27194-1_2
33. Xiong, J., Huang, C.-R.: The synaesthetic and metaphorical uses of 味 *wei* 'taste' in Chinese Buddhist Suttras. In: PACLIC-30, Seoul (2016)
34. Xiong, J., Huang,C.-R.: The hardness of determination and reassurance: a corpus-based study of 硬 *yìng*. Paper presented at the 18th Chinese lexical semantics workshop (CLSW), Leshan, China (2017)
35. Zhao, Q., Xiong, J., Huang, C.-R.: 赵青青,熊佳娟,黄居仁. 通感、隐喻与认知——通感现象在汉语中的系统性表现与语言学价值 Linguistic Synaesthesia, Metaphor and Cognition: the systematicity and significance of linguistic synaesthesia in Chinese. To Appear in *Zhongguo Yuwen* 《中国语文》 (to appear)
36. Zhao, Q., Huang, C.-R., Long, Y.: Synaesthesia in Chinese: a corpus-based study on gustatory adjectives in Mandarin. Linguistics **56**, 1167 (2018)

37. Zhao, Q., Huang, C.-R.: 赵青青,黄居仁. 2018. 现代汉语通感隐喻的映射模型与制约机制 A Study on the Mapping Model and Underlying Mechanisms of Synaesthetic Metaphors in Mandarin.《语言教学与研究》Language Teaching and Linguistic Studies. 01(no. 189), pp. 44–55 (2018)
38. Zhao, Q., Huang, C.-R.: From linguistic synaesthesia to embodiment: asymmetrical representations of taste and smell in Mandarin Chinese. Paper presented at the 18th Chinese lexical semantics workshop (CLSW), Leshan, China (2017)

Grammaticalization of *Shuo* and *Jiang* in Singapore Mandarin Chinese: A Spoken-Corpus-Based Study

Jingxia Lin(✉)

Nanyang Technological University, 48 Nanyang Avenue, Singapore 639818, Singapore
jingxialin@ntu.edu.sg

Abstract. This study investigates the extended grammatical uses of the speech act verbs 说 *shuō* 'say' and 讲 *jiǎng* 'say' in Singapore Mandarin Chinese (SMC). With data from a contemporary spoken corpus, the study finds that while both 说 and 讲 are major speech act verbs in SMC, 说 has been more grammatically expanded than 讲 not only in SMC, but also in its counterparts, namely other Mandarin varieties and Chinese dialects. The extension has been motivated by both language-external and language-internal factors. The findings of this study will contribute not only to the typology of speech act verbs and their grammaticalization in general, but also to the study of language variations and changes.

Keywords: Speech act verbs · Singapore Mandarin · Complementizer

1 Introduction

The extended uses of speech act verbs (or SAY verbs) have been discussed in a good number of literature on a variety of languages. For the Chinese language, it has been observed that different dialects tend to adopt different speech act verbs, e.g., 说 'say' in the Northern, 话 'say' in the Southern, and 讲 'say' in the middle [1]. Moreover, these speech act verbs have undergone different degrees of grammaticalization and have acquired different functions, e.g., as a complementizer, a topic marker, or a conjunction [2–4, among others].

Contemporary Singapore Mandarin Chinese (SMC) shares the major linguistic features with Mainland China Mandarin Chinese (MMC), but exhibits a variety of features that are to a great extent either triggered by the properties of SMC itself or motivated by language contact to local dominant languages such as English and Malay and local Chinese dialects such as Min (Southern Min, Teochew, Hainanese, etc.) and Cantonese [5]. The two major speech act verbs 说 *shuō* and 讲 *jiǎng* in SMC are among the ones that show special features different from the other varieties of standard Mandarin, e.g., MMC and Taiwanese Mandarin Chinese (TMC). For instance, while both 说 and 讲 can serve as discourse markers, in expressions such as 说/讲真的 'honestly speaking' and (我)跟你说/讲 'let me tell you', SMC prefers 讲 *jiǎng* over 说 *shuō*, whereas MMC has an opposite preference.

J.-F. Hong et al. (Eds.): CLSW 2018, LNAI 11173, pp. 82–90, 2018.
https://doi.org/10.1007/978-3-030-04015-4_7

Furthermore, in SMC, 说 frequently occurs after another verb and functions as a complementizer to turn an independent sentence into an object clause. As illustrated in (1a) and (1b) respectively, 说 introduces 每天都吃很多 'eat (it) a lot every day' and 我们女人的疑心病很重 'we women are paranoid' as the objects of the verbs 建议 'suggest' and 觉得 'think'. However, neither the 讲 in SMC nor 说/讲 in MMC is commonly found in such a use.

1. a. 其实我也不**建议说**每天都吃很多因为它是一种高能量的嘛 (xmbdwt4-ep7)
   'Actually, I don't suggest that you eat a lot everyday because it is high-caloric.'
   b. 所以你们男人就**觉得说**我们女人的疑心病很重 (jxhxdbt-ep5)
   'So, you guys think that we women are paranoid.'

There are relatively few studies that focus on the meanings, functions, and distributions of 说 and 讲 in SMC, or compare these two with their counterparts in other varieties of Mandarin or Chinese dialects. This study aims to fill this gap with a spoken-corpus-based investigation of 说 and 讲 in SMC. By comparisons with MMC and Chinese dialects, this study proposes that the speech act verb 说 in SMC has grammaticalized to a further degree than its counterparts and cognates. Furthermore, this study argues that the variations that SMC displays are triggered by both language external and internal factors.

The paper is structured as follows: Sect. 2 presents the extended uses of 说 and 讲 in SMC. In Sect. 3, this paper focuses on their uses as a (semi-)complementizer and discusses the motivations that may have led to the special features exhibited by 说 and 讲 in SMC. Section 4 concludes the whole study.

2 说 and 讲 in SMC

2.1 Extended Uses of Speech Act Verbs in Chinese Dialects

Speech act verbs have been observed to undergo grammaticalization in many languages in the world. (2) presents the possible functions of grammaticalized speech act verbs found in Chinese dialects, including Taiwanese Southern Min, Cantonese, and Beijing Mandarin Chinese [4].[1]

2. a. quotative marker or complementizer; marker of embedded questions
   b. conditional conjunction
   c. reason or purpose conjunction
   d. causal conjunction
   e. topic marker
   f. discourse marker at clause-initial or clause-final positions

[1] See Chappell [4] for a summary of all functions from studies such as Lord [6], Hock [7], Saxena [8], and Heine and Kuteva [9].

2.2 Grammaticalization of 说 and 讲 in SMC

In SMC, both 说 and 讲 are frequently used as speech act verbs. The functions of 说 and 讲 in SMC will be examined based on a corpus of contemporary Spoken Singapore Mandarin Chinese. The spoken corpus consists of around 0.54 million of Chinese characters transcribed from five local variety shows (46 episodes in total) broadcasted between the years 2012 and 2015. The corpus finds 1,658 instances of 说 and 1,085 instances of 讲, with the former approximately 1.5 times more frequent than the latter. This study randomly selected about 30% of the samples, i.e. 500 instances of 说 and 300 instances of 讲 for a close examination.

As shown in Table 1, the usages of 说 and 讲 can be classified into four major types according to their functions identified from the corpus examples: (a) as a speech act verb; (b) as part of a lexical word; (c) as part of a grammatical sequence; (d) as a (semi-) complementizer. All functions in (2) are possible for 说 in SMC, but not necessarily with 讲 in SMC. The rest of this section will introduce the similarities and differences between 说 and 讲.

Table 1. Functions of 说 and 讲 in SMC

Speech act verb		208 (41.6%)	210 (70%)
As a part of a lexical word		35 (7%)	35 (11.7%)
As a part of a grammatical sequence	(i) Topic marker	11 (2.2%)	9 (3%)
	(ii) Sentential adverbial	9 (1.8%)	3 (1%)
	(iii) Discourse marker of self-evident assertion, warning, etc.	41 (8.2%)	43 (14.3%)
	(iv) Conjunction introducing condition, purpose, reason, etc.	84 (16.8%)	0 (0%)
(Semi-)complementizer		112 (22.4%)	0 (0%)
Total		500 (100%)	300 (100%)

Table 1 shows that 说 and 讲 in SMC share several major functions. First, both 说 and 讲 can be used as a speech act verb. They can take an object (3a) or introduce a direct or a reported speech (3b, 3c). They behave like typical verbs in that they can be negated (e.g., 不说 'not to say'), reduplicated (e.g., 说说 'say a bit'), suffixed with aspectual markers (e.g., 说着 'saying'), or take a resultative complement (e.g., 说出来 'speak out').

3. a. 你其实你不用说太多话 (jxhxdbt-ep8)
   'You… actually you do not need to say much.'
   b. 她一直说我只要名牌包包 (jxhxdbt-ep5)
   'She kept saying 'I only want designer bags.''
   c. 他还说我是上天赐给他的礼物 (jxhxdbt-ep4)
   'He said I am the gift from the heavens for him.'

Second, both 说 and 讲 are also found as a morpheme in lexical words such as 说话/讲话 'say', 说法 'explanation', and 讲解 'explanation; to explain'. Third, as shown in (c) of Table 2, both 说 and 讲 can occur in fixed collocations to perform a variety of functions: (i) as a topic marker, e.g., 对女生来说 'as for girls' and 对我来讲 'as for me', (ii) as a sentential adverbial, e.g., 总的来说/一般来讲 'generally speaking', (iii) as a discourse marker (e.g., 我跟你讲/跟你说 'let me tell you') to express speaker's self-assertion (4a) or warning (4b).

4. a. 你会后悔的，我跟你讲 (xfz8z-ep5)
   'You will regret it. I say to you.'
   b. 我要吐了，我跟你讲快吐了 (xfz8z-ep1)
   'I'm going to vomit. I say to you. I'm going to vomit.'

Nonetheless, differences are also found between the two speech act verbs. Here I highlight three of the major ones. First, while both can function as speech act verbs, the majority of 讲 (70%) is used as a speech act verb, whereas the same only goes for less than half (41.6%) of 说. Second, as presented in Table 1, 说 can collocate with a variety of conjunctions introducing clauses such as condition (如果说/比方说 'if X'), purpose (所以说 'so that X'), and reason (因为说 'because X'), but 讲 is not found in such collocations. Third, a good number of 说 (22.4%) is found as a (semi-)complementizer, but 讲 does not have such a use. All these three differences suggest that 说 is used less often as a verb and more as a functional word, and 说 has acquired more grammatical functions than 讲. In other words, 说 has travelled much further than 讲 in the path of grammaticalization. Due to the constraints of space, the next section will only discuss in more detail the third difference between 说 and 讲 in SMC, i.e. as a (semi-)complementizer.

3 说 and 讲 as Complementizers in SMC

3.1 Speech Act Verbs Functioning as Complementizers

The grammaticalization of speech act verbs into a complementizer has been observed in different languages, particularly the language families in South and Southeast Asia and Africa [4]. Where Chinese is concerned, Chappell points out that the speech act verbs in Taiwan Southern Min, Taiwanese Mandarin, and Beijing Mandarin have reached an advanced stage of grammaticalization, those in Cantonese and Hakka are more at the incipient stage, whereas MMC and other dialects such as Shanghainese Wu and Changsha Xiang are seldom found with any complementizer [4].

Both Fang [3] and Chappell [4] propose that speech act verbs in Chinese dialects undergo two major stages on the way of grammaticalization into complementizers.[2] Take Fang's [3] investigation of 说 in Beijing Mandarin as an example. At the first stage, 说 occurs after another speech act verb and functions as a semi-complementizer, e.g., "告诉我 'tell me' + 说 + clause" in (5a). At this stage, either the speech act verb and its object (e.g., 告诉我) or 说 can be deleted without affecting the meaning. At the second stage, 说 occurs after a non-speech act verb and functions as a complementizer, e.g., 认为 'think' + 说 + clause in (5b). At this point, 说 no longer expresses any speech act. Furthermore, only 说, but not the matrix verb 认为, can be deleted without affecting the meaning.[3]

5. a. 到了前两天，他忽然来了，**告诉我说**，他 在别处借着银子了, 这个银子他不用了。(谈论新篇) [3]
   'Two days ago, he came suddenly and told me that he managed to borrow money from somewhere else and did not have to use this money.'
   b. 到了前两天，他忽然来了，**告诉我说**，他 在别处借着银子了, 这个银子他不用了。(谈论新篇) [3]
   'There are many people who think that their unemployment is not their responsibility but rather an issue that should be solved by the government.'

Chappell [4] proposes an implicational hierarchy of verb types that may co-occur with complementizers. As illustrated in (6), the hierarchy consists of five types of verbs from left to right. If a verb type in the hierarchy can co-occur with a complementizer, the verb types on the left of the given verb type can also co-occur with the complementizer. The hierarchy also indicates that the more grammaticalized a complementizer is, the more verb types it can co-occur with. For instance, a complementizer that can co-occur with Type (a–d) has reached a higher degree of grammaticalization than a complementizer that can only co-occur with Type (a–c).

6. (a) speech act verbs < (b) cognition and perception verbs < (c) stative and emotion verbs < (d) modal verbs < (e) factive verbs in general

[2] Fang [3] and Chappell [4] adopt different terms for the grammatical status of speech act verbs at different stages of grammaticalization. According to Fang [3], the speech act verbs become a quotatative marker in the first stage and a semi-complementizer in the second stage, but according to Chappell [4], the speech act verbs are considered a semi-complementizer in the first stage, and a complementizer in the second stage. This study follows [4].

[3] In addition to the two stages, Fang's [3] study of Beijing Mandarin proposes a third stage, where 说 occurs after a noun and functions to introduce an appositive clause for the noun. For instance, the clause 上电视演戏 'act on TV' in (i) is appositive of the noun 机会. While being linguistically interesting, in these cases, 说 functions as a complementizer that links a noun complement with a noun, which thus differs from Fang's [3] first two stages where 说 links a verb complement with a verb. In addition, because 说 in SMC is not found as a noun clause complementizer, such a function will not be explored in more detail in this paper.

(i) 好容易有个机会, **说**上电视演戏, 结果她还不让去 [3]
'Finally, there was an opportunity that I could act on TV, but she did not allow me to do so.'

According to Chappell [4], the verb types in (6) are found to collocate with quotative complementizers in a variety of languages across various language families like Tibeto-Burman, Indo-Iranian, Dravidian and Malayo-Polynesian (see more in [4]). Of the two standard Mandarin (MMC and TMC) and eight Chinese dialects (Southern Min, Cantonese, Beijing Mandarin, Sixian Hakka, Changsha Xiang, Nanchang Gan, Shanghainese Wu, and Huojia Jin) that Chappell [4] has investigated, the speech act verb 讲 (pronounced as *kóng*) in (Taiwanese) Southern Min has grammaticalized to the highest degree. It is found to co-occur with verbs from Type (a–d), that is, speech act verbs, cognition and perception verbs, stative and emotion verbs, and modal verbs. On the contrary, the speech act verbs in MMC and a few Chinese dialects (Xiang, Gan, Wu, and Jin) have not been grammaticalized to any degree and they typically do not co-occur with any verb type in (6).

3.2 Speech Act Verbs Functioning as (Semi-)complementizers in SMC

As presented in Table 1, of the 500 instances of 说 in SMC, 22.4% (i.e. 112 instances) function as a (semi-)complementizer. Among them, two instances are identified where 讲 and 说 form a (semi-)complementizer compound. In the following, I will first introduce the 110 cases where 说 alone is used as a (semi-)complementizer before discussing 讲说.

Table 2 presents the types of verbs that can occur before the (semi-)complementizer 说 in SMC. Recall that in Chappell's [4] study, 讲 in Taiwanese Southern Min is, by far, the most grammaticalized complementizer among all Mandarin varieties and dialects investigated, but it is only found to co-occur with four types of verbs in (6), i.e. Types (a-d). Table 2 thus suggests that 说 in SMC is much more grammaticalized than 讲 in Taiwanese Southern Min; 说 not only is found with all the five verb types in (6), but also has been extended to collocating with common action verbs such as 导致 'cause' (7a), 试过 'try' (7b), and 确保 'ensure' (7c), i.e. type (f) in Table 2. The extension to common action verbs suggests that 说 has further generalized and productively functions as a complementizer that links a clause with a matrix verb.

Table 2. Types of verb that occur before (semi-)complementizer 说

Verb type	**Example**	**Freq.**
Speech act verbs	讲 'say', 问 'ask', 投诉 'complain', 提到 'mention', 承认 'admit'	18 (16.4%)
Cognition/ perception verbs	觉得 'feel', 发现 'find', 以为 'think', 想 'think'	25 (22.7%)
Stative/ copular/ emotion verbs	代表 'mean', 是 'is', 担心 'worry'	39 (35.5%)
Modal verbs	想 'want', 不会 'will not', 可以 'can'	15 (13.6%)
Factive verbs	知道 'know', 误解 'misunderstand'	7 (6.4%)
Common action verbs	导致 'cause', 试过 'try', 确保 'ensure'	6 (5.5%)
Total		110 (100%)

Another interesting use of the speech act verbs in SMC is the amalgamation of 讲 and 说 into a compound (semi-)complementizer. As introduced earlier, 讲 in SMC is not used as a complementizer. However, two instances exist for when 讲 and 说 have become a compound and carry the function of a (semi-)complementizer. The two instances are given in (8). In (8a), the main VP 通知往生者 'inform the dead' that by itself expresses a speech act, so the presence of 讲说 is optional and it only functions as a (semi-)complementizer. In (8b), the factive verb 知道 is the matrix verb, and 讲说 should be analyzed as a complementizer that introduces the clause object of the matrix verb.[4]

7. a. 我就是觉得是一个基因的关系所以这会**导致说**他们在情感理解度会比较细腻一些。(jxhxdbt-ep2)
   'I indeed think it is something genetic, so that it causes a consequence that they are relatively more sensitive in understanding emotions."
   b. 你要**确保说**这段感情是可以持续下去而不是约出来然后是个一夜情。(jxhxdbt-ep8)
   "You should ensure that this relationship can potentially evolve into something lasting instead of just being a one-night stand."
   c. 那有没有**试过说**你们在洗的时候啊，纽扣啊、拉链啦，还是什么东西洗掉了，你们会负责?(mcskcs-ep1)
   "Have you tried to take the responsibility for the buttons, zippers, or others that fall off during laundry?"
8. a. 我们要**通知往生者讲说**要迁移他出来，到新的地方去了。(mcskcs-ep3)
   'We need to inform the dead that we are going to move him out to a new place.'
   b. 所以看的话，我们大概就**知道讲说**这年份的话，就是大概多久的时间了。(mcs-kcs-ep3)
   'So we may know how long it has been by taking a look at it.'

3.3 Factors Motivating the Extended Uses of 说 and 讲 in SMC

In the previous sections, it is shown that in SMC, 说 has become more grammatical than 讲. This section argues that the extended uses are motivated by both language-external and language-internal factors.

As introduced in Sect. 1, while SMC shares with major linguistic features with MMC, it has also been influenced by local languages and dialects. Where language-external factors are concerned, the contact of SMC with Southern Min is probably the major reason for the grammatical extension of 说 in SMC. However, it should be noted that while both MMC and Southern Min have been involved in the case of the speech act verbs in SMC, neither of them plays the sole or the dominant role.

---

[4] Note that the corpus examples include another 11 cases where 说 and 说 occur together, but in these cases, the two do not form a compound; rather, 讲 functions as a speech act verb and 说 as a semi-complementizer, as in (i).

(i) 你跟小玲讲说她那个裙子太短 (jxhxdbt-ep6)
'Please tell Xiao Ling that her dress is too short.'

According to previous studies ([4], cf. [10, 11]), 说 in MMC is the major speech act verb but it has not yet started developing the function of being a complementizer. On the contrary, 讲 is the major speech act verb in Southern Min, and as shown in Chappell [4], it is the most grammaticalized speech act verb in all the Chinese dialects that she investigated. In this sense, if SMC was heavily influenced by MMC, 说 in SMC would have not grammaticalized because its counterpart 说 in MMC is not grammaticalized. On the other hand, if SMC was heavily influenced by Southern Min in this regard, it would have been 讲, rather than 说, in SMC that acquired the function of complementizer, because of how 讲 is the major speech act verb and how grammaticalized it is in Southern Min. Therefore, this study proposes that the grammaticalization of 说 in SMC has been induced by the interactions between MMC and Southern Min: SMC took the verb form 说 from MMC but followed 讲 in Southern Min in terms of grammaticalization.

In addition to the external factors, SMC also exhibits features that can only be ascribed to language-internal factors, that is, the motivation that leads to variations and changes by the properties of a language itself and no obvious external factor is identifiable in the process. As introduced in Sect. 3.3, 说 in SMC has grammaticalized to a degree that is higher than all other Chinese varieties, as it can co-occur with the broadest range of verbs. Therefore, even though 说 in SMC may have started its grammaticalization process following 讲 in Southern Min, it has surpassed the latter on the path of grammaticalization. Furthermore, the compound (semi-)complementizer 讲说 has not been observed in any other Mandarin varieties or Chinese dialects, which is thus probably a feature that is unique developed in SMC. As no language contact or other external factors are clearly identifiable, both the processes, the grammaticalization beyond 讲 in Southern Min and the formation of the compound (semi-)complementizer, could be consequences of the internal development of SMC.

4 Conclusion

This study investigates the extended grammatical uses of speech act verbs 说 and 讲 in SMC. It finds that 说 has been more grammatically extended than 讲 and proposes that the extension is likely to have been motivated by both language-external and language-internal factors. Nonetheless, this study has only covered 30% of the database available, more findings may be yielded when more data are analyzed. Furthermore, due to the limitation of space, this study has not discussed in more depth a few equally significant issues, including both the verbal and grammatical uses of 讲 in SMC and the discourse functions of 说 and 讲 in SMC. These issues will be explored in future studies.

Acknowledgements. The study is supported by Ministry of Education Academic Research Fund Tier 1 (RG145/15) from Singapore and the National Social Sciences Foundation for National Key Project (16ZDA209) from China.

References

1. Wang, W: Diachronic evolution and synchronic distribution of "shuo-type verbs" in Chinese (汉语"说类词"的历时演变与共时分布). Zhongguo Yuwen (中国语文) **295**(4), 329–342 (2003)
2. Dong, X.: Lexicalization of X shuo ("X 说"的词汇化). Lang. Sci. (语言科学) **3**(2), 46–57 (2003)
3. Fang, M.: Grammaticalization of shuo in Beijing Mandarin: from lexical verb to subordinator (北京话里"说"的语法化——从演说动词到从句标记). J. Chin. Dialects (中国方言学报) **1**, 107–121 (2006)
4. Chappell, H.: Variation in the grammaticalization of complementizers from verba dicendi in Sinitic languages. Linguist. Typology **12**(1), 45–98 (2008)
5. Lin, J., Shi, D., Jiang, M., Huang, C.-R.: Variations in world Chineses. In: Huang, C., Meisterernst, B., Jing-Schmidt, Z. (eds.) The Routledge Handbook of Applied Chinese Linguistics. Routledge, London (2018)
6. Lord, C.: Evidence for syntactic reanalysis: from verb to complementizer in Kwa. Chic. Linguist. Soc. **12**, 179–191 (1976)
7. Hock, H.: The Sanskrit quotative: a historical and comparative study. Stud. Linguist. Sci. **12** (2), 37–96 (1982)
8. Saxena, A.: The case of the verb "say" in Tibeto-Burman. Berkeley Linguist. Soc. **14**, 375–388 (1988)
9. Heine, B., Kuteva, T.: Language Contact and Grammatical Change. Cambridge University Press, Cambridge (2005)
10. Sui, L.: The grammatical markers shuo and dao (语法标记说和到). J. PLA Univ. Foreign Lang. (解放军外国语学院学报) **30**(4), 19–22 (2007)
11. Xuan, Y.: On a new usage of "shuo" ("说"的一种新用法——可观叙述标记词). Chin. Linguist. (汉语学报) **34**(2), 28–35 (2011)

Internal Structures and Constructional Meanings: '*Da-X-da-Y*' and Its Related Constructions in Mandarin Chinese

Chiarung Lu[1(✉)], I-Ni Tsai[2], I-Wen Su[1], and Te-Hsin Liu[2]

[1] Graduate Institute of Linguistics, National Taiwan University, Taipei 10617, Taiwan
{chiarung, iwensu}@ntu.edu.tw

[2] Graduate Program of Teaching Chinese as a Second Language, National Taiwan University, Taipei 10617, Taiwan
{initsai, tehsinliu}@ntu.edu.tw

Abstract. Adopting the theoretical framework of Construction Grammar, the present paper aims to examine the internal structures and constructional meanings of six Mandarin idiomatic prefabs: *da-X-da-Y* 'big-X-big-Y', *da-X-xiao-Y* 'big-X-small-Y', *xiao-X-xiao-Y* 'small-X-small-Y', *da-X-wu-Y* 'big-X-no-Y' and *wu-X-wu-Y* 'no-X-no-Y'. The analysis has not only identified five constructional meanings among them, but confirmed the weightiness of semantic integration between lexical and constructional senses. The semantic map approach is further applied to characterize these sense relations in illustration of any multiple inheritance nested among distinct constructional meanings. For instance, the sense of intensification or emphasis is prominent in parallel constructions: meanings inherited from the reduplication structure. On the contrary, non-parallel constructions may carry such senses as overallness, equivalence, contrast, or serve a subjunctive mood.

Keywords: Chinese four-character idioms · Construction · *Da-X-da-Y*
Quadrisyllabic idiomatic expression · Semantic map

1 Introduction

Four-character idiomatic expressions, aka QIE (Quadrisyllabic Idiomatic Expression), are so culturally tinged that they have turned into a linguistic feature of Mandarin Chinese, eventually coming along as an abiding issue in Chinese linguistic theory. From the perspective of the history of Chinese languages, Mandarin has developed from monosyllabic to disyllabic. To this point, the structure of four-character expressions can be seen as an extension of disyllabic words [1]. If disyllabic words are taken as a unit, then, a four-character expression can either function as a complete sentence or

This paper is partially supported by research grant from the Ministry of Science and Technology, Taiwan (Project number: 105-2420-H-002-009-MY2). The authors would like to express their gratitude for this support.

J.-F. Hong et al. (Eds.): CLSW 2018, LNAI 11173, pp. 91–106, 2018.
https://doi.org/10.1007/978-3-030-04015-4_8

express a proposition. In general, four-character expressions are richly found in historical stories and classic words [2, 3]. Indeed, those with historical stories are the most typical QIEs, while investigation of those without stories has nonetheless been carried out, leading to later studies on the complex internal structures of latter QIEs [4, 5]. Some previous studies focused on the categorizations of QIEs [2, 3], and others on the teaching strategies of them [6]. This study, however, addresses itself to analyzing QIEs from a different perspective by probing into their constructional meanings using a construction-grammar approach.

Lu et al. [7] conducted a detailed analysis of Chinese QIEs (i.e., *yi-X-#-Y* 'one X number Y') and proposed a constructional network of this *yi-X-#-Y* group. It was found that the constructional network forms and emerges as a result of the interpretation of both constructional meaning and lexical meaning. Indeed, Chinese native speakers interpret the meaning of a QIE out of this complex combination. For instance, the polysemy level of *yi-X-#-Y* 'one X number Y' would rise when the contrast between the first number (in first position) and the other number (in third position) appears to increase. Although the above-mentioned study can be illuminating, further investigations are required to validate its generality.

This present study brings six groups of QIEs (i.e., *da-X-da-Y* 'big-X-big-Y', *da-X-xiao-Y* 'big-X-small-Y', *xiao-X-xiao-Y* 'small-X-small-Y', *xiao-X-da-Y* 'small-X-big-Y', *da-X-wu-Y* 'big-X-no-Y', and *wu-X-wu-Y* 'no-X-no-Y') to the examination of constructional meanings, each characterizing a clear syntactic form. Moreover, after a detailed discussion of their lexical senses and constructional meanings, it aims to account for their complicated interactions by means of the semantic map approach.

This paper is organized as follows. Section 1 is introduction. Section 2 reviews key papers on idioms. Section 3 addresses data and methodology, spelling out the sources of the data and selection criteria. Section 4 presents our data analysis, based on forms and meanings of individual constructions. Section 5 discusses the underlying mechanisms in the constructional network and the interaction between construction and compositionality. The concluding remarks are found in the last section.

2 Literature Review

As mentioned earlier, a four-character idiom is defined as a chunk composed of four characters, which carries a specific communicative function or a conventional meaning unpredictable from its components. On that account, studies on the compositionality and metaphoricity of English idioms [8, 9] may lend important insights to the analysis of Chinese idioms. Also, previous studies on the syntactic structures of Chinese idioms are believed to contribute significantly to the analysis of the internal structures of Chinese idioms. In this section, we inquire briefly into the literature on compositionality of idioms, construction grammar, internal structures of Chinese idioms, and the semantic map approach.

2.1 Compositionality of Idiom

"Compositionality" must be well taken into account in analyzing idioms. In the framework of generative grammar, word meanings are held to be conventional and not predictable from syntactic rules. When words combine to form a sentence, the syntactic structures generate meanings. However, such a framework cannot account for the fact that idioms contain more than one word but are not predictable from syntactic structures. To provide an explanation, some researchers proposed Construction Grammar to address the issue of idiomaticity. Fillmore et al. [10] argued that there is a positive correlation between semantic transparency and idiomatic compositionality. That is, although the semantics of decoding idioms is opaque, the semantic transparency of encoding idioms is comparatively higher so that meanings of the latter are easier to derive from their internal components.

Some psycholinguistic studies examine the issue of semantic composition from the perspective of reaction time. Swinney and Cutler [11] proposed the lexical representation hypothesis, arguing that idioms are non-compositional in nature and their retrieval process is similar to that of words. Put alternatively, the reaction time for a native speaker to process "to break the ice" should be shorter than that of "to break the glass." However, this hypothesis fails to explain why the reaction time for "to pop the question" is shorter than "to kick the bucket" provided that they both belong with idioms. To answer this question, Gibbs and Nayak [8] put forward the idiom decomposition hypothesis, which draws attention to the idiosyncrasy of internal properties of an idiom. In fact, idioms, such as "to pop the question," contain more decomposable elements than others so that their semantic transparency appears to be greater than that of such idioms as "to kick the bucket," whose composite meaning is not predictable from its components. Tinone and Connine [12] struck a middle ground indicating that idioms are compositional sequences, and, at the same time, are conventional products. They argued that two types of interactions should emerge during the retrieval of the individual sense of components in an idiom. One type holds that if the idiom is decomposable, then the individual sense of each component contributes to the interpretation of the overall meaning of that idiom. The other type, however, runs the opposite way: If the meaning of an idiom is opaque, then the individual sense of a component will impair the understanding of the whole idiom.

2.2 The Internal Structure of Chinese QIEs

Hu [13] (p. 302) and scholars such as Liu and Xing [14] categorized Chinese QIEs into two types: parallel and non-parallel. The former can be illustrated by *tian-fan-di-fu* 天翻地覆 'sky-turn-earth-cover; heaven and earth turning upside down' where *tian-fan* and *di-fu* share similar syntactic structures, namely, paralleled and symmetric. The latter can be realized by *xiong-you-cheng-zhu* 胸有成竹 'chest-have-mature-bamboo, meaning 'to have a well-considered plan', which contains a relatively complete syntactic structure (i.e., subject, predicate and object). Tsou [5] conducted a series of research on four-character idioms and proposed a special term to catalog these idioms, namely, QIE (Quadrisyllabic Idiomatic Expression). A QIE consists of four syllables and boasts parallel and repetition as its two salient features in terms of structure.

According to Tsou [5], QIEs with a parallel structure account for 35% of all QIEs: e.g., *long-fei-feng-wu* 龍飛鳳舞 'dragon-fly-phoenix-dance; lively and vigorous flourishes in calligraphy' and *feng-qi-yun-yong* 風起雲湧 'wind-rise-cloud-scud; rolling on with full force'. QIEs with a modification structure account for 21.5%: e.g., *da-qian-shi-jie* 大千世界 'big-thousand-world; the boundless universe'. Other QIEs with a subject-predicate structure make up 17.5%: e.g., *ni-niu-ru-hai* 泥牛入海 'mud-ox-enter-sea; like a clay ox entering the sea, gone without return'. Lastly, QIEs with a predicate-object structure make up 15%: e.g., *yi-jue-ci-xiong* 一決雌雄 'one-decide-female-male; fight a decisive battle'. Furthermore, according to the the statistical result, based on *The Modern Dictionary of Idioms* published in 1994, Liu and Xing [14] reported that out of 12,703 idiom entries, 39.2% belongs with symmetric structure, which is similar to Tsou's [5] finding (i.e., 35%).

No consensus has been reached on how to categorize the internal structures of Chinese QIEs. For instance, in *A General Introduction to Modern Chinese* [15], QIEs have been divided into two types: parallel and non-parallel. The parallel type is sorted into four subtypes: subject-predicate (e.g., *long-fei-feng-wu* 龍飛鳳舞), predicate-object (e.g., *gu-ming-si-yi* 顧名思義), modification (e.g., *xing-feng-xie-yu* 腥風血雨), and juxtaposition (e.g., *qing-hong-zao-bai* 青紅皂白). On the other hand, the non-parallel type embraces five subtypes: subject-predicate (e.g., *ye-lang-zi-da* 夜郎自大), predicate-object (e.g., *yi-xiang-tian-kai* 大同小異), modification (e.g., *jin-shui-lou-tai* 近水樓台), pivotal (e.g., *ren-zei-zuo-fu* 認賊作父), and serial (e.g., *yao-dao-bing-chu* 藥到病除). Another approach categorizes QIEs in terms of their semantic senses, which oftentimes results in fuzzy boundaries and overlapping categories. These categories are hypernymy (e.g., *san-jiao-jiu-liu* 三教九流), old Chinese sayings (e.g., *san-si-er-xing* 三思而行), cultural norms (e.g., *san-cong-si-de* 三從四德), cultural scripts (e.g., *san-guo-qi-men* 三過其門), synonymy combination (e.g., *shuo-san-dao-si* 說三道四), and antonymy combination (e.g., *san-chang-liang-duan* 三長兩短). Yet another study characterizes these QIEs using "quasi-fixed structures" [16]. Hence, the five basic patterns: open slots in first and third syllables (e.g., *X-lai-Y-qu* 'X-come-Y-go' as in *zou-lai-zou-qu* 走來走去), open slots in second and fourth syllables (e.g., *ban-X-ban-Y* 'half-X-half-Y' as in *ban-xin-ban-yi* 半信半疑), open slots in first and last syllables (e.g., *X-bu-ke-Y* '(too much) X-(so that) no-possible-Y' as in *gao-bu-ke-pan* 高不可攀), embedded chunks (e.g., *bu-ke-XY* 'not-possible-XY' as in *bu-ke-li-yu* 不可理喻), and one fixed syllable (e.g., *XY-ru-Z* 'XY-as (if)-Z' as in *yi-pin-ru-xi*一貧如洗).

2.3 Construction Grammar and Idioms

Moon [17] (p. 161) posited that an entrenched linguistic chunk can be taken as an important constraint in the process of idiom production where a kind of idiomatic schema may start to take shape. Fillmore et al. [10] (p. 516) also argued that the proliferation and productivity of idioms lies in basic structural conventions, resulting from the multi-operations of syntactic, semantic and pragmatic phases. Studies based on frame semantics usually aim at telling apart the different functions from syntactic, semantic, and pragmatic perspectives, and at figuring out the senses of specific structural regularity and their constructions. Goldberg [18] defined "construction" not only as a meaningful pair of form and meaning, but as essential important element for constituting linguistic structures. She pointed out that in English exist a variety of grammatical phenomena that cannot be explained by considering lexical properties or syntactic rules alone. Idioms are indeed built up by specific constructions. Also, Bybee [19] proposed several tiers of construction according to differing degrees of conventionality and substitutability. In this notion, the most abstract one should lie in the syntactic configuration such as the ditransitive construction [V NP_1 NP_2], where a sense of *giving* is generated. The most concrete tier contains abundant prefabs, a type of construction in Bybee's definition, which consist of specific lexemes. Thus, a prefab is a chunk, ready-made for retrieval from memory at any time.

Along this line, some researchers have attempted to apply Construction Grammar to Chinese linguistics. For instance, Su [4] analyzed the constructional meanings of idiomatic expressions such as *X-lai-X/Y-qu* 'X-come-X/Y-go', *bu-X-bu-Y* 'not-X-not-Y', and *bu-X-er-Y* 'not-X-but-Y'. Using empirical evidence, she argued that it is necessary to analyze constructional meanings in a systematic manner, because the full interpretation of an idiom cannot be attained by calculating the sum of its internal components. She also pointed out that Chinese four-character idioms carry not only conventional constructional meanings but specific pragmatic functions, which accords with the basic tenets of Construction Grammar.

Lu et al. [7] further analyzed the constructional meanings of Chinese QIE *yi-X-#-Y* 'one-X-#-Y', where # represents numbers. They found that *yi-X-#-Y* indeed consists of several construction subgroups such as *yi-X-yi-Y* 'one-X-one-Y', *yi-X-er-Y* 'one-X-two-Y', and *yi-X-qian-Y* 'one-X-thousand-Y'. These subgroups constitute a constructional network as shown in Fig. 1. The *yi-X-yi-Y* construction has more constructional meanings as compared with other constructions, resulting in its high productivity in actual use. In *yi-X-er-Y, er* 'two' is the double of one; therefore, it has *double* as one of its constructional meanings. Besides, *er* happens to be both a cardinal number (i.e., two) and an ordinal number (i.e., second) in Chinese, so it suggests a sense of doubled or repeated emphasis in this construction. For instance, *yi-gan-er-jing* 一乾二淨 'one-clean-two-clean; extremely clean' contains a disyllabic word *ganjing* 'clean' as its semantic root and a repeated emphasis as its constructional meaning. Similarly, *yi-X-qian-Y* 'one-X-thousand-Y' has a constructional sense of contrast due to the contrastive nature between the numbers: one and thousand. Besides, the number *one* is polysemous in nature, which leads to the constructional polysemy of *yi-X-yi-Y.*

In addition to the constructional network, Lu and colleagues also proposed several observations of the internal structures of *yi-X-#-Y*. Firstly, most of the components in the *yi-X-#-Y* QIEs are parallel and symmetrical. Secondly, the syntactic structure of non-parallel QIEs is highly likely to assume the relation of topic and comment. For instance, in *yi-shi-er-niao* 一石二鳥 'one-stone-two-bird; (kill) two birds with one stone', the first unit of this idiom *yi-shi* 'one stone' serves as a cue for the context or as a topic, and the second unit the comment, conforming to the fact that Mandarin Chinese is a topic prominent language [20]. Thirdly, the polysemicity of *yi-X-#-Y* varies with the contrastive degree between the first syllable *one* and the third syllable *number* (#). As a result, the polysemicity of the *yi-X-#-Y* construction may ease off when the number in the third position increases. For instance, *yi-X-yi-Y* 'one-X-one-Y' can trigger off such constructional senses as each (every), repetition, distribution, whole,

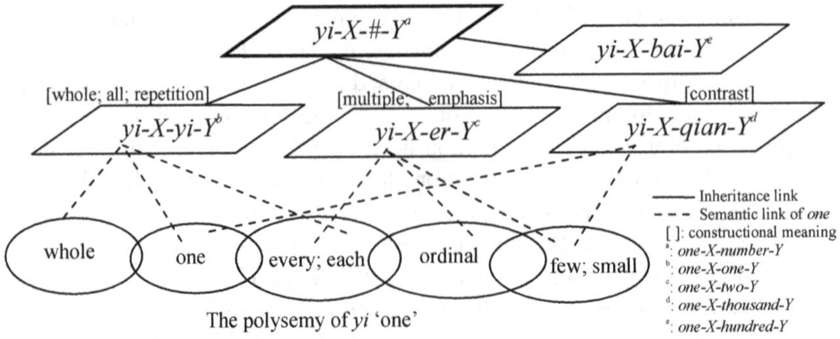

Fig. 1. The constructional network of *yi-X-#-Y* QIE (translated from Lu et al. [7])

one, and a few because *one* may serve many functions: cardinal number *one*, ordinal number *first,* each, whole, and few. On the contrary, in *yi-X-er-Y* 'one-X-two-Y', the *two* is 'doubled *one'*, which gives rise to the emergence of such interpretations as multiple, emphasis, repetition, etc. In *yi-X-qian-Y* 'one-X-thousand-Y', the first *one* merely refers to the number *one*, and from this appreciable difference between *one* and *thousand* comes forth a salient sense of "contrast." As for the non-parallel QIEs, the word order should correspond to the cognitive features of Mandarin Chinese in general. Notwithstanding that the result of their study is inspiring, more empirical data are needed to examine its general application in accounting for the meaning of Chinese QIE constructions. This paper is thus intended to provide further empirical data in examination of the constructional meanings of Chinese QIEs.

2.4 The Semantic Map Approach

The semantic map approach, proposed by Haspelmath [21], is a theoretical framework that can be used to cross-linguistically examine the similarities and differences within a particular concept or lexical item in terms of its functional range. It is defined as "a geometrical representation of functions in 'conceptual/semantic space' that are linked by connecting lines and that constitute a network." [21] (p. 213). Functions or senses appearing in a given semantic map have not come as *a priori* design but as emergent properties from real data. They are the result of empirical trial and error. If a function can be found in multiple languages, then it may serve as a universal function of that particular lexical item. A well-cited example is the analysis of English preposition *to*. In the semantic map of *dative*, English *to* has such functions as recipient, experiencer, direction, and purpose. French preposition *à*, on the other hand, has functions of recipient, experiencer, predicative possessor, and direction. These similarities and differences can be shown in the same semantic map where the semantic ranges of English *to* and French *à* overlap with each other. On this account, the semantic map can be effective and efficient in characterizing the semantic ranges of some particular units. The study adopts this approach to compare the constructional meanings of different *da-X-da-Y* constructions.

3 Data and Methodology

This study starts with a collection of QIE examples to be examined. The materials used herein are collected from representative online dictionaries of idioms: Dictionary of Chinese Idioms website[1], compiled by National Academy for Educational Research, Taiwan, and Online Dictionary of Idioms[2], China. Firstly, we searched for and confirmed the meanings of all QIEs that come in the forms of *da-X-da-Y* 'big-X-big-Y', *da-X-xiao-Y* 'big-X-small-Y', *xiao-X-xiao-Y* 'small-X-small-Y', *xiao-X-da-Y* 'small-X-big-Y', *da-X-wu-Y* 'big-X-no-Y', and *wu-X-wu-Y* 'no-X-no-Y'. Since these constructions contain specific lexical items, they are then treated as prefabs in nature [22]. As suggested in Bybee [22] (p. 79), "the lexical items that occur in a construction contribute to the meaning of the construction and help to determine its function and distribution in discourse." Next, we manually sorted through these prefabs by examining the senses of not only the first syllable *da* 'big', *xiao* 'small', and *wu* 'no' but also the third syllables, in an attempt to discern whether these lexical items are polysemous or not. Then, we inquired into the sense relations (i.e., hypernymy, synonymy, antonymy) and the semantic field between X and Y. After that, we analyzed all the combination patterns among *da-X, xiao-X, wu-X, da-Y, xiao-Y,* and *wu-Y*. Their sense relations were later studied with instances obtained from aforementioned online sources. Lastly, we examined the gestalt meanings of the composite *da-X-da-Y* QIE series.

4 Data Analysis

This section presents the analysis of the constructional meanings of the six prefabs of *da-X-da-Y* 'big-X-big-Y', *da-X-xiao-Y* 'big-X-small-Y', *xiao-X-xiao-Y* 'small-X-small-Y', *xiao-X-da-Y* 'small-X-big-Y', *da-X-wu-Y* 'big-X-no-Y', and *wu-X-wu-Y* 'no-X-no-Y'. Prefabs are constructions containing particular lexical items. The internal structures of these prefabs are specifically explored below.

4.1 Da-X-da-Y 'Big-X-Big-Y'

There are 24 *da-X-da-Y* QIEs in our data, where most X and Y slots end up in the same semantic field. Some of them may share similar semantic traits while others appear to be antonymous. These instances can be further divided into two subtypes according to their constructional meaning. Table 1 shows that if X and Y are synonyms or belong in the same semantic field, *da-X-da-Y* may prompt a sense of "emphasis" in this particular QIE, as realized in the example of *da-ji-da-li* 大吉大利 'big-luck-big-benefit', which means extremely lucky. When X and Y are antonyms, the *da-X-da-Y* construction then induces a sense of "wholeness" to its QIE. For instance, *da-qi-da-luo* 大起大落 'big-rise-big-fall' may allude to the whole process of one's career. Indeed, *Da-qi-da-luo* not

[1] Dictionary of Chinese Idioms website (http://dict.idioms.moe.edu.tw/cydic/index.htm).

[2] Online Dictionary of Idioms website (http://cy.5156edu.com; http://cy.hwxnet.com/).

only highlights the degree of the ups and downs of the career, but calls attention to the experiencing of the whole process of a particular event.

Table 1. The constructional meanings of *da-X-da-Y*

Type	Constructional meaning	Token (%)	Example
1	Emphasis: XY: a. Near synonymy	12 (50%)	大搖大擺 *da-yao-da-bai* 'big-sway-big-swing; come/go swaggeringly'
	b. Same semantic field	9 (37.5%)	大吃大喝 *da-chi-da-he* 'big-eat-big-drink; binge-eating'
2	Overall XY: antonymy	2 (8.3%)	大起大落 *da-qi-da-luo* 'big-rise-big-fall; the whole process of ups and downs'
3	N/A (Others)	1 (4.2%)	
	Total	24 (100%)	

4.2 Da-X-xiao-Y 'Big-X-small-Y'

Thirteen *da-X-xiao-Y* QIEs are found in our data (see Table 2). Since *da* 'big' and *xiao* 'small' are conventionally viewed as antonyms, the contrastive meaning is prominent, leading to two potential readings: overallness (when applied to antonyms) and contrast (when applied to a topic-comment structure). Furthermore, when X and Y are near synonyms, this *da-X-xiao-Y* construction may also induce a kind of emphasis. More details will be discussed in 5.4.

Table 2. The constructional meanings of *da-X-xiao-Y*

Type	Constructional meaning	Token (%)	Example
1	Emphasis: XY: Near synonymy	3 (23%)	大驚小怪 *da-jing-xiao-guai* 'big-surprise-small-excite; get excited over a little thing'
2	Overall: XY: Same semantic field	3 (23%)	大街小巷 *da-jie-xiao-xiang* 'big-street-small-lane; everywhere'
3	Equivalence: XY: Antonymy	1 (7.5%)	大同小異 *da-tong-xiao-yi* 'big-same-small-different; almost equivalent'
4	Contrast: XY: Miscellaneous	6 (47%)	大材小用 *da-cai-xiao-yong* 'big-talent-small-use; put fine timber to petty use'
	Total	13 (100%)	

4.3 Xiao-X-xiao-Y 'Small-X-small-Y'

Due to the effect of reduplication, the constructional meaning of *xiao-X-xiao-Y* 'small-X-small-Y' behaves similarly to that of *da-X-da-Y* 'big-X-big-Y', both conveying a sense of emphasis, although the former actually foregrounds the aspect of small scale (see examples in Table 3).

Table 3. The constructional meanings of *xiao-X-xiao-Y*

Type	Constructional meaning	Token (%)	Example
1	Emphasis: XY: a. Near synonymy	2 (28.6%)	小恩小惠 *xiao-en-xiao-hui* 'small-favor-small-favor; tiny faovr'
	b. Same semantic field	4 (57%)	小頭小臉 *xiao-tou-xiao-lian* 'small-head-small-face; delicate appearance'
2	N/A (Others)	1 (4.2%)	
	Total	7 (100%)	

4.4 Xiao-X-da-Y 'Xiao-X-big-Y'

There are sixteen *xiao-X-da-Y* QIEs in our data (see Table 4). Similar to *da-X-xiao-Y* 'big-X-small-Y', the contrastive sense is prominent due to the antonymous nature between *da* 'big' and *xiao* 'small', which accounts for 68% of the examples. When X

Table 4. The constructional meanings of *xiao-X-da-Y*

Type	Constructional meaning	Token (%)	Example
1	Contrast: XY: a. Antonymy	6 (37.5%)	小屈大伸 *xiao-qu-da-shen* 'small-bend-big-extend; bend first but greatly extend later'
	b. Miscellaneous	5 (31.25)	小題大作 *xiao-ti-da-zuo* 'small-topic-big-issue; make a mountain out of a molehill'
2	Equivalence: XY: Antonymy	1 (6.25%)	小異大同 *xiao-yi-da-tong* 'small-difference-big-same; almost equivalent'
3	Subjunctive: XY: Miscellaneous	2 (12.5%)	小懲大誡 *xiao-cheng-da-jie* 'small-punish-big-amend; A stumble may prevent a fall everywhere'
4	N/A (others)	2 (12.5%)	
	Total	16 (100%)	

and Y appear as antonyms, the construction then prompts the sense of contrast. For instance, *xiao-qu-da-shen* 小屈大伸 'small-bend-big-extend; bend first but greatly extend later' carries the sense of "then" (temporal sequence) and the sense of "but" (contrast). However, when obvious sense relations do not exist between X and Y, the QIE tends to be interpreted as a case of topic and comment. For instance, in *xiao-ti-da-zuo* 小題大作 'small-topic-big-react; make a mountain out of a molehill', *ti* 'topic' is not related to *zuo* 'react' in any particular sense, so *xiao-ti* 'small topic' can be viewed as a topic phrase, and *da-zuo* 'big reaction' a comment phrase.

Note that the topic-comment structure is a more abstract schema that underlies many constructions. For instance, although *xiao-cheng-da-jie* 小懲大誡 'small-punish-big-amend; A stumble may prevent a fall everywhere' is classed as a case of subjunctive mood (if ~then~) based on the temporal iconicity principle, it can also be treated as a topic-comment structure: topic ("small punishment") + comment ("big amending"), meaning 'then it will serve as a big warning for the future'. Moreover, it is found that *da* 'big' and *xiao* 'small' may register differing levels of polysemicity in themselves and thus can induce certain metonymic meanings. They may not only indicate size or scale, but hint at such senses as trivial detail, small error, and petty official. For instance, *xiao-lian-da-fa* 小廉大法 'small-integrity-big-law' can be interpreted as "if a petty official conforms to work ethics, then the senior officer will respect the law."

4.5 Da-X-wu-Y 'Big-X-no-Y'

Da 'big' and *xiao* 'small' are adjectives of size, scale, and dimension. When the size decreases to zero, it turns out to be none, or nothing which is *wu* 無 in Chinese. In order to fully investigate the properties of the *da-X-da-Y* groups, this study has also investigated the *da-X-wu-Y* QIEs. Our result shows that the sense of contrast features most prominently among the *da-X-wu-Y* QIEs (see Table 5).

Table 5. The constructional meanings of *da-X-wu-Y*

Type	Constructional meaning	Token (%)	Example
1	Contrast: XY: a. Same semantic field	1 (12.5%)	大車無輗 *da-che-wu-ni* 'big-car-no-clamps for crossbar of carriage; A big car without a clamps'
	b. Miscellaneous	4 (50%)	大言無當 *da-yan-wu-dang* 'big-speech-no-adequacy; speak loud but without adequacy'
2	Equivalence: XY: Antonymy	2 (25%)	大公無私 *da-gong-wu-si* 'big-public welfare-no-selfish; great public welfare without selfishness'
3	N/A (others) Total	1 (12.5%) 8 (100%)	

4.6 Wu-X-wu-Y 'no-X-no-Y'

Since *wu-X-wu-Y* 'no-X-no-Y' has a parallel structure akin to those of *da-X-da-Y* 'big-X-big-Y' and *xiao-X-xiao-Y* 'small-X-small-Y', they are found to share such similar constructional senses as emphasis or overallness when collocating with antonyms. The major difference among them lies in where X and Y assume antonymous roles: The lexical meaning *wu* 'none; no' will give the construction a reading of "none (of the whole process)." Therefore, *wu-tou-wu-wei* 無頭無尾 'no-head-no-tail' does not refer to the state of having no heads or tails, but rather, it signifies a state of not having anything throughout the whole process. *Wu-shi-wu-fei* 無是無非 'no-right-no-wrong', therefore, can mean "amoral." Another difference resides in the part of speech of *wu* 'no', which normally acts as a predicate. Therefore, *wu-X-wu-Y* can also be treated as a subjunctive clause ('if no X, then no Y'). For instance, *wu-quan-wu-yong* 無拳無勇 can be understood as "(if one has) no fists (strength), then (one has) no bravery."

Table 6. The constructional meanings of *wu-X-wu-Y*

Type	Constructional meaning	Token (%)	Example
1	Emphasis: XY: a. Near synonymy	25 (39.6%)	無憂無慮 *wu-you-wu-lu* 'no-worry-no-concern; without any worries and concern'
	b. Same semantic field	15 (23.8%)	無聲無息 *wu-sheng-wu-xi* 'no-sound-no-air; without any sound or motion'
2	Overall XY: antonymy	11 (17.4%)	無頭無尾 *wu-tou-wu-wei* 'no-head-no-tail; without beginning or end'
3	Subjunctive: XY: Miscellaneous	4 (6.4%)	無拳無勇 *wu-quan-wu-yong* 'no-fist-no-courage; be lacking both in strength and in courage'
4	N/A (Others)	8 (12.8%)	
	Total	63 (100%)	

5 Discussion

Based on the analysis of the internal structures and constructional meanings of these six prefabs, this section presents discussions from different angles of vision. We focus mainly on three perspectives: distribution of constructional meanings, inheritance structure of constructions, and interaction between lexical semantics and construction.

5.1 Da-X-da-Y QIEs and Construction

As analyzed in Sect. 4, there appear to be five primary constructional meanings in the six QIE prefabs, namely, emphasis, overallness, equivalence, contrast, and subjunctive mood. See Table 7 for the distribution and summary of the five senses.

Table 7. The distribution and summary of these six QIE constructions

Constructional meaning	XY (sense relation)	da-da-	da-xiao-	xiao-xiao-	xiao-da-	da-wu-	wu-wu-	Sum
Emphasis	Near synonymy	✓	✓	✓			✓	4
	Same semantic field	✓		✓			✓	3
Overall	Antonymy	✓					✓	2
	Same semantic field		✓					1
Equivalence	Antonymy		✓		✓	✓		3
Contrast	Antonymy				✓			1
	Same semantic field					✓		1
	Miscellaneous		✓		✓	✓		3
Subjunctive	Miscellaneous				✓		✓	2

Note that the data categorized in the "others" are left out because their constructional meanings are difficult to arrive at. It is obvious that when the first and third syllables assume the same words, namely, forming a parallel structure, the constructional sense of emphasis stands out, especially where X and Y appear as near-synonyms or belong in the same semantic field. Since the sense of emphasis is shared by four constructions (especially, the parallel types: *da-X-da-Y*, *xiao-X-xiao-Y*, and *wu-X-wu-Y*), it can be taken as the fundamental constructional sense that underlies these QIEs. In fact, it is a well-acknowledged fact that parallel structures tend to gain differing abstract senses due to their repetition patterns as specified in the iconicity principle of language [24]. According to Haiman [24], reduplication usually contributes to such senses as intensity, plurality, and repetition. These abstract senses tie in with the notion of Construction Grammar in that they can be seen as the constructional meanings. The sense of contrast is also prevalent. It can be found in three constructions: *da-X-xiao-Y*, *xiao-X-da-Y*, and *da-X-wu-Y*. This sense emerges from the contrast between the lexical meanings of *da* 'big', *xiao* 'small' and *wu* 'no'.

If X and Y are antonymous to each other, then an overall sense emerges. If the first and third syllables are antonyms in nature, then by collocating with another pair of complementary antonyms, this particular QIE will induce a sense of equivalence, as in *da-tong-xiao-yi* 大同小異 'big-same-small-difference; almost the same' or *xiao-yi-da-tong* 小異大同 'almost the same'. Note that although the two QIEs may carry the same propositional meanings, their foci indeed differ from each other due to different designs of linear sequencing, performing a kind of figure-ground alternation. Tai [25, 26] argued that compared to English as an agent-oriented language, Chinese is a patient-oriented language, which means that the focus in Chinese may be found in the latter part of a sentence. Therefore, the two QIEs can be interpreted as "almost the same with a bit difference," or "despite a little difference, it is almost the same." In this way, the interpretation of a four-character idiom (QIE) can be quite complicated. Also, a sense of contrast or subjective mood can emerge due to the first and third syllables that assume antonymous roles. The constructional meanings of these six QIEs can be further illustrated in Fig. 2, showing how they are related with each other in terms of the semantic map approach.

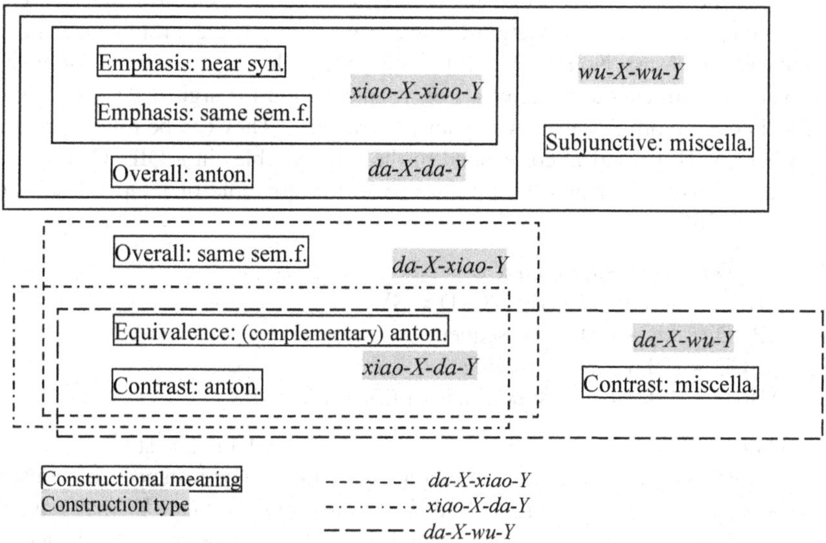

Fig. 2. The semantic map of constructional network of *da-X-da-Y* QIE series

In addition to the sense of emphasis triggered by parallel QIEs, the sense of contrast may stand out as a salient constructional meaning in non-parallel ones if X and Y are not near synonyms. Note that family resemblance is found among the six QIE types. The parallel QIEs take emphasis as their core constructional meaning. However, the prominent meaning of non-parallel QIEs is the sense of contrast. If a non-parallel structure collocates with complementary antonymous words, it then induces a sense of equivalence instead.

5.2 The Inheritance Structure of QIE Construction

In Pustejovsky's theory of Generative Lexicon [23], a lexical item is supposed to be specified with at least four structures, i.e., argument structure, event structure, qualia structure, and the lexical inheritance structure. Among them, the lexical inheritance structure is defined as the "identification of how a lexical structure is related to other structures in the type lattice, and its contribution to the global organization of a lexicon" (p.61). In this paper, we found there exist identical features between the lexical inheritance structure and the constructional inheritance structure in that lower level items (e.g., the subordinate) may share certain common features found in upper level items (e.g., the superordinate). For instance, the abstract constructional meaning of repetition is inherited by many reduplicated forms, words, or even QIEs. Thus, the sense of emphasis in *da-X-da-Y*, *xiao-X-xiao-Y*, and *wu-X-wu-Y* may originate from this reduplication construction.

In fact, QIEs not only inherit the sense of repetition or emphasis from reduplication construction, but they also inherit other constructional meanings. These are genuinely abstract in nature. In his seminal works on Chinese syntax, Tai has figured out at least six important principles of conceptualization specific to the Chinese language. These include: Temporal Sequence, Action-Result, Part-whole, Topic Prominence, Patient Prominence, and Mass Nouns [25, 26]. These principles of conceptualization may trigger some constructional meanings. For instance, Tsou [5] argued that QIEs has at least five internal morphological and syntactic structures. They can be roughly realized in (1) where A, B, C, and D correspond to the four syllables in a QIE. Of these five constructions abovementioned, (1c) conforms to the principle of temporal sequence causality [25, 26].

(1) a. ABCD = ABC + D/AB + CD = NP
b. ABCD = A + B+CD/AB + C+D = SV
c. ABCD = AB + CD = VP sequence
d. ABCD = AB + CD = coordination
e. ABCD = AB + CD = subordination (Tsou [5] p. 48)

In addition to (1) proposed by Tsou [5], it is found in this study the "topic-comment" structure is also prominent among other QIEs. For instance, the constructions of *xiao-X-da-Y* 'small-X-big-Y' and *da-X-xiao-Y* 'big-X-small-Y' may have this "topic-comment" reading. *Da-cai-xiao-yong* 大材小用 usually refers to "a talented man being appointed to an easy job", which means a big fish in a small pond. It also can be interpreted as follows. The first unit *Da-cai* can be viewed as a topic: "as for the man with great capacity" while the second unit *xiao-yong* serves as the comment to the topic: "he has been given an unimportant position." Although this study focuses primarily on *da-X-da-Y* construction groups, many instances of these QIEs still feature the basic patterns as AB + CD. They naturally inherit the constructional meanings of temporal causality [25, 26] (e.g., 1c), juxtaposition (e.g., 1d), or even contrast (e.g., 1e).

5.3 The Interaction Between Lexical Meaning and Construction

At least five abstract constructional meanings are found among the six Chinese QIE constructions, i.e., *da-X-da-Y* groups and their instances. Since constructional meanings are usually schematic and abstract in nature, lexical semantic input is thus crucial in helping obtain the overall meaning of a QIE construction. This accords with Goldberg's [18] notion of the English ditransitive construction [V NP_1 NP_2]. The constructional meaning of [V NP_1 NP_2] is giving; in other words, X CAUSES Y to RECEIVE Z. However, if the verb slot takes verbs of refusal (e.g., refuse, deny) to signify the negation of transfer, the ditransitive sentence will result in a non-giving action. For instance, even if the same construction *da-X-xiao-Y* can be applied to *da-tong-xiao-yi* 大同小異 'almost equivalent' and *da-cai-xiao-yong* 大材小用 'put fine timber to petty use', the overall meanings of these QIEs will differ from each other because their collocates display different sense relations. Our interpretation of a particular QIE always depends on the result of the interaction between the constructional meaning and the lexical meaning. Moreover, the semantic transparency of a QIE must also rely on a speaker's background knowledge of the QIE. For instance, it would be difficult to correctly interpret *xiao-lian-da-fa* 小廉大法 'small-integrity-big-law' if one is clueless about the implied senses of *xiao* (small: petty official) and *da* (big: senior official). The actual interpretation of this QIE is "if a petty official conforms to work ethics, then the senior officer will respect the law."

6 Concluding Remarks

Lu et al. [7] proposed the constructional network of a set of QIE *yi-X-#-Y*, based on Construction Grammar. This paper uses further empirical data to examine and substantiate the validity of its observations. Our findings confirm the generality of constructional meanings to research Chinese QIEs. Also, we have identified the crucial contributions of lexical semantics to the QIE research. That is to say, a well interpreted QIE results from an integrated understanding of both the lexical side, e.g., sense relations, and the structural side, e.g., constructional meanings. Moreover, cultural background knowledge is also crucial in the process of interpretation. To better explain our findings, a semantic map of the six constructional meanings is presented to catalog their senses and distances of meaning. It is clearly indicated in this semantic map that the sense of intensification or emphasis is prominent in parallel types. These are inherited meanings from the reduplication structure. Non-parallel constructions are, by comparison, more difficult to detect. They could carry such senses as overallness, equivalence, contrast, or even subjunctive mood as a consequence of complicated interplay between lexical semantics and constructional meanings. To fully analyze the constructional meaning of a QIE is a task not only difficult but also strenuous and complicated; however, if Chinese QIEs can be systematically studied, piece by piece, then the overall picture of the mysterious cultural, linguistic heritage can be gradually revealed in the future.

References

1. Cheng, X.: Studies on Chinese Historical Disyllabic Compounds. The Commercial Press, Beijing (2003). (程湘清. *漢語史書複音詞研究*. 北京: 商務印書館, 2003)
2. Fu, Z.: Modern Chinese Vocabulary. Beijing University Press, Beijing (2003). (符淮青. *現代漢語詞彙*. 北京: 北京大學出版社, 2003)
3. Ge, B.: Chinese Morphology. Foreign Language Teaching and Research Press, Beijing (2006). (葛本儀. *漢語詞彙學*. 北京: 外語教學與研究出版社, 2006)
4. Su, I.W.: Why a Construction—that is the question! Concentric Stud. English Lit. Linguist. 28(2), 27–42 (2002)

5. Tsou, B.K.: Idiomaticity and classical traditions in Some East Asian languages. In: Proceedings of the 26th Pacific Asia Conference on Language, Information and Computation (PACLIC 26), pp. 39–55 (2012)
6. Luk, R.W.P., Ng, A.B.Y.: Computer-assisted learning of Chinese idioms. J. Comput. Assist. Learn. **14**, 2–18 (1998)
7. Lu, C., Liu, T.H., Su, I.W., Tsai, I.N.: The Polysemy of the Four-Character Idiomatic Construction 'yi-X-#-Y' in Mandarin Chinese, at the 18th Chinese Lexical Semantics Workshop, in Sichuan, China. (May, 18–20) (呂佳蓉, 劉德馨, 蘇以文, 蔡宜妮: 論漢語四字格「一 X#Y」的構式網絡, (CLSW2017))
8. Gibbs, R.W., Nayak, N.: Psycholinguistic studies on syntactic behavior of idioms. Cogn. Psychol. **21**, 100–138 (1989)
9. Gibbs, R.W., Nayak, N., Cutting, C.: How to kick the bucket and not decompose: analyzability and idiom processing. J. Mem. Lang. 28, 576–593 (1989)
10. Fillmore, C.J., Kay, P., O'Connor, M.C.: Regularity and idiomaticity in grammatical constructions. Case Let Alone Lang. **64**(3), 501–538 (1988)
11. Swinney, D.A., Cutler, A.: The access and processing of idiomatic expressions. J. Verbal Learn. Verbal Behav. **18**, 523–534 (1979). https://doi.org/10.1016/S0022-5371(79)90284-6
12. Tinone, D.A., Connine, C.M.: On the compositional and noncompositional nature of idiomatic expressions. J. Pragmat. **31**, 1655–1674 (1999)
13. Hu, Y.: Modern Chinese. Xinwenfeng Publisher, Taipei (1992). (胡裕樹. 1992. *現代漢語*,台北: 新文豐)
14. Liu, Z., Xing, M.: The semantic symmetrical features of four-character idioms in Chinese and their effects on cognition. Chinese Teach. World 1, 77–81 (2000). (劉振前, 邢梅萍. 2000. 漢語四字格成語語義結構的對稱性和認知, *世界漢語教學*, 1: 77-81)
15. Shao, J.: A General Introduction to Modern Chinese, 2nd edn. Shanghai Education Publisher (2007). (邵敬敏. *現代漢語通論*. 2nd edn, 上海教育出版社)
16. Chen, C., Li, C.: Studies on the Quasi-fixed Structures in Modern Chinese. Shanghai Xuelin Publisher, Shanghai (2012). (陳昌來, 李傳軍. *現代漢語類固定短語研究*. 上海學林出版社)
17. Moon, R.: Fixed Expressions and Idioms in English. Oxford University Press, Oxford (1998)
18. Goldberg, A.: Constructions: A construction Grammar Approach to Argument Structure. University of Chicago Press, Chicago (1995)
19. Bybee, J.: From usage to grammar: the mind's response to repetition. Language **82**(4), 711–733 (2006)
20. Li, C., Thompson, S.: Mandarin Chinese: A Functional Reference Grammar. University of California Press, Berkeley (1981)
21. Haspelmath, M.: The geometry of grammatical meaning: semantic maps and cross-linguistic comparison. In: Tomasello, M. (ed.) New Psychology of Language, vol. 2, pp. 211–242. Lawrence Erlbaum, London (2003)
22. Bybee, J.L.: Language, Usage and Cognition. Cambridge University Press, New York (2010)
23. Pustejovsky, J.: The Generative Lexicon. MIT Press, Cambridge (1995)
24. Haiman, J.: The iconicity of grammar: isomorphism and motivation. Language **56**(3), 515–540 (1980)
25. Tai, J. –H.Y.: Temporal Sequence and Chinese Word Order. In: Haiman, J. (ed.) Iconicity in Syntax: Proceedings of a Symposium on Iconicity in Syntax, J. Benjamins, Amsterdam, 49–72 (1985)
26. Tai, J.-H.Y.: Conceptual structure and conceptualization in Chinese. Lang. Linguist. **6**(4), 539–574 (2005)

Quantifier *měi* and Two Types of Verbal Classifiers in Mandarin Chinese

Hua-Hung Yuan(✉)

School of Foreign Languages, Xiangtan University, Hunan, China
yuan.huahung@gmail.com

Abstract. This paper discusses the quantifier *měi* in Mandarin Chinese, especially its co-occurrence with two types of verbal classifiers (Cl_V), which individualize event-denoting expressions at phase level, such as *xià*, and at occasion level, such as *cì*, *huí* in terms of verbal plurality in the framework of Cusic [1]. The sequence *měi*-Cl_V can appear in two types of structures: (i) *měi*-V-Num(eral)-Cl_V and (ii) *měi*-(Num-)Cl_V, and both require the co-occurrence of an adverb, *jiù* or *dōu* in the sentence. It is claimed that according to the co-occurrence with the adverb, *jiù* or *dōu*, the *měi*-quantification over VPs involves different types of pairing relation between *měi*-Cl_V-N/VP and the VP after the adverb.

Keywords: Distributive quantifier · *měi* · Distributivity · Verbal plurality
Verbal classifier · Mandarin chinese

1 Introduction

This paper focuses on quantification of *měi* over eventualities, especially when *měi* co-occurs with Numerals (Num) and Verbal classifiers (Cl_V).

The quantifier *měi* can be situated along different positions in a sentence: within an DP, or as a modifier to a VP or a CP. Within an DP, *měi* is a determiner before a [Num-Cl N] sequence, as in (1a)–(1b). *Měi* can also appear before a VP, specifically gé (隔), as in (1c), and as a modifier to VP *féng* (逢) 'meet' in a CP, marked by a temporal subordinator *(de)shí(hòu)* ((的)時(候)) 'while', as in (1d).

J.-F. Hong et al. (Eds.): CLSW 2018, LNAI 11173, pp. 107–125, 2018.
https://doi.org/10.1007/978-3-030-04015-4_9

(1) a. 每一個人都交了一份報告
Měi-yī-gè rén dōu jiāo-le yī-fèn bàogào
every-one-Cl person all hand-in-Acc[1] one-Cl report
'Everyone handed in a report.'

b. 每三個學生交一份報告
Měi-sān-gè xuéshēng jiāo yī-fèn bàogào
every-three-Cl student hand-in one-Cl report
'Students hand in a report per group of three.'

c. 每隔三公尺
měi gé sān-gōngchǐ
every separate three-meter
'every three meters'

d. 每逢春節((的)時(候))
Měi féng chūnjiē ((de-)shí(hòu))
every meet new-year while
'Every time when it is Chinese new year'

In this paper, I will show the quantifier *měi* functions in the verbal domain in the same way with its quantification in the nominal domain, especially the structures *měi*-V-Cl_V and *měi*-(Num-)Cl_V-VP, parallel to [*měi*-Num-Cl_N-N].

1.1 Discussion in the Literature

The quantification of *měi* over eventualities has not been studied as much as the quantification over individuals. Xing [2] lists the combinations of *měi*, Cl_V and VPs, which are *měi*-Cl_V, *měi*-Num-Cl_V, *měi*-Cl_V-VP and *měi*-Num-Cl_V-VP, as illustrated in (2).

(2) a. 每回都是他掏錢買瓜子
Měi-huí *dōu* *shì tā tāo* *qián* *mǎi guāzǐ*
every time all be he take money buy seed
'Every time it is him that paid for melon seeds.'

b. 每一趟都撲了空
Měi-yī-tàng *dōu pū-le* *kōn*
every-one-time all pounce-Acc empty
'Every time he came for nothing.'

c. 他每回來我們家，總提著一筐…
Tā ***měi-huí*** *lái* *wǒmen jiā,* *zǒng* *tí-zhe* *yī-kuāng*
he every-time come our home always carry-Prog one-Cl
'Every time he went to our house, he carried al ways a bucket of…'

d. 每一次技術革命之後，都要伴隨…
Měi-yī-cì *jìshù* *gémìng* *zhī-hòu,* *dōu yào bànsuí*
every-one-time technique revolution after all will accompany
'Every time after a technique revolution, it is accompanied…'

Zhang [3] explains that the structures in (2) express repetition of events. Huang and Shi [4] notice the VP introduced by *měi*-Cl_V, denoting events can be suffixed by aspectual markers, *le* and attached by a resultative verb *wán* only and the VP contains preferably a verb and a bare NP object, as (3) shows.

(3) 每次幹完活，總(/都)要單獨留下多呆一會
Měi-cì *gàn-wán-huó, zǒng (/dōu) yào dāndú liú-xià* *duō* *dāi yī-huì*
Every-time do-finish-work always/all will alone stay-down more stay one-moment
'Every time when he finished the work, he always stayed alone for a while.'((29d) in Huang and Shi [4])

Xing [2] points out that in *měi*-VP-Cl_V, an adverb, either *dōu* (/*zǒng*) (4a) or *jiù* (/ *biàn*) must be used (4b).

(4) a. 每發現一次異常現象,都(/總)要做複雜的計算
Měi *fāxiàn* ***yī-cì*** *yìcháng xiànxiàng,* *dōu (/zǒng)* *yào zuò fúzáde jìsuàn*
every discover once abnormal situation all always will do complicated calculate
'Every time he discovered an abnormal case, he had to make a complicated calculation.'

b. 每擰一次便(/就)流出一公升左右的清水
Měi *nǐng* ***yī-cì*** *biàn (/jiù)* *liú-chū yī-gōngshēng zuǒyòu de qīng-shuǐ*
every tighten once then then pour-outone-litre around *de* clear-water
'Every time the faucet got tightened, around one litre of clear water would pour out.' ((73) and (78) in Xing [2])

However, I observe that the co-occurrence of *dōu* (*/zǒng*) or *jiù* is necessary not only in the above structure but also in [*měi*-Num-Cl_V]-VP structure, as in (5). This is not explained by the above researches.

(5) a. 每次幹完活，就要單獨留下多呆一會
Měi-cì *gàn-wán-huó,* *jiù* *yào dāndú liú-xià duō dāi yī-huì*
Every-time do-finish-work then will alone stay-down more stay one-moment
'Every time he finished the work, he would stay alone for a while.'

b. 每一次技術革命之後，就要伴隨...
Měi-yī-cì *jìshù gémìng zhī-hòu,* *jiù* *yào bànsuí*
every-one-time technique revolution after then will accompany
'Every time after a technique revolution, it is accompanied…'

1.2 Research Questions

From the above, it can be observed that the quantification with *měi* over eventualities is complex and it deserves to be more studied. The proposal aims to answer the following questions:

(i) How does *měi* function when it co-occurs with Cl_V?
(ii) How does *měi* quantify over eventualities?
(iii) How do the co-occurrences of *měi-dōu* and *měi-jiù* differ from each other?

I will adopt the notion of verbal plurality in the framework of Cusic [1] to analyze the quantification with *měi* in verbal domain, especially for the distinction between two types of Cl_V, such as *cì* (次) and *xià* (下). In Sect. 2, I will present the verbal plurality in the framework of Cusic [1], and some properties of Cl_Vs in Chinese. In Sect. 3, I will analyze the quantifier *měi* when it co-occurs with Cl_Vs in terms of verbal plurality.

2 Verbal Plurality

In this section, I will introduce the three levels of verbal plurality in the framework of Cusic [1] and the Cl_Vs in Chinese correlated to verbal plurality and the co-occurrence of *mĕi*-Cl_Vs.

2.1 Cusic [1]

According to Cusic [1], verbal plurality can occur at three different levels, phases, events and occasions. The three different levels are illustrated in his examples below.

(6) The mouse nibbled the cheese. (plurality of **phases**)
(7) The mouse nibbled the cheese again and again on Thursday. (plurality of **events**)
(8) Again and again, the mouse nibbled the cheese on Thursday. (plurality of **occasions**)

Phases refer to the plurality of event-internal parts. In Mandarin Chinese, some verbs, like *kĕn*, *qiāo*, *ké sòu*, and so on can express phases of an event. (See Lamarre [5], Chan and Yuan [6])

(9) 啃兩口/一下麵包
kĕn liăng-kŏu /yī-xià miànbāo
nibble two-bite one-Cl_V bread
'nibble two bites/a bit bread'

Events can be pluralized by some adverbs, e.g. *again and again* in (7). In Chinese, such adverbs as *pínpín* and *yīzài(-dì)* 'repeatedly', as in (10) pluralize events in one single occasion, *tīng yănjiăng*, marked by the temporal subordinator *-shí*. (see Yuan and Chan [7])

(10) 昨天他聽演講時, 頻頻/ 一再(地)點頭
Zuótiān tā tīng yănjiăng shí, pínpín / yīzài(-dì) diăntóu
yesterday he listen speech while repeatedly repeatedly nod 'Yesterday, he repeatedly nodded while listening to the [same] speech.'

Occasions are larger than events and each occasion must occur within different time frames. Yuan and Chan [7] indicate the difference with events (E) and occasions (O) in Chinese, illustrated in the ambiguous example, (11).

(11) 約翰生了三年的病
Yuēhàn sheng-le sān-nián de bìng
John fall-Acc three-year *de* ill
'John fell ill for three years'
(a) The illness of John lasted 3 years. (1O,1E)
(b) John fell ill several times over a period of 3 years. (1O, Many E)

In Chinese, Cl_Vs count actions and events. (Chao [8], Lü [9], Paris [10, 11] among others). Zhang [12] points out that the event-external type of Cl_Vs, such as *cì*, *huí* counts verbal units at occasion level while the event-internal type of Cl_Vs, like *quán*, *xià*, *bāzhǎng*, *sheng*, etc…counts units at phase level in the sense of Cusic [1].

(12) 他打了我兩次 (昨天打了一次,今天打了一次)
*Tā dǎ-le wǒ liǎng-**cì** (zuótiān dǎ-le yī-**cì** jīntiān dǎ-le yī-**cì**)*
he beat-Acc I twice yesterday beat-Acc once today beat-Acc once
'He beat me two times. (He beat me once yesterday and once today.)' ((9) in Zhang [12])

(13) 他打了我兩拳 (#昨天打了一拳,今天打了一拳)
*Tā dǎ-le wǒ liǎng-**quán** (#zuótiān dǎ-le yī- **quán**, jīntiān dǎ-le yī- **quán**)*
he beat-Acc I twice-Cl_V yesterday beat-Acc one-Cl_V today beat-Acc onc- Cl_V
'He punched me two times. (#He punched me yesterday and today.)'

As an occasion-level Cl_V (Cl_V-O), *cì* captures the disconnectedness parameter mentioned by Cusic [1], as in (12) because two occasions of punching event denoted by *liǎng-cì* 'two-time' are distinct. As a phase-level Cl_V (Cl_V-P), *quán* shows its connectedness characteristic (Cusic [1]), as in (13) since event-internally, *liǎng-quán* 'two-punch' can only indicate two continuous phases within one punching event. (See Zhang [12]).

Therefore, the hierarchy between occasions and phases can be shown in (14) below, which states there are two separate occasions and in each occasion, Mary hit/punched/slapped Xiaoming twice.

(14) 前兩次/回吵架時,瑪莉打了小明兩下/拳/巴掌
*Qián liǎng-**cì /huí** chǎojià shí, Mǎlì dǎ-le Xiǎomíng liǎng-**xià /quán/bāzhǎng***
Last two- -Cl_V-O fight while Marybeat-Acc X.M two -Cl_V-P
'Mary and XM fought for two times. Each time when Mary and XM fought, she hit XM two times/punched two times/ slapped two times.

Cusic [1] discusses about verbal plurality in different predicate classes based on Vendler's four classes of predicates: activity, state, accomplishment, achievement. At the time of Cusic [1], the Vendler's classification did not include semelfactives, but it has been argued that the fifth type of predicate should be added[1]. Thus, the five types of predicates for Chinese (see also Smith [13]) are displayed and the possible co-occurrence with Cl_Vs below.

[1] For instance, Lamarre [5] (2015, p. 234) notes: "The term *semelfactive* denotes events which happen only once, i.e. punctual, single-stage events, and is usually opposed to iterative, a term used for events which occur several times.".

(15) a.小明肚子餓了三次/*三下 (Stage-level state)
*Xiǎomíng dùzǐ è-le sān-**cì** /*sān-**xià***
X.M tummy hungry-Acc three- Cl_V-O three-Cl_V-P
'XM was hungry for three times.'

b.小明游了三次/*三下/一下泳 (Activity)
*Xiǎomíng yóu-le sān-**cì** /*sān-**xià**/yī-**xià** yǒng*
X.M swim-Acc three- Cl_V-O three-Cl_V-P one-Cl_V-P swim
'XM swan three times.'

c.小明啃了三次/三{口/下}麵包 (Semelfactive)
*Xiǎomíng kěn-le sān-**cì** /*sān-{**kǒu**/**xià**} miànbāo*
X.M nibble-Acc three-Cl_V-O three-Cl_V-P bread
'XM nibbled the bread three times/with three bites.'

d.小明洗了{三次/*三下}五件衣服{三次/* 三下} (Accomplishmnt)
*Xiǎomíng xǐ-le {sān-**cì** /*sān-**xià** } wǔ-jiàn yīfú {sān-**cì** /*sān-**xià** }*
X.M wash-Acc three-Cl_V-O three Cl_V-P five-Cl clothes three-Cl_V-O three Cl_V-P
'XM washed five pieces of clothes three times.'

e.小明{三次/*三下}把球打進湖裡{三次/*三下} (Achievement)
*Xiǎomíng {sān-**cì** /*sān-**xià** }bǎ qiú dǎ-jìn hú-lǐ {sān-**cì** /*sān-**xià** }*
X.M three- Cl_V-O three Cl_V-P O.M ball hit-into lake-inside three-time three Cl_V-P
'XM hit the ball into the lake three times'

Event-external, Cl_V-Os are compatible with the five types of predicates and pluralize the predicates at occasion level. However, only semelfactives can be compatible with Cl_V-Ps. Cusic [1] relates the verbal plurality with the boundedness of predicates: activities, states and accomplishments are plural because they are characterized as bound while achievements are singular due to its expression of change of state. The accomplishment is internally plural but externally singular because the accomplished accomplishment is bounded, which is countable. The boundness of predicates is compatible with Cl_V-O, i.e *cì*, not Cl_V-P, as the contrast illustrated in (15). This also shows the Cl_Vs are bound and disconnected. Chan and Yuan [6] think that semelfactives have natural internal parts, countable that can be counted by Cl_V-Ps, such as *kǒu*, *xià* in (15c) (see also Zhang [12]) while activities that don't have natural internal parts cannot be counted by the general Cl_V-P *xià*, as in (15b). However, even phases are countable, semelfactives can be bound only while the whole process of action is ended and are pluralized at occasion level by Cl_V-Ps.

In the next section, I will present the syntactic properties of the two types of Cl_Vs.

2.2 Syntactic Positions of Cl_Vs

Cl_Vs can occur to the right (R), or the left (L) of a predicate, or between a verb and its complement (M(iddle)). Zhang [12] shows the position contrast of Cl_V-Os and Cl_V-Ps by (16)–(17).

(16) 大林曾經 ^{OK}三次 ^{L}看過 ^{OK}三次 ^{M}那部電影 ^{OK}三次 ^{R}
Dàlín céngjīng ^{OK}***sān-cì***^{L} *kàn-guò* ^{OK}***sān-cì***^{M} *nà-bù diànyǐng* ^{OK}***sān-cì***^{R}
D.L ever three-Cl_V-O see-Exp three-Cl_V-O that-Cl movie three-Cl_V-O
'DL saw that movie three times before.'

(17) 大林曾經*三拳 ^{L}打過*三拳 ^{M}玉如 ^{OK}三拳 ^{R}
Dàlín céngjīng ****sān-quán***^{L} *dǎ-guò* ****sān-quán***^{M} *Yùrú* ^{OK}***sān-quán***^{R}
D.L ever three-Clv-P beat-Exp three-Clv-P Y.R three-Clv-P
'DL punched Yuru three times before.'

Cl_V-Os can be put at the three positions, R, L and M while Cl_V-Ps can be at R position only, rejecting L and M positions. However, I claim that it is needed to see their co-occurrence with Cl_Vs at all possible positions since Cl_V-P is compatible with semelfatives (15c) and activities (15b), which are referred to verbs with a cognate object, such as *yóuyǒng*, *késòu*. The Cl_V-Ps cannot appear at R position, which is against the analysis of Zhang [12] when the predicates contain a cognate object, as (18)–(19) show and the sole position of Cl_Vs is M ((15b)–(15c)).

(18) 小明游了泳$^{??}$三次 ^{R}/* 一下 ^{R} (Activity)
Xiǎomíng yóu-le yǒng$^{??}$***sān-cì***^{R} /****yī-xià***^{R}
X.M swim-Acc swim three-Cl_V-O one-Cl_V-P

(19) 小明啃了麵包$^{?}$三次 ^{R}/*三{口/下}^{R} (Semelfactive)
Xiǎomíng kěn-le $^{?}$***sān-cì***^{R} /****sān-{kǒu/xià}***^{R} *miànbāo*
X.M nibble-Acc three-Cl_V-O three -Cl_V-P bread
Intended: 'XM nibbled bread three times.'

Cl_V-Os are at R position when the predicate is a state (15a), an accomplishment (15b) and an achievement (15c). Since accomplishment is V-O structured, Cl_V-O can be at M position (15d), which is not preferred.

Měi quantifies over NP with nominal Cls, as in the sequence [*měi*-(Num-)Cl]. It can quantify over verbal units at occasion level and at phase level with Cl_Vs in at least two structures: (i) *měi*-(Num-)Cl_V or (ii) *měi*-V-Num-Cl_V. Now I start with (i).

(i) ***měi*-(Num-)Cl_V**: When *měi* modifies Cl_Vs, the sequence *měi-cì* and *měi-xià* cannot be situated at R, L and M positions, as in (20).

(20) *小明(每次/{口/下})啃了每次/{口/下}麵包
Xiǎomíng měi-cì/ {kǒu/xià} kěn-le měi-cì /{kǒu/xià} miànbāo
X.M every- Cl_V-O Cl_V-P nibble-Acc every- Cl_V-O Cl_V-P bread

Měi-cì or *měi-xià* forms a constituent and it can be used as a pronoun, as in (21) to replace the mentioned events or phases described by the predicate in (15c). As a pronoun, *měi-cì* or *měi-xià* must be the subject of the predicate and co-occurs with *dōu*, as illustrated in (21)–(22).

(21) 每次/每{口/下}都讓牙齒很痛
Měi-cì* / *měi-{kǒu/xià}* *dōu *ràng yáchǐ hěn tòng*
every-Cl_V-O every Cl_V-P all make teeth very pain
'Every time (of biting bread)/Every bite hurts his teeth.'

(22) *每次/每{口/下} 讓牙齒很痛
****Měi-cì* / *měi-{kǒu/xià}*** *ràng yáchǐ hěn tòng*
every- Cl_V-O every Cl_V-P make teeth very pain

Only *měi-cì*, not *měi-xià* can precede VP and forms a temporal subordinate clause in which the marker ((*de*-)*shí* (*hòu*)) can be omitted, as (23)–(24) show. This shows the distinction between Cl_Vs at phase and occasion level. *Cì* is a Cl_V at occasion level so as to be able to individualize and count an event at occasion level, which is evidenced by the omitable ((*de*-)*shí* (*hòu*)), an indicator of occasion. *Xià* is a Cl_V at phase level, which counts phases within an event so that it cannot co-occur with the occasion indicator ((*de*-)*shí* (*hòu*)).

(23) 每次啃麵包((的)時(候))
Měi-cì *kěn miànbāo ((de-)shí (hòu))*
every-Cl_V-O nibble bread while
'Every time XM bites bread'

(24) *每下/口啃麵包((的)時(候))
****Měi-xià/ kǒu*** *kěn miànbāo ((de-)shí (hòu))*
every-Cl_V-P nibble bread while

The constituent *měi-cì* or *měi-xià* can be NP that is modified by VP, as (25) shows. *Měi*-Cl_V sequence must be preceding the cognate NP object.

(25) a.小明啃的$^?$每次{口/下}麵包…
Xiǎomíng kěn-de $^?$***měi-cì*** ***{kǒu/xià}*** *miànbāo*
X.M nibble *de* every-Cl_V-O Cl_V-P bread

b. 小明啃的每一次{口/下}麵包…
Xiǎomíng kěn-de ***měi- yī-cì*** ***{kǒu/xià}*** *miànbāo*
X.M nibble *de* every-one-Cl_V-O -Cl_V-P bread
'Every bite of bread nibbled by X.M'

However, it can be observed when *měi* -Cl_V-N modified by VP, it prefers to co-occur with the numeral *yī*, as illustrated in (25b). When the predicate is an activity, like *yóuyǒng*, as in (26), the cognate object cannot be separated from its verb and the presence of numeral *yī* is needed while *měi* and Cl_V co-occur.

(26) 小明游泳的每(*一)次/*下
Xiǎomíng yóuyǒng de ***měi (-*yī)-cì*** ***/*-xià***
X.M swim *de* every one-Cl_V-O Cl_V-P
For *měi-cì* :'Every time of X.M's swimming'
For *měi-xià*: impossible

Another distinction between Cl_V-Os and Cl_V-Ps is shown when *měi*-Cl_V precedes the modified NP, as in (26). Cl_V-P *xià* counting phases, internal parts of the event cannot go out of VP shell, *kěn-miànbāo* while Cl_V-O *cì* counting occasions of the event denoted by *kěn-miànbāo* is outside of VP shell.

(27) 小明每次/{*口/*下}啃的麵包
Xiǎomíng ***měi-cì*** ***/{*kǒu /*xià}*** *kěn de miànbāo*
X.M every-Cl_V-O Cl_V-P nibble *de* bread
For *měi-cì*: 'Bread that XM nibbles every time'
For *měi-xià*: impossible

Měi-Cl_V-O can count occasions because the predication is viewed as an occasion and it can be expressed by a nominalized VP, such as *kěn-miànbāo* or *yóuyǒng* in (28). In such case, *měi* must precede the numeral *yī*, before Cl_V-O and the relator *de* must correlate *měi*-NP and the predicate. However, Cl_V-P cannot quantify phases denoted by a nominalized VP, as illustrated in (29).

(28) 每(*一)次的啃麵包/游泳
*Mĕi (-*yī)-cì /*-xià de kĕn miànbāo / yóuyŏng*
Every one-Cl_V-O Cl_V-P de nibble bread swim
'Every time of nibbling bread/ of swimming'

(29) *每一下的啃麵包
**Mĕi-yī-xià* de kĕn miànbāo*
Every-one-Cl_V-P de nibble bread

(ii) ***mĕi*-V-Num-Cl_V**: *mĕi* quantifies over an occasion or a phase with the structure while *mĕi*-VP co-occurs with another V-Num-Cl_V structure and adverb *jiù*, as in (4b) and (30) or with adverb *dōu*-VP, as in (4a) and (31).

(30) 小明每出一拳,對手就後退(*一步)
*Xiăomíng **mĕi** chū yī-quán, duìshŏu jiù hòutuì (*yī-bù)*
X.M every hit one-Cl_V-P opponent then back one-pace
'As long as XM hit one punch, his opponent backed a pace.'

(31) 小明每出一拳,對手*(都)無法招架
*Xiăomíng **mĕi** chū yī-quán, duìshŏu *(dōu) wúfă zhāojià*
X.M every hit one-Cl_V-P opponent all unable deal
'Every punch that XM hit made his opponent unable to deal with.'

In the next section, I will propose my analysis of quantification of *mĕi*.

3 My Analysis

The quantifier *mĕi* expresses plurality. Firstly, I will introduce two types of distributivity induced by the quantifier *mĕi* that Yuan [14, 15] analyzes. Secondly, I will discuss the types of *mĕi*-quantification over VPs, i.e. (i) *mĕi*-V-Num-Cl_V and (ii) *mĕi*-(Num-)Cl_V.

3.1 Yuan [14, 15]

Yuan [14, 15] shows *mĕi*-quantification in the nominal domain involves two relationships according to the sentence structure. *Mĕi*-Num-Cl_N-N can co-occur either with *dōu* and a VP, as in (32) or with a VP including a Num-NP, as in (33).

(32) 每一(/*三)個學生都交兩份報告
Měi-*yī (/*sān)-gè xuéshēng* **dōu** *jiāo liǎng-fèn bàogào*
Every-one three-Cl student all hand-in two-Cl report
'Every student handed in two reports.'

(33) 每三個學生交兩份報告
Měi-sān-*gè xuéshēng jiāo* ***liǎng-fèn bàogào***
Every-three-Cl student hand-in two-Cl report
'Students handed in two reports per group of three.'

I argue that as a plurality marker, *měi* functions differently in these two *měi* structures: in *měi-dōu* structure ([MD]), *měi* pluralizes the single entity in the NP subject (32) whereas in *měi*-Num-Cl without *dōu* in co-occurrence ([M-Num]), *měi* pluralizes at group level in the NP subject, i.e. the group of three students in (33). The [MD] differs from ([M-Num]) syntactically and semantically. (i) Num must be one (32) in [MD] while Num must be larger than one (33) in [M-Num]; (ii) [MD] in which *dōu* is quantificational expresses a universal quantification, which is proven by the possible modification with *jǐhū* 'almost' showing its exhaustiveness while [M-Num] is not, as (34) illustrates.

(34) a.幾乎每一個學生都交兩份報告
Jǐhū ***měi***-*yī-gè xuéshēng dōu jiāo liǎng-fèn bàogào*
almost every-one-Cl student all hand-in two-Cl report
'Almost every student handed in two reports.'

b.*幾乎每三個學生交兩份報告
Jǐhū* ***měi-sān*-*gè xuéshēng jiāo liǎng-fèn bàogào*
almost every-three-Cl student hand-in two-Cl report

(iii) VP in [MD], seen as an event denotes a property while VP in [M-Num] is not because the former can be integrated into the focus form, *shì…de*, which shows it is attributive to the NP subject of the predicate.

(35) a.每一個學生都是交兩份報告的
Měi-*yī-gè xuéshēng dōu shì jiāo liǎng-fèn bàogào de*
every-one-Cl student all be hand-in two-Cl report *de*
'It is true that every student has handed in two reports.'
'Every student handed in two reports.'

b. *每三個學生是交兩份報告的
****Měi-sān***-*gè xuéshēng shì jiāo liǎng-fèn bàogào de*
Every-three-Cl student be hand-in two-Cl report *de*

(iv) [M-Num] indicates the distributivity between the Num-NP subject and Num-NP object, between nominal individuals, as the sentential negation *bù shì* illustrated in (36b). Since [MD] is a universal quantification, the sentential negation over it (36a) shows only a part of individuals concern the predication.

(36) a.不是每一個學生都交兩份報告; 有的交了 有的沒有
Bù shì *měi-yī-gè xuéshēng dōu jiāo liǎng-fèn bàogào*;
neg be every-one-Cl student all hand-in two-Cl report
yǒu-de jiāo-le, yǒu-de méiyǒu
some hand-in-Acc some neg
'It is not the case that every student handed in two reports. Some of them did; some did not.'

b.不是每三個學生交兩份報告 是每三個交兩份/是三份
Bù shì *měi-sān-gè xuéshēng jiāo liǎng-fèn bàogào*
neg be every-three-Cl student hand-in two-Cl report
'It is not the case that the students of a group of three hands in two reports.'
shì měi-sān-gè jiāo liǎng-fèn / shì sān-fèn
be every-three-Cl hand-in two-Cl be three-Cl
'It's a group of three handed in two reports.' 'It's three reports per group.'

[MD] and [M-Num] are different due to their different denotations: the former expresses the VP attributing to each individual denoted by the *měi*-NP subject and the latter indicates the pairing relation between the groups of individuals denoted by *měi*-NP subject and Num-NP object. This distinction helps to analyze *měi*-quantification over VPs, especially when Cl_Vs are served.

As I have shown in the above sections *měi* pluralizes at occasion or phases according to the Cl_V-O or Cl_V-P when *měi* co-occurs with Cl_Vs in at least two structures: (i) *měi*-(Num-)Cl_V or (ii) *měi*-V-Num-Cl_V.

3.2 *měi*-V-Num-Cl_V

In this section, I will treat *měi* when it is used in a coordinate sentence, [*měi*-V-Num-Cl_V, VP]. The first clause, *měi*-V-Num-Cl_V must co-occur with one of the adverbs, *dōu* or *jiù* in the second clause of the coordinate sentence. I will apply the analysis of [MD] and [M-Num] on this types of sentences of *měi*.

Firstly, *měi* pluralizes phases (37) or occasions (38) below when it co-occurs with the second clause which is composed of *jiù* and a [V-Num-N] sequence.

(37) 小明每走百步,(就)拍一張照片,共拍了一百張
*Xiǎomíng **měi** zǒu bǎi-bù, (**jiù**) pāi yī-zhāng zhàopiàn, gòng pāi-le yī-bǎi zhāng*
X.M every walk one-pace then shoot one-Cl photo total shoot-Acc one-hundred Cl
'XM shoot a photo every hundred steps and he shoot one hundred photos totally.'

(38) 今年秋天每下一場雨,氣溫 (就)下降一度, 現在都 5 度了
*Jīnnián qiūtiān **měi** xià yī-chǎng yǔ, qìwēn (**jiù**) xiàjiàng yī-dù,*
this-year autumn every fall one-Cl_V-O rain temperature then lower one-degree
xiànzài dōu 5 dù le
now already 5 degree F.P
'This autumn, every time it rained, the temperature lowered one degree.'

In [M-Num] over NPs (33), *měi* pluralizes over a group of three entities, seen as a unit. In the same way, *měi* pluralizes the spatial or temporal interval denoted by Num-Cl_V-N, which is the unit of pluralization, e.g. one hundred paces in (37) and the temporal interval between two occasions of raining in (38). Each interval is paired with an entity denoted by the Num-Cl-N in the coordinate clause, i.e. one photo in (37) and one degree in (38). The pairing is realized due to the sentence structure, coordination of two Num-Cl-N sequence which are connected by the adverb *jiù*, a logic operator. This indicates that the first mentioned action will trigger the second one in the structure, which ensures the pairing relation.

In addition, *měi* not only pluralizes the intervals but also organizes them one after another on a spatial or temporal axis and displays a cumulative effect, which is shown by the total number of calculation.

However, when *měi* pluralizes over phases (39) and occasions (40) with the co-occurrence of *dōu*, Num-Cl-N is not necessarily present in the second clause.

(39) 小明每走一(/*兩)步都心驚膽跳
*Xiǎomíng **měi** zǒu **yī** (/*liǎng)-bù **dōu** xīn-jīng-dǎn-tiào*
X.M every walk one two- pace all scare
'Every time XM moved a pace, he felt scared.'

(40) 每下一(/*兩)場雨都把空氣洗淨了一點
***Měi** xià yī (/*liǎng)-chǎng yǔ, **dōu** bǎ kōngqì xǐjìng-le yī-diǎn*
Every fall one two-Cl_V-O rain all O.M air clean-Acc a-little
'Every time it rains, the air got washed a little.'

Compared with [MD] in the nominal domain, *měi* pluralizes a single interval (and two intervals combined as one not allowed) in (39)–(40), as *měi* pluralizes a single entity in (32). In the coordinate sentence, the VP after *dōu* denotes a property and it is attributed to the *měi*-Num-Cl_V-N in the first clause. Each interval marked by *měi*, e.g. one hundred paces (39) and the time between two occasions of raining (40) is paired with a property denoted by the VP in the second clause. Also, *měi* does not bring about any cumulative effect in this type of sentences.

The two types of *měi*-V-Num-Clv structure can be written as below.

(41) ***měi***-V-Num-Cl_V-N, ***jiù*** -V-Num-Cl_N-N
(42) ***měi***-V-Num-Cl_V-N, ***dōu*** -V-(Num-Cl_N)-N

In the next section, I will analyze *měi*-(Num-)Cl_V structure.

3.3 *měi*-(Num-)Cl_V

In this section, I show the sequence *měi*-(Num-)Cl_V that introduces a verbal unit in a simple sentence and in a complex sentence.

(i) ***měi*-(Num-)Cl_V** in a simple sentence. While *měi-xià* at phase level and *měi-cì* at occasion level function as a pronoun, the *měi*-Cl_V sequence prefers to be the subject of the predicate, as in (21), instead of being an object (20) (see Sect. 2.2). However, I notice that as a pronoun, *měi*-Cl_V can co-occur with *dōu* only, instead of *jiù*, as the contrast between (43) and (21) shows.

(43) *每(一)次/{口/下}就讓牙齒很痛
*****Měi**-(yī-)cì/{kǒu/xià}* ***jiù*** *ràng yáchǐ hěn tòng*
every-Cl_V-O Cl_V-P then make teeth very pain

This shows *měi*-(Num-)Cl_V, as a pronoun can only express the pairing between *měi*-NP and VP denoting a property. Likewise, while *měi-yī*-Cl_V-O quantifies over a nominalized VP (28), the adverb *dōu*, not *jiù* must co-occur, as illustrated in (44).

(44) 每一次的游泳都/*就很有意思
Měi-yī-cì *de yóuyǒng* ***dōu*** / ****jiù*** *hěn yǒu yìsī*
every-one-Cl_V-O *de* swim all then very have meaning
'Every time of swimming is interesting.'

(ii) ***měi*-(Num-)Cl_V** in a complex sentence. The adverb *jiù* or *dōu* is needed since *měi*-Cl_V-O introduces a subordinate clause marked by the temporal subordinator, (*de-*) *shí* (*hòu*) in the main clause, as (45) shows.

(45) 小明每次肚子餓<u>(的)時(候)</u>,都/就吃薯片
Xiǎomíng ***měi-cì*** *dùzǐ è* <u>*(de)shí(hòu)*</u>, ***dōu*** /***jiù*** *chī shǔpiàn*
X.M every-Cl_V-O tummy hungry while all then eat chip
'Every time XM is hungry, he eats chips.'

In this section, I will focus on the structure *měi*-Cl_V-O in a complex sentence since Cl_V-P is not able to occur at occasion level (see 2.2). The analysis of [MD] and [M-Num] can be applied for NPs here, in which are involved the two types of pairing.

(a) **Two distinct types of [*měi*-Cl_V-VP]**: Two tests can help to show the differences between the two structures, [*měi*-Cl_V-VP, *dōu*-VP] and [*měi*-Cl_V-VP, *jiù*-VP]. The adverbial modification with *jīhū* 'almost' in (46) reveals that [*měi*-Cl_V-VP, *dōu*-VP] expresses the exhaustiveness while [*měi*-Cl_V-VP, *jiù*-VP] fails to do so.

(46) 小明<u>幾乎</u>每次肚子餓(的)時(候), ^OK^都/*就/^OK^總是吃薯片
Xiǎomíng <u>jīhū</u> ***měi-cì*** *dùzǐ è (de)shí(hòu),* ^{OK}***dōu/*jiù*** /^{OK}***zǒngshì*** *chī shǔpiàn*
X.M almost every-Cl_V-O tummy hungry while all then always eat chip
For [*měi*-Cl_V-VP, *dōu*/*zǒngshì*-VP]:'Almost every time XM is hungry, he eats chips.'
For [*měi*-Cl_V-VP, *jiù*-VP]: **impossible**

Due to its exhaustiveness, [*měi*-Cl_V-VP, *dōu*-VP] is a universal quantification over VPs, at occasion level. That's why the adverb *dōu* in (45)-(46) can be alternated by *zǒngshì* 'always'.

Also, the sentential negation *bù shì* in (47) differentiates between the two complex sentences of [*měi*-Cl_V-VP] by giving different implications.

(47) 小明<u>不是</u>每次肚子餓(的)時(候),**都/就**吃薯片
Xiǎomíng <u>bù shì</u> ***měi-cì*** *dùzǐ è (de)shí(hòu),* ***dōu /jiù*** *chī shǔpiàn*
X.M neg be every-Cl_V-O tummy hungry while all then eat chip
'It is not the case that every time XM is hungry, he eats chips.'

The sentential negation over [*měi*-Cl_V-VP, *dōu*-VP] indicates only parts of occasions denoted by *dùzǐ è* is associated with the occasions of eating chips, as its implication illustrated in (48). Nevertheless, *bù shì* negation concerns the logic relation between the subordinate clause [*měi*-Cl_V-VP] and the main clause [*jiù*-VP], as the implication in (49) shows.

(48) 有時候也吃別的東西
yǒushíhòu yě chī bié-de dōngxī
sometimes also eat other thing
For [*měi*-Cl_V-VP, *dōu*-VP]: 'Sometimes he eats other things (than chips.)'

(49) 是不餓的時候也吃薯片
shì bù è (de)shí(hòu) yě chī shǔpiàn
be neg tummy while also eat chip
For [*měi*-Cl_V-VP, *jiù*-VP]: 'It is that when he is not hungry, he eats chips too.'

In [MD] structure, the VP after *dōu* is seen as a property that attributes to the NP quantified by *měi*. In the same way, in the universal quantification of [*měi*-Cl_V-VP, *dōu*-VP], the occasion denoted by the VP after *dōu* is attributive to the occasion pluralized by *měi*.

As for [*měi*-Cl_V-VP, *jiù*-VP], *jiù* implicates the logic relation in the complex sentence: the subordinate clause [*měi*-Cl_V-VP] is sufficient for the main clause [VP]. The optional presence of connector *zhīyào* 'as long as' in (50) can evidence for the sufficient condition held when the adverb *jiù*, not *dōu* co-occurs with [*měi*-Cl_V-VP] subordinate clause (Yuan [14]).

(50) 小明每次只要肚子餓(的)時(候),*都/^{OK}就吃薯片
Xiǎomíng ***měi-cì*** *zhī yào dùzǐ è (de)shí(hòu),* ****dōu*** */*^{OK}***jiù*** *chī shǔpiàn*
X.M every-Cl_V-O as long as tummy hungry while all then eat chip
'Every time, as long as XM is hungry, he eats chips.'

In sum, [*měi*-Cl_V-VP, *dōu*-VP] expresses a universal quantification over occasions, between the subordinate clause [*měi*-Cl_V-VP] and the main clause [VP]. [*měi*-Cl_V-VP, *jiù*-VP] indicates *měi* pluralizes over occasions where the sufficient condition of the main clause [VP] is the subordinate clause [*měi*-Cl_V-VP].

(b) **Predicate types in [*měi*-Cl_V-VP]**. Bound and viewed as a point, the Cl_V-O, *cì* is able to integrate all types of predicates, states (44) and activities, semelfactives, accomplishments and achievement (51) into it. This Cl_V-O describes a single occasion of an event (disconnectedness parameter of occasions, Cusic [1]).

(51) 每次游泳/咳嗽/洗五件衣服/胃病發作((的)時(候))
Měi-cì yóuyǒng /késòu /xǐ wǔ-jiàn yīfú /wèi bìng fāzuò ((de)shí (hòu))
Every-Cl_V-O swim cough wash five clothes stomach illness occur while
'Every time [he] swims/coughs/washes five pieces of clothes/gets stomach ache.'

The temporal subordinator (*de-*)*shí*(*hòu*) indicates formally an occasion, by making a state verb, like *dùzìè* in (44) bound and locating it at a single time frame. In the complex sentence (51), the co-occurrence of the adverb *dōu* or *jiù* is necessary. However, it is found that when the predicate is an activity, as in (52) following *měi-cì*, the co-occurrence of *jiù* is not perfectly acceptable.

(52) 小明每次游泳,^{OK}都/$^{??}$就會頭痛
Xiǎomíng ***měi-cì*** *yóuyǒng,* ^{OK}***dōu*** */*$^{??}$***jiù*** *huì tóutòng*
X.M every-Cl_V-O swim all then will headache
'Every time X.M swims, he gets headache.'

The presence of *jiù* is perfect only when the predicate is aspectually marked as resultative, V-*wán*, as in (53) in the subordinate clause.

(53) 小明每次游完泳,^{OK}都/^{OK}就會頭痛
Xiǎomíng ***měi-cì*** *yóu-**wán**-yǒng,* ^{OK}***dōu*** */*^{OK}***jiù*** *huì tóutòng*
X.M every-Cl_V-O swim-finish all then will headache
'Every time XM finishes swimming, he has headache.'

As [M-Num] over NPs, *měi* pluralizes at group level of *měi*-NPs. While *měi* pluralizes over occasions marked by Cl_V, occasions are bound and the internal parts within an occasion is not viewed. The resultative suffix in (53) indicates the end of the whole process within the said occasion. This can be contrasted by an occasion of a semelfactive verb in (54) having natural internal parts.

(54) 小明每次咳嗽完,??就會頭痛
Xiǎomíng ***měi-cì*** *késòu-wán,* ??***jiù*** *huì tóutòng*
X.M every-Cl_V-O cough-finish then will headache
'Every time XM finishes coughing, he gets headache.'

Even the verb is marked as resultative, the process of action may not finish so that the occasion of getting headache is not ensured. This accounts for the case of accomplishment type in (55). The entire process is ended and this leads the occasion of telling mother to take place.

(55) 小明每次洗完五件衣服,OK就會告訴媽媽
Xiǎomíng ***měi-cì*** *xǐ-wán wǔ-jiàn yīfú,* OK ***jiù*** *huì gàosù māmā*
X.M every-Cl_V-O wash-finish five-Cl clothes then will tell mother
'Every time XM finishes washing five pieces of clothes, he will tell his mother.'

The pairing between *měi-cì*-VP and *jiù* –VP shows that the occasion denoted by VP after *jiù* can take place only while the entire process of VP introduced by *měi-cì* finishes. Due to its operational property, the adverb *jiù* ensures the pairing relation between the two clauses in the complex sentence. While the adverb *dōu*, which is quantificational is used in the complex sentence of *měi-cì*, VP after *dōu* is a viewed as property and attributed to *měi-cì*-VP, in which whether the entire process is ended is not important to the predication.

4 Conclusion

I have discussed the types of verbal plurality, phases, events and occasions in the framework of Cusic [1]. In Chinese, the two types of Cl_Vs: phase-type, such as *xià*, *quán*, *bù* and so on and occasion-type, such as *cì*, *huí*, *chǎng*, etc… can mark different levels of plurality in verbal domain. Following Yuan [14, 15], I analyzed *měi* quantification over phases and occasions which are used in two types of structures: (i) *měi*-V-Num-Cl_V and (ii) *měi*-(Num-)Cl_V. Both types can co-occur with the adverb, *jiù* or *dōu* and indicate different types of pairing relation. With *jiù*, *měi*-(Num-)Cl_V is the sufficient condition of the VP after *jiù* and the latter is ensured to be paired with the verbal unit denoted by *měi*-Cl_V-N. With *dōu*, the complex sentence of *měi*-(Num-)Cl_V expresses a universal quantification at occasion level, in which the VP after *dōu*, seen as a property, is attributed to the unit denoted by *měi*-Cl_V-N.

References

1. Cusic, D.: Verbal Plurality and Aspect, Ph.D. dissertation. Stanford University, Stanford (1981)
2. Xing, F.X.: *Mei* and some Sentences Relative to it, MA thesis. Henan University (2008) (邢凤翔.每及相关句式.河南大学.硕论)
3. Zhang, N.X.: The Related Research of 'Mei+Number' Structure, MA thesis. Jilin University (2015) (张楠溪.每+数量"结构的相关表达研究.吉林大学.硕论)
4. Huang, Z.H., Shi, D.X.: Mei-construction in quantification over events. Chin. Teach. World **2013**(3), 305–318 (2013). (黄瓒辉,石定栩.量化事件的"每"结构.世界汉语教学). (in Chinese)
5. Lamarre, C.: Chinese semelfactives and body movements. In: Xu, D., Fu, J. (eds.) Space and Quantification in Languages of China, pp. 233–247. Springer, Cham (2015). https://doi.org/10.1007/978-3-319-10040-1_12
6. Chan, D.K.G., Yuan, H.H.: Verbal Plurality: A View from Mandarin Chinese, M.S. The 29th Paris Meeting on East Asian Languages, Paris (2016)
7. Yuan, H.-H., Chan, D.K.G.: Verbal plurality of frequency adverbs in mandarin chinese: the case of *cháng* and *chángcháng*. Chinese Lexical Semantics. LNCS (LNAI), vol. 10085, pp. 483–496. Springer, Cham (2016). https://doi.org/10.1007/978-3-319-49508-8_46
8. Chao, Y.R.: A Grammar of Spoken Chinese. University of California Press, Berkeley (1968)
9. Lü, S.X.: Modern Chinese: 800 Words, Revised edition. The Commercial Press, Beijing (1999) (吕叔湘.现代汉语八百词(增订本).北京:商务印书馆)
10. Paris, M.-C.: Problèmes de syntaxe et de sémantique en linguistique chinoise. Institut des Hautes Etudes Chinoises. Collège de France, Paris (1981)
11. Paris, M.-C.: Verbal reduplication and verbal classifiers in Chinese. In: Cao, G., Chappell, H., Djamouri, R., Wiebusch, T. (eds.) Breaking Down the Barriers: Interdisciplinary Studies in Chinese and Beyond, pp. 257–278. Academia Sinica, Taipei (2013)
12. Zhang, N.: The syntax of event-internal and event-external verbal classifiers. Studia Linguistica **71**(3), 266–300 (2017)
13. Smith, C.: Aspectual viewpoint and situation type in Mandarin Chinese. J. East Asian Linguis. **3**, 107–146 (1994)
14. Yuan, H.H.: Quelques aspects de la quantification en chinois mandarin: pluralité et distributivité, Ph.D. dissertation, Université Paris-Diderot (2011)
15. Yuan, H.-H.: Distributive quantifier *mĕi* in mandarin Chinese. Chinese Lexical Semantics. LNCS (LNAI), vol. 10709, pp. 97–111. Springer, Cham (2018). https://doi.org/10.1007/978-3-319-73573-3_8

Research on Basic Vocabulary Extraction Based on Chinese Language Learners

Zimin Wang(✉), Huizhou Zhao, Junping Zhang, and Caihong Cao

Beijing Language and Culture University, Beijing, China
wangzm000@qq.com, zhaohuizhou@blcu.edu.cn,
jpzhang0315@126.com, hdxiaoxi@163.com

Abstract. The basic vocabulary of language teaching is an important resource for use in the classroom, and for the compilation of teaching materials. In this paper, a hypothesis was proposed that every Chinese learner has a fuzzy set of Chinese basic vocabularies in their minds. We investigate 309 Chinese language learners and require them to automatically output their own basic words. We put forward a model for extracting basic words based on the above data. Through continuous improvement, we have achieved positive results and established the basic vocabulary knowledge base of Chinese language learners. This resource will provide a strong support for the vocabulary teaching and textbook compilation.

Keywords: Mental wordlist · Common-used word · Word order
Positional interval

1 Introduction

The basic vocabulary of language teaching is an important resource for use in the classroom, and for the compilation of teaching materials. At present, it is very difficult for us to filter the basic words which we really need to learn in our daily life, because of the limitation of a large scale corpus.

Regarding common words, scholars use statistical techniques to extract basic words. For example, there is an important resource named the modern Chinese Frequency Dictionary, in the field of teaching. It uses a word's frequency and distribution to calculate the usage degree for the first time which it has been used, as a standard to measure the common words. Also, the first 8000 of the wordlist with the highest usage level is compiled, which is mainly considered the classification and discourse of corpus.

Researchers also explored the relationship between frequency, distribution rate, text, and word length. In the same "usage", the higher the frequency, the lower the distribution rate (Su 2007). There is a dependency relationship between the frequency and the length of words. The longer the vocabulary is, the lower the frequency is in the text. Both are inversely proportional (Deng and Feng 2013). Another idea put forward was that of the knowledge base of common words, which is a function of corpus and coverage coefficient (Yu and Zhu 2015). Even a new method was proposed, namely to acquire a teaching thesaurus combined with word frequency and time span (Wang 2010). The above methods provide a good reference for the extraction of basic words.

J.-F. Hong et al. (Eds.): CLSW 2018, LNAI 11173, pp. 126–135, 2018.
https://doi.org/10.1007/978-3-030-04015-4_10

Students are the main body of Chinese classroom teaching. How do they think about the basic word? What are the basic words in their minds? What are the differences in basic vocabulary output among different Chinese language learners? They are questions worthy of discussion. If we can investigate and collect basic vocabulary in their minds, it will be a good supplement to the existing large-scale corpus.

Therefore, this paper will collect and extract the basic vocabulary in their minds of Chinese language learners, so as to establish and improve the basic vocabulary extraction model, and related basic wordlist for language teaching. The rest of the paper is organized as follows. In Sect. 2, we describe a survey of the basic wordlist. In Sect. 3, we present a priority model of the basic word. In Sect. 4, we explore the improvement of model. Finally, we conclude with a summary and an outline of further research.

2 The Survey of the Basic Wordlist

Supposing every Chinese learner with a certain Chinese knowledge has a vague set of words in their minds, which we call the mental wordlist. Because each person has different understanding, the content of the mental wordlist will also be different. The purpose of our research is to enable students to output their mental wordlist in a certain period of time. If we can collect enough data, we would be able to draw a Chinese learner's vocabulary star map. We will find the brightest word stars through statistical methods and develop a knowledge base for language teaching.

This paper investigates the senior Chinese language learners from the College of Chinese Studies of Beijing Language and Culture University, and guides them to take the initiative to output their basic vocabulary in the classroom. The Questionnaire is designed as appendix.

There are two notable characteristics here, namely, the full development of the students' imagination and, at the same time, the reduction of any manual intervention by the survey itself. According to previous investigations, the subjects often draw a tick in the sequence of words given, where many subjective factors are added to the questionnaire and the subjects are only a process of selection, only passive participation.

In order to ensure subjects maintain originality, we do not give the students any reference data. We only let them output the 300 basic words on their existing knowledge instead. The vocabulary output time is about 50–70 min.

We initially process 309 test papers, which come from Beijing Language and Culture University. The grade distribution of the students is shown in Fig. 1.

From the above figure, it can be seen that we mainly take senior students as the object of investigation, and the grade three students ranked first. The total number was 101 and 45, accounting for 32.69%, 14.56%. Grade four students ranked second, the number of 84 people, 54, accounting for 27.18% and 17.48% of the total. The students in grade two were the last, the total number was 25, accounting for 8.09% of the total. The choice of senior students is mainly due to the higher grades, and the deeper understanding of language learning. Moreover, they have their own consideration when outputting vocabularies.

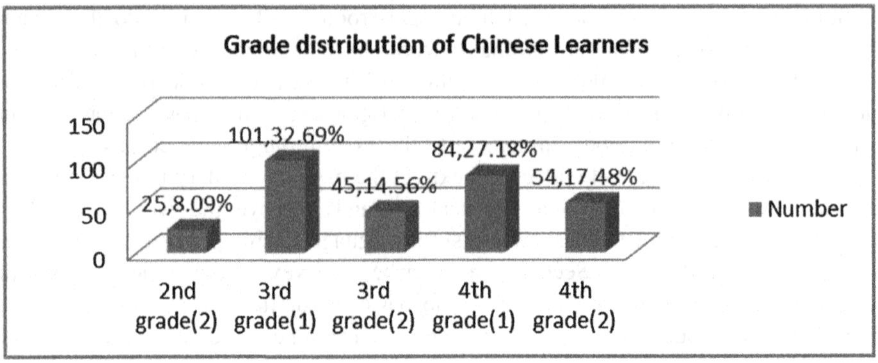

Fig. 1. Grade distribution of Chinese language learners

The paper also investigates the ratio of male to female, as shown in the following Fig. 2.

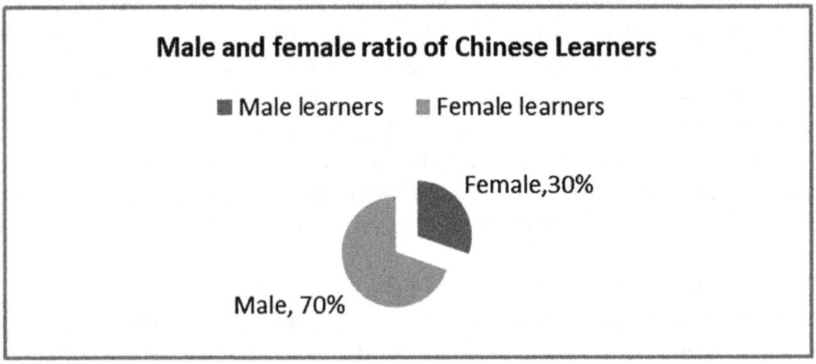

Fig. 2. Male and female ratio of Chinese language learners

According to the data collected, girls are 70%, boys are 30%, and girls are far more than boys. Gender differences may lead to different understanding of basic words and the specific situation needs to be further studied.

The length of learning Chinese is closely related to the ability of students to export vocabulary independently. The data above shows that most students' grades are consistent with the length of time learning Chinese, but there are exceptions. The details are shown in the following Fig. 3.

The learning time of Chinese language learners is different. The number of Chinese language learners was the largest in 3–4 years, with a total number of 108, accounting for 34.95% of the total number. The number of Chinese language learners in 4–5 years ranks second and is 85, accounting for 27.51% of the total. Chinese language learners with 2–3 years rank third, with a total number of 59, accounting for 19.09% of the total.

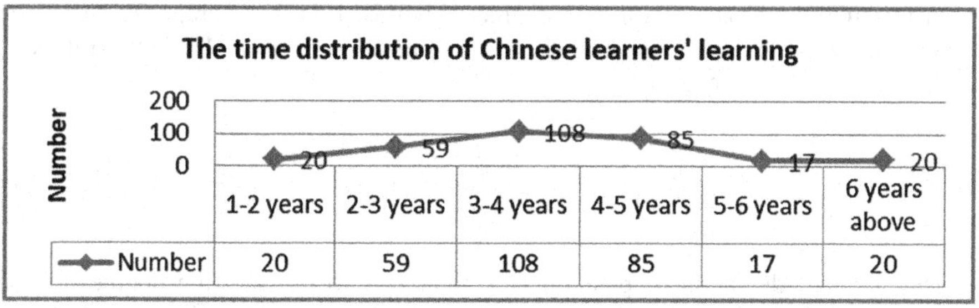

Fig. 3. The time distribution of Chinese language learners

In addition, there are 5–6 or more than 6 years of Chinese language learners, the number is 17, 20, accounting for 5.5% and 6.47% of the total respectively.

For Chinese language learners over 4 years, they may have had Chinese learning experiences in their own countries before entering undergraduate studies. However, no matter how long the time is, they can smoothly upgrade and enter senior high school, which shows that learners have strong learning ability.

And with the increase of grade, the experience of language learning will increase. For beginners, they should have their own thoughts on what they should learn most.

3 The Design of the Common Degree Order Model of the Basic Word

Frequency and coverage are the most important parameters to measure whether a word is commonly used or not. While considering the frequency of words, scholars often consider the number of texts in which those words appear, that is, text coverage.

The 300 basic words designed in this paper require that words should not be repeated. A word can only appear once in a text, and the frequency and number of basic words are exactly the same. At this time the coverage rate of this paper can be ignored.

In addition to the spatial distribution of words, there is the order of time output. At the beginning of the survey, we took full account of the time sequence of words, that is, the words position and Chinese language learners' output sequence in unit time.

The survey is based on the basic vocabulary output of time units. We suppose that the 300 words are a continuous node appearing on the time series. The words' different positions determine the mental importance of the Chinese learner.

Therefore, this paper takes positional information in unit time as an important parameter to measure basic words.

We will determine the basic ordering problem through frequency, word output position, word stability and so on. The common degree order model is designed as follows:

$$U = \frac{\mathrm{F}}{Stdev(K)} \quad (1)$$

In formula (1), U is the common degree of words. F is the average frequency of words, *stdev*(k) is the word standard deviation of position. In formula (2) "*n*" refers to the number of average frequency $\bar{k}$.

$$Stdev(K) = \sqrt{\frac{\sum(k - \bar{k})^2}{n - 1}} \tag{2}$$

The standard deviation of position is a parameter to measure the degree of dispersion of words. The greater the variance of a word's output sequence from Chinese language learners, the more unstable the distribution. The common degree of U is proportional to the frequency of words, which is proportional to the number of Chinese language learners to vote, which means that the more the number of votes, the higher the ranking of the basic word. At the same time, the common degree of U is inversely proportional to the standard deviation of position, which is inversely proportional to the consistency of the positional information output by the Chinese language learners. The higher the positional consistency is, the higher the ranking of the basic words is.

4 Experimental Data and Model Improvement

After organizing the data, we compute the following parameters in our model: Freq, Distinct_freq, Avg(Pos), StDev(Pos) and U. Freq is the frequency of a word, Distinct_freq is the distinct frequency of a word and they both represent F in the model. Avg(Pos) is the average position which is $\bar{k}$ in the model. StDev(Pos) is the word standard deviation of position which is *Stdev(K)* in the model. In some questionnaires, there exists a same word at different position, so we use two frequency-related parameters: Freq and Distinct_freq. For example, $\text{Freq}_{老师} = 254$ and $\text{Freq}_{汉语} = 203$. There is one questionnaire containing two "老师" and four questionnaires containing two "汉语". We clean the duplicate word in the same questionnaire, only keep the foremost one which has the least position number, and the position numbers of the words, which behind the dropping words, are not adjusted. After this data cleaning step, $\text{Distinct\_freq}_{老师} = 253$ and $\text{Distinct\_freq}_{汉语} = 199$. Our model will use Distinct_freq as the F parameter to compute the U, which is a word common degree. Next, we improve model by analyzing the experimental data, in order to make the result close to people's experience.

In total, we got 11,026 different words from the 309 questionnaires. Table 1 shows the top 8 words in descending order by U, which is computed based on formula (1).

In Table 1, "老师","学习","手机","汉语" and "我" are all basic words in people's minds. They all have higher frequency and better position average. So it is reasonable to put them in higher order. But the frequency of "五官","素食" and"业绩" are all 2. They should not be the basic words.

Why do these 3 words have higher U? Because their StDev(Pos) is less. This means the word position numbers in different questionnaires are very close. For a higher frequency word, although the word position numbers are not very large, the StDev(Pos) of the word may be larger. That because we use the original position numbers to

Table 1. Experimental result based on word common degree order model

Word	Freq	Distinct_freq	Avg(Pos)	StDev(Pos)	U_order
老师	254	253	54.5511811023622	60.9387314496646	4.14914376993723
学习	217	217	42.9493087557604	53.8417796261998	4.0303274057161
手机	252	249	79.9761904761905	71.9461910800545	3.48526535197493
汉语	203	199	64.9310344827586	71.1614060798491	2.92030989723659
我	182	174	41.3516483516484	67.5569534436974	2.85470194744869
五官	2	2	246.5	0.707106781186548	2.82842712474619
素食	2	2	57.5	0.707106781186548	2.82842712474619
业绩	2	2	131.5	0.707106781186548	2.82842712474619

compute StDev(Pos). Take "老师" as an example, 253 subjects vote this word, but the 253 position numbers are very different and StDev(Pos) is more than 60. In order to reduce StDev(Pos) of the higher frequency words, we separate the 300 position points into zones and the positions in each zone have the same position number. We separate the 300 positions into 6 zones and each zone has 50 points. We call these position numbers interval position numbers. Table 2 shows the top 10 words in descending order by U, which is computed based on formula (1) with interval position numbers.

The result in Table 2 is better than in Table 1. The top 10 words are "学习", "老师", "手机", "我", "你好", "汉语", "朋友", "时间", "妈妈" and "爸爸". These top 10 words are all higher frequency words and their StDev(Pos) are less too. Take these words as basic words, as they are fully conformed to people's experience.

Table 2. Experimental result based on word common degree order model, formula (1) with interval position numbers.

Word	Freq	Distinct_freq	Avg(Pos)	StDev(Pos)	**U_order**
学习	217	217	1.53917050691244	0.981111073419004	221.177811441667
老师	254	253	1.70866141732283	1.15317219280233	219.507620584057
手机	252	249	2.15873015873016	1.36497273683906	183.61346255499
我	182	177	1.6043956043956	1.23377085257582	163.506156092183
你好	158	157	1.41772151898734	1.0600756485049	153.349345149686
汉语	203	201	1.89655172413793	1.36944663646787	153.079628856423
朋友	215	213	2.30697674418605	1.51586552630804	143.943444586023
时间	203	199	2.41871921182266	1.39909600763832	141.459374439466
妈妈	210	210	2.18095238095238	1.49820276625764	140.167943037883
爸爸	203	202	2.17733990147783	1.47858603105189	137.530904382781

But we also need to adjust the order of these 10 words. For instance, $\mathrm{Distinct\_freq}_{老师} = 253$ and Distinct_freq = 217, but "学习" is in the first order and "老师" is in the second order. With the increase in the number of "老师" voters, there is also an increase in StDev(Pos). In the word common degree order model, formula (1), we only consider the relation of frequency and the standard deviation of position; and not consider the weight of these two parameters. Based on the experiment result of "学习" and "老师", we think the frequency parameter is more important than the parameter of positional standard deviation. So we modify our word common degree order model to formula (3).

$$U' = \frac{F^2}{Stdev(Pos)} \tag{3}$$

In formula (3), numerator F^2 highlights the important role of frequency in our model. Table 3 shows the top 10 words in descending order by U, which is computed on formula (3).

Table 3. Experimental result based on improved word common degree order model.

Word	Freq	Distinct_freq	Avg(Pos)	StDev(Pos)	**U'_order**
老师	254	253	1.70866141732283	1.15317219280233	55535.4280077664
学习	217	217	1.53917050691244	0.981111073419004	47995.5850828417
手机	252	249	2.15873015873016	1.36497273683906	45719.7521761925
汉语	203	201	1.89655172413793	1.36944663646787	30769.005400141
朋友	215	213	2.30697674418605	1.51586552630804	30659.9536968229
妈妈	210	210	2.18095238095238	1.49820276625764	29435.2680379555
我	182	177	1.6043956043956	1.23377085257582	28940.5896283164
时间	203	199	2.41871921182266	1.39909600763832	28150.4155134538
爸爸	203	202	2.17733990147783	1.47858603105189	27781.2426853217
你好	158	157	1.41772151898734	1.0600756485049	24075.8471885007

The above words in Table 3 are "老师", "学习", "手机", "汉语", "朋友","妈妈", "我", "时间", "爸爸" and "你好". Compared with Table 2, we see the following differences. (1) The orders of "老师" and "学习" have been exchanged, the higher frequency word "老师" ranks first, and "学习" ranks second. (2) The orders of "汉语"、"朋友"、"妈妈" move forward, and "你好" fell to 10th order.

In the traditional language concept, "你好" is a phase not a word. But in the language learners' mind, "你好" is a primary and higher frequency expression in

Chinese language. So we think of “你好” as an independent chunk and put it in the basic words set. There are many similar chunks in Chinese teaching, and we will determine their orders according to our model. That also exactly reflects the uniqueness of vocabulary oriented to language teaching.

Meanwhile, “妈妈” has the prior order over ““我" and "爸爸"”, which reflects the importance of “妈妈” in the learners’ minds.

These ten words in Table 3, "老师", "学习", "手机", "汉语", "朋友","妈妈", "我", "时间", "爸爸" and "你好" are the most important vocabularies in learners’ minds. “老师”, “学习”, "手机" and "汉语" reflect the learners’ learning life. “学习” is their task, “老师” is the person who teaches them, “汉语” is the object which they learn and “手机” is an important tool in their life. Another characteristic of this word list is that there are five words related to people. They are "老师", "朋友", "妈妈", "我" and "爸爸". “Teacher, friend, me, mom, Dad” is the most important figure who constitutes learner’s social relationship. Therefore, they are recognized as basic words by Chinese language learners.

But it is worth noting that the order of "老师" and "朋友" are prior to “order of "妈妈", "我" and "爸爸", This could be that classroom is the test site, where the subjects first think of “老师” and “朋友”. Of course 妈妈", "我" and "爸爸 are also important. Totally, the result in Table 3 reflects the characteristic of the learners’ basic words.

In order to understand the rationality of the order of basic words, we display the positional distribution of the top 3 words "老师", "学习" and "手机" in the following zones in Fig. 4.

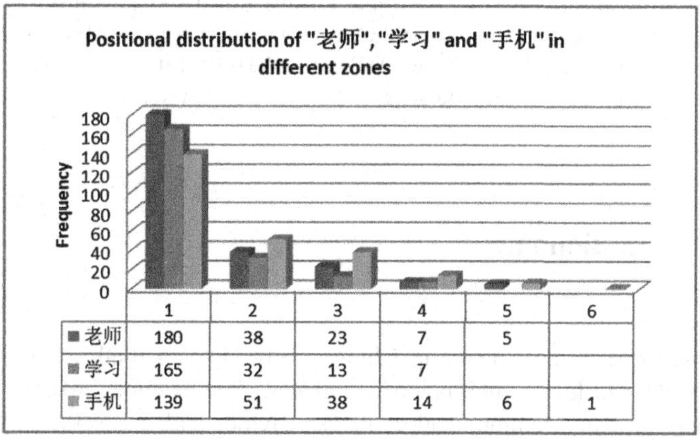

	1	2	3	4	5	6
■ 老师	180	38	23	7	5	
■ 学习	165	32	13	7		
■ 手机	139	51	38	14	6	1

Fig. 4. Positional distribution of "老师", "学习" and "手机" in different zones.

In Fig. 4, we can intuitively see the frequencies of the 3 words in different 6 position zones. All these 3 words have the largest numbers in zone 1 (original position number: 1 to 50), they are 180, 165 and 139. The frequencies of “学习” are both 0 in zone 5 and 6 (original position number: 201 to 300). This phenomenon shows that

"学习" is very important, and if a learner outputs "学习", the original position is less than 201. Although "手机" has higher frequency than "学习", the position of "手机" is more dispersive, distributing in 6 zones. This illustrates that learners have different identification of "手机", so the position of output varies with different degrees. In zone 1, the frequency of "手机" is lower than "老师", so "手机" is in the third order. The distribution differences of words in different zones verify the rationality of our word common degree order model.

5 Conclusions

This paper collects the mental words of the Chinese language learners and presents the method and model for ordering basic words list, based on the investigation of 309 Chinese language learners. The word common degree experiment has achieved positive results, by setting the positional zone and adjusting the weight of the parameter. Meanwhile, we construct the learners' basic wordlist which is language teaching oriented.

This paper only contains a small amount of survey data. In the future, we will gather the mental words of thousands of Chinese language learners and teachers. We will build a hierarchical word list for Chinese teaching as a second language. At the same time, we will also compare and analyze the existing authoritative vocabulary syllabus and further verify the validity of our hierarchical word list.

Acknowledgments. The work was supported by Funding Project of Education Ministry for Development of Liberal Arts and Social Sciences (16YJA740036); the support program of young and middle-aged backbone teachers for Beijing Language and Culture University; Wu Tong Innovation Platform of Beijing Language and Culture University (supported by the Fundamental Research Funds for the Central Universities (16PT03, 14YJ160502)). The authors also gratefully acknowledge the helpful comments and suggestions of the reviewers, which have improved the presentation.

Appendix. Questionnaire

Dear classmates:

With your experience in learning Chinese, how do you think are the 300 most commonly used words for international students? For example, words concerning learning, survival, daily communication, daily activities and so on. Please fill in your own ideas in the form. Thank you for your cooperation.

……									

References

Institute of language teaching, Beijing Language and Culture University.: Modern Chinese Frequency Dictionary. Beijing Language and Culture University Press, Beijing (1986)

Deng, Y., Feng, Z.: A quantitative linguistic study on the relationship between word length and word frequency. J. Foreign Lang. **3**, 29–39 (2013)

Chinese Test Center.: The Syllabus of Graded Words and Characters for Chinese Proficiency (Revised). Economics Science Press (2001)

Office of Chinese Language Council International, Department of Social Sciences of Ministry of Education of the People's Republic of China.: The Graded Chinese Syllables, Characters and Words for the Application of Teaching Chinese to the Speakers of Other Languages. Beijing Language and Culture University Press, Beijing (2010)

Development of Word Frequency Statistics: Liu Hongbo. Library Inf. **2**, 13–19 (1991)

Su, X.: The Role of Quantitative Method in Lexical Research and Frequency Level Statistics, vol. 2, pp. 118–124. Yangtze River Academic (2007)

Su, X.: Comparative study of GOTCFL and the glossaries in two textbooks. Appl. Linguist. **2**, 103–111 (2006)

Wang, Z.: The statistical research on diachronic changes of the common wordlist for Chinese teaching. TCSOL Stud. **4**, 49–55 (2010)

Yu, S., Zhu, X.: Quantitative lexicon study and knowledge base construction for commonly used words. J. Chin. Inf. Process. **3**, 16–20 (2015)

Chinese Emotion Commonsense Knowledge Base Construction and Its Application

Liang Yang(✉), Fengqing Zhou, Hongfei Lin, Jian Wang, and Shaowu Zhang

School of Computer Science and Technology, Dalian University of Technology, Dalian, China
{liang,hflin,wangjian,zhangsw}@dlut.edu.cn

Abstract. Commonsense knowledge usually exists in standard human to human communication, and it is very helpful to most of natural language processing works. However, Chinese commonsense knowledge, especially emotion commonsense knowledge, is still an urgent demand. In this paper, we try to construct a Chinese emotion commonsense knowledge base, which optimizes the existed structure of emotion commonsense knowledge base. First, emotion commonsense are collected and extracted from corpus, then HowNet and Tongyici Cilin are used to expand its scale, finally manually labeled and verified annotation quality are completed. The experiment results on the corpus and dataset show that the Chinese emotion commonsense knowledge base is helpful to improve the results of text polarity and emotion classification to some degree and it can be used in other emotion analysis work.

1 Introduction

Sentiment analysis, also called opinion mining, is the field of study that analyzes people's opinions, sentiments, appraisals, attitudes and emotions toward entities and their attributes expressed in written text. Regarding the name of the field, sentiment analysis or emotion analysis is used almost exclusively in industry, whereas both opinion mining and sentiment analysis are commonly employed in academia, such as web page comment analysis, public opinion analysis and so on [1]. At present, there are several types of methods for text sentiment or emotion analysis: statistics methods, such as lexicon based method [2]; methods based on context semantic feature mining [3]; machine learning methods, such as neural network [4]. Although, these methods can solve the problem preliminarily, it is still hard to analyze the emotions more correctly in the texts without guidance of external knowledge. Meanwhile, the massive user-generated contents (UGC) in the era of Web 2.0 sometimes have data noise and limited emotion words, hence, the contents are more ambiguous and complex than before, which brings new challenges to sentiment or emotion analysis.

By now, the majority of knowledge base research focuses on English, such as lexicon construction, which aims to capture the polarity of each word. Chinese, as another important language, still has very limited knowledge resources for emotion analysis, so there is an urgent demand for this work, especially the knowledge base for commonsense knowledge.

J.-F. Hong et al. (Eds.): CLSW 2018, LNAI 11173, pp. 136–146, 2018.
https://doi.org/10.1007/978-3-030-04015-4_11

Commonsense knowledge usually exists in standard human to human communication, and it has always been the research hotspot in the field of artificial intelligence. Commonsense knowledge also plays an important role in making the computers inherit the human knowledge, which has been widely applied in expert system and question and answer system. Commonsense knowledge usually stores in the form of a commonsense knowledge base: WordNet, Cyc and ConceptNet are typical commonsense knowledge bases for English, while HowNet and Pangu (盘古) knowledge base are the representatives for Chinese. But not all the commonsense knowledge bases mentioned above contain emotion categories and strength, so they cannot be used for text emotion analysis. However, commonsenses are closely related to emotion states in our daily life, and an example sentence is as follows:

Chinese: “"五星级酒店桌子上却是一层灰！"”
English: “Dust is on the table in 5 stars Hotel!”

In this sample sentence, there is no emotion lexicon, but we can find that the writer expresses a negative emotion to the hotel. Therefore, it can be inferred that introducing emotion commonsense knowledge can improve the effect of text emotion analysis to some extent.

In this context, Chen et al. [5] sets up a Chinese emotion commonsense base, including the rule base and the case base. An instance is represented by quintuple. But this type of representation cannot cover the commonsense knowledge with complex sentence structures. Based on Chen's work, we take dependency syntactic parsing into consideration, and convert a quintuple form into a binary syntactic structure for a single word, such as “verb + nouns”, “nouns + adjectives”, which improves the accuracy and extensibility of commonsense knowledge expression. In order to obtain commonsense resources to construct emotion commonsense knowledge base, following work has been done: firstly, verb-object structure and subject-predicate structure are extracted from the Chinese emotion corpus [6], and emotion collocation and the combination of product attributes and evaluation words are also collected; secondly, HowNet and Tongyici Cilin are used to achieve extension for the knowledge base; finally, manually labeled emotion information and verified annotation quality are completed.

The structure of this paper is as follows: Sect. 2 illustrates how to construct the Chinese emotion commonsense knowledge base; Sect. 3 explains the applications of emotion commonsense knowledge; Sect. 4 shows the experiment results and analysis; Sect. 5 comprises concluding remarks and future directions.

2 Construction of Binary Chinese Commonsense Knowledge

Commonsense knowledge has following characteristics: (1) big scale; (2) lack of regularity; (3) difficult to define the boundary; (4) many statements used to describe the word are only vague, time-varying and so on. Emotion commonsense, as a category of commonsense knowledge, also has the same characteristics. Due to the existence of these characteristics, a single word normally cannot be used to express commonsense in an accurate and complete way, and it is difficult to provide a unified description for emotion commonsense. Hence, we try to use a binary structure to represent emotion commonsense as an attempt.

2.1 The Representation of Binary Emotion Commonsense Knowledge Base

We define the following framework to represent the detailed description of an emotion commonsense. The specific framework of an emotion commonsense C is as follows:

$$C = (C_{\text{Emotion}},\ C_{\text{Subject}},\ (C_{\text{Passive}},\ C_{\text{Attention}}),\ C_{\text{Conditions}})$$

Where C_{Emotion} is the emotion category of a commonsense [7]; C_{Subject} is emotion holder, including emotion agent and recipient (of action); C_{Passive} is a passive sign (0 is active, 1 is passive, and the default value is 0); $C_{\text{Attention}}$ is the part of commonsense; $C_{\text{Conditions}}$ represents time and space conditions.

The binary emotion commonsense knowledge $C_{\text{Attention}}$ is a form of two-word structure. The reason why a commonsense is represented by two words is that it is relatively simple, intuitive and convenient for application. In addition, using only one word can lead to lack of information, which cannot express the commonsense comprehensively. While the information of word pairs is relatively abundant, this can illustrate a commonsense well. For example, a verb-object phrase or a subject-predicate phrase can fully express an event as well as the emotions related to it. Here is a sample sentence.

Chinese: “"小明在生日当天收到了许多礼物。"”
English: “Xiao Ming received many gifts on his birthday.”

In the sample sentence, it contains emotion commonsense “receive gift”, and emotion category of it is “happy”. We can also find out that any single word in this sentence cannot express the emotion category of “happy”. Hence, the general expression of the commonsense is as follows:

(("乐", "小明", (1, ("收到","礼物")), "生日当天"))
(“happy”, “Xiao Ming”, (1, (receive, “gift”)), “birthday”)

2.2 Emotion Commonsense Extraction

The content of binary emotion commonsense knowledge base mainly consists of four parts: verb-object structure, subject-predicate structure, emotion collocation, and some combinations of attributes and evaluation words in product reviews.

With the help of Harbin Institute of Technology’s language and technology platform LTP, dependency sentence parsing of the emotion corpus is carried out, and the main principle is the dependency parsing based on graph model (graph-based parser). Using syntactic parsing method can identify Chinese text in verb-object structures, subject-predicate structure relationship, and syntactic structure on LTP platform. The following part will briefly introduce how to extract the emotion commonsense knowledge from the corpus.

Verb-Object Structure: A verb and a noun can form a verb-object structure, and the verb-object structure can be used as a simplified expression of an event. As the sample sentence mentioned above, there are more than one element in this event. From emotion perspective, the verb-object structure "receive" and "gift" can express emotion of this specific event well. An event is a form of expression of emotion commonsense. When an accident happens, people will have feelings of sadness and fear. When receiving gifts, people will have happy feelings. As a simplified description of an event, the verb-object structure can be used to represent an emotion commonsense. After manually labeling verb-object structures, we can use it as a complete commonsense for emotion commonsense knowledge.

Subject-Predicate Structure: It is similar with verb-object structure, and it can also be seen as a simplified expression of events, such as "blood pressure" and "rising", which can form a subject-predicate structure for emotion knowledge and express fear. The same as verb-object structure, it needs to be obtained from emotion corpus by using syntactic analysis.

Emotion Collocation: It is a common phenomenon in Chinese. Emotion collocation indicates that the collocation containing emotion factors, the main manifestation of which is that certain emotion words with different words will produce different emotions. For example, "rise" and "score", it will produce positive emotion, but "rise" and "house price" will produce negative emotion. It is obvious that the feelings of these collocations could be judged by commonsense knowledge, so emotion collocation is also one of constitutes in emotion commonsense knowledge base. Thus, by using graph method, these emotion collocations can be captured to a large degree.

Attributes and Evaluation Words Combinations: Online product reviews also contain emotion commonsense, such as a combination of a product attribute and an evaluation word. In the combination of "size" and "small", only the word "small" cannot be used to judge the emotion. But combinations can be used to express certain emotions, such as the "size" and "small" can describe the portability of mobile phones, and it expresses positive emotions. By constructing the bipartite graph between product attributes and evaluation words [6], pairs of attributes and evaluation words can be mined, and then be integrated into emotion commonsense knowledge after annotation.

2.3 Extension of Binary Chinese Emotion Commonsense Knowledge Base

Considering the size of the corpus and the domains of product attributes and evaluation words (mainly in the field of IT and Finance), the binary Chinese emotion commonsense knowledge base mentioned above is limited in scale and the coverage is not comprehensive enough. In order to further expand the scale and increase the coverage, we need to extend the knowledge base.

In order to extend knowledge base, the synonym forest and HowNet are adopted. When apply synonym forest, we extend a word simply with its synonym, which can avoid noise introduction. When HowNet is implemented, we mainly use the concept of a word, as well as the upper and lower information on the corresponding word.

By using above two resources, we achieve the extension work. After expansion of the binary emotion commonsense base, there are 8100 emotion common senses included. The proportion of its components is shown in Table 1.

Table 1. The proportion of binary emotion commonsense knowledge base and examples

Modules		Scale	Examples
Binary emotion commonsense knowledge base	Subject-predicate or verb-object structure	13%	Ordi((“judge”, “fair/just”), “joy”)
	Emotion collocation	62%	Emo_Col((“stock”, “drop/bearish”), “sadness”)
	Attribute and evaluation word	10%	Attr_Eval((“appearance”, “artful”), “joy”)
	Extension part	15%	Attr_Eval((“fungal”, “infections”), “fear”)

3 Application of Binary Chinese Commonsense Knowledge

Text emotion analysis has always been the focus of text mining research. The polarity analysis only needs to classify the tendency of text to be positive or negative, while text emotion analysis needs to analyze the specific emotion of texts, which is more detailed than polarity analysis. At present, there are a few public emotion corpuses for Chinese. In order to validate the effect of binary emotion commonsense knowledge in emotion and polarity analysis, experiments are implemented on Chinese emotion corpus [6] and Chinese sentiment mining corpus [8].

3.1 Emotion Analysis on Emotion Corpus

We apply emotion commonsense knowledge base on Chinese emotion corpus to verify its effectiveness on text emotion analysis. Corpus includes script, literature, primary school texts, fairy tales, blogs and microblogs. There are 1355 articles and 50 thousand sentences, including three parts, namely sender, keywords and emotion.

The emotion tag of this corpus is based on sentence units, and emotion category of the annotation is consistent with the emotion category in Chinese emotion lexicon [7]. The emotion commonsense knowledge base maintains the same emotion category.

For sentence level emotion analysis, the baseline experiment is lexicon based method, which uses Chinese emotion lexicon as an external dictionary. Due to the purpose of this experiment is to verify the role of the emotion commonsense base in emotion analysis, in this paper, we don’t emphasis the study of models or methods, which are relatively complex, but we use a certain sliding window to analyze the sentence emotion based on matching of emotion commonsense knowledge.

According to the method mentioned above, the emotional score f_{ei} of class i is shown in formula (1).

$$f_{e_i} = \begin{cases} f_{e_i} + 1 & \exists w_j \in V_{e_i} \\ f_{e_i} - 1 & w_j \in V_{e_i} \text{ and } \exists w_x \in \{w_{j-d}, \ldots w_{j-1}\}, w_x \in V_{nw} \end{cases}. \quad (1)$$

Each parameter of Eq. (1) is as follows: e_i is emotion of class i; V_{ei} is the emotion lexicon set of class i in emotion ontology; V_{nw} is the negative vocabulary set; w_j is the j th word in the current sentence; w_x is the negative word appearing in the window size d before the current word w_j.

$$f'_{e_i} = \begin{cases} f'_{e_i} + 1 & \exists (w_1, w_2) \in V_{c_i} \text{ and } w_1, w_2 \in \text{Sub}_j \\ f'_{e_i} - 1 & (w_1, w_2) \in V_{c_i}, w_1, w_2 \in \text{Sub}_j \text{ and } \exists w_x \in Sub_j, w_x \in V_{\text{nw}} \end{cases}. \quad (2)$$

When using emotion commonsense for emotional analysis, V_{ci} is an emotion commonsense set of the i th emotion class in binary emotion commonsense knowledge base. Sub_j is a sub clause of current sentence. (w_1, w_2) is an emotion commonsense in binary emotion commonsense knowledge base. w_x still expresses negative words.

For each sentence in the corpus, firstly, we adopt the emotion lexicon ontology [7] to recognize emotion words; secondly, we check the negative words in a fixed window. If there is a negative word within the window of an emotion ontology, then reduce the count of this emotion category by 1; the final emotion category of a sentence relies on the largest proportion of the emotion words in one specific class. But if the number of emotion words in some categories is the same, the emotion category of this sentence is decided by the emotion words near the end of the sentence.

The method of using binary emotion commonsense is the same as the method of using emotion ontology, and in this part an emotion commonsense is equivalent to an emotion ontology. If a sentence does not contain emotion words or emotion commonsense, the sentence is neural.

After obtaining the results based on emotion lexicon and emotion commonsense respectively, we merge the two methods in the following way.

First of all, we recognize emotion lexicon and emotion commonsense in each sentence; secondly, we calculate the score of emotion lexicon and emotion commonsense in different emotion categories, and get the score of each emotion category by adding the scores from each part ($f_{ei} + f'_{ei}$); finally, we select the highest score of the emotion categories as the emotion category of the sentence.

3.2 Polarity Analysis on Product Reviews

Polarity analysis is a binary classification, which tries to classify the polarity of each document with a tag, such as positive or negative. Just like the emotion analysis part, we still focus on the effect of the emotion commonsense base, and continue using the sliding window method to match the emotion lexicon and emotion commonsense, and then judge the polarity.

However, the categories of emotion lexicon are more than two categories (positive and negative). Hence, we map emotion categories into polarities, and the corresponding relationship between emotion categories and polarities is shown in Table 2.

Table 2. Polarity and emotion categories

Polarity	Emotion categories
Positive	Happy, admire
Negative	Angry, sad, fear, hate, surprise

When using lexicon based method to determine text polarity, we first split a document into sentences, and then identify the emotion lexicon in the document, finally calculate the number of emotion words in two categories. When one emotion word corresponding to positive appears once, the contribution value to the "positive" emotion score F_+ is 1. Similarly, if it is a negative emotion word, the contribution of "negative" emotion words to F_- is also 1. The treatment of negative words is the same as the processing way in the text mentioned above. The final polarity of a sentence is the difference between the "positive" score and the "negative" score. The formula for calculating polarity score is shown in formula (3), and the polarity P is shown in formula (4). When the positive and negative scores are the same, the polarity of the sentence is determined by the polarity of the emotion word near the end of the sentence.

$$F = F_+ - F_- = \sum_{e_i \in e_+} f_{e_i} - \sum_{e_i \in e_-} f_{e_i}. \tag{3}$$

In formula (3), e_+ is positive emotion; e_- is negative emotion; F_+ is positive emotion score, F_- is negative emotion score; F *is* the total polarity score.

$$P = \begin{cases} \text{positive} & F > 0 \\ \text{negative} & F < 0 \\ \text{polarity of the last emotion} & \\ \text{word in the sentence} & F = 0 \text{ and } F_+ \neq 0,\ F_- \neq 0 \\ \text{neutral} & F_+ = F_- = 0 \end{cases}. \tag{4}$$

The algorithm used binary commonsense to determine text polarity is similar to the lexicon methods, and it is shown in formula (5).

$$F' = F'_+ - F'_- = \sum_{e_i \in e_+} f'_{e_i} - \sum_{e_i \in e_-} f'_{e_i}. \tag{5}$$

When the two methods are merge, we only need to calculate the polarity score of the two methods separately (F and F′). The merging way of the two methods is the same as formula (4).

4 Experiments Results and Analysis

4.1 Experiment of Emotion Analysis

The main purpose of the emotion analysis experiment is to verify the role of the emotion commonsense knowledge base in emotion analysis. The experiment corpus uses the Chinese emotion corpus [6]. The experiment is carried out at the sentence level, and the accuracy of 7 kinds of emotion analysis is calculated respectively. Calculation formula of the correct rate is as follows:

$$\text{Accuarcy} = \frac{\text{the correct number in one emotion class}}{\text{the total number of this emotion class}} \times 100\%. \tag{6}$$

The benchmark experiment is lexicon based method of emotion analysis, and the proposed method is based on emotion commonsense and emotional lexicon. The results of the experiment are shown in Fig. 1.

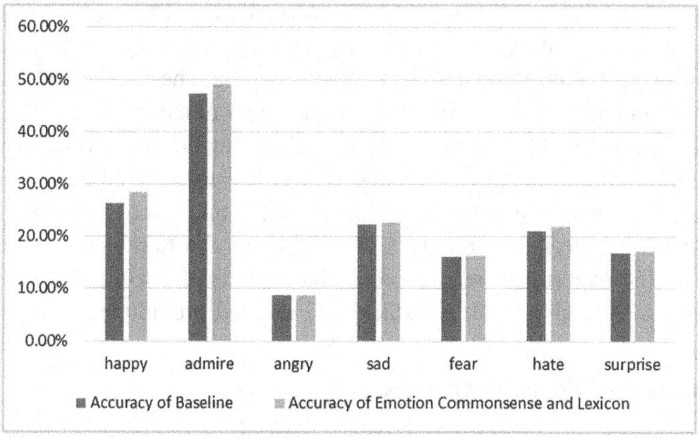

Fig. 1. Experiment results of emotion analysis

From Fig. 1 we can see that the accuracy is imbalanced in different emotion categories, and this is mainly caused by the inhomogeneous distribution of all kinds of emotion words in the corpus. After adding the emotion commonsense, most of the accuracy rates have been improved.

Due to the limited coverage of emotion commonsense in emotion corpus, the improvement of accuracy is not obvious in some emotion categories. For some sentences do not contain emotion commonsense, it cannot determine their emotions with emotion commonsense knowledge base. Therefore, the following experiments extract sentences, which contain emotion commonsense in the corpus to further verify its effectiveness, and the experiment results are shown in Fig. 2.

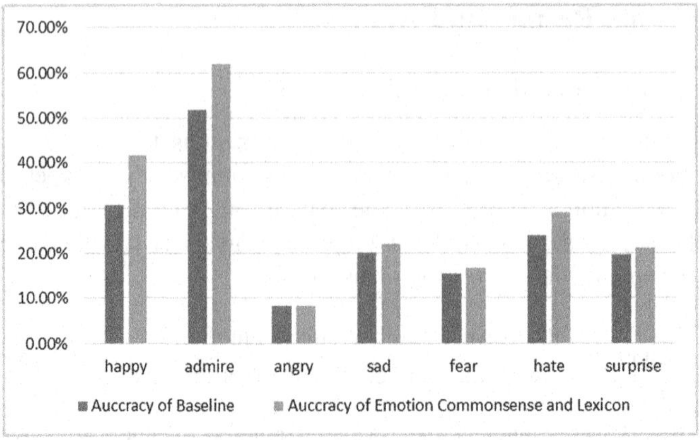

Fig. 2. Emotion analysis results of sentences with emotion commonsense

From Fig. 2 we can see that the accuracy results of the sentence with emotion commonsense have obvious improvement compared with the baseline method. Meanwhile, due to the different distributions of emotion commonsense knowledge, the improvement of each emotion category is also different. The increase of "happy" and "admire" emotion categories are relatively higher than others.

Generally speaking, the accuracy rate is still not ideal. On one hand, many sentences of some emotion categories are closely related to their context; On the other hand, the method adopted in this paper can be revised and improved. But the study of emotion analysis has verified effectiveness of Chinese emotion commonsense knowledge base, and the experiment results prove that it is helpful to improve the accuracy rate of text emotion analysis, which is also as expected previously.

4.2 Experiment of Polarity Analysis

The polarity analysis experiment is mainly to verify the role of emotion commonsense in text polarity classification. The public dataset, which consists of hotel reviews [8], has 4000 reviews, 2000 positive comments and 2000 negative comments. We use traditional metric including precision, recall rate and F1 to evaluate the classification results. The benchmark method is still using emotion lexicon only, and the compared method is the combination of emotion lexicon and emotion commonsense. The experiment results of polarity analysis are shown in Fig. 3.

Although the source of Chinese emotion commonsense is the emotion corpus, from Fig. 3 we can still find that after taking emotion commonsense into consideration, the results of precision (P), recall (R) and F1 score are improved in both positive and negative categories compared with the baseline. It is proved that the Chinese emotion commonsense knowledge base has a certain universality for the Chinese public emotion analysis corpus, and it can be widely used in Chinese text emotion analysis.

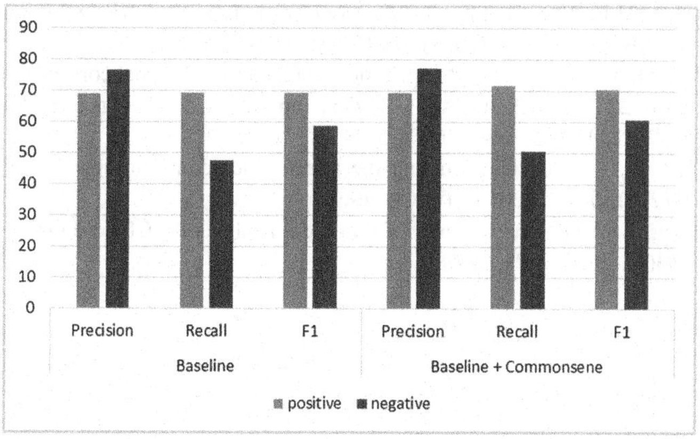

Fig. 3. Experimental results of polarity analysis

5 Conclusion

This paper mainly constructs a binary emotion commonsense knowledge base, including verb-object structure, subject-predicate structure, emotion collocation, and attribute and evaluation collocation and so on. In order to validate the effectiveness of emotion commonsense knowledge, experiments are carried out on Chinese emotion corpus and other public datasets. Considering the emotion commonsense knowledge, the experiment results improved, which indicates that it can be used as an auxiliary resource for emotion analysis. For future work our goal is to study multiple emotions commonsense, to further expand emotion commonsense knowledge base, and use knowledge base to improve results of emotion or sentiment analysis.

Acknowledgement. This research is supported by the National Natural Science Foundation of China (No: 61702080), the Fundamental Research Funds for the Central Universities (No. DUT17RC(3)016), Postdoctoral Science Foundation of China (2018M631788).

References

1. Liu, B.: Sentiment analysis: mining opinions, sentiments, and emotions. Comput. Linguist. **42** (3), 1–4 (2016)
2. Pang, B., Lee, L., Vaithyanathan, S.: Thumbs up? sentiment classification using machine learning techniques. In: Proceedings of the ACL-02 Conference on Empirical Methods in Natural Language Processing, vol. 10, pp. 79–86. Association for Computational Linguistics (2002)
3. Xu, L.H., Lin, H.F.: Discourse affective computing based on semantic features and ontology. J. Comput. Res. Dev. **44**(S2), 356–360 (2007). (in Chinese)
4. Jiang, L., Yu, M., Zhou, M., et al.: Target-dependent Twitter sentiment classification. In: Proceedings of the Association for Computational Linguistics: Human Language Technologies, pp. 151–160 (2011)

5. Chen, J.M., Lin, H.F.: Constructing the affective commonsense knowledgebase. J. China Soc. Sci. Tech. Inf. **28**(4), 492–498 (2009). (in Chinese)
6. Yang, L., Lin, H.: Construction and application of Chinese emotional corpus. In: Ji, D., Xiao, G. (eds.) CLSW 2012. LNCS (LNAI), vol. 7717, pp. 122–133. Springer, Heidelberg (2013). https://doi.org/10.1007/978-3-642-36337-5_14
7. Xu, L.H., Lin, H.F., et al.: Constructing the affective lexicon ontology. J. China Soc. Sci. Tech. Inf. **27**(2), 180–185 (2008). (in Chinese)
8. Tan, S., Zhang, J.: An empirical study of sentiment analysis for Chinese documents. Expert Syst. Appl. **34**(4), 2622–2629 (2008)

A Comparable Corpus-Based Study of Three DO Verbs in Varieties of Mandarin: 從事 *congshi*, 做 *zuo* and 搞 *gao*

Menghan Jiang(✉) and Chu-Ren Huang(✉)

Department of CBS, The Hong Kong Polytechnic University, Hong Kong, China
menghan.jiang@connect.polyu.hk,
churen.huang@polyu.edu.hk

Abstract. In this study, we adopt a comparable corpus-based approach to investigate variations of three DO verbs in Mandarin Chinese: 做 *zuo* 'do', 搞 *gao* 'do' and 從事 *congshi* 'be engaged in'. Mandarin Chinese is unique in having three light verbs with bare meaning. The interesting and challenging facts about these three DO verbs are that: first, their usages can be differentiated even though they share the bare minimal meaning of 'to do'; and second, their ranges of usages vary in different varieties of Chinese. How can the complex differentiations of these three verbs within one variety and across different varieties be accounted for with the minimal shared meaning? We tackle this challenge applying functions from Chinese Word Sketch to effectively identify the subtle differences among near-synonyms and their usage variations among different varieties with explicit semantic cues. This study thus underlines the contribution of empirical approaches when there is very little intuition to rely on.

Keywords: DO verbs · Corpus-based approach · Language variation

1 Introduction

In Modern Chinese, the verbs 做 *zuo* 搞 *gao* and 從事 *congshi* share the function of English verb DO and are typically used to define one another in dictionary glosses [1, 2]. This is quite unique since a DO verb is supposed to be the lighted verb without any substantive meaning and the eventive meaning comes from its complements without (much) contribution from the light verb. For instance, 做研究 is considered to be (almost) totally synonymous to the verb 研究. Given the lack of semantic content, the uses of these three verbs are often interchangeable, as predicted. E.g. 從事/做/搞研究 *congshi/zuo/gao yanjiu*,'do research'. However, they are not interchangeable all the time. E.g. 從事/搞/*做養殖業, *congshi/gao/*zuo yangzhiye* 'engaged in breeding', *從事/?搞/做買賣 *congshi/*gao/zuo maimai*'engaged in business' [3, 4]. Given the 'bare' meaning of these three verbs, then, what is the lexical semantic motivation that allows speakers to use them differently?

Furthermore, the usages of these three verbs are not identical in different Mandarin. Previous scholars [1, 5, 6] observed many differences in usages of these DO verbs in different Mandarin varieties. For instance, 從事 *congshi* in Taiwan Mandarin can take

J.-F. Hong et al. (Eds.): CLSW 2018, LNAI 11173, pp. 147–154, 2018.
https://doi.org/10.1007/978-3-030-04015-4_12

complements denoting negative events such as 勾當 *goudang* 'shady business' and 性交易 *xingjiaoyi* 'sex trade', while such complements are seldom found in Mainland Mandarin. Assuming that such distributional and collocational differences arose from the different meanings and semantic constraints, how can we account for the full range of complex variations when the lexical meaning(s) of these verbs are already bare?

2 Previous Studies on 做 *zuo*, 搞 *gao* and 從事 *congshi*

Although some studies can be found on these three words respectively [1, 2], very few has focused on the differentiation and identification of them, let alone the verb variations between different variants of Mandarin. Wang [4] describes the (dis)-similarity of 做 *zuo* and 搞 *gao*. He summaries that both 做 *zuo* and 搞 *gao* can take a very wide range of complements, including verbal and nominal. The syntactic collocations of these two verbs are very similar, except for the position of the theme of taken complement. The difference between 做 *zuo* and 搞 *gao* mainly lies in that 做 *zuo* can use preposition to introduce the theme, as in 對數據做分析 *dui shuju zuofenxi* for_data_do_analyze 'analyze the data', while 搞 *gao* cannot (e.g., *對數據搞分析 **duishuju gaofenxi* for_data_do_analyze 'analyze the data').

In this study, we are taking a comparable corpus-based approach, aiming at (a) differentiating these three verbs in Mainland Mandarin; (b) identifying the similarities and differences of each verb in two varieties, i.e., Taiwan Mandarin and Mainland Mandarin.

In terms of the semantic property of these three verbs, since these three verbs themselves are semantically impoverished, they themselves usually do not contain eventive or contentive information. The most important predicative information mainly comes from their taken complements. With respect to syntactic collocation, we find these verbs are very similar in syntactic behavior (i.e. their syntactic function, whether it can take aspectual marker, the sentential type they can occur in), while vary a lot in their taken complements (i.e. what complements can they take). Therefore, the focus of our study is to look at the taken complements of 從事 *congshi*, 做 *zuo* and 搞 *gao* in both Mainland Chinese and Taiwan Mandarin Chinese.

3 Data Analysis

The data for this study was extracted from Annotated Chinese Gigaword corpus [7], which was collected and available from LDC and contains over 1.1 billion Chinese words, consisting of 700 million characters from Taiwan Central News Agency and 400 million characters from Mainland Xinhua News Agency. Variety internal comparison (i.e. the differentiation among these three verbs in one variety) as well as variety external comparison (i.e. differentiation between different varieties) will be conducted.

3.1 Differentiation of 做 *zuo* 搞 *gao* and 從事 *congshi* in Mainland Mandarin

The function of word sketch in the sketch engine is used to examine the syntactic collocation for each word. The word sketch is a one-page, automatic, corpus-derived summary of a word's grammatical and collocational behavior. Its collocates are grouped according to grammatical relations in which they occur. In our study, we selected the 50 most frequently occurred complements for each verb. Appendix 1 shows the 50 most frequently occurred complements/objects taken by Mainland 從事 *congshi*.

Through an overview of the data, it is obvious to see that the complements of 從事 *congshi* are very limited in number and type. Most of them are nous refers to profession and career, therefore the complement usually has the suffix 業 *ye* 'trade'.

For these collocations, if we replace 從事 *congshi* by 做 *zuo*, more than 50% (29/50) of the replaced constructions are not natural. Different from 從事 *congshi*, the complements taken by 做 *zuo* are usually verbs/deverbal nouns which refers to specific event or action like 研究 *yanjiu* 'research'/設計 *sheji* 'design'/交易 *jiaoyi* 'trade', as shown in Appendix 2.

Different from 做 *zuo*, all the 50 most frequently complements taken by 從事 can also be taken by 搞 *gao*, without changing the meaning of the whole construction. (e.g., 搞電子商務/從事電子商務 *gao/congshi dianzi shangwu* do_electronic_commerce 'engage in e-commerce'; 從事水產養殖業/搞水產養殖業 *congshi/gao yanzhiye* do_aquaculture 'engage in aquaculture').

Based on the syntactic collocation shown by the large-scale corpus, we can summarize as 從事 *congshi* and 搞 *gao* are syntactically more similar, while 做 *zuo* tends to co-occur with different types of complements.

As can be seen from Appendix 3, the complements can only be taken by 做 *zuo* usually refer to specific telic events which have an endpoint and always requires certain outcome. For example, some of the constructions are accomplishment events like 做記錄 *zuo jilu* 'make record' and 做對比 *zuo duibi* 'make comparison', while most of the taken complements are activity like 報告 *baogao* 'report', 計畫 *jihua* 'plan', 論述 *lunshu* 'dissertate'. In other words, the complements taken by 做 *zuo* usually refers to dynamic process instead of state.

It would be clearer if we compare the usages of 做 *zuo* and 搞 *gao*, even when taking the same complements, their event structures are different. As the example given by Diao [1] in (1):

(1) 做錄音---他在現場做錄音---? 他在現場搞錄音
zuo luyin — ta zai xianchang zuo luyin — ?ta zai xianchang gao luyin
'make sound recording — he is recording sound on site'
搞錄音---他是搞錄音的---? 他是做錄音的
gao luyin – ta shi gao luyin de – ?tashi zuo luyin de
'make sound recording – he is a sound recordist'

The construction 做錄音 *zuo luyin* 'make sound recording' refers to a specific event that the subject is making record and this event requires certain outcome (like a CD or tape). In contrast, 搞錄音 *gao luyin* just implicates that the profession of the subject is a sound recordist. A locative modification can be inserted (e.g., 在現場 *zai xianchang* 'on site') before 做錄音 to specify the event (e.g., 他在活動現場做錄音 *ta zai huodong xianchang zuo luyin* 'He is making sound recording on site').

Moreover, when the three verbs all take the same complement 研究 *yanjiu* 'research', the meaning of the whole construction are also different. 做研究 *zuo yanjiu* 'conduct research' refers to a specific event while 搞研究 *gaoyanjiu* 'conduct research' and 從事研究 *congshi yanjiu* 'conduct research' usually refers to long-term career or profession (i.e. He is a researcher). Therefore, the progressive marker 正在 *zhengzai* and location marker 辦公室 'office' can be used to test their event structure, since 正在 *zhengzai* is usually compatible with dynamic process (shown in (2)).

(2) 他正在辦公室做研究
ta zhengzai bangongshi zuo yanjiu
'He is doing research in the office now'
? 他正在辦公室搞研究
ta zhengzai bangongshi gao yanjiu
'He is doing research in the office now'
*他正在辦公室從事研究
ta zhengzai bangongshi congshi yanjiu
'He is doing research in the office now'

As examples shown above, 做研究 *zuo yanjiu* as an activity event can co-occur with 正在 *zhengzai* and location, while 從事研究 *congshi yanjiu* as a state cannot compatible with it.

With respect to 搞 *gao*, the corpus data shows that it can take a much wider range of complements, the most frequently occurred ones are shown below.

Among all the 50 most frequently occurred complements of 搞 *gao*, 23 examples cannot be taken by 從事 *congshi* while 13 tokens cannot be taken by 做 *zuo*. This may help to explain why In Chinese traditional grammar, 搞 *gao* is called 萬能動詞 *wanneng dongci* 'universal verb'. It is 'universal' in the sense that it can be used to replace a variety of verbs under different contexts. It has a wider range than 從事 *congshi* and 做 *zuo* in taking complements.

Summary
Based on the analysis above, it is clear to see that 從事 *congshi* and 搞 *gao* are often interchangeable. For complements taken by 從事 *congshi*, almost all of them can also be taken by 搞 *gao*. 搞 *gao* has a much wider range in usage in the sense that it can take a much wider range of complements.

做 *zuo* behaves the most differently from 搞 *gao* and 從事 *congshi* in the sense that it seldom take nouns which refer to profession or career (a state). Instead, it usually takes verb or deverbal noun which refers to specific event or action, with a dynamic process. This event usually requires telic point or an outcome.

3.2 Comparison Between Taiwan and Mainland Mandarin

To identify the variation differences between different variants of Chinese, a random sample of 200 sentences for each of the three verbs was extracted from both Mainland Mandarin sub-corpus and TW Mandarin sub-corpus. Specific usages (i.e. usages can only be detected in one variety) in each variety have been annotated.

3.2.1 從事 *congshi* in Mainland and Taiwan Mandarin

TW 從事 *congshi* and Mainland 從事 *congshi* are very similar in usage. Specific usages can only be found in Taiwan corpus. For example, 從事 *congshi* in TW can take informal event complements such as 休閒娛樂 *xiuxian yule* "entertainment", 散步等運動 *sanbu deng yundong* "do exercises like take a walk", as well as complements denoting negative events such as 性交易 *xing jiaoyi*, 色情行業 *seqing hangye*, "sex trade", etc. In contrast, 從事 *congshi* in Mainland can only take formal or positive event as its complement (e.g., 從事國事訪問 *congshi guoshi fangwe* 'have a state visit'), and this is consistent with the result shown in Huang el al. [8].

3.2.2 做 *zuo* in ML and TW Chinese

Our data shows that the event complements of Mainland 做 *zuo* are limited. Among 200 sentences we have annotated, 72 are 做工作 *zuo…gongzuo* 'do…work'. The only specific usage is 做…努力 *zuo…nuli* 'take efforts'.

Different from Mainland 做 *zuo*, TW 做 *zuo* can take a much wider range of complements. Among the 200 sentences, only 7 are 做工作 *zuo…gongzuo*. Plenty of specific usage can be found, 做答覆 *zuodafu* 'to reply', 做以上的表示 *zuo yishang biaoshi* 'make statement', 做人身攻擊 *zuo renshengongji* 'to make a personal attack', 做澄清 *zuo chengqing* 'to clarify', 做接觸 *zuojiechu* 'to touch', 做衝刺 *zuo chongci* 'to sprint', 做競賽 *zuo jingsai* 'to participate in the competition'.

The comparison of TW and ML 做 *zuo* shows that TW 做 *zuo* is semantically more bleached (light in meaning) in the sense that it can take a much wider range of complements. Therefore, for most of the specific complements taken by TW 做 *zuo*, they are often taken by other light verbs in ML. For example, 做答覆 *zuo dafu* is seen as 進行答覆 *jinxing dafu* in ML Chinese, 做人身攻擊 *zuo renshengongji* is 進行人身攻擊 *jinxing renshen gongji*, 做澄清 *zuo chengqing* is 進行澄清 *jinxing chengqing*, 做考慮 *zuo kaolv* is always used as 加以考慮 *jiayi kaolv*, 做接觸 *zuo jiechu* is 進行接觸 *jinxing jiechu*, 做競賽 *zuo jingsai* is 進行競賽 *jinxing jingsai* in ML Mandarin. This may show that 做 *zuo* in TW tend to be used as the default light verb.

3.2.3 搞 *gao* in ML and TW Chinese

When it comes to 搞 *gao*, our annotated results show that Mainland 搞 *gao* can take a variety of complements, and plenty of specific usages can be found. The semantic domains of these complements are also very diverse, which is consistent with our findings in the above section. According to SUMO (Suggested Upper Merged Ontology) [9], 傾銷 *qingxiao* 'dump', 直銷 *zhixiao* 'direct sales', 批發 *pifa* 'wholesale', 銷售 *xiaoshou* 'sales' and 貿易 *maoyi* 'trade' belong to the domain of selling; while 運輸 *yunshu* 'transportation', 販運 *fanyun* 'transport goods for sale', 航運 *hangyun* 'shipping' belong to the domain of transportation, and also 製作 *zhizuo* 'manufacture', 加工 *jiagong* 'process', 設計 *sheji* 'design' belong to the concept of making.

In contrast, the complements of TW 搞 *gao* are very limited in types. More than 90% complements are political event (and also related to ML context). The specific complements mostly refer to specific political event of Taiwan and can only be appeared in the negative context. For example, 搞形式主义/和平演变/分裂/抹黑 *gao xingshizhuyi/heping yanbian/fenlie/mohei* do_formalism/peaceful evolution/dispute/

throw-mud 'take formalism approach/make peaceful evolution/cause state disrup tion/throw mud'.

In general, for 做 *zuo* and 搞 *gao* in both Mainland and Taiwan, we can summarize as the usage of Taiwan 做 *zuo* is semantically much lighter than its Mainland counterparts, in the sense that it can take a much wider range of complements under different context. While in Mainland, 搞 *gao* may be semantically more bleached than its Taiwan counterparts, because Taiwan 搞 *gao* can barely be used in other context except for political context with the negative meaning.

4 Conclusion

In this study, we differentiate three DO verbs in Mandarin Chinese 從事 *congshi*, 做 *zuo* and 搞 *gao,* both in terms of their collocational constraints and their usage variations in different varieties of Chinese. By examining their differences in the taken complements as well as the event structure, we also identify the variation differences for each corresponding verb between Mainland and Taiwan. We show that, with the bare meaning of these light verbs, they differ from either other in terms of the event types they select. Similarly, by alternations of the groupings, different event types, varieties of Chinese also use these DO verbs differently. We show that, with the assistant of large-scale comparable corpus, a study of near synonyms share bare meaning is possible even though there is very little 'meaning' or intuition to rely on.

Appendix

Appendix 1. The 50 most frequently occurred complements taken by 從事 *congshi*

研究 *Yanjiu*	第三產業 *disanchanye*	活動 *huodong*	業務 *yewu*	工作 *gongzuo*	第二職業 *di'er zhiye*
運動 *yundong*	種植業 *zhongzhiye*	農副產品 *nongfuchanpin*	服務業 *fuwuye*	房地產 *fangdichan*	創作 *chuangzuo*
交易 *Jiaoyi*	職業 *zhiye*	農業 *nongye*	建築業 *Jianzhu ye*	科研 *keyan*	公務 *gongwu*
漁業 *Yuye*	作業 *zuoye*	商業 *shangye*	貿易 *maoyi*	農牧業 *nongmuye*	建築 *Jianzhu ye*
旅遊業 *lvyouye*	設計 *sheji*	事業 *shiye*	產業 *chanye*	文學 *wenxue*	養殖業 *Yangzhiye*
社區服務 *shequfuwu*	訓練 *xunlian*	教育 *jiaoyi*	副業 *fuye*	種養業 *zhongyangye*	生意 *shengyi*
加工業 *Jiagongye*	客運 *keyun*	工商業 *gongshangye*	家政服務 *jiazheng fuwu*	行業 *hangye*	運輸業 *Yunshuye*
製造業 *zhizaoye*	電子商務 *dianzi shangwu*	工種 *gongzhong*	畜牧業 *xumuye*	庭院經濟 *tingyuan jingji*	商貿 *Shangmao*
體育活動 *tiyu huodong*	環保產業 *huanbaochanye*				

Appendix 2. The 50 most frequently occurred complements taken by 做 *zuo*

手術 *Shoushu*	文章 *wenzhang*	生意 *shengyi*	貢獻 *gongxian*	工作 *gongzuo*	報告 *baogao*	實驗 *shiyan*
試驗 *Shiyan*	嘗試 *changshi*	規定 *guiding*	小買賣 *xiaomaimai*	宣傳 *xuanchuan*	記錄 *jilu*	買賣 *Maimai*
交易 *Jiaoyi*	學問 *xuewen*	演講 *yanjiang*	保證 *baozheng*	解釋 *jieshi*	研究 *yanjiu*	人工呼吸 *rengonghuxi*
調查 *Diaocha*	翻譯 *fanyi*	統計 *tongji*	評價 *pingjia*	評論 *pinglun*	小本生意 *xiaoben shengyi*	總結 *Zongjie*
訓練 *xunlian*	限制 *xianzhi*	報導 *baodao*	決策 *juece*	規劃 *guihua*	對比 *duibi*	保障 *baozhang*
計畫 *Jihua*	決定 *jueding*	尿檢 *niaojian*	後勤 *houqin*	論述 *lunshu*	抵押 *diya*	設計 *Sheji*
分析 *Fenxi*	測試 *ceshi*	建設 *jianshe*	科研 *keyan*			

Appendix 3. Complements can only be taken by 做 *zuo*

手術 *shoushu*	文章 *wenzhang*	貢獻 *gongxian*	報告 *baogao*	嘗試 *changshi*	規定 *Guiding*
記錄 *Jilu*	演講 *yanjiang*	保證 *baozheng*	解釋 *jieshi*	評價 *pingjia*	評論 *Pinglun*
總結 *zongjie*	限制 *xianzhi*	決策 *juece*	對比 *duibi*	保障 *baozhang*	計畫 *Jihua*
決定 *jueding*	論述 *lunshu*	抵押 *diya*			

References

1. Diao, Y.: Research on Delexical Verb in Modern Chinese (現代漢語虛義動詞研究). Liaoning Normal University Press, Dalian (2004)
2. Du quner. Form verbs in modern Chinese (现代汉语形式动词研究), Master's dissertation, Shanghai Normal University (2010)
3. Huang, C.R., Lin, J.X., Jiang, M.H., Xu, H.Z. Corpus-based study and identification of Mandarin Chinese light verb variations. In: COLING Workshop on Applying NLP Tools to Similar Languages, Varieties and Dialects, Dublin (2014)
4. Jian, W.: Comparison and Collocation of "Gan, Gao, Zuo", ("干, 搞, 做" 的詞語搭配範圍及其詞義對比) Chin. Teach. Overseas (*海外華文教學*)2, 48–53 (2002)
5. Huang, C.-R., Lin, J.: The ordering of Mandarin Chinese light verbs. In: Ji, D., Xiao, G. (eds.) CLSW 2012. LNCS (LNAI), vol. 7717, pp. 728–735. Springer, Heidelberg (2013). https://doi.org/10.1007/978-3-642-36337-5_73

6. Jiang, M.H., Shi, D.X., Huang, C.R.: Transitivity in light verb variations in Mandarin Chinese–a comparable corpus-based statistical approach. In: Proceedings of the 30th Pacific Asia Conference on language, information and computing. Seoul, Korea (2016)
7. Huang, C.R.: Tagged Chinese Gigaword Version 2.0. Philadelphia: Lexical Data Consortium, University of Pennsylvania (2009). ISBN 1-58563-516-2
8. Huang, C-R., Lin, J., Zhang, H.: World Chinese's based on comparable corpus: the case of grammatical variations of jinxing. *《澳门语言文化研究》*, pp. 397–414. (2013)
9. Niles, I., Pease, A.: Towards a standard upper ontology. In: Proceedings of the international conference on Formal Ontology in Information Systems, vol. 2001, pp. 2–9. ACM (2001)

From Near Synonyms to Power Relation Variations in Communication: A Cross-Strait Comparison of “Guli” and “Mianli”

Xiaowen Wang[1,2] and Chu-Ren Huang[3(✉)]

[1] School of English and Education, Guangdong University of Foreign Studies, Guangzhou, China
200611520@oamail.gdufs.edu.cn

[2] National Experimental Teaching Center of Simultaneous Interpreting, Guangdong University of Foreign Studies, Guangzhou, China

[3] Department of Chinese and Bilingual Studies, The Hong Kong Polytechnic University, Kowloon, Hong Kong SAR, China
churen.huang@polyu.edu.hk

Abstract. This paper proposes a new approach to the study of stance differences in different speaking communities based on comparable corpus-based study of near synonyms. In particular, we study the differences in stance implications of the same pair of near synonyms of two varieties of Mandarin Chinese cross the strait: in Taiwan and Mainland China. We show that important communication frame differences such as interpersonal power relation can be encoded lexically and sharing same lexical forms that express different power relations can lead to barriers in communication. More specifically, our study of the uses of near synonyms 鼓勵 “guli” and 勉勵 “mianli” adopts both verbal semantic representation of MARVS theory and functional communication theory of Systemic Functional Linguistics. The stance differences in terms of implication of interpersonal relation variations in Taiwan and Mainland China are represented and accounted for in MARVS. Our study synergizes the verbal semantic representation of MARVS theory with the functional communication theory of Halliday’s Systemic Functional Linguistics, especially in terms of tenor and modality. Our results also suggest that comparable corpus-driven, lexical semantics based approaches can provide a strong foundation for stance detection and classification of different communities.

Keywords: Near synonyms · MARVS · Interpersonal meaning
Comparable corpus

1 Introduction

Near synonyms in Mandarin Chinese, especially verbs, have been the focus of past studies. It has been argued that the “syntactic behaviors of verbs are semantically determined” [1, p. 57], hence comparing the syntactic differences of synonym verbs can effectively reveal semantic differences between the verbs [1]. Since such comparison cannot be based on intuition, the corpus-based approach following the Module-Attribute

J.-F. Hong et al. (Eds.): CLSW 2018, LNAI 11173, pp. 155–166, 2018.
https://doi.org/10.1007/978-3-030-04015-4_13

Representation of Verbal Semantics (MARVS) theory [7, 11–13] has been shown as a new, powerful approach to explore semantic representations of near synonyms [8].

In particular, as cross-strait communication has become more frequent, scholars [8, 9] have compared lexical correspondences in Taiwan and Mainland China following the MARVS approach. However, little attention has been paid to the variations of interpersonal relations in terms of how near synonyms are used in these two different speech communities. To fill this gap, this paper tries to apply MARVS theory in cross-cultural comparison of synonyms "mianli" and "guli"in Taiwan and Mainland China. In the comparison, we draw on Halliday's [3–5] Systemic Functional Linguistics (SFL) to explore the interpersonal variations in MARVS representations of the two verbs used in Taiwan and Mainland China. In order to get evidence, the two sub-corpora of Gigaword Corpus [2, 10] – Gigaword_XIN and Gigaword_CNA are used as corpora for the study, and Chinese Sketch Engine [13] is used as the query tool.

In terms of natural language processing and computational linguistics, detection and classification of stance in terms of interpersonal relation vis-à-vis positions on certain issues have been a hot and challenging topic (e.g., [16, 17]). However, with the exception of Hasan and Ng [6], such studies do not typically apply lexical semantic theories. Studies so far also focused on stances of individuals, not the collective stance of a community, which should be critical in understanding and resolution of conflict between different cultural, ethnical, or social groups. We believe our study based on comparable corpus of two Mandarin speaking communities can make important contributions to future language technology for collective stance identification.

2 Research Questions

The following research questions are explored in this paper:

(1) What are the event representations for "guli"and "mianli" used in Taiwan and Mainland China?
(2) Are there any differences in terms of interpersonal relations of these two words in Taiwan and Mainland China? And if so, how can these differences be represented in the event representations of "guli"and "mianli"?

3 Theoretical Framework

3.1 MARVS Theory

MARVS theory [12] is a practical approach to interpret the grammatical behaviors of verbs. It is advanced in comparison to traditional semantic theories in that it views verb sense as eventive information. The semantic representation of a verb has two modules: event modules and role modules, both bearing its internal attributes.

There are five "atomic event structures" [11, p. 26]:

(1) . Boundary (including a Complete Event)
Boundary is an event module that can be identified with a temporal point and that must be regarded as a whole.
(2) / Punctuality
Punctuality is an event module that represents a single occurrence of an activity that cannot be measured by duration.
(3) ///// Process
Process is an event module that represents an activity that has a time course.
(4) _____ State
State is a homogeneous event module in which the concept of temporal duration is irrelevant.
(5) ^^^^^ Stage
Stage is an event module consisting of iterative sub events. [11, p. 26]

According to MARVS theory, the event-internal attributes are "properties that can be assigned to an event, and they are motivated by cognitive necessity and supported by linguistic data" [12, p. 301]. Besides, the ROLE modules include two parts: the focused roles (participants) of an event and the role-internal attributes, the latter being "the semantic properties of the participants, such as [sentience], [volition], [affectedness], and so forth" [12, p. 301].

However, we think there still needs a systematic way to capture internal attributes. Therefore, we try to draw on one of the language metafunctions in SFL – interpersonal meaning, to capture role-internal attributes and make comparisons between Taiwan and Mainland China for the uses of near synonyms.

3.2 Systemic Functional Linguistics and Interpersonal Meaning

Halliday [4, 5] 's SFL tries to detect the context of language use through the study of register, which includes field, tenor and mode. He proposes that there are three metafunctions of language which correspond to the three components of register – interpersonal meaning corresponding to tenor, experiential meaning corresponding to field, and textual meaning corresponding to mode. Here we only focus on tenor and its related interpersonal meaning to help us explore the role internal attributes of the synonyms under study. Tenor is defined as "the cluster of socially meaningful participant relationships, both permanent attributes of the participants and role relationships that are specific to the situation, including speech roles, those that come into being through the exchange of verbal meanings" [3, p. 143]. Interpersonal meaning, which realizes tenor, is about our use of language "to interact with other people, to establish and maintain relations with them, to influence their behavior, to express our own viewpoint on things in the world, and to elicit or change theirs" [18, p. 28]. In SFL, the interpersonal meaning can be realized by some grammatical systems, such as mood and modality. For mood, there are four types: statement, question, offer and command. For modality, "the area of meaning that lies between yes and no – the intermediate ground between positive and negative polarity" [5, p. 356], there are modal verbal operators which can be categorized into high, median, and low values:

"High: must, ought to, need, has to, is to
Median: will, would, shall, should
Low: may, might, can, could" [5, p. 362]

4 Research Methodology

The current study is based on the sub-corpora of Chinese Gigaword Corpus – Gigaword_XIN (XIN) and Gigaword_CNA (CNA). The former includes collected news texts from the Xinhua News Agency of Beijing (382,881,000 tokens), and the latter from Central News Agency of Taiwan (735,499,000 tokens).

The Sketch Engine, "a corpus processing system developed in 2002" [13–15], is used as the query tool for the two sub corpora. We use functions like KWIC concordances, word sketch, and sketch differences in the Sketch Engine for our analysis of the near synonyms in the two sub-corpora.

5 Analysis and Findings

5.1 Overall Distribution of "Guli" and "Mianli" in CNA and XIN

Since CNA and XIN have different sizes, we firstly searched for the frequencies of "guli" and "mianli" in CNA and XIN, and then compared their frequency distribution through log-likelihood values (See Table 1) in the two sub-corpora. The results clearly show that in comparison to Mainland China, "guli" is highly significantly underused, and "mianli" is highly significantly overused in Taiwan.

We will try to interpret the reasons for the uneven distribution with reference to the event and role attributes below.

Table 1. Overall distribution of the word "guli" and "mianli" in CNA and XIN – comparison of log-likelihood values

Word	Freq. in CNA	Freq. in XIN	Log-likelihood	Sig.
鼓勵（guli）	61427	34883	166.92	0.000 *** -
勉勵（mianli）	8451	2214	935.49	0.000 *** +

5.2 Event Module: Structure and Attributes

After running CQL query in Sketch Engine, we got the concordances for "mianli" and "guli" collocated with "buduan" (continuously) and/or "yizhi" (constantly) in CNA and XIN. We also find that the event structure of "guli" belongs to process, as it refers to a kind of activity that can be modified by adverbs signaling temporal duration, such as "buduan" (0.22 per million in CNA, 0.09 per million in XIN), and/or "yizhi" (0.31 per million in CNA, 0.16 per million in XIN), and sometimes can be measured by time duration such as years. It is a kind of inchoative process, because the duration is typically characterized by time duration "...yilai" (since ...), which means that the beginning point of the process is clear but the ending point is not.

However, for "mianli", it is similar to "guli" in that it is inchoative. But it tends to be a punctuality event in XIN, as it is an activity that is rarely modified by durative adverbs such as "buduan" (0.014 per million in CNA, 0.008 per million in XIN) and "yizhi" (0.007 per million in CNA, 0.005 per million in XIN). For the internal attributes of the event, both events can be controlled and are used to motivate people toward a positive objective.

Therefore, the event structure and event internal attributes can be tentatively presented as:

In Taiwan:

guli ./////[control] [positive polarity]
mianli ./////[control] [positive polarity]

In the Mainland:

guli ./////[control] [positive polarity]
mianli ./[control] [positive polarity]

5.3 Role Module: Roles and Attributes

Tenor and Roles. In order to work out the structure of the role module, we look into the tenor in the context where the two words are used, i.e., who can be the typical subjects and objects. The following figures show the "sketch differences" results of "guli" and "mianli" in CNA and XIN in Sketch Engine, including the general differences (Fig. 1), and the "only patterns" of "guli" (Fig. 2) and "mianli" (Fig. 3).

However, there are sharp differences between CNA and XIN as well: In CNA there is a widely acceptable range for agents and patients of "mianli", so the hierarchy distance concerned is not as high as that in XIN. For subjects, the "only patterns" for "mianli" in XIN only include individuals who are political leaders (e.g., Jiang Zemin) in Mainland China, but those in CNA include not only individual political leaders in Taiwan (e.g., Lian Zhan), but also the renowned scholar Li Yuanzhe (0.034 per million), who is a Noble prize winner, as well as the generic expression "dajia" (a group of people), and the self reference "ziwo" (oneself, ourselves). The concordance results of "mianli" collocated with "dajia" (0.11 per million) and "ziwo" (0.05 per million) within 3 tokens on its left in CNA are shown in Figs. 4 and 5 respectively. For objects, patients such as students ("tongxuemen", "xueyuan") and graduates ("biyesheng") are more oriented to the continuum of "mianli" in CNA, whereas graduates ("biyesheng") are obviously oriented to "guli" in XIN (See Fig. 1). The "only patterns" for "mianli" (Fig. 3) in Taiwan include a wider range than the Mainland: patients for "mianli" in XIN include people in military or political sense ("renmin", "guanbing", "tongzhi" etc.) in the Mainland, but CNA include students in lower grades ("xuedi", "xuemei") and players ("duiyuan") additionally.

CNA

鼓勵/勉勵 **gigaword2cna freq = 61427/8451**

Common patterns

鼓勵 21 14 7 0 -7 -14 -21 勉勵

Subject	1180	1588	0.5	4.9
他	72	431	19.0	39.9
她	21	42	15.6	21.1
總統	8	113	1.7	20.1
精神	9	7	9.9	7.3
他們	7	5	6.1	3.6

Object	44045	6363	4.4	4.5
同仁	164	[illegible]	22.3	49.0
大家	587	405	35.9	47.3
同學們	15	52	17.5	43.3
畢業生	[illegible]	147	18.5	41.0
同學	72	134	19.7	40.6
民眾	2590	57	40.2	9.8
台商	817	26	38.9	11.9
企業	1570	10	38.4	1.7
他們	745	380	29.3	37.2
年輕人	217	31	35.4	22.8
學子	160	67	34.7	35.3
廠商	846	10	34.4	3.6
學員	45	80	14.7	32.8
業者	932	21	32.5	6.4
國人	316	87	32.1	29.1
學生	984	221	31.9	28.5
小朋友	135	84	24.7	31.7
企業界	175	19	30.9	16.7
師生	69	62	19.5	30.0
員工	380	136	26.2	28.1
選手	231	165	17.4	28.1
市民	338	11	27.6	6.4
農民	275	8	27.2	5.5
官兵	35	[illegible]	12.4	27.1
中小企業	200	11	26.9	9.1

SentObject_of	2328	64	3.4	0.7
希望	628	21	45.1	22.5
不忘	20	7	27.2	26.2

Modifier	11741	1561	3.3	3.1
互相	32	[illegible]	24.1	49.4
相互	[illegible]	[illegible]	23.4	46.9
並	624	370	34.4	44.4
也	1225	477	37.7	42.3
予以	121	14	29.6	16.1
要	407	14	29.0	7.8
多所	30	11	28.7	24.4
會	405	10	26.8	4.9
來	249	106	22.0	26.5
不斷	74	8	24.1	11.6
一再	55	12	22.8	16.3
則	138	62	18.1	22.5
更	99	31	20.1	19.4
還	122	21	17.7	12.5
常	24	6	16.6	11.8
當面	12	6	15.8	15.7
經常	22	5	14.7	9.8
曾	79	13	14.6	9.6
都	105	18	14.0	9.9
仍	59	16	11.6	11.0
一起	9	7	6.1	10.8

Modifies	504	32	0.0	0.0
話	22	8	24.4	22.6

XIN

鼓勵/勉勵 **gigaword2xin freq = 34883/2214**

Common patterns

鼓勵 21 14 7 0 -7 -14 -21 勉勵

Object	24236	1855	4.4	5.1
大家	[illegible]	[illegible]	27.8	59.6
他們	933	371	35.5	44.8
企業	2247	8	36.3	0.6
同學們	23	25	20.7	33.7
畢業生	113	5	26.2	8.5
工作者	87	47	17.2	25.8
官兵	20	[illegible]	6.5	25.4
學生	271	30	24.8	17.0
健兒	24	20	14.7	24.4
年輕人	55	6	22.9	12.1
青年人	31	6	21.8	14.8
留學生	19	17	10.9	20.8
職工	209	20	20.5	12.6
運動員	192	42	20.4	20.3
人員	467	49	20.4	14.7
群眾	301	28	20.2	12.8
青年	80	45	10.4	20.1
孩子們	30	14	15.9	19.6
她	150	23	19.3	15.4
青少年	91	15	18.7	14.6
員工	49	8	18.2	12.6
她們	35	9	16.8	14.8
學員	15	10	9.9	16.1
學子	21	7	16.0	15.2
大學生	53	8	13.9	9.8

Subject	438	486	0.3	4.8
他	[illegible]	[illegible]	5.1	42.1
他們	9	11	9.9	11.0

Modifier	4313	145	2.7	1.4
互相	70	23	35.2	36.7
還	437	35	35.8	25.6
相互	91	13	31.3	23.8
也	189	7	27.1	11.0
曾	11	8	7.5	16.4

Fig. 1. A comparison of the "sketch differences" results of "guli" and "mianli" in CNA and XIN in Sketch Engine

CNA

"鼓勵" only patterns

PP_和	122	79.9
外商	11	24.3
掌聲	6	20.5
企業	7	12.3

PP_以	101	6.1
方式	9	14.6
市場	8	11.7

Object	44045	4.4
民間	1955	53.0
外商	738	48.6
私人	286	42.2
久任	22	31.3
人們	91	28.7
士氣	128	28.3
外人	70	26.5
作用	198	26.3
外資	224	25.3
民間團體	71	25.3
台胞	43	24.8
私營企業	40	23.9

SentObject_of	2328	3.4
無異	63	48.0
旨在	79	42.6
繼續	315	42.3
在於	98	38.2
設法	57	32.7
需要	89	27.2
包括	133	26.4
意在	11	24.5
用來	24	24.5
有助於	32	24.1
肯定	34	24.0
不宜	22	23.7

Modifier	11741	3.3
以資	194	65.5
變相	147	51.4
應	717	41.0
多	298	37.7
不	1057	36.2
將	1298	35.8
應該	220	34.7
間接	73	34.3
給他	26	30.8
予	92	28.3
儘量	47	27.8
一直	110	27.6

PP_自	12	2.4
美	6	19.1

PP_在	273	2.2
泰	6	17.6
台商	8	14.2
青年	6	12.0
國內	6	9.1
學生	6	9.0
台灣	10	7.4
美國	8	7.2
大陸	8	6.6
地區	5	3.8

Subject	1180	0.5
獎金	23	22.8
政府	127	22.3
掌聲	11	20.2
獎狀	7	18.9
大陸	69	17.0
港府	8	15.9
方式	30	15.6
我們	17	15.3
政策性	5	14.2
北京市	5	12.5
措施	13	10.7
中共	22	10.1

Modifies	504	0.0
掌聲	31	37.6
態度	39	28.3
立場	29	23.1
作用	17	22.8
方式	33	20.8
項目	15	17.3
事	16	16.8
方向	11	15.7
心情	7	15.7
誘因	5	15.7
作法	9	15.0
電話	10	14.5

XIN

"鼓勵" only patterns

Object	24236	4.4
外商	983	51.9
自謀職業	98	42.6
私人	158	40.0
農民	867	33.4
冒尖	19	31.9
中小企業	155	30.9
獎	121	30.8
企業家	197	30.7
下崗職工	146	29.9
私營企業	102	29.0
政策	663	28.4
台商	105	27.3

PP_以	40	4.3
企業	5	9.2

SentObject_of	1010	4.1
旨在	226	58.8
繼續	354	50.7
在於	45	34.3
有利於	50	30.9
包括	61	26.0
堅持	36	21.4
意在	8	21.4
有助於	17	21.1
希望	33	18.2
不忘	5	14.9
同意	11	14.5
致力	8	14.1

PP_在	228	3.1
領域	16	19.4
海外	6	13.5
國外	5	12.7
地區	10	9.3
企業	5	4.7

Modifier	4313	2.7
要	549	40.7
以資	22	38.8
應	181	38.3
將	534	35.7
了	373	34.2
動搖	36	33.9
應該	85	32.5
大力	122	31.6
進一步	180	30.9
應當	62	29.3
予以	55	28.8
並	133	28.6

Subject	438	0.3
中方	25	30.2
政府	53	19.8
北京市	13	18.3
措施	15	14.2
系列	11	14.1
政策	14	12.4
我們	10	12.4
深圳	5	10.4
大陸	5	9.6
國家	18	9.6

Modifies	128	0.0
掌聲	15	29.8
產業	11	16.6
話	5	14.7
項目	11	14.0
能源	5	13.2
作用	6	11.0

Fig. 2. A comparison of the "only patterns" of "guli" in CNA and XIN in Sketch Engine

CNA

"勉勵" only patterns

Subject 1588		4.9
黃大洲	21	22.8
自我	17	21.4
郝柏村	17	20.1
呂秀蓮	16	18.1
蘇貞昌	11	17.2
大家	20	16.9
尤清	10	16.7
廖永來	8	16.2
連戰	25	16.2
許水德	10	16.1
阮	7	15.8
李遠哲	9	15.6

Object 6363		4.5
軍官兵	15	20.7
隊員們	6	19.4
全體	36	17.2
隊員	18	16.7
學妹	5	16.6
學弟	6	16.3
後備軍人	7	14.4
全黨	6	14.3
眾人	5	11.4
新鮮人	5	11.2
國手	8	11.0
村里長	5	10.0

XIN

"勉勵" only patterns

Object 1855		5.1
指戰員	13	22.8
官兵們	9	18.7
戰線	12	16.2
老同志	5	12.5
同志	16	10.4
全體	5	6.7
年	9	3.0
人民	8	0.9
全國	5	0.5

Subject 486		4.8
江澤民	23	21.6
李鵬	15	19.2
周南	5	18.9
伍紹祖	6	18.9
胡錦濤	10	18.3
李嵐清	6	14.7
她	10	13.4
李瑞環	5	13.3
主席	15	12.1
同志	9	11.0
總理	10	10.3

Modifier 145		1.4
語重心長	6	28.1
親切	5	20.6

Fig. 3. A comparison of the "only patterns" of "mianli" in CNA and XIN in Sketch Engine

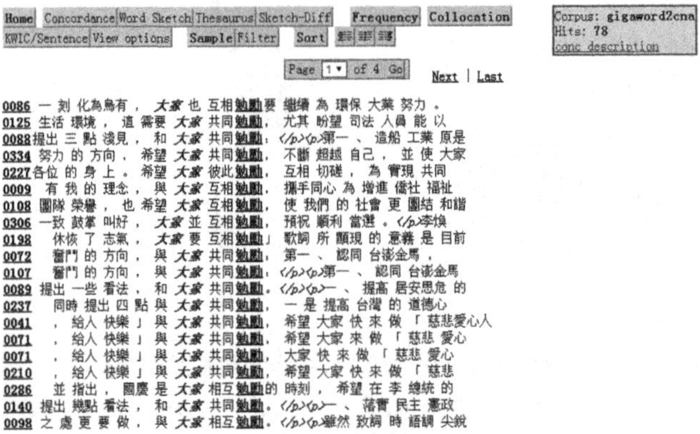

Fig. 4. The concordance results for "mianli" collocated with "dajia" on the left in CNA (extract)

Modality and Role Internal Attributes. For the modifiers shown in the sketch results for "mianli" in XIN (Figs. 2 and 3), high and median value modal verbal operators "yao", " ying", "yinggai", "yingdang" are "only patterns" collocated with "guli", rather than "mianli". The modal verbal operators "ying" and "yinggai" are "only patterns" collocated with "guli" in CNA as well, but "yao" is not included in the "only patterns" in CNA. There are 29 instances for the collocation of "mianli" with the modal verbal operator "yao" in CNA (0.039 per million). However, in XIN there are only 6 instances (0.016 per million) in which "yao" is collocated with "mianli". Furthermore, we can also tell from the log-likelihood values for collocation of "guli", "mianli" with modal verbal operators in CNA and XIN (shown in Table 2) that a role-internal attribute for "mianli" is that obligations are not supposed to be imposed over the agent to carry out this event in XIN, whereas in CNA obligations can be imposed over the agent to do so. This also indicates a higher hierarchy attribute inherently coded in the word "mianli" used in the Mainland than in Taiwan.

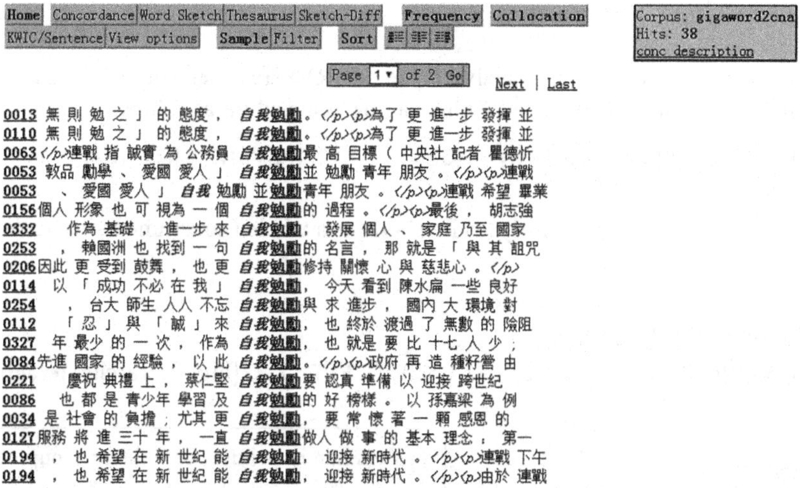

Fig. 5. The concordance results for “mianli” collocated with “ziwo” on the left in CNA (extract)

Table 2. Log-likelihood values for collocation of “guli”, “mianli” with modal verbal operators in CNA and XIN

Word	Freq. in CNA	Freq. in XIN	Log-likelihood	Sig.
應該 鼓勵	523	159	38.53	0.000 *** +
應該 勉勵	11	0		+
應當 鼓勵	32	62	39.17	0.000 *** -
應當 勉勵	0	1		-
應 鼓勵	720	182	86.52	0.000 *** +
應 勉勵	15	0		+
要 鼓勵	413	551	210.85	0.000 *** -
要 勉勵	29	6	5.10	0.024 * +

6 Discussion

Based on the above data and analysis, the MARVS representations of "guli" and "mianli" in Taiwan and Mainland China can be summed up as follows:

guli ./////**[control][positive polarity]** <AGENT, PATIENT, EVENT > **[eventive]**

AGENT: predominantly leading body as a whole (government, party, we...)

<u>"mianli" in Mainland China:</u>

./ **[control][positive polarity]**<AGENT, PATIENT, EVENT >|| [high hierarchy] **[eventive]**

AGENT: predominantly individual political leader in Mainland China

PATIENT: predominantly political or military group of people ("renmin", "guanbing", "tongzhi", etc.)

<u>"mianli" in Taiwan:</u>

./////**[control][positive polarity]**<AGENT, PATIENT, EVENT >|| [hierarchy]**[eventive]**

AGENT: predominantly individual political leader and renowned scholar in Taiwan, as well as "dajia" and "ziwo"

PATIENT: predominantly political, millitary, academic, or sports group of people

We found no salient differences in the MARVS representations of "guli" in Taiwan and Mainland China, but there are significant contrasts for the use of "mianli". It is shown that the main differences are in terms of interpersonal power relations: while "mianli" in Taiwan is a "process" event that involves both moral and actual authority over the patient, "mianli" in the Mainland tends to be a punctuality event that involves an actual governing authority. For instance, whereas famous individuals with academic fame or authority typically use "mianli" rather than "guli" to encourage students in Taiwan, their counterparts in the Mainland tend to use "guli" instead. People sometimes "mianli" each other and "mianli" themselves in Taiwan, but people in the Mainland use "guli" instead in those cases. The use of "mianli" in Mainland China, however, requires that the agent have direct governing authority over the patient. And in particular, the event being advised is often related to that particular authority. In other words, "mianli" in Mainland Chinese usage represents a specific stance and requires a special power relation between the agent and patient.

Given the power relation constraint of "mianli" in Mainland usage, the overall distributional disparity of overuse of "mianli" in Taiwan is easily explained. Since the Taiwan usage has neutral stance and does not have the power relation constraint, it is relatively free and allows wider ranges for subjects and objects.

7 Conclusion

Our study shows that although the core meanings of the synonyms "guli"and "mianli" in Mainland China and Taiwan are basically the same, they are used to express different stances and hence imply different interpersonal power relation. This is an important dimension of lexical semantic relation for differentiating minimal near synonym pairs which has not been typically represented in previous literature. Such relations have been well-studied in pragmatics and functional frameworks such as Halliday's SFL, particularly from the perspectives of tenor and its associated interpersonal meaning. We attempt to incorporate this dimension to MARVS. SFL insights have helped us to interpret roles and internal attributes of the role module, thereby enriching the MARVS theory by adding an attribute of interpersonal relation. It might also be possible to adopt other metafunctions in SFL to link the semantic representation of a word to the situational and socio-cultural context in which it is used. Our study shows the importance of considering the social and cultural context in the study of word semantics representation. It indicates that MRAVS representations of a verb can not only predict its grammatical behaviors but also reflect the cultural norms by which the word is used.

Last, but not the least, our study shows that lexical semantic representation of near synonyms can be rich in stance related information. In addition, using near synonyms as basis for study based on comparable corpora can contribute to identification and comparison of collective stances of different speaking communities. This suggests a brand new and potentially very fruitful direction of stance detection studies with high impact.

Acknowledgments. This research is funded by the Science and Technology Project of Guangdong Province, China (2016A040403113), and the Center for Institutional Discourse Studies of Guangdong University of Foreign Studies.

References

1. Chief, L.-C., Huang, C.-R., Chen, K.-J., Tsai, M.-C., Chang, L.-L.: What can near synonyms tell us? Int. J. Comput. Linguist. Chin. Lang. Process. **5**(1), 47–59 (2000). https://doi.org/10.30019/IJCLCLP.200002.0003
2. Graff, D., Chen, K.: Chinese Gigaword LDC2003T09. Linguistic Data Consortium, Philadelphia (2003). https://catalog.ldc.upenn.edu/LDC2003T09
3. Halliday, M.A.K.: Language as Social Semiotic: The Social Interpretation of Language and Meaning. Edward Arnold, London (1978)
4. Halliday, M.A.K.: An Introduction to Functional Grammar. Arnold, London (1994)
5. Halliday, M.A.K.: An Introduction to Functional Grammar. Foreign Language Teaching and Research Press, Beijing (2000)

6. Hasan, K.S., Ng, V.: Frame semantics for stance classification. In: Proceedings of the Seventeenth Conference on Computational Natural Language Learning, pp. 124–132. (2013)
7. Hong, J.-F., Ahrens, K., Huang, C.-R.: Event structure of transitive verb: a MARVS perspective. Int. J. Comput. Process. Lang. **24**(1), 37–50 (2012). https://doi.org/10.1142/S179384061240003X
8. Hong, J.-F., Huang, C.-R.: A corpus-based approach to the discovery of cross-strait lexical contrasts. Lang. Linguist. **9**(2), 221–238 (2008). (in Chinese)
9. Hong, J.-F., Huang, C.-R., Xu, M.-W.: A study of lexical differences between China and Taiwan based on the Chinese Gigaword Corpus. In: Proceedings of the Conference on Computational Linguistics and Speech Processing (ROCLING 2007), pp. 287–301 (2007)
10. Huang, C.-R.: Tagged Chinese Gigaword Version 2.0. LDC2009T14. Linguistic Data Consortium, Philadelphia (2009). https://catalog.ldc.upenn.edu/LDC2009T14
11. Huang, C.-R., Ahrens, K., Chang, L.-L., Chen, K.-J., Liu, M.C., Tsai, M.-C.: The module-attribute representation of verbal semantics: from semantics to argument structure. Int. J. Comput. Linguist. Chin. Lang. Process. **5**(1), 1–79 (2000). https://doi.org/10.30019/IJCLCLP.200002.0002
12. Huang, C.-R., Hsieh, S.-K.: Chinese lexical semantics: from radicals to event structure. In: Wang, W.S.-Y., Sun, C. (eds.) The Oxford Handbook of Chinese Linguistics, pp. 290–305. Oxford University Press, New York (2015)
13. Huang, C.-R., et al.: Chinese Sketch Engine and the extraction of grammatical collocations. In: Proceedings of the Fourth SIGHAN Workshop on Chinese Language Processing, pp. 48–55. (2005)
14. Kilgarriff, A., Rychlý, P., Smrz, P., Tugwell, D.: The Sketch Engine. In: Proceedings of EURALEX. Lorient, France (2004)
15. Kilgarriff, A., Tugwell, D.: Sketching words. In: Corréard, M.-H. (ed.) Lexicography and Natural Language Processing: A Festschrift in Honour of B.T.S. Atkins, pp. 125–137. Euralex, Grenoble (2002)
16. Mohammad, S., Kiritchenko, S., Sobhani, P., Zhu, X., Cherry, C.: SemEval-2016 task 6: detecting stance in tweets. In: Proceedings of the 10th International Workshop on Semantic Evaluation (SemEval-2016), pp. 31–41 (2016)
17. Somasundaran, S., Wiebe, J.: Recognizing stances in online debates. In: Proceedings of the Joint Conference of the 47th Annual Meeting of the ACL and the 4th International Joint Conference on Natural Language Processing, vol. 1, pp. 226–234. Association for Computational Linguistics, Stroudsburg (2009)
18. Thompson, G.: Introducing Functional Grammar. Foreign Language Teaching and Research Press, Beijing (2000)

Exploring and Analyzing the Contact-Induced Semantic Transferring Cases Based on a Sanskrit-Chinese Parallel Corpus

Bing Qiu(✉)

College of Humanities and Social Sciences,
Beijing Language and Culture University, Beijing, China
sukhii@163.com

Abstract. Semantic transferring is a special way of producing the new senses of words in the process of language contact. From the perspective of Sanskrit-Chinese language contact, a parallel corpus of Sanskrit and Chinese languages was established and two categories of semantic transferring cases were brought into discussion to analyze their respective motivation. Various cases were provided to illustrate the conditions, processes and results of semantic transferring, which is a cross-language phenomenon that can only be investigated by comparing two languages in detail. Semantic transferring, as a special linguistic phenomenon, can reflect the similarities and differences between the mechanisms of lexical representation across different languages to a certain extent.

Keywords: Semantic transferring · Sanskrit-Chinese language contact
Parallel corpus · Buddhist sutra literature

1 Introduction

The evolution of word senses and the underlying mechanisms are one of the fundamental topics in lexical semantics. Among the varied types of the semantic changes, we will focus on a specific and distinctive way of producing new senses of words which usually occurs in the process of language contact. Since such kind of contact-induced semantic change is related to semantic linking among languages, it is thus named semantic transferring, semantic borrowing or functional transferring and has attracted increasing attention from the academia in recent years [1].

Language contact has likely been ubiquitous throughout much of human language history [2, 3]. Translation is regarded as an important category of language contact [4, 5]. Some typical semantic transferring phenomena originated in the process of translation. When a text is translated from a source language (SL) into a target language (TL) by bilingual translators, suppose there is a word S in SL which has a sense S_a and a word T in TL which has a sense T_a, satisfying the condition $S_a = T_a$. Thus, the translators treat the word T as the translation equivalent of the word S. In other words, the semantic structure of the word S is linked to that of the word T. Now suppose the

J.-F. Hong et al. (Eds.): CLSW 2018, LNAI 11173, pp. 167–174, 2018.
https://doi.org/10.1007/978-3-030-04015-4_14

word S has another sense S_b different from its former sense S_a. Motivated by the psychological mechanism of analogy, individuals may impose the sense S_b on the word T, resulting in the word T obtaining a new sense T_b, as shown in Fig. 1. Here the senses T_b and T_a are not necessarily related by semantic extension.

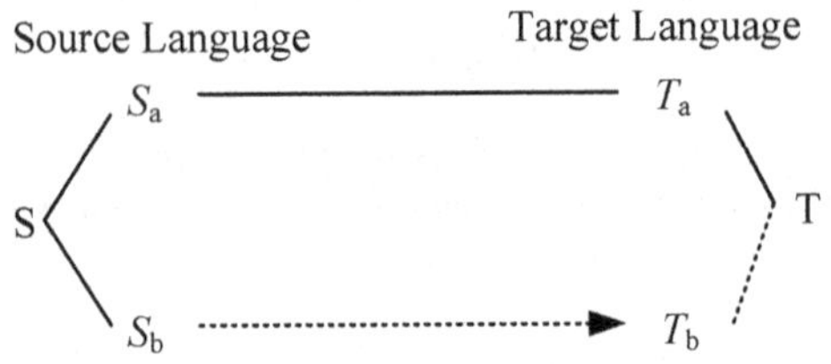

Fig. 1. An illustration of semantic transferring.

Semantic transferring is one of the most complicated language phenomena worth being studied. It can possibly affect the target language to a certain degree and such influence on the target language is not easily to be explained without the evidence from language contact.

The influence of Sanskrit on Middle Chinese in the process of language contact, and more specifically, in the procedure of translation during the Middle Ages, has been noticed by many scholars [6–10]. Here the term Middle Chinese is defined as the historical variety of Chinese from Northern and Southern Dynasties to around Tang Dynasty. Since East Han Dynasty, Buddhist ideologies had been imported into China mainly through translations of Buddhist sutras from foreign languages (for the major part Sanskrit) into Chinese, which occurred mostly in the age of Middle Chinese. The translation of Buddhist scriptures into Chinese is regarded as the only large-scale interlingual rendition in the history of translation prior to the 19th century.

Since the introduction of Buddhism into China, the translation of Buddhist scriptures into Chinese had continued for about a millennium. The Chinese Buddhist scriptures preserved until the present time contain about 70 million Chinese characters. In such a large corpus of Chinese Buddhist scriptures, how to systematically collect and then study the cases of semantic transferring, especially those translated from Sanskrit Buddhist scriptures, is still a difficult problem. One of the fundamental reasons is the lack of an annotated parallel corpus.

Aiming at the aforementioned problems, we have established a parallel corpus of Sanskrit and Chinese languages. Based on the corpus, we will discuss some semantic transferring cases collected from *Buddhacarita*, including both the original Sanskrit version and its Chinese translation namely 佛所行贊 (Fo Suo Xing Zan in pinyin, abbr. FSXZ). From the perspective of Sanskrit-Chinese language contact, we will present two categories of semantic transferring cases and determine their respective motivation, which will better the understanding of certain lexical phenomena in Middle Chinese.

2 Background and Related Work

The significance of the research work on language contact, especially on semantic transferring, is partly due to the specialty of Middle Chinese. The long-lasting procedure of translating Buddhist scriptures from foreign languages covered the whole span of Middle Chinese. During the long period of such large-scale translations, a new language variety was thus developed, comprising both linguistic features of Chinese and those of foreign languages, especially Sanskrit, which not only stimulated the production of numerous new lexicons, but also changed some important Chinese grammatical structures. The Chinese translations of Buddhist scriptures constitute a typical product of language contact based on the translation of documents.

Sutra translation is the process and result of converting Sanskrit-based languages into Chinese, aiming at finding the equivalents in Chinese to reproduce all the grammatical and lexical features in the source works as accurately as possible. In order to achieve equivalence between the Sanskrit and Chinese texts, translators were bound to translate the characteristics of the Sanskrit words equivalently into Chinese, thus forming a peculiar vocabulary of the Buddhist sutra literature, different from that of the native Chinese literature.

Chinese-translated Buddhist scriptures are rather special in nature because of the tremendous difference between the translators' mother tongues and the Chinese language, as well as the uneven levels of the translators' Chinese proficiency and so on. As a product of language contact, the language of Chinese-translated Buddhist scriptures is mixed both in vocabulary and grammar with non-Chinese ingredients. Zürcher [6] concluded:

> *"As early as the third century AD a distinctly Chinese Buddhist 'scriptural style' had developed, as different from Chinese secular literature as from its Indian prototypes; in its turn it became frozen into a kind of canonical language and divorced from the living language. Several forces were at work in shaping the terminological and stylistic conventions of this vast literature: the persisting influence of the Indian original; the influence of classical Chinese; the role of the translator's personal inventivity in creating new forms and ways of expressions or in borrowing them from other sources."*

In consideration of the special nature of the Chinese-translated Buddhist scriptural language, we need to adopt the method to conduct the parallel comparative analysis of the Chinese Buddhist scriptures and the original Sanskrit texts. Some scholars have adopted this method to carry out their research work, such as [11, 12].

As one of the fastest-growing methodologies in contemporary linguistics, corpus linguistics has now become mainstream and corpus-based research is increasingly influential in many areas of linguistic study. However, bilingual corpora with both Chinese texts and their Sanskrit parallel texts are too scanty to support the research objects of Chinese as well as general language contact theories.

3 Semantic Transferring Cases and Their Discussion

The Sanskrit version of *Buddhacarita* and its Chinese translation *FSXZ* are the ideal language materials to support mutual annotations between Sanskrit and Chinese. *Buddhacarita* was originally written by Aśvaghoṣa, a philosopher, poet and dramatist of ancient Indian Buddhism in the first century AD. It was the first Kāvya in the history of Indian Sanskrit literature. During the Northern and Southern Dynasties, it was translated into Chinese and had a very positive impact on Chinese literature.

Buddhacarita has a well-collated Sanskrit text. We had spent years to align and annotate Sanskrit and Chinese texts in the word level to support a word-to-word comparison between the source language and the target language. An example of the internal data structure for the aligned and annotated texts is shown in Fig. 2.

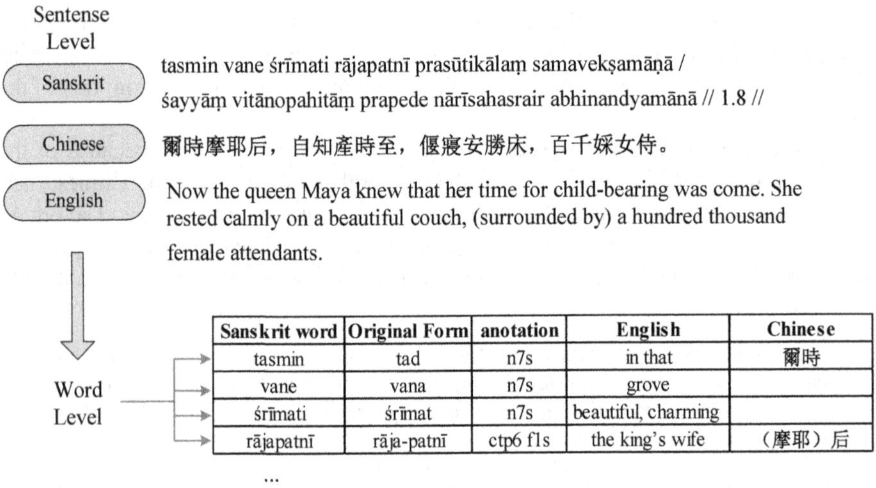

Sanskrit word	Original Form	anotation	English	Chinese
tasmin	tad	n7s	in that	爾時
vane	vana	n7s	grove	
śrīmati	śrīmat	n7s	beautiful, charming	
rājapatnī	rāja-patnī	ctp6 f1s	the king's wife	（摩耶）后

Fig. 2. Internal data structure of the parallel texts of *Buddhacarita*.

The aligned parallel corpus will be part of the database of Chinese Buddhist translation and their Sanskrit parallels [13].

The aforementioned corpus makes it possible to systemically collect the semantic transferring cases in *FSXZ*. Several typical cases in which new senses of words were produced by semantic transferring, will be presented and discussed in this section.

These typical cases can be divided into two categories.

Those in the first category A are based on the same cognitive object, the same cognitive capacity, and the same psychological association. It seems reasonable to have the new meaning derived from the original meaning of the Chinese word. The cases of the category A are discussed as follows.

3.1 軟 (*ruan* in pinyin)

斯由貪欲生，軟中上差降。（《佛所行贊》）

(These are all generated by greed, divided into low, medium and superior grades.)

In native Chinese literature, the original meaning of the Chinese word "軟" (*ruan*) is soft, as opposed to "硬" (*ying* in pinyin, literally, hard). In *FSXZ*, there is a special meaning of "軟" (*ruan*), which collocates with "中" (*zhong* in pinyin) and "上" (*shang* in pinyin). In this context, "軟中上" means "low-grade", "medium-grade" and "high-grade" respectively. "軟" (*ruan*) means "feeble, low-grade". This special new meaning is also commonly seen in other Chinese-translated Buddhist literature, such as in "此菩薩以軟中上心, 除害過罪" (《大寶積經》)[1] and "是菩薩知諸性軟中上差別相" (《大方廣佛華嚴經》)[2]. In Chinese, the original meaning of the word "軟" (*ruan*) can also be extended to indicate the following three meanings: (1) gentle; (2) no strength; (3) without hard tactics, just to carry out peacefully. The word "軟" (*ruan*) with the meaning "low" only appears in Chinese Buddhist scriptures, with no trace in the native literature of the same period. Based on Sanskrit-Chinese parallel corpus, the Sanskrit equivalent of "軟" (*ruan*), "mṛdu", has two senses: "soft, delicate, tender" and "weak, feeble". The former meaning "soft" is equivalent to that of the Chinese word "軟" (*ruan*). By semantic transferring, the latter meaning "weak, feeble" was imposed on the Chinese word "軟" (*ruan*). Therefore, the fact that "軟" (*ruan*) was used to mean "weak" or "low" in Buddhist literature can be explained by semantic transferring.

From the point of semantic development, it is possible and reasonable for the Chinese word "軟" (*ruan*) to extend and evolve from its original meaning of "soft" to the new meaning of "low, weak". In fact, the Chinese word "軟" (*ruan*) did obtain the extended meaning of "weak" and "low", yet not until the time of modern Chinese.

Another example, the Chinese word "边" (*bian* in pinyin) is discussed below.

3.2 邊 (*bian* in pinyin)

無生老病死，無地水火風，亦無初中邊。（《佛所行贊》）

(Not old and sick, no fire and water, no beginning, middle and end.)

In this case, the word "邊" (*bian*) means "end". In native Chinese literature, the original meaning of the Chinese word "邊" (*bian*) is "boundary". The original meaning of "邊" (*bian*) can also be extended to indicate the meanings "border" and "side". However, we have not found any occurrence of the word "邊" (*bian*) meaning

---

[1] Translated by Dharmarakṣa in the Western Jin Dynasty. The sentence means that this Bodhisattva uses the high, the medium and the low ranks of the heart to remove evil.

[2] Translated by Buddhabhadra in the Eastern Jin Dynasty. The sentence means that The Bodhisattva knows that the essence of different things is divided into inferior, medium and superior.

"end" in native Chinese literature. This special and new meaning of "邊" (*bian*) only appears in the Chinese Buddhist scriptures. Based on our Sanskrit-Chinese parallel corpus, "anta", the Sanskrit equivalent of "邊" (*bian*), has two senses: "limit, boundary" and "end, end of life". The former was usually translated as "邊" (*bian*) or "邊際" (*bian ji*). In this sentence, "邊" (*bian*) in "初中邊" (*chu zhong bian*) means "後" (end), collocating with "初" (*chu*, literally, beginning) and "中" (*zhong*, literally, middle). It was also commonly used in other Buddhist literature, such as in "如似大海水, 初中及邊際, 等同於一味" (《大莊嚴論經》)[3]. The fact that "邊" (*bian*) means "end" can be attributed to semantic transferring. The word "anta" in Sanskrit has two senses, and through translation, its sense "end" was imposed on the Chinese word "邊" (*bian*).

Those in the second category B are based on semantic analogy, actually a type of "false analogy". Words with one common sense are falsely believed to have all their senses the same, misleading language users to impose a new sense on the corresponding word in a groundless manner. Due to differences in language and cultural background, some new meanings are not possibly derived from the original meanings of the Chinese words.

3.3 月光 (*yue guang* in pinyin)

事火奉諸神，叉手飲月光，恒水沐浴身，法水澡其心。（《佛所行贊》）

(Worship gods, clap hands, drink soma, take a bath with Ganges water, clean heart with Dharma.)

Based on our Sanskrit-Chinese parallel corpus, the word "月光" (*yue guang*) in this case refers to "soma wine". Its Sanskrit equivalent "soma" has two senses: "juice", a liquid used in the sacrificial rituals, nowadays known as soma wine, and "the moon or the moon god". The word "月光" (*yue guang*) was first used in translation to represent the sense "the moon", but the translator also imposed the sense "soma wine" on it. As a result, the Chinese word was endowed with this new sense. In native Chinese literature, Chinese word "月光" (*yue guang*) only has the meaning of "moonlight" and will never obtain such a new meaning of "soma wine" if only based on Chinese culture.

3.4 宮殿 (*gong dian* in pinyin)

無量諸天人，乘宮殿隨送。（《佛所行贊》）

(A large number of immortals take the car of the god.)

In native Chinese literature, the original meaning of the Chinese word "宮殿" (*gong dian*) is "the palace of an emperor". Here the word "宮殿" (*gong dian*) refers to "the car of god". The Sanskrit equivalent of the Chinese word "宮殿" (*gong dian*), "vimāna", has two senses: "the car of god" and "the palace of an emperor". When

[3] Translated by Kumārajīva in Yao Qin. The sentence means that just like the sea, the taste is the same regardless of the middle front or the back.

translating the scriptures, the translator imposed the sense "the car of god" on the Chinese word "宫殿" (*gong dian*). As a result, in Chinese-translated Buddhist literature, "宫殿" (*gong dian*) obtains the new meaning "the car of god".

4 Conclusion

Word senses are always in constant evolution: some senses disappear while some new senses arise. The most important way to generate new senses is to extend from the old senses through metaphor or metonymy. However, such extension is not the only way to develop new senses of words. Semantic transferring is a special way of producing new senses of words in the process of language contact.

Although semantic transferring is an infrequent phenomenon, it is of great research significance for both textual criticism and the explanation of certain words as well as for the theoretical development of language contact. In the process of language contact, when an extended sense of the source language word is rendered into its target language counterpart, the target language word will obtain a new sense, which displays translation equivalence at the semantic level.

At the same time, the phenomenon of semantic transferring can also reflect the similarities and differences between the mechanisms of lexical representation across different languages to a certain extent. In the above discussion, we have employed some example cases to further the study on the conditions, processes and results of semantic transferring, which is a cross-language phenomenon that can only be investigated by comparing two languages in detail. Semantic extension exists in all languages. In different languages, words of the same original meaning may have the same extended meanings as well, based on the same cognitive object, the same cognitive capacity, and the same psychological association, such as the word "軟" (*ruan*) and its Sanskrit counterpart. But due to the differences in language type and cultural background, their extension patterns and association mechanisms vary greatly from one another. Take the word "宫殿" (*gong dian*) as an example. Its Sanskrit equivalent is "vimāna", originally meaning "chariot of the gods". Later a new sense "palace" emerged because this Sanskrit word was often used to describe something like a house or palace. However, due to the differences between Chinese and Indian cultures, such semantic extension could hardly be established in the Chinese language. Another example is "月光" (*yue guang*). Its Sanskrit equivalent, "soma", originally referred to a liquid used in sacrificial rituals to worship the moon or the moon god, and as a result, it obtained the extended sense "the moon or the moon god". However, in the Chinese lexical system, there hardly existed any semantic relations between the moon and the soma wine. It shows that the new senses of the Chinese words "宫殿" (*gong dian*) and "月光" (*yue guang*) resulted from the influence of the Indian culture and the original Sanskrit scriptures, rather than the semantic extension rules within the Chinese language itself.

In addition, we have established a prototype of bilingual corpus which aligns the Sanskrit texts and their Chinese parallels in the word level. It is proved to be both feasible and efficient to collect the semantic transferring cases together with other language contact interfering phenomena based on the corpus.

Acknowledgments. The work was supported by the National Social Science Foundation of China (Grant No. 16BYY143). The author would also like to thank the national youth talent support plan in the Ten Thousand Talent Program.

References

1. Zhu, G.: More examples of semantic transfer in Buddhist scriptures translation [佛經翻譯中的詞義移植補例]. Stud. Lang. Linguist. **35**(04), 107–111(2015). (in Chinese)
2. Thomason, S.G., Kaufman, T.: Language Contact. Edinburgh University Press, Edinburgh (2001)
3. Heine, B., Kuteva, T.: Language Contact and Grammatical Change. Cambridge University Press, Cambridge (2005)
4. Kranich, S.: Translations as a locus of language contact. In: House, J. (ed.) Translation: A Multidisciplinary Approach. Palgrave Advances in Language and Linguistics. Palgrave Macmillan, London (2014)
5. Malamatidou, S.: Understanding translation as a site of language contact. Target. Int. J. Transl. Stud. **28**(3), 399–423 (2016)
6. Zürcher, E.: A new look at the earliest Chinese Buddhist texts. In: Shinohara, K., Schopen, G. (eds.) From Benares to Beijing: Essays on Buddhism and Chinese Religion. Mosaic Press, Oakville-New York-London (1991)
7. Zhu, Q.: Translation of Buddhist scriptures in translation and its impact on Chinese vocabulary [佛經翻譯中的仿譯及其對漢語詞彙的影響]. The Study of Middle and Modern Chinese, Series 1. Shanghai Education Press, Shanghai (2000)
8. Zhu, Q.: Buddhism Mixed Chinese [佛教混合漢語初論]. Discussion of Linguistics [語言學論叢], vol. 24, The Commercial Press, Beijing, (2001)
9. Qiu, B.: The study on the historical motivation of the polysyllablization in Medieval Chinese [中古漢語詞彙複音化的歷史動因]. J. Chongqing Univ. Technol. (Humanit. Soc. Sci. Ed.) [重慶理工大學學報(社會科學)], 83–88 (2013)
10. Qiu, B.: Retrospect and prospect of studies on the polysyllablization of middle Ancient Chinese Vocabulary [中古漢語詞彙複音化研究回顧與展望]. J. Ningxia Univ. (Humanit. Soc. Sci. Ed.) [寧夏大學學報(社會科學)], 56–60 (2013)
11. Karashima, S.: A Comparative Study of "Prajna Parauta" and "Translated Verse"—A Comparative Study of "Prajna Parauta" with Parasol and Vatican [《道行般若經》和"異譯"的對比研究——《道行般若經》與異譯及梵本對比研究], Studies on the History of Chinese Language, the 4th series. [《漢語史研究集刊》], Bashu Publishing House, Chengdu, China (2001)
12. Chu, T.: The source of the "monk" and its evolution ["和尚" 的語源及其形義的演變]. Linguist. Res. [語言研究], **1**, 83–90 (2002)
13. Huangfu, W., Zhu, Q., Qiu, B.: Construction of a bilingual annotated corpus with Chinese Buddhist translation and their Sanskrit parallels. In: 2016 International Conference on Asian Language Processing (IALP), pp. 108–111 (2016)

The Adjective "*dà* (big)" and Grammatical Analysis of "*dà*+N" Structure

Qiang Li(✉)

College of Liberal Arts, Shanghai University, Shanghai, China
leeqiang2222@163.com

Abstract. Adjectives can be semantically classified into intersective adjectives, which modify the whole object referred by nouns, and non-intersective adjectives, which can also modify the characteristic function of semantic structure in nouns, so ambiguous interpretation appears. The adjective "*dà*" (big) is consistent with the above-mentioned adjective classification. "*dà*" indicating large size is an intersective adjective, while "*dà*" indicating degree is a non-intersective adjective. Some significant differences in syntactic performance exist in "*dà*+N" structure with different semantic usages. In addition, nouns have descriptive and hierarchical semantic features, which causes the different semantic interpretation of "dà" in "*dà zhuōzi*" (big table) and "*dà bèndàn*" (big idiot). Moreover, the hierarchical property of nouns is consistent with the measurable concept of adjectives. Hence, the semantic structure of nouns can be described formally.

Keywords: (non-)intersective adjective · "*dà*" · "*dà*+N" structure
Description · Hierarchy

1 Introduction

The adjective "*dà*" (big) means that in terms of volume, area and so forth, the general standard or the object being compared is exceeded. "*dà*" (big) initially belongs to the conceptual category in spatial material domain, such as "*dà xiāngzi*" (big box) and "*dà dìfang*" (large place). Under the circumstance of metaphor, the usage of "*dà*" gradually spreads from the spatial material domain to more abstract conceptual domains such as audio domain, visual domain, and temporal domain, and its meaning changes, such as "*yīnyuè shēngyīn dà*" (music is loud). "*dàhóngdàzǐ*" (big red and big purple), "*dàbáitiān*" (daytime), in which "*dà*" no longer means large in size or area but has an enhancement in degree.

The above usage of "*dà*" can be simply summarized into two types: volume and degree. Starting from the semantic classification of adjectives, this paper discusses the

This research is sponsored by the Youth Fund Project of Humanity Social Science Research of Ministry of Education "Interactive Study on the Conceptual Semantic Construction and Grammatical Structure Realization of Chinese Nouns" and "2018 Shanghai Training Funding Program for Young Teachers". We hereby express our sincere thanks.

J.-F. Hong et al. (Eds.): CLSW 2018, LNAI 11173, pp. 175–184, 2018.
https://doi.org/10.1007/978-3-030-04015-4_15

two usages of "*dà*", focusing on the grammatical nature of "*dà*+N" structure, and analyzes the semantic difference and source of "*dà*+N" structure.

2 The Semantic Classification of Adjectives

According to the meaning of adjectives when they modify nouns, [1] divided adjectives into three categories: a. **intersective adjective**. Object referred by an adjective-noun combination is the intersection of objects referred by the adjective and noun, for example, ||carnivorous N||=||carnivorous||$\cap$||N||. Such adjectives also include "sick, blond, rectangular" and so on. b. **subsective adjective**. Object referred by an adjective-noun combination is a true subset of object referred by the noun, for example, ||skillful N||$\subset$||N||. Such adjectives also include "typical, recent, good, perfect". c. **privative adjective**. Object referred by an adjective-noun combination is no longer the object referred by the noun, so the intersection with the noun is an empty set, such as ||former senator||$\neq$||former||$\cap$||senator||, ||former senator||$\not\subset$||senator||,||counterfeit N||$\cap$||N||=$\varnothing$. Similar adjectives also include "past, imaginary, would-be, pseudo-".

It is worth noting that when some adjectives enter a particular syntactic structure, ambiguous interpretation appears. These adjectives look like both the intersective adjective and non-intersective adjective. For example [2]:

(1) a. Olga is a beautiful dancer.
→ Olga is beautiful and Olga is a dancer.
→ Olga dances beautifully.
b. Peter is an old friend.
→ Peter is old and Peter is a friend.
→ The friendship is old with Peter as a friend.

In sentence (1a), "beautiful" can refer to dancer's face or dance. The former interpretation is the intersective usage, while the latter is the non-intersective usage, which is somewhat similar with subset adjectives. That is to say, dancers who dance beautifully are the true subset of the big collection of dancers. Similarly, the adjective "old" in sentence (1b) can refer to the age of the friend or the long relationship as a friend. The former interpretation is the intersective usage, and the latter interpretation is the non- intersective usage.

Faced with the ambiguous interpretation of adjectives, [2] argued that adjectives can be dichotomy, that is, there are two kinds of adjectives with different syntactic and semantic types: intersective adjectives and non-intersective adjectives. The intersective adjective is extensional and shows as a predicate conjunction when combined with nouns. Its semantic function is to describe the nature of individuals. For example, when "beautiful dancer" means "dancer who is beautiful", the adjective "beautiful" refers to things with nature of beauty, indicating the attribute of dancer. This can be expressed formally as:

beautiful dancer → λx [beautiful' (x) & dancer' (x)]

Non-intersective adjectives are intensional. When combined with nouns, their semantic effects are the limits of nature of individuals. For example, when "beautiful dancer" means "dance beautifully", the adjective "beautiful" describes the dancer's dancing behavior. This can be expressed formally as:

beautiful dancer → beautiful' (^dancer')

Therefore, some adjectives are divided into these two categories. For example, "aged" is an intersective adjective, and "former" is a non-intersective adjective. Some adjectives have two properties, such as "old" and "beautiful". They can be divided into old_1 and old_2, $beautiful_1$ and $beautiful_2$, corresponding to different usage and semantic interpretation respectively.

Unlike the above-mentioned analysis method in [2, 3] suggested that the ambiguous interpretation should not be attributed to the syntactic and semantic features of adjectives, but mainly to nouns (individual or individual behavior), which are modified by adjectives. Therefore, in addition to object argument, he assumed that some nouns have event argument *e*, which can be directly modified by adjectives. For example, the semantic type of noun "dancer" is $<x, e>$, in which *x* is the agent of *e* and *e* refers to the dancing event. Thus, in "beautiful dancer", an ambiguous interpretation occurs when the adjective modifies the object argument and event argument respectively. Taking the above (1a) as an example, the two semantic interpretations can be expressed as:

(2) a. ∃*e* [**dancer** (o, *e*) & **beautiful** (*e*)]
→ Olga dances beautifully.
b. ∃*e* [**dancer** (o, *e*) & **beautiful** (o)]
→ Olga is beautiful and Olga is a dancer.

On the contrary, the following example (3) has only one semantic interpretation, because the adjective only modifies the event argument in the semantic structure of "smoker".

(3) Laia is an occasional smoker.
→ Laia smokes occasionally.
∃*e* [**smoker** (l, *e*) & **occasional** (*e*)]

In short, in the face of ambiguous structures such as "beautiful dancer", there exist two explanations: one is that adjectives can be divided into intersective adjectives and non-intersective adjectives, and different meanings occur when different types of adjectives and nouns combine. The other is to treat the adjectives in a unified way, enrich the semantic structure of nouns and emphasize that the ambiguity stems from different parts of the semantic structure of nouns.

3 Two Senses of "*dà*" and the Syntactic Behavior of "*dà*+N" Structure

As an adjective, the basic usage of "*dà*" is to indicate size, area or volume related to space, such as "*dà zhuōzi*" (big table), "*dà fángjiān*" (big room) and "*dà chuáng*" (big bed). Then "*dà*" gradually means an abstract scale, such as "*dà shìgù*" (big accident), "*dà tóuzī*" (big investment), "*dà xūqiú*" (big demand). Another use of "*dà*" is to express degree, such as "*dà shǎguā*" (big fool), "*dà bèndàn*" (big idiot), "*dà chīhuò*" (big eater). These two sorts of "*dà*+N" structure have many syntactic and semantic differences.

Adjective "*dà*" indicating large size can modify objects at the material level and things at the abstract level. The general material nouns, nouns that represent abstract things or events, and nouns that represent weather condition can be modified by "*dà*". The "*dà*+N" structure with this usage has the following grammatical features:

① "*dà*" as a modifier has the use of scale enhancement, and "*xiǎo*" (small) can also be used as a modifier to convey the opposite meaning of "*dà*". For instance:

大桌子-小桌子	大床-小床
big table – small table	big bed – small bed
大房间-小房间	大电视-小电视
big room – small room	big TV – small TV

② "*dà*" can be used as a modifier for nouns or as a predicate component. The senses of "*dà*+N" and "N+*dà*" are basically the same. For instance:

大桌子-桌子大	大床-床大
big table – table is big	big bed – bed is big
大房间-房间大	大电视-电视大
big room – room is big	big TV – TV is big

③ "*dà*+N" structure indicating large scale can be modified by degree adverbs. For instance:

很大的桌子	很大的床	很大的房间	很大的电视
very big table	very big bed	very big room	very big TV

Adjective "*dà*" that conveys degree meaning approximates the degree adverb "*hěn*"(very) in meaning and usage. Whether "*dà*" modifies adjectives or verbs, it means degree enhancement. For example, "*dàhóngdàzǐ*" (big red and big purple) is similar to "very red and very purple", which means "beyond the general degree of red and purple colors, reaching a deep red and purple state"; "*dàfùdàguì*" (big rich and expensive) is "very rich and very expensive", which means "exceed the general level of wealth". Another example is "*dàxiào*" (big laugh), which means that the degree of laugh is deep, and it is not a general smile. "*dàchīdàhē*" (big eating and drinking) means that the frequency of eating and drinking is high and the amount of food is large. It has exceeded the frequency and quantity of eating and drinking by ordinary people. In addition to verbs and adjectives, in some "*dà*+N" structures, "*dà*" also indicates an increase in degree, such as "*dà bèndàn*" (big idiot) and "*dà shǎguā*" (big fool), which mean that someone has the attribute of "idiocy/fool" to a very deep degree. "*dà*" has the function of quantifying the "idiocy/fool" attribute. This type of "*dà*+N" structure has three characteristics in terms of grammatical performance:

① There is an imbalance between the use of "*dà*" and "*xiǎo*". Only "*dà*" as a modifier has a usage of degree enhancement, while "*xiǎo*" as a modifier cannot indicate a low degree. "*dà*" and "*xiǎo*" no longer constitute an antonym. For instance:

小笨蛋	小傻瓜	小英雄	小天才
small idiot	small fool	small hero	small genius

Adjective "*xiǎo*" is either an intimate expression, or indicates young age, small size, but has nothing to do with degree.

② "*dà*" with the degree use can only act as an attribute, not as a predicate alone, and cannot act as a predicate together with "*shì*"(is), "*kànsì*"(like). For instance:

*笨蛋大	*傻瓜大	*英雄大	*天才大
*笨蛋是/看似大	*傻瓜是/看似大	*英雄是/看似大	*天才是/看似大

idiot is/looks like big fool is/looks like big
hero is/looks like big genius is/looks like big

③ "*dà*+N" structure with enhanced degree is no longer modified by the general degree adverbs but can be combined with "*chāojí*" (super) to form a fixed expression. For instance:

*很大的笨蛋	*很大的傻瓜	*很大的英雄	*很大的天才
very big idiot	very big fool	very big hero	very big genius
超级大笨蛋	超级大傻瓜	超级大英雄	超级大天才
super big idiot	super big fool	super big hero	super big genius

The adjective "*dà*" that expresses scale has a degree usage, which exists not only in Chinese but also in other languages, hence it is a universal commonality in languages. [4] pointed out that adjectives with degree have two characteristics: a. adjectives indicating degree can only appear at the attributive position, but not at the predicate position (or after nouns); b. "dà" can indicate a heavy degree, but "xiǎo" cannot indicate a light degree. For instance:

(4) ENGLISH

a. that big stamp-collector
#that stamp-collector is big.

b. George is a big idiot.
#George is a small idiot.

(5) SPANISH

a. Pedro es un gran idiota. # Pedro es un idiota grande.
Pedro is a great idiot Pedro is a idiot great
'Pedro is very idiotic.' 'Pedro is idiotic and physically large.'

b. #Pedro es un pequeño idiota
Pedro is a small idiot
'Pedro is an idiot and physically small.'

(6) POLISH

a. wielki idiota #idiota wielki
great idiot idiot great
'someone very idiotic' 'an idiot who is physically large'

b. #maly idiota
small idiot
'an idiot who is physically small'

(7) GERMAN

a. #Dieser Idiot ist gro
this idiot is big

b. # Floyd ist ein kleiner Idiot.
Folyd is a small idiot
'Floyd is and idiot and physically small.'

(8) HEBREW

a. #ha-idyot hu gado
the idiot HU big

b. #George hu idyot katan.
George HU idiot small

4 "*dà*" as an Intersective and Non-intersective Adjective

From the perspective of intersection and non-intersection, "*dà*" that indicates size belongs to intersective adjectives, while "*dà*" that indicates degree belongs to non-intersective adjectives. Because "*dà zhuōzi*" (big table), "*dà diànshì*" (big TV) can be formally represented as the intersection of adjectives and nouns, such as "*dàzhuōzi*" → λx [*dà* (x) & *zhuōzi* (x)]". However, "*dà shǎguā*" (big fool), "*dà bèndàn*" (big idiot) cannot be formally represented as the intersection of adjectives and nouns, for example, the intersection object referred by "big thing" and "fool" is not the object referred by "big fool", in which "*dà*" is the intrinsic attribute of "*bèndàn*".

[5, 6] pointed out that the semantic structure of noun is a semantic network formed by the interrelation of its component or function, and the network contains four aspects:

(1) nouns can be described and the characteristic function f of an attribute can be provided.
(2) for the specified description of a time period i, when the characteristic function f exists can be provided.
(3) for a possible world w, it can let us know whether the characteristic function f exists in the real world, or that the characteristic function f in other imaginary worlds is not necessarily wrong;
(4) a dynamic assignment function g allows us to determine the true value of the final formula formed by each momentum associated with a specific thing in the model.

Bouchard argued that the reason why an adjective-noun combination is ambiguous is the result of the interaction of adjectives and nouns in different parts or the overall meaning of nouns. When adjectives are associated with the overall semantic network of nouns, adjectives have intersective usage. When adjectives are only associated with some part of the semantic network of nouns, adjectives have non-intersective usage. For example, in "a perfect scoundrel", the characteristic function f of the noun "soundrel" is "*huài*" (bad), which is the limited descriptive object of the adjective. In "the future president", the semantic description of "future" is that it provides the existence period, in which there is an event that allows someone to be described as a president. In "a false eyelash", relative to "eyelash" (*jié máo*) in the real world, the object of the entire structure is valid and correct in the possible world. In "an alleged Communist", the "Communist" takes a false value because of the semantic function of "alleged".

The modifying relation between adjectives and nouns can explain the semantic differences between the two structures in the following French:

(9) a. un {mangeur/ fumeur/ buveur} gros
a eater/smoker/drinker fat
'a fat eater/smoker/drinker'
b. un gros {mangeur/ fumeur/ buveur}
a fat eater/smoker/drinker
'a {big/ heavy} {eater/smoker/drinker}

The adjective "gros" in French means "beyond the general standard in capacity and volume", and the pre- and post-placement of the modified nouns will produce different semantic interpretations. In case (9a), the adjective is placed after the noun and modifies the semantic network of the noun as a whole. The whole structure means "eater/smoker/drinker is very fat". In case (9b), the adjective is placed before the noun, and modifies the characteristic function of the semantic network of the noun, then "gros" no longer means "fat", but means that the degree is heavy, and the whole structure has the meaning of "eat/pump/drink much". Therefore, under the meaning of "capacity above the general standard", the adjective "gros" is embodied in two different semantic facets: size meaning and degree meaning.

Similarly, the semantic difference between "*dà zhuōzi*" (big table), "*dà diànshì*" (big TV) and "*dà shǎguā*" (big fool), "*dà bèndàn*" (big idiot) can also be explained by the above-mentioned noun semantic network. The "*dà*" (big) in "*dà zhuōzi*" (big table) and "*dà diànshì*" (big TV) modifies "*zhuōzi*" (table), "*diànshì*" (TV) as a whole, indicating that the size is large. The "*dà*" (big) in "*dà shǎguā*" (big fool) and "*dà bèndàn*" (big idiot) modifies the characteristic functional component "*shǎ*" (fool), "*bèn*" (idiocy), thus indicating the heavy degree of this feature.

5 Description and Hierarchy of Nouns

It can be seen from the above analysis that there is a semantic difference between "*dà*" (big) in "*dà zhuōzi*" (big table) and "*dà bèndàn*" (big idiot). The former represents scale and the latter represents degree. Besides, this semantic difference is caused by the different semantic structure of nouns modified by "*dà*" (big). Nouns such as "*zhuōzi*" (table) are modified as a whole, and the semantic features contained in nouns such as "*bèndàn*" (idiot) are modified. Then, when the adjective "*dà*" (big) modifies "*zhuōzi*" (table) and "*bèndàn*" (idiot), different semantic structures can be chosen.

Closely observing "*zhuōzi*" (table) and "*bèndàn*" (idiot), we will find that the former is a concrete noun and the latter is an abstract noun. The semantic components contained in concrete nouns and abstract nouns are very different. [7] pointed out that there are two kinds of semantic components in nouns: related semantic component and descriptive semantic component. The related semantic component is objective content that restricts noun's connotation. It shows the related semantic features of nouns, so it is the part of nouns' semantic features that represent the "element", such as genus, structure, material, purpose, quantity, time, location. The descriptive semantic component is evaluative content that describes and modifies noun's connotation. It reveals the descriptive semantic features of nouns, and thus is the part of nouns' semantic features that represent property, such as attribute, feature, relation, specific performance. Taking "zhuōzi" (table) and "bèndàn" (idiot) as examples, their interpretations in Modern Chinese Dictionary (6th edition) are as follows [8]:

【桌子】家具，上有平面，下有支柱，在上面放东西或做事情。

[*zhuōzi*] (table) a kind of furniture which has planes and pillars, and has the function of putting things and doing things on it.

"Furniture" is a generic category, "has planes and pillars" is the structure and "putting things and doing things on it" is the use. These are related semantic components, only showing the elements of "*zhuōzi*", and don't describe the property.

【笨蛋】蠢人。
[*bèndàn*] (idiot) stupid man.

"Man" is a generic category, which is the related semantic component. "Stupid" is the attribute of "idiot" and is the descriptive semantic component.

Nouns are not only descriptive but also hierarchical. According to [7], descriptive semantic components can be summed up as the property of nouns, which contain measurement meaning in degree, so they are graded in their meaning. For example, "*bèndàn*" (idiot) means the degree of idiocy, "*fěnsī*" (fan) means the degree of love, and "*yīngxióng*" (hero) means the degree of braveness. In contrast, the meaning of nouns such as "*fángzi* (house), *yǐzi* (chair), *píngguǒ* (apple)" has a clear boundary. For nouns such as "*bèndàn* (idiot), *fěnsī* (fan), *yīngxióng* (hero)", the definition of their meaning depends on speaker's subjective evaluation, space and time environment and standard of comparison [9]. Therefore, the degree adverbs "*bǐjiào* (relative), *xiāngdāng* (quite), *hěn* (quite), *tài* (very), *fēicháng* (very), *gèng* (more)" are often used to modify hierarchical nouns, such as "*X比Y更笨蛋*" (X is more stupid than Y), "*很/非常英雄*" (very heroic), "*相当美女*" (pretty beautiful).

This hierarchy of nouns is consistent with the degree concept of adjectives. Different from numerical value in nouns and verbs, adjectives are mainly with non-numerical measurement, because adjectives have no definite joint points and boundaries, usually represent fuzzy properties and states and cannot be expressed in a definite amount, such as "*hěn* (very), *bǐjiào* (comparative), *gèngjiā* (more), *zuì* (most)". [10] argued that adjectives could be divided into two categories: quantitative adjectives and non-quantitative adjectives. Quantitative adjectives refer to words such as "*yoūyì* (excellent), *guīlì* (magnificent), *xuěbái* (snow-white)", which represent "quantity" or "quantity point", and thus they are bounded. Non-quantitative adjectives refer to "*féi* (fat), *xīn* (new), *gānjìng* (clean)", which can be marked by degree words. They represent "quantity" and therefore are unbounded.

For this measurable feature of adjectives, in the framework of degree semantics, [11–13] indicated that adjectives have the semantic function of measuring the attribute from individuals to adjectives. For example, the semantic function of adjective "tall" can be formally described as:

$$[[\text{tall}]] = \lambda x.\iota d\ [x \text{ is d-tall}] = \text{tall}$$

The sentence "Clyde is tall" is usually understood as "Clyde is higher than ordinary people", because it is possible to assume that there is a degree head POS in front of "tall". The meaning of this POS can be expressed as:

$$[[\text{POS}]] = \lambda g \lambda x.\ \text{standard}\ (g) \leq g(x)$$
$$[[\text{POS}]]\ ([[\text{tall}]]) = \lambda x.\ \text{standard}\ (\text{tall}) \leq \text{tall}(x)$$

Because the semantic structure of adjectives and nouns is hierarchical, the meaning of noun "*shǎguā*" (idiot) can be described in the same way:

$$[[\text{idiot}]] = \lambda x.\iota d\ [x \text{ is d- idiot}] = \text{idiot}$$

In the sentence "Clyde is an idiot", a degree head POS can also be assumed before "idiot", which can be played by "*dà* (big)", so "*dà* (big)" becomes a modifier with degree meaning, and the whole meaning of "big idiot" can be described as:

$$[[\text{big}]] = \lambda g \lambda x.\ \text{standard}\ (g) \leq g(x)$$
$$[[\text{idiot}]] = \lambda x.\iota d\ [x \text{ is d- idiot}] = \text{idiot}$$
$$[[\text{big}]]\ ([[\text{idiot}]]) = \lambda x.\ \text{standard}\ (\text{idiot}) \leq \text{idiot}\ (x)$$

6 Conclusion

Adjectives can be semantically divided into intersective adjectives and non-intersective adjectives. When intersective adjectives such as "aged, sick" are combined with nouns, the overall semantic network of nouns is modified, while when non-intersective adjectives such as "old, beautiful" modify nouns, not only the object as a whole can be modified, but the characteristic function of nouns' semantic structure can be modified. Thus, ambiguous interpretation appears, such as "She is a beautiful dancer".

The Chinese adjective "*dà*" (big) is consistent with the above classification of adjectives. Generally speaking, "*dà*" has two different uses: scale and degree. "*dà*" with the scale use belongs to the intersective adjective, while "*dà*" with the degree use is a non-intersective adjective. There are some significant differences in the syntactic representation of "*dà*+N" structure consisted of "*dà*" with different semantic usages.

Nouns have descriptive and hierarchical semantic features, which causes the adjective "*dà*" in "*dà zhuōzi*" (big table) and "*dà bèndàn*" (big idiot) different. The former represents scale meaning, and the latter expresses degree meaning. In addition, this hierarchy of nouns is consistent with the degree concept of adjectives, so nouns can be formally described in the framework of degree semantics.

References

1. Partee, B., Kamp, H.: Are there privative adjectives? In: Conference on the philosophy of Terry Parsons, University of Massachusetts, Amherst, 7–8 February 2003
2. Siegel, M.: Capturing the Adjective. Doctoral dissertation, University of Massachusetts, Amherst (1976)
3. Larson, R.: Events and modification in nominals. In: Strolovitch, D., Lawson, A. (eds.) Proceedings of Semantics and Linguistic Theory VIII, pp. 145–168. CLC Publications, Ithaca (1998)
4. Morzycki, M.: Degree modification of gradable nouns: size adjectives and adnominal degree morphemes. Nat. Lang. Seman. **17**(2), 175–203 (2009)
5. Bouchard, D.: The distribution and interpretation of adjectives in French: a consequence of Bare Phrase Structure. Probus **10**, 139–183 (1998)
6. Bouchard, D.: Adjectives Number and Interfaces. Elsevier, Oxford (2002)
7. Shi, C.H.: The descriptive features of nouns and the probability of adverbs modifying nouns. Stud. Chin. Lang. **3**, 212–224 (2001). (in Chinese)
8. Institute of Linguistics in Chinese Academy of Social Sciences: Modern Chinese Dictionary, 6th ed. The Commercial Press, Beijing (2012). (in Chinese)
9. Luo, Q.P.: Gradable nouns and the degree interpretations of "Da+NP" constructions. Chin. Lang. Learn. **3**, 43–52 (2016). (in Chinese)
10. Zhang, G.X.: The Function and Cognition of Adjectives in Modern Chinese. The Commercial Press, Beijing (2006). (in Chinese)
11. Kennedy, C.: Projecting the Adjective: The Syntax and Semantics of Gradability and Comparison. Doctoral dissertation, UC Santa Cruz (1997)
12. Kennedy, C.: Vagueness and grammar: the semantics of relative and absolute gradable adjectives. Linguist. Philos. **30**(1), 1–45 (2007)
13. Kennedy, C., McNally, L.: Scale structure, degree modification and the semantics of gradable predicates. Language **81**, 345–381 (2005)

Acquiring Unaccusative Verbs in a Second Language: An L1-Mandarin L2-English Learner Investigation

Yu-Leng Lin(✉)

Department of Foreign Languages and Literature, Feng Chia University, No. 100 Wenhwa Rd., Seatwen, Taichung 40724, Taiwan
ylenglin@fcu.edu.tw

Abstract. This study investigates English unaccusative verbs, definiteness, and word order in native Mandarin speakers whose second language is English. The goal of the paper is to see how L1 Mandarin influences speakers' learning of the unaccusative structure in English. I propose two hypotheses. Hypothesis (a) proposes that participants judge raised internal arguments as more acceptable than in-situ internal arguments because both indefinite and definite internal arguments are always allowed to move to a subject position (i.e., raise) in Mandarin. Hypothesis (b) proposes that unaccusative constructions where a definite internal argument remains in situ are less acceptable than those where an indefinite one remains in situ because, in Mandarin, only an indefinite internal argument is allowed to remain in situ. The findings support hypothesis (a) but not (b).

Keywords: Unaccusative verbs · Definiteness · Word order · L2 acquisition

1 Introduction

This study investigates English unaccusative verbs, definiteness, and word order in native Mandarin speakers whose second language is English. The goal of the paper is to see how Mandarin influences speakers' acquisition of the English unaccusative structure.

According to Yuan [1: 279], in Mandarin, if an internal argument in an unaccusative structure is indefinite, it can either move to a subject position, as in (1a), or remain in situ, as in (1b). However, if an internal argument is definite, it must move to a subject position, as in (1c); otherwise, it will be ungrammatical, as in (1d).

(1) Indefinite vs. Definite [1: 279]

(a)上個月，三艘船在這個海域沉了。

shang	ge	yue	,	san	sou	chuan
last	CL	month		**three**	**CL**	**ship**
zai	zhe	ge	hai	yu	chen	le
in	this	CL	sea	area	**sink**	PFV

'Last month, three ships sank in this area of the sea.'
(indefinite & raised)

J.-F. Hong et al. (Eds.): CLSW 2018, LNAI 11173, pp. 185–191, 2018.
https://doi.org/10.1007/978-3-030-04015-4_16

(b)上個月，在這個海域沉了三艘船。

shang	ge	yue	,	zai	zhe	ge
last	CL	month		in	this	CL
hai	yu	chen	le	san	sou	chuan
sea	area	**sink**	PFV	**three**	**CL**	**ship**

'Last month, three ships sank in this sea area.'
(indefinite & in situ)

(c)上個月，那艘船在這個海域沉了。

shang	ge	yue	,	na	sou	chuan
last	CL	month		**that**	**CL**	**ship**
zai	zhe	ge	hai	yu	chen	le
in	this	CL	sea	are	**sink**	PFV

'Last month, that ship sank in this sea area.'
(definite & raised)

(d)*上個月，在這個海域沉了那艘船。

*shang	ge	yue	,	zai	zhe	ge
last	CL	month		in	this	CL
hai	yu	chen	le	na	sou	chuan
sea	area	**sink**	PFV	**that**	**CL**	**ship**

'Last month, that ship sank in this sea area.'
(definite & in situ)

2 Experiment

The goal of the experiment was to test whether definiteness (indefinite article vs. definite article) and word order (remain in situ vs. raise) influence how native Mandarin speakers learn the accusative structure in English. This section introduces the method.

2.1 Design

The grammaticality judgment task is set up with a 2 × 2 design: definiteness × word order, as shown in Table 1:

There are two types of unaccusative constructions: causative constructions and inchoative constructions. In order to avoid noise, this study focused only on inchoatives. Eight inchoative unaccusative verbs were selected: *break*, *melt*, *boil*, *freeze*, *collapse*, *spill*, *sink*, and *rot*. Thus, eight concrete token sets (32 test sentences in total) were generated. In addition to the test sentences, there were 32 fillers of four types: number agreement, articles, conjunction with transitive verbs, and passives (i.e., 8

Table 1. Definiteness × Word order

Word order	Definitiveness: INDEFINITE	Definiteness: DEFINITE
Raised	(1) Because of the earthquake **a window broke**	(2) Because of the earthquake **the window broke**.
In situ	(3) *Because of the earthquake **broke a window**.	(4) *Because of the earthquake **broke the window**.

fillers for each condition). In total, four lists were generated, in order to use a Latin square design.

The test sentences and the fillers were pseudo-randomized. For each list, each participant would see 8 test sentences and 32 fillers in a questionnaire. The questionnaire adopted a Likert scale from 1–5, where 5 indicates *definitely agree* (for a perfectly normal sentence which is well-formed and natural sounding) and 1 indicates *definitely disagree* (for a sentence which makes no sense, and is badly formed). Forty sentences were counterbalanced.

2.2 Subject

Twenty-four native Taiwan Mandarin speakers were recruited on-line. A control group of four native English speakers was also recruited.

2.3 Procedure

Subjects received an initial e-mail from the main investigator to make sure they were willing to participate in this study. If they agreed, they were asked to complete a consent form, and then open an Excel file with two sheets: a sheet contained the instructions and personal information survey. The other sheet contained 40 test sentences. After signing the consent form, they read the instructions and filled in their personal information about their age, language background, and linguistics courses taken before. They then read the 40 English sentences (8 test sentences + 32 fillers) without looking up any words in the dictionary, and finished the whole questionnaire without interruption. They then sent both the consent form and Excel file back to the main investigator.

3 Results

The results are summarized in Table 2 and displayed graphically in Fig. 1. First, it appears that participants judged raised internal arguments as more acceptable than in-situ ones, with a mean acceptability of 3.69, 3.77 (in situ) > 2.17, 2.04 (raised). However, items in the definite & raised condition were slightly more acceptable than those in the indefinite & raised condition (mean acceptability 3.77 > 3.69). Second, items in the definite & in situ condition were slightly less acceptable than those in the indefinite & in situ condition (mean acceptability 2.04 < 2.17).

Table 2. Mean scale for Definiteness × Word order for native Mandarin speakers

Word order	Definitiveness: INDEFINITE	Definiteness: DEFINITE
Raised	(1) Because of the earthquake **a window broke** (3.69)	(2) Because of the earthquake **the window broke**. (3.77)
In situ	(3) *Because of the earthquake **broke a window**. (2.17)	(4) *Because of the earthquake **broke the window**. (2.04)

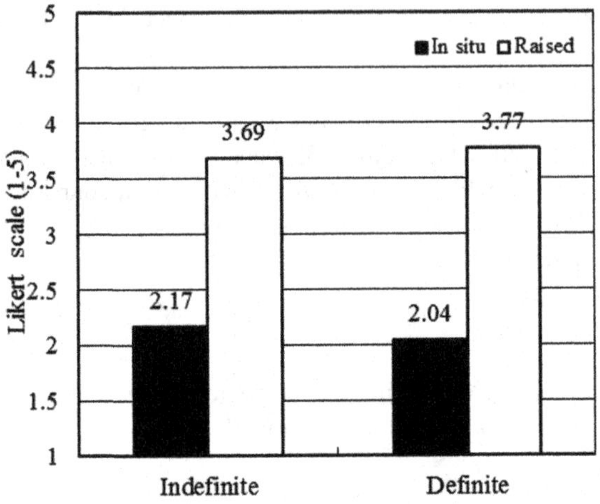

Fig. 1. Acceptability of definiteness and word order in native Mandarin speakers

The main effect of "WORD_ORDER" was highly significant ($x^2 = 54.93$, $df = 2$, $p_{\text{two-tailed}} < 0.001$). Examining both Table 4 and Fig. 1, the main effect of "WORD_ORDER" indicates that the raised condition was more acceptable than the in-situ condition. No other main effect or interaction was found.

Ordinal logistic regression was used because the dependent variable (acceptability Likert scale points) can be treated as 'ordered' levels [2]. The analysis was done using the R package *Design* [3].

The dependent variable was the acceptability data from "SCALE" (from 1 to 5), and the independent variables were word order and definiteness. Two independent variables were nominal. "WORD_ORDER" was "RAISE" for the raised condition, and

Table 3. Ordinal logistic regression: effects and interaction

	χ^2	d.f.	Pr(> F)
DEFINITENESS	0.05	2	0.9753
WORD_ORDER	54.93	2	<0.0001***
DEFINITENESS: WORD_ORDER	0.02	1	0.8914

'***': $p < .001$, '**': $p < .01$, '*': $p < .05$, '.': $p < .1$

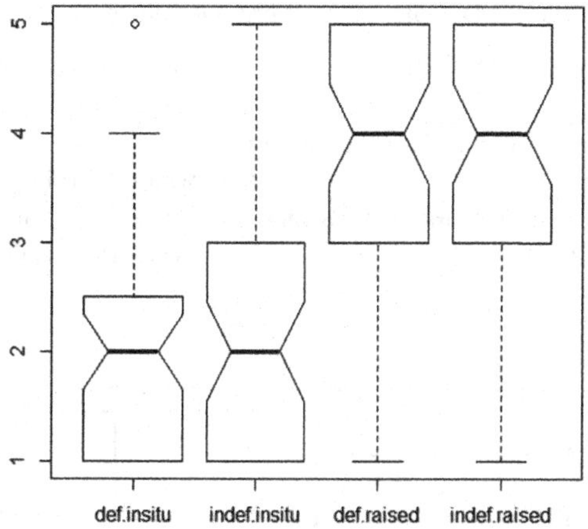

Fig. 2. Definiteness and word order in native English speaker

was "IN_SITU" for the in-situ condition. "DEFINITENESS" was "DEFINITE" for the definite condition, and was "INDEFINITE" for the indefinite condition.

The results are displayed in Table 3 and plotted graphically in Fig. 2.

4 General Discussion and Implications

As mentioned in the introduction, two hypotheses and their possible results were proposed. *Hypothesis (a)* proposed that participants would judge items in the raised condition as more acceptable than those in the in-situ condition. The basis for this hypothesis is that both indefinite and definite internal arguments can raise in Mandarin. *Hypothesis (b)* proposed that a definite internal argument remaining in situ would be less acceptable than an indefinite one. The basis for this hypothesis is that in Mandarin, definite internal arguments must raise; only indefinite internal arguments are allowed to remain in situ.

The empirical results support *hypothesis (a)*. In Mandarin, only indefinite arguments can remain in situ. If this Mandarin unaccusative structure affects how native Mandarin speakers learn English unaccusative verbs, then the results should show that in situ arguments would be less acceptable than raised ones. This asymmetry is indeed borne out in the results.

Nevertheless, since no interaction between "WORD_ORDER" and "DEFINITENESS was found, this suggests that the current empirical results did not offer positive evidence to support *hypothesis (b)*.

In order to figure out why the interaction was absent, I also looked at the data obtained from the four native English speakers. The native English speakers also showed a similar pattern, as shown in Table 4 and Fig. 3: the raised condition was more acceptable than the in-situ condition. Note that the number of native Mandarin and English speakers was not equivalent (24 vs. 4), since English speakers simply

Table 4. Mean scale for Definiteness × Word order for native Mandarin speakers

Word order	Definitiveness: INDEFINITE	Definiteness: DEFINITE
Raised	(1) Because of the earthquake **a window broke** (4.50)	(2) Because of the earthquake **the window broke**. (4.83)
In situ	(3) *Because of the earthquake **broke a window**. (2.67)	(4) *Because of the earthquake **broke the window**. (2.17)

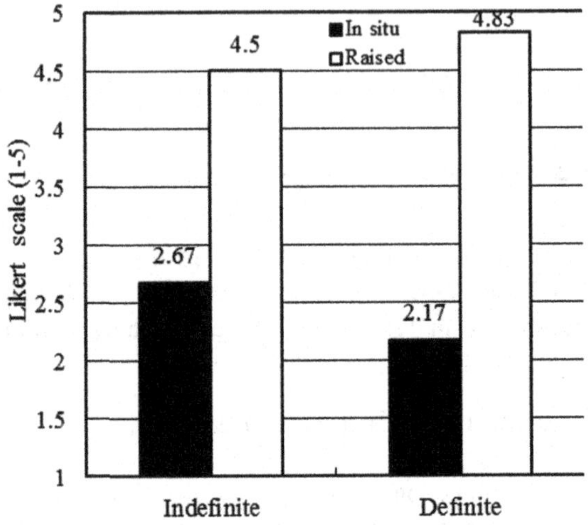

Fig. 3. Acceptability of definiteness and word order in native English speakers

served as a control to confirm that the grammaticality of sentences conformed to native speakers' intuition.

Along the same lines, what does it imply if both native Mandarin and English speakers show similar patterns for English unaccusative verbs, and how do we figure out this puzzle? Further study is needed to see if Mandarin unaccusative verbs also show a similar pattern to native Mandarin speakers. If only native Mandarin speakers show a preference for indefinite & in situ items over definite & in situ items, it suggests that the native Mandarin speakers recruited in this study had actually learned the English unaccusative structure, so they showed the same pattern as the native English speakers. If both English and Mandarin unaccusative structures show no significant interaction between definiteness and word order, it suggests that Yuan [1] 's claim might be wrong. If so, this would further explain why the effect of "DEFINITENESS" was absent in the current study.

One thing to consider in future investigation is that Mandarin does not have a distinction between *a* and *the*; it might therefore be desirable to use non-article ways of showing definiteness (e.g., proper names) in the test sentences. English proficiency might also play a role in the results. L1 Mandarin participants should be classified into groups based on their proficiency in L2 English. Sample size can also be increased in future work.

Acknowledgments. Thanks to Ailís Cournane for assisting me in checking the grammaticality of the English test sentences and fillers and recruiting four native English pilot participants.

References

1. Yuan, B.: Acquiring the unaccusative/unergative distinction in a second language: evidence from English-speaking learners of L2 Chinese. Linguistics **37**(2), 275–296 (1999)
2. Baayen, H.: Analyzing Linguistic Data: A Practical Introduction to Statistics Using R. Cambridge University Press, Cambridge (2008)
3. Harrell, F.: Regression Modeling Strategies, pp. 18–24. Springer, New York (2001). https://doi.org/10.1007/978-1-4757-3462-1

A Referendum Is a Forward-Moving Object or a Bundled Object?

Ren-feng Duann[1(✉)], Kathleen Ahrens[2], and Chu-Ren Huang[3]

[1] Center for General Education, National Taitung University, Taitung City, Taiwan
rduann@nttu.edu.tw

[2] Department of English, The Hong Kong Polytechnic University, Kowloon, Hong Kong
kathleen.ahrens@polyu.edu.hk

[3] Department of Chinese and Bilingual Studies, The Hong Kong Polytechnic University, Kowloon, Hong Kong
churen.huang@polyu.edu.hk

Abstract. This article analyzes how a referendum is represented through the use of conceptual metaphors in two major newspapers in Taiwan, the *Liberty Times* and the *United Daily News*. The analysis indicates that a general schema for the referendum A CAUSER CAUSES AN OBJECT TO MOVE OR STOP, which is further divided to the forward-moving and stopping sub-schemas, can be retrieved from the metaphors used. Moreover, it shows that three expressions for the forward-moving sub-schema, as lexicalized in the LEGISLATION domain, are predominant in the representation of the referendum. With the inevitability to use the general schema, the two newspapers take strategies to elaborate or neutralize the effects embedded in the schema, so as to transmit their respective political stances.

Keywords: Referendum · Conceptual metaphor · Taiwan

1 Introduction

Metaphor as a discourse device interacting with political agenda has been attracting scholars' attention for decades, e.g. [1, 2]. This paper, focusing on a referendum held in Taiwan, aims to reveal how two newspapers' utilization of metaphors for an identical political event transmit their respective political agenda and to reveal how the metaphors work on the conceptual level. By analyzing the corpora drawn from the *Liberty Times* and the *United Daily News*, which reflect two opposing political stances in Taiwan, we argue that a general schema can be retrieved from the top two source domains. Moreover, despite the use of the same general schema, each newspaper employs a variety of strategies to enhance or cancel the general schema.

This article aims to find the answers to the following two research questions:

1. What are the conceptual metaphors for the referendum and what is the general schema retrieved from the metaphors?
2. How does the general schema work under the constraints of the political agenda reflected in the newspapers?

J.-F. Hong et al. (Eds.): CLSW 2018, LNAI 11173, pp. 192–201, 2018.
https://doi.org/10.1007/978-3-030-04015-4_17

We will briefly illustrate the political context in Taiwan and the background information of the referendum in Sect. 2, and the theoretical background in Sect. 3. The data and method will be described in Sect. 4, followed by the analysis and discussion in Sect. 5. Section 6 concludes the research.

2 The Political Context in Taiwan

Taiwan is an arena where two national identities compete: Chinese national identity, promoted by the pan-blue camp centering around the Chinese Nationalist Party (i.e. Kuomintang, henceforth KMT); and Taiwanese national identity, advocated by the pan-green camp with the Democratic Progressive Party (DPP) at its core. The former camp takes a softer policy towards the People's Republic of China (PRC), and the latter advocates Taiwan independence from China, be it Republic of China (ROC) or PRC. The diverging national identities and tenets of the two political camps are correspondingly echoed by two major newspapers in Taiwan: the *United Daily News* (UDN) and the *Liberty Times* (LT), with the former aligning itself with the pan-blue camp and the latter with the pan-green camp [3]. They thus can be regarded as channels through which the two political camps respectively voice and transmit their political agenda.

The referendum at issue, joining the UN under the name 'Taiwan', was proposed as a result of the international predicament Taiwan had been facing. The establishment of the PRC has caused Taiwan's loss of a substantial number of diplomatic allies, and the PRC's replacement of the ROC in the UN in 1971. The 'One-China' principle has isolated the ROC and driven it out of most international organizations [4], despite its importance in the international economy.

The UN membership has been an unresolved issue for the ROC/Taiwan since 1971 due to the PRC's opposition. On June 18, 2007, Chen Shui-bian, the then incumbent President of the ROC, expressed his hope that a referendum on joining the UN under the name 'Taiwan' would be held concurrently with the 2008 Taiwan Presidential Election. This proposal gained support from the advocates of Taiwan independence, while it was challenged and criticized by those who claimed that Chen was using it as a means both to mobilize the pro-independence DPP as the election approached, and to dodge problems such as the recession in the economy and the corruption of himself and his family members. This referendum,[1] having earned sufficient public endorsement, took place alongside the 2008 Taiwan Presidential Election, but was declared invalid because the voter turnout, 35.82%, was lower than the required 50%.

[1] The wording of the referendum question, National Referendum Proposal No. 5, is translated by Lu [9] as follows: In 1971, the People's Republic of China joined the United Nations, replacing the Republic of China and making Taiwan an international orphan. Do you agree that the government, in a strong expression of the will of the Taiwanese people and in order to elevate Taiwan's international status and promote its international participation, should join the United Nations under the name 'Taiwan'?

3 Theoretical Consideration

The conceptual metaphor theory proposed by Lakoff and Johnson [5] has underscored two aspects of metaphor: (a) it is pervasive in everyday life, and (b) it is deeply rooted in language, thought and action. This theory has changed the way metaphor is defined: instead of merely an embellishment in language, it is a constitutive part of thought, which helps people understand and experience the world.

Quasi-ubiquitous in language, thought and action, conceptual metaphors can pass unnoticed. Chilton and Lakoff [6] argued that metaphors function as powerful tools to define what is taken as 'reality'. This very nature of metaphor provides the text producer with a good way to guide the reader because the underlying ideology transmitted through the text may be overlooked if the reader is unaware of it. The text producer can persuade the reader to take one stance rather than another and s/he can bypass the 'boomerang effect' brought about by highly charged language/images [7]. Metaphor is thus frequently used in political discourse because the behavior at the core of politics involves persuasion [8].

We argue that, when an identical event is represented as a variety of metaphors, a general schema can be retrieved from these metaphors. Moreover, the political stance behind the text producer will influence whether the general schema is elaborated or neutralized.

4 Data and Method

The data under analysis consists of editorials related to the referendum on joining the UN under the name 'Taiwan' (henceforth the UN membership referendum) from the *United Daily News* (UDN) and the *Liberty Times* (LT), spanning from June 19, 2007, when the then President's proposal of the referendum appeared in Taiwan's newspapers, to March 23, 2008, one day after the referendum was held. The size of the LT corpus is 49,753 and that of the UDN corpus is 45,649 words.

Setting 入聯 'joining the UN', 公投, acronym of 'referendum' in Chinese and 公民投票 'referendum' as the search words of the target domain, we then search for the conceptual metaphors for this referendum.

In terms of linguistic metaphor identification, we apply the metaphor identification procedure [10] modified to suit Chinese texts. Consider Extract 1 as an illustration:

Extract 1

A REFERENDUM IS A JOURNEY

政府尤須抵抗各種外來壓力，激勵國人的國家意識，讓以台灣名義加入聯合國的公投案一舉過關, …

'The government especially needs to resist pressure from outside and to raise people's awareness of state, so that *the referendum on joining the UN under the name of Taiwan* can **pass the pass** at a blow….' (LT2007/10/03)

The referendum in Extract 1 is represented as the agent of the process 過關, which is defined in the MOE dictionary as follows:

(i) 度過關隘。如：我們的船馬上就要過關了。To pass the pass (i.e. the location in a range of mountains of a geological formation that is lower than the surrounding peaks). E.g. *Our ship is going to pass the pass.*
(ii) 比喻及格、合格。如：你的口試過關了。Metaphorical use: To pass. E.g. *You pass your oral exam.*
(iii) 度過困難。如：困難重重，恐怕很難過關。Go through difficulties. E.g. *There are so many difficulties. It may be hard to go through all these difficulties.*

A comparison among the three senses indicates that (i) was more physical than (ii) and (iii) because it refers to an agent's physical movement through a location. We thus choose (i) as the basic meaning of 過關. Based on a method assisted by an online dictionary, we justify the metaphoricity of tokens identified.

The identified linguistic metaphors are then grouped, and a source domain is determined for each group.

5 Results

The general information about the two corpora is presented in Table 1. The JOURNEY metaphor ranks the highest in the LT corpus and the PHYSICAL OBJECT tops in the UDN corpus. Interestingly, the JOURNEY metaphor ranks the second highest in the UDN corpus and the PHYSICAL OBJECT the second highest in the LT corpus. Moreover, the two corpora differ in the usages and rankings of the rest metaphors. Due to the space limit, we only focus on the JOURNEY and PHYSICAL OBJECT metaphors.

A close examination of the JOURNEY and PHYSICAL OBJECT metaphors enables us to retrieve a general schema out of the two source domains. With the lexeme 推動 'to propel' in the PHYSICAL OBJECT domain and the lexemes 過關 'to pass a pass' and 通過 'to pass' in the JOURNEY domain, we retrieve the general schema of the referendum: A CAUSER CAUSES AN OBJECT TO MOVE OR STOP. With the activation of this schema, both newspapers represent the referendum as a forward-moving object, despite their diverging intentions: the LT emphasizes that the referendum is nothing but a legislative process, but the UDN intends to offset the effects brought about by this schema through a variety of strategies, e.g. representing the referendum as an object tied up with another object, which will be discussed in Sect. 5.3.

When an object is set in motion and moves forward, it may encounter obstacles and/or finally stops. We thus divide the discussion of this general schema into two parts: the forward-moving and the stopping sub-schemas.

5.1 The Forward-Moving Sub-schema

This sub-schema is mainly realized through the use of 推動 'to propel', 通過 'to pass' and 過關 'to pass the pass'. 推動 is defined as 推進啟動 'to propel/to set… in motion' in the MOE dictionary. With the lexeme, the referendum is propelled along a forward-

Table 1. The conceptual metaphors for the UN referendum in LT and UDN

Corpus	LT	Incidence (%)	UDN	Incidence (%)
Source domain	No. of tokens		No. of tokens	
Journey	62	**43.36**	48	**17.98**
PHYSICAL OBJECT	38	**26.57**	61	**22.84**
PERSON	28	18.88	22	8.24
WIN/LOSE	6	4.20	10	3.75
COMBAT	3	2.10	16	5.99
LOCATIO	2	1.40	14	5.24
STOCK EXCHANGE	1	0.70	10	3.75
MEDICINE	1	0.70	4	1.49
CRIME	0	0	28	10.49
ORGANISM	0	0	17	6.37
FOOD	0	0	8	2.99
BALLOON	0	0	6	2.25
NATURE	0	0	6	2.25
DRAMA	0	0	5	1.87
TOY	0	0	4	1.50
GAMBLE	0	0	2	0.75
Others	3	2.10	6	2.25
Total	143	100	267	100

moving path with an inherent goal. As shown in Extract 2, the referendum is represented as the patient being propelled:

Extract 2

台灣七成以上的主流民意支持台灣加入聯合國，政府推動入聯公投乃反映民眾的心聲。

70% of the mainstream public opinion support Taiwan's joining the UN. Therefore, that the government **propels** *the UN referendum* reflects aspiration of the public. (LT2007/10/30)

The representation of the referendum as a forward-moving object in the JOURNEY domain is mainly realized through the lexical items 通過 'to pass' and 過關 'to pass the pass'. When the object is set in motion, it moves on, and it 通過 'pass (through)' or 過關 'pass the pass', both of which are prominent metaphorical expressions in this subschema (Extracts 3 and 4).

Extract 3

入聯公投之舉行與通過，可以讓世人更加看清，陳總統的努力背後有強大的民意後盾

That *the UN referendum* is to be held and **to pass** enable the world to see clear the great support behind President Chen's back. (LT2007/07/25)

Extract 4

「入聯公投」過關的陳水扁必藉此全力綁架民進黨

If *the UN referendum* **passes the mountain path**, Chen Shui-bian will abduct the DPP with this. (UDN2007/12/15)

Overall, the following conceptual mappings are revealed: A REFERENDUM IS A MOVING OBJECT; THE AGENT INSTIGATING THE REFERENDUM IS THE AGENT PROPELLING/SETTING THE OBJECT IN MOTION; THE REFERENDUM BEING VALID AND PASSING IS THE MOVING OBJECT PASSING THROUGH/PASSING THE PASS.

The predominant use of these three lexemes is attributed to the fact that they are lexicalized expressions in legislative processes, as evidenced in the Word Sketch of the Chinese Gigaword [11].[2]

We argue that whether a metaphorical expression is lexicalized in a domain is consequential because, on the one hand, a lexicalized metaphorical expression can pass unnoticed by the reader, and on the other hand, its occurrence is inevitable when a newspaper talks about an issue in the domain. To the newspaper which supports this referendum, i.e. the LT, using these expressions declares that this referendum is no more than an ordinary legislative process, as they frequently collocate with statues and bills. We believe it is the reason why 36% of all the metaphorical expressions (52 out of 143 tokens) are these three lexemes in the LT corpus.

The lexicalization of the lexemes in the legislative process also makes it inevitable for the UDN to use them. Despite the inevitable use of the lexemes, the UDN corpus takes several strategies to neutralize the effects brought about by these lexemes. It reduces the incidence of the lexemes realizing the forward-moving object, which is why only 9.74% (26 out of 267 tokens) of all the metaphorical expression are these lexemes. It also increases its use of the stopping sub-schema, and resorts to other metaphors to re-direct the readers' attention, which will be discussed in details in the following sections.

[2] The Word Sketch of the Sketch Engine (https://the.sketchengine.co.uk/ipauth/) presents how a word behave, e.g. as a subject or an object, in a sentence. According to the Word Sketch of the Chinese Gigaword, the grammatical objects of 推動 include 民主改革 'democratic reforms', 憲政改革 'constitutional reform', 政策 'policy', 計畫 'scheme', 方 案 'plan', 法案 'bill', etc., and the grammatical subject of this process includes the unit of legislation or implementation: e.g. 政府 'government', 部會 'ministries and councils', etc. The grammatical subjects of 通過 'to pass (through)' contain 法案 'bill', 條例 'statute', 修正案 'amendment', 決議 'resolution', 草案 'draft', etc. Regarding 過關 'to pass the pass', expressions in the lawmaking field such as 延任案 'extension case', 覆議案 'reconsideration case', etc., are dominant. It is obvious that these three lexemes are widely used and lexicalized in the LEGISLATION domain.

5.2 The Stopping Sub-schema

The stopping sub-schema can be further divided into two types: voluntary and involuntary. The voluntary stopping is realized through the use of 下車 'to get off'; the involuntary type, indicating the stopping caused by a counterforce, is realized through a series of compounds initiated with 阻 'to obstruct', such as 阻力 'drag', 阻撓 'to impede', 阻擋 'to stop', 阻止 'to stop', and lexemes such as 制止 'to restrain', 牽制 'to impede', 設置障礙 'to set up an obstacle', 提高門檻 'to raise the threshold', and 脫鉤 'to unhook'. The LT employs the involuntary type solely while both types occur in the UDN corpus.

The involuntary stopping in the LT corpus indicates that it is the pan-blue camp or the KMT, the PRC, and/or the US, which draws back the moving object or deliberately sets up the impediments. The moving object is thus kept from moving forward successfully or even halted. Extract 5 shows that the pan-blue camp, opposed to this referendum, sets up hindrance and raises the threshold against the referendum, which prevents the referendum from passing through smoothly.

Extract 5

何以藍營非要堅持二階段投票？其中實暗藏不可告人的動機，即為民進黨所提出的「討黨產」,「入聯」等公投案製造障礙，使之門檻提高，無法順利通過。

'Why did the pan-blue camp insist on two-stage voting? There is a motivation, to **set up hindrance and to raise the threshold** against the *referendum* on claiming the property from the KMT and *the UN referendum* so as to prevent both from passing through.' (LT2007/12/20)

The UDN corpus also employs the involuntary stopping mostly, but in a way different from that of the LT corpus. The UDN corpus employs 脫鉤 'to unhook', a lexeme presupposing the referendum as a car hooked together with another car: the presidential election (Extract 6). When a car is unhooked from the rest of the train, it stays at the same place. The UDN, representing the referendum as an unhooked car which does not go anywhere, avoids pointing out the agent who actually unhooks the car. This bypasses the discussion about the one responsible for stopping the referendum's movement.

Extract 6

...因此，公投與大選脫鉤的主張，對全民或綠營而言，皆具完全的正當性

... Therefore, the contention that *the UN referendum* and the election **should be unhooked** is full of legitimacy to either the general public or the green camp. (UDN2008/02/24)

Aside from the involuntary type, the UDN also employs the voluntary stopping. By using 下車 'to get off' with the referendum as the agent, the UDN implies the referendum is going to stop on its own as a natural course, as shown in Extract 7:

Extract 7

其實，「入聯公投」走到今日，已在「下車」狀態… (UDN2008/02/19)
Actually *the UN referendum,* walking so far, is in the state of **getting off**….

The analysis of the stopping sub-schema reveals that different aspects and types of stopping have been selected in the representations. For the involuntary stopping, the conceptual parings in the LT are DIFFICULTIES ARE OBSTACLES, and THE AGENT CAUSING THE DIFFICULTIES ARE THE AGENTS SETTING UP THE OBSTACLES. However, the UDN does not employ these pairings. Instead, representing the referendum as a car, the UDN conveys that the moving object stops not because it encounters obstacles on the way, but because it is disconnected from the whole train, and the agent unhooking it is left unmentioned. Therefore, in the conceptual pairings A REFERENDUM IS A CARRIAGE OF A TRAIN, THE CANCELLED REFERENDUM IS AN UNHOOKED CARRIAGE are obvious in the UDN corpus, but THE AGENT CANCELLING THE REFERENDUM IS THE AGENT UNHOOKING THE CARRIAGE is missing. Regarding the voluntary stopping in the UDN corpus, the referendum is represented as a passenger who is about to get off, and the conceptual pairings are A REFERENDUM IS A PASSENGER and THE CANCELLATION OF THE REFERENDUM IS THE PASSENGER ALIGHTING.

The two corpora's diverging uses of the stopping sub-schema shows the constraints caused by the two newspapers diverging political stances. As referendum is a form of direct democracy, which is a way to make up the insufficiency of representative democracy and is highly recognized in democratic states, those who are in the way or stop a referendum are likely to be regarded as those who repress the development of democracy and thus are negatively evaluated. Like the forward-moving sub-schema, the stopping subgroup facilitates both newspapers to express their distinctive viewpoints toward the referendum. The LT ascribes the blame to the pan-blue camp or the KMT, the PRC, and the US by representing them as the agent who deliberately set up obstacles or hold back the referendum. As a result, they are negatively labeled. The UDN takes a different strategy in the use of this sub-domain. By omitting the agent who unhooks the referendum or describing the referendum in the state of getting off on its own, the UDN directs the attention away from the one responsible to stop the referendum.

5.3 A REFERENDUM IS A BUNDLED OBJECT

Aside from the forward-moving object retrieved from the PHYSICAL OBJECT metaphor, this metaphor also shows other aspects in the two corpora. Due to the space limit, we focus on the 'bundle' aspect, which, we argue, functions to reduce the effect brought about by the inevitable use of the lexemes for the forward-moving object.

The bundle aspect is realized mainly through the construction 公投綁大選 'the referendum bundled together with the presidential election', as in Extract 8 below:

Extract 8

「入聯公投」亦原有正面寓意，但亦因陳水扁不可信任，多數國人不贊同「公投綁大選」。

The UN referendum also has positive connotation. However, because Chen Shui-bian is not trustworthy, the majority of the people do not support '*the UN referendum* **bundled together with** the election'. (UDN2008/02/29)

The lexeme 綁 is defined as 'to fasten or tie up with a rope/cord' in the MOE Dictionary. When two or more things are tied together, they form a bundle. When a bundle is carried or moved, the parts of the bundle are carried or moved as a whole. There is little flexibility in the parts of the bundle. When the notion of bundle comes to the referendum and the election, we claim that this lexeme conveys the mutual constraints between the referendum and the election aside from indicating the two events to be held simultaneously. The constraints embedded in the construction leave no flexibility to either the referendum or the presidential election. The conceptual pairings thus generated are CONSTRAINT IS BUNDLE, TWO EVENTS HELD SIMULTANEOUSLY ARE TWO OBJECTS BUNDLED TOGETHER.

While occurring in the UDN corpus 23 times, this construction occurs in the LT corpus once only. We argue it is the notion of 'constraint' embedded in this lexeme which keeps the LT corpus from using it as frequently as the UDN corpus does. The LT corpus uses alternative ways to talk about the referendum and the presidential election to be held on the same day. Rather than 公投綁大選, the LT corpus uses 合併/一併舉行'merged', and 同時舉辦 'to be held simultaneously', and none of these compounds are found in the UDN corpus. The incidence of this construction in the two corpora reveals the seemingly neutral construction is actually laden with negative value. The LT corpus avoids using the construction, leading to only one occurrence of this construction, or 0.65% of all the metaphorical expressions. Compared with the LT corpus, the UDN corpus employs 23 times, or 8.52% of all the metaphorical expressions.

6 Concluding Remarks

We have analyzed how a referendum is represented through the use of conceptual metaphors in two major newspapers which hold opposing political stances in Taiwan, the LT and the UDN. The analysis indicates that a general schema for the referendum A CAUSER CAUSES AN OBJECT TO MOVE OR STOP, which is further divided to the forward-moving and stopping sub-schemas, can be retrieved from the metaphors used. Moreover, it shows that three expressions for the forward-moving sub-schema, as lexicalized in the LEGISLATION domain, are predominant in the representation of the referendum. With the inevitability to use the general schema, we have explicated how the two newspapers take strategies to elaborate or neutralize the effects embedded in the schema, which is motivated by the newspapers' diverging political stances.

Acknowledgments. The authors would like to thank Prof. Meichun Liu and the anonymous reviewers for their constructive comments and suggestions. The second author would like to acknowledge partial funding support from Hong Kong University Grant Council General Research Fund Grant #1240014. All remaining errors are our own.

References

1. Charteris-Black, J.: Britain as a container: immigration metaphors in the 2005 election campaign. Discourse Soc. **17**, 563–581 (2006)
2. Chiang, W.-y., Duann, R.-f.: Conceptual metaphors for SARS: 'war' between whom? Discourse Soc. **18**, 579–602 (2007)
3. Su, H.-y.: Fourth estate and public interest: news media in the Post War Taiwan, 1949–2004 (第四權與公共利益：戰後台灣的新聞媒體, 1949 ~ 2004). M.A. Thesis, National Taiwan University (2004)
4. Liao, F.-T.: Name rectification of Taiwan: the analysis of international dimension (台灣正名：國際面向之分析). Think Tank Forum of New Century **19**, 11–20 (2002)
5. Lakoff, G., Johnson, M.: Metaphors We Live By. University of Chicago Press, Chicago (1980)
6. Chilton, P., Lakoff, G.: Foreign policy by metaphor. In: Schaffner, C., Wenden, A.L. (eds.) Language and Peace, pp. 37–59. Harwood Academic Publishers, Singapore (1995)
7. Mio, J.S.: Metaphor and politics. Metaphor Symb. **12**, 113–133 (1997)
8. Semino, E.: Metaphor in Discourse. Cambridge University Press, Cambridge (2008)
9. Lu, M.: Referendum: referendums fail to meet thresholds. Taipei Times, Sunday, March 23, 6 (2008)
10. Pragglejaz Group: MIP: a method for identifying metaphorically-used words in discourse. Metaphor Symb. **22**, 1–40 (2007)
11. Huang, C.-R.: Tagged Chinese Gigaword Verion 2.0. Lexical Data Consortium, University of Pennsylvania, Philadelphia (2009)

A Cognitive Study on Modern Chinese Construction "V-lai-V-qu"

Xiaolong Lu(✉)

University of Hawaii at Manoa, Honolulu, USA
collinlew007@gmail.com

Abstract. As a commonly-used construction in modern Chinese, X-lai (come)-X-qu (go) comes from classical Chinese and it is still widely used in both oral and written Chinese today. In this paper we focus primarily on the construction where two Xs belong to the same monosyllable verb (V-lai-V-qu). Based on previous studies, we use theories of cognitive linguistics to explain the syntactic and semantic features of this construction, as well as the different frequencies of its variants. We hope this study can bring new insights to the exploration of cognitive mechanisms in researches of the similar Chinese verbal constructions.

Keywords: V-lai-V-qu · Syntactic distribution · Semantic features Cognitive linguistics · Frequency

1 Introduction

The four-character Chinese structure X-lai (come)-X-qu (go), as a specific verbal construction, originates from classical Chinese. As a form and meaning pairing (Goldberg 2003) [1], it bears some typical features, such as the high frequency of use, the parallel structure with stabilized meaning but varied form, which has been explored in previous studies (Liu 1999; Li 2002; Liu 2004; et al.). Generally, from the part of speech, the word X can mainly be a noun, a verb, an adjective or a quantifier, such as "chun (spring)-lai-qiu (autumn)-qu", "zou (walk)-lai-zou-qu", "zhi (straight)-lai-zhi-qu", "yi (one)-lai-er (two)-qu"; from the number of syllables, two Xs can be either monosyllables or bisyllables at the same time, such as "pao (run)-lai-pao-qu" and "zheteng (toss)-lai-zheteng-qu"; from the lexical meaning, the two Xs can be identical, related or opposite, the corresponding cases are "si (think)-lai-xiang (think)-qu", "mei (eyebrow)-lai-yan (eye)-qu", "ming (bright)-lai-an (dark)-qu".

In this paper we aim to reanalyze the case where two Xs in the construction belong to the *same monosyllabic verb*, which is the *V-lai-V-qu* construction. Based on Liu (1999) [2], we firstly conclude that there are four variants in this construction with two different meanings included:

(1) Displacement in "V1-lai-V1-qu" (1a) and "V1-qu-V1-lai" (1b);
(2) Non-displacement in "V2-lai-V2-qu" (2a) and "V2-qu-V2-lai" (2b).

J.-F. Hong et al. (Eds.): CLSW 2018, LNAI 11173, pp. 202–224, 2018.
https://doi.org/10.1007/978-3-030-04015-4_18

Compare the following examples:

(1) a. Women chulai de shihou, qiaojian ni jia nazhi da

1PL get-out ASSOC when see 2SG house that-CL big

huanggou zai menkou *zou-lai-zou-qu.*

yellow-dog PREP doorway walk-come-walk-go

"When we got out, (we) saw that big yellow dog walking back and forth at the doorway of your house." (cf. BCC)

b. Wo zai yangtai shang wang-le-you-wang, zai loudao zhong

1SG PREP balcony on look-PFV-again-look PREP corridor in

zou-qu-zou-lai, zai louti li shang-shang-xia-xia, liu-shen-wu-zhu.

walk-go-walk-come PREP stairs in go-up-and-down out of one's mind

"I had looked again and again on the balcony, (then) walked back and forth in the corridor, (then) went up and down in the stairs, I was out of my mind." (cf. BCC)

(2) a. Ruguo ni yiding yao wo cai shi shui shang le tamen, wo

if 2SG must require 1SG guess EM who hurt PFV 3PL 1SG

xiang-lai-xiang-qu ye zhi you liangge ren.

think-come-think-go EM only have two-CL people

"If you must require me to guess who has hurt them, I (can guess) only the two people (suspects) after thinking back and forth." (cf. BCC)

b. Wo huixiang zhe fuqin yisheng de xingwei, *xiang-qu-xiang-lai,* hai

1SG recall IMP father lifetime ASSOC behavior think-go-think-come EM

zhen rang wo xiangqi fuqin de yixie shi.

really let 1SG remember father ASSOC some affairs

"I was recalling my father's behaviors in his lifetime, I thought back and forth, which really let me remember some affairs about my father." (cf. CCL)

From the above, we can see that "zou (walk)-lai-zou-qu" in (1a) can be interchanged with "zou (walk)-qu-zou-lai" in (1b), the meaning of V1 (zou) can express a kind of spatial displacement or movement. By the same token, "xiang (think)-lai-xiang-qu" in (2a) can be replaced by "xiang (think)-qu-xiang-lai" in (2b), the meaning of V2 (xiang) cannot show the spatial displacement but an abstract action. Besides, the meaning and usage of the two pairs of constructions ("V-lai-V-qu" and "V-qu-V-lai") could remain the same. By analyzing data from BLCU Chinese Corpus (BCC) and Center for Chinese Linguistics Corpus (CCL) in the mainland China, we then propose new insights on this construction by using a cognitive and constructionist approach, and try to explain the psychological and social mechanisms reflected in the variants of "V-lai-V-qu".

2 Literature Review

Former researches on this construction have been carried out from multiple aspects, with a focus on the syntactic and semantic analysis plus cognitive explanations. Therefore, a comprehensive picture can be drawn for the research on "V-lai-V-qu" from diachronic and synchronic perspectives. However, there are still some unsettled problems to be considered.

As for the syntactic research, one issue is about the syntactic distribution of this construction. Li (2002) [3] states that the construction "V-lai-V-qu" can mainly serve as predicate in a sentence, and both Liu (2004) [4] and Hu (2012) [5] claim that this construction can also serve as attribute, adverbial and complement in a sentence; Yang (2012) [6] and Zhou (2017) [7] also take subject and object into consideration. Also, most of researchers consider the two words "lai" and "qu" should belong to directional verbs (Li 2002; Liu 2004; Zhou 2017). According to the definition of directional verb in Huang and Liao (2007: 11) [8], we know that "lai" and "qu" belong to monosyllabic directional verbs which can typically show the trend of reverse actions. Usually, the syntactic distribution of directional verbs is to serve as directional complements which are attached to verbs, hence the word "lai" and "qu" can exist in many Chinese verb-complement structures such as "dai (bring)-lai", "na (take)-qu", "de (get)-lai", "shi (lose)-qu", "jin (enter)-lai", "chu (exit)-qu", "shang (go up)-lai", "xia (go down)-qu", "guo (come)-lai", "hui (return)-qu" etc., to express the tendency of reverse actions. Another is about the syntactic insufficiency. Previous studies (Li 2002; Zhou 2017) show that in most cases the construction "V-lai-V-qu" needs be followed by a clause to make sure a complete meaning of the whole sentence, in this sense this construction has a feature of syntactic insufficiency which means it can not be used alone in the sentence. And its following clause can be divided into different categories like result clause, cause clause, purpose clause, etc., in different contexts. But so far people haven't explained why this construction often needs to be followed by a clause to make a complete meaning for the sentence.

Regarding the semantic research, one question is about the classification of V-element. Liu (1999) has classified the meaning of V-element as “motional” and “non-motional”, such as “zou (walk)-lai-zou-qu” and “chang (sing)-lai-chang-qu”, the same idea is shared in Li (2002), Liu (2004) and Zhou (2017). Liu (1999) also notes that some non-physical verbs, like “xiang (think)” and “kan (look at)” can be filled in “V-lai-V-qu” pattern, later Zhang (2007) [9] adds the emotional verbs like “ai (love)-lai-ai-qu” into non-physical verbs. Importantly, Liu (1999) has found that state and achievement verbs can rarely be inserted into the whole pattern by referring to Vendler’s (1967) [10] verb classification, this is because the construction “V-lai-V-qu” has a progressive meaning, this meaning is only supported by non-stative and non-instantaneous verbs. At last, she preliminarily concludes that some state verbs like “mei (be beautiful)”, and achievement verbs like “si (die)”, cannot be filled into the whole construction, but we have found these seemingly unqualified verbs could be filled into the construction in some cases by reanalyzing relative cases in Chinese corpora, so what is the reason? Noticeably, Zeng (2008) [11] finds that the meaning of V-element has been weakened in some cases like “shuo (speak)-lai-shuo-qu” and “jiang (speak)-lai-jiang-qu”, they are more likely to be discourse markers in the contexts, and the same viewpoint can be also shared in Liu (2004). Another is about the constructional meaning. Liu (1999) considers the construction “V-lai-V-qu” has two meanings: (1) when the V-element is motional, the whole meaning of the construction is to show a repeated motion in the opposing direction; (2) when the V-element is non-motional, the whole meaning of the construction is to show a continuous or repeated activity. The same idea can be also shared in Liu (2004), Zhang (2007), Zeng (2008) and Hu (2012). Especially, Liu (1999) notices that sometimes the construction “V-lai-V-qu” expresses a reciprocal meaning, this idea is also encoded as an alternate repetition in Yang (2012) and Zhou (2017). And Liu (1999) also emphasizes that the construction may have a reciprocal meaning when the V-element is transitive and accompanied with a plural subject, she concludes that it’s the transitivity variables of the whole clause that triggers this reciprocal reading. Li (2002) and Zeng (2008) adds that in some cases the meaning of “V-lai-V-qu” can be weakened, just like the mentioned “shuo (speak)-lai-shuo-qu”, which does not show a meaning of repeated action but show a meaning of summary as a kind of textual function. However, there’s no study about the semantic differences among the four construction variants such as “V1-lai-V1-qu”, “V1-qu-V1-lai”, “V2-lai-V2-qu” and “V2-qu-V2-lai”, and also we still don’t know exactly how to differentiate the structure between construction “V1-lai-V1-qu” and “V2-lai-V2-qu”.

For the cognitive mechanisms embodied in this construction. Liu (1999) maintains that the word “lai (come)” and “qu (go)” undergo the process of grammaticalization and metaphorization from spatial to aspectual domain, and she draws a schema which is about a reciprocal relation between A participant and B participant (two ending points), to express the idea that the spatial directionality is mapped unto the relational directionality. Zeng (2008) points out that the concept of “V-lai-V-qu” can be expanded from space to time, which means humans use the concept of spatial motion to express the concept of time change, as one of their basic cognitive abilities, which can be related with *Conceptual Metaphor*. Zhou (2017) outlines two schemas (from the space domain to the time domain) by combining *Causal Chain Model* with *Source-Path-Destination Schema.* But these studies haven’t yet explained how the metaphorical mappings work among different variants of "V-lai-V-qu" in details. Particularly, Zhou also mentions that the order of "lai" and "qu" in the construction is influenced by (1) spatial order, consequently the word "lai" and "qu" can be interchanged in example (1) to express the same idea; (2) temporal order, hence the time word "chun (spring)" should often precede the time word "qiu (fall)" in the construction "chun-lai-qiu-qu"; (3) social cognition, such as the tendency of self-centeredness and empathy in human behavior, in this way the frequency of "zou (walk)-lai-zou-qu" is much higher than that of "zou (walk)-qu-zou-lai", this concerns the concept of *Sequencing Iconicity* [12]. Moreover, she notices that compared with the concept of "X-lai" and "X-qu", as a kind of one-way displacement or change, "X-lai-X-qu" has more language units, which can express a more complicated concept: a repetitive motion or change. In this regard, we have found that in some cases "V-lai-V-qu" and "V-qu-V-lai" can be linked together to emphasize the repetition of action showed by V, but previous studies have not paid attention to this phenomenon as well as its explanations. Besides, we can find the different frequencies of internal categories of "V-lai-V-qu" in Zhou (2017), but she didn't clearly explain the generic mechanism (how the variants of this construction are related to each other) from a cognitive perspective.

The main research questions in this paper can be listed as follows:

(1) What are the semantic differences among the four construction variants: "V1-lai-V1-qu", "V1-qu-V1-lai", "V2-lai-V2-qu" and "V2-qu-V2-lai"? Is there any difference in the syntactic components between "V1-lai-V1-qu" and "V2-lai-V2-qu"?
(2) How the theories of cognitive linguistics can be used to explain the phenomenon that the construction "V-lai-V-qu" and "V-qu-V-lai" can be linked together to emphasize the repetition of action in some cases?
(3) Why some state verbs like "zhi (straightforward)" and achievement verbs like "si (die)" can be inserted into the whole construction?
(4) Why the construction "V-lai-V-qu" must be followed by a clause to make the meaning of the whole sentence complete in most cases?
(5) How do metaphorical mappings work specifically among different variants of the construction "V-lai-V-qu"?
(6) How to explain different frequencies of variants of the construction "V-lai-V-qu" from a cognitive perspective?

3 Research Method

Based on corpora, we conduct qualitative and quantitative analysis in BCC and CCL corpora where all the examples come from. We adopt a cognitive-functional approach to explain how the theories of iconicity, conceptual metaphor and prototype category work in this construction. The approach of comparative analysis can be also used when studying different construction variants.

4 Syntactic Analysis

Based on previous studies, we mainly analyze the components and syntactic distribution of the construction "V-lai-V-qu", the relative position of "lai" and "qu", and the concept of cognate constructions in this section.

4.1 Component Analysis

The Chinese construction "V-lai-V-qu", as a kind of parallel structure, combines the same two Vs with "lai" and "qu", to emphasize that the action denoted by V is persistent. Therefore, the whole meaning of the construction "V-lai-V-qu" conveys a dynamic event, and its structural focus lies in V. From historical syntax, Cao (1995) [13] and Ōta (2004) [14] contend that the part of speech of "lai" and "qu" can be changed from notional verbs to directional verbs, and these two directional verbs often attach to the two Vs (notional verb) as directional complements in the construction. In this sense both "V1-lai" and "V1-qu" are verb-complement (VC) patterns, they can be combined into the whole parallel construction "V1-lai-V1-qu". From prosodic syntax, the natural foot of "V1-lai-V1-qu" is [2 + 2] because we can easily sense that there's an obvious pause between "V1-lai" and "V1-qu" when reading the whole construction. Therefore, we consider this construction "V1-lai-V1-qu" as a kind of combined verb-complement structure, and the pattern "V1-lai" and "V1-qu" can be taken as independent constituents in examples like "zou (walk)-lai", "fei (fly)-qu", "song (send)-lai", "ji (mail)-qu", "qiang (rob)-lai", "na (take)-qu", "piao (float)-lai", "tao (flee)-qu", etc.

However, for another variant "V2-lai-V2-qu", it works like a gestalt that has an integrated meaning: the whole meaning is more than the sum of the parts. "V2-lai" and "V2-qu" are unacceptable in modern Chinese, such as "*xiang (think)-lai", "*ma (scold)-qu", "*chi (eat)-lai", "*ai (love)-qu", "*xiao (smile)-lai", "*xue (study)-qu", etc., because they are not independent syntactic units, nor can they be used alone. Instead, they can make sense only in their combined form, such as "xiang-lai-xiang-qu (think back and forth)", "ma-lai-ma-qu (scold back and forth)", "chi-lai-chi-qu" (eat back and forth), "ai-lai-ai-qu (love back and forth)" and so on. In this sense, we can not grammatically take the VC constituent as an independent unit in the whole construction, thus making the structure of "V2-lai-V2-qu" less intuitional compared with the former one.

4.2 Relative Positioning of "Lai" and "Qu"

Through the corpus analysis we have found that the directional verb "lai" and "qu" are interchangeable in most cases[1] like in the above example (1) and (2), we can also use "zou (walk)-qu-zou-lai" and "xiang (think)-qu-xiang-lai" to express the same meaning. This phenomenon can be also seen from a, b, c in (3), which shows the

[1] The case where "lai" and "qu" are interchangeable in "V-lai-V-qu" (V is monosyllabic) has the number of 2278 out of 5897 (about 38.6%) cases in BCC Corpus, while the number of "V-qu-V-lai" (V is monosyllabic) is only 97 out of 380 (25.5%) cases in BCC Corpus, among these 97 cases, "lai" and "qu" are interchangeable most of the time.

construction "V2-lai-V2-qu" is the same as "V2-qu-V2-lai".

(3) a. Tamen *suan-qu-suan-lai* bu huasuan, suoyi zhi mai le

3PL count-go-count-come not cost-effective so only buy PFV

yixie mianbao.

some bread

"They didn't feel it was cost-effective after counting back and forth, so they only bought some bread." (cf. CCL)

In this case both "suan (count)-qu-suan-lai" and "suan (count)-lai-suan-qu" can make sense because they have the same meaning which is about counting something back and forth. So the changing order of "lai" and "qu" in the construction can not change the meaning of the whole sentence.

b. Wo shougou le, zheyang *pian-qu-pian-lai* de ganqing, you

1SG have-had-it CRS this fool-go-fool-come ASSOC emotion there-be

biyao zai yanxu-xiaqu ma?

necessity again continue-RVC Q

"I have had it for this emotion which can be fooled back and forth, is there any necessity (for us) to continue it again?" (cf. BCC)

In this case both "pian (fool)-qu-pian-lai" and "pian (fool)-lai-pian-qu" are to show that the speaker's emotion has been fooled again and again by someone, which is unacceptable and unbearable to the speaker. The changing position in "lai" and "qu" cannot alter the whole meaning of the construction.

c. Xiangzhang yi kaikou jiuyao pai wo chu wushi,

Township-head when open-mouth be-going-to assign 1SG pay fifty-RMB

shuo-qu-shuo-lai haishi chu sishi-kuai.

speak-go-speak-come still pay forty-RMB

"When the township head opened his mouth, he was going to assign me to pay fifty RMB (for something), after speaking back and forth, (he still wants me to) pay forty RMB." (cf. BCC)

In this case both "shuo (speak)-qu-shuo-lai" and "shuo (speak)-lai-shuo-qu" can show the meaning that the township head has spoken to the speaker for many times, but there's no big change on his decision. As a result, we can change the position of "lai" and "qu" to express the same idea with different construction forms.

But in the following (4) to (7), “lai” and “qu” are not interchangeable, we should only put the word “qu” before the word “lai” in the construction because of specific context, which determines the order of spatial motion and restricts the number of round trips to only one round in the meaning of this construction. We can clearly see the ending point and initial point of the trip embodied in the context. See below:

(4) Na difang sui bu shen yuan, ta shi *zou-qu-zou-lai* de,

That place although not so far 3SG EM walk-go-walk-come ATTR

huidao jia yijing liudian-duo le.

come-back home already over-six o’clock CRS

“Although that place was not so far, she did walk here and then walk back home, when she came back home, it was already over six o’clock.” (cf. BCC)

In this case the context determines the word order that “qu” is before “lai” in the construction, because of the fact that she can only walk to that place first, and then walk back home. In this process, there’s only one round trip.

(5) Cong zheli dao yuemiao *tai-qu-tai-lai* xuyao shiliang yinzi.

From here to Yue-Fei-Temple carry-go-carry-come need ten-CL silvers

“You need to pay ten silvers for the cost of carrying you from Yue Fei Temple to this place.” (cf. BCC)

In this case the situation is the same as in (4) because of the fact that it’s necessary to be carried to Yue Fei Temple first, and to be carried back, the order of “qu” and “lai” is fixed in the context. There is also only one round trip in this process.

(6) Xianzai ganghao shier-dian wo ganggang tingjian zhong qiao guo, ni

Now just twelve-o’clock 1SG just-now hear clock strike EXP 2SG

zhunshi *fei-qu-fei-lai* de.

must fly-go-fly-come ATTR

“Now it’s just twelve o’clock, I heard the clock strike just now, you must fly to that place and fly back.” (cf. BCC)

In this case, it emphasizes that the person (you) walks to that place and comes back so fast that the speaker thinks the person must fly during the trip, which is for only one round.

(7) Ni ruguo qu tushuguan jieshu, keyi yong kuaidi

2SP if go to library borrow-books can use express-delivery

ji-qu-ji-lai, ji yitang buguo liangmaowu.

mail-go-mail-come mail one-CL no-more-than a-quarter

"If you go to the library to borrow books, you can use express delivery to mail to the library and mail your books back, the trip can cost you no more than a quarter." (cf. BCC)

In this case, it emphasizes that the person (you) should use express delivery to mail to the library first and then to get his or her books back via mail, this process also requires only one round trip.

4.3 Syntactic Distribution

By analyzing the data in Zhou (2017), we can see that among all the syntactic distributions of "V-lai-V-qu" (including "V1-lai-V1-qu" and "V2-lai-V2-qu"), the total proportion of the predicates counts up to 74.2%, with the ratio of attributives (about 6.8%) and the ratio of adverbials (about 5.5%) followed by. This shows it is most common that the construction serves as predicates (see most cases in 1-7), followed by attributives and adverbials, examples can be seen below.

(8) Chitang-bian you yixie *fei-lai-fei-qu* de qingting.

Along the pond there be some fly-come-fly-go ASSOC dragonfly

"Along the pond there are some dragonflies flying back and forth." (cf. BCC)

In this case, the construction "fei (fly)-lai-fei-qu" serves as an attributive to modify the noun "qingting (dragonfly)", to show the current status (dynamic) of these dragonflies.

(9) Ta duan zhe yiwan miantiao zai jiaoshi li *zou-lai-zou-qu* de chi.

3SP hold IMP one-CL noodle PREP classroom in walk-come-walk-go C eat

"He holds a bowl of noodles in the classroom, eating with walking back and forth." (cf. BCC)

In this case, the construction "zou (walk)-lai-zou-qu" serves as an adverbial to modify the verb "chi (eat)", to show the way he is eating the noodles.

4.4 The Concept of Cognate Structure

If we take a close look at the internal structure of the construction "V-lai-V-qu" (the V-element is monosyllabic), we can find that it can be classified into different patterns according to the semantics of V-element. These patterns are still widely-used in modern Chinese, the following three patterns include:

(1) Pattern 1: two Vs are both semantically-identical monosyllabic verbs (two Vs share the same form).
Example: "da (hit)-lai-da-qu", "jiao (yell)-lai-jiao-qu", "chi (eat)-lai-chi-qu", "pao (run)-lai-pao-qu", "chao (quarrel)-lai-chao-qu", "pan (expect)-lai-pan-qu", " du (gamble)-lai-du-qu", "ji (push)-lai-ji-qu", etc.;
(2) Pattern 2: two Vs are both semantically-related monosyllabic verbs (two Vs have different forms).
Example: "fei (fly)-lai-wu (dance)-qu", "fan (turn over)-lai-gun (roll)-qu", "zheng (dispute)-lai-qiang (grab)-qu", "chuan (cross)-lai-cha (interpose)-qu", "piao (drift)-lai-fu (float)-qu", "yao (shake)-lai-huang (waggle)-qu", "beng (bounce)-lai-tiao (jump)-qu", "si (reflect)-lai-xiang (think)-qu", etc.;
(3) Pattern 3: two Vs are both semantically-opposite monosyllabic verbs (two Vs have different forms).
Example: "huo (live)-lai-si (die)-qu", "tui (push)-lai-la (pull)-qu", "ai (love)-lai-hen (hate)-qu", "cun (save money)-lai-qu (draw money)-qu", "kai (open)-lai-guan (close)-qu", "he (unify)-lai-fen (separate)-qu", "mai (buy)-lai-mai (sell)-qu", "ju (get together)-lai-san (fall apart)-qu", etc.

We know that all these patterns, which share some common grounds in their features, are semantical categories of the construction "V-lai-V-qu", and the order of frequency can be shown by searching BCC Corpus:

Pattern 1 (66.8%) > Pattern 2 (21.8%) > Pattern 3 (11.4%)

Therefore, we call these patterns "cognate structures" to show they are from a common framework "V-lai-V-qu", relative explanations can be shown in the following cognitive part.

5 Semantic Interpretation

Previous studies tell us that the notional verb "lai" and "qu" can be changed into directional verbs because their notional meanings have been weakened gradually in the development of "V-lai-V-qu" (Li 2002; Liu 2004; Zeng 2008). Besides, the semantic features of V-element in this construction can be described as [+Atelic], [+Durative], [+Dynamic]. And also the constructional meaning of "V-lai-V-qu" can be divided into three parts (Liu 1999; Li 2002; Zhang 2007; Yang 2012; Zhou 2017):

(1) V1-lai-V1-qu: a repeated spatial motion in opposing directions.
Eg. zou (walk)-lai-zou-qu, ban (carry)-lai-ban-qu, tiao (jump)-lai-tiao-qu, etc.;
(2) V2-lai-V2-qu: a continuous or repeated temporal activity.
Eg. xiang (think)-lai-xiang-qu, chi (eat)-lai-chi-qu, ai (love)-lai-ai-qu, etc.;

(3) Both: reciprocal activity or alternate repetition (V-element is transitive and accompanied with a plural subject).
Eg. ji (crowd)-lai-ji-qu, ma (scold)-lai-ma-qu, ti (kick)-lai-ti-qu, etc.

Now we further focus on the semantic features of “V-lai-V-qu” with examples found in the BCC and CCL Corpus.

Initially, from the above we know that the V-element in the construction “V1-lai-V1-qu” and “V1-qu-V1-lai” can show a visible motion (displacement), see example (1); while the V-element in the construction “V2-lai-V2-qu” and “V2-qu-V2-lai” can show an invisible motion (non-displacement), see example (2).

Besides, from the number of round trips, we know that in (1) even if the event “zou-lai-zou-qu” means walking for many times, it should contain at least two rounds ($R \geq 2$) based on our experience. Similarly, in (2) the event “xiang-lai-xiang-qu” also includes at least two rounds ($R \geq 2$), it means a person should think about something back and forth, not just for one time.

Finally, from two ending points in the motion event this construction has displayed, in (1) and (2) we can hardly sense there are two ending points in the context of the construction “zou-lai-zou-qu” (V1-lai-V1-qu) and “xiang-lai-xiang-qu” (V2-lai-V2-qu), but in the following three examples (a, b, c) in (10), we can find two clear ending points in each event shown by each context:

(10) a. Ta jingchang zai Beijing he Shanghai zhijian *fei-lai-fei-qu*

3SP often PREP Beijing and Shanghai between fly-come-fly-go

“He often flies back and forth between Beijing and Shanghai (by airplane).”

In this sentence, the action verb “fei” has two clear ending points: Beijing and Shanghai.

b. Xiaoming fanhou zai chufang he keting *zou-lai-zou-qu*

3SP after-dinner PREP kitchen and living room walk-come-walk-go

“Xiaoming walked back and forth between kitchen and living room after dinner.”

In this sentence, the action verb “zou” has two clear ending points: “chufang (kitchen)” and “keting (living room)”.

c. Xiaowang chang zai liangge gongchang zhijian *pao-lai-pao-qu*

3SP often PREP two-CL factory between run-come-run-go

“Xiaowang often runs back and forth between the two factories.”

In this sentence, the action verb “pao” has two clear ending points: the two “gongchang (factories)”.

(all cf. online data)

By searching online data like examples in (10), we can conclude that sometimes the construction "V1-lai-V1-qu" has two clear ending points because of its context. Here is a table to show the semantic features in different variants of "V-lai-V-qu".

Table 1. The semantic features of different variants

Examples \ Variants	V1 is monosyllabic		V2 is monosyllabic	
Features	V1-lai-V1-qu	V1-qu-V-lai	V2-lai-V2-qu	V2-qu-V2-lai
Conditions	1a, 10, 14 (a, b, c)	1b, 4, 5, 6, 7, 11	2a, 3 (a, b, c), 8	2b, 3 (a, b, c), 9
Rounds	+ ($R \geqslant 2$)	+ ($R \geqslant 1$)	+ ($R \geqslant 2$)	+ ($R \geqslant 2$)
End Points	+ / -	+ / -	-	-
Displacement	+	+	-	-

6 Cognitive Mechanism

In what follows we will mainly refer to the theory of quantitative iconicity, conceptual metaphor, image schema, construction coercion and prototype category to help explain the unsettled issues by proposing the following cognitive mechanisms.

6.1 Quantitative Iconicity

Judging from the following cases in BCC Corpus, we see that the construction "V-lai-V-qu" and "V-qu-V-lai" can be linked together in one sentence to show the same meaning with an emphasis on the repetition of V, thus we have this verbal construction "V-lai-V-qu, V-qu-V-lai"[2]. Compared with the single use of "V-lai-V-qu" or "V-qu-V-lai", the linguistic units used to express ideas in this linking construction are more complex, so the information processed and decoded is more abundant in this way. The meaning of this linking construction has been extended from semantics to pragmatics, not only does it lead to a rhythmical and continuous manner in reading, but also it highlights the speaker's emotional tendency especially for negative attitude in some situations. On this account, more information or concepts can be conveyed by using this linking construction. This basically conforms to the *Quantity Principle* in *Iconicity* proposed by Haiman (1985a: 147) [15], which means that the formal complexity should correspond to the conceptual complexity. Example a, b, c in (11) can explain

[2] Even if we only find 5 corresponding cases in BCC Corpus, some verbs like "da (hit)", "xiang (think)", "ai (love)", "tui (push)", "ku (cry)", "jiang (speak)", "fan (grub)" and so forth, can be found in the spoken Chinese online, this shows that people tend to use this pattern to emphasize the repetitive action represented by the V-element.

this principle in details.

(11) a. Laoyu Jiandao le Xiang-Shizhang, que wu-lun-ru-he ye ba huati che-bu-dao

3SG meet PFV 3SG but in any case EM BA topic talk-not-to

fangzi shangqu, *rao-lai-rao-qu*, *rao-qu-rao-lai.*

house on talk in circles talk in circles

"(When) Mr. Yu met Mayor Xiang, in any case he could not talk on the topic of house (directly) but talked in circles (firstly)."

b. Ta kaishi rao zhe nage yuanzi zou, *zou-lai-zou-qu*, *zou-qu-zou-lai,*

3SG begin around IMP that-CL yard walk walk-come-walk-go walk-go-walk-come

xiang yizhi kunshou.

"He began to walk around that yard, he walked back and forth, just like a trapped beast."

c. Liangtao bieshu moxing zuowan bei haizimen *bai-lai-bai-qu,*

Two-CL villa model last-night BEI children place-come-place-go

bai-qu-bai-lai, *bai-lai-bai-qu,* *bai-qu-bai-lai,* jiupa

place-go-place-come place-come-place-go place-go-place-come be afraid that

tianxia bu renao.

world not lively

"Last night two sets of villa modals had been placed back and forth by children, who were afraid that the world was not lively (enough)."

(all cf. BCC)

As we can see in example (11a), the construction variant "rao-lai-rao-qu" and "rao-qu-rao-lai" are linked together to emphasize the durability of the action "rao", and also the author tends to criticize the way of Laoyu's speaking by conveying a kind of dissatisfied attitude in the linking construction. In example (11b) we see that the linking construction "zou-lai-zou-qu" and "zou-qu-zou-lai" can not only emphasize the repetition of action "zou", but also show a sort of good-for-nothing attitude to his walking behavior, because he looks like a trapped beast and can not get out of the plight. From example (11c) we find that more than two "V-lai-V-qu" constructions can be used together to put emphasis on the repetition of action verb "bai", but the author tends to be fed up with the situation that children place their villa models so often that they have made some noise in the house, this attitude of antipathy can be drawn from the passive voice shown in the BEI construction and the ironical meaning expressed in the positive adjective "renao" in the sentence.

6.2 Metaphorical Mapping

If we pay close attention to the meaning of different variants in the construction "V-lai-V-qu", we will find there are three different metaphorical mappings that exist among these variants. Lakoff and Johnson (1980: 63–64) [16] have made the definition for metaphorical mapping that it is the systematic set of correspondences that exist between constituent elements of the source and the target domain. Here the source domain is the conceptual domain from which we draw metaphorical expressions, and the target domain is the conceptual domain that we try to understand. Let's see how the conceptual metaphor works by comparing these constructions with each other.

6.2.1 From Spatial Displacement to Concept of Quantity

From the construction "V1-lai-V1-qu" and "V1-qu-V1-lai" we see that V-element is to show a concrete and visible action, like "pao (run)-lai-pao-qu" and "piao (float)-qu-piao-lai", and also we have mentioned that "lai" and "qu" belong to monosyllabic directional verbs which show the trend of reverse action. Consequently we can see a clear denotation of spatial movement in these constituents. But when these constituents combine to form a whole part, the concept of quantity can be activated, that is, the constructional meaning is to show the times of spatial action "V1-lai-V1-qu", in some cases like (4) to (7) the number of times can be counted as only one (Round = 1), as described in Table 1, but in most cases like (8), (9), (10), the number of times can be uncountable, so more than two times of "V1-lai-V1-qu" can happen (Round $\geq$ 2), as also illustrated in Table 1. Here the source domain that shows the spatial displacement, has been mapped into the target domain that shows the concept of quantity, which is how metaphorical mapping works between the construction "V1-lai-V1-qu" and "V1-qu-V1-lai". We use solid arrow to represent the two opposing directions of the concrete or visible V1. Here is the image schema (Fig. 1).

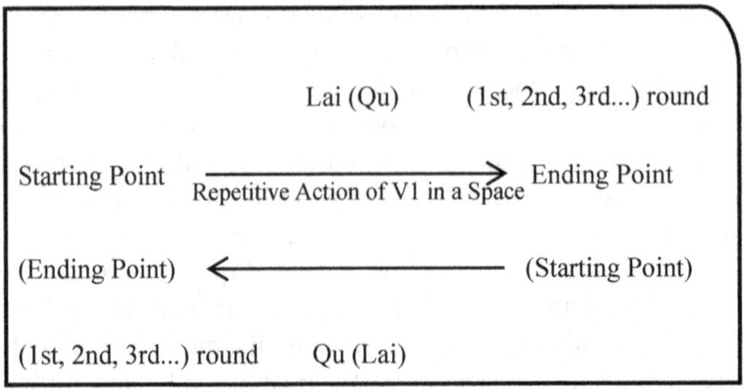

Fig. 1. Mapping from spatial displacement to quantity (round times)

6.2.2 From Temporal Non-displacement to Concept of Quantity

From the construction "V2-lai-V2-qu" and "V2-qu-V2-lai" we know that the V-element can express mental and invisible action (non-displacement), like "xiang (think)-lai-xiang-qu" and "pian (cheat)-qu-pian-lai", here the word "lai" and "qu" can show a kind of opposing directions of abstract action. But when these constituents are filled into the whole construction, the constructional meaning is to show the number of times the abstract action (taken as a temporal event) "V2-lai-V2-qu" has occurred, in this sense the concept of quantity can be activated in this construction. Here the source domain shows a temporal (duration of time) meaning and the target domain shows the concept of quantity, it is a metaphorical mapping from the source domain to the target domain. This shows how the metaphorical mapping works between the construction "V2-lai-V2-qu" and "V2-qu-V2-lai". Let's see the following image schema (Note that in this situation no spatial displacement can be shown by the construction, we hereby use dotted arrow to represent the two opposing directions of the abstract or invisible V2) (Fig. 2).

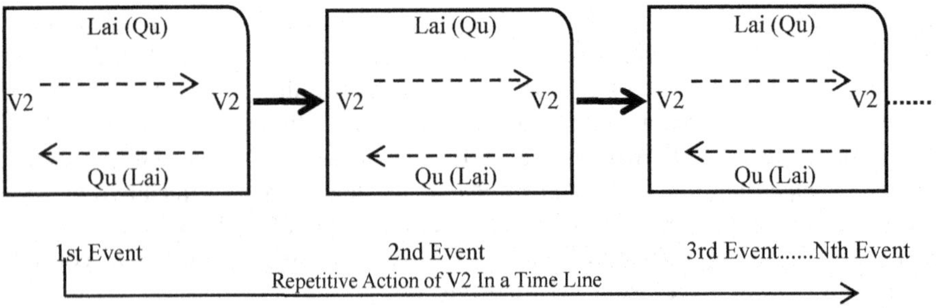

Fig. 2. Mapping from temporal non-displacement to quantity (event times)

6.2.3 From Spatial Concept to Temporal Concept

From Liu (1999) we know that the linguistic analogy can be seen from the construction "V1-lai-V1-qu" to "V2-lai-V2-qu" in the historical development of "V-lai-V-qu", the displacement verb (V1) can be replaced by non-displacement verb (V2) to produce large numbers of constructions which contain the abstract actions like "xiang (think)", "ai (love)", "shuo (speak)", etc. This is because language needs to be rich in people's communication to express more abstract and complex concepts, from the perspective of social usage. Now we can clearly see that the construction "V1-lai-V1-qu" or "V1-qu-V1-lai" can emphasize a kind of spatial concept, because the verb V1 in the construction can show concrete movement in the space. While the construction "V2-lai-V2-qu" or "V2-qu-V2-lai" can emphasize a kind of temporal concept, because we can not see any concrete movement in the verb V2 and it mainly focuses on times of abstract actions, usually these continuous times are not countable but they can express the duration of time when taking them as a whole event. Here the source domain contains the spatial concept and the target domain contains the temporal concept, it's safe to say that the space is mapped into the time from the construction "V1-lai-V1-qu" to "V2-lai-V2-qu". This is how metaphorical mapping works between "V1-lai-V1-qu" and "V2-lai-V2-qu". See the figure below (Fig. 3).

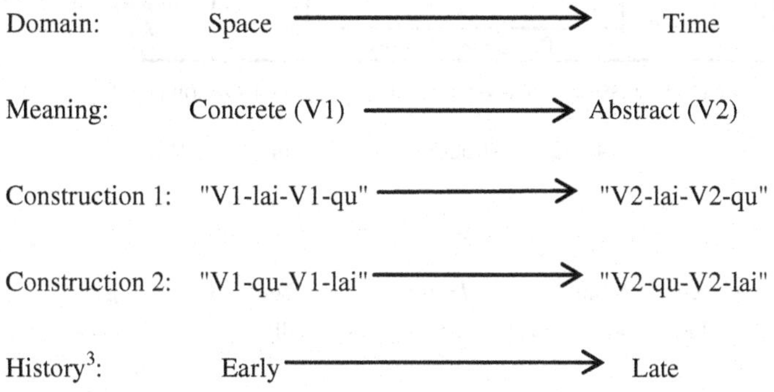

Fig. 3. Mapping from spatial concept to temporal concept. [3](In the historical development of "V-lai-V-qu", the time V1 appears is earlier than V2's, and the construction "V2-lai-V2-qu" is very likely to develop from the construction "V1-lai-V1-qu" because of the extended meaning of the V-element. Details can be seen in Li (2002) and Liu (2004))

6.3 Event Structure Metaphor

As previously noted in Sect. 2, sometimes the construction "V-lai-V-qu" has a syntactic insufficiency, which means that it should be followed by a clause to make sure a complete meaning in a sentence. Like some examples in (2) and (3), this construction "V-lai-V-qu", as a predicate, must be followed by a clause to express the result of the event the construction shows, that is, we can not end with "V-lai-V-qu" in a sentence because the meaning of the sentence has not been completed without mentioning the following parts, this is to show the syntactic insufficiency. Noticeably, Zhou (2017) has proposed that the ratio of syntactic insufficiency for the construction "V-lai-V-qu" is

71.7%, and resultative clause can take up the most part (42.7%) among all the follow-up clauses in the sentences involving this construction.

Based on *Event Structure Metaphor* (Lakoff 1993) [17] we know that progress made is distance traveled or distance from goal. Here the source domain "distance from travel destination" has been mapped into the target domain "progress" made in our life. On this account, when the subject makes something in progress, it's just like a half-way travel in a long journey, there should be two results: finished travel or unfinished travel. Correspondingly, the event embodied by the construction "V-lai-V-qu" emphasizes an ongoing process because of its repetitive action, which can semantically activate possible follow-up events which contain the results of this process. This event-activation mechanism is well explained by *Event Structure Metaphor*, and there should be two different results in the process "V-lai-V-qu" has expressed: finished goal (12a) or unfinished goal (12b). In this regard we could vividly image that the syntactic distribution of the construction "V-lai-V-qu" can be mapped onto the travelling event in our life. See Fig. 4 below:

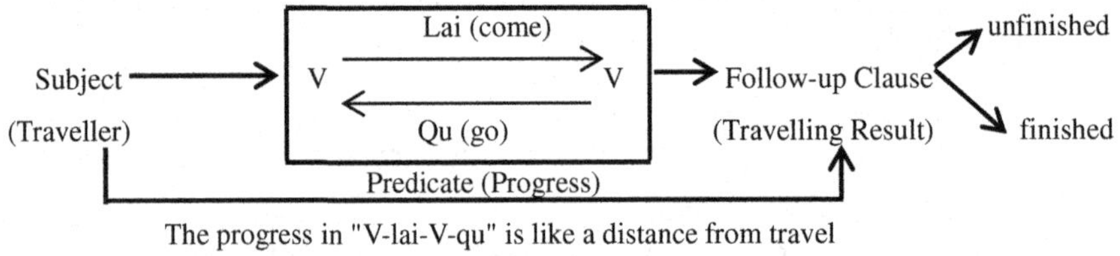

Fig. 4. Event structure metaphor in "V-lai-V-qu"

(12) a. Zhe yu zai shuili *tiao-lai-tiao-qu,* zuihou cong yu-gang tiao-le-chulai.
This fish PREP water jump-come-jump-go finally PREP fish-tank jump-PFV-RVC

"This fish is jumping back and forth in the water, finally it jumped out of the fish tank."

b. Wo *xiang-lai-xiang-qu,* xiang-buchu hai you shenme banfa neng cha-qing zhejianshi.
1SG think-come-think-go think-RVC also have what idea can find-out this-CL-thing

"I have thought back and forth and cannot think out what kind of idea I also have to find out this thing."

(all cf. CCL)

From (12a) we can clearly see that the clause following "tiao-lai-tiao-qu" shows that the fish can finally jump out of the fish tank after trying again and again, while in (12b) the clause following "xiang-lai-xiang-qu" shows that "I" cannot think out another idea even if "I" have thought for many times. Here we see that "V-lai-V-qu" can lead to a finished goal in (12a) while it can also lead to an unfinished goal in (12b).

6.4 Construction Coercion

As mentioned earlier in Sect. 5, only non-telic, non-instantaneous, and non-stative verbs can be filled into the construction "V-lai-V-qu" in most cases, like "zou (walk)" in (1) and "xiang (think)" in (2), they are durable verbs which don't contain the meaning of results. However, we have found that some achievement verbs can be also filled into this construction by reanalyzing BCC Corpus. This phenomenon can be shown in the following example a, b, c in (13), the verb "si (die)", "jia (marry)", "yun (swoon)" and "bian (change)" are all instantaneous and telic verbs, but why these verbs can get the licence to fill in this construction? According to the *Override Principle* proposed by Michaelis (2004) [18] we know that if a lexical item is semantically incompatible with its syntactic context, the meaning of the lexical item conforms to the meaning of the structure in which it is embedded. This is a kind of *Construction Coercion*, which means the whole construction has the power to change or suppress the semantic features of its lexical items. Here we see that the meaning of the verb "si (die)" originally is to show an instantly-completed action, but it has been coerced into a durable activity in order to be compatible with the constructional meaning, which is to show a continuous or repeated activity in "si-lai-si-qu". The sentence in (13a) tells us that the five protagonists who have died for many times can still come up throughout the story of the animation, and we know that usually the protagonists can not die easily on TV. Similarly, in example (13b) the verb "jia (marry)" is coerced into a durable activity under the control of the constructional meaning, because the context tells us that the woman is so fickle in her love that she used to marry different men. And in example (13c) the verb "yun (swoon)" is coerced into a durable activity because the constructional meaning of "yun-lai-yun-qu" is to show a continuous event, the meaning of a single lexical item should conform to the whole meaning of the construction where it's embedded. Last, the verb "bian (change)" in example (13d) shows that under the influence of the constructional meaning, its lexical meaning has changed from an achievement action to a durable event, which means the goals can been changed constantly during the process of plan making, till the final decision could be made.

(13) a. Dongmanban kan de wo hao jiujie, wuge zhujue

animation-version watch C 1SG very entangled five-CL protagonist

buting de *si-lai-si-qu*, wo juede fangqi dongmanban,

ceaselessly C die-come-die-go 1SG think give-up animation-version

kan dianyingban.

watch movie-version

"I am very entangled with the animation version in the watching, (because) the five protagonists had died back and forth ceaselessly, I think (I have to) give up this animation version and to watch the movie version instead."

b. Wo dasuan dui Wengege cong-yi-er-zhong, cai bu yao xue na

1SG plan to 3SG single-minded EM not want follow that

nvren *jia-lai-jia-qu*, jian yige ai yige.

woman marry-come-marry-go meet one-CL love one-CL

"I plan to be single-minded to brother Wen, I don't want to follow that woman, (because she has) married back and forth and she used to fall in love with different men when meeting."

c. Wo he ta goutong de shihou, ta yong hen fuza de gainian

1SG and 3SG communicate ASSOC when 3SG use very complex ASSOC concept

ba wo rao de *yun-lai-yun-qu* de.

BA 1SG confuse C swoon-come-swoon-go ATTR

"When I was communicating with her, she used some very complex concepts to make me so confused that I swooned back and forth."

d. Ni suo ding de naxie mubiao, shi-guo-jing-qian,

2SP SUO set ASSOC those goal time-pass-circumstance-change

zong ye *bian-lai-bian-qu,* daotoulai bing mei you zongzhi.

always EM change-come-change-go in the end EM not have purpose

"As time passed and circumstance changed, those goals you have set for yourselves can always be changed back and forth, which means you will not have a purpose in the end."

(all cf. BCC)

6.5 Cognate Mechanism

According to the theory of *Prototype Category* in cognitive psychology, Rosch (1973) [19] have pointed out that the prototype is a stimulus, which takes a salient position in the formation of a category as it is the first stimulus to be associated with that category, and prototype is the most central member of a category. In this way we use the theory to reconsider the lexical meaning of this construction, and find that some constructions belong to the same family if they are closely related in their meanings and forms, because they have the features of *Family Resemblance* (Wittgenstein 1953) [20]. But the categories of these constructions should have a fuzzy boundary which is the semantic transition existing between typical ones and non-typical ones, the typical constructions as the prototype are core members and non-typical ones are peripheral members in the construction family.

It is clear that we have mentioned that the framework "V-lai-V-qu" contains three different patterns based on semantic relations between two V elements (see 4.4), and we know that the different frequencies exist in different patterns. Now it's time to consider the pattern 1 in the construction "V-lai-V-qu" can be the prototype in the category, because it has the highest frequency of use, which means people prefer to use this pattern to express the concept of repetition in most cases. Based on the theory of *Prototype Category*, we can conclude that this pattern belongs to typical members of "V-lai-V-qu" family and should lie in the center of category (core), with pattern 2 and pattern 3 (periphery) followed by in the order of the framework. Hence we can see that the three patterns are closely related in meaning and form but share a fuzzy boundary between each other's meanings. See Fig. 5.

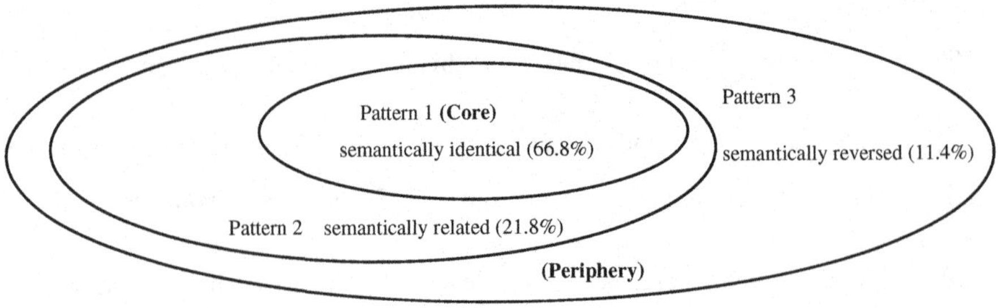

Fig. 5. Prototype category of "V-lai-V-qu" (V is monosyllabic)

7 Conclusion

Above all, although the construction "V-lai-V-qu" has been elaborately described in terms of syntax, semantics and cognitive study so far, some different aspects still need to be further explored. One aspect is to do typological analysis of similar constructions across different languages, like English construction "V back and forth", or comparative studies on relative Chinese constructions like "V-shang (up)-V-xia (down)", "V-jin (enter)-V-chu (exit)" and "V-qian (front)-V-hou (back)". Another is to demonstrate if the potential relationship among these different constructions like "A-lai-A-qu", "N-lai-N-qu" and "V-lai-V-qu" could be predicted from the perspective of grammaticalization[3].

We hope this study can bring new insights to the exploration of cognitive mechanisms in relative researches. We also believe the study of verbal constructions will inspire us to broaden and deepen functional-cognitive approaches in the field of Cognitive Linguistics and Construction Grammar in the long run.

1 Abbreviations

1SG 1st person singular

1PL 1st person plural

2SG 2nd person singular

2PL 2nd person plural

3SG 3rd person singular

3PL 3rd person plural

[3] By searching for relative cases in BCC modern Chinese corpus we find that the total number of frequencies of "A-lai-A-qu" and "N-lai-N-qu" is no more than 400 but the number of "V-lai-V-qu" is almost 2200. However, we can also see some "A-lai-A-qu" constructions like "ming (bright)-lai-an (dark)-qu", "qiao (artful)-lai-miao (artful)-qu", "gao (high)-lai-di (low)-qu", etc., and some "N-lai-N-qu" constructions like "zhao (morning)-lai-mu (evening)-qu", "si (silk)-lai-xian (thread)-qu", "chun (spring)-lai-dong (winter)-qu" in classical Chinese corpus.

PREP Preposition

CL Classifier

PST Past tense

NEG Negator

PASS passive

IMP Imperfective

EM Emphasis marker

EXP Experiential

Q Question Marker

MOOD Modal particle

SUO Functional particle *suo*

BA *Ba*-construction

BEI *Bei*-construction

RVC Resultative Verb Complement

C Complimentizer *de*

CRS Current Relevant State *le*

PFV Perfective *le*

ASSOC Associative *de*

CSC Complex stative construction *de*

ATTR Attributive *de*

References

1. Goldberg, A.E.: Constructions: a new theoretical approach to language. Trends Cogn. Sci. **7** (5), 219–224 (2003)
2. Liu, M.: Reciprocal marking with deictic verbs come and go in Mandarin. In: Frajzyngier, Z., Curl, T.S. (eds.) Reciprocals: forms and functions, pp. 123–132. John Benjamins Publishing Company, Amsterdam (1999)
3. Li, J.: "V-lai-V-qu" geshi jiqi yufahua (On the Structure "V-lai-V-qu" and its Grammaticalization). Yuyan Yanjiu (Linguist. Study) **47**, 63–69 (2002). [In Chinese]
4. Hu, W.: "A-Lai-B-Qu" gongshi yu lishi yanjiu (A Synchronic and Diachronic Study of "A-Lai-B-Qu"). Yunnan Shifan Daxue Xuebao (Duiwai Hanyu Jiaoxue Yu Yanjiu Ban). J. Yunnan Normal Univ. (Teaching and Research of Chinese as A Foreign Language) **10**(6), 30–39 (2012). [In Chinese]

5. Liu, Z.: Jindai hanyu zhong de "V-lai-V-qu" geshi kaocha (Investigating "V-lai V-qu" in the Modern Chinese). Guhanyu Yanjiu (Res. Ancient Chin. Lang.) **65**, 74–78 (2004). [In Chinese]
6. Yang, D.: Zaiyi "V-lai-V-qu" ji yu zhi xiangguan de geshi (On "V-lai-V-qu" and Other Relevant Constructions). Shijie Hanyu Jiaoxue (Chin. Teach. World) **26**, 198–208 (2012). [In Chinese]
7. Zhou, H.: Duidie kuangjia "X-lai-X-qu" de yufahua he xiucihua (The Grammaticalization and Rhetoricalization of the Stack Frame "X-lai-X-qu"). Dangdai Xiuci Xue (Contemp. Rhetoric) **199**, 24–34 (2017). [In Chinese]
8. Huang, B., Liao, X.: Xiandai hanyu (xiace) [Modern Chinese (partII)]. Higher Education Press, Beijing (2007). [In Chinese]
9. Zhang, H.: Tan "V-lai-V-qu" (On "V-lai-V-qu"). J. Shandong Normal Univ. (Humanities and Social Sciences) **210**, 64–68 (2007). [In Chinese]
10. Vendler, Z.: Linguistics in Philosophy. Cornell University Press, Ithaca (1967)
11. Zeng, C.: Yetan "V-lai-V-qu" geshi jiqi yufahua (On the Construction "V-lai-V -qu" and its Grammaticalization). Yuyan Jiaoxue yu Yanjiu (Lang. Teach. Linguist. Stud.) **06**, 22–29 (2008). [In Chinese]
12. Haspelmath, M.: Frequency vs. iconicity in explaining grammatical asymmetries. Cogn. Linguist. **19**(1), 1–33 (2008)
13. Cao, G.: Jindai hanyu zhuci (Modern Chinese Auxiliary Words). Language & Culture Press, Beijing (1995). [In Chinese]
14. Ōta, T.: Zhongguoyu lishi wenfa (A Historical Grammar of Modern Chinese), trans. by Jiang, Shaoyu & Xu Changhua. Peking University Press, Beijing (2003). [In Chinese]
15. Haiman, J.: Natural Syntax: Iconicity and Erosion. Cambridge University Press, Cambridge (1985)
16. Lakoff, G.: Metaphors We Live By. The University of Chicago Press, Chicago (1980)
17. Lakoff, G.: The contemporary theory of metaphor. In: Ortony, A. (ed.) Metaphor and Thought, vol. 2, pp. 202–251. Cambridge University Press, Cambridge (1993)
18. Michaelis, L.A.: Type shifting in construction grammar: an integrated approach to aspectual coercion. Cogn. Linguist. **15**(1), 1–67 (2004)
19. Rosch, E., Mervis, C.B.: Family resemblances: studies in the internal structure of categories. Cogn. Psychol. **7**(4), 573–605 (1975)
20. Wittgenstein, L.: Philosophical Investigations. Blackwell Publishing, Hoboken (2001)

A Study on the Type Coercion of the Causer of Chinese Causative Verb-Resultative Construction Based on the Generative Lexicon Theory

Yiqiao Xia[1] and Daqin Li[2(✉)]

[1] School of Communication and Animation, Qingdao University of Science and Technology, Laoshan District, Qingdao 266061, China
xiayiqiao58@126.com

[2] Faculty of Literature and Law, Communication University of China, Chaoyang District, Beijing 100024, China
liidaaqiin@163.com

Abstract. Based on the qualia structure and co-composition of Generative Lexicon Theory, as well as the Light Verb Theory, this paper analyzes the logical metonymy and the acceptability of an expression as a causer. We find out that the NP expression of the causer of the event in the Causative resultative construction undergoes an event coercion. Thus the NP does not represent an entity but an event, in order to adapt to the causative event schema. We also find out that the qualia unification of the NP and the VP has a great influence on the acceptance of the causer as well. This paper puts forward an unified interpretation model for the diverse sources of the causer.

Keywords: Verb-Resultative Construction · Causative · Causer Type coercion

1 Introduction

In the causative construction, the causer brings about changes of the causes. The analysis of the causer involves the understanding of the semantic relationship of the arguments governed by the Verb-Resultative Construction in Mandarin Chinese. Therefore, the description and interpretation of the causer is key to studying the semantic features and syntactic structure of the Verb-Resultative Construction.

Scholars have elaborated on the multiple sources of the causer, but nobody has discussed the reason of the diverse sources of the causer. This paper attempts to provide an unified interpretation model for this phenomenon based on the type coercion theory of the Generative Lexicon Theory. Because the causer is the initiator of the causal relation, all of the semantic components of the causing event can act as a causer. So this can explain why so many semantic components can be used as a causer in the causative construction. Therefore, when we analyze the semantic type of the causer, all the semantic components of the causing event should be considered.

J.-F. Hong et al. (Eds.): CLSW 2018, LNAI 11173, pp. 225–235, 2018.
https://doi.org/10.1007/978-3-030-04015-4_19

2 Logical Metonymy and Event Coercion

2.1 The Difference Between Logical Metonymy and Conceptual Metonymy

Logical metonymy is an important semantic combination phenomenon, which means that the syntactic argument of a word seems to be different from the logical form of that argument. For instance:

1. a. John began the book.
   b. John began to write/to read the book.
2. a. Books bored me.
   b. My reading books bored me.

The verb *begin* in the first sentence above is supposed to take an object that represents an action. However, the *book* refers to an entity, so it does not meet the requirement of the semantic type of the object that *begin* takes. In this case, a type mismatch appears, and the typing requirements specified by the verb *begin* are satisfied just in case the type of the NP is coerced to an event function. Pustejovsky [1] called it *type coercion.*

TYPE COERCION is a semantic operation that converts an argument to the type which is expected by a function, where it would otherwise result in a type error. The NP *book* is coerced to the appropriate type required by its governing verb, in this case an event. What makes coercion possible in this case is the availability of the selected type, given as part of the NP's qualia structure, indicating, for example, that the NP's TELIC role is the event function of reading, while its AGENTIVE role is an event function of writing. The result of applying this coercion operator to an NP is effectively to create an extension of the NP meaning, namely a metonymic reconstruction. In the case of the NP the *book*, for example, the coercion operator provides two event function interpretations, namely, reading the book and writing the book. These interpretations are generated by virtue of the type of the selected complement and availability of such types in the qualia structure of the complement itself.

There is a difference between the logical metonymy and the conceptual metonymy. The logical metonymy is a semantic operation that converts an argument to the appropriate type required by its governing verb, for instance, an entity represents an event, and the entity and the event are not in the same category. However, the conceptual metonymy is another situation, we substitute A for B, and A and B are in the same category, such as an entity represents another entity (e.g. an author represents his works) or an event represents another event (e.g. a foreground event represents a core event).

2.2 Event Coercion

Type coercion theory is the latest theory that interprets the logical metonymy. Type coercion is a semantic operation that converts an argument to the type which is expected by a function, where it would otherwise result in a type error. Based on the qualia structure and co-composition of the Generative Lexicon Theory, we find out that the NP expression of the causer of the event in the Causative resultative construction undergoes an event coercion. Thus the NP does not represent an entity but an event, in order to adapt to the causative event schema. This kind of operation is called event coercion. Logical metonymy as an event coercion is a kind of type coercion.

According to the Generative Lexicon Theory, the logical metonymy is caused by the mismatch of the semantic type and it can be explained by the semantic generative mechanism of type coercion. Considering that the complement to *begin* is actually an event of some sort, and the NP *the book* does not satisfy the type required by the predicate *begin*, as in the sentence 1a, the type mismatch appears. The verb coerces the NP into an event denotation, one which is available from the NP's qualia structure through qualia projection. There are two event readings associated with this NP, namely the values of the AGENTIVE and TELIC qualia roles.

In the past, scholars mainly discussed the type coercion of the verb and its complement [2, 3]. This paper aims to interpret the type coercion of the subject and its predicate based on the Generative Lexicon Theory. As a kind of causative expression, the VRC is a binary event structure constituted of 2 subevents, a causing event e_1 and a resulting event e_2, and the initial event e_1 is headed.

The causer of the VRC that expresses causative meaning is supposed to be a causing event. However, the expression of the causer is a NP that represents an entity, and does not meet the requirement of semantic type of the causer. In this case, the type mismatch occurs, and the NP undergoes a type shifting. In the VRC, the event verb coerces an entity-denoting NP into an event as a resolution to the predictable type mismatch. In order to highlight the important information of the causative event, such as the agent, the object, and the means of the event, etc., the expression that represents the entity is used as the causer in the sentence. In this sense, the *event-coercion* is a mechanism of semantic decompression.

The NP *clothes* does not satisfy the type required by the predicate, as in the example below, the verb coerces the NP *clothes* into an event denotation, one which is available from the NP's qualia structure through qualia projection. There are two event readings associated with this NP, namely, the values of the AGENTIVE and TELIC qualia roles.

What makes coercion possible in this case is the availability of the selected type, given as part of the NP's qualia structure, indicating, for example, that the AGENTIVE role for *clothes* is the event function of sewing.

In the case of the NP *the clothes*, for example, the coercion operator provides an event function interpretation, namely, sewing clothes. The interpretation is generated by virtue of the type of the selected complement and availability of such types in the qualia structure of the NP itself. For example (Figs. 1 and 2):

3.衣服缝累了我。
yifu feng lei le wo
(Sewing clothes makes me tired.)

[<PRO [DO]*yifu*(clothes) > CAUSE <*wo*(I)BECOME *lei le*(tired) >] (1)

衣服 *yifu* (*clothes*)

ARGSTR = [ARG_1=x:phys_obj; D-ARG_1=y:mass]

QUALIA = [CONST=y; FORMAL=x; TELIC= *wear*, cov*er up embarrassment*, *against the cold*, *sunscreen*, *radiation protection* (e_2,z,x); AGENTIVE=*sew*, *make*, *wash*_act(e_1,w,y)]

Fig. 1. The lexical representation for the noun *yifu* (clothes)

缝 *feng* (*sew*)

ARGSTR = [ARG_1=x:human; ARG_2=y: *fabric*]

QUALIA = [FORMAL= *put together*; AGENTIVE=*sew*_act(e_1,w,y)]

Fig. 2. The lexical representation for the verb *feng* (sew)

Event coercion is realized by the AGENTIVE role of the *clothes*. The AGENTIVE role for the NP *clothes* projects the activity of *sewing clothes* to the interpretation of the subjective noun. The deep structure of the sentence is *I sewed clothes and it made me tired*. In other words, the entity-denotation is used to express an event *I sew clothes*.

The event coercion requires the NP and the verb to work together: The event predicate activates a semantic pattern containing an implicit verb, which is actually a light verb v[DO]; the AGENTIVE role or the TELIC role of the subjective noun unifies with the qualia structure of this verb; then the implicit verb becomes a concrete verb which is associated with the NP. There are two factors contributing to the interpretation of the implicit verb, namely, the qualia structures associated with the subjective NP and the predicate.

In this sentence, the light verb DO is embodied in the context as *sew*, and the deep structure of the sentence is *I sewed clothes and it made me tired*. The AGENTIVE role of the *clothes* may be *sew* or *make*, while the TRUE ARGUMENT of the ARGSTR of the predicate *sew* is the fabric. In this way, the subjective noun *clothes* is associated with the predicate. The scheme of the event coercion of the clothes is shown below (Fig. 3).

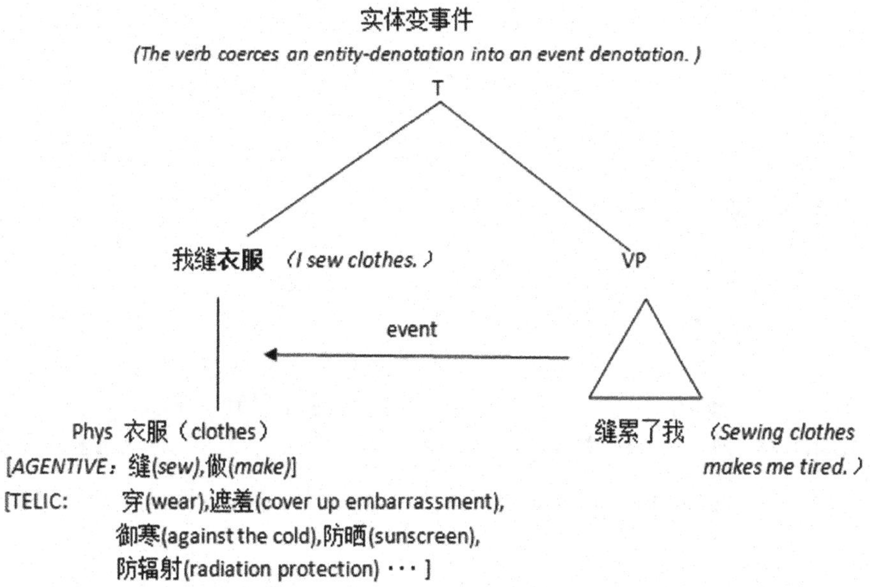

Fig. 3. The scheme of the event coercion of the *yifu* (clothes)

In addition, there are three examples that are shown below (Figs. 4 and 5):

4.蛋糕做累了我。
dangao zuo lei le wo
（Making cakes makes me tired.）

$$[\ <\text{PRO[DO]}\mathit{dangao}(\text{Cake}) > \text{CAUSE} < \mathit{wo}(\text{I})\text{BECOME}\ \mathit{leile}(\text{tired}) >\ ] \quad (2)$$

$$\begin{bmatrix} \text{蛋糕}\ \ \mathit{dangao}(\mathit{cake}) & \\ \text{ARGSTR} = \begin{bmatrix} \text{ARG}_1\text{=x:food\_ind} \\ \text{D-ARG}_1\text{=y:mass} \end{bmatrix} & \\ \text{QUALIA} = \begin{bmatrix} \text{CONST=y} \\ \text{FORMAL=x} \\ \text{TELIC=}\mathit{eat}(e_2,z,x) \\ \text{AGENTIVE=}\mathit{make}\text{\_act}(e_1,w,y) \end{bmatrix} & \end{bmatrix}$$

Fig. 4. The lexical representation for the noun *dangao* (cake)

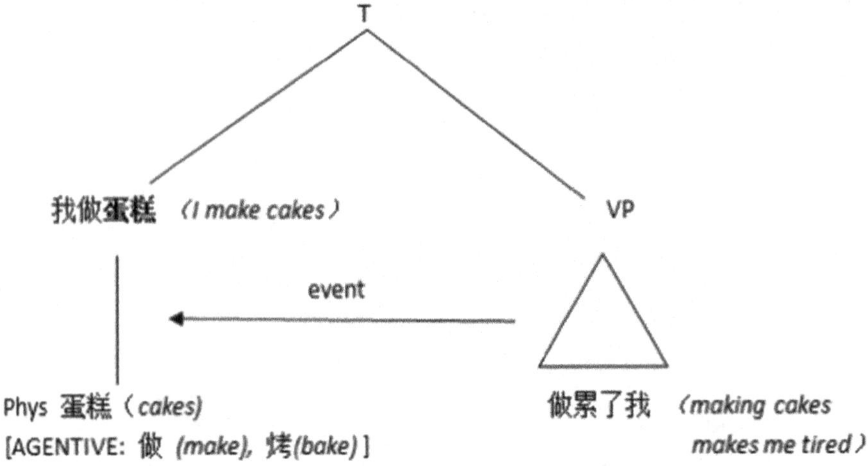

Fig. 5. The scheme of the event coercion of the *dangao* (cake)

5.蛋糕吃腻了我。
dangao chini le wo
(I am sick of eating cakes.)

$$[<\text{PRO[DO]}\textit{dangao}(\text{Cake}) > \text{CAUSE} < \textit{wo}(\text{I})\text{BECOME } \textit{ni le}(\text{sick}) >] \quad (3)$$

As in the example above, the AGENTIVE role of the cake is *zuo* (make), which is associated with the verb *zuo* (make), so the deep semantic structure of the sentence is *Making cakes makes me tired* (Fig. 6).

In the example 5 the TELIC role of the cake is *chi* (eat), which is associated with the verb *chi* (eat), so the deep semantic structure of the sentence is *I am sick of eating cakes* (Figs. 7 and 8).

6.这种书读傻了孩子。
zhezhong shu du sha le haizi
(Reading this kind of book makes the child become stupid.)

[<PRO[DO]这种书(*book*)>CAUSE<孩子(*child*) BECOME傻了(*stupid*)>]. (4)

The deep semantic structure of the sentence above is *reading this kind of book makes the child become stupid*, and the TELIC role of the *book* is *for people to read*, which unifies with the ARGSTR of the predicate *read*.

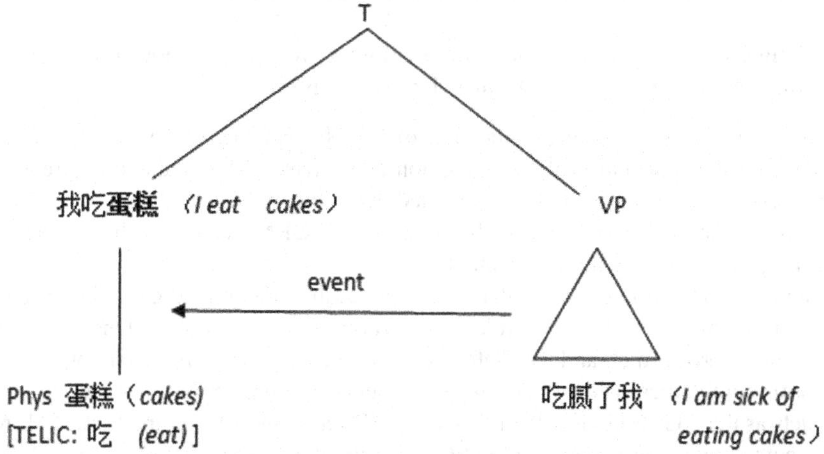

Fig. 6. The scheme of the event coercion of the "蛋糕" *(cake)*

$$\left[\begin{array}{l} \text{书}\,\textit{shu}\,(\textit{book}) \\ \\ \text{ARGSTR} = \left[\begin{array}{l} \text{ARG}_1\text{=x:information} \\ \text{ARG}_2\text{=y:phys\_obj} \end{array}\right] \\ \text{QUALIA} = \left[\begin{array}{l} \text{information} \cdot \text{phys\_obj\_lcp} \\ \text{FORMAL=hold(y,x)} \\ \text{TELIC=}\textit{read}\text{(e,w,x} \cdot \text{y)} \\ \text{AGENTIVE=}\textit{write}\text{\_act(e}_1\text{,w,y)} \end{array}\right] \end{array}\right]$$

Fig. 7. The lexical representation for the noun *shu* (book)

书*shu* (*book*)
FORMAL = *artifact* − *publication*(X•Y)
CONST = *paper*(X)•inf *ormation*(Y)
TELIC=(*readerA*)*read*(Y)
AGENTIVE=(*authorB*) ⟹ *press*(C)
write *publish*
partnership

Fig. 8. The lexical representation for the noun *shu* (book)

3 The Acceptability of an Expression as a Causer

3.1 The Great Influence of the Qualia Unification of the NP and the VP on the Acceptance of an Expression as a Causer

The paper analyses the qualia unification of the NP and the VP, which has a great influence on the acceptance of an expression as a Causer. The qualia structure of the expression as a causer is highly correlated with the qualia structure of the verb. The TELIC role of the NP more likely matches the FORMAL role of the VP, and the NP acting as a causer is more acceptable.

The co-composition of the qualia structures results in a derived causative meaning of the VP, where the AGENTIVE role of the action verb *she* (shoot) matches that of the complement verb *si* (die), and the FORMAL role of the action verb *she* (shoot) matches that of the complement verb *si* (die). In consequence, the AGENTIVE role of the action verb acts as the AGENTIVE role of the entire VP *shesi* (shoot), and the FORMAL role of the complement verb acts as the FORMAL role of the entire VP *shesi* (shoot). And according to the qualia unification, the TELIC role of the noun *jian* (arrow) is to cause death or injury, which unifies with that of the VP. So the *jian* (arrow) acts as a causer in the causative event is more acceptable. For example:

7. a.霍去病用乱箭射死了老虎。
   huo qubing yong luanjian shesi le laohu
   (Huo qubing shot the tiger with arrows.)
   b.乱箭射死了老虎。
   luanjian shesi le laohu
   (The arrows shot the tiger.)
8. a.顽皮的孩子用足球砸碎了食堂的玻璃。
   wanpi de haizi yong zuqiu zasui le shitang de boli
   (The naughty child smashed the glass of the canteen with a football.)
   b.足球砸碎了食堂的玻璃。
   zuqiu zasui le shitang de boli
   (The football smashed the glass of the canteen.)
9. a.药毒死了农妇的丈夫。
   yao dusi le nongfu de zhangfu
   (The medicine poisoned the husband of the peasant woman.)
   b.老鼠药毒死了农妇的丈夫。
   laoshuyao dusi le nongfu de zhangfu
   (The rat poison poisoned the husband of the peasant woman.)
   c.剧毒老鼠药毒死了农妇的丈夫。
   judu laoshuyao dusi le nongfu de zhangfu
   (The highly toxic rat poison poisoned the husband of the peasant woman.)

In 7b the TELIC role of the *jian* (arrows) is to shoot people or animals, which makes the arrows act as a causer of death more acceptable. In 8b the TELIC role of the *zuqiu* (soccer) is not to smash the object, which makes the soccer act as a causer less acceptable. In 9a the TELIC role of the *yao* (medicine) is to cure disease rather than make people sick or die, which makes the medicine act as a causer of death less acceptable. The TELIC role of the *laoshuyao* (rat poison) in 9b and the *judu laoshuyao* (highly toxic rat poison) in 9c are to make rats sick or die, which makes them act as a causer of death more acceptable. So the *laoshuyao* (rat poison) and the *judu laoshuyao* (highly toxic rat poison) acting as a causer of death respectively in the sentence are more acceptable than the *yao*(medicine).

3.2 The More Information the Expression Provides, the More Qualified It Is Likely to Be

The more information the expression provides, the more qualified it is likely to be. For example:

10. a.数学老师用那些难题考倒了所有的学生。
shuxue laoshi yong naxie nanti kaodao le suoyou de xuesheng
(Those difficult problems that the math teacher put forward baffled all the students.)
b.那些难题考倒了所有的学生。
naxie nanti kaodao le suoyou de xuesheng
(All the students were stumped by those difficult problems.)
11. a.数学老师用那些题目考倒了所有的学生。
shuxue laoshi yong naxie timu kaodao le suoyou de xuesheng
(Those problems that the math teacher put forward baffled all the students.)
b.那些题目考倒了所有的学生。
naxie timu kaodao le suoyou de xuesheng
(All the students were stumped by those problems.)

In 10b the TELIC role of the *nanti* (difficult problems) makes students more likely to fail the exam, which makes the difficult problems act as a causer of *kaodao (*failing the exam) more acceptable. In 11b the TELIC role of the *timu* (problems) is to check their mastery of knowledge, which makes it act as a causer of *kaodao (*failing the exam) less acceptable. The *nanti* (difficult problems) acting as a causer of *kaodao* (failing the exam) is more acceptable, because it is more specific than the "problem".

3.3 The More Significant Impact the Expression Has on the Patient, the More Qualified It Is Likely to Be

The more significant impact the expression has on the patient, the more qualified it is likely to be. In contrast, the NP below do not have a direct effect on the patient, and thus it can not act as a causer. In addition, the qualia structure of the NP is not unified with the qualia structure of the VP in the following sentences. For example:

12. a.我用课本捅开了大门。
wo yong keben tongkai le damen
(I opened the door with the textbook.)
b.? 课本捅开了大门。
?keben tongkai le damen
(? The textbook opened the door.)
13. a.姐姐洗被子洗湿了布鞋。
jiejie xi beizi xi shi le buxie
(The sister washing the quilt made the shoes wet.)
b.*被子洗湿了布鞋。
**beizi xi shi le buxie*
(*The quilt made the shoes wet.)

The qualia structure of the *shu* (book) is not unified with the qualia structure of the *tongkai* (open) in 12b. And The qualia structure of the *beizi* (quilt) is not unified with the qualia structure of the VP *xishi* (washing-wet) in 13b. Both of them do not have a direct effect on the recipient, and thus they can not act as a causer.

In summary, we find out that the acceptability of the expression of the causer is closely related to the following aspects: the more information the expression provides, the more qualified it is likely to be; the more significant impact the expression has on the patient, the more qualified it is likely to be; the qualia unification of the NP and the VP has a great influence on the acceptance of the causer.

4 Conclusion

Based on the qualia structure and the co-composition of the Generative Lexicon Theory, as well as the Light Verb Theory, we find out that the acceptability of the expression of the causer is closely related to the following aspects: the more information the expression provides, the more qualified it is likely to be; the more significant impact the expression has on the patient, the more qualified it is likely to be; the qualia unification of the NP and the VP has a great influence on the acceptance of the causer.

We also find out that the NP representing an entity acts as the causer in the sentence, in order to highlight the important information of the causative event, such as the *agent*, the *object*, and the means of the event, etc. And the NP expression of the causer of the event in the Causative resultative construction undergoes an event coercion. Thus the NP does not represent an entity but an event, in order to adapt to the causative event schema. This kind of operation is called event coercion. Logical metonymy as an event coercion is a kind of type coercion. The logical metonymy is a semantic operation that converts an argument to the appropriate type required by its governing verb, for instance, an entity represents an event. In this sense, the *event coercion* is a mechanism of semantic decompression. So the logical metonymy is caused by the mismatch of the semantic type and it can be explained by the semantic generative mechanism of type coercion.

This paper puts forward an unified interpretation model for the diverse sources of the causer. Because the causer is the initiator of the causal relation, all of the semantic components of the causing event can act as a causer. So this can explain why so many semantic components can be used as a causer in the causative construction. Therefore, when we analyze the semantic type of the causer, all the semantic components of the causing event should be considered.

Acknowledgment. This research was supported by the Social Science Funding project of Qingdao University of Science and Technology "A Study on Causative meaning of Verb-Resultative Construction in Mandarin Chinese Based on the Generative Lexicon Theory and the Minimalist Program" (2017). We hereby express our sincere thanks.

References

1. Pustejovsky, J.: The Generative Lexicon. MIT Press, Cambridge (1995)
2. Jiang, D.: Types and constructions of exocentric adjectives in Tibetan. In: Sun, M. et al. (eds.) CCL and NLP-NABD 2015. LNAI, vol. 9427, pp. 167–179. Springer, Heidelberg (2015). https://doi.org/10.1007/978-3-319-25816-4_14
3. Song, Z.Y.: The latest developments of generative lexicon theory. J. Lang. **44**, 1–14 (2011). The Commercial Press, Beijing
4. Pustejovsky, J., Elisabetta, J.: An Introduction to Generative Lexicon Theory. Oxford University Press, Oxford (2012)
5. Pustejovsky, J.: Type theory and lexical decomposition. In: Pierrette, B., Hitoshi, I., Kyoko, K., Chungmin, L. (eds.) Advances in Generative Lexicon Theory, pp. 9–38. Springer, Heidelberg (2013)
6. Pustejovsky, J.: Type construction and the logic of concepts. In: Pierrette, B. (ed.) The Language of Word Meaning, pp. 91–123. Cambridge University Press, Cambridge (2001)

Towards a Lexical Analysis on Chinese Middle Constructions

Lulu Wang(✉)

Department of Linguistics, Communication University of China, Beijing 100024, China
lulu.wang@cuc.edu.cn

Abstract. This paper aims to provide a formal analysis on Chinese middle constructions in a lexical approach. In analyzing the middle constructions, there are two prominent issues that are discussed: (1) how does the transitive complex predicate become intransitive in the middle constructions? (2) how to assign the semantic roles to the logical object and the implicit argument? To answer the first question, the study makes use of the argument composition technique to append the arguments together in HPSG (Head-driven Phrase Structure Grammar). Then this study makes use of a flat semantics analysis within the MRS (Minimal Recursive Semantics) framework to constrain the semantic relations. The analysis shows that a lexical approach can deal with the syntax-semantics interface issues of the middle constructions with complex predicates.

Keywords: Chinese middle constructions · Lexical representation Syntax-Semantics interface · MRS · HPSG

1 Introduction

Middles are believed to behave intermediately between the active and passive voice in many languages. Mandarin middles, such as (1a), are constructed in a similar way.

(1) a. 衣服 洗-好 了
clothes wash-done PERF.ASP
'The clothes have been washed.'

b. 我 洗-好 衣服 了
I wash-done clothes PERF.ASP
'I have washed my clothes.'

c. 衣服 被 我 洗-好 了
clothes BEI I wash-done PERF.ASP
'The clothes are washed by me.'

Since Chinese is a language following the SVO order, (1b) and (1c) are typical active and passive sentences. Compared to them, (1a) is a typical middle construction, where the logical object '衣服' (clothes) is in the sentence-initial position, and the logical subject '我' (I) is implicit, while the transitive predicate '洗-好' (washed) as in (1b) becomes intransitive in (1a), which expresses the 'state' of the subject NP. But

J.-F. Hong et al. (Eds.): CLSW 2018, LNAI 11173, pp. 236–244, 2018.
https://doi.org/10.1007/978-3-030-04015-4_20

how does the transitive predicate become intransitive in middle constructions? Moreover, how to assign the semantic roles to the logical object and the implicit argument? To answer these two questions, the study needs to analyze the relationship between the syntactic configuration and the semantic constraints of the argument taking predicates.

The paper is thus organized as follows: to start with, this study compares the different types of the middles, and the general features of the construction are summarized at the end of this section. In the following, the paper discusses the pros and cons of the two representative articles in analyzing the middle formation. The detailed analysis is given in Sect. 4, in which the paper analyzes the syntactic aspects of middles within HPSG and their semantic relations in MRS. A short conclusion is given in the end.

2 Phenomenon

So far, there are four most notable middle constructions that are suggested from earlier works [1–5]. It turns out that the differences mostly lie in the type of the predicates. The common feature of these predicates is that they are decomposable into one monosyllable verb and other constituents, which are illustrated in the following:

- 'V-起来' [1-2]

  (2) a. 这 本 书 读-起来 很 容易
  this CL book read-becoming very easy
  'This book reads easily.'

  b. 这 本 书 很 容易
  this CL book very easy
  'The book is very easy.'

  c. 他 跑-起来 很 快
  he run-becoming very fast
  'He runs very fast.'

- 'A-V' [3]

  (3) 这 个 面包 很 好-吃
  this CL bread very good-eat
  'This bread tastes very good.'

- 'V-A' [4]

  (4) 衣服 洗-好 了
  clothes wash-done PERF.ASP
  'The clothes have been washed.'

- '给-VP' [5]

  (5) 米饭 给 *(妈妈) 煮-糊 了
  rice GEI *(mom) cook-overcooked PERF.ASP
  'The rice was overcooked *(by mom).'

To note that, it is suggested that 'V-起来' is a 'dummy middle' construction [3], because the predicate '读-起来' can be omitted, as in (2b), and the logical subject '他' can be an agent, as in (2c). In addition, the 'A-V' construction is also problematic.

That is because predicates '好-吃' as 'A-V' are predicative adjectives, which are totally intransitive. In contrast, the other two types as in (4) and (5) share more features with middles in other languages, which are listed as follows:

(a) the logical objects ('衣服' and '米饭') are in the subject positions;
(b) the logical subjects ('妈妈') are implicit or suppressed;
(c) the transitive predicates ('洗-好' and '煮-糊') appear intransitive;
(d) the predicates denote some properties ('好' and '糊') of the subjects.

Further, the predicates are constituted as pairs of a monosyllable verb and a predicate adjective. And they could be classified as accomplishment verbs [6, 7]: [verb CAUSE pre-adj]. The verbal part is transitive action verb ('洗', '煮') and the predicate adjective ('好', '糊') is the result of the action.

3 Previous Studies on Middle Formation

Concerning the derivation of Mandarin middles, there are debates on the syntactic or presyntactic approach. In the following, this chapter introduces their suggestions and discusses their pros and cons.

3.1 The Presyntactic Approach

It is argued that the patient NP in a grammatical subject position is base-generated as external argument of the middle verb and that the logical subject of the middle verb is suppressed and present only at some presyntactic structure [4]. In short, middles like (1a) can be derived by the following lexical rules [4].

- Assign *arb* or *indef* to the external theta-role;
- Externalize (direct theta-role);
- Semantics: passives;
- Condition: the predicate has a high degree of transitivity.

This study agrees with the lexical approach to Chinese middles, but the above formation is not very clear to answer the following questions: firstly, the first two rules assign a generic or existential interpretation to the implicit argument and then externalize the direct theta-role of the verb. This process apparently conflicts with the claim that the patient NP is base-generated as external argument and the theta criterion.

Accordingly, it is necessary to make sure of the mapping of the theta-roles to the syntactic configuration. This study prefers a decomposable account of the complex predicate, and the theta-roles mapping to the relevant part of the complex predicate should be specified.

Next, it denotes the semantics as passive [4]. This assumption is not accurate. As Fagan [8] notes that 'middles are used to convey certain properties of their subjects…', the semantics of Chinese middles lies in the resultative part of the predicate, which is mostly filled by the predicative adjective. This can also be supported by the difference between middles and short passives.

(6) a. 衣服 洗-好 了
clothes wash-good PERF.ASP
'The clothes have been washed.'
b. ?衣服 被 洗-好 了
clothes BEI wash-good PERF.ASP
'The clothes are washed.'
(7) a. ?衣服 洗-坏 了
clothes wash-bad PERF.ASP
b. 衣服 被 洗-坏 了
clothes BEI wash-bad PERF.ASP
'The clothes are destroyed by washing.'

The slight difference between the two above examples is related to the meaning of passive. As Chinese passives require adversative meaning in the sentence, it is preferred to express the positive sentence without '被'. In this case, middle construction in (6a) is sounder with the positive adjective '好' (good), and short passive in (7b) is more acceptable with negative adjective '坏' (bad). Moreover, the two constructions also differ in information structure. That is because, middles are the answers to the question like (8a), while passives are the answers to (8b). The former one focuses on the property of the subject, but the latter one emphasizes the verbal action.

(8) a. 衣服 洗-得 怎么样 了?
clothes wash-DE how PERF.ASP
'How is the clothes-washing going?'
b. 衣服 怎么 坏 的?
clothes how bad DE
'How did you ruin the clothes?'

The last condition is vague too. It is true that the predicates in middles are in the high level of transitivity since the subject is affected by the predicate, which also includes a change of state. However, just as the vagueness of the concept of 'affectedness', this feature is not adequate to decide which predicate can be the predicate in middles. Rather, this study can specify the predicate in the lexicon that if it can be used in the middle construction.

3.2 The Syntactic Approach

It is claimed that '给-VP' is a typical middle construction, because '给' requires a semantic component 'external force' [5]. As middles require implicit argument, they believe the external force relates to the implicit agent. Thus, they assume '给' is obligatory in middle construction and sentences like (5) are not middles, but ergative. This paper agrees with the idea of '给-VP' as middles, but their account of ergative without '给' is not strong enough.

(9) a. 米饭 *自己 煮-糊 了
rice itself cook-overcooked PERF.ASP

b. 船 自己 沉 了
boat itself sink PERF.ASP
'The boat sank.'

(9b) is a typical ergative sentence, because the verb '沉' (sink) expresses the action itself without having a separate subject. However, the verb in (9a) is not deliberately or intentionally done by the doers, which is a typical feature of the middle construction.

The second issue is the middle formation, which is based on the 'small clause' account in Government and Binding theory [5]. To take (2) for example, since small clause lacks of complementizer and an inflection, the subject '米饭' (rice) of the small clause must move out of the clause to receive case and avoid violating the Case Filter Condition. And the predicate '糊' (overcooked) must also move out of the clause and combine with the main verb '煮' (cook) as a compound verb '煮-糊' (cook-overcooked) as the follows:

(10) a. [VP cook [SC rice overcooked]]
b. [IP rice$_i$ [VP cook [SC t$_i$ overcooked]]
c. [IP rice$_i$ [VP cook-overcooked$_j$ [SC t$_i$ t$_j$]]

As it is shown above, the syntactic formation requires NP-movement of the subject of the small clause, as well as the raising and combining the predicate. This is surely a strong account only if the main verb can take the other constituents as a small clause. However, based on the evidence below, the main verb '煮' (cook) cannot take small clauses as objects, but only undergoing entities.

(11) a. *我 煮-了 [米饭 糊 了]
I cook-ASP rice overcooked PERF.ASP
b. 我 煮-了 米饭
I cook-PERF.ASP rice
'I have cooked the rice.'

Hence, this paper prefers a lexical approach, rather than the syntactic one. To make the lexical one clearer, the next chapter will describe the syntactic and semantic properties of both the construction and the constituents within the construction in the next section.

4 A Lexical Account of Chinese Middles

In this section, the study gives a lexical account for the middle constructions with complex predicates. The syntactic structure is formalized within the framework of HPSG and particularly is integrated with the technique of argument composition. As for the semantics, the minimal recursive grammar (MRS) is adopted as a working grammar.

4.1 Complex Predicates

This paper reduces the complex predicates to verb-adjective pairs. The verbal part is a transitive verb and the other part is restricted to the predicative adjective. As the adjective functions as the predicate, not adjunct, this study suggests that the verbal part subcategorizes for the adjective via the argument composition technique in Head-driven Phrase Structure Grammar (HPSG) [9].

In the syntactic level, the verbal part as the matrix verb selects two NPs, together with the adjective part. For example, '洗' (wash) subcategorizes for an agent and a patient in active sentences. But in the middle construction, the agent is suppressed and the patient is in the subject position. There is also no object in the middle construction, which is taken by the adjective part instead.

(12) a. 妈妈 洗 衣服 了
mother wash clothes PERF.ASP
'Mother has washed the clothes.'
b. ?衣服 洗 了
clothes wash PERF.ASP
c. 衣服 洗-好 了
clothes wash-good PERF.ASP
'The clothes have been washed.'

The sentence in (12b) is questionable without the adjective part. This shows that the adjective predicate is required within the complex predicate. Then this is an extra valency of the adjective predicate with the double valences of the verbal part. For example, both the verbal part and the adjective select '衣服' (clothes) as an argument in addition with the implicit argument of 'someone'. This phenomenon is like the English VP-complement and German verb cluster, which is known as the 'incoherent' construction.

Hence, this paper adopts the argument composition mechanism to analyze the above complex predicate in Chinese. The mechanism is illustrated by the following formation, where the predicator consists of the verbal complement followed by the list of dependents of that same complement [10], which is shown in below (Fig. 1).

To take '洗' (wash) as an example, its lexical entry is described as follows (Fig. 2).

$$\left[\textbf{SUBCAT}\ \boxed{1} \oplus \left\langle \left[\textbf{V}\ \left[\textbf{SUBCAT}\ \boxed{1}\ \textit{list(synsem)}\right]\right] \right\rangle \right]$$

Fig. 1. The argument composition mechanism

$$\begin{bmatrix} \text{PHON}\left\langle x\check{i} \right\rangle \\ \text{SYN|LOC} \begin{bmatrix} \text{HEAD} \begin{bmatrix} \textit{verb} \\ \text{SUBJ } \boxed{2} \end{bmatrix} \\ \text{SUBCAT } \boxed{1} \oplus \left\langle \begin{bmatrix} \text{SYN|LOC} \begin{bmatrix} \text{HEAD } \textit{pred-adj} \\ \text{SUBCAT } \boxed{1} \\ \text{SUBJ } \boxed{2} \end{bmatrix} \end{bmatrix} \right\rangle \end{bmatrix} \end{bmatrix}$$

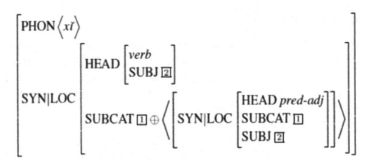

Fig. 2. The lexical entry of '洗' (wash)

4.2 Semantic Constraints

It is suggested that the main semantic properties of middles lie in the following three features [11]:

(a) implicit argument may appear overtly (in English, German and French) or existentially (in French);
(b) middles are noneventive, which do not describe actual events;
(c) middles are used to convey certain properties of their subjects.

Similarly, this study claims that Chinese middles with complex predicates also have these three properties. The following data support the first feature of the generical and existential nature of the implicit argument.

(15) a. 对于任何人来说，这些衣服洗好了
'As for anyone, these clothes have been washed.'
b. 对于某人来说，这些衣服洗好了
'As for someone, these clothes have been washed.'

This feature can also be clearly represented by the formal logic expression.

(16) a. (∀x1|people (x1)) (∃x2|衣服 (x2)) 洗-好 (x1, x2)
b. (∃x1|people (x1)) (∃x2|衣服 (x2)) 洗-好 (x1, x2)

In short, this paper assumes that the implicit argument (logical subject) is specified by the semantic restriction. Since the implicit argument is sup-pressed in the sentence, it is semantically underspecified. Then concerning the noneventive feature, this study does not take it as a requirement, because it makes no difference in Mandarin middles. Rather, the study pays more attention to the predicates, which require the semantic role mapping to the syntactic configuration. In detail, the verbal part takes an agent and a patient. The adjective takes only the theme. Since the patient and the theme refers to the same word, a flat semantics is required to capture the co-index relation between the semantic roles. This constraint can be easily described by the shared HANDLE values in MRS, which is shown in the following (Fig. 3).

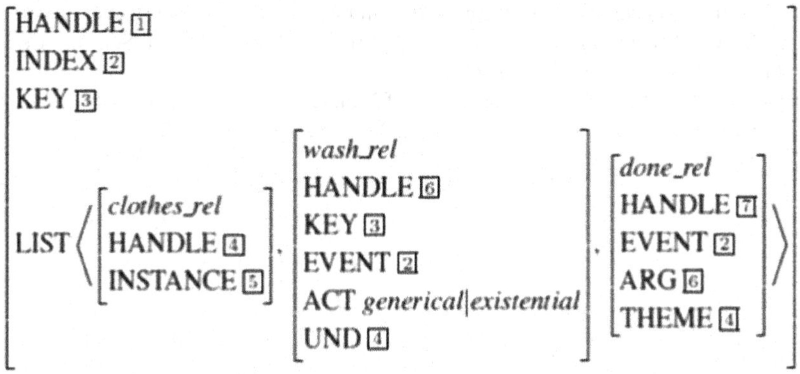

Fig. 3. The MRS for ‘衣服洗好了’ (The clothes have been washed.)

5 Conclusion

This paper has proposed a lexical analysis of Chinese middle constructions with complex predicates. To build up a formal grammar of the middle constructions, this study makes use of the argument composition technique to formalize the internal structure of the complex predicates; and a flat semantic account of structure sharing and underspecification of the semantic role mapping relations. The result shows that the lexical approach is reliable in dealing with the complicated syntax-semantics interface issues of the middle constructions with complex predicates.

Acknowledgments. Thanks are due to the anonymous reviewers of CLSW 2018 for the comments and the Research Projects of Communication University of China (CUC16B09, CUC18JL104) for the support. Special thanks go to Junping Zhang for her help in delivering the speech.

References

1. Sung, K.: Case assignment under incorporation. Ph.D. thesis, University of California at Los Angeles (1994)
2. Ji, X.: The middle construction in English and Chinese. Master’s Thesis, The Chinese University of Hong Kong (1995)
3. Furukawa, Y.: On the middle construction of modern Chinese. Chin. Linguist. **2**, 22–32 (2005)
4. Ting, J.: The middle construction in Mandarin Chinese and the presyntactic approach. Concentric: Stud. Linguist. **32**, 89–2006 (2006)
5. Shen, Y., Sybesma, R.: The derivational relation between the syntactic marker ‘给’ and several verbal constructions. Stud. Chin. Lang. (2010). (in Chinese)
6. Vendler, Z.: Verbs and times. Philos. Rev. **66**, 143–160 (1957)
7. Van Valin, R.D.: A synopsis of role and reference grammar. In: Advances in Role and Reference Grammar. John Benjamins Publishing Company, Amsterdam (1993)
8. Fagan, S.M.B.: The English Middle. Linguist. Inq. 181–203 (1988)

9. Hinrichs, E., Tsuneko, N.: Linearizing AUXs in German Verbal Complexes (1994)
10. Kathol, A., Przepiorkowski, A., Tseng, J.: Advanced topics in HPSG. In: Complex Predicates in Nonderivational Syntax (2000)
11. Fagan, S.M.B.: The Syntax and Semantics of Middle Constructions: A Study with Special Reference to German. Cambridge University Press, Cambridge (1992)

A Study of Color Words in Tang Poetry and Song Lyrics

Ying Yang, Zhijun Zheng, and Yanqiu Shao(✉)

Information Science School,
Beijing Language and Culture University, Beijing 100083, China
yqshao163@163.com

Abstract. Throughout history, litterateurs have always attached great importance to the use of color words in their works. Tang poetry and Song lyrics, the most brilliant parts of Chinese literature history, are perfect examples in using color words to create artistic conception and express the thoughts and feeling. In this paper, high-frequency color words that appear in "All-Tang Poetry" (The collection of ancient Chinese poetry in 618–907 A.D.) and "All-Song Poetry" (The collection of ancient Chinese lyrics in 960–1279 A.D.) are chosen as research objects, and the optimal algorithm is employed to study the collocation of the color words in Tang poetry and Song lyrics by comparing the effects of PMI and Word2vec extraction collocation. The detailed analysis of works of twenty poets in Tang and Song Dynasties are also carried out from both macro and micro perspectives, from the use of color words in "All-Tang Poetry" and "All-Song Poetry" to that specific works. As a result, most *"白 (white)"* in Tang poetry expresses frustration or sadness. *"红 (red)"*, the most popular word used in Song lyrics, expresses femininity, indicating that *"诗言志，词抒情 (Tang Poetry expresses aspiration and ambition, and Song lyrics express personal emotions between lovers.)"*.

Keywords: Tang poetry and Song lyrics · Color · Quantitative analysis
Collocation

1 Introduction

"The sense of color is the most popular form of common aesthetics [1]." and plays an important role in art. Since ancient times, litterateurs have been depicting images and expressing feelings using color words. Tang poetry and Song lyrics, as a vital part in Chinese literary history, are renowned for their use of color words. For example, the Chinese character *"白 (white)"*, *"红 (red)"*, *"绿 (green)"* were used in *"孤屿含霜白，遥山带日红 (The mountains are covered with white frost, and the distant peaks reflect the afterglow of the sun.)"* and *"绿杨芳草几时休，泪眼愁肠先已断 (When will the green poplar grass decay? My heart was already broken with tears in my eyes.)"*.

In these poems, a variety of different Chinese characters are often used to illustrate the same color, for example, *"红 (red)"*, *"朱 (vermilion)"*, *"丹 (scarlet)"*, *"绛 (magenta)"* and *"绯 (crimson)"* all refer to different categories of red. Although all words

J.-F. Hong et al. (Eds.): CLSW 2018, LNAI 11173, pp. 245–255, 2018.
https://doi.org/10.1007/978-3-030-04015-4_21

express the same color, there are subtle semantic differences among them and they appear in different collocations. Study of these nuances can help us better understand how poets express their emotions.

Numerous scholars have studied the use of color words in Tang poetry and Song lyrics, such as Cheng [2] who studied from the semantic perspective, Xu [3] from the cultural perspective, and Gu [4] from the translation perspective. This paper first selects representative colors with high frequency in “All-Tang Poetry” and “All-Song Poetry” as research objects, then investigates the similarities and differences in the use of colors between Tang poetry and Song lyrics, and uses PMI to extract color collocations for further analysis. The corresponding conclusion indicates the view that *“诗言志，词抒情 (Tang Poetry expresses aspiration and ambition, and Song lyrics express personal emotions between lovers.)”*.

2 High-Frequency Colors in Tang Poetry and Song Lyrics

In this paper, words in Tang Poetry (42,979) and Song lyrics (21,050) are sorted in descending order of frequency and words representing color are selected from the top 300 words (see Tables 1 and 2).

Table 1. The colors in the top 300 words of “All-Tang Poetry”

Color	白 (white)	金 (golden)	青 (blue, black or green)	红 (red)	黄 (yellow)	碧 (emerald)	绿 (green)	翠 (viridis)
Sort	31	55	59	152	155	241	245	271
Frequency	9183	7013	6719	4179	4048	2832	2807	2558

Table 2. The colors in the top 300 words of “All-Song Poetry”

Color	红 (red)	金 (golden)	青 (blue, black or green)	翠 (viridis)	黄 (yellow)	绿 (green)	碧 (emerald)	白 (white)	银 (sliver)	粉 (pink)
Sort	26	34	63	75	84	88	127	142	287	295
Frequency	5380	4701	3539	3282	3111	3043	2429	2225	1268	1226

Considering the existence of synonyms in Tang poetry and Song lyrics, for instance, *“红 (red)”*, *“朱 (vermilion)”*, *“绛 (magenta)”*, *“绯 (crimson)”* and *“丹 (scarlet)”* all express the meaning of red. Based on that, Figs. 1 and 2 are obtained by combining and processing the data from Tables 1 and 2.

Tang poetry usually conveys ambitions of intellectuals, while Song lyrics express poets’ tenderness. These two completely different emotions differ greatly in the use of color words. For example, as seen from Figs. 1 and 2, color words with the highest frequency in “All Tang Poetry” is *“白 (white)”*, and in “All Song Poetry” is

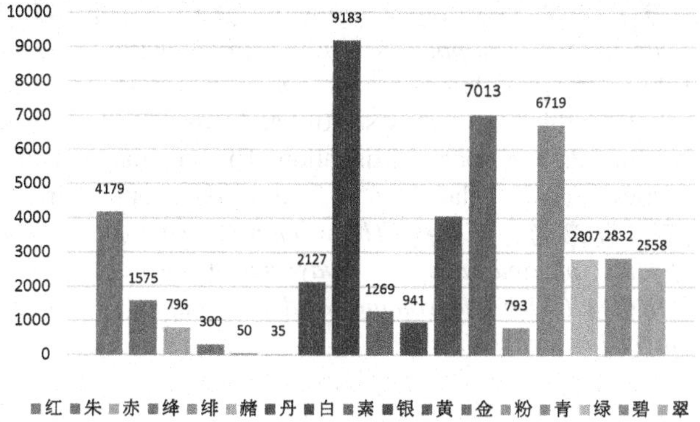

Fig. 1. Distribution of high frequency color words in "All Tang Poetry"

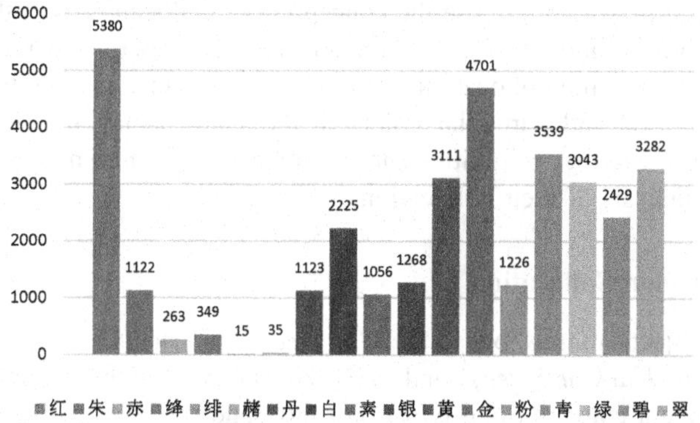

Fig. 2. Distribution of high frequency color words in "All Song Poetry"

"红 (red)". "白 (white)" in Tang poetry mostly refer to poets' lament for lost time, grief over the ups and downs of careers, and frustration for failing to realize lofty aspirations. *"红 (red)"* in the Song lyrics is always used to describe flowers and girls. Specifically, *"白 (white)"* expresses two different emotions in Tang poetry. One signifies fresh and bright feelings, while the other represents dignified and deep feelings. For the first meaning, the lighthearted emotions are often used in describing sceneries. For example, in the poem named *《金陵城西楼月下吟》 ("Reciting Poetry in the West Tower of Jinling City under Moonlight")*, the word *"白 (white)"* runs through the whole work. The poem reads: *"金陵夜寂凉风发，独上高楼望吴越。白云映水摇空城，白露垂珠滴秋月。(On a quiet night in Jinling, I climb the tall building alone to view the scenery of Wu Yue. White clouds droop, water shakes the empty city, and white dew are like drops of water from the autumn moon.)"* The *"白云" ("white clouds")* and *"白露" ("white dew")* added freshness to this poem. For the second meaning, just like what Li He wrote in *《寒江吟》 ("Recite the Cold Water of the River"): "冬至日光白，始知阴气凝。(He saw that the sun was no longer shining, so he knew that the weather became cold.)"*

and in *《灞上轻薄行》("A Leisurely Journey")*, *"此中生白发，疾走亦未歇 (He fought for his ideals and never stopped, so his hair turned white.)"*. *"白日光" ("White light")* is bright, but *"阴气" ("Yin Qi" here expresses a dark and oppressive atmosphere)* is very heavy, which expresses sorrow and dissatisfaction in his career [5]. These *"白 (white)"* words revel poets' frustration. The vast majority of *"红 (red)"* in the Song lyrics is related to flowers or girls, such as *"一曲啼乌心绪乱，红颜暗与流年换 (The woman played a guzheng tune on spring day, with the feeling of time passing away and beauty no longer existing.)"*, *"半妆红豆,各自相思瘦 (When the woman was dressing up, she remembered red bean and missed her lover far away.)"*.

3 Color Collocation in Tang Poetry and Song Lyrics

The study of collocation has always been a traditional topic in western vocabulary research. The first person to propose the conception of collocation is Firth (1957). The use of color words is indispensable when tracing the imagery and rendering atmosphere. By combining the collocations and colors, this paper intends to find out the most frequently used and particular colors in the Tang poetry and Song lyrics. Its purpose is to compare the similarities and differences of color synonyms through the extraction and analysis of their collocations.

3.1 Extract Color Collocation

The research objects in this paper are: *"红(red)"*,*"白 (white)"*,*"黄 (yellow)"*,*"粉 (pink)"*,*"青 (blue, black or green)"* and *"绿 (green)"*. Among these colors, *"红 (red)"* is the most frequent color in Song lyrics. For thousands of years, from state affairs to folklore, red holds an irreplaceable place in traditional Chinese culture. *"白 (white)"* is the most frequent color in Tang poetry, and it is also one of the traditional Five Colors but with a completely opposite meaning from *"红 (red)"*. So in this part we select color collocation of *"红 (red)"* and *"白 (white)"*.

By analyzing the frequency of words extracted from the left and right windows of color keywords, it turns out that most of the high-frequency combinations are in accordance with the word specification. However, depending on the word frequency only can not accurately extract all words that matches the color word. The commonly used improvement methods include the introduction of external dictionaries and the calculation of relevance. Yet the method of introducing an external dictionary is over-dependent on the quality of the dictionary, and its portability is poor. Therefore, this method is not employed in this paper. Instead, two main methods of correlation calculation, PMI and Word2Vec are adopted and by analyzing and comparing the two experimental results, the optimal results are selected as the following analyzed data.

3.1.1 PMI

In the relevant applications of data mining or information retrieval, the PMI [6–8] indicator is often used to measure the correlation between two things and defined as follows:

$$PMI(w_i, c_j) = log_2 \frac{p(w_i, c_j)}{p(w_i)p(c_j)} \quad (1)$$

In formula (1), $p(w_i, c_j)$ represents the probability of the target word w_i (color word) and the context word c_j appearing in the corpus simultaneously; $p(w_i)$ represents the probability of the target word w_i appearing in the corpus; $p(c_j)$ represents the probability of the context word c_j appearing in the corpus. PMI shows that the correlation between the target word w_i and the context word c_j is not only related to the probability of co-occurrence between them, but also to the probability of each other, which makes up for the disadvantage of relying only on co-occurrence word frequency to calculate correlation.

3.1.2 Word2Vec

Statistical linguistics generally study the relationship between words by discrete rather than intrinsic connections between words. Word2vec [9–11], launched by Google in 2013, is an efficient and open-source tool for representing words as real-valued vectors. With deep learning, it simplifies the processing of text content into vector (k-dimension) operations through training, and the similarity in vector space can be used to represent the semantic similarity of text. This method can fill the semantic gap between pocket words and to some extent, explore the internal semantic relationship between words.

The contents and titles containing *"红 (red)"* in Tang poetry and Song lyrics are extracted. Base on these data, the correlation between the top 200 words with the highest frequency and the color keywords are calculated via PMI and Word2Vec, and the top 100 words are selected as the relevant collocation of the color keywords according to the correlation. Through manual screening, 80% of the relevant collocations selected by PMI are found to be reasonable, but only 65% of the relevant collocations selected by Word2Vec meet the requirements. The reason for this phenomenon is the insufficient data and the scattered word distribution, which limits the performance of Word2Vec. Therefore, PMI algorithm is chosen for this experiment for collocation extraction.

3.2 Examples of Color Collocation

According to the frequency distribution of color words shown in Figs. 1 and 2, *"白 (white)"* has the highest using frequency in "All Tang Poetry" whereas *"红 (red)"* in "All Song Poetry". Taking the synonymous expressions of *"白 (white)"* and *"红 (red)"* into account, this experiment selects the specific expression of *"白 (white)"* for the collocation study by using the words *"白 (white)"* and *"素 (plain-colored)"*, at the same time, and selects the specific expression of *"红 (red)"* for the collocation study by using the words *"红 (red)"* and *"朱 (vermilion)"*. PMI method is used to statistically analyze the top 20 collocations that are most closely related to the words *"白 (white)"* and *"素 (plain-colored)"* in "All-Tang Poetry". And the top 20 collocations that are most closely related to the words *"红 (red)"* and *"朱 (vermilion)"* in "All-Song Poetry".

From Table 3, we can see that in ancient Chinese, both *"白 (white)"* and *"素 (plain-colored)"* can indicate the meaning of *"white"*, so their usages are similar in some respects. For instance, *"白 (white)"* and *"素 (plain-colored)"* are often used in combination with other morphemes or word collocations to form a compound. When *"白 (white)"* and *"素 (plain-colored)"* are combined with other words, they always present at the beginning, and in most cases, belong to the complex word formation with modifier-head construction, i.e. *"白 (white)"* + noun, or *"素 (plain-colored)"* + noun, such as *"白鹇"*, *"白袷"* and *"白纻"*; *"素柰"*, *"素莲"* and *"素云"*. Besides that, they can also form up, verb-object compounds such as ""*镊白" (夹取白须," clip off a white beard)* and *"点素, (点染绢素 dye the plain-colored silk).*

Table 3. Color synonyms *"白 (white)"* and *"素 (plain-colored)"* in "All-Tang Poetry"

X白	贞白	洁白	太白	镊白	煮白*	斑白	弄白*	李白	虚白	骑白*
X素	点素	将素*	映素*	拂素*	出素*	成素*	为素*	见素*	明素*	清素
白X	白鹇	白皙	白蝙*	白袷	白纻	白鼻	白苎	白刃	白璧	白蘋
素X	素貌	素柰	素莲	素沙	素帝	素云	素锦	素传*	素雪	素华

Note: No match with the * mark

In addition to similar usages, in terms of their different meanings, the word *"白 (white)"* also has a joint type when it is combined with other morphemes or words to form a compound word, that is, two similar roots that have the same meaning constitute a word, *"贞白"* and *"洁白"*. The word *"素 (plain-colored)"* in Tang poetry is mostly related to women. For example, *"素貌"* means face without makeup which especially refers to a female's face. *"素手"* in Li Shanpu's poem *《贫女》("the Poor Girl")*, as well as in *《三月三日》("March 3rd")* written by Bai Juyi, describes girl's slim and white hands.

Table 4 shows that in Song lyrics *"红 (red)"* and *"朱 (vermilion)"* are often combined with other morphemes or word collocations to form a compound. When *"白 (white)"* and *"素 (plain-colored)"* are combined with other words, they always present at the beginning of the phrase, i.e. *"红 (red)"* + noun, or *"朱 (vermilion)"* + noun. For example, *"红靴"*, *"红绫"*, *"红豆"* and *"朱扉"*, *"朱槿"*, *"朱邸"*. As for *"红 (red)"* alone, it is commonly used in Song lyrics as a metaphor for flowers, e.g. *"残红"* and *"乱红"*, both of which indicate faded flowers, and *"繁红"*, flourishing flowers. *"红 (red)"* is interpreted as *"赤帛之色 (a color mixture of both white and red)"*,which is closed to pink in *《说文解字》("Explaining Graphs and Analyzing Characters")*, the first Chinese dictionary, compiled by Xu Shen, 121 A.D. Compared with *"朱 (vermilion)"*, *"红 (red)"* presents a kind of flexibility and is more used to depict flowers. *"红 (red)"* is also used as a metaphor for *"血 (blood)"* in the Song lyrics, such as *"猩红 (bloodred)"*, which is between red and orange, and *"啼红"* is also called

"啼血". It means continuous mournful sobbing until the throat is bleeding. Neither *"红 (red)"* in *"猩红"* nor in *"啼红"* stands for the traditional sense of red. It refers to dark red like the color of blood. In terms of *"朱 (vermilion)"*, it is interpreted as *"赤心木，五行属木 (red heart wood, one of the five elements–wood)"*. Therefore, *"朱 (vermilion)"* used in ancient Chinese normally describe the color of buildings or part of a building, and it is regarded as a positive color. *"朱邸"* refers to the princes' house with doors in *"朱 (vermilion)"* color. *"朱扉"* is also interpreted as a door in *"朱 (vermilion)"* color, and *"朱牖"* is explained as a window in *"朱 (vermilion)"* color.

Table 4. Color synonyms *"红 (red)"* and *"朱 (vermilion)"* in "All-Song Poetry"

X 红	江红*	猩红	摇红*	残红	乱红	繁红	嫣红	蒸红*	题红*	啼红
X 朱	研朱	损朱*	餍朱	返朱*	扃朱*	薇朱*	茫朱*	薄朱*	捐朱*	挽朱*
红 X	红靴	红盐	红豆	红绫	红蕖	红蓼	红药	红旌	红牙	红尘
朱 X	朱扉	朱槿	朱夏	朱邸	朱雀	朱索	朱牖	朱燎	朱楹	朱绂

Note: No match with the * mark

4 Specific Use of Colors

From the perspective of the development law of literature, representative works can reflect the literary characteristics of specific historical periods. Therefore, famous poets of Tang and Song dynasties are selected to investigate the use of colors.

4.1 Colors in Poetry Works

According to the research results of Wang [12, 13], this paper selects the works of the ten famous poets in Tang and Song dynasties respectively, to study the high-frequency color words in their works. Due to the difference in the number of works, it is impossible to directly compare the number of color words occurrences. Therefore, the frequency of color words is divided by the number of works of poets respectively to obtain the frequency of each color word in the poet's works. And the frequency results are expanded by one hundred times.

As shown in Fig. 3, the use of color words in the poems of ten famous poets in Tang Dynasty presents certain rules. From the macro trend of the graph, the ten poets have some similarity in the use of color words, *"白 (white)"* is the color favored by all ten poets, especially by Li Bai, Liu Yuxi and Bai Juyi. The use frequency of *"白 (white)"* in Li Bai's works is significantly higher than that of other poets. Among Li Bai's nearly 1,000 poems, *"白 (white)"* appears for 570 times. Everything in Li Bai's eyes can be whitened, as we can see in Li Bai's verses *"且放白鹿青崖间 (Herding white deer in the green cliffs for the time being.)"*, *"白首太玄经 (He devoted all his life to reading. Although his hair was white, he was still writing Tai Xuan Jing.)"*, *"乌啼白门柳 (It's the white willow tree with the crowing birds.)"* and so on. As Yuan [14] put it, "perhaps because Li Bai likes things that are bright and clean, the most used color word in his poems is white. In his creative writing, almost everything can be white." By classifying the *"白 (white)"* in Li Bai's poetry, it is found that Li Bai's *"白 (white)"*, in addition to its original meaning "white", also contains the emotion of sadness or ethereal. For example, in Li Bai's poem *《古诗三十九首》("Thirty-nine Ancient Poems")*, the *"白 (white)"* of *"白日掩徂晖，浮云无定端 (The sun conceals the brilliance of the sunset, and there is no fixed place for the clouds.)"* expresses the sadness because sunset is covered by clouds. In Li Bai's poem *《书情赠蔡舍人雄》("a Poem to the Friend Cai Xiong")*, the *"白 (white)"* of *"白璧竟何辜，青蝇遂成冤 (The flies have smeared the white jade. Li Bai compares himself with white jade here and expresses his situation of being slander by villains.)"* shows his lamentation with a sense of frustration, helplessness and fear. And in Li Bai's other poem *《望终南山寄紫阁隐者》("a Poem Sent to the Recluse in the Zhongnan Mountain")*, the *"白 (white)"* of *"有时白云起，天际自舒卷 (There were white clouds floating above the sky, and they stretched freely in the sky.)"* reflects the poet's indulgence in natural sceneries [15].

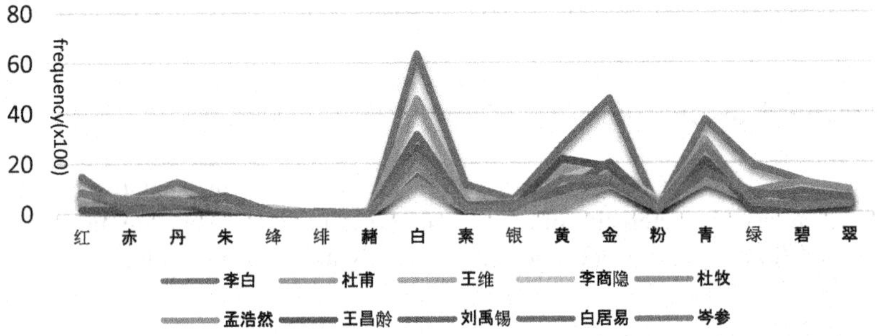

Fig. 3. The color distribution in the works of representative poets in Tang dynasty

In order to better reflect the use of *"白 (white)"* in representative works of the poet, this paper specifically studied the top five highest frequency collocations with *"白 (white)"*. They are *"白鹇 (silver pheasant)"*, *"白纻 (white ramie)"*, *"白皙 (fair-skinned)"*, *"白髭 (shirahige)"* and *"白蘋 (white apple)"*. *"白鹇"* is a kind of bird with gorgeous mane hair and white feathers. In ancient times, it was embroidered on the clothes of senior officials. *"白纻"* could refer to the robe made by white ramie, which was worn by ancient scholars when they did not get any titles in the national examination. *"白蘋"* is a kind of plant which blooms in the late summer and early fall. Its color is pure and white, which symbolizes elegance. The ten poets mentioned above are either working in the government or looking forward to being able to serve for the government and devote themselves to the battlefield. This also represents the values of mainstream intellectuals at that time. These phrases can be used when expressing determination to build a successful career, ups and downs in their life, and praise for noble interests. Therefore, the phrases above reflect the inner world of the poets to some extent.

Figure 4 shows the use of color words by ten famous poets in Song dynasty and also presents certain rules. The macro trends in the distribution of the use of color words are basically the same. The frequencies of the use of *"红 (red)"* and *"金 (golden)"* are relatively high, and the frequencies of the use of *"赤 (dark red)"*, *"绯 (crimson)"*, and *"赭 (ochre)"* are relatively low. In order to find out why the poets of Song lyrics prefer the words *"红 (red)"* and *"金 (golden)"*, the paper specifically studied the top five highest frequency collocations with *"红 (red)"* and *"金 (golden)"* (as shown in Table 5).

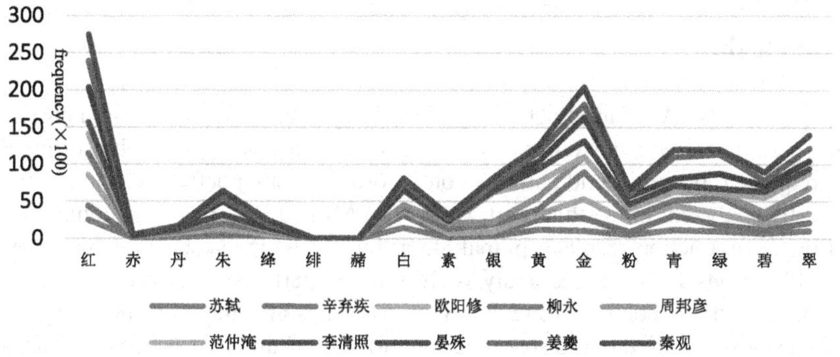

Fig. 4. The color distribution in the works of representative poets in Song dynasty

Table 5. Collocations with *"红 (red)"* and *"金 (golden)"* in the works of ten poets of Song lyrics

红	红绡	姹红	红旌	红蓼	红萼
金	金銮	金钏	金粟	金盆	金齑

In the table above, *"红绡"* refers to a kind of red silk fabric; *"姹红"* is often interpreted as a blooming flower. *"金銮"* means the decoration of the emperor's chariots and horses; *"金钏"* and *"金粟"* are names of jewelry; *"金齑"* refers to delicate food which are cut into small pieces.

Based on the data, most of the collocations with *"红 (red)"* refer to flowers and plants. Most of the collocations with *"金 (golden)"* are related to luxurious decorations and feasts. The original function of Song lyrics is to entertain guests so it is not surprising that there are a lot of collocation related to flowers, trees and entertainment in Song lyrics.

4.2 Comparison of Colors in the Works of Famous Poets

In terms of similarities, the use frequency of *"金 (golden)"* and *"黄 (yellow)"* in the Tang poetry and Song lyrics are relatively high, while that of *"绛 (magenta)"* and *"绯 (crimson)"* are relatively low.

In terms of differences, the most frequently used color in Tang poetry is *"白 (white)"*, while that in Song lyrics is *"红 (red)"*; when expressing the same color "green", Tang poetry commonly used *"碧 (emerald)"*, while Song lyrics mostly used *"翠 (viridis)"*; compared with Tang poetry, *"银 (sliver)"* is used more frequently in Song lyrics.

In general, the color in Tang poetry expresses the poet's depression, while the color in Song lyrics describes the life full of beauties and enjoyments.

5 Conclusion

This paper selects "All-Tang Poetry" and "All-Song Poetry" as the research corpus. In the first part, high-frequency color words are chosen as research subject by sorting their word frequency. In the second part, the color words of Tang poetry and Song lyrics are specifically analyzed. In the third part, values of PMI and Word2vec are compared and based on the extraction results, optimal algorithm (PMI) is chosen to extract specific color collocations for semantic analysis. In the last part, uses of color words in the works of ten famous poets of Tang and Song dynasties are studied respectively, and a statistical study is carried out to show the similarities and differences between Tang and Song lyrics in color use. The experiment verifies that as for the extraction of short Tang poetry and Song lyrics texts, the traditional method is more suitable for collocation than mainstream word vectors. Meanwhile, we find that *"白 (white)"* is frequently used in Tang poetry, whereas in Song lyrics *"红 (red)"* are more common. This finding is in line with the mainstream view that *"诗言志，词抒情(Tang Poetry expresses aspiration and ambition, and Song lyrics express personal emotions between lovers.)"*.

Acknowledgments. This research was funded by the National Natural Science Foundation of China (No. 61872402), Humanities and Social Science Planning (No. 17YJAZH068) supported by the Ministry of Education and the Graduate Innovation Fund (No. 18YCX004) supported by Beijing Language and Culture University. We hereby express our sincere thanks.

References

1. Central Compilation and Translation Bureau: Karl Marx and Frederick Engels. People's Publishing House, vol. 13, p. 145 (1962)
2. Cheng, J.: A study on the meaning of monosyllabic color words in the category of "black" in the Tang poetry. J. Qinghai Normal Univ. Philos. Soc. Sci. **39**(06), 115–121 (2017)
3. Xu, C.: Cultural Analysis of "green" Color Combination Words in Ancient Poetry. Yunnan Normal University, Kunming (2008)
4. Gu, C.: Studies on Color Images in Tang and Song Poetry and Their Translation. Liaoning Normal University, Dalian (2010)
5. Xuan, Y.: Emotional expression of "white" in Tang poetry. Master **16**, 80–81 (2010)
6. Yuan, L.: A word clustering algorithm based on mutual information. Syst. Eng. **26**(5), 120–122 (2008)
7. Wang, Z., Wu, Z., Hu, F.: Calculation of emotional polarity of words based on HowNet and PMI. Comput. Eng. **38**(15), 187–189 (2012)

8. Ma, H., Z, Z., Xuefeng, Z., Zhao, X., Su, F.: Synonymous extraction combining latent semantic analysis and point mutual information. Comput. Knowl. Technol. Acad. Exch. **1**, 128–132 (2014)
9. Bengio, Y., Ducharme, R., Vincent, P., Janvin, C.: A neural probabilistic language model. J. Mach. Learn. Res. **3**, 1137–1155 (2003)
10. Handler, A.: An empirical study of semantic similarity in WordNet and Word2Vec. University of New Orleans Theses and Dissertations (2014)
11. Luo, J., Wang, Q., Li, Y.: Word clustering based on Word2vec and semantic similarity. In: China Automation Society Control Theory Specialized Committee, China Institute of systems engineering. The thirty-third China control conference paper (A volume). China Automation Society Control Theory Specialized Committee, China Institute of Systems Engineering, p. 5 (2014)
12. Wang, Z.: The ranking of Tang poetry. **12**(1), 10–13 (2013)
13. Wang, Z., Yu, Y., Guo, H.: The ranking of Song Ci poetry. **1**(1), 15–17 (2012)
14. Yuan, X.: History of Chinese literature. **7**(1), 153–154 (2005)
15. Hua, Z., Ye, J.: An analysis of implication of "white" in Li Bai's poetry. Author **10**, 136–137 (2011)

A SkE-Assisted Comparison of Three "Prestige" Near Synonyms in Chinese

Longxing Li[1,2(✉)], Chu-Ren Huang[1], and Xuefeng Gao[1]

[1] Department of Chinese and Bilingual Studies, The Hong Kong Polytechnic University, Hong Kong, China
yb67707@umac.mo, churen.huang@polyu.edu.hk, gaoxuefeng0812@163.com

[2] Department of English, University of Macau, Macao, China

Abstract. The discrimination of near synonyms is one of the most important research areas in lexicology and lexical semantics. Traditional comparative studies of near synonyms are mostly introspection-based and corpus-based, both having disadvantages. Sketch Engine (SkE), a tool designed to automatically obtain grammatical and collocational relations of target words from huge amount of data, helps to avoid subjectivity and solves the problem of utilizing the massive amount of data efficiently. By making use of various functions of Chinese Word Sketch (CWS), this paper distinguishes three Chinese synonymous words *mingwang*, *shengwang* and *weiwang* and finds that *shengwang* and *weiwang* are closer in meaning and more similar in grammatical features. Our comprehensive detailed examination of similarities and differences between the three words through CWS will shed light on Chinese lexicography, near synonym discrimination as well as Chinese vocabulary teaching and learning.

Keywords: Chinese Word Sketch · Near synonym discrimination
Mingwang · *Shengwang* · *Weiwang*

1 Introduction

Discrimination of near synonyms is an important but difficult task in teaching Chinese as a foreign language and even as a native language. The precise use of synonyms plays a significant role in idiomatic spoken and written expression. To facilitate learners' acquisition of Chinese synonyms, many scholars have conducted studies with different methods. Wang and Huang [1] summarized two stages that the academia has gone through regarding the methods used in distinguishing synonyms. The first stage is the manual data collection stage, relying on researchers' introspection and experience. The second is the corpus-based stage which obtains KWIC from a corpus and requires a big amount of human resources to process the huge number of data. The corpus-based approach has been adopted by many scholars to solve the difficult problem of distinguishing synonyms [2–6]. However, previous research tends to be subjective and limits their attention to individual pairs of synonyms, neglecting the utilization of the innovative corpus query tool Word Sketch and the formation of a systematic framework for synonym discrimination. Being able to obtain grammatical and collocational relations

J.-F. Hong et al. (Eds.): CLSW 2018, LNAI 11173, pp. 256–266, 2018.
https://doi.org/10.1007/978-3-030-04015-4_22

of the target words and reflect the differences and features between synonyms through huge amount of authentic data, Word Sketch Engine is regarded as the tool in the third stage of synonym discrimination [1].

Academia Sinica, in collaboration with the SkE team, developed Chinese Word Sketch (CWS). Because of its good performance in corpus linguistics, SkE and CWS have been applied to many studies [7–9]. However, the potential of SkE revealed by Ge [10] has not been full tapped. Thus, this article attempts to discriminate at one time through CWS three Chinese synonymous words, namely 名望 *mingwang*, 聲望 *shengwang* and 威望 *weiwang*, and find out their lexical and grammatical features as well as their similarities and differences. The detailed demonstration and explanation of the process is expected to provide Chinese language learners and educators a way of explorative autonomous learning with the assistance of CWS and corpora. The paper is organized as follows: Sect. 2 examines the basic meanings of the three words in dictionaries and their distribution in the Chinese Gigaword corpus; Sect. 3 is devoted to a thorough investigation of the three words' behavior and the cross-Strait comparison of each words; Sect. 4 is a summary of the whole paper.

2 Three Words in Dictionary and Corpora

As shown in Table 1, the meanings of the three words in dictionaries are very similar to each other and hard to distinguish, with *prestige* as the shared corresponding word in English. Obviously, the dictionary explanation is far from enough for learners to tell the nuances between these words. In addition, the three words have not been studied together so far. Therefore, the following parts will be devoted to a detailed examination of the three words utilizing Chinese Gigaword corpus via CWS.

Table 1. Explanation of *mingwang, shengwang* and *weiwang* in the dictionary

	現代漢語詞典(第 7 版) The Contemporary Chinese Dictionary (The 7th Edition)	新時代漢英大詞典 New Age Chinese-English Dictionary
名望 *mingwang*	好的名声；声望：頗有~	prestige, renown
聲望 *shengwang*	为众人所仰望的名声：國際~/~日隆	popularity, prestige, repute
威望 *weiwang*	声誉和名望：國際~	prestige

This article makes use of the part-of-speech tagged Chinese Gigaword corpus data (Gigaword2all, 831,748,000 words), which is composed of three sub-corpora of news texts from Central News Agency in Taiwan (Gigaword2cna, 501,456,000 words), Xinhua News Agency in Mainland (Gigaword2cna, 311,660,000 words), and Lianhe Zaobao in Singapore (Gigaword2zbn, 18,632,000 words) [11]. While the search from Gigaword2all finds that the frequency of *shengwang, weiwang* and *mingwang* ranks from high to low, the frequency of the same word used in Taiwan and Mainland is quite different. The frequency of *mingwang* and *weiwang* per million words in Taiwan corpus is lower than in Mainland corpus. However, *shengwang* is another way around, with its frequency about 7.8 times higher than that of Mainland, which also contributes to its high frequency in Gigaword2all. For Gigaword2xin, *weiwang* has the highest frequency, with *shengwang* and *mingwang* following behind, which is in concordance with that of BCC corpus [12]. Compared with the somewhat even distribution of the three words in Mainland, the use of *shengwang* in Taiwan is dominant, reflecting the preferences and different word usages between Taiwan and Mainland (Table 2). The following sections compare at first the three words in Gigaword2all corpus to present their similarities and differences in terms of lexical and grammatical relations, and then try to identify some features of each word use across the strait.

Table 2. Frequency of *mingwang*, *shengwang* and *weiwang* in corpora

	名望 *mingwang*		聲望 *shengwang*		威望 weiwang	
Corpora	freq.	freq./million	freq.	freq./million	freq.	freq./million
Gigaword2all	417	0.50	9297	11.18	1631	1.96
Gigaword2cna	164	0.33	8540	17.03	509	1.02
Gigaword2xin	225	0.72	683	2.19	1087	3.49
BCC	1530	1.53	2981	2.98	3263	3.26

3 CWS-Assisted Comparison

3.1 Obtaining Similar Words from *Thesaurus*

The *Thesaurus* function within CWS can automatically generate similar words for target words. We set *Maximum number of items* to 20 and then click the button *Show Similar Words*, the results are produced. The six most similar words for each target word are shown in Table 3. Although *weiwang* is the most similar word to *mingwang*, their similarity is only 0.158. However, the similarity between *weiwang* and *shengwang* is 0.254. It is inferred that *shengwang* and *weiwang* are closer semantically and grammatically, which will be further explored and confirmed through *Sketch Diff.*

3.2 Obtaining Grammatical Patterns Through *Word Sketch*

The Word Sketch function helps to illustrate the relations the target word has and the salient words within the relation. We set the *minimum frequency* at 5, input each word and click *Show Word Sketch*, then the results are produced. As shown in Table 4, there are more grammatical patterns for *shengwang* and *weiwang* than for *mingwang*.

However, this does not mean *mingwang* has no such relation like *and/or*. If we set the *minimum frequency* lower, other relations may emerge. For instance, words like

Table 3. Similar words of *mingwang, shengwang* and *weiwang*

名望 mingwang		*聲望 shengwang*		*威望 weiwang*	
similar word	similarity	similar word	similarity	similar word	similarity
威望 weiwang	0.158	支持率 zhichilv support rate	0.394	威信 weixin prestige	0.384
愛澳 ai'ao love macao	0.144	支持度 zhichidu support degree	0.297	聲譽 shengyu reputation	0.266
盛譽 shengyu great fame	0.142	聲譽 shengyu reputation	0.286	聲望 shengwang	0.254
權勢 quanshi power	0.129	知名度 zhimingdu popularity	0.265	信譽 xinyu credit	0.235
名氣 mingqi reputation	0.126	聲勢 shengshi momentum	0.258	可信度 kexindu trustworthiness	0.234
建樹 jianshu attainment	0.12	威望 weiwang	0.254	公信力 gongxinli credibility	0.232

Table 4. Grammatical patterns of *mingwang, shengwang* and *weiwang*

	Possession[a]	Possessor	Object_of	Subject_of	A_Modifier	N_Modifier	Modifies	Measure	and/or
mingwang	√	√	√			√	√		
weiwang	√	√	√	√	√	√	√	√	√
shengwang	√	√	√	√	√	√	√		√

[a] *Possession* represents the objects belonging to the target words, like cover belongs to the book in the expression *書的封面* (shu de fengmian, the cover of the book). The *Possession* results of the three target words produced by CWS are incorrect. For example, CWS treats *領導人* (*lingdaoren*, *leader*) as a possession of *威望* (*weiwang*, authority), which is illogical. In the article, we cleared the mistakes and combined *Possession* and *Possessor* to form the category of possessive relations.

影響力 *yingxiangli influence*, 地位 *diwei status* and 聲譽 *shengyu fame* emerge in the *and/or* relation for *mingwang* at the *minimum frequency* of 2. As for *shengwang* and *weiwang*, their *and/or* relation is more salient, collocating with nouns as 地位 *diwei status*, 資歷 *zili qualification*, 成就 *chengjiu achievement*, and 能力 *nengli capacity*. Meanwhile, *mingwang* seldom has adjective modifiers and is rarely used as a subject. In contrast, *shengwang* and *weiwang* usually find adjective modifiers like 崇高 *chonggao lofty* and 高 *gao high*, and subjects like 提高 *tigao improve* and 下降 *xiajiang fall*.

Table 4 also reveals that *shengwang* can be "measured". However, the quantifiers generated by the SkE like 位 *wei*, 個 *ge*, 種 *zhong*, 所 *suo*, 年 *nian*, 項 *xiang* are mismatches in most cases. For instance, in sentence (1), 位 *wei* is not a quantifier of *shengwang*, but of *social democrat*. The same is true for *mingwang* and *weiwang* if we lower the *minimum frequency* to produce results in *Measure*.

(1) 培瑞斯 是 一 **位** 聲望 不 佳 的 社會民主黨員。
Péiruìsī shì yī ***wèi*** *shēngwàng bù jiā de shèhuìmínzhǔdǎngyuán*
Perez BE one **CL** reputation NEG good DE Social Democrat.
Perez is **a** Social Democrat with poor reputation.

After examining manually the generated quantifiers for the three words, we conclude that the three words rarely have quantifiers. 種 (*zhong, type/kind*) in sentence (2) is the quantifier which can collocate with *shengwang* and *weiwang*, while 項 (*xiang, item*) is found in only one case collocating with *shengwang*. No quantifier matches with *mingwang* in the corpus.

(2) 他 沒有 那 **種** 威望。
tā méiyǒu nà ***zhǒng*** *wēi wàng*
he NEG has that **CL** authority
He does not have that **type** of authority.

3.3 Obtaining *Common Patterns* and *Only Patterns* via *Sketch Diff*

The *Sketch Diff* function can compare two words at a time, generating common patterns and exclusive patterns of each pair. We keep the default setting of the *minimum frequency* at 5, *maximum number of items in a grammatical relation of the common block* at 25, and *maximum number of items in a grammatical relation of the exclusive block* at 12, and click *Show Diff* button. Common patterns and only patterns of *mingwang* and *weiwang* are illustrated in Table 5 as an example. Although the listed words can collocate with both target words, their tendency is different. The color chain from green to red (left to right) indicates the tendency, which means the greener a word is, the more likely it collocates with *mingwang*.

After comparing the target words two by two, we synthesize the results and present their common and only patterns in Tables 6, 7, 8 and 9. As for their common patterns shown in Table 6, it is found that: (1) *Shengwang* and *weiwang* share common patterns in seven out of the eight grammatical relations, which is in consistence with the inference through *Thesaurus* in Sect. 3.1; (2) The three words are similar in three aspects, i.e., all of them may have possessive relation with 人士 *renshi personnage,* 人 *ren person,* 他 *ta he*; they can be the objects of 享有 *xiangyou enjoy* and 具有 *juyou possess*; and they can all be modified by noun modifier 社會 *shehui society*. The common collocations of the three words can be regarded as a starting point for learners in learning the three words and a must for learners to acquire, suggesting instructors in making decisions on vocabulary teaching syllabus.

Table 5. Common patterns of *mingwang* and *weiwang*

名望 *mingwang* 21 14 7 0 -7 -14 -21 威望 *weiwang*				
Patterns	Freq.		Salience[a]	
	mingwang	*weiwang*	*mingwang*	*weiwang*
Possession	**192**	**211**	**18.0**	**3.6**
人士 renshi personnage	18	5	18.3	7.6
人 ren person	8	5	8.2	5.2
Possessor	**27**	**391**	**2.5**	**6.7**
他 ta he	9	33	16.0	17.6
Object_of	**70**	**709**	**1.2**	**2.2**
享有 xiangyou enjoy	8	250	23.6	68.3
具有 juyou possess	5	18	13.1	17.1
N_Modifier	**40**	**326**	**0.5**	**0.7**
社會 shehui society	5	9	11.2	9.3

[a] Salience is the *MI log Frequency*, please refer to the *Statistics used in SkE* for detail via: https://www.sketchengine.co.uk/documentation/statistics-used-in-sketch-engine/#top.

Table 6. Common patterns of *mingwang, shengwang and weiwang*

Grammatical relations	*Mingwang & shengwang*	*Mingwang & weiwang*	*Shengwang & weiwang*	all
Possession	人士 personage, 專家 expert, 律師 lawyer, 大學 university, 人 person	人士 personage, 人 person	政治家 politician, 人士 personnage, 領袖 leader, 人 person	人士 personage, 人 person
Possessor	他 he	他 he	他 he, 個人 individual, 總統 president, 自己 self, 黨 party, 聯合國 UN, 政府 government	他 he
Subject of_			提高 improve,高 high	
Object of_	享有 enjoy, 具有 possess, 素有 always have, 負 carry	享有 enjoy, 具有 possess	享有 enjoy, 具 possess, 提高 improve, 提升 raise, 使 make, 具有 possess, 樹立 set up, 擁有 own, 有損 harm, 建立 establish, 贏得 win, 利用 use, 建立起 set up, 損害 harm, 降低 lower, 領導 lead	享有 enjoy, 具有 possess
N_Modifier	職業 occupation, 社會 society	社會 society	國際 international, 政治 political, 個人 individual, 社會 society, 道德	社會 society
			virtue, 國家 national, 政府 government	
A_Modifier			崇高 lofty,高 high	
and/or			資歷 qualification, 地位 status,成就 achievement, 能力 capability, 權力 power	

Sharing similarities as shown above, the three words also differ in many ways. By looking at the only patterns of each pair, we can find the unique features of each word. To make clear their differences, we classify the eight patterns of grammatical relations into three categories, i.e., possessive relation, noun-verb relation, and modifying relation. After getting the results and removing the mistakes generated by the tool, we extract the unique patterns of each word in comparison of another two and list the collocated words in order of salience.

Table 7. Only patterns of *mingwang, shengwang* and *weiwang* in possessive relation

	Words with possessive relation
ming wang	知識分子 intellectual, 專家 expert, 律師 lawyer, 演員 actor, 大學 university, 活佛 living buddha, 企業 enterprise, 商人 businessman, 教練 coach
sheng wang	報紙 paper, 保守黨 conservative, 柯林頓 Clinton, 工黨 Labor Party, 布希 Bush, 週刊 weekly, 裴洛 Pellew, 梅傑 Major, 杜爾 Dole, 密特朗 Mitterrand, 居貝 Juppé, 巴拉杜 Balladur, 董建華 Tung Chee-hwa, 泰晤士報 The Times, 個人 individual, 葉爾勤 Yeltsin, 政客 politician, 新聞報 Die Presse, 獎項 award
weiw ang	領導人 leader, 鄧小平 Deng Xiaoping, 政治家 politician, 黨 party, 自己 own, 聯合國 UN, 個人 individual, 我國 my country, 中國 China, 東盟 ASEAN, 俄羅斯 Russia, 祖國 motherland, 領袖 leader, 科學家 scientist, 老人 elder, 同志 comrade

Possessive Relation. It is noticed from Table 7 that *mingwang* tends to have possessive relation with nouns of occupations, *shengwang* with media, political parties and influential politicians, and *weiwang* with political leaders, international organizations and particular countries.

Verb-Noun Relation. This category of grammatical relation, target words as subjects or objects, in fact reflects their collocation with verbs. It can be seen from Table 8 that *mingwang* has the least number of unique collocated verbs, *weiwang* has more and *shengwang* has the most. Closer observation reveals the features of the verbs collocated with each word. *Shengwang* can collocate with verbs signifying both the rising and falling of name, which shows that the polarity of *shengwang* is neutral and that it can standard for both positive and negative fame. This contrasts clearly with *mingwang* (*name-fame*) and *weiwang* (*compelling-fame*), both representing only positive fame. As for *weiwang*, it seems it needs efforts to gain and maintain since it is often found as the object of 樹立 *shuli set up*, 建立 *jianli establish*, 贏得 *yingde win* and 維護 *weihu maintain*. The generalization that *shengwang* is the only near synonym which can represent both positive and negative fame is important and explains why it is less likely to collocate with established authority or respected entities. Besides, the seemingly arbitrary collocation of *shengwang* with foreign persons and organizations can also be easily explained, as it is much easier to criticize the reputation of non-local entities.

Modifying Relation. Different features of the three words can be found from their special adjective and noun modifiers listed in Table 9. *Mingwang* has only one unique noun modifier, which is 職業 *zhiye occupation*. Most adjective modifiers of

Table 8. Only patterns of verb-noun relation

	Object of_	Subject of_
mingwang	有 have, 負 possess	
shengwang	提升 raise, 重振 rebuild, 拉抬 lift, 挽回 redeem, 使得 make, 提振 raise up, 負 possess, 恢復 recover, 有助於 help, 扭轉 reverse, 提昇 promote, 累積 accumulate, 挽救 save, 打擊 strike	跌到 fall to, 如日中天 like the sun at high noon, 跌至 fall to, 落在 fall, 下降 decline, 上升 raise, 低落 fall down, 降 fall, 提升 lift, 超前 surpass, 攀升 ascend, 下挫 slump, 下跌 drop
weiwang	寄托 rely on, 缺乏 lack, 增強 strengthen, 維護 maintain, 借 make use of, 取得 gain	

Table 9. Only patterns of modifying relations

	Adjective modifiers	Noun modifiers
mingwang		職業 occupation
shengwang	低落 low, 如日中天 high noon, 搖搖欲墜 tumbledown, 不振 sluggish, 下跌 falling, 相當 quite, 低 low, 一定 certain, 下滑 sliding, 下降 decline	工黨 Labor Party, 保守黨 Conservative Party, 布希 Bush, 柯林頓 Clinton, 學術 academia, 宮澤 Miyazawa, 民調 poll, 政治 politics, 民間 folk, 巴拉杜 Balladur, 裴洛 Pellew, 內閣 cabinet
weiwang	巨大 tremendous	美商 American businessman, 法國 France, 政壇 political circle, 美國 US

shengwang are those indicating its status (high/low) or fluctuation (rising/falling), while a majority of its noun modifiers are proper nouns of certain Parties or politicians. As for *weiwang*, while it shares two adjective modifiers, 高 *gao high* and 崇高 *chonggao lofty, with shengwang*, it features nations and political issues as its noun modifiers.

3.4 Cross-Strait Comparison

Previous section has compared the frequency of each word between Mainland and Taiwan sub-corpora. In this section, we will explore further the cross-strait similarities and differences in the usage of each word. Gigaword Corpus has been utilized to study the differences of words used in Mainland and Taiwan in previous study [13]. What they compare are certain pairs of words of a similar concept in the two areas, like 警察 *jingcha* police and 公安 *gong'an public security* or 做 *zuo* do and 搞 *gao do*. However, due to the limitation of CWS, there is no way to eliminate the overlapping use of the words at both sides of the Taiwan Strait. The SkE team has developed Bilingual Word Sketch, a function which can compare a pair of equivalent words in two different language corpora such as *house* in English and *haus* in German [14]. We creatively apply this function in comparing each target word in this study to examine the similarities and differences between the two varieties of Mandarin Chinese. Take *mingwang* as an example, we at first select *GigaWord 2 Corpus: Mainland, simplified*, click *Word Sketch* and input the simplified "声望" in *Word form*, then select *Chinese Traditional* as the comparing "language" in *Bilingual word sketch*, choose the comparable corpus of *GigaWord 2 Corpus: Taiwan, traditional* and type "聲望" in the *lemma* column. After clicking *Show word sketch*, the result is presented in one page with the same gramrel listed side by side. The result is then analyzed in accordance with the classification of grammatical relations proposed in the previous section of the study.

Mingwang, having no big difference in frequency between the two corpora, differs mainly in its possessor and when it serves as an object. The most frequent possessors of *mingwang* in Mainland are 專家 *zhuanjia expert,* 人士 *renshi personage,* 知識分子 *zhishifenzi intellectual,* 演員*yanyuan actor/actress,* 活佛 *huofo living buddha,* 律師 *lvshi lawyer,* 學者 *xuezhe scholar*, etc., while in Taiwan, they are 律師 *lvshi lawyer,* 學府 *xuefu institution of higher learning*. It collocates with 卓有 *zhuoyou possess* in Mainland and with 素有 *suyou always have* and 深具 *shenju enjoy* in Taiwan when it is used as an object.

Table 10 shows that the collocation of *shengwang* is diverse and much richer in Taiwan than in Mainland especially in regard to its adjective modifiers. This again seems to stem from the fact that it can be used to both positive and negative fame (as clearly shown by its subject_of usage and usages in Taiwan), yet in Mainland usage, positive adjectives are strongly preferred. As for its relation to verbs, a feature is shared across both regions. When it is used as an object, it mostly collocates with verbs indicating the subjects' status of owning or their intention of raising or gaining *shengwang*, while it serves as the subject, *shengwang* is more dynamic, raising and falling to different degrees.

Table 10. Comparison of *shengwang* between Mainland and Taiwan

	Mainland	Taiwan
Noun-verb relation	Object_of: 享有 enjoy, 有助於 be conducive to, 具 have, 提高 raise, 贏得 gain, 擁有 possess, 具有 have, 利用 make use of Subject_of: 日增 raise daily, 大跌 plunge, 跌倒 fall down, 跌至 fall to, 下降 fall, 上升 raise, 提高 improve	Object_of: 重振 revitalize, 具 have, 挽回 save, 享有 enjoy, 拉抬 lift, 提高 raise, 有損 harm, 提振 raise up Subject_of: 大跌 plunge, 領先 lead, 扶搖直上 skyrocket, 下降 fall, 跌倒 fall down, 滑落 slide, 回升 recover, 墜 fall, 跌落 fall, 上升 raise, 跌至 fall to, 下挫 slump
Adj modifier	高 high, 崇高 lofty	高 high, 崇高 lofty, 相當 considerable, 低落 downcast, 下跌 falling, 下降 falling, 如日中天 like the sun at high noon, 不振 at a low ebb, 低 low, 一定 certain, 落後 backward, 搖搖欲墜 toppling

As for *weiwang*, possessors of it in Mainland are mostly nations, international organizations and China itself: 黨 *dang party,* 自己 *ziji own,* 我國 *woguo our country,* 聯合國 *lianheguo UN,* 俄羅斯 *eluosi Russia,* 東盟 *dongmeng ASEAN,* 個人 *geren individual,* 祖國 *zuguo motherland,* 共和國 *gongheguo republic*, whereas it is 鄧小平 *Deng Xiaoping,* 自己 *ziji own,* and 領導人 *lingdaoren leader* in Taiwan. It is worth mentioning that Deng Xiaoping, as the paramount leader of the People's Republic of China and the "chief architect" of China's reform and opening-up, not being found as the possessor of *weiwang* in the Mainland corpus, occurs 11 times in Taiwan corpus, showing Taiwan media's concern of his huge impact on the island and in the Greater China region. With a majority of *weiwang*'s possessors being countries, international organizations and China in Mainland and individuals and leaders in Taiwan respectively, it reflects the two regions' differences on the media concern, culture, ideology, political system and international outlook, etc. Due to the limited space, we cannot provide more detailed analysis, yet the tentative findings so far clearly illustrated the potential of SkE as a tool for critical discourse analysis.

4 Conclusion

Through utilizing various functions of SkE, this paper extracted rich distributional information on the linguistic behavior of the three target near synonyms, leading a detailed elaboration of the nuances among them as well as comparisons of their usages in Mainland and Taiwan. In conclusion, the three near synonyms demonstrate significant differences in possessive relation, noun-verb relation, and modifying relation. By applying the new bilingual word sketch function creatively to cross-strait comparison of the same word, subtle differences are demonstrated, which enhances our understanding of Chinese varieties and facilitates cross-strait communication. Though the differences seem to be highlighted, it is not to deny the similarities among the target words and across the Strait. Through thesaurus, grammatical pattern distribution and word sketch, *shengwang* and *weiwang* are shown to share more common contexts. Yet other usages contrasts showed that *shengwang*, by far the most frequent word among the three, also has the wider range of grammatical patterns owing to its representing of both positive and negative fames. Thus, another advantage of SkE is revealed, which is to cross-check the findings obtained through different SkE functions to draw reliable conclusion. This study is expected to provide implication for the future comparative lexical studies, learning and teaching of Chinese near synonyms as well as dictionary and thesaurus compiling. What needs to be done in the future is to improve the correctness of the automatically generated results and to fully tap the potential of the tool to transcend the boundary of near synonym discrimination and establish a comprehensive and systematic framework for SkE-assisted lexical semantic study.

Acknowledgments. This work is supported by the Joint Supervision Scheme with the Chinese Mainland, Taiwan and Macao Universities sponsored by the Hong Kong Polytechnic University (Project No. G-SB97).

References

1. Wang, S., Huang, C.R.: Word sketch lexicography: new perspectives on lexicographic studies of Chinese near synonyms. Lingua Sinica **3**(1), 1–22 (2017)
2. Gao, X.F., Lee, Y.M.: A corpus-based analysis of near-synonymous sentence-final particles in Mandarin Chinese: "*bale*" and "*eryi*". In: Proceedings of the 31st Pacific Asia Conference on Language, Information and Computation (PACLIC31) (2017)
3. Liu, M.C., Chiang, T.Y., Chou, M.H.: A frame-based approach to polysemous near-synonymy: the case with Mandarin verbs of expression. J. Chin. Lang. Comput. **15**(3), 137–148 (2005)
4. Chang, C.W.: A corpus-based lexical semantic study of Mandarin verbs of hanging: on the near synonym set: Guà, Xuán, Diào. MA thesis, National Chiao Tung University, Hsinchu (2015)
5. Zhang, W.X., Qiu, L.K., Song, Z.Y., Chen, B.Y.: Corpus-based quantitative analysis on stylistic difference of Chinese synonyms. Chin. Lang. Learn. **3**, 72–80 (2012). (in Chinese)
6. Chung, S.F.: A corpus-based analysis of "create" and "produce". Chang Gung J. Humanit. Soc. Sci. **4**(2), 399–425 (2011). (in Chinese)
7. Huang, C.R., et al.: Chinese sketch engine and the extraction of grammatical collocations. In: Proceedings of the Fourth SIGHAN Workshop on Chinese Language Processing, pp. 48–55 (2005)
8. Zhang, L.: The application of sketch engine in teaching collocations and synonyms. CAFLE **2**, 75–78 (2008). (in Chinese)
9. Wang, S., Huang C.R.: Apply Chinese word sketch engine to facilitate lexicography. In: Deny, A., Nur, W., Lilla, M. (eds.) Lexicography and Dictionaries in the Information Age: Selected Papers from the 8th ASIALEX International Conference, pp. 285–292 (2013)
10. Ge, X.H.: Core functions and application prospects of sketch engine. TEFLE **04**, 23–30 (2017). (in Chinese)
11. Huang, C.R.: Tagged Chinese Gigaword version 2.0 (2009). https://catalog.ldc.upenn.edu/LDC2009T14.
12. Xun, E., Rao, G., Xiao, X., Zang, J.: The construction of the BCC corpus in the age of big data. Corpus Linguist. **1**, 93–118 (2016). (in Chinese)
13. Hong, J.F., Huang, C.R.: A corpus-based approach to the discovery of cross-strait lexical contrasts. Lang. Linguist. **9**(2), 221–238 (2008). (in Chinese)
14. Kovář, V., Baisa, V., Jakubíček, M.: Sketch engine for bilingual lexicography. Int. J. Lexicogr. **29**(3), 339–352 (2016)

"Zuì(the Most)+Noun" Structure from the Perspective of Construction Grammar

Bin Yang(✉)

Institute for Big Data and Language Education,
Beijing Language and Culture University, Beijing, China
alexyang1991@163.com

Abstract. "最[Zuì](the most)+Noun" structure is widely used, and yet runs counter to traditional grammar rules. In order to explore the theoretical basis of this construction, the paper analyzes "最[Zuì](the most)+Noun" structure from the perspective of the construction coercion mechanism. The research shows that "最[Zuì](the most)+Noun" is a non-common construction structure in the intermediate state of schematic construction and entity construction. The fundamental motivation of construction coercion effect lies in interface conflict, including the contradiction and discord among the syntactic, semantic and pragmatic levels. Meanwhile, construction prototype, cognitive context and use frequency exert an influence on the process of construction coercion effect of "最[Zuì](the most)+Noun" structure.

Keywords: "最[zuì](the most)+noun" · Construction grammar
Construction coercion effect

1 Introduction

In traditional grammar, nouns cannot be modified by adverbs. However, "最(the most) +Noun" structures, such as 最中国("the most China"), 最小说("the most novel") are increasingly used in real life. While it is true that the "最(the most)+Noun" structure is still a non-common phenomenon compared with common language phenomenon, the in-depth study of this structure can help to reveal the motivation, formation mechanism, and the influence factors of construction coercion effect of non-common construction. Based on the investigation, there is not enough research on this construction in academic fields. Chai [5] made the first exploration in this field and comes to the conclusion that "最(the most) can modify some nouns". Wang [13] explains the validity of the construction from grammatical and semantic levels respectively. Jia [7] illustrates the reasons that "最(the most)" can be followed by nouns with construction grammar theory, however the research method still focuses on the discussion of examples and lacks data support from quantitative investigation.

The paper will discuss the formation mechanism and general rule of "最(the most) +Noun" structure using both quantitative data from the perspective of the construction grammar and construction coercion theory.

J.-F. Hong et al. (Eds.): CLSW 2018, LNAI 11173, pp. 267–276, 2018.
https://doi.org/10.1007/978-3-030-04015-4_23

2 Motivation Analysis on Construction Coercion of "最(the Most)+Noun" Structure

In the 1990s, Fillmore [4], Goldberg[1] and Paul [8] proposed "construction grammar" and created the construction grammar theory, deriving from the framework semantics of Fillmore [3]. Research relating to construction grammar has continued to develop, spanning a thirty year period. Goldberg [2] puts forward the theoretical concept of "cognitive construction grammar". Shi [9] believes that "the research based on construction concept is becoming the 'famous discipline' in the study of linguistics both at home and abroad".

2.1 "最(the Most)+Noun" Structure and Construction Coercion Effect

Construction grammar is formed in opposition of cognitive linguistics to generative grammar. Unlike generative grammar, it puts forward a new understanding in the concept of combining form and meaning, which emphasizes that the whole entity is larger than the sum of its parts, and the understanding of the relationship between the whole and the parts thus represents an important breakthrough in generative grammar. At the same time, construction grammar emphasizes that the initial unit of language is "construction", which is a very important basic concept in construction grammar. Any non-common structure can be called construction, including phonemes, words, morphemes, chunks, sentences, and discourses. The "最(the most)+Noun" discussed in this paper is also one of these constructions.

The "最(the most)+Noun" is a non-common construction in the intermediate state between schematic construction and entity construction. Schematic construction originates from abstracting linguistics rules, such as "X V-ed Y PP". The entity construction is the concrete linguistic expression, such as in "the most beautiful", "I have had dinner" and so on. The "最(the most)+Noun" structure has both "最(the most)" with concrete examples and "noun" with abstract meaning. Therefore, it can be regarded as a construction in the intermediate state. The non-common construction is a concept corresponding to the common construction, which is an unconventional construction in a language system. In non-common construction, the relationship between the whole and the parts is often incongruous, which is illustrated by the constituent components of construction and construction as a whole. For example, they conflict with each other at the semantic level. Generally speaking, a component cannot be part of the construction if it is extremely incompatible with the whole construction. Obviously, the "最(the most)" and "Noun" of "最(the most)+Noun" is incompatible with the whole construction, but because of construction coercion effect, this structure can exist.

The construction coercion is defined when the overall construction oppresses components, and then the components are endowed with semantic features of construction [10]. In this process, the semantic features and functions of components will be oppressed by the whole construction, gradually obtaining the semantic features and functions of the whole. The result of "subduing" is consistency and coordination between components and the whole construction.

2.2 Formation of "最(the Most)+Noun" Structure and Its Interface Conflict

"The formation and application of construction are the result of the interaction of features among different linguistic interfaces" [11]. Interface conflict is the precondition and fundamental motivation for the generation of "最(the most)+Noun", that is to say, the main reason for construction coercion is the conflict and incongruity of the "最(the most)+Noun" between the syntactic level and the semantic level, or the syntactic level and the pragmatics level. The "最(the most)" and the "Noun" cannot combine in the syntactic level, but because some nouns have special semantic features, they can be harmonized by the whole structure. Under the effect of construction coercion, the semantic features of components are highlighted, and the incongruous semantic features are hidden. Ultimately, "最(the most)" and the "Noun" reach a harmonious relationship at the syntactic and semantic level. In the pragmatic level, there may also be some conflicts in the syntax and semantic level because of the special needs of expression. When this occurs, the construction coercion will highlight a particular pragmatic function of the noun and weaken the conflict parts, ultimately achieving coordination in all three levels.

(1) 谈到对儿子学古诗的看法时，张玫说："现在儿子的课本里没有古诗词。我希望他能背诵一些古诗，因为那是中文最精华的部分。但是，现在我自己都背不下来几首了，也不会讲解古诗，真不知道该怎么去教他。" *When it comes to the opinion on her son learning ancient poem, Zhang Mei said, "There are no ancient poems in my son's textbook now. I hope he can recite some ancient poems, because that is "the most essence" part of Chinese. But even I cannot recite any poems now, nor can I explain ancient poetry. I really don't know how to teach him.* (From "people. cn")

(2) "故宫讲坛"正以最故宫、最学术、最亲民的方式、吸引更多公众的目光，让观众徜徉在故宫的文化殿堂，感悟故宫文化的魅力、学术的神圣和故宫人的敬业。 *The "Palace Museum Forum" is attracting much more public attention because its "the most Palace Museum", "the most academy" and the most popular methods, and let the audience wander in the cultural hall of the Palace Museum, as well as understanding the charm of the culture, the sanctity of the academy and the devotion of the employees.* (From "health. people. cn")

In example (1), the 精华(essence) in 最精华("the most essence") is a noun in Chinese. In Modern Chinese Dictionary (Sixth Edition), it is interpreted as "the most important and best part". Obviously, 精华(essence) causes the conflict between the semantic level and the syntactic level in the whole construction. Since 精华(essence) has the features of "the most important and best" in semantic meaning, it highlights the semantic features of "importance" and "good", and conceals the attribution of "part of things" in the whole construction.

In example (2), 故宫(Palace Museum) and 学术(academy) in 最故宫("the most Palace Museum") and 最学术("the most academy") are both nouns. The analysis of 学术(academy) is the same as that of 精华(essence) in example (1), and to avoid redundancy the paper won't say anymore on this particular construction. 故宫(Palace Museum) is a place name, which can be understood as "with the characteristics of the

Palace Museum". Here, the reasons 故宫(Palace Museum) can work cohesively in the structure of 最故宫("the most Palace Museum") are as follows. On the one hand, 故宫 (Palace Museum) has a special pragmatic function in the sentence. In Chinese, 最故宫 ("the most Palace Museum"), 最学术("the most academy") and 最亲民(the most popular) form parallel structures, which provides a sense of unity. If this expression is changed as "with the characteristics of the Palace Museum", the original sense will disappear. On the other hand, 故宫(Palace Museum) is also influenced by the context. Because of the strong contextual effect, readers will not be aware of the disharmony; they may even think it is very appropriate. Therefore, 故宫(Palace Museum) enters the 最故宫("the most Palace Museum") structure as a pragmatic function. Since 故宫 (Palace Museum) has no special semantic features, 最故宫("the most Palace Museum") shows the conflict between pragmatic, syntactic as well as semantic levels, and simultaneously demonstrates construction coercion.

3 Construction Prototype of "最(the Most)+Noun" and Its Influence on Construction Coercion

3.1 Prototype Analysis of "最(the Most)+Noun" Structure

The prototype effect of category is based on modern categorization theory, which holds that all categories are prototypical and have typical members, sub typical members and marginal members. To analyze the category prototype effect of "最(the most)+Noun", the paper considers it as a category, and therefore finds the typical, sub typical and marginal members. Starting with the typical member, this paper will inspect the prototype in order to gain a deeper understanding of its influence on construction coercion.

In order to gain a more scientifically sound study on the prototype and members of "最(the most)+Noun", the paper makes the research of "最(the most)+X(all the words)" in text corpus(about 300 million words in total) of the People's Daily in Dynamic Circulation Corpus (DCC) from 2011 to 2016. The paper has collected all the words that can enter "最(the most)+X" structure, in which 1231 adjectives (number of words) account for almost half of all words. The specific numerical values are as follows.

In Table 1, the number and proportion of nouns are basically consistent with previous studies of grammar. Adjectives account for 49.51% of the total, while the proportion of verbs is 32.46%. Idioms and nouns of locality only account for 6.44% and 3.25% respectively. To be sure, there are not many words of these two categories in modern Chinese, especially nouns of locality. However, these 81 words cover almost all the nouns of locality in modern Chinese, thus their proportion is relatively greater. There are only 141 nouns, accounting for a small proportion compared with the large cardinal number of modern Chinese nouns. There are fewer kinds of multi-category words, but since most of them have adjective features, they are easily used in this construction. The temporal word is the most rare with only one example.

Therefore, the typical members of the "最(the most)+X" should include adjectives. The sub typical members include verbs, nouns of locality, idioms, and multi-category words. The marginal members include nouns and temporal words. After specific

Table 1. Words number and proportion of "X" in "最(the most)+X" structure

Part of speech	Number of words	Proportion	Examples
Adjective	1231	49.51%	重要(important), 早(early)
Verb	807	32.46%	关心(care), 需要(need)
Idiom	160	6.44%	引人注目(attract sb.'s attention), 激动人心(arouse sb.'s feeling)
Noun	141	5.67%	前沿(forefront), 小说(novel)
Noun of locality	81	3.25%	前面(front), 北(north)
Multi-category word	65	2.61%	关键(vital), 理想(ideal)
Temporal word	1	0.04%	秋天(autumn)
Total	2486	1	

investigation of multi-category words, it is found that except 本能(instinct, with features of noun and adverb) and 根源(root, with features of both noun and verb), the remaining multi-category words have adjective features, which account for 96.92% in all multi-category words, and most of them have the features of nouns and adjectives with a total of 60 cases. This implies that the nouns that can enter "最(the most)+Noun" structure may have a higher tendency of inter-category. Due to the typicality of adjectives, the paper will construct prototype constructions with adjectives as the origin and theoretical coordinates.

Thus, the study demonstrates that the origin of "最(the most)+Noun" is 最(the most)+property adjective.

A point worth emphasizing is that adjectives include property adjectives and state adjectives. Although 最笔直(the most straight), 最雪白(the most snow-white) and 最冰冷(the most cold) also exist, the state adjectives such as 笔直(straight) and 雪白(snow-whit) are generally made up of a morpheme of degree meaning followed by a monosyllabic property adjective. Since "最(the most)" can modify all property adjectives, the adjectives can be simplified as property adjectives based on the principle of simplification.

3.2 Influence of "最(the Most)+Noun" on Construction Coercion

The prototype construction is the restoration result of "最(the most)+Noun", and also the destination of construction coercion on "最(the most)+Noun". The distance between target construction and prototype construction affects the force of construction coercion on "最(the most)+Noun". "Distance" refers to the distance between "nouns" in "最(the most)+Noun" and "property adjective" in prototype construction. The closer the "distance" is, the closer the semantic meaning will be. Additionally, "nouns" that are more harmonious with the whole construction makes the construction easier to generate.

At the same time, if the "distance" is close, the large force of construction coercion is unnecessary. Since the main function of the construction coercion is to stimulate its semantic features, the nouns with close "distance" have similar semantic features to "property adjective", and they still can form construction without larger force of construction coercion; and vice versa.

The influence of "prototype construction" on construction coercion is closely related to the nouns in "最(the most)+Noun". The paper has counted the nouns that can enter into "最(the most)+Noun" structure in People's Daily during the past 6 years (from 2011 to 2016), and has classified them according to their meanings. The table is as follows.

In Table 2, the proportion of abstract noun is 78.72%, which shows that abstract nouns are more likely to enter the "最(the most)+Noun" structure than concrete nouns. Most abstract nouns tend to have semantic features of measurement, while adjectives usually represent property, which are characterized by measurement. Therefore, abstract noun is closest to "property adjective" in the prototype construction, and the "prototype distance" is relatively close to it. Thus, as the constituent elements, abstract noun enters the "最(the most)+Noun" and is in harmony with the overall construction, and the force of the construction coercion is not so great.

Table 2. Noun classification of "最[zui](the most)+Noun" structure

Classification		Number of words	Semantic features	Examples
Concrete noun	Noun of persons and objects	25	Connotation meaning	妈妈(Mother), 草根(Grass root), 泥土(Soil)
	Place name	5	Connotation meaning	中国(China), 巴西(Brazil), 杭州(Hangzhou)
Abstract noun		111	Measurement meaning	基层(Primary level), 精华(Essence), 学术(Academy)

Specifically, nouns can be divided into two categories: one is the noun of persons and objects, such as 爷们(true man) and 泥土(soil). Such words are often concrete with rich meaning of their internal contents, can be adequately described and have descriptive semantic features. For example, when seeing or hearing the word 泥土(soil), people think of soil in real life, it is therefore associated with simple and unadorned content. The second category is place name. Five place names have entered the construction, which are 中国(China), 江南(Jiangnan), 河南(Henan), 巴西(Brazil) and 杭州(Hangzhou). There are a few reasons that these names can enter the construction. The first reason is that they have their own characteristics and rich connotation compared with other geographical names. The second reason is the influence of their use frequency. 巴西(Brazil) and 杭州(Hangzhou) are very representative, as they enter the construction because of popular social events, all of which will be explained in detail later. Since concrete nouns have a far distance from the "property adjective" of the prototype construction, they are very incompatible with the whole construction when they enter the "最(the most)+Noun". In order to achieve coordination with the whole construction, a strong construction coercion mechanism is needed to stimulate and highlight the meaning of the connotation, which produces the association from "soil" to "simple". In this way, the goal of converging with the prototype can be reached.

4 Influence Factors Analysis of "最(the Most)+Noun" Structure

Shi [10] considers that "construction coercion effect is influenced by specific language structure relationships, use frequency and cognitive context." Next, the paper will analyze the factors that influence the construction coercion process of "最(the most) +Noun" from cognitive context and use frequency.

4.1 Influence Analysis of Cognitive Context on Construction Coercion

The paper has investigated the influence of context on acceptability through the acceptability questionnaire of "最(the most)+Noun" construction. The questionnaire is divided into two parts. The first part includes 25 structures which combine "noun" and "最(the most)", while the second part is about sentences including these 25 structures with a higher level of context. The grade is from 1 to 5, where a higher score means the word is more acceptable. A total of 51 questionnaires are collected in the survey, of which 44 are valid.

Through the statistical analysis of the questionnaire, the paper confirms that the cognitive context does have an impact on the process of construction coercion, that is to say, "context effect" does exist in the process of construction coercion, and it has a positive effect. The more contextual information provided, the greater the contextual effect, and thus the more acceptable the construction will be. Moreover, the higher the acceptability of construction is, the more successful the construction coercion is. Table 3 shows the acceptability of some constructions. It is easy to see that the values with context are higher than those without context. It shows that the acceptability of construction is improved by context, which indirectly promotes the process of construction coercion.

Table 3. Average value of acceptability of some constructions with context and without context

Construction	Without context	Context
最妈妈("the most mother")	1.64	3.14
最泥土("the most soil")	1.48	3.11
最右翼("the most right wing")	3.45	4.3
最少年("the most teenager")	3.32	3.7
最国家("the most country")	1.89	3.43
最捷径("the most shortcut")	3.14	3.55
最中国("the most China")	3.48	4.05
最江南("the most Jiangnan")	2.48	3.68
最末期("the most final stage")	3.57	4.43
最原初("the most primary")	3.39	3.98

In addition, we have also found several noteworthy phenomena.

First, the acceptability of different types of "最(the most)+Noun" structure is obviously different in situations without context. The highest degree of acceptance is the 最前沿("the most forefront"), which is 4.95, and the lowest is the 最泥土("the most soil"), whose acceptance degree is 1.48. Through calculating the average value of the construction acceptance for two types of nouns, it is found that the average acceptance of "最(the most)+concrete noun" is 2.71, and the average acceptance of "最(the most)+abstract noun" is 4.11, which is much higher than the former.

Second, the acceptance degree is directly proportional to the number of words and total frequency. In Table 4, the number of words, total frequency and average acceptance of "最(the most)+concrete noun" are 30, 73, and 2.71 respectively, while these three of the "最(the most)+abstract noun" are 111, 2973, and 4.11 respectively. The number of words and total frequency of "最(the most)+concrete noun" are less and the average acceptance is lower, while the number of words and total frequency of "最(the most)+abstract noun" are much higher, and the average acceptance is also very high. Shi [10] points out that "construction coercion, productivity and acceptability are three sides of a problem". The number of words and total frequency can partly represent the productivity of the construction. The higher productivity is, the higher acceptability will be, and the more natural the resulting construction coercion structure will be.

Table 4. Number of words, frequency and average acceptance of "最(the most)+Noun"

Classification		Number of words		Total frequency		Average acceptance
Concrete noun	Noun of persons and objects	25	30	65	73	2.71
	Place name	5		8		
Abstract noun		111		2973		4.11
Total		141		3046		3.41

4.2 Influence Analysis of Use Frequency on Construction Coercion

The use frequency refers to the use degree of a certain construction in language and social life. The use frequency of a word indicates that people use this construction more commonly, and it is much more popular in society. The use frequency can indirectly influence the process of construction coercion effect, by promoting or slowing down the process of construction coercion, and thereby influence the nouns entering the "最(the most)+Noun" structure. It is necessary to point out that the "use frequency effect" does not apply to all nouns. Some nouns cannot enter the "最(the most)+Noun" structure through the mechanism of construction coercion even if their use frequency is high. It is clear that a higher use frequency can improve people's acceptance. This improvement of acceptance can stimulate the construction coercion effect on semantic and pragmatic features of the noun, which highlights some elements while simultaneously hides others, and then shortens the "distance" between the noun parts of the target structure and the prototype construction. Thus, construction coercion is finished and "最(the most) +Noun" structure can be formed.

The use frequency of nouns used as constituent elements is also related to the frequency of whole constructions. The most typical example is 最巴西("the most Brazil") and 最杭州("the most Hangzhou"). The search indexes(搜索指数) of 巴西 (Brazil) and 杭州(Hangzhou) in "Baidu Index" are as follows (Fig. 1).

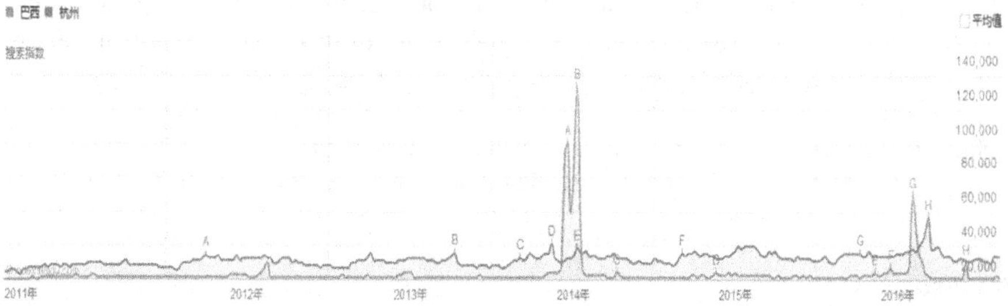

Fig. 1. Average value(平均值) in Baidu indexes of 巴西(Brazil) and 杭州(Hangzhou)

In this figure, the blue curve shows the change for 巴西(Brazil) search index, and the green curve shows the change for 杭州(Hangzhou) search index. There are three obvious peaks on the blue curve, which are A (2014.6.19), B (2014.7.20) and G (2016.8.4). Corresponding to their dates, the peak of A and B occur at the time of the Brazil World Cup, and the peak of G occurs during the Rio Olympic Games. The peak value of the green curve is H (2016.9.8), during which the G20 summit was held in Hangzhou. Obviously, hot social events have led to an increase in the use frequency of these nouns. At the same time, news on social media and public articles on WeChat have used the expression of 最巴西("the most Brazil") and 最杭州("the most Hangzhou") around these search peaks. The People's Daily used the 最巴西("the most Brazil") on August 6, 2016 and August 7, 2016. It is the Olympic Games that led to the rapid formation of 最巴西("the most Brazil") structure. If the Olympic Games were not held in Rio, other constructions may have resulted, and 最巴西("the most Brazil") would be delayed until the next hot social spot. In other words, the process would not have been so rapid.

That is to say, the occurrence of hot social events raises people's attention to some nouns, especially place names, which results in higher use frequency of nouns. At the same time, more and more people are starting to use "最(the most)+Noun" for other purposes such as publicity, which accelerates the process of construction coercion and makes such non-common constructions come into being quickly.

5 Conclusion

Through the analysis of the motivation and process of "最(the most)+Noun" construction coercion from the perspective of construction grammar, the paper finds that the interface conflict is the precondition and fundamental motivation for the formation of "最(the most)+Noun", i.e., the main reason lies in the conflict and incongruity of the "最(the most)+Noun" structure at the syntactic, semantic and pragmatic level. Different interfaces form a stable interaction relationship in the process of construction coercion of "最(the most)+Noun". At the same time, the construction prototype effect, cognitive context and use frequency influence the process of construction coercion of "最(the most)+Noun".

Acknowledgement. This paper is supported by the Fundamental Research Funds for the Central Universities, and the Research Funds of Beijing Language and Culture University, 17YCX128.

References

1. Goldberg, A.E.: Constructions: A Construction Grammar Approach to Argument Structure. The University Chicago Press, Chicago (1995)
2. Goldberg, A.E.: Constructions at Work: The Nature of Generalization in Language. Oxford University Press, Oxford (2006)
3. Fillmore, C.J:. Frame Semantics. In: Linguistic Society of Korea, Linguistics in the Morning Calm. Hanshin Publishing Co., Seoul (1982)
4. Fillmore, C.J: Construction Grammar. Course Reader for Linguistics 120A. University of California, Berkeley (1990)
5. Chai, S.: Can "最[zui](the most)" only modify adjectives? Bull. Chin. Lang. Teach. **8**, 30–32 + 29 (1980). (柴世森."最"只能修饰形容词吗?.语文教学通讯, 1980, 8:30–32 + 29.) [In Chinese]
6. Jia, J.: A study of the superlative construction of "最 (the most) XX". J. Hainan Normal Univ. (Soc. Sci.). **3**, 96–101 (2014). (贾君芳. 试论极性程度构式"最XX". 海南师范大学学报, 2014,3:96–101.) [In Chinese]
7. Paul, K.: Construction grammar. In: Verschueren, J., et al. (ed.) Handbook of Pragmatics: Manual. John Benjamins Publishing Co., Amsterdam (1995)
8. Shi, C.: Basic concept and research path of interactive construction grammar. Contem. Rhetoric **2**, 12–29 (2016). (施春宏.互动构式语法的基本理念及其研究路径.当代修辞学, 2016,2:12–29.) [In Chinese]
9. Shi, C.: Linguistics value of the construction coercion analysis. Contem. Rhetoric **2**, 12–28 (2015). (施春宏.构式压制现象分析的语言学价值. 当代修辞学,2015,2:12–28.) [In Chinese]
10. Shi, C., et al.: The theoretical thinking on second language acquisition of Chinese constructions. Lang. Teach. Linguist. Stud. **5**, 34–48 (2017). [In Chinese]
11. Wang, X.: On "最[zui](the most)+AB (noun)". J. Fuyang Normal Univ. (Soc. Sci. Ed.) **5**, 1–3 (2002) (王希杰."最 + AB(名词)"说.阜阳师范学院学报(社会科学版),2002,5:1–3) [In Chinese]

Buddhist Influence on Chinese Synesthetic Words—A Case Study of 味 Wèi in the Āgamas and Indigenous Chinese Literature

Jiandao Shi(✉) and Jianxun Shi

Noble Path Buddhist Education Fellowship, Towaco, USA
jiandao.shi@gmail.com, jianxun.shi@gmail.com

Abstract. This study examines whether Chinese synesthetic words that are composed of 味 *wèi* 'taste' were influenced by the spread of Buddhism to China through the translation of Buddhist texts into Chinese. Many terms of 味 *wèi* found in the Chinese Āgamas go beyond the gustatory field, e.g., the taste of material form and the taste of feeling. To confirm that these terms are derived from their source language, the parallel Pāli texts of the Āgamas are used to identify the original terms of *wèi*. By doing so, this study reveals the essential meanings of *wèi* in the Āgamas, which are employed as a yardstick to determine whether they influenced the *wèi* terms found in Chinese literature across different periods of time. The results show that translated Buddhist texts influenced the Chinese language regarding synesthetic words, as exemplified by the case of *wèi*.

Keywords: Synesthetic words · Metaphor · Translation of buddhist texts Archaic chinese

1 Introduction

This article is regarded as a probe for the project *From Synesthesia to Cross-cultural Representation of Cognition: A Lexical Semantic Study of Translated Buddhist Texts*.[1] Focusing on the Chinese character 味 *wèi* 'taste' [1], this paper compares and contrasts synesthetic terms that are composed of *wèi* in the Āgamas[2] to those that appear in native Chinese literature. The result of this investigation reveals whether foreign cultures, that is, Indic languages and Indian culture in ancient times, influenced Chinese synesthesia through the translation of Buddhist scriptures into Chinese and the spread of Buddhism in China.

The Buddhist literature used in this study includes the four Āgamas [3] and the four Pāli Nikāyas of the Theravāda school [4], which are the primary textual resources of Early Buddhism. On the other hand, the native Chinese literature is based on the three

[1] This project is supported by the Chiang Ching-kuo Foundation, Grand Recipients, 2016–2017.
[2] Āgama, literally means "transmitted teachings". It is a term indicating the sūtras, consisting of teachings handed down from the past [2, p. 83]. The Āgamas used in this paper refer to the four Chinese Āgamas.

J.-F. Hong et al. (Eds.): CLSW 2018, LNAI 11173, pp. 277–293, 2018.
https://doi.org/10.1007/978-3-030-04015-4_24

subcorpora of the *Academia Sinica Ancient Chinese Corpus*[3], i.e., the (1) Academia Sinica Tagged Corpus of Old Chinese (from Pre-Qin to Pre-Han) [5], (2) Middle Chinese subcorpus (from Late Han to the Six Dynasties) [6], and (3) Early Mandarin Chinese subcorpus (from Tang to Ching) [7]. We searched for synesthetic *wèi* terms throughout these three corpora to investigate their diachronic development paying special attention to situations before and after the introduction of Buddhism into China.

Synesthesia, literally meaning joined senses, refers to cross-sensory experiences that can occur in a neuro-cognitive phenomenon; for example, a person can taste a shape. As in neuro-cognitive synesthesia, linguistic synesthesia indicates a linguistic device that causes a perceptual experience involving multiple senses, as exemplified by "sweet voices", in which "sweet", a gustatory word, modifies the auditory "voice". In other words, synesthesia describes linguistic phenomena that express a certain sensory domain communicated through the concept of another sensory domain [8]. Based on the crucial nature of synesthesia, our criteria for data extraction regarding the synesthetic term *wèi* are that all *wèi* words simply used in their dominant sensory field—that is, for indicating the taste of food, savoring, etc.—are excluded.

Moreover, in linguistic studies, whether synesthesia is comparable to metaphor remains undecided. This paper does not address this issue, but phrases that are metaphorical expressions are not considered full-fledged synesthetic terms. For example, in the Āgamas the Buddha said, "Just as the taste of the great ocean is salty, my dispensation is the same, that is, without desire is the taste; the taste of enlightenment (覺味, *jue-wèi*), taste of extinguishment (息味, *xī-wèi*), and taste of the path (道味, *dào-wèi*) [is the taste]."[4] Here, 覺味 *jue-wèi*, 息味 *xī-wèi,* etc., are not fully developed synesthetic terms because they are metaphorical expressions in the sense that they compare the salty taste of the ocean to the nature of Buddhism. In contrast, a fully developed synesthetic phrase refers to expressions possessing the Chinese character *wèi* but whose meaning has nothing to do with the taste of food and whose context is not related to any metaphor. For example, one text in the Āgamas says, "When a baby girl is born, her parents are unhappy, which is the first point. Second, while the parents are nurturing this baby girl and looking at her, they do not get any taste (滋味, *zī-wè*i)."[5] The *zī-wèi* in this quotation does not refer to the taste sensed by the parents' mouths but to their emotion resulting from looking at their girl child. Such an expression, not metaphorical or relevant to food, is a well developed synesthetic term; thus, it is the focal interest of this paper.

[3] All quotations of Chinese literature are from the database except those noted.

[4] MĀ 35: 如大海水鹹, 皆同一味…我正法律亦復如是, 無欲爲味, 覺味, 息味及道味. (CBETA, T01, no. 26, p. 476c11–12).

[5] T 143: 一者, 女人初生墮地, 父母不喜; 二者, 養育視無滋味. (T02, 886a 12).

2 Synesthetic Wèi Term in the Āgamas and Their Origins

Searching the word *wèi* in the Āgamas yields 1307 results. However, only 32 terms match our focal interest of synesthesia, after excluding those that are simply related to food and taste. To confirm these terms came from their source language, the parallel Pāli texts of the Āgamas are used to identify the original meaning of *wèi* in Indic languages and Indian culture. Surprisingly, we found that the Chinese character *wèi* could be translated from at least three identified sources in Pāli: *rasa*, *assāda*, and *byañjana*. These three Pāli words appear in different scenarios in the Pāli Nikāyas. Based on the explanations given by The Pāli Text Society's *Pāli-English Dictionary* (PED) [9], each of the three is analyzed accordingly, and their translations in the Āgamas are listed.

The first Pāli word *rasa* means "that which is connected with the sense of taste". It is the most basic word that denotes the meaning of taste and conveys more meanings than the other two Pāli words. According to the PED, *rasa* has five explanations:

(1) the sense object of the tongue.
Rasa refers to the sense object of the tongue, which often appears together with the other five sense objects. This definition is the most common meaning of *rasa* in Buddhist texts, as one example reads, 舌嘗味 *shé-cháng-wèi* 'tongue perceives taste'. However, this meaning has nothing to do with synesthesia; thus, all related terms are excluded.

(2) the sense of taste, especially as in quality and personal accomplishment.
The most common term is *rasagga*, the highest taste, which is usually related to one of the 32 significant marks of the Buddha. In the Āgamas, the translation of *rasagga* is 第一味 *dì-yī-wèi* 'the top-most taste'.

(3) an object or act of enjoyment, a sensual stimulus, or material enjoyment.
Rasa, usually in its plural form, imparts the meaning of enjoyment; as one text says, "A monk should not sleep on a luxury bed, not use embellished clothing, and not attach to the taste while eating (不著味 *bù-zhuó-wèi).*"[6] Here, in Chinese, 不著味 *bù-zhuó-wèi* can literally mean "not attach to the taste" and "not attach to the enjoyment" while eating.

(4) a substance; metaphorically, a flavor.
The fourth meaning of *rasa* given here goes beyond the sense domain of taste. An example of the first meaning found in the Āgamas reads, "Such as someone plants a seed of a bitter fruit and irrigates it whenever necessary. The seed gets the *wèi* of the earth, water, fire, and air."[7] In this context, the *wèi* of the earth, water, fire, and air (地味 *dì-wèi* 'the taste of the earth', 水味 *shuǐ-wèi* 'the taste of the water', 火味 *huǒ-wèi* 'the taste of the fire', 風味 *fēng-wèi* 'the taste of the air') obviously does not indicate the flavor of the four primary material elements in Buddhism. Here, the *wèi* refers to the substance of the earth, water, fire, and air, which is the material foundation in which the plant grows. The next meaning of *rasa* conveys

[6] T 20: 沙門不得安臥好床, 衣不文綵, 食不著味. (CBETA, T01, no. 20, p. 261b2–3).

[7] SĀ 788: 譬如苦果, 種著地中, 隨時溉灌, 彼得地味, 水味, 火味, 風味. (CBETA, T02, no. 99, p. 204b16–18).

its metaphorical sense of "flavor, relish, pleasure." For instance, a verse in the Āgamas reads, "The taste of serenity and calmness! When one knows its taste of detachment and has detached from flaming evil, he/she drinks the taste of Dharma joy."[8] Thus, the taste, *wèi,* is used in this verse as a metaphorical expression of flavor and pleasure. Similar examples found in the Āgamas include 法味 *fă-wèi* 'taste of Dharma', 甘露味 *gān-lù-wèi* 'taste of nectar', 覺味 *jue-wèi* 'taste of enlightenment', 道味 *dào-wèi* 'taste of the path', and so on.

(5) a fine substance, semi-solid semiliquid substance, extract, delicacy, fineness, or dust.
This meaning is particularly exemplified by 地味 *dì-wèi* (*rasapaṭhavī*), which means savory earth. This *dì-wèi* is different from that mentioned above. It is edible and was the food for ancient people according to the legend of evolution recorded in the Nikāyas (DN 27) and Āgamas (DĀ5, MĀ 154), which says, "At that time, 地味 *dì-wèi* 'savory earth' appeared on the surface of the ground. It has the color and taste just like curd and butter. Its taste is like honey".[9]

The PED also mentioned two other meanings of *rasa*: one refers to flavor in drama, and the other is terminology used exclusively in Abhidhamma that emphasizes the "essential property" in style or in philosophy. Although there seems to be no such case in the Āgamas, these two meanings of *rasa,* together with the above five, indicate that in addition to its basic meaning of taste, *rasa* can be further extended to show positive emotion, e.g., flavor, enjoyment, and substance or essence. Interestingly, the former is notable in the Āgamas but is mostly relevant to the next Pāli word *assāda.*

The second Pāli word related to Chinese *wèi* is *assāda*. The PED explains *assāda* as "taste, sweetness, enjoyment, satisfaction". Compared to *rasa*, it is particularly affiliated with the Buddhist doctrine on the triad of *assāda, ādīnava,* and *nissaraṇa* (味患離, *wèi-huàn-lí*), which literally means 'taste/gratification, danger, and escape'. In the context of the triad of 味患離 *wèi-huàn-lí*, we find various synesthetic terms such as 色味 *sè-wèi* 'taste of form', 欲味 *yù-wèi* 'taste of desire', 受味 *shòu-wèi* 'taste of feeling', and 痛味 *tòng-wèi* 'taste of pain', depending on the different objects given in the texts.

What does *assāda, wèi,* mean in the scriptures? The Buddha explains 欲味 *yù-wèi* 'taste of desire' as follows: "What is the taste of desire? Through the five kinds of sensual desire, if pleasure and joy arise [in the mind], which is the taste of desire."[10] In the same text, an example is given to illustrate 色味 *sè-wèi* 'taste of form': "When a girl is fourteen or fifteen years old, her physical beauty is in the prime time. On account of her beauty, depending on her loveliness, pleasure and joy arise [in one's mind], which

[8] SĀ 978: 寂靜止息味, 知彼遠離味, 遠離熾然惡, 飲以法喜味. (CBETA, T02, no. 99, p. 253c15–16).

[9] T 23: 時, 地上自然生地味, 譬如白酥上肥, 其地味色如是也, 其味譬如蜜. (CBETA, T01, no. 23, p. 305b13–14).

[10] MĀ 99: 云何欲味? 謂因五欲功德, 生樂生喜, 極是欲味. (CBETA, T01, no. 26, pp. 584c29–585a2).

is the taste of form and no others could be it."[11] Moreover, 欲味 *yù-wèi* 'taste of desire' is explained as follows:

> "There are five kinds of sensual desire which are lovely, pleasing and rejoicing. [Because of] being associated with desire, they make people happy. What are those five? That is, the eyes cognize physical form; the ears cognize sound; the nose cognizes smells; the tongue cognizes taste, and the body cognizes contact. Because of these [desire], the king and king's retinue are happy and joyful. That is the taste of desire and no others could be it."[12]

From the definition of *assāda* given above, it can be concluded that the Chinese expression of "so and so *wèi*" is whatever makes people happy, joyful, and pleased. Thus, if a person is happy due to desire, the person has the taste of desire. If a person's joy is aroused by a kind of feeling, this joy is the taste of the feeling. The interpretation of "so and so *wèi*" is applied to other synesthetic terms under this category.

In addition to the triad of *assāda, ādīnava,* and *nissaraṇa*, another Chinese translation of *assāda*—味著 *wèi-zhuó* 'to taste and attach'—can be found in the Āgamas. It appears in elaborations of the teaching of Dependent Origination and how suffering results from the contact of sense organs and sense objects. In the context, phrases such as 味著顧念 *wèi-zhuó-gù-niàn* '[one] tastes and attaches [any] contemplation' and 取法味著 *qǔ-fǎ-wèi-zhuó* 'grasping a thing, one tastes and attaches' are found. A remarkable point about these translations is that *assāda* is a noun but 味著 *wèi-zhuó* are verbs. This feature is discussed below.

The third Pāli word that is relevant to *wèi* is *byañjana* (or *vyañjana*). According to the PED, it has three meanings: (1) it denotes an attribute, a distinctive mark, sign, or characteristic; (2) it refers to a letter (of a word) especially in contrast to *attha*, meaning; and (3) it means a condiment, curry.

Byañjana in the sense of the first two is translated as 相 *xiàng* 'distinctive mark' and 文 *wén* 'letter or word' in the Āgamas, but surprisingly, many cases are also translated as *wèi*, which is relevant to the third meaning. For example, *byañjana* is usually used in statements such as the following: "*bhikkhu cakkhunā rūpaṃ disvā na nimittaggāhī hoti nānu<u>byañjana</u>ggāhī*" (AN 4.14), which means, "Having seen the form by eyes, a monk does not grasp the mark and inferior marks" (*byañjana*). Its parallel Chinese translation is "眼已見色, 不受相, 不觀相 *yǎn-yǐ-jiàn-sè, bù-shòu-xiàng, bù-guān-xiàng*" (EĀ 2.11). By comparison, *byañjana* in this statement is translated as 相 *xiàng* 'feature'. The modern Western translator Bhikkhu Bodhi translates *byañjana* in this sentence as "features"[13], which agrees with 相 *xiàng* in Chinese. However, instead of 相 *xiàng*, more cases of *byañjana* in similar sentences are rendered into Chinese as *wèi* in the Āgamas. In other words, 不觀相 *bù-guān-xiàng* 'not contemplating the mark' (*nānubyañjanaggāhī*) has 不味色 *bù-wèi-sè* 'not tasting

[11] *Ibid.*: 云何色味? 若刹利女, 梵志, 居士, 工師女, 年十四五, 彼於爾時, 美色最妙, 若因彼美色, 緣彼美色故, 生樂生喜, 極是色味無復過是. (CBETA, T01, no. 26, p. 585c17–20).

[12] MĀ 100: 有五欲功德, 可愛可念, 歡喜, 欲相應而使人樂, 云何爲五? 謂眼知色, 耳知聲, 鼻知香, 舌知味, 身知觸, 由此令王及王眷屬得安樂歡喜, 摩訶男, 極是欲味無復過是. (CBETA, T01, no. 26, p. 586b18–22).

[13] Bhikkhu Bodhi translated it: "A bhikkhu does not grasp its marks and features." [10, p. 402].

the form' as its corresponding translation.[14] Regarding the Pāli statement quoted above and its resemblances, only one case of *byañjana* is rendered into 相 *xiàng* 'mark' in the Āgamas as mentioned here. By contrast, *wèi* renditions occur at least ten times.

In the Āgamas, we also find that *wèi* is another translation of *byañjana* instead of 文 *wén* 'character, letter' in its second meanings given by the PED, in the stock sentence, "*So dhammaṃ deseti ādikalyāṇaṃ majjhekalyāṇaṃ pariyosānakalyāṇaṃ sātthaṃ sabyañjanaṃ*", which means, "He teaches the Dhamma good in the beginning, good in the middle, and good in the end, with the right meaning and phrasing". The Pāli phrase *sātthaṃ sabyañjanaṃ is translated as* 'with the right meaning and phrasing', which is in accordance with the PED and other Western translators' interpretations.[15] On the Chinese side, a corresponding translation, 有義有文 *yǒu-yì-yǒu-wén* 'possessing meaning and possessing letter', can be found in the Āgamas,[16] which also conforms to the meaning given by the PED. However, we find even more cases in which *wèi* has replaced 文 *wén* as the Chinese translation of *byañjana* in similar stock phrases such as 善義善味 *shàn-yì-shàn-wèi* 'good meaning and good taste' and 義味具足 *yì-wèi-jù-zú* 'possessing complete meaning and taste'. Since both translations, 文 *wén* and 味 *wèi,* exist in the Āgamas, it is interesting to see their respective occurrences.

The phrase 有義有文 *yǒu-yì-yǒu-wén* appears 30 times in the Āgamas, all from the same translator, Saṃghadeva in the Eastern Jin Dynasty. Meanwhile, for the translation of *wèi*, 義味具足 *yì-wèi-jù-zú* has 19 results, only one of which was translated by Saṃghadeva; others came from Buddhayaśas and Zhu Fonian. 善義善味 *shàn-yì-shàn-wèi* has 18 results, all of which came from Gunabhadra. 義味清淨 *yì-wèi-qīng-jìng* 'meaning and taste [are] clear and pure' occurs five times, and this translation is also from Buddhayaśas and Zhu Fonian. Overall, 42 cases of *byañjana* are translated *wèi* by various translators; by contrast, 30 examples are translated into 文 *wén* 'letter'. This statistic shows that translators of the Chinese Āgamas were dichotomous in interpreting *byañjana,* but contemporary Western translators of the Pāli texts hardly translate it into anything related to taste.

The interpretation of *byañjana* as *wèi* is significant and surely has a certain influence on Chinese. First, when *byañjana* is translated into *wèi* a slight change in meaning occurs. The phrase 有義有文 *yǒu-yì-yǒu-wén* conveys that the Buddha's teachings have both meaning (substantive content) and literary grace. Such an interpretation agrees with its original context, which refers to two aspects of the Buddha's teaching—*attha* and *byañjana* as presented in Pāli texts. By contrast, 有義有味 *yǒu-yì-yǒu-wéi* means that the Buddha's doctrine has meaning (有義 *yǒu-yì*), which makes the listener feel wonderful or relish it (有味 *yǒu-wéi*). In this translation, *wèi* performs as an adjective modifying the Buddha's teaching and describing the audiences' psychological response while listening, although it originally modifies only the former matter. Furthermore, we can classify the resemblances of the stock phrase 有義有味 *yǒu-yì-yǒu-wén* into two

[14] MĀ 80: 若眼見色, 然不受相, 亦不味色 (CBETA, T01, no. 26, p. 553a13–14). Also seen in MĀ 144, 146, 182, 187.

[15] Ñāṇamoli Thera translated it as "letter" [11, p. 3] and Bhikkhu Bodhi as "phrasing" [12, p. 677].

[16] For example, MĀ 132: 彼若說法, 初妙, 中妙, 竟亦妙, 有義有文. (CBETA, T01, no. 26, p. 623a21–22).

groups: one is the translation that separates 義 and 味 by another character, e.g., 善義善味 *shàn-yì-shàn-wèi*, and the other combines these two words, e.g., 義味具足 *yì-wèi-jù-zú*, 義味清淨 *yì-wèi-qīng-jìng*. The phrase 義味 *yì-wèi* in the latter group would be confusing for Chinese readers because it looks like 法味 *fă-wèi* 'taste of Dhamma', 覺味 *jue-wèi* 'taste of enlightenment', and 道味 *dào-wèi* 'taste of the path', as mentioned previously in the explanation of *rasa*. In other words, Chinese readers tend to interpret 義味 *yì-wèi* as "the taste of meaning", just as they perceive the metaphorical and abstract meanings of 法味 *fă-wèi*, 覺味 *jue-wèi*, etc. Consequently, the fact that 義味 *yì-wèi* indicates two things is likely to be ignored without referring to the specific context of its source language.

To this extent, the meanings of the three Pāli words and their relevant Chinese translations have been discussed. Their individual features have also been revealed. Significantly, two more points should be disclosed. First, the part of speech in some cases was changed after translation into Chinese. Although all three Pāli words—i.e., *rasa*, *assāda*, and *byañjana*—are nouns and most of the Āgamas translators retained this part of speech, some translators changed them into verbs. For instance, at the beginning of EĀ 21.9, *wèi* (*assāda*) appears as a noun and literally means the taste/flavor in such phrases such as 何味 *hé-wèi* 'what taste', 色味 *sé-wèi* 'taste of form', and 欲味 *yù-wèi* 'taste of desire'.[17] However, in the conclusion of the same text, *wèi* becomes a verb that literally means "to perceive the flavor of something" and helps to construct various V-O phrases such as 味欲 *wèi-yù* 'to taste the desire', 味色 *wèi-sé* 'to taste the form', and 味痛 *wèi-tòng* 'to taste the pain'.[18] Such a translation phenomenon also occurs in *byañjana* terms, especially exemplified by the phrase 味色 *wèi-sé* in the context that advises monks not to taste (*byañjana*) the form when the eyes see the form. Similarly, the phrase 味著 *wèi-zhuó* 'to taste and attach' is translated from *assāda* and becomes a verb in Chinese translation, such as the two examples mentioned previously: 味著顧念 *wèi-zhuó-gù-niàn* '[one] tastes and attaches [any] contemplation' and 取法味著 *qŭ-fă-wèi-zhuó* 'grasping a thing, one tastes and attaches'.

In addition to the change in part of speech, a deviation from source language occurs when in some of the Āgamas texts the term *wèi* occurs without the three corresponding Pāli words or in other connections to the meaning of taste in their parallel texts in Pāli. As exemplified by SĀ 244, we see several occurrences of 味著 *wèi-zhuó* in the statement that defines the hook of Māra[19] as the attachment occurring between the six sense organs (i.e., eye, ear, nose, tongue, body, and mind) and the six sense objects (i.e., form, sound, fragrance, taste, physical contact, and mental objects).[20] Compared with its two parallel texts in Pāli, SN 35.114-115, no word corresponds to *rasa*, *assāda*, or *byañjana*, but six adjectives describe how lovely and attractive each of the sense

[17] EĀ 21.9: 欲有何味…色有何味…痛有何味…若復於此五欲之中, 起苦樂心, 是謂欲味. (CBETA, T02, no. 125, p. 605a2–6).

[18] *Ibid.*: 我今比丘! 以說著欲, 味欲, 欲爲大患, 復能捨者; 亦說著色, 味色, 色爲大患, 能捨離色; 以說著痛, 味痛, 痛爲大患. (CBETA, T02, no. 125, p. 606b23–25).

[19] Māra is the Buddhist 'Tempter-figure'. He appears in the texts both as a real person and as a personification of evil and passions of the totality of worldly existence and of death [13].

[20] SĀ 244: 眼味著色, 是則魔鉤, 耳味著聲, 是則魔鉤, 鼻味著香, 是則魔鉤, 舌味著味, 是則魔鉤, 身味著觸, 是則魔鉤, 意味著法, 是則魔鉤. (CBETA, T02, no. 99, p. 58c11–14).

objects is, and three verbs report how happy and attached people feel when the sense organs contact the sense objects.[21] The message delivered by the six adjectives and the three verbs resembles the definition of 欲味 *yù-wèi* 'taste of desire' given in MĀ 99, that is, the pleasure and joy that arise owing to sensual desire. By counterchecking MN 13, the parallel Pāli text of MĀ 99, we find the same six adjectives used in SN 35.114-115. MN 13 also mentions that people who perceive lovely sense objects generate joy. Thus, we may conclude that the Chinese word *wèi* in the Buddhist context has the meaning of giving rise to joy and happiness, which motivates people to pursue it. This meaning is explicitly delivered in the Buddhist teaching of 味患離, *wèi-huàn-lí* 'taste/gratification, danger, and escape', as mentioned previously. Consequently, this doctrine might have imprinted in the Chinese translators' minds; then they imposed the doctrinal point on the Chinese *wèi*. We find several examples in which *wèi* is affiliated with joy and happiness, such as 養育無味 *yǎng-yù-wú-wèi*, 'bringing up tastelessly/joylessly', 視無滋味 *shì-wú-zī-wèi* 'looking at [the person] without flavor/pleasure', 受味甚少 *shòu-wèi-shèn-shǎo* 'receiving little flavor/pleasure', and 欲猶少味 *jù-yóu-shào-wèi* 'desire is as little relish'. We have a better understanding of *wèi* in both its explicit and implicit senses when it appears in the Āgamas even without their parallel Pāli scriptures.

At this point, we have explored the multiple explanations of *wèi* with its three corresponding Pāli words, *rasa*, *assāda*, and *byañjana.* To summarize, three points are made regarding the features of *wèi* presented in its source language and the possible influence on the Chinese language caused by the usage of *wèi* in the Āgamas.

1. The metaphorical usage of *rasa* has introduced some abstract or even abstruse terms associated with *wèi* into the Chinese language, such as 法味 *fǎ-wèi*, 道味 *dào-wèi*, and 覺味 *jue-wèi*. As mentioned in the section explaining *rasa,* the term refers to the sense object of the tongue, then extends to indicate the substance of things and even abstract senses of flavor and the relish people appreciate yet find difficult to express literally.
2. Although various *wèi* phrases regard metaphorical expressions, some phrases, as exemplified by 義味 *yì-wèi,* in the source language are not used metaphorically. Similarly, 句味 *jù-wèi*[22] 'phrases and letters' (*pada-byañjana*) tends to be mistaken for a metaphorical term, that is, 'the taste of sentences', by Chinese readers. In some cases, not only have they been misunderstood grammatically in the Buddhist context but also their original meanings have changed when they are applied by Chinese people in a non-Buddhist context. For instance, 風味 *fēng-wèi* is a technical term indicating 'the essence of the wind/air', one of the four basic elements in the Buddhist scriptures, but it is conventionally apprehended as the flavor of food or the characteristic, style, or quality of something in Chinese literature.

[21] The six adjectives in Pāli are *iṭṭhā, kantā, manāpā, piyarūpā, kāmūpasaṃhitā,* and *rajanīyā* (desirable, lovely, agreeable, pleasing, sensually enticing, and tantalizing); the three verbs are *abhinandati, abhivadati,* and *ajjhosāya tiṭṭhati* (seeks delight in them, welcomes, and remains holding to them). The translation refers to Bodhi [14, p. 1187].

[22] SĀ2 192: 希有瞿曇! 汝及弟子, 義與義句, 及與句味, 所說之事, 等無差別. (CBETA, T02, no. 100, p. 443c-4-5).

3. Although *wèi* has multiple senses, as demonstrated previously, the most significant one is its doctrinal definition in the Buddhist scriptures, which is the happiness and joy one has whenever one's sense organs contact sense objects. We compare this definition to the usage of *wèi* in local Chinese. If native Chinese people did not use *wèi* in the same sense of its doctrinal definition before the introduction of Buddhism into China but have applied it accordingly since then, we can conclude that the translation of Buddhist scriptures affects the usage of *wèi*.

3 Definitions Given by the Chinese Dictionary

After the exploration of *wèi* in the Āgamas with comparison to its three corresponding Pāli terms in their source language, we analyze the synesthetic *wèi* terms in the Chinese literature. Before our survey in the corpus of Chinese literature, we introduce how Chinese people use the word *wèi* by consulting three dictionaries: the *Great Old Chinese Dictionary* (GOCD) 古漢語大詞典 [15], the *Ancient Chinese Dictionary* (ACD) 古代漢語詞典 [16] and the *Great Chinese Dictionary* (GCD) 漢語大字典 [17]. The explanations listed below come from the first dictionary, supplemented with the other two references.

The GOCD lists four meanings for different applications of *wèi*:

1. 滋味 *zī-wèi* 'the taste of food' such as sweet, salty, or sour; 氣味 *qì-wèi* 'smell of food'. Because of the affiliation with food, this meaning of *wèi* can extend to indicate dishes, e.g., 韓非子 *Han-fei-zi*: "While one eats, one does not have two dishes (二味 *èr-wèi*). While sitting, one does not sit on two mats"[23].
2. 意味 *yì-wèi* 'meaning'; 趣味 *qù-wèi* 'fun'. As 言語無味 *yán-yǔ-wú-wèi,* it literally means one's speech is tasteless, but it denotes that the talk is senseless and not fun.
3. 辨味 *biàn-wèi* 'distinguishing the taste'. An example in 列子 *Liè-zǐ* reads, "有味味者 *yǒu-wéi-wéi-zhě* 'there is distinguishing what is tasted'". The former *wéi* performs as the verb 'to distinguish various flavors'. The action of distinguishing the taste can further refer to 'studying and comprehending something' as exemplified by 體味 *tǐ-wèi*.
4. A quantifier of Chinese herbal medicine, e.g., 一味藥 *yī-wèi-yào* 'one kind of herbal medicine'.

In addition to the above meanings, the ACD differentiates the third meaning given by the GOCD into two entries: one is associated with 'discriminating and tasting food', e.g., 品味 *pǐn-wèi* 'to taste', and the other is to 'comprehend or to appreciate something' with the example of 玩味 *wán-wèi* 'ruminating', as the quotation in 呂氏春秋 *Lǚ-shì-chūn-qiū* reads, "Therefore, when one is in the disorder and hubbub, one must ruminate (*wèi*) on the situation.[24]" In addition, the ACD has an entry of 意義 *yì-yì* 'meaning' and 旨趣 *zhǐ-qù* 'purpose, essential idea', as exemplified by the statement in 文心雕龍 *Wén-xīn-diāo-lóng*: "That is, though what has gone is old, the meaning (*wèi*)

[23] 韓非子: 食不二味, 坐不重席.

[24] 呂氏春秋: 故訩訩之中, 不可不味也.

of its remains is revived daily."[25] This meaning is similar to 意味 *yì-wèi* 'meaning' in the GOCD, but the ACD does not include any interpretation of *wèi* with regard to 趣味 *qù-wèi* 'interest'. The last dictionary, GCD, does not provide any new meaning of *wèi* but gives more examples for the entry of 意義 *yì-yì* and 旨趣 *zhǐ-qù*. For instance, in 晉書 *Jin-shu*: 潛心道味 *qián-xīn-dào-wèi* 'diving one's mind into the *wèi* of Dao'; 紅樓夢 *Hóng-lóu-mèng* reads, "Pages full of silly litter. Tears a handful sour and bitter. All a fool the author hold, but their zest (*wèi*) who can unfold."[26] [19]

In sum, according to all three Chinese dictionaries, we conclude five applications and meanings of *wèi* in agreement with the division of 意味 *yì-wèi* and 趣味 *qù-wèi*. Although only one dictionary lists 趣味 *qù-wèi*, this application appears frequently in local literature, especially in Early Mandarin Chinese, which can be seen in later sections. Next, we extract synesthetic terms of *wèi* from the corpora of Old, Middle, and Early Mandarin Chinese literature, and compare the results with the Āgamas.

4 Synesthetic *Wèi* Terms in Old Chinese

To prove any effect of the translation of Buddhist scriptures on the Chinese language, we must first find differences between Chinese literature written before and after Buddhism's introduction. Therefore, it is crucial to know when Buddhism was transmitted to China. Many legends report various accounts of Buddhism's introduction into China; one even proposes that Buddhism came to China at the time of Emperor Qin Shi Huang, which is not accepted by Buddhist scholars. As far as concrete evidence is concerned, 後漢書 *Hòu-hàn-shū* records that Chu Wangying (41-70 CE), the king of Chu, worshipped the sacred temple of the Buddha and supported the preparing of Buddhist banquets for laypeople and monks. This record shows that by Late Han, Buddhism was introduced into China, as proved by the worship of the Buddha and the occurrence of two Buddhist proper nouns: 伊蒲塞 *yī-pú-sài* 'Buddhist laypeople' (*upāsaka*) and 桑門 *sāng-mén* 'monastic' (*samaṇa*). In addition, the historical book reports another two proofs of the fact that Buddhism was popular in Late Han: a Daoist scholar Xiang Kai noted characteristics of Buddhism in his memorial to the emperor,[27] and he documented a Buddhist legend about a pretty woman sent by the god to seduce the Buddha.

Another temporal point that requires consideration in our study is when the Āgamas were translated into Chinese. According to the *Authority Database of Buddhist Tripitaka Catalogues* [18], the translation dates of the four Chinese Āgamas spread from the Eastern Jin Dynasty (397 CE) to the Dynasty of Liu Song (431 CE). Although the translation dates are later than the Late Han Dynasty, if we include the translations of independent scriptures, we can even trace them back to Late Han.

The assumption that Buddhism entered in the Late Han Dynasty is relatively conservative. Although the time of Buddhism's introduction is not settled, the division

[25] 文心雕龍: 是以往者雖舊, 餘味日新.

[26] 紅樓夢: 滿紙荒唐言, 一把辛酸淚, 都云作者癡, 誰解其中味.

[27] 後漢書: 此道清虛, 貴尚無爲, 好生惡殺, 省慾去奢.

of Pre-Han and the Late Han Dynasty serves as a watershed in Chinese language history, as it is used as a reference to divide the corpora of Old from Middle Chinese. Presumably, the period of Old Chinese, from Pre-Qin to Pre-Han, is mostly before the introduction of Buddhism. However, the influence of cultural contact on language might occur earlier than the official record, such as the evidence mentioned above. Some *wèi* terms endowed with Buddhist features might appear in Pre-Han literature. To avoid missing any important clues, we mark and pay special attention to the search results from the Pre-Han Dynasty.

From the *Academia Sinica Tagged Corpus of Old Chinese*, 562 terms of *wèi* are retrieved. Nonetheless, only 6 results (1%) match our study's requirement, after removing 3 results categorized as "not fully developed" synesthetic terms and other non-synesthetic terms. The 6 synesthetic *wèi* terms are listed in the following table (Table 1).

Table 1. Synesthetic *wèi* terms in Old Chinese

Dynasty	Literature	Part of speech	Quotations	Meaning of *wéi*
Qin	呂氏春秋	v.	故喣喣之中，不可不味也	study and comprehend
Pre-Han	史記	n.	馮公之論將率，有味哉！有味哉	meaning and fun
Pre-Han	史記	v.	其推轂士及官屬丞史，誠有味其言之也	admire [what being said]
Pre-Han	春秋繁露	v.	亦有名為弒君而罪不誅者，逆而距之，不若徐而味之	study and comprehend
Pre-Han	淮南子	v.	脩務者，所以為人之於道未淹，味論未深，見其文辭，反之以清靜為常，恬淡為本	study and comprehend
Pre-Han	說苑	v.	故使人味食然後食者，其得味也多；使人味言然後聞言者，其得言也少	study and comprehend

In observing the above table, three points are remarkable: (1) The synesthetic usage of *wèi* is rare in Old Chinese, but more than 80% (5/6) of the synesthetic terms are located Pre-Han, which is close to or even at the dawn of Buddhism's introduction. (2) More than 60% (4/6) of the examples are affiliated with the meaning of 體味 *tǐ-wèi* 'studying and comprehending something', which is extended from distinguishing the taste of food. (3) Two findings located Pre-Han are similar to the definition of *wèi* given in the Āgamas, i.e., "giving rise to joy and happiness". One is 有味哉 *yǒu-wèi-zāi* in the second quotation; apparently, *wèi* expresses the compliment, "What a meaningful and interesting [talk]!" The other is 味其言 *wèi-qí-yán* in the third quotation, which is tricky. The *wèi* is used here as a verb, but the meaning of "studying and comprehending something" doesn't fit in the context. As annotated by Yan Shigu, the commentator of this work in the Tang Dynasty, 有味 *yǒu-wèi* here conveys, "one's words are quite beautiful." Extending Yan's comment further, 誠有味其言 *chéng-yǒu-wèi-qí-yán* means, '[he] sincerely admires one's words' or, '[he] sincerely feels one's talk is beautiful.' Thus, the two examples of *wèi* carry the sense of appreciation and delight. They might have been influenced by Buddhist culture as indicated by the facts that no such usage was found previously and they were written close in time to the official record of Chu Wangying's worship and support of Buddhism.

5 Synesthetic *Wei* Terms in Middle Chinese

The translation of Buddhist texts into Chinese is a prominent phenomenon in Middle Chinese (from Late Han to the Six Dynasties), but this section focuses on extracting relevant terms from local Chinese literature. Thus, excluding all Chinese translations of Buddhist scriptures, 251 *wèi* terms are obtained from the *Academia Sinica Tagged Corpus of Middle Chinese*. However, only 10 of them (4%) match our criteria of synesthetic terms, as listed in Table 2.

In Middle Chinese, the synesthetic usage of *wèi* evolved, and the Buddhist impact on it was more clearly evident than before. Four points help to analyze Table 2: (1) The greatest difference between the results of Middle and Old Chinese is the appearance of abstract terms such as 風味 *fēng-wèi* 'taste of atmosphere' and 玄味 *xuán-wèi* 'profound meaning/profound taste'. In addition, the term 氣味 *qì-wèi* in Old Chinese refers to 氣 *qì* and 味 *wèi*; the former means the 'smell' of something. However, the sixth quotation here is used as a synesthetic term describing a person's condition, which is abstract and difficult to express literally. (2) Interestingly, the meanings of 風味 *fēng-wèi* and 氣味 *qì-wèi* in the table transcend the explanations given by the three Chinese dictionaries consulted. *Wèi* in these two terms refers to the characters, properties, and natures of certain objects, which is similar to the fourth meaning of *rasa* explained previously, i.e., indicating the substance of a certain thing. (3) In addition, *wèi* terms mostly appeared in disyllabic forms in Middle Chinese, as exemplified by 鑽味 *zuān-wèi* 'to drill the taste', 諷味 *fěng-wèi* 'to recite and taste', and 追味 *zhuī-wèi* 'to recall the taste', where *wèi* means 'studying and comprehending'. By comparison, the same meaning is expressed with simply the one character *wèi* in Old Chinese. This phenomenon concurs with a recognized effect of Buddhism on the emergence of large numbers of disyllabic words in the Chinese language [20, p. 18]. (4) In the quotation "我皇帝深味大乘" *wǒ-huáng-dì-shēn-wèi-dà-shèng,* the meaning of *wèi* carries more senses than "studying and comprehending" in Old Chinese. In this context, *wèi* should be interpreted as "to like, love" and 深味 *shēn-wèi* means 'to love deeply'. Such an application blended into the sense of appreciation and delight conveyed by *wèi* in Buddhist doctrine.

Table 2. Synesthetic *wèi* terms in Middle Chinese

Dynasty	Literature	Part of speech	Quotations	Meaning of *wéi*
Song of the Southern dynasties	世說新語	v.	莊子逍遙篇，舊是難處，諸名賢所可鑽味……支卓然標新理於二家之表，立異義於眾賢之外，皆是諸名賢尋味之所不得	study and comprehend
		v.	閑習禮度，不如式瞻儀形。諷味遺言，不如親承音旨	study and comprehend
		v.	諸人追味餘言	study and comprehend
		n.	支道林喪法虔之後，精神賨喪，風味轉墜	condition of the person
		n.	余與夫子，交非勢利，心猶澄水，同此玄味	profound meaning/purpose
Jin	新校搜神記	n.	雖強語笑，無復氣味也	state, condition
Eastern Wei	洛陽伽藍記	v.	我皇帝深味大乘，遠求經典，道路雖險，未敢言疲	like, prefer
Northern Qi	顏氏家訓	n.	至於陶冶性靈，從容諷諫，入其滋味，亦樂事也	feeling or meaning
		v.	簡文吟詠，不能忘之，孝元諷味，以為不可復得……常以謝詩置几案間，動靜輒諷味	study and comprehend
		n.	大同以末，斯風頓盡。然而此樂愔愔雅致，有深味哉	profound meaning/feeling

6 Synesthetic Wèi Terms in Early Mandarin Chinese

A search for *wèi* in the *Academia Sinica Tagged Corpus of Early Mandarin Chinese* (from Tang to Ching) yields 515 results. While 168 (33%) of them are regarded as synesthesia, many of them are commonly used in modern Chinese. This finding shows that synesthetic *wèi* terms increased significantly after Middle Chinese. In addition, several new terms are found in Early Mandarin Chinese, which are listed along with the number of occurrences: 況味 *kuàng-wèi* 'taste of a certain state' (1), 意味 *yì-wèi* 'meaning' (3), 詩味 *shī-wèi* 'poetic taste' (3), 趣味 *qù-wèi* 'fun' (14), 玩味 *wán-wèi* 'to contemplate, to appreciate' (1), 無味 *wú-wèi* 'boring, tasteless' (10), 一味 *yī-wèi* 'one taste, simply' (67), 有味 *yǒu-wèi* 'with taste, interesting' (4), 品味 *pǐn-wèi* 'to taste, or [one's] taste' (1), and 法味 *fǎ-wèi* 'taste of Dharma' (7). In comparison to the results from the first two periods, the number of cases that appeared then also increased at this stage, such as 氣味 *qì-wèi* 'smell, style' (6) and 風味 *fēng-wèi* 'flavor, quality' (5). In addition to the development of the synesthetic *wèi* revealed by the statistic, another four points are noteworthy in Early Mandarin Chinese.

(1) In Early Mandarin Chinese, the metaphorical usage of *wèi* in an abstract sense, such as 道味 *dào-wèi* 'taste of the path' or 法味 *fǎ-wèi* 'taste of Dharma' in the Āgamas, grew greatly by contrast to the resemblances found in Middle Chinese; such an application did not exist in Old Chinese.

(2) The meanings and applications of the terms 氣味 *qì-wèi* 'smell' and 滋味 *zī-wèi* 'flavor' became more extensive. Both originally referred to smell and flavor associated with food in Old Chinese. In Middle Chinese literature, their meanings changed to indicate an abstract state or even the feeling one gets from reading an article. In Early Mandarin Chinese, they were applied even more extensively in vernacular writings such as Chan literature and novels. Exemplified by 祖堂集 *Zu-tang-ji,* the earliest historical book of Chan in existence today, 氣味 *qì-wèi* extended from 'smell' to indicate the Buddhist spirit and essence in an abstract sense in the phrase 法中無氣味 *fǎ-zhōng-wú-qì-wèi* 'no smell/spirit in the Dharma'. Another example quoted from 儒林外史 *Rú-lín-wài-shǐ* reads, 和老弟氣味還投合 *hé-lǎo-dì-qì-wèi-hái-tóu-hé* 'yet being in harmony with [your] personality, bro'; such an application is popularly used in the contemporary abbreviated idiom 氣味相投 *qì-wèi-xiāng-tóu* '[people] have the same taste' or '[friends] attracted to each other by common qualities'. For 滋味 *zī-wèi*, it seemingly became an ordinary phrase referring to a person's feeling, as seen in two examples from vernacular novels in the Ching Dynasty. One example is quoted from 紅樓夢 *Hóng-lóu-mèng*: "These words are plain when you just heard, but recalling them makes you feel interesting (有滋味 *yǒu-zī-wèi)*".[28] Another one is in 岐路燈 *Qí-lù-dēng*: "[He] had already seen the variants [of playing cards] before the noon, and got some feeling (滋味 *zī-wèi*)."[29]

(3) In Early Mandarin Chinese, *wèi* clearly denotes something that is interesting or fun, thereby bringing about happiness and joy, as applied in the terms 趣味 *qù-wèi*, 有味 *yǒu-wèi*, and 無味 *wú-wèi.* This denotation is in line with the doctrinal definition of *wèi* in the Āgamas and continues to reside in modern Chinese, as in the dictionary definition of the term 趣味: "what makes people happy and bring up interest" [21, p.1075]. Although this sense of *wèi* appeared before Early Mandarin Chinese, it obviously increased at this stage. In Old Chinese, two instances occur—有味哉 *yǒu-wèi-zāi* 'very interesting' and 味其言 *wèi-qí-yán* 'to admire/appreciate his talk'—both of which are located in the same Pre-Han book. In Middle Chinese one case occurs: 深味大乘 *shēn-wèi-dà-chéng* 'deeply found of Mahāyāna'. In Early Mandarin Chinese, these cases increase to 28. Because the occurrences of *wèi* denoting what brings about happiness and joy significantly grow after the introduction of Buddhism into China, Buddhism likely affected this usage of *wèi.* Although two similar examples appeared in Chinese

[28] 紅樓夢: 這幾句話雖是淡的, 回想卻有滋味.

[29] 岐路燈: [他]午前早已看那搭配變化, 有些滋味.

literature Pre-Han, they were close to the introduction of Buddhism, and no antecedent for them is found in China. Thus, to argue that *wèi* in the sense of interesting or fun originally existed in the Chinese language is weaker than to assume it was influenced by Buddhist culture.

(4) Special attention should be paid to the differentiation between 意味 *yì-wèi* and 義味 *yì-wèi* because they resemble each other in sound and meaning. 意味 *yì-wèi* first appeared in Early Mandarin Chinese literature with 3 results that denote 'meaning' in the same sense; it is still used in Modern Mandarin and even in contemporary Japanese. On the other hand, 義味 *yì-wèi* occurred much earlier in translations of Buddhist scripture in Middle Chinese, mostly from Eastern Jin to Liu Song, and appears twice in two official history books composed in Tang, 晉書 *Jìn-shū* and 隋書 *Suí-shū*, according to the *Scripta Sinica database* [22]. But it existed neither in Old Chinese literature nor in Middle Chinese according to the *Academia Sinica Ancient Chinese Corpus*. As mentioned previously, 義味 *yì-wèi* in the Āgamas actually refers to two matters of the Buddha's teaching: 'meaning and phrasing.' The term was invented to translate Buddhist scriptures and is particular to the Buddhist context. However, 義味 *yì-wèi* would be easily interpreted as 'taste of meaning' or simply 'meaning' by Chinese people, as illustrated by two examples from the Tang Dynasty. One is quoted from 晉書 *Jìn-shū*: 造數萬言, 皆有義味 *zào-shuò-wàn-yán-jiē-yǒu-yì-wèi* '[he] wrote tens of thousands of words which all had a taste of meaning [22]; the other is from 隋書 *Suí-shū*: 深明義味 *shēn-míng-yì-wèi* 'deeply understanding the meaning' [22]. Neither case is in the Buddhist context, but they are related to Confucianism and Daoism, respectively. As time goes by, in the sense of 'meaning,' 意味 *yì-wèi* seems to replace 義味 *yì-wèi* and resides in Modern Mandarin; consequently, the latter is rarely visible today.

7 Conclusion

The investigation of *wèi* terms in the translation of Buddhist scriptures, i.e., the Āgamas, and in indigenous Chinese literature shows that Buddhism affected the synesthetic use of *wèi* in the Chinese language. The respective ratios of the synesthetic *wèi* words appearing in the three periods of Chinese are 1.6% (9/562) in Old Chinese, 4% (10/251) in Middle Chinese, and 32.6% (168/515) in Early Mandarin Chinese. As shown by the data extraction of the synesthetic *wèi* terms from the three corpora, the synesthetic usage of *wèi* rarely existed in Old Chinese literature, which was mostly written before Buddhism was introduced into China, but the usage appeared later, around the time Buddhism entered into China and grew rapidly after the Tang Dynasty, the golden era of the development of Chinese Buddhism. The Buddhist impact on the synesthetic usage of *wèi* is summarized in the following three aspects:

(1) The metaphorical usage of the Pāli word *rasa* introduced synesthetic *wèi* terms such as 覺味 *jue-wèi* 'taste of enlightenment', 道味 *dào-wèi* 'taste of the path', and 法味 *fǎ-wèi* 'taste of Dharma' into Chinese, which might have stimulated the emergence of terms such as 玄味 *xuán-wèi* and 品味 *pǐn-wèi* in Middle Chinese.

Because the usage of these terms did not appear in Old Chinese and because of their similarity to Buddhist terms, Buddhism appears to have influenced the synesthetic *wèi* terms in Chinese.

(2) In addition, the meaning of *wèi* is enriched by the Buddhist teaching of "taste (*assāda*), danger, and escape", which defines *wèi* as whatever gives rise to happiness and joy. This synesthetic usage of *wèi* is rarely found in Old Chinese, but in Early Mandarin Chinese, the usage increased greatly, as shown in the discussion above. Today, many synesthetic terms of *wèi* entail the sense of giving rise to happiness and joy, either explicitly or implicitly.

(3) 風味 *fēng-wèi* and 義味 *yì-wèi* originated from translations of the Āgamas but were then adopted into Chinese, and their original meaning in the Buddhist context was changed. 風味 *fēng-wèi* has become a term referring to the abstract sense of certain matters such as flavor, personality, and quality; it is rarely known as a Buddhist jargon today. A more complicated case is 義味 *yì-wèi*, which was originally the translation associated with *byañjana.* Because it literally reads as "the taste of meaning", it might have introduced the sense of 'meaning' into the word *wèi*, as explained by Chinese dictionaries. However, when its associated term 意味 *yì-wèi* appeared in Early Mandarin Chinese, 義味 *yì-wèi* seems to have been replaced and is rarely seen today.

Overall, this study is a successful probe of the Buddhist influences on the development of synesthesia in the Chinese language in terms of the method applied and the results revealed. Moreover, it urges the necessity of comparative research between Chinese translations of Buddhist scriptures and corresponding texts in their source languages regarding how translations of Buddhist scriptures affected the Chinese language.

References

1. Xiong, J., Huang, C.R.: The synaesthetic and metaphorical uses of 味 *wei* 'taste' in Chinese Buddhist Sutras. In: PALIC30, Kyunhee University, Seoul Korea (2016)
2. Hirakawa, A.: A History of Indian Buddhism: From Śākyamuni to Early Mahāyāna, Motilal Barnarsidass Publication (1993)
3. Chinese Buddhist Electronic Text Association (CBETA). http://cbetaonline.dila.edu.tw/zh/T0001_001
4. Burmese edition of Pāli Tipitaka, Chatta Saṅgayana CD (CSCD). http://www.tipitaka.org/romn/
5. Academia Sinica Tagged Corpus of Old Chinese. http://lingcorpus.iis.sinica.edu.tw/ancient/
6. Academia Sinica Tagged Corpus of Middle Chinese. http://lingcorpus.iis.sinica.edu.tw/middle/
7. Academia Sinica Tagged Corpus of Early Mandarin Chinese. http://lingcorpus.iis.sinica.edu.tw/early/
8. Zhao, Q., Huang, C.-R., Lee, Y.-S.: From linguistic synaesthesia to embodiment: asymmetrical representations of taste and smell in Mandarin Chinese. Chinese Lexical Semantics. LNCS (LNAI), vol. 10709, pp. 420–427. Springer, Cham (2018). https://doi.org/10.1007/978-3-319-73573-3_38

9. Pāli Text Society. The Pāli Text Society's Pāli-English dictionary (PED), London, 1921–1925. http://dsal.uchicago.edu/dictionaries/Pali/
10. Bodhi, B.: The Numerical Discourses of the Buddha: A Translation of the Aṅguttara Nikāya. Wisdom Publications, Boston (2012)
11. Thera, Ñ.: Raṭṭhapāla Sutta: A Discourse from Majjhima Nikāya. BPS, Kandy (1980)
12. Bodhi, B.: The Middle Length Discourses of the Buddha: A new Translation of the Majjhima Nikāya. Wisdom Publications, Boston (1995)
13. Buddhist Dictionary, Nyanatiloka Thera. https://what-buddha-said.net/library/pdfs/Nyanatiloka_Buddhist_Dictionary.pdf
14. Bodhi, B.: The Connected Discourses of the Buddha: A Translation of the Saṃyutta Nikāya. Wisdom Publications, Boston (2000)
15. Gu hanyu da cidian 古漢語大詞典 [the Great Old Chinese Dictionary]. Shanghai cishu chubanshe faxingsuo 上海辞書出版社發行所, Shanghai cishu chubanshe 上海辞書出版社 (2001)
16. Gudai hanyu cidian 古代漢語詞典 [the Ancient Chinese Dictionary]. Gudai hanyu cidian bianxiezu 古代漢語詞典編寫組, Shangwu yinshuguan 商務印刷館 (2005)
17. Hanyu da zidian 漢語大字典 [the Great Chinese Dictionary] Sec. ed. Hanyu da zidian bianji weiyuanhui 漢語大字典編輯委員會, Chengdu: Sichuan cishu chubanshe 四川辭書出版社 (2010)
18. Authority Database of Buddhist Tripitaka Catalogues. http://dev.dila.edu.tw/authority/catalog/?fromInner=CA0004098
19. Joly, H.B. (trans.): The Dream of the Red Chamber. Tuttle Publishing, North Clarendon, VT (2010)
20. Liang, X.-H. 梁曉虹: "Fojiao yu hanyu" 佛教與漢語 [Buddhism and Chinese]. In: Yuwen Tiandi 語文天地 19, vol. 3, pp. 15–22 (1992)
21. Xiandai hanyu cidian 現代漢語詞典 [The Modern Chinese Dictionary]. Zhongguo shehui kexuyuan yuyan yanjiusho cidian bianjishi 中國社會科學院語言研究所詞典編輯室, Shangwu yinshuguan 商務印書館 (2005)
22. The Scripta Sinica database. http://hanchi.ihp.sinica.edu.tw/ihp/hanji.htm

The Semantic Differences and Substitution Restrictions of *-Zhe*(着) and *Zhengzai*(正在)

Jie Fan[1,2(✉)] and Chong-ming Ding[2]

[1] College of Humanities, Xihua University, Chengdu 610039, Sichuan, People's Republic of China
fanjie_219@qq.com

[2] College of Chinese Language and Culture, Beijing Normal University, Beijing 100875, People's Republic of China

Abstract. The substitution of *-zhe*(着) and *zhengzai*(正在) is influenced by the temporal meaning, aspectual meaning and the verb situation. This paper analyzes the differences of *-zhe* and *zhengzai* in detail in these three areas above, and finds out some meanings and usages of them, which rarely be mentioned in the prior literature. The temporal and aspectual meaning of *-zhe* and *zhengzai* are quite different. It is proposed that *-zhe* represents aspectual meaning while *zhengzai* mainly represents temporal meaning. *-Zhe* can not only indicate progressive, continuous and frequentative aspect of single event, but also indicate plural event and habitual events. The core meaning of *zhengzai* is concurrence, which means the process of change occurs simultaneously with the corresponding event. Only in two occasions can *-zhe* and *zhengzai* substitute with each other. One is when *-zhe* and *zhengzai* represent progressive aspect plus process verb. The other is when they represent frequentative aspect plus instantaneous verb. In the rest of situations *-zhe* and *zhengzai* are not mutually replaceable.

Keywords: *-zhe*(着) · *zhengzai*(正在) · Temporal meaning
Aspectual meaning · Collocation restriction of verbs · Substitution condition

1 Introduction

The semantic difference of *-zhe*(着) and *zhengzai*(正在) is an important problem in the research of modern Chinese. The view that both *-zhe* and *zhengzai* indicate progressive aspect is accepted widely. In addition to the similarity, there are a lot of differences between the two words in semantics and usage. Some literature studied specifically or involved in the problem of *-zhe* and *zhengzai*, such as [1–5]. These studies discussed the two words from the different viewpoints, such as scope, focusing degree, pragmatics, and verb selectional restriction, etc., and gained many useful views. But it is not comprehensive systematic enough and cannot fully indicate the semantic differences and the substitution condition of *-zhe* and *zhengzai*.

Through analyzing the substitution of the two words, this paper reveals that the substitution condition of *-zhe* and *zhengzai* is very complex: in some occasions, "*zhengzai*+V" cannot be replaced with "V-*zhe*", for example (1)[1]; in some occasions,

[1] In addition to the individual examples written by ourselves, the examples in this paper are from CCL corpus of Peking University and BCC corpus of Beijing Language University.

J.-F. Hong et al. (Eds.): CLSW 2018, LNAI 11173, pp. 294–310, 2018.
https://doi.org/10.1007/978-3-030-04015-4_25

"V-*zhe*" cannot be replaced with "*zhengzai*+V", for example (2); in some occasions, both of the two phrases can be used but the meaning of sentences are different, for example (3); and in the other occasions, the two groups of sentences with *-zhe* and *zhengzai* are same meaning, for example (4).

(1)a.*Yixie bu fuhe suzhi jiaoyu yaoqiu, weibei jiaoyu*
some not conform quality-oriented education requirements, break education
guilvde wenti zhengzai zhubu dedao jiuzheng.
rule problems is being gradually gain resolution.
Some problems that do not conform to the requirements of quality-oriented education and break the rules of education are being gradually corrected.

b.*Zhezhong wangshang jiaoxue zhengzai zhubu fazhan cheng*
This kind of online teaching is gradually develop become
renmen yuanyi jieshoude you yizhong banxue moshi.
persons be will to accept another kind run a school mode.
This kind of online teaching is gradually developing another school running mode that persons are willing to accept.

c.*Zhishi jingji, xinxi jingjide shidai zhengzai daolai.*
Knowledge economy, information economy era is coming.
The era of knowledge and information economy is coming.

(2)a.*Buduide zhuangbei jidu quefa, henduoren dou haishi*
Troops' equipment extremely scarce, many people all still
yong-zhe yixie zhiliang bugao de bingren.
using some quality not good weaponry.
The troop's equipment is extremely scarce, and many people still use the inferior quality weapons.

b.*Buyude Hezhe Zu guniang chuanqi piaoliangde huase lianyiqun, chi-zhe*
Fishing Hezhen girls wearing pretty floral dress, eating
dami, baimian he gese ziji zhongzhide shucai.
rice, wheat and all kinds of planted by themselves vegetables.
The Hezhen fishing girls wearing pretty dress eat delicate food and all kinds of vegetables planted by themselves.

c.*Ta faxian youde yuanshi shehui zhong, renmen zai chongmide shihou, shi*
He find some in primitive society, people when trash rice, is
yimian chongmi, yimian chang-zhe seqingde geyao.
on one hand trash rice, on the other hand singing pornographic songs.
He discovered that in some primitive societies, people always sang the pornographic songs when they trashed the rice.

(3)a.*Ta fu-zhe laonainai.≠Ta zhengzai fu laonainai.*
She holds granny.≠She is holding granny.
She holds the granny.≠She is holding the granny.

b. *Ta wan-zhe yao.≠Ta zhengzai wan yao.*
She bent waist .≠She is bending her waist.
She bent her body.≠She is bending her body.

c.*Ta hong-zhe lian.≠Ta zhengzai honglian.*

She red face.≠She is getting red face.
Her face is red.≠Her face is getting red.

(4)a. *Dangshi dage zhengzai ban Tianjin Jiaoan.*
That time big brother was dealing with Tianjin Church case.
——*Dangshi dage ban-zhe Tianjin jiaoan.*
That time big brother was dealing with Tianjin Church case.
At that time, big brother was dealing with the case of Tianjin Church.

b. *Cheng Jingdong ye zuozai nali, zhengzai anwei ta gugu.*
Cheng Jingdong also sit at there, was comforting his aunt.
——*Cheng Jingdong ye zuozai nali, anwei-zhe ta gugu.*
Cheng Jingdong also sit at there, was comforting his aunt.
Cheng Jingdong was sitting there, comforting his aunt.

c. *Weier fushen zai chezhao xia, jiancha-zhe shenme.*
Weier bent at car cover under, was inspecting something.
——*Weier fushen zai chezhao xia, zhengzai jiancha shenme.*
Weier bent at car cover under, was inspecting something.
Weier was inspecting something under the car cover with bending his body.

d. *Wo xianzai tongshi chuli-zhe sange fangmiande shiqing.*
I now same time am dealing with three aspects business.
——*Wo xianzai zhengzai tongshi chuli sange fangmiande shiqing.*

I now am same time dealing with three aspects business. Now I'm dealing with three aspects businesses at the same time.

From example (1) to (3), What is the restriction for the substitution? Why can the replacements of example (4) be established?

The previous studies found that both *-zhe* and *zhengzai* contribute to the aspectual meaning primarily, and the differences of them are mainly embodied in aspect. But this paper reveals that the differences of *-zhe* and *zhengzai* are in both aspect and tense, which are the important basis of substitution of *-zhe* and *zhengzai*.

This paper analyzes the meanings of *-zhe* and *zhengzai* in aspect and tense, and discusses the semantic differences in detail. In order to exclude the influence of special sentence patterns on semantics and pragmatics, "V-*zhe*" imperative sentence, "V-*zhe*" existential sentence, "V_1-*zhe* V_2" serial verbs sentence and other special sentence patterns are excluded from the discussion.

2 The Aspect and Tense of *-Zhe*

2.1 The Aspect of *-Zhe*

It is consensus that *-zhe* can indicate progressive and continuous, but through the analysis of corpus we found that *-zhe* can represent more aspectual meanings. In this article, the aspects of *-zhe* are divided into two categories. One is single event that limits strictly the verb situations. The other is plural event that doesn't require specific verb situations and expresses meaning depending on context auxiliary.

2.1.1 The Aspect of Single Event

"V-*zhe*" can represent three basic aspects that indicate different stages in action. The verb situation is the key point of the three aspectual meanings. We describe the three aspects through the verb (phrase) "wanyao (bend)".

(5)a.*Kangfu xunlian shi ta bugan dadong, zhineng*
Rehabilitation training time she dare not move vigorously, can just
Manman-de *wan-zhe yao*.
slowly bending her waist.
She did not dare to move vigorously during the rehabilitation exercise, but could only bend slowly.

b.*Weile lianhao yige xiayao dongzuo, ta zhengge*
In order to exercise well one back bending motion, she the whole
Shangwu dou butingde *wan-zhe yao*.
morning all time ceaselessly bending her waist.
In order to practice a low back action, she kept bending all morning.

c.*Tade bei yijing gouloule, zoulushi yizhi* *wan-zhe yao*.
Her back already rickets, as walking always bending her waist.
Since her back is rickets, she has to keep bending her waist when she walks.

The phrase "wan-*zhe* yao (bending)" represents different aspects by *-zhe* tagging "wanyao (bend)". (5a) is progressive aspect representing the process of one time of "wanyao (bend)", (5b) is frequentative aspect representing the repeated "wanyao (bend)", (5c) is continuous aspect representing the continued state after the change. The internal process of "wan-*zhe* yao (bending)" can be shown as following:

The "a" in Fig. 1 indicates the process of one time "bending", the "b" indicates repeated "bending" more than one time, and the "c" indicates the stative process after the change of "bend". The three stages indicate the three basic aspects represented by the phrase of "V-*zhe*", which are progressive, frequentative and continuous. These three aspects are single event that require explicit verb situations.

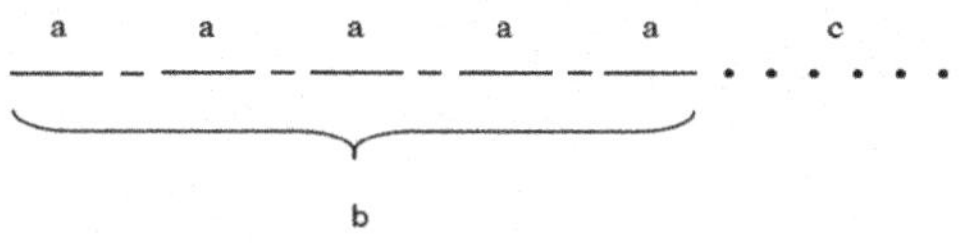

Fig. 1. Three aspectual meanings of "wan-zhe yao"

Stage a (progressive aspect): "V-*zhe*" means the progressive aspect of single action or activity. The stage a is a continuous process, which requires the verb is continuous and dynamic, for example "chi-*zhe* (eating)" "du-*zhe* (reading)" "xie-*zhe* (writing)" "pao-*zhe* (running)" "bianzhi-*zhe* (knitting)" "taolun-*zhe* (discussing)", etc.

Stage b (frequentative aspect): "V-*zhe*" means the frequentative aspect. The stage b is a process of repeated activities. There are two categories of verbs that can co-occur with -*zhe*. Continuous verb plus -*zhe* means the repeated processes, such as "wan-*zhe* yao", and instantaneous verb with -*zhe* represents the repeated activities, for example "beng-*zhe* (jumping)" "tiao-*zhe* (jumping)" "qiao-*zhe* (knocking)" "pai-*zhe* (patting)", etc.

Stage c (continuous aspect): "V-*zhe*" means continuous aspect that is a steady state after the change of action or activity. There are three kinds of verbs can indicate continuous aspect with -*zhe* in this stage, which are process verb[2], transition verb and state verb. The examples for continuous aspect are shown as below (Table 1).

Table 1. The verb situations of "V-*zhe*" in stage c

Verb Situations	Examples of "V-*zhe*"
Process verbs	"chuan-*zhe* (wearing)" "zuo-*zhe* (sitting)" "xie-*zhe* (written)" "ke-*zhe* (carved)" "bianzhi-*zhe* (knitted)"
Transition verbs	"gua–*zhe* (hanging)" "gai-*zhe* (covered)" "fang-*zhe* (lying)"
State verbs	"ai-*zhe* (loving)" "chou-*zhe* (worrying)" "danyou-*zhe* (wearing)"

In short, verbs can co-exist with -*zhe* must possess at least one of the three stages mentioned above. If it possesses two or more stages, the "V-*zhe*" will be ambiguous. For example, many process verbs plus -*zhe* may have ambiguity, such as "chuan-*zhe*" "xie-*zhe*" "ke-*zhe*" and "bianzhi-*zhe*". In the appropriate context, "V-*zhe*" can not only express the progressive aspect (stage a) in dynamic process, but also express the continuous aspect (stage c) after the action completed.

2.1.2 The Aspect of Plural Event

2.1.2.1 General Plural Event

In many cases, "v-*zhe*" is able to represent plural event constituted with single events. These single events are usually in different space or time. Such as:

[2] According to the theory of [6], this paper divides the verb situations into three categories: process, transition and state.

(6)a. *"9.18"qianxi, zai Zhongguo dongbei zhepian heitudi shang,*
On the eve of "9.18"Emergency, in Northeast China, the black land,
bansui hanzhe xuehelei de gesheng, renmen fenfen yi
following with blood and tears songs, people one after another in
gezhong fangshi jinian-zhe "nage beicande shihou".
a variety of ways commemorating "that miserable time".
On the eve of "9.18"Emergency, in the black land of Northeast China, people were commemorating "that miserable time" with the songs of blood and tears in a variety of ways.
b. *Meige wangchao zai tianzhi shuifa shang jinxing-zhe gezhonggese de douzheng.*
Each dynasty on land system tax law doing all kinds of struggles.
Each dynasty had been struggling on land system and tax law in all kinds of ways.

In the case of (6), "jinian-*zhe* (commemorating)" and "jinxing-*zhe* (doing)" do not mean a single event, but rather indicate the repeated single events that usually span time and space, and the subjects of the single events must be different.

2.1.1.2 Habitual Plural Event

The further development of the general plural event will lead to the habitual meaning. The so-called "habitual aspect" refers to a regular situation. In English, it is represented by present tense or "used to". In Chinese, it is more common to use frequency adverbs, state verbs or bare verbs to represent the habitual aspect. For example:

(7)a. *Canjia gongzuo qian wo yizhi zai xuexiao dushu.*
Take part in work before I all the time at school study.
I had been studying at school all the time before I took part in the work.
/ *Ta jingchang guanggu zhejia shudian.*
He often patronize this bookstore.
He often patronizes this bookstore.
/ *Xiao Wang huihui kaihui dou chidao.*
Xiao Wang every time meeting always be late.
Xiao Wang is late for every meeting always.
b. *Ta zhegeren ai da xiaobaogao.*
/ He a guy like sneak.
He's a guy who likes sneaking.
/ *Lao Wang xihuan da taijiquan.*
Lao Wang like practice shadowboxing.
Lao Wang likes practicing shadowboxing.
/ *Ta jiu hao chi liangkou haode.*
He just like eat some tasty.
He just likes to eat some tasty food.
c. *Wo zhu xuexiao sushe. / Ta chouyan./ Wo airen qizixingche shangban.*
I live in school dormitory./ He smoke./ My lover by bike to work.
I live in school's dormitory./ He smokes./ My lover goes to work by bike.

In addition, there is a large number of "V-*zhe*" express the habitual aspect in the corpus. When the plural event occurs regularly over a period of time, the habitual aspect comes out. For example (6a), the event extended from "one commemorative" to "annual commemorative", which possess the two conditions of regularity and high frequency. Another example is (2) at the beginning of the paper.

(2)a.*Buduide zhuangbei jidu quefa, henduoren dou haishi*
Troops' equipments extremely be short of, many people all still
yong-zhe yixie zhiliang bugaode bingren.
using some quality not good weaponry.
The troop's equipment is extremely scarce, and many people still use the inferior quality weapons.

b.*Buyude Hezhe Zu guniang chuanqi piaoliangde huase lianyiqun, chi-zhe*
Fishing Hezhen girls wearing pretty floral dress, eating
dami, baimian he gese ziji zhongzhide shucai.
rice, wheat and all kinds of planted by themselves vegetables.
The Hezhen fishing girls wearing pretty dress eat delicate food and all kinds of vegetables planted by themselves.

c.*Ta faxian youde yuanshi shehui zhong, renmen zai chongmide shihou, shi*
He find some in primitive society, people when trash rice, is
yimian chongmi, yimian chang-zhe seqingde geyao.
on one hand trash rice, on the other hand singing pornographic songs.
He discovered that in some primitive societies, people always sang the pornographic song when they trashed the rice.

No matter expresses general plural event or habitual aspect, the "V-*zhe*" means events occurring repeatedly. The difference between them is that the general plural event merely emphasizes the objective fact have occurred, while the habitual aspect possesses predictability. For example, in (2a), "use the inferior quality weapon" is a predictable phenomenon; in (2b), it has become normal that a fishing girl can eat delicate food; in (2c), it is not hard to know that people sing pornographic songs when they trashed the rice in the primitive society.

It should be said that the "habitual event" is a subordinate category of plural event. When the habitual aspect spans the eventual boundaries and the granularity of events diminishes with the homogeneity rising, the habitual aspect is close to a state; when the events completely vanish, the "V-*zhe*" habitual aspect is close to a property. Such as:

(8)a. *Zhe chaiyi chi-zhe guanfan, ban-zhe guanshi.*
The officer eating official food deal with official affairs.
The officer takes official meals and deals with official affairs.

b. *Ta suiran bita xiao yisui, dan zongshi xiangge jiejie yiyang aihu-zhe ta.*
She although than him young one year, but always like a elder sister take care of him
Although she is one year younger than him, she always takes care of him like an elder sister.

c. *Renzhen de dushu shi yizhong renshi huodong, xunlian-zhe women shibie, panduan laizi daqianshijie de gezhong xinxi fuhao.*
Serious reading is a kind of cognitive activity, train us identify, judge from the world all kinds of information symbols.
Serious reading is a cognitive activity that trains us to identify and judge all kinds of information symbols from the world.

It is difficult to distinguish specific event from example (8), as "eating official meals" is hard to say it's how many times to eat, "take care of him" can not be understood as "take care of him for many times". The phrase of "xunlian-*zhe* (train)" in (8c) is not a event but a comment of "serious reading". The "V-*zhe*" has gradually lost its eventual meaning in habitual sense. Even if *-zhe* is removed, the meaning of sentence does not change. It can be seen that there are different degrees in the habitual aspect, including the habitual event, the habitual state and the habitual property.

The *-zhe* indicates the meaning of habitual, which is related to the context and the property of *-zhe* itself. Firstly, context provides more broad background knowledge for people to judge the situation, such as (8a). The native speakers know that "eating official meals" dose not mean "eating official food", but means "for the public service to make a living". "Eating official meals" is not a single event or plural event, but a habitual occupation. Sometimes the mismatch between the context and event is a hint, such as "he washes the dishes in the kitchen" and "he washes the dishes in New York". The scene of the previous sentence matches the event and the latter does not. The "wash dishes" in the "kitchen" is likely to represent a single event, and the latter "wash the dishes" and "New York" do not match the general background knowledge. This mismatch provides a hint that "wash the dishes" may not refer to a particular event, but refers to a habitual situation even an occupation. Therefore, the latter sentence provides a background knowledge or a space-time range to help people judge whether a sentence expresses a specific event or a habitual situation.

Secondly, the habitual aspect indicated by *-zhe* usually cross time and space. Especially in descriptive languages, the event or situation is not so strongly related to the real world. Speaker (writer) or listener (reader) are standing in a separated view of events or situations, and the time range of *-zhe* is almost unrestricted. Shi [4] also expressed a similar view that the time range of *-zhe* can be extended from the past and the present to the future. The spacial and temporal range of plural event and habitual aspect are deep, and the property of *-zhe* corresponds to this.

Through the analysis above, we can see that the aspect of *-zhe* includes two situations: the aspect of single event and plural event. The progressive, continuous and frequentative aspects involved more in the prior studies, but the aspects of plural event are seldom mentioned. According to a ascending in homogeneity and a descending in granularity of events, there is a continuum of the aspect meaning of the plural event: the general plural event - the habitual event - the state of the habitual-property.

2.2 The Tense of "-*Zhe*"

The -*zhe* does not represent temporal meaning as indicating a single event. The single event of "V+*zhe*" is less related to reality, and there is no definite time point. "Mama zai chufang zuo-*zhe* fan. (Mom's cooking in the kitchen.)" is more like describing a scene, and the time of the scene needs to be judged by context.

The temporal meaning of -*zhe* is mainly reflected in the habitual plural event. The time of "V+*zhe*" extends from the past to the present even to the future. If there is a time word in a sentence, the time is indicated by the time word; if there is no time information in sentence, the "V+*zhe*" generally expresses the present situation. Take the previous sentences as examples:

(9)a. *Meige wangchao zai tianzhi shuifa shang jinxing-zhe gezhonggese de douzheng.*
Each dynasty on land system tax law doing all kinds of struggles.
Each dynasty had been struggling on land system and tax law in all kinds of way.

b. *Zhe zuo mingchengde zhuyao jiedaoshang zhijin benpao-zhe yizhong*
This famous city main streets up to now running a kind of
laoshi dianche.
old tram.

On the main streets of this famous city, a kind of old trams are running up to now.

c. *Cong ta nashi yihou, Yadian-de qingnian jiu beisong-zhe Hema,*
From his time after, Athens young people already reciting Homer,
er zhe chengwei tamen jiaoyuzhong zui zhongyao-de bufen.
and that become their education most important part.
From then on, young people in Athens were reciting Homer, which became the most important part of their education.

d. *Zhe chaiyi chi-zhe guanfan, ban-zhe guanshi.*
The officer eating official food deal with official affairs.
The officer takes official meals and deals with official affairs.

(10)a. *Ta suiran bita xiao yisui, dan zongshi xiangge jiejie yiyang*
She although than him young one year, but always like a elder sister
aihu-zhe ta.
take care of him
Although she is one year younger than him, she always takes care of him like an elder sister.

b. *Renzhen de dushu shi yizhong renshi huodong, xunlian-zhe women*
Serious reading is a kind of cognitive activity, train us
shibie, panduan laizi daqianshijie de gezhong xinxi fuhao.
identify, judge from the world all kinds of information symbols.
Serious reading is a cognitive activity that trains us to identify and judge all kinds of information symbols from the world.

The "V-*zhe*" indicates different time information in examples (9) and (10). The four sentences in example (9) have time information, in (9a) "every dynasty" indicates that "douzheng (struggle)" is a historical events, which happened in the past; (9b) "up to now" shows that "trams running" occurs from the past to now; (9c) "from then on" indicates that the starting point of "reciting Homer" is in the past, and the end of the event does not show in the sentence; in (9d) "chaiyi" is a historical word, so it is possible to speculate that "take official meals and deal with official" is a past events. There are no clear time words in the sentences of example (10). In (10a) the event may be the present situation; (10b) indicates a sense of axiom, and the events of "V-*zhe*" are set up from the past to the present and future. It can be seen that, "V-*zhe*" seldom indicates the specific time, even in the expression of habitual events, the effect of "V-*zhe*" on the absolute time is also very limited.

3 The Aspect and Tense of *Zhengzai*

3.1 The Tense of *Zhengzai*

There are not many syntactic means to express tense in modern Chinese. The more general way is to use time adverbs, time nouns or context to express the temporal information. *Zhengzai* as an adverb has a clear function on expressing temporal meaning.

The temporal meaning of "*zhengzai*+V" is "happening at the same time". No matter if there are other events in the sentence, the time of "*zhengzai*+V" is always occurring at the same time with a corresponding time. If there is no reference time in the sentence, *zhengzai* occurs simultaneously with the time of speech. For example, "Mama *zhengzai* zuofan (Mun is cooking)", the time of "*zhengzai* zuofan (Mum is cooking)" is the speech time. If there is a reference time in the sentence, *zhengzai* occurs simultaneously with the reference event. In "wo jinmenshi, Mama *zhengzai* zuofan (when I enter the door, Mum is cooking)", the time of "*zhengzai* zuofan (Mum is cooking)" is located at "I enter the door". The main function of "*zhengzai*+V" is to specify time information.

Due to the restriction of corresponding event, the time span of "*zhengzai*+V" is corresponding to the time span of reference events. The events described by *zhengzai* may be small or big, but they are always restricted by the corresponding events. Therefore, the time range of *zhengzai* is relatively narrow. At the same time, the temporal meanings of *zhengzai* are different in diverse styles. In a style with strong relevance to the speaker, there is no other reference time in the sentence, and *zhengzai* points to the time of speech, such as dialogues, news reports, and other languages. Such as:

(11)a. "*Mama* *zhengzai* *zuofan*."
Mum was cooking.
Mum was cooking.
b. "*Laoshi* *zhengzai* *pigai* *zuoye*."
The teacher was correct homework.
The teacher was correct students' homework.
c. "*Wo fumu* *zhengzai* *nao lihun,* *wo buwang* *zheyang*."
My parents are do divorce, I not want that.
My parents are getting divorced, and I don't want that.
d. *Guoji shehui* *zhengzai* *jinxing yichang* *xinjishu* *geming*.
International community are doing a new technological revolution.
A new technological revolution is being carried out in the international community.
e. *Beijingshi* *xuanbu* *zhengzai* *yanjiu* *shi'ernian* *yiwujiaoyu de*
Beijing announce was studying twelve-year compulsory education
shishi zhunbei.
implementation
Beijing announced that it was studying the implementation of the twelve-year compulsory education.
f. *Jiji xinlixue* *shi* *meiguo* *xinlixuejie* *zhengzai* *xingqi-de* *yige*
Positive psychology is American psychology are emerging a
xinde yanjiu *lingyu*.
new research field.
Positive psychology is a new research field in American psychology.

The first three sentences in (11) occurred in dialogues, and the time of "*zhengzai* +V" is speech time. The last three sentences are in news reports and scientific documents, the "*zhengzai*+V" refers to the time of passage. The dialogues in novel and the scripts in film are not related to the real time, but imitate the daily dialogues. Therefore, "*zhengzai*+V" is also pointing to the speech time.

In narrative style, events occur in fictional scenes or in the past, there is no strong relevance to the speaker and listener. The time of "*zhengzai*+V" point to the time of the narration if there is no reference time, or point to the time of reference if there is the time of reference. Examples as below.

(12)a. *Yici wo zhengzai qiaodixia shuidajiao, guolai yige daizhe yanjing de*
Once I was under the bridge sleeping, come a wearing glasses
zhishifenzi muyang de ren.
intellectual looks like man.
Once I was sleeping under the bridge, a man looks like a intellectual who was wearing glasses was coming.

b. *Fanza-de qidong gongzuo he zheliangge weiji shijian,*
The complicated start-up work and these two crisis events,
rang guge zhengzai sunshi baogui-de shichang fen'e.
make Google was losing valuable market share.
The complicated start up works and these two crises were making Google lose valuable market share.

c. *Kangzhan shiqi, jiefangqu-de shixue gongzuozhe*
During the War of Resistance against Japan, Liberated Area historians
zhengzai litu yong Makesi zhuyi yanjiu jindaishi zhuwenti.
were trying with Marxism study modern history various problems.
During the War of Resistance Against Japan, historians in Liberated Area were trying to study the problems of modern history with Marx doctrine.

d. *Zhuyao you shangren, baomaishang, shougonggongchangzhu, nongchangzhu*
Mainly with businessmen, buyers, handwork men, farmers
zucheng de chengxiang zichanjieji zhengzai xingcheng, qizhong
composed urban and rural bourgeoisie was taking shape, in which
shangye zichanjieji zhan shouyao diwei.
commercial bourgeoisie play a leading role.
The urban and rural bourgeoisie, which was mainly composed of businessmen, buyers, handwork men and farmers, was taking shape, with the commercial bourgeoisie playing a leading role.

In (12a), "once" describes an event in the past; in (12b), Li Kai-fu reviewed the "ICP licence disturbance", and "the loss of market share" occurred after the licence disturbance; in (12c), there is a clear time information, the War of Resistance Against Japan period; in (12d), there is no time information, but the words as "hand workers" and "Bourgeoisie" indicate the past. In this style, the time is mainly provided by contextual discourse, and "*zhengzai*+V" refers to reference time.

3.2 The Aspect of *Zhengzai*

The aspect of "*zhengzai*+V" is much simpler than "V-*zhe*". Back to the three stages shown in Fig. 1, only in stage a and b can "V-*zhe*" be replaced by "zhengzai+V". It can be seen that "*zhengzai*+V" can represent the progressive and frequentative aspect, but can not represent continuous aspect. At the same time, the "V-*zhe*" can not be replaced by "*zhengzai*+V" in plural event, which means "*zhengzai*+V" can not represent the aspect of plural event. The aspect of *zhengzai* is mainly characterized by two points: change and process.

3.2.1 The Changes—*Zhengzai* Play Role at the Stage of Change

Zhengzai usually plays a role in the stage of change. This is an important characteristic of *zhengzai* different from "*-zhe*". The problem, as shown in example (3), is:

Ta hong-zhe lian.≠Ta zhengzai honglian.
Her face is red.≠Her face is getting red.
Ta dun-zhe.≠Ta zhengzai (wangxia)dun.
She is squatting.≠She's squatting down.
Ta fu-zhe laonainai.≠Ta zhengzai fu laonainai.
She holds the granny.≠She is holding the granny.

In the sentences of "ta *zhengzai* honglian" "ta *zhengzai* (wangxia)dun" and "ta *zhengzai* fu laonainai", the "*zhengzai*+V" is a sign of change. Here, the "V-*zhe*" has ambiguity, which can indicate not only the progressing stage of "a", but also the continuous stage of "c". In order to avoid ambiguity, "*zhengzai*+V" and "V-*zhe*" have focused on different function. "*zhengzai*+V" indicates progressive aspect on stage "a", and "V-*zhe*" indicates continuous aspect on stage "c". "Ta hong-*zhe* lian" shows the blushing state after her face turn red. "Ta dun-*zhe*" "Ta fu-*zhe* laonainai" are the same, which is shown in Fig. 1.

The semantic of *Zhengzai* is incompatible with state verb, but sometimes we can see some state verbs used with *zhengzai*, such as "renshi (to know)" "liaojie (to understand)" "fachou (worry)"and "shuxi (be familiar with)". Because these verbs can indicate both action and state, they can co-exist with *zhengzai* representing a process of change. The two meanings of these verbs in the modern Chinese Dictionary (Seventh Edition) are interpreted as follows:

Liaojie: (1)know clearly. (state verb)
*wo liaojie nide xinqing/*zhengzai liaojie*
I know your situation/*to be knowing
(2)inquire; investigate. (process verb)
liaojie yixia zhege ren/zhengzai liaojie
get to know the man/be inquiring

Renshi: (1)It can be sure that a person or thing is a person or thing rather than something or someone else. (state verb)
*Wo renshi zhezhong caoyao/*zhengzai renshi*
I know this herb-medicine/*to be knowing
(2)Understand and master objective things through practice(process verb)
Renshi shijie, gaizaoshijie/zhengzai renshi
Cognize the world and transform the world/be cognizing

Shuxi: (1)know clearly. (state verb)
*hen shuxi/*zhengzai shuxi*
be familiar with/*be familiaring with
(2)cognize, inquire. (process verb)
shuxi yixia chengdi/zhengzai shuxi
familiarize yourself with the playing field/being familiar with

In the interpretations above, these state verbs possess two meanings that one is process and the other is state. The meaning of "*zhengzai*+V" is process rather than state in fact. It shows that *zhengzai* can not represent the continuous of state, but mainly indicates the process of change. It's not hard to say that indicating change is a important characteristics of "*zhengzai*+V".

3.2.2 The Process—*Zhengzai* Can Make the Moment Change to Be Process

Zhengzai acts on instantaneous transition and makes it process. Such as the phenomenon at the beginning of the article (1):

(1)a. *Yixie bu fuhe suzhi jiaoyu yaoqiu, weibei jiaoyu*
some not conform quality-oriented education requirements, break education
guilvde wenti zhengzai zhubu dedao jiuzheng.
rule problems is being gradually gain resolution.
Some problems that do not conform to the requirements of quality-oriented education and violate the rules of education are being gradually corrected.

b. *Zhezhong wangshang jiaoxue zhengzai zhubu fazhan cheng*
This kind of online teaching is gradually develop become
renmen yuanyi jieshoude you yizhong banxue moshi.
persons be will to accept another kind run a school type.
This kind of online teaching is gradually developing another school running mode that adults are willing to accept.

c. *Zhishi jingji, xinxi jingjide shidai zhengzai daolai.*
Knowledge economy, information economy era is coming.
The era of knowledge and information economy is coming.

The "*zhengzai*+V" in these examples can not be replaced by "V-*zhe*". According to previous studies, the typical instantaneous verbs can not co-occur semantically with *zhengzai* and "-zhe". But the reality is that, in addition to the above examples, there are a large number of instantaneous verbs that can co-occur with *zhengzai*, such as "*zhengzai* miewang (being perished)" "*zhengzai* siqu (dying)" "*zhengzai* huimie (being destroyed)" "*zhengzai* pomie (being broken)" "*zhengzai* xiaoshi (be disappearing)" "*zhengzai* fenlie (being split)" "*zhengzai* gaibian (is changing)" "*zhengzai* tigao (be improving)" "*zhengzai* jinbu (be progressing)" and so on. "*Zhengzai*+V" represents a sense of change when it co-occurs with these verbs. There are two different situations:

3.2.2.1 *Zhengzai*+ "Gradual Change Meaning" Instantaneous Verbs

"tigao (improve)" "gaijin (make better)" "jinbu (progress)" "youhua (make better)"

Although these verbs are instantaneous (transition) verbs, they can be repeated because they indicate gradual change. One time of "tigao (improve)" is instantaneous, but many times of "tigao (improve)" can be regarded as a process. Therefore, this kind of instantaneous verbs are compatible with *zhengzai* in semantics. This category of "*zhengzai*+V" can collocate with "buduan (continuous)" "chixu (continuous)" or "zhujian (gradual)" indicating the continuous changes, such as "*zhengzai* buduan jinbu (be continuously progressing)" "*zhengzai*i chixu youhua (be continuously making better)" "*zhengzai* zhujian gaishan (is gradually improving)" and so on.

3.2.2.2 *Zhengzai*+ "Qualitative Change Meaning" Instantaneous Verbs

"huimie (destroy)" "miewang (perish)" "xiaoshi (disappear)" "siqu (dye)" "pomie (break)"

This kind of verbs represent qualitative change of things, which can't repeat and are incompatible semantically with *zhengzai*. But in fact, qualitative change does not happen abruptly, and there will be a process of change accumulation before the transition. In the previous view, when we understood instantaneous verbs, we mainly emphasized the moment of transition instead of paying attention to the stage of approaching the critical point. *Zhengzai* highlights the process before the critical point, which extends the usage of the instantaneous verb. Such as "*zhengzai* siqu (dying)" is a stage of progressive death before death; "*zhengzai* fenlie (splitting)" is a stage of progressive division before the division; "*zhengzai* miewang (being perished)" and "*zhengzai* xiaoshi (disappearing)" are same situation. This usage is an important difference between *zhengzai* and *-zhe*.

In general, the sequence of *zhengzai* acting on Fig. 1 is in the following three stages: a → b → c. The stage a indicating progressive aspect is most free, and the most important function of *zhengzai* is to indicate the change (dynamic process). It is limited when *zhengzai* indicates the stage b, which can only represent the repeated action of the single event, but can not represent the repetition of plural event. It does not represent the stage c indicating the continuous after the movement. The basic aspect of *zhengzai* is to indicate the process of change.

4 The Substitution Conditions of *-Zhe* and *Zhengzai*

4.1 The Semantic Differences of *-Zhe* and *Zhengzai*

Through the analysis above, we can see that the grammatical function of *-zhe* and *zhengzai* have each emphasis on different points. *-Zhe* emphasizes aspect mainly. Only when it represents habitual aspect, *-zhe* can express the temporal meaning. The time span of the "V-*zhe*" is long, in which *-zhe* relatively indicates a stable stage of action, state and event. No matter dynamic or static, *-zhe* represents a sense of "no change".

It is relatively prominent that *zhengzai* indicates temporal meaning, which means "simultaneous occurrence". And the aspectual meaning of *zhengzai* is "the process of change". The core semantics of *zhengzai* is simultaneity of process of change and the corresponding time (Table 2).

Table 2. Differences of *zhengzai* and *-zhe*

	-zhe	*zhengzai*
Tense or aspect	aspect	tense
Variability and stability	stability	variability
Space-time range of event	long	short

4.2 Substitution Conditions of *-Zhe* and *Zhengzai*

The semantic differences influence the collocation of *-zhe* and *zhengzai* with different verbs. According to the theory of [6], this paper divides verb situations into three categories.

State, [STATIC]+[CONTINUOUS]
Process, [-STATIC]+[CONTINUOUS]
Transition, [-STATIC]+[-CONTINUOUS]

There are several kinds of verbs that can match with *-zhe*. The verbs that can express one of the five aspects can be used with *-zhe,* including but not limited the continuous verbs. It includes most of the state verbs and all process verbs, and some transition verbs.

The verbs that can be used with *zhengzai* are mainly the process verbs. In addition to the frequentative, the transition verb (instantaneous verb) plus *zhengzai* indicates the process of change (progressive).

The substitution conditions of *-zhe* and *zhengzai* are the semantic differences in the aspect and tense. When the semantics and the verb situations are same, *-zhe* and *zhengzai* can be replaced by each other. The comparison between Tables 3 and 4 shows the situations are very limited, in which *-zhe* and *zhengzai* can be replaced. When they represent progressive aspect plus a process verb and represent frequentative aspect plus a transition verb in single event, *-zhe* and *zhengzai* can be replaced by each other. The reason is that these two situations are overlapping parts of the aspectual meaning of *-zhe* and *zhengzai,* as the shadow marks in Tables 3 and 4.

Table 3. The restrictions of verb selection of *-zhe*

Aspect of *-zhe*		State	Process	Transition
Single event	Progressive		+	
	Frequentative		+	+
	Continuous	+	+	+
plural event	General		+	+
	Habitual	+	+	+

Table 4. The restrictions of verb selection of *zhengzai*

Aspect of *zhengzai*	State	Process	Transition
Progressive		+	+
Frequentative			+

5 Conclusion

The semantic differences between *-zhe* and *zhengzai* lies in tense and aspect. *-Zhe* indicates mainly aspectual meaning, while *zhengzai* represents both temporal and aspectual meaning. In terms of aspect, *-zhe* can not only indicate the progressive, continuous and frequentative of single events, but also represent plural event and habitual aspect. And *zhengzai* indicates progressing of change, which highlights the process of instantaneous verb. In terms of tense, *zhengzai* indicates the speech time or reference time, which means "occurs simultaneously". The main function of "*zheng-zai*" is to specify time information.

The substitution conditions of *-zhe* and *zhengzai* are influenced mainly by aspectual meaning. Only in two situations are *-zhe* and *zhengzai* interchangeable. One is when *-zhe* and *zhengzai* represent progressive aspect plus process verb, and the other is when they represent frequentative aspect plus instantaneous verb. In the rest of situations, *-zhe* and *zhengzai* are not mutually replaceable. According to the differences of meanings and usages of *-zhe* and *zhengzai*, maybe it can be proposed that *-zhe* is an aspect mark while *zhengzai* is a tense-aspect mark.

References

1. Chen, Y.M.: Adverb "在" and particle "着$_1$". Chin. Lang. Learn. **4**, 10–14 (1999)
2. Xiao, X.Q.: A comparative study of the functions of *zheng* (*zai*), *zai* and *-zhe*. Stud. Lang. Linguist. **4**, 27–34 (2002)
3. Chen, Q.R.: Focality and subjectivity in Chinese progressive and imperfective aspect. Chin. Teach. World **4**, 2, 22–31 (2003)
4. Shi, Y.Z.: The different functions of progressive aspectual markers. Chin. Lang. Learn. **3**, 14–24 (2006)
5. Wang, Y.: Event decomposition and the semantic durativity. Doctoral dissertations of Peking University, Beijing (2011)
6. Pustejovsky, J.: The syntax of event structure. Cognition **41**, 47–81 (1991)

The Expressive Content of the Ad-Adjectival *tai* 'too' in Mandarin Chinese: Evidence from Large Online Corpora

Qiongpeng Luo(✉) and Fan Liu

School of Liberal Arts, Nanjing University, Nanjing 210023, China
qpluo@nju.edu.cn, fanliu_ling@foxmail.com

Abstract. There are two competing analyses for the semantics of the ad-adjectival modifier *tai* 'too' in Mandarin Chinese. On the homophonous account, there are two *tai*s: one *tai* is a canonical degree adverb, while the other is a subjective intensifier expressing the speaker's evaluation. On the unified account, *tai* is essentially a degree adverb, and the subjective evaluation of *tai* is attributed to pragmatic inferencing in the pragmatic domain. Both of these accounts face empirical challenges. An alternative analysis in the multidimensional, use-conditional framework is proposed. On the present account, the meanings of *tai* operate on two dimensions: in the descriptive (truth-conditional) dimension, *tai* contributes some degree-related semantics, while in the expressive (use-conditional) dimension, *tai* contributes some expressive meaning expressing the speaker's subjective (mostly negative) evaluation towards *x* holding to a high degree. Data from large collections of online commodity reviews (more than 12,000 reviews; over 335,000 characters) provides quantitative support for this multidimensional analysis.

Keywords: The ad-adjectival modifier *tai* 'too' · Multidimensional semantics Online commodity reviews · Expressive content

1 Introduction

In this paper, we use large collections of online commodity reviews to investigate the relationship between use conditions and semantic content. Our case in point is the ad-adjectival modifier *tai* 'too' in Mandarin Chinese. The semantics of *tai* has been a subject of controversy in the literature. There are two opposing views on the market. One view argues that *tai* is homophonous, actually, there are two *tai*s: tai_1 is a pure degree word, while tai_2 is a subjective intensifier, mostly, if not always, expressing the speaker's negative evaluation ([6, 7], a. o.). The other view takes a unified approach, claiming that *tai* is essentially a degree word, and the flavor of subjective intensification is the result of pragmatic inferencing such as conversational implicatures in the pragmatic domain (see [3, 12]). The locus of variation between these two analyses lies in how to deal with the subjective flavor of *tai*: is the subjective evaluation a part of the lexical meaning of *tai* or is it just some conversational implicature in the pragmatic domain?

In this paper, we present a novel solution to this problem in the multidimensional, use-conditional framework as proposed by [4, 5, 8, 11], among others. Unlike the

J.-F. Hong et al. (Eds.): CLSW 2018, LNAI 11173, pp. 311–320, 2018.
https://doi.org/10.1007/978-3-030-04015-4_26

traditional truth-conditional semantics, in the multidimensional semantics, meanings operate on different dimensions. Thus, an utterance may express both an at-issue (truth-conditional) content in the descriptive dimension and an expressive (use-conditional) content in the expressive dimension. Informally, the expressive meaning is like "double assertion", or some side comment by the speaker. The truth- and use-conditional contents thus receive a unified logical treatment in this framework. Following this line of thought, we propose that the subjective flavor of *tai* should be analyzed as the expressive content in the expressive dimension. Such said, *tai* is a mixed expressive that has some multidimensional semantics: in the descriptive dimension, it is a degree word expressing an entity x exceeding a high standard, while in the expressive dimension, it conveys the speaker's evaluation toward x exceeding a high standard, which the speaker judges to be excessive. We show that this analysis receives some quantitative support from large online corpora extracted from commodity reviews on the website.

2 Review of Existing Accounts

As mentioned above, the lexical semantics of *tai* has been a hotly debated issue in the literature (cf. [6, 7, 9, 12], among many others). Roughly, the existing accounts can be divided into two approaches, i.e., the homophonous one and the unified one. The former was proposed by [6, 7, 9], among others, whereas the latter was developed by [12]. In this section, we provide a brief review of these accounts.

[7] claims that *tai* is homophonous, that is, there are two *tai*s in Mandarin Chinese. When modifying an adjective ADJ, tai_1 expresses some entity x holding to an excessive degree of ADJ-ness, and this reading is usually associated with unsatisfactory or negative contexts, as shown in (1); while tai_2 is a canonical degree adverb that expresses some entity x holding to a high degree, as shown in (2).

(1) a. 文章不能太长
Wenzhang buneng tai chang
Papers cannot TAI long
'Papers cannot be too long.'

b. 写得太简单了
xie de tai jiandan le
write DE TAI easy SFP[1]
'The writing is too simple.'

(2) a. 太好了！
Tai hao le!
TAI good SFP
Lit.: 'Too great!'

b. 最近我太忙
Zuijin wo tai mang
recently I TAI busy
'I am too busy recently.'

In line with [7]'s homophonous treatment, [6] further differentiates *tai* by the adjectives it modifies. When *tai* modifies an appreciative or positive adjective, such as *baogui* 'valuable', *guangrong* 'honorable' or *ke'ai* 'lovely', it expresses some positive evaluation of the speaker. By contrast, when *tai* modifies a pejorative or negative adjective, such as *leng* 'cold', *xiao* 'small', *weixian* 'dangerous' or *cuxin* 'too careless', it basically strengthened the negative meaning, and expresses the negative evaluation of the speaker.

Unlike the homophonous, ambiguous treatment, [12] proposes that there is no substantive ambiguity between the excessive and degree readings. [12] argues instead that *tai* is essentially a degree adverb expressing some entity *x* exceeding a certain standard. As for the subjective evaluation, [12] argues that it arises from pragmatic inferencing in the pragmatic domain, just like conversational implicatures. This pragmatic content of *tai* is triggered and reinforced by its frequent uses with social or normal conventions, and is both dynamic and temporary, regulated by social or discourse factors.

To summarize, both of the approaches have observed that *tai* has a degree component. The locus of variation between them lies in how to cope with the subjective evaluation expressed by *tai*. So far, there has been no consensus regarding whether the subjective, excessive interpretation should be treated as a separate meaning or as some side effect of pragmatic inferencing in the pragmatic domain. In the following sections, we will present a novel solution to this problem in the multidimensional, use-conditional framework.

3 A Multidimensional Analysis

3.1 Some Empirical Observations

As noted above, the two analyses diverge on how to deal with the subjective evaluation of *tai*. In this subsection, we will conduct a more comprehensive examination of the empirical data. We show that the subjective flavor of *tai* is conventional, rather than conversational such that it is detachable and cannot be defeasible from a particular context. The subjective meaning of *tai* does not like the canonical pragmatic meaning which arises from inferencing of conversational implicatures.

First, the subjectivity of *tai* is detachable, and does not vary from context to context. '*tai* + AP' consistently expresses some entity *x* exceeding an excessive degree, regardless of the contexts.

(3) a. 晚上东西吃太多了。(BLCU Chinese Corpus, henceforth BCC)
Wanshang dongxi chi tai duo le.
evening stuff eat TAI much SFP
'In the evening, (someone) has eaten too much.'

b. 前面小胡子那桌，也有人过来交头接耳，只可惜声音太小。(BCC)
Qianmian xiaohuzi na zhuo, ye you ren guolai jiaotoujieer, zhi kexi shengyin tai xiao.
Front Xiaohuzi that table also have people come whisper only pity voive TAI small
'(As for) Xiaohuzi's table in the front, some people came to whisper unfortunately, the volume was too low.'

c. 您对那个可爱的孩子真是太严厉了一点。(BCC)
Nin dui na ge ke'ai de haizi zhenshi tai yanli le yidian.
you to that CL lovely DE kid truly TAI strict ASP bit
'You have truly been a bit strict with that lovely kid.'

Typical pragmatic inferencing such as conversational implicatures, as is well-known, is non-detachable, and can be cancellable from particular contexts, and varies from context to context. As shown by the following examples, the subjective evaluation expressed by *tai* cannot be canceled from the contexts.

(4) a. 晚上东西吃太多了，#可是我很舒服。
Wanshang dongxi chi tai duo le, #keshi wo hen shufu.
evening stuff eat TAI much SFP but I very comfortable
'In the evening, I have eaten too much, # but I felt comfortable.'
b. 前面小胡子那桌，也有人过来交头接耳，只可惜声音太小，#但我还是听到了。
Qianmian xiaohuzi na zhuo, ye you ren guolai jiaotoujieer, zhi kexi shengyin tai xiao, #dan wo haishi tingdao le.
Front Xiaohuzi that table also have people come whisper only pity voive TAI small but I still hear SFP
'(As for) Xiaohuzi's table in the front, some people came to whisper; unfortunately, the volume was too low, # but I still heard what they are talking.'

Second, the use conditions of *tai* is conventional such that they are subject to some conventional restrictions of language. Normally, when people make an evaluation, the object under evaluation must be identifiable. Otherwise, the evaluation cannot take place. The same restriction applies to *tai*. [6] observes that "*tai* +AP" cannot modify indefinite, non-specific nouns. Consider:

(5) a. *我们昨天去参观了一所太好的学校。
*Women zuotian qu canguan le yi suo tai hao de xuexiao.
we yesterday go visit ASP one CL TAI good DE school
Lit.: 'We visited a too good school.'
b. *前面来了一位太矮的人。
*Qianmian lai le yi wie tai ai de ren.
ahead come ASP one CL TAI short DE people
Lit.: 'A too short man comes in front of us.'

Additionally, [6] points out that *tai* cannot be used to describe individual-level or habitual events, as shown below:

(6) a. *王教师今天整整一天都太忙。
*Wang jiaoshi jintian zhengzheng yi tian dou tai mang.
Wang teacher today whole one day all TAI busy
'Teacher Wang has been too busy for the whole day today.'
b. *她常常情绪太低落。
*Ta changchang qingxu tai diluo.
she usually mood TAI low
'Her mood is usually too low.'

Third, compared to canonical degree adverbs like *hen* 'very', *tai* cannot occur in the immediate scope of conditionals, *yes-no* questions, imperatives and *wish* modals, see (7). However, (7) becomes felicitous when *tai* is substituted by the neutral degree word *hen.* This indicates that the subjective evaluation of *tai* is conventional rather than conversational.

(7)a. *如果晓丽太聪明的话，她爸爸会很高兴。
*Ruguo Xiaoli tai congming dehua, tai baba hui hen gaoxing.
If Xiaoli TAI smart SFP she dad will very happy
'If Xiaoli were too smart, her father will be very happy.'
b. *你最近太忙吗？
*Ni zuijin tai mang ma?
you recently TAI busy SFP
'Are you too busy recently?'

We conclude that besides expressing some entity *x* holding to a high degree, *tai* also contributes an expressive content describing the speaker's heighted emotion towards *x* exceeding an excessive degree. This subjective evaluation of *tai* is conventional, and should be treated on a par with conventional implicatures, rather than conversational implicatures.

3.2 A Multidimensional Account

Recall that *tai* cannot occur in the immediate scope of negations, conditionals, questions, etc. These contexts are all entailment-cancelling ones. To be precise, these contexts are all non-veridical ones. A non-veridical context is the context where the truth of the proposition cannot be asserted. The definition of (non-)veridicality is provided as below (1: true; 0: false):

(8) (Non)veridicality
(i) Let O be a monadic sentential operator. O is veridical iff $Op=1 \Rightarrow p=1$, otherwise O is nonveridical;
(ii) A nonveridical operator O is averidical iff $Op=1 \Rightarrow p=0$.

Tai's systematic resistance to being embedded in nonveridical contexts has placed it in parallel with speaker-oriented, evaluative adverbs (see [2]) and expressive items (see [10]). Most of the speaker-oriented, evaluative adverbs cannot occur in the semantic scope of nonveridical operators. The following examples (9) and (10) are from [2] and [11] respectively:

(9) a. Unfortunately, John disappeared.
b. *John didn't unfortunately disappeared.
c. *Has he unfortunately disappeared?
d. *If he has unfortunately disappeared,…
(10) a. *He isn't fucking calm.
b.* Is he fucking calm?

To capture the semantics of expressive items such as *damn*, *fucking*, [10, 11] propose a multidimensional semantics of conventional implicatures (CIs). Conventional implicatures are non-truth-conditional inferences that are not derived from the pragmatic principles (maxims of quality, quantity, manner and relevance), but are simply attached by convention to particular lexical items. Potts makes a further step by arguing that CIs are expressive content, and as such they can also be semantically computed. Expressive items, as CI-triggers, express the speaker's heightened emotional state. The meaning of a sentence that contains an expressive item is thus bi-dimensional in the sense that it expresses both an at-issue content in the descriptive (truth-conditional) dimension and a CI content in the expressive dimension. Inspired by this analysis, we take *tai* to contribute some expressive content in the expressive dimension. As a consequence, the meaning conveyed is speaker-oriented and cannot be contradicted in the same manner as asserted meaning ([8] have identified several such subjective ad-adjectival modifiers that have bi-dimensional meanings). This provides a straightforward account of the distributional pattern of *tai*, esp. its systematic resistance to being embedded in nonveridical contexts.

Following this line of thought, we propose that *tai* encodes some sort of bi-dimensional meanings. In the descriptive dimension, *tai* is a degree adverb that modifies gradable adjectives. Hence, "*tai* + ADJ" denotes that the ADJ-ness of some entity x exceeds a certain standard (related to the speaker's expectation). In the expressive dimension, *tai* expresses the speaker's heighted emotion towards some entity x holding to such a high degree that exceeds the permissible maximum in the current context of utterance. The excessive degree usually leads to some negative consequence. A multidimensional semantics of *tai* is provided in (11), where the two components are separated by the diamond sign ✧. Moreover, the truth conditions of "*tai* + AP" are demonstrated as (12), adopting the bullet • as a metalogical symbol to separate the descriptive content from the expressive (conventional implicature) content in Potts's style. $\mathbf{EXCESS_S}$ means the speaker (s) judges the d of G-ness that x holds to be excessive.

(11)

$$[[tai]] = \begin{cases} \text{Descriptive dimension: } \lambda G \lambda x \exists d[G(d)(x) \wedge d > !s] \\ \diamond \\ \text{Expressive dimension: } \lambda G \lambda x.\exists d[G(d)(x) \wedge d > !s] \rightarrow \mathbf{EXCESS_S}((G)(d)(x)) \end{cases}$$

(12) ⟦*tai* AP⟧ is true iff:

(i) Descriptive dimension: $\exists d\ [d > !s\ \&\ [\![AP]\!](x)(d)]$

(ii) Expressive dimension: $\exists d\ [d > !s\ \&\ [\![AP]\!](x)(d)] = 1 \rightarrow \mathbf{EXCESS_s}((G)(d)(x))$

(iii) Multidimensional meaning: $\exists d\ [d > !s\ \&\ [\![AP]\!](x)(d)] \bullet \exists d\ [d > !s\ \&\ [\![AP]\!](x)(d)] = 1 \rightarrow \mathbf{EXCESS_s}((G)(d)(x))$

Unlike the existing analyses, this account treats the expressive content as a part of *tai*'s lexical semantics. To illustrate, consider (13). (13) has some bi-dimensional meanings. In the descriptive dimension, it states that the beauty of Xiaoli exceeds a certain standard. In the expressive dimension, it conveys the message that this degree of beauty has exceeded the degree that most partners could possibly hold, thus leading to an excessive, negative evaluation. This subjective meaning is a conventional implicature of *tai*.

(13) 晓丽太漂亮了，不好找对象。
Xiaoli tai piaoliang le, buhao zhao duixiang.
Xiaoli TAI beautiful SFP not.easy find partner
'Xiaoli is too beautiful to find any partner.'

This multidimensional account predicts that *tai* will be more likely to occur in the contexts in favor of negative evaluation than the contexts of positive evaluation. In the following section, we provide some quantitative evidence for this from large collections of online commodity reviews.

4 A Corpus Study

4.1 Methodology and Data

In this section, we use large online corpora extracted from the commodity reviews to investigate the distributional and use conditions of *tai* (following the methodology as proposed by [1]). Normally, commodity reviews are classified into five categories, from the highest (5-star) rating to the lowest (1-star) rating, that is, from the positive polar to the negative polar. Different semantic analyses of *tai* lead to different predictions regarding the distributional and use conditions. There are three possibilities. (i) If *tai* is homophonous, the occurrences of *tai* in all rating categories should be balanced. (ii) If *tai* is essentially a degree adverb, and the excessive semantics is due to pragmatic inferencing such as conversational implicatures, we should not expect any significant difference in the occurrences of *tai* in positive and negative reviews. (iii) If the lexical meaning of *tai* is multidimensional, where the expressive content is part of *tai*'s lexical semantics, the occurrences of *tai* in negative reviews should be statistically more significant than its occurrences in positive reviews, since 'excess' always leads to negative evaluation. Different predictions per different semantic analyses are summarized in Table 1:

Table 1. Different predictions per different semantic analyses

	Semantic analyses	Predictions
I	Homophonous: two *tai*s a. 'excessively'; b. intensifier	Balanced distribution in all rating categories
II	Unified: *tai* is a degree adverb	Balanced distribution in positive and negative reviews
III	Multidimensional: descriptive ♢ expressive	Occurrences in negative reviews is statistically more significant than in positive reviews

To make the samples substantial, we selected 25 best-selling items from the websites of jd.com (i.e., Chinese Amazon), and collected a text of over 335,000 characters with more than 12,000 reviews (roughly 2,500 reviews for each rating category). The commodity items are carefully chosen to balance the gender preference. The items are listed in Table 2.

Table 2. The list of commodity items surveyed

	Male	Female
Strong preference	Mobil engine oil, Septwolves leather suits, Durex condoms	Perfect aloe gel, Paradise three folding umbrella, Nanjiren thermal underwear
Weak preference	Swiss army backpack, Binge watch	Pampers diapers, Pigeon nipples
Neutral	Huawei smartphone, Apple MacBook, Fort Oude milk, Deerma delmar humidifier, Midea drinking fountains, TP-LINK router, Kawasaki badminton, Mi mobile power, Dove chocolate, *Modern Chinese Dictionary*, Centrum vitamin tablets, Lock Lock mug, October rice, 3 M masks	

Ignoring the nonsense or unreasonable reviews through the careful filter (e.g. posting review for bonus, mismatch of the content and the rating), we finally selected more than 12,000 reviews from a pool of 8.22 million ones of the 25 items listed in Table 2.

4.2 Results and Discussion

The result is provided in Table 3. It demonstrates that the frequency of occurrences of *tai* in lower-graded reviews significantly exceeds its frequency of occurrences in higher-graded reviews

Table 3. The distributions of *tai* in online commodity reviews

	5 star	4 star	3 star	2 star	1 star	Total
Reviews	2500	2080	2500	2500	2500	12,080
tai AP	121	100	230	501	913	1,865
Characters	65,644	39,542	65,560	66,594	97,680	335,020

The frequency and log-odds distribution formulae are shown in (14a–b), where Count(x_n, R) is the number of tokens of x_n (a word-string of length n) in rating category R, and $count_n$(R) is the number of tokens of word-strings of length n in rating category R. Figure 1 shows the frequency and log-odds of *tai* in online reviews. It is worth noting that the two methods lead to the same result.

The result clearly shows that the distribution of *tai* in negative reviews (one- and two-star ratings) is statistically more significant than its distribution in positive reviews (four- and five-star ratings) and neutral ones (three-star ratings). Actually, its

(14) a. Frequency distribution

$\text{frequency}(X_n, R) = \text{count}(X_n, R) / \text{count}_n(R)$

b. Log-odds distribution

$\text{log-odds}(X_n, R) = \ln(\text{count}(X_n, R) / (\text{count}(X_n, R) - \text{count}_n(R)))$

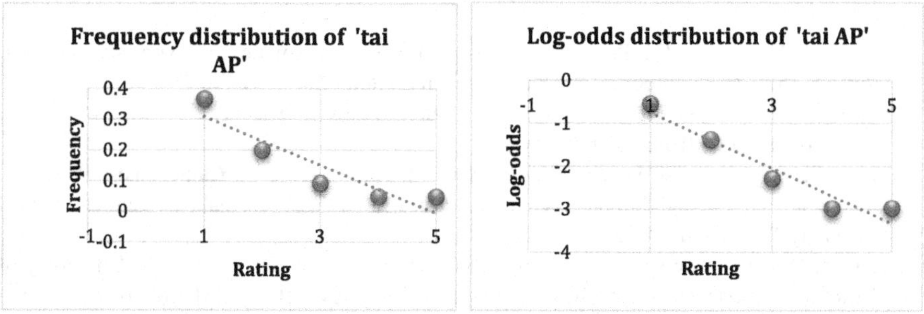

Fig. 1. Frequency and log-odds distributions of *tai* in online reviews

occurrences in one-star rated reviews equals the sum of its occurrences in all other reviews (i.e., 913 vs. 121 + 100 + 230 + 501). If we take the two-star rated category as a negative one, then the ratio between the occurrences of *tai* in negative reviews and its occurrences in positive reviews is more significant: (913 + 501)/(121 + 100 + 230) = 3.135, which means it is 3.135 times more likely for *tai* to appear in a negative review than in a positive review. This ratio is statistically significant. This result provides solid quantitative support for the multidimensional semantics of *tai*, which takes the negative evaluation to be part of its semantics (in the expressive dimension).

5 Conclusion

This paper uses large online corpora from commodity reviews to investigate the distributional and use conditions of *tai*. The data demonstrates that the frequency of occurrences of *tai* in lower-graded reviews is significantly larger than that in other higher-graded ratings. This result provides quantitative evidence for a multidimensional semantic analysis of *tai*, namely, *tai* has some conventional implicature that expresses the speaker's negative evaluation towards some entity's degree exceeding a certain standard that the speaker judges to be 'excessive'. This expressive content is conventional rather than conversational, and should not be confused with typical pragmatic inferencing such as conversational implicatures. Multidimensional Semantics, when supplemented by (almost freely accessible) large online corpora, proves to be a very useful tool to investigating the semantics of subjective intensifiers which would be formally inscrutable otherwise.

Acknowledgments. This work is supported by the National Social Science Fund of China under grant #16BYY006 to Qiongpeng Luo, the Postgraduate Education Reform Project of Jiangsu Province under grant #KYZZ16_0016 and DFG-SFB 991 to Fan Liu. We thank the audience at CLSW 2018 for helpful comments and feedback. All errors remain our own.

References

1. Constant, N., Davis, C., Potts, C., Schwarz, F.: The pragmatics of expressive content: evidence from large corpora. Sprache Datenverarbeitung **33**, 5–21 (2009)
2. Ernst, T.: Speaker-oriented adverbs. Nat. Lang. Linguist. Theory **27**, 497–544 (2009). https://doi.org/10.1007/s11049-009-9069-1
3. Grice, P.: Studies in the Way of Words. Harvard University Press, Cambridge (1989)
4. Gutzmann, D.: Use-conditional Meaning: Studies in Multidimensional Semantics. Oxford University Press, Oxford (2015)
5. Kaplan, D.: The meaning of *ouch* and *oops*. Howison lecture delivered at the University of California at Berkeley (2004). https://www.youtube.com/watch?v=iaGRLlgPl6w
6. Lu, J.: The teaching and analysis of *tai*. Chin. Teach. World **2**, 74–81(2000). (Guanyu 'tai' zi jiegou de jiaoxue yu yanjiu. Shijie Hanyu Jiaoxue). (in Chinese)
7. Lü, S.: The Eight Hundred Words in Modern Chinese. The Commercial Press, Beijing (1999). (Xiandai Hanyu Babai Ci). (in Chinese)
8. Luo, Q., Wang, Y.: when degree meets evaluativity: a multidimensional semantics for the ad-adjectival modifier *hăo* 'well' in Mandarin Chinese. Chinese Lexical Semantics. LNCS (LNAI), vol. 10085, pp. 472–482. Springer, Cham (2016). https://doi.org/10.1007/978-3-319-49508-8_45
9. Ma, Z.: The distribution of degree adverbs in comparatives. Chin. Teach. World **2**, 81–86 (1988). (Chengdu fuci zai biaoshi chengdu bijiao de jushi zhong de fenbu qingkuang kaocha. Shijie Hanyu Jiaoxue). (in Chinese)
10. Potts, C.: The Logic of Conventional Implicature. Oxford University Press, Oxford (2005)
11. Potts, C.: The expressive dimension. Theor. Linguist. **33**, 165–197 (2007). https://doi.org/10.1515/TL.2007.011
12. Zhang, Y.: On Adverbs in Mandarin Chinese. The Sanlian Press, Shanghai (2010). (Xiandai Hanyu Fuci Fenxi). (in Chinese)

A Survey of the Compatibility of *Laizhe* with the MARVS Model of Event Types

Tong Mu[1] and Yu-Yin Hsu[2(✉)]

[1] Faculty of Humanities, The Hong Kong Polytechnic University, Kowloon, Hong Kong SAR, China
tony.mu@connect.polyu.hk

[2] Department of Chinese and Bilingual Studies, The Hong Kong Polytechnic University, Kowloon, Hong Kong SAR, China
yyhsu@polyu.edu.hk

Abstract. Previous studies have shown that *laizhe* can be compatible with some types of verbs, and that it is related to a certain concept of past tense. However, there is no consensus about the exact conditions that allow *laizhe* to surface in a sentence. This study argues that simply examining verbal semantics is insufficient to identifying the use and functions of *laizhe*, and instead investigates them from the perspective of MARVS-theory event types. This new approach establishes that predicates compatible with *laizhe* often express an event from a prior time point that, while recent, is still different from the time of the conversation. Thus, two fundamental attributes are needed to account for the distribution of *laizhe*: that is, the timing of the expression of (1) temporal gaps, and/or (2) different stage-level properties associated with the subject of a sentence.

Keywords: *Laizhe* · Verb types · Situation aspects · MARVS theory Event states

1 Introduction

Prior studies have drawn various conclusions about the meanings and functions of the word *laizhe* in colloquial Chinese. For example, Chao [1, 2] has described *laizhe* as a sentence final particle (SFP) expressing the recent past, while Chen [3] has claimed that it can be treated as an aspect marker. However, as the following literature review makes clear, there is a current scholarly consensus that the semantic nature of *laizhe* is partly similar to SFPs such as *le* and *ne*, but quite different from aspect markers such as *zhe*, *le* and *guo*, insofar as the interpretation of *laizhe* interacts with the whole event that a sentence describes, rather than with the verb alone. Assuming, with Chao [1, 2], that *laizhe* is an SFP, the present study seeks to identify the function and interpretations that *laizhe* contributes to a sentence by examining the event types in Xu's [14] fine-grained extension of Huang et al.'s [6] model-attribute representation of verbal semantics (MARVS).

J.-F. Hong et al. (Eds.): CLSW 2018, LNAI 11173, pp. 321–333, 2018.
https://doi.org/10.1007/978-3-030-04015-4_27

2 Background

Despite most of the prior research on *laizhe* having concentrated on the characteristics and semantics of verbs, no consensus has been reached on the exact types of verbs that can be compatible with *laizhe* in a sentence. Vendler [12] used three parameters (i.e., telic, dynamic, and durative) to distinguish four situational classes of verbs, i.e., state, activity, accomplishment, and achievement. In a similar vein, Ōta [8] argued that *laizhe* is only compatible with verbs expressing durative meanings, including instantaneous, stative, and durative verbs (see Zhang [15] for a similar claim). That is, he argued that only verbs containing the [+durative] feature can co-occur with *laizhe*. Following Vendler's [12] framework, He [5] argued that only the activity class is compatible with *laizhe*. However, we propose that simply relying on Ōta's [8] and Vendler's [12] verb-type classifications cannot fully capture the use of *laizhe*.

Durative verbs as discussed by Ōta [8] are related to three of the four classes of verbs in Vendler's [12] theory, since the latter's [+durative] feature represents whether a situation takes time or not, and thus is inherent in the state, activity, and accomplishment classes. However, in contrast to what Ōta [8] proposed, the present authors have observed that accomplishment verbs (such as *chi* 'eat') are never compatible with *laizhe* (e.g., (1)), despite such verbs being categorized as [+durative].

(1) * 他吃一個麵包來著。

However, Vendler's [12] classification scheme is not capable of fully capturing the use of *laizhe* either. For instance, verbs like *kanjian* 'see' and *si* 'die' are both accomplishment verbs and are both categorized as [−durative]; yet, as shown in examples (2a) and (2b), *kanjian* is compatible with *laizhe*, but *si* is not. In other words, whether a predicate has a [+durative] feature cannot explain the rules governing the use of *laizhe*, contrary to what Ōta [8] and Zhang [15] suggest; nor can this feature alone explain differences in the perceived correctness and incorrectness of the sentences in (1–2).

(2) a. 我剛才看見他來著。

b.* 他昨天晚上死來著。

The contrast between (2a) and (2b) also renders untenable He's [5] proposal that only Vendler's [12] activity class of verbs is compatible with *laizhe*. In fact, Vendler's [12] state-class verbs (e.g., *xing* 'name') can also be compatible with *laizhe*, as shown in (3).

(3) 他以前姓張來著，現在改跟他媽媽的姓了。

Xie [13] has proposed that *laizhe* can only co-occur with verbs that have a [+telic] feature; and Song [11], that *laizhe* cannot be compatible with so-called "one time" verbs, which describe actions that occur very quickly. In addition to Vendler's [12] four classes of verbs, a fifth – semelfactive – has commonly been used by other scholars [4, 9] in regard to events that take a very short period of time (for instance, *kesou* 'cough', and *zhayan* 'blink') and are thus defined as [+dynamic], [−telic], and

[+durative]. We found that semelfactive verbs in Chinese are compatible with *laizhe*, as shown in (4), although this phenomenon has not been discussed in previous studies. Certainly, because the "one-time" semelfactive verb *zhayan* has a [−telic] feature, yet is compatible with *laizhe*, both Xie's [13] and Song's [11] proposals are untenable as general rules.

(4) 他剛才眨眼來著，雖然只眨了一下。

In brief, previous studies on *laizhe* have mostly focused on what types of verbs can co-occur with it, but have yielded contradictory results. This suggests that *laizhe* might usefully be studied from perspectives that transcend verbal semantics: for instance, how it interacts with whole events [16] or what it contributes to the interpretation of whole sentences.

Luo [7] has proposed that the main function of *laizhe* is to describe a past event that was followed by a time gap, and that it is this gap's existence that licenses the use of *laizhe* in a sentence about such an event. In Fig. 1's depiction of such a *laizhe* sentence, AA refers to a past event that encoded a starting point A and an end-point B. This past event occurred before speech time (ST), and there was a temporal gap between B and ST; and for Luo [7], it is this temporal gap that licenses *laizhe*'s use in a sentence.

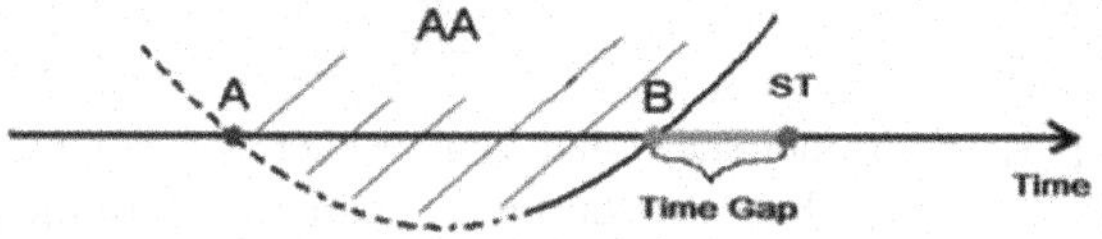

Fig. 1. Representation of time in a *laizhe* sentence (Luo 2012)

Nonetheless, some real-world examples suggest that *laizhe* is not always used in reference to a past event. That is, one may use it to describe observations concurrent with ST. For example, after the context (5a) 'You know what? That man standing over there is really weird', one can utter a sentence containing *laizhe* like (5b) '(Since earlier on to now,) he keeps winking!' Examples like (5) suggest that defining the use of *laizhe* as only denoting the past is not tenable.

(5) a. 你知道嗎？站在那裡的那個男人好奇怪。

b. 他(從剛剛到現在)一直眨眼來著！

Therefore, to investigate the distribution and functions of *laizhe* and its compatibility with various types of predicates, the present study will focus on event types. Huang et al.'s [6] MARVS theory proposes that verbs' meanings are represented through five event modules: boundary, process, stage, state, and punctuality. Based on MARVS, Xu [14] proposed a theory of linguistic event types in an attempt to account for the whole aspectual meanings of clauses. Specifically, this involved combining the viewpoint aspect [9] and the situation aspect [12] to develop five main classes and 19 sub-classes of linguistic events. The remainder of this paper will focus on the interaction between *laizhe* and the 19 MARVS-based linguistic-event types that Xu [14] identified. We will argue that (1) a temporal gap between the speech time and the event described, and (2) a stage-level difference associated with the subject described in a sentence between the reference time (RT) of an event and ST are the two factors that determine whether *laizhe* can be used in a sentence. We will also show that the use of *laizhe* is not licensed only by a specific tense concept (e.g., past-tense events), but can also be used in atelic or hypothetical situations, contrary to Luo's [7] proposal.

3 Event Types and *Laizhe*

The following five subsections discuss the use of *laizhe* in sentences representative of Xu's [14] five main classes of linguistic events: static state, dynamic state, change of state, semelfactive, and accomplishment.

3.1 Static State

For Xu [14], the static state has four sub-classes: instant, delimitative, inchoative, and cessative. We will show that when a temporal gap and/or a stage-level difference is available in a sentence, *laizhe* can be used; and will also indicate instances concerning how the use of *laizhe* differs from that of SFP *le*.

Instant Static State

According to Xu [14], the instant static state is a speaker's viewpoint arising suddenly at the moment of ST, and in which the starting or ending point of the static state is not encoded. We can observe that an instant static state is not compatible with *laizhe*, as shown in (6a), because RT and ST overlap, i.e., there is no temporal gap. Thus, instant static state alone cannot denote any different stage-level property from what was delivered at ST. However, if a temporal adverbial is added, as in (6b), the sentence becomes acceptable.

(6) a. * 他很瘦來著。

b. 他以前很瘦來著，現在居然變胖了。

In (6b), the event *ta hen shou* 'he was thin' refers to a static state in the RT, due to the past-tense adverbial *yiqian* 'in the past'. Thus, considered as a whole sentence, (6b) indicates a stage-level property that differs from the property described at ST, i.e., *xianzai juran pang le* 'he is actually fat now'.

The instant static state includes a subtype, habitual events [14], which we note are not compatible with *laizhe* unless a temporal adverbial is added. In (7a), the habitual predicate *xidu* 'take drugs' denotes a current property, i.e., no temporal gap, and we would therefore predict that *laizhe* would not be allowed in this sentence. In (7b), however, the adverbial *qianjinian* 'several years ago' in the first clause indicates an RT different from ST, causing the whole sentence to denote a stage-level property different from the event indicated at ST (i.e., the second clause). Therefore, this sentence is grammatical despite its inclusion of *laizhe*.

(7) a.* 他吸毒來著。

b. 他前幾年還吸毒來著，現在已經戒毒了。

Examples like (6–7) indicate that temporal gaps and differences in stage-level properties are both relevant to the use of *laizhe* in sentences. Nonetheless, we found that they are not always indispensable properties of grammatical *laizhe* sentences. For example, in (8), the static-state predicate *houhui* 'regret' is associated with both RT and ST, and does not seem to indicate any different stage-level property; yet, the sentence is still grammatical. Possibly, this is because the meaning of *houhui* 'regret' often implies a change in the speaker's view of something that occurred in the past; and this change of opinion might be why one can use *laizhe* in this context, i.e., to rhetorically emphasize how regretful one feels at the current time about a past event.

(8) 借錢給他這件事，我去年後悔來著，現在我仍然後悔。

Delimitative Static State

Xu's [14] delimitative static state is a static state bounded by a clear starting-point and end-point. Sentences expressing a delimitative static state are compatible with *laizhe*. The sentence in (9), for instance, denotes a state of event (i.e., the first clause, 'Last time he was sick for about two months') that is different from the state described in ST (i.e., the second clause, 'now he's recovered but is still weak'). In other words, sentences with the delimitative static state describe multiple, temporally distinct events.

(9) 他上次病了兩個月來著（，現在病雖然好了身體還是很虛弱)。

Inchoative Static State

In Xu's [14] inchoative static state – also categorized as an achievement class by Vendler [12] – only the starting point of the static state is described. It is not compatible with *laizhe*. As example (10a) shows, *bing* 'be sick' is an open and unbounded state that does not express any temporal gap, and which alone cannot express stage-level differences associated with a state at ST. Sentences about static states, however, are compatible with the SFP *le*, as shown in (10b), because *le* adds the meaning 'change of state' to the inchoative static state [10].

(10) a * 他病來著。

b. 他病了。

Cessative Static State

According to Xu [14], the cessative static state represents a period of static state of which only the end point is discussed; and it too is categorized as an achievement class in Vendler's [12] theory. However, the cessative static state also represents the beginning of a new state. As shown in (11a), this type of state (e.g., *hao* 'recover') is incompatible with *laizhe*. Again, we speculate that this ungrammaticality can be explained by the lack of a temporal gap and/or stage-level differences between any state in a prior RT and what an event at ST expresses in such a sentence. Like the inchoative static state in (10b) above, the cessative is compatible with the SFP *le* in (11b), because the internal end point expressed by the cessative static state matches the 'change of state' meaning that *le* expresses.

(11) a. * 他傷口好來著。

b. 他傷口好了。

3.2 Dynamic State

Xu's [14] dynamic state is also divided into four sub-classes: instant, bounded, inceptive, and terminative. We will show that, while these sub-classes all encode event boundaries differently, only the inceptive dynamic state requires a clearly marked end point of a state within a sentence; and as such, it is the only sub-class of the dynamic state that often disallows the use of *laizhe* while being used alone in a sentence, for reasons that will be explored below. Dynamic state's other three sub-classes can naturally incorporate the required temporal differences between an RT and the ST, and thus are compatible with *laizhe*.

Instant Dynamic State

The instant dynamic state represents a snapshot of a dynamic state at an RT that overlaps the ST [14], but unlike its counterpart the instant static state, it is compatible with *laizhe* without any need to add a past temporal adverbial. For example, the sentence 'He is eating sushi' in (12a) describes an ongoing event; however, when *laizhe* is added to the end of that sentence, as in (12b), the RT of the sushi-eating event no longer overlaps with the ST, but moves backward to a specific time point prior to the beginning of ST. The sentence in (12b) thus describes eating that occurred before the event described in its second clause, 'the phone suddenly rings'. The change of interpretations between (12a) and (12b) is particularly interesting, because it indicates the *laizhe*'s function of creating a temporal gap between RT and ST. In other words, the existence of the *laizhe* clause renders the event's original RT to one that is different from ST, thus creating stage-related differences among the events being described.

(12) a. 他正在吃壽司。

b. 他正在吃壽司來著，突然電話響了。

Bounded Dynamic State

The bounded dynamic state, which is also known in Vendler's [12] theory as activity, denotes a process that occurs entirely within a specified period of time [14]. Similar to the delimitative static state, it has both an intrinsic starting point and an intrinsic end point, even though such event boundaries may not be explicitly described in a given sentence. The bounded dynamic state is compatible with *laizhe*, as in (13). The sentence in (13a) describes an event, 'He runs every morning', that has no definite beginning or end, whereas in (13b), a running event is described with specific time points: i.e., 'Yesterday afternoon between 3 pm and 5 pm, he had been running'. In other words, having intrinsic beginning and end points, the bounded dynamic state exhibits its own reference interval, and thus, the RT of this type of dynamic state is always different from its ST, i.e., intrinsically conveys temporal gap; and thus, it allows the use of *laizhe*.

(13) a. 他早上跑步來著。

b. 昨天下午三點到五點，他一直跑步來著。

Inceptive Dynamic State

The inceptive dynamic state expresses events with only a starting point [14], and we found it to be incompatible with *laizhe*. In the sentences in (14a) and (14b), 'He started running' and 'The audience started clapping', as is usual for the inceptive dynamic state, the action is assumed by default to continue to ST, and does not contain a temporal gap and/or any stage-level difference.

(14) a. * 他開始跑步來著。

b. * 台下響起掌聲來著。

However, if the inceptive dynamic state in a sentence is tied to a specific RT that is different from any part of the dynamic state in ST, that sentence becomes compatible with *laizhe*. For example, in the sentence in (15a), the speaker utters a dynamic state in the first clause, 'He started running last Friday'; and while this clause by itself would imply that the event it describes has continued to ST, the sentence's second clause indicates that 'but after doing it a few days, he doesn't run any more', a state of affairs that is presumed to continue to ST. The differences between the actual current situation and the event described in the first clause, constituting both a temporal gap and a stage difference, make *laizhe* appropriate in this sentence (cf. (14a)); and the contrast between (15b) and (14b) demonstrates the same point.

(15) a. 他上個星期五開始跑步來著，這還不到一個星期他就堅持不下去了。

b. 台下剛剛響起掌聲來著，也不知道為什麼，突然就鴉雀無聲了。

Terminative Dynamic State

Terminative dynamic state represents only the end of a dynamic event [14]. For instance, the first clause in (16), 'He just stopped running', is compatible with *laizhe*. In general, the end of a state prior to ST portends the beginning of a new state. In other words, we see the terminative as intrinsically exhibiting a temporal gap and allowing stage-level differences; and these properties make this type of dynamic state readily compatible with *laizhe*.

(16) 他才剛停止跑步來著，天就下起了大雨。

3.3 Change of State

Change of state refers to a instantaneous change from one state into another [14], and has four sub-classes: static-static; dynamic-dynamic; static-dynamic; and dynamic-static. The following subsections will show that within-type state changes – i.e., from static to static, or from dynamic to dynamic – are not compatible with *laizhe*; whereas state changes that are also typal, i.e., from static to dynamic or dynamic to static, are compatible with it.

Static-Static Change

In change from one static state to another [14], the first-described static state has already changed into a new state which continues from a prior RT to ST; and therefore, such changes are irreversible. For example, in (17a), 'he died' means that the state of the subject 'he' had changed from alive to dead, and that this change cannot be undone. In (17b), 'he won' means the state of the subject 'he' has arrived at the situation of winning, and can no more 'un-win' than the subject in (17a) can 'un-die'. In events like those in (17), the changes of state last up to ST, and their irreversible characteristics prevent the described event from providing either any temporal gap or any stage differences. Thus, such sentences are not compatible with *laizhe*.

(17) a. * 他死來著。

b. * 他贏來著。

Dynamic-Dynamic Change

Change from one dynamic state to another [14], like static-static change, is irreversible. As such, we would predict that dynamic-dynamic change of state cannot provide a temporal gap or stage differences, and therefore that sentences expressing it will not be compatible with *laizhe*. This is borne out in (18). In (18a) a computer "has been turned on and been running" and (18b) a car "has been speeded up and continued running".

(18) a. * 電腦啟動好來著。

b. * 汽車提速到一百二十邁繼續行駛來著。

Static-Dynamic Change

An instantaneous change from a static state to a new dynamic state [14] is similar to the two previously discussed types of change of state, in that the process of change involved is complete. However, the grounds of a static-dynamic change (i.e., the earlier, static state) and its results (i.e., the later, dynamic state) may exhibit either a partial temporal overlap or stage-level differences emerge across two states. Thus, unlike the prior two subtypes of state change, static-dynamic state change can license the use of *laizhe*. In (19), for example, both the static state *gaoxing* 'being happy', and the dynamic state *guzhang huanhu* 'clap and cheer' occur in a very short period of time. The sentence descries two different types of stage-level properties of the subject. Therefore, static-dynamic changes of state can provide the stage differences that are the preconditions for *laizhe* surfacing in a sentence.

(19) 我們高興得鼓掌歡呼來著。

Dynamic-Static Change

Lastly, a process of change from a dynamic state to a static state [14] is exemplified in (20a), in which the dynamic state *zhanggao* 'grow tall' is succeeded by the static state *bu zhang le* 'not growing any more'; this provides a temporal gap between a prior RT, for the dynamic state, that is different from the static state expressed in ST. The differences between these dynamic and static states also create stage differences associated with the subject. Therefore, such sentences are compatible with *laizhe*, as also demonstrated in (20b) and (20c).

(20) a. 他過去幾年一直長高來著，現在不長了。
b. 他剛剛寫完作業來著。
c. 我聽見你的聲音來著。

3.4 Semelfactive

As explained in Sect. 2, above, semelfactive events take a very short time [4, 9], and sentences expressing the semelfactive are compatible with *laizhe*, as shown in (21a), 'He had been winking'. Despite their brevity, it should be noted that semelfactive situations are complete dynamic-state processes. Such situations can be repeated and create multiple distinct states across multiple RT. It is noteworthy that, if such a dynamic process is modified by an action-measure phrase such as *yixia* 'one time', the sentence it is in becomes incompatible with *laizhe*, as in (21b): 'He winked at me one time.' This may be because the whole process of such a semelfactive dynamic state falls in the scope of the modifying measure 'one time' and is considered ended at the reported RT, and therefore the ending state of the subject is perceived to be the same from RT to ST; thus, it cannot provide stage-level differences, and is not compatible with *laizhe*. Interestingly, if such an event containing an action-measure phrase is paraphrased into a parenthetical adverbial clause modifying such a dynamic state, as in (21c) – 'He just winked at me (, although it only happened once, but I seemed to understand what he thought) – such a sentence becomes compatible with *laizhe*.

(21) a. 他一直眨眼來著。

b. 他剛剛對我眨了一下眼(*來著)。

c. 他剛剛對我眨眼來著 (雖然只是一下，但我好像明白了他的意思)。

3.5 Accomplishment

Accomplishment is divided into six sub-classes, the first of which is also known simply as accomplishment. The other five are the instant-dynamic, inceptive, terminative, completive, and bounded-dynamic states of accomplishment [4].

For example, the first sub-class, accomplishment, refers to a process with a final state that can be either dynamic or static. As shown in (22), this sub-class is not compatible with *laizhe*.

(22) a. 他跑了五公里。

b. 他啟動了一個程序。

c. * 他跑了五公里來著。

d.* 他啟動了一個程序來著。

The instant-dynamic state of accomplishment describes an single time-point within a dynamic state of accomplishing an action (e.g., the fifth of eight bites taken as part of a wider process of eating something). Its incompatibility with *laizhe* is demonstrated by (23).

(23) 他正在吃一個麵包(*來著)。

The third sub-class, inceptive accomplishment, describes the beginning state of an accomplishment action (e.g., *kaishi xiou qiao* 'start to fix a bridge'), and an event related to this type of state is likewise incompatible with *laizhe*.

(24) 他開始修一座橋(*來著)。

The fourth sub-class, terminative accomplishment, indicates an abnormal interruption of accomplishment, irrespective of whether the final state is realized. As shown in (25), '[For some reason] he is not continuing to write that book anymore', this type of accomplishment is also not compatible with *laizhe*.

(25) 他不再寫那本書(*來著)。

The fifth sub-class, completive accomplishment, describes the ending of accomplishment (e.g., *gai hao* 'finish building' in (26)). Again, it is not compatible with *laizhe*.

(26) 他蓋好那座橋(*來著)。

The sixth sub-class, bounded-dynamic accomplishment, denotes part of a process of accomplishment (e.g., *xie san ge xiaoshi* 'write for three hours'), but differs from the bounded dynamic state discussed above (e.g., (13)). Whereas bounded-dynamic accomplishment does not contain a natural end point, and the described state can last continuously to ST, bounded-dynamic (non-accomplishment) events encode an intrinsic endpoint. Therefore, bounded-dynamic accomplishment is also incompatible with *laizhe*, as shown in (27).

(27) 他今天寫作業寫了三個小時(*來著)。

In short, no sub-class of accomplishment is compatible with *laizhe*, perhaps due to their shared focus on the final state denoted in ST. In other words, we speculate that because accomplishment describes events that have already ended, but whose final states still prevail at the time of the utterance, it cannot provide a temporal gap between any potential RT and ST, and does not express any stage differences. Table 1 below summarizes the results that we have presented in Sect. 3.

Table 1. The summary of the compatibility of *laizhe* with the MARVS Model of event types (√ indicates *laizhe* can surface in such types of events)

		Linguistic event types	*Laizhe*
1	I. Static state	instant static state - - -	√
2		delimitative static state |- - -|	√
3		inchoative static state|- - -	
4		cessative static state - - -|	
5	II. Dynamic state	instant dynamic state ~ ~ ~	√
6		bounded dynamic state |~ ~ ~|	√
7		inceptive dynamic state |~ ~ ~	√
8		terminative dynamic state ~ ~ ~|	√
9	III. Change of state	state-static change - - -|- - -	
10		dynamic-dynamic change ~ ~ ~|~ ~ ~	
11		static-dynamic change - - -|~ ~ ~	√
12		dynamic-static change ~ ~ ~|- - -	√
13	IV. Semelfactive	semelfactive |~|	√
14	V. Accomplishment	accomplishment |~ ~ ~|===	
15		instant dynamic state of accomplishment ~ ~ ~	
16		inceptive of accomplishment |~ ~ ~	
17		terminative of accomplishment ~ ~ ~|	
18		completive of accomplishment ~ ~ ~|===	
19		bounded dynamic sate of accomplishment |~ ~ ~|	

4 Conclusion

In this study, we have argued that *laizhe* should not be defined by tense, by the temporal boundaries of an event, or by verbal semantics. Instead, we suggest that one or both of two attributes are needed if *laizhe* is to surface in a sentence: that is, a temporal gap between RT and ST, and different stage-level properties associated with the subject in the event described. This view is capable of accounting not only for seemingly contradictory sentences found with the same verb, but also for why *laizhe* occurs in sentences with a wide variety of verb types. In particular, we found that *laizhe* is compatible with nine of the 19 linguistic event types in Xu's [4] system, and that it cannot co-occur with the other 10 types, for the reasons discussed in Sect. 3, above.

This study has also empirically confirmed Chao's [1, 2] suggestion that to be compatible with *laizhe*, as one of the criterion is that predicates should describe an event in the recent past (relative to ST), thus creating a fairly small temporal gap between the described event in RT and observable reality in ST. Moreover, those predicates that are compatible with *laizhe* often denote stage-level properties associated with the subject that present differences in the state expressed at ST. If a sentence contains no such difference, or if a change associated with an event it describes is permanent, that sentence will not be compatible with *laizhe*. For example, as we showed in Sect. 3, the instant static state is a homogeneous state without either temporal gaps or stage-level differences; and as such, it can only be made compatible with *laizhe* via the addition of a past temporal adverbial.

In sum, having examined the previous proposals about the meaning and functions of *laizhe*, we have provided a new perspective for explaining its distribution and the factors that drive its compatibility with various types of event states. Future studies could usefully adapt our methodology to studies of other SFPs in Chinese languages, and thus help to build a unified framework capable of accounting for how different SFPs contribute to the interpretation of events and to cognition of their temporal sequencing.

Acknowledgments. We would like to thank Chu-Ren Huang and Niina Zhang for their insightful comments and suggestions. We are also grateful to the reviewers and the audience of the 19TH Chinese Lexical Semantics Workshop (CLSW 2018) for their comments. Any errors and inadequacies that remain are exclusively our own.

References

1. Chao, Y.R.: Beijing, Suzhou, Changzhou yuzhuci de yanjiu. J. Tsinghua Univ. **2**, 865–917 (1926). [in Chinese]
2. Chao, Y.R.: A grammar of spoken Chinese. University of California Press, Los Angeles (1965)
3. Chen, Q.R.: The development of Chinese particle laizhe and subjectivization. Stud. Chin. Lang. **4**, 308–319 (2005)
4. Comire, B.: Aspect: An Introduction to the Study of Verbal Aspect and Related Problems. Cambridge University Press, Cambridge (1976)

5. He, B.Z.: A synchronic account of laizhe. J. Chin. Teachers Assoc. **33**, 99–114 (1998)
6. Huang, C.R., Ahrens, K., Chang, L.L., Chen, K.J., Liu, M.C., Tsai, M.C.: The module-attribute representation of verbal semantics: from semantics to argument structure. Int. J. Comput. Linguist. Chin. Lang. Process. **5**(1), 19–46 (2000)
7. Luo, S.: Final particle laizhe. Master thesis, The Hong Kong Polytechnic University, Hong Kong (2012). [in Chinese]
8. Ōta. T.: A history grammar of modern Chinese. Konan Shoin, Tokyo (1947)
9. Smith, C.S.: The Parameter of Aspect. Kluwer Academic Publishers, Dordrecht (1991)
10. Soh, H.L., Gao, M: Perfective aspect and transition in Mandarin Chinese: an analysis of double-le sentences. In: Proceedings of the 2004 Texas Linguistics Society Conferences, pp. 107–122 (2006)
11. Song, Y.Z.: Temporal particle de and laizhe. Stud. Chin. Lang. **4**, 113–125 (1981). [in Chinese]
12. Vendler, Z.: Verbs and times. Philos. Rev. **66**(2), 143–160 (1957)
13. Xie, C.M.: On telicity and temporal-aspectual properties of laizhe. Chin. Teach. World **4**, 491–502 (2015). [in Chinese]
14. Xu, H.Z.: The Chinese aspectual system. Doctoral thesis. The Hong Kong Polytechnic University, Hong Kong (2015)
15. Zhang, Y.S.: On the tense auxiliary term laizhe. J. Dali Teacher Coll. **48**, 61–67 (2003). [in Chinese]
16. Zhu, D.X.: Lectures on Grammar. Commercial Press, Beijing (1982). [in Chinese]

The Comparative Construction and the Evolution of "过于" [guò yú]

Qi Rao[1,2], Hui Li[3], Mengxiang Wang[2], and Youjie Zheng[4(✉)]

[1] School of Chinese Language and Literature, Central China Normal University, Wuhan, China
qirao@Pku.edu.cn
[2] MOE Key Laboratory of Computational Linguistics, Central China Normal University, Wuhan, China
MengxiangWang1984@Pku.edu.cn
[3] Institute of Applied Linguistice Ministry of Education, Beijing, China
islihui@foxmail.com
[4] School of Foreign Studies, Huanggang Normal University, Huanggang, China
YoujieZheng@163.com

Abstract. "过于"[guò yú](excessively) is a typical adverb in modern Chinese, but in the early history of Chinese language, it was not a word but a cross layer syntactic structure. This shows that in the whole process of Chinese evolution, "过于" [guò yú] as a case has experienced the evolution from non-word to word. This article firstly studies the character of "过于" [guò yú] in different historical periods, depicts the word formation process of "过于" [guò yú](excessively); The second, the paper discusses the motivation and the mechanism of "过于" [guò yú] to be word; After the discussion the motivation and mechanism of "过于" [guò yú](excessively), the paper explores the word formation of "过于" [guò yú] (excessively) as a comparison and as an adverb respectively. The article finally claims the comparative construction is the important syntactic soil for "过于" [guò yú] to be a word, and with the procedure there emerged the semantic prosody of emotion in the pragmatic level.

Keywords: "过于"[guò yú] · Word · Language evolution · Construction

1 Introduction

"过于" [Guò yú] (excessively) is a very common adverb in modern Chinese. According to the adverb classification constructed by (Zhang 2010), it should be included in the subcategory of the degree adverbs [1]. Modern Chinese Dictionary (7th edition) explains "过于" [guò yú](excessively) as an expression for too much in degree and quantity, which indicates that the degree adverb of "过于" [guò yú](excessively) has something in common with "过分" [guò fèn](excessive) and "太" [tài](very) in semantics [2].

The existing researches on "过于" [guò yú] (excessively) have mainly formed two specific discussion ideas: The first one tries to compare with other degree adverbs such as "过" [guò] (excessive),"过分" [guò fèn] (excessive), "太" [tài] (Zhang 2008; Zhang

J.-F. Hong et al. (Eds.): CLSW 2018, LNAI 11173, pp. 334–346, 2018.
https://doi.org/10.1007/978-3-030-04015-4_28

2014) [3, 4]; The second is the historical investigation on the process of how "过于" [guò yú] has come into being a degree adverb. Chen (2006) pointed out that "过于" [guò yú] (excessively) as a degree adverb firstly appeared in Ming dynasty and became very common in Qing dynasty [5]. But different from this, Chen [6] claimed it was not late than Tang dynasty that it had been used as a degree adverb, and he discussed a little about the formation motivation of "过于" [guò yú](excessively) to be a degree adverb. Some other discussions did not examined exclusively the case of "过于" [guò yú], but they investigated the sources and the formations for the classical words of "X (monosyllabic)+yú" in modern Chinese by a group of cases. These studies are consistent that the monosyllabic preposition "于" [yú](excessively) experienced the procedure of grammaticalization in Chinese change and it became a quasi-affix, which induced a phenomenon of fossilization with adjacency items.

Obviously, the above mentioned researches about "过 于" [guò yú], greatly enriched our understanding about the character, syntactic semantic function, origin and formation of this word from many aspects. However, there are still some room for further exploration, such as it is not clear enough to show the procedure of "过于" [guò yú] (excessively), as a degree adverb, and the causes of the formation are not well explained, both problems are what this paper tries to answer.

2 Historical Investigation on "过于" [guò yú]

In this section, we investigate the character and function of "过于" [guò yú](excessively), mainly according to the perspective of different historical stages of Chinese, which are the pre-Qin Chinese period (B.C. 21th century- B.C.221 years), the Middle Ancient Chinese age (B.C.202–589 years) and the modern Chinese period (581–1911 years).

2.1 The Nature and Function of "guò yú" in the Pre-qin Chinese Period

"过于" [Guò yú], in the pre-Qin Chinese period was a non-phrase structure which constituted by a content verb "过" [Guò] and a preposition "于" [yú]. During this period, the frequency of adhesive co-occurrence of "过" [Guò] and "于" [yú] was low. According to statistics, it has appeared 14 times in the corpus of Peking University (CCL) and 11 times in the full-text database of Chinese. From the perspective of function, there were mainly three grammatical functions of "过 于" [guò yú](excessively), in the pre-Qin period, which were the result of interactive matching between different meanings of the verb "过" [Guò] and various grammatical functions of the preposition "于" [yú]. As follow:

A. To constitute a location argument

（1）昔者晋公子重耳出亡，**过于**曹。（《韩非子・十过》）

[xī zhě jìn gōng zǐ zhòng ěr chū wáng , **guò yú** cáo.]（*hán fēi zǐ · shí guò*）

(The former prince of Jin zhonger went into exile and passed the Nation of Cao.)

（2）异日，君**过于**康庄.（《晏子春秋・问下》）

[yì rì, jūn guò yú kāng zhuāng.] *(yàn zi chūn qiū · wèn xià)*

(Another day, Duck Huan of Lu passed the highway.)

B. To constitute an object argument

（3）有善于前，有**过于**后。（《商君书・赏刑》）

[yǒu shàn yú qián, yǒu guò yú hòu].（*shāng jūn shū · shǎng xíng*）

(Good deeds have been done before, faults have been committed later.)

（4）宁**过于**君子，而毋失于小人。（《管子・立政》）

[níng guò yú jūn zǐ，ér wú shī yú xiǎo rén] .（*guǎn zi· lì zhèng*）

(Would rather offence the gentleman than make mistake with the villain.)

C. To constitute an object argument

（5）而君之禄位贵盛，死家之富**过于**三子。（《战国策・秦策三》）

[ér jūn zhī lù wèi guì shèng , sǐ jiā zhī fù guò yú sān zi .]（*zhàn guó cè · qín cè sān*）

(Your noble status, high salary and private wealth are greater than that of three persons.)

（6）今君以贤**过于**尧、舜, 彼且胡可开说哉？（《吕氏春秋・壅塞》）

[jīn jūn yǐ xián guò yú yáo shùn , bǐ qiě hú kě kāi shuō zāi ?.]（*lǚ shì chūn qiū · yōng sè*）

(Now Prince of Qi thinks he is wiser than Yao and Shun, how can he listen to other's advice?)

Which meant to make a comparison between two object arguments and indicates that "X was greater than Y", here the antecedent components usually were monosyllable adjectives, and the comparative construction provided the syntactic context for it to show the comparison in character or situation.

Together, "过于" [guò yú](excessively), in above examples are cross-layer structures constituted by the verb "过" [guò] and the preposition "于" [yú], which formed the same structure of "V+P+N" in syntax where "过" [Guò] worked as the predicate with three senses as "to go by", "to commit a fault" and "to exceed", and "于[yú] +x" worked as the complements of the predicate. The components "曹[cáo] / /康庄[kāng zhuāng]" followed by "于[yú]" in (1) (2) were location arguments, in which "过" [guò] means "to go by"; The components "后[hòu] /君子[jūn zǐ]" followed by "于[yú] " were object arguments, in which "过[guò]" means "commit a fault"; Two object arguments in (5) and (6) showed the degree of comparison in "富" [fù] and "贤[xián]", in which "过[guò] " means "exceed ".

"过[guò]" means "degree", originated from 辵 (chuò, walk one moment and stop the next), which could be construed as "there had been" *说文解字(Shuowen-Jiezi)*, annotation by 段玉裁 (Duan Yucai).*释言(Shì Yán)* (Interpretation of the words) explains it as "post, and 邮亭[yóu tíng]" (post-houses) are places where people go by, and trespass mail are someone's faults. Those explanations indicates that "过[guò]" in the Pre-Qin literatures was a polysemic verb, whose original meaning was "to go by", the senses of "to commit a faultand" to compare with were construed by the original meaning of "go by". The procedure could be interpreted as the following figures (Fig. 1).

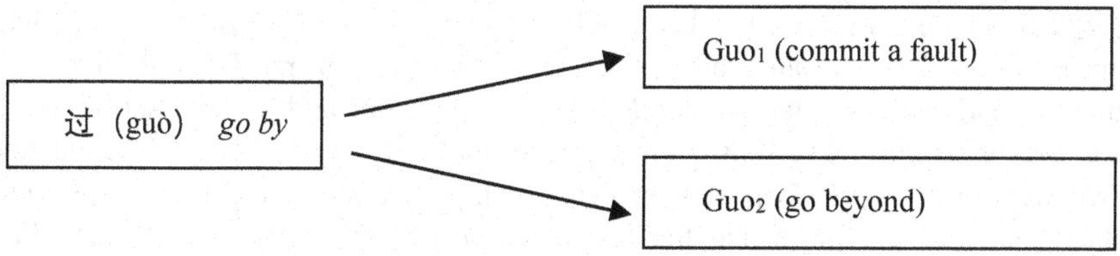

Fig. 1. The semantic evolution of "过"[guò]

2.2 The Nature and Function of "过于" [guò yú] in the in the Middle Ancient Times

In the Middle Ancient Times the nature and grammatical function of "过+于" [guò +yú] continued to maintain the usage frame in the pre-Qin stage, but there were two new changes: the first is that it began to take a shape of a word in character, and the second the priority distribution with the thematic role collocation with "过于" [guò yú] (excessively) began to change in grammatical functions.

2.2.1 Beginning to Take a Shape of a Word

The first step is to discuss the beginning to take a shape of a word. Most "过于" [guò yú](excessively), in this stage were still "cross layer structures" in nature, in which "于" [yú] worked as markers for non-core arguments and "过于" [guò yú] sprang up to begin to take a shape of a word. We can compare two examples (7) (8).

（7）夫万物凡事**过于**大，末不反本者，殊迷不解，故更反本也。（《太平经•丙部》）

[fū wàn wù fán shì guò yú dà, mò bù fǎn běn zhě, shū mí bù jiě, gù gèng fǎn běn yě .](*tài píng jīng · bǐng bù)*

(Therefore, if there were something that exceeded Heaven, that's to say they would had lost themselves. Without understanding this point, it is harder to know the truth.)

（8）天从今以往，大疾人为恶，故夫君子乃当常**过于**大善，不宜**过于**大恶。（《太平经•己部》）

[tiān cóng jīn yǐ wǎng, dà jí rén wéi è, gù fū jūn zi nǎi dàng cháng guò yú dà shàn, bù yí guò yú dà è.]*(tài píng jīng)*

(From now on, Heaven is greatly worried about man's evil deeds, so a gentleman should always do good, not great evil things.)

《太平经》*(Taiping Jing, Scripture of The Great Peace)* was written in the late Eastern Han Dynasty, 《抱朴子》*(Bao Puzi)* was written in the period of East Jin Dynasty, both were Taoism literatures. The follow-up arguments of "于"[yú] in (7) (8) had not been the classic location and object arguments in the Ancient Times. In (7) the follow-up component of "于" [yú] was a NP, "大" [dà] was a Taoism terminology, therefore, "于" [yú] worked as a basic standard for comparative sentence to make a comparison. While there are two ways to understand (8), "大善" [dà shàn] and "大恶" [dà è] followed by "于" [yú] may be regarded as not only a NP, but also an AP. Right-Reading *太平经*(Taiping Jing, Scripture of The Great Peace) written by "于"[yú] Liming explains them as "a good people and the evil one". Read and Interpret Taiping Jing Today written by Yang Jilin explains them as "the kind behavior and the evil action" [7, 8]. The two explanations make sense in meaning, thus "过于" [guò yú] could be understood in two ways: [guò +[yú AP]] or [[guò yú]+AP]. This ambiguous state is the critical syntactic environment in which the lexicalization of "过于" [guò yú] occurs. From existing literatures, we can read examples in Bao Puzi which was Taoism literature written in about 4th Century as follows:

（9）人生之为体，易伤难养，方之二木，不及远矣，而所以攻毁之者，**过于**刻剥，剧乎摇拔也。（《抱朴子•内篇》）

[rén shēng zhī wèi tǐ, yì shāng nàn yang, fāng zhī èr mù, bù jí yuǎn yǐ, ér suǒ yǐ gōng huǐ zhī zhě, guò yú kè Bō, jù hū yáo bá yě .] *(bào pǔ zǐ · nèi piān)*

(So is true of the human body, which is extremely vulnerable and difficult to be recuperated. And compared with hibiscus and willows, the vitality of human life is far less, which is more serious than the cutting of trees and more severe than the shaking of trees.)

(9) should be the earliest example to prove that "过于" [guò yú] had become a word, in which "过于" [guò yú] combined with the two-syllable adjective "刻薄" [kè bō], this is the origin of the typical syntactic function of "过于" [guò yú] as a adverb. At the same time, "过于" [guò yú] also appeared at the initial position of a clause. Take (10) (11) as examples,

（10）**过于**庖牺，多于老氏，皆当贬也。（《抱朴子•外篇》）

[guò yú páo xī，duō yú lǎo shì，jiē dàng biǎn yě .] *(bào pǔ zǐ • wài piān)*

(Your words are beyond Fuxi, and are more than five thousand words speech of Laozi, both should have been denied by caning.)

（11）陛下五让，**过于**许由四矣。（《前汉纪•孝文皇帝纪》）

[bì xià wǔ ràng ,guò yú xǔ yóu sì yǐ .] *(qián hàn jì • xiào wén huáng dì jì)*

(Your Majesty has given up the throne for five times, which is 4 times more than Xuyou.)

In (10) (11) both "过于" [guò yú] at the initial position of a clause mean to make a comparison, "yú" is the basic standard of the comparative sentence, while the first comparison items in two examples are zero-anaphora in text. Dong (2011) pointed out that due to the restriction of prosody, the lexicalized cross-layer structure was generally located at the beginning of a sentence, which was likely to be a transitional environment [9]. For more evidence, there are occasional examples of "guò yú" as a word in *HanShu • Yan Shigu Notes* written not late than Tang dynasty.

(12) 宫室百官同制京师，可谓撟扗过其正矣。［师古曰："撟与矫同。扗，曲也。正曲曰矫。言矫秦孤立之败而大封子弟，过于强盛，有失中也。"］

[gōng shì bǎi guān tòng zhì jīng shī, kě wèi jiāo kuáng guò qí zhèng yǐ. shī gǔ yuē: "jiāo yù jiǎo tòng. Kuáng, qǔ yě. zhèng qǔ yuē jiǎo. yán jiǎo qín gū lì zhī bài ér dà fēng zǐ dì, guò yú qiáng sheng, yǒu shī zhōng yě.]

If to compare it with the origin text in *HanShu*, there is no such an example to show "过于" [guò yú] had become a word. It is only in the notes for *HanShu* in subsequent generations that the interpreter mentioned that "过于" [guò yú](excessively), was a word in their line clip notes, which just proved that it was the result of language evolution. But it should be pointed out that "guò yú" in the stage was in the cross situation among a word and a non-word in language unit. To prove the situation, we make a statistics by all data in CCL, there are only 4 "过于" [guò yú], that could be judged as words in total 78 instances, the distribution could be described as following figures (Fig. 2).

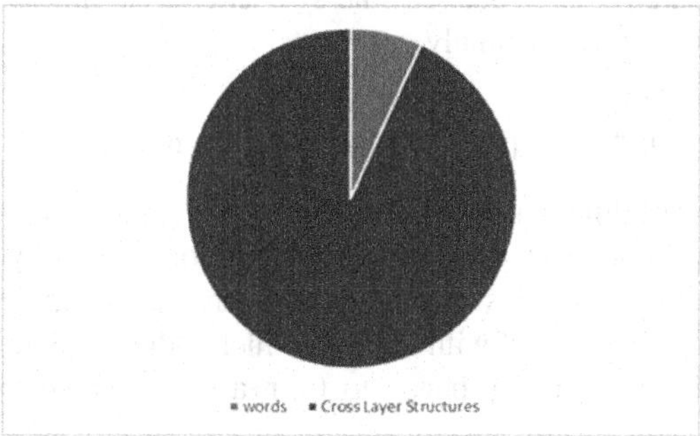

Fig. 2. The nature distribution of "过于" [guò yú] (excessively) in middle ancient times

2.2.2 Diachronic Change of Arguments Collocation

While the meanings of "过" [guò] was changing, the priority of combination with different arguments also changed. In above discussion, we described a collocation frame for the combination of "过于" [guò yú](excessively), with the subsequent arguments, which indicates the various syntactic possibilities of "过于" [guò yú] in sentences. But with the further investigating, there is still unclear about the priority based on the various syntactic possibilities of "过于" [guò yú]. For the purpose, we use the data from both CCL and the full database of Chinese to make a statistics about the collocation distribution of combination between "过于" [guò yú] and different kinds of arguments from the pre-Qin to the six dynasties, the specific situation is as the following table (Table 1):

Table 1. "过于" [guò yú] in middle ancient times

The historical period	Location arguments	Objects arguments	Comparative basic standard
The pre-Qin stage	9	3	2
The western and eastern han periods	2	3	41
The period of the six dynasties	1	1	19

It can be seen from the above table that from the pre-qin to the six dynasties, the distribution of "过于" [guò yú] and the subsequent arguments experienced an evolutionary process from introducing a location to the basic comparative standard as one fell, and another rose. In the pre-Qin stage, to introduce location argument was the key point, and after the Western and Eastern Han periods, the quantity of the subsequent constituted as location arguments decreased a lot, the subsequent arguments of "过于" [guò yú]" steadily indicated the object arguments, which was used to express the comparison between X and Y in quantity and degree. The change like this in syntax provided the ground for high frequency fossilization of "过于" [guò yú], and we conclude that the comparative sentence was the syntactic environment in which the word of "过于" [guò yú] was formed finally.

2.3 Investigation on "过于" [guò yú] Since Modern Times

Though it was in the Middle Ancient Times that "过于" [guò yú](excessively), began to form a word, there was not such a steady tendency to form a word yet. While it were in the Ming and the Qing dynasties that there were an increasing frequency for "过于" [guò yú](excessively), to be used with AP/VP, which indicates that it was during those period that "过于" [guò yú] really began to form a word. There are instances as following types.

2.3.1 "过于" [guò yú] +AP

(13) 此时已过于惨烈。（《万历野获编》）

[cǐ shí yǐ guò yú cǎn liè.] *(wàn lì yě huò biān)*

(At that time it was already very miserable and horrifying)

(14)特疏谏止，云恐所司承望意旨，**过于**严切，未免忠邪并斥，且引汉唐宋钩党之事为鉴。（《万历野获编》）

[tè shū jiàn zhǐ, yún kǒng suǒ sī chéng wàng yì zhǐ, guò yú yán qiè, wèi miǎn zhōng yé bìng chì, qiě yǐn hàn táng sòng gōu dǎng zhī shì wèi jiàn.] *(wàn lì yě huò biān)*

(Special suggestion was presented to the emperor on purpose to stop it, which said “the correspondent government agencies would deal with affairs according to the emperor’s will, and it would be too strict, because such actions would admonish unavoidably both the royal and the evil, and cliques in Han dynasty, Tang dynasty and Song dynasty would be cited as the reference to prove it.”) *(wàn lì yě huò biān)*

Due to the restriction of rhythm coordination, “过于” [guò yú](excessively), usually was followed by adjectives or adjective phrases with double syllables, but sometimes it was followed by the adjectives or adjective phrases with more than three syllables, such as:

(15) 只见沈仲思向他说道：“这件事儿实是我自家不好，**过于**大意了些，虽然付了他六千洋钱，却是我亲手交与月娥。（《九尾龟》）

[zhǐ jiàn shěn zhòng sī xiàng tā shuō dào:” zhè jiàn shì er shí shì wǒ zì jiā bù hǎo, guò yú dà yì le xiē, suī rán fù le tā liù qiān yáng qián, què shì wǒ qīn shǒu jiāo yǔ yuè é.]*(jiǔ yǐ guī)*

(Shen Zhongsi said to him:”It’s really my own fault, I was too careless, though I paid him 6,000 flat silver, and I gave it to Yue-E with my own hand.) (*The Nine-tailed Turtle*)

(16) 不怕得罪太太说，他老人家**过于**忠厚些，太太是惊天动地的大才，想算着那们可成就，就只管奉行。（《绿野仙踪》）

[bù pà dé zuì tài tai shuō, tā lǎo rén jiā guò yú zhōng hòu xiē, tài tai shì jīng tiān dòng dì de dà cái, xiǎng suàn zhe nà men kě chéng jiù, jiù zhǐ guǎn fèng xíng.] *(lǜ yě xiān zōng)*

(Don’t be afraid to offend the old lady, and to be frank she is too loyal, she is a real talent, as soon as we think of her accomplishments, we just do what she says)(lǜ yě xiān zōng) *(Walking in The Green Field)*

2.3.2 “过于” [guò yú] +VP

(17) 侍臣奏曰：“陛下年过六旬，不宜**过于**哀痛”。（《三国演义》）

[shì chén zòu yuē: "bì xià nián guò liù xún , bù yí guò yú āi tòng." xiān zhǔ yuē: " èr dì jù wáng ,zhèn ān rěn dú shēng ! ″.] *(sān guó yǎn yì)*

(The courtier said to the emperor: "Your Majesty is over sixty, and don't be too sad.") (*Romance of the Three Kingdoms)*

陪伴的臣子禀奏说："皇上您已经超过六十岁了，不要过分的伤心了。

（18）狄友苏，你也**过于**无用！（《醒世姻缘传》）

[dí yǒu sū , nǐ yě guò yú wú yòng！.] *(xǐng shì yīn yuán zhuàn)*

(Di Yousu, you are too insignificant!)

Sometimes "过于" [guò yú](excessively), was followed by phrases with three and four syllables.

（19）四爷蒋平道："五弟未免**过于**心高气傲，而且不服人劝。小弟前次略略说了几句，险些儿与我反目"。（《七侠五义》）

[sì yé jiǎng píng dào :"wǔ dì wèi miǎn guò yú xīn gāo qì ào, ér qiě bù fú rén quàn. xiǎo dì qián cì lüè lüè shuō le jǐ jù, xiǎn xiē er yù wǒ fǎn mù.] *(qī xiá wǔ yì)*

(Fourth Elder Jiangping said: "The fifth brother is too proud and refuses to other advice. I gave him some advice some days ago, and then he almost regarded me as an enemy.)

"过于"[guò yú](excessively) might be followed by clauses.

（20）那尹先生摇着头道:"姑娘，你也莫**过于**小看了我尹其明！"（《侠女奇缘》）

[nà yǐn xiān sheng yáo zhe tóu dào: "gū niang，nǐ yě mò guò yú xiǎo kàn le wǒ yǐn qí míng! .] *(xiá nǚ qí yuán)*

(Mr Yin shook his head and said: "Girl, you should not have been be less dismissive of me Yin Qiming!".)

（21）她两个两张粉脸，泛四朵桃花，一齐说道："这是我两个的不是，话**过于**说得急了！"（《侠女奇缘》）

(They both were pink faces, which looked like four peach blossoms, they said together: "It's our faults, the speech was too hasty.")

In the above sections, we investigated the diachronic evolution situation of "过于" [guò yú] in details. In the following sections, we mainly discuss the evolution mechanism and the motivation of "过于" [guò yú] to be a word.

3 The Mechanism by Which "过于" [guò yú] Evolved into a Word

3.1 Two Steps Development Process of Forming a Word

The transition from the typical cross-layer structure of "verbs+prepositions" in the pre-Qin period to the stable adverb in the Ming and Qing dynasties is the result of the interaction between "过" [guò] and "于" [yú] on the basis of the historical evolution of their respective semantic and syntactic functions. In general, the transition is a process of two steps development: the first step is that "于" [yú] had finished the grammaticalization process from a verb to a preposition. But with the appearance of a new emerging preposition of "在" [zài] after "于" [yú] the Han dynasty, the function of as a preposition became weaker and weaker during a long time in the Middle Ancient Times Chinese, the typical syntactic presentation was that the ability to match the location arguments had been restrained by "在" [zài], which indicated the tendency of further grammaticalization of "于" [yú]. Hoppor and Traugort [10] proposed a cline of grammaticalization:

content word > grammatical word > clitic > inflectional affix

On typology Chinese is a analytical and isolated language, thus Chinese grammatical words or clitics would not further evolve into an inflectional affix but fuse together with adjacent items to form a new lexical items [11]. According to the actual situation of Chinese, proposed a revised cline of grammaticalization:

content word > grammatical word > in-word morpheme

But it is important to note that the process from grammatical words to in-word morphemes did not happen overnight. From the historical evolution situation, the process of the second step is unclear. Is it the process that after typical lexical words with "于" as "过于" [guò yú](excessively), had fossilized as a word, "于" [yú] finished the evolution from a preposition to an in-word element? Or is it the process that "于" [yú] further grammaticalized into an in-word element and then fused with monosyllabic words as to "过" [guò] form a word? In short, is it lexicalization before grammaticalization, or grammaticalization before lexicalization? This problem is hard to answer or prove in a Chinese diachronic study. But what it tells is that the process shows the interpenetration of lexicalization and grammaticalization, which indicates that lexicalization and grammaticalization are not reversible from the side to another.

3.2 Inducing Mechanism: Reanalysis

In the process of forming the word "过于" [guò yú] (excessively), two possible explanations allow the formal structure of it can be analysed as [guò+[yú+NP]] and [[guò+[yú+AP]] and the deep structure of [[guò+[yú+AP]] can be reanalysed as [[guò+yú]+AP]], which is the critical condition for "过于" [guò yú] to be a word. However, it is not enough to just have a reanalysis, if the candidate items for lexicalization could not acquire enough pragmatic power and make the innovative reanalysis become a conventional unique one, it was still hard to cause a word finally.

3.3 Pluralistic Integration

Forming a word of "过于" [guò yú] (excessively), is the result of integration induced by many factors, it is very hard to say which factor is dominant one, and which one is secondary. At first, on the rhythm disyllable "过于" [guò yú] (excessively), is a typical foot, which meets the requirement of the minimal prosodic word in Chinese. This provides the possibility for "过于" [guò yú](excessively), to form a word. Next, "过于" [guò yú] (excessively), had a high-frequency of co-occurrence in the critical syntactic context, which made it very easy to package the chunk of "过于" [guò yú] in cognition. From the beginning to form a word around the 3rd century AD to be a stable word in the 15th–16th century, it experienced a long time of accumulation. The reason why it was so late to become a word is that it had been seeking for the conventional pragmatic force by the frequency ratio.

4 The Motivation of "过于" [guò yú] Evolving into a Word

From the pre-Qin period to the six-dynasties period, the priority sequence of subsequent arguments of "过于" [guò yú] had changed, the change was from the location arguments to the object arguments which expressed the meaning of comparison, the consequence of the evolution of the priority argument category was that the comparison sentence became the syntax context for "过于" [guò yú]. The change became the key point for "过于" [guò yú] to be a word. (1) the first stage: a comparison of degree; (2) the second stage: from the degree to the character; (3) the second stage is the extended transfer of combinatorial domains brought by metaphor. Peng [12, 13] made a very significant observation on the grammaticalization candidate, in fact the same situation is also true in lexicalization. The occurrence of lexicalization is not only the matter of its constituent parts, but also closely related to its language environment. Himmelmann [14] proposed an environment-based view of grammaticalization, which includes three levels:

A. The constitute of host class: An→An+X;
B. The change of syntactic context: Xn→Xn+X;
C. The change of semantic -pragmatic context: Kn→kn+X;

On the basis of Himmelmann's analysis model, we can see how the lexicalization of "过于" [guò yú] happened. In the second stage, "过于" [guò yú] (excessively), realized the category transfer of the constitute of host class, the constitute of host class subsequent "于" [yú] shifted from the "degree" to the "character", while the syntactic construction of the comparative sentence still was playing the "grandfather effect", which was still making a comparison on the quantity of "character".

At the same time, the syntactic context also accelerated the extended transfer, the priority of the subsequent arguments category had been shifted from NP to VP and AP, which was a cognitive metaphor procedure. In the comparative construction, NP that could get into the "过于[guò yú] +NP" usually was a personal noun, which showed the constructional meaning that X was greater than Y, here "过于" [guò yú], was used to describe the sense relation between X and Y. The transfer from NP to VP and AP was the relation similarity projected from the register of personal noun to the character register or the mental activity register, that's to say, the key constructional meaning implicated was projected into two new registers.

The third stage: the mental fulfillment of latter-comparative items. In the process of being a word for "过于" [guò yú], there was the change of semantic -pragmatic context. In the stage, the syntactic context of "过于" [guò yú](excessively), changed in some degree, which was mainly reflected on the syntactic context—the form of comparative sentence changed, and the latter-comparative item did not appear in the form any more. But, this change did not mean that there was no the latter-comparative item and the sentence was not a comparative sentence, in fact the latter-comparative item was here by the way of the mental fulfillment. Meanwhile, the construction register—the constructional meaning of quantity relative ratio still had "grandfather effect", which had syntactic functions of coercion and overlooking. Only when the meaning-form pair of "过于" [guò yú](excessively), became stable in the syntactic context, could it be concluded that the key semantic and syntactic functions of "过于" [guò yú](excessively), have formed stably in Modern Chinese.

5 The Conclusion

The thesis starts to investigate "过于" [guò yú](excessively), from the early pre-qin dynasty and extends to the end of Qing Dynasty. The study found that although there were signs of it to be a word in the Middle Ancient Chinese Times, this did not mean that it had become a stable word. It was during the Ming and the Qing Dynasty periods that "过于" [guò yú](excessively), had been a real stable word. This indicates that there is a relative synchronic level, for a certain specific language unit, in which level exists characters of various lingual units, and words and non-word units co-exist here. On the another hand, the situation shows that word segmentation is still a difficult problem in deep-processing the historical data.

The evolution procedure of "过于" [guò yú] (excessively) as a word indicates that the shift procedure from a non-word unit to a word was deeply influenced by its syntactic context. In Chinese evolution procedure, both the antecedent constitute and the latter constitute have experienced obvious change, and at the same time the comparative construction has obtained the function of overlooking.

Acknowledgments. Project Supported by the National Natural Science Foundation of China (No. 61602040), China Postdoctoral Science Foundation (No. 2017M1004), China National Language Commission Foundation (No. Wt135-27).

References

1. Zhang, Y.S.: The nature, scope and classification of adverbs in modern Chinese. Stud. Lang. Linguist. **39**(2), 51–63 (2000)
2. Institute of Language, Chinese Academy of Social Sciences (eds). Modern Chinese Dictionary, 7th edn. The Commercial Press, Beijing (2016)

3. Jiahe, Z.: Grammatical and Functional differences of degree adverb “guo” and “guoyu”. J. Soc. Sci. Jiamusi Univ. **28**(5), 60–62 (2010)
4. Yanjun, Z.: The comparative analysis of excessive degree adverbs “Guoyu” and “Guofen”. Chin. Lang. Learn. **39**(2), 74–79 (2014)
5. Chen, Q.: Study on the Adverbs of Degree in Modern Chinese. Sichuan Bashu Press, Chengdu (2006)
6. Cheng, H.: The bleaching process of the adverb “guo yu”. J. Mudanjiang Coll. Educ. **17**(5), 30–31 (2008)
7. Liming, Y.: Taiping Jing Zheng Du (Right Reading Scripture of The Great Peace). Bashu Publishing House, Chengdu (2001)
8. Jilin, Y.: Taiping Jing Jin Du Jin Yi (Read and Interpret Taiping Jing Today). Hebei People’s Publishing House, Shijiazhuang (2002)
9. Dong, X.: Lexicalization: The Origin and Evolution of Chinese Disyllabic Words (Revised Edition). The Commercial Press, Beijing (2011)
10. Hopper, P.J., Traugott, E.C.: Grammaticalization, pp. pp. 7–11. Cambridge University Press (2003)
11. Fuxiang, W.: Some typological features in the grammaticalization changes of Chinese. Chin. Lang. **18**(5), 484–494 (2005)
12. Rui, P.: A preliminary examination of the expansion effect of grammaticalization. Chin. Linguist. **31**(1), 50–64 (2009)
13. Rui, P.: Critical frequency and noncritical frequency: the frequency grammaticalization relationship revisited. Chin. Lang. **13**(4), 3–18 (2011)
14. Himmelmann, N.P.: Lexicalization and grammaticalization: opposite or orthogonal? In: Bisang, W., Himmelmann, N.P., Wiemer, B. (eds.) What Makes Grammaticalization-A Look from Its Fringes and Its Components, pp. 23–25. Mouton de Gruyter, Berlin & New York (2004)

On the Condition of X in "fei X bu ke" Constructions

An Analysis Based on the BCC Corpus

Peicui Zhang[1(✉)], Lei Wang[1], and Wentong Sun[2]

[1] Henan University, Kaifeng, China
zhangpeicui@aliyun.com, 1418458965@qq.com
[2] Zhengzhou Chenggong University of Finance and Economics, Zhengzhou, China
swt1215@163.com

Abstract. Prosody plays an important role in Chinese studies. This can be observed not only in word building but also in constructions' formation. By analyzing the 1120 results of the "fei X bu ke" construction via the BCC corpus, it is discovered that no matter from the amount of use or from the average frequency of use of the construction, the quadrisyllabic "fei X bu ke" construction takes a dominant position, that is, the monosyllabic X is preferred to form the construction. In order to explicate the reason, this paper attempts to analyze the preference of syllables of X in the "fei X bu ke" construction from the perspective of prosody.

Keywords: "fei X bu ke" construction · Corpus · Prosody

1 Introduction

"fei X bu ke" (非X不可) is a construction widely used in Modern Chinese with its own specific features. This language pattern is solidified after long time of use frequency and is in possession of semantic and syntactic features of its own. Previous studies deal with this construction from various perspectives, which can be summarized as follows:

In the first instance, some scholars make a comprehensive analysis on this construction from the perspective of diachronic evolution, semantic condition and pragmatic function. For example, Zhang (1992) takes "fei X bu ke" as one of the sentence patterns of "fei X bu Y" and classifies this construction into four categories in terms of the development path of "fei X bu Y": double negative type, solidified grammaticalized type, implicit abbreviation type and restricted condition type. The semantics of "fei X bu Y" can be further classified into necessity of intension, necessity of situation and necessity of deduction in terms of expression. "fei X bu ke" is a subtype of the solidified grammaticalized pattern "fei X bu K". Guo (1999) views "fei A bu B" as a type of complex sentence in ancient Chinese in expression of conditional relations, which grows into three forms from the Pre-Qin Period to modern times. He makes a specific analysis on the emergence and development of "fei A bu B" in terms of four chronological phases in his paper. Wu (2003) treats "fei X bu Ke" as one of the double

J.-F. Hong et al. (Eds.): CLSW 2018, LNAI 11173, pp. 347–357, 2018.
https://doi.org/10.1007/978-3-030-04015-4_29

negative patterns, grouping it into intensive type in terms of the force of the tone. Hong and Dong (2004) explore "fei X bu ke" from the perspective of historical evolution and grammaticalization and take subjectivity as one type of motivation of grammaticalization. He believes that this language pattern is a construction of subjective expression from the very beginning and its subjective expression gives birth to a new usage by the end of the Qing Dynasty: a usage of emphasis on the subjective wishes in terms of the deduction and emphasis of the necessity of objective truth on the basis of which the function of this construction is grammaticalized. Wang (2008) makes an analysis of the presence and absence of "bu ke" in the structure of "fei VP bu ke" from the perspective of expression and points out that the presence and absence of "bu ke" is regulated by some rules and makes an in-depth depiction and analysis on the rules and causes. Zhang (2016) points out five phases of "fei X bu Y" on the basis of the emergence and development of this language pattern and deems that this language pattern, which originally expresses double expressions, grows into utterances that express single proposition later on. X evolves into a predicative constituent from a substantive constituent and the structure of "fei X bu ke" is characterized by solidification and boundedness, which fulfills the grammaticalization of "fei X bu Y".

Secondly, Yang (2002) and Wan (2006) make an in-depth analysis on the meanings of "fei X bu ke" from the perspective of teaching Chinese as a foreign language, explore the impacts exerted by meanings on the grammar and put forward effective teaching methods. Yang (2015) makes a comprehensive survey on "fei X bu Y" and relevant constructions in terms of corpus statistics and finds that the relevant constructions of "fei X bu Y" are "fei X bu xing", "fei X bu cheng", "fei X bu zhong" and "fei X". Each construction has different usages with the difference of X. The utilization frequency and syntactic functions of these usages are not completely identical.

Thirdly, Cheng (2001) and Long (2012) make an analysis on "fei X bu ke" from the perspective of construction. Cheng believes that the basic meaning of "fei X bu ke" is "must, have to", with the variation between subjectivity and objectivity in different context. He believes that the "X" which is negated by "fei" in the construction is generally an action, and the construction uses "bu ke" to illustrate that it is impossible or unviable without such action or behavior. The meaning of this construction makes X imply or refer to the relevant actions or behaviors when X is a nominal. Long points out from the perspective of construction grammar that "fei X bu ke" is in effect a construction that expresses irrealis events.

Cheng (2011) makes a constructional analysis on three common language patterns "fei X bu VP", "fei X bu ke/xing/cheng" and "fei dei X" that belong to the language pattern "fei X bu Y" from the perspective of constructional contrast analysis. He unveiles the semantic and syntactic differences and similarities of these three constructions and makes a detailed contrastive analysis on both "非X不可 fei X bu ke" and "非X才可 fei X cai ke" to find out the differences and similarities between them. Wang (2017) makes a detailed description of "fei X bu Y" and "fei X cai Y" respectively and makes an in-depth analysis on their differences and similarities from the perspectives of syntax, semantics and pragmatics, which are eventually put into the practice of teaching Chinese as a foreign language.

Previous studies mainly concern themselves with the origin, syntax and semantics of "fei X bu ke" with the ignorance of the preference of number of characters of X in the construction, which will be discussed intensively in this paper. We will gather the statistical results of "fei X bu ke" appearing in literary works by virtue of BCC corpus and then make an analysis of the constitutional condition of X.

2 A Constitutional Analysis of X

"fei X bu ke" is a language pattern with comparatively higher frequency of usage in the construction "fei X bu Y". It is inclusive of two constants ("fei" and "bu ke", which have been grammaticalized into a modal particle) and a variable X. It can either serve as a constituent in a sentence or act as an embedded clause in complex sentences on account of its high degree of solidification.

This paper makes a corpus analysis on the construction "fei X bu ke" in terms of the BCC corpus of Beijing Language and Culture University. We have found that the variables that follow "fei" are mainly predicative constituents (谓词性成分), including monosyllabic verbs (e.g., 非死不可 fei si bu ke, 非去不可 fei qu bu ke, etc.), disyllabic verbs (e.g., 非知道不可 fei zhidao bu ke, 非解决不可 fei jiejue bu ke, etc.), verb-object phrases (e.g., 非动手不可 fei dong shou bu ke, 非送命不可 fei song ming bu ke, etc.), and verb-complement phrases (e.g., 非弄清楚不可 fei nong qingchu bu ke, 非晕过去不可 fei yun guoqu bu ke, etc.). Besides, the variables can either be substantive constituents (体词性成分) that can be represented by nominals both nouns (e.g., 非钱不可 fei qian bu ke, etc.) and pronouns (非你不可 fei ni bu ke, 非他不可 fei ta bu ke, etc.) or idioms (成语, e.g., 非粉身碎骨不可 fei fen-shen-sui-gu bu ke, 非一败涂地不可 fei yi-bai-tu-di bu ke, etc.). Semantically, this construction expresses that the strong subjective wishes on the part of the speakers of participants or signifies the necessity of situation and deduction objectively. The distribution property of constitutional types of X is illustrated as Fig. 1:

1447 results are derived when we type "fei X bu ke" into the input box below the self-defined "literature" in the BCC corpus of Beijing Language and Culture University and 1120 results show up after screening. Figure 1 indicates that X is primarily used as a predicative constituent in "fei X bu ke", due to the fact that the adverbial nature of "fei" requires that X should be a verb, whether "fei" is used as a negative adverb in its primitive stage, a positive commentary adverb in the subsequent stage or a modal adverb. For example:

We can firstly classify the predicative constituents into verbs (动词) and verbal phrases (动词性短语) in terms of Table 1, from which Fig. 2 can be derived. Obviously, the number of verbs is roughly two times the number of phrases. That is to say, X is primarily used as a verb in literary works when it serves as a predicative constituent. Figure 2 is represented as follows:

The predicative X can be further classified into monosyllabic verb (单音节动词), disyllabic verb (双音节动词), verb-object phrase (动宾短语) and verb-complement phrase (动补短语) according to the Table above. A survey of the number of all types of constituents that make appearance in literary works gives birth to the following figure:

Figure 3 indicates that the number of X, when it acts as monosyllabic verbs, is comparable with the number of X when serves as disyllabic verbs. However, the number of verb-object phrases is much more than the number of verb-complement

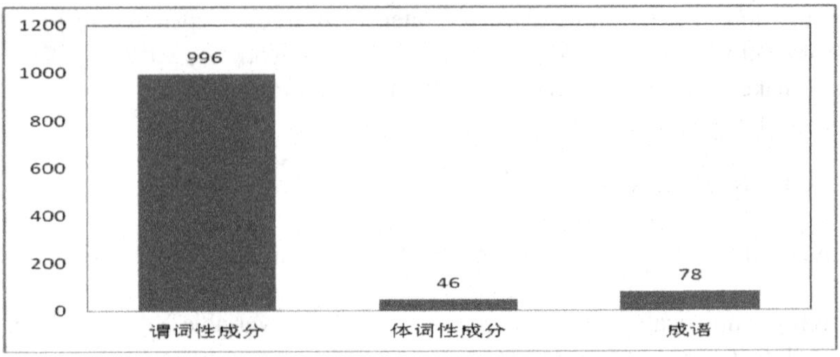

Fig. 1. The distribution property of constitutional types of X

Table 1.

fei si bu ke 非死不可	fei daying bu ke 非答应不可	fei dong shou bu ke 非动手不可	fei qi-si bu ke 非气死不可
fei qu bu ke 非去不可	fei huiqu bu ke 非回去不可	fei chi-kui bu ke 非吃亏不可	fei lei-si bu ke 非累死不可
fei zou bu ke 非走不可	fei jinqu bu ke 非进去不可	fei chu luanzi bu ke 非出乱子不可	fei nong qingchu bu ke 非弄清楚不可
fei shuo bu ke 非说不可	fei zhidao bu ke 非知道不可	fei chu renming bu ke 非出人命不可	fei duo qilai bu ke 非躲起来不可

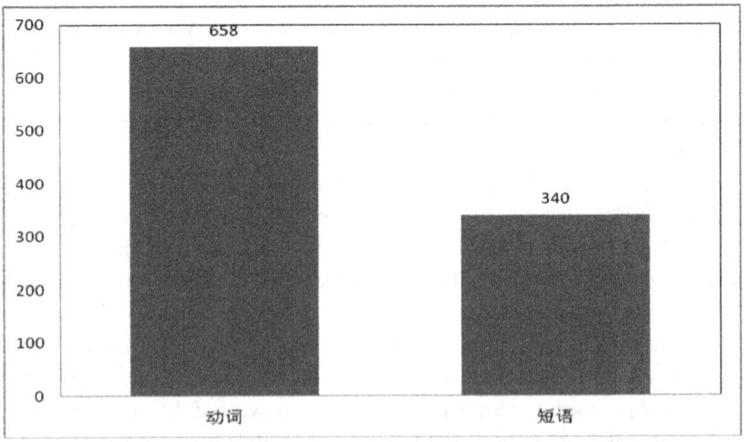

Fig. 2. Classification of predicative constituents into verbs and verbal phrases

phrases. As the occurrence frequency of all types of specific verbs and phrases varies, the average frequency of all types must be figured out before we come to a more precise conclusion.

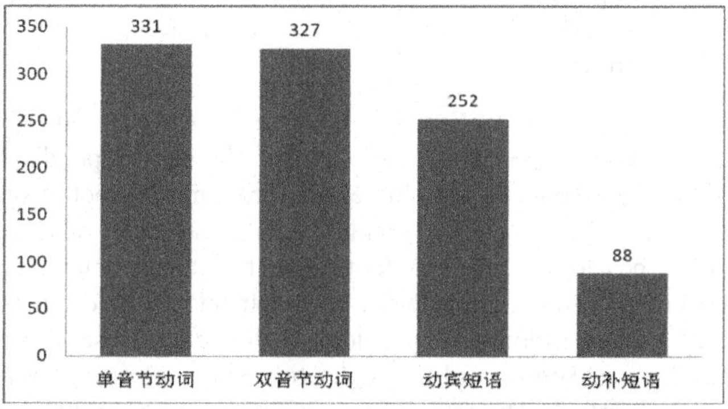

Fig. 3. Classification of predicative constituents

It can be seen from Fig. 4 that the average use frequency of monosyllabic verbs is approximately four times the use frequency of disyllabic verbs in terms of their average use frequency, though their number of occurrence is roughly identical. And the use frequencies of verb-object phrases and verb-complememt phrases are much lower than that of the monosyllabic verbs. The use frequency of the expression “非死不可 fei si bu ke” reaches up to 2285 times, and the highest use frequency of other expressions are 118 times (非答应不可 fei daying bu ke), 205 times (非动手不可 fei dong shou bu ke) and 48 times (非弄清楚不可 fei nong qingchu bu ke) respectively.

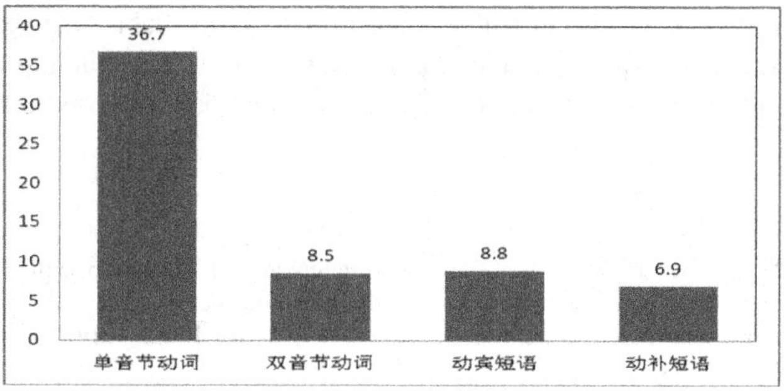

Fig. 4. Average use frequency of monosyllabic verb (单音节动词), disyllabic verb (双音节动词), verb-object phrase (动宾短语) and verb-complement phrase (动补结构)

We can say that the use frequency of monosyllabic X is much higher than that of disyllabic words. Then what is the reason for such a high use frequency of monosyllabic X? Prosody may help to offer us a way out.

3 Prosodic Interpretation of "fei+X+bu ke"

3.1 Theoretical Interpretation

Four-character patterns are widely used in Chinese, which is in effect a product of prosodic operation. Feng (2000, 2009) believes that Chinese adopts disyllabic foot, a phenomenon caused by the fact that Chinese shifts from moraic foot to syllabic foot in history. As the simplification of the complex syllabic structure of ancient Chinese, syllabic foot has to be adopted as moraic foot cannot be realized in monosyllables. This conversion has brought huge impact to the development of Chinese language in that disyllabic words occupy a dominant position in Modern Chinese all on account of lexical disyllabification. Some words, though non-disyllabic, assume a two-character rhythm in natural utterances (Huang and Liao 1981; Liu and Xing 2003), for example:

(1) ji xing xie |[1]dian →ji xing # xie dian (畸形鞋|店→畸形#鞋店)
(2) wu |fei bing | niu→wu fei # bing niu[2] (无|肺病|牛→无肺#病牛)
In fact, the effect of prosody is so powerful that it surpasses the constraints of construction. Sometimes the structures and orders of languages have to be readjusted in order to achieve grammaticality and fluency. For example:
(3) bei | si chuan lu→si chuan # bei lu (北|四川路→四川#北路)
(4) zhi | bian ji bu→bian ji # zhi bu (支|编辑部→编辑#支部)
(5) zhi | dian ying pian | chang→dian ying # zhi pian chang (制|电影片|厂→电影#制片厂)
(6) shou | huo che piao | chu→huo che # shou piao chu (售|火车票|处→火车#售票处)

Lexical disyllabification in Chinese required by prosody is realized by the fact the basic words (prosodic words) in Chinese are primarily disyllabic. However, although words in Chinese are mainly disyllabic, units larger than words (such as constructions and idioms) tend to be larger than two syllables. The prosodic patterns suitable for them

---

[1] In this paper, "|" signifies the division of syntactic structure and "#" is used to segment prosodic foot. "|" alone means that the syntactic structures and the prosodic foot overlap with each other. "#" is used when any inappropriateness shows up. Besides, "*" is used to signify that the pause in the phrase or word is unacceptable.

[2] This phrase comes from Chao (1968). Chao caught sight of a board which read "无肺病牛 wu fei bing niu", which had the meaning of "bulls without lung diseases". However, many people who caught sight of it may utter it as "无肺-病牛 wu fei-bing niu", which has a meaning roughly interpreted as "infected bulls without lungs". In actual fact, under such specific context, though this phrase was uttered with a two-character rhythm, people realized the ungrammaticality of such mode of utterance and re-uttered the phrase as "无-肺病牛 wu-fei bing niu" right away. This can also serve as a piece of evidence for the phenomena such as "鸟兽散 niao shou san" that show up later in this paper, a rejection exerted by the semantic meanings toward prosody.

are trisyllabic, quadrisyllabic, penta-syllabic, etc. As for the construction "fei+X+bu ke", quadrisyllabic pattern is the most popular one and has the highest use frequency.

Why quadrisyllabic patterns are the most frequently used prosodic patterns in Chinese? Here two constraints are at work. One is the economy principle, the other being prosodic constraint. Trisyllabic patterns cannot form feet despite their superficial economy. Though a large number of supra-feet formed by trisyllables make appearance in Chinese (Feng 1996, 2009), it is an actual fact that the supra-foot serves as a last resort. The realization condition for supra-feet is that in a language string, when the operation of the standard footing is completed, the residual monosyllabic constituents (if there were any) will attach themselves to their adjacent feet to form trisyllabic feet (Feng 1996: 163). Thus, quadrisyllabic patterns become the optimal choice on account of their conciseness in form, which is consistent with the requirement of economy. Besides, it is able to contain two feet, which conforms to the prosodic constraint.

3.2 Further Evidence

In actual fact, other types of constituents also favor four-character constructions apart from "fei+V+bu ke". Analyses and comparisons are also made when X serves as pronouns.

46 results are derived after our searching and screening in BCC corpus when X serves as a substantive constituent. Among these results, we get 10 results when X is a personal pronoun (ni 你, ta 他, wo 我, ta 她, tamen 他们, women 我们, nimen 你们, with comparatively high use frequency, as shown in Fig. 5.

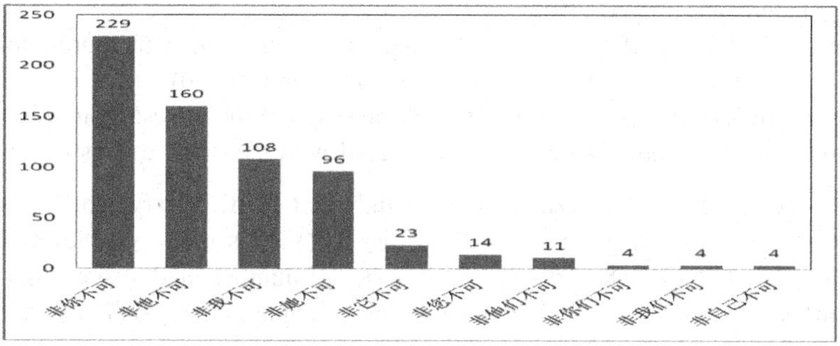

Fig. 5. Relative use frequency of the 10 results

Figure 5 shows the relative use frequency of the 10 results, among which the use frequency of singular pronouns (ni 你, ta 他, wo 我, ta 她) are much higher than that of the plural pronouns (tamen 他们, women 我们, nimen 你们). In the other 36 non-personal pronoun results, "fei ci bu ke 非此不可" have the highest use frequency (161 times), which is still lower than that of "fei ni bu ke 非你不可" when X serves as a personal pronoun. The results are shown as Fig. 6:

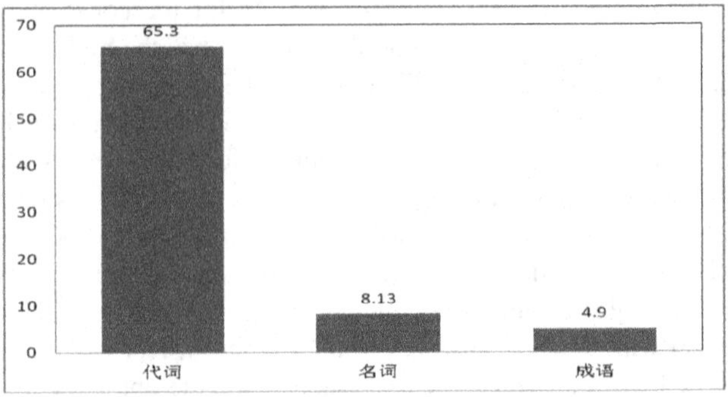

Fig. 6. Average use frequency of X as pronoun (代词), noun (名词) and idiom (成语)

Figure 6 shows the average use frequency of X when it serves as a pronoun, a noun and an idiom respectively in literary works. It indicates that though the number of pronouns is much lesser than that of nouns (on account of their own restrictions), the use frequency shows a completely reversed picture. Though the number of idioms is more than that of substantive constituents, the use frequency of idiom is the lowest among the three types of constituents.

We can come to the following conclusions after we compare the average use frequencies of X in "fei X bu ke" when it serves as a substantive constituent and an idiom respectively in literary works:

(1) X has the highest use frequency when it serves as a pronoun, though the numbers of pronouns are limited (10);
(2) The use frequency of a nominal X is only 1/8, compared with a pronominal X, though the utilization number of nouns is much greater (36).
(3) The use frequency of X when it serves as an idiom is the lowest though its overall number is comparatively high (78), compared with substantive constituents.

We have the following results of the number of X in literary works when we classify pronouns into singular pronouns (代词单数) (X is monosyllabic) and plural pronouns ((代词复数)) (X is disyllabic) in terms of numbers and also classify nouns into monosyllabic nouns (单音节名词) and poly-syllabic nouns (多音节名词):

Figure 7 shows that though the number of pronouns is comparatively small (due to the constraints of their own), the number of singular pronouns is larger than that of plural pronouns. As for nouns, the number of monosyllabic nouns is 1/5 of the number of poly-syllabic nouns. The corresponding average frequency of use is represented by Fig. 8, which indicates that the average use frequency of singular pronouns is 30 times that of plural pronouns and the average use frequency of monosyllabic nouns is 10 times that of poly-syllabic nouns.

It can be proved that monosyllabic words are the best candidates for the construction of "fei X bu ke", whether they be monosyllabic verbs, singular pronouns or monosyllabic nouns. Though some of them may be less in number than their disyllabic counterparts, they have a comparatively higher use frequency.

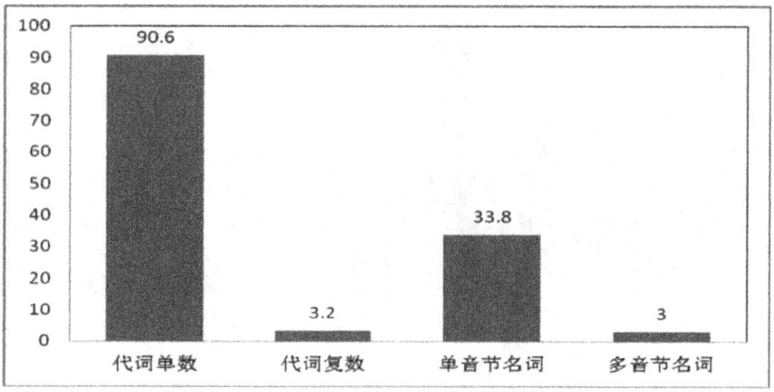

Fig. 7. The number of singular and plural pronouns and the number of monosyllabic and polysyllabic nouns

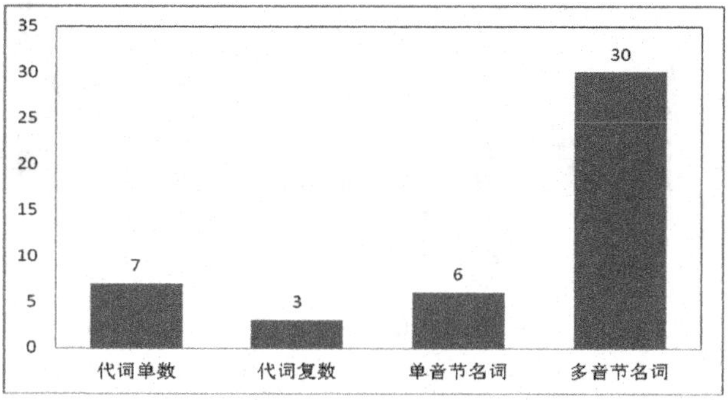

Fig. 8. Average use frequency of singular and plural pronouns as well as singular and plural nouns

4 Conclusion

This paper makes an in-depth analysis of the construction "fei X bu ke" through the BCC corpus in Beijing Language and Culture University. X in the construction may serve as predicative constituents, substantive constituents and idioms. We have found that X occupies the dominant position in the construction when it is predicative (illustrated by Fig. 1). Figure 9 shows the numbers of the various types of constituents that show up in literary works and Fig. 10 is concerned with the average frequencies of their occurrence.

However, the average use frequency of monosyllabic verbs is more than 4 times that of disyllabic verbs. As for the verbal phrases, though the number of verb-object phrases is roughly as three times as that of verb-complement phrases, they have roughly the same average use frequency. Under the light of prosodic syntax put forward by Feng (2009), this paper holds that X enjoys the highest popularity and has the highest use frequency when it is monosyllabic, which is tantamount to say that when

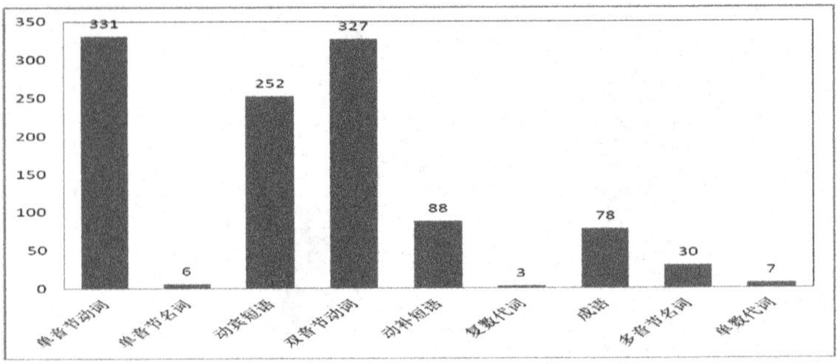

Fig. 9. The numbers of the various types of constituents that show up in literary works

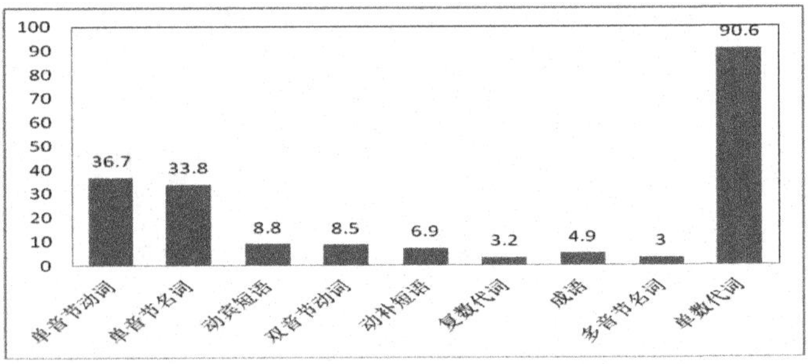

Fig. 10. The average frequencies of their occurrence

"fei X bu ke" is quadrisyllabic. Verification is also made through the average use frequency of X when it serves as substantive constituents.

Figure 1 indicates that X is the least in number when it serves as substantive constituents (46). We classify X into pronouns (10) (whose number is highly restricted) and nouns (36) in terms of parts of speech. But the average use frequency of the pronouns is eight times that of nouns. We derive the following results after we classify pronouns in terms of numbers: 6 singular pronouns (你 ni, 他 ta, 我 wo, 她 ta, 它 ta, 您 nin), 1 singular reflexive pronoun (自己 ziji) and 3 plural pronouns (他们 tamen, 你们 nimen, 我们 women). The average use frequency of singular pronouns (90.6) is as 28 times as that of plural pronouns (3.2). That is, X has the highest use frequency when it serves as monosyllabic pronouns. The same conclusion can also be applied to the case of nouns. If we classify nouns into monosyllabic nouns (6) and poly-syllabic nouns (30), the average use frequency of monosyllabic nouns (33.8) is almost 10 times that of poly-syllabic nouns (3).

In a word, X is primarily predicative when "fei X bu ke" is used in literary works, and monosyllabic verbs occupy a dominant position when it comes to the average use frequency. As for the substantive constituents and idioms that are less in number, both singular pronouns (90.6) and monosyllabic nouns (33.8) occupy a predominant position, with the average use frequency of plural pronouns (3.2), poly-syllabic nouns

(3) and idioms (4.9) all less than 5 times. That is to say, monosyllabic words are most favored by the construction "fei X bu ke", which is decided by the prosodic properties of language. The comparatively high use frequency of monosyllabic verbs in the construction has something to do with the adverbial property of "fei".

Acknowledgments. We would like to express our sincere gratitude to the anonymous CLSW reviewers for their comments of the argumentation and language in this paper. The usual disclaimers apply. The study is supported by the Humanities and Social Sciences by the Ministry of Education (14YJC740115).

References

Cheng, X.: On "fei…bu ke". Lang. Plan. **1**, 33 (2001)

Cheng, Y.: A study of "fei X bu Y" and the relevant constructions. Master Thesis of Shanghai Normal University (2011)

Feng, S.: On the "Prosodic Words" in Chinese. Chin. Soc. Sci. **1**, 161–176 (1996)

Feng, S.: Historical origin of Chinese disyllabification. Mod. Chin. Stud. **1**, 123–138 (2000)

Feng, S.: Interactions Between Morphology, Syntax and Prosody in Chinese (revised and enlarged edition). Beijing University Press, Beijing (2009)

Guo, P.: The emergence and development of "fei X bu B". J. Cent. China Norm. Univ. (Humanities and Social Sciences) **3**, 51–56 (1999)

Hong, B., Dong, Z.: Historical evolution and grammaticalization of the expression "fei X bu ke". Stud. Chin. Lang. **3**, 253–261 + 287–288 (2004)

Huang, B., Liao, X.: Modern Chinese. Gansu People's publishing House (1981)

Long, Y.: An constructional analysis of "fei X bu ke". J. Sichuan Univ. Arts Sci. **1**, 117–119 (2012)

Liu, Z., Xing, M.: Symmetry in phonological patterns in four-character idioms and cognition. Lang. Teach. Linguist. Stud. **3**, 48–57 (2003)

Wan, Q.: An semantic analysis of "fei X bu K". Mod. Chin. **2**, 88–90 (2006)

Wang, C.: On the occurrence and non-occurrence of the "bu ke" in "fei X bu ke" and the grammaticalization of "fei" in the Construction "fei+VP+buke". Stud. Chin. Lang. **2**, 109–119 + 191 (2008)

Wang, R.: The comparative study of the construction "fei X bu Y" and "fei X cai Y". Master Thesis of Jilin University (2017)

Wu, S.: Reconsider double negative. J. Hubeei Inst. Natl. (Philoso. Soc. Sci.) **2**, 107–111 (2003)

Yang, D.: A study of the constructions associated with "fei X bu ke". J. Int. Chin. Teach. **3**, 79–87 (2015)

Yang, Y.: The semantic types of "fei X bu ke" and its pragmatic teaching. Chin. Lang. Learn. **1**, 57–60 (2002)

Zhang, X.: An analysis of the diachronic evolution path of "fei X bu Y". Mod. Chin. (Lang. Stud. Ed.) **7**, 72–75 (2016)

Zhang, Y.: "fei X bu Y"and relevant sentence patterns. J. Xuzhou Teach. Coll. **2**, 36–40 (1992)

Chao, Y.-R.: A Grammar of Spoken Chinese. University of California Press, Berkeley (1968)

A Corpus-Based Lexical Semantic Study of Mandarin Verbs: *Guān* and *Bì*

Meng-Chieh Lin[1] and Siaw-Fong Chung[2(✉)]

[1] Master's Program of Teaching Chinese as a Second Language, National Chengchi University, Taipei, Taiwan
104161007@nccu.edu.com

[2] Department of English, National Chengchi University, Taipei, Taiwan
sfchung@nccu.edu.com

Abstract. This is a corpus-based study of the near-synonymous pair *Guān* 關 and *Bì* 閉 in Mandarin. We adopt the Module-Attribute Representation of Verbal Semantics (MARVS) to analyze the differences between this pair of words. There are three shared senses: 'to close the opening of a specific object' (hereafter 'close an opening'), 'to stop a machine by using a switch' (hereafter 'stop a machine'), and 'to close stores or agencies' (hereafter 'close a store'). The event of 'close an opening' in *Guān* 關 is a composite event of a dual process-state, while *Bì* 閉 is a composite event of a completive resultative. The event relating to 'stop a machine' was not found for *Bì* 閉. The events of 'close a store' for both *Guān* 關 and *Bì* 閉 are simplex events of an inchoative state. However, *Guān* 關 often appears in collocates such as *Guānchǎng* 關廠, while *Bì* 閉 has collocates such as *Bìguǎn* 閉館. It is also discovered that *Guān* 關 emphasizes not only the process of the activity but also the state after the activity. However, *Bì* 閉 emphasizes only the state after the activity.

Keywords: Near-synonyms · *Guān* 關 · *Bì* 閉 · MARVS · Event structure

1 Introduction

Antonyms are words that have opposite meanings. There are different types of antonyms. For example, complementary pairs (*Shēng* 生: *Sǐ* 死) or gradable pairs (*Gāo* 高: *Ǎi* 矮). The antonyms of *Kāi* 開 can be both *Guān* 關 and *Bì* 閉; therefore, *Guān* 關 and *Bì* 閉 form a pair of synonyms, or words with close but not entirely the same meaning. Synonyms are not always exchangeable because they have differences in meaning (semantic) or sentence structure (syntax). The use of *Guān* 關 and *Bì* 閉 in Taiwan can be contrasted as follows. First, it is common to use *Guān*dēng 關燈 (turn off the light) and *Guān*mén 關門 (close the door); at the same time, it is not allowed to say * *Bìdēng* 閉燈 or * *Bìmén* 閉門. Second, it is usual to say *Bìzuǐ* 閉嘴 (shut up) and *Bìmù* 閉幕 (a closing (ceremony)), but it's not acceptable to say **Guānzuǐ* 關嘴and **Guānmù* 關幕. In order to find the differences between this pair of synonyms, we refer to dictionary meanings. The *Dictionary of Chinese Synonyms* 《漢語近義詞辭典》 [7] indicates that the meaning of "close an opening", *Guān* 關 is used the most often; *Bì* 閉 is used more often with body parts such as *Zuǐ* 嘴 (mouth) and *Yǎnjīng* 眼睛

J.-F. Hong et al. (Eds.): CLSW 2018, LNAI 11173, pp. 358–371, 2018.
https://doi.org/10.1007/978-3-030-04015-4_30

(eyes). In another reference, the *1700 Groups of Frequently Used Chinese Synonyms* 《1700對近義詞與用法對比》 [10] distinguishes the differences of *Guān* 關 and *Bì* 閉 with an English explanation: There are five English explanations of *Guān* 關. Namely, shut and close, turn off, (off a business) close down, shut in or lock up and barrier or a critical juncture. However, *Bì* 閉 is not provided with English explanations. These two reference books about Chinese synonyms merely provide descriptive explanations about the pair of synonyms *Guān* 關 and *Bì* 閉. Also, we found there are 16 senses for *Guān* 關 and nine senses for *Bì* 閉 in the *Chinese WordNet*[1]. *Chinese WordNet* (hereafter *WordNet*) is a lexical database which provides complete specific senses of words. *WordNet* provides more senses than the above two reference books, but what it provides is quite vague. The limited information is not sufficient to distinguish the differences between *Guān* 關 and *Bì* 閉.

The research questions are as follows:

1. What are the distributional patterns of *Guān* 關 and *Bì* 閉 in the corpus?
2. What are the differences in usage between their shared senses?
3. Are there any restrictions in the highly frequent senses of *Guān* 關 and *Bì* 閉?

These questions will be answered by analyzing the differences between *Guān* 關 and *Bì* 閉 using the *Academia Sinica Balanced Corpus of Modern Chinese*[2] (*Sinica Corpus*) from Taiwan.

2 Literature Review

Dai [3] employs a componential analysis (sememe analysis) and image schema theory to analyze a group of synonyms with the meaning of 'closure': *Guān* 關, *Bì* 閉 and *Hé*合. A sememe is a semantic unit of meaning conveyed by a morpheme. Seme is a basic or minimal unit of meaning; two or more semes existing together in a more complex unit of meaning comprise a sememe. (Schleiner [8]) The meaning of closure in *Guān* 關 is a metonym form of its original meaning of the noun 'latch'. Since the latch is a device to lock a door, the door must be in the closed position after it is locked; as a result, the concept of using the device to lock the door has become the action of closing the door. Based on this, Dai [3] suggests that the semantic feature of *Guān* 關 is linkage. As for *Bì* 閉, the ancient Chinese dictionary *Shuowenjiezi* 《說文解字》[3]states that *Bì* 閉 also means 'to close the door.' So the initial meaning of *Bì* 閉 would be doors or windows that has been closed. While the doors or windows remain closed, the indoor and outdoor space is cut off; therefore, the core meaning is 'separation and cut off'. In short, the sememe of *Guān* 關 from the componential analysis are [+closure][+linkage][-separation][-integration]; the sememe of *Bì* 閉 are [+closure][-linkage][+separation][-integration]. In addition, Dai [3] also indicates which object

[1] Chinese WordNet: http://lope.linguistics.ntu.edu.tw/cwn2.

[2] Academia Sinica Balanced Corpus of Modern Chinese: http://asbc.iis.sinica.edu.tw/index_readme.htm.

[3] Shuowenjiezi 《說文解字》: http://www.zdic.net/z/swjz/.

collocates can be placed after the verbs by contrasting three typical examples among *Guān* 關, *Bì* 閉 and *Hé* 合 which were *Guānmén* 關門 and *Bìmén* 閉門; Bìyǎn 閉眼 and *Héyǎn* 合眼; and *Bìkǒu* 閉口 and *Hékǒu* 合口. In contrasting *Guānmén* 關門 and *Bìmén* 閉門, it is stated that those two were to close the door; however, the semantic profiles are not the same. *Guānmén* 關門 puts emphasis on the action of closing, making the previous state (opening state) different from the latter state. *Bìmén* 閉門 focuses on the state in which the inside and outside are separated after closing. Inside couldn't communicate with outside, so inside couldn't be influenced by outside either. For that reason, there are words like *Bìménsīguò* 閉門思過 (shut oneself up and ponder over one's mistake) and *Bìméngēng* 閉門羹 (cold-shoulder treatment). However, those contrasts are not attested to in corpora. This study intends to investigate the distributional patterns from corpora and re-examine the differences between the two verbs.

As for corpus-based studies, Tsai [9], Huang and Chen [6], and Hsu and Chung [4] employ different corpus methods to analyze synonyms. Chu-Ren et al. [5] proposes the Module-Attribute Representation of Verbal Semantics (MARVS) to express every event structure of each sense of the verb by presenting information from the argument structure, functional distribution, and collocation of the verb to differentiate the semantic features of the compared verbs. Ideally, each sense of every verb has its individual event structure which is composed of inherent attributes, namely, verbs with different senses will have different eventive information. Our study applies MARVS to analyze the differences between this pair of synonyms.

3 Methodology

First, the data are collected from the *Academia Sinica Balanced Corpus of Modern Chinese* (hereafter *Sinica Corpus*). All single and multiple character words containing *Guān* 關 and *Bì* 閉 are extracted. Second, the concordance lines are analyzed according to the senses of *Guān* 關 and *Bì* 閉 in the Chinese Wordnet. Third, MARVS is employed to discuss the syntactic functions, semantic roles and event structures of both *Guān* 關 and *Bì* 閉 in order to determine the differences between the two synonyms.

4 Analysis and Discussion

4.1 Morphological Form

The extracted single (single-character) and multiple (compound) words containing *Guān* 關 and *Bì* 閉 are shown in Table 1. A total of 482 instances are found in the single-character words of *Guān* 關; deducting one instance which is duplicated, there are 481 instances in total. The original instances in compounds of *Guān* 關 are 22,202. After deleting 138 duplicated instances, 298 proper nouns and eight instances with tagging errors, we extract a total of 22,202 instances. The original number of the single words from the *Sinica Corpus* for *Bì* 閉 are 90 instances; at the same time, the number of compounds are 1,026 instances; removing ten duplicated instances and eight instances that are tagged incorrectly, a total of 1,015 instances of *Bì* 閉 in compounds are found.

In order to see the compound word combinations formed by *Guān* 關 and *Bì* 閉, this study refers to Chung's [2] methodology of sorting the Chinese five elements; analysis of their positions in two-character expressions and three-character expressions are carried out as shown in Table 2. A question mark indicates a character.

In Table 2, the use of *Guān* 關 and *Bì* 閉 in expressions with two- to three-characters is shown. From Table 2, we can see that both *Guān* 關 (95.44%) and *Bì* 閉 (87.88%) appear most often as two-character expressions. *Guān* 關 compounds appearing in the initial composition (關?) are the highest; they reach 54.49%. On the other hand, the compounds of *Bì* 閉 appear the highest (60.1%) in the final composition (?閉). The instances of three-character expressions are less than 10% for both *Guān* 關 and *Bì* 閉; therefore, the analysis below will not discuss three-character compounds as they are not in the scope of our research.

The following analysis of *Guān* 關 and *Bì* 閉 two-character compounds will be analyzed based on 250 tokens taken randomly from the corpus. As the single characters are fewer than 250 tokens, we analyze the number that we retrieve from the corpus. In total, there are 481 tokens of single-character words and 500 tokens of compounds with *Guān* 關. Ninety tokens of single characters and 500 tokens of compounds with *Bì* 閉 are analyzed.

4.2 Senses

This study refers to the senses from *Wordnet*. There are 16 senses of *Guān* 關, including six verbal senses, seven noun senses, and three senses of measure words; on the other hand, there are nine senses of *Bì* 閉, and all are verb senses. *Guān* 關 and *Bì* 閉 are synonyms when they act as verbs, so while sorting instances, we put the usage of a noun and its measure word together. The way to sort compounds is to see what literal meaning *Guān* 關 and *Bì* 閉 express in the corpus. We calculate the number of single-character words and compounds for both *Guān* 關 and *Bì* 閉.

In Table 3, we can see that *Guān* 關 in single-character words is used most often as a noun or measure word (30.77%). Removing the usage as a noun or measure word, we see the first six meanings of the verbs with the highest number of senses is 'to isolate the object mentioned later in the specific space so that it cannot leave' (29.73%), and the second highest is 'to close stores or agencies' (11.85%). In compounds, the highest number of senses of *Guān* 關 is 'specific objects involve the objects mentioned later' (56.2%); the second highest is a noun or measure word, and the instances in the remaining five senses of compounds are less than 5%. In both single-character words and compounds, *Bì* 閉 appears most often as the sense of 'an object's two components can be combined and tightly coupled'; there are 75.56% in single-character words and 24.8% in compounds. In the compounds of *Bì* 閉, except for the above senses, the number of 'to describe an opening or passage of a particular object is enclosed, usually for doors and windows' is the same as 'two components of an object can be combined and tightly coupled'.

Table 1. Numbers of instances from the Sinica Corpus

	*Guān*關		*Bì*閉	
	Token	%	Token	%
Single-character words	481	2.12%	90	8.14
Compound	22,202	97.88%	1,015	91.86
In total	22,683	100%	1,105	100%

Table 2. *Guān* 關and *Bì* 閉 combinations in the Sinica Corpus

		*Guān*關		*Bì*閉	
		Token	Percentage	Token	Percentage
Two-character expression	**Initial: C?** (e.g.,: 關係 'relationship', 閉嘴 'shut up')	12,098	54.49%	282	27.78%
	Final: ?C (e.g.,: 公關'public relation', 倒閉'close down')	9,092	40.95%	610	60.10%
Three-character expression	**Initial: C??** (e.g.,: 關鍵性'criticality', 閉幕式'closing ceremony')	483	2.18%	32	3.15%
	Medial: ??C (e.g.,: 總開關 'main switch', 關禁閉 'put in confinement')	49	0.22%	2	0.20%
	Final: ?C? (e.g.,: 指關節 'knuckle', 自閉兒 'autistic child (ren)')	480	2.16%	89	8.77%
Total		22,202	100%	1,015	100%

From Table 3, we can find that there are three shared senses in *Guān* 關 and *Bì* 閉: 'to close the opening of a specific object, usually used with doors or windows', 'to stop a machine by using a switch,' and 'to close stores or agencies'. *Guān* 關 and *Bì* 閉 are distributed differently among single-character words and compounds. *Guān* 關's single-character words are the most in the sense of 'to close the opening of specific object, usually used with doors or windows' and 'to stop a machine by using a switch'. There are no instances of 'to stop a machine by using a switch' for *Bì* 閉. In the sense of 'to close stores or agencies', *Bì* 閉's compounds occur with a higher frequency than those of *Guān* 關.

Table 3. *Guān* 關 and *Bì* 閉 from the Sinica Corpus correspondence to senses in Wordnet

	Senses	Single-character words	Compound
Guān 關	**1. To close the opening of a specific object, usually used with doors or windows**	**50 (10.4)**	**4(0.8)**
	2. To stop a machine by using a switch	**24(4.99)**	**5(1)**
	3. To close a store or agency	**57(11.85)**	**4(0.8)**
	4. To lower the operational settings of the aforementioned objects with the switch	6(1.25)	0
	5. To isolate the object mentioned later in the specific space so that it cannot leave	143(29.73)	1(0.2)
	6. Specific objects involve the objects mentioned later	53(11.01)	281(56.2)
	7. As a noun or measure word	148(30.77)	205(41)
	In total	481(100%)	500(100%)
閉 *Bì*閉	**1. To close the opening of specific object, usually used with doors or windows**	**7(7.78)**	**56(11.2)**
	2. Describe an opening or passage of a particular object that is enclosed, usually for doors or windows	2(2.22)	124(24.8)
	3. An object's two components can be combined and tightly coupled	68(75.56)	124(24.8)
	4. Describe the two parts of an object are tightly combined	3(3.33)	22(4.4)
	5. To stop a machine by using a switch	**0**	**0**
	6. To use the switching device to make a carrier pipe close and not circulate	4(4.44)	3(0.6)
	7. To close stores or agencies	**6(6.67)**	**107(21.4)**
	8. Event or state is terminated at a specific point in time	0	40(8)
	9. Stop talking or singing	0	24(4.8)
	In total	90(100%)	500(100%)

4.3 Syntactic Function and Argument Structure

There are three shared senses in *Guān* 關 and *Bì* 閉. From the distributions of *Guān* 關 and *Bì* 閉, we found instances of *Bì* 閉 that mean 'to stop a machine by using a switch' and 'to close stores or agencies' are fewer than *Guān* 關. However, *Guān* 關 and *Bì* 閉 have almost the same proportion while they mean 'to close the opening of a specific object.'

Guān 關 is used as a predicate in terms of its syntactic function, as in example (1). There is a small number of instances of it appearing as an attribute, as in (2). Compared to *Guān* 關, the situation of *Bì* 閉 being used as an attribute is higher, as in (3) (Table 4).

Table 4. Syntactic function and argument structure

	To close the opening of a specific object (*Guān* 關: 54 instances, *Bì* 閉: 45 instances)			**To stop a machine by using a switch** (*Guān* 關: 29 instances, *Bì* 閉: 0 instance)			**To close stores or agencies** (*Guān* 關: 61 instances, *Bì* 閉:12 instances)		
	Predicate	Attribute	Nominalization	Predicate	Attribute	Nominalization	Predicate	Attribute	Nominalization
Guān 關	49 (90.7)	5 (9.3)	0	26 (89.7)	3 (10.3)	0	44 (72.2)	16 (26.2)	1 (1.6)
Bì 閉	35 (77.8)	9 (20)	1 (2.2)	0	0	0	7 (58.3)	3 (25)	2 (16.7)

(1)
不能 【關】了 前門 又【關】後門
bùnéng *Guān* le qiánmén yòu *Guān* hòumén
cannot close *le* front door and close back door
(You) cannot close the front door and then close the back door.

(2)
準確 迅速 控制 開 的 時間 與【關】的時間
zhǔnqiè xùnsù kòngzhì kāi de shíjiān yǔ *Guān* de shíjiān
accurately rapidly control open *de* time and close *de* time
Control the opening time and closing time accurately and rapidly.

(3)
大千 好像 久 【閉】 籠中 的 鳥
Dàqiān hǎoxiàng jiǔ *Bì* lóngzhōng de niǎo
Daqian (feel)like long-time close in the cage *de* bird
It seems like Daqian is a bird that has been closed in a cage for a long time.

The first and second senses of *Bì* 閉 from Table 3 are 'an opening or passage of a particular object that is enclosed'; the difference between them is that the second sense focuses on 'describe'; hence, the data with this semantic meaning belongs to this sense, and they both perform as attributes in terms of their syntactic function (as did the third and fourth sense).

In the shared senses of *Guān* 關 and *Bì* 閉, there are different argument structures. The participant roles for the sense 'to close the opening of a specific object' are both agent and theme. The similarity of the property of the theme is quite high; most are doors or windows. When we compare *Guān* 關 and *Bì* 閉's differences in this shared sense, we find that *Guān* 關 usually appear with the pattern of single-character words, and it can accompany different complements to express the procedure of closing a window, as in (4). *Bì* 閉 appears the most often in a compound pattern; the usage in this sense tends to be in written form and it appears as a fixed usage, as in (6) and (7). *Bì* 閉 could not express the progressive process in this sense. It could only be instantaneous, as in (5). In this sense, the agent makes the theme move; it can use *ba*-structure (把字句) and *bei*-structure (被字句, passive structure)to indicate the relationship between agent and theme. Therefore, *Guān* 關 in this meaning is grammatically correct, but *Bì* 閉 is not.

(4)
把 窗戶 【關】 小
bǎ chuānghù *Guān* xiǎo
Ba window close small
Close the window a little. (gradually make the gap smaller)

(5)
*把 窗戶 【閉】 小
bǎ chuānghù *Bì* xiǎo
Ba window close small
*Close the window a bit.

(6)
只要 能夠 【閉戶】 讀書 就 好了
zhǐyào nénggóu *Bìhù* dúshū jiù hǎo le
as long as be capable of close windows study *jiu* be fine
As long as (I) can close windows and study, then it would be fine.

(7)
張愛玲 【閉門】 不見
Zhāng àilíng *Bìmén* bújiàn
Zhang Ailing close door not see (not meet)
Zhang Ailing closed the door and refused to meet.

(8)
今天 回去 馬上 把 店門 給 【關】 了
jintiān huíqù mǎshàng bǎ diànmén gěi *Guān* le
today go back immediately Ba door Gei close le
(I) will close the door as soon as I go back.

The sense of 'to stop a machine by using a switch' also needs two participant roles: causer and theme. However, there are no instances of *Bì* 閉 in the *Sinica Corpus*, so we can conclude that speakers in Taiwan use *Bì* 閉 to convey the meaning of 'to stop a machine by using a switch'.

The sense of 'to close stories or agencies' needs a participant: theme. In the *Sinica Corpus*, *Guān* 關 appears most often in the collocation *Guānchǎng* 關廠 and *Guānchǎng xiēyè* 關廠歇業. However, *Bì* 閉 appears in compounds in the *Sinica Corpus* the most often; we find 107 instances in total, of which there are 104 instances in which the pattern is '?閉'. For this reason, *Bì* 閉 mostly plays as a complement in the predicate-complement pattern, and it usually gives voice to a negative semantic, as in (9) and (10).

(9)
耀元 電子場 突然 【倒閉】
Yàoyuán diànzichǎng túrán *dǎobì*
Yaoyuan (name) electronics factory suddenly close down
Yaoyuan electronics factory was closed down suddenly.

(10)
票號、 銀行、 當鋪 一律 【歇閉】。
piàohào yínháng dàngpù yílǜ *xiēbì*
exchange shop bank pawnshop uniformly rest
All of the exchange shops, banks and pawnshops were rested uniformly.

Table 5. Event type of 'close an opening' and 'close a store'

Sense	To close the opening of a specific object (close an opening)		To close stores or agencies (close a store)	
Near-synonyms	*Guān* 關	*Bì* 閉	*Guān* 關	*Bì* 閉
1. Time duration	✓ e.g., (11a)	✓ e.g., (12a)	✓ e.g., (13a)	✓ e.g., (14a)
2. Endpoint [le了]	✓ e.g., (11b)	✓ e.g., (12a)	✓ e.g., (13b)	✓ e.g., (14b)
3. Process [zhèngzài正(在)]	✓ e.g., (11c)	✗ e.g., (12b)	✗ e.g., (13c)	✗ e.g.,. (14c)
4. Continuous state	✓ e.g., (11d)	✓ e.g., (12c)	✗ e.g., (13c)	✗
Event type	Composite Event: Dual Process-State •/////•——	Composite Event: Completive Resultative /•——	Simplex Event: Inchoative State (Effect State) •——	Simplex Event: Inchoative State (Effect State) •——

4.4 Event Types

After searching for the data in the *Sinica Corpus* to ascertain the distribution of *Guān*關 and *Bì* 閉, we find that there are no instances of the second sense 'to stop a machine by using a switch' in *Bì* 閉. Therefore, we will not discuss *Bì* 閉's event type in the following section. Only two other senses will be discussed (Table 5).

In the first shared sense: 'close an opening', the event type in *Guān* 關 is a dual process-state of a composite event. It can denote two event modules: the progress as in (11c) or the state after the action has been accomplished as in (11d). However, two of the modules cannot emerge at the same time. This shows that *Guān* 關 not only places emphasis on the process of the action, it also lays emphasis on the state after the action has been accomplished. The event type of *Bì* 閉 is a completive resultative of a composite event. It focuses on the state after closing the opening of a specific object as in (12c), so the event puts particular emphasis on the result.

(11a)
窗戶 【關】 了 三天 都 沒 打開
chuānghù *Guān* le sān tiān dōu méi dǎkāi
window closed *le* three days all not open
The window has been closed for three days and it has not been opened.

(11b)
他 提早 把 店門 【關】 了
tā tízǎo bǎ diànmén *Guān* le
he early *ba* shop door close *le*
He closed the store early.

(11c)
我 在 【關】 窗戶
wǒ zài *Guān* chuānghù
I *zai* closing window
I am closing the window.

(11d)
【關】 著 窗 等 到 天亮
Guān zhe chuāng děng dào tiānliàng
close *zhe* window wait until daybreak
Close the window and wait until daybreak.

(12a)
曹 老 先生 的 木門 一連 【閉】了 兩天
Cáo lǎo xiānshēng de mùmén yìlián *Bì* le liǎng tiān
Cao old man 's wooden door in a row close *le* two days
Mr. Cao's wooden door has been closed for two days in succession.

(12b)
*他 正在【閉】 窗戶
tā zhèngzài *Bì* chuānghù
he *zhengzai* close window
*He is closing window.

(12c)
他的門 一直 【緊閉】著
tāde mén yìzhí jǐn*Bì* zhe
his door continuously tightly close *zhe*
His door has been continuously closed.

Another shared sense in *Guān* 關 and *Bì* 閉 is 'close a store'. No matter whether for *Guān* 關 or *Bì* 閉, the event type is a simplex event which denotes an inchoative state (effect state). They both indicate the state after the stores or agencies stopped operation at some time point, so they can use the endpoint (了*le*) as in (13b) and (14b). In the 'close a store' sense, this pair of near-synonyms does not have a difference in the event type; however, there are some differences in the usage of collocation. The idiomatic collocation of *Guān* 關 is *Guānchǎng* 關廠; at the same time, the idiomatic collocation of *Bì* 閉 is *Bìguǎn* 閉館 as in (14a) and (14b).

(13a)
塔爾寺 一 【關】就是 二十 餘 年
tǎěrsì yì *Guān* jiùshì èrshí yú nián
Ta'er temple as soon close as twenty more than years
Ta'er temple had closed for more than twenty years.

(13b)
所有的 店 都 【關】了。
suǒyǒu de diàn dōu *Guān* le
all *de* stores all close *le*
All stores have been closed.

(13c)
*業者 在 【關廠】
yàzhě zài *Guānchǎng*
operator *zai* shut down a factory
*Operator is shutting down factory.

(14a)
吉美 【閉館】 至 兩千年。
jíměi *Bìguǎn* zhì liǎngqiān nián
Jimei close the building until two thousand year
Jimen (*a name*) has been closed until year 2000.

(14b)
這裡 已經 【閉館】 了
zhèlǐ yǐjīng *Bìguǎn* le
here already close *le*
It has already closed.

(14c)
*吉美 正在 【閉館】
jíměi zhèngzài *Bìguǎn*
Jimei zhengzai close
*Jimei is closing.

4.5 The Differences in Highly-Frequent Senses

In order to see which meanings *Guān* 關 and *Bì* 閉 use more often, we observe the highest distributions of *Guān* 關 and *Bì* 閉 in the *Sinica Corpus*. In the single-character words, *Guān* 關's highly-frequent sense is 'to isolate the object mentioned later in the specific space so that it cannot leave'; the instances in this sense appear with time or location, and it can appear as a *ba*-sentence or *bei*-sentence (passive sentence). We can see that *Guān*關's sense mostly works as an agent that does something to the theme, as in (15) and (16).

(15)
把 我自己 一個人 【關】在 廁所 中
bǎ wǒzìjǐ yígerén *Guān* zài cèsuǒ zhōng
ba myself alone close in toilet inside
(I) Keep myself alone in the toilet.

(16)
我 一個人 被【關】在 廁所 中
wǒ yígerén bèi *Guān* zài cèsuǒ zhōng
I alone *bei* close in toilet inside
I was closed in the toilet alone.

(17)
請 你 把 眼睛【閉】起來
qǐng nǐ bǎ yǎnjīng *Bì* qǐlái
please you *ba* eyes close up
Please close your eyes.

(18)
*你的 眼睛 被【閉】起來。
nǐde yǎnjīng bèi *Bì* qǐlái
your eyes *bèi* close up
*Your eyes were being closed.

In the single-character words of *Bì* 閉, the highly-frequent sense is 'an object's two components can be combined and are tightly coupled'. The relation between closing an object and its components is 'the part-the whole'. These kinds of instances can only use *ba*-sentences instead of *bei*-sentences, as in (17) and (18). From Table 3, we can see that in all *Bì* 閉's senses, there are several meanings which indicate 'describe'. Therefore, compare to *Guān* 關, *Bì* 閉 is used as a description or indicates the state more often.

5 Conclusion

This paper aims to determine the differences between the near-synonyms of *Guān* 關 and *Bì* 閉 through a corpus. Both *Guān* 關 and *Bì* 閉 appear as compounds most often. *Guān* 關 and *Bì* 閉 have the same event type in the sense of 'close a store'; however, their idiomatic collocations are different. In the *Sinica Corpus*, the words conveying this meaning are mostly *Guānchǎng* 關廠 and *Bìguǎn* 閉館. In the sense of 'close an opening', the event type of *Guān* 關 is a dual process-state of a composite event. It can express not only the process that the theme closes but also the state after the theme has been closed. The event type of *Bì* 閉 in the 'close an opening' is a completive resultative of a composite event. Its semantics focuses on the continuously closed state after the accomplished movement of closing.

In addition, to classify the instances extracted from the *Sinica Corpus*, we can see that the highly-frequent sense of *Guān* 關 is 'to isolate the object mentioned later in the specific space so that it cannot leave'; it can be used with *ba*-sentences and *bei*-sentences. This is because the senses of *Guān* 關 almost all have the meaning of the agent to do something to the theme to make the theme change. The highly-frequent sense of *Bì* 閉 is 'an object's two components can be combined and are tightly coupled'; the relation between the object and components are 'the part-the whole', so it can use the *ba*-sentence but not the *bei*-sentence. Finally, we find that *Bì* 閉 is used more often to describe the state after the movement.

This study discusses the pair of Chinese near-synonyms *Guān* 關 and *Bì* 閉. However, because the data we extract from the *Sinica Corpus* are mostly from Taiwan, it can only reflect the different usages in Taiwan. Furthermore, this corpus-based study uses a large number of instances as an analytical basis, attempting to find modules in the usage of natural language. The instances we collect from the corpus are limited.

References

1. Chang, L., Chen, K.J., Huang, C.R.: A lexical-semantic analysis of Mandarin Chinese verbs: representation and methodology (漢語動詞詞彙語意分析:表達模式與研究方法). Int. J. Comput. Linguist. Chine. Lang. Process. **5**(1), 19–46 (2000)
2. Chung, S.F.: A corpus-based study on figurative language through the Chinese five elements and body-part terms. Int. J. Comput. Linguist. Chin. Lang. Process. **14**(2), 221–236 (2009)
3. Dai, X.-X.: Semantics features of modern Chinese synonymous verbs *guan1*, *bi4*, *he2* (現代漢語近義動詞「關、閉、合」區別性語意特徵分析). Unpublished Master Thesis, Hebei Normal University, Hebei (2011)
4. Hsu, Y.-F., Chung, S.-F.: A corpus-based study of Chinese soaking verbs *Jin*4 and *Pao4* (中文「泡」、「浸」之辨析——以語料庫爲本). In: The Proceedings of the 12th Chinese Lexical Semantics Workshop, pp. 301–308, (2011)
5. Huang, C.-R., et al.: The module-attribute representation of verbal semantics: from semantics to argument structure. Int. J. Comput. Linguis. Chin. Lang. Process. **5**(1), 19–46 (2000)
6. Huang, Y.-C., Chen, X.-Y.: A lexical-semantic analysis of Mandarin Chinese near-synonym pair 'fang4' and 'bai3' (說「放」和「擺」:從事件訊息結構和身體動作動詞的詞彙語義進行初探). J. Chin. Lang. Teach. **3**(1), 27–44 (2005)
7. Ma, Y.-H., Ying, Z.: Dictionary of Chinese Synonyms (漢語近義詞辭典). Beijing University Press, Beijing (2002)
8. Schleiner, L.: Cultural Semiotics, Spenser, and the Captive Woman. Lehigh University Press, Bethlehem (1995)
9. Tsai, M.-C.: "Convenient" during the process or as a result—event structure of synonymous stative verbs in TCSL (過程方便，結果便利——狀態動詞事件結構與近義詞教學). J. Chin. Lang. Teach. **8**(3), 1–22 (2011)
10. Yang, J.-Z., Jia, Y.-F. (eds.): 1700 groups of frequently used Chinese synonyms (1700對近義詞語用法對比). Beijing Language and Culture University Press, Beijing (2009)

Information-Seeking Questions and Rhetorical Questions in Emotion Expressions

Helena Yan Ping Lau(✉) and Sophia Yat Mei Lee

Department of Chinese and Bilingual Studies, The Hong Kong Polytechnic University, Kowloon, Hong Kong
helena.lau@connect.polyu.hk, ym.lee@polyu.edu.hk

Abstract. This paper explores the interaction between emotions and two types of questions, namely information-seeking questions and rhetorical questions. Corpus data shows that rhetorical questions (60.3%) are more frequently used in social media than information-seeking questions (39.7%). Of the two types of questions, approximately 94% of rhetorical questions are used to express emotions, while only 23% of information-seeking questions contain emotions. Given that rhetorical questions do play an important role in emotion expressions, we examine the interaction between rhetorical questions and emotions in terms of question type. Various syntactic structures are proposed for the identification of different emotions. We believe that the linguistic account of different types of rhetorical questions in emotion expressions will paint a fuller picture of the nature of emotion.

Keywords: Emotion expression · Information-seeking question
Rhetorical question

1 Introduction

Information-seeking questions (IQs) generally aim to elicit an answer, while rhetorical questions (RQs), expecting no answer, aim to achieve a pragmatic goal, such as to emphasize, to persuade, to show emotions etc. [5, 21]. As a form of figurative language, rhetorical questions usually imply meaning that goes beyond the literal. It is generally believed that rhetorical questions are a rather productive means of expressing or evoking emotions, in particular the negative ones [8, 14, 21]. Yet, it has been a challenging task to distinguish rhetorical questions from information-seeking questions, as both of them have the structure of a question. In addition, given that figurative language is frequently used for emotion expressions [7, 8, 10–12], the disregard for the interaction between rhetorical questions and emotions has greatly restricted the classification and detection of emotions.

This paper aims to study the use of information-seeking questions and rhetorical questions in social media, and explore the interaction between rhetorical questions and emotions in terms of question type. We propose various syntactic structures that can be used to identify different emotions.

J.-F. Hong et al. (Eds.): CLSW 2018, LNAI 11173, pp. 372–380, 2018.
https://doi.org/10.1007/978-3-030-04015-4_31

2 Related Work

Rhetorical questions are generally regarded as an effective persuasive device [5, 18]. As a form of figurative language, rhetorical questions are sometimes studied in a more general way. A great deal of work indicated that figurative language is commonly used to express emotions [7, 8, 10–12], especially the intense ones [4, 6]. [21] examined the discourse goals of eight types of figurative devices, namely hyperbole, idiom, indirect request, irony, understatement, metaphor, rhetorical questions, and simile. They found that rhetorical questions are used to express both positive and negative emotions, with the latter being more frequent. [15] investigated people's emotion reactions to different figurative devices. They showed that rhetorical questions are used to alert or challenge addressee's problem or behavior. Therefore, rhetorical questions are prone to evoke negative emotions, such as *anger*, *disgust*, and *contempt*. In addition, speakers of rhetorical questions appear to feel more negative emotions than that of other figurative devices. Rhetorical questions are also perceived as having very negative intent. Lee [14] suggested that there is a close interaction between figurative language and emotion. She found that about one-third of the social media posts contain figurative devices, among which rhetorical questions are the most frequently used one (37%). She illustrated that rhetorical questions are particularly productive in evoking negative emotions, i.e. *sadness* and *anger*.

Despite the important role rhetorical questions play in emotion expressions, existing classification models have mainly developed for other forms of figurative language, such as irony and sarcasm [2, 9, 20]. The automatic identification of rhetorical questions has received little attention [1, 19], let alone the distinctive structures of rhetorical questions for the identification and detection of different emotions.

3 Corpus Data and Annotation

The corpus was made up of 8,529 posts randomly extracted from *Sina Weibo*, one of the most popular social media sites in China [13]. Each post contains no more than 140 characters, and emoticons are taken into account for the annotation.

The corpus was annotated by two annotators. Five basic emotions were annotated in each post, namely *happiness*, *sadness*, *anger*, *fear*, and *surprise*. Some posts contain more than one emotion, and all of them were labelled. For the identification of the use of information-seeking questions and rhetorical questions, all the 8,529 posts were read through. For each post that contains both emotion and question, annotators would be asked to determine whether or not the tagged emotion is concerned with the question identified. If not, the question would be regarded as "no emotion". According to Lee [14], questions can roughly be categorized into open question and closed question. She further classified the questions into 10 subtypes, including A-not-A, alternative, echo, particles, *wh*-questions and so on. Although both information-seeking questions and rhetorical questions contain open and closed questions, only rhetorical questions were further classified as our preliminary observation suggests that most information-seeking questions do not express emotions. In addition to the 10 subtypes proposed in Lee [14],

4 were added, given the existence of other types of rhetorical questions, including *which*, *where*, *when* and *others*.

In Chinese, open questions refer to questions with *wh*-words such as *why*, *what*, *how*, etc., and they aim to elicit an open-ended answer. Closed questions refer to questions represented in the form of A-not-A structure, alternative, echo, particle or other question words that require a pre-determined answer. A-not-A questions are formed with an affirmative and its negative counterpart juxtaposed, and the respondent can choose either the affirmative or its negative counterpart as the answer [16]. Consider (1).

(1) 你喜不喜歡台灣菜？
(Do you like Taiwanese food?)

Alternative questions explicitly provide two or more possible options which are mostly connected by the morpheme 還是 (or), as in (2).

(2) 你喜歡台灣菜還是日本菜？
(Do you like Taiwanese food or Japanese food?)

Echo questions have the form of a declarative sentence but end with a question mark in the written form. Particle questions refer to questions that end with a sentence-final particle, such as 嗎, 呢. Rhetorical interrogation markers such as 難道, 何必 etc. are grouped into *others*.

4 Data Analysis

4.1 Inter-annotator Agreement

In order to evaluate the annotation tasks, two annotators were asked to annotate the same set of data which comprises 500 posts. Table 1 shows the inter-annotator agreement calculated using Cohen's Kappa coefficient. The Kappa scores for both emotion annotation and question type annotation are high, indicating that the quality of annotation is satisfactory. Apart from that, the agreement of question type annotation is higher than emotion annotation. This may be attributed to the fact that emotions are subjective in nature, but question types are not.

Table 1. Inter-annotator agreement

	Kappa score
Emotion	0.663
Question type	0.918

4.2 Corpus Analysis

Of the 8,529 posts, 3,671 posts (43%) do not contain any emotions, while 5,137 emotions are identified in 4,858 posts (57%). That means, some posts express more than one emotion. Among the five emotions, *happiness* has the highest frequency (49.7%), followed by *sadness* (25.5%), *anger* (12.4%), *surprise* (7.4%), and *fear* (4.9%).

The total number of questions identified is 900, among which 357 (39.7%) are information-seeking questions and 543 (60.3%) are rhetorical questions. Figure 1 shows the distribution of emotions per question type. This is calculated relative to the total number of each question type.

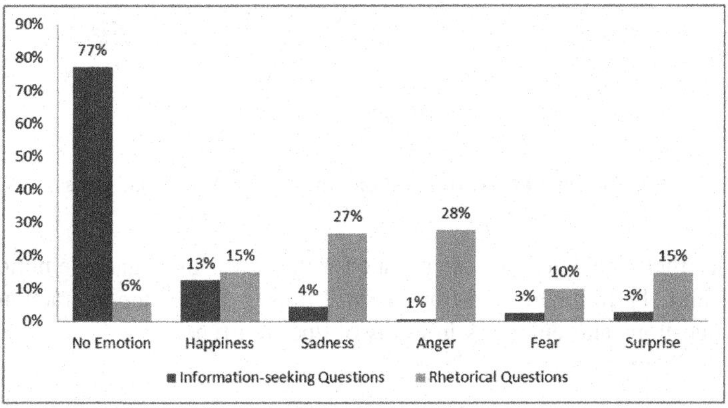

Fig. 1. Emotion expressed using information-seeking questions and rhetorical questions

From Fig. 1, we can see that a lot more than half (77%) of information-seeking questions are not associated with any emotions, and less than a quarter of them express *happiness*. The remaining 11% are used to express *sadness* (4%), *fear* (3%), *surprise* (3%), and *anger* (1%). As for rhetorical questions, the vast majority (94%) of them do evoke emotions. Unlike information-seeking questions, rhetorical questions have a tendency to express negative emotions, especially *anger* (28%) and *sadness* (27%). The *happiness* and *surprise* emotions account for 15% of rhetorical questions respectively. *Fear* has the weakest connection (10%) with rhetorical questions, which may be due to the small number of posts containing *fear*. In order to compare the role information-seeking questions and rhetorical questions play in emotion expressions, Fig. 2 shows the distribution of question type per emotion in all posts.

Figure 2 is calculated relative to the total number of posts of a given emotion type. On one hand, Fig. 2 shows that information-seeking questions are not often used to express emotions. Among the emotions, *fear* is most frequently expressed via information-seeking questions, accounting for only 4%. On the other hand, Fig. 2 shows that rhetorical questions are rather productive in expressing emotions as more than one fifth of posts containing *anger*, *fear*, and *surprise* are expressed by means of rhetorical questions. The *anger* emotion has the greatest tendency (24%) to be expressed via rhetorical questions, followed by *surprise* (22%), *fear* (22%), *sadness* (11%), and *happiness* (3%).

In sum, Figs. 1 and 2 not only demonstrate the significant role rhetorical questions play in expressing emotions as compared to information-seeking questions, they also

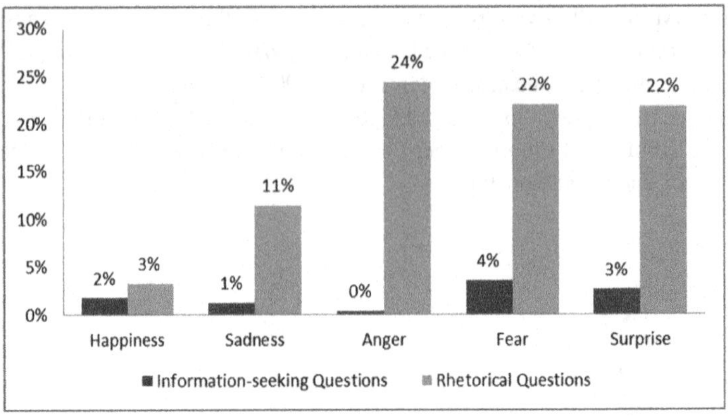

Fig. 2. Distribution of question type per emotion in all posts

illustrate that rhetorical questions are productive in expressing negative emotions which is in line with [21]. In the next section, we will further discuss the interaction between rhetorical questions and emotions in terms of question type.

5 Interaction Between Rhetorical Questions and Emotions

Lee [14] indicated that rhetorical questions are the most frequently used figurative devices for evoking emotions. Although the distribution of rhetorical questions was shown, the study focused more on the general picture of the use of various figurative devices, such as metaphor etc. Hence, only a small number of rhetorical questions (i.e. 38 tokens) were identified and the scattered distribution could not clearly show the correlation between each type of rhetorical questions and emotions. Therefore, we further classify the 543 rhetorical questions into 14 subtypes, as shown in Table 2.

Table 2. Distribution of types of rhetorical questions used

	Series of Q	Close class question					Open class question								**Total**
		A-not-A	Alternative	Echo	Particle	Others	How	How many/much	What	Which	Who	Why	Where	When	
No emotion	1	7	0	2	10	1	2	0	5	0	0	3	2	0	**33**
Happiness	5	27	0	2	14	4	7	0	7	0	2	15	1	0	**84**
Sadness	11	17	4	0	27	5	15	5	25	0	5	34	1	1	**150**
Anger	39	6	1	20	37	4	5	0	12	1	7	21	3	0	**156**
Fear	11	6	2	1	5	1	8	0	13	0	0	5	4	0	**56**
Surprise	9	0	2	15	22	9	3	2	10	0	0	11	0	0	**83**
Total	**76**	**63**	**9**	**40**	**115**	**24**	**40**	**7**	**72**	**1**	**14**	**89**	**11**	**1**	**562**

Table 2 shows that different types of rhetorical questions may show different preferences for a particular emotion. While more than a half of the posts containing a series of questions are used to express *anger*, only a couple of them are used to express *happiness*, and the rest are almost evenly distributed for the expressions of *sadness*, *fear*, and *surprise*. [5] mentioned the use of clustering of rhetorical questions as "…in each case the question is re-stated for emphasis, in slightly different form. This makes for a stronger impact on the hearer; a strategy that most likely would be unnecessary if these were simply informational questions, but is a highly effective device for persuasion… (p. 734)". Lee [14] regarded it as the strategy writers use to draw readers' attention to their strong emotions. Consider (3).

(3) 學校你是要把我趕盡殺絕嗎？停電？你居然停電？你居然停電了？？？涼快，涼快，涼快 [微風]
(Does this school trying to kill me or something? It went out of electricity? Seriously? It's out of electricity??? Cool down, cool down, cool down [breeze])

In (3), the rhetorical questions are restated to emphasize the fact that the electricity has been turned off. The writer intentionally used a series of questions to increase the emotion intensity which cannot be reached by stating only once. [3] defined *anger* as "the response to interference with our pursuit of a goal we care about…(p. 365)". Thus, the purpose of the use of a series of questions is to vent one's anger to someone who evokes the emotion.

As for closed questions, particle questions are most frequently used to form rhetorical questions, one-third of which are used to express *anger*. Among the five emotions, *anger* is often expressed in the pattern of "還…….嗎?", as in (4).

(4) 如果每件事我們都能自己完成那還用你教嗎，那你早就下崗了
(If we can accomplish everything on our own, why would we even need you? You'd have been sacked long ago)

Although this pattern may also appear in posts of other emotions, the use of 還 in rhetorical questions shows a tendency toward *anger*. [17] indicated that the use of 還 in rhetorical question is not to make objective statements but to express one's attitude and make the statement even stronger. It reflects how well a fact is established to the writer. To the writer in (4), students being incapable of accomplishing everything on their own is understandable as it is 你 (your) responsibility to teach them. This kind of rhetorical questions is uttered when what other people do does not reach the writer's standard or live up to his expectation. This explains the strong correlation between the pattern and *anger*.

"Declarative + 好嗎/麼/嘛" is another frequent pattern used to express *anger*, as in (5).

(5) 我真是討厭死夏天多蟲的季節了好麼！！
(I really hate summer and all the bugs so damn much, okay??)

In (5), 好麼 is obviously not a question used to seek information, but to highlight how much the writer hates summer. This pattern is occasionally found to express *happiness* as in (6), and rarely, if not never, found to express other emotions. It is observed that the semantic polarity of the verb(s) or adjective(s) in the declarative sentence may give some hints about the emotion expressed. That is, rhetorical questions are likely used to express *happiness* (/*anger*) when there is one or more than one positive (/negative) verb or adjective found in this kind of sentences.

(6) [愛你]今晚還是很炫酷的好嗎
([Love you] We actually showed off a lot tonight, okay?)

"Declarative + question word" can also be found in A-not-A questions. Among those A-not-A forms in "declarative + A-not-A", 有沒有[1] and 好不好 are the most common ones. While the latter does not have a clear semantic orientation pointing to a particular emotion, the former tends to associate with *happiness*, as in (7).

(7) 我瘦了，有木有。[哈哈][哈哈][哈哈][哈哈]
(I lost weight, yea? [haha][haha][haha][haha])

In (7), the writer used 有木有 to "re-confirm" the statement he made. In fact, the writer holds firm to his belief that he did lose some weight as hinted by the period and emoticons he used. Although an answer may be given in spoken context, most readers would not bother to comment on this kind of questions in social media platforms. Hence, the purpose of the question is to restate the statement that the writer is confident of or happy with.

"Rhetorical interrogation" markers including 難道, 豈, 何必, 何苦 are labelled as *others*. Among these markers, 難道 tends to correlate with *surprise*. All of the tokens of 豈 appear in the structure of "豈 + 不", expressing either positive or neutral emotion (i.e. *happiness* and *surprise*). 何必 and 何苦 are typically used for evoking negative emotions, with the former indicating both *anger* and *sadness*, and the latter *sadness*.

Among the six subtypes of open questions, four of them including *how*, *how many/much*, *what*, and *why* have a strong connection with *sadness*. *Who* question is an indicator of *anger*, *sadness*, and occasionally *happiness* whereas *where* is more evenly used in evoking various emotions (except for *surprise*). *Which* and *when* are rarely used to form rhetorical questions.

As for *how* questions expressing *sadness*, about one-fifth of the posts are formed with "……是有多……", as in (8).

(8) 又是同一家麵館，同一張桌子，同一碗麵。我是有多沒創意。。。多愛念舊。
(It's the same noodle restaurant, same table and same bowl of noodles. How dull am I…how nostalgic.)

In (8), the writer grumbles about himself being so dull and nostalgic. Although this pattern can also be used to express other emotions, it is observed that if the subject is the first-person pronoun 我 (I) or in its possessive form 我的 (my), the sentence is likely expressing *sadness*. In (8), the writer is discontented with what he did but is not being able to take control of or willing to change.

W*hat* questions are quite often used for expressing *sadness* and *fear*. We observe that 怎麼辦 demonstrates a close relationship with both *sadness* and *fear*, comparing to

[1] 有木有 is often found in Weibo as a netizen transformation of 有沒有.

the other three emotions. Yet, 怎麼辦 used for the expression of *sadness* and *fear* cannot be distinguished without understanding the situation provided in the context. Examples are exemplified as in (9) and (10).

(9) 吃了八個鍋貼感覺剛開胃怎麼辦！想要更多！
(Feels like I just started after eight dumplings, what should I do! Craving for more!)

(10) 睡不著睡不著睡不著怎麼辦 [衰]
(Can't fall asleep, can't fall asleep, can't fall asleep, what should I do [sad])

Although both (9) and (10) pose a rhetorical question with 怎麼辦, the expressed emotions are different. (9) is tagged as *fear* because the writer can have some more just if he wants to, and 怎麼辦 only implies that he fears that he may have to take the consequence of having more. (10) is labelled as *sadness* because the writer is suffering from insomnia helplessly. Thus, the use of 怎麼辦 can help identify and distinguish *sadness* and *fear* from the other emotions, but more tokens are needed to investigate what kind of contextual information we need to discriminate *sadness* and *fear*.

Why questions are the most frequently used open questions and approximately 40% of *why* questions are in the form of "why + (…) + 這/那麼". The tendencies of this pattern being used for each emotion in descending order are as follows: *sadness* (38%), *anger* (26%), *happiness* (24%), *surprise* (9%), and *fear* (3%). The statistics are of concern to automatic emotion classification. We found that the adjective(s) following 這 / 那 麼 may help determine what emotion the rhetorical question expresses. Consider (11).

(11) 為什麼感覺這麼鬧心這麼煩
(Why am I feeling so hectic and annoyed)

(11) is annotated as *anger* as suggested by the adjectives 鬧心 (hectic) and 煩 (annoyed) following 這麼. It is also observed that if the subject refers to the writer himself, the emotion expressed is likely a negative one, such as *sadness* or *anger*.

6 Conclusion

In this paper, we identify the use of information-seeking questions and rhetorical questions in emotion expressions. Results show that 94% rhetorical questions are used to express emotions, while only 23% of information-seeking questions are associated with emotions. We demonstrate that different types of rhetorical questions may have different preferences for a particular emotion. In addition, various syntactic structures of different types of rhetorical questions are proposed for emotion identification. We believe that the linguistic account of rhetorical questions in emotion expressions will provide a clearer picture of the nature of emotion.

Acknowledgements. This work is supported by a General Research Fund (GRF) project sponsored by the Research Grants Council (Project No. B-Q50Z) and a PolyU Faculty Research Grant (Project No. 1-ZEVK).

References

1. Bhattasali, S., Cytryn, J., Feldman, E., Park, J.: Automatic identification of rhetorical questions. ACL **2**, 743–749 (2015)
2. Davidov, D., Tsur, O., Rappoport, A.: Semi-supervised recognition of sarcastic sentences in twitter and amazon. In: Proceedings of the 14th Conference on Computational Natural Language Learning, pp. 107–116 (2010)
3. Ekman, P., Cordaro, D.: What is meant by calling emotions basic. Emot. Rev. **3**(4), 364–370 (2011)
4. Fainsilber, L., Ortony, A.: Metaphorical uses of language in the expression of emotions. Metaphor Symb. **2**(4), 239–250 (1987)
5. Frank, J.: You call that a rhetorical question?: forms and functions of rhetorical questions in conversation. J. Pragmat. **14**(5), 723–738 (1990)
6. Fussell, S.R.: The use of metaphor in written descriptions of emotional states. Unpublished manuscript, Carnegie Mellon University (1992)
7. Fussell, S.R., Moss, M.M.: Figurative language in emotional communication. In: Social and Cognitive Approaches to Interpersonal Communication, pp. 113–141 (1998)
8. Gibbs, R.W., Leggitt, J.S., Turner, E.A.: What's special about figurative language in emotional communication. In: Fussell, S.R. (ed.) The Verbal Communication of Emotions: Interdisciplinary Perspectives, pp. 125–149. Lawrence Erlbaum Associates, Mahwah (2002)
9. González-Ibánez, R., Muresan, S., Wacholder, N.: Identifying sarcasm in twitter: a closer look. In: Proceedings of the 49th Annual Meeting of the Association for Computational Linguistics: Human Language Technologies: Short Papers, vol. 2, pp. 581–586 (2011)
10. Kövecses, Z.: Emotion Concepts. Springer, New York (1990). https://doi.org/10.1007/978-1-4612-3312-1
11. Kövecses, Z.: Metaphor and Emotion: Language, Culture, and Body in Human Feeling. Cambridge University Press, Cambridge (2003)
12. Lakoff, G., Johnson, M.: Metaphors We Live by. University of Chicago Press, Chicago (1980)
13. Lee, S.Y.M.: A linguistic analysis of implicit emotions. In: Lu, Q., Gao, H. (eds.) CLSW 2015. LNCS (LNAI), vol. 9332, pp. 185–194. Springer, Cham (2015). https://doi.org/10.1007/978-3-319-27194-1_19
14. Lee, S.Y.M.: Figurative language in emotion expressions. In: Wu, Y., Hong, J.F., Su, Q. (eds.) CLSW 2017. LNCS (LNAI), vol. 10709, pp. 408–419. Springer, Cham (2018). https://doi.org/10.1007/978-3-319-73573-3_37
15. Leggitt, J.S., Gibbs, R.W.: Emotional reactions to verbal irony. Discourse Process. **29**(1), 1–24 (2000)
16. Li, C.N., Thompson, S.A.: Mandarin Chinese: A Functional Reference Grammar. University of California Press, Berkeley (1981)
17. Liu, F.-h.: The scalar particle hai in Chinese. Cahiers de linguistique-Asie orientale **29**(1), 41–84 (2000)
18. Petty, R.E., Cacioppo, J.T., Heesacker, M.: Effects of rhetorical questions on persuasion: a cognitive response analysis. J. Pers. Soc. Psychol. **40**(3), 432 (1981)
19. Ranganath, S., Hu, X., Tang, J., Wang, S., Liu, H.: Identifying rhetorical questions in social media. In: ICWSM, pp. 667–670 (2016)
20. Reyes, A., Rosso, P., Veale, T.: A multidimensional approach for detecting irony in twitter. Lang. Resour. Eval. **47**(1), 239–268 (2013)
21. Roberts, R.M., Kreuz, R.J.: Why do people use figurative language? Psychol. Sci. **5**(3), 159–163 (1994)

Verbal Plurality of Frequency Adverbs in Mandarin Chinese: The Case of *Tōngcháng* (通常)

Daniel Kwang Guan Chan[1(✉)] and Hua-Hung Yuan[2]

[1] Centre for Language Studies, National University of Singapore, Singapore 117572, Singapore
daniel.chan@nus.edu.sg

[2] School of Foreign Languages, Xiangtan University, Xiangtan, Hunan, China
yuan.huahung@gmail.com

Abstract. This paper concerns the adverb, *tōngcháng*, which can be placed in the topic position, at the beginning of a sentence or in the preverbal position. It will be analyzed as a verbal plurality marker at the occasion level in the framework of Cusic [1]. We will identify the adverb in these two positions as having different semantic properties, namely habituality and iterativity, as defined Bertinetto and Lenci [2]. We will demonstrate the function of *tōngcháng* when co-occuring with NP subjects with individual or kind denotation.

Keywords: Verbal plurality · Frequency adverbs · Mandarin chinese
Habituality · Iterativity

1 Introduction

This paper aims to understand how the adverb, *tōngcháng* functions. It is usually analysed in the same manner as other frequency adverbs, such as *jīngcháng*, *shícháng*, *wángwǎng*, *shíshí* and so on in the sinologist literature. For example, Zou [3], Shi, Hu [4] think that these adverbs are classified as "adverbs of medium frequency" (中頻副詞). Other authors, like Zhou [5] and Zhang [6], claim that *tōngcháng* expresses a higher frequency of actions – labelled "adverb of high frequency"(高頻副詞) – than *cháng*, *jīngcháng, chángcháng,* which are "adverbs of medium frequency"(中頻副詞). Similarly, He [4] calls it an "adverb of higher frequency" (較高值頻率副詞). Zhou [5], [7] and Guan [8] claim that the presence of *tōngcháng* is constrained by the co-occurrence of a temporal or locative phrase in the VP, which distinguishes it from another adverb of frequency, such as *chángcháng* (cf. (1)).

J.-F. Hong et al. (Eds.): CLSW 2018, LNAI 11173, pp. 381–395, 2018.
https://doi.org/10.1007/978-3-030-04015-4_32

(1) a. 約翰*通常/常常遲到'
Yuēhàn ****tōngcháng /chángcháng*** *chídao*
John usually often late (intended: John is usually late.) /John is late often.'

b. 約翰星期一通常遲到
Yuēhàn xīngqīyī ***tōngcháng*** *chídào*
John Monday usually late
'John is usually late on Monday.' (Zhou [5])

Shi, Hu [4] (2004, p. 10) claim that both *tōngcháng* and *chángcháng* express a frequency of events (事件頻度), as opposed to adverbs that express a frequency of actions (動作頻度), like *lǚlǚ*, *zàisān* 'repeatedly', without giving further explanations. Chen, Ren [9] notice that *tōngcháng* can be put in two positions which give rise to different meanings to the sentence: before and after the NP subject in a sentence (2).

(2) a.高大的人通常容易给人憨厚的印象
Gāodà-de rén ***tōngcháng*** *róngyì gěi rén hānhòu-de yìnxiàn*
Tall person usually easy give person simple-and-honest image
'Tall persons usually give a simple and honest impression to others.' (Chen, Ren [9], (23) and (25))

b. 通常我只看一小會兒風景
Tōngcháng *wǒ zhī kàn yī xiǎo huìér fēngjǐng*
Usually I only look one little moment scene
'Generally, I look at scenery for an instant…'

They explain that when *tōngcháng* appears before the NP subject, a comment is made over the whole sentence, but when the adverb appears after the NP subject, then a regularity of the occurrences of an action is expressed (see also Lü [10], Zhou [7], He [11]). On the other hand, Guan [8] indicates more precisely habituality. However, it is not shown how *tōngcháng* is syntactically and semantically different when appearing in each of the two positions. Also, it is still unknown why it is necessary to distinguish between "frequency of events" and "frequency of actions"?

We found that when *tōngcháng* in (2a) is placed before the subject as in (3), i.e. the typical topic position in Mandarin, the adverb can denote "habituality".

(3) 通常高大的人容易给人憨厚的印象
Tōngcháng *gāodà-de rén róngyì gěi rén hānhòu-de yìnxiàng*
usually tall person easy give person simple-and-honest image
'Usually, tall persons give a simple and honest impression to others.'

Nevertheless, Guan [8] does not define what "habituality" is and in what way *tōngcháng* expresses habituality in the sentence. In addition, *tōngcháng* can co-occur with the VP without locative or temporal phrase, like in (2a) and (3), thereby falsifying Zhou [5] and Guan [8]'s claim. Finally, we notice that the NP subject in (2a) and (3), *gāodà de-rén* 'tall person' is a kind-denoting and the type of predicate co-occurring with it is different from a NP subject of individual denotation, like in (1b) and (2b). Thus, we think that *tōngcháng* deserves to be analysed in more depth and detail.

1.1 Research Questions

From the above, it is clear that *tōngcháng* shows some differences when it is placed before and after the NP subject. In this paper, we seek to find out:

(i) How does *tōngcháng* pluralize over VP? Specifically, at what level of the VP?
(ii) Does *tōngcháng* function in the same way when it appears before and after the NP subject?
(iii) How does *tōngcháng* quantify when it co-occurs with an individual-denoting and kind-denoting NP subject?

In this paper, the *tōngcháng* before the NP subject will be named as the topical *tōngcháng*, or *tōngcháng*$_{\mathrm{TOP}}$, because it appears in the typical topic position of Mandarin Chinese sentences; when it occurs after the NP subject it will be called preverbal *tōngcháng*, *tōngcháng*$_{\mathrm{PrV}}$, which appears at the canonical position of adverbs. In order to distinguish the two types of *tōngcháng*, we give it two translations in English: 'generally' for *tōngcháng*$_{\mathrm{TOP}}$ and 'usually' for *tōngcháng*$_{\mathrm{PvV}}$.

The two *tōngcháng* are different because they are associated with two different denotations (see Yuan and Chan [12]). Since *tōngcháng*$_{\mathrm{TOP}}$ is a topic, it is a reply to a known information, as (4) shows.

(4) a. 游泳和跑步，瑪莉做哪種運動？
Yóuyǒng hé pǎobù, Mǎlì zuò nǎ-zhǒng yùndòng?
Swim and jog Mary do which kind sport
'Swimming and jogging, which one does Mary do?'

b. 通常瑪莉會去游泳 而不是去跑步
Tōngcháng *Mǎlì huì qù yóuyǒng ér bù-shì qù pǎobù*
Generally Mary will go swim but not-be go jog
'Generally, Mary will go swimming, not go jogging.'

Because *tōngcháng*$_{\mathrm{PrV}}$ is linked with an explicit or implicit topic, (5b) is plausible because the topic as in (5a) is presupposed.

(5) a.說到運動 / 如果要做運動的話
Shuō dào yùndòng /rúguǒ yào zuò yùndòng de-huà
Speak arrive sport if want do sport if
'Speaking of exercise/ If she does exercise,'

b. 瑪莉**通常**會去游泳, 有時也會去跑步
Mǎlì ***tōngcháng*** *huì qù yóuyǒng, yǒushí yě huì qù pǎobù*
Mary usually will go swim sometimes also will go jog
'Mary will usually go swimming and will go jogging sometimes.'

In order to discuss the semantics of frequency involved in the use of these two *tōngcháng*, it is first necessary to consider the broader notion of "verbal plurality" (Cusic [1]). In Sect. 3, we will identify the properties of the two *tōngcháng* positions, and the expression habituality and iterativity, as proposed by Bertinetto and Lenci [2]. In Sect. 4, we will analyse *tōngcháng* in both positions when they co-occur with a kind-denoting NP subject.

2 Verbal Plurality Marker

In this paper, we propose to analyse *tōngcháng* as a marker of "**verbal plurality**" (Cusic [1]), a broad semantic category for describing the multiplicity of actions. In Chan and Yuan [13], frequency adverbs *jīngcháng* and *chángcháng* are considered as markers of verbal plurality at the occasion-level. As a result, *tōngcháng* is treated in the same manner as *jīngcháng* and *chángcháng* because *tōngcháng* denotes multiple occasions of an event, as (6)–(7) show.

(6) {通常}他{通常}抓我的右手 (每次都抓得我好)
{Tōngcháng}*tā****{tōngcháng}*** *zhuā wǒde yòu shǒu (měi-cì dōu zhuā dé wǒ hǎo tòng)*
Generally he usually grab my right every-time all grab get me very painful
'{generally,} He {usually} grabbed my right hand. (Every time, I was in pain from the grabbing.).'

(7) 他抓我的右手. (#每次都抓得我好痛).
Tā zhuā wǒde yòu shǒu (#měi-cì dōu zhuā dé wǒ hǎo tòng)
he grab my right hand every-time all grab get me very painful
'He grabbed my right hand. (#Every time, I was in pain from the grabbing.)

Syntactically, *tōngcháng* appears in the same paradigm with other adverbs of frequency, as *jīngcháng, chángcháng,* as in (8).

(8) 保羅**通常/經常/常常**在公園跑步
Bǎoluó ***tōngcháng /jīngcháng/chángcháng*** *zài gōngyuán pǎobù*
Paul usually regularly often at park jog
'Paul usually/regularly/often goes jogging at the park.'

They share some syntactic properties: occupying the preverbal position and operating rightward, over the VP. Unlike *jīngcháng* and *chángcháng*, *tōngcháng* can be placed in the topic position, at the beginning of a sentence.

(9) {***經常/*常常**}**通常**保羅在公園跑步 ***{*jīngcháng/*chángcháng}***
tōngcháng *Bǎoluó zài gōngyuán pǎobù* regularly often
usually Paul at park jog 'Generally, Paul goes jogging at the park.'

The focus construction, *shì...de*, can show the barrier between *tōngcháng* and the VP. *tōngcháng*$_{\mathrm{TOP}}$, and *tōngcháng*$_{\mathrm{PrV}}$, since both cannot enter into the phrase of *shì... de*, as (10) - (11) illustrate.

(10) a.保羅{**通常/經常/常常**}是在公園跑步的
*Bǎoluó **tōngcháng/jīngcháng/chángcháng** shì zài gōngyuán pǎobù de*
Paul usually regularly often be at park jog *de*[1]
'Paul usually/regularly/ often jogs at the park.'
'It is at the park that Paul usually/regularly/often jogs.'

b. *保羅是{**通常/經常/常常**}在公園跑步的
Bǎoluó shì {tōngcháng/jīngcháng/chángcháng**} zài gōngyuán pǎobù de*
Paul be usually regularly often at park jog *de*

(11) a.{***經常/*常常**}**通常**是保羅在公園跑步的 {***jīngcháng/*chángcháng**}
***tōngcháng** Bǎoluó shì zài gōngyuán pǎobù de* regularly often
usually Paul be at park jog *de* 'Generally, Paul jogs at the park.'

b.*是**通常**保羅在公園跑步的
Shì **tōngcháng Bǎoluó zài gōngyuán pǎobù de*
be usually Paul at park jog *de*

Moreover, like *jīngcháng* and *chángcháng, tōngcháng*$_{\mathrm{PvV}}$ quantifies rightward, over the VP and induces the multiple occurrences of VP, as in (8) and (10a). *Tōngcháng*$_{\mathrm{TOP}}$ also operates rightward over the occurrence of jogging at the park, as in (9) and (11a), and it states a generalization of Paul. When a contrary occurrence of VP, like (12) can be uttered, following (8)–(10a) and (11a). This shows *tōngcháng*'s rightward quantification.

(12) 但今天是在學校跑步
Dàn jīntiān shì zài xuéxiào pǎobù
but today be at school jog
'but today, it is at school that he jogged.'

From the above demonstration, we can see the scope of *tōngcháng* is determined by its syntactic position, at the topic position or at preverbal position, so does the scope of pluralization.

In next section, we will show *tōngcháng* is a verbal plurality marker at the occasion level.

2.1 Occasion-Level Verbal Plurality

In Cusic's framework, verbal plurality can occur at different levels: phases, events and occasions. We will then apply several tests to show that *tongcháng* is an "occasion-level verbal plurality marker". (Yuan and Chan [14]).

We will now demonstrate, through a comparison between *tōngcháng* on one hand, and *pínpín* (頻頻) on the other hand, that the former should be analysed as a marker of verbal plurality at the occasion level, while the latter is a marker of verbal plurality at the event level.

Firstly, *tōngcháng* **cannot co-occur with durational complements**, unlike *pínpín* (see (13)-(14)). This is because the durational complement in these sentences only specify the duration of single events only, but not of occasions (see (15)).

(13) *他不說話，只是**通常**點頭，點了十五分鐘
Tā bú shuōhuà, zhǐshì* ***tōngcháng* *diǎn tóu, diǎn-le shíwǔ fēnzhōng*
he neg speak only usually nod head nod-Acc fifteen minute

(14) 他不說話，只是**頻頻**點頭，點了十五分鐘
Tā bú shuōhuà, zhǐshì ***pínpín*** *diǎn tóu, diǎn-le shíwǔ fēnzhōng*
he neg speak only repeatedly nod head nod-Acc fifteen minute
'Not saying a word, he only nodded and nodded for fifteen minutes'

(15) 他(*天天) 點頭，點了十五分鐘
*Tā (*tiāntiān) diǎn tóu, diǎn-le shíwǔ fēnzhōng*
he day-day nod head nod-Acc fifteen minute
'He nodded for fifteen minutes.'
(Intended: 'He nodded daily for fifteen minutes')

Secondly, *tōngcháng* **cannot modify the verb of a sentence if only a single, unique occasion is being described**. Hence, while the sentence in (16) describes what happens across several different speech-listening occasions, (17) is unacceptable because the use of the demonstrative determiner restricts the reference to a single speech-listening occasion, and is in conflict with the function of *tōngcháng*.

(16) {**通常**}他上課時{**通常**}會打瞌睡
*{**Tōngcháng**} tā shàngkè shí {**tōngcháng**} huì dǎ-kēshuì*
generally he in-class while ususally will doze-off
'{Generally},He {usually} dozed off while being in [**different**] class.'

(17) *{**通常**}他<u>那次</u>上課時{**通常**}會打瞌睡
{Tōngcháng**} tā <u>nà-cì</u> shàngkè shí {**tōngcháng**} huì dǎ-kēshuì*

The adverb *pínpín*, however, does not have this problem because it only induces a plurality of events within the same occasion: examples (18) and (19) describe a person who nods repeatedly or frequently within a same speech occasion.

(18) 他上課時**頻頻**打瞌睡
Tā shàngkè shí ***pínpín*** *dǎ-kēshuì*
he in-class while repeatedly doze-off
'He repeatedly dozed off while being in [the same] class.'

(19) 他<u>那次</u>上課時頻頻打瞌睡
Tā <u>nà-cì</u> shàngkè shí ***pínpín*** *dǎ-kēshuì*
he that time in-class while repeatedly doze-off
'He often dozed off whil being in class that time.'

Thirdly, ***tōngcháng*** **can scope over a temporal adverbial describing the set of occasions**, once again proving that *tōngcháng* is marker of verbal plurality at the occasion level. Hence, (20) has an interpretation equivalent to that of (21) above. This is in contrast with *pínpín*, which is clearly a marker of verbal plurality at the event level only (compare 18–19).

(20) {**通常**}他{**通常**}上課時打瞌睡
*{**Tōngcháng**} tā {**tōngcháng**} shàngkè shí dǎ-kēshuì*
generally he usually in-class while doze-off
'{Generally, he {usually} dozed off while being in [**different**] class.'

(21) *他**頻頻**上課時打瞌睡
Tā **pínpín shàngkè shí dǎ-kēshuì*
he repeatedly in-class while doze-off (Intended:
'He repeatedly dozed off while being in different class.')

Finally, in order for plurality to be applied at the occasion-level of eventualities, it must be possible to perceive the reference time as a duration in which the multiple occasions can likely occur. Hence, to express that one has had multiple occasions of taking the wrong bus in one's youth, *tōngcháng* can be used (see (22)), but if the time span considered is only one day, then *tōngcháng* is not natural (see (23)) and *pínpín* is used instead (see (24)).

(22) 小时候 {$^?$**通常**}他{**通常**}會搭錯車
*Xiǎoshíhòu {$^?$**tōngcháng**} tā {**tōngcháng**} huì dā cuò chē*
When-young generally he usually will take wrong bus
'{Generally},when he was young, he {usually} took the wrong bus.'

(23) ??昨天{**通常**}他{**通常**}會搭錯車
*??Zuótiān {$^?$**tōngcháng**} tā {**tōngcháng**} huì dā cuò chē*
yesterday generally he usually will take wrong bus
(Intended: 'Yesterday, {generally}, he {usually} took the wrong bus.')

(24) 昨天他**頻頻**搭錯車
*Zuótiān, tā **pínpín** dā cuò chē.*
yesterday he repeatedly take wrong bus
'Yesterday, he repeatedly took the wrong bus.'

In sum, we have established that *tōngcháng* is a verbal plurality marker, and that it applies on the occasion level only, i.e. *tōngcháng* quantifies only over occasions. The pluralization by *tōngcháng* can be expressed by the structure below.

(25) **VPL** , S **VPL** VP
$\textit{tōngcháng}_{\text{TOP}}$ S $\textit{tōngcháng}_{\text{PvV}}$ VP

2.2 Type of Predicate

In this section, we will show that *tōngcháng* co-occurs with predicates bound by time or locative phrases, i.e. stage-level predicates (SLP). Individual-level predicates (ILP) describe a property of an entity, which is atemporal i.e. *having green eyes* while SLPs indicate a transitory stage of an entity, varied with time, i.e. *doing exercise*. This has been discussed in Kratzer [15].

ILPs are not compatible with *tōngcháng, jīngcháng* and *chángcháng* and this type of predicates cannot be pluralized, which makes distinct occasions of a state of an entity, as (26) illustrates.

(26) *瑪莉{**經常/常常/通常**}有綠眼睛
Mǎlì ***{jīngcháng/chángcháng/tōngcháng}*** *yǒu lǜ yǎnjīng*
Mary regularly often usually have green eyes

Predicates modified by time or locative adverbs, as in (26), are SLPs, because they are bounded temporally or spatially (see Kratzer [15]). SLPs are compatible with these three frequency adverbs.

(27) OK小明{**經常/常常/通常**}早上/在健身房運動
OK*Xiǎomíng****{jīngcháng/chángcháng/tōngcháng}***
X.M regularly often usually
zǎoshàng /zài jiànshēnfáng yùndòng
morning at gym do-exercise
'Xiaoming regularly/often/usually does exercise at gym.'

An occasion can take place at an indicated time or location only, which delimits naturally the boundary of an occasion and temporal intervals between occasions. An occasion is viewed as bounded in time and as a point on the time axis. However, how do we account for the co-occurrence of VP *yùndòng* 'exercise', as in (27), with *tōngcháng*?

(28) 小明 OK經常/OK常常/*通常運動
Xiǎomíng{OK***jīngcháng***/OK***chángcháng/*tōngcháng***} *yùndòng*
X.M regularly often usually do-exercise
'Xiaoming regularly/often does exercise.'

In (28), a SLP without time or spatial modification is not able to be pluralized by *tōngcháng* because the occasion cannot be seen as bounded. This is not the case when *jīngcháng* and *chángcháng* pluralize over the same SLP since the two adverbs can view the predicate as bounded. This makes a major difference of the two adverbs in relation to *tōngcháng* in terms of sensitivity to predicate types.

Let us see more examples to show the pluralization expressed by frequency adverbs when combined with bounded occasions. In (29), the three adverbs cannot pluralize over the occasion denoted by the modified VP, *wǎnshàng xiě liǎng-piān zuòwén* due to the lack of boundary markers. When the indefinite determinant *yī-gè* defines the time adverb *wǎnshàng*, as in (30), the former is shifted to a boundary of the occasion where the action of writing two compositions takes place. Therefore, *yī-gè wǎnshàng xiě liǎng-piān zuòwén* is taken as a marked occasion and *yī-cì* 'one-time', the sequence of one and the verbal classifier *cì* 'time', interchangeable here, as in (30), also marks the boundary of the occasion.

(29) *小明{**經常/常常/通常**}晚上寫兩篇作文
****Xiǎomíng{jīngcháng/chángcháng/tōngcháng}****wǎnshàng xiě liǎng-piān zuòwén*
X.M regularly often usually evening write two-Cl composition

(30) 小明{**經常/常常/通常**}{一個晚上/一次}寫兩篇作文
Xiǎomíng ***{jīngcháng/chángcháng/tōngcháng}***
X.M regularly often usually
{yī-gè wǎnshàng/yī-cì } xiě liǎng-piān zuòwén
one-Cl evening once write two-Cl composition
'Xiaoming regularly/often/usually writes two compositions one night/once.'

Since *tōngcháng* pluralizes only occasions denoted by temporally or spatially modified SLP, this leads a regular repetition of an occasion. The adverb *tōngcháng* itself does not describe the regularity of occasions. From this point of view, *tōngcháng* is different from *jīngcháng* and *chángcháng*.

In sum, the frequency adverbs pluralize over an occasion viewed as bounded, and for *tōngcháng*, occasions must be marked either by time or locative phrases.

3 Semantic Properties: Habitual and Iterative

We present two types of verbal plurality, "habituality" and "iterativity", as defined by Bertinetto and Lenci [2], and then argue in favour of the hypothesis that the verbal plurality markers $tōngcháng_{\mathrm{TOP}}$ and $tōngcháng_{\mathrm{PrV}}$ mark "habituality" and "iterativity" respectively.

Bertinetto and Lenci [2] state that habituality is a presupposition of a "more or less regular iteration of an event" and amounts to generalizations about the occurrences of a situation while iterativity only expresses a plurality of occurrences of a situation within a determined time period. Habituality involves iterativity, and iterativity is a component of habituality.

Bertinetto and Lenci highlight that there are four features distinguishing habituality from iterativity: (i) numerical specifiability, (ii) temporal localisation, (iii) time-frame, and (iv) determinability of the framing adverbial. The four properties that distinguish habituality from iterativity are summarised below:

(31) Properties of habituality and iterativity

	Iterative	**Habitual**
Numerical specifiability	+ specifiable	– specifiable
Temporal localisation	only past- and future-referring	all temporal domains
Time-frame	strictly delimiting	vaguely delimiting
Determinability of framing adverbial	potentially determinable	non-determinable

Based on this differentiation, we hypothesise that ***tōngcháng*$_{TOP}$ marks habituality, while *tōngcháng*$_{PrV}$ marks iterativity**.

Preliminary evidence for the above-mentioned hypothesis comes from the co-occurrence with a habituality adverb, as shown in (32).

(32) 一般來說，{*通常}保羅{通常}在公園跑步
*Yībān-lái-shuō, {*tōngcháng} Bǎoluó {tōngcháng} zài gōngyuán pǎobù*
Generally speaking generally Paul usually at park jog
'Generally speaking, Paul usually goes outdoors for a jog.'

Tōngcháng$_{PrV}$ can co-occur with the habituality adverb, *yibanlaishuo* while *tōngcháng*$_{TOP}$ excludes it because they are both situated at the topic position and deliver the same meaning.

The time frame for iterative sentences can be strictly delimiting while that of habitual sentences is preferably not delimiting:

(33) 去年，{??通常}瑪莉{通常}在家吃晚餐
Qù-nián, {??tōngcháng} Mǎlì {tōngcháng} zài jiā chī wǎncān
last year generally Mary usually at home eat dinner
'Last year, {generally}, Mary {usually} had dinner at home.'

Also, the multiplicity of occurrences is numerically specifiable in an iterative sentence but not in a habitual sentence:

(34) 談到購物，{*通常}保羅{通常}會去法國。他已經去了二十次了。
*Tán-dào gòuwù, {*tōngcháng} Bǎoluó {tōngcháng} huì qù fǎguó*
Talk-arrive shopping generally Paul usually will go France
Tā yǐjīng qù-le èrshí-cì le
he already go-Acc twenty-time FP.
(a) With ***tōngcháng*$_{TOP}$**: (impossible reading)
(b) With ***tōngcháng*$_{PrV}$**: 'Talking about shopping, Paul usually went to France. He has gone a total of 20 times' (iterative)

To sum up, *tōngcháng*$_{TOP}$ marks habituality, while *tōngcháng*$_{PrV}$ marks iterativity respectively. In fact, the two semantic denotations of *tōngcháng*, habituality and iterativity come from the scope effect of *tōngcháng*. This is an important finding, because it is basically at odds with what has been said in the literature: *tōngcháng*$_{PrV}$ marks habituality and *tōngcháng*$_{TOP}$ states a generalization of the referent. (see Guan [8], Lü [10]).

4 Co-occurrence with Kind-Denoting NP

A problem that has remained unresolved is how *tōngcháng* functions when it co-occurs with a kind-denoting NP subject. We show that when the NP subject is kind-denoting and individual-denoting, *tōngcháng* operates its quantification in the same way, i.e. rightward quantification at the occasion level.

In Mandarin Chinese, a sentence as (35) states a generalization over the species, dogs and the bare NP subject *gǒu* 'dog' receives a kind-referring interpretation. (see Li [16]) The predicate *chī ròu* 'eat meat' describes a characterizing property of its NP subject.

(35) 狗吃肉
Gǒu chī ròu
dog eat meat
'Dogs eat meat.'

Tōngcháng can co-occur with the kind-denoting NP subject, as in (36)–(37).

(36) 狗**通常**吃肉
*Gǒu **tōngcháng** chī ròu*
dog usually eat meat
'Dogs usually eat meat.'

(37) **通常**狗吃肉
***Tōngcháng** gǒu chī ròu*
Generally dog eat meat
'Generally, dogs eat meat.'

The adverb is often considered as a marker of characterizing sentences to make a sentential genericity. (See Li [16], Krifka et al. [17]) Here, the predicate *chī ròu* 'eat meat' is SLP which defines a property of the NP subject on one hand, and *tōngcháng* expresses a generalization of patterns of occasions of the kind-denoting NP on the other hand.

In Sect. 2.2, we showed that *tōngcháng* has to co-occur with a temporally or spatially modified SLP. However, now we understand that while the NP subject is a kind-denoting one in a lexical generic sentence, a SLP without modification can co-occur with *tōngcháng*. Therefore, we modify the condition of requirement of predicate types. See (25), the structure of VPL, *tōngcháng*.

(25) **VPL** , S **VPL** VP
tōngcháng$_{TOP}$ S *tōngcháng*$_{PvV}$ VP

When *tōngcháng* pluralizes the VP whose NP subject is individual-denoting, as in (8), (16) and (20), the VP must be a temporally or spatially modified SLP. Since *tōngcháng* can also pluralize the VP whose NP subject is kind-denoting, as in (36)–(37), the VP can be SLP, which denotes a general property. When the NP subject is individual-denoting, it is the subject of each occasion denoted by [*tōngcháng* –VP], which means the multiple occasions with the same subject. However, when the NP subject is kind-denoting, how do we account for the multiple occasions denoted by [*tōngcháng*–VP] where VP is a SLP, since the subject refers to a plurality of entities which is interpreted as a kind denotation? How do we explain that the NP is a plural one and its predication which is pluralized by the VLP? To solve this puzzle, we will apply the notion of "plural predication" that Landman [18] uses. Landman [18] distinguishes two manners of predication, singular predication and plural predication. Singular predication attributes a singular predicate to a singular NP argument (subject) while plural predication attributes a plural predicate distributively to a sum of singular entities.

Now we return to our VLP, *tōngcháng*. We have shown that as VLP, *tōngcháng*$_{\mathrm{TOP}}$ and *tōngcháng*$_{\mathrm{PrV}}$ quantify rightward at the occasion level. We apply this rule of quantification in (36)–(37). In (36), *tōngcháng*$_{\mathrm{PrV}}$ pluralizes over the predication, *chī ròu* 'eat meat' and it forms a plural predication as a unit, [Pl-Pred] (see Landman [18], Yuan [19]). This plural predication is attributed to the kind-denoting NP subject, dog, which is viewed as a set containing individual dogs and in the set of [Pl-Pred], each single predication of 'eat meat' is attributed to an individual dog, which makes multiple occasions of 'dog eats meat'. Since the [Pl-Pred] is applied to many of the individuals in the set of dog-kind, but not all individuals, due to the NP dog being outside of the scope of *tōngcháng*$_{\mathrm{PrV}}$, (36) asserts that in the set of dog-kind, most of individual dogs eat meat. In other word, there are individual dogs that don't eat meat in the set of dog-kind. The entailment of (36) is shown in (38) in which the second NP dog is referred to a specific dog, my dog, which is individual-denoting. Since [Pl-Pred] cannot be applied to a sub-set of dog-kind, (39) is not plausible as an entailment of (36).

(38) 狗**通常**吃肉，但我的狗不吃肉
Gǒu ***tōngcháng*** *chī ròu, dàn wǒ-de gǒu bù chī ròu*
dog usually eat meat but my dog neg. eat meat
'Dogs usually eat met. But my dog does not eat meat.'

(39) …, # 但有些種類的狗不吃肉
…, # dàn yǒuxiē zhǒnglèi de gǒu bù chī ròu
but some kind of dog neg. eat meat
'…. But there are some kinds of dogs that don't eat meat.'

Now, since *tōngcháng*$_{\mathrm{TOP}}$ pluralizes the whole constituents at its right, the kind-denoting NP subject dog is under its scope and it pluralizes over occasions denoted by the predication attributed to a set of dog-kind. In other word, (37) indicates the plurality of kinds of dogs in which each kind of dogs eat meat. The entailment of (37) shows that there are some kinds of dogs that don't eat meat, as (40) illustrates. Due to the pluralization over the kind-level of NP, the individual dog, such a specific dog that doesn't eat meat cannot be entailed, as in (41).

(40) **通常**，狗吃肉，但有些種類的狗不吃肉
Tōngcháng, *gǒu chī ròu, dàn yǒuxiē zhǒnglèi de gǒu bù chī ròu*
Generally dog eat meat but some kind of dog neg. eat meat 'Generally, dogs eat meat. But there are some kinds of dogs that don't eat meat.'

(41) …, #但我的狗不吃肉
…, #dàn wǒ-de gǒu bù chī ròu
but my dog neg. eat meat
'… .But my dog does not eat meat.'

The above account can be supported by the test with the focus marker, *shì*, as (42)-(43) illustrate. The NP subject before *tōngcháng*$_{\mathrm{PrV}}$ is not able to be focused with the *shì*, as in (42) while the one after *tōngcháng*$_{TOP}$ can be focused, which indicates another kind of animal, as in (43).

(42) *是狗**通常**吃肉
Shì gǒu **tōngcháng chī ròu*
be dog usually eat meat

(43) 通常是狗吃肉，而不是羊
***Tōngcháng** shì gǒu chī ròu, ér bù shì yang*
Generally be dog eat meat but neg. be sheep
'Generally, it is dogs that eat meat, not sheep.'

The same analysis for *tōngcháng* can apply to the sentences with kind denoting NPs subjects, like (44).

(33) 去年，{??**通常**}瑪莉{**通常**}在家吃晚餐
*Qù-nián, {??**tōngcháng**} Mǎlì {**tōngcháng**} zài jiā chī wǎncān*
last year generally Mary usually at home eat dinner
'Last year, {generally}, Mary {usually} had dinner at home.'

The NP subject is a modified one and it denotes a class of entities with the same features. We can predict the result of pluralization with *tōngcháng*$_{PrV}$ (45) and *tōngcháng*$_{TOP}$ (46).

(45) 會叫的狗**通常**不咬人，但也有會叫的狗咬人
*Huì jiào de gǒu **tōngcháng** bù yǎo rén, dàn yě yǒu huì jiào de gǒu yǎo rén*
know bark de dog usually neg. bite person but also have know bark de dog bite person
'Dogs that bark usually don't bite, but among the dogs that bark, there are some that bite.'

(46) **通常**會叫的狗不咬人
***Tōngcháng** huì jiào de gǒu bù yǎo rén*
Generally know bark de dog neg. bite person
'Generally, dogs that bark don't bite.'

Tōngcháng$_{PrV}$ pluralizes over the predication *bù yǎo rén* while *tōngcháng*$_{TOP}$ pluralizes over occasions of dogs that bark but don't bite. The entailments of (45)–(46), which are shown in (45) and (47), show that the adverb *tōngcháng*'s scope interaction with the NP subjects.

(47) 不會叫的狗會咬人
Bù huì jiào de gǒu huì yǎo rén
Neg. know bark de dog know bite person
'Dogs that don't bark bite.'

The test with the focus marker, *shì*, can help to show whether the NP subject is in the scope of the adverb or not, as (48)–(49) indicate. As we predict, the NP subject can be focused by *shì* when it co-occurs with *tōngcháng*$_{TOP}$, instead of *tōngcháng*$_{PrV}$.

(48) **通常**，是會叫的狗不咬人，而不是不會叫的狗
__Tōngcháng__, shì huì jiào de gǒu bù yǎo rén, ér bù shì bù huì jiào de gǒu
Generally be know bark de dog neg. bite person but neg. be neg. know bark de dog
'Generally, it is dogs that bark that don't bite, instead of dogs that don't bark.'

(49) *是會叫的狗通常不咬人
**Shì huì jiào de gǒu __tōngcháng__ bù yǎo rén*
be know bark de dog usually neg. bite person

To sum up, we showed that *tōngcháng*$_{\mathrm{TOP}}$ and *tōngcháng*$_{\mathrm{PrV}}$ pluralize always over the constituents on their right side when both co-occur with a kind-denoting NP subject, as established previously in Sect. 2. *tōngcháng* functions identically whether the NP subject is kind-denoting or individual-denoting.

5 Conclusion

In this paper, we showed that *tōngcháng* is a verbal plurality marker at the occasion level, in the sense of Cusic [1]. This adverb can be placed in two positions, namely, the topic position, which is at the beginning of a sentence, and the preverbal position. The adverb *tōngcháng* in both positions functions in the same way, which is to quantify rightward. The scope varies according to its positions. In the topic position, *tōngcháng* takes scope over the whole sentence; while in the preverbal position, it takes scope over the VP only. As a result of scope effect of the adverb, *tōngcháng* gives rise to different semantic denotations. The adverb *tōngcháng* in the topic position marks habituality while *tōngcháng* in the preverbal position marks iterativity. The occasion-level plurality marker, *tōngcháng* operates in the same way when it co-occurs with NP subjects with individual denotation and those with kind denotation.

References

1. Cusic, D.: Verbal Plurality and Aspect. Ph.D. dissertation. Stanford University, Stanford (1981)
2. Bertinetto, P.M., Lenci, A.: Habituality, pluractionality, and imperfectivity. In: Binnick, R.I. (ed.) The Oxford Handbook of Tense and Aspect. Oxford University Press, New York (2012)
3. Zou, H.Q.: The scope and types of frequency adverbs. Chin. Teach. World **77**, 36–45 (2006). (邹海清:频率副词的范围和类别, 世界汉语教学) (in Chinese)
4. Shi, J.S., Hu, X.P.: Types of adverbs of verbal quantification and their selection. Linguist. Res. **2**, 9–14 (2004). (史金生, 胡晓萍. 动量副词的类别及其选择性, 语文研究 2004(2), 9–14)

5. Zhou, X.B.: Classification of frequency adverbs and usage rules. J. East China Normal Univ. Humanit. Soc. Sci. **4**, 116–119 (1999). (周小兵. 频度副词的划类与使用规则华东师范大学学报(哲学社会科学版))
6. Zhang, Y.S.: The Analysis of Modern Chinese Adverbs. Xuélín, Shànghǎi (2000) (张谊生《现代汉语副词探索》上海:学林出版社)
7. Zhou, X.B.: *chángcháng* and *tōngcháng*. Lang. Teach. Linguist. Stud. 1994(4) (1994). (周小兵. “常常” 和 “通常”，《语言教学与研究》)
8. Guan, H.Z.: A study on the frequency adverbs in modern Chinese, PhD dissertation. Jilin University (2015) (关黑拽. 现代汉语频度副词研究, 吉林大学博论)
9. Chen, Y.X., Ren, H.B.: A comparative analysis on *chángcháng* and *tōngcháng*. Modern Chin. **2**, 50–53 (2010). (陈玉潇 任海波,"常常"和"通常"的比较分析.《现代语文：下旬．语 言研究》2010(2), 50-53)
10. Lü, S.X.: Xiandai Hanyu Babaici (Modern Chinese: 800 words, revised edition). The Commercial Press, Beijing (1999) (吕叔湘.现代汉语八百词(增订本).北京:商务印书馆)
11. He, S.B.: Research based on data on frequency adverbs in modern Chinese, M.A. thesis, Nanjing Normal University (2006) (何淑冰.基于统计的现代汉语频率副词研究,南京师范大学)
12. Yuan, H.H., Chan, D.K.G.: The verbal plurality of adverb: the case of *tōngcháng* ‘usually/generally’ in Mandarin Chinese, M.S. The 28th Paris Meeting on East Asian Linguistics, Paris (2015)
13. Chan, D.K.G., Hua-Hung, Y.: On the semantic functions and denotations of *jīngcháng* (经常) and *chángcháng* (常常). Chinese Lexical Semantics. LNCS (LNAI), vol. 10709, pp. 112–123. Springer, Cham (2018). https://doi.org/10.1007/978-3-319-73573-3_9
14. Yuan, H.-H., Chan, D.K.G.: Verbal plurality of frequency adverbs in Mandarin Chinese: the case of cháng and chángcháng. In: Dong, M., Lin, J., Tang, X. (eds.) CLSW 2016. LNCS (LNAI), vol. 10085, pp. 483–496. Springer, Cham (2016). https://doi.org/10.1007/978-3-319-49508-8_46
15. Kratzer, A.: Stage-level/individual-level predicates. In: Carlson, G., Pelletier, F.J. (eds.) The Generic Book, pp. 125–175. University of Chicago Press, Chicago (1995)
16. Li, J.: Predicate type and the semantics of bare nouns in Chinese. In: Xu, L.J. (ed.) The referential properties of Chinese noun phrases, pp. 61–84. Ecole des Hautes Etudes en Sciences Sociales, Paris (1997)
17. Krifka, M., et al.: Genericity: an introduction. In: Carlson, G., Pelletier, F.J. (eds.) The Generic Book, pp. 1–124. University of Chicago Press, Chicago (1995)
18. Landman, Fred.: Events and Plurality: The Jerusalem Lectures, Studies in Linguistics and Philosophy, vol. 76. Kluwer, Dordrecht (2000)
19. Yuan, H.H.: Quelques aspects de la quantification en chinois mandarin: pluralité et distributivité, Ph.D. dissertation, Université Paris-Diderot (2011)

A Comparative Analysis of Level 1 of the ICCLE and Learners' Basic Mental Lexicon

Caihong Cao[1(✉)], Junping Zhang[1], Huizhou Zhao[2], and Zhimin Wang[1]

[1] School of Chinese Studies, Beijing Language and Culture University, Beijing 100083, China
hdxiaoxi@163.com, jpzhang0315@126.com, wangzm000@qq.com

[2] School of Information Science, Beijing Language and Culture University, Beijing 100083, China
zhaohuizhou@blcu.edu.cn

Abstract. This study makes a comparison between the level 1 word list of the ICCLE issued by Hanban and the learners' Basic Mental Lexicon (BML). The results show that 80 words in the ICCLE are verified, meaning they are also found in the BML, accounting for 53.3% of the 150 words. In terms of parts of speech, nouns have the biggest difference with 30.36%, while verbs, adverbs and phrases have the smallest difference at 3.57%. Classifiers, interjections, and auxiliaries are not found in the BML. In regard to the topics, the degree of attention and emphases in the two lists differ. The ICCLE emphasizes the function words in achieving grammar integrity, whereas students focus on learning words related to their daily life. Finally, the results are discussed and corresponding suggestions are put forward to guide the practice of the international teaching of Chinese.

Keywords: Level one words of the ICCLE · Basic mental lexicon
Comparative analysis

1 Introduction

Chinese commonly used words are an important basis for Chinese learning, classroom teaching, textbook writing, and Chinese language ability examinations. Therefore, compiling the list of commonly used words is "a very significant project" [1]. Commonly used words play a pivotal role in the construction of general language knowledge base [2]. Chinese scholars have made some achievements in the study of common vocabulary, such as "The List of Three Thousand Common Words in Mandarin" (普通

Source of Funding: Supported by Science Foundation of Beijing Language and Cultural University (supported by "the Fundamental Research Funds for the Central Universities") (Approval number: 16PT03 and 18YJ080110).

J.-F. Hong et al. (Eds.): CLSW 2018, LNAI 11173, pp. 396–407, 2018.
https://doi.org/10.1007/978-3-030-04015-4_33

话三千常用词表, 1959), "List of Common Words for Teaching Chinese as a Foreign Language" (对外汉语教学常用词表, 1986), "Dictionary of Modern Chinese High Frequency Words" (现代汉语常用词词频字典, 1989), "Chinese Proficiency Vocabulary and the Outline of Chinese Characters" (汉语水平词汇与汉字大纲, 1992), and "The Graded Chinese Syllables, Characters and Words for the Application of Teaching Chinese to the Speakers of Other Languages" (汉语国际教育用音节汉字词汇等级划分, 2010), and many other dictionaries of common vocabulary. The publication of these common word lists has played a great role in promoting the development of Chinese language education. However, these studies of vocabulary are all based on data from published newspapers, books, textbooks, or radio and television dialogues etc. [3]. Of course, researchers can expand their corpora to bring their vocabulary closer to reality, reflecting the real demand for words. However, whether the resulting common vocabulary can truly meet the needs of the learners and reflect the most necessary words of the learners will need to be tested and verified by the learners. If the published lists of common words cannot be verified by the learners, then these word lists are just part of a "Glossary of Published Words". Several Chinese researchers have keenly aware of this need for a learners' test for verification and have appealed and affirmed this research at some conferences. At present, some linguists have already built a corpus of spoken Chinese by recording private conversations [4]. No scholars have yet studied this issue from the perspective of the language learners. Therefore, this research is aimed specifically at this issue.

The National Hanban Office launched "the International Curriculum for Chinese Language Education (国际汉语教学通用课程大纲)" in 2008 (Abbr. ICCLE). Since its publication, this curriculum has been "translated into 45 languages and widely used all over the world, and has played an important guiding role in the teaching of the Chinese language at home and abroad" [5]. At the same time, in order to "better plan and guide the design of Chinese courses, the compilation of teaching materials, and the ability evaluations etc." [5], the National Hanban Office has revised the ICCLE and published the revised version in May 2014 in order to "adapt to the new changes in the international teaching situation of Chinese and summarize the research results of Chinese teaching in a timely manner" [5]. Since the syllabus is "the results and experience of international Chinese teaching at the present stage" [5] and has great influence on Chinese teaching in the world, it should be tested more prudently. Hence this study will examine the level one words of the ICCLE to see whether it meets the learning needs of the learners by using the learners' mental lexicon as a measuring tool. Therefore, this study first obtains the basic vocabulary that the learners must learn in their daily life by means of a questionnaire, thus forming a summary table of foreign students' basic mental lexicon (Abbr. BML), and then tests its effectiveness by using Zipf's law. If the results pass the test, we can extract the basic mental lexicon of the foreign students and use this word list as a measuring tool to compare the vocabulary in the ICCLE. The results of analysis are then drawn and discussed so as to put forward corresponding suggestions for teaching and textbook writing, thereby guiding the international Chinese Teaching practice.

2 Research Methodology and Data

2.1 Data Collection

The researchers used questionnaires to obtain the basic mental lexicon of international students studying in China who are learners of Chinese as a second language. For the questionnaire, see Fig. 1.

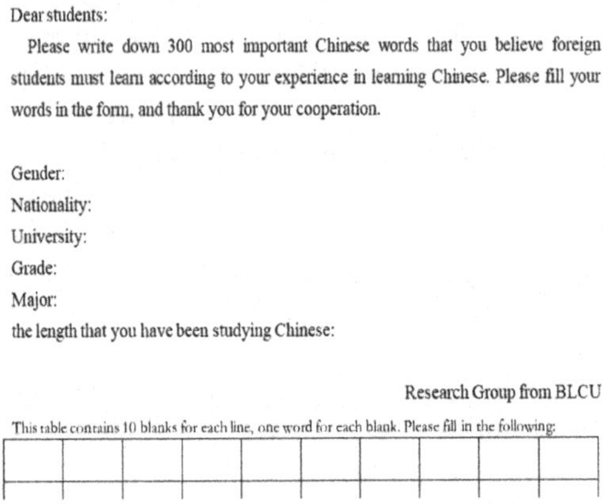

Dear students:

Please write down 300 most important Chinese words that you believe foreign students must learn according to your experience in learning Chinese. Please fill your words in the form, and thank you for your cooperation.

Gender:
Nationality:
University:
Grade:
Major:
the length that you have been studying Chinese:

Research Group from BLCU

This table contains 10 blanks for each line, one word for each blank. Please fill in the following:

Fig. 1. Basic mental lexicon questionnaire

The premises of the questionnaire are: (1) there is a Chinese mental lexicon in every Chinese language learner's mind, which varies from person to person. To answer the question "what are the most commonly used words in daily life?", we must extract the first Chinese words that foreign students think of, as they can be regarded as the most necessary mental lexicon for the students, then those words that have been filled in the questionnaires which produce the highest frequencies form the basic mental lexicon of the objects. (2) According to the law of large numbers in Statistical Science, when the number of investigations obtained in a random state reaches a certain amount, the results can reflect the overall characteristics of the study object. Therefore, the final sample of the mental lexicon can be regarded as the basic mental lexicon of Chinese learners.

Based on the above premises, this study requires the students to fill in the most basic Chinese words that they think are the most needed in their actual daily life. At the same time, we determined the confidence level of the questionnaire to be 95%; the overall standard deviation of the sample is set to 0.4-0.5, and the sample error is 5%. Under these research conditions, the number of samples needed to be investigated was 245–384.

This study conducted a cluster sampling questionnaire of 309 Chinese language students from more than 30 countries from sophomore to senior year of the undergraduate school of Chinese studies in Beijing Language and Culture University in September 2016 and September 2017 respectively. In light of the fact that the junior and senior year students who have been learning Chinese for 3–4 years not only have enough Chinese vocabulary to complete the 300 word questionnaire, but also have rich learning experience and memory for the words that should be mastered by beginners, they are the main respondents of the investigation. The length of time spent learning Chinese is shown in Fig. 2, of which 108 spent 3–4 years, accounting for 35%; of those who spent 4–5 years, 27.5%; 2–3 years, 19.1%; the proportion of learners who spent less than 2 years or more than 6 years is 6.5%.

A total of 10447 words were collected from the questionnaire, and the average frequency of each word, the average position of the words in the list and its positional

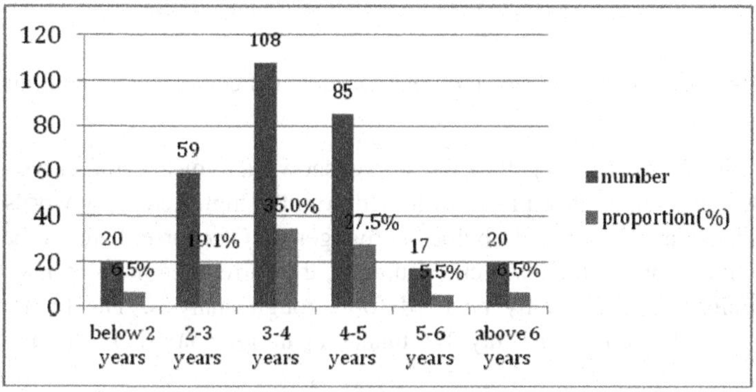

Fig. 2. Number of years spent learning Chinese

variance were also calculated[1].

2.2 Validation of the Research Data

Whether the data collected by the investigation is scientific or not, and whether or not we can use it as an effective measurement tool requires further verification of the data. Thus it is necessary to examine convergence of the data to see if it is consistent with the common linguistic features of the language.

Zipf's law is one of the three laws in quantitative linguistics. The law describes that in the absence of human intervention, the distribution of the two variables, word frequency and the descending order of words according to frequency, exhibits an inverse function shape or curve. The formula is:

$$f_r = k \times r^{-1} \tag{1}$$

Where f_r is the word frequency, r is the order of words frequency, and k is a constant. This law has proven to be widespread in linguistics [6]. Therefore, according to this law, we examine the mental lexicon of foreign students collected from the questionnaire. We get the relationship diagram of the two variables. (See Fig. 3).

[1] The relevant data of this study can be provided in accordance with requirements.

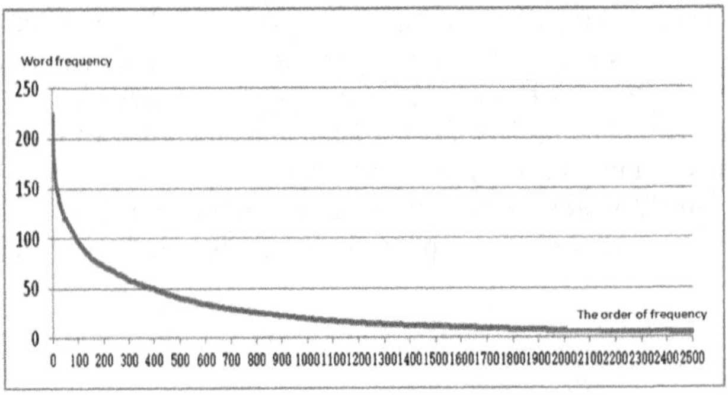

Fig. 3. The relationship between word frequency and its frequency order in mental lexicon

From Fig. 3, we can see that the curve shows a typical Zipf curve, which is completely consistent with Zipf's law. In addition, the high frequency words collected from the questionnaire showed obvious convergence. Of course, here we believe that due to the limitations of the research conditions, the current learner's mental lexicon is only preliminary and can only be used for a rough analysis. The higher accurate comparison needs the further study, but this comparative analysis is still a meaningful attempt.

In general, this study holds that the results of the mental lexicon questionnaire carried out according to the law of large numbers are effective. The results of this questionnaire can be used as a scientific basis for further extracting the BML based on the learners and for measuring the other word lists to reflect the needs of the learners.

3 The Distribution Characteristics of Mental Lexica

3.1 The Basic Mental Lexicon

In order to conduct a learner mental measurement of the ICCLE, we need to establish their basic mental lexicon (BML), and then the degree of matching is calculated and analyzed accordingly. In this study, the first group of words is arranged in descending order according to their frequency. We sort them out according to the frequency of 10447 words so as to take the top 150 words with the highest frequency as the final results. This paper refers to the first 150 words as the basic mental lexicon, and some of these words are in Table 1.

Table 1. The basic mental Lexicon based on the learners' answers

Order	Words	Part of speech	Order	Words	Part of speech	Order	Words	Part of speech
1	lǎoshī (老师)	n.	51	wèntí (问题)	n.	101	rènshì (认识)	v.
2	shǒujī (手机)	n.	52	yùndòng (运动)	n.	102	shítáng (食堂)	n.
3	xuéxí (学习)	v.	53	bǐ (笔)	n.	103	chī (吃)	v.
4	péngyǒu (朋友)	n.	54	gēgē (哥哥)	n.	104	yīnwèi (因为)	con.
5	shíjiān (时间)	n.	55	guójiā (国家)	n.	105	tā (她)	pron.
46	mèimei (妹妹)	n.	96	xiūxí (休息)	v.	146	fùxí (复习)	v.
47	dōngxī (东西)	n.	97	hǎo (好)	adj.	147	yīshēng (医生)	n.
48	kěyǐ (可以)	v.	98	yǐzi (椅子)	n.	148	shūbāo (书包)	n.
49	shēnghuó (生活)	n.	99	mǐfàn (米饭)	n.	149	fúwùyuán (服务员)	n.
50	mǎi (买)	v.	100	duì (对)	adj.	150	hěn (很)	adv.

3.2 A Comparative Analysis of Parts of Speech Between the Basic Mental Lexicon and ICCLE

3.2.1 Comparison of the Number and Composition of Words in Different Parts of Speech

If we compare the level one words of the ICCLE with the BML, we find that in the first level of the ICCLE, there are 11 parts of speech (See Table 2), but only 8 in the BML as there are no classifiers, auxiliaries, or interjections. Both include phrases[2]. Out of the commonly shared parts of speech, the amount of words of each part of speech and the choice of words differ, among which nouns differ the most. For example, the number of nouns in level one of the ICCLE is 61, whereas the BML has 78. The difference between the two lists is 17 words, and the contribution to the difference of the two word lists is 28.33%, which is the main source of the difference in parts of speech. Adjectives and numerals tie for second, with a difference of 8 words, each making the difference contribution rate 13.33%. In the third and fourth positions are pronouns and classifiers, respectively, of which pronouns differ by 7, accounting for 11.67%, and classifiers differ by 6, accounting for 10%. The parts of speech with the least difference are verbs, adverbs, interjections and phrases, differing with only 1–2 words. It is worth noting that the reasons for the difference in these parts of speech in the two word lists are different.

[2] The phrases have been placed in the part of speech column for convenience.

Table 2. Difference in parts of speech between the BML and the ICCLE

Order	Part of speech	BML		Level one of the ICCLE		Discrepancy	
		Number	Proportion (%)	Number	Proportion (%)	Discrepancy in number[a]	Proportion[b] (%)
1	Nouns	78	52.00	61	40.67	17	28.33
2	Verbs	35	23.33	33	22.00	2	3.33
3	Adjectives	17	11.33	9	6.00	8	13.33
4	Pronouns	8	5.33	15	10.00	−7	−11.67
5	Conjunctions	4	2.67	1	0.67	3	5.00
6	Numerals	2	1.33	10	6.67	−8	−13.33
7	Adverbs	2	1.33	4	2.67	−2	−3.33
8	Classifiers	0	0.00	6	4.00	−6	−10.00
9	Interjections	0	0.00	1	0.67	−1	−1.67
10	Auxiliaries	0	0.00	4	2.67	−4	−6.67
11	Phrases	4	2.67	6	4.00	−2	−3.33
12	Total	150	100.00	150	100	60[c]	100.00

[a]The positive sign indicates that the number of BML words is more than the number of words in the level 1 word list of the ICCLE. A negative sign would mean the opposite.

[b]Take the ratio of the absolute value of the difference in quantity to the total difference. The meaning of the sign is the same as the quantity.

[c]Take the absolute value of the number difference and add the total.

Most of the lexical discrepancies are due to the different number of words, while the discrepant classifiers, interjections and auxiliaries are only found in the ICCLE, not the BML. That is to say, none of the language-learning students choose these words from these parts of speech.

In Table 2, we can see that the top four parts of speech in the ICCLE are nouns, verbs, pronouns, and numerals, while most of the parts of speech in the BML are nouns, verbs, adjectives, and pronouns. Comparing the two word lists, we find that there are many more pronouns, numerals and classifiers in the ICCLE than in the basic mental lexicon, while the BML has more nouns, adjectives and conjunctions than the ICCLE.

In addition to the difference in the number of parts of speech, the two word lists differ in terms of the composition of words (See Fig. 4). The two word lists produce a total of 210 words, of which 80 words are common, accounting for 53.3% of 150 words, and the number of different words is 70, accounting for 46.7%.

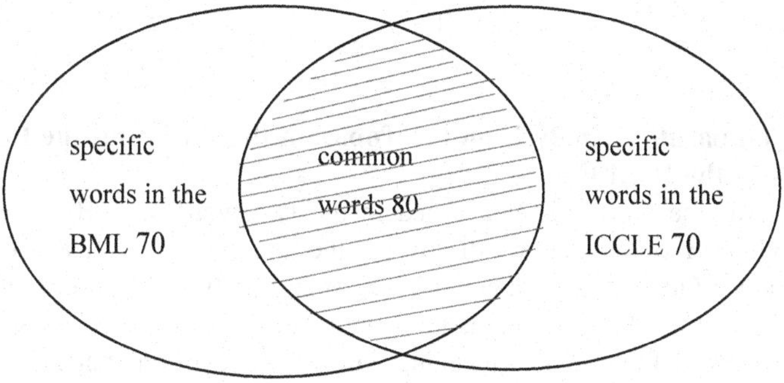

Fig. 4. Composition of BML and level 1 of the ICCLE

The parts of speech with the most overlapping words are adverbs, adjectives, verbs, pronouns and phrases, accounting for 50%, 44.44%, 43.75%, 43.75% and 37.50% of the words from each part of speech respectively. The parts of speech with the greatest difference in the number of words are the classifiers, conjunctions, interjections and auxiliaries.

The reason for the difference in conjunctions is that the selection of the conjunctions is completely different between the two word lists, while the classifiers, the interjections and the auxiliary words have a great difference because the students did not choose any of these words, so in these cases the difference is as high as 100%. In addition, it was unexpected to see numerals, whose difference is also significant, reaching 80%, as shown in Table 3.

Regarding the numerals, researchers generally believe that the numbers one to ten in Chinese should be the most basic words and should be learned together, but this intuitive feeling is not recognized by the learners, and the questionnaire data reveals that even the ordering of the two numbers "one" and "ten" in 150 words is also very low, 142 and 143 respectively. If the mental lexicon is further extended to 300 words, the middle numbers may be included, but learners' cognitive order and importance are still not the same.

Table 3. Comparison between the composition of the BML and the ICCLE

Order	Part of speech	Common words	Specific words in the BML	Specific words in the ICCLE	Ratio of common words (%)	Ratio of discrepancy words (%)
1	Nouns	36	41	24	35.64	64.36
2	Verbs	21	14	13	43.75	56.25
3	Adjectives	8	9	1	44.44	55.56
4	Pronouns	7	1	8	43.75	56.25
5	Numerals	2	0	8	20.00	80.00
6	Adverbs	2	0	2	50.00	50.00
7	Classifiers	0	0	6	0.00	100.00
8	Conjunctions	0	4	1	0.00	100.00
9	Interjections	0	0	1	0.00	100.00
10	Auxiliaries	0	0	4	0.00	100.00
11	Phrases	3	2	3	37.50	62.50
12	Total	79	71	71	35.75	64.25

3.2.2 A Comparative Analysis on the Topics in the BML and the Level One Words in the ICCLE

We further examine the topics concerned in the two word lists. By classifying the words according to topic types, we discovered the topic features of the two word lists. The words are divided into 6 categories: learning, emotion, life, time, quantity and grammatical function. Among them, the grammatical functional class is defined as "words having no definite lexical meaning, but that have a grammatical or functional meaning".

Comparing the two word lists, we can see that they are concerned with the same topics, but their focus and degree of concern differ. The students obviously pay much more attention to learning than the researchers do (See Table 4). From Table 4, we can see that aside from some basic common words such as lǎoshī (老师, teacher), tóngxué (同学 classmate), xuéshēng (学生 student), xuéxiào (学校 school), xuéxí (学习 learning), tīng (听 listening), shuō (说 speaking), dú (读 reading), xiě (写 writing), kàn (看 see), shū (书 book) and hànyǔ (汉语 Chinese), the words the experts chose based on text research has only one selected word, namely zì (字 Chinese character), while the students' BML includes the other 19 words. These words demonstrate that students pay more attention to learning, not only being concerned with the usual learning of phrases and words like "shàngkè (上课 have a class), xiàkè (下课 dismiss the class), kǎoshì (考试 examination) and zuòyè (作业 homework) chídào (迟到), bǐ (笔 pen)", but also the difficulty of learning and hard work "wèntí (问题 queation), nán (难 difficulty), róngyì (容易 easy), zhīdào (知道 knowing), míngbái (明白 understanding), duì (对right), nǔlì (努力 study hard)", and various relationships within the study environment, such as "lǎoshī (老师 teacher), tóngxué (同学 classmate), xuéshēng (学生 student)," as well as the learning environment itself, with words like "dàxué (大学 university), jiàoshì (教室 classroom), bàngōngshì (办公室 office)etc." They may go further in their contemplations about learning, “yǔyán (语言 language), wénhuà (文化 culture)”, and the future of learning, such as “bìyè (毕业 graduation)”. Connecting with the word “gōngzuò (工作 work)” in life category, we can see that students are also very concerned about the future, the completion of learning.

Table 4. Comparison of learning category between the BML and ICCLE

Common words	Specific words in the BML	Specific words in level 1 of the ICCLE
lǎoshī (老师), tóngxué (同学), xuéxiào (学校), xuéxí (学习), xuéshēng (学生), tīng (听), shuō (说), dú (读), xiě (写), kàn (看), shū (书), hànyǔ (汉语)	shàngkè (上课), xiàkè (下课), zuòyè (作业), kǎoshì (考试), bǐ (笔), chídào (迟到), nán (难), róngyì (容易), wèntí (问题), míngbái (明白), zhīdào (知道), duì (对), nǔlì (努力), dàxué (大学), jiàoshì (教室), bàngōngshì (办公室), yǔyán (语言), wénhuà (文化), bìyè (毕业)	zì(字)

In the category of the emotion and the relationship, the students’ perspectives are flat, using self-centered words such as “bàba (爸爸 father), māmā (妈妈 mother), jiějiě (姐姐 elder sister), mèimei (妹妹 younger sister), gēgē (哥哥 elder brother) and dìdì (弟弟 younger brother)”, emotional words “kuàilè (快乐 happy), kāixīn (开心 joyful), gāoxìng (高兴 cheerful), xiǎng (想 miss), jiā (家 home) and yīnyuè (音乐 music)”, openness and the future “nǐhǎo (你好 Hello), xīwàng (希望 hope)”,and the non-social “zìjǐ (自己 self)”. The words chosen by the researchers are relatively overlooked, as they focus on hierarchical relationship words “érzi (儿子 son), nǚ’ér (女儿 daughter)”, social terms “xiǎojiě (小姐 Miss), xiānshēng (先生 Mr.)”, home life “gǒu (狗 dog), māo (猫 cat)”, manners “qǐng (请 please), bùkèqì (不客气 my pleasure), méiguānxì (没关系 no worries)”,social contact “wǒmen (我们 we)”.

In terms of daily life, students are concerned with aspects of their daily lives, such as eating “shítáng (食堂 cafeteria), chīfàn (吃饭 eat), kāfēi (咖啡 coffee)”, accommodations “sùshè (宿舍 dormitory), fángjiān (房间 room)”, attire “piàoliang (漂亮 beautiful), yīfú (衣服 clothes)”, travel by “zǒu (走 walk), dìtiě (地铁 subway), zìxíngchē (自行车 bicycle)”, using items “shǒujī (手机 cell phone), diànhuà (电话 telephone), go to “chāoshì (超市 supermarket), yínháng (银行 bank), jīchǎng (机场 airport)”, and others, such as “zhōumò (周末 weekend), yùndòng (运动 sports), xiūxí (休息 rest), shēnghuó (生活 life), qián (钱 money), fúwùyuán (服务员 waiter), mǎi (买 buy), mài (卖 sell), guì (贵 expensive), piányí (便宜 cheap)”, and even, they focus more on themselves, such as “shēntǐ (身体 body), yǎnjīng (眼睛 eyes), tóufǎ (头发 hair) and shǒu (手 hands)”. Moreover, in the students’ BML, words are more concrete and related to their daily life, such as “chāoshì (超市 supermarket), shítáng (食堂 cafeteria), yínháng (银行 bank), jīchǎng (机场 airport)”, while the ICCLE words are "fàndiàn (hotel 饭店), shāngdiàn (商店 store), qiánmiàn (前面 front), hòumiàn (后面 back), lǐ (里 inside)",the ICCLE drinks "chá (茶 tea)" and the students drink "kāfēi (咖啡 coffee)",the ICCLE focuses on the abstract "rén (人person)", while the students focus on the concrete "shēntǐ (身体 body)". Learners are very concerned about things related to the modern lifestyle, such as "shǒujī (手机 mobile phones), wēixìn (微信 WeChat[3]), dìtiě (地铁 subway), chāoshì (超市 supermarkets)", but the same words are not found in the ICCLE.

The words in the time category are also different. The students' mental lexica have the words "shíjiān (时间 time), zǎoshang (早上 morning), wǎnshàng (晚上 evening), hòutiān (后天 the day after tomorrow), dōngtiān (冬天 winter), xiàtiān (夏天 summer)", while the ICCLE has "shíhòu (时候 when), diǎn (点 hour), fēnzhōng (分钟 minute), shàngwǔ (上午 morning), zhōngwǔ (中午 noon), xiàwǔ (下午 afternoon), xīngqī (星期 week), hào (号 day)". In regard to time related words, students focus on a larger time range, while the ICCLE is more specific.

The difference in quantitative words is much unexpected. It is generally considered that 1–10 are the most basic numerals and should be learned together, but this intuitive feeling is not recognized by the learners. Only "yī (一 one)" and "shí (十 ten)" enter the top 150 words of the BML and even the ordering of the two numbers "one" and "ten" in 150 words is also very low, 142 and 143 respectively. If the mental lexicon is further extended to 300 words, the middle numbers may be included, but learners' cognitive order and importance are still not the same. As for the classifiers, the ICCLE gives 4 commonly used classifiers, "gè (个 a), běn (本 book), kuài (块 block), suì (岁 years old)", but none of the classifiers can be found in the top 150 words of the BML.

The words in the grammatical function category occupy the large proportion in the ICCLE. In addition to the common words of the two lists, the ICCLE also has the words "de (的 of), dōu (都 all), hé (和 and), huì (会 can), le (了 past tense marker), ma (吗 particle used for asking questions), ne (呢 similar to "what about…?"), nà (那 that), zhè (这 this), xiē (些 some), jiào (叫 name), shì (是 is)". These words are necessary to construct a grammatically correct sentence, but the mental lexicon does not include these words, and even when the mental lexicon is expanded to 300 words we find these words are still not in the top chosen words by the students. Students only chose words like "yīnwèi (因为 because), suǒyǐ (所以 therefore), dànshì (但是 but), rúguǒ (如果 if), yào (要 want), juédé (觉得 think)".

4 Conclusion

Through the above data analysis of the ICCLE and the BML, we have drawn the following basic conclusions.

1. Generally speaking, the words in the ICCLE can only roughly reflect learners' studying needs. Therefore, it is necessary to give full play to the initiative of teachers, allowing them to prepare lessons carefully, timely adding the relative new words reflecting the latest living conditions and mental states of students so that

[3] The word "WeChat" can be found in the top 300 words of the BML.

students can feel the congruency and assistance from the knowledge they have learned match their growth and cognitive needs.

2. The perspectives of the two lists are completely different. So the choice of words in the ICCLE or text-based research focus more on the integrity and standardization of language ontology, while learners are more concerned with their own learning and survival needs. Although we can't deny the serviceability of the research results, which implies that both the ICCLE and the teaching materials should focus primarily on meeting the needs of the users, this article does not propose that we should adhere exclusively to the learners' needs and only choose the words they would choose themselves. Obviously, the words chosen by the students relate well to daily life, but not enough attention is given to the function words. This is important to note because Chinese uses function words as an essential means of grammatical relations [7]. If you do not have these grammatical functions, then it would be hard to imagine what the results of learning would be. Hence, we should combine the characteristics of the language itself with the learning needs of learners, taking both aspects into account.

References

1. Zhao, J., Zhang, B., Cheng, J.: Some suggestion on the revision of the outline of the graded vocabulary for HSK. J. Chin. Teach. World (2003). https://doi.org/10.13724/j.cnki.ctiw.2003.03.012
2. Yu, S., Zhu, X.: Quantitative Lexicon study and knowledge base construction for commonly used words. J. Chin. Inf. Process. 16–20 (2015)
3. Huang, C., Li, J.: The Corpus Linguistics. The Commercial Press, Beijing (2002)
4. Deng, Y., Feng, Z.: A quantitative linguistic study on the relationship between word length and word frequency. J. Foreign Lang. **36**(3), 29–38 (2013)
5. Confucius Institute Headquarters/Hanban: International Curriculum for Chinese Language Education. Beijing Language and Culture University Press, Beijing (2014)
6. Liu, H.: An Introduction to Quantitative Linguistics. The Commercial Press, Beijing (2017)
7. Wenhua, Lv.: Teaching Grammar of Chinese as a Foreign Language. Beijing University Press, Beijing (2015)

Toward a Unified Semantics for *Ū* in *Ū* + Situation in Taiwan Southern Min: A Modal-Aspectual Account

Jiun-Shiung Wu(✉) and Zhi-Ren Zheng

Institute of Linguistics, National Chung Cheng University,
168, University Road, Minhsiung, Chiayi County 621, Taiwan
Lngwujs@ccu.edu.tw, kuraltarkey@gmail.com

Abstract. *Ū* in *ū* + situation in Taiwan Southern Min has been noted, in the literature, to express multiple readings. In this paper, we argue for a modal-aspectual account for *ū*. The semantics of *ū* includes an epistemic modal base, a modal force – necessity, and an affirmative ordering source, which orders possible worlds based on the number of propositions affirmed to be true. Furthermore, *ū* performs event realization, with complications concerning atelic situations.

Keywords: ū · Affirmative ordering · Taiwan Southern Min · Modal-aspect
Event realization

1 Introduction

Ū, which literally means 'have, exist', can go with a situation in Taiwan Southern Min (for short, TSM). It receives much attention, e.g. [5, 7–9, 19, 20, 29–31], and so forth.

In addition to possessive and existential readings, as demonstrated in (1a, b), *ū* can also present a situation, as in (2).

(1) a. guá ū sann-koo gîn.
I have three-CL[1] money
'I have three dollars.'
b. tsù-lāi ū lâng-kheh.
house-inside have guest
'There are guests in the house.'

[1] The abbreviations used in this paper include: CL for classifier, Poss for possessive marker, Prc for a sentential particle, Prg for the progressive marker.

J.-F. Hong et al. (Eds.): CLSW 2018, LNAI 11173, pp. 408–422, 2018.
https://doi.org/10.1007/978-3-030-04015-4_34

(2) a. guá ū bué tiō kàu-siū-ê tsheh.
I have buy Tio Professor-Poss book
'I indeed bought Prof. Tio's book.'

b. i ū tsia̍h-hun.
he have smoke
'He indeed smokes.'

c. hue ū âng.
flower have red
'The flower is indeed red.'

d. tsit-tiâu kiô ū tsi̍t-pah kongtsioh tn̂g.
this-CL bridge have one-hundred meter long
'This bridge is as long as one hundred meter.'

In terms of temporal readings, the examples in (2) show a wide variety: (2a) receives a past tense reading, (2b) a characterizing reading, (2c, d) a present tense reading. On the other hand, [7] refers to (2b) as emphatic, (2c) as aspectual-assertive, and (2d) as approximative. [7] does not take (2a) into consideration. [31] classifies (2a) as aspectual-existential, and (2c) as emphatic. [31] does not consider (2b) and (2d).

In this paper, we discuss what the semantics of *ū* is so that it can express different temporal readings and a variety of readings, such as an assertive reading, aspectual reading, or emphatic reading, as discussed in the literature.

This paper is organized as follows. In Sect. 2, we briefly review related literature. We point out their strength and weakness. In Sect. 3, data is presented and a modal-aspectual account is argued for. Section 4 concludes this paper.

2 Literature Review

There have been abundant studies on *yǒu*[2] in Chinese southern dialects, and on *ū* in Southern Min and TSM.

[5] discusses the functions of *yǒu*. Four types are identified: (i) *yǒu* + dynamic predicate, expressing certainty of realization, (ii) *yǒu* + static predicate, affirming the realization of a state, (iii) *yǒu* + dynamic predicate, affirming the realization of an event to denote a characterizing reading, and (iv) *yǒu* + dynamic predicate, confirming the realization of a resultative state or the completion of a change of state. TSM does not allow for (iv).

[7–9] examine *ū* in TSM, among other things. [8] defies the idea that *ū* is a past-tense marker, and suggests that *ū* and its negative form *bô* serve as modals which assert the actual happening of an event.

[2] Please note that the character for *ū* in Southern Min and TSM is 有, which is pronounced as *yǒu* in Mandarin Chinese. Because this character has different pronunciations in different Chinese dialects, we use *yǒu* as a cover term. When discussing Southern Min or TSM, we use *ū*.

[19] suggests the following. Serving as a verb, *ū* denotes (i) possession, (ii) existence, (iii) listing, and (iv) quantity or comparison. As an adjective, *ū* describes quantity or quality. As an auxiliary verb, *ū* confirms realization of an event or a state. As an adverb, *ū* is placed before a verb to express quantity or quality.

[29] discusses *yǒu* in Taiwan Mandarin and Chinese dialects from a historical point of view. It is suggested that *yǒu* undergoes a semantic change from possession (*yǒngyǒu*) to presentation (*cúnyǒu*) and finally to existence (*cúnzài*). It is further suggested that completion and assertion are derived from this line of semantic change.

[30] discusses the interaction of *ū* in TSM with different situation types. Going with an activity, *ū* expresses actual happening of the activity, but not completion. Going with an accomplishment with a quantized direct object, *ū* denotes the culmination of the quantized event. Two possibilities surface when *ū* goes with an achievement. An achievement that describes a simple instantaneous event cannot go with *ū*. On the other hand, an RVC achievement can go with *ū* to denote the completion of the achievement. Finally, *ū* goes with a state to emphasize on or confirm the state.

[31] proposes that *ū* in Southern Min has five usages: (i) existential, (ii) possessive, (iii) presentational, (iv) existential-aspectual and (iv) emphatic. It is proposed that the existential-aspectual reading and emphatic reading of *ū* come from the sense 'existence'. *Ū* confirms the existence of an event. Because it is not possible to confirm an event that does not exist, *ū* naturally goes with a past event. Emphatic *ū* is semantically equal to existential-aspectual *ū* because in both usages *ū* confirms an eventuality that has happened. This eventuality can be an event, a state, or an abstract property.

All these studies are enlightening in that: (i) they conduct a complete observation of the possible readings of *ū* and/or (ii) the interaction between *ū* and situation types is observed, such as [30, 31], etc.

However, no account is provided for how the different temporal readings are derived and where the emphatic reading comes from. Hence, more detailed examination is called for.

3 Intensification and Event Realization

In this section, we, first, point out that the emphatic reading discussed in the previous studies is, in fact, intensification, i.e. the speaker uses *ū* to intensify the degree of his/her affirmativeness toward the truth of a proposition. And then we propose that *ū* performs event realization, c.f. [1, 2, 21], and so on. We also discuss a variety of readings expressed by *ū* + activity and *ū* + progressive event and explain how these readings are derived. Finally, we combine the ideas presented and propose a modal-aspectual semantics for *ū*.

3.1 Intensificaiton

One interesting question to ask is how a sentence with *ū* is different from one without *ū*. That is, how does (3a) differ from (3b), given the diverse proposals in the literature?

Obviously, assertion is not the difference because (3a) is also asserted, according to [25–27], who propose that uttering a declarative sentence performs the speech act of assertion.

(3) a. i siá tsi̍t-tiunn phue.
he write one-CL letter
'He wrote a letter.'
b. i ū siá tsi̍t-tiunn phue.
he have write one-CL letter
'He indeed wrote a letter.'

We argue that the difference between (3a) and (3b) lies in the degree of the speaker's affirmativeness toward the truth of a proposition. Using *ū* to present a sentence, the speaker shows a higher degree of his/her affirmativeness toward the truth of the proposition, compared to using a sentence without *ū*. The proposal that *ū* expresses a higher degree of the speaker's affirmativeness is explicitly revealed in the following conversation.

(4) A: a-bîn siá tsi̍t-pún tsu.
A-bîn write one-CL book
'A-bîn wrote a book.'
B: ū-iánn, bô-iánn?
true false
'Really?'
A: ū-lah, i ū siá tsi̍t-pún tsu!
have-Prc he have write one-CL book
'Really. He indeed wrote a book!'
B: tsiànn ê?
real Prc
'Really??'
A: i tsua̍t-tuì ū siá tsi̍t-pún tsu!
he absolutely have write one-CL book
'He absolutely did write a book!'

The conversation (4) clearly shows different degrees of the speaker's affirmativeness toward the truth of a proposition. A states that A-bin wrote a book. This proposition is asserted to be true, since it is a declarative sentence with no modal in it. B questions A's statement. A uses *ū* to show a higher degree of his/her affirmativeness than when he/she utters the first sentence. To put it differently, A intensifies the degree of affirmativeness. B questions A again. A uses *tsua̍t-tuì* 'absolutely' plus *ū* to show a much higher degree of his/her affirmativeness than when he/she utters the second sentence with *ū* only.

The reading of different degrees of the speaker's affirmativeness toward the truth of a proposition is why the literature on *ū* suggests that *ū* has an emphatic reading. [7] proposes an assertive reading for *ū* but the classification in [7] does not include an emphatic reading, while [9] includes an emphatic reading for *ū*. Since all declarative sentences are asserted, the semantic function of *ū* is not to perform assertion. Otherwise, in (4), the first utterance of A cannot be distinguished from his/her second one. Furthermore, the examples of an assertive reading in [7] are very similar to examples of an emphatic reading in [31]. Hence, we conclude that an emphatic reading and an assertive reading are two different ways to describe the same semantic behavior of *ū*. In our analysis, both the emphatic reading and the so-called assertive reading express a higher degree of the speaker's affirmativeness toward the truth of a proposition, that is, an intensification reading.

The above proposal might raise the following questions. First, in terms of the degree of speaker's commitment toward the truth of a proposition, a true proposition is the strongest one. Why can a degree adverb such as *tsuȧt-tuì* 'absolutely' or *ū* as argued above further increase the speaker's commitment?

It is accurate that uttering a declarative sentence indicates that the speaker has committed himself/herself to the truth of the proposition. However, a speaker can always use some device to emphasize. As pointed out in the related literature, *ū* can express an emphatic reading. (4) shows that there can be different degrees of emphasis on the truth of the proposition. When a speaker utters a declarative sentence without a modal or an emphatic device, e.g. the first utterance of A in (4), the speaker commits himself/herself to the truth of the proposition. In his/her second utterance, A uses *ū* to emphasize on the truth of the proposition expressed by his/her first utterance. In A's third utterance, *tsuȧt-tuì* 'absolutely' plus *ū* is used to make an emphasis stronger than his/her second one. We argue that, by different degrees of emphasis, the speaker expresses different degrees of his/her affirmativeness.

Therefore, as far as the first question goes, the speaker commits himself/herself to the truth of a proposition when the proposition is uttered as a declarative sentence without a modal or an emphatic device. Under this circumstance, there is no degree difference with respect to the speaker's commitment. However, the speaker is always allowed to show different degrees of his/her affirmativeness, by using an emphatic (intensification) device.

Second, if *ū* expresses an intensification reading, what if when *ū* occurs in an interrogative sentence? Does *ū* really express an emphatic reading? Concerning this question, we argue for two points. First, in (4), if *ū* is removed from the second utterance of A, then the conversation becomes infelicitous. This supports our argument that *ū* expresses an intensification reading. Second, one can question the affirmativeness of truth of a proposition. The sense of affirmativeness (intensification or emphasis) is weakened when affirmativeness is questioned. The same reasoning applies to the following scenario. If one asks, "Is the boy very tall?", the high degree of tallness expressed by the degree modifier *very* is weakened, because *very tall* is questioned.

The proposal that emphasis stands for a higher degree of the speaker's affirmativeness toward the truth of a proposition suggests that the semantic function of emphasis is similar to that of intensification. A typical example of intensifiers is *very* in English. In the sentence *John is very tall*, there is no doubt that John is tall but the intensifier *very* increases the degree of John's tallness. Emphasis is one type of intensification. When a speaker makes an emphasis on that a proposition is true, he/she increases the degree of his/her affirmativeness toward the truth of the proposition. That is, in a sense, emphasis is a kind of intensification.

The speaker expresses his attitude toward a proposition when (s)he intensifies the degree of his/her affirmativeness toward a proposition. Modality is often considered as the speaker's attitude toward a proposition, e.g. [23] Therefore, we propose a modal semantics for $\bar{u}$. [16, 17] proposes that the semantics of a modal expression includes a modal base, an ordering source and a modal force.

First, we propose a new ordering source: an affirmative one. An affirmative ordering source orders possible worlds according to the number of propositions affirmed to be true in a world. We use $\leq_{\text{AFFIRM}}$ to represent an affirmative ordering source:

(5) a. For all w, $w' \in$ W: $w \leq_{\text{AFFIRM}} w'$ iff, when a proposition p is affirmed to be true in w', then p is also affirmed to be true in w.
b. For all w, $w' \in$ W: $w \leq_{\text{AFFIRM}} w'$ iff [p: p is affirmed to be true in w'] $\subseteq$ [p: p is affirmed to be true in w]

(5a) and (5b) are two different ways to define an ordering source. (5a) is [24]'s style and (5b) is [16]'s. Both say the same thing: w and w' are two possible worlds. w is as good as or better than w' in terms of an affirmative ordering source if and only if the number of propositions which are affirmed to be true in w is the same as or greater than the number of propositions which are affirmed to be true in w'.

The affirmative ordering proposed here is not very different from other ordering sources proposed in [16, 17]. An ordering can be based on a variety of sources. For example, we can order possible worlds based on belief, and this is referred to as a doxastic ordering source. That is, affirmativeness is to an affirmative ordering source as belief is to a doxastic one.

Furthermore, the modal force for $\bar{u}$ is necessity, parallel to an epistemic necessity modal. An epistemic necessity modal expresses a high degree of confidence toward a stipulation, while a possibility one denotes a low degree. Since $\bar{u}$ describes a high degree of affirmativeness, we argue that its modal force is necessity.

Finally, we propose that $\bar{u}$ has an epistemic modal base, i.e. a set of possible worlds where propositions are true, according to the speaker's knowledge. Combining the modal base, ordering source and modal force together, we define the semantics of $\bar{u}$ as follows:

(6) a. $[\![\bar{u}]\!]$:
Modal base: epistemic
Ordering source: affirmative
Modal force: necessity
b. First attempt:
Suppose that $f(w)$ is an epistemic modal base and $g(w)$ is an affirmative ordering source.
$[\![\bar{u}(p)]\!] = 1$ iff $\forall u \in \cap f(w)\ \exists v \in \cap f(w)$ such that $v \leq_{g(w)} u$ and $\forall z \in \cap f(w)$: if $z \leq_{g(w)} v$, then $z \in p$.

(6b) is very similar to the definition of human necessity as in [16] and of necessity in [17], except for that the ordering source is identified as an affirmative one in the semantics of $\bar{u}$.

When an epistemic modal base is ordered by an affirmative ordering, the result is a series of worlds ordered based on the number of propositions affirmed to be true. An epistemic modal base contains worlds where propositions are true, according to the speaker's knowledge. Taking a step further, we suggest that, among the propositions which are true according to the speaker's knowledge, some are known to be affirmed to be true, while the others are simply known to be true. When an affirmative ordering source orders an epistemic modal base, the worlds where propositions are simply known to be true are ruled out because these worlds do not contain propositions known to be affirmed to be true and cannot be ordered. Let's call the result of an epistemic modal base ordered by an affirmative ordering source an 'affirmative epistemic modal base'.

Hence, in plain English, (6b) says the following. When *ū* is used to present a proposition *p*, then *ū*(*p*) means: for all possible worlds *u* in an affirmative epistemic modal base, there is another possible world *v* in the same modal base, and *v* is at least as good as *u* with respect to the affirmative ordering source. For all possible worlds *z* in the modal base, if *z* is at least as good as *v* in terms of the affirmative ordering source, then *p* is true in *z* as well.

To put it in a very simplified way, when *p* is affirmed to be true in all possible worlds equal to or better than some possible world, the degree of affirmativeness is high and *ū* is used. The idea here is parallel to epistemic necessity. Suppose that the epistemic modal base is ordered according to a doxastic ordering source. In the same simplified way, when a proposition is believed to be true in all possible worlds (in the epistemic modal base) beyond a certain world, the certainty of the proposition believed to be true is high and an epistemic necessity modal is used.

To sum up, we propose a modal semantics for *ū*. It has an epistemic modal base, an affirmative ordering and necessity as its modal force.

3.2 Event Realization

In addition to denoting intensification, *ū* has a seeming contradictory temporal behavior: it can express a completive (past) reading, a present tense reading, a characterizing reading, and a progressive reading, etc. See the examples below.

(7) a. guá ū siá tsi̍t-pún tsheh.
I have write one-CL book
'I indeed wrote a book.'

b. hue ú âng.
flower have red
'The flower is indeed red.'

c. i ū tsia̍h-hun.
he have smoke
'He (indeed) smokes.'

d. I ū lit tshuē thâu-lōo.
he have Prg look.for job
'He is indeed looking for a job.'

(7a) has a completive (past) reading. (7b) has a present tense reading. (7c) expresses a characterizing reading. And, (7d) denotes a progressive reading. (7d) contains a progressive marker *lit*, but the other three examples do not contain anything that seems to provide information to infer the temporal location of these examples. So, how does *ū* produce such a variety of temporal readings?

[1, 2] shed some light here. [1, 2] examine German, Inukititut and Russian, and find that the aspectual properties of clauses in these languages rely on the telicity of the propositions described by clauses. Basically, a telic event is preferably correlated with the perfective aspect, while an atelic situation with the imperfective aspect. This correlation is referred to as event realization: for a telic event to be realized, the perfective aspect is required, whereas for an atelic situation to be realized, the imperfective aspect is necessary. [21] applies the idea proposed in [1, 2] to the perfective *le* in Mandarin Chinese.

The proposals of [1, 2, 21] seem applicable to (7a-b). In (7a), *guá siá tsít-pún tsheh* 'I write a book' is telic and therefore *ū* gives this sentence a perfective reading, while in (7b) *hue âng* 'flower (be) red' is atelic and hence *ū* gives it an imperfective reading. As a result, (7b) gets a present-tense reading.

But, the story does not end here. There are atelic situations that do not behave like (7b) when they go with *ū*. Let's look at the following examples.

(8) a. i ū tsiảh-hun.
he have smoke
'He (indeed) smokes.'
b. i ū ūn-tōng.
he have work.out
'He (indeed) works out.'
c. i ū lit tshuē thâu-lōo.
he have Prg look.for job
'He is indeed looking for a job.'
d. i ū lit ūn-tōng.
he have Prg work.out
'He is indeed working out (as a habit).'

(8a, b) receive a characterizing reading, that is, these two sentences describe a characteristic or a habit of the subjects'. (8c) has an ongoing reading, while (8d) expresses a characterizing reading, as well. If we examine the examples in (8) more closely, we can find that all of the predicates in (8a-d) are activities and (8c, d) are activities presented by the progressive aspect marker *lit*.

So, why does a state plus *ū* get a present tense reading but activities presented by *ū* have diverse temporal readings? We argue that this difference lies in that a state can be true of an instant, while an event cannot.[3] A state can be true of an instant. *Ū* associates a state with the imperfective aspect, and this state is true of the speech time. This is how a present tense reading is derived for (8b).

Ū also associates an activity to the imperfective aspect. However, an activity cannot cumulate at an instant and hence cannot get a present tense reading. Then, what kind of temporal reading can *ū* + activity get? [3, 4, 10, 12, 13], and so on, shed some light on this question. These studies all suggest that cross-linguistically imperfective marking is used on episodic predicates to express a characterizing reading. Let's look at a very interesting pair of examples.

(9) a. i ū kóng huat-bûn.
he have speak French
'He does speak French.'
b. *i ū bat huat-bûn.
he have know French

[18] claims that *speak French* can denote either an episodic reading or a characterizing reading, while *know French* has only a characterizing reading. Taking *ū* into consideration, as illustrated in (9), we find that, in TSM, only a predicate which allows for an episodic reading can go with *ū* to express a characterizing reading. In (8a, b), *tsia̍h-hun* 'smoke' and *ūn-tōng* 'work out' can refer to individual situations and hence are compatible with an episodic reading. When they go with *ū*, just like (9a), the sentences get a characterizing reading.

As for (8c), an activity presented by the progressive aspect is also atelic, as evidenced by Imperfective Paradox. (8c) does not need event realization based on the telicity of this situation because a progressive aspect marker is explicitly present. As argued in [32], the progressive aspect marker presents an event ongoing at an instant, while the durative aspect marker describes a situation lasting over an interval. Along the same line, the TSM progressive aspect marker *lit* can be argued to present an event ongoing at instant, presumably the speech time. Therefore, (8c) gets an ongoing reading.

However, (8d) complicates the situation. (8d) also contains the progressive aspect marker, but it gets a characterizing reading. We argue for two points for the temporal interpretation of *lit* + activity. First, world knowledge plays a significant role here. Looking for a job is less likely to be a characteristic of someone than smoking/working out, though not completely impossible. It is plausible to give *looking for a job* a characterizing reading if we add an adverb of frequency such as *tiānn-tiānn* 'often':

---

[3] In fact, this is why in English a state presented by the simple present tense gets a present reading, but an event presented by the simple present tense gets a characterizing reading, e.g. [11]. See below.
(i) a. John believes that he is very smart.
b. John wakes up at six.
In (ia), *believe* is a state, which can be true of an instant, and therefore (ia) gets a present reading, where the proposition *John believe that he is very smart* is true of the speech time. On the other hand, *wake up* is dynamic and can cannot cumulate at an instant. Hence, the simple present tense cannot give it a present reading. Instead, (ib) gets a characterizing reading.

(10) i ū tiānn-tiānn lit tshuē thâu-lōo.
he have often Prg look.for job
'He is, indeed, often looking for a job.'

Second, *lit* + activity can be viewed in two different, but related, ways: it is ongoing, and it is dynamic and atelic. When *lit* + activity expresses an event ongoing at an instant, event realization is not required since *lit* indicates the progressive aspect. As a result, *ū* + *lit* + activity gets an ongoing interpretation. On the other hand, if *lit* + activity is treated as an atelic dynamic event, then according to our above discussion on *ū* + activity, which is also an atelic dynamic event, *ū* + *lit* + activity gets a characterizing reading.

There is another complication with activities. That is, some activities plus *ū* do not get a characterizing reading, but a past reading. Moreover, the same activity plus *ū* is underspecified with respect to a past reading and a characterizing reading, pending additional information, e.g. world knowledge/pragmatics, contextual information, etc. For example,

(11) a. A-bîn tsa-hng ū tsia̍h-hun.
A-bîn yesterday have smoke
'A-bîn indeed smoked yesterday.'
b. i ū mā sian-sinn.
he have scold teacher
'He scolded the/a teacher.'
c. i ū tiānn-tiānn mā sian-sinn.
he have often scold teacher
'He often scolds the/a teacher.'

In (11a), with *tsa-hng* 'yesterday', the sentence gets a past reading, rather than a characterizing reading. In (11b), although *mā sian-sinn* 'scold the/a teacher' is an activity, the sentence gets a past reading. On the other hand, in (11c), with *tiānn-tiānn* 'often', the sentence gets a characterizing reading.

Why is this so? [15] is enlightening on this seeming arbitrary phenomenon. Although an activity is generally considered as open-ended because it does not have a natural final endpoint, e.g. [28], [15] suggests that all activities come to an end. This statement is realistic because it takes energy for an activity to continue and no energy can last forever. We refer to the idea of [28] about an activity as idealistically atelic because [28] talks about the inherent property of an ideal activity, and that of [15] as realistically bound because [15] considers the issue whether a dynamic event can realistically last forever.

These two views interact with *ū* and two different temporal readings are derived: if an activity is considered (idealistically) open-ended, then *ū* correlates it with the imperfective aspect and hence a characterizing reading is derived. Nevertheless, if an activity is treated as (realistically) bounded, *ū* associates it with the perfective aspect and therefore a perfective reading is produced.

This underspecification can be resolved by means of world knowledge/pragmatics or contextual information. For example, in the real world, *tsiȧh-hun* 'smoke' and *ūn-tōng* 'work out' are more likely to be someone's habit than *mā sian-sinn* 'scole the/a teacher'. That is, the former two activities tend to be atelic, but the latter is inclined to be bounded/episodic, and hence (8b, d) get a characterizing reading, but (11b) gets a perfective reading.

Contextual information, such as other words in the sentences, can help with underspecification resolution as well. For example, in (11a), *tsa-hng* 'yesterday' provides a bounded past time. For an activity to be true of the bounded time period, it naturally comes to an end. As a result, (11a) gets a perfective reading. On the other hand, in (11c), *tiānn-tiānn* 'often' provides an unbounded time span and hence an activity easily gets a characterizing reading. Hence, (11c) gets a characterizing reading.

The above proposal of underspecification resolution by world knowledge and/or pragmatics is actually further supported by the following examples.

(12) A-tiong ū tsiȧh bí, A-hue ū tsiȧh mī.
A-tiong have eat rice A-hue have eat noodles
'A-tiong ate rice, and A-hue ate noodles.'

Some native speakers suggest that (12) gets only a past reading, but not a characterizing reading. But, what if we replace *bí* 'rice' or *mī* 'noodles' with *gû bah* 'beef' or even *káu bah* 'dog meat'? If we do the substitution, the sentence immediately gets a characterizing reading! As evidenced by this example and by the suggested substitution, the proposal that world knowledge/pragmatics plays a role is further supported!

To summarize, we argue that *ū* performs event realization, along the lines of [1, 2, 21]. When *ū* presents a telic event, the event is associated with the perfective aspect. When *ū* presents an atelic situation, the situation is correlated with the imperfective aspect. If the atelic situation is a state, a present tense reading is derived because a state can be true of an instant, including the speech time. If the atelic situation is an activity, either a characterizing reading or a past reading is derived because an activity can be regarded either as idealistically atelic or realistically bound. If the atelic situation is *lit* + activity, either an ongoing reading or a characterizing reading is yielded because *lit* + activity can be viewed as an ongoing event or an atelic dynamic event. In other words, when the situation in *ū* + situation is an activity or *lit* + activity, the sentence is temporally underspecified. This underspecification is resolved by world knowledge/pragmatics.

Before concluding this section, we would like to discuss a possible alternative analysis to *ū* when *ū* goes with a state. Some might suggest that *ū* has a function similar to a degree modifier, such as *tsiok* 'very', based on the following examples.

(13) a. *hue âng.
flower red
b. hue ū âng.
flower have red
'The flower is indeed red.'
c. hue tsiok âng.
flower very red
'The flower is red.'
d. huā *(hěn) hóng. (Mandarin Chinese data)
flower *(very) red
'The flower is red.'

In (13), *ū* seems to behave parallel to degree modifier *tsiok* 'very' when it goes with an adjective. An adjective cannot stand alone in a sentence, unless it goes with *ū* or a degree modifier. Chinese adjectives behave the same in that a degree modifier must appear with an adjective, as shown in (13d). [22] discusses Chinese examples of this type and proposes that *hěn* 'very' in Chinese is the overt realization of *pos*, the positive morpheme discussed in [14]. One might suggest that *ū* is also an overt realization of *pos* in TSM since it is also required in (13b), just like *tsiok* 'very' in (13c). However, this suggestion is not accurate. *Ū* in examples such as (13b) does not describe the degree of the adjective. See the example below.

(14) hue ū âng, tsí-sī bô tsin âng.
flower have red just not very red
'The flower is indeed red. It's just not very red.'

As (14) shows, *ū* does not specify that the degree of *redness* is greater than some standard. Then, what does *ū* do here, in addition to expressing the speaker's higher degree of affirmativeness? [6] has a very interesting idea about degree modification in Chinese. He proposes that degree modifier *hěn* 'very' in Chinese serves to anchor an adjective on the timeline. *Ū* performs event realization and associates a state with the imperfective aspect so that a temporal reading can be decided for the sentence. This is why *ū* is obligatory in (13b). Without *ū*, the adjective is not aspectually realized and hence not temporally anchored. A degree modifier, such as *tsiok* 'very', performs tense anchoring, but it cannot intensify the affirmativeness toward the truth of a proposition.

This proposal that *ū* performs event realization (and therefore can anchor a situation temporally) might attract a very interesting question: if temporal anchoring is involved in *ū* + state, why can temporal phrases such as *tsit-má* 'now' not serve the same purpose to make *tsit-má hue âng* 'now flower(s) red' grammatical? It is plausible that temporal phrases do not perform temporal anchoring at all. Not just in TSM, temporal phrases do not conduct temporal anchoring in Mandarin Chinese as well. If the analysis is on the right track that *hěn* 'very' performs temporal anchoring in Mandarin Chinese, then the fact that *xiànzài huā hōng* 'now flower(s) red' is not good suggests that temporal phrases cannot execute temporal anchoring.

Then, what is the function of temporal phrases? While temporal phrases do not perform temporal anchoring, they may serve as a Topic Time (TT) in a sentence, at least in Mandarin Chinese and TSM. Event realization relates a situation to a TT according to the telicity of the situation, based on [1, 2, 21]. If a sentence contains a state and a temporal phrase, but does not have an event realization operator, then we cannot decide how the state is related to the TT. This might be the reason why *tsit-má hue âng* 'now flower(s) red' in TSM and *xiànzài huā hōng* 'now flower(s) red' in Mandarin Chinese are not good.

To sum up, in this section, we argue that *ū* executes event realization in the sense of [1, 2, 21]. Going with a telic event, *ū* associates the event with the perfective aspect and a sentence receives a completive (past) reading. Presenting an atelic situation, *ū* correlates the situation with the imperfective aspect. If the atelic situation is a state, a present tense reading is derived because a state can be true of an instant, including the speech time. If the atelic situation is an activity, either a characterizing reading or a past reading is derived because an activity can be regarded either as idealistically atelic or realistically bound. If the atelic situation is *lit* + activity, either an ongoing reading or a characterizing reading is yielded because *lit* + activity can be viewed as an ongoing event or an atelic, dynamic event. That is, when the situation in *ū* + situation is an activity or *lit* + activity, the sentence is semantically underspecified. This underspecification can be resolved by world knowledge/pragmatics.

3.3 A Model-Aspectual Semantics

Incorporating the above discussions on intensification and on event realization of *ū*, we propose *ū* has the following semantics:

(15) Final attempt:
Suppose that $f(w)$ is an epistemic modal base and $g(w)$ is an affirmative ordering source.
$[\![\bar{u}(p)]\!] = 1$ iff $\forall u \in \cap f(w)$, $\exists v \in \cap f(w)$ such that $v \leq_{g(w)} u$ and $\forall z \in \cap f(w)$:
if $z \leq_{g(w)} v$, then $z \in \mathscr{R}(p)$.

(15) is identical to (6b), except for the final line. Instead of the proposition *p* presented by *ū* being true in *z*, *ū* specifies that the proposition *p* must undergo event realization. We use $\mathscr{R}$ to represent the event realization operator. The semantic function of $\mathscr{R}$ is as discussed in Sect. 3.2.

4 Conclusion

In this paper, we argue that *ū* in *ū* + situation in TSM has a modal-aspectual semantics. Its modal semantics is as follows. The modal base is an epistemic one, where propositions are true or are affirmed to be true, according to the speaker's knowledge. The ordering source is affirmative. An affirmative ordering source orders possible worlds according to the number of propositions affirmed to be true in a world. Its modal force is necessity. This modal semantics is where the emphatic (assertive) reading of *ū* comes from.

Furthermore, *ū* performs event realization. *Ū* associates a telic event with the perfective aspect and the sentence receives a completive (past) reading. *Ū* connects an atelic situation to the imperfective aspect, and the temporal reading of such a sentence depends on the dynamicity of the predicate. If the main predicate is a state, a present tense reading is produced, because a state can be true of an instant, including the speech time. On the other hand, when the main predicate is dynamic, i.e. an activity, the sentence gets either a characterizing reading or a past reading, because an activity is treated either as idealistically atelic or realistically bound. Moreover, an activity presented by the progressive aspect marker *lit* can be regarded as an ongoing event or an atelic, dynamic one. Such a sentence gets an ongoing reading or a characterizing reading. World knowledge and/or pragmatics help to identify an appropriate reading.

References

1. Bohnemeyer, J., Swift, M.: Default aspect: the semantic interaction of aspectual viewpoint and telicity. In: Proceedings of Perspectives on Aspect. Institute of Linguistics, Utrecht (2001)
2. Bohnemeyer, J., Swift, M.: Event realization and default aspect. Linguist. Philos. **27**(3), 263–269 (2004)
3. Bybee, J., Dahl, Ö.: The creation of tense and aspect systems in the languages of the world. Stud. Lang. **13**, 51–103 (1989)
4. Bybee, J., Perkins, R., Pagliuca, W.: The Evolution of Grammar: Tense, Aspect and Modality in the Languages of the World. University of Chicago, Chicago (1994)
5. Chen, Q.-R., Wang, J.-H.: On the multifunctionality of *you* in Southern Chinese dialects. Yǔyán jiāxué yǔ yánjì (Teaching and Research of Language) **2010**(4), 47–55 (2010)
6. Chen, Y.-L.: Degree modification and tense anchoring in Mandarin. In: Online Proceedings of NACCL22 & IACL18, pp. 117–129. Ohio State University, Columbus (2010)
7. Cheng, R.L.: Taiwanese Ū and Mandarin YOU. In: Taiwanese and Mandarin Structures and Their Development Trends in Taiwan, Temporal and Spatial Relations, Questions and Negatives in Taiwanese and Mandarin, Yuan-Liu, Taipei, vol. III, pp. 191–230 (1997a [1981])
8. Cheng, R. L.: Tense interpretation of four Taiwanese modal verbs. In: Taiwanese and Mandarin Structures and Their Development Trends in Taiwan, Temporal and Spatial Relations, Questions and Negatives in Taiwanese and Mandarin, Yuan-Liu, Taipei, vol. III, pp. 19–36 (1997b [1978])
9. Cheng, R.L.: Táiyǔ hé huáyǔ de shíduàn-shítài xìtǒng (the phase of Taiwanese and Mandarin Chinese: Tense and Aspect). In: Taiwanese and Mandarin Structures and Their Development Trends in Taiwan, Temporal and Spatial Relations, Questions and Negatives in Taiwanese and Mandarin, Yuan-Liu, Taipei, vol. III, pp. 73–161 (1997c [1992])
10. Comrie, B.: Aspect: An Introduction to the Study of Verbal Aspect and Related Problems. Cambridge University Press, Cambridge (1976)
11. Comrie, B.: Tense. Cambridge University Press, Cambridge (1985)
12. Deo, A.: Tense and aspect in Indo-Aryan languages: variation and diachrony. Ph.d. Dissertation. Stanford University, Stanford (2006)

13. Deo, A.: Temporal genericity and the contribution of imperfective marking. In: Proceedings of the 10th Symposium on Logic and Language, pp. 109–118. Research Institute for Linguistics, Hungarian Academy of Sciences and Theoretical Linguistics Program, Eöströs Loránd University, Budapest (2009)
14. Kennedy, C.: Vagueness and grammar: the semantics of relative and absolute gradable adjectives. Linguist. Philos. **30**(1), 1–45 (2007)
15. Klein, W., Li, P., Hendriks, H.: Aspect and assertion in Mandarin Chinese. Nat. Lang. Linguist. Theory. **18**(4), 723–770 (2000)
16. Kratzer, A.: The notional category of modality. In: Eikmeyer, H., Reiser, H. (eds.) Words, Worlds and Context, pp. 38–74. Walter de Cruyter, Berlin (1981)
17. Kratzer, A.: Modality. In: von Stechow, A., Wunderlich, D. (eds.) Semantics: An International Handbook of Contemporary Research, pp. 639–650. de Gruyter, Berlin (1991)
18. Krifka, M., Pelletier, F.J., Carlson, G.N., ter Meulen, A., Chierchia, G., Link, G.: Genericity: an introduction. In: Carlson, G.N., Pelletier, F.J. (eds.) The Generic Book, pp. 1–124. University of Chicago, Chicago (1995)
19. Li, R.: Mǐnnánhuà 'ū' hé 'bô' (ū and bô in Southern Min). Fújiàn Shīfàn Dàxué Xuébào (J. Fujian Normal University) **2**, 76–83 (1986)
20. Lien, C.: Middles in Taiwanese Southern Min: the interface of lexical meaning and event structure. Lingua **120**, 1273–1287 (2009)
21. Lin, J.-W.: Temporal reference in Mandarin Chinese. J. East Asian Linguist. **12**, 259–311 (2003)
22. Liu, C.-S.L.: The positive morpheme in Chinese and the adjectival structure. Lingua **120**, 1010–1056 (2010)
23. Marques, R.: On the selection of mood in complement clauses. In: Hogeweg, L., de Hoop, H., Malchukov, A. (eds.) Cross-linguistic Semantics of Tense, Aspect and Modality. John Benjamins, London (2009)
24. Portner, P.: Modality. Cambridge University Press, Cambridge (2009)
25. Searle, J.R.: A taxonomy of illocutionary acts. In: Grunderson, K. (eds.) Minnesota Studies in the Philosophy of Science: Language, Mind and Knowledge, vol. 9, pp. 344–369 (1975)
26. Searle, J.R.: A classification of illocutionary acts. Lang. Soc. **5**(1), 1–23 (1976)
27. Searle, J.R., Vanderveken, D.: Speech acts and illocutionary logic. In: Vanderveken, D. (ed.) Logic, Thought and Action, pp. 109–132. Springer, The Netherlands (2005 [1985])
28. Smith, C.: The Parameter of Aspect, 2nd edn. Kluwer Academic, Dordrecht (1997)
29. Tsai, W.-T.D.: *You* 'have' in Taiwan Mandarin and dialects—on the social and historical aspects of grammatical theories. Tsinghua J. Chin. Stud. **32**(2), 495–528 (2002)
30. Tsao, F.-F.: On three aspect-related morpheme *'U', '∅', 'A'* in Taiwanese Minnan. Tsinghua J. Chin. Stud. **28**(3), 299–334 (1998)
31. Tsao, F.-F., Cheng, Y.: Tán mǐnnányǔ 'ū' de wǔ zhǒng yòngfǎ (On the five usages of *ū* in Southern Min). Zhōngguó yǔwén yánjiù (Studies on Chinese Languages) **11**, 155–167 (1995)
32. Wu, J.-S.: Semantic difference between the two imperfective markers in Mandarin and its implications on temporal relations. J. Chin. Linguist. **35**(2), 372–398 (2007)

Right Dislocation in Cantonese: An Emotion-Intensifying Device

Sophia Yat Mei Lee and Christy Choi Ting Lai(✉)

Department of Chinese and Bilingual Studies,
The Hong Kong Polytechnic University, Kowloon, Hong Kong
ym.lee@polyu.edu.hk, laichristy@gmail.com

Abstract. This paper explores the emotive function of Cantonese right dislocation based on language samples in a large spoken Cantonese database. Right dislocation is found to be highly associated with emotion expressions. In particular, explicit emotion words always appear in the first part of right dislocation. We argue that right dislocation is used as a focus marking device for highlighting emotion information and intensifying emotions. Therefore, right dislocation can serve as one of the linguistic cues for identifying implicit emotions.

Keywords: Right dislocation · Emotion expression · Cantonese

1 Introduction

This paper investigates the emotive function of right dislocation (RD), a non-canonical word order, in Cantonese spoken discourse. We argue that RD is frequently used as a linguistic device by speakers to highlight emotion information.

RD refers to the sentence construction in which some syntactic components are dislocated from the sentence beginning or internal position to the end of the sentence. Cantonese is known for its flexibility in terms of the syntactic categories of dislocated elements, which may include nouns, verbs, adverbs, connectives, modals and adverbial clauses [2–4, 15]. An example of Cantonese RD is given below:

(1) 好失望呀,, 我覺得
'I am very disappointed'

Conversational utterances are often found in which some elements are dislocated to the utterance final position after the sentence final particle (SFP). This phenomenon has been studied by a number of researchers from different perspectives, i.e. syntactic and grammatical constraints [2, 3, 9]; pragmatic functions [22]; information structure [7, 12] and conversation analysis [15]. Research to date has generally lent support to the claim that RD is a focus marking device motivated by time pressure in conversation. The emotive function of RD has been observed and mentioned briefly in the literature [4, 7]. However, to the best of our knowledge, there is no work focusing on the emotive function of RD yet. This paper aims to address the following questions:

J.-F. Hong et al. (Eds.): CLSW 2018, LNAI 11173, pp. 423–430, 2018.
https://doi.org/10.1007/978-3-030-04015-4_35

(1) How frequently is RD associated with emotion expression in Cantonese?
(2) What types of emotion are more commonly expressed through RD?
(3) How is RD used to express emotions?

Section 2 gives an overview of the previous studies in relation to emotion expression and RD in different languages. Section 3 describes the methodology of the present work including the database where the speech sample is drawn. Section 4 presents the analysis and results. Section 5 discusses how RD is used to intensify emotions with examples. Section 6 concludes the paper.

2 Related Work

RD was initially proposed by Chao [1] as "afterthought", referring to the unplanned content that was added to a completed sentence. Packard [20] has argued that it is actually a left dislocation in which the focus information in the sentence has undergone a left dislocation movement to the sentence initial position. Other terms for this construction include "transposition" [13], "dislocation" [12], "focus-fronting" [16, 22], and "incremental sentences" [14, 15]. Liang [12], Zhang and Fang [22] suggested that RD mainly occurred in conversation. Due to the lack of planning time in conversational communication, speakers tend to place the most important information in the initial position of a sentence, and then fill in the less important information at the end. A conversation analytic account was adopted in Luke [15]. Luke observed that RD performs a variety of discourse functions, such as intensification, emphasis, clarification etc. RD in monologues was investigated by Lai [7]. The study suggested that the use of RD is influenced by genre type, information pressure and speakers' assumption of shared knowledge. It was also observed in the study that RD is often used by Cantonese speakers to express emotions.

The affective function of RD in Mandarin Chinese was first discussed in Guo [4]. Based on children's speech data, the study examined RD utterances with dislocated noun phrases. Three main types of RD were classified: (i) zero anaphoric, (ii) elaborations, and (iii) reduplications. The zero anaphoric and elaborative types of RD were found to be mainly used for statement purposes, while reduplications mainly served the functions of questioning, ridiculing and reprimanding. It was proposed that Mandarin RD is a grammaticalized device to serve affective function, in particular, commonly being used to express the speaker's negative feelings.

Similar observations were made in Japanese by Ono [18]. Despite the rigidity of SOV constituent order in Japanese, RD with non-predicate final is commonly found in conversational discourse. Ono and Suzuki [19] argued that RD is a "planned" production rather than a repair device since there is no prosodic break between the main clause and the dislocated elements in most RDs. An inspection on the RDs revealed that adjectives and nouns most frequently appear in the main clause of RDs, and they often directly express emotion. Similar to Mandarin Chinese, the results suggested that Japanese RD is grammaticalized to express the speaker's emotion. Emotion is a driving force in the creation of RD in Japanese.

The affective function of Cantonese RDs was statistically examined in Lai et al. [6]. The study investigated the use of RDs in different genres in relation to emotion expression. Although the association between the two was not statistically significant, the result showed that RD is used more frequently when a speaker talks about an emotional topic (i.e. personal recount) than an emotion-neutral topic (i.e. procedural description). It is also worth noting that the "emotion expression" in the study only refers to explicit emotion whereas emotion words, such as "happy", "sad", were explicitly used. However, emotion may be conveyed implicitly without saying emotion words. This paper aims to investigate both explicit and implicit emotions expressed in Cantonese RDs.

3 Methodology

3.1 Corpus Data

The data of this study were drawn from a spoken Cantonese database recently made available in the public domain, i.e. Cantonese AphasiaBank [5]. Cantonese AphasiaBank contains speech samples elicited from various narrative tasks of native speakers of Cantonese including 144 neurologically unimpaired male and female native Cantonese speakers of varied ages and education levels. Participants were asked to (1) narrate an important event in their life; (2) tell two highly familiar stories—"The Hare and the Tortoise" and "The Boy who Cried Wolf"—with picture cues; (3) describe three pictures and a photo; and (4) describe the procedure of making a ham and egg sandwich. There was no bias on the emotion types of the topics. However, the contents in task (1) and (2) were believed to be more emotional compared to task (3) and (4). The language samples were orthographically transcribed with part-of-speech (POS) annotation. The transcriptions are formatted using the Codes for the Human Analysis of Transcripts (CHAT) [17]. The database contains about 155,500 words in all the transcripts, with 38 different word types (POS).

3.2 Identification of RD

Instances of RD were identified from the database manually. The present study follows criteria for identifying RD mentioned in Cheung [2] and Liang [12]. Structurally, RD takes the form of [α (SFP), β], where α and β refer to components of a clause. We will refer to α as the host; and β as the tail in this paper. If there is a sentence final particle (SFP), it must appear between the host and tail. SFP is not obligatory although it is commonly found in RD [12]. Semantically, the tail should be able to form a complete clause with the host when the clause is in a canonical word order. Phonetically, there is no noticeable pause between the main clause and the dislocated element, and the dislocated element is always said in a fast tempo [12].

3.3 Emotion Annotation

The unit for emotion analysis includes five clauses: the two clauses preceding the RD, the RD clause, and the two clauses following the RD. For each RD unit, with reference to the Chinese emotion taxonomy proposed by Lee [10], we analyze if there is emotion. Following Lee [10], five basic emotions are annotated, namely *happiness, sadness, fear, anger*, and *surprise*. If there is a presence of emotion, we annotate whether it is explicit or implicit emotion. Explicit emotion refers to the presence of emotion-related information denoted by emotion keywords. Implicit emotion refers to the emotion-related information that requires inference or connotation instead of being conveyed by emotion keywords [11]. Emotion keywords include three types: emotion words, emotion related words and emotion-laden words. Following Pavlenko [21], emotion words are the words that directly refer to particular affective states ('happy', 'angry') or process ('to worry', 'to rage'), and function to either describe ('she is sad') or express them ('I feel sad'). Emotion-related words ("tears", "tantrum", "to scream") are words that describe behaviors related to particular emotions without naming the actual emotions. Emotion-laden words are words that do not refer to emotions directly but instead express ("jerk", "loser") or elicit emotions from the speakers ("cancer", "malignancy"). The position of emotion keywords is also examined.

4 Data Analysis

A total of 204 instances of RD were identified from the database. Among all the RDs, 132 tokens (64.7%) are found to convey emotions. The total number of emotions identified is 142, given some RDs involved more than one emotion. 90 emotions are expressed explicitly, which means there are emotion words, emotion related or emotion-laden words; while 52 emotions are expressed implicitly. In terms of emotion types, *sadness* occurred most frequently, followed by *happiness, anger*, and *surprise*, the least frequently occurring is being *fear*. Table 1 shows the distribution of explicit and implicit emotions.

We also examined the position where the emotions are shown. For explicit emotions, the majority of emotion keywords (79%) are found inside the RD utterance. The remaining are shown to evenly precede and follow the RD utterance. In a RD, over 93% (66 instances) of emotion keywords appear in the first part of RD (host) as in (2).

Table 1. Distribution of explicit and implicit emotions

Emotions	Frequency		Total no. of emotion
Sadness	Explicit	Implicit	
Happiness	37	19	56 (39%)
Anger	23	9	32 (23%)
Surprise	17	9	26 (18%)
Fear	4	12	16 (11%)
Total	9	3	12 (8%)

(2) 係最感動最開心嘅,, 我覺得
'I feel it is the most touching and happiest (event).'

The distribution of implicit emotions is more spread out. Although RD still contains the highest frequency (33%) of implicit emotions, the utterances before and after RD also involve a considerable amount of emotion expression. Interestingly, the data show that speakers generally use more utterances to convey implicit emotion than explicit emotion. 23% of implicit emotions take more than one utterance to express, as in example (3), which convey sadness throughout the clauses by describing a series of thoughts. In (4), the speaker expresses surprise and happiness implicitly by recalling a surprising birthday celebration event.

唔想出聲, 唔想出街
(3) 好攰,, 成日都會
咩都無動力嘅
'Do not want to make a sound or go out, (I am) always feeling tired, do not want to speak, no intention to (do) anything.'
突然拎個蛋糕出嚟同我慶祝
(4) 即係係估唔到嘅,, 完全
仲同我一齊切蛋糕
'Suddenly (he) took out a cake to celebrate with me. I didn't expect that at all. He even cut the cake with me' (Table 2).

Table 2. Distribution of emotions in positions

Positions	Frequency	
	Explicit	Implicit
Pre-RD	7 (8%)	14 (27%)
Post-RD	6 (7%)	9 (17%)
RD [Host] [Tail]	71 (79%) [66] [5]	17 (33%) [13] [4]
More than one utterance	6 (7%)	12 (23%)
Total	90	52

Regarding the linguistic structure of RD, we identified some verbs and adjectives that often appeared in the host; and they are closely connected with emotions, as shown in Table 3.

For the tail, the slot is mostly occupied by pronoun, demonstrative, connective, or adverb elements (Table 4).

Table 3. Words with emotion in RD host

Emotions	Words appeared in RD Host
Happiness	開心, 喜悅, 好運, 笑, 舒服, 好彩, 驕傲, 感動, 感激, 感恩, 興奮, 激動
Sadness	心痛, 後悔, 慘, 無助, 難過, 喊,傷心, 失望, 尷尬, 狼狽 , 沮喪
Anger	抵死, 麻煩, 反感, 憤怒, 嬲, 搞錯, 深深不忿, 後悔, 激氣
Fear	弊, 死 , 慘 , 驚, 虛脫, 冷汗, 震
Surprise	點知/點不知 , 嘩/哇, 咦, 吖, 原來, 特別, 好彩, 估唔到, 意料之外, 驚喜

Table 4. Words in RD tail

	Words appeared in RD Tail
Pronoun	我, 佢
Demonstrative	嗰日, 哩次
Connective	所以, 但係, 不過
Adverb	梗係, 真係, 已經

5 Discussion

The quantitative results in this study have shown that RD is frequently used together with emotion keywords. These emotion keywords usually appear in the host, which is an assumed position for placing the focus or important information [7, 12]. We propose that RD is a linguistic device to highlight and intensify emotion information. This feature of RD is even more prominent when explicit emotion is conveyed. In canonical word order, emotion words usually appear in the post-verbal position like in (5).

From the information structure perspective, this type of clause is categorized as 'sentence-focused' or 'predicate-focused' [8]. Sentence-focused refers to a construction where both subject and predicate are in focus; predicate-focused usually refers to the topic-comment construction in which the predicate is in focus. If the speaker only wants to focus on certain emotion, in addition to vocally stressing on the element, he/she can re-order the constituent to achieve this purpose. By pre-posing the emotion words in the utterance initial position as in (6), the clause is a marked focus construction in which the host receives focus and the emotion information is thus highlighted. (6) gives an impression that the emotion is intense and the speaker is eager to express it out. Comparing to (5), the emotion in (6) is being intensified when it occupied the focus position. The pattern of (6) as "degree adverb + emotion word + (SFP), subject + verb" is commonly observed in the data. This might suggest that RD has been conventionalized as an emotion intensification device. It may also explain the high frequency of co-occurrence of RD and emotion words.

(5) 我覺得好開心呀
'I feel very happy'
(6) 好開心呀,, 我覺得
'I feel very happy'

The emotion-highlighting function of RD is less relevant to implicit emotion which is shown in two aspects: (1) a relatively small proportion of implicit emotion (37%) was detected in RDs; (2) it is scattered in several clauses instead of solely showing in RD. The first phenomena may be due to the lack of research on this topic which has restricted an accurate detection of implicit emotions [11]. However, RD still has a role in expressing implicit emotions. For instance, it is observed that the speaker may highlight the event that causes emotion in RD as in (7), which describes a traffic incident in which *fear* is implicitly noted.

(7) 嗰啲燈啱啱又轉埋
趴喺度,, 我起唔切身
架巴士會撞死我㗎嘞,, 已經諗住
應該無辦法喇

'The (traffic) light has just turned, I was still lying on my stomach and couldn't get up. I thought the bus would run over me. There is no way out.'

Two RD clauses are used in (7): 趴喺度 'I was still lying on my stomach' describes a dangerous situation; and 架巴士會撞死我㗎嘞 'the bus will run over me'. Both can be seen as the cause of *fear*. By dislocating the cause of emotion into the focus position, the implicit *fear* emotion is being intensified and highlighted. Implicit emotion has always been difficult to detect since there is no explicit cue. With the findings of the present work that right dislocation is highly collocated with emotion, right dislocation can serve as one of the linguistic cues for identifying implicit emotions.

6 Conclusion

The affective function of RD has been observed in the literature. This study is the first to examine how emotions are expressed in naturally-occurring speech samples. We propose that RD is used to highlight and intensify emotion information as a focus marking device. The host is the favorite position of Cantonese speakers to express explicit emotions. The occurrence of RD can also serve as one of the linguistic cues for implicit emotion identification. The findings in this study enhance the current understanding of linguistic representation of emotion expressions, with a focus on word order in particular.

Acknowledgments. This work is supported by a General Research Fund (GRF) project sponsored by the Research Grants Council (Project No. B-Q50Z) and a PolyU Faculty Research Grant (Project No. 1-ZEVK).

References

1. Chao, Y.R.: A Grammar of Spoken Chinese. University of California Press, Berkeley (1968)
2. Cheung, Y.L.: A study of right dislocation in Cantonese. Unpublished M.Phil. thesis, The Chinese University of Hong Kong, Hong Kong (1997)
3. Cheung, Y.L.: Dislocation focus construction in Chinese. J. East Asian Linguist. **18**, 197–232 (2009)
4. Guo, J.: From information to emotion: the affective function of right-dislocation in Mandarin Chinese. J. Pragmat. **31**(9), 1103–1128 (1999)
5. Kong, A.P.-H., Law, S.-P., Lee, A.: Toward a multi-modal and multi-level analysis of Chinese aphasic discourse. A grant funded by the National Institutes of Health, USA (2010)
6. Lai, C.T., Law, S.P., Kong, A.P.H.: A quantitative study of right dislocation in Cantonese spoken discourse. Lang. Speech **60**(4), 633–642 (2017)
7. Lai, C.T.: A quantitative study of information structure and right dislocation in Cantonese spoken discourse. M.Phil Thesis, The University of Hong Kong (2015)
8. Lambrecht, K.: Information Structure and Sentence Form: Topic, Focus, and the Mental Representations of Discourse Referents. Cambridge University Press, Cambridge (1996)
9. Law, A.: Right dislocation in Cantonese as a focus-marking device. UCL Working Papers in Linguistics vol. 15, pp. 243–275 (2003)
10. Lee, S.Y.M.: A linguistic approach to emotion detection and classification. Dissertation, The Hong Kong Polytechnic University (2010)
11. Lee, S.Y.M.: A linguistic analysis of implicit emotions. In: Lu, Q., Gao, H. (eds.) Chinese Lexical Semantics. LNCS (LNAI), vol. 9332, pp. 185–194. Springer, Cham (2015). https://doi.org/10.1007/978-3-319-27194-1_19
12. Liang, Y.: Dislocation in Cantonese: sentence form, information structure, and discourse function. Unpublished doctoral dissertation, University of Hong Kong, Hong Kong (2002)
13. Lu, J.: 漢語口語句法裡的易位現象 [The phenomenon of inversion (of sentence parts) in syntax of spoken Chinese]. Zhongguo yuwen (Chin. Lang. Writ.) **154**, 28–41 (1980)
14. Luke, K.K.: 說延伸句 [On incremental sentences]. In: Yuwen, Z. (ed.) Academic Papers for Celebrating the 50th Anniversary of Zhongguo yuwen (Chinese Language and Writing), pp. 39–48. The Commercial Press, Beijing (2004)
15. Luke, K.K.: Dislocation or afterthought? A conversation analytic account of incremental sentences in Chinese. Discourse Processes. **49**(3–4), 338–365 (2012)
16. Luke, K.K., Zhang, W.: Retrospective turn continuations in Mandarin Chinese conversation. Pragmat. Q. Publ. Int. Pragmat. Assoc. **17**(4), 605–636 (2007)
17. MacWhinney, B.: The CHILDES Project: Tools for Analyzing Talk. Lawrence Erlbaum Associates, Mahwah (2000)
18. Ono, T.: An emotively motivated post-predicate constituent order in a 'strict predicate final' language. In: Suzuki, S. (ed.) Emotive Communication in Japanese, pp. 139–154. John Benjamins, Amsterdam (2006)
19. Ono, T., Suzuki, R.: Word order variability in Japanese conversation: motivations and grammaticization. Text Interdiscip. J. Study Discourse **12**(3), 429–446 (1992)
20. Packard, J.L.: A left-dislocation analysis of 'afterthought' sentences in Peking Mandarin. J. Chin. Lang. Teach. Assoc. **21**(3), 1–12 (1986)
21. Pavlenko, A.: Emotion and emotion-laden words in the bilingual lexicon. Biling. Lang. Cogn. **11**(2), 147–164 (2008)
22. Zhang, B., Fang, M.:《漢語功能語法研究》[Studies in Chinese Functional Grammar]. Jiangxi Education Publishing House, Nanchang (1996)

The Constructional Form of Meaning and the Difficulty Level of Definition in Chinese Compound Words

Enxu Wang[1(✉)] and Yulin Yuan[2]

[1] International School of Education and Exchange, Jinan University, No. 336 Nanxinzhuang West Road, Shizhong District, Jinan 250022, China
Wangbush000@126.com

[2] Department of Chinese Language and Literature, Peking University, No. 5 Yiheyuan Road, Haidian District, Beijing 100871, China
yuanyl@pku.edu.cn

Abstract. Most of the meanings of Chinese compound words are opaque. How to define the meaning of compound words, there is no good methods. With the predication and the undergraded predication theory, this paper analyzes the semantic construction of compound words and summarizes more than 20 semantic constructional forms. On this basis, we further analyzes the definition difficulty of compound words and divides it into four levels: level 0 means the meaning is easiest to define; level 1 is easier to define; level 2 is difficult to define; and level 3 is the most difficult to define. We hope this paper can contribute to solve the definition problem of Chinese compound words.

Keywords: Compound words · Constructional form of meaning
Definition difficulty

1 Introduction

Most of the meanings of Chinese compound words are opaque. How to define the meaning of compound words, there is no good methods. Scholars noticed that the construction of Chinese compound words is the same as the sentence structure basically [1–6]. Therefore, we can analyze the construction of compound words with reference to sentence structure. According to reference [7: 86], in Chinese compound words, the number of "pianzheng(modifier-center)" (including attribute-centered and adverbial-centered) structure is the largest, the "zhuwei(subject-predicate)" structure and "shubu (predicate - complement)" structure is the second, and the "lianhe(coordinate)" structure and "dongbin(verb-object)" structure is the least. The concrete data are as follows:

(1) The structural form of disyllabic compound words
  a1. "dingzhong(attribute-centered)" structure(44.9%): nainiu(milking cow), ruzhu (porket), hushi(nurse), lingtu(territory), jikan(quarterly), chaguan(tea house), tonglv(verdigris), kongjun(air force)…
  a2. "zhuangzhong(adverbial-centered)" structure(10.9%): jiafang(visit to the parents of schoolchildren), susuan(calculate quickly), nushi(glare at), banshu

J.-F. Hong et al. (Eds.): CLSW 2018, LNAI 11173, pp. 431–444, 2018.
https://doi.org/10.1007/978-3-030-04015-4_36

(write on a blackboard), yunji(gather), zuodeng(sit back and wait), ciliao(-magnetic therapy), daoli(do a handstand), xiuxiang(don't think about)…

b. "lianhe(coordinate)" structure(21.8%): jiaoxue(teaching and studying), chengsong(praise), tingxie(dictation), qifei(take off), anwei(comfort), haowu (likes and dislikes), enyuan(feeling of gratitude or resentment), chunchi(labial and teeth), heshan(rivers and mountains), tiandi(sky and land)…
c. "dongbin(verb-object)" structure(19%): xiche(clean cars), xiahai(go to sea), tucun(strive for survival), xianliang(limit the quantity of), chuangyou(create excellence), yiwei(translocation), dongshen(set out), guanjia(keep the house), jiangong(make great contributions), huxi(kneecap)…
d. "shubu(predicate-complement)" structure (2.4%): lengque(cool down), tigao (raise), renqing(see clearly), ganlie(crack), weisuo(recoil), songdong(come loose), xunfu(tame), tuifan(overturn), quanxiang(induce someone to surrender), tiaoyun(mix well)…
e. "zhuwei(subject-predicate)" structure (1%): xingji(short-tempered), guzhe (fracture), lianhong(blush), xintiao(palpitate), renwei(man-made), richu(sunrise), dizhen(earthquake), qiduan(shortness of breath), weiyi(shift), zhibian (qualitative change), renjun(per capita)…

The compound words of the same structure often have the same constructional form of meaning. Generally speaking, the compound words of "dingzhong(attribute-centered)" structure has the same constructional form, which is "+ de(of) +"; and the "zhuangzhong(adverbial-centered)" structure has the same constructional form, which is "zhuang(adverbial) + (de(of)) + zhong(center)". However, knowing these is neither enough to define the meaning of the compound words nor to distinguish the subtle semantic differences between the different compound words within the same structure. For example, "nainiu" and "niunai" have the same structure, which is "dingzhong (attribute-centered)" structure, and the same constructional form of meaning, which is "+ de(of) +", but their meanings are different. The former is "channai(produce milk) + de(of) + muniu(cow)"; the latter is "muniu(cow) + chan(produce) + de(of) + nai(milk)". In order to distinguish the subtle semantic differences among the different compound words, it is necessary to refine the subordinate classification of the constructional form of meaning and let each compound word have a corresponding constructional form of meaning and definitional mode.

2 The Constructional Form of Meaning in Compound Words

Analyzing the semantic structure of sentences, it usually starts with predicate structure. A predicate structure may contain only predicates and arguments, such as "dizhen le(it has earthquaked)", "muniu xia duzi(the cow produces calf)" or "Xiao Zhang song Xiao Li yi ben shu(Xiao Zhang sends Xiao Li a book)". Sometimes it may also contain a predicate structure. Making a predicate structure included in another predicate structure, there are two ways: one is to downgrade the status of predicate structure and make it become an (subject /object) argument. Such as "the Jin Dynasty persuades Yue Fei to surrender". In this sentence, "(that) Yue Fei surrender" is a downgraded predicate structure which acts as the object argument of the predicate structure "the Jin Dynasty persuades…". The other way is to further downgrade the status of predicate structure and make it become a feature which acts as the syntactic attribute, adverbial or complement component. Such as "they marry in a church", in this sentence, "in the church" is a predicate structure which acts as the syntactic adverbial component of "marry" [8].

Analyzing the construction of word meaning, it can also start with predicate structure. Using the predicate structure or downgraded predication, reference 5 analyzed the semantic structure of compound words. This paper will analyze its semantic constructional form. According to our investigation, there are 8 types of semantic constructional forms in "dingzhong(attribute-centered)" compound words:

(2) The constructional form of meaning in "dingzhong(attribute-centered)" compound words
   a. ding(attribute) + de(of) + zhong(center). e.g. 【jiachan(family property)】 jiating(family) + de + caichan(property)
   b. ding(attribute) + V + de(of) + zhong(center). e.g. 【niunai(milk)】 muniu(-cow) + chan(produce) + de + nai(milk)
   c. V + ding(attribute) + de(of) + zhong(center). e.g. 【ruzhu(porket)】 chi(eat) + nai(milk) + de + xiaozhu(piggy)
   d. ding(attribute) + N + de(of) + zhong(center). e.g. 【hushi(nurse)】 huli(nursing) + bingren(patient) + de + ren(person)
   e. N + ding(attribute) + de(of) + zhong(center). e.g. 【lingtu(territory)】 guojia (state) + lingyou(possess) + de + tudi(land)
   f. the predicate structure that contains "ding(attribute)"[1] + V + de(of) + zhong (center). e.g. 【jikan(quarterly)】 an(according to) jidu(quarter) + chuban(pubulish) + de + kanwu(journal)
   g. V + the predicate structure that contains "ding(attribute)" + de(of) + zhong(-center). e.g. 【chaguan(teahouse)】 gong(offer) + keren(guest) hecha(drink tea) + de + difang(place)
   h. the predicate structure that contains "ding(attribute)" + de(of) + the predicate structure that contains "zhong(center)" + N. e.g. 【tonglv(verdigris)】 zai(on) tong(copper) biaomian(surface) + shengcheng(come into being) + de + lv(-green) + xiu(rust)

By this method, we further analyze the rest compound words, and get the semantic constructional forms as follows:

[1] What the "predicate structure that contains X" refers to in this paper is a predicate structure X is contained in another predicate structure or downgraded predication. In general, there are two kinds of "predicate structure that contains X": one is the preposition-object structure, such as "he marries in a church", where 'in the church" is a predicate structure, which is contained in the predicate structure of "he marries…"; the other is the predicative component or predicate structure, such as "it is a place for guests to drink tea", where "guests drink tea" is a predicate structure, which is contained in the downgraded predication structure of "it is a place for…".

2.1 The Constructional Form of Meaning in "Zhuangzhong (Adverbial-Centered)" Compound Words

Differing from "dingzhong(attribute-centered)" compound words, the constructional form of meaning in "zhuangzhong(adverbial-centered)" compound words is relatively simple, which can be summarized into 4 types:

Type one: zhuang(adverbial) + (de(of)) + zhong(center). For example:

(3) 【buduan(ceaselessly)】 bu(-less) + jianduan(cease)
【nushi(glare at)】 fennu(rage) + de + kanzhe(seeing)
【wujie(misunderstand)】 cuowu(wrong) + de + lijie(understand)

Type two: zhuang(adverbial) + zhe(-ing) + zhong(center). Here, the "Zhuang(adverbial)" is a verbal component, which indicates the accompanying state of "zhong (center)". For example:

(4) 【zuodeng(wait for)】 zuo(sit) + zhe + dengdai(wait for)
【kusu(complain tearfully)】 ku(cry) + zhe + sushuo(complain)

Type three: the predicate structure that contains "zhuang(adverbial)" + (de (of)) + zhong(center). In form, the predicate structure that contains "zhuang(adverbial)" is expressed by "on/at/in/from/to + adverbial" or "by means of/through/via + adverbial". In function, the predicate structure that contains "zhuang (adverbial)" indicates time, location, way, tool, material etc. For example:

(5) 【banshu(write on the blackboard)】 zai(on) + heiban shang(blackboard) + shuxie (write)
【kanshou(instruction via periodicals)】 yi(by) jifa(send) kanwu(periodicals) + de (of) fangshi(means) + jiaoshou(teach)

Type four: xiang(like) + zhuang(adverbial) + nayang(as) + zhong(center). Here, "zhuang(adverbial)" is usually a nominal component, which indicates what the action looks like. For example:

(6) 【yunji(gather)】 xiang(like) + yun(cloud) + nayang(as) + juji(gether) zai yiqi (together)
【huore(fiery)】 xiang(like) + huo(fire) + nayang(as) + zhire(broiling)

2.2 The Constructional Form of Meaning in "Lianhe (Coordinate)" Compound Words

The constructional form of meaning in "lianhe(coordinate)" compound words can be summarized into 4 types: (A, B represent the structural components of compound word)

Type one: AB = (especially refer to) A or B. For example:

(7) 【jiaoxue(teaching and studying)】 (especially refer to) teaching
【anwei(safety and danger)】 especially refer to danger

Type two: AB = A + and/or + B. For example:

(8) 【chunchi(labial tooth)】 zuichun(labial) + and + yachi(tooth)
【chengbai(success or failure)】 chenggong(success) + or + shibai(failure)

Type three: AB = A + and + B, used to refer to C or used as a metaphor for C. Besides the basic meaning of "A + and + B", there is a new meaning which derives from "A + and + B". For example:

(9) 【heshan(rivers and mountains)】 "he(rivers)" + and + "shan(mountains)", used to refer to territory
【fengyu(wind and rain)】 "feng(wind)" + and + "yu(rain)", used as a metaphor for hard environment

2.3 The Constructional Form of Meaning in "Dongbin (Verb-Object)" Compound Words

The constructional form of meaning in "dongbin(verb-object)" compound words is relatively simple, which can be summarized into 2 types:

Type one: dong(verb) + bin(object). Sometimes we need to make up some attribute, adverbial or complement for "bin(object)". For example:

(10) 【xiche(clean cars)】 qingxi(clean) + cheliang(car)
【tucun(strive for survival)】 mouqiu(strive for) + guojia huo mingzu(country or nation) de(of) shengcun(survival)

Type two: (refer to) dong(verb) + bin(object) + de(of) + N. Here, these compound words seemed to be "dongbin(verb-object)" structure. Actually, they have become "dingzhong(attribute-centered)" structure, used to refer to agent, tool, time, place, result, etc. For example:

(11) 【guanjia(housekeeper)】 (refer to) guanli(manage) + jiawu(housework) + de + ren(person)
【huxi(kneepad)】 (refer to) baohu(protect) + xiguanjie(knee) + de + yongpin (appliance)

2.4 The Constructional Form of Meaning in "Shubu (Predicate-Complement)" Compound Words

According to the difference between the subject and object of action, we can summarize the semantic constructional form of "shubu(predicate-complement)" compound words into 3 types:

Type one: shu(predicate) + bu(complement). Here, the subject of "shu(predicate)" and "bu(complement)" is the same, so does the object (if there is). For example:

(12) 【buru(step into)】 zou(step) + jin(into)
【laozhao(get the opportunity)】 lao(get) + dao(get)(opportunity, benefit, etc.)

Type two: yin(because) shu(predicate) + er(so) bu(complement). There is a causal relationship between "shu(predicate)" and "bu(complement)", and the subject of "shu (predicate)" and "bu(complement) " may be the same or may be different. For example, the subject of “weisuo(flinch)” is the same, while the subject of “ganlie(seasoning crack)” is different:

(13) 【weisuo(flinch)】 yin(because) haipa(fear) + er(so) tuisuo(flinch)
【ganlie(seasoning crack)】 yin(because) ganzao(dry) + er(so) liekai(crack)

Type three: tongguo(by means of) shu(predicate) + shi(cause) N + bu(complement). There is a causative relationship between “shu(predicate)” and “bu(complement)”, where the object of “shu(predicate)” is the subject of “bu(complement)”. For example:

(14) 【xunfu(tame)】 tonguo(by means of) xunyang(domesticate) + shi(cause) ta (it) + shuncong(obey)
【gaizheng(correct)】 tonguo(by means of) xiugai(revise) + shi(cause) ta(it) + zhengque(right)

2.5 The Constructional Form of Meaning in “Zhuwei (Subject-Predicate)” Compound Words

The number of “zhuwei(subject-predicate)” compound words is the least, and be limited by a variety of conditions: the object of that the “zhu(subject)” refers to is usually inanimate, and the transitivity and uncontrollability of “wei(predicate)” is relatively low [9]. In “zhuwei(subject-predicate)” compound words, there are two constructional forms of meaning.

Type one: zhu(subject) + wei(predicate), which is usually used to define the “zhuwei(subject- predicate)” compound words. For example:

(15) 【xingji(impatient)】 xingqing(disposition) + jizao(impatient)
【guzhe(fracture)】 gutou(bone) + zheduan(break) huo(or) suilie(fracture)

Type two: zhu(subject) + wei(predicate); refer to… Here, these compound words have not only original meanings but also extended meanings. The original meaning is used to describe the physical changes of human organs, and the extended meaning is used to describe the emotional and psychological changes caused by the physical changes. For example:

(16) 【xintiao(heartbeat)】 xinzang(heart) + tiaodong(beat), zhi(refer to) yin(because) qingxu(emotion) jidong(excitement) er(so) xin(heart) tiao(beat) jiakuai(faster)
【lianhong(blush)】 lianse(face) + bianhong(blush), duo(usually) zhi(refer to) haisao(feel ashamed)

3 The Difficulty Level of Definition in Compound Words

It is the meaning of structural components and structural relationship that is the basis of the semantic construction of compound words. According to this basis, this paper divides the definition difficulty of compound words into 4 levels.

3.1 Level 0

Here, the definition difficulty of compound words is the lowest. The meaning of compound word can be deduced from the meaning of its structural components and structural relationship. Such situation often can be found in "zhuwei(subject-predicate)" and "lianhe(coordinate)" compound words. For example:(the meaning of structural components is abbreviated to SC, and the meaning of structural relationship is abbreviated to SR)

(17) word SC SR definition

【*guzhe*】 *gutou /zheduan zhu + wei gutou zheduan huo suilie*
(bone /break subject-predicate the bone breaks or fractures)
【*chunchi*】 *zuichun /yachi A + he + B zuichun he yachi*
(labial /tooth A + and + B labial and tooth)

Why is the definition difficulty of the "zhuwei(subject-predicate)" and "lianhe(-coordinate)" compound words the lowest?This is related to the structural characteristics of compound words.

Firstly, let`s look at "zhuwei(subject-predicate)" compound words. Because the subject argument is an external argument, whose semantic relation with the predicate is loosely, it is not easy to combine into a "zhuwei(subject-predicate)" compound word with the predicate [9]. But if the relationship between the subject and the predicate is close, and when we mention a subject which can make us associate a related action or mention an action which can make us associate a related subject, they are easy to co-exist and easy to combine into a "zhuwei(subject-predicate)" compound word. Taking "shanbeng(landslide)" as an example, when mentioning the action "beng(slide)" which can make us associate its related subject "shan(mountain)", so "beng(slide)" and "shan (mountain)" are easy to combine together. Another example is "xintiao(heartbeat)", when we mention the subject "xin(heart)" which can make us associate its related action "tiaodong(beat)", so they are easy to combine into a compound word. The investigation of corpus also proves that most of the relationships between the subject and the predicate of "zhuwei(subject-predicate)" compound words are close. Such as "richu(sunrise)", "riluo(sunset)", "dizhen(earthquake)", "taidong(fetal movement)", "bisai(nasal congestion)", "guzhe(fracture)", "touteng(headache)", "lianhong(blush)", "xinfan(be vexed)", "qijue(breathless)", "zhibian(qualitative change)", "weiyi(displacement)". For this reason, it is easier to define "zhuwei(subject-predicate)" compound words.

Then, look at "lianhe(coordinate)" compound words. If we divide the lexical relationship into rapports syntagmatiques and rapports associatifs, the reason of which the definition difficulty of "zhuwei(subject-predicate)" and "lianhe(coordinate)" compound words is lowest is different. As for the former, it is the rapports syntagmatiques that causes "zhuwei(subject-predicate)" compound words easier to define. As for the later, it is the rapports associatifs(synonymy, analogy and antisense) that causes "lianhe (coordinate)" compound words easier to define.

In addition to the above evidence, there is another evidence can prove "lianhe (coordinate)" compound words are mainly relate to rapports associatifs rather than rapports syntagmatiques. The compound words formed by the rapports syntagmatiques are restricted by the word order, and the word orders of compound words are relatively fixed, only few of them are homo-morpheme inverse order words. In contrast, the compound words formed by the rapports associatifs are flexible in the word order, and lots of them are homo-morpheme inverse order words. Through a corpus investigation, this paper finds that most of homo-morpheme inverse order words are "lianhe(coordinate)" compound words. Such as "liqi(strength) - qili(strength)", "jidu(envy) - duji (envy)", "xiaofang(imitate) - fangxiao(imitate)", "fenhao(the least bit) - haofen(the least bit)", "fafen(exert oneself) - fenfa(exert oneself)", "caijian(tailor) - jiancai(tailor)", "jiansuo(reduce) - suojian(reduce)", etc. [10].

3.2 Level 1

Here, the definition difficulty of compound words is relatively low. To define these compound words, we need to supplement a semantic component which relates to structural components besides the meanings of structural components and structural relationship. The semantic component that need to be supplemented is usually predicate or argument. For example:(the meaning that relates to structural relationship is abbreviated to SR)

(18) word SC SR relate to SC definition

(18) word	SC	SR	relate to SC	definition
【*ruzhu*】	*ruzhi/ xiaozhu*	*ding + de + zhong*	*chi*	*chi nai de xiaozhu*
	(milk / piglet	attribute + of + center	eat	suckling pig)
【*qifei*】	*kaishi/ feixing*	*dong + bin*	*feiji*	*(feiji) kaishi feixing*
	(begin to / fly	verb-object	plane	planes begin to fly)

3.3 Level 2

Here, the definition difficulty of compound words is relatively high. To define these compound words, we need to supplement at least two semantic components that relate to structural components besides the meanings of structural components and structural relationship. The semantic components that need to be supplemented can be predicates, arguments or modifiers, restrictive, complementary elements. For example:

(19) word SC SR relate to SC definition

(19) word	SC	SR	relate to SC	definition
【*daiyv*】	*daizi / yv* (ribbon/fish)	*ding + de + zhong* attribute + of + center	*waixing/xiang* shape / like	*waixing xiang daizi de yv* A fish shaped like a ribbon)
【*shibu*】	*shiwu/ buchong* (food/ supplement	*zhuang+ zhong* adverbial+ center	*yong../yingyang* by.../ nutrition	*yong shiwu buchong yingyang* supplement nutrition with food)

What we have defined above is the original meaning. Sometimes defining the extended meaning of compound words should also be on the basis of the meanings of structural components and structural relationship. Slightly differing from the original meaning, when defining the extended meaning, the meaning of structural relationship of compound words will be changed. For example:

(20) word SC SR relate to SC definition

(20) word	SC	SR	relate to SC	definition
【*jiangong*】	*jiandu / gongren* (supervise/ worker	*dong +bin→ ding +zhong* verb + object →attribute + center	*fuze / laodong / ren* be responsible for / labor / person	*fuze jiandu gongren laodong de ren* a person who is responsible for supervising the labor of the workers)
【*jianzhi*】	*jian / zhi* (cut / paper	*dong+bin→ ding+ zhong* verb + object →attribute + center	*yong.../zuo pin* by.../ works	*yong zhi jianchu de zuopin* a works that cuts out of paper)

3.4 Level 3

Here, the definition difficulty of compound words is the highest. There are 2 reasons responsible for the highest definition difficulty:

The first one is the Extension of Meaning. To define the extended meaning, we need to refer to the original meaning [11]. Comparing the following words:

(21) word original meaning semantic relation extended meaning

(21) word	original meaning	semantic relation	extended meaning
【*lianhong*】	*lianse bian hong* (the face turns red	*haixiu shi lianse hui bian hong* the face turns red when it is ashamed	*duo zhi haixiu* especially refer to shyness)
【*zhaoya*】	*niao shou de jianzhua he liya* (the sharp claws and teeth of birds and animals	*keyi liyong de gongju* tools that can be used	*biyu huairen de zougou huo bangxiong* a metaphor for a bad man's dog or accomplices)

Obviously, without considering the original meaning, it is difficult to clarify the extended clues of the meaning, and it is difficult to define the extended meaning of compound words. After considering the original meaning, the extended clues of the meanings are clear, and it is easier to define the extended meaning of compound words. Such as "lianhong(flash)", its original meaning is "the face turns red". Because people`s faces usually turn red when they are shy, the compound word "lianhong(flash)" derives a new meaning used to refer to shyness.

The second reason is the constructional form of meaning is complicated. Taking nouns for example, according to this paper`s investigation, the meanings of nouns include more than one aspect. To define these compound words, we can use the method of Qualia Role distribution. If the compound word is a natural noun, it is necessary to define its constitutive role(abbr. CON) and telic role (abbr. TEL); if it is an artificial noun, it is necessary to define its agentive role(abbr. AGE) and telic role [12]. Taking the "shui(water) X" compound word as an example:

(22) a. natural noun: need to define its CON and TEL

【*shuiguo*(fruit)】 *han shuifen jiaoduo de* $_{\text{CON}}$ 、*ke shengchi de* $_{\text{TEL}}$ *zhiwu guoshi*。*Ru li*、*pingguo*、*boluo deng*。

(The fruit of an edible $_{\text{TEL}}$ plant with more water $_{\text{CON}}$. Such as pears, apples, grapes, pineapples, and so on.)

【*shuijing*(crystal)】 *wuse touming de shiying* $_{\text{CON}}$ *jingti*。*Ke yonglai zhizuo guangxue yiqi*、*gongyipin deng* $_{\text{TEL}}$。

(A colorless and transparent quartz $_{\text{CON}}$ crystal, which can be used to make optical instruments, arts and crafts and so on $_{\text{TEL}}$.)

b. artificial noun: need to define its AGE and TEL

【*shuichuang*(waterbed)】 *chuangdian li chong shui de* $_{\text{AGE}}$ *chuang*。*Liyong shui de fuli tuoqi renti, shi ren gandao shushi* $_{\text{TEL}}$.

(A bed in which the mattress is filled with water $_{\text{AGE}}$. Use the buoyancy of water to lift up the human body and make people feel comfortable $_{\text{TEL}}$.)

【*shuigang*(water vat)】 *chengshui de* $_{\text{TEL}}$ *rongqi,duo yong taotu shaozhi. er cheng* $_{\text{AGE}}$,*kou da di xiao,cheng yuangu xing* $_{\text{FOR}}$。

(Containers for holding water $_{TEL}$ are mostly made of clay $_{AGE}$, with large mouth, small bottom and round drum shape $_{FOR}$.)

Of course, what is said above is only a tendency. When defining a specific compound words, which Qualia Role need or need not to define usually varies with the compound words. Such as "shuigang(water vat)", in addition to define its AGE and TEL, we also need to define its formal role(abbr. FOR), such as "kou da di xiao, cheng yuangu xing".

Table 1. A comparison of the constructional form of meaning and the difficulty level of definition in Chinese compound words

	The constructional form of meaning	The difficulty level of definition	Example
dingzhong (attribute-centered)	1. ding(attribute) + de(of) + zhong(center)	Level 0	【*jiachan*】 *jiating + de + caichan*
	2. ding(attribute) + V + de (of) +zhong(center)	Level 1	【*niunai*】 *muniu + chan + de + nai*
	3. V + ding(attribute) + de (of) + zhong(center)		【*ruzhu*】 *chi + nai + de + xiaozhu*
	4. ding(attribute) + N + de (of) + zhong(center)		【*hushi*】 *huli + bingren + de + ren*
	5. N + ding(attribute) + de (of) + zhong(center)		【*lingtu*】 *guojia + lingyou + de + tudi*
	6. the predicate structure that contains "ding (attribute)" + V + de (of) + zhong (center)	Level 2	【*jikan*】 *an jidu + chuban + de + kanwu*
	7. V + the predicate structure that contains "ding (attribute)" + de (of) + zhong(center)		【*chaguan*】 *gong + keren hecha + de + difang*
	8. the predicate structure that contains "ding (attribute)" + de(of) + the predicate structure that contains "zhong (center)" + N		【*tonglv*】 *tong biaomian + yanghua shengcheng + de + lv + xiu*
	# referring to the original meaning; refer to /A metaphor for …	Level 3	【*majia*】 *zhi + meiyou xiuzi he lingzi + de + shangyi*

(*continued*)

Table 1. (*continued*)

	The constructional form of meaning	The difficulty level of definition	Example
zhuangzhong (adverbial-centered)	9. zhuang(adverbial) + (de (of)) + zhong(center)	Level 0	【*buduan*】 *bu + jianduan*
	10. zhuang(adverbial) + zhe (-ing) + zhong(center)	≈ Level 1	【*zuodeng*】 *zuo + zhe + dengdai*
	11. xiang(like) + zhuang (adverbial) + nayang (as) + zhong(center)	Level 2	【*yunji*】 *xiang + yun + nayang + juji zai yiqi*
	12. the predicate structure that contains “zhuang (adverbial)” + (de (of)) + zhong(center)		【*banshu*】 *zai + heiban shang + shuxie*
	# referring to the original meaning; refer to /A metaphor for …	Level 3	【*fengxing*】 *biyu + hen kuai de liuxing kailai*
lianhe (coordinate)	13. AB = (especially refer to) A or B	Level 0	【*jiaoxue*】 zhi *jiao (shu)*
	14.AB = A + (and/or +)B		【*chengsong*】 *chengzan + songyang*
	# AB = A + B, refer to /A metaphor for C	Level 3	【*heshan*】 *he + he + shan, jie zhi + guojia de lingtu*
dongbin (verb-object)	15. dong(verb) + bin (object)	Level 0	【*xiche*】 *qingxi + cheliang*
	16. (refer to) dong (verb) + bin(object) + de (of) + N	≈ Level 2	【*guanjia*】 *(zhi) guanli + jiawu + de + puren*
	# referring to the original meaning; refer to /A metaphor for …	Level 3	【*guanshui*】 *zhi + xiang luntan guanzhu wu yiyi de tiezi*
shubu (predicate-complement)	17. shu(predicate) + bu (complement)	Level 0	【*buru*】 *zou + jin*
	18. yin(because) shu (predicate) + er(so) bu (complement)	≈ Level 1	【*ganlie*】 *yin ganzao + er liekai*
	19. tongguo(by means of) shu(predicate) + shi(cause) N + bu(complement)	≈ Level 2	【*xunfu*】 *(tongguo) xunhua + shi ta + shuncong*
	# referring to the original meaning; refer to /A metaphor for …	Level 3	【*chongdan*】 *biyu + ganqing deng zai yiding tiaojian xia bei jianruo*

(*continued*)

Table 1. (*continued*)

	The constructional form of meaning	The difficulty level of definition	Example
zhuwei (subject-predicate)	20.zhu(subject) + wei (predicate)	Level 0	【*xingji*】 *xingqing* + *jizao*
	# referring to the original meaning; refer to /A metaphor for …	Level 3	【*lianhong*】 *lianse* + *bian hong, duo zhi* + *haisao*

4 Conclusion

As discussed above, the meaning construction of compound words is regular. The main rules are as follows: (1) the meaning construction of compound words is in accord with the sentence structure. When grasping the rules of sentence structure, we will basically grasp the construction rules of compound word meanings. (2) It is the meaning of structural components and structural relationship that is the basis of compound words definition. On this basis, we can define the simple meaning(Level 0) of compound words directly; supplementing some meaning components related to structural components, we can define the relatively complicated meaning(Level 1, 2) of compound words. Referring to the original meaning, we can define the highly complicated meaning(Level 3) of compound words. (3) In compound words, the complexity of the meaning construction is proportional to the definition difficulty. The simpler the meaning construction is, the lower the definition difficulty is; and vice versa. For further details, see Table 1:

Annotation: In Table 1, the main constructional form of compound words meaning is numbered by 1,2,3…20, and their corresponding difficulty level is 0–2. Differing from level 0–2, level 3 has no unified constructional form. In order to distinguish it from Level 0–2, this paper marked it with "#".

Acknowledgments. This paper is supported by the Key Project of Research Institute of Humanities & Social Science of National Ministry of Education "A study of lexical semantic knowledge representation and its computing system under Chinese parataxis grammar framework", the Youth fund of the Ministry of Education "A study of the theory and method of the definition of Chinese Dictionary", the National Basic Research Program of China (2014CB340502), the Project of the National Language Commission (YB135-45), and Shandong Province Social Science Fund (16CZWJ31). The anonymous experts of CLSW2018 put forward many valuable comments. Here, we express our sincere thanks!

References

1. Chao, Y.: Mandarin Primer: An Intensive Course in Spoken Chinese. Harvard University Press, Harvard (1948)
2. Lu, Z., et al.: Chinese Word Formation. Science Press, Beijing (1957). (In Chinese)
3. Zhu, D.: Lectures on Grammar. The Commercial Press, Beijing (1982). (In Chinese)
4. Tang, T.: The incorporation phenomenon of Chinese grammar (Part I). Tsinghua J. Taiwan. **1–2** (1991). (In Chinese)
5. Zhu, Y.: A study of the semantic word-formation of Chinese compound words (doctoral dissertation). East China Normal University, Shanghai (2003). (In Chinese)
6. Xiufang, D.: Lexicalization: The Origin and Evolution of Chinese Disyllabic Words, rev. Edn. The Commercial Press, Beijing (2011). (In Chinese)
7. Yuan, C., Huang, C.: A study of Chinese morpheme and word formation based on Morpheme Data Bank. Chin. Teach. World **2**, 8–13 (1998). (In Chinese)
8. Leech: Semantics. Translated by Li Ruihua. Shanghai Foreign Language Education Press, Shanghai (1987/2008). (In Chinese)
9. Xiufang, D.: The conditional restriction of the subject-predicate compound word lexicalization. J. Southwest Univ. Natl. **4,** 303–307 (2002). (In Chinese)
10. Wang, Y.: Study on the disyllabic coordinator compound words in modern Chinese (master`s dissertation). Guangxi Normal University, Guilin (2011). (In Chinese)
11. Guo, Z.: Historical Semantics, rev. edn. China Publishing House, Beijing (1986/2005). (In Chinese)
12. Enxu, W., Yuan, Y.: The Qualia role distribution in word meaning and its influence on the word interpretation. J. Foreign Lang. **2**, 21–31 (2018). (In Chinese)

A Corpus-Based Study on the Semantic Prosody of Quasi-Affix "Zu"

Yueming Du[1,2], Bihua Wang[1,2], and Lijiao Yang[1,2](✉)

[1] Institute of Chinese Information Processing, Beijing Normal University, Beijing, China
dddydym@yeah.net, 282843696@qq.com, yanglijiao@bnu.edu.cn

[2] UltraPower-BNU Joint Laboratory for Artificial Intelligence, Beijing Normal University, Beijing, China

Abstract. Semantic prosody has been a hot issue in corpus linguistics since it has been put forward in the early 1990s. Some theories suggest that some words in specific context are subject to semantic inflection. However, this paper argues that semantic prosody appears in not only collocation, but also words and their internal affixes. In this paper, we chose the most commonly used quasi-affix "Zu" as the research object. Our study explores the semantic prosody tendencies of "X_zu" and analyzes the cognition mechanism of the words constructed as "X_zu". The analysis shows that the words of "X_zu" implicating negative meanings appear more frequently than those with positive ones based on a large scale corpus.

Keywords: Semantic prosody · Semantic inflection · Quasi-affixes

1 Introduction

With the development of society, new things are emerging endlessly. In order to meet the needs of times progress, language need a more flexible method to refer to these new things, which promotes the development of word formation. As one of the most productive ways of forming words, affixation drives the emergence of a large number of new words and phrases. Affixes can be divided into two types: one is called typical affixes, such as Lao-, A-, -Zi, -Tou, -Er, -Hua, -Xing and so on, whose position have been fixed and the meaning of these affixes have tended to be invariant after the neologism formed. The other is non-typical affixes. This kind of affixes has flocked to the crowd of word-building in recent years, and we call them quasi-affixes.

This paper gets the foundation from Key Project of the National Language Committee, Revision of the Standard of POS tag of contemporary Chinese for Information Processing (ZDI135-42).

J.-F. Hong et al. (Eds.): CLSW 2018, LNAI 11173, pp. 445–453, 2018.
https://doi.org/10.1007/978-3-030-04015-4_37

1.1 Research Status and Related Review

In the 1940s, Shuxiang Lv put forward the "approximate suffix" in his work *Essentials of Chinese Grammar*, which could be regarded as a primary research of quasi-affixes. However, the concept didn't arouse much attention at that time. In the 90s, some work focused on the rationality of quasi-affixes in the perspective of social development and language features. Related well-known works in this period are Hu (1955) and Chen (2001). However, the discussion of quasi-affixes did not jump out the macroscopic view. At the beginning of this century, many researches about quasi-affixes have been published, such as the work of Shi (2002), whose paper discussed the instantiation of quasi-affixes. He took two quasi-affixes ("-Jie" and "-Tan") as examples to explore the vacancy and occupying problem of words, revealing the factors that restrict those phenomena. Liu (2008) studied burgeoning affix "-Men" from the perspective of generation and evolution, structure and function, usage and expression. Although case study got more attention, research of characteristics of quasi-affixes and its inherent semantic meaning need more work to carry forward.

In this study, we focus on the words "X_zu", and try to explore the semantic prosody and the semantic inflection produced by quasi-affix "-Zu".

1.2 The Theoretical Basis of the Research: Semantic Prosody Theory

In structuralist phonetics, phonemes are regarded as discrete and divisible units. Firth suggested that phoneme analysis should cross various levels of discourse structure, which improved the traditional method, and finally set up rhythmic phonology through rhythmic analysis method.

Sinclair, a student of Firth, had adopted the views of Firth and creatively introduced his theory into semantic analysis. Then in 1993, Louw put forward the term of "Semantic Prosody" formally in his paper. It is generally believed that semantic prosody is a kind of special collocation. Some words always attract specific semantic features within certain linguistic units. They are gradually influenced with a sort of semantic atmosphere, producing specific shades of meaning and pragmatic meaning.

Semantic prosody can be roughly divided into three types: positive semantic prosody, neutral semantic prosody and negative semantic prosody. Within positive semantic prosody, most of the words attracted by the key words have strong tendency of being positive, which makes the unit a positive semantic atmosphere. Negative semantic prosody is on the opposite. Key words within the neutral semantic prosody not only attract some positive meaning words, but also attract some negative or neutral meanings, thus forming an intricate semantic atmosphere.

1.3 Research Methods and Significance

Our paper combined data-based and data-driven approach, then randomly selected 4000 sentences in BCC corpus and counted the collocation words with the help of Antconc3.4.4. Antconc is an open source software developed by Laurence Anthony, which can be used for word retrieval, collocation extraction, keyword extraction, word cluster extraction and so on. By using random sorting function of BCC corpus, the first 1000 sentences containing affix "Zu" were selected to carry out the related research.

Traditional quasi-affixes study focus more on its semantic and process of grammaticalization. We tried to integrate related theories of semantic prosody on this basis in order to provide a new perspective on modern linguistics.

On the other hand, most of the previous researches of semantic prosody were based on the combination of word collocation and semantic inflection. However, we believe that there ought to be a certain similarity between the word formation and phrase collocation, that is, the semantic prosody of the affixes is likely to be transferred to word through semantic contamination to make the word have a certain emotional tendency.

2 The Semantic Prosody Research on Words "X-Zu"

Chinese Net-speak words have been produced rapidly with the development of internet technology. We found that quasi-affix "Zu" was very active in Chinese Net-speak words, and the usage of this quasi-affix on the internet was gradually normalized. Some related researches about "X_zu" not only focused on language structure but also reflected great concern on social psychology and social background of this issue. The researchers explained how this quasi-affix was produced and why it became more popular (Liang 2007). Besides this, Standardization of "X_zu" was also discussed by Zhao (2007). In general, those researches paid more attention on external language instead of the interior of language.

We studied different types of "X_zu", analyzed the semantic prosody of this quasi-affix from its colligation, and examined the semantic prosody's distribution of each type.

There are 1000 sentences containing affix "Zu", which are selected to carry out the related research from BCC.

2.1 The Colligation Types of the Words "X-Zu"

We used Antconc to process 1000 sentences selected from the corpus, then classified the words and phrases formed by the quasi-affix "Zu" as follows:

(1) N + "zu": the nouns in Chinese can be combined with "Zu" to refer to a group of people with common characteristics. There are 451 cases of this colligation in the corpus of investigation, and some examples are as follows:
   A. "Xiao piao zu" ("校漂族") and "yi zu" ("蚁族") have different behavioral characteristics and causes, which cannot be described and studied as the same group.
   B. As he likes to get together with his friends, and rushes to pay for the meal every time, he is totally a "yue guang zu" ("月光族").

(2) V + "zu": There are 337 cases of this colligation in the corpus of investigation, and some examples are as follows:

A. It was surprised that he didn't find a job after graduation and felt at ease to be a "ken lao zu" ("啃老族").
B. They are "shang ban zu" ("上班族") in Japanese women who are so different from our understanding.
C. We will probably become "kong gui zu" ("恐归族") by the end of a year.

(3) Adj + "zu": Adjectives can be matched with the quasi-affix "Zu" to form words. There are 337 cases in the data which can be divided into two types:
A. The second flattering type we talk about is "yin xian zu" ("阴险族"). These people are not as easy to distinguish as the first type, and they always have bad temper behind their smiling faces and you can never tell if they tell the true.
B. *The angel not online* reveals the current situation and essence of Chinese network of erotic field. With a bold writing style and common perspective, it exposes the real mentality of erotic industry practitioners and shapes the image of "she hui kong xu zu" ("社会空虚族").

(4) ADV + V + "zu": In this kind of colligation, the adverb can be used directly with the verb, then associate the phrase with the combination of the quasi-affix "Zu". The proportion of this colligation is smaller than others, and the adverb is always temporal adverb or always brings negative meaning. There are 40 examples of the colligation in the investigate corpus which are as follows:
A. Having no boyfriend might not be that bad, even the "bu hun zu" ("不婚族") has become popular nowadays.
B. Three kinds of diet soup are customized to lose weight and strongly recommended for those "jiu zuo zu" ("久坐族").

(5) letter + "zu": In this kind of colligation, "Zu" can be added directly to the English alphabet and there are 15 cases of the colligation in our corpus. The example are as follows:
A. The trademark of "OL zu" ("OL族"): cocoon-like red cashmere coat, straight bang and the most popular high-heeled shoes of this winter make a typical "OL zu" look, confident, neat and sweet.

(6) overlapping words + "zu": Except for the above colligation, "Zu" can be added behind overlapping words. This kind of colligation firstly reduplicate the intrinsic component and then add the quasi-affix "Zu" to constituent the word. There are 25 cases of this colligation in the corpus investigated. Its proportion is not large and some examples are given as:
A. It is worth mentioning that, through the depiction of a group of self strengthening youngster, the film makes a perfect interpretation of the personality of the most influential "ben ben zu" ("奔奔族").
B. English certifications, computer ones and driver's license tend to be regarded as the important "amulet" when college graduates apply for a job. Which lead to the "ben ben zu" ("本本族") who pursuits all kinds of certifications blindly.

2.2 A Quantitative Study on the Semantic Prosody of Words with Quasi-Affix "Zu"

By statistical analysis, we quantified the semantic prosody of the above colligations. As Table 1 shows, we find that the the N + "zu" takes the largest proportion in the collected corpus. The nouns in this kind of colligation are always common nouns with simple meaning, such as "dian nao zu" ("电脑族"), which refers to a group of people with same profession or characteristics. From the perspective of semantic prosody, most of these words tend to be neutral, because their etyma are mostly concrete nouns without commendatory or derogatory colors. The other part of nouns presents some complications, it mainly uses the pattern of metaphor, such as "yue guang zu" ("月光族"), "yi zu" ("蚁族"), "tiao zao zu" ("跳蚤族") and so on. Most of these words tend to be derogatory, that is to say, they tend to reveal the helplessness of the users. The helplessness has no obvious commendatory or derogatory meaning, but implies subjective attitude of the speaker like sympathy, regret or powerlessness. For instance, "di tan zu" ("地摊族") indirectly conveys the meaning of low wages and low social status. Although this meaning is not easy to tell and some what unobtrusive, we believe it is what the speakers mostly meant to convey to readers.

Table 1. The colligation and semantic prosody of words "X_zu".

	Positive	Neutral	Negative
N + zu	60	202	189
V + zu	45	60	232
A + zu	53	34	50
ADV + V+zu	6	31	3
Letter + zu	0	15	0
overlapping words + zu	15	0	5
total	179	342	479

The highest frequency of word formed by the colligation "V + zu" in corpus are "shang ban zu" ("上班族"), "da gong zu" ("打工族"), "bao zou zu" ("暴走族"), "kong gui zu" ("恐归族") and "ken lao zu" ("啃老族"). Except for "shang ban zu" ("上班族") and "da gong zu" ("打工族"), most of words semantic prosody tend to be negative, basically revealing the sympathy or opposition of the speaker (author) to such people.

Compared with the former ones, the proportion of "A + zu" is much smaller. From the perspective of semantic prosody, the number of positive and the one of negative semantic prosody are unbiased. From perspective of semantic prosody, "A + ADV + zu" and "letter +zu" are almost all neutral semantic prosody. From a pragmatic point of view, they are only a kind of reference to certain groups of people.

The minimum words with quasi-affix "Zu" in corpus such as "overlapping words + zu" are simple in construction but rich in semantics. For example, "ben ben zu" ("奔奔族") refers to the generation born in 1975 to 1985. They are always active on the road of business, but at the same time, they are the most stressful generation, and they are constantly under pressure. "Ben ben zu" ("本本族") refers to those who think highly of pursuing certificates and diplomas in their life. Because these two cases are the only samples we could collect from the corpus, we did not put further effort in "overlapping words + zu" out of its rare occurrence.

In general, most of the words "X_zu" have negative semantic prosody. Formally, the number of positive semantic prosody is less than its negative counterpart, and that is true for almost all subcategories of "X_zu" (except for "letter + zu" and "overlapping words + zu").

3 The Cognitive Basis of the Words of "X_Zu"

3.1 Conceptual Metaphor

As a Quasi-affix, "Zu" is used to refer to the group of people with the same attributes or same characteristics. From the words of "X_zu", the semantic prosody of those words mainly depends on that of "Zu". In order to further clarify the rationale for formation of semantic rhyme, we analyze it from cognitive perspective. Here we divided the cognitive formation of "X_zu" into two kinds of circumstances, one of which is the conceptual metaphor. The second is metonymy.

The construction of the human concept system is inseparable from cognition. In this kind of cognition, the most basic one is conceptual metaphor. In process of cognition, people often make use of that familiar, tangible, and concrete concepts to understand unfamiliar, intangible, and abstract concepts, thus interrelationship between different concepts is formed. Conceptual metaphor is the cross-domain mapping in the conceptual system. It always uses one conceptual domain to understand another conceptual domain. The words of "X_zu" also do that.

Through the specific corpora, we can see that there are a class of words in the words of "X_zu", such as "yi zu" ("蚁族") 、"xiang ri kui zu" ("向日葵族"). The formation of these words is inseparable from metaphor.

"Yi zu" ("蚁族"), which is used to refer to "low-income groups of college graduates", is the fourth most vulnerable group after the three disadvantaged groups (farmers, migrant workers, laid-off workers). The typical characteristics of "yi zu" ("蚁族") are: receiving a good education, living in rural-urban fringe zone, and getting a small salary but best hope for future. They are "weak but strong". According to a relevant research, ants are the most powerless but intelligent species among many species. The characteristics of "ants" and that of "college graduates" have corresponding mapping relationships. The living state of ants in the source domain is projected together with the living state of college graduates in the target domain into a synthetic space, thereby creating a layered structure "yi zu" ("蚁族"). The word vividly reflects the real living circumstance of college graduates – low income and dwelling narrowness.

"Xiang ri kui zu" ("向日葵族") is a word of the Internet language which has been popular these years, referring to a group of people who can always discover tiny happiness. The typical characteristics it has are as follows: able to discover tiny happiness; having no ambitious; easy to find the good side of things; resistance to stress and resistance, insensitive feelings of negative emotions; grateful; passionate about life. It is obvious that these features are very similar to the characteristics of the plant "Sunflower", that is, always facing the sun and sunshine. The metaphorical spatial mapping is similar to "yi zu" ("蚁族"), projecting from two originally different source domain into a composite space, which vividly reflects a group of optimists who keep positive attitude towards their life.

Moreover, the source domain and target domain have the same semantic features. In other words, semantic features are the basis for establishing the synthesis space. Therefore, the semantic prosody of the source domain and the semantic prosody of the target domain are also projected into the synthesis space. For example, the positive semantic prosody in "xiang ri kui zu" ("向日葵族") is related to the semantic prosody of the sunflower itself.

3.2 Metonymy

Since 1980s, with the development of cognitive linguistics, academic community has developed a different understanding of the nature and mechanism of metonymy. Most important point is that metonymy is the same as metaphor, it means that metonymy is not just a language expression, but also a way of thinking and a cognitive process.

Contrary to the cross-domain mapping of metaphors, metonymy is a conceptual mapping that occurs in the same cognitive domain. From a cognitive point of view, the attention when people learn something is largely paid on the salient or prominent features of the thing itself, i.e. the formation of words by means of metonymy is somewhat similar to the relationship between the whole thing and the focus part. Since the characteristics of "partial" are more significant, the name of "partial" is used to refer to "the whole thing". Constructing words through metonymy is also a major way in the cognitive field. The premise of metonymy is that in the process of metonymy the correlation between source and target domains is also based on the prominent of the matter.

As far as the words of "X_zu" is concerned, the path of metonymy is roughly the same as above. For example, "dian nao zu" ("电脑族") refers to those people who use computers all day long. The remarkable feature of such kind of people is "using computers"; "di tan zu" ("地摊族") refers to those street vendors who has a small salary, inferior social status, brave the wind and dew; "jiu zuo zu" ("久坐族") refers to those kind of office workers who is sitting the whole day.

From the perspective of the semantic prosody of the words " X_zu", the dip of the semantic prosody is always accompanied with them. The early types of the semantic prosody of words "X_zu" are the same as emerging words of later. Negative semantic prosody of the word "zu" itself is roughly in the same cognitive domain as the group pessimistic property of the words " X_zu". The same kind of attributes attract each other. As a result, the word "zu" becomes gradually popular and grows into a unique phenomenon of Chinese language. In the analysis from previous section, we can see that the earlier "X_zu" words (e.g. "shang ban zu" ("上班族"), "xue sheng zu" ("学生族"), etc.) all contain some negative semantic prosody. Since the negative tendency settled from the beginning, words constructed later easily falls into the same pattern, which explains why the new words are more likely to be negative ones. We do believe that there must be some reasons causing that language phenomenon and needed to be study in the future.

The words "X_zu" through the metonymy mechanism can not only expand the number of original word, but also make its meaning become more stable (i.e. which means groups with common characteristics or attributes) through the continuous metonymy and expansion.

4 Conclusion

Based on the corpus, this paper took the words "X_zu" and its semantic prosody as the research object. In order to explore the unique attributes of this linguistic phenomenon, we first analyzed the semantic prosody of words quantitatively and qualitatively. We divided the words "X_zu" into six types of colligation, analyzing high-frequency words and the semantic prosody of each type. According to analysis, we found that the words formed by this quasi-affix were all affected by the semantics of "Zu" in the process of communication, which resulted in three types of semantic prosody: positive, negative and neutral.

According to quantitative analysis, the words of "X-zu" basically reflects a user's sympathy, pessimism or helplessness, and its semantic prosody tends to be relatively negative. Even if the pre-added roots convey a neutral meaning, after being combined with "Zu", most of them turn to express negative meanings. For example, "di tan" ("地摊族") in the word of "di tan zu" is a neutral etymon, but it is used to refer to the way of supplement families by struggling with life helplessly, which includes a kind of negative semantic prosody.

Moreover, from the perspective of cognition, we made a rough analysis of the semantic prosody of the words "X_zu", focusing more on the causes of meaning of the "X_zu". From the perspective of metaphor, formation of its semantic prosody is mainly due to the source domain and target domain, so they can be projected together to the third synthetic space, and has a specific semantic prosody. From the perspective of metonymy, the prominence of things is the basis for formation of metonymy. The prominence of semantic features is "representation", and the prominence of semantic prosody is its "essence".

The internet language has flourished as the Internet evolves, so that a large number of words with quasi-affixes have sprung up, such as "X_chi", "X_mi", "X_kong", etc. Chinese words are all influenced by the semantics of their quasi-affixes to some extent, so the words themselves also carry some semantic prosody. This paper tries to use the words "X_zu" as an example to explore the relationship between the semantic prosody and the quasi-affixes inside such words. We hope that our work will be helpful for future research in this field.

Acknowledgments. This work is supported by National Language Committee Research Program of China (No. ZDI135-42), and Research & development of question answering for intelligent robots (230200001).

References

Shi, C.: On JIE and TAN. Chin. Lang. Learn. **01**, 9–15 (2002)
Liu, Y.: On X-MEN. Chin. Linguist. **04**, 80–86 (2008)
Liang, Y.: Analysis of the phenomenon of 'X-ZU'. Sci. Educ. Artic. Collect. **09**, 183 (2007). https://doi.org/10.3969/j.issn.1672-7894.2007.25.148
Zhao, G.: Linguistic analysis of "X_zu". J. Yunan Norm. Univ. (Teach. Res. Chin. Foreign Lang. Ed.) **06**, 86–89 (2007)
Zhao, J.: Analysis and comparion on new words "X_zu", "X_ke", "X_you". Huazhong University of Science and Technology (2012). https://doi.org/10.7666/d.y2077450
Meng, Z., Wei, N.: Research on semantic prosody of academic texts: attributes, features and methods. J. PLA Univ. Foreign Lang. **03**, 14–22 (2015)
Wei, N.: General method of semantic prosody research. Foreign Lang. Teach. Res. **04**, 300–307 (2002). https://doi.org/10.3969/j.issn.1000-0429.2002.04.010
Zhang, Y.: An overview of 20-year research on semantic prosody based on corpus. Foreign Lang. Res. **06**, 23–28 (2012). https://doi.org/10.3969/j.issn.1005-7242.2012.06.004
Wan, W.: The research on semantic prosody of adverb of degree which denotes a less degree in Modern Chinese Peking University (2012)
Cao, T., Mo, W.: Semantic analysis of network new words "X Men". J. Hunan Univ. Sci. Technol. (Soc. Sci. Ed.), 122–124 (2012). https://doi.org/10.3969/j.issn.1672-7835.2012.01.025
Zhang, J.: Analysis of the "X" in the "X_zu" words. Mod. Chin., 143–145 (2010). https://doi.org/10.3969/j.issn.1008-8024-c.2010.06.053
Wang, Z., Zhang, Y.: The theory of semantic prosody. Tongji Univ. J. Soc. Sci. Sect. (2009). https://doi.org/10.3969/j.issn.1009-3060.2005.04.014
Liu, D.: Study of modern Chinese quasi-affix and its cognitive aspect. Jinan University (2015)
Sun, J.: A cognitive semantic study of English and Chinese quasi-affixes. Hunan Normal University (2013)
Jia, Z.: Study of quasi-affix in Chinese in the cognitive aspects. Northwest Normal University (2011)
Yuan, Y.: Conceptual metonymy in Chinese and its grammatical consequences. Lang. Teach. Linguist. Stud. **01**, 30–43 (2018)
Chen, G.: Chinese Lexical Theory. Xue Llin Publishing House (2001)
Hu, F.: Modern Chinese Grammar Exploration. Oriental Bookstore (1955)

Placement Verbs in Chinese and English: Language-Specific Lexicalization Patterns

Meichun Liu(✉) and Jui-Ching Chang

Department of Linguistics and Translation,
City University of Hong Kong, Hong Kong, China
meichliu@cityu.edu.hk, showtheray@gmail.com

Abstract. This study aims to show that language-specific distinctions of lexicalization patterns are crucial to verbal semantic studies by examining the differences of Placement verbs in English and Chinese. It argues that cross-linguistic transference of lexical knowledge should not be made without a detailed analysis of seemingly corresponding verbs in different languages. It also probes into the long-debated issue on how languages conceptualize a common event type with distinct lexical and grammatical realizations. By conducting a contrastive study of the lexicalization patterns of placement verbs in Chinese and English, it is proposed that, while a placing event is conceptually universal in taking the basic semantic components of Agent, Theme, Location, and Path, placement verbs in Chinese and English vary in their lexical origins, level of specificity and morpho-semantic subtypes. It is shown that placement verbs are lexicalized and categorized in language-specific ways that have typological implications. Ultimately, the study sheds new light on class-specific, cross-linguistic comparisons.

Keywords: Placement verbs · Lexicalization pattern · Verbal semantics
Language-specific distinction · Chinese and English

1 Introduction

How a given event or state is conceptualized by speakers from various cultural and linguistic backgrounds has been a long-debated issue in linguistics and cognitive science. Some scholars argue that different languages may share a similar conceptualization pattern since the semantic structures of a basic-level event should share a common ground, as a universal 'prototype' for the event [1]. Other schools of thought, such as the Sapir-Whorf hypothesis [2, 3], stand in the opposite side proposing that different languages may adopt different strategies in conceptualizing and understanding the world. There are also viewpoints that lie in between, incorporating the two extremes (e.g., [4, 5]).

A direct way to probe into the question can be done with a cross-linguistic comparison of lexicalization patterns, which can help to reveal in what way and to what extend languages are similar or distinctive to each other. In this study, we conduct a class-specific comparison of the lexicalization pattern of placement verbs (PL verbs) in Chinese and English. Placing is one of the most basic domains of experience.

J.-F. Hong et al. (Eds.): CLSW 2018, LNAI 11173, pp. 454–466, 2018.
https://doi.org/10.1007/978-3-030-04015-4_38

The experiential domain of placement, such as 'putting a book on the table' and 'putting a pen in the pencil box', is cognitively fundamental for all speakers. Thus, the linguistic means of coding such a fundamental event may help re-veal the language-specific distinctions, if any. The way placement is conceptualized is manifested through its lexicalization pattern in the verbal lexicon. In other words, verbal semantic distinctions realized in placement verbs may provide a window to the fundamental differences of conceptual frameworks between languages.

In the following, a brief review of the semantics of placement event is given in Sect. 2; Sect. 3 outlines the three major differences in lexicalization patterns between Chinese and English Placement verbs; and Sect. 4 concludes the study with a summary and discussion of its implication.

2 Semantics of Placement

A placement event, or putting event, as termed in some studies, can be defined as "deliberately placing an object somewhere under manual control" [6: 10], and is universally encoded with the four basic semantic components: Motion, Figure, Path, and Ground [7]. Although placing is mundane for human cognition as it can be acquired early in childhood [8], it is proposed that languages have different ways of 'framing' the essential components. That is, while Motion is generally encoded with the verb, there is a coding distinction among 'satellite-framed languages' such as English, in which Path is encoded by a satellite (i.e., prepositional phrase) and 'verb-framed languages' such as Spanish, in which Path is lexicalized into the verb itself, as illustrated in (1) and (2). On the other hand, Chinese, while Talmy [9] takes it as Satellite-framed and Tai [10] argues that it is verb-framed, can be viewed as an 'equipollently-framed language', in which serial verb construction is used [11–14],[1] as illustrated in (3):

(1) Satellite-framed (e.g., English)
I $\text{put}_{\text{Motion}}$ the pencil in_{Path} the box.
(2) Verb-framed (e.g., Spanish)
$\text{Mete}_{\text{Motion+Path}}$ el lapiz en la caja
'(Someone) insert the pencil at the box.'
(3) Equipollently-framed (e.g., Chinese)
我把鉛筆放$_{\text{Motion}}$進$_{\text{Path}}$盒子裡
'I put the pencil in the box'

[1] It is still debatable among scholars about the specific framing type Chinese belongs to. Counter to Slobin's [13] proposal that Chinese is equipollently-framed, Talmy [9] classified Chinese as a satellite-framed language, taking the path markers in Chinese as 'prepositions'. However, Tai [10], based on the fact that Chinese resultative complement is verb-rooted, argued that Chinese is primarily verb-framed and only secondarily satellite-framed. See the references cited above for details of discussion.

The typological differences show that while the semantic components of placing may be similar, they may be encoded by different linguistic devices. The coding distinctions are manifested at both the lexical and syntactic levels. In verb-framed languages, verbs themselves are lexicalized with the essential information of motional Path. Thus, in Spanish, it tends to use *mete* 'insert' or *entrar* 'enter' that specifies the path contour, rather than a path-neutral verb such as English *put* that needs a satellite-PP to specify the path contour.

PL verbs in Chinese and English also involve motional path. Besides the typological difference in framing schemes, it has been observed that the prototypical members of PL verbs, i.e., English *put* and Chinese *fàng* 放, differ in their semantic scopes and constructional associations [15, 16]. While English *put* is restricted to denoting a mere placement event, occurring only with locative prepositions *on/in/at* but not with source marker *from* or goal marker *to*, Chinese *fàng* 放 'place, put' encompasses a wider range of usage, capable of collocating with both source and goal markers (*cóng* 從 'from' and *dào* 到 'to') and aligning more with caused-motion verbs such as *bān* 搬 'move' in highlighting a path (把書放到/搬到桌上 'place/move the book to the table'), as given in (4). While both verbs are used in an agentive-transitive pattern as in (4), the Chinese *fàng* 放 can also describe the spatial position of the moved entity in Figure-anchored stative expression or Ground-anchored locative inversion, indicating a spatial configurational relation; but the English *put* cannot appear in these constructions without a passivized form [17, 18], as given in (5):

(4) a. 我把書放在桌上 → I put the books on the table.
b. 我把書從地上放到桌上 → *I put the books from the ground to the table.
c. 我把書搬到/放到桌上 → I moved/*put the books to the table.

(5) a. 書放在桌上 → The books were placed/*placed on the table.
b. 桌上放著書 → On the table were placed/*placed the books.

These examples indicate that PL verbs in Mandarin encode a motion-triggered causal chain of three potential stages: caused-to-move, caused-to-be and the resultative state of spatial configuration [16]. The preliminary study paves the way for further exploration of lexical specificities that are characteristic of PL verbs in the two languages. In the next section, we will discuss the cross-linguistic variations in lexical origin, level of specificity and morpho-semantic subtypes.

3 Lexicalization of Placement Verbs in Chinese and English

In this section we examine the similarities and differences in the lexicalization patterns of PL verbs in Chinese and English. Three dimensions are discussed: posture- vs. non-posture based lexical source; informatively light vs. heavy verbs; morpho-semantic coding of manner vs. result.

3.1 Posture- vs. Non-posture-Based Placement

In English, PL verbs show a posture-based pattern of lexicalization. English has four basic PL verbs *put*, *place*, *set*, and *lay*, among which *set* and *lay* are derived from the verbs *sit* and *lie*, which denote the common postural states of humans [19]. This posture-based lexicalization pattern is well-observed not only in English, but also in other Germanic languages, such as Dutch and Swedish. For example, similar to English, the basic Dutch PL verbs *zetten* 'set' and *leggen* 'lay', are derived from posture verbs *zitten* 'sit' and *liggen* 'lie', respectively. Thus, PL verbs in these languages are also termed as 'caused-posture' verbs, as they are the causative counterparts of posture verbs [20]. This posture-based strategy is cognitively fundamental and sensible as it takes bodily experiences that are most familiar to humans as the basis of conceptualizing and lexicalizing the act of placing external entities [21].[2]

However, in Chinese, a different strategy is adopted. Firstly, typical Chinese PL verbs, such as *fàng/bǎi/shè/zhì*放/擺/設/置, do not originate from posture verbs. The original meaning of *fàng* 放 may refer to a kind of hand movement, as the radical of *fàng* 放 is *pū* 攴, which means 'knock by hand'; and in *Shuowen Jiezi* (說文解字), *fàng* 放 means 'release or banish (someone from a place to another)'. Similarly, *bǎi* 擺 is also a hand movement, as it is formed with *shǒu* 手 'hand' as its radical. It is clear that these prototypical placement verbs in Chinese are movement-based rather than posture-based. The only exception may be the verb *lì*立, which is a more archaic form and used more restrictively as a posture or placement verb.[3]

Secondly, Chinese posture verbs cannot be used to denote the act of placing, as shown in (6) and (7). This is supported with evidence from corpus distribution: in Sinica Balanced Corpus,[4] all three cardinal posture verbs *zuò/zhàn/tǎng*坐/站/躺 are found to denote human postures, as given in Table 1.

(6) a. 我坐在桌上
'I sat on the desk.'
b. *我把電腦坐在桌上
'I set the PC on the desk.'

(7) a. 我躺在床上.
'I lay on the bed.'
b. *我把衣服躺在床上
'I lay the clothes on the bed.'
c. 我把衣服平放在床上
'I lay the clothes on the bed.'

[2] Note that English *put* is not derived from posture verb but from *putten* 'push' in Middle English and therefore it can be viewed as also a movement-based placement verb. In this sense, English is slightly different from other Germanic languages in which the posture-based pattern is adopted predominantly.

[3] The verb *lì*立 'stand' is originally a verb of human posture and can also be used to denote placement as in 我把書立在桌上 stood the book on the table.' But as an archaic form, it is less prototypical as a posture verb since it cannot be used to denote 'assuming posture' (**他立了起來 He stood up.').

[4] http://asbc.iis.sinica.edu.tw/.

Table 1. Distribution of posture vs. placement uses of ***zuò/zhàn/tǎng*** 坐/站/躺 in Sinica Corpus

	Posture	Placement
zuò 坐	807	0
zhàn 站	667	0
tǎng 躺	352	0

In (7c), when denoting the equivalent of 'lay (caused to lie)', Chinese has to use a Manner-Verb compound *píng-fàng* 平放 'flat-put', to indicate the act of 'placing something horizontally'. In addition, given the posture-based lexicalizing strategy in English, English posture verbs can be directly used to predicate inanimate entities in locative constructions, without using passivized forms, as in (8).

(8) a. The book lies on the table.
    b. On the table lies the book.

This shows that English posture verbs provide the essential conceptual base for lexicalizing placement events as well as spatial configurational states. In contrast, Chinese placement verbs are lexically independent and distinct from posture verbs, as they are motion-triggered and encode a wider range of eventive structure from caused motion to placement to spatial configuration.

In sum, the posture-based pattern of conceptualizing and lexicalizing PL verbs, found in English along with other Germanic languages, is not adopted in the Chinese way of lexicalization; instead, Chinese exhibits a movement-based lexicalization pattern.

3.2 Level of Specificity

In this section, we compare Chinese and English placement verbs in terms of level of semantic specificity or informativeness. Verbs that are semantically underspecified can be applied to a wider range of expressions and thus are termed as 'general purpose verbs' or 'light verb'; on the other hand, 'heavy verbs' are semantically more specified or highly informative and can only be applied to a more limited range of context [22–24]. Languages vary in terms of how they lexicalize the level of specificity in their verbal lexicon. Both Chinese and English lexicalize informationally light as well as heavy PL verbs,[5] but show different modes of distributions. We will discuss light verbs first, and then heavy verbs.

3.2.1 Light Verbs

In English, *put* is generally considered as a light verb, as [6: 10] states, "*put*" is typically described as a "light verb" with relatively little meaning beyond its schematic

[5] Not all languages show the differences between 'light verbs' vs. 'heavy verbs' in placement. For example, Tzeltal, a Maya language, has been reported habitually using more than sixty lexicons in denoting various types of placement events in terms of the spatial-configurational states and therefore is argued as a language without light verb [25].

sense of "caused motion/change of location." Slobin *et al.* [12] echoes this view with supporting data from children's speech. They further proposed that this is a distinctive feature of English from other Germanic languages such as German. German speakers make finer categorization of placement events since they tend to differentiate the situations in which a Figure is placed horizontally or vertically, with commonly used verbs such as *legen* 'lay' or *stellen* 'make stand'. That is to say, German speakers prefer to use lexically more specified verbs to describe 'caused-posture' that results in a certain spatial-configurational orientation of the placed entity. Compared to German, English tend to use the semantically generic verb *put*, to denote placement regardless of the spatial-configurational state of the Figure to the Ground, as given in Fig. 1.

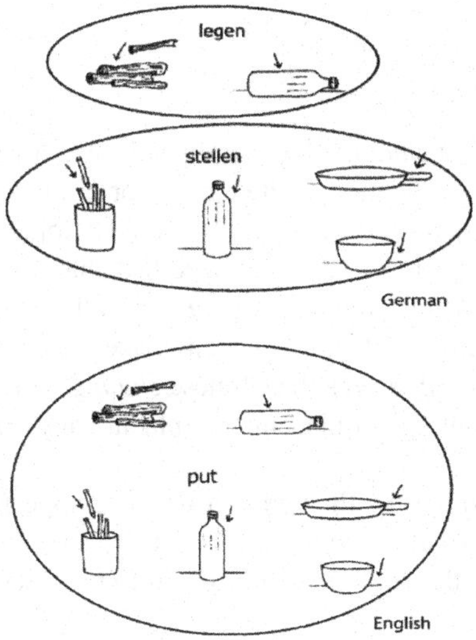

Fig. 1. German vs. English placement categories [12: 153]

In this regard, Chinese and English are typologically alike: in Chinese, the verb *fàng* 放 put, place' can also be characterized as a light verb [14]. There is no spatial configurational implication attached to it under the non-posture-based strategy. Moreover, *fàng* 放 used not only to denote the hand movement of putting, but to cover a wide range of meaning extensions, as exemplified in (9).

(9) a. 我把一半的錢放在銀行
'I store half of our money in the bank.'
b. 攤販把蔥放在較隱密處
'The vender hides the green onions in the covert place'
c. 商人將總部放在台灣
'The business set the headquarter in Taiwan.'

Each use of *fàng* 放 (9) can be replaced with another verb which is more specified in meaning: for example, it can be substituted with *cún* 存 store' in (9a), *cáng* 藏 hide' in (9b), and *shèzhì* 設置 set' in (9c). That is, *fàng* 放 is an informationally light verb of placement, which is semantically underspecified in its characterization of the involved components (figure, ground, path, goal), and thus can be used more freely in denoting various types of placing.

Besides *fàng* 放 another Chinese verb - *zhuāng* 裝 'load or fill' - is relatively 'light' compared to its English counterparts. The verb is semantically underspecified in coding different types of moved entities, and it can correspond to a number of English verbs that are rather distinct in meaning, such as *load*, *pack*, *fill*, *package*, as given in (10).

(10) a. 我把貨物裝到推車上
'I loaded the goods onto the trolley.'
b. 我把衣服裝進箱子裡
'I packed my clothes into the box.
c. 我把咖啡裝到瓶子裡
'I filled the bottle with coffee.'

The examples show that *zhuāng* 裝 generally subcategorizes a Container-Containee relation without further specification of the manner or means: "trolley, box, and bottle" are all container-like, which can take less-constrained Containee, be it solid or fluid. The meaning of *zhuāng* 裝 is surely more specified than that of the prototypical PL verb *fàng* 放 as the uses of *zhuāng* 裝 in (9) can all be replaced by *fàng* 放 But compared to English verbs of loading which makes a distinction on the types of Containee (load goods vs. fill water), the Chinese *zhuāng* 裝 is semantically 'lighter' as it profiles a generalized subtype of placement – placing any kind of Containee into any kind of Container.

In sum, the categorization of PL verbs in Chinese appears to be less fine-grained than their English counterparts in view of the fact that there is a more generic term or hypernym for describing the subtype of placement, i.e., placing into a Container.

3.2.2 Heavy Verbs

With regard to heavy PL verbs, they are semantically more restricted and informative, such as English *insert* and Chinese *chā* 插 which are manner-specific in requiring a narrow opening of the ground with a thin figure to denote 'tight-fitting' placement. Moreover, there are some intriguing subtypes of PL verbs in English with a relatively high level of specificity in depicting the Figure, Ground, or Instrument. According to [17], there are 'butter verbs' (e.g., *butter*, *seed*, *poster*) with further specified Figure, 'pocket verbs' (e.g., *pocket*, *bottle*, *box*) with further specified Ground, and 'funnel verbs' (e.g., *funnel*, *spoon*, *hammer*) with further specified Instrument, as given in (11) to (13), respectively.

(11) I *buttered* the toast. (i.e. I put butter on the toast.)
(12) I *pocketed* the change. (i.e. I put the change in her pocket.)
(13) I *funneled* the mixture into the bottle. (i.e. I use funnel to put the mixture into the bottle.)

In Levin's terms, these verbs "have zero-related nominals"; they originate from nouns that refer to the specified Figure (*butter*), Ground (*pocket*), or Instrument (*funnel*). This shows that English PL verbs are relatively more flexible in their lexical origins and placing-relevant nouns can be type-shifted into verbs with incorporated information from the nominal source. These types of verbs are highly specific in semantics and thus highly restricted in use.

In contrast, this N-to-V lexicalization pattern of PL verbs is rarely found in Chinese. The Chinese counterparts of examples (11) to (13) can only be expressed with a lighter PL verb, such as *tú* 塗 spread, spray' or *zhuāng* 裝 load, fill', as given in (14) to (16).

(14) I buttered the toast:
  a. 我塗了奶油在這片麵包上
  b. *我奶油了這片麵包
(15) I pocketed the change:
  a. 我裝了零錢在口袋裡
  b. *我口袋了零錢
(16) I funneled the mixture into the bottle:
  a. 我用漏斗把混合液裝到瓶子裡
  b. *我漏斗了混合液到瓶子裡

As shown above, Chinese is in general less flexible in allowing direct shift of nouns into PL verbs. However, there are still few cases that show N-to-V shift, as exemplified in (17).

(17) a. 他把車身漆為白色
  'He painted the car into white (with paint)'
  b. 他把垃圾鏟到推車裡
  'He shovels the garbage into a cart.'
  c. 他盛了一碗湯
  'He bowled a cup of soup'
  d. 他把色彩塗在畫布上
  'He paints the colors on the canvas.'

In (17a), *qī* 漆 paint', can be used as either a noun or a verb. The verb *qī* 漆 is originally a noun referring to coatings and then used as a PL verb, but it only takes cognate NP-objects such as *yóuqī* 油漆 or *yánliào* 顏料 e.g., 漆油漆 In (17b), the use of *chǎn* 鏟 shovel' is similar to English *funnel* in (13); *chǎn* 鏟 originally refers to 'shovel', and used here as a verb denoting an event of 'placing by shoveling,' in which a shovel is used as the instrument. The verb *chéng* 盛 ladle out' as given (17c) is also derived from a nominal origin referring to a kind of 'sacrificial utensil/bowl/cup'. When it is used as a verb, it denotes only the meaning of 'putting food/soup in a bowl/cup' whereby both the figure and ground are fixed in type. However, *chéng* 盛 different from English 'pocket' verbs, which have 'zero-related nominals', since *chéng* is no longer used as a noun in Modern Chinese. The nominal origin of *chéng* 盛 is already lost by giving its way to the verbal use. Similar to *chéng* 盛 the verb *tú* 塗 paint' in (17d) is originally a noun referring to 'mud'; but it has lost its nominal use and no longer refers to mud. These Chinese verbs are different from English '*butter* verbs' that are predominantly used as a nominal. Based on the cases of *chéng* 盛 and *tú* 塗 it can be observed that the Chinese N-to-V lexicalization pattern can be considered as resulting from 'lexical diffusion' [26–28]: While they are originally used as nouns, they have lost their nominal meanings and used mainly as verbs in contemporary Chinese.

In sum, in terms of level of specificity, English productively lexicalizes noun-incorporated verbs: It makes finer distinctions in the domain of placement and contain highly-specified subtypes of PL verbs as those illustrated in (11) to (13), namely, 'butter verbs' (Figure-specified), 'pocket verbs' (Ground-specified), and 'funnel verbs' (Instrument-specified); and these kinds of verbs are productive. Chinese, on the other hand, uses semantically lighter verbs for these expressions and has much less noun-derived PL verbs, and adopts this N-to-V pattern as lexical diffusion.

3.3 Lexicalizing the Resulting State

In this section, we discuss how English and Chinese differ in terms of the way 'result' is lexicalized.

In English PL verbs, there is a class of '*fill* verbs', as Levin proposed that "these verbs typically describe the resulting state of a location as a consequence of putting something on/in it" [17: 120]. Two examples of such verbs are given in (18).

(18) a. *He filled the bottle with apple juice.*
b. *He soaked the dog with water.*

These verbs focus more on the resulting state in relation to the affected object. For the use of *fill* in (18a), the bottle (Container) must be full, and for the use of *soak* in (18b), the dog (Containee) must be totally wet. Note that in terms of locative alternation (*unto* vs. *with* variants), these verbs can only occur in the *with* variant (*I filled the bottle with water*), taking the Containee-Figure as the instrument marked by the preposition *with* and the Container-Ground as the direct object. They are said to lexically encode a 'holistic' effect [17, 29]. For these 'result-incorporated' PL verbs, they may each has a 'manner-incorporated' counterpart. *Fill* in (18a) could be contrasted with *pour*, which simply denote the action of pouring liquid into the container; and *soak* in (18b) with *splash/spill*, which semantically focus more on the manner of action instead of resulting state of the location. Broadly speaking, English verbal lexicon in general displays a bipartite distinction between manner vs. result verbs [30–32]. Manner verbs specify a manner of carrying out an action (e.g., *pound, sweep*), while Result verbs specify the result of an action (e.g., *cover, empty, clean*). Such a dichotomy gives rise to two subclasses of verbs in the same frame, as illustrated in Table 2.

Table 2. Manner verbs vs. Result verbs

	Manner	Result
Verbs of removing	Shovel	Empty
Verbs of killing	Stab	Kill
Verbs of putting	Pour	Fill

However, due to typological differences, Chinese does not use simple PL verbs to denote result; instead, it resorts to the morphological device of Resultative-Verb Compound (RVC) (or Verb-Result, V-R compound) to encode the resulting state [33]. The Chinese counterparts of *fill* and *soak* are *zhuāng-mǎn* 裝滿 'pour-full' and *jìn-shī* 浸濕 'soak-wet', both of which are bi-syllabic V-R compounds. Syntactically, the Chinese expressions of result involve the use of the co-verb BA followed by the affected object, as given in (19).

(19) a. 他把瓶子裝滿蘋果汁
'He filled the bottle with apple juice.'
b. 他把狗浸濕在水裡
'He soaked the dog with water.'
c. 他把小孩用毛毯包住
'He swaddled the baby with a blanket.'
d. 他把窗戶用毛巾遮住
'He covered the windows with towels.'

With different morpho-constructional devices, Chinese shows a different lexicalization means of encoding the result of placing. While English has clearly lexicalized a class of result-encoded '*fill* verbs', Chinese has no such lexical equivalents except for using V-R compounds with a V indicating the manner of placing and a R indicating the result of being 'full'. A consequence of this lexical strategy is that the event of 'fill' can be expressed with a variety of V-elements followed by the designated R-element *mǎn* 滿 'full', such as ***zhuāng/fàng/dào/zhēn/zhù+mǎn***裝/放/倒/斟/注+滿 'load/put/pour/pour (wine)/fill'.

What's interesting is that this lexical semantic variation may cause problems for Chinese learners of English verbs. Since Chinese students may not have a clear idea about the distinction of manner vs. result verbs, they may use *fill* as a manner verb similar to *load*, and utter odd sentences such as **Please fill water for me*, mistaking *fill* as equivalent to the Chinese verb *zhuāng* 裝 'load', a semantically light verb denoting the general manner of putting some containee into a container. The lexical 'slicing' of meanings in PL verbs vary cross-linguistically, which is responsible for problems in language learning.

In addition, as observed above, English *fill*-verbs must take the *with*-variant, in which Figure is expressed as Instrument (*fill the bottle with water*). In Chinese, it is also possible to express the Figure as Instrument with an instrument marker *yòng* 用 (20); however, for some verbs, it is the Ground, instead of the Figure, that is encoded as Instrument, as seen in (21) below. The corpus distribution of Figure-as-Instrument vs. Ground-as-instrument in Chinese Gigaword[6] is shown in Table 3.

(20) Figure as Instrument
a. 他用易燃的液體淋濕自己
'He soaked himself with flammable liquids'
b. 他用一條大毛巾將新生兒包住
'He swaddled the new-born baby with a blanket.'

[6] Chinese Gigaword is a corpus of 1.4 billion words (https://catalog.ldc.upenn.edu/ldc2011t13)

Table 3. Distribution of Figure-as-Instrument vs. Ground-as-Instrument in PL compounds (in Chinese GigaWord)

	línshī 淋濕	*bāozhù* 包住	*zhuāngmǎn* 裝滿	*sāimǎn* 塞滿
Figure-as-instrument	4	27	1	0
Ground-as-instrument	0	0	23	4

(21) Ground as Instrument
a. 他用袋子裝滿泥土
#'He fill the bag with mud'
b. 他用杯子盛滿香檳
#'He fill the glass with champagne.'

As we can see in (21), Ground can also be expressed as Instrument with *yòng* 用 'use'; and the tendency is quite clear from the corpus distribution. What is revealed here is that, English *fill*-verbs are quite homogeneous in use as they semantically profile the resulting state in relation to the Ground. But in Chinese, the resultative state can be described in alternative ways with two different viewpoints: a result pertaining to the Ground with the Figure as Instrument (*用水灌入抽水機* 'fill the pump with water'), or a result pertaining to the Figure with the Ground as Instrument (用瓶子裝滿水 # 'fill up water with the bottle'). It shows that there are language-specific ways of profiling the semantic roles with different arrangements.

4 Conclusion

In this study, we have provided a detailed comparison of the lexicalization patterns of placement verbs in Chinese and English. It shows in what ways PL verbs in the two languages vary in terms of lexical origins, semantic specificity and slicing of sub-classes. First, Chinese and English adopt different strategies in conceptualizing and lexicalizing PL verbs: while most PL verbs in English (e.g., *set* and *lay*) are posture-based, Chinese PL verbs are mostly motion-based and use patterns similar to caused-motion verbs. Secondly, PL verbs in the two languages differ in fine-tuned levels of semantic specificity: Chinese PL verbs tend to be lexically under-specified and informationally light without further characterizing the semantic restriction of Figure/Ground/Instrument. As a result, there are less noun-incorporated PL verbs in Chinese. In English, a clear distinction can be made between Manner vs. Result verbs and finer characterization may be found in subclasses of PL verbs, which depict varied features of Figure, Ground, Instrument, Manner, or Result. Such verbs include '*butter* verbs', '*pocket* verbs', and '*funnel* verbs', which are highly restricted and informative in meaning. Lastly, Chinese and English apply different morphological patterns in encoding the result of placing. While English may incorporate the resulting state into a single verb such as the '*fill/wet*' subtype, Chinese uses V-R compounds to denote an action+result, and thus lacks fully lexicalized equivalents to 'fill' verbs.

In conclusion, the study offers a detailed cross-linguistic comparison of verbal semantic distinctions in the lexicalization patterns for the class of placement verbs. It suggests that language-specific properties need to be teased out before we can make theoretical generalizations or annotational decisions to represent lexical information for further applications. Such an approach may help to detect cross-linguistic variations and shed new light on how different conceptual models and strategies may be adopted by different languages in lexicalizing fundamental event types other than placement.

References

1. Rosch, E., Mervis, C.B.: Family resemblances: studies in the internal structure of categories. Cogn. Psychol. **7**, 573–605 (1975). https://doi.org/10.1016/0010-0285(75)90024-9
2. Sapir, E.: Language: An Introduction to the Study of Speech. Harcourt Brace and Company, New York (1921)
3. Whorf, B.: Language, Thought, and Reality: Selected Writings of Benjamin Lee Whorf. In: Carroll, J.B. (ed.) Technology Press of MIT, Oxford, UK (1956)
4. Regier, T.: The Human Semantic Potential. The MIT Press, Cambridge (1996)
5. Levinson, S.C., Meira, S.: The language and cognition group: 'natural concepts' in the spatial topological domain-adpositional meanings in crosslinguistic perspective: an exercise in semantic typology. Language **79**(3), 485–516 (2003). https://doi.org/10.1353/lan.2003.0174
6. Bowerman, M., Gullberg, M., Majid, A., Narasimhan, B.: Put project: the cross-linguistic encoding of placement events. In: Majid, A. (ed.) Field Manual, vol. 9, pp. 10–24. Max Planck Institute for Psycholinguistics, Nijmegen (2004). https://doi.org/10.17617/2.492916
7. Talmy, L.: Semantics and syntax of motion. In: Kimball, J. (ed.) Syntax and Semantics, vol. 4, pp. 181–238. Academic Press, New York (1975)
8. Pinker, S.: Learnability and Cognition: The Acquisition of Argument Structure. MIT Press, Cambridge, MA (1989)
9. Talmy, L.: Towards a Cognitive Semantics, 2 vols. MIT Press, Cambridge, MA (2000)
10. Tai, J.H.-Y.: Cognitive relativism: resultative construction in Chinese. Lang. Linguist. **4**(2), 301–316 (2003)
11. Talmy, L.: Path to realization: a typology of event conflation. Proc. Berkeley Linguist. Soc. **17**, 480–520 (1991)
12. Slobin, D.I., Bowerman, M., Brown, P., Eisenbeiß, S., Narasimhan, B.: Putting things in places: developmental consequences of linguistic typology. In: Bohnemeye, J., Pederson, E. (eds.) Event Representation in Language and Cognition, pp. 134–165. Cambridge University Press, New York (2010). https://doi.org/10.1017/cbo9780511782039.007
13. Slobin, D.I.: The many ways to search for a frog: linguistic typology and the expression of motion events. In: Strömqvist, S., Verhoeven, L. (eds.) Relating Events in Narrative: Typological and Contextual Perspectives, vol. 2, pp. 219–257. Lawrence Erlbaum Associates, Mahwah, NJ (2004)
14. Chen, J.: "She from bookshelf take-descend-come the box": encoding and categorizing placement events in Mandarin. In: Kopecka, A., Narasimhan, B. (eds.) Events of Putting and Taking: A Crosslinguistic Perspective, pp. 37–54. John Benjamins, Amsterdam (2012)
15. Liu, M., Chang, J.-C.: From placement to positioning – spatial configuration verbs in Mandarin. Paper presented IACL 25, Budapest, Hungary, 25–27 June 2017
16. Liu, M., Chang, J.-C.: From caused-motion to spatial configuration: placement verbs in Mandarin. Language & Linguistics **20**(1) (forthcoming)

17. Levin, B.: English Verb Classes and Alternations: A Preliminary Investigation. University of Chicago Press, Chicago (1993)
18. Chen, Y.-L.: On Syntax and Semantics of Placement Verbs in Mandarin Chinese. M.A. Thesis. National Cheng Kung University, Tainan (2009)
19. Pauwels, P.: Put, Set, Lay, and Place: A Cognitive Linguistic Approach to Verbal Meaning. Lincom, Munich (2000)
20. Lemmens, M.: Caused posture: experiential patterns emerging from corpus research. In: Gries, S., Stefanowitsch, A. (eds.) Corpora in Cognitive Linguistics: Corpus-Based Approaches to Syntax and Lexis, pp. 261–296. Mouton de Gruyter, Berlin (2006)
21. Newman, J. (ed.): The Linguistics of Sitting, Standing, and Lying. John Benjamins, Amsterdam, Philadelphia (2002). https://doi.org/10.1075/tsl.51
22. Clark, E.V.: Discovering what words can do. In: Farkas, D., Jacobsen, W.M., Todrys, K.W. (eds.) Papers from the parasession on the lexicon, pp. 34–57. Chicago Linguistic Society, Chicago, IL (1978)
23. Ninio, A.: Model learning in syntactic development: intransitive verbs. Int. J. Biling. **3**(2&3), 111–131 (1999). https://doi.org/10.1177/13670069990030020301
24. Maouene, J., Laakso, A., Smith, L.B.: Object associations of early-learned light and heavy english verbs. First Lang. **31**(1), 109–132 (2011). https://doi.org/10.1177/0142723710380528
25. Brown, P.: Verb specificity and argument realization in Tzeltal child language. In: Bowerman, M., Brown, P. (eds.) Crosslinguistic Perspectives on Argument Structure: Implications for Language Acquisition, pp. 167–189. Lawrence Erlbaum Associates, Hillsdale (2008). https://doi.org/10.4324/9780203826218
26. Chen, M.Y., Wang, W.S.-Y.: Sound change: actuation and implementation. Language **51**(2) 255–281 (1975). https://doi.org/10.2307/412854
27. Ogura, M., Wang, W.S.-Y: Lexical diffusion in semantic change: with special reference to universal changes. Folia Linguistica Historica **29**, 29–74 (1995). https://doi.org/10.1515/flih.1995.16.1-2.29
28. Tottie, G.: Lexical diffusion in syntactic change: frequency as a determinant in the development of negation in English. In: Kastovsky, D. (ed.) Historical English Syntax, pp. 439–467. Mouton de Gruyter, Berlin (1991)
29. Dowty, D.: The garden swarms with bees' and the fallacy of 'argument alternation'. In: Ravin, Y., Laecock, C. (eds.) Polysemy: Theoretical and Computational Approaches, pp. 111–128. Oxford University Press, Oxford (2000)
30. Levin, B., Rappaport Hovav, M.: Argument Structure. Cambridge University Press, Cambridge (2005)
31. Rappaport Hovav, M., Levin, B.: Building verb meanings. In: Butt, M., Geuder, W. (eds.) The Projection of Arguments: Lexical and Compositional Factors, pp. 97–134. CSLI Publications, Stanford (1998)
32. Rappaport Hovav, M., Levin, B.: Reflections on manner/result complementarity. In: Rappaport Hovav, M., Doron, E., Sichel, I. (eds.) Lexical Semantics, Syntax, and Event Structure. Oxford University Press, Oxford, UK (2010). https://doi.org/10.1093/acprof:oso/9780199544325.001.0001
33. Li, C.N., Thompson, S.A.: Mandarin Chinese: A Functional Reference Grammar. University of California Press (1981)

A Study on Lexical Ambiguity in Mandarin Chinese

Jia-Fei Hong(✉)

National Taiwan Normal University, Taipei, Taiwan
jiafeihong@ntnu.edu.tw

Abstract. This study explored lexical ambiguity in Mandarin Chinese. Previous studies have concentrated on the lexical ambiguity resolution of nouns and verbs in the sentential context, while others presented different results for ambiguity resolution in English and Italian. Based on [1] study, which focused on the cognitive processing of strong bias words in the sentential context, the current study proposed two modular and interactive hypotheses and designed two experiments—a production test and a YES-NO test—to distinguish lexical and metaphorical bias found in Mandarin Chinese. This article would present the results of the two experiments, followed by a discussion of the related senses of lexical ambiguity in Mandarin Chinese.

Keywords: Mandarin chinese · Lexical ambiguity · Literal senses Metaphorical senses

1 Introduction

This study used the Chinese Gigaword Corpus [2] and Chinese Word Sketch (http://wordsketch.ling.sinica.edu.tw/) to retrieve data for the experimental materials. Based on [1] study on the cognitive processing of strong bias words in the sentential context, the results of which verified the modular and interactive hypotheses proposed, the current study designed two experiments—a production test and a YES-NO test—to distinguish sense bias of lexical ambiguity in Mandarin Chinese.

This article will first present a review of previous studies on lexical ambiguity, followed by the hypotheses and research questions for the current study. Then, the article will discuss the Chinese Gigaword Corpus and how Chinese Word Sketch was used to select the data for the experimental materials. Next, original data from the Chinese Gigaword Corpus will be presented. Finally, the results from the two experiments will be presented, and the conclusion section will discuss the related senses of lexical ambiguity in Mandarin Chinese.

2 Previous Studies

Previous studies on lexical ambiguity have focused on the resolution of nouns and verbs [3, 4], the sentential context [1, 3, 5–7], and the different results of ambiguity resolution in English and Italian [8, 9]. The current study focused on four studies on lexical ambiguity— [1, 3, 4], and [8] —in designing its experimental materials.

J.-F. Hong et al. (Eds.): CLSW 2018, LNAI 11173, pp. 467–477, 2018.
https://doi.org/10.1007/978-3-030-04015-4_39

In [1], two major hypotheses were proposed to investigate lexical ambiguity, the modularity hypothesis and the interactive hypothesis. According to the modularity hypothesis, all meanings of lexical ambiguity are accessed regardless of the preceding sentential context, while the interactive hypothesis proposed that context plays a role in lexical ambiguity resolution, where both context and meaning frequency influence lexical ambiguity resolution.

In addition, the modularity hypothesis suggested that in the multiple access condition, all meanings are accessed immediately and automatically. However, the results showed that 1500 ms after the onset of ambiguity, lexical selection occurred [1]. The ordered access condition was similar to the multiple access condition in postulating a lack of influence on the preceding sentential context, so more frequent meanings were accessed faster. The interactive hypothesis predicted that even with shorter visual target presentation times, lexical access would still be influenced by context. The results showed that visual target presentation times of less than 1000 ms allowed for multiple access of ambiguous meanings, but visual target presentation times of 1500 ms or greater showed priming effects for only contextually appropriate meanings. This might indicate that the longer processing time allowed for access to occur and then a meaning to be chosen.

In another study [3], the author explored the possibility of the susceptibility of verbs to semantic change, which allowed the sentential context to influence their lexical access. The study also found that the lexical access system operated independently of the preceding sentential context.

In [4], they discussed the theoretical issues in constructing a lexical semantic theory to distinguish polysemy and homonymy, as well as metaphor and metonymy, and the implications of constructing a theoretical model that made possible the calculation of word senses.

In the final study [8], there were two basic theoretical models of lexical ambiguity resolution, context-dependent and context-independent. The context-dependent model was compatible with language processing, while the context-independent model was compatible with modular language processing. The implications for lexical ambiguity resolution extended not only to the nature of the language processing system but also to the makeup of the underlying cognitive architecture that supports language.

3 Hypotheses and Research Questions

The current study employed two hypotheses: (I) the most frequent primary meanings of lexically ambiguous words will always be comprehended and produced more quickly than less frequent meanings; and (II) the primary meanings or concepts of lexically ambiguous words will be chosen first.

The three research questions in this study are: (1) which words have a strong literal bias or a strong metaphorical bias; (2) which senses show a strong bias for lexically ambiguous words; and (3) were the primary meanings of the lexically ambiguous words chosen first? This study designed a production test and a YES-NO test to examine these research questions.

4 Chinese Gigaword Corpus and Chinese Word Sketch

The Chinese Gigaword Corpus contains about 1.1 billion Chinese characters, including more than 700 million characters from Taiwan's Central News Agency and nearly 400 million characters from China's Xinhua News Agency. Before loading Chinese Gigaword into Sketch Engine, all simplified characters were converted into traditional characters, and the texts were segmented and POS-tagged using the Academia Sinica segmentation and tagging system [10]. The segmentation and tagging were performed automatically, with automatic and partially manual post-checking. The precision accuracy was estimated to be over 95% [11].

Two challenges to corpus-based computational approaches to linguistic analysis are acquiring enough data to show linguistic distributions and designing efficient tools to extract linguistically significant generalizations from vast amounts of data. About [12], the authors developed Sketch Engine to facilitate the efficient use of gargantuan corpora. Sketch Engine (SKE, also known as Word Sketch Engine) is a novel Corpus Query System incorporating word sketches, grammatical relations, and a distributional thesaurus.

The advantage of using Sketch Engine as a query tool is that it focuses on the grammatical context of a word instead of just listing an arbitrary number of adjacent words. To show the cross-lingual robustness of Sketch Engine, as well as to propose a powerful tool for collocation extraction based on a large-scale corpus with minimal pre-processing, Chinese Word Sketch (CWS) was constructed by loading the Chinese Gigaword Corpus into SKE [13]. All the components of SKE were implemented, including *Concordance*, *Word Sketch*, *Thesaurus*, and *Sketch Difference*.

5 Data Collection

This study used the Chinese Word Sketch Search Engine to retrieve data from the Chinese Gigaword Corpus. This search engine focused on verbal words as the key-words and then found their argument role (i.e., object). Compound words were the stimuli in this study, for example, the verbs *pao1* (拋) and *pan1* (攀) and their "object" argument roles *xiu4 qiu2* (繡球) and *gao1 feng1* (高峰) formed the compounds *pao1 xiu4 qiu2* (拋繡球) and *pan1 gao1 feng1* (攀高峰).

80 different verbs were selected from the Chinese Gigaword Corpus, along with their collocations, to form the Verb + Noun construction and all had lexically ambiguous senses. Moreover, from the same corpus, 40 fillers with the Verb + Noun construction and only one lexical sense were also obtained.

6 Methodology

To test the related senses of lexical ambiguity in Mandarin Chinese, two experiments were run in this study. The first one was a production test and the second one was a YES-NO test. In the production test, 80 lexical ambiguity words were divided into two groups based on bias words, and 40 stimuli (20 literal bias words and 20 metaphorical bias words) from the analysis results were used. In the YES-NO test, the participants were asked to choose "YES" or "NO" for the relation between one word with the other concept. The YES-NO test was a without-context test.

6.1 Experiment 1: Production Test

In the production test, the same materials were used to design two different sorting order questionnaires to ensure that all the participants comprehended all the lexically ambiguous words in the two different questionnaires. This assured that useful data could be obtained regarding literal bias and metaphorical bias.

6.1.1 Participants

Twenty-two undergraduate students (mean age = 20.2 years; SD = 1.5 years; range = 18 to 24 years; female = 16; male = 6) from National Taiwan University participated in the production test. They were all native Mandarin Chinese speakers, were right-handed, and had no linguistics background knowledge.

6.1.2 Materials

All materials for the production test were taken from the Chinese Gigaword Corpus using CWS. The focus was on verbs as the keywords and their argument role (i.e., object), as well as lexically ambiguous words with the Verb + Noun construction. A total of 80 items, all of which were lexically ambiguous words in Mandarin Chinese, such as 吃火鍋 (*chi1 huo3 guo1*, 'to eat boiled food') and 丟飯碗 (*diu1 fan4 wan3*, 'to lose one's job'), were collected.

6.1.3 Procedure

In Experiment 1, the production test, two different questionnaires were designed using the same materials. The only difference between them was sorting order. This design ensured that all the participants comprehended all the lemmas to obtain useful results. All the participants were asked to write down all the possible senses for each lemma according to the instructions in Fig. 1 below:

問卷一共有 80 題中文的詞彙。每個題目裡都有一個詞彙。請你在看過詞彙之後，根據你的語感，寫下這個詞彙所有的意義。首先，先寫下第一個想到的意義，並請標注數字 1；然後，再寫下第二個想到的意義，並標注數字 2，以此類推。請就你所知道的，盡量寫下來，並請依序排列。舉例如下：

導火線
1. 事件發生的直接原因。
2. 點燃炸彈爆炸的引線。
3. 造成雙方關係緊張、對立的作戰區。

Fig. 1. Instructions for Experiment 1, the production test

Before the production test, 22 questions were analyzed to find out whether the items were lexically biased or metaphorically biased. Moreover, the 80 items were divided into two groups—literal bias and metaphorical bias—as shown in Fig. 2 below:

• 吃火鍋	• 丟飯碗
• 刮鬍子	• 炒魷魚
• 擦屁股	• 放鴿子
• … …	• … …

Fig. 2. Literal bias word group (left) and metaphorical bias word group (right)

6.1.4 Analysis

After running the production test, two bias word groups from the 80 items were ascertained, including 21 items of literal bias words and 56 items of metaphorical bias words. To determine the stimuli of the lexical ambiguity words for the YES-NO test, 20 items from the 21 literal bias words and 20 items from the 56 metaphorical bias words were selected. For the 20 literal bias words, their frequency range was from 1 token to 428 tokens based on the Chinese Gigaword Corpus, with an average of 107.95 tokens and a percentage of over 64%. For the 20 metaphorical bias words, based on the Chinese Gigaword Corpus, their frequency range was from 30 tokens to 427 tokens, with an average of 105.9 tokens and a percentage of over 60%. A t-test compared the literal senses of the literal bias words with the metaphorical senses of the metaphorical bias words and found that the p value was 0.477975 ($p > 0.05$), which was not significant, meaning that all situations for the literal bias word group and the metaphorical bias word group were controlled (Table 1).

Table 1. The results of Experiment 1, the production test

	Literal bias	Metaphoric bias
Freq. range--- based on Chinese Gigaword Corpus	1 ~ 428	30 ~ 427
Average	107.95	105.9
Percentage	> 64%	> 60%
T-test	p = 0.477975 (p>0.05), No significant	

The bias word group analysis in the production test found a distribution of literal sense and metaphorical sense for the literal bias words and literal sense and metaphorical sense for the metaphorical bias words. In Table 2 below, columns B, D, H, and J show the tokens for the literal sense and the metaphorical sense of each literal and metaphorical bias word in the same situation, while columns C, E, I, and K show the percentage of literal sense and metaphorical sense for each literal and metaphorical bias word. The percentages of 10 literal sense items and 12 metaphorical sense items were above 80%.

Table 2. Analysis of the production test by bias word group

	A	B	C	D	E	F	G	H	I	J	K
1	Lemma---Literal bias						Lemma---Metaphoric bias				
2		Literal sense		Metaphoric sense				Literal sense		Metaphoric sense	
3	收紅包	14	63.64%	8	36.36%		挖牆根	8	36.36%	14	63.64%
4	搶鏡頭	14	63.64%	8	36.36%		吐口水	7	31.82%	15	68.18%
5	編故事	14	63.64%	8	36.36%		坐板凳	7	31.82%	15	68.18%
6	攀高峰	14	63.64%	8	36.36%		抱大腿	7	31.82%	15	68.18%
7	搓湯圓	16	72.73%	6	27.27%		斬雞頭	7	31.82%	15	68.18%
8	鑽空隙	16	72.73%	6	27.27%		跳火坑	7	31.82%	15	68.18%
9	夾娃娃	17	77.27%	5	22.73%		種草莓	7	31.82%	15	68.18%
10	抬轎子	17	77.27%	5	22.73%		踢皮球	6	27.27%	16	72.73%
11	塞牙縫	17	77.27%	5	22.73%		碰釘子	4	18.18%	18	81.82%
12	獵人頭	17	77.27%	5	22.73%		找台階	3	13.64%	19	86.36%
13	吃火鍋	18	81.82%	4	18.18%		丟飯碗	2	9.09%	20	90.91%
14	吹喇叭	18	81.82%	4	18.18%		炒魷魚	2	9.09%	20	90.91%
15	刮鬍子	18	81.82%	4	18.18%		砸飯碗	2	9.09%	20	90.91%
16	搭架子	18	81.82%	4	18.18%		灑熱血	2	9.09%	20	90.91%
17	擦屁股	18	81.82%	4	18.18%		放鴿子	1	4.55%	21	95.45%
18	倒垃圾	19	86.36%	3	13.64%		咬耳朵	1	4.55%	21	95.45%
19	啃骨頭	19	86.36%	3	13.64%		欠東風	0	0.00%	22	100.00%
20	戴帽子	19	86.36%	3	13.64%		背黑鍋	0	0.00%	22	100.00%
21	包粽子	20	90.91%	2	9.09%		賣關子	0	0.00%	22	100.00%
22	做記號	21	95.45%	1	4.55%		翻舊帳	0	0.00%	22	100.00%
23		17.2	78.18%	4.8	21.82%			3.65	16.59%	18.35	83.41%

In Experiment 1, the production test, among the 22 participants, 17.2 (78.18%) chose the literal sense of the literal bias words, 4.8 (21.82%) chose the metaphorical sense of the literal bias words, 18.35 (83.41%) chose the metaphorical sense of the metaphorical bias words, and 3.65 (16.59%) chose the literal sense of the metaphorical bias words. A t-test compared the two bias groups and found that the p value was 0.082094 ($p > 0.05$), which was not significant, meaning that all conditions were controlled in both the literal and the metaphorical word groups, as shown in Table 3 below:

Table 3. Statistics for the production test by bias word group

	Literal bias		Metaphoric bias	
	Literal Sense	Metaphoric Sense	Literal Sense	Metaphoric Sense
Average	17.2 (78.18%)	4.8 (21.82%)	3.65 (16.59%)	18.35 (83.41%)
T-test	p = 0.082094 (p>0.05), No significant			

6.2 Experiment 2: YES-NO Test

6.2.1 Participants

Twenty right-handed undergraduates (mean age = 21.1 years; SD = 2.0 years; range = 19 to 27 years; female = 13; male = 7) with no history of psychiatric or neurological illnesses and who were native Chinese speakers participated in the YES-NO test. None of the 20 participants took part in Experiment 1 or any other related experiments in this study

6.2.2 Materials

Eighty items were presented as the experimental stimuli in the YES-NO test, which were the same as those from the production test. Forty items were the stimuli (20 literal bias words and 20 metaphorical bias words) and 40 items were fillers, all of which had a Verb + Noun construction and only one lexical sense. In addition, to test the correlation of the experimental stimuli, other concept words were needed, which were taken from the primary meanings of the words in the production test, and all were revised into two characters, such as 工作 ('job'), 食物 ('food'), and so on. In the literal bias word group, there were three verb concept words (e.g., three each for 食物, 'food') and different concept words for each word. In the metaphorical bias word group, there were also three verb concept words (e.g., three each for 工作, 'job') and different concept words for each word. Furthermore, different concept words were obtained for each word in the filler word group.

6.2.3 Procedure

In Experiment 2, the YES-NO test, the stimuli were selected from the production test, resulting in 20 literal bias words and 20 metaphorical bias words selected from 77 lexical ambiguity words. Moreover, based on the Chinese Gigaword Corpus, the 20 literal bias words and 20 metaphorical bias words showed a higher frequency. The 20 participants were asked to choose "YES" or "NO" regarding the correlation between the first lemma and the second concept, as shown in Fig. 3 below:

問卷一共有80題中文的問句，每個題目裡分別有兩個概念。請你在看過詞組之後，根據你的語感，決定每題裡的概念與概念之間是否相關，然後圈選作答。請你一定要在是或否之間圈選你覺得最適當的答案。舉例如下：

1→ 請問，「講八卦」和「明星」這兩種概念是否相關？··(是)·否··

2→ 請問，「戴項鍊」和「檯燈」這兩種概念是否相關？···是(·否)·

Fig. 3. Instructions for Experiment 2, the YES-NO test

Before the YES-NO test, the participants' performance in distinguishing the two bias word groups (i.e., literal and metaphorical) from the 80 items presented as stimuli was analyzed.

6.2.4 Analysis

After the production test, a YES-NO test was run. The experimental stimuli of the YES-NO test were presented in the same way as in the production test. In Table 4, columns B, D, H, and J show tokens for the YES and NO answers for each literal and metaphorical bias word in the same situation, while columns C, E, I, and K show the percentage of YES and NO answers for each literal and metaphorical bias word. The percentages of 14 literal bias items and 19 metaphorical bias items were above 80%. Worthy of mention is 獵人頭 (*lie4 ren2 tou2*/ 'to hunt a head or to search for talent'), which received 50% of the YES answers and 50% of the NO answers. The reasons for these results may have been a poorly designed second concept used to examine its correlation or that the literal sense and the metaphorical sense of 獵人頭 were equally used in conversation; nevertheless, the lexical ambiguity word 獵人頭 was equally comprehended.

Table 4. Analysis of the YES-NO test by bias word group

	A	B	C	D	E	F	G	H	I	J	K
1		Literal bias						Metaphoric bias			
2	Lemma	Yes		No			Lemma	Yes		No	
3	飆人頭	10	50.00%	10	50.00%		挖牆角	14	70.00%	6	30.00%
4	塞牙縫	12	60.00%	8	40.00%		跳火坑	16	80.00%	4	20.00%
5	搶鏡頭	13	65.00%	7	35.00%		欠東風	17	85.00%	3	15.00%
6	鑽空隙	15	75.00%	5	25.00%		吐口水	17	85.00%	3	15.00%
7	倒垃圾	15	75.00%	5	25.00%		灑熱血	18	90.00%	2	10.00%
8	啃骨頭	15	75.00%	5	25.00%		踢皮球	19	95.00%	1	5.00%
9	搓湯圓	17	85.00%	3	15.00%		找台階	19	95.00%	1	5.00%
10	擦屁股	18	90.00%	2	10.00%		翻舊帳	19	95.00%	1	5.00%
11	包粽子	19	95.00%	1	5.00%		抱大腿	19	95.00%	1	5.00%
12	吃火鍋	19	95.00%	1	5.00%		丟飯碗	20	100.00%	0	0.00%
13	抬轎子	19	95.00%	1	5.00%		咬耳朵	20	100.00%	0	0.00%
14	編故事	19	95.00%	1	5.00%		賣關子	20	100.00%	0	0.00%
15	搭架子	19	95.00%	1	5.00%		碰釘子	20	100.00%	0	0.00%
16	做記號	20	100.00%	0	0.00%		炒魷魚	20	100.00%	0	0.00%
17	收紅包	20	100.00%	0	0.00%		背黑鍋	20	100.00%	0	0.00%
18	夾娃娃	20	100.00%	0	0.00%		坐板凳	20	100.00%	0	0.00%
19	戴帽子	20	100.00%	0	0.00%		種草莓	20	100.00%	0	0.00%
20	吹喇叭	20	100.00%	0	0.00%		砸飯碗	20	100.00%	0	0.00%
21	攀高峰	20	100.00%	0	0.00%		放鴿子	20	100.00%	0	0.00%
22	刮鬍子	20	100.00%	0	0.00%		斬雞頭	20	100.00%	0	0.00%
23		17.5	87.50%	2.5	12.50%			18.9	94.50%	1.1	5.50%

In Experiment 2, the YES-NO test, among the 20 participants, 17.5 (87.50%) chose YES for the literal bias words, 2.5 (12.50%) chose NO for the literal bias words, 18.9 (94.50%) chose YES for the metaphorical bias words, and 1.1 (5.50%) chose NO for the metaphorical bias words. Moreover, all 20 participants chose NO for all the filler question sentences. A t-test compared these two bias groups and found that the p value was 0.041452 ($p < 0.05$), which was significant, meaning that when the participants examined the lexically ambiguous words, they distinguished a strong sense bias in both the literal and the metaphorical word groups, as shown in Table 5 below:

Table 5 Statistics for the YES-NO test by bias word group

	Literal bias		Metaphoric bias	
	Yes	No	Yes	No
Average	17.5 (87.50%)	2.5 (12.50%)	18.9 (94.50%)	1.1(5.50%)
T-test	p = 0.041452 (p>0.05), Significant			

7 General Discussion

The results of the production test and the YES-NO test showed that the literal sense of the bias words and the metaphorical sense of the bias lemmas were distributed. Experiment 1, the production test, confirmed that 20 literal bias words and 20 metaphorical bias words used as the experimental stimuli in this study were carefully controlled. Moreover, 10 items of literal sense were above 80% in the literal bias word group and 12 items of metaphorical sense were above 80% in the metaphorical bias word group, which suggests that the balance between these groups was controlled.

In Experiment 2, the YES-NO test, there was the relation between one word with the other concept, as the primary meanings of the lexically ambiguous words were chosen first. Moreover, the difference between the words with a literal bias and a metaphorical bias and those with a strong sense bias among the lexically ambiguous words was ascertained.

Another finding was that the literal primary concepts had a strong bias for literal words and the metaphorical primary concepts had a strong bias for metaphorical words, which corresponds to the hypotheses in this study—the most frequent primary meanings of the lexically ambiguous words were comprehended and produced more quickly than less frequent meanings, and the primary meanings or concepts of the lexically ambiguous words were chosen first.

8 Conclusion and Future Work

The two experiments in this study found strong literal bias senses and strong metaphorical bias senses in the lexically ambiguous words in Mandarin Chinese, which resulted in their primary meanings being chosen first. It was also found that the Chinese Gigaword Corpus and Chinese Word Sketch provided a superior database and search engine functions, respectively, for the selection of the experimental materials and controlling the experimental stimuli frequency.

Further studies should use the same materials to examine the literal bias context, metaphorical bias context, and neutral context; in addition, they should focus on additional strong bias items. Finally, regarding literal bias words, more items should be included in the search to select more appropriate words, which would result in better performance in comprehending lexically ambiguous words.

Acknowledgements. This research is supported by the Ministry of Science and Technology, Taiwan, R.O.C., under Grant no. MOST 107-2410-H-003-053. I also would like to thank Prof. Kathleen Ahrens for her feedback on this paper.

References

1. Ahrens, Kathleen: The effect of visual target presentation times on lexical ambiguity resolution. Lang. Linguist. **7**(3), 677–696 (2006)
2. Lexical Data Consortium.: Chinese Gigaword Corpus 2.5. http://www.ldc.upenn.edu/Catalog/CatalogEntry.jsp?catalogId=LDC2005T14 (2005)
3. Ahrens, Kathleen: On-line sentence comprehension of ambiguous verbs in Mandarin. J. East Asian Linguis. **10**(4), 337–358 (2001)
4. Lin, C., Ahrens, K.: Calculating the number of senses: implications for ambiguity advantage effect during lexical access. In: H.Y. Tai, Y.L. Chang (eds.), Proceedings of the Seventh International Symposium on Chinese Languages and Linguistics, pp. 141–155. National Chung-Cheng University, Chai-yi (2000)
5. Li, Ping: Crosslinguistic variation and sentence processing: the case of Chinese. In: Hillert, D. (ed.) Sentence Processing: A Cross-Linguistic Perspective, pp. 35–53. Academic Press, San Diego, CA (1998)
6. Li, P., Yip, M.C.: Lexical ambiguity and context effects in spoken word recognition: evidence from Chinese. In: G. Cottrell (ed.) Proceedings of the 18th Annual Meeting of the Cognitive Science Society, pp. 228–232 (1996)
7. Li, Ping, Yip, Michael C.: Context effects and processing of spoken homophones. Read. Writ.: Interdiscip. J. **10**, 223–243 (1998)
8. Ahrens, Kathleen: Lexical ambiguity resolution: languages, tasks and timing. In: Hillert, Dieter (ed.) Sentence Processing: A Cross-Linguistic Perspective, pp. 11–31. Academic Press, San Diego, CA (1998)
9. Tabossi, Patrizia, Zardon, Filmmaker: Processing ambiguous words in context. J. Mem. Lang. **32**, 359–372 (1993)
10. Huang, C.-R., Chen, K.-J., Hsieh, S.-K.: Mandarin Chinese Words and Parts of Speech: A Corpus-Based Study. Routledge (2017)
11. Ma, W.-Y., Huang, C.-R.: Uniform and effective tagging of a heterogeneous giga-word corpus. Presented at the 5th International Conference on Language Resources and Evaluation (LREC2006). Genoa, Italy, 24–28 May 2006
12. Kilgarriff, A., Rychlý, P., Smrz, P., Tugwell, D.: The sketch engine. Proceedings of EURALEX. Lorient, France. http://www.sketchengine.co.uk/ (2004)
13. Kilgarriff, A., Huang, C.-R., Rundell, M., Rychlý, P., Smith, S., Tugwell, D., Dhonnchadha, E.U.: Word sketches for Irish and Chinese. Presented at corpus linguistics 2005, Birmingham, UK, 14–17 July 2005

The Dynamic Evolution of Common Address Terms in Chinese Based on Word Embedding

Yingdi Jiang[1,2], Zhiying Liu[1,2], and Lijiao Yang[1,2](✉)

[1] Institute of Chinese Information Processing, Beijing Normal University, Beijing, China
201621090024@mail.bnu.edu.cn, {liuzhy,yanglijiao}@bnu.edu.cn
[2] UltraPower-BNU Joint Laboratory for Artificial Intelligence, Beijing Normal University, Beijing, China

Abstract. Common address terms as an important part of daily communication have been studied with qualitative methods. Inspired by previous methods, this paper proposes a novel method based on word embedding to study the dynamic evolution of common address terms in Chinese. In particular, we first obtained the relevant words of address terms by calculating the distance between word embeddings based on *People's Daily Corpus* (1948–2017), then studied the laws of semantic changes of fictive kinship terms and non-kinship terms which belong to common address terms in Chinese through the related words. The results showed that there were significant differences between them.

Keywords: Common address terms · Word embedding · Semantic change

1 Introduction

The word "称谓(chengwei)" is originally derived from *Hou Hanshu. The Contemporary Chinese Dictionary (6th edition)* defines an address term as "a general term referring to a name derived from relatives, identities, occupations, or other relationships", such as father, master, factory director, etc. Address terms, as one of commonly-used social address terms, are widely used in social interpersonal communication among people with different ages, genders, occupations and identities.

There are two types of common address terms in Contemporary Chinese: fictive kinship terms and non-kinship terms. Fictive kinship terms derive from kinship terms which are used by people without kinship to call each other to narrow the distance between them, such as "大哥(dage)", "大姐(dajie)", "大爷(daye)", "大妈(dama)", "叔叔(shushu)", "阿姨(ayi)". Generally, this kind of address terms is stable, and the meanings will not change greatly in the short time. Non-kinship terms are relatively polite terms used among unfamiliar people, for example, "小姐(xiaojie)", "先生(xiansheng)", "同志(tongzhi)", "师傅(shifu)", "太太(taitai)", "美女(meinv)", "帅哥(shuaige)". Using these non-kinship terms can let us communicate in an appropriate way, i.e. not too intimate but very polite. However, non-kinship terms are greatly influenced by the society, and their semantics may expand, shrink, shift, or even disappear completely after a certain historical stage.

J.-F. Hong et al. (Eds.): CLSW 2018, LNAI 11173, pp. 478–485, 2018.
https://doi.org/10.1007/978-3-030-04015-4_40

2 Related Work

The address terms as an important part of daily communication have been studied with qualitative methods. *Erya Shiqin,* as the earliest monograph on the kinships, recorded the kinship terms of Pre-Qin from the aspects of clans, maternal kinsfolk, wife's kinsfolk and marriage kinsfolk. In recent years, many scholars have conducted research on the meanings, usages and changes of address terms from different perspectives.

On the one hand, address terms were studied as a whole. *Address Terms in Chinese* written by Zhao Yuanren described the Chinese address terms system in detail. Dong et al. [1] explained the usage and diachronic changes of address terms. Lou [2] analyzed the semantic features of address terms and described the similarities and differences between Chinese and English appellations. Zheng [3] introduced the generalization phenomenon, missing link and unconventional usages of common address terms and clarified their rules for the changes. Qi [4] analyzed the semantic fission phenomenon of common address terms based on prototype theory in cognitive linguistics. These studies explored the overall development of common address terms from various dimensions. Unfortunately, most of them are lack of support from large-scale corpora and quantitative discussions.

On the other hand, address terms were studied from a micro perspective. Zhu [5] investigated the meaning, usage, distribution and social characteristics of the address term "师傅(shifu)". Hu et al. [6] focused on the development and changes of the semantic function and pragmatic condition of "同志(tongzhi)". Fan et al. [7] summarized the semantic connotations and semantic features of "小姐(xiaojie)". Chen [8] studied the term "先生(xiansheng)" and its composite address term, summarized their meanings and structural forms. Li [9] discussed the usage of "太太(taitai)" from the principle of power relations and balance relations in social communication. Ji [10] summarized and predicted development trend of "阿姨(ayi)" by using a combined analysis method. However, they separate common address terms from each other and fail to discuss whether these address terms influence each other in the process of evolution or not.

Much influenced by political, economic, socio-cultural, environmental and other external factors, the meanings of the common address terms change in the dynamic process. The study of common address terms is of great importance to the development of lexicology and pragmatics. In addition, it will benefit to the study of the development of Chinese vocabulary.

This paper tries to conduct a detailed exploration of the semantic changes and rules of common address terms for decades based on *People's Daily Corpus* (1948–2017) by using the method of word embedding.

3 Corpus and Method

3.1 Corpus

Considering *People's Daily* is an authoritative and comprehensive daily newspaper with long time of publication and can well reflect the usage of words in the contemporary era, we used it to investigate common address terms. We divided *People's Daily Corpus* from 1948 to 2017 into seven parts by decades, (i.e. 1948–1957, 1958–1967, 1968–1977, 1978–1987, 1988–1997, 1998–2007, 2008–2017).

3.2 Method

One-hot Representation is the most commonly-used word representation method in Natural Language Processing (NLP) where each word is represented as a vector with high dimension. The dimension of this vector is the size of the word list. The dimension value of the current word is 1 and other dimension values are 0. For example, in the four-dimensional space of "漂亮(beautiful)", "美丽(pretty)", "回家(go home)" and "放假(holiday)", the vectors can be expressed as [1 0 0 0] [0 1 0 0] [0 0 1 0] [0 0 0 1] respectively. The method is very simple. Nevertheless, these words are isolated from each other and it is hard to see whether the meanings between words are related from the vector.

With the development of deep learning, Distributed Representation [11] is used to represent words: Word Embedding. It represents a word as a low-dimensional real vector, such as [0.693, 0.921, −0.324, 0.658, …]. The distance of the vectors in space can be calculated by Euclidean distance, Hamming distance, Cosine distance, etc. For example, cosine distance is measured by the angle between two vectors in vector space. The smaller the angle between two vectors, the higher the similarity. Therefore, the distance between "漂亮(beautiful)", "美丽(pretty)" must be less than "回家(go home)" and "放假(holiday)" under normal circumstances. Word embedding has been widely used to measure the semantic similarity in recent years.

Word2vec is a tool developed by Google in 2013 to calculate word embedding. It can train words into word embeddings based on large-scale data sets and measure the semantic similarities between words. It mainly adopts CBOW model and Skip-gram model [12]. In this paper, we used a Python module named gensim to train word embeddings and calculate the distances between words.

4 Evolution of Common Address Terms

4.1 Non-kinship Terms

Non-kinship terms such as "小姐(xiaojie)", "先生(xiansheng)", "女士(nvshi)" and "美女(meinv)" have been in dynamic development, and their related words changed greatly from 1948 to 2017, indicating that the semantic scope and users of these words are constantly being adjusted (Table 1).

Table 1. The evolution of related words of "同志(tongzhi)", "小姐(xiaojie)", "美女(meinv)", "帅哥(shuaige)" and "姑娘(guniang)".

Non-kinship terms	"tongzhi" (同志)	"xiaojie" (小姐)	"meinv" (美女)	"shuaige" (帅哥)	"guniang" (姑娘)
1948-1957	首长 0.53 同学 0.51 战友 0.51 乡亲 0.49 干部 0.48 老工友 0.48 工友 0.48 大夫 0.47 休养员0.47指战员 0.46	太太 0.82 公子 0.77 老爷 0.69 绅士 0.69 少爷 0.68 丫头 0.67 大姐 0.66 小丑 0.66 姥姥 0.65 骑士 0.65	书签 0.65 剧照 0.64 鸳鸯 0.64 水彩画 0.62 牡丹 0.63 风景画 0.62 肖像画0.62写生 0.61 静物 0.61 模特儿 0.61	无	少女 0.83女孩子 0.82 小伙子0.82小姑娘0.76 老大娘0.75小孩子0.72 女人 0.70老妈妈 0.70 娃娃 0.70男孩子 0.69
1958-1967	副统帅0.59同学 0.57 乡亲 0.53 首长 0.52 支委 0.51 战友 0.51 长辈 0.48 大夫 0.48 陈云 0.48 工友 0.48	太太 0.85 公子 0.82 少爷 0.72 绅士 0.70 老爷 0.67 财主 0.65 书生0.65老爷太太 0.65 姨 0.64 道士 0.63	珠宝 0.61 禽兽 0.60 贝壳 0.59 毛发 0.59 财宝 0.58 水獭 0.58 鹦鹉 0.58 犀牛 0.57 猴子 0.57 魔术 0.57	无	小伙子0.82小姑娘0.80 女孩子0.72老妈妈0.70 老大妈0.70 娃娃 0.69 少女 0.69 牧人 0.68 老人 0.67 猎手 0.67
1968-1977	支委 0.61 同学 0.57 老师傅0.54成员 0.53 战友 0.52 常委 0.48 首长 0.48 组员 0.48 委员 0.48 乘务员0.45	太太 0.78 女士 0.71 埃米・马科斯 0.69 老爷太太 0.68 王公 0.58 伍兹 0.58 权贵 0.56 教士 0.56	毒牙 0.61 贝壳 0.60 阿谀奉承0.58封官0.58 弹弓 0.57 小恩 0.56 废铜 0.55 风雅 0.55 铁棍 0.55 玉米秸 0.55	无	小伙子 0.79女将 0.68 娃娃 0.66 孩子 0.66 钻工 0.64 乡亲 0.62 采油工 0.62老汉 0.61 小青年0.61小伙伴0.61
1978-1987	首长 0.59 同学 0.57 老干部0.55董老 0.55 秦邦宪0.54何叔衡0.53 老帅 0.53 干部 0.53 叶帅 0.51 大姐 0.51	太太 0.74 女士 0.65 女郎 0.64 大哥 0.64 阿姨 0.62 掌柜 0.62 老板 0.62 孙儿 0.61 三毛 0.61 老太太 0.61	女郎 0.68 仕女 0.68 美人 0.67 模特儿 0.67 裸体 0.67 水墨 0.66 嫦娥 0.64 维纳斯 0.64 蝴蝶 0.63 饰 0.63	无	小伙子0.82小姑娘0.82 少女 0.73 小伙 0.69 女孩子0.68老太太0.67 农妇 0.67小青年 0.66 庄稼汉 0.66娃儿 0.66
1988-1997	李明瑞 0.60 聂帅 0.59 老帅 0.58 刘伯承 0.57 老干部 0.56 叶帅 0.56 田家英 0.56 董老 0.55 张云逸 0.54陈云李0.53	服务员0.73导游 0.71 女士 0.69 空姐 0.69 售货员 0.67男士 0.64 女郎 0.64 老板 0.63 店主 0.63 导医 0.62	美人 0.76 情人 0.68 西施 0.68 黛玉 0.66 孙悟空0.65仙鹤 0.64 张飞 0.64 仙子 0.64 美貌 0.63 秋菊 0.63	荡妇 0.76如梦令 0.75 阿拉木汗0.74活络片0.74 板鞋舞 0.73 菊豆 0.72 陈炜 0.72 萨特热 0.72 从军记 0.72筷子舞 0.72	小伙子 0.85小姑娘 0.81 小伙 0.77 少女 0.72 女孩子 0.70妹子 0.69 女孩 0.68 后生 0.67 小伙儿 0.67农妇 0.67
1998-2007	总书记 0.61 邝 0.57 刘伯承 0.56张云逸 0.56 文选 0.55 老干部 0.54 共产党员0.50董必武0.50 缪孝恩 0.50李立三 0.50	女士 0.75 大妈 0.66 师傅 0.64 先生 0.64 老伯 0.64售货员 0.64 大爷 0.63营业员 0.63 店主 0.63 太太 0.61	女郎 0.71 侠客 0.70 小丑 0.67 西施 0.66 淑女 0.66 大腕 0.66 帅哥 0.66 歌星 0.66 秀 0.65 裸体 0.65	小燕子0.68龙凤呈祥0.66 达达 0.66 美女 0.66 腕儿 0.65天女散花 0.65 帅气 0.65 小夜曲 0.65 洋娃娃 0.65奥特曼 0.65	小伙子0.83小姑娘0.79 小伙 0.79 少女 0.74 汉子 0.69 小伙儿 0.69 女孩子0.69女孩 0.68 骑手 0.67 女人 0.65
2008-2017	总书记 0.66张云逸 0.58 老干部 0.55张闻天 0.54 何叔衡 0.53赵紫阳 0.52 刘伯承 0.52文选 0.51 党外人士0.50革命家0.50	女士 0.83 阿姨 0.77 老伯 0.75 大姐 0.72 大妈 0.72 先生 0.72 大爷 0.71 老太 0.71 丽萍 0.69 一鸣 0.68	帅哥 0.71 民族风 0.62 哒 0.62 萌萌 0.62 炫 0.62 卖萌 0.61 网名 0.60 吴菊萍 0.59 凤姐 0.59 红衣 0.59	美女 0.71 网名 0.62 女郎 0.61 女孩儿 0.61 萌萌 0.60 昵称 0.60 模特 0.60 雅号 0.59 比基尼 0.59虾米 0.59	小伙子 0.87小伙 0.83 小姑娘 0.78小伙儿 0.77 女孩 0.75 汉子 0.71 男孩 0.69 女孩子 0.68 女孩儿 0.67女人 0.67

The word "同志(tongzhi)", with a strong revolutionary and political implication, began to be used as an address term after the 1st National Congress of the Communist Party of China. The members of the party called each other "同志(tongzhi)". Judging from the existing corpus, "同志(tongzhi)" was used in all ages, genders, and occupations from 1948 to 1967. It could be used not only for members of the party and the troop such as "首长(shouzhang)", "干部(ganbu)" and "战友(zhanyou)", but also for "同学(tongxue)", "工友(gongyou)", "乡亲(xiangqin)" and "大夫(daifu)". In other words, users could call each other "同志(tongzhi)" unless they were enemies of different classes. The corpus of 1968–1977, which roughly covered the period of the Cultural Revolution, showed that the use of "同志(tongzhi)" was limited, and most of the relevant words were "支委(zhiwei)", "常委(changwei)" and "首长(shouzhang)". However, owing to the end of the Cultural Revolution, the scope of use of "同志(tongzhi)" was confined to political party again, and most of the words which were close to it in the vector space are the names of the prestigious members in the party.

The word "小姐(xiaojie)" has appeared in a similar context with "公子(gongzi)", "老爷(laoye)", "绅士(shenshi)", "财主(caizhu)" and "权贵(quangui)" for a long time, and they are highly correlated. It was not until the end of the Cultural Revolution that "小姐(xiaojie)" became popular, like "女士(nvshi)", "阿姨(ayi)" and "老板(laoban)", meant the name of a young woman or an unmarried woman. The corpus of 1988–2007 showed that the use scope of "小姐(xiaojie)" suddenly expanded. The women who were in the service fields such as "服务员(fuwuyuan)", "空姐(kongjie)", "导游(-daoyou)", "营业员(yingyeyuan)" and "售货员(shouhuoyuan)" all could be called as "小姐(xiaojie)". However, the use of "女士(nvshi)", "太太(taitai)" changed little. The corpus after 2008 reflected that "小姐(xiaojie)" had gradually been abandoned by professional women and once again been an ordinary address term. Reasons for this change cannot be known through related words. According to practical experience, "小姐(xiaojie)" may be gradually contaminated with the implication of pornography. Therefore, "小姐(xiaojie)" is no longer used frequently. The change of "小姐(xiaojie)" can also be verified by the frequency information obtained from the BCC corpus of Beijing Language and Culture University (Fig. 1).

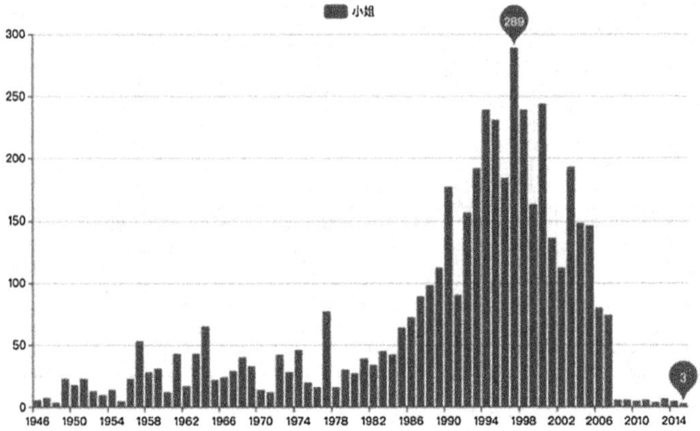

Fig. 1. Frequency of "小姐(xiaojie)".

4.2 Fictive Kinship Terms

The address terms "叔叔 (shushu)" and "阿姨(ayi)", "大哥(dage)", "大姐(dajie)", etc., which are transformed from kinship terms, are quite different from non-kinship terms. As shown in Table 2, most of the related or similar words of fictive kinship terms are kinship terms or other fictive kinship terms.

The related words of fictive kinship terms didn't change greatly in the past 70 years. But the stability of this kind of address terms is not absolute, and its semantic scope changed slightly.

In 1948–1967, "阿姨(ayi)" which was defined as mother's sister was more closely related to kinship terms, like "姑姑(gugu)", "妈妈(mama)", "爸爸(baba)", etc. At that time, it was not a common address terms literally because its meaning depended on blood relationship. The data after 1968 showed that the use scope of "阿姨(ayi)" was no longer limited to blood relations. Besides the members of blood relations, it also included occupation terms such as "列车员(liecheyuan)" and unrelated terms such as "老乡(laoxiang)", "乡亲(xiangqin)" and "病友(bingyou)". It referred to the person of the same age as user's mother. The reason why "阿姨(ayi)" became a common address term was probably that "太太(taitai)" and "小姐(xiaojie)" were abandoned during the Cultural Revolution, and "阿姨(ayi)" as a common address term for an adult woman filled the gap in female address terms in time. Additionally, similar change happened within the term "叔叔(shushu)". But due to the existence of "先生(xiansheng)" and "师傅(shifu)" in male address terms, its scope of use was narrowed to some extent.

Table 2. The evolution of related words of "阿姨(ayi)", "叔叔 (shushu)", "大哥(dage)" and "大姐(dajie)".

Fictive kinship terms	"ayi" (阿姨)	"shushu" (叔叔)	"dage" (大哥)	"dajie" (大姐)
1948-1957	姑姑 0.81 妈妈 0.76 叔叔 0.75 孩子 0.75 小朋友 0.74 弟妹 0.74 小孩子0.73老婆婆 0.73 娃娃 0.73 老娘 0.72	姑姑 0.77 阿姨 0.75 妈妈 0.74 爸爸 0.69 伯伯 0.69 大哥 0.67 老大娘0.67小朋友0.66 休养员0.65老大爷0.64	哥哥 0.80 大爷 0.78 妈 0.78 老伴 0.78 大嫂 0.78 姐姐 0.78 娘 0.77 爷爷 0.76 大伯 0.76 爸爸 0.76	大嫂 0.79 大叔 0.79 大爷 0.78 大娘 0.77 老头 0.77 太太 0.75 老汉 0.73 奶奶 0.73 大哥 0.73 大妈 0.73
1958-1967	妈妈 0.78 叔叔 0.77 娃娃 0.74 大婶 0.74 小朋友 0.74大姐 0.73 爸爸 0.73 婶婶 0.73 孩子 0.72 大娘 0.72	阿姨 0.77 大哥 0.74 爸爸 0.74 妈妈 0.71 哥哥 0.69 姐姐 0.67 婶婶 0.67 大姐 0.67 老爷爷0.64老奶奶0.64	大姐 0.83 爸爸 0.82 爷爷 0.82 大伯 0.79 妈妈 0.78 妈 0.78 大爷 0.78老爷爷 0.77 姐姐 0.77 爹 0.76	大妈 0.84 大哥 0.83 大娘 0.83 大爷 0.81 大婶 0.79 大伯 0.78 大叔 0.77 大嫂 0.76 妈妈 0.76 老爹 0.75
1968-1977	小朋友 0.75 叔叔 0.75 老乡 0.66 列车员 0.65 话务员 0.64 婶婶 0.63 孩子 0.63 儿孙 0.62 乡亲 0.62 大嫂 0.61	阿姨 0.75 妈妈 0.63 老乡 0.62 爸爸 0.62 孩子 0.61 小朋友 0.60 大叔 0.60 亲人 0.59 大嫂 0.58 姐姐 0.58	爷爷 0.74 祖母 0.73 爸爸 0.70 妈 0.70 谭家进 0.70哥哥 0.69 公公 0.69 大伯 0.69 祖父 0.69 爹 0.68	大叔 0.76 大伯 0.73 大妈 0.72 大嫂 0.72 老汉 0.72 大爷 0.70 大娘 0.69 学良 0.69 妈 0.69 妈妈 0.67
1978-1987	叔叔 0.82 奶奶 0.76 爷爷 0.75 大婶 0.74 妈妈 0.73 病友 0.70 大嫂 0.70 伯伯 0.70 姐姐 0.69 大人 0.69	阿姨 0.82 妈妈 0.76 爷爷 0.73 奶奶 0.71 大哥0.70小朋友 0.69 伯伯 0.69 姐姐 0.68 爸爸 0.67 大婶 0.67	爷爷 0.80 舅舅 0.79 大妈 0.79 外婆 0.79 姑姑 0.78 哥哥 0.78 大伯 0.78 姐夫 0.78 奶奶 0.77 姐姐 0.77	伯伯 0.80 奶奶 0.73 大娘 0.70 大爷 0.69 宝珊 0.69 大妈 0.69 爷爷 0.69 大伯 0.68 老总 0.68 妈妈 0.67
1988-1997	叔叔 0.86 妈妈 0.82 爷爷 0.79 奶奶 0.78 爸爸 0.74 姐姐 0.73 大妈 0.72 伯伯 0.72 妹妹 0.72 嫂子 0.71	阿姨 0.86 妈妈 0.81 爷爷 0.80 奶奶 0.77 爸爸 0.76 哥哥 0.74 大哥 0.73 妈 0.72 伯伯 0.72 姐姐 0.71	嫂子 0.79 爹 0.78 大叔 0.78 爸 0.77 妈 0.77 外甥 0.76 闺女 0.76 奶奶 0.76 哥哥 0.76 大伯 0.76	伯伯 0.77 王老 0.71 爷爷 0.70 世昌 0.69 邓 0.68 妈妈 0.67 奶奶0.67老先生 0.66 老总 0.66 聂帅 0.65
1998-2007	叔叔 0.84 姐姐 0.79 妈妈 0.77 大妈 0.77 伯伯 0.76 大娘 0.76 大姐 0.76 奶奶 0.76 大婶 0.75 大嫂 0.74	阿姨 0.84 姐姐 0.75 妈妈 0.74 哥哥 0.73 爸爸 0.73 妹妹 0.72 爷爷 0.72 外甥 0.71 奶奶 0.69 光美 0.69	姐姐 0.74 嫂子 0.73 大姐 0.72 伯伯 0.71 儿媳妇0.71父亲 0.70 哥哥 0.70 舅舅 0.69 太太 0.69 妈 0.69	伯伯 0.81 大娘 0.77 姐姐 0.77 阿姨 0.76 大爷 0.75 老太 0.74 大妈 0.74 老伯 0.74 奶奶 0.73 练贤 0.72
2008-2017	大爷 0.88 大妈 0.87 大姐 0.87 老伯 0.83 大娘 0.83 老太 0.82 伯伯 0.78 师傅 0.77 小姐 0.77 女士 0.75	伯伯 0.78 爷爷 0.76 奶奶 0.75 姐姐 0.74 大哥 0.74 妈妈 0.74 姥姥 0.74 爸爸 0.73 嫂子 0.72 哥哥 0.71	大嫂 0.82 伯伯 0.81 大姐 0.79 嫂子 0.78 大娘 0.77 大叔 0.77 大伯 0.76 闺女 0.76 太太 0.75 姐姐 0.75	阿姨 0.87 大娘 0.85 大爷 0.84 老伯 0.83 大妈 0.81 老太 0.81 大哥 0.79 伯伯 0.79 老汉 0.79 大嫂 0.77

5 Asymmetry in Common Address Terms

In this paper, we take "美女(meinv)" and "帅哥(shuaige)" as examples to analyze asymmetry in common address terms.

"美女(Meinv)" has been in existence since 1948, referring to the beautiful young woman. In the corpus of 1948–1967, "美女(meinv)" did not become a real address term, because it was far from people's daily life. Instead, it had similar contexts with "剧照(still photo)", "水墨画(ink painting)", "珠宝(jewel)", etc. Moreover, due to some historical reasons, it was closer to a number of derogatory words such as "毒

(malicious)" and "阿谀奉承(flattery)" in 1968–1977. The corpus of 1978 to 1997 showed that "美女(meinv)" represented a beautiful woman who was recognized by everyone, for example, "黛玉(daiyu)", "西施(xishi)" and "嫦娥(chang'e)". It was associated with film and television programs after 1998. In particular, the corpus of 2008 reflected that the word "美女(meinv)" has been generalized into a common address term (Table 3).

Table 3. Symmetrical vocabulary of "美女(meinv)" and "帅哥(shuaige)".

Equation	男人 - 女人 + 美女=?	女人 - 男人 + 帅哥=?
Year	Related Words	Related Words
1948-1957	书签 0.513276	无
1958-1967	财宝 0.525324	无
1968-1977	衣物 0.493220	无
1978-1987	裸体 0.577556	无
1988-1997	情人 0.610015	如梦令 0.709601
1998-2007	侠客 0.646105	小燕子 0.664614
2008-2017	帅哥 0.664278	美女 0.689834

The word "帅哥(shuaige)" which is symmetrical with "美女(meinv)" did not appear until 1988, At the beginning of its appearance, it was not close to "美女(meinv)" in vector space. The two words established a relationship in 1998–2007, and quickly became the most symmetrical words in 2008–2017. Figure 2 shows the frequency of appearance of "美女(meinv)" and "帅哥(shuaige)" in BCC corpus from 1946 to 2014.

In addition, the word embedding can be analogized. For instance, the famous equation "King - Queen = Man – Woman" can be transformed into "King - Man + Woman = Queen". In fact, these words cannot be added or subtracted. The reason why this equation is established is that king is related to man and queen is related to woman in vector space. Based on this, we can get the word that is most relevant to "Man" and most symmetrical with "美女(meinv)" through the equation "Man-Woman + meinv", and the word which is most relevant to "帅哥(shuaige)" and most symmetrical with "Woman" through the equation "Woman - Man + shuaige". Thus, we concluded that the two words were not truly symmetrical until 2008.

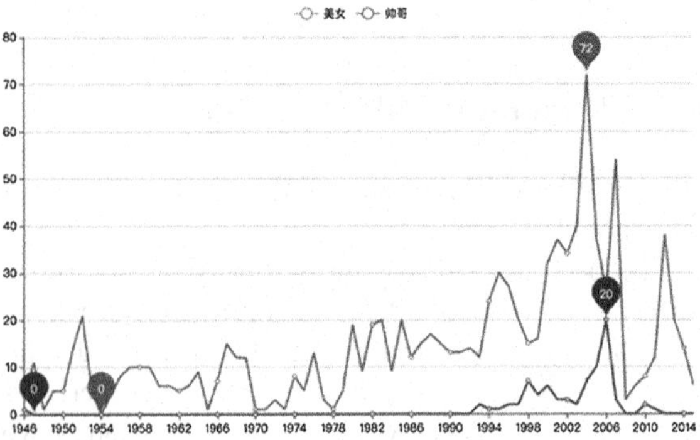

Fig. 2. Frequency comparison between "美女(meinv)" and "帅哥(shuaige)".

6 Conclusions

In this paper, word embeddings were used to study the dynamic evolution of common address terms in Chinese. We first obtained the relevant words of address terms by calculating the distance between word embeddings, then studied the rules of semantic changes of fictive kinship terms and non-kinship terms. Finally, we concluded that common address terms derived from kinship terms were very different from those from non-kinship terms, got the formation time of the symmetry between common address terms by analogy, made some new discoveries which were neglected before.

Acknowledgments. This work is supported by National Language Committee Research Program of China (No. ZDI135-42), Research and Development of Question Answering for Intelligent Robots (230200001) and China Scholarship Council.

References

1. Dong, Y., Niu, A.: The common social titles in Chinese and their diachronic changes. J. Lanzhou Polytech. Coll.E **13**, 50–53 (2006) (In Chinese)
2. Lou, F.: A semantic study of Chinese common address terms. Zhejiang University (2007) (In Chinese)
3. Zheng, J.: Research on Chinese address terms. Shandong University (2009) (In Chinese)
4. Qi, S.: An Analysis of semantic fission of Chinese common address terms based on prototype theory. Northeast Normal University (2011) (In Chinese)
5. Zhu, W.: Investigation on usage of "Shifu". Linguist. Res., 44–47 (1984) (In Chinese)
6. Hu, F., Hu, Y.: On semantic function and pragmatic constraints of "Tongzhi". J. East China Norm. Univ. **32**, 114–118 (2000) (In Chinese)
7. Fan, X., Hu, F., Lin, J., Ma, X.: The pragmatics, geographic distribution and developing trend of application "Xiaojie". Appl. Linguist., 41–47 (2004) (In Chinese)
8. Chen, H.: A study of the address terms of "Xiansheng". Wuhan University (2005) (In Chinese)
9. Li, C.: The meaning of usage theory of address terms. Rhetoric Learning (2005) (In Chinese)
10. Ji, D.: The cognitive development of the address terms of "A yi": based on the method of associative collocation analysis. Appl. Linguist., 44–50 (2014) (In Chinese)
11. Hinton, G.E.: Learning distributed representations of concepts. In: Proceedings of the Eighth Annual Conference of the Cognitive Science Society, vol. 1 (1986)
12. Mikolov, T., Chen, K., Corrado, G., Dean J.: Efficient estimation of word representations in vector space. arXiv preprint arXiv: 1301.3781 (2013)

Arguments of the Disposal Construction in Hainan Min

Hui-chi Lee(✉)

National Cheng Kung University, Tainan 701, Taiwan
hclee6@mail.ncku.edu.tw

Abstract. This paper studies the disposal construction in Hainan Min, especially focusing on its argument structure. The *ɓue* construction in Hainan Min corresponds to the *ba* construction in Mandarin. Unlike the multiple arguments of *ba* in Mandarin, the object and subject of *ɓue* have some semantic restrictions. After examining different thematic roles on the arguments of *ɓue*, the result shows that the animacy feature of *ɓue* object affects the grammaticality of *ɓue* sentences. Furthermore, the thematic role of object of *ɓue* is mostly Patient, and the subject of *ɓue* is Agent. Following Dowty's (1991) proto-roles of Patient and Agent, this paper shows that the object of *ɓue* tends to match the properties for proto-role of Patient and the subject of *ɓue* tends to match the properties for proto-role of Agent. The arguments of the disposal construction in Hainan Min are strongly associated with the s-selection of the word *ɓue*.

Keywords: Disposal construction · Argument structure · Hainan Min

1 Introduction

The present study aims to explore the semantic properties of subject and object of the verb *ɓue* in Hainan Min, a branch of Min dialects and spoken on Hainan Island. The *ba* construction in Mandarin has been widely studied (e.g. Wang 1954; Chao 1968; Hashimoto 1971; Li and Thompson 1981; Huang 1982; Li 1990). The previous studies of *ba* generally explore the categorical status of *ba*, the semantic/pragmatic properties of the object of *ba* and the syntactic structure of the *ba* sentences. Corresponding constructions in Taiwan Southern Min and Hakka are also explored (e.g. Lien 2002; Tsao 2005; Endo 2016), while the disposal construction in Hainan Min (*ɓue* construction) is often neglected by linguists. Only one piece of literature, Lee (2009), provides references of the *ɓue* construction. In addition to describing the distribution and characteristics of the *ɓue* construction, Lee (2009) also compares the *ba* construction over three different Chinese dialect, Mandarin, Southern Min and Hainan Min. Based on Lee's (2009) syntactic findings, this paper mainly focuses on the semantic properties of subject and object of the verb *ɓue*. We found that the animacy feature plays an important role for the arguments of the disposal construction in Hainan Min.

J.-F. Hong et al. (Eds.): CLSW 2018, LNAI 11173, pp. 486–493, 2018.
https://doi.org/10.1007/978-3-030-04015-4_41

2 Semantic Features of Object of *ɓue*

The animacy feature and thematic roles of the object of *ɓue* are tested in this section.

2.1 Animacy Feature [−animate]

The verb *ɓue* cannot accept its object with [+animate] feature, as shown in (1a). However, it is very common in Mandarin to have a [+animate] object for the word *ba*, as shown in (1b). In Hainan Min, the [+animate] object is only acceptable in a sentence without *ɓue*, as in (1c).

(1) a. *Bue^{42} kia^{21} ɓong^{42} hi^{21} lai^{22}.
hold son hold rise come
'Hold my son up.'
b. Ba erzi bao qi lai.
hold son hold rise come
'Hold my son up.'
c. Bong^{42} kia^{21} hi^{21} lai^{22}.
hold son rise come
'Hold my son up.'

When the object is [−animate], it can be allowed to occur following the verb *ɓue*, as in (2).

(2) Ah^{3}-ta^{44} ɓue^{42} ɗoh^{5} suah^{5} heh^{5} la^{11}.
Ta hold table wipe clean PERF
'A-Ta wiped the table clean.'

In addition to the nouns conveying [+animate] features, we also test nouns expressing body parts to examine their acceptability in the *ɓue* construction. The data with finger nail and eye in (3)–(5) are not accepted.

(3) *Mai^{21} ɦam^{11} gua^{21} ɓue^{42} siu^{21}-kah^{5} ka^{44} ɗe^{21}.
mother call 1SG hold finger.nail cut short
'Mother asks me to cut my nail short.'
(4) *I^{44} ɓue^{42} i^{44} kai^{22} siu^{21} liau^{44} na^{11}-ku^{11} ka^{44}-to^{44}.
3SG hold 3SG MOD hand stain very dirty
'He stained his hands very dirty.'
(5) *Bue^{42} mak^{3}-tseng^{44} gut^{3} hu^{11} la^{11}.
hold eye close go PERF
'He closed the eyes.'

In addition to the body parts, the noun conveying animals and insects/worms are also tested as follows.

(6) *Bue^{42} io^{22} ɓien^{11}-seng^{22} lang^{21}.
hold sheep become wolf
'He changed the sheep into a wolf.'

(7) *Kong^{44} ɓue^{42} koi^{44}-bo^{21} hai^{22} la^{11}.
grandfather hold chicken-female kill PERF
'The grandfather killed the hen.'
(8) *I^{44} ɓue^{42} hang^{22} nam^{11} ɦat^{3} la^{11}.
3SG hold insect play tired PERF
'He played the insect and got tired.'

The examples from (1)–(8) show that nouns with the [+animate] feature, including body parts, animals and insects, are not allowed to occur at the object position of *ɓue*. Notice that eggs are not assumed to be with [+animate] feature, because they can be accepted in the *ɓue* construction, as in (9).

(9) I^{44} ɓue^{42} dziak^{3} kai^{22} nui^{42} tiak^{5} ɓeh^{5} la^{11}.
3SG hold one CL egg throw broken PERF
'He broke an egg.'

2.2 Theta Role: Patient

The most common theta role of the *ɓue* object is Patient. Patient undergoes a visible physical change in state, while Theme does not share the feature [+ change] (cf. Rozwadowska 1988). For example, the verbal complements *loh*^{3} 'fall' in (10) and *ɓai*^{44} 'damage' in (11) indicate the change state.

(10) Gua^{21} ɓue^{42} phang^{44}-tiu^{44} liah^{3} loh^{3}.
3SG hold bee.lair catch fall
'I took down the honeycomb.'
(11) I^{44} ɓue^{42} i^{21} tse^{42} ɓai^{44} la^{11}.
3SG hold chair sit damage PERF
'He broke the chair by sitting on it.'

2.3 Theta Role: Instrument

Instrument is something that may cause an action indirectly. While not many data with Instrument object, we find that the Instrument theta role is accepted in the *ɓue* construction.

(12) Gua^{21} ɓue^{42} sio^{44} ɗui^{11} tun^{21} uai^{44} nang^{22}.
1SG hold gun toward exact bad person
'I held my gun towards the bad guy.'

2.4 Theta Role: Theme

Unlike Patient object (e.g. (2), (10), (11)), the Theme object does not undergo a change. In addition, Theme object is not accepted in the *ɓue* construction, as in (13)–(16).

(13) *Gua^{21} ɓue^{42} le^{44}-ɗo^{11} toh^{5} ɗa^{44}-ki^{44} kai^{22} su^{11}.
1SG hold here do self MOD home
'I consider here as my own home.'

(14) *Gua²¹ ɓue⁴² ɦang²² ti⁴⁴ o²¹-tsiop³ la¹¹.
1SG hold Tang poem learn PERF
'I have learned the Tang poems.

(15) *Gua²¹ ɓue⁴² tiom⁴⁴ lai⁴² kai²² ue⁴⁴ kong²¹ sut⁵ lai²².
1SG hold heart in MOD word say out come
'I said the words in my heart out.'

(16) *Gua²¹ ɓue⁴² tse²¹ phien⁴⁴ bun²²-tsiang⁴⁴ mo⁴⁴ bat⁵ la¹¹.
1SG hold this CL article see know PERF
'I read the article and understood it.'

2.5 Theta Role: Location

Like Theme object and Instrument object, the Location object does not occur often in the *ɓue* construction, and it is not fully accepted by the language consultant, as in (17).

(17) ?Bue⁴² huang⁴⁴ pho⁴⁴ ɗou⁴⁴ tsiang¹¹ siu⁴⁴.
hold barren hill all plant tree
'He planted trees on the barren hill.'

2.6 Theta Role: Experiencer

Experiencer is an entity that can perceive a sensory impression. Experiencer object is not allowed in the *ɓue* construction, as in it is not fully accepted by the language consultant, as in (18).

(18) *Bue⁴² ɗu²¹ kia⁴⁴ ɗit⁵ ɦo¹¹-toh⁵ kin²¹-tsiang⁴⁴.
hold 2SG scare extent that nervous
'The thing scared you and made you nervous.'

The most common theta role for the object of *ɓue* is Patient. Instrument object does not occur frequently. Theme object, Locàtion object and Experience object are not fully accepted or even not allowed in Hainan Min.

3 Semantic Features of Subject of *ɓue*

Unlike the object of *ɓue*, the animacy feature does not affect the subject of *ɓue*. The thematic roles of the subject are tested in this section.

3.1 Theta Role: Agent

Based on Fillmore (1968), Agent is the typically animate perceived instigator of the action. Agent subject is the most common subject of the verb *ɓue*. The majority of the subject of *ɓue* plays the Agent thematic role.

(19) Ko⁴⁴-hiang²² ɓue⁴² ua²¹ phah⁵ ɓeh⁵ la¹¹.
sister hold bowl hit broken PERF
'My sister broke the bowl.'

(20) I^{44} ɓue^{42} ɓeh^{3} tua^{21} liau^{44} ou^{44} liau^{21}.
3SG hold white paper stain black finish
'He stained the piece of white paper black.'

(21) I^{44} ɓue^{42} ɓok^{5}-hau^{22} kak^{3} ɗu^{42} hou^{22}-tih^{5}.
3SG hold ax put at ground
'He put the ax on the ground.'

(22) I^{44} ɓue^{42} hap^{5}-ɗang^{22} mo^{44} dziak^{3} si^{11}.
3SG hold contract see one CL
'He checked contract for one time.'

3.2 Theta Role: Experiencer

The Experiencer subject of *ɓue* is not acceptable in Hainan Min, as in (23).

(23) *I^{44} ɓue^{42} tse^{21} ku^{11} ue^{42} tio^{42} liau^{21} dziak^{3} e^{44}.
3SG hold this CL word think PERF one CL
'He considered the words for a while.'

3.3 Theta Role: Instrument

The Instrument subject of *ɓue* is not acceptable in Hainan Min, as in (24).

(24) *Do^{44} ɓue^{42} ɗe^{44} kuah^{5} ɓeh^{3} la^{11}.
knife hold bag cut break PERF
'The knife cut the bag broken.'

3.4 Theta Role: Causer

The Causer subject of *ɓue* is not acceptable in Hainan Min, as in (25).

(25) *Ue^{21} ɓue^{42} su^{11} ɗou^{44} tio^{44} heh^{5} la^{11}.
fire hold house all burn clean PERF
'The fire burned the house out

3.5 Theta Role: Theme

The Theme subject of *ɓue* is not acceptable in Hainan Min, as in (26).

(26) *No^{42} tsiang^{44} tsiu^{21} ɓue^{42} i^{44} im^{21} tui^{11} la^{11}.
two CL wine hold 3SG drink drunk PERF
'Two glasses of wine made him drunk.'

3.6 Theta Role: Time and Location

The Time/Location subject of *ɓue* is not acceptable in Hainan Min, as in (27).

(27) *Ke^{11}-hi^{22} ɓue^{42} kia^{21} ɗou^{44} nam^{11} huang^{22} la^{11}.
holiday hold kid all play crazy PERF
'The holidays made the kids play crazily.'

In summary, the thematic role for the subject in the *ɓue* construction only accepts Agent, rather than Experiencer, Causer, Theme and Time/Location.

4 Proto-Roles of Object and Subject of *ɓue*

After testing the argument structure of the verb *ɓue*, we found that the semantic properties of the object and subject fit Dowty's (1991) proto-role properties for the Patient and Agent roles. Firstly, the object of *ɓue* only allows Patient and Instrument thematic roles, and it basically matches the properties for patient proto-role proposed by Dowty as in (28).

(28) Properties for Patient proto-role (Dowty 1991):
a. undergoes change of state
b. incremental theme
c. causally affected by another participant
d. stationary relative to movement of another participant

The most common thematic role of the object of *ɓue* is Patient and it is often followed by a verbal complement indicating the state of change. For example, the second verb *de*^{21} 'short' and *ti*^{21} 'dead' in the verbal sequences *ka*^{44} *de*^{21} 'cut short' and *hai*^{22} *ti*^{21} 'kill dead' perform the function of verbal complement which refers to the change of state. The incremental theme is an NP that plays a part in determining the telicity of certain events (cf. Dowty 1991; Krifka 1992; Ramchand 1997; Tenny 1992). For example, in the sentence *John ate an apple*, the NP *an apple* is the incremental theme because every subpart of the apple corresponds to a subpart of the event of eating the apple. In addition, the object of *ɓue* is often affected by the subject of *ɓue*. For example, in the sentence like *Ko*^{44}*-hiang*^{22} *ɓue*^{42} *ua*^{21} *phah*^{5} *ɓeh*^{5} *la*^{11} 'My sister broke the bowl,' the object *ua*^{21} 'bowl' is affected by the subject *ko*^{44}*-hiang*^{22} 'sister' because the sister broke the bowl. Lastly, the object of *ɓue* is often relative to movement of the subject of *ɓue*. For example, in the sentence like *I*^{44} *ɓue*^{42} *ɓok*^{5}*-hau*^{22} *kak*^{3} *du*^{42} *hou*^{22}*-tih*^{5} 'He put the ax on the ground,' the object *ɓok*^{5}*-hau*^{22} 'ax' is moved by the subject *i*^{44} 'he/she' because he/she moved the ax. From the above discussion, the object of *ɓue* fits the four properties for Patient proto-role proposed by Dowty (1991).

On the other hand, the subject of *ɓue* also mostly matches the properties for Agent proto-role of Dowty (1991), as in (29).

(29) Properties for Agent proto-role (Dowty 1991):
a. volitional involvement in the event or state
b. sentience (and/or perception)
c. causing an event or change of state in another participant
d. movement (relative to the position of another participant)

Firstly, the subject of *ɓue* is often volitionally involved in the event or state. For example, in the sentence like *I*^{44} *ɓue*^{42} *ɓok*^{5}*-hau*^{22} *kak*^{3} *du*^{42} *hou*^{22}*-tih*^{5} 'He put the ax on the ground,' the subject *i*^{44} 'he/she' volitionally put the ax on the ground. Secondly, the subject of *ɓue* is often volitionally involved in the event or state. For example, in the sentence like *I*^{44} *ɓue*^{42} *hap*^{5}*-ɗang*^{22} *mo*^{44} *dziak*^{3} *si*^{11} 'He checked contract for one time,' the subject *i*^{44} 'he/she' is with sentience and perception because *i*^{44} 'he/she' can see and read. Thirdly, the subject *ɓue* can cause an event of change of state in the object of *ɓue*. For example, in the sentence like *Ko*^{44}*-hiang*^{22} *ɓue*^{42} *ua*^{21} *phah*^{5} *ɓeh*^{5} *la*^{11} 'My sister broke the bowl,' the subject *ko*^{44}*-hiang*^{22} 'sister' causes the object of *ɓue* to be broken and causes the change of state of the object, *ua*^{21} 'bowl.' Lastly, the subject of *ɓue* can make a movement (relative to the position of the object of *ɓue*). For example, in the sentence like *I*^{44} *ɓue*^{42} *ɓok*^{5}*-hau*^{22} *kak*^{3} *ɗu*^{42} *hou*^{22}*-tih*^{5} 'He put the ax on the ground,' the subject *i*^{44} 'he/she' causes the movement of the object of *ɓue*, the ax. In summary, the subject of *ɓue* matches the properties for Agent proto-role.

Notice that the *ɓue* construction only allows Agent role to serve as its subject. The object of *ɓue* tends to be Patient. The s-selection of agent can be referred to Sybesma's (1992) two types of *ba* sentences: "canonical *ba* sentences" and "causative *ba* sentences." The former expresses sentences with animate agent subjects; the latter expresses sentences with inanimate causer subjects. According to Sybesma's typology, the *ɓue* construction in Hainan Min belongs to the canonical *ba* sentence group. The s-selection of the word *ɓue* remains in Hainan Min, and this makes the disposal construction in Hainan Min very different from the word *ba* in Mandarin.

This paper provides the argument properties of *ɓue* in the disposal construction and shows that the word *ɓue* strongly s-selects its object and subject. In addition, the animacy feature of the object affects grammaticality of the *ɓue* construction. These semantic properties of arguments of the disposal construction make Hainan Min very unique among Chinese languages.

References

Chao, Y.: A Grammar of Spoken Chinese. University of California Press, Berkeley (1968)

Dowty, D.R.: Thematic proto-roles and argument selection. Language **67**, 547–619 (1991)

Endo, M.: The semantic property of the subject of the disposal construction in Taiwanese Hailu Hakka. J. Taiwan. Lang. Lit. **11**(2), 169–197 (2016)

Fillmore, C.: The case for case. In: Bach, E., Harms, R. (eds.) Universals in Linguistic Theory, pp. 1–88. Holt, Rinehart and Winston, New York (1968)

Hashimoto, Y.: Mandarin syntactic structures. Unicorn **8**, 1–149 (1971)

Huang, J.: Logical relations in Chinese and the theory of grammar. Doctoral dissertation, MIT, MA (1982)

Krifka, M.: Thematic relations as links between nominal reference and temporal constitution. In: Sag, I., Szabolcsi, A. (eds.) Lexical Matters, pp. 29–54. CSLI Publications, Stanford (1992)

Lee, H.: On the object marker BUE in Hainan Min. Lang. Linguist. **10**(3), 471–487 (2009)

Li, A.: Order and Constituency in Mandarin Chinese. Kluwer, Dordrecht (1990)

Li, C., Thompson, S.: Mandarin Chinese: A Functional Reference Grammar. University of California Press, Berkeley (1981)

Lien, C.: Grammatical function words Qi, Du, Kong, Jia, Jang and Li in Li Jing Ji and their development in Southern Min. In: Ho, D. (ed.) Dialect Variations in Chinese, pp. 179–216. Institute of Linguistics, Academia Sinica, Taipei (2002)

Ramchand, G.: Aspect and Predication. Clarendon Press, Oxford (1997)

Rozwadowska, B.: Thematic restrictions on derived nominals. In: Wilkins, W. (ed.) Syntax and Semantics, Thematic Relations, pp. 147–165. Academic Press, San Diego (1988)

Sybesma, R.: Causatives and accomplishments: the case of the Chinese ba. Doctoral dissertation, Leiden University, Leiden (1992)

Tenny, C.: The aspectual interface hypothesis. In: Sag, I., Szabolcsi, A. (eds.) Lexical Matters, pp. 1–27. CSLI Publications, Stanford (1992)

Tsao, F.: Ka in Taiwan Southern Min and object preposing. Chin. Linguist. **9**, 21–30 (2005)

Wang, L.: Zhongguo yufa lilu [Theory of Chinese Grammar]. Zhonghua Shuju, Beijing (1954)

Applications of Natural Language Processing

A Study on Automatic Recognition of Chinese Sentence Pairs Relations Based on CNN

Xuejing Zhang[1], Xueqiang Lv[1], Qiang Zhou[2,3](✉), and Tianke Wei[1]

[1] Beijing Key Laboratory of Internet Culture and Digital Dissemination Research, Beijing Information Science and Technology University, Beijing 100101, China
[2] Beijing National Research Center for Information Science and Technology (BNRist), Beijing 100084, China
zq-lxd@mail.tsinghua.edu.cn
[3] Research Institute of Information Technology, Center for Speech and Language Technology (RIIT, CSLT), Beijing 100084, China

Abstract. The sentence pairs relations of Chinese discourse play an important role in many natural language processing tasks. Automatic recognition the sentence pairs relations will effectively improve the performance of tasks such as automatic writing and text generation. Among sentence pairs relations, coordination as the double-nucleus relation is the most widely distributed one. In order to automatically identify the double-nucleus relations, this paper combines convolutional neural network and word sequence features, synthetically takes into account the semantic and structural characteristics, and add attention to dig the double-nucleus relations. Experiments show that this method can effectively identify the double-nucleus relations, and the method is portability.

Keywords: Recognition of Chinese sentence pairs relations · CNN Attention · Double-nucleus

1 Introduction

The recognition of sentence pair relations is very important in many natural language processing tasks. For example, machine translation, automatic segmentation of text paragraphs or sentence groups, automatic generation of text summaries, and so on. Generally, the sentence pair relation is divided into explicit relation and implicit relation. When clear coherent words exist between sentences which means an explicit relation, the recognition of the sentence pair relation is easier. However, most of the sentence pairs do not have a coherence word, the implicit relation can be identified only by the deep analysis of the semantic relation between the sentences. How to identify these implicit relations between sentences has become the focus of researches. The identification of implicit sentence pair relations is often regarded as a task of classification. Methods such as naive Bayes [1], maximum entropy [2] and support vector machine (SVM) [3] were used to handle this task. Most of the traditional text representation methods are "Bag-of-words model". That means only the frequency of words appearing in the text is considered, and the sequence information is not taken into account. Traditional methods can

J.-F. Hong et al. (Eds.): CLSW 2018, LNAI 11173, pp. 497–508, 2018.
https://doi.org/10.1007/978-3-030-04015-4_42

also use N-gram methods, but this can lead to sparse problems. With the rapid development of deep learning, neural network model has gradually entered the vision of researchers, it has good performances in many fields. Recurrent neural network (RNN) [4] was used to improve the performance of sentence pair relation recognition. And a structure of convolutional neural network (CNN) [5] was improved and proposed a stacking gated neural network structure. This work studied the implicit relations between discourse sentences, and divided them into four categories to further refined the implicit relations. The experimental result on the Penn Discourse Treebank (PDTB) showed the average accuracy of the four groups reached 51.35%. And the author continued to study the implicit relation between discourse sentences by using adversarial connective-exploiting networks, and made new progress [6].

In Chinese, parallel relation, selection relation, undertake relation and flowing relation occupy the overwhelming majority. Improving the recognition rate of these four relation will effectively advance the research progress of sentence pair relation recognition. For the parallel relation, undertake relation and flowing relation (Flowing relation in Chinese is a kind of spoken language phenomenon, It is fluent and does not use or rarely use a conjunctive as a formal marker), they all have one thing in common, that is, the two coherent sentences do not have a focus and share the main purpose. This paper defined such a pair as a double–nucleus pair. This problem is similar of paraphrase identification (PI) and textual entity (TE). In the tasks of PI and TE, this paper compared various neural network models, the performance of CNN is relatively better than others. Therefore, this paper chooses CNN as the basic model. Of course, the effective feature is also important. For the recognition of double-nucleus explicit sentence pairs, this paper used the traditional word sequence features. For the recognition of implicit relation, besides the basic semantic information, this paper also considered the vector similarity between sentence pairs. So that the correct recognition rate of double-nucleus sentence pairs can be improved.

In the following sections, related work is described in Sect. 2, and Sect. 3 introduces the model of double-nucleus sentence relations in detail, Sect. 4 shows experimental results and analysis. The last section is the conclusion and prospect.

2 Related Work

In Chinese, there are few researches on the recognition of paratactic complex sentences pair relation than analysis of traditional sentence pair relations. SVM was used to classify the paratactic complex sentences, and the researchers selected subject, predicate and other features in sentences to propose a sentence pair relation research based on the subject-predicate knowledge [7]. The recognition of paratactic complex sentences relation was realized by the methods of sentence similarity, maximum common substrings, predicate perimeter matching length and repetition of specific words, especially the unsupervised methods reduced the need of annotation [8]. In English sentence pair relations studies, there are few papers aiming to deal with paratactic structures, and most of them tried to identify the traditional types of sentence pair relations automatically. Paratactic relation is just one of the types of relations. Generally, sentence pair relation recognition is regarded as a classification task, which needs to select a suitable classifier and features. At present, deep learning includes CNN and RNN. CNN has certain advantages in identifying the structure of target, while RNN has advantages in sequence recognition because of its memory module. CNN and RNN also have been applied in many natural language processing applications. A study [9] summarized the effects of CNN and RNN on emotional analysis, sentence classification, entity identification, question answering system and so on. It was concluded that CNN had a certain advantage in sentence pair recognition and RNN had an advantage in serialization tasks such as named entity recognition and contextual Q&A. As a result, this paper chose CNN to identify the relationship between the double-nucleus sentence pairs.

CNN was used to classify sentences [10], which showed the advantages of CNN in sentence classification tasks. And an attended-based convenient network (ABCNN) [11] was proposed which achieved good results on many datasets in the task of sentence pair relations recognition. This work used CNN as the basic model and improved the convolution layer directly by adding attention mechanism in the input layer, then they added attention mechanism in the convolution layer to improve tasks performance. Their experiments in answer selection (AS) on WiKiQA, paraphrase identification (PI) using MSRP and textual entity (TE) on SenEval Task have all achieved good results, especially in PI. The discourse relation language models (DRLM) proposed [4] also classified the sentence pair relations by using the long short-term memory (LSTM) model [12], and used two vectors to represent the context environment. One vector represented the context of the word level within the sentence, and the other vector was the context between the pairs. The two vectors were combined linearly. And the model achieved good results on the PDTB dataset.

To sum up, the previous researches on the identification of sentence pair relations in English are quite adequate, while the identification of sentence pair relations in Chinese remains to be explored. Many methods of solving English problems are not entirely applicable to Chinese studies. To some extent, many methods can also solve the problem of sentence pair relations recognition in Chinese discourse, but the effect is not remarkable. In addition, CNN has a significant effect on the task of sentence pair relations recognition. And the double-nucleus sentence pair occupies the overwhelming majority in all the sentences. Correctly identifying the double-nucleus sentence pairs will pave the way for the recognition of the implicit sentence pair relations. Therefore, this paper used CNN to identify the double-nucleus sentence pairs in Chinese, and integrates the double-nucleus sentence pairs' significant features in structure and semantics to improve the recognition accuracy of the double-nucleus sentence pairs' implicit and explicit relations.

3 Model Design

3.1 Models of Word Vector

As the basic of some neural network models, word vector determines the performance of a model to a certain extent. In order to get a good performance, this paper studied the word vector from different aspects, and explored the effects of corpus scale, data domain and dimension of the word vector. First of all, this paper collected the corpus of news, Baidu Encyclopedia, Wikipedia, Sina Weibo and so on, and this paper used the skip-gram model to train word vectors of different dimensions. The dataset of NLPCC-ICCPOL [13] was used to evaluate, which means 500 word pairs randomly selected from 10,000 words was used to calculate the similarity, so as to complete the evaluation of word vectors. In this paper, the best performance word vector was used as the input of neural network.

3.2 Introduction of Task

The task of this paper is to realize the double-nucleus sentence pair relations recognition of Chinese discourse, the two adjacent clauses is combined into a pair and used as input for neural network model. And they are divided into two categories: parallel relation, selection relation, and undertake relation was classified as nucleus-nucleus (N-N), and flowing relation is time-time (T-T). Because the flowing relation is mostly time-coherent, which is different from the relation of parallel relation, selection relation, and undertake relation, but it still belongs to the category of double-nucleus. These two types of double-nucleus sentences are closely related to each other, and they are easy to be confused and difficult to distinguish. Therefore, this paper synthesizes the information of structure and semantics to distinguish N-N and T-T.

In this paper, we improved ABCNN model [11]. ABCNN used two layers of CNN, and attention mechanism was added to the first CNN layer, which expanded the input into two channels. That means the matrix A was computed first, then the attention map of the two sentences is computed separately. The formula for A_{ij} is as follows:

$$A_{i,j} = match - score\left(F_{0,r}\,[:,i],\ F_{1,r}[:,j]\right) \tag{1}$$

A_{ij} represented the match_score of the word i in sentence 1 to the word j in sentence 2 and was calculated using the Euclidean distance. Then the two matrices W_0 and W_1 were multiplied by A and A^T respectively to obtain the same feature graph as the original feature matrix. The specific formula is as follows:

$$\mathrm{F}_{0,a} = W_0 \cdot A^T,\ \mathrm{F}_{1,a} = W_1 \cdot A \tag{2}$$

In the second CNN layer, when the attention matrix A was calculated, the two attention weight vectors for two sentences needed to be calculated. And the pooling layer method is modified, which was no longer a simple average pooling, but was calculated based on the calculated attention weight vector.

The author proposes that ABCNN model had a good performance in dealing with PI or TE tasks. For example, sentence 1 is “a football is played by more than one people” and sentence 2 is “some people are playing football”. It is necessary to use the word i in sentence 1 to match the score of the word j in sentence 2. This pair of sentences is very similar in structure and semantics. ABCNN can make good use of its semantic information when dealing with these pairs. These are also useful when dealing with our task.

PI and TE tasks are similar to the double-nucleus sentence pair recognition task, but there are some differences. In the double-nucleus sentence pairs, there are a lot of structural features that can show the relations between the two sentence pairs, but these significant features cannot be used very well when using the neural network model. In addition, CNN has many problems. For example, when the sentence is too long or too short, the performance is poor. The length of sentences is very unstable, and this problems often appear in the task of identifying the relations of the double-nucleus sentences. In order to identify the double-core sentence pair relations more accurately, it is necessary to design a model suitable. Based on the ABCNN model, this paper combined the peculiar features of the double-nucleus sentence pair relations, and designed a neural network model, double-nucleus attention based convolutional neural network (DABCNN) which is more suitable for the task in this paper to improve the performance.

3.3 DABCNN Design

The automatic recognition method of parallel relation is mainly to calculate the similarity of sentences. When using neural network, models hardly can make full use of semantic information. And once the sentence is too long, the neural network will lose lots of information. When the sentence is too short, the neural network cannot learn enough features. Therefore, this paper used traditional statistical-based method to select features aimed to compensate for the deficiency of neural networks. In addition, the double-nucleus sentence pair relations also has obvious structural features. For example, here are usually conspicuous conjunctions, like "not only, but also", "on the one hand, on the other hand" and so on. These conjunctions can show the relations between sentence pairs.[1] Therefore, the traditional statistical methods can be used to statistic these salient features, and then be incorporated into the neural network model to help achieve the recognition of the relations between the double-nucleus sentences. Specific features are shown in the Table 1.

The discrete feature matrix composed of these words was also used for convolution and pool operation. Then the obtained features are stitched with other features in the full connection layer, and the new joint features can be used to classify the sentence pair relations. In addition, for the double-nucleus implicit relation, the structure between the sentences and the semantics are characteristic which are more obvious. Therefore, the similarity between sentences is of great help to the identification of parallel relation. For the calculation of sentence similarity, the method [8] was used. In semantic, the basic unit of a sentence is word, and a sentence is an ordered set of words, clause S1(w1,w2,...,wn), clause S2(w'1, w'2, . . ., w'm) were used to constructed word similarity matrix (n $\times$ m). The elements of the matrix are the similarity of the corresponding words in the two clauses. The specific formula is as follows:

$$\mathrm{M}[i][j] = \begin{cases} 1 & if\left(w_i = w_j'\right) \\ sim\left(w_i, w_j'\right), & if\left(w_i.pos = w_j'.pos \,\&\, pos \in \{v, n, a\}\right) \\ 0 & \text{other} \end{cases} \quad (3)$$

[1] The detail can be seen from "Tsinghua Syntactic Tree-Annotation Standard", a technical report of Research Institute of Information Technology, Center for Speech and Language Technology.

Table 1. Features of words used in classification of double-nucleus sentences

Feature name	Value
"co-existent" conjunction	(0/1)
"simultaneous" conjunction	(0/1)
"alternate" conjunction	(0/1)
"co-enumeration"conjunction	(0/1)
"time coherence" conjunction	(0/1)
"spatial coherence" conjunction	(0/1)
"relevance" conjunction	(0/1)
"optional" conjunction	(0/1)
"restricted" conjunction	(0/1)
"preferred" conjunction	(0/1)
"direct quote" structure	(0/1)

The w.pos denotes the part of speech of the word w, the formula for the similarity between sentences is as follows:

$$\mathrm{score}_1 = \mathrm{sim}(\mathrm{S}_1, \mathrm{S}_2) = \frac{\sum_{i-1}^{n} \max_{j=1}^{m} M[i][j]}{n} \tag{4}$$

$$\mathrm{score}_2 = \mathrm{sim}(\mathrm{S}_1, \mathrm{S}_2) = \frac{\sum_{j-1}^{m} \max_{i=1}^{n} M[i][j]}{m} \tag{5}$$

The similarity between the two sentences is calculated by (score 1 + score 2)/2. Summarizing the above methods, this paper combined ABCNN with word features and sentence similarity features, and used the DABCNN model to classify the relations between the double-nucleus sentence pairs. The structure of DABCNN is as follow (Fig. 1).

The input layer consisted of sentence matrix composed of word continuous vectors and sentence matrix composed of word discrete features. And there were four matrices obtained from one sentence pair. In the first layer of DABCNN, the four matrices were convoluted and pooled. In the second layer of feature processing, only the continuous feature matrix was used to mining the coherence relation. In the full connection layer, the continuous word features, the discrete features and the sentence similarity features were stitched together into a new feature vector. Finally, we used softmax for classification.

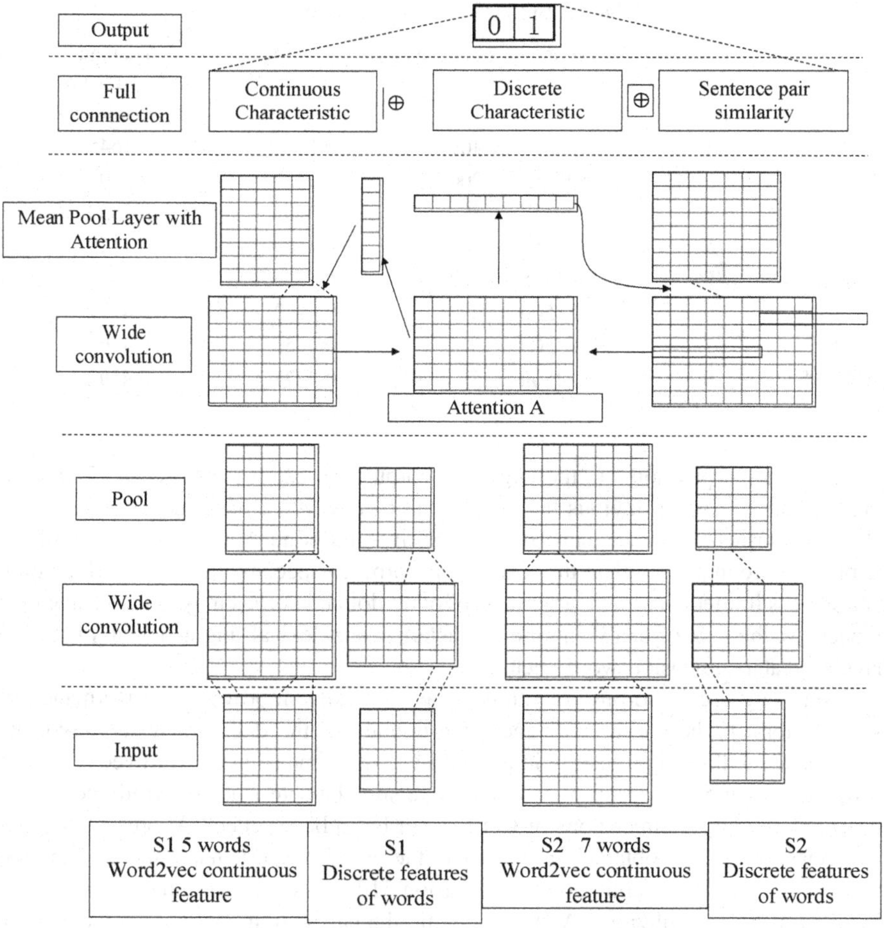

Fig. 1. Structure of DABCNN

4 Experimental Results

4.1 Evaluation Experiment of Word Vector

The corpus of training word vector are from Wikipedia, Sina Weibo and News. The Spearman's rank correlation coefficient[2] and Pearson correlation coefficient[3] were used for evaluation, the results are shown in the Table 2.

By comparing these word vectors based on Wikipedia, we can find that the scale of train data and the dimension of word vector both determine the performance of word vector. And the scale of train data has a more powerful influence than dimension.

[2] https://baike.baidu.com/item/spearman相关系数/7977847?fr=aladdin.

[3] https://baike.baidu.com/item/皮尔森相关系数/4222137?fr=aladdin.

Table 2. Evaluation results of word vector

Corpus	Number	Vocab	Dimension	Spearman correlation coefficient	Pearson correlation coefficient
Wikipedia	1	460824	400	0.1715	0.1645
	2	598454	200	0.2297	0.2605
	3	669217	200	0.2657	0.2659
News & Weibo	4	912253	200	0.4129	0.4129
	5	**1002405**	**300**	**0.4395**	**0.4479**
News & Weibo &Wikipedia	6	1682500	200	0.4303	0.4397
	7	1682500	256	0.4355	0.4464
	8	**1682500**	**512**	**0.4477**	**0.4502**

For the same corpus domain, the larger the corpus, the better performance. The same domain corpus has an obvious help on the task, however it has a negative influence when the corpus not in the same domain. So in some kind, the domain purity of the corpus is more important than the scale of the corpus. Especially in the task which train data scale is limited, adding a large scale of other domain corpus may lead to a negative impact. As the task of analyzing the characteristics of lexical linguistics, it's better to have a greater dimension word vector.

Using large-scale corpus for training can generally improve the performance of word vectors. If the corpus is in the same domain as the data which task used, the performance will be significantly improved. And the dimension of word vectors needs to be more than 50, especially when the linguistic characteristics of word vectors are measured, the larger dimensions of word vector has a better effect. At present, a better performance can be obtained only when the word vectors have more than 200 dimensions. The dimension 256 and dimension 512 are better than dimension 300, but the difference is not obvious. And considering the calculation complexity, we can not only consider "the bigger the better". In this paper, the word vector of number 5 and number 8 were selected for the evaluation and used of the following neural network models.

4.2 Data Setting

In this paper, all the complex sentences are extracted from Tsinghua Chinese Treebank (TCT) [14], and the experiment was based on relations among the clauses in the complex sentences. Specific data are shown below (Table 3).

Table 3. Experimental data setting

Class	N-N	T-T
Sum	7132	27847
Train data	5857	22278
Test data	1275	5569

4.3 Experimental Results and Analysis

When the ABCNN was trained with number 5 word vector, the results of the various relations are as follows:

From the Table 4, it can be concluded that there are lots of T-T relation in training corpus, and the correct rate is 79.9%. The accuracy of N-N relation is 76% and lower than T-T. But the overall accuracy is 79.2% because of the large occupation of T-T.

Table 4. ABCNN experimental results (300 dimensions)

Class	N-N	T-T	Num/Acc
Sum	7132	27847	34979
Train data	5857	22278	28135
Test data	1217	4933	6150
Correct data	925	3946	4871
Acc	**0.760**	**0.799**	**0.792**

The DABCNN was used with word features and similarity features, and the results are as follows:

The results in Table 5 shows the DABCNN model improved the effects of both relations of double-nucleus sentence pair.

Table 5. DABCNN experimental results (300 dimensions)

Class	N-N	T-T	Num/Acc
Sum	7132	27847	34979
Train	5857	22278	28135
Test	1217	4933	6150
Correct	975	4060	5035
Acc	**0.801**	**0.823**	**0.819**

This paper compared several cases of ABCNN wrong prediction and DABCNN correct prediction, the results is shown as Table 6:

Table 6. Analysis of experimental data (300 dimensions)

Order	Tag	ABCNN	DABCNN	S1	S2
1	N-N	T-T	N-N	In May 1967, the Red Guards of many secondary schools organized the "Mao Zedong Thought Propaganda Corps" 一九六七年五月，许多中学红卫兵组织"毛泽东思想宣传队"	I had a "Red Guard drama troupe" with a couple of my friends as well. 我和几个同伴也拉了个"红卫兵话剧团"
2	N-N	T-T	N-N	No professional titles 一没有专业职称	and no academic works. 二没有学术著作

(continued)

Table 6. (*continued*)

Order	Tag	ABCNN	DABCNN	S1	S2
3	N-N	T-T	N-N	He doesn't leave the bedroom, 大门不出	not to mention goes out 二门不迈
4	N-N	T-T	N-N	How to make life worthwhile, 怎样让人生活得有价值	and how to help readers, contribute to society and people, 怎样对读者有帮助，对社会、对人民有贡献
5	T-T	N-N	T-T	Her eyes are slender like beans, 她的眼睛是细长的有如豆角	her thick red spindle lips were tightly closed. 厚而红的梭形嘴唇紧闭着
6	T-T	N-N	T-T	I went back in a hurry and ate my meal, 我回去匆忙扒拉完了饭	then ran to the courtyard door. 又跑到院门

From Table 6, when the relation between sentences is explicit, there are more obvious conjunctions and play an active role in identify, such as the case 1 and 2 in Table 6. When the sentence pair structure is too short or too long, and there is no definite conjunction word, the neural network can not learn the features between the sentence pair very well. At this time, the sentence pair is divided into N-N by the sentence similarity, such as case 3, 4. And sentence pairs in case 5 and 6 are more like the flow relation of action or description rather than parallel relation in case 2 and 3. After using the DABCNN model, the result was corrected.

The length of sentence influences the performance of a model. So this paper analyzed the performance of DABCNN model in different sentences length, and the results are shown in the Fig. 2:

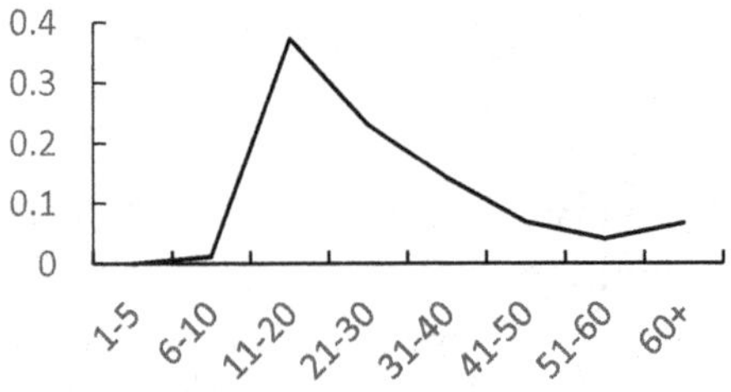

Fig. 2. Correct rate of prediction for different sentence lengths

Figure 2 shows when the sentence length is less than 10 or more than 60, the correct rate of predicted labels is very limit. How to solve the influence of sentence length is a difficult problem to solve, and our next step is to study this issue.

In order to compare the influence of different word vectors, this paper chose the number 8 word vectors to carry out the experiment. The experimental results of each model are as Table 7:

Table 7. DABCNN experimental results (512 dimensions)

Class	N-N	T-T	Num/Acc
Sum	7132	27847	34979
Train data	5857	22278	28135
Test data	1217	4933	6150
Correct data	980	4080	5060
Acc	**0.805**	**0.827**	**0.823**

The results in Table 7 shows that in the 512 dimensions word vector, the accuracy of each category and the whole accuracy have been slightly improved. However, combined with the computational cost and training time of the model, these effects can almost be ignored. Therefore, it is not a good choice to increase dimension and domain of the word vector.

At the same time, the DRLM model was compared with the DABCNN model. The DRLM model was modified based on LSTM in order to identify the sentence pair relations. This paper compared the performance of DABCNN and DRLM on the 300 dimensions word vector, and used the same training and test dataset, the results are as shown in the Table 8. The experimental results verified the superiority of DABCNN in the task of sentence pair relations recognition.

Table 8. Comparison of DABCNN Model and DRLM Model (300 Dimensions)

Class	Train	Test	Acc
DABCNN	28135	6150	0.819
ABCNN	28135	6150	0.792
DRLM	28135	6160	0.765

5 Conclusion

This paper proposed a method of automatic recognition of sentence coherence in Chinese discourse, especially classified double-nucleus sentence pairs by CNN and attention mechanism. And this paper fully mining sentence pair coherence by fusing word features, and analyzed the differences and connections between the two types of double-nucleus sentence pairs in semantics and structure. In addition, this paper evaluated a series of word vectors to illustrate the importance of word vectors for natural language processing. Finally, experimental results show that using DABCNN model can effectively improve the performance of relations between the two types of double-nucleus sentence pairs. With the addition of word features, the two types of double-nucleus sentence pairs can also be distinguished in structure. The automatic recognition of the double-nucleus sentence pairs, which occupy a large majority in the Chinese sentence coherence relationship, is completed.

Of course, this paper has shortcomings, such as when dealing with the sentences which are very disproportionate in the structure the effect is not good enough. In this situation, it is easy to lose the important information of the long sentence. Besides, how to classify the coherent relation of single-nucleus sentence pairs will be the focus of our work.

Acknowledgements. This work was supported by grants from National Natural Science Foundation of China (No.61433018, No.61373075), National Natural Science Foundation of China (No.61671070), National Language Committee Major Project (No.ZDI135-53), and Beijing Advanced Innovation Center for Imaging Technology (No.BAICIT-2016003).

References

1. McCallum, A., Nigam, K.: A comparison of event models for naive bayes text classification. In: AAAI-98 Workshop on Learning for Text Categorization, vol. 752, pp. 41–48 (1998)
2. Berger, A.L., Pietra, V.J.D., Pietra, S.A.D.: A maximum entropy approach to natural language processing. Comput. Linguist. **22**(1), 39–71 (1996)
3. Cortes, C., Vapnik, V.: Support-vector networks. Mach. Learn. **20**(3), 273–297 (1995)
4. Ji, Y., Haffari, G., Eisenstein, J.: A latent variable recurrent neural network for discourse relation language models. arXiv preprint arXiv:1603.01913 (2016)
5. Qin, L., Zhang, Z., Zhao, H.: A stacking gated neural architecture for implicit discourse relation classification. In: EMNLP, pp. 2263–2270 (2016)
6. Qin, L., Zhang, Z., Zhao, H., et al.: Adversarial connective-exploiting networks for implicit discourse relation classification. arXiv preprint arXiv:1704.00217 (2017)
7. Zhou, W., Yuan, C.: Automatic recognizing of complex sentences with coordinating relation. Appl. Res. Comput. **3**, 764–766 (2008). (in Chinese)
8. Wu, Y., Shi, J., Wan, F.: Automatic identification of Chinese coordination discourse relation. Acta Scientiarum Naturalium Universitatis Pekinensis. **49**(1), 1–6 (2013). (in Chinese)
9. Yin, W., Kann, K., Yu, M., et al.: Comparative study of CNN and RNN for natural language processing. arXiv preprint arXiv:1702.01923 (2017)
10. Kim, Y.: Convolutional neural networks for sentence classification. arXiv preprint arXiv: 1408.5882 (2014)
11. Yin, W., Schütze, H., Xiang, B., et al.: ABCNN: attention-based convolutional neural network for modeling sentence pairs. arXiv preprint arXiv:1512.05193 (2015)
12. Hochreiter, S., Schmidhuber, J.: Long short-term memory. Neural Comput. **9**(8), 1735–1780 (1997)
13. Wu, Y., Li, W.: Overview of the NLPCC-ICCPOL 2016 shared task: Chinese word similarity measurement. In: Lin, C.-Y., Xue, N., Zhao, D., Huang, X., Feng, Y. (eds.) ICCPOL/NLPCC -2016. LNCS (LNAI), vol. 10102, pp. 828–839. Springer, Cham (2016). https://doi.org/10.1007/978-3-319-50496-4_75
14. Qiang, Z.: Annotation scheme for Chinese treebank. J. Chin. Inf. Process. **18**(4), 1–8 (2004). (in Chinese)

A Classification Method for Chinese Word Semantic Relations Based on TF-IDF and CNN

Teng Mao, Yuanyuan Peng, Yuru Jiang(✉), and Yangsen Zhang

Institute of Intelligent Information Processing, Beijing Information Science and Technology University, Beijing, China
yurujiang@126.com

Abstract. The classification of semantic relations between words is an important part of semantic analysis in natural language research. The automatic achievement of this classification is of significance to construction of the Knowledge Graph and Information Retrieval. In NLPCC2017 shared task on Chinese Word Semantic Relations Classification, the semantic relations have been classified into four categories: synonym, antonym, hyponymy and meronym. This paper presents a classification method for Chinese word semantic relations based on TF-IDF and CNN, and uses words' literal and semantic features. Four new literal features are proposed including whether a word is part of another word and the ratio of their common substring. The extraction of semantic features is a four-step process— training a vector model of words on BaiduBaike Corpus, selecting a set of words most related to a given word from BaiduBaike based on TF-IDF, constructing a vector matrix for the set of related words, and using CNN to get the semantic features of the given word from the vector matrix. The experiment on the NLPCC2017 dataset demonstrates that the F_1-score is up to 83.91%, which proves effective to eliminate the influence of the OOV words.

Keywords: Semantic relations · CNN · TF-IDF

1 Introduction

With the development of Natural Language Processing (NLP) technology, how to make the computer truly understand the natural language has become an important research direction. The identification of semantic relations is a key step for the computer to understand natural language. It can help computers extract basic information of texts, construct semantic networks and identify text implication relations [1, 2]. It can also be used in many research fields, such as Information Retrieval, Knowledge Graph construction, etc. Some scholars have constructed semantic dictionaries to show the semantic relation between words. For example, Wordnet [3] developed by the Cognitive Science Laboratory of Princeton University, organizes English words as a collection of synonyms, uses vocabulary concepts to represent synonym sets, and establishes a variety of semantic relations between sets; HowNet [4] uses the concept represented by Chinese as the description object, and describes the semantic relation of concept-concept and attribute-concept with a limited set of semantic primitives.

J.-F. Hong et al. (Eds.): CLSW 2018, LNAI 11173, pp. 509–518, 2018.
https://doi.org/10.1007/978-3-030-04015-4_43

"Synonym CiLin" [5] and "Chinese Concept Dictionary" [6] also described the semantic relation between words in different degrees.

Knowledge extracted from dictionaries is accurate, but their construction is time-consuming. And with the evolution of cyberculture, many new words appear in the network and many traditional words have been given new meanings. But the existing semantic dictionaries can't adapt to these changes in time. Therefore, it would be very meaningful to make full use of the huge amount of internet resources to automatically recognize semantic relations.

Some evaluation activities have been held on recognition of semantic relations. For example, the NLPCC 2012 shared task on Chinese word semantic relation extraction, which was to find the synonyms and hyponyms of a given word; the NLPCC 2017 shared task on Chinese word semantic relation classification [7], in which the semantic relation of a given word pair is classified into synonym, antonym, hyponym, and meronym. For the NLPCC 2017 shared task, this paper uses the literal structure of words to extract literal features, uses TF-IDF and CNN to extract semantic features. And with these two types of features, it classifies the semantic relations into four types of semantic relations as mentioned above.

2 Related Work

The semantic relations of words can be directly acquired from dictionary resources and some online resources, For instance, we can use "Synonym CiLin" to confirm whether words have synonymous relation. However, this way is limited by the size of dictionary. If words do not appear in the dictionary (OOV words), their semantic relation can't be judged. Therefore, scholars have carried out a lot of research work that is not entirely depending on dictionary resources. The current recognition methods of semantic relations can be divided into pattern matching methods and statistics-based methods.

For the pattern matching methods, a certain number of pattern matching rules are defined for each semantic relation, and then these rules are used to match word pairs in existing corpus. Hearst and Marti [8], the first one to use pattern matching, have obtained pairs of words with hyponym relations. Defining 3 pattern matching rules through manual observation, they used these rules to extract word pairs whose semantic relation is hyponym. They extracted other rules from these pairs of words to get more new word pairs. Although the method of pattern matching can obtain word pairs directly from the corpus, it cannot guarantee that the obtained semantic relation of word pairs is correct. In addition, due to the usage of Chinese is very flexible, pattern matching method has low coverage and high cost of migration to the new field.

For the statistical method, firstly, it makes a statistical analysis of the various characteristics of vocabulary, and then uses clustering or classification methods to deter-mine the semantic relation between words. From the perspective of lexical semantics, contexts and spatial structures, Lei and Cungen [9] proposed a set of features which can be used to verify hyponym relation between word pairs. Hu and Sui [10] used vector based method to obtain the hyponym word in computer field. Zhang and Wang [11] used RNN (Recurrent Neural Network) to learn the potential features of vocabulary and sentence, and used these features to identify the semantic relations between nouns existing in the same sentence. Statistical method can make use of lexical semantic information. In view to its good portability, it also can be used in different training corpus.

In the NLPCC2017 shared task, Changliang and Teng [12] proposed a se-mantic relation classification system by using dictionary resources, word vectors and linguistic knowledge, and the F_1-score was up to 85.90%. Shijia et al. [13] classified the semantic relation of given word pairs by word vector and CNN (Convolutional Neural Network), and the F_1-score was 76.80%. Although the above two methods have obtained good F_1-score, they can't handle the OOV problem.

Based on all above, this paper uses statistical methods to extract literal features and semantic features to classify semantic relations. In order to eliminate the influence of OOV, online resources, such as BaiduBaike[1], are used as corpus when extracting words' semantic features.

3 The Method for Chinese Word Semantic Relations Based on TF-IDF and CNN

The classification method for Chinese word semantic relations proposed in this paper consists of three parts: the extraction of Literal Feature (LF), the extraction of Semantic Features (SF) and the selection of classifier.

This paper first trains a vector model of words on BaiduBaike Corpus. When a pair of word is given, the TF-IDF is used to select a set of related words for each word from the BaiduBaike, and two vector matrix are constructed for two sets of related words; the Semantic Features are drawn from vector matrix for each word by using CNN, and then splice of Semantic Features of each word are to be classified. On the other hand, this paper also extracts Literal Features to classify, such as the length of word pairs, the ratio of common substring, etc. Finally, two classification results are polled and merged to get the final classification results.

Figure 1 is the overall framework of the classification method. The following part of this section is a detailed description of the extraction methods of Literal Features and Semantic Features, and the selection of classifier.

3.1 Extraction Literal Features

This paper have extracted 210,000 pairs of word that have synonymous, antonym, hyponym and meronym relations from HowNet, WordNet, Synonym CiLin and Chinese Concept Dictionary. By the analysis of these word pairs and NLPCC data sets, it is found that the literal structure of Chinese words can reflect the semantic relationship between words. Zhou et al. [14] extracted features, such as the length of words, the length difference between words, and the number of repeated words as the literal features of words. This paper proposes another four literal features. One of these features is whether a word is part of another word which can reflect the semantic relationship between words, such as <风扇(fan), 电风扇(electric fan)>. In addition,

[1] https://baike.baidu.com/.

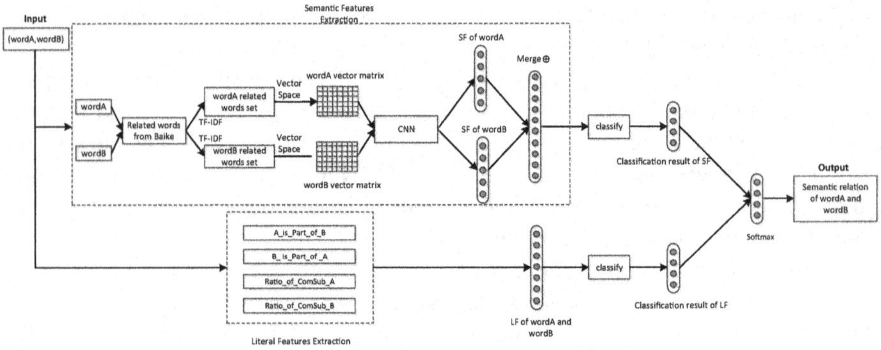

Fig. 1. The overall framework

the ratio of the length of common substring of two words to the length of one of them can also be helpful to this task. For example, in word pair <**花(flower),** 樱花(sakura) >, the common substring is "花(flower)", and the ratio of "花(flower)" to "花(flower)" is 100%, and the ratio of "**花(flower)**(flower)" to "樱花(sakura)" is 50%, so the semantic relation between them is likely hyponym or meronym. In word pair <**梨花(pear flower), 樱花(sakura)**>, the ratio for each word is equal to 50%, and the semantic relation between them is likely synonymous.

As for word pair <word A, word B> , this paper extracts 11 features as literal features which are shown in Table 1. These features are divided into two groups LF1 (features used in other work) and LF2 (features proposed in this paper).

3.2 Semantic Features Extraction

In order to obtain Semantic Features of a given word, four steps of work have been done. Firstly, a word vector model is trained on BaiduBaike Corpus; secondly, the related words set of a given word is obtained by TF-IDF; third the word vector matrix of a given word is constructed with the previous two sources. The matrix can be regarded as a given word's semantic representation, the matrix is represented as: $SenMatrix \in R^{n \times m}$, where n is the number of related words, and m is the word vector dimension. Finally, the semantic feature vector of a given word is obtained by CNN from the word vector matrix.

Training Word Vector: This paper have crawled 15.13 million BaiduBaike entries, and have used the jieba segmentation tool[2] to segment word. Then this paper have used word2vec module in gensim[3] to train word vector on the segmented BaiduBaike corpus. In the training process, the CBOW algorithm is selected; the word vector dimension is set to 200; the minimum word frequency is 5; and the context window is 5.

[2] https://pypi.python.org/pypi/jieba/.

[3] https://radimrehurek.com/gensim/moels/word2vec.html.

Table 1. Literal features

Group	Feature name
LF1	Length_of_A
	Length_of_B
	DiffLength_of_AB
	Union_Number_of_AB
	Intersection_Number_of_AB
	Is_Same_of_prefix
	Is_Same_of_suffix
LF2	**A_is_Part_of_B**
	B_ is_Part_of _A
	Ratio_of_ComSub_A
	Ratio_of_ComSub_B

Constructing Related Word Set: TF-IDF can reflect the importance of a word for a document in a corpus [15]. Yutao et al. [16] used the TF-IDF to extract text keywords for text classification and achieved a good results. Therefore, this paper uses TF-IDF to extract the most related words set of a given word from its BaiduBaike entry which is detailed descriptions of this word. For a given word, this paper takes the topN words with high TF-IDF value to construct the related word set. Taking "钢笔(pen)" as an example, the top-9 words and their TF-IDF values are shown in Table 2 and these words are strongly correlated with "钢笔(pen)".

Table 2. Related words of "壶盖(pot lid)

壶盖(pot lid)

"

Related words	钢笔 (pen)	墨水 (ink)	上墨 (inking)	书写 (write)	笔杆 (penholder)	金笔 (fountain pen)	墨囊 (ink sac)	钢笔尖 (pen nib)	品牌 (brand)
TF-IDF	0.132	0.1	0.064	0.045	0.031	0.028	0.024	0.018	0.015

In addition, there are some words without BaiduBaike entries. For a word without BaiduBaike entry, this paper extracts a certain number of sentences containing it from BaiduBaike pages as the word's context information, and then uses TF-IDF to obtain related words set of it. Taking "钢笔(pen)" as an example, the final calculation results of it are shown in Table 3.

Table 3. Related words of "壶盖(pot lid)壶盖(pot lid)
"

Related words	壶盖 (pot lid)	壶 (pot)	壶口 (pot mouth)	壶嘴 (pot spout)	盖 (lid)	茶壶盖 (teapot lid)	茶壶 (teapot)	壶把 (pot handle)	砂壶 (sand-fired pot)
TF-IDF	0.227	0.108	0.028	0.027	0.027	0.025	0.024	0.021	0.018

Extracting Semantic Features: With a strong descriptive ability in many applications, CNN can very well extract the high-dimensional features of the data [17]. In the field of Natural Language Processing, Kim [18] used CNN for text classification tasks and achieved good results. This paper also uses CNN to extract semantic features of a given word. First, this paper uses word vectors to convert related words set of the given word to SemMatrix, and then uses CNN to extract higher-level semantic feature vectors from SemMatrix. The basic structure of CNN used in this paper is shown in Fig. 2.

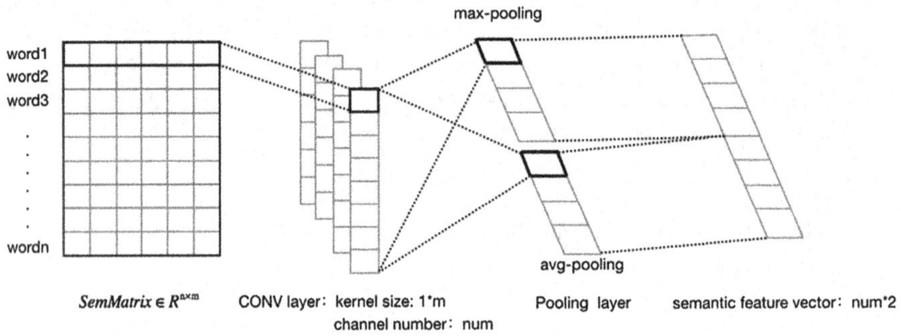

Fig. 2. The basic structure of CNN

It is noteworthy that for the given word pair, this paper extracts semantic features of each word, then splices the two groups of semantic features, and finally obtains semantic features vector of the given word pair.

Selecting Classifier: Softmax classifier is used to classify literal features and semantic features respectively extracted in Sects. 3.1 and 3.2. Then two classification results are combined to obtain final result.

4 Experiment

4.1 Dataset Selection

This paper have extracted 210,000 word pairs whose semantic relations are one of the four types of NLPCC 2017 shared task from four dictionary resources. Taking BaiduBaike as concerned, this paper deletes those word pairs containing a word or two that do don't exist in BaiduBaike. 110,000 word pairs were left as experimental dataset samples. However, there are serious imbalance problems in the experimental dataset samples. The number of synonymous word pairs is far more greater than other relations, and the number of meronym word pairs is the least. Therefore, according to the number of meronym word pairs, we randomly extract 2000 word pairs for each type of semantic relations. They are used as train data (OURDIC) in this paper. There are 2000 word pairs (NLPCCDIC) in the NLPCC2017 shared task, with 2905 words and 198 words without BaiduBaike entries. The state of datasets used in this paper is shown in Table 4.

Table 4. The list of datasets

Num \ Dataset Relation	NLPCCDIC	OURDIC
synonym	500	2000
antonym	500	2000
hyponymy	500	2000
meronym	500	2000
SUM	2000	8000

4.2 Experimental Results and Analysis

During the experiment, this paper randomly selects 90% data of data set as the train-ing set and 10% data as the test set; in the setting of experimental parameters, n is 20, m is 200, num is 4, dropout in CNN is set to 0.2, Adam optimizer is used and F_1-score is used as evaluation indicator. In order to compare and analyze the effects of different features on the results, this paper have used different combinations of features to do the experiments, and the results are shown in Table 5.

As can be seen from Table 5, the semantic features play a dominant role for the entire system. The four word features proposed in this paper can also significantly improve the experimental result. However the experiment result is influenced by different dataset to some extent.

Table 5. F1–value when using different features

Feature / Dataset	LF		SF	LF+SF
	LF1	LF1+LF2		
NLPCCDIC	36.20%	45.00%	67.87%	72.36%
OURDIC	34.90%	36.50%	86.37%	89.62%
NLPCCDIC+ OURDIC	32.24%	33.94%	85.23%	87.05%

Table 6 shows the classification effect of each type of semantic relation in the third data set (NLPCCDIC+OURDIC). The method proposed in this paper can achieve good results for each relation, among which the classification result of hyponymy relation is the best.

Table 6. Experiment results of different semantic relation

Indicator / Semantic relation	Precision	Recall	F_1-score
synonym	89%	75%	82%
antonym	81%	91%	86%
hyponymy	93%	89%	91%
meronym	87%	94%	90%

In order to compare with other participating teams of the NLPCC2017 shared task, this paper randomly divides the NLPCCDIC into ten parts, using nine of them and OURDIC as the training set and the remaining as the test set. F_1-score is up to 83.91%. Comparing with the result from teams that didn't using dictionary resources, the result is improved by 7%.

Finally, a specific experiment on word pairs that don't have BaiduBaike entry has carried and the F_1-score is 72.36%. It shows that using sentences containing given word as word context to construct related words set can also obtain semantic information, but it is not as good as constructing a related words set from the text describing given word.

5 Conclusion

This paper proposes a classification method to solve the classification problem of Chinese Word Semantic Relations. The method is based on TF-IDF and CNN. It uses TF-IDF to extract related words set from BaiduBaike corpus and uses CNN to extract semantic information from the lexical semantic matrix constructed by related words set.

Semantic Features and Literal Features of the word are combined together to classify semantic relations. Our experimental results show that this method has certain advantages. It can solve the problem of OOV words to a certain extent, so that it is not affected by the dictionary resources and the word vector list. In addition, the semantic information extraction model constructed in this paper is helpful for text classification, text similarity calculation and other natural language processing tasks.

However, this method proposed here has some shortcomings. For example, the information of polysemy words in BaiduBaike entries are not taken into account; there is no better way to create related words set for words that do not appear in BaiduBaike entries. Further study of this paper could focus on the above shortcomings and find ways to deal with polysemous words or construct better semantic representations of words.

Acknowledgements. This work was supported by grants from National Nature Science Foundation of China (No. 61602044), National Nature Science Foundation of China (No. 613 70139), Scientific Research Project of Beijing Educational Committee (No. KM201711232022).

References

1. Girju, R., Nakov, P., Nastase, V., Szpakowicz, S., Turney, P., Yuret, D.: Classification of semantic relations between nominals. Lang. Resour. Eval. **43**(2), 105–121 (2009)
2. Hendrickx, I., Su, N.K., Kozareva, Z., Nakov, P., Pennacchiotti, M., Romano, L., et al.: SemEval-2010 task 8: multi-way classification of semantic relations between pairs of nominals. In: The Workshop on Semantic Evaluations: Recent Achievements and Future Directions, pp. 94–99 (2009)
3. Miller, G.: WordNet: an on-line lexical database. Int. J. Lexicogr. **3**(4), 235–244 (1990)
4. Zhengdong, D., Qiang, D.: A study of the HowNet and the Chinese language. Contemporary Linguist. **3**(1), 33–44 (2001)
5. Jiaju, M.: Synonym CiLin. Shanghai Lexicographical Publishing Press, Shanghai (1985)
6. Jiangsheng, Y., Shiwen, Y.: The structure of the Chinese concept dictionary. J. Chin. Inf. Process. **16**(4), 12–20 (2002)
7. Wu, Y., Zhang, M.: Overview of the NLPCC 2017 shared task: chinese word semantic relation classification. In: Huang, X., Jiang, J., Zhao, D., Feng, Y., Hong, Y. (eds.) NLPCC 2017. LNCS (LNAI), vol. 10619, pp. 919–925. Springer, Cham (2018). https://doi.org/10.1007/978-3-319-73618-1_81
8. Hearst, M.A.: Automatic acquisition of hyponyms from large text corpora. In: Proceedings of the International Conference on Computational Linguistics, pp. 539–545 (1992)
9. Lei, L., Cungen, C.: A method of verifying hyponymy relations based on mixed features. Comput. Eng. **34**(14), 12–13 (2008)
10. Hu, Y., Sui, Z.: Extracting hyponymy relation between Chinese terms. In: Asia Information Retrieval Symposium, vol. 4993, pp. 567–572 (2008)
11. Zhang, D., Wang, D.: Relation classification via recurrent neural network. Comput. Sci. (2015). https://arxiv.org/abs/1508.01006
12. Li, C., Ma, T.: Classification of Chinese word semantic relations. In: Huang, X., Jiang, J., Zhao, D., Feng, Y., Hong, Y. (eds.) NLPCC 2017. LNCS (LNAI), vol. 10619, pp. 465–473. Springer, Cham (2018). https://doi.org/10.1007/978-3-319-73618-1_39

13. Shijia, E., Jia, S., Xiang, Y.: Study on the Chinese word semantic relation classification with word embedding. In: Huang, X., Jiang, J., Zhao, D., Feng, Y., Hong, Yu. (eds.) NLPCC 2017. LNCS (LNAI), vol. 10619, pp. 849–855. Springer, Cham (2018). https://doi.org/10.1007/978-3-319-73618-1_74
14. Zhou, Y., Lan, M., Wu, Y.: Effective semantic relationship classification of context-free Chinese words with simple surface and embedding features. In: Huang, X., Jiang, J., Zhao, D., Feng, Y., Hong, Y. (eds.) NLPCC 2017. LNCS (LNAI), vol. 10619, pp. 456–464. Springer, Cham (2018). https://doi.org/10.1007/978-3-319-73618-1_38
15. Leskovec, J., Rajaraman, A., Ullman, J.D.: Mining of massive datasets: data mining, pp. 1–17 (2011)
16. Yuntao, Z., Gong, L., Yongcheng, W.: An improved TF-IDF approach for text classification. J. Zhejiang Univ. Sci. A **6**(1), 49–55 (2005)
17. Razavian, A.S., Azizpour, H., Sullivan, J., Carlsson, S.: CNN features off-the-shelf: an astounding baseline for recognition, pp.512–519 (2014)
18. Kim, Y.: Convolutional neural networks for sentence classification. Eprint Arxiv (2014)

Research on Question Classification Based on Bi-LSTM

Qian Zhang, Lingling Mu(✉), Kunli Zhang(✉), Hongying Zan, and Yadi Li

School of Information Engineering, Zhengzhou University, Zhengzhou 450001, Henan, China
{iellmu, ieklzhang}@zzu.edu.cn

Abstract. Question classification plays an important role in question answering (QA) system, and its results directly affect the quality of QA. Traditional methods of question classification include rule-based methods and statistical machine learning methods. They need to manually summarize rules or extract the features of questions. The rule definition and feature selection are subjective and one-sided, which are not conducive to fully understand the semantic information of questions. Based on the above problem, this paper proposes a question classification model based on Bi-LSTM. This model combines words, part of speech (POS) and position information of words to generate embedded representation of words, and uses Bi-LSTM to classify questions. The method can efficiently extract the local features of questions and simplify feature engineering. The accuracy of coarse-grained classification on the question classification data set of Harbin Institute of Technology (HIT) has reached 92.38%.

Keywords: QA system · Deep learning · Question classification Bi-LSTM

1 Introduction

QA system can answer users' questions in accurate and concise natural language, which generally includes three modules: question understanding, information retrieval and answer extraction. Question understanding is the first step in QA system, which can be divided into three parts: question classification, keyword extraction and keyword expansion [1]. The question classification is an important part among them. The goal of question classification is to assign a category to each question, and this category represents the type of answer to a question [2]. Question classification in QA system has two main functions. On the one hand, it can effectively reduce the search space and time of answers. On the other hand, it can formulate different answer extraction strategies based on the types of questions. Therefore, question classification performance affects the performance of QA system to a large extent [3].

Traditional question classification methods include rule-based and statistical machine learning. Rule-based approaches construct question classification rules manually or semi-automatically, which are time-consuming and difficult to guarantee the

J.-F. Hong et al. (Eds.): CLSW 2018, LNAI 11173, pp. 519–531, 2018.
https://doi.org/10.1007/978-3-030-04015-4_44

completeness of rules. The methods based on statistical machine learning need to define the features of questions manually, and then select a machine learning model for classification. Common features include POS, named entities, central words, syntactic structures and semantic relations [4–8]. In order to obtain the features of questions, it is generally necessary to complete the Natural Language Processing (NLP) tasks such as POS tagging, syntactic analysis and semantic analysis on questions. The accuracy of these NLP tasks has great impact on the accuracy of question classification. In addition, artificial rules and feature selection have certain subjectivity, and it is difficult to ensure the completeness of rules and features, which might result the failure to fully understand the semantics of questions.

In recent years, deep learning has been widely used in the field of NLP. Some researchers have used deep learning to explore question classification and have achieved certain results [2, 9]. Long short term memory (LSTM) and Convolutional Neural Network (CNN) with better flexibility are two common deep learning frameworks. They can extract the potential syntactic and semantic features of questions by self-learning, which are more conducive to the representation and understanding of questions, and effectively simplify manual extraction of features in traditional machine learning. Zhou et al. [2] integrated words, POS and word weights into embedded representation of words and used Bi-directional LSTM (Bi-LSTM) to classify English questions. Li et al. [9] proposed an improved model that combined the advantages of LSTM and CNN to enhance learning of word senses and deep features. Although the methods adopted by the above scholars have made up for some shortcomings in traditional machine learning, there are some deficiencies. The word weight extracted by Zhou et al. [2] has good performance on English questions, but its influence on Chinese questions is not obvious. Although combining the advantages of LSTM and CNN, the model proposed by Li et al. [3] also has three shortcomings. Firstly, using two models makes algorithm with high time complexity. Secondly, the unidirectional LSTM model can only be introduced from the previous information, but sometimes it is not enough to just look at the preceding words. For example, in the sentence "*世界上主要有哪些宗教 (what are the main religions in the world?)*", it is difficult to judge the question category if only considering "*世界 (the world)*" without the word "*宗教 (religion)*" in the back. Finally, the AdaDelta method used in the gradient updating has very good acceleration effect in the early and middle training phases. However, AdaDelta repeatedly shakes around the local minimum after entering the local minimum minefield in the later stage of training.

In order to overcome the deficiencies mentioned above, this paper proposes a question classification model based on Bi-LSTM, which integrates word vectors, POS and the position of words into embedded representation of words, uses Bi-LSTM to automatically learn the semantic representation of questions, and uses Adam algorithm to complete gradient updating. The Adam algorithm can quickly converge and quickly find the correct target direction in the parameter updating and minimize the loss function in the maximum extent. At last, questions are classified by SoftMax function.

2 Related Work

Early question classification mainly used rules-based approaches, such as DIOGENE [10] system and NUS [11] system. These methods extract the special question words (such as "*why*", "*where*"), the common question words (such as "*what*") and the nouns closest to the question words as features and judge the types of questions according to the combination rules of feature words. However, these methods often consume a lot of human resources and lack flexibility.

Statistical machine learning is another way of question classification, which has been used for a long time. This method needs to manually define question features, and then to select a machine learning model for classification. The common machine learning models in question classification are Bayesian model [12–14], maximum entropy model (ME) [15] and supported vector machine (SVM) model [6, 7]. Li et al. [6] used the X^2 statistic to select the upper concept in WordNet to selectively expand the vocabulary in questions, and its accuracy of the coarse-grained classification reached 91.60% on the UIUC dataset [7]. Zhang et al. [7] used the tree kernel function to enable SVM [16] to take advantage of the syntactic structures of questions. The accuracy of the coarse-grained classification reached 90.0% on the TREC QA track[1] dataset. Zhang et al. [12] simplified the classification of questions by using the irrelevance of words. The coarse-grained classification accuracy conducted on HIT's Chinese question dataset reached 72.4%. Tian et al. [13] improved question classification based on self-learning rules and Bayesian model, and coarse-grained classification was conducted on HIT's Chinese question sets with the accuracy of 84%. Wen et al. [14] extracted the main stems, interrogative words and subsidiary components of questions as features for classification, and the classification accuracy of coarse-grained reached 86.62% on the Chinese question sets provided by HIT and Chinese Academy of Sciences (CAS). Sun et al. [15] presented a new method of feature extraction, which used HowNet as a semantic resource. The classification accuracy of coarse-grained reached 92.18% on the Chinese question sets provided by HIT and CAS. In order to get question features, the above methods generally need to complete NLP tasks such as POS tagging, syntactic analysis and semantic analysis. The accuracy of these NLP tasks has great impact on the accuracy of question classification.

In recent years, deep learning models have achieved significant progress in some areas such as computer vision [17], speech recognition [18] and NLP. Kim et al. [19] used CNN to extract features and applied them to the classification tasks in multiple NLP fields. They have achieved good results on MR[2], SST-2 (See Footnote 3), SST-1[3], subj TREC[4], CR[5], and MPQA[6] data sets. Li et al. [9] presented an autonomous learning framework with hybrid LSTM and CNN to learn question features. The classification

[1] http://trec.nist.gov/.

[2] https://www.cs.cornell.edu/people/pabo/movie-review-data/.

[3] http://nlp.stanford.edu/sentiment/Data.

[4] http://cogcomp.cs.illinois.edu/Data/QA/QC/.

[5] http://www.cs.uic.edu/~liub/FBS/sentiment-analysis.html.

[6] http://www.cs.pitt.edu/mpqa/.

accuracy of coarse-grained reached 93.08% on the Chinese question sets provided by HIT, NLPCC 2015 QA and Fudan University. Zhou et al. [2] presented Bi-LSTM classification model based on word, POS and word weight. Its classification accuracy of coarse-grained reached 94.0% on the TREC QA dataset (See Footnote 5).

3 Question Classification Based on Bi-LSTM

3.1 LSTM and Bi-LSTM Models

LSTM is a recurrent neural network (RNN), which can remember long-term information to avoid long-term dependence problem that RNN cannot solve. The key part of LSTM is the memory unit, which controls the reading and writing of information by using the input gate i_t, the forget gate f_t and the output gate o_t. The input gate controls the amount of new information input to the memory unit, the forget gate controls the information through the memory unit, and the output gate controls output information. LSTM neuronal structure is shown in Fig. 1, and the specific calculation formula is shown as Eqs. (1–6):

$$i_t = \sigma(W_i x_t + U_i h_{t-1} + b_i) \tag{1}$$

$$f_t = \sigma(W_f x_t + U_f h_{t-1} + b_f) \tag{2}$$

$$o_t = \sigma(W_o x_t + U_o h_{t-1} + b_o) \tag{3}$$

$$g_t = \tan\mathrm{h}(W_g x_t + U_g h_{t-1} + b_g) \tag{4}$$

$$\mathrm{c_t} = i_t * g_t + f_t * c_{t-1} \tag{5}$$

$$h_t = o_t * \tan h(c_t) \tag{6}$$

Where h_t is the output of LSTM unit, σ is the activation function sigmoid, * indicates the point multiplication between vectors, t is the time step. The input gate i_t, the forget gate f_t and the output gate o_t depend on the previous state h_{t-1} and the current input x_t, the extracted feature g_t is used as candidate storage units, c_t is the current storage unit.

Although single direction LSTM model can avoid long-term dependence problem, it can only capture the characteristics of the previous word. In order to fully utilize the contextual information of words, Bi-LSTM utilizes both the previous and the future context by processing the sequence on two directions, and generates two independent sequences of LSTM output vectors. The addition of output vectors is input to the Max Pooling layer to generate sentence representation.

3.2 Question Classification Model Based on Bi-LSTM

Question classification model based on Bi-LSTM is shown in Fig. 2, which mainly consists of three modules: corpus preprocessing, word embedding and classification.

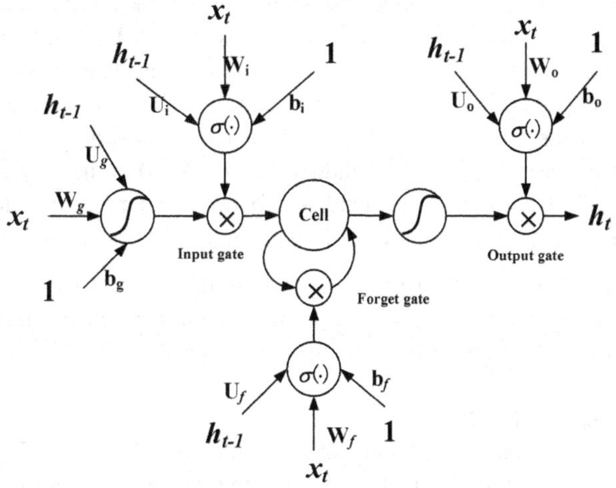

Fig. 1. LSTM neuronal structure

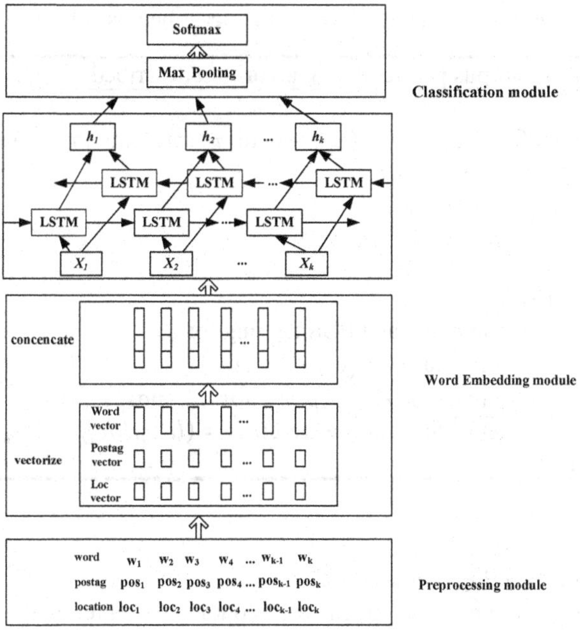

Fig. 2. Bi-LSTM question classification model

The function of corpus preprocessing module is mainly to complete the preprocessing of the raw corpus, which includes word segmentation, POS tagging, etc. The preprocessing model generates the word sequence $S_i = (w_0, w_1, \ldots, w_k)$, the POS sequence $POS_i = (pos_0, pos_1, \ldots, pos_k)$ and the word position sequence $LOC_i =$

$(loc_0, loc_1, \ldots, loc_k)$ for the *i-th* question, where k is the number of words in the question, w_j is the *j-th* word in the question, pos_j is the *j-th* POS, loc_j is the *j-th* word position. The word embedding module mainly completes feature vectorization and feature vectors concatenating. Firstly, w_j, pos_j and loc_j are vectorized respectively, and then their vectors are concatenated to generate word embedding. The classification module mainly consists of Bi-LSTM hidden layer, Max Pooling layer and SoftMax layer. The Bi-LSTM hidden layer calculates forward and reverse state of questions through three gate functions, obtains the forward output $h_j^{\sim}$ and the reverse output $h_j^{'}$, and then adds $h_j^{\sim}$ and $h_j^{'}$ together to get the output h_j. The Max Pooling layer gets the maximum of the output of the hidden layer and generates question representation. The SoftMax layer uses question representation for classification.

3.2.1 Preprocessing Module

In the classification model, the quality of data directly affects the classification performance [20]. As the basic unit of questions, the words store the main features of questions. In addition, word location and POS information are also important for question classification. In the preprocessing module, this paper considers three kinds of position information: "*beginning*", "*middle*" and "*end*", which are represented by "*1, 2, 3*" respectively. The preprocessing algorithm is described as follows:

Algorithm 1: Corpus preprocessing algorithm described

Input:

Question set $Q = \{Q_1, Q_2, \ldots, Q_n\}$, where n represents the number of questions in a question set

Output:

Q_i, POS_i, LOC_i .

Process:

while $0 < i \leq n$:

word segmentation and POS tagging for Q_i

generate $Q_i = (w_0, w_1, \ldots, w_k)$

generate $POS_i = (pos_0, pos_1, \ldots, pos_k)$

get position sequence $LOC_i = (loc_0, loc_1, \ldots, loc_k)$

End while

3.2.2 Word Embedding Module

Word embeddings as dense low-dimensional continuous representation of words can effectively represent semantic and grammatical information of words [21]. The word embedding module is mainly composed of feature vectorization and feature vectors concatenating. Firstly, w_j, pos_j, loc_j of output sequence S_i, POS_i, LOC_i of the preprocessing module are vectorized to get word vector $V_j^w = (\gamma_0, \gamma_1, \ldots, \gamma_m) \in R^m$, POS vector $V_j^p = (\eta_0, \eta_1, \ldots, \eta_n) \in R^n$ and location vector $V_j^l = (\lambda_0, \lambda_1, \ldots, \lambda_l) \in R^l$. Then the word embedding vector $X_j = (x_0, x_1, \ldots, x_d) \in R^d$ is obtained by concatenating V_j^w, V_j^p, V_j^l, where $d = m + n + l$. The concatenating equation is shown as Eq. (7):

$$X_j = (x_0, x_1, \ldots, x_d) = \left[V_j^w, V_j^p, V_j^l\right] = (\gamma_0, \gamma_1, \ldots, \gamma_m, \eta_0, \eta_1, \ldots, \eta_n, \lambda_0, \lambda_1, \ldots, \lambda_l) \tag{7}$$

Word embedding generation algorithm for the *i-th* question is described as follows, where k is the words length of the *i-th* question.

Algorithm 2: Word embedding algorithm described

Input:
word sequence $S_i = (w_0, w_1, \ldots, w_k)$,
POS sequence $POS_i = (pos_0, pos_1, \ldots, pos_k)$,
word position sequence $LOC_i = (loc_0, loc_1, \ldots, loc_k)$

Output: $X = (X_0, X_1, \ldots, X_k)$

Process:
While $0 \le j < k$:
    to vectorize w_j, to get $V_j^w = (\gamma_0, \gamma_1, \ldots, \gamma_m)$,
    to vectorize pos_j, to get $V_j^p = (\eta_0, \eta_1, \ldots, \eta_n)$
    to vectorize loc_j, to get $V_j^l = (\lambda_0, \lambda_1, \ldots, \lambda_l)$
    $X_j = [V_j^w, V_j^p, V_j^l]$
End while

3.2.3 Classification Module

The classification module is composed of three parts: Bi-LSTM hidden layer, Max Pooling layer and softmax layer. Firstly, X_j generated from word embedding module is used as the input of Bi-LSTM hidden layer and is calculated forward and backward through three gates. The forward output is $h_j^{\sim}$ and the reverse output is $h_j^{'}$. Then $h_j^{\sim}$ and $h_j^{'}$ are summed to get the output of Bi-LSTM hidden layer, the formula is shown as Eq. (8):

$$h_j = h_j^{\sim} + h_j^{'} \tag{8}$$

The *i-th* question obtains an output matrix $H_i = (h_{i0}, h_{i1}, \ldots, h_{ik})$ through the Bi-LSTM hidden layer, where h_{ij} represents Bi-LSTM hidden layer output corresponding to $X_j (0 \le j < k)$, k is the length of the *i-th* question. H_i is used as the input of Max Pooling layer to generate the representation of the *i-th* question, and its calculation equation is shown as Eq. (9):

$$f_i = \max_j (h_{ij}) \tag{9}$$

Questions are classified by softmax layer as Eq. (10):

$$h_\theta(f_i) = \begin{bmatrix} p\left(y^{(i)} = 1\right)|f_i, \theta \\ p\left(y^{(i)} = 2\right)|f_i, \theta \\ p\left(y^{(i)} = 3\right)|f_i, \theta \\ \cdot \\ \cdot \\ \cdot \\ p\left(y^{(i)} = m\right)|f_i, \theta \end{bmatrix} = \frac{1}{\sum_{j=1}^{m} e^{\theta_j^T f_i}} \begin{bmatrix} e^{\theta_1^T f_i} \\ e^{\theta_2^T f_i} \\ \cdot \\ \cdot \\ \cdot \\ e^{\theta_m^T f_i} \end{bmatrix} \tag{10}$$

Where m is the number of categories, model parameters are $\theta_1, \theta_2, \ldots, \theta_m \in R^{n+1}$. The classification algorithm is described as follows:

Algorithm 3: Classification algorithm described

Input:
the word embedding sequence of the i-th question: $X = (X_0, X_1, \ldots, X_k)$
Output: $h_\theta(f_i)$
Process:
1. while 0h$j < k$:
   For each word embedding X_j:
   Calculate X_j forward to get $h_j^{\sim}$ calculate X_j backward to get h_j'
   $h_j = h_j^{\sim} + h_j'$
   End while
2. $H_i = (h_{i0}, h_{i1}, \ldots, h_{ik})$
3. $f_i = \max_j(h_{ij})$
4. $h_\theta(f_i) = \begin{bmatrix} p\left(y^{(i)} = 1\right)|f_i, \theta \\ p\left(y^{(i)} = 2\right)|f_i, \theta \\ p\left(y^{(i)} = 3\right)|f_i, \theta \\ \cdot \\ \cdot \\ \cdot \\ p\left(y^{(i)} = m\right)|f_i, \theta \end{bmatrix} = \frac{1}{\sum_{j=1}^{m} e^{\theta_j^T f_i}} \begin{bmatrix} e^{\theta_1^T f_i} \\ e^{\theta_2^T f_i} \\ \cdot \\ \cdot \\ \cdot \\ e^{\theta_m^T f_i} \end{bmatrix}$

---

4 Experiment and Result Analysis

4.1 Question Classification System

To classify questions, firstly, we need to know what types of questions exist. The types of questions are determined by the classification scheme. Information Retrieval and Social Computing Center of HIT defines the Chinese question classification scheme based on some existing QA systems, the characteristics of dividing things in the real world and the characteristics of Chinese. This classification scheme is widely adopted by scholars [9]. This paper adopts the scheme to mark questions on coarse-grained categories. Table 1 shows the hierarchical classification scheme of HIT's question classification, including seven coarse categories: *description, human, location, number, time, entity and unknown*. Each coarse category defines some sub-categories according to actual situations. There are totally 84 small categories.

4.2 Dataset

This paper uses the HIT Question Classification Dataset. There are 6,296 questions in this dataset, 4,981 questions in the training set and 1,315 questions in the test set. The question distribution of the dataset is shown in Table 2.

4.3 Experimental Parameters Setting

This paper uses the fixed length of questions, which is set to the maximum length. The insufficient length is filled with "*0*". The dimensions of word vectors, POS vectors, and word position vectors are randomly initialized by 150, 100 and 100 respectively. The Bi-LSTM hidden Layer consists of 100 LSTM units. The learning rate adaptive optimization algorithm (Adam) is used to update the parameters. The batch training method is adopted during training, and the batch size is 128. The maximum number of training rounds for network training is set to 2000. In each round of training, the dropout rate of the dropout method is 0.4.

4.4 Experimental Result

This paper uses three kinds of evaluation criteria: accuracy (A), recall rate (R), and F1 value (F1) [22] to evaluate the effect of word location on each category. The results are shown in Table 3. For convenience, the model of "*Bi-LSTM + Word + POS*" is denoted by "*model1*", "*Bi-LSTM + Word + POS + Word Location*" is denoted by "*model2*".

According to Table 3, the micro-average accuracy of coarse-grained without word location feature is 90.27%. After word location feature is integrated, the micro-average accuracy is 92.38%. This shows that adding word location feature to the word embedding generation process improves the classification performance. Moreover, as can be seen from Table 3, the word location feature significantly improves the results of class "*human*" and "*entity*", and the accuracy increased by 9.5% points and 5.9% points respectively. This is because the positions of keywords that determined whether the question belongs to the "*human*" class or "*entity*" class are more obvious. For example, "*HP是哪个公司的简称?? (which company is HP's abbreviation?)*"

The keywords "*公司 (company)*" and "*简称 (abbreviation)*" in the sentence have the same POS and different locations. The keyword "*简称 (abbreviation)*" is one of the features of the "*description*" class. If the position of the keyword is not considered, it is not easy to determine the category of this question. Therefore, the keyword position becomes the key to correctly determine the category of questions. From Table 4, it can be seen that the effect of word positions of "*number*" class is not obvious. This is

Table 1. HIT's question classification scheme

Coarse classification	Fine classification
Description	Abbreviation, expression, meaning, mode, reason, definition, judgment, other
Human	Specific human, organization groups, human descriptions, other
Location	Universe, city, continent, country, province, river, lake, mountains, ocean, islands, buildings, address, other
Number	Temperature, area, volume, weight, speed, frequency, distance, amount of money, quantity, order, multiple, percentage, number, length of time, range, other
Time	Year, month, day, season, era, week, day, holiday, time, time range, other
Entity	Substance, animals, plants, microorganisms, bodies, materials, clothing, food and medicine, currency, bills, languages, events, diseases, works of art, services, liberal works, academic disciplines, planning programs, laws and regulations, job titles, occupations Industry, Symbols, Rewards, Criminal Law, Categories, Rights and Duties, Colors, Religions, Sports, Entertainment, Terms, Other
Unknown	unknown

Table 2. Distribution of training questions and test questions

Dataset	Description	Human	Location	Number	Entity	Time	Unknown
Train set	786	333	936	1076	1242	598	10
Test set	153	178	390	244	194	153	3

Table 3. The effect of word location feature on each category

Category	Model1			Model2		
	A (%)	R (%)	F1 (%)	A (%)	R (%)	F1 (%)
Description	83.87	84.97	84.42	86.36	86.93	86.64
Human	84.04	88.76	86.33	93.49	88.76	91.06
Location	95.80	87.69	91.57	96.24	91.79	93.96
Number	96.57	97.54	97.14	96.75	97.54	97.14
Entity	75.23	84.54	79.61	81.08	92.78	86.54
Time	94.04	92.81	93.42	95.97	93.46	94.70

because the questions in the "*number*" class contain entities with obvious characteristics such as "*area*", "*zip code*", "*number*", and "*area code*". Therefore, adding location information has no obvious effect on numeric question classification.

The results of coarse-grained question classification based on different methods are shown in Table 4.

Table 4. Chinese question coarse-grained classification work comparing

	Feature	Model	Data size	Class number	Data name	A (%)
Wen et al. [15]	Trunk + question word + accessory components	Bayes	9,600	7	References [13] + CAS question set	86.62
Tian et al. [14]	Self-learning rules	Bayes	4,280	6	HIT question set	84.00
Sun et al. [16]	Question word + syntactic structure + question intention words + the first sememe	ME	5,613	7	HIT and CAS question set	92.18
Zhang Yu et al. [13]	Word +POS + TF-IDF	Bayes	4,280	7	HIT question set	72.40
Yu et al. [20]	Word +POS + Chunks syntactic feature +implicit semantic feature	SVM	1,500	6	Chinese question set	88.70
maximum entropy [10]	Word vector	ME	6,296	7	HIT question set	88.75
Li et al. [9]	Self-learning feature	LSTM + CNN	9,600	6	HIT question set +NLPCC2015 + Fudan University question set	93.08
Methods of this paper	Word +POS + word location	Bi-LSTM	6,296	7	HIT question set	92.38

Traditional methods mostly used manual strategies to formulate feature extraction, which had some limitations and lack flexibility. The method of this paper makes up for the shortcomings of traditional learning methods, and the accuracy of coarse-grained classification of questions is 3.6 percentage points higher than traditional methods. According to Table 4, the question classification model proposed in this paper has not yet reached the best classification result. The possible reasons are as follows. The amount of experimental data used in this paper is small, but the number of parameters in the Bi-LSTM model is large. It is difficult to train a better classifier when the experimental data is small. Li Chao et al. [9] combined the advantages of both unidirectional LSTM and CNN. They used more training data to autonomously learn the deep syntactic and semantic features of questions, which can train classifiers with better performance.

5 Conclusion

For question classification, this paper used Bi-LSTM to classify questions. The question classification model based on Bi-LSTM is divided into three modules for classification. The preprocessing module is mainly to preprocess the raw corpus and generate word sequences, POS sequences and word position sequences after processing. The word embedding generation module combines word vector, POS vector and position vector to produce the embedded representation of words. The classification module first generates the distributed representation of words through the hidden layer of Bi-LSTM, then generates the representation of questions via the Max Pooling layer, finally classifies questions in the softmax layer. Experiments on the question classification datasets of HIT showed that the accuracy reached 92.38%. This shows that the question classification method based on Bi-LSTM can improve the performance of questions under the condition that it is unnecessary to make complex feature rules. However, the classification accuracy of "*description*" class and "*entity*" class needs further improvement. This is because there are fewer corpora for "*description*" class and "*entity*" class, while other classes have relatively more corpora, which can better train the model. Therefore, in order to solve this problem, in addition to collecting and marking more data, the features extracted from this paper can be applied to a variety of deep learning methods to fully understand the semantics of questions. This will be the focus of the next step.

References

1. Zheng, F.S., Liu, T., Qin, B., et al.: Overview of question-answering. J. Chin. Inf. **16**(6), 46–52 (2002)
2. Zhou, X.P.: Research on question classification based on deep learning. Harbin Institute of Technology (2016)
3. Zhen, L.H., Wang, X.L., Yang, S.C.: Overview on question classification in question—answering system. J. Anhui Univ. Technol. (Nat. Sci. Edn.) **32**(1), 48–54 (2015). (In Chinese)
4. Li, W.: Question classification using language modeling. CIIR Technical report (2007)
5. Li, X., Roth, D.: Learning question classifiers. In: COLING-2002, pp. 556–562 (2012)
6. Li, X., Du, Y.P., Huang, X.J., et al.: Question classification using syntactic and semantic information. In: National Conference on Information Retrieval and Content Security (2004). (In Chinese)
7. Zhang, D., Lee, W.S.: Question classification using support vector machines, pp. 26–32. ACM (2003)
8. Dan, R., Small, K.: The role of semantic information in learning question classifiers. In: Conference First International Joint Conference on Natural Language Processing, pp. 184–187 (2004)
9. Li, C., Chai, Y.M., Nan, X.F., et al.: Research on question classification method based on deep learning. Comput. Sci. **43**(12), 115–119 (2016). (In Chinese)
10. Magnini, B., Negri, M., Prevete, R., et al.: Mining knowledge from repeated co-occurrences. DIOGENE at TREC 2002 (2002)
11. Yang, H., Chua, T.S., Wang, S., Koh, C.K: Structured use of external knowledge for event-based open domain question answering. In: Proceedings of the 26th annual international ACM SIGIR conference on Research and development in information retrieval, pp. 33–40. ACM (2003)
12. Zhang, Y., Liu, T., Wen, X.: Modified Bayesian model based question classification. J. Chin. Inf. Process. **19**(2), 101–106 (2005). (In Chinese)

13. Tian, W.D., Gao, Y.Y., Zu, Y.L.: Question classification based on self-learning rules and modified Bayes. Res. Comput. Appl. **27**(8), 2869–2871 (2010). (In Chinese)
14. Wen, X., Zhang, Y., Liu, T., et al.: Syntactic structure parsing based Chinese question classification **20**(2), 35–41 (2006). (In Chinese)
15. Sun, J.G., Cai, D.F., Lv, D.X., et al.: HowNet based Chinese question automatic classification. J. Chin. Inf. Process. **21**(1), 90–95 (2007). (In Chinese)
16. Yu, Z.T., Fan, X.Z., Guo, J.Y.: Chinese question classification based on support vector machines. J. South China Univ. Technol. (Nat. Sci. Edn.) **33**(9), 25–29 (2005). (In Chinese)
17. Krizhevsky, A., Sutskever, I., Hinton, G.: ImageNet classification with deep convolutional neural networks. In: Advances in Neural Information Processing Systems 25, pp. 1106–1114 (2012)
18. Graves, A., Mohamed, A.R., Hinton, G.: Speech recognition with deep recurrent neural networks. In: 2013 IEEE International Conference on Acoustics, Speech and Signal Processing (ICASSP), pp. 6645–6649. IEEE (2013)
19. Kim, Y.: Convolutional neural networks for sentence classification. Eprint Arxiv (2014)
20. Pang, B., Lee, L.: A sentimental education: sentiment analysis using subjectivity summarization based on minimum cuts. In: Proceedings of the 42nd annual meeting on Association for Computational Linguistics, p. 271. Association for Computational Linguistics (2004)
21. Zong, C.Q.: Statistical Natural Language Processing. Tsinghua University Press, Beijing (2013). (In Chinese)
22. Hochreiter, S., Schmidhuber, J.: Long short-term memory. Neural Comput. **9**(8), 1735–1780 (1997)

Optimizing Relation Extraction Based on the Type Tag of Named Entity

Yixing Zhang, Yangsen Zhang(✉), Gaijuan Huang, and Zhengbin Guo

Beijing Information Science and Technology University, Beijing 100192, China
yixingzhang1994@163.com, zhangyangsen@163.com, guozhengbin11@163.com, hgj@bistu.edu.cn

Abstract. Using the named entity's type tag to construct a unique vector for a class of named entities can solve the problem that named entities are too scattered in the semantic space. In the relation extraction task, the relation of the specified entity pair in each sentence needs to be extracted. However, the general deep learning model cannot reflect the usefulness of the entity pair and its type tag effectively. In order to solve this problem, this paper studies the characteristics of named entity's type tag, and proposes a word vector optimization relation extraction model and a parallel structure optimization relation extraction model based on the type tags of named entities. Experiments on COAE 2016 task 3 show that the parallel structure optimization model based on the named entity's type tag improves the relation extraction effect effectively.

Keywords: Named entity · Relation extraction · Deep learning

1 Introduction

The explosive growth of Internet information has made it difficult for traditional information retrieval methods to meet the needs of people to obtain accurate information. In order to allow users to obtain new information and knowledge faster and easier, in 2012, Google announced that it would reintegrate the world's information based on Knowledge Maps and build a new generation of search engines. To construct the knowledge map, the extraction of entity relation is a very important step. The structured knowledge bases such as Baidu baike and Wikipedia can provide a large amount of high availability data for knowledge maps, but more unstructured data contains more rich and timely information [1]. Therefore, how to extract entity relations from unstructured data is a key issue that needs to be studied.

Entity relation extraction emphasizes how to extract the semantic relation between the two pairs of entities in the sentence [2]. We extract entities and relations to construct a semantic network and further assist in retrieval techniques.

The study of English entity relation extraction was carried out earlier, and there were evaluation conferences such as ACE and TAC-KBP. In terms of Chinese entity relation extraction, there are few related open corpora, and the research is relatively slow. However, some evaluation conferences have begun to pay attention to this field, for example, the 2016 COAE relation extraction evaluation task [3].

J.-F. Hong et al. (Eds.): CLSW 2018, LNAI 11173, pp. 532–541, 2018.
https://doi.org/10.1007/978-3-030-04015-4_45

Entity relation extraction, includes unsupervised relation extraction and supervised relation extraction. Unsupervised relation extraction is also called open relation extraction. Currently, auxiliary information such as dictionaries, syntactic analysis, and relative position of words are mainly used to rank candidate relations through rules-based methods. Supervised relation extraction first needs to determine the relation category, and then trains the relation classification model by manually labeling the relational corpus. Finally, the relation between the entities in the sentence is identified by the relation classification model. At present, the effect of unsupervised relation extraction is relatively poor and supervised relation extraction methods have the disadvantages of less corpus and low coverage of relation types [4]. This paper focuses on the issue of supervised relation extraction.

2 Related Work

At present, there are three main methods of supervised entity relation extraction: pattern matching, machine learning and deep learning.

Pattern matching methods generally customize templates based on keywords, type tag, and syntactic analysis, and use the customized templates to implement entity relation extraction. However, this method has some inherent deficiencies, such as the limited number of templates that are customized, narrow coverage, and the existence of template matching errors. Therefore, the pattern matching methods usually only serve as a supplementary method.

The method of machine learning is to treat entity relation extraction as a classification problem. And, we usually implement the extraction of entity relations based on features. The features mainly include the following three types: lexical features, syntactic features, and semantic features. The lexical features include entity order, inter-entity distance, entity-to-context, etc.; syntactic features include syntax analysis tree, dependency syntax, etc.; semantic features include semantic roles and semantic dependencies, etc. At present, Support Vector Machine (SVM) method can obtain relatively good results than the traditional classification method. On the basis of the lexical features and the original features of the entity, Guo et al. propose a method of extracting entity relations based on syntactic features and semantic features [5]. In the proposed method, it incorporates features such as dependency syntax relations, core predicates, and semantic role annotation. Wan et al. combine machine learning methods with rules, and propose a Chinese implicit entity relation extraction method based on the "company verbs" [6]. This method can use explicit entity relations to achieve implicit entity relation extraction through reasoning.

The deep learning method is to acquire the feature automatically by neural network, and to excavate the semantic relation in the sentence. Deep learning models include CNN (Convolutional Neural Network), RNN (Recurrent Neural Network) and so on. CNN can be used to model the combinational features of words. It is often applied to text classification in NLP, such as sentiment analysis, spam recognition, and topic classification. However, the CNN convolution operation will lose the position information of the words, and the RNN can better handle the sequence data, that is, the order of the words. Rong et al. propose a multichannel convolutional neural network model, which uses multiple channels to represent more semantic information and more distinguishing features of sentences. And this method can enhance the ability to express natural language [7]. Wang et al. add category keywords on the basis of convolutional neural networks to make up for the inadequacies of neural network auto learning features [8]. Sun et al. based on the shortest dependent path and LSTM method, make full use of the dependency analysis to represent the text [9].

3 Methodology

3.1 Entity Relation Extraction Based on Deep Learning

In the field of Chinese text processing, the input to the CNN or RNN model is a word vector or a character vector. Word vector is represented by a low dimensional real number vector. This way of expression solves the dimension disaster problem and can express the semantic similarity between words by the distance of vectors. For example, Word2vec uses Continuous Bag of Words (CBOW) and Skip-gram language models to learn related knowledge of the word through the context of a word.

Entity relation extraction method based on CNN model, firstly uses pre-trained word vectors to generate corresponding word vector matrix for each sentence, then gets semantic features through calculation of convolution layer and pooling layer, finally, inputs the extracted features into fully connected layer and uses softmax classifier to classify the relation [10].

The hidden layer nodes of the RNN model are connected, and the information of the previous node can be passed forward. Therefore, the input of the hidden layer at each moment includes the input at the moment and the output at the previous moment. Entity relation extraction based on RNN model also uses word vector to generate sentence vector matrix, and then inputs the matrix to RNN model. Finally, fully connected layer and softmax classifier can be used to classify relations. In addition, there are many optimized models for RNN. For example, the bidirectional RNN model can acquire future knowledge and combine sentence context information to solve the problem that RNN can only trained by historical information. Conventional recurrent neural networks cannot effectively solve long distance dependence problems. The Long Short-Term Memory (LSTM) and Gated Recurrent Unit (GRU) models are used to control the amount of historical information and current information through a special gate structure to avoid long-distance dependence issues. Because the GRU algorithm simplifies the LSTM algorithm, the LSTM effect is slightly higher than the GRU algorithm, but it takes longer training time.

In the deep learning model, the L1 norm, L2 norm, and dropout methods are usually used to solve the problem of overfitting. Norm regularization is a method of parametric norm penalty; Dropout method refers to using a random method when training the model, so that some hidden layer nodes do not work temporarily. When the next training data arrives, the random process continues.

3.2 Entity Relation Extraction Based on Type Tag Features

Named entities are one of the important carriers of textual information and an important part of information extraction systems. For example, named entity recognition plays an important role in the knowledge map. The establishment of entity relation triples requires the identification of named entities. Named entity recognition also plays an important role in information retrieval and summarization.

Named entities include personal names, place names, organization names, proper nouns, time, quantity etc. It is a concept that is distinguished by name. The "雷军" (Lei Jun) and "北京" (Beijing) are one of the instance of personal name and place name respectively. In relation extraction, the identification of named entities has a great impact on the effect of extraction. For example, in the relation between a person and a graduate school, "雷军毕业于武汉大学" (Lei Jun graduated from Wuhan University) and "刘强东毕业于中国人民大学" (Liu Qiangdong graduated from Renmin University of China). Both of these examples belong to the relation between "people" and "school". However, both "雷军" (Lei Jun) and "刘强东" (Liu Qiangdong) are the semantic roles of "people". This will lead to two problems, (1) The training complexity of the model will be increased, and the effect of relation extraction will be reduced, (2) If a new name appears, it does not appear in the training corpus, which may lead to the failure of relation extraction. In addition, these issues will also appear in relations such as the person's birth time (person-time), the founder of an organization (organization-person), and so on.

Therefore, through the use of named entity recognition and the entity's type tag, it can improve the effect of relation extraction. For example, a person-to-person relation has husband-wife relation and parent-child relation. Suppose we know that the result of the named entity recognition is two names. If other common nouns are "wife" or "husband", it usually indicates that the entity is a husband and wife relation. However, if it is a "child" or "father", it will indicate that the relation between the entities is a parent-child relation. Therefore, on the basis of the original text, the named entity is replaced by the named entity's type tag, and the semantic representation is learned by CNN or RNN model, and finally the relation classification is performed.

3.3 Entity Relation Extraction Based on Deep Learning and Type Tag Features

The input of the deep learning model CNN and RNN is a sentence. For each entity pair in the sentence, it is usually represented by <e1>entity1</e1> and <e2>entity2</e2>. However, neither CNN's convolution operation nor RNN's historical information transmission can make the model use entity information effectively. For example, " 李明带他的妻子张华去了他的母校清华大学" (Li Ming took his wife Zhang Hua to his alma mater-Tsinghua University). In this sentence, there are multiple named entities "李明" (Li Ming), "张华" (Zhang Hua), and "清华大学" (Tsinghua University), that is, there are multiple entity relations. However, there must be only one kind of entity relation for any two entities. However, the traditional deep learning model cannot reflect which entity pairs need to be extracted. Therefore, how to strengthen the ability of the model to identify entity pairs is very important.

Because the entity disperses the semantics of its type tag, and the entity's type tag can represent this entity, this article uses the entity's type tag to express its semantics. We construct a type tag vector for a person's name, place name, organization name, proper noun, time, and quantity, and use a 6-dimensional one-hot vector to represent each kind of type tag.

This paper studies the relation extraction optimization based on the entity's type tag. In the deep learning model, there are two main optimization methods, optimization of word vector representing and optimization of deep learning model structure.

The optimization of the word vector representing is to optimizing the expression of the word vector by adding some auxiliary information on the basis of the trained word vector. In this paper, auxiliary information refers to the type tag of the named entity. We add its type tag vector to the original vector. The model structure is shown in Fig. 1.

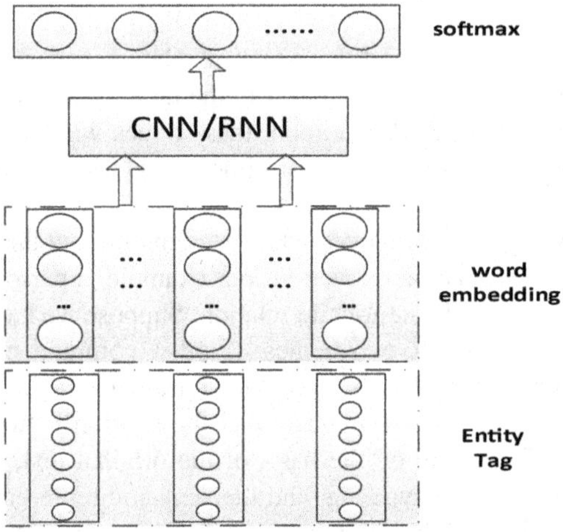

Fig. 1. Word vector optimization relation extraction model

In this paper, the optimization of model structure uses the parallel structure model to design two deep learning models, and the two models achieve different functions respectively. Finally, the two outputs are combined or added as new outputs. In this paper, we design a model to enhance the effect of entity pair's type tag. Through the parallel structure model, a deep learning model learns the semantic representation of the sentence, and another deep learning model learns the semantics of the specified entity pair, and then we stitch the results together. And finally the fully connected layer and softmax are used to classify relations. The model structure is shown in Fig. 2.

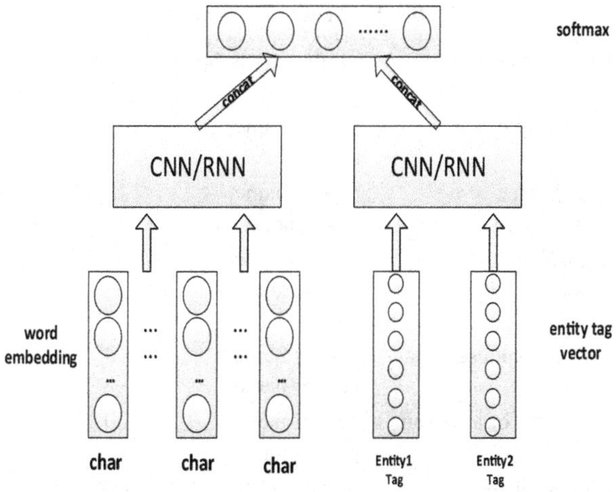

Fig. 2. Parallel structure optimization relation extraction model

4 Result and Analysis

4.1 Data Set

This experiment uses the corpus of COAE 2016 task 3 for the entity relation extraction. And the data set includes 988 training data and 483 test data. The details of the task data are shown in Table 1.

4.2 Experimental Procedure

Step1: We separate the training set by the word, and train the word vector;
Step2: The input sequence of the model is Constructed for the training set and the test set respectively;
Step3: We construct neural network model and determine model parameters (word vector dimension = 256, hidden layer nodes = 128, dropout = 0.3, batch number = 32, sentence interception length = 60);
Step4: We use 90% of the data as the training set for training (The number of training times for each model is 100.) and 10% of the data as the validation set.
Step5: We use the test set to get the evaluation index of accuracy, recall rate, F1 value.

4.3 Comparing the Effect of Different Types of Named Entities

First of all, we use named entity recognition and entity's type tag tagging tool to recognize the entity's type tag in the sentence, and most of the entities can be tagged with these tools, but there will still be some error. For example, some longer name may be divided into multiple words. Each word has a corresponding type tag, and the most frequently occurring type tag may be used. In this way, some entity's type tag will be

Table 1. Detail of task data

Relation category	Relation description	Entities' type tag	Number of training sets	Number of testing sets
cr2	The birthday of a person	person name, time	199	101
cr4	The birthplace of a person	person name, place name	28	11
cr16	The graduate school of a person	person name, organization name	100	52
cr20	A person's spouse	person name, person name	90	46
cr21	The children of a person	person name, person name	200	99
cr28	Executive of the organization	organization name, person name	200	102
cr29	Number of employees in the organization	organization name, quantity	49	18
cr34	The founder of the organization	organization name, quantity	110	47
cr37	The headquarters of the organization	organization name, place name	12	7

tagged wrongly. Therefore, this article adopts the input method of word vector, and uses the corresponding symbol for each named entity. In addition, because the entity marked with <e1><e2> is more important in the sentence, we have manually proofread the entity's type tag. In this paper, we use the word vector to represent the text, and each type of entity is represented by its type tag, for example, the person's name is represented by "human".

In this paper, we design several groups of experiments, using CNN, LSTM, GRU three models for comparison. The results are evaluated by F1 values. Each experiment is based on the replacement of marked entity's type tag. And, in the experiment, we replace one type tag (person name, place name, organization name, proper noun, time, time + quantity) each time. The experimental results are shown in Table 2.

According to the experimental results, the LSTM and GRU models are all optimized models of the RNN. Their performance are similar and both of them are better than CNN. However, CNN model has more advantages in the case of extracting local semantics. It captures high-level features of different levels of texts through different convolution kernels or convolution kernels with different dimensions. The corpus used in this article is composed of short sentences and the semantic relation is relatively simple. It can not exert the advantages of CNN model and is more suitable for RNN model. Based on the CNN model, the effect of replacing different type tag is improved compared with the effect of the original corpora. Because the amount of data in each relation of the corpus is not balanced, the effect of each type tag is different. And, a

Table 2. Effect of different types of named entities

Data	Model		
	CNN	LSTM	GRU
Raw data	0.6518	0.7314	0.7286
Replace the person name	0.6559	0.6915	0.7029
Replace the place name	0.6957	0.6911	0.6898
Replace the organization name	0.6684	0.6748	0.6932
Replace the proper noun	0.6722	0.6960	0.6790
Replace the time	0.6502	0.7067	0.6810
Replace the time and the quantity	0.6812	0.7120	0.7386
Replace all the entities	0.7123	0.7171	0.7092

certain type of entity will appear in different entity relations, which will reduce the effect of the entity type. For example, in the training corpus, the person's name appears in 7 kinds of entity relations. CNN experimental results also show that its improvement is low. Finally, compared with the original corpus, the experimental effect of the CNN model is improved after replacing the entity's type tag, but the effect of LSTM and GRU is decreased. It shows that the replacement of the entity's type tag has different effects on the deep learning model, which requires us to study the mechanism of more models.

4.4 Comparison Based on the Type Tag of Named Entity

Based on CNN, LSTM and GRU models and named entity's type tag, two optimization model are designed. The one is word vector optimization relation extraction model (entity_w2v), the other is parallel structure optimization relation extraction model (entity_parallel). The entity_w2v model is based on the trained word vector and adds the additional information of the entity's type tag. Because the experimental method in this paper uses six kinds of named entities, each word vector will be additionally added with a six-dimensional one-hot vector. The entity_parallel model refers to adding a parallel deep learning model based on the original model. The input is the type tag vector of the entity pair, and finally we concatenate the output of the two models as the final semantic representation.

Based on the experimental results of COAE-2016, the CNN model (proposed by Sun Jiandong) and the strengthened category keyword CNN model (proposed by Wang Linyu) are compared with the models mentioned in this paper. The experimental result are shown in Table 3. According to the experimental results, it can be seen that the entity_w2v model is not effective because the added one-hot type tag vector is sparse, resulting in limited optimization. As for CNN model, the effect of entity_parallel model is better than the Sun Jiandong's method and slightly lower than Wang Linyu' method. About LSTM model, the entity_parallel model achieves the best results, better than the two CNN models mentioned above. And compared with the original LSTM model, the improvement in performance is 6.96%. This shows that this article proposes a parallel structure optimization method based on the named entity's type tag, which has an improving effect on entity relation extraction.

Table 3. Comparison of different neural network models

Model	CNN	LSTM	GRU
Jiandong Sun	0.6480	-	-
Linyu Wang	0.775	-	-
Original model	0.6518	0.7314	0.7286
This paper (entity_w2v)	0.6554	0.7247	0.7152
This paper (entity_parallel)	0.7718	0.8010	0.7893

5 Conclusion

In view of the fact that the traditional deep learning model can not effectively use the entity pairs and its type tag, we first compare the role of different types of entities in relation extraction, and then propose two deep learning optimization models based on entity's type tag. The experimental results show that the parallel structure optimization model based on the named entity's type tag has an improved effect on the relation extraction.

Our main work in the future includes the following:

(1) We will continue to optimize the CNN model and consider adding a segmented convolutional neural network (PCNN) model [11] for relation identification.
(2) Based on the LSTM and GRU models, we will consider how to introduce the attention mechanism into the relation classification [12].
(3) CNN and RNN models have different semantic expressions. Considering how to combine the two models for relation classification is our next research point.

Acknowledgments. This work was supported by grants from National Nature Science Foundation of China (No. 61772081), National Nature Science Foundation of China (No. 61602044), and Scientific Research Project of Beijing Educational Committee (No. KM201711232022).

References

1. Liu, J., Liu, Y., Duan, H., Liu, Y., Qin, Z.: Knowledge graph construction technology. J. Comput. Res. Dev. **53**(3), 582–600 (2016). (in Chinese)
2. Yang, J., Yu, Q., Guan, Y., Jiang, Z.: An overview of research on electronic medical record oriented named entity recognition and entity relation extraction. Acta Autom. Sin. **40**(8), 1537–1562 (2014). (in Chinese)
3. Sun, J., Gu, X., Li, Y., Xu, W.: Chinese entity relation extraction algorithms based on COAE2016 datasets. J. Shandong Univ. (Nat. Sci.) **52**(9), 7–12+18 (2017). (in Chinese)
4. Lin, Y., Shen, S., Liu, Z., Sun, M.: Neural relation extraction with selective attention over instances. In: Proceedings of ACL 2016, Germany, pp. 2124–2133 (2016)

5. Guo, X., He, T., Hu, X., Chen, Q.: Chinese named entity relation extraction based on syntactic and semantic features. J. Chin. Inf. Process. **28**(6), 183–189 (2014). (in Chinese)
6. Wan, C., Gan, L., Jiang, T., Liu, D., Liu, X., Liu, Y.: Chinese named entity implicit relation extraction based on company verbs. Chin. J. Comput., 1–24 (2017). (in Chinese). http://kns.cnki.net/kcms/detail/11.1826.TP.20170601.1915.002.html
7. Rong, B., Fu, K., Huang, Y., Wang, Y.: Relation extraction based on multi-channel convolutional neural network. Appl. Res. Comput. **34**(3), 689–692 (2017). (in Chinese)
8. Wang, L., Wang, L., Zheng, T.: Entity relation extraction based on convolutional neural network and keyword strategy. Pattern Recogn. Artif. Intell. **30**(5), 465–472 (2017). (in Chinese)
9. Sun, Z., Gu, J., Yang, J.: Chinese entity relation extraction method based on deep learning. Comput. Eng. **44**(9), 164–170 (2018). (in Chinese)
10. Zeng, D., Liu, K., Lai, S., Zhou, G., Zhao, J.: Relation classification via convolutional deep neural network. In: Proceedings of COLING 2014, Ireland, pp. 2335–2344 (2014)
11. Zeng, D., Liu, K., Chen, Y., Zhao, J.: Distant supervision for relation extraction via piecewise convolutional neural networks. In: Proceedings of EMNLP 2015, Portugal, pp. 1753–1762 (2015)
12. Wang, H., Shi, J., Zhang, Z.: Text semantic relation extraction of LSTM based on attention. Appl. Res. Comput. **35**(5),1417–1420+1440 (2018). (in Chinese)

Answer Ranking Based on Language Phenomenon Recognition

Han Ren[1], Jing Wan[2], Yafeng Ren[3], and Wenhe Feng[1(✉)]

[1] Laboratory of Language Engineering and Computing, Guangdong University of Foreign Studies, Guangzhou 510420, China
hanren@gdufs.edu.cn, wenhefeng@gmail.com

[2] Center for Lexicographical Studies, Guangdong University of Foreign Studies, Guangzhou 510420, China

[3] Collaborative Innovation Center for Language Research and Services, Guangdong University of Foreign Studies, Guangzhou 510420, China

Abstract. Answer Ranking is one of the core tasks in Question Answering, which greatly depends on the performance of answer ranking. This paper introduces an approach of answer ranking based on language phenomenon identification, that is, identifying language phenomena between a question and its answer sentence candidates, then computing entailment confidence score between the question and each candidate. Finally, an answer ranking is made according to such scores. This paper also introduces a joint model for both language phenomenon identification and entailment recognition task, in order to avoid error propagation to some extent, and make the two tasks learn to each other for a better overall performance as well. Experimental results show that the joint learning of language phenomenon identification and entailment recognition is an effective way for answer ranking.

Keywords: Answer ranking · Language phenomenon
Recognizing Textual Entailment · Joint learning

1 Introduction

Answer ranking, which refers to the sorting of answer sentences from retrieved sentences, is one of the core issues in question answering. Answer ranking aims to output an answer list, in which more possible answer sentences take in the front positions [1].

There are, generally, two strategies for answer ranking: pipeline and end-to-end learning. Pipeline models pick out most possible answer sentences using miscellaneous approaches such as syntactic parsing, semantic similarity and pattern matching, and then extract answer nuggets from them [2], while end-to-end approaches directly compute the similarities between a question and the answer nuggets [3]. Such approaches, however, have low performances when questions and answer sentences are very dissimilar due to different words and their syntactic relations. Such questions and answer sentences, in fact, have complex semantic relations, which need to be captured by deep semantic analysis and rich background knowledge.

J.-F. Hong et al. (Eds.): CLSW 2018, LNAI 11173, pp. 542–550, 2018.
https://doi.org/10.1007/978-3-030-04015-4_46

To solve this problem, some researchers employ Recognizing Textual Entailment (RTE), which is a general framework of semantic inference and widely used in many natural language processing applications, such as question answering, multi-document summarization and information extraction [4, 5]. By this idea, question analysis and answer extraction in question answering can be transformed to the judgment of entailment relations between questions and answer sentences [6]. Since the aim of RTE is to analyze deep semantic relations between two texts, it contribute to bridging the semantic gap between a question and its answer sentence.

In this paper, we propose an RTE based approach for answer ranking. Following the RTE framework [7], each question is viewed as H(hypothesis), while each answer sentence is viewed as T(text), and the aim is to judge if T semantically entails H: it means that the answer sentence holds the answer nugget for the question if so, and the answer sentence does not contain the answer nugget for the question if not.

Textual entailment involves multiple inference relations, such as coreference, apposition and syntactic alternation. To investigate inference relations in RTE tasks, some research efforts have been made to sort inference phenomena in RTE data, and build annotation frameworks as well as resources of such phenomena [8–10]. Take the following text pair as an example:

T: *Who is the founder of the context-free grammar?*

H: *Chomsky proposed the generative grammar theory.*

There are two kinds of inference phenomena in the above example: one is **lexical entailment** for *founder* in T and *proposed* in H, and the other is **hypernymy** for *context-free grammar* in T and *generative grammar theory* in H. Acquiring inference phenomena is helpful to understand complex semantic relations between T and H, which will contribute to achieving a better performance for RTE. Ren et al. proposed an approach to recognize language phenomena, including 19 entailment phenomena and 9 contradiction ones [11]. Following this idea, we proposed an joint model to recognize language and entailment relation for answer ranking. The aim of the joint model is to avoid error propagation and improve the performance by mutual learning. Experimental results show that the approach performs efficiently for answer ranking.

The rest of the paper is organized as follows. Section 2 gives related work of answer ranking. Section 3 describes the joint model in detail. Section 4 gives experimental results and discussion. Finally, the conclusion and the future work are given in Sect. 5.

2 Related Work

Traditional question answering use multiple retrieval technologies for answer ranking. Most of them are bag-of-words methods [12], which treat questions and answer texts as a set of discrete words and rank answers with the amount of semantically relevant words and phrases. Such methods do not take the relationship between words, thus can not detect structurally semantic information.

Recent research on question answering focuses on semantic analysis approaches, such as parsing syntactic and semantic relations in questions and answer sentences [13], and mapping texts into a semantic graph to bridge the semantic gap between a question and its answer candidate [14]. Another way is knowledge-based question answering, that is, using knowledge graphs to detect semantic relations between questions and answer sentences [15]. To avoid complex feature engineering and get better performances, some researchers use deep learning approaches, e.g., Li et al. [3] build a CNN-based end-to-end model to acquire answers directly. However, those approaches achieve low performances when dealing with the questions containing complex semantic relations.

Some researchers move their attention to deep semantic inference in order to improve the performance of question answering. Harabagiu et al. [6] proposed a classification model for recognizing textual entailment. The model is used in question expansion, document retrieval and answering extraction and the system greatly outperformed the baseline system. The experiment proved the efficiency of entailment recognition technologies to question answering. As a new direction, entailment recognition is concerned by many question answering researchers, and fine-grained entailment recognition approaches are focused on, such as language phenomenon identification [11, 16].

3 The Approach

3.1 Answer Ranking Based on Language Phenomenon

The answer ranking model implemented contains two subtasks: language phenomenon identification and textual entailment recognition. The former one is to find answer sentence candidates from retrieved documents, and the latter one is to rank those candidates to find most possible answer sentences. More specifically, first, we recognize language phenomena in a question(H) and each sentence(T) from retrieved documents, then compute entailment scores for each (T, H). Finally, a ranking list is built according to those entailment scores and scores over threshold values are picked out. For factoid questions, we use the expected answer type of each question to extract answer nuggets; for complex ones, those sentences are directly outputted as the answers.

3.2 The Joint Model

Since our goal is to judge entailment in texts using inference phenomena, we can employ a pipeline framework, that is, identifying language phenomena at the first stage, then classifying entailment classes based on the results of language phenomenon identification at the second stage. However, the performance of the first stage greatly impact the performance of the second stage, which may cause error propagation.

To avoid this problem, Ren et al. [11] proposed a joint approach to combine inference phenomenon identification and entailment recognition into one model. By this approach, such two subtasks can learn each other and will benefit the overall performance as well. In such approach, language phenomenon and entailment recognition are learned in a united model:

$$\begin{aligned} Score_{joint}(t,h,p,c) &= Score_{phe}(t,h) + Score_{ent}(t,h,p) \\ &= w_{phe \oplus ent} \cdot f_{phe \oplus ent}(t,h,p,c) \end{aligned} \tag{1}$$

where p is the inference phenomenon set, c is the entailment class of the text pair (t, h), $Score_{phe}(\cdot)$ and $Score_{ent}(\cdot)$ are the models for inference phenomenon identification and entailment recognition, respectively. f is the joint vector including all features for two subtasks, and w is the weighting vector.

Such model, however, is a linear one, which may lead to low performance in the case of complex feature space. For a better performance, the random forest, a non-linear model, is employed in this paper to deal with the joint learning task. Our consideration is that: (1) random forest is suitable for such tasks of rich features. As a matter of fact, there are over 40 features for language phenomenon identification and over 20 features for entailment recognition (described in Sect. 3.3), although some of these features are same for the two subtasks. Random forest is able to deal with features of such scale without feature selection. (2) Random forest is suitable for such tasks of multiple outputs. In this task, the output is actually a Cartesian product of language phenomenon type and entailment class, which may produce over 100 types of output, hence the model needs to deal with the problem of data sparse. (3) Random forest achieves a robust performance in the case of bias data. In fact, the occurrence of some language phenomena is much higher than other language phenomena in the training and test data, which may lead to low performance if the model is not robust enough.

The ability of generalization is one of the most important factor for machine learning models. As to random forest, correlation variables greatly impact the generalization ability. In order to minimize correlation degree over variables, we can maximize the differences of trees in random forest, that is, each decision tree recognizes language phenomena as few as possible. To this end, features of recognizing single language phenomenon are expected to equally distributed in decision trees.

We employ features from [11] to build the random forest. Such features can be classified as three types: specific language phenomenon identification features(F_S), general language phenomenon identification features(F_G) and entailment recognition features(F_E), all of which will be described in the following subsection. In particular, the first type of features is to detect single language phenomenon in our approach, thus we need to equally distribute them in decision trees.

The construction algorithm of the random forest is described as follows:

Algorithm 1. Random Forest Construction

Input: training data *D*, random forest scale *K*, F_S, F_G, F_E, feature amount for decision trees *n*

Output: random forest *R*

Algorithm:

1. sample *K* training subset with bootstrap algorightm;
2. for *i* = 1 to *K*
   1) stochastically select *m* features from F_S and *n-m* features from F_G+F_E to combine a new feature subset f_i, $n \ll |F_S| + |F_G| + |F_E|$;
   2) build a decision tree t_i using the *i* training subset and the feature subset f_i;
   3) add t_i to R.

For prediction, a voting procedure is carried out via *K* decision trees and the class with the highest voting result is the final decision for a test data.

3.3 Features

Three types of features are employed in our model for training and prediction. The first type of features is specific language phenomenon identification feature, the second one is general language phenomenon identification feature and the third one is entailment recognition feature. All these features come from [11]. Features of the first type aim to identify single language phenomenon, while features of the second type help to identify language phenomenon by featuring text fragments having language phenomenon as well as their contexts.

Specific Language Phenomenon Identification Features. A heuristics has been defined to build these features in [11]. If a rule is matched, it probably means that the text holds the corresponding language phenomenon. The heuristics needs support from rich background knowledge, such as Tongyici Cilin, HowNet, Wikipedia, syntactic resources and a geographic ontology [17]. In the approach, a word embedding-based method [18] is also used to identify *lexical_entailment* phenomenon.

General Inference Phenomenon Identification Features. These features aim to feature text fragments having language phenomenon as well as their contexts. We select some features that much impact the performance than others from [11] and build a subset, listing as follows (Table 1):

where + and − means the left and right word, ↑ and ↓ means the syntactic parent and children, *pos* means Part-Of-Speech, *len* means the length to the syntactic root, *role* means semantic constituent, *sib* means the siblings. $C(\cdot)$ judges if the two tokens are identical and $S(\cdot)$ computes the similarity of two sets derived from the two tokens. Note that one of the two tokens may missing; in such cases the feature value is 0.

Table 1. General language phenomenon identification features

Feature	Description
$C(x+1, y+1)$	judges if the right two words of x and y are same
$C(x-1, y-1)$	judges if the left two words of x and y are same
$C(x_{\uparrow}, y_{\uparrow})$	judges if the two parents of x and y are same
$C_{pos}(x+1, y+1)$	judges if the two POS of the right words of x and y are same
$C_{pos}(x-1, y-1)$	judges if the two POS of the left words of x and y are same
$C_{pos}(x_{\uparrow}, y_{\uparrow})$	judges if the two POS of the parents of x and y are same
$C_{len}(x_{\uparrow}, y_{\uparrow})$	judges if the two values of routes from x and y to their roots are same
$S(x_{\downarrow}, y_{\downarrow})$	the overlapping degree of the children of x and y
$S_{sib}(x, y)$	the overlapping degree of the sibling of x and y

Entailment Recognition Features. The goal of these features is used for the overall entailment recognition. Such features come from [19], which includes string, structure and linguistic features.

4 Experimental Results and Analysis

The data in this experiment comes from the Chinese QA track in NTCIR-5 challenge, including 200 Chinese questions of 9 factoid question types. The document set is CIRB040r Chinese corpus from NTCIR, including 901,446 documents. For language phenomenon recognition training and prediction, we use Chinese RTE evaluation data from NTCIR-11 RITE-3 track, which includes 581 training text pairs and 1200 test pairs, each of which contains a text and a hypothesis, a language phenomenon class label and an entailment class label.

The experiment metrics are accuracy ratio(Acc.) and MRR. The first one computes the ratio of correct answers over answer candidates in the top of the ranking list, while the second one considers how many correct answers are there in the top n of the ranking list. In the second metric, R represents the answer is right and it can be inferred from the document where the answer exists, while U represent the answer is right but it cannot be inferred from the document where the answer exists. In the experiment, we evaluate MRR values of top 5 answers.

Five experiments are set. The first one (svm) employs an SVM classifier with entailment recognition features to classify text pairs and use the sigmoid function to transform the output values to entailment scores. The second one (pipeline+F_S+F_E) uses the pipeline method, that is, using two random forest models to recognize language phenomenon and entailment class respectively for answer ranking. The third one (joint+F_S+F_E) uses the joint model with specific language phenomenon features and entailment recognition ones. The last one (joint+F_S+F_G+F_E) is the system of this paper, which uses the joint model with all the feature mentioned in this paper for answer ranking. We also build a baseline system, which is our participating system in NTCIR

[20]. Such system adopts pattern matching to extract answers by defining patterns for each type of questions. Experimental results are shown in Table 2.

Table 2. Experimental results.

	Acc.(R)	Acc.(R+U)	MRR(R)	MRR(R+U)
baseline	0.285	0.31	0.3225	0.3456
svm	0.325	0.36	0.3755	0.4019
pipeline+F_S+F_E	0.345	0.38	0.3858	0.4261
joint+F_S+F_E	0.36	0.39	0.4017	0.4383
joint+F_S+F_G+F_E	**0.375**	**0.41**	**0.4125**	**0.4460**

It can be seen from the results that:

(1) The answer ranking approach based on language phenomenon recognition outperforms the pattern matching approach. In comparison with the baseline, the svm system achieves an increasing 4% performance of Acc.(R), 5% of Acc.(R+U), 5.3% of MRR(R) and 5.63% of MRR(R+U).
(2) It is efficient to improve the performance of RTE by identifying language phenomena in texts. In comparison with the svm system, the system of this paper (joint +F_S+F_G+F_E) achieves an increasing 5% performance of Acc.(R), 5% of Acc.(R +U), 3.7% of MRR(R) and 4.41% of MRR(R+U).
(3) The joint model outperforms the pipeline one in this experiment. In comparison with the system (pipeline+F_S+F_E), the system (joint+F_S+F_E) achieves an increasing performance in every metric. It indicates that the two subtasks of language phenomenon recognition is a correlative task for textual entailment recognition and answer ranking.
(4) The general features for entailment recognition help to improve the performance of answer ranking according to the experimental results of the two joint systems: in comparison with the system (joint+F_S+F_E), the system (joint+F_S+F_G+F_E) achieves an increasing performance in every metric.

5 Conclusion

This paper introduces a joint approach to incorporate inference phenomenon identification and entailment judgment for answer ranking. In this approach, random forest is used to build a non-linear learning model to predict entailment class and inference phenomena by employing features from such two tasks. The approach not only helps to rank answer for question answering, which is approved on the experiments, but also contributes to exploring a way to better understand semantic relations in texts.

Acknowledgements. This work is supported by Natural Science Foundation of Hainan (618MS086), Special innovation project of Guangdong Education Department (2017KTSCX064), National Natural Science Foundation of China (61402341) and Bidding Project of GDUFS Laboratory of Language Engineering and Computing (LEC2016ZBKT001, LEC-2016ZBKT002).

References

1. Ren, H.: Recognizing textual entailment and its application in question answering. Doctoral Thesis, Wuhan (2011)
2. Wu, Y., Zhao, J., Duan, X., Xu, B.: A survey of question answering technologies and evaluation approaches. J. Chin. Inf. Process. **19**(3), 1–13 (2005)
3. Li, D., Wei, F., Zhou, M., Xu, K.: Question answering over freebase with multi-column convolutional neural networks. In: Proceedings of the 53rd Annual Meeting of the Association for Computational Linguistics (2015)
4. Dagan, I., Dolan, B.: Recognizing textual entailment: rational, evaluation and approaches. Nat. Lang. Eng. **15**(4), i–xvii (2009)
5. Androutsopoulos, I., Malakasiotis, P.: A survey of paraphrasing and textul entailment methods. J. Artif. Intell. Res. **38**(1), 135–187 (2010)
6. Harabagiu, S., Hickl, A.: Methods for using textual entailment in open-domain question answering. In: Proceedings of ACL 2006, Sydney, Australia (2006)
7. Dagan, I., Glickman, O.: Probabilistic textual entailment: generic applied modeling of language variability. In: Proceedings of PASCAL Workshop on Learning Methods for Text Understanding and Mining, Grenoble, France (2004)
8. Bentivogli, L., Cabrio, E., Dagan, I., Giampiccolo, D., Leggio, M.L., Magnini, B.: Building textual entailment specialized data sets: a methodology for isolating linguistic phenomena relevant to inference. In: Proceedings of the International Conference on Language Resources and Evaluation, Valletta, Malta (2010)
9. Kaneko, K., Miyao, Y., Bekki, D.: Building Japanese textual entailment specialized data sets for inference of basic sentence relations. In: Proceedings of the 51st Annual Meeting of the Association of Computational Linguistics, Sofia, Bulgaria (2013)
10. Sammons, M., Vydiswaran, V.G.V., Roth, D.: Ask not what textual entailment can do for you…. In: Proceedings of the Annual Meeting of the Association for Computational Linguistics, Uppsala, Sweden (2010)
11. Ren, H., Li, X., Feng, W., Wan, J.: Recognizing textual entailment using inference phenomenon. In: Proceedings of the 18th Lexical Semantics Workshop, Leshan, pp. 274–283 (2017)
12. Bascaldi, D., Paolo, R.: A bag-of-words based ranking method for the Wikipedia question answering task. In: Proceedings of Cross-Language Evaluation Forum Workshop (2006)
13. Katz, B., Borchardt, G., Felshin, S.: Syntactic and semantic decomposition strategies for question answering from multiple resources. In: Proceedings of the AAAI 2005 Workshop on Inference for Textual Question Answering, pp. 35–41 (2005)
14. Jurczyk, T., Choi, J.D.: Semantics-based graph approach to complex question-answering. In: Proceedings of NAACL-HLT 2015 Student Research Workshop, pp. 140–146 (2015)
15. Bao, J., Duan, N., Yan, Z., Zhou, M., Zhao, T.: Constraint-based question answering with knowledge graph. In: Proceedings of COLING 2016, the 26th International Conference on Computational Linguistics, pp. 2503–2514 (2016)

16. Huang, H.-H., Chang, K.-C., Chen, H.-H.: Modeling human inference process for textual entailment recognition. In: Proceedings of the 51st Annual Meeting of the Association for Computational Linguistics, Sofia, Bulgaria (2013)
17. Jiang, M., Xiao, S., Wang, H., Shi, S.: An lexical semantic similarity approach based on Hownet. J. Chin. Inf. Process. **22**(5) (2008)
18. Ren, H., Wu, H., Tan, X., Wang, P., Wan, J.: The WHUTE system in NTCIR-11 RITE task. In: Proceedings of the 11th NTCIR Conference, Tokyo, Japan (2014)
19. Matsuyoshi, S., et al.: Overview of the NTCIR-11 Recognizing Inference in TExt and Validation (RITE-VAL) task. In: Proceedings of the 11th NTCIR Conference, Tokyo, pp. 223–232 (2014)
20. Ren, H., Ji, D., He, Y., Teng, C., Wan, J.: Multi-strategy question answering system for NTCIR-7 C-C task. In: Proceedings of the 7th NTCIR Workshop, Tokyo, pp. 49–53 (2008)

Text Rewriting Pattern Mining Based on Monolingual Alignment

Yuxiang Jia(✉), Lu Wang, and Hongying Zan

School of Information Engineering, Zhengzhou University, Zhengzhou, China
{ieyxjia,iehyzan}@zzu.edu.cn, 1187978223@qq.com

Abstract. Text rewriting pattern mining was important for stylistic change detection and machine (aided) writing. This paper combined monolingual sentence alignment and monolingual word alignment for text rewriting pattern mining. Edit distance was used to compute sentence similarity for sentence alignment, and a log-linear modification of IBM Model 2 was used for word alignment. We built a rewriting corpus of Jin Yong's novels, on which quantitative and qualitative experiments were carried out. Rewriting patterns were extracted and classified, including function word usages and some content word usages, which reflected the stylistic shift of the author.

Keywords: Text rewriting pattern · Corpus stylistics
Monolingual sentence alignment · Monolingual word alignment

1 Introduction

Rewriting was an important process when we wrote something. We may write several drafts before the camera ready paper was submitted. A novel may be revised by the author several years later, or simplified for teenage readers. We may also rewrite our essays to correct grammatical errors. When we got different editions of a novel, we could investigate the stylistic change of the author. With text revisions, rewriting patterns could be mined to guide human writing or machine writing.

Ho [1] studied corpus stylistics based on two editions of a novel. After computing chapter similarity between two editions, chapters that had been greatly changed were determined and qualitative studies were carried out on those chapters. In Chinese, Jin Yong was the most famous martial arts novel writer. Three different editions were published for all his 15 novels and much work had been done on the edition comparison [2, 3]. Zhang et al. [4, 5] annotated a corpus of revisions for argumentative writing study, detecting revised sentences and classifying them into different rewriting purposes. Tan et al. [6] defined significant change as meaning altering change, and detected significant change in versioned sentences of software requirement specification documents.

Monolingual sentence alignment was the basic step for rewriting detection. Different from bilingual sentence alignment, sentence similarity computation was the key point for monolingual sentence alignment. Levenshtein distance (Edit distance) [7], TF-IDF, or SimHash could be used to compute sentence similarity, while global sentence order in the text should also be considered [8, 9].

J.-F. Hong et al. (Eds.): CLSW 2018, LNAI 11173, pp. 551–558, 2018.
https://doi.org/10.1007/978-3-030-04015-4_47

This paper introduced monolingual word alignment [10] into rewriting pattern mining. For modified sentences, after word alignment, words and their revisions would be extracted and counted. The most frequent word pairs reflected the rewriting patterns. We used Jin Yong's novels as our dataset, investigating linguistic changes between editions.

The rest of this paper was organized as follows. Section 2 described the rewriting pattern mining process, including monolingual sentence alignment algorithm and monolingual word alignment method. Section 3 gave the quantitative and qualitative experiments and analysis. Conclusions were given in Sect. 4.

2 Text Rewriting Pattern Mining Approach

The process of rewriting pattern mining was shown in Fig. 1. The original text and its revision were split into sentences. Then sentence alignments were constructed and classified in the monolingual sentence alignment step. Monolingual word alignment was applied to aligned sentence pairs of '*Modify*' category. Lastly, frequent aligned word pairs were extracted as the rewriting patterns.

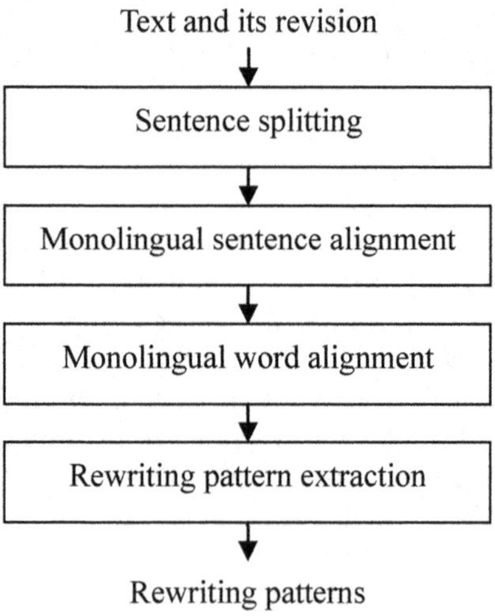

Fig. 1. Rewriting pattern mining process

2.1 Monolingual Sentence Alignment

The monolingual sentence alignment algorithm was shown as algorithm 1. The input was the sentence sequences of two text versions. The output was the aligned sentence pairs and corresponding categories. There were four categories, *Keep*, *Modify*, *Delete* and *Add*. *Keep* meant the sentence was unchanged. It was *Modify* when the sentence similarity was greater than the threshold *th* but smaller than 1. When the sentence similarity was smaller than the threshold *th*, the sentence in version1 was deleted

(*Delete*) or the sentence in version2 was added (*Add*). Levenshtein distance was employed to compute sentence similarity. Sentence length was counted as the number of characters in the sentence. As was shown in formula 1, the scope of sentence similarity was between 0 and 1.

$$\mathrm{sim}(s_1, s_2) = 1 - \frac{\mathrm{LevenshteinDistance}(s_1, s_2)}{\max(\mathrm{length}(s_1), \mathrm{length}(s_2))} \tag{1}$$

Algorithm 1: Monolingual Sentence Alignment

```
Input:
 Sentence sequence of text version1: {sen_1i}, 1 ≤ i ≤ m
 Sentence sequence of text version2: {sen_2j}, 1 ≤ j ≤ n
Output:
 Sentence alignment and category: S = {(i, j, label)}, 0 ≤ i ≤ m, 0 ≤ j ≤ n
 label ∈ {Keep, Modify, Delete, Add}
Initialize S = Φ
for i = 1 ··· m
    for j = 1 ... n
        Computing sentence similarity sim(sen_1i, sen_2j)
    end for
end for
for i = 1 ... m
    j = argmax_k sim(sen_1i, sen_2k)
    if sim(sen_1i, sen_2j) < th then (i, 0, Delete) ∪ S
    else if sim(sen_1i, sen_2j) = 1 then (i, j, Keep) ∪ S
    else (i, j, Modify) ∪ S
end for
for j = 1 ... n
    i = argmax_k sim(sen_1k, sen_2j)
    if sim(sen_1i, sen_2j) < th then (0, j, Add) ∪ S
    else if sim(sen_1i, sen_2j) = 1 then (i, j, Keep) ∪ S
    else (i, j, Modify) ∪ S
end for
```

2.2 Monolingual Word Alignment

For a pair of aligned sentences of category '*Modify*', we took the original sentence as a sentence of the source language and the modified sentence as a sentence of the target language. Then we could use bilingual word alignment tools for monolingual word alignment. Figure 2 showed an example of the monolingual word alignment. We could see that the word "我"/I was changed to "俺"/I in the revised sentence while all other words kept unchanged.

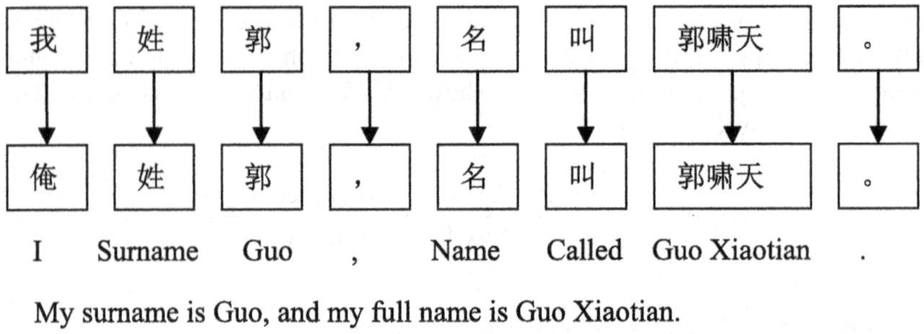

Fig. 2. Monolingual word alignment example

Rewriting could be considered as paraphrasing which needed fewer reordering operations than cross-lingual translation. For monolingual word alignment, we used fast_align [11], a simple, fast, and effective reparameterization of IBM model 2, achieving better performance than IBM model 4 on several large-scale translation tasks.

3 Experiments and Analysis

3.1 Dataset

We collected two editions of Jin Yong's novels from http://www.jinyongwang.com/, version 2 and version 3. Experiments were carried out on two novels, "射雕英雄传"/Legends of the condor heroes 1 (LCH1) and "神雕侠侣"/Legends of the condor heroes 2 (LCH2). There were 40 chapters each in both LCH1 and LCH2. Chapters were directly aligned in version 2 and 3. Levenshtein distance was used to compute the chapter similarity between the two versions. The smaller the similarity was, the greater

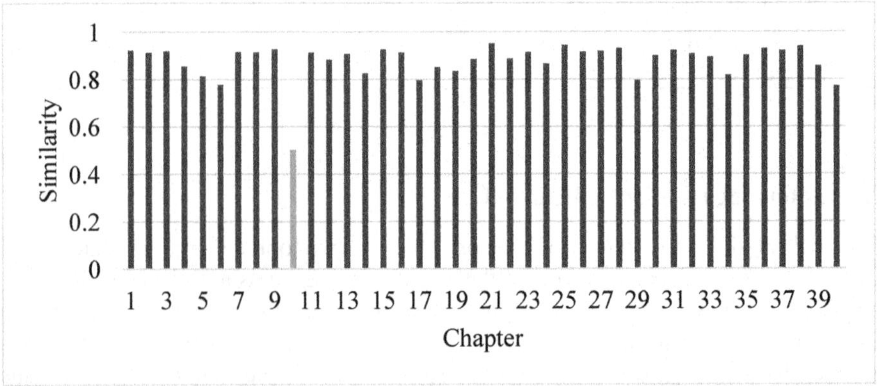

Fig. 3. Chapter similarity of LCH1

the chapter was modified. As was shown in Fig. 3, chapter 10 was changed the most in LCH1.

We chose chapter 10 of LCH1 to tune parameters and test performance of sentence alignment and word alignment. As was shown in Table 1, Ver2 had 587 sentences while Ver3 had 927. After manual alignment, we totally had 985 aligned sentence pairs, including four categories. For the 279 *Modify* sentence pairs, we further built word alignment gold standard data for word alignment evaluation. All the datasets were independently annotated by three annotators and conflict annotations were solved by discussion.

Table 1. Number of sentence and aligned sentence pair

Ver2	Ver3	Keep	Modify	Delete	Add	Total
587	927	227	279	66	413	985

3.2 Monolingual Sentence Alignment Result

Precision (P), Recall (R) and F1 measure (F1) were used to evaluate both sentence alignment and word alignment. Based on the LCH1 chapter 10 data, Fig. 4 showed the variation of values of the three metrics with the change of threshold *th*. The best performance (F1 = 91.91%) was achieved with *th* of 0.4. So we set *th* = 0.4 for later experiments.

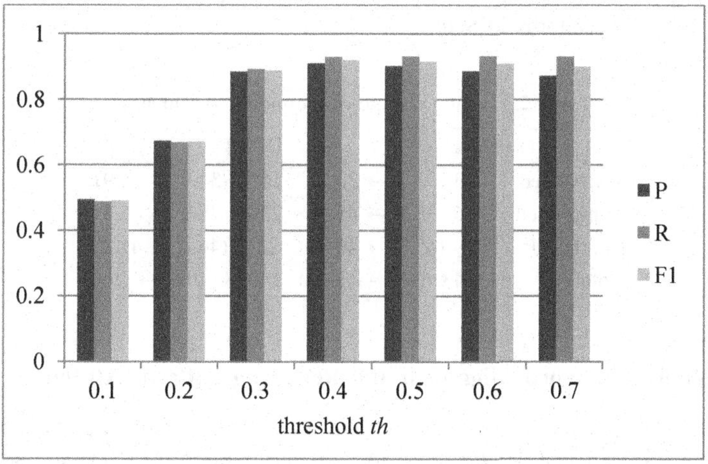

Fig. 4. Sentence alignment performance with different threshold *th*

Applying algorithm 1 to each chapter, we had aligned sentences and their categories. Figure 5 showed the sentence alignment category distribution of each chapter in

LCH1. We could see that most sentences were unchanged (*Keep*) or modified (*Modify*), and only a fraction of sentences were deleted (*Delete*) or added (*Add*).

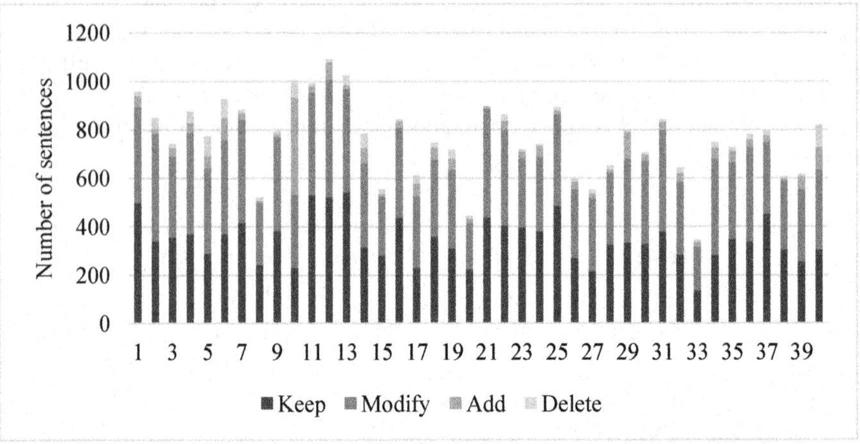

Fig. 5. Sentence alignment category distribution of each chapter in LCH1

For the modified (*Modify*) sentences, we closely looked at the sentence length (number of characters) change. Table 2 showed the sentence number and the average sentence length change. As could be seen, many more sentences were shortened than lengthened, and the average sentence length became smaller. It was a characteristic of the rewriting of Jin Yong's novels from version 2 to version 3, as was proved by the extracted rewriting patterns in Sect. 3.3.

Table 2. Length change of the modified sentences

	LCH1	LCH2
Unchanged	5813 (33.3 → 33.3)	5664 (34.9 → 34.9)
Lengthened	2286 (38.2 → 45.1)	2208 (38.9 → 45.5)
Shortened	5649 (45.2 → 40.7)	6226 (46.4 → 41.8)
Total	13748 (39.0 → 38.3)	14098 (40.6 → 39.6)

3.3 Monolingual Word Alignment and Rewriting Pattern Extraction

Fast_align was used for word alignment and all parameters were set by default. The aligned sentence pairs of *Modify* were used as the training data. Table 3 showed the performance of the word alignment model trained on LCH1.

We computed the frequency of the aligned word pairs and from frequent aligned word pairs we got rewriting patterns. Table 4 showed some rewriting patterns extracted from LCH1 and LCH2, including five types of patterns, a short description and examples for each pattern. Most patterns were about function word usages, which

Table 3. Word alignment performance

P	R	F1
91.98%	85.38%	88.56%

reflected the stylistic change of the author. Still some patterns were about content words, like person names, etc. The 'Shorten' type explained the shortened length of the modified sentences.

Table 4. Some rewriting patterns from LCH1 and LCH2

Type	Description	Examples: Ver2→Ver3(frequency)
Era	Word or word form changing with era	的/DE→地/DI(1040) 甚么/what→什么/what(978) 罢/BA→吧/BA(409) 干么/what→干吗/what(93) 教/by→叫/by(108) 斗然/suddenly→陡然/suddenly(64) 胡涂/confused→糊涂/confused(38)
Synonym	One2many, many2one, and one2one substitution of synonyms	被/by→给/by(325) 被/by→为/by(118) 被/by→让/by(73) 被/by→遭/by(40) 和/with→跟/with(68) 与/with→跟/with(63) 若是/suppose→倘若/suppose(81) 无/not→没/not(52)
Shorten	Words substituted by short synonym for simplification	虽然/although→虽/although(156) 却是/but→却/but(143) 只见/see→见/see(138) 仍是/still→仍/still(130) 只是/just→只/just(93) 又是/again→又/again(78) 竟然/unexpectedly→竟/unexpectedly(73) 也是/also→也/also(73) 都是/all→都/all(72) 急忙/hastily→忙/hastily(53) 一个/one→个/one(53) 眼见/see→见/see(46) 没有/not→没/not(44) 知道/know→知/know(36)
Person	Person names changing for some reasons, like real person with the same name existing in the history	法王/Buddha→国师/Teacher of the emperor(927) 尹志平/Yin Zhiping→甄志丙/Zhen Zhibing(165) 马光佐/Ma Guangzuo→麻光佐/Ma Guangzuo(134) 史孟捷/Shi Mengjie→史少捷/Shi Shaojie(30) 吕文德/Lv Wende→吕文焕/Lv Wenhuan(30) 尹赵二人/Yin&Zhao→甄赵二人/Zhen&Zhao(24)
Others	Content words, dialect words, etc.	匕首/dagger→短剑/dagger(57) 我/I→俺/I(3)

4 Conclusions

We combined monolingual sentence alignment and monolingual word alignment to mine text rewriting patterns. Levenshtein distance was used to compute sentence similarity for sentence alignment. A log-linear modification of IBM Model 2 was applied to monolingual word alignment. Experiments were carried out on Jin Yong's novels. Some rewriting patterns were extracted, including function word usages and content words, which reflected the stylistic shift of the author. Next, we would apply this approach to other text domains, like scientific papers and HSK compositions.

Acknowledgments. We thank Qian Wang and Yue Zhang for their helpful discussions on literary computing. We are grateful to the anonymous reviewers for constructive advices to improve this paper. This work is partially supported by grants from the National Natural Science Foundation of China (No. 61402419) and the National Social Science Foundation of China (No. 14BYY096).

References

1. Ho, Y.: Corpus Stylistics in Principles and Practice: A Stylistic Exploration of John Fowles' The Magus. A&C Black (2011)
2. Lan, D.H., Cao, L.Y.: On the new revised version of Jin Yong's novels. J. Hangzhou Dianzi Univ. (Soc. Sci.) **6**(1), 57–61 (2010). (in Chinese)
3. Xue, D.C.: The edition research of the legend of the condor heroes. Henan University (2011). (in Chinese)
4. Zhang, F., Litman, D.: Sentence-level rewriting detection. In: Proceedings of the Ninth Workshop on Innovative Use of NLP for Building Educational Applications, pp. 149–154 (2014)
5. Zhang, F., Hashemi, H.B., Hwa, R., et al.: A corpus of annotated revisions for studying argumentative writing. In: Proceedings of the 55th Annual Meeting of the Association for Computational Linguistics (Volume 1: Long Papers), pp. 1568–1578 (2017)
6. Tan, P.P., Verspoor, K., Miller, T.: Structural alignment as the basis to improve significant change detection in versioned sentences. In: Proceedings of the Australasian Language Technology Association Workshop 2015, pp. 101–109 (2015)
7. Navarro, G.: A guided tour to approximate string matching. ACM Comput. Surv. **33**(1), 31–88 (2001)
8. Nelken, R., Shieber, S.M.: Towards robust context-sensitive sentence alignment for monolingual corpora. In: Proceedings of EACL 2006, pp. 161–168 (2006)
9. Barzilay, R., Elhadad, N.: Sentence alignment for monolingual comparable corpora. In: Proceedings of EMNLP 2003, pp. 25–32 (2003)
10. Liu, Z.Y., Wang, H.F., Wu, H., et al.: Collocation extraction using monolingual word alignment method. In: Proceedings of EMNLP 2009, vol. 2, pp. 487–495 (2009)
11. Dyer, C., Chahuneau, V., Smith, N.A.: A simple, fast, and effective reparameterization of IBM model 2. In: Proceedings of NAACL 2013, pp. 644–648 (2013)

Sense Group Segmentation for Chinese Second Language Reading Based on Conditional Random Fields

Shuqin Zhu[1,2](✉), Jihua Song[1](✉), Weiming Peng[1](✉), and Jingbo Sun[1]

[1] College of Information Science and Technology, Beijing Normal University, Beijing 100875, China
{songjh, pengweiming}@bnu.edu.cn, 201721210040@mail.bnu.edu.cn

[2] Teachers' College of Beijing Union University, Beijing 100011, China
sftzhushuqin@buu.edu.cn

Abstract. Second language reading is an important task for second language learners, and sense group reading training can quickly improve a learner's reading speed. In this paper, we consider text containing syntactic information as experimental data. Sense group segmentation is converted to the problem of sequence annotation, and automatic sense group segmentation is completed based on conditional random fields (CRF). This method provides an auxiliary segmentation approach by which information technology can assist international Chinese teaching.

Keywords: Sense group segmentation · Second language reading
Conditional random fields

1 Introduction

Reading is the main means of obtaining information and knowledge from written language. Second language reading is an important task for second language learners. A sentence can be divided into several segments according to its semantic and syntactic structure. Each independent segment expresses a relatively complete meaning, and each segment is called a sense group. A sense group can be a word, phrase, or clause in a compound sentence. The meaning of a sentence can be understood by combining sense groups [1]. In the field of linguistics, "/" is typically used to divide sense groups. For example, the sentence "马丽原来学的是艺术专业 (Mary originally majored in art)" is divided into "马丽原来学的 / 是艺术专业". A sense group can express a relatively complete meaning, and reading with the sense group as the unit of view is a necessary condition for good reading ability in any language.

In [1], the effect of sense group reading training on rapid reading ability was observed and analyzed. The results showed that the reading speed of the experimental group was significantly improved. The primary textbook on Chinese newspaper reading provided sense group segmentation for every sentence, as shown in Fig. 1 [2].

J.-F. Hong et al. (Eds.): CLSW 2018, LNAI 11173, pp. 559–569, 2018.
https://doi.org/10.1007/978-3-030-04015-4_48

Sense group reading training helps learners to quickly retrieve and extract language units, and reduce difficulty in language acquisition. After a great deal of reading training, these language units become meaningful for learners and help them to enhance their reading speed.

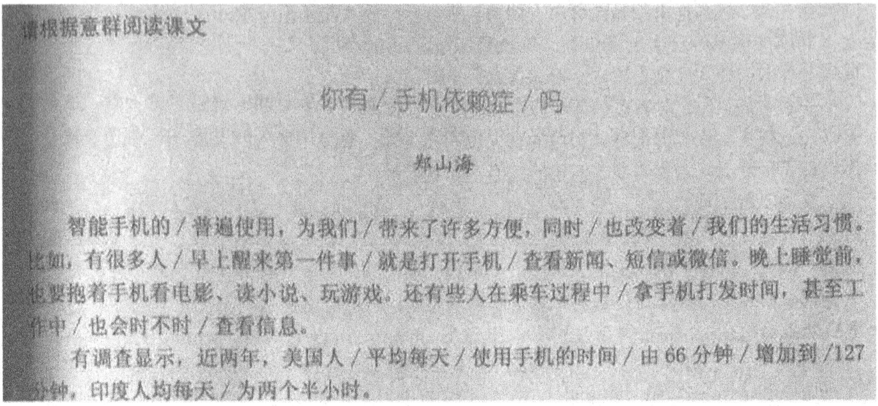

请根据意群阅读课文

你有 / 手机依赖症 / 吗

郑山海

智能手机的 / 普遍使用，为我们 / 带来了许多方便，同时 / 也改变着 / 我们的生活习惯。比如，有很多人 / 早上醒来第一件事 / 就是打开手机 / 查看新闻、短信或微信。晚上睡觉前，也要抱着手机看电影、读小说、玩游戏。还有些人在乘车过程中 / 拿手机打发时间，甚至工作中 / 也会时不时 / 查看信息。

有调查显示，近两年，美国人 / 平均每天 / 使用手机的时间 / 由 66 分钟 / 增加到 /127 分钟，印度人均每天 / 为两个半小时。

Fig. 1. Sense group segmentation of a textbook

Although sense group reading can quickly improve a learner's reading speed, only language teachers are concerned about this. As mentioned in [3], a rhythm group is a language fragment based on Chinese characters, in which phonology, semantics, and syntax are integrated into Chinese language flow. The concept of a rhythm group describes a hierarchical unit in Chinese language teaching, which is similar to the concept of a sense group in our paper. In [3], the basic principles to be followed when a rhythm group is divided were also proposed:

(1) Semantic integrity
Chinese has evolved from monosyllabic words to disyllabic words, and cohesive words are no longer separated. The integrity of the semantics is the basic principle for a rhythm group.

(2) Symmetric and neat
A pause in language teaching helps Chinese learners to understand, and its tone is symmetrical and restrained, which can express the normal meaning of language in a clear and precise manner. Rhythm group segmentation in language teaching should follow the symmetrical and neat principle, to reflect the internal syntactic combination.

(3) 7 ± 2
Miller's human brain information processing experiment demonstrated that a human brain's short-term information memory capacity is "7 ± 2" which was a milestone in the study of short-term memory. In [3], a large number of written

papers were quoted to prove the specific value of the number “7” in Chinese. According to this principle, a clause of fewer than seven syllables is no longer divided, and a sentence with more than seven syllables is typically divided into two or three parts of roughly equal length.

From these principles, it can be seen that there is a great deal of subjectivity in sense group segmentation, and language teachers perform sense group segmentation in an artificial manner, which is time-consuming, laborious, and inefficient. In the field of computer information processing, few people pay attention to sense group segmentation. At present, there are no studies that are using information technology to assist sense group segmentation and apply it to teaching. In [4], text classification was completed by extracting sense groups instead of words as characteristic values. The researchers performed syntactic analysis based on the existing mature dependency analysis system, and the extraction rules of the sense group were set according to the result of dependency parsing, and the sense groups of sentences were extracted using the rules. In [5], the clause in a sentence was regarded as a sense group, and the sentence was divided into sense groups using the comma and semicolon. This definition is different from the general definition of linguistics, and we do not provide a discussion in this paper.

In this paper, we attempt to provide a tool for international Chinese teachers to assist sense group segmentation. This method uses text containing syntax tagged information as experimental data, and the CRF method to complete the automatic sense group segmentation. This method provides an auxiliary method for sense group segmentation, which provides an idea for information technology to assist international Chinese teaching.

2 Sentence-Based Treebank and Experimental Data Acquisition

Sense group segmentation criteria and processes are related to syntactic structure. The main syntactic structure of Chinese information processing includes phrase structure, dependency structure, and sentence-based syntax. An analysis of phrase structure and dependency structure has demonstrated a binary relation. For sense group segmentation, a large amount of sentence pattern information is needed, and binary relation is unfavorable for sense group segmentation.

For this study, we chose the sentence-based treebank constructed by the language and text resources research center of Beijing Normal University. The first reason for this choice is that the sentence-based treebank was based on sentence-based syntactic theory proposed by Jinxi Li, which originated from teaching, and had a natural connection to teaching grammar. It had been formalized, and can be used for computer analysis and processing. The second reason is the actual practical application. Although automatic syntactic analysis has made great progress, it is far from practical. Chinese second language reading is oriented to teaching, and the demand for the accuracy of text is high. The sentence-based treebank based on international Chinese textbooks, has been completed the detailed processing of text, and can meet high requirements.

Additionally, sense group segmentation standards established by language educators are qualitative and fuzzy in execution. Standards of computer-aided sense group segmentation are definitely related to syntax. Therefore, for this study, we chose the sentence-based treebank with syntactic structure information to conduct the experiment.

The sentence-based treebank used a diagrammatic analysis method to analyze and annotate the sentence, as shown in Fig. 2. Sentence components (subject, predicate, object, attribute, adverbial, and complement) were directly tagged. The subject, predicate, and object were all above the trunk line, and were the main components of the sentence. The attribute, adverbial, and complement were located below the trunk line, and were the additional components of the sentence. The long horizontal line in Fig. 2 was the benchmark used to observe the hierarchy of the sentence. The sentence components attached to the same horizontal line belonged to the same level. The annotation results were stored in XML format, and the diagram and XML can be converted in a bidirectional manner. In the XML, the subject <sbj>, predicate <prd>, object <obj>, adverbial <adv>, and complement <cmp> were at the same level of the hierarchy, and were all the children of <xj>. The attribute <att> was lower in the hierarchy. The attribute and central word were siblings. In complex predicate sentences composed of multiple predicates, the front and back predicates were also arranged in turn. If a component can be extended to a VP (verb phrase) structure with a predicate kernel, then a new hierarchy was produced on the basis of <prd> (e.g., the attribute of "影响" is "非常不好的"), as shown in Fig. 2. For more details, please see [6].

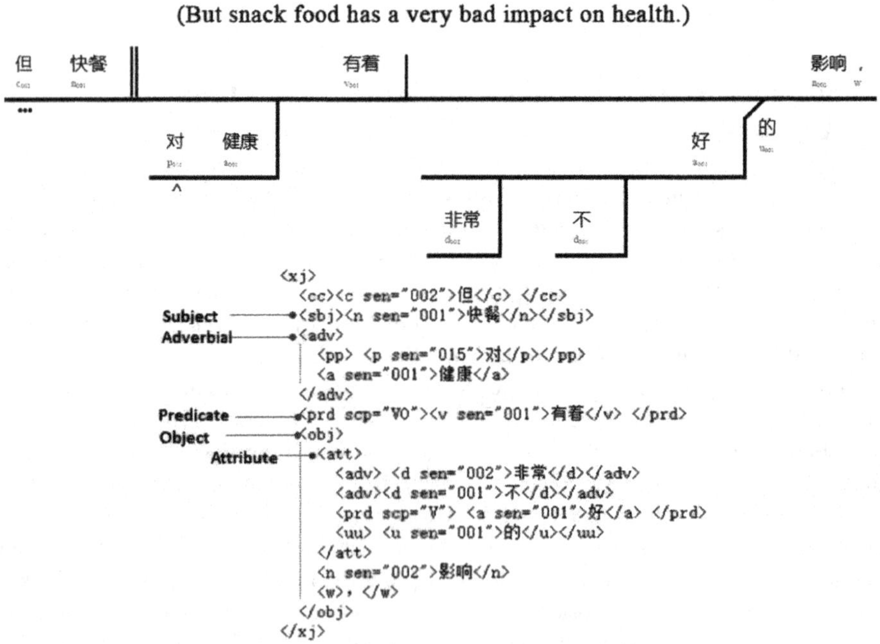

Fig. 2. Diagrammatic style and corresponding XML structure

The raw corpus was exported from two textbooks in the treebank: “Reading Newspapers to Learn Chinese—primary” (word count 8,688, sentence count 271) and “Intermediate course experiencing Chinese— 1” (word count 6,641, sentence count 215). The raw corpus was in text format, which did not contain tagging information, such as syntax and part of speech, and did not interfere with artificial sense group segmentation. The tagging staffs were two master’s degree candidates who were native Chinese speakers. First, they were informed of the segmentation principle, and then they completed the segmentation independently. They discussed segmentation inconsistencies and determined a segmentation approach. Finally, Chinese teaching experts were invited to proofread the segmentation results, which were the experimental data used in this paper. We did not consider segmentation caused by rhythm and rhetoric. We drew on the principle of sense group segmentation proposed by Haiyan Liu (2016) mentioned above, and the effect of segmentation was as follows:

马丽毕业于 / 一所美国大学。因为 / 在中国的留学经历，这个典型美国女孩 / 现在的生活，每天都与中文、中国文化 / 和中国人有关。马丽原来学的 / 是艺术专业，这让她 / 对中国汉字产生了 / 浓厚的兴趣。“中国字 / 真是太美了，” 马丽说，她从大学一年级 / 就开始学习中文，自己对说汉语 / 和写汉字 / 都非常着迷。

(Mary graduated from an American university. Because of the experience of studying in China, the typical American girl’s present life involves relating to the Chinese language, Chinese culture and Chinese people every day. Mary originally studied art, which made her interested in Chinese characters. “Chinese words are really beautiful,” Mary said. She began to learn Chinese in the first year of college. She was fascinated by speaking Chinese and writing Chinese characters.)

The annotation data (XML file) with syntax and other information from the two textbooks (“Reading Newspapers to Learn Chinese—primary” and “Intermediate course experiencing Chinese— 1”) was exported from the sentence-base treebank. These data together with syntactic annotation information, corresponded to the text that resulted from artificial sense group segmentation, and they both formed the experimental data used in this study.

3 Sense Group Segmentation Based on CRF

The purpose of this paper is to explore the relationship between syntactic structure and sense group segmentation. The relationship does not conform to a simple one-to-one rule, but is a combination of many factors; hence, the automatic learning algorithm was selected. CRF is a type of machine learning algorithm that considers context and has good learning ability [7]. Therefore, we based sense group segmentation on CRF in this paper.

3.1 Principle of CRF

CRF is a sequence-marking recognition model based on statistical methods, and was proposed by Lafferty et al. in 2001. In this paper, the problem of sense group segmentation was converted to the problem of sequence annotation, and CRF was used to solve the problem of sense group segmentation.

In the CRF model, given an observed sequence of sentences $S = (s_1, s_2, \ldots s_m)$ the corresponding annotation sequence is $Y = (y_1, y_2, \ldots y_m)$ output. The goal of CRF is to determine the sequence of Y that maximizes the following formula:

$$P(Y|S) = \frac{1}{Z_s} \exp\left[\sum_i \sum_j W_j f_j(y_{i-1}, y_i, S)\right], \tag{1}$$

Where $f_j(y_{i-1}, y_i, S)$ denotes the characteristic functions of the observation sequences, and typically takes Boolean values. $W = (\omega_1, \omega_2, \ldots \omega_m)$ is the weight value that corresponds to each characteristic function after the model is trained. The maximum likelihood method is generally used for the estimation of W, and to avoid overfitting, the Gauss prior is generally added to the parameters. Z_s is a normalization factor, and

$$Z_s = \sum_y \exp\left[\sum_i \sum_j W_j f_j(y_{i-1}, y_i, S)\right] \tag{2}$$

3.2 Feature Selection

The learning and prediction of CRF was conducted on multiple features of a sample. It was necessary to select various features that influenced sense group segmentation, and add these features to the feature template. The threshold was set to *K* so that the system selected features that appeared more than *K* times in the training corpus. In this paper, the experimental results demonstrate that the best value was two. Through the analysis of the corpus for which sense group segmentation was complete, we found that the main factors affecting sense group segmentation were as follows:

(1) Size of the sense group
The word is the basic unit of automatic analysis of Chinese syntax and semantics, and sense group segmentation is a further processing of words. The main unit of Chinese sense group segmentation is the word. Constrained by the limitation of short-term information capacity, there is a certain restriction on the size of the group when conducting sense group segmentation.

(2) Syntactic feature
To a large extent, a sense group is based on the syntactic structure of a sentence. A sense group is a type of natural pause formed by the syntactic structure itself, which reflects the syntactic relationship between words and phrases. Segmentation has a certain regularity, and the location of segmentation is different for different syntactic structures. This position is also related to the length of the syntactic component.

(3) Syntactic hierarchy
When performing sense group segmentation, the context syntactic hierarchy of the current word has a significant influence on the current word. The syntactic hierarchy of words that are located around the current word has a direct impact on whether the word is segmented or not. The position at which the hierarchy changes is the location of sense group segmentation.

Based on the above analysis, we classify the main factors that affected sense group segmentation into three categories: atomic features, compound features, and dynamic features. The following, "马丽 原来 学 的 / 是 艺术专业, (Mary originally majored in art)" is an example of feature selection.

(1) Atomic features
To make full use of factors such as the word itself, syntactic feature, and syntactic hierarchy feature, an atomic feature template can be used, as shown in Table 1. An atomic feature template only considers a class of factor that affects sense group segmentation, which is, in fact, a function of the context of the current field.

Table 1. Atomic feature template

Number	Template	Explanation
1	L(n), $n \in \{-2, -1, 0, 1, 2\}$	The length of the current word and the length of the two words in the front and back
2	S(n), $n \in \{-2, -1, 0, 1, 2\}$	The syntactic component of the current word and the syntactic components of the two words before and after the current word
3	H(n), $n \in \{-2, -1, 0, 1, 2\}$	The syntactic hierarchy of the current word and the syntactic hierarchy of the two words before and after the current word

For example, for current field "的," atomic feature template $S(-1)$ can be instantiated into a two-value function as shown in the following formula:

$$f_S(Y, X, i) = \begin{cases} 1, & S(-1) = \text{"prd"} \ \textit{and} \ Y = \text{"F"} \\ 0, & \textit{otherwise} \end{cases} \quad (3)$$

The expression indicates that the function value is 1 only when the syntactic component of the preceding word is "prd" and the current word is the location of sense group segmentation.

(2) Compound features
In many cases, it is difficult to use only atomic feature templates to fully describe some of the complex phenomena in the language. By combining various atomic templates, we form a number of compound feature templates to represent more complex and nonlinear contextual information, as shown in Table 2.

Table 2. Compound feature template

Number	Template	Explanation
1	$S(n)S(n+1),\ n \in \{-2,\ -1, 0, 1, 2\}$	Syntactic component combination of two consecutive words
2	$S(n)S(n+1), S(n+2), n \in \{-2,\ -1, 0\}$	Syntactic component combination of three consecutive words
3	$H(n)H(n+1),\ n \in \{-2,\ -1, 0, 1, 2\}$	Syntactic hierarchy combination of two consecutive words
4	$H(n)H(n+1),\ H(n+2),\ n \in \{-2,\ -1, 0\}$	Syntactic hierarchy combination of three consecutive words

For example, for current field "的," compound feature template $H(0)H(1)$ can be instantiated into a two-value function, as shown by the following formula:

$$f_H(Y, X, i) = \begin{cases} 1, & H(0) = \text{"2"}\ and\ H(1) = \text{"1"}\ \ and\ Y = \text{"F"} \\ 0, & otherwise \end{cases} \tag{4}$$

The expression indicates that the function value is 1 only when the syntactic hierarchy of the current word is "2," the syntactic hierarchy of the following word is "1," and the current word is the location of sense group segmentation.

(3) Dynamic features
The sense group mark of the preceding words is also very important information. Generally, a short term after a sense group cannot represent a sense group.

3.3 CRF Model Training

In this paper, the CRF++ V0.58 toolkit was used to train and test the model. The details are as follows:

(1) The toolkit required training and testing files to contain multiple tokens, where each token contained multiple columns. Each token had to be written on one line, with space or tab interval between columns. The sequence of tokens could form a sentence, with a blank line between sentences, and the last column was the correct annotation of the CRF for training.
According to the above CRF feature selection, we combined the XML file and tagged sense group segmentation text, and obtained experimental data that conformed to the format requirements, as shown below. The first column represents the word length; second column represents the syntactic component; third column represents the syntax hierarchy; and fourth column indicates whether the word is segmented, where "B" indicates that there is no segmentation after the word, "F" indicates that there is segmentation after the word, and "K" indicates punctuation.

2 sbj 2 B （马丽）
2 adv 2 B （原来）
1 prd 2 B （学）
1 uv2 F （的）
1 prd 1 B （是）
4 obj 1 B （艺术专业）
1 ， 1 K （，）

(2) The number of occurrences of each feature in the training corpus was calculated, and features with occurrences less than or equal to K were filtered out. In the experiment, we choose K = 2.
(3) The initial value of each feature weight was 9. The LBFGS algorithm was used to train parameters until convergence. The default threshold was 0.0001.

4 Experimental Results and Analysis

We used 10-fold cross-validation to conduct an open test. Each word corresponded to "B" or "F," which indicates a two-classification problem, where "F" corresponds to a positive example and "B" corresponds to a negative example. We used four indicators to evaluate sense group segmentation: precision rate P, accuracy rate A, recall rate R, and F value. The calculation methods are as follows:

$$P = TP/(TP + FP)$$

$$A = (TP + TN)/(TP + FN + FP + TN) \tag{5}$$

$$R = TP/(TP + FN)$$

$$F\text{-value} = \frac{2PR}{P + R}$$

TP: true positive; FP: false positive; FN: false negative; TN: true negative.
The results of the experiment are shown in Table 3.

Table 3. Experimental results

Precision rate	Accuracy rate	Recall rate	F-Value
76%	92%	71%	73%

The accuracy rate of the experimental results was relatively high, which indicates that the algorithm was relatively narrow, and the restrictions were clearer. The algorithm was suitable for some scenarios, but it could not cover all cases. The position of segmentation was almost always correct. The recall rate was low, which indicates that some locations were not segmented, and the sense group chunks were large. As shown in Table 4, there is a manual segmentation behind the "来“, .cbut no segmentation by computer.

Table 4. Result demonstration

Word length	Syntactic component	Syntactic hierarchy	Text	Manual tag	Experimental result
2	adv	1	三年	B	B
1	ff	1	来	F	B
6	sbj	1	中国收养中心	F	F
2	adv	1	一直	B	B
1	adv	1	在	B	B
3	prd	1	关心着	B	B
3	obj	1	小凯丽	B	B
1	,	1	,	K	K

By analyzing these positions of sense group segmentation, some of the characteristics shown in Table 5 were found.

Table 5. Position analysis

Position	Characteristic
Subject	If the subject is a pronoun, it usually does not segmented, and there is a significant segmentation after the long subject
Object	The object after a verb is long, there is a segmentation before the object If the object is modified by the indefinite number phrase such as "one" or "some", the segmentation appears after the indefinite number phrase
Attribute	If the attributive is longer, the attributive far away from the central word is divided, and the attributive close to the central word must not be divided
Adverbial	When the adverbial is longer, the adverbial is divided
Complement	When the complement is long, the complement is divided before the complement
Parallel	There is segmentation between the long parallel components
Transition	There is a cut in the turning of meaning

5 Conclusions

In this paper, sense group segmentation was based on the sentence-based treebank with which the syntactic structure analysis of the text had been completed. Based on text that was tagged using manual sense group segmentation, model training was first conducted, and automatic sense group segmentation was completed using the obtained model. This method provides an idea for sense group segmentation, and a feasible method to assist international Chinese teaching.

In this paper, for the problem of automatic sense group segmentation, teachers needed to modify the segmentation manually. As an auxiliary tool for language teachers, most of the sense group segmentation was completed; only a few corrections needed to be made by the teachers. Additionally, sense group segmentation considers only syntax rather than semantics. In future work, we will consider sense group segmentation that combines phonology, syntax, and semantics.

References

1. Zhongxin, D., Yaohua, H.: A study on the effect of meaningful chunk reading training upon the improvement of fast reading. J. Beijing Radio Telev. Univ. **48**(3), 45–49 (2008)
2. Chengnian, W.: Reading Newspaper and Learning Chinese. Beijing University Press, Beijing (2015)
3. Haiyan, L.: The enlightenment of Tang Tong's view of Chinese on Chinese teaching and research. In: The Frontier of Language and Literature (Series sixth). Knowledge Industry Press, Beijing (2016)
4. Li, Z., Yi, J.: Sense group categorization algorithm for Chinese text. Comput. Eng. **39**(8), 204–208 (2013)
5. Bin, G., Xiaoping, Y., Jianlin, Z., Zhongxia, Z.: Chinese micro-blog sentiment orientation identification based on sense group partition. J. Chin. Inf. Process. **29**(3), 100–105 (2015)
6. Peng, W., Song, J., Sui, Z., Guo, D.: Formal schema of diagrammatic Chinese syntactic analysis. In: Lu, Q., Gao, H.H. (eds.) CLSW 2015. LNAI, vol. 9332, pp. 701–710. Springer, Heidelberg (2015)
7. Jing, X., Xiaoping, Y.: Topic clues extraction of network news based on conditional random fields. J. Chin. Inf. Process. **31**(3), 94–100 (2017)

Multi-perspective Embeddings for Chinese Chunking

Chen Lyu, Bo Chen(✉), and Donghong Ji

Collaborative Innovation Center for Language Research and Services, Guangdong University of Foreign Studies, Guangzhou 510420, China
{lvchen1989,dhji}@whu.edu.cn, cb9928@gmail.com

Abstract. Chunking is a crucial step in natural language processing (NLP), which aims to divide a text into syntactically correlated but non-overlapping chunks. The task is typically modeled as a sequence labeling problem. Various machine learning algorithms, such as Conditional Random Fields (CRFs) and Support Vector Machines (SVMs), have been successfully used for this task. However, these state-of-the-art chunking systems largely depend on hand-crafted appropriate features. In this paper, we present a recurrent neural network (RNN) framework based on multi-perspective embeddings for Chinese chunking. This framework takes the character representation, part-of-speech (POS) embeddings and word embeddings as the input features of the RNN layer. On top of the RNN, we use a CRF layer to jointly decode labels for the whole sentence. Experimental results show that various embeddings can improve the performance of the RNN model. Although our model uses these embeddings as the only features, it can be successfully used for Chinese chunking without any feature engineering efforts.

Keywords: Chinese chunking · Embeddings
Recurrent neural networks · Conditional Random Fields

1 Introduction

Syntactic chunking is also called shallow parsing, and it aims to divide a text into syntactically correlated non-overlapping chunks [1]. Most previous work formalized Chinese chunking as a sequence labeling problem. Various machine learning algorithms, such as Conditional Random Fields (CRFs) and Support Vector Machines (SVMs), have been applied to this task and achieve promising results [14,15].

The rapid development of deep learning for natural language processing [9,10,12,18] brings hope for possibly alleviating the problem of manual feature efforts. Different from the traditional one-hot representation, it provides a different approach that automatically learns latent features as distributed dense vectors. Neural networks, including non-linear feed-forward networks and recurrent neural networks (RNNs) [5], can learn feature representation and capture semantic information for natural language.

J.-F. Hong et al. (Eds.): CLSW 2018, LNAI 11173, pp. 570–579, 2018.
https://doi.org/10.1007/978-3-030-04015-4_49

In this paper, we propose a recurrent neural network architecture based on multi-perspective embeddings for Chinese chunking. Our neural network method can be successfully used for this task without any hand-crafted features. On one hand, to capture character information of words, we used an attention model to encode a word into its character-level representation. On the other hand, the part-of-speech (POS) information of words helps Chinese chunking, and we used POS embeddings to represent POS information. We combined the character-level representation, POS embeddings and word embeddings, and then fed them into the RNN layer as the input features. On top of the neural network architecture, we used a CRF layer to jointly decode labels for the whole sentence.

We evaluated our model through two commonly used data sets - CTB4 and CTB6. Experimental results show that the character-level representation and POS embeddings both can improve the performance of the RNN model. Although our model uses character embeddings, POS embeddings and word embeddings as the only features, the bidirectional gated RNN model achieves comparable performance for Chinese chunking.

2 Related Work

Chunking research started with English, with the CoNLL-2000 organizing a shared task for system comparison [16]. The data set used for English chunking was automatically generated from the Penn Treebank. Most previous work modeled chunking as a sequence labeling problem. Classification models, including SVMs [6] and other classifiers [19], have been applied to English chunking. Kudo and Matsumoto [7] combined multiple SVMs classifiers and achieved the best performance in the CoNLL-2000 shared task. Sequence labeling models, such as CRFs, were also widely used for chunking, and gave state-of-the-art results [13].

Similar approaches, including SVMs and CRFs, were also applied to Chinese chunking [14,15]. Chen et al. [2] used CTB4 as a standard benchmark to compare the performances of several state-of-the-art models for Chinese chunking, and proposed ensemble voting methods to improve the performance.

Most previous work performed chunking with hand-designed features. Zhou et al. [20] utilized rich features for Chinese chunking and achieved state-of-the-art performance. This system designed almost 30 feature templates, including chunk-level features. Most of their features are based on words within chunks, such as the first word and the last word of the chunk. Lyu et al. [11] performed character-level Chinese chunking. The character-level chunking system was based on the transition-based framework and performed word segmentation, POS tagging and chunking jointly. The success of these chunking systems largely depend on manually designed features.

3 Methods

3.1 Overall Architecture

Figure 1 illustrates the overall architecture of our approach. Given an input sentence, an attention model is used to compute the character-level representation of the word based on the character embeddings. Then we combine the character representation, POS embeddings and word embeddings to get the feature representation of each word in the sentence.

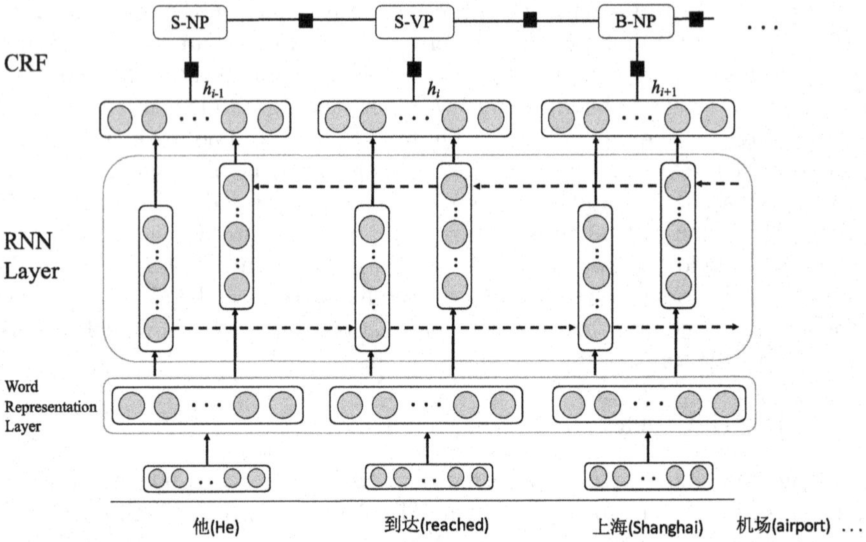

Fig. 1. The overall architecture of our model.

The extracted features of each word are then passed through the RNN hidden layer, which is designed to combine the local and contextual information of a word. The bidirectional RNN can be also used in this layer. A nonlinear hidden layer f_1 follows to form more complex features automatically. Finally, the output vectors of the neural network are fed into a CRF layer.

3.2 Input Layer

Given an input sentence s as an ordered list of m words $\{w_1, w_2 \ldots w_m\}$, the input representation $\boldsymbol{x}$ of the RNN layer is computed based on the character embeddings, POS embeddings and word embeddings.

To obtain the character representation of the word w_i, we denote the character sequence of w_i with $\{c_1, c_2 \ldots c_n\}$, where c_j is the jth character. The character embedding lookup table function $\boldsymbol{e}_c$ is used to map each character c_j into its character embedding $\boldsymbol{e}_c^j$. Then we use an attention model to combine the character embeddings $\{\boldsymbol{e}_c^1, \boldsymbol{e}_c^2 \ldots \boldsymbol{e}_c^n\}$ for w_i. In this model, $\boldsymbol{R}_c^i = \sum_{j=1}^{n} a_c^j \odot \boldsymbol{e}_c^j$, where $\boldsymbol{R}_c^i$ is the character representation of w_i, a_c^j is the weight for $\boldsymbol{e}_c^j$, $\odot$ is the Hadamard product function and $\sum_{j=1}^{n} a_c^j = 1$.

Each a_c^j is computed based on both the word embedding of the current word w_i and the representation of characters around the current character $\boldsymbol{e}_c^j$.

$$\boldsymbol{h}_c^j = tan(W_c(\boldsymbol{e}_c^{j-2} \oplus \boldsymbol{e}_c^{j-1} \oplus \boldsymbol{e}_c^j \oplus \boldsymbol{e}_c^{j+1} \oplus \boldsymbol{e}_c^{j+2}) + b_c) \quad (1)$$

$$t_c^j = exp(W_t \boldsymbol{h}_c^j + U_t \boldsymbol{e}_w^i + b_t) \tag{2}$$

$$a_c^j = \frac{t_c^j}{\sum_{j=1}^{n} t_c^j} \tag{3}$$

where $\oplus$ is the vector concatenation function and $\boldsymbol{e}_w^i$ is the embedding of the current word w_i. W_c, W_t, U_t, b_c and b_t are mode parameters.

The word embedding lookup table function is used to map each word into its word embedding $\boldsymbol{e}_w^i$, and the POS embedding lookup table function is used to map the POS of each word into its POS embedding $\boldsymbol{e}_p^i$. Then we combine the character representation $\boldsymbol{R}_c^i$, POS embedding $\boldsymbol{e}_p^i$ and word embedding $\boldsymbol{e}_w^i$ to form the representation $\boldsymbol{R}^i$: $\boldsymbol{R}^i = \boldsymbol{R}_c^i \oplus \boldsymbol{e}_p^i \oplus \boldsymbol{e}_w^i$.

Finally, the input representation $\boldsymbol{x}$ of the RNN layer is computed by a window function: $\boldsymbol{x}_i = \boldsymbol{R}_{i-2} \oplus \boldsymbol{R}_{i-1} \oplus \boldsymbol{R}_i \oplus \boldsymbol{R}_{i+1} \oplus \boldsymbol{R}_{i+2}$.

3.3 Recurrent Neural Networks

The RNNs in this section are neural networks, which have recurrent connections and allow a form of memory. The Elman-type RNN computes compositional vector representations for the input word sequences. These representations are then used as features to predict the label of each token in the sentence.

Although Elman-type RNN can, in principle, model long range dependencies, training them is difficult in practice, likely due to the vanishing and exploding gradient problem.

In this paper, we can also apply Gated RNN (GRNN) to this task. GRNN is an extension of the Elman-type RNN, and the recurrent layer in GRNN is constituted with the gated recurrent units (GRUs) [3]. The GRU processes inputs with update gate and input gate. Similar to the long short-term memory (LSTM) unit, the GRU has been shown to be able to capture long range dependencies. Compared with the LSTM, the Gated RNN does not have a separate cell, and is much simpler to compute.

The hidden state in RNNs at time t only captures information from the past. However, both past (left) and future (right) information can be beneficial for our task. To incorporate the future and past information, we use bidirectional RNNs in our framework. We combine the features from the forward and backward RNNs by a hidden layer f_1. The final output h_t is computed as follows:

$$h_t = tanh(W_f[\overrightarrow{h_t}; \overleftarrow{h_t}] + b_f) \tag{4}$$

where $\overrightarrow{h_t}$ is the forward RNN and $\overleftarrow{h_t}$ is the backward RNN. W_f and b_f denote the weight matrix and bias vector in the hidden layer f_1.

The output feature representation h_t is then fed into the CRF layer. For a given input sentence, we model the chunking label sequence jointly using a CRF [8], considering the correlations between labels in neighborhoods.

3.4 Training

We use max likelihood objective to train our model. Given the training examples set $\mathcal{B}$, the log-likelihood objective function is defined as:

$$L(\Theta) = \frac{1}{|\mathcal{B}|} \sum_{(x_n, y_n) \in \mathcal{B}} logP(y_n|x_n) + \frac{\lambda}{2} \parallel \Theta \parallel^2 \tag{5}$$

where Θ is the set of model parameters, $logP(y_n|x_n)$ is the log probability of y_n and λ is a regularization parameter.

To maximum the objective, we use online learning to train our model, and the AdaGrad algorithm [4] is used to update the model parameters. The parameter update at time t for the j-th parameter $\theta_{j,t}$ is defined as follows:

$$\theta_{j,t} = \theta_{j,t-1} - \frac{\alpha}{\sqrt{\sum_{\tau=1}^{t} g_{j,\tau}^2}} g_{j,t} \tag{6}$$

where α is the initial learning rate, and $g_{j,\tau}$ is the subgradient for the j-th parameter at time τ.

4 Experiments

4.1 Experimental Settings

Data. Unlike English chunking, there is not a most commonly used benchmark corpus for Chinese chunking. We follow Chen et al. [2] in dataset selection and chunk type definition. The chunking corpus can be extracted from CTB4 with a public tool. We conducted our experiments on the CTB4 corpus following previous studies on Chinese chunking [2,20]. We split the corpus according to previous work, using files (FID from 301–325) from the training set as the development set from the training set. In addition, we also conducted experiments on CTB6 and split the corpus according to the official documentation. Table 1 shows the statistics of the two data sets.

Table 1. Statistics of the datasets.

	Training	Dev	Test
CTB4			
Sentences	9543	352	5290
Words	232079	6821	165857
CTB6			
Sentences	23418	2079	2795
Words	641366	59955	81576

Parameters. The pre-trained word embeddings were trained on Chinese Gigaword corpus (LDC2011T13). We used ZPar to segment the raw corpus and the word2vec tool [17] is used to train word embeddings.

Character embeddings and POS embeddings were randomly initialized with uniform samples from range $[0, 1]$ and we set the dimension of these embeddings to 30.

For each neural layer in our neural network model, parameters W and b were randomly initialized with uniform samples from $[-\sqrt{\frac{6}{nr+nc}}, +\sqrt{\frac{6}{nr+nc}}]$, where nr and nc are the number of rows and columns of W. The initial learning rate for AdaGrad was set to 0.01 and the regularization parameter was set to 10^{-8}.

We set the dimension of the single RNN hidden layer h_1 and the hidden layers f_1 to 100. Tuning the hidden layer sizes can not significantly impact the performance of our model.

Evaluation Metrics. We evaluated the results in the same way as the CONLL2000 shared task, using precision P and recall R. The F1 score is given by $F1 = 2PR/(P + R)$.

4.2 Main Results

Table 2 presents our results on the CTB4 and CTB6 data sets. The models used in the experiments include RNN, bidirectional RNN (BRNN), Gated RNN (GRNN) and bidirectional Gated RNN (BGRNN). Word embeddings are used in our experiments without fine-tuning.

Table 2. Results on the CTB4 and CTB6 data sets.

System	CTB4 (P/R/F1)	CTB6 (P/R/F1)
RNN	91.39/91.16/91.27	93.62/93.24/93.43
BRNN	91.75/91.52/91.63	94.14/93.39/93.76
GRNN	91.89/91.14/91.52	93.69/93.35/93.52
BGRNN	**91.91/91.61/91.76**	**94.26/93.54/93.90**

As shown in Table 2, the BGRNN model outperforms other models on both corpora. BGRNN outperforms RNN with the gains of 0.49% on CTB4 and 0.47% on CTB6.

When we compare the RNNs with their bidirectional counterparts, we can see that the bidirectional improves the performance. BGRNN significantly outperforms GRNN with the gains of 0.43% on CTB4 and 1.21% on CTB6. Compared with RNN, BRNN improves the F1 score with the gains of 0.36% on CTB4 and 0.33% on CTB6.

4.3 Effects of Character Representation

Figure 2 shows the effects of character representation in our RNN framework on both data sets. Character embeddings are randomly initialized and they are fine-tuned in our experiments.

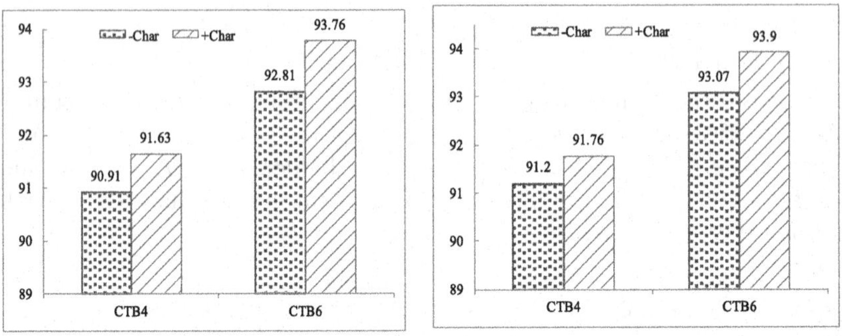

(a) BRNN. (b) BGRNN.

Fig. 2. Effects of character representation. +Char - with character representation; −Char - without character representation

As shown in Fig. 2, we observe an essential improvement on both data sets. Compared with the model without character representation, the model with character representation improves the F1 score with the gain of 0.72% on CTB4 and 0.95% on CTB6 by BRNN. It demonstrates the effectiveness of character representation for Chinese chunking.

4.4 Effects of POS Embeddings

Figure 3 shows the effects of POS embeddings in our models on both data sets. POS embeddings are randomly initialized and they are fine-tuned in our experiments.

As shown in Fig. 3, POS embeddings can improve the Chinese chunking performance on both data sets. Compared with the model without POS embeddings, the BGRNN model with POS embeddings improves the F1 score with the gain of 14.15% on CTB4 and 8.43% on CTB6.

4.5 Comparison with Previous Systems

Table 3 illustrates the results of our model on the CTB4 corpus, together with previous top performance systems for comparison. Chen et al. [2] compared the performance of some state-of-the-art machine learning models, including SVMs, CRFs, transformation-based learning and memory-based learning for Chinese chunking on the CTB4 corpus. Furthermore, they proposed ensemble voting methods to improve performance. The results of CRFs-based and SVMs-based

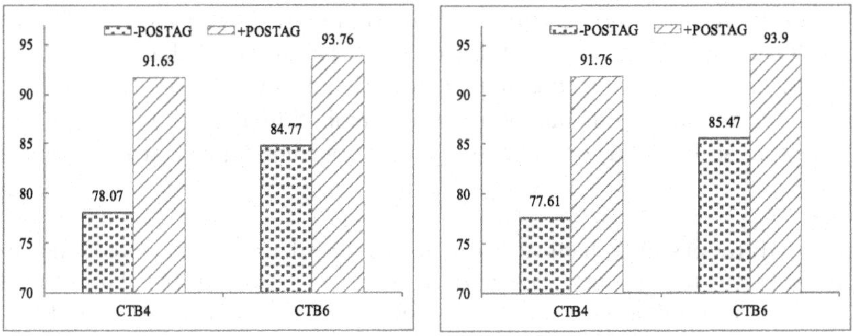

(a) BRNN. (b) BGRNN.

Fig. 3. Effects of POS embeddings. +POSTAG - with POS embeddings; −POSTAG - without POS embeddings

chunking systems are taken from Chen et al. [2]. Zhou et al. [20] utilized rich features for Chinese chunking and achieved state-of-the-art performance. The performance of these systems depends on manually extracted features.

Table 3. Results of our model on the CTB4 corpus, together with previous top performance systems

Method	P/R/F1
CRFs	91.47/90.01/90.74
SVMs	92.03/90.91/91.46
Voting [2]	92.40/90.97/91.68
Zhou [20]	**92.54/91.68/92.11**
BGRNN	**91.91/91.61/91.76**

As shown in Table 3, our BGRNN model outperforms other chunking systems, including SVMs, CRFs and Voting methods. Although our RNN-based models only use character representation, POS embeddings and word embeddings as input features, the BGRNN model achieves comparable performance for Chinese chunking without manual feature engineering.

5 Conclusions

In this paper, we present a multi-perspective embeddings based RNN framework for Chinese chunking. This framework utilizes a multi-perspective embeddings based method to get the input representation for the RNN layer, which is computed based on the character embeddings, POS embedding and word embeddings. On top of the RNN layer, we use a CRF layer to jointly decode labels for the whole sentence.

We evaluated our model through two commonly used copora - CTB4 and CTB6. Experimental results on both corpora demonstrate that character-level representation and POS embeddings can both improve the performance of the RNN model. Although our model uses these embeddings as the only features, it can be successfully used for Chinese chunking without any feature engineering efforts.

Acknowledgments. We thank all reviewers for their detailed comments. This work is supported by the Science and Technology Project of Guangzhou (No. 201704030002), the National Natural Science Foundation of China (No. 61772378, 61702121) and Humanities and Social Science Foundation of Ministry of Education of China (16YJCZH004).

References

1. Abney, S.P.: Parsing by chunks. In: Berwick, R.C., Abney, S.P., Tenny, C. (eds.) Principle-Based Parsing. SLAP, vol. 44, pp. 257–278. Springer, Dordrecht (1991). https://doi.org/10.1007/978-94-011-3474-3_10
2. Chen, W., Zhang, Y., Isahara, H.: An empirical study of Chinese chunking. In: Proceedings of the COLING/ACL on Main Conference Poster Sessions, pp. 97–104. Association for Computational Linguistics (2006)
3. Cho, K., van Merriënboer, B., Bahdanau, D., Bengio, Y.: On the properties of neural machine translation: encoder-decoder approaches. In: Syntax, Semantics and Structure in Statistical Translation, p. 103 (2014)
4. Duchi, J., Hazan, E., Singer, Y.: Adaptive subgradient methods for online learning and stochastic optimization. J. Mach. Learn. Res. **12**, 2121–2159 (2011)
5. Elman, J.L.: Finding structure in time. Cogn. Sci. **14**(2), 179–211 (1990)
6. Kudo, T., Matsumoto, Y.: Chunking with support vector machines. In: Proceedings of the Second Meeting of the North American Chapter of the Association for Computational Linguistics on Language technologies, pp. 1–8. Association for Computational Linguistics (2001)
7. Kudoh, T., Matsumoto, Y.: Use of support vector learning for chunk identification. In: Proceedings of the 2nd Workshop on Learning Language in Logic and the 4th Conference on Computational Natural Language Learning-Volume 7, pp. 142–144. Association for Computational Linguistics (2000)
8. Lafferty, J.D., McCallum, A., Pereira, F.C.N.: Conditional random fields: probabilistic models for segmenting and labeling sequence data. In: Proceedings of ICML 2001, pp. 282–289 (2001)
9. Lin, Y., Liu, Z., Sun, M.: Neural relation extraction with multi-lingual attention. In: Proceedings of the 55th Annual Meeting of the Association for Computational Linguistics (Volume 1: Long Papers), Vancouver, Canada, pp. 34–43. Association for Computational Linguistics, July 2017. http://aclweb.org/anthology/P17-1004
10. Lyu, C., Chen, B., Ren, Y., Ji, D.: Long short-term memory RNN for biomedical named entity recognition. BMC Bioinform. **18**(1), 462 (2017)
11. Lyu, C., Zhang, Y., Ji, D.: Joint word segmentation, POS-tagging and syntactic chunking. In: Proceedings of the Thirtieth AAAI Conference on Artificial Intelligence, pp. 3007–3014. AAAI Press (2016)

12. Mikolov, T., Sutskever, I., Chen, K., Corrado, G.S., Dean, J.: Distributed representations of words and phrases and their compositionality. In: Advances in Neural Information Processing Systems, pp. 3111–3119 (2013)
13. Sha, F., Pereira, F.: Shallow parsing with conditional random fields. In: Proceedings of the 2003 Conference of the North American Chapter of the Association for Computational Linguistics on Human Language Technology-Volume 1, pp. 134–141. Association for Computational Linguistics (2003)
14. Tan, Y., Yao, T., Chen, Q., Zhu, J.: Chinese chunk identification using SVMs plus sigmoid. In: Su, K.-Y., Tsujii, J., Lee, J.-H., Kwong, O.Y. (eds.) IJCNLP 2004. LNCS (LNAI), vol. 3248, pp. 527–536. Springer, Heidelberg (2005). https://doi.org/10.1007/978-3-540-30211-7_56
15. Tan, Y., Yao, T., Chen, Q., Zhu, J.: Applying conditional random fields to Chinese shallow parsing. In: Gelbukh, A. (ed.) CICLing 2005. LNCS, vol. 3406, pp. 167–176. Springer, Heidelberg (2005). https://doi.org/10.1007/978-3-540-30586-6_16
16. Tjong Kim Sang, E.F., Buchholz, S.: Introduction to the CoNLL-2000 shared task: chunking. In: Proceedings of the 2nd Workshop on Learning Language in Logic and the 4th Conference on Computational Natural Language Learning-Volume 7, pp. 127–132. Association for Computational Linguistics (2000)
17. Word2vec. https://code.google.com/archive/p/word2vec/. Accessed 5 Jan 2018
18. Zhang, M., Zhang, Y., Fu, G.: Transition-based neural word segmentation. In: Proceedings of the 54th Annual Meeting of the Association for Computational Linguistics (Volume 1: Long Papers), pp. 421–431. Association for Computational Linguistics, Berlin, August 2016. http://www.aclweb.org/anthology/P16-1040
19. Zhang, T., Damerau, F., Johnson, D.: Text chunking based on a generalization of winnow. J. Mach. Learn. Res. **2**, 615–637 (2002)
20. Zhou, J., Qu, W., Zhang, F.: Exploiting chunk-level features to improve phrase chunking. In: Proceedings of the 2012 Joint Conference on Empirical Methods in Natural Language Processing and Computational Natural Language Learning, pp. 557–567. Association for Computational Linguistics, Stroudsburg (2012)

Applying Chinese Semantic Collocation Knowledge to Semantic Error Reasoning

Yangsen Zhang(✉), Wenjie Wei, Ruoyu Chen, and Gaijuan Huang

Institute of Intelligent Information Processing, Beijing Information Science and Technology University, Beijing 100192, China
zhangyangsen@163.com, wei_wjl228@163.com, chenruoyu@bistu.edu.cn, huang_gj@163.com

Abstract. The knowledge of Chinese semantic collocation plays an important role in Chinese semantic understanding. Based on the investigation of the existing semantic collocation knowledge base, this article proposes a method of constructing the Chinese semantic collocation knowledge base which combines dependency parsing with HowNet. Based on the analysis of the existing semantic collocation relationship, the method extracts the collocation relation in the corpus by dependency parsing, and then the semantic information of the collocation knowledge base is generalized based on the sememe information in HowNet. A three-layer semantic collocation knowledge base is constructed. At the same time, based on the semantic collocation knowledge base, a Chinese semantic error detection algorithm is designed and implemented, and its effectiveness is verified by experiments. The semantic collocation knowledge base based on dependency parsing and HowNet is less dependent on word distance and can better deal with the long-distance semantic collocation in text.

Keywords: Chinese semantic collocation knowledge base · Text error detection · HowNet · Dependency parsing · Chinese semantic error reasoning

1 Introduction

The knowledge base of Chinese semantic collocation is the basis of studying text semantic, and its application field is very broad. It is mainly used in information retrieval, machine translation, text proofreading and other fields.

In the field of information retrieval, the semantic relationship can reflect the degree of consistency between the user search words and the text to be checked, and the accuracy of information retrieval can be improved significantly by adding the semantic relationship analysis. Liu [1] used the TF-IDF algorithm to calculate the feature weights, and with the help of HowNet to analyze the semantic relationship between words, proposed a text similarity weighting algorithm based on HowNet semantic similarity, which considered the semantic relationship between feature items. It can effectively improve the accuracy of Chinese text classification; In the field of machine translation, semantic relationship reflect the degree of mutual substitution between words in the text. Deng [2] constructed a Bayesian word sense disambiguation

J.-F. Hong et al. (Eds.): CLSW 2018, LNAI 11173, pp. 580–591, 2018.
https://doi.org/10.1007/978-3-030-04015-4_50

classifier based on semantic information and applied it to machine translation to improve the accuracy of translation. In the field of Chinese text proofreading, Chinese text proofreading is different from English text proofreading because of its inherent characteristics. Chinese text proofreading is an analytical process based on three levels of word, grammar and semantics. The study of word and grammatical level has been more adequate, and good results have been achieved [3–7]. But there are still a lot of semantic level errors in the Chinese text, such as: "他那崇高的革命品质经常浮现在我的脑海中."(His lofty revolutionary quality often emerges in my mind.), in which the collocation of subject "品质"(quality) and the predicate "浮现"(emerges) does not conform to semantic norms. So far, there has been no mature solution to such error that the words in Chinese text are correct, the syntactic structure is complete, but does not conform to the semantic collocation criterion at the semantic level. Therefore, in this article, a Chinese semantic collocation knowledge base is constructed, based on which the computer can detect semantic collocation errors in Chinese text just like humans.

2 Related Work

At present, there are three methods for extracting collocation pairs as follows: (1) the method based on extraction rules; (2) the method based on statistics; (3) the method of combining rule and statistics. Most of the studies are mainly based on statistical methods, and combined with grammar, syntactic rules or semantic knowledge of linguistics to filter the extracted collocations.

Guan [8] adopted a rule-based extraction method when constructing the word collocation knowledge base, put forward seven kinds of specific rules from three aspects of following Verb-Noun, Noun-Verb and Adjective-Noun, to construct the knowledge base of collocation of words. Quan [9] proposed a method for automatically obtaining collocation based on statistical model. This method is divided into two steps: the first step is to extract the candidate set of collocation from the corpus, the second step is to select candidate words with a certain collocation strength by using six statistical indexes: word frequency statistics, average and variance, mutual information, cubic mutual information, hypothesis test and cost criteria. Fan [10], aiming at the problem of domain term extraction, proposed an algorithm for extracting domain terms and constructed a corresponding extraction system from the angle of lexical degree and domain degree by using the method of combining rules with various statistical strategies.

Xu [11] proposed a method to construct the word relevance semantic database based on vector space model. When constructing the semantic database, various factors that influence the semantic relations between words such as the co-occurrence frequency, the average appearance distance, the information entropy and the single character semantic information are considered. A large number of corpus texts are iteratively learned, and the elimination algorithm is introduced in the learning process. Liang [12] first encoded semantic knowledge with the help of Tongyici Cilin (A Dictionary of Synonyms), defined the coding form of semantic collocation, and use this coding method to assign the appropriate semantic class to the node words instance in the two-words collocation knowledge base. Then the collocation words in the collocation instance are assigned appropriate semantic classes. Finally, the final semantic collocation knowledge base is obtained by merging and counting all the semantic collocations. The methods proposed in the above literatures cannot detect long distance semantic collocation errors. Therefore, this article proposes a method to construct the knowledge base of Chinese semantic collocation, which combines dependency parsing with HowNet. The method is less dependent on the distance of words, and the knowledge base can be used to analyze the semantic collocation of long distance words in the text.

3 Construction of Chinese Semantic Collocation Knowledge Base

The construction of Chinese semantic collocation knowledge base needs to be considered from two angles of word structure information and semantic information. The corresponding collocation pairs are extracted by using the structural information between words, and the semantic information between words is used to generalize the collocation of words on the basis of collocation of words, so as to realize the expansion of collocation of words at the semantic level. In this article, the dependency tree library is used to extract the structural information of words, and the semantic information of collocation is extended based on HowNet knowledge base.

3.1 Analysis of Semantic Collocation Relationship Between Words

According to the relevant theories of word collocation in linguistics and the analysis of common error text information in large-scale corpus, we find that the common types of semantic collocation errors which are as follows:

(1) **Subject-predicate mismatches**

Example 1: 石头吃了一个面包. (The stone ate a loaf of bread.)

Analysis: the subject "石头" (stone) and the predicate "吃" (eat) do not match

(2) **Verb-object mismatches**

There are two kinds of cases: ① the verb is in front and the object is behind; ② the object is in front, while the verb is in the back, it is also called the pre-object relation.

Example 2: 他戴着靴子出门了. (He went out wearing his boots.)

Analysis: This is a normal verb-object collocation, where the verb "戴" (wear) and object "靴子" (boots) mismatches.

Example 3: 他什么饭都喝. (He can drink whatever bread.)

Analysis: In this case, the object "饭" (bread) is put in front of the verb "喝" (drink), but the verb "喝" (drink) and the object "饭" (bread) are mismatched.

(3) **Subject-object mismatches**

Example 4: 该厂狠抓生产质量，重视企业文化，十几年来培养了一批技术骨干， 所生产的内衣产量成为全国同行业销售额率先突破十亿大关的一个著名品牌. (The factory pays close attention to the quality of production and attaches great importance to corporate culture. Over the past decade, it has trained a group of technical backbones. The output of underwear produced by the factory has become a famous brand in the same industry.)

Analysis: The subject "产量" (output) and the object "品牌" (brand) do not match

(4) **Modifier-headword mismatches**

There are three main cases of improper collocation of modifier-headword: ① attributive-headword mismatches; ② adverbial-headword mismatches; ③ headword-complement mismatches.

Example 5: 自己有双聪明的手, 什么都能造出来. (He has a pair of clever hands and can make anything.)

Analysis: This kind belongs to attributive-headword collocation is improper, among them attributive "聪明" (clever) and headword "手" (hand) collocation is improper.

Example 6: 菲戈射门射得很正确. (Figo shot the ball right.)

Analysis: This belongs mismatch of headword-complement, in which the verb "射" (shoot) and the adjective "正确" (right) are mismatched, so the word "正确" (right) should be changed to "准确" (accuracy).

3.2 The Collocation Extraction of Words Based on Dependency Tree Library

Based on the analysis of the common dependency relationship between words, we adopt the syntactic analysis function of the language cloud developed by Harbin Institute of Technology and 863 standard Part-of-speech (POS) set, make a syntactic analysis to the corpus of the people's daily, extract the POS information, dependency relationship of each sentence in the corpus, and build the dependency tree library of the corpus. For example, for the sentence "这位饱经风霜的老人将出现在体育馆" (The weather-beaten old man will appear in the gymnasium), its dependency syntactic analysis graph is shown in Fig. 1.

(1) POS and location tagging.

[1]这/r [2]位/q [3]饱经风霜/I [4]的/u [5]老人/n [6]将/d [7]出现/v [8]在/p [9]体育馆/n [10] 。/wp

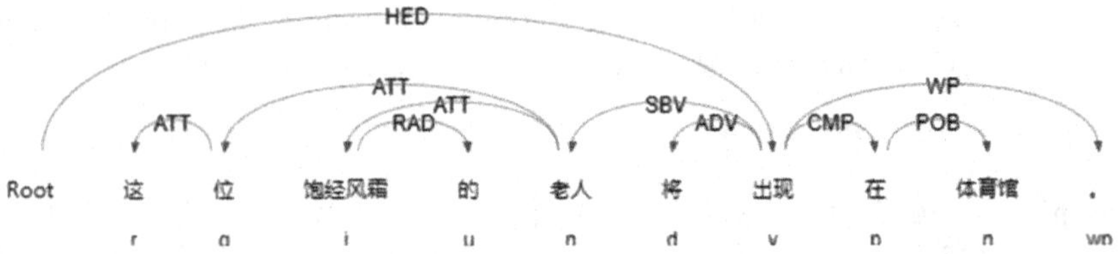

Fig. 1. The dependency syntactic analysis graph. In the Fig. 1, r, q, i etc. are POS information. HED, ATT etc. are dependence relationship.

(2) Dependency relationship analysis results.

Root→出现(HED)	[1] 这← [2] 位(ATT)	[2] 位← [5] 老人(ATT)
[3] 饱经风霜→ [5] 老人(ATT)	[4] 的← [3] 饱经风霜(RAD)	[5] 老人← [7] 出现(SBV)
[6] 将← [7] 出现(ADV)	[7] 出现→ [8] 在(CMP)	[8] 在→ [9] 体育场(POB)

Among which:
HED represents the core relationship; ATT represents the attributive-headword relationship; RAD represents the right adjunct relationship; SBV represents the subject-verb relationship; ADV represents the adverbial-headword structure; CMP represents the verb-complement structure; POB represents the preposition-object relationship.

The dependency tree library describes the dependencies collocation relationship in the sentences. In this article, XML is used to store the dependency collocations. The specific storing format is shown in Table 1.

Table 1. Dependency tree library storing sample

```
<sent id="0" cont="这位饱经风霜的老人将出现在体育馆。">
<word id="0" cont="这" pos="r" parent="1" relate="ATT" >
<word id="1" cont="位" pos="q" parent="4" relate="ATT" >
<word id="2" cont="饱经风霜" pos="i" parent="4" relate="ATT">
<word id="3" cont="的" pos="u" parent="2" relate="RAD">
<word id="4" cont="老人" pos="n" parent="6" relate="SBV">
<word id="5" cont="将" pos="d" parent="6" relate="ADV">
<word id="6" cont="出现" pos="v" parent="-1" relate="HED">
<word id="7" cont="在" pos="p" parent="6" relate="CMP">
<word id="8" cont="体育馆" pos="n" parent="7" relate="POB">
<word id="9" cont="。" pos="wp" parent="6" relate="WP">
</sent>
```

In this sample of dependency collocations storage, each word gives the ID of its parent node, such as the parent node ID of the word “饱经风霜” (weather-beaten) is 4. The word for ID = 4 is “老人” (old man), therefore, “饱经风霜” (weather-beaten) and “老人” (old man) has the dependency relationship.

3.3 Construction of Word Collocation Knowledge Base

In this article, the word semantic collocation knowledge base is divided into four sub-libraries: subject-predicate collocation knowledge base, verb-object collocation knowledge base, subject-object collocation knowledge base and modifier-headword collocation knowledge base. The construction methods of each sub-library are as follows:

(1) **Construction of subject-predicate collocation knowledge base**

After syntactic analysis, the subject-predicate relationship has been marked in the syntax analysis tree, so only the subject- predicate relationship in the parse tree need to be extracted and stored in the SBV library.

(2) **Construction of verb-object collocation knowledge base**

The two cases of the verb-object relationship are also marked in the syntactic parse tree, so only the verb-object relationship and the pre-object relationship in the parse tree need to be extracted and stored in the VOB library.

(3) **Construction of subject-object collocation knowledge base**

Since there is no subject-dependent collocation relationship in the syntactic parse tree, further extraction is needed with the help of correlation relations. The specific extraction steps are as follows:

Step1: first find the subject-predicate collocation relationship, assign the subject to N1, assign the predicate to S, and turn to Step2.
Step2: if there is a verb-object collocation relationship with S as a verb, assign the object to N2 and turn to Step3. Otherwise, stop.
Step3: store N1 + N2 as the subject-object collocation into the SOB library, stop.

(4) **Construction of modifier-headword collocation knowledge base**

There are three cases between modifier-headword, which correspond to ATT, ADV and CMP, which only need to be extracted from syntactic parse tree and store them into MOC library.

3.4 Extraction of Semantic Information of Words

Because of the limitation of the size and domain of the corpus, the collocations of words constructed have great limitations, and it is difficult to express all the linguistic phenomena. In this article, we use HowNet to generalize the word collocation knowledge base. In HowNet, we define the sememe as the most basic, non-divisible, the smallest semantic unit, and all the concepts can be expressed as sememe. That is to say, the finite sememe set is used to describe the relationship between concepts, and between attributes of concepts, which coincides with the generalization of collocation, finite sememe collocations are used to represent infinite word collocations. Therefore, we use HowNet to transform word collocations into corresponding sememe collocations, but not all word collocations can be converted into sememe collocations in the process of generalization. If all words are translated into their sememe without restriction, it will lead to some wrong collocations. In order to solve this problem, we use the index of *limited divergence*, which is defined as follows:

Definition 1: The ratio of the number of words which has same sememe with the word i and collocated with the word j and the number of all words which have the same sememe with the word i, known as the *limiting divergence*, was denoted as W, and the formula for the *limiting divergence* is as shown in formulas (1) and (2):

$$W = \frac{\sum_{i=1}^{n} F_{ij}}{SUM_i} \tag{1}$$

$$F_{ij} = \begin{cases} 1 & \text{j is collocation word and the sememe is same as } i \\ 0 & \text{Other cases} \end{cases} \tag{2}$$

Where word i is the translated word,j is the collocation word, W is the *limiting divergence* and SUM_i is the total number of words which have the same sememe with word i in the semantic collocation knowledge base, $\sum_{i=1}^{n} F_{ij}$ is the total number of words which has same sememe with word i and collocated with word j. If $W = 1$, It is proved that all the words which have same sememe with word i can be matched with word j; The closer the W value approaches 1, the higher the accuracy of using the semantic collocation to replace the word collocation; Conversely, most of the words whose sememe same as word i cannot be collocated with word j.

3.5 Construction of Word Semantic Collocation Knowledge Base

(1) Construction of semi-sememe collocation knowledge base

The semi-sememe collocation knowledge base is constructed by transforming one word in the collocation pair into a sememe and then forming a new collocation with the other word. The following is illustrated by taking verb-object collocation as an example: First, take the verb as the transformation word and the object as the collocation word to carry on the semi-sememe transformation. Then the *limiting divergence* W is calculated according to the formulas of (1) and (2), and if W > α, it is transformed into semi-sememe collocation. Through relevant experiments, when α is 0.12, the best result is obtained. Another three semi-sememe collocation knowledge bases are constructed by the same method.

(2) Construction of all-sememe collocation knowledge base

Since the semi-sememe collocation has already transformed one of the words into the sememe, it only needs to transform the other word, that is to say, the words that have been transformed into the sememe is regarded as collocation word, the untransformed word is used as the transformed word, and α is also chosen as the threshold, transform into a collocation library at the all-sememe level.

In order to reduce the redundancy of the knowledge base, the collocation that has been transformed into the all-sememe and semi-sememe is deleted from the semi-sememe and word collocation knowledge base respectively, then the final semantic knowledge base is obtained. The structure of the final semantic collocation knowledge base is shown in Fig. 2.

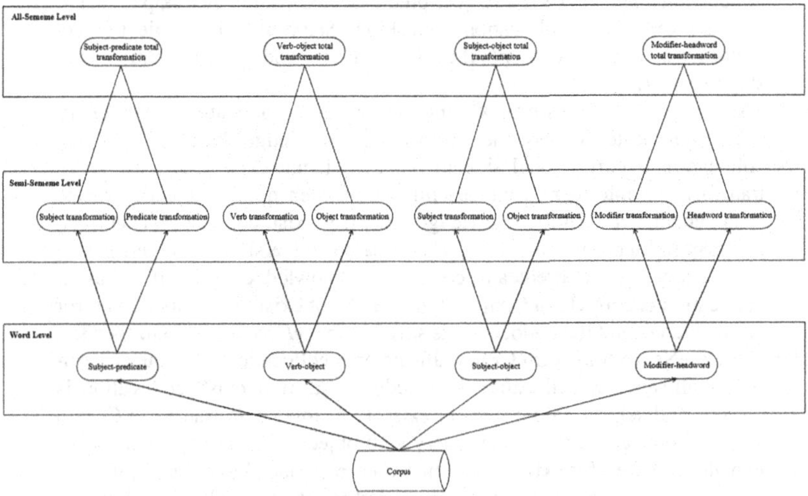

Fig. 2. Architecture of collocation knowledge Base.

4 Appling Semantic Collocation Knowledge Base to Semantic Error Reasoning

4.1 Semantic Error Reasoning Based on Semantic Collocation Knowledge Base

Semantic errors refer to the errors that are correct in the word representation and complete in the syntactic structure, but do not conform to the semantic collocation norms at the semantic level. The common types of errors are shown in the correlation analysis in Sect. 3.1. For these problems, most researchers built semantic collocation knowledge base through rules and statistics. However, it is found that this method does not consider the semantic limitation between words.

In order to solve the above problems, a semantic collocation error reasoning algorithm is constructed based on the three-layer semantic collocation knowledge base. The specific algorithm process is described as follows:

Input: Text to be proofread *T*, Semantic Collocation Knowledge Base.
Output: Proofreading results.

Step1: Call the Harbin Institute of Technology working language cloud platform to carry out syntactic analysis for the text *T*;

Step2: Obtain the collocations of subject-predicate, verb-object, subject-object and modifier-headword, then put them in collocation list *L*;

Step3: Scan list *L*, if empty, skip to Step8; otherwise, scan the list *L* to get a collocation pair Ci, if Ci is a subject-predicate collocation, then skip to Step4, if Ci is a verb-object collocation, then skip to Step5, if Ci is a subject-object collocation, then skip to Step6, if Ci is a modifier-headword collocation, then skip to Step7;

Step4: Use HowNet to transform Ci into all-sememe collocation, then query subject-predicate all-sememe collocation knowledge base, if it exist, collocation is correct, and skip to Step3; if it not exist, Use HowNet to transform Ci into semi-sememe collocation, then query subject-predicate semi-sememe collocation knowledge base, if it exist, collocation is correct, and skip to Step3; if it not exist, The sememe conversion is not performed, then query subject-predicate collocation knowledge base, if it exist, collocation is correct, and skip to Step3; If it not exist, the collocation error is considered, and the collocation is saved to the *wL* list and skip to Step3;

Step5: Use HowNet to transform Ci into all-sememe collocation, then query verb-object all-sememe collocation knowledge base, if it exist, collocation is correct, and skip to Step3; if it not exist, Use HowNet to transform Ci into semi-sememe collocation, then query verb-object semi-sememe collocation knowledge base, if it exist, collocation is correct, and skip to Step3; if it not exist, The sememe conversion is not performed, then query verb-object collocation knowledge base, if it exist, collocation is correct, and skip to Step3; If it not exist, the collocation error is considered, and the collocation is saved to the *wL* list and skip to Step3;

Step6: Use HowNet to transform Ci into all-sememe collocation, then query subject-object all-sememe collocation knowledge base, if it exist, collocation is correct, and skip to Step3; if it not exist, Use HowNet to transform Ci into semi-sememe collocation, then query subject-object semi-sememe collocation knowledge base, if it exist, collocation is correct, and skip to Step3; if it not exist, The sememe conversion is not performed, then query subject-object collocation knowledge base, if it exist, collocation is correct, and skip to Step3; If it not exist, the collocation error is considered, and the collocation is saved to the *wL* list and skip to Step3;

Step7: Use HowNet to transform Ci into all-sememe collocation, then query modifier-headword all-sememe collocation knowledge base, if it exist, collocation is correct, and skip to Step3; if it not exist, Use HowNet to transform Ci into semi-sememe collocation, then query modifier-headword semi-sememe collocation knowledge base, if it exist, collocation is correct, and skip to Step3; if it not exist, The sememe conversion is not performed, then query modifier-headword collocation knowledge base, if it exist, collocation is correct, and skip to Step3; If it not exist, the collocation error is considered, and the collocation is saved to the *wL* list and skip to Step3;

Step8: Read out *wL* in turn and mark red in proofread text according to position information, and stop;

4.2 Semantic Error Reasoning Experiment Results and Analysis

In order to verify the semantic collocation knowledge base constructed in this article and its role in the semantic error reasoning, we use Java to implement semantic error reasoning algorithm on the eclipse development tool.

There are no public data sets for semantic collocation error detection in this field, therefore the researchers build their own test sets. This paper collects 200 incorrect-sentence revision questions for primary and secondary school and 10 essays for primary school as a test set which contains 230 semantic collocation errors. The focus of this article is to introduce construction method of Chinese semantic collocation knowledge base, while semantic collocation errors reasoning is only used to verify the validity of the constructed semantic collocation knowledge base. Therefore, this article does not in-depth research on semantic error detection algorithm, and the relevant study of semantic error detection algorithms can be found in the article published by the author in the journal of computer science [13]. In literature [13], we obtain a recall ratio of 93.3% and accuracy of 83.3% in semantic error detection. The error reasoning detection algorithm adopted in this article is relatively simple, as described in Sect. 4.1, recall rate, accuracy rate and F1 value of corresponding experiments are shown in Table 2.

Table 2. Experimental results of semantic error detection

Total number of actual errors	Total number of detected errors	The real number of errors	Recall	Accuracy rate	F1 measure
230	270	206	89.57%	76.30%	82.32%

It can be seen from the above experiment that the semantic collocation knowledge base constructed in this article is very effective. The experimental results of semantic error reasoning are not as good as those given in literature [13], because this article emphasizes the construction method of the semantic collocation knowledge base and does not in-depth research on semantic error detection algorithm, also does not take into account the relevant semantic context knowledge, meanwhile the selected corpus is small in scale (about 13 million the People's Daily corpus) which mainly relates to politics, so the experimental results can validate the effectiveness of the method in this article. The following are some examples of the experiments in this article:

Example 7: 我们戴着太阳好不好?(Shall we wear the sun?)

Analysis: In this case, the predicate "戴" (wear) and the object "太阳" (sun) are mismatched. Errors similar to this case can be detected correctly using the semantic error inference algorithm designed in this article. However, as for the semantic collocation errors that need to be detected in combination with specific context, this article has not conducted in-depth research, so it may not be detected, just as shown in Example 8.

Example 8: 同学们选我当班长是对自己的信任. (The students chose me as monitor because of their trust in themselves.)

Analysis: This sentence has the former context setting that "classmates chose me as the monitor", then it must be trust in me rather than themselves. However, this system does not consider the context, so the semantic collocation error in this sentence is not detected.

Although this article is unable to detect the context-related semantic errors, it have a good effect on the collocation errors with long intervals of words, just as shown in Example 9.

Example 9: 现在我又看到了那阔别多年的乡亲、那我从小就住惯了的山区特有的石头和茅草搭成的小屋、那崎岖的街道、那熟悉的可爱的乡音. (Now I have seen the folks who have been away for many years, the unique stone and thatched cottages that I used to live in when I was a child, the rugged streets, familiar and lovely local accents.)

Analysis: For such a long sentence, the existing research methods are difficulty to detect its semantic collocation errors, however, in this article, based on the dependency syntactic, using dependency parsing can get a result that there is a parallel relationship between "小屋" (cottages), "街道" (streets) and "乡音" (accents). Because "看" (seen) and "小屋" (cottages) have verb-object relationship, we can infer that "看" (seen) and "乡音" (accents) also have verb-object relationship. Therefore, using the semantic collocation knowledge base constructed in this article, we can detect that "看" (seen) and "乡音" (accents) are mismatched.

The above results show that the semantic collocation knowledge base constructed in this article is effective and can be used as a reference for semantic error inference.

5 Conclusion

Based on dependency syntax and HowNet, this article detailly introduced the method of constructing a three-layer Chinese semantic collocation knowledge base, applied it to the reasoning of Chinese semantic error, and good results have been achieved. However, due to the fact that syntactic analysis and HowNet knowledge base are unable to analyze specific context and domains, it may lead to poor effect in dealing with some problems based on specific context and domains. In the later study, we will try to add context analysis module and domain analysis module in language analysis process, and establish various contextual and domain knowledge bases, so that the computer can act as human to take into account contextual and domain factors and then implement semantic inference based on context and domain analysis.

Acknowledgements. This work was supported by grants from National Nature Science Foundation of China (No.61772081), Science and Technology Development Project of Beijing Municipal Education Commission (No. KM201711232014, No. KM201711232022).

References

1. Liu, H.L., Du, K., Qing, C.X.: Research on Chinese text categorization based on semantic similarity of HowNet. New Technol. Libr. Inf. Serv. **31**(2), 39–45 (2015). (in Chinese)
2. Deng, L.: Chinese Word Sense Disambiguation Based on Semantic. Harbin University of Science and Technology (2015). (in Chinese)
3. Yeh, J.F., Chen, W.Y., Su, M.C.: Chinese spelling checker based on an inverted index list with a rescoring mechanism. ACM Trans. Asian Low-Resour. Lang. Inf. Process. **14**(4), 1–28 (2015). https://doi.org/10.1145/2826235
4. Liu, L.L., Cao, C.Y.: Chinese real-word error automatic proofreading based on combining of local context features. Sci. J. Comput. Sci. **43**(12), 30–35 (2016). (in Chinese)
5. Xiong, J., Zhang, Q., Hou, J., et al.: Extended HMM and ranking models for Chinese spelling correction. In: Cips-Sighan Joint Conference on Chinese Language Processing, pp. 133–138 (2014)
6. Zhang, Y.S., Cao, Y.D.: A hybrid model of combining rule-based and statistics-based approaches for automatic detecting errors in Chinese text. J. Chin. Inf. Process. **20**(4), 1–9 (2006)
7. Liu, X., Cheng, F., Duh, K., et al.: A hybrid ranking approach to Chinese spelling check. ACM Trans. Asian Low-Resour. Lang. Inf. Process. **14**(4), 16 (2015). https://doi.org/10.1145/2822264
8. Guan, J., Xie, W., Zhang, Y.S.: Construction and application of semantic collocation knowledge base based on multiple knowledge bases. J. Comput. Eng. Des. **34**(6), 2136–2140 (2013). https://doi.org/10.3969/j.issn.1000-7024.2013.06.045. (in Chinese)
9. Quan, C.Q., Liu, H., He, T.T.: Analysis and comparison about the approaches of collocation retrieval based on statistical model. J. Appl. Res. Comput. **22**(9), 55–57 (2005). https://doi.org/10.3969/j.issn.1001-3695.2005.09.017. (in Chinese)
10. Fan, M.J., Zhang, Y.S., Duan, D.S.: Domain-specific terms extraction algorithm research based on combination of statistics and rules. J. Appl. Res. Comput. **33**(8), 2282–2285 (2016). https://doi.org/10.3969/j.issn.1001-3695.2016.08.009. (in Chinese)
11. Xu, N.X., Zou, H.M.: Constructing semantic library to reflect word interrelationship. J. Shanghai Jiaotong Univ. **42**(7), 1129–1132 (2008). (in Chinese)
12. Liang, W.J., Zheng, F.B., Du, Y.: Design and implementation of collocation repositories in Chinese intelligent input method based on grammar and semantics. J. Comput. Eng. Des. **30**(21), 5003–5006 (2009). https://doi.org/10.7666/d.y910703. (in Chinese)
13. Zhang, Y.S., Zheng, J.: Study of semantic error detecting method for Chinese text. Chin. J. Comput. **40**(4), 911–924 (2017). https://doi.org/10.11897/SP.J.1016.2017.00911. (in Chinese)

Resolution of Personal Pronoun Anaphora in Chinese Micro-blog

Yuanyuan Peng, Yangsen Zhang(✉), Shujing Huang, Ruoyu Chen, and Jianqing You

Institute of Intelligent Information Processing,
Beijing Information Science and Technology University, Beijing, China
pengyy0322@163.com, zhangyangsen@163.com,
479624895@qq.com, ruoyu-chen@foxmail.com,
yjq@bistu.edu.cn

Abstract. Anaphora resolution plays an important role in Chinese micro-blog information mining. Based on the linguistic features of personal pronouns in Chinese micro-blog texts, this paper proposes a multi-strategy method for the resolution of personal pronoun anaphora. Firstly, according to part of speech tagging and named entity recognition, personal pronouns and their candidate antecedents are extracted from Chinese micro-blog texts, and the rules for judging the consistency between a personal pronoun and its antecedents in grammar, semantics, gender and singular-plural are established. The antecedents which are inconsistent with the personal pronoun in these four aspects are preliminarily filtered, and Candidate Set 1 of antecedents is obtained. Then, SVM is used to classify the antecedents in Candidate Set 1, and the antecedents which have certain anaphoric relations with the current personal pronoun are selected to construct Candidate Set 2 of antecedents. Finally, by combination of the four linguistic characteristics of grammatical role, co-occurrence relation, reference distance and appositive dependency, the best antecedent is found out from Candidate Set 2 through the priority selection policy. At the same time, a strategy of extending antecedent is provided to solve the problem that the antecedent of the pronoun can't be found according to the above method. In this paper, the validity of the proposed method is verified by using NLPCC2013 micro-blog corpus as the experimental data set. The experimental results show that the F value of the proposed method is 91.7% in Chinese micro-blog texts.

Keywords: Anaphora resolution · Personal pronoun · Candidate antecedent SVM · Priority selection policy

1 Introduction

Anaphora is a common linguistic phenomenon in natural languages. In order to reduce redundancy and make contents coherent and clear, people use a large number of pronouns to connect discourses. However, these pronouns make it difficult for computers to process natural languages. So anaphora resolution has become an important

J.-F. Hong et al. (Eds.): CLSW 2018, LNAI 11173, pp. 592–605, 2018.
https://doi.org/10.1007/978-3-030-04015-4_51

task for natural language processing. In linguistics, the noun or the noun phrase referred to by a pronoun is called an antecedent. The purpose of anaphora resolution is to find the antecedents of pronouns.

There are many anaphoric phenomena in Chinese micro-blog texts, which have brought difficulties for the research works of topics detection, sentiment analysis, opinion leaders mining and personalized recommendation. Therefore, the anaphora resolution in micro-blog texts is important for the information mining of Chinese Micro-blog. There are many types of anaphora in Chinese, including personal pronoun anaphora, demonstrative pronoun anaphora, noun phrase anaphora, event anaphora and zero anaphora [1]. This paper focuses on the resolution of personal pronoun anaphora in Chinese micro-blog texts.

2 Related Work

Fan [2] was the earliest researcher of anaphora resolution in the Chinese text. He realized the resolution of pronoun anaphora in his human-machine dialogue system. At the same time, he pointed out that anaphora resolution was a thorny issue. Due to the lack of background knowledge, it was difficult for computers to formulate explicit rules to resolve anaphora accurately. Nevertheless, in recent years, a variety of methods for anaphora resolution have been put forward.

(1) *Rules-based Methods*: Filtering rules were proposed by Lee [3], which were only applied to English texts. The complexity of Chinese and the small scale of 'HowNet' and 'Tongyici Cilin', brought difficulties in calculating the semantic similarity between a pronoun and its candidate antecedent. Based on Lee's research, Zhang [4] used part of speech tagging and named entity recognition to extract pronouns, and designed two rules to judge the singular and plural forms of pronouns for improving the accuracy of anaphora resolution. Zhou [5] believed that semantic information was very important for resolution, according to Lee's study, he proposed a new model, added a semantic layer, and introduced Web semantic knowledge to expand the small Chinese knowledge bases.

(2) *Rules and Machine Learning Methods*: Li [6] combined decision tree and priority selection approach to implement the resolution of personal pronoun anaphora. Firstly, he used POS consistency, gender and singular-plural features to train the decision tree. And then, he designed a priority selection policy by integrating two factors of frequency and reference distance to improve the anaphora resolution performance. Dong [7] modified the above model, replaced POS consistency with semantic consistency, and applied maximum entropy theory to solve this problem.

(3) *Rules and Semantic Method*: On the basis of Dong's research, Zhang [8] formulated appositive rules to filter candidate antecedents, and used synonym recognition algorithm to calculate the semantic relevance between a pronoun and its candidate antecedent, and the most relevant antecedent was selected as the final result.

(4) *Semantic and Syntactic Methods*: Xu [9] used syntactic structure, semantic context and case frame to realize the resolution of the third personal pronoun anaphora. Wang [10] proposed a strategy based on sentence categories, who formulated 14

exclusion rules and locally optimal solution to resolve personal pronoun anaphora. Song [11] proposed a strategy for Chinese pronoun anaphora resolution based on SVM, and employed grammatical role features and the similarity between a pronoun and its candidate antecedent, whose experimental result showed that these semantic and syntactic features were effective.

All the methods above are concerned with formal texts, which are not suitable for social short texts such as micro-blog texts. In the study of pronoun anaphora resolution in social short texts, Zhang [12] proposed a strategy based on the multi-level information, including grammar, semantics and pragmatics. His experimental result showed that this method could achieve good results. In this paper, we analyze the linguistic features of personal pronouns in Chinese micro-blog texts, and propose a multi-strategy method for the resolution of personal pronoun anaphora.

3 The Linguistic Features of Personal Pronouns in Chinese Micro-blog

There are lots of personal pronouns in Chinese micro-blog texts, and these pronouns contain many anaphoric relations. If we want to mine and understand the semantic information in micro-blog texts, anaphora resolution is the first step. Their linguistic features in Chinese micro-blog texts are introduced in the following sections.

3.1 The Types of Personal Pronouns

Personal pronouns can be divided into three types: the first personal pronoun, the second personal pronoun and the third personal pronoun. In Chinese micro-blog texts, the first personal pronoun mainly includes '我(I or me)', '咱(I or me)', '俺(I or me)', '咱们(we or us)', '我们(we or us)', the second personal pronoun includes '你(you)', '你们(plural of 'you')', '您(show respect for 'you')', and the third personal pronoun includes '他(he or him)', '她(she or her)', '它(it)', '她们(they, gender: female)', '他们(they, gender: male)', '它们(they, plural of 'it')'.

3.2 The Types of Anaphoric Relations

According to whether the pronoun's antecedent occurs in micro-blog texts, anaphoric relations can be divided into the internal anaphora and the external anaphora. The internal anaphora means that the pronoun's antecedent occurs in the original text. As shown in Example 1, we can find the antecedent of '她(her)' is '张檬(Zhang Meng)'. The external anaphora means the pronoun's antecedent doesn't occur in the original text. From Example 2, we can't identify which noun is the antecedent of '她(her)'. According to whether the pronoun represents a specific person or thing, anaphoric relations can be divided into the definite anaphora and the indefinite anaphora. Example 1 is the definite anaphora, because '她(her)' represents a specific person, Example 3 is the indefinite anaphora, because '我们(we)' doesn't represent a specific person.

*Example 1:*一直以来就不太看好张檬，总觉得她拍的戏看起来怪怪的. (I don't like Zhang Meng. I feel her performance is strange.)

Example 2: 现代服装比古代服装更适合她. (The modern dress is more suitable for her than the ancient one.)

Example 3: 六一节今天估计最开心的不是儿童，而是商家，他们大赚六一财，但是我们要呼吁的是商家要诚信经商. (On Children's Day, the happiest people are not children but businessmen, who make huge profit through this festival. So we need to appeal to them for integrity management.)

3.3 Pseudo Personal Pronoun

Micro-blogs, belonging to colloquial expression, contain many pseudo personal pronouns which are similar to personal pronouns but do not refer to anything, such as '花他几年时间(take years)', '管他三七二十一(in spite of anything)'. In order to eliminate the effects of these words, we construct a pseudo personal pronoun vocabulary.

4 Resolution of Personal Pronoun Anaphora

Based on the above linguistic features of personal pronouns in Chinese micro-blog texts, we propose a multi-strategy method for the resolution of personal pronoun anaphora. Firstly, the micro-blog text is preprocessed. Secondly, the rules for judging the consistency between a personal pronoun and its antecedents in grammar, semantics, gender and singular-plural are established. The antecedents which are inconsistent with the current personal pronoun in these four aspects are preliminarily filtered, and Candidate Set 1 of antecedents is obtained. Then, SVM is used to classify the antecedents in Candidate Set 1, and the antecedents which have certain anaphoric relations with the current personal pronoun are selected to construct Candidate Set 2 of antecedents. Finally, four linguistic characteristics of grammatical role, co-occurrence relation, reference distance and appositive dependency are combined to make the priority selection policy, and the best antecedent from Candidate Set 2 is found out through the priority selection policy. When we can't find the personal pronoun's antecedent according to the above method, we use the strategy of extending antecedent to supplement the antecedent. The process is discussed in the following sections.

4.1 Micro-blog Preprocessing and the Antecedents Candidate Set 1 Establishing

Since the informal nature of micro-blog texts bring difficulties to anaphora resolution, we need to preprocess these texts. Firstly, we remove the meaningless symbols, emoticons, URLs, duplicate symbols, pseudo personal pronouns, and convert the traditional Chinese into simple Chinese. Secondly, we use NLPIR to segment micro-blog texts and tag POS. At last, we use the tool developed by Stanford University to realize named entity recognition, grammatical role recognition and noun phrase extraction. Based on these works, we extract personal pronouns, nouns and noun phrases, and regard nouns and noun phrases as candidate antecedents.

On the basis of micro-blog preprocessing, we design some rules for judging the consistency between a personal pronoun and its antecedents in grammar, semantics, gender and singular-plural, and then use these rules to filter antecedents which are inconsistent with the personal pronoun so that we can establish Candidate Set 1 of antecedents. The rules are shown as follows.

(1) Grammatical consistency rule

The dialogue discourses often appear in micro-blog texts, and the first and second personal pronouns are commonly used in these dialogues. Based on dialogue features, we formulate the following rules.

Rule 1: When the first personal pronoun is singular and appears in quotes, we can check if the structures of '<person>+verb' and '<person>+':"' exist before the quotes. When one of the structures is present and '<person>' is a noun or noun phrase, we take '<person>' as the first personal pronoun's antecedent; if it is a personal pronoun, we take its antecedent as the first pronoun's antecedent. In Example 4, '<person>' is '他', which is a personal pronoun. So '我' and '他' have the same antecedent, and the antecedent is '王明(Wang Ming)'.

Example 4 王明工作了一天, 他说: "我需要休息". (Wang Ming worked all day, he said 'I need a rest'.)

Rule 2: When micro-blog texts have one of the following structures: '<person1>+verb+<content1>,<person2>+verb+<content2>' and '<person1>+verb+<person2>+':'+<content1>,<person2>+verb+<person1>+':'+<content2>'. If the second personal pronoun appears in '<content1>', and '<person2>' is a noun or noun phrase, we can take '<person2>' as the second personal pronoun's antecedent; if '<person2>' is a personal pronoun, we take its antecedent as the second personal pronoun's antecedent.

(2) Semantic consistency rule

Semantic representations can be divided into two classes, one of which represents individuals, and the other represents impersonal things. In personal pronouns, '我, 俺, 他, 她, 我们, 俺们, 他们, 她们' represent individuals, '它, 它们' represent impersonal things. With the help of 'HowNet' and Named entity recognition, we can classify candidate antecedents into two representations, individuals and impersonal things. Firstly, we search the semantic representations of candidate antecedents in 'HowNet', and use their semantic representations to classify them. When we can't find the representation, we use named entity recognition to extract. If candidate antecedents belong to names, they represent individuals; if they belong to places or agencies, they represent impersonal things. After classification, we compare the semantic consistency between a personal pronoun and its candidate antecedents, and the candidate antecedents which differ from the personal pronoun in semantic representation are filtered.

(3) Gender consistency rule

Gender consistency between the personal pronoun and its candidate antecedent is an important influential factor in anaphora resolution. Based on micro-blog texts, we select a series of words with obvious gender feature to construct a male lexicon and a female lexicon. Male lexicon contains '先生(gentleman)', '兄弟(brother)', '儿子(son)' and so on. Female lexicon contains '母亲(mother)', '小姐(lady)', '妞(girl)', '妹(sister)', '姑(aunt)', '妻子(wife)' etc. According to the two lexicons, we can filter candidate antecedents that differ from the personal pronoun in gender.

(4) Singular-plural consistency rule

The singular and plural form of personal pronouns could be distinguished easily. The singular personal pronouns include '我', '俺', '他', '她', '它'; the plural personal pronouns include '我们', '他们', '她们', '咱'. The singular and plural form of candidate antecedents need to be analyzed on a case-by-case basis. When candidate antecedents represent a single concept such as a name, a place or an agency, they belong to the singular form. When candidate antecedents represent group concept such as '父母(parents)', '夫妻(couple)', '姐妹(sisters)', '哥俩(brothers)', they belong to the plural form. We can also distinguish their forms by quantifiers before them. According to the singular-plural consistency rule, we can filter candidate antecedents which differ from the personal pronoun in singular-plural.

4.2 Classification Model Based on SVM

Anaphora resolution can be regarded as a binary classification problem. We use SVM to classify the antecedents in Candidate Set 1 of antecedents, and find out the antecedents which have certain anaphoric relations with the current personal pronoun to construct Candidate Set 2 of antecedents. The SVM model is a statistical method based on the theory of VC dimension and the principle of structural risk minimization, which transforms the classification of sample space into a convex quadratic programming problem and obtains the optimal hyperplane by learning from sample space. Suppose the sample point is $\left(x_{i,}y_i\right), i = 1, 2, \cdots, m, x \in R^n, y \in (+1, -1)$, m is the number of samples, n is the input dimension. When the training samples can be separated, the optimal hyperplane is showed as Eq. (1):

$$w \cdot x + b = 0. \tag{1}$$

w is the normal vector, b is the intercept, at this time, the distance between the positive and negative classes and the hyperplane is maximized. When the training samples are not separable, we introduce slack variable ξ_i. The optimization problem can be expressed as Eq. (2):

$$\min \frac{||w||^2}{2} + C\sum_{i=1}^{m} \xi_i. \tag{2}$$

C is the penalty coefficient, $C \geq 0, y_i(w \cdot x_i + b) \geq 1 - \xi_i,\ \xi_i \geq 0,\ i = 1, 2, \cdots, m$. Lagrange Duality Theorem is used to solve the dual problem, and the solution of the original problem is obtained.

In order to construct a classification model, we extract the features of personal pronouns and candidate antecedents, and normalize them. We constantly adjust the kernel functions and parameters of the SVM model according to the training samples, and get the best classification model by learning samples. The feature selection, the kernel function and parameter selection are shown below.

Feature Selection. According to micro-blog texts, we extract eight features between the personal pronoun and its candidate antecedent, and build a representation model. These eight features are as follows:

(1) *Singular-plural.* If the personal pronoun and its candidate antecedent are the same in singular-plural, the feature value is 1; if we can't identify the form of the personal pronoun or candidate antecedent, the feature value is 0.
(2) *Semantics.* If the personal pronoun and its candidate antecedent are the same in semantic representation, the feature value is 1; if the representation of the personal pronoun or candidate antecedent is unclear, the feature value is 0.
(3) *Personal pronoun gender.* If the personal pronoun refers to female, the feature value is 2; if the personal pronoun refers to male, the feature value is 1; if we can't identify its gender, the feature value is 0.
(4) *Candidate antecedent gender.* The method for dealing with the feature value is the same as personal pronoun gender.
(5) *Reference distance.* We take candidate antecedent as the unit of reference distance. If there are more than five candidate antecedents between the personal pronoun and its candidate antecedent, the feature value is 1; otherwise, the feature value is 0.
(6) *Grammatical role of personal pronoun.* Personal pronouns can be divided into three types: subject, object and attributive. If the personal pronoun is the subject, the feature value is 1; if it is the object, the feature value is 2; otherwise, the feature value is 3.
(7) *Relative position.* If the candidate antecedent appears before the personal pronoun, the feature value is 1; otherwise, the feature value is 0.
(8) *Position of personal pronoun.* When the personal pronoun is at the beginning of a sentence, the feature value is 0; when it is in the middle of the sentence, the feature value is 1; and when it is at the end of the sentence, the feature value is 2.

The Kernel Function and Parameter Selection. The selection of the kernel functions and parameters has an important influence on the performance of the SVM classification model. The common kernel function is:

Linear kernel function:

$$\mathrm{K}(x, z) = x^T \cdot z. \tag{3}$$

Polynomial kernel function:

$$\mathrm{K}(x, z) = \left(\gamma\left(x^T \cdot z\right) + 1\right)^d. \tag{4}$$

Gauss kernel function:

$$\mathrm{K}(x, z) = exp\left(-\gamma||x - z||^2\right). \tag{5}$$

x and z are samples; γ and $d$are kernel functions' parameters. Linear kernel function, as shown in Function (3), is the inner product in the original space. It is usually used in the case that the number of feature vectors is almost the same as the samples' size. When the samples in the original vector space are linearly separable, Linear kernel function can get a good result. When the samples are not linearly separable, we can map the samples in the original vector space to a high-dimensional vector space by kernel function, and classify them by Polynomial kernel function or Gauss kernel function. We will discuss the selection process of the kernel functions and parameters in experiments.

4.3 Priority Selection Policy

The results of classification model based on SVM may not be unique, a personal pronoun may refer to multiple antecedents. We combine four linguistic characteristics of grammatical role, co-occurrence relation, reference distance and appositive dependency, and make the priority selection policy to find out the best antecedents from candidate set 2 of antecedents.

We assign candidate antecedents' scores by the above factors, and select the candidate antecedent with the highest score as the antecedent. The candidate antecedent's score can be divided into four parts, they are RoleScore, ArrScore, DisScore and AppScore. We will introduce how to get the scores.

If a candidate antecedent is the subject, RoleScore's value is 1; otherwise, its value is 0. For example '有店家告诉记者，他们主要是回收塑料袋 (Shopkeepers told the reporter that they usually recycled plastics)', '店家(Shopkeepers)' is the subject of the sentence, its RoleScore is 1, and '记者(reporter)' is the object, its RoleScore is 0.

A sentence can be separated into short sentences by punctuation. If the personal pronoun and its candidate antecedent exist simultaneously in the short sentence, we regard there is a co-occurrence relation between them. If the personal pronoun and its candidate antecedent have a co-occurrence relation, the candidate antecedent's ArrScore is 0; otherwise, the ArrScore is 1. For example '张檬英语写作很好，老师对她评价很高 (Zhang Meng English writing is good, our teacher speaks highly of her)', '张檬(Zhang Meng)' and '她 (her)' don't have the co-occurrence relation, the ArrScore of "张檬" (Zhang Meng) is 1, '老师(teacher)' and '她(her)' have the co-occurrence relation, the ArrScore of '老师(teacher)' is 0.

We take the number of candidate antecedents between the personal pronoun and its candidate antecedent as the reference distance. The shorter the reference distance is, the more likely the candidate antecedent is the result. If the reference distance is 0, DisScore is 0; otherwise, DisScore is the inverse of the reference distance.

When the personal pronoun and the candidate antecedent are appositive, the candidate antecedent's AppScore is 2; otherwise, the AppScore is 0. By using appositive language, the performance of anaphora resolution can be improved.

The sum of RoleScore, ArrScore, DisScore and AppScore is the score of the candidate antecedent. We select the candidate antecedent with the highest score as the antecedent of the personal pronoun.

4.4 The Strategy of Extending Antecedent

When we can't find the antecedent of the personal pronoun according to the above method, we propose a strategy of extending antecedent to solve the problem. We formulate two extending policies.

Policy 1: When the structure of '@+<name>' appears in sentences, we extract '<name>', and regard it as a candidate antecedent.

Policy 2: When we can't find the personal pronoun's antecedent in sentences, we mine the potential antecedent from other micro-blogs within the same topic. In this policy, we select the most frequent noun phrase in this topic as the candidate antecedent.

5 Experiment

In order to validate the proposed method for anaphora resolution, we have done the following experiments: (1) Comparison experiment of SVM classification model based on different kernel functions and parameters; (2) Comparison experiment of different methods for personal pronoun anaphora resolution.

5.1 Datasets and Evaluation Criterion

We selected 1000 micro-blogs from the shared task of NLPCC 2013 as the experimental corpus. There were 1095 personal pronouns in this corpus, including 569 the first personal pronoun, 185 the second personal pronoun and 341 the third personal pronoun.

We used Precision, Recall and F measure to evaluate the performance of the proposed method. The evaluation criterion formulas are as follows:

$$Precision(P) = \frac{\text{number of pronoun resolved}}{\text{number of pronoun extracted by the system}} \times 100\%. \quad (6)$$

$$Recall(R) = \frac{\text{number of pronoun resolved}}{\text{total number of pronoun}} \times 100\%. \quad (7)$$

$$F\ measure = \frac{2 \times P \times R}{P + R} \times 100\%. \quad (8)$$

5.2 The Process of Personal Pronoun Anaphora Resolution

Input: A sentence in Chinese micro-blog texts.
Output: The pairs of personal pronouns and their antecedents.

Step1: Preprocess the sentence, find its personal pronouns, and extract nouns or noun phrases as candidate antecedents.

Step2: Analyze each of the personal pronouns. If the personal pronoun is the first personal pronoun, skip to Step3; if it is the second personal pronoun, skip to Step4; if it is the third personal pronoun, skip to Step5.

Step3: If the personal pronoun is singular form and appears in quotes, use Rule1 from grammatical consistency rule; if it is singular form and isn't in quotes, its antecedent is blogger; otherwise, skip to Step6.

Step4: If the personal pronoun appears in quotes, use Rule2 from grammatical consistency rule; if the sentence contains '@', use Policy1 from the strategy of extending antecedent; otherwise, skip to Step6.

Step5: If the second pronoun is the beginning of the sentence, use Policy2 from the strategy of extending antecedent; otherwise, skip to Step6.

Step6: Use the rules to filter the inconsistent antecedents, and construct Candidate Set 1 of antecedents. And then, use SVM to classify the antecedents in candidate set 1, and select the antecedents which have certain anaphoric relation with the current personal pronoun to construct Candidate Set 2 of antecedents. Finally, use the priority selection policy to select the best antecedent from Candidate Set 2. If there is no antecedent for the personal pronoun, skip to Step7; otherwise, skip to Step8.

Step7: Use the strategy of extending antecedent to find the antecedent for the personal pronoun. Then skip to Step8.

Step8: Output the result.

5.3 Performance Comparison of SVM Classification Model Based on Different Kernel Functions

For the three different kernel functions in Eqs. (3)–(5), the range of C of linear kernel function was set to $\{2^{-10}, 2^{-8}, \ldots, 2^{0}\}$, the range of C of Polynomial kernel function and Gauss kernel function was set to $\{2^{-5}, 2^{-3}, \ldots, 2^{15}\}$, the range of γ was set to $\{2^{-15}, 2^{-13}, \ldots, 2^{3}\}$, and the range of d was set to $\{1,2,3,4\}$. The results of different parameters are showed in Fig. 1.

Figure 1 shows experimental results of three kernel functions. The abscissa of the graph is C, the ordinate is γ of the kernel function, and the curves are the contour of the average accuracy of the cross-validation when different parameters are selected. Figure 1(a) shows the performance of the model with Linear kernel function on the training samples. We can find that it increases with penalty coefficient, and the highest

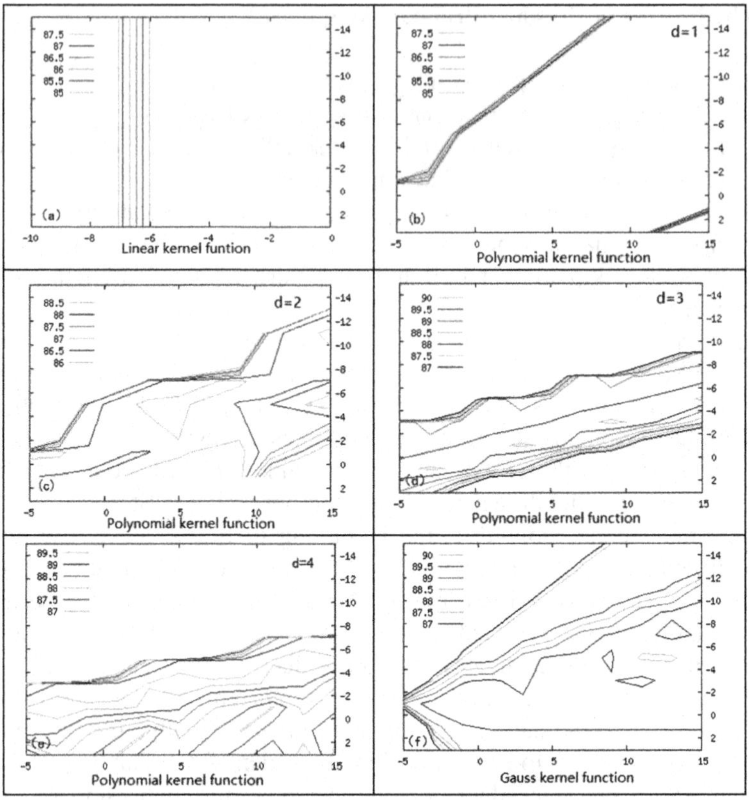

Fig. 1. Experimental results of different kernel functions

accuracy is 87.25%. Figure 1(b)–(e) show the performance of the model by using Polynomial kernel function on the training samples. The accuracy first increases then decreases. When *d* is *3*, the accuracy is highest and up to 90.07%. Figure 1(f) shows the performance of the model by using Gauss kernel function on the training samples. The accuracy is 90.07%. It can be seen that Polynomial kernel function is equivalent to Gauss kernel function. Owing to the existence of an over fitting phenomenon, the best parameter combinations of each kernel is tested on the test set to verify their generalization capability.

Table 1 shows that the accuracy of Polynomial kernel function is higher than Gauss kernel function in the test set. We chose Polynomial kernel function and defined *d*'s value as 3 for all concerned.

Table 1. Kernel function parameters and experimental results.

Kernel function	d	C	γ	Accuracy of train set	Accuracy of test set
Polynomial	3	0.125	2	90.07%	**90.24%**
Gauss	–	2048	0.03125	90.07%	90.03%

5.4 Performance Comparison of Different Methods

In order to verify the effectiveness of the multi-strategy method for personal pronoun anaphora resolution, we combined different methods and constructed 5 comparative experiments, including RP, RPA, RSP, [12], and PSPA. RP was a method combining rules and the priority selection policy. RPA combines rules, the priority selection policy and the strategy of extending antecedent. RSP combines rules, SVM model and priority selection policy. RSPA is the proposed method in this paper. The results of different experiments are shown in Table 2. FPP represents the first personal pronoun, SPP the second personal pronoun, TPP the third personal pronoun, and APP represents all types of personal pronouns.

Table 2. Resolution results of different methods.

Method		RP	RPA	RSP	[12]	RSPA
Precision	FPP	97.72%	97.72%	97.72%	97.13%	97.72%
	SPP	46.26%	66.67%	67.82%	83.72%	83.91%
	TPP	67.91%	68.85%	71.65%	87.72%	87.85%
	APP	79.35%	83.07%	84.15%	92.21%	92.27%
Recall	FPP	97.19%	97.19%	97.19%	97.13%	97.19%
	SPP	45.40%	64.32%	65.41%	75.79%	80.54%
	TPP	68.04%	68.92%	71.55%	86.55%	86.80%
	APP	79.36%	82.83%	83.84%	90.55%	91.14%
F measure	FPP	97.45%	97.45%	97.45%	97.13%	97.45%
	SPP	45.97%	65.47%	66.59%	79.56%	82.19%
	TPP	67.97%	68.88%	71.60%	87.13%	87.32%
	APP	79.36%	82.95%	83.99%	91.37%	**91.70%**

As shown in Table 2, we can find that Precision, Recall and F measure of the first personal pronoun anaphora resolution are the highest, and the results of RP, RPA, RSP and PRSA are the same. The reason may be that the first personal pronouns' antecedents generally refer to the bloggers themselves and that they can be resolved easily. In RPA, the evaluation indexes are higher than RP, from which we could conclude that the strategy of extending antecedent is beneficial to the performance of anaphora resolution. And the evaluation indexes of RSP are higher than RP, which shows that the method based on SVM is better than rules and the priority selection policy. Compared to these methods, our method shows a great superiority in personal pronoun anaphora resolution.

6 Summary

In this paper, we proposed a multi-strategy method for the resolution of personal pronoun anaphora in Chinese micro-blog texts. Firstly, we have preprocessed the micro-blog texts. Secondly, we have designed four consistency rules including grammar, semantic, gender and singular-plural to filter the antecedents which are inconsistent with the personal pronoun in these four aspects, and Candidate Set 1 of antecedents has been established. Thirdly, we have extracted eight features to represent the anaphoric relations between a personal pronoun and candidate antecedents from Candidate Set 1, using SVM to classify the antecedents in candidate set 1, and found out the antecedents which have certain anaphoric relations with the current personal pronoun in order to construct Candidate Set 2 of antecedents. Finally, we have used the priority selection policy to select the best antecedent of the personal pronoun. When we can't find the personal pronoun's antecedent according to the above method, the strategy of extending antecedent has been used to supplement the antecedent. The proposed method has combined different policies to realize anaphora resolution, and the experimental results have shown that it is effective and practical.

In the future, there will be two points which can be improved: (1) the noun phrase extracting method in text preprocessing; (2) the assigned score of four factors in the priority selection policy.

Acknowledgements. This work was supported by grants from National Nature Science Foundation of China (No. 61772081), Science and Technology Development Project of Beijing Municipal Education Commission (No. KM201711232014, No. KM201711232022).

References

1. Gao, J.W.: Study of key problems on Chinese anaphora resolution. Soochow University (2012). (in Chinese), https://doi.org/10.7666/d.y2120835
2. Fan, J.Y., Xu, Z.M.: Research on natural language understanding and modern linguistics. Lang. Res. **5**, 7–22 (1983). (in Chinese)
3. Lee, H., Peirsman, Y., Chang A., et al.: Stanford's multi-pass sieve coreference resolution system at the CoNLL-2011 Shared Task, Portland, Oregon, pp. 28–34 (2011)
4. Zhang, X., Wu, C., Zhao, H.: Chinese coreference resolution via ordered filtering. In: Joint Conference on EMNLP and CoNLL-Shared Task. Association for Computational Linguistics, Jeju, Republic of Korea, pp. 95–99 (2012)
5. Zhou, X.Y., Liu, J., Shao, P., et al.: Chinese anaphora resolution based on multi-pass Sieve model. J. Jilin Univ. **46**(4), 1209–1215 (2016). (in Chinese). https://doi.org/10.13229/j.cnki.jdxbgxb201604029
6. Li, G.C., Luo, Y.F.: Chinese pronominal anaphora resolution via a preference selection approach. J. Chin. Inf. Process. **19**(4), 24–30 (2005). (in Chinese), https://doi.org/10.3969/j.issn.1003-0077.2005.04.004
7. Dong, G.Z., Zhu, Y.Q., Cheng, X.Y.: Research on personal pronoun anaphora resolution in Chinese. Appl. Res. Comput. **28**(5), 1774–1776 (2011). (in Chinese), https://doi.org/10.3969/j.issn.1001-3695.2011.05.051

8. Zhang, W.Y., Li, C.H., Zhong, Z.M.: Resolution of Chinese personal pronouns with combination of semantics and rules. Data Acquis. Process. **32**(1), 149–156 (2017)
9. Xu, M., Qiu, Y.H., Wang, N.Z.: A multi-strategy solution to the problem of Chinese reference. In: Chinese Academic Conference on Machine Learning (2000). (in Chinese)
10. Wang, H.F., He, T.: Research on Chinese pronominal anaphora resolution. Chin. J. Comput. **24**(2), 136–143 (2001). (in Chinese)
11. Song, W., Qin, B., Lang, J., Liu, T.: Combining syntax and word sense for Chinese pronoun resolution. J. Chin. Inf. Process. **22**(06), 8–13 (2008). (in Chinese), https://doi.org/10.3969/j.issn.1003-0077.2008.06.002
12. Zhang, Y., Liang, L., Hou, M., et al.: The characteristics and resolution strategies of personal pronouns in topic based micro-blog. J. Hainan Univ. **32**(2), 119–126 (2014). (in Chinese)

Automatic Chinese Nominal Compound Interpretation Based on Deep Neural Networks Combined with Semantic Features

Huayong Li, Yanqiu Shao(✉), and Yimeng Li

Information Science School, Beijing Language and Culture University,
Beijing 100083, China
yqshao163@163.com

Abstract. The present paper reports on the results of the automatic interpretation of Chinese nominal compounds using CNN-Highway network model combined with semantic features. Chinese nominal compound interpretation is aimed to identify semantic relations between verbal nouns like "*采集处理*" (data acquisition and processing), and "*污染处理*" (wastewater treatment). The main idea is to define a set of semantic relations of verbal nouns and use deep neural network classifier with semantic features to automatically assign semantic relations to nominal compounds. Experiment shows that our model achieves 84% F1-score on the test dataset. Convolutional layer plus highway network combined with semantic features architecture can effectively solve the problem of Chinese nominal compound interpretation.

Keywords: Nominal compound interpretation · Highway network
CNN

1 Introduction

The automatic semantic dependency analysis of nominal phrases such as "*饮料/n 质量/n 监督/v 抽查/v*" (the supervision and spot check of beverage quality), "*文化/n 展示/v 活动/v 开幕式/n*" (the opening ceremony of cultural exhibition) and "*商业/n 调查/v 统计/v 工作/v*" (business investigation and statistical work) is a difficulty in Chinese due to the fact that verbs in Chinese can be nominalized without inflection. However, an important step towards being able to ascertain sentence meaning is to analyze the meaning of such compounds more generally.

Interpretation of nominal compounds is highly dependent on lexical information. One of the themes of SemEval-2007 is the interpretation of nominalizations and studies conducted by using different methods indicate the importance of lexical resources. So we explore the possibility of using deep neural classifier combined with existing handcrafted semantic knowledge-base (SKCC, Semantic Knowledge-base of Contemporary Chinese) for the purpose of identifying the semantic relation between two "verbs" of a nominal compound. We design a semantic feature extractor that automatically extracts semantic features from SKCC. We then incorporate these semantic features into the neural network and use the neural network model to categorize the relationships.

J.-F. Hong et al. (Eds.): CLSW 2018, LNAI 11173, pp. 606–614, 2018.
https://doi.org/10.1007/978-3-030-04015-4_52

The remainder of the paper is structured as follows: previous related work to the automatic classification of compound relations, semantic relations that hold between verbal nouns, the classifier to determine the relations, the evaluation of the results and some conclusion.

2 Related Work

We focus on the methods that analyze semantic relations in nominal compounds. Rosario and Hearst [1] use a machine learning algorithm and a domain-specific lexical hierarchy, achieving more than 60% accuracy on a dataset with 16 semantic relations.

Hearst and Fillmore [2] continue the study by placing the words from a two-word compound from biomedical domain into categories, and then using this category membership to determine the relations that hold between nouns, obtaining classification accuracy of approximately 90% on a dataset with 35 semantic relations.

Girju [3] use machine learning tools such as SVM to explore noun relations with attributes extracted from ComLex and VerbLex. It turns out that SVM achieves the highest accuracy of 72% on a dataset with 35 semantic relations.

Nastase [4] use the machine learning tools such as decision trees, instance-based learning and SVM, with attributes respectively extracted from WordNet and corpus. The F-measure reaches a maximum of 82.47% on a dataset with 5 semantic relations after the introduction of the WordNet word meaning.

Tratz and Hovy [5] use Maximum Entropy Classifier and SVM multiclass to classify semantic relations between English noun compounds and obtain an accuracy of 79.3% and 79.4% respectively. Their dataset comprises 17509 compounds with a new taxonomy of 43 semantic relations.

Dima and Hinrichs [6] use neutral network classifier implemented in the Torch7 scientific computing framework for the automatic classification of noun compound semantic relations. The F-measure reaches a maximum of 79.48% on a dataset with 12 semantic relations.

3 Semantic Relations

The Chinese nominal compounds such as "*学生 /n 申诉 /v 处理 /v 制度 /n*" (processing system of student's appeal) and "*疾病 /n 预防 /v 控制 /v 中心 /n*" (centers for disease control and prevention) are a common linguistic phenomenon. Because there is no inflection in Chinese, the part-of speech taggers of the verbal nouns are also "verbs", which poses a difficulty for automatic acquisition of semantic relations. The original semantic labels are from BLCU-HIT Semantic Dependency Graph [7], on the basis of which we find that there are four kinds of relations that hold between the verbal nouns [8]. Table 1 describes the details of the four types of semantic relationships that we define.

Table 1. Four types of semantic relationships

Label	Relation	Definition	Examples
Pat	Case relation	One of the verbal noun is an object of the other	*污染处理* (pollution treatment)
Desc	Attribute modifier	One of the verbal noun is a modifier of the other	*上网服务* (Internet service)
Coo	Coordinating relation	The two verbal nouns function equally syntactically	*预防控制* (prevention and control)
Mann	Adverbial modifier	The verbal noun describes the manner of the action	*跨境采访* (cross border interview)

4 Dataset

The dataset for the present study consists of 2000 nominal compounds. These compounds are automatically extracted from BLCU-HIT Semantic Dependency Graph Bank and Dynamic Circulation Corpus (DCC) and then checked manually. We run a part-of-speech tagger on LTP (Language Technology Platform) and a program that extracts only sequences of units tagged as nouns and verbs. The data are further inspected manually to create a dataset of only compounds with two consecutive verbal nouns.

The original data set is not balanced with the number of samples in each semantic relationship varying greatly, which brings new difficulties to our classification model. Most machine learning algorithms work best when the number of instances per class is approximately equal. When the number of instances of a class far exceeds that of other classes, the performance of the machine learning algorithm drops drastically [9].

We use the SMOTE algorithm to balance the dataset. SMOTE algorithm is an improvement based on random oversampling algorithm [10]. The basic idea of SMOTE algorithm is to analyze a few samples and add them to the data set according to a few samples of artificial synthetic new samples. The SMOTE algorithm generates a new sample rather than an instance of a copy by random sampling, thus alleviating the problem of over fitting.

In the end we got a training set of 2000 pieces of data and a test set of 200 pieces of data. Both training data sets and test data sets are balanced data sets. The detailed classifications of data sets are in Table 2:

5 Method

5.1 The Model Architecture

The input of the model are nominal phrases. Firstly, nominal phrases, such as “数据收集处理” (data acquisition processing), are divided into lists consisting of three

Table 2. The classifications of datasets

	Category	Number (pieces)
Training data set	Obj	500
	Coo	500
	Desc	500
	Mann	500
Test data set	Obj	50
	Coo	50
	Desc	50
	Mann	50

words: $[noun, verb_1, verb_2]$ (e.g. "data", "acquisition", "processing"). Then the list is put to a data preprocessor which is used to extract 8 semantic features based on SKCC and transform the input word into the index of the word in the vocabulary. Lastly, the output information of the data preprocessor will be put into the CNN-Highway network model.

As is illustrated in Fig. 1. the model consists of 4 parts. The first part is an embedding layer, which is a two-dimensional matrix with the size of $voca * dim$. The second part is a convolutional layer, the size and number of whose filter are $3 * dim$ and 256 respectively. Then convolutional layer's output will be put to a deep highway network where they are combined with semantic features. At last, the highway network's output will be put into the softmax layer in order to obtain classification results.

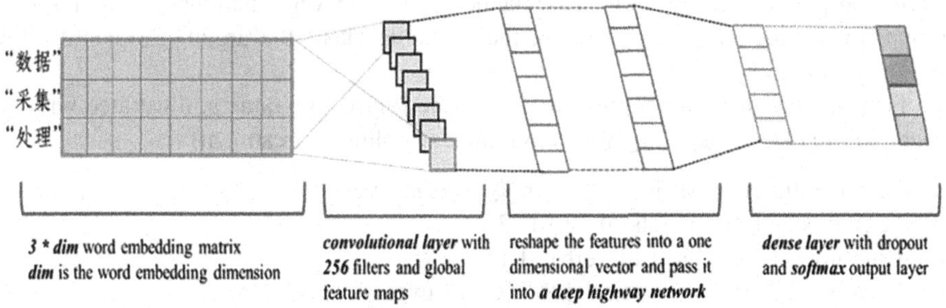

Fig. 1. The CNN-highway network architecture

5.2 Word Embedding

In the first level of the model we convert the input word to word embedding, which is the n-dimensional real-valued vector mapping function: $W : D \rightarrow R^n$. Given a noun phrase containing three words $[noun, verb_1, verb_2]$, every word in it will be converted into a real-valued vector R^n and as a result, the input of this word sequence will be converted to a sequence of real-valued vectors: $\left[R^{noun}, R^{verb1}, R^{verb2}\right]$.

Word embeddings learned from significant amounts of unlabeled data are far more satisfactory than the randomly initialized embeddings. We train a $voca * dim$ word vector using gensim's word2vec algorithm [11] with 100 GB Chinese corpus that includes Sogou news, Baidu encyclopedia and online novels. The word embedding is represented in the model as a two-dimensional matrix W. The i-th row of the word embedding matrix corresponds to the i-th word in the vocabulary.

When the nominal phrases are entered into the model, we look up W to extract the word vector representation. In the training process of the model, the embedding layer W is trainable, which means W will be updated with the training process, so that the quality of word embedding can be improved.

5.3 Semantic Features

The nominalizations can keep the original argument structure, so we can utilize this property to ascertain the semantic relation between verbal nouns. Semantic information plays an important role in the classification of semantic relations.

So we combine the deep neural classifier with semantic information from SKCC. The Semantic Knowledge-base of Contemporary Chinese (SKCC) is a large scale of bilingual semantic resource developed by Chinese Department of Peking University. It provides quite amount of semantic information such as semantic classification and collocation features for 66539 Chinese words and their English counterparts. It has three dictionaries including noun, adjective and verb. Each dictionary is organized in hierarchy with respect to semantic classes. Nouns are divided into four general semantic classes: entity, abstraction, time and space, and each of the category is further divided into multiple subcategories. The noun dictionary has three components: the word, the part of speech and the semantic class. The verb dictionary is a six-point group: the word, the part of speech, the semantic class, the argument quantity, the subject and the object.

For each nominal compound, we extract the following features, illustrated with an example "垃圾/n 污染/v 处理/v"(environment pollution treatment):

a. the semantic class of the verb1-"污染": Other events;
b. the number of arguments of verb1: 2;
c. if the noun is an object of verb1: 1 (Yes);
d. the semantic class of verb2-"处理": Other events;
e. the number of arguments of verb2: 2;
f. if the object of verb2 contains "abstraction": 1(Yes);
g. if the noun is an object of verb2: 1 (Yes);
h. if the objects of verb1 and verb2 has intersection: 1(Yes).

5.4 Convolutional Layer

The CNN model is the most commonly used neural network model in image recognition, especially for two-dimensional images. Convolution operation can effectively extract the features within the filter window [12].

Because words can be mapped as a real-valued vector by word embedding, phrases or sentences composed of multiple words can be arranged into a two-dimensional numerical matrix. At this point we can use the convolution operation to extract the global features of the word within the context window. Experiments show that the CNN model can effectively solve the task of phrase or sentence information extraction.

We can use multiple filters so that the global characteristics of a phrase can be extracted from multiple perspectives. In our model, we use multiple full-window-sized filters whose shape is $3 * dim$ and dim represents the dimension we embed in terms of words. We use 256 filters to extract as many global features as possible. The convolutional layer does not use padding, so the output of each filter is a scalar. The entire convolution output is 256 scalars. Then we use the reshape operation to get a one-dimensional vector as the input feature for the next layer.

Since the filter's window size is large enough, we dropped the pooling layer. The model directly puts the extracted features into the deep highway network.

5.5 Highway Network

Highway network is an approach to optimizing networks and increasing their depth [13]. Highway networks use learned gating mechanisms to regulate information flow, inspired by LSTM. The gating mechanisms allow neural networks to have paths for information to follow across different layers. In a dense neural network, input x multiply a weight W_x and added to a bias b, then pass through an activation function H such that:

$$y = H(W_x * x + b) \tag{1}$$

Highway network additionally define two non-linear transforms g_T and g_C as follows:

$$g_T = sigm(W_T * x + b_T) \tag{2}$$

$$g_C = sigm(W_C * x + b_C) \tag{3}$$

$$y = H(W_X * x + b) \odot g_T + x \odot g_c \tag{4}$$

W_T and b_T are the weight matrix and bias vector for the transform gate. W_C and b_C are the weight matrix and bias vector for the carry gate.

In our model, we input word embedding features into a deep highway network. Using highway, we can use a deeper network structure to fully extract the relationship between word embedding features. And it is easy to train a deep highway network.

In our model, highway network is followed by two dense layers, with 100 neurons and 30 neurons. At the same time, we add a dropout layer for each dense layer to avoid overfitting. At the end of the model, we use the softmax layer as the output layer and cross entropy as the loss function.

6 Experiments

6.1 The Evaluation Standard

Since the classification task of semantic relations is a multiclass classification task, we do not directly use the accuracy as the evaluation criteria. In order to be able to accurately evaluate the performance of the classification model, we calculate Precision, Recall, F1-score for each semantic relationship. Finally, we calculate the macro averaged precision, recall and F1-score, and use the macro averaged F1-score as the evaluation criteria for the classification task as follows:

$$F_{marco} = \frac{F_{Obj} + F_{Coo} + F_{Desc} + F_{Mann}}{4}$$

6.2 Results and Analysis

We test the model's classification performance on a dataset that is balanced using the SMOTH algorithm. We use a training set containing 2000 data to train the model and test the final performance on a test set containing 200 pieces of data.

As shown in Table 3, the neural network model with the semantic features converged finally achieved better classification performance: the macro averaged F1 score reach 0.84. In the Coo classification, the model achieves the best F1 score: 0.85. Mann classification get the best Precision: 0.91. As for the Obj classification and Coo classification, the model achieves the best Recall: 0.88. Relatively speaking, our model still needs to improve the identification of the Obj classification, which F1 score is the lowest.

Table 3. Performance of the CNN-highway network

Category	Precision	Recall	F1 score
Obj	0.76	0.88	0.81
Coo	0.83	0.88	0.85
Desc	0.87	0.80	0.83
Mann	0.91	0.78	0.84
Macro-average	0.84	0.83	0.84

In order to better compare the performance of the model, we tested different classification algorithms/models on the same dataset. We implemented a simple classifier based purely on linguistic rules and tested rule-based classification performance. At the same time, we compared the classification performance of neural network model without using semantic features.

As shown in Table 5, the classification performance of neural networks (using semantic features and not using semantic features) is superior to the classification model based purely on linguistic rules, which proves that the neural network model has strong non-linear fitting ability. Neural network model can map complex non-linear relationship, with strong robustness, memory, and strong self-learning ability. Neural network model does not require expensive manual rules extraction, and avoid the interference of human factors.

At the same time, it can be seen in Table 4 that the neural network using the semantic features has a significant improvement over the performance of the neural network model without using the semantic features. Semantic features respectively increase F1 score of Obj class, Coo class, Desc class and Mann class by 0.08, 0.10, 0.13 and 0.03. It turns out that semantic information helps improve the performance of deep neural network classifier in this case. Since our data set is small, the model also needs to be tested on a larger dataset to further analyze performance.

Table 4. Performance of various models

Algorithms	F-Obj	FCoo	FDesc	FMann	Fmacro
Based on the rules	0.65	0.64	0.68	0.58	0.64
Neural Network	0.73	0.75	0.80	0.81	0.77
Neural network + Semantic features	0.81	0.85	0.83	0.84	0.84

7 Conclusion

In this paper, we exploit a CNN-Highway network combined with semantic features for semantic relation classification of Chinese Nominal Compounds. Experiments show that the CNN-Highway network can extract global features of the nominal phrases and has a strong learning ability. Our model achieves 84% F1-score on the test data set. Additionally, our experimental results show that: (1) our model is far superior to rule-based classifiers; (2) the model obtains a significant improvement when semantic features are added.

Acknowledgments. This research was funded by the National Natural Science Foundation of China (No.61872402), the Humanities and Social Science Planning (No.17YJAZH068) supported by the Ministry of Education and the Graduate Innovation Fund (No.18YCX008) supported by Beijing Language and Culture University. We hereby express our sincere thanks.

References

1. Rosario, B., Hearst, M., Fillmore, C.: The descent of hierarchy, and selection in relational semantics. In: Meeting on Association for Computational Linguistics, pp. 247–254. Association for Computational Linguistics, Philadelphia (2002)
2. Rosario, B., Hearst, M., Fillmore, C.: Classifying the semantic relations in noun compounds via a domain-specific lexical hierarchy. In: Lee, L., Harman, D. (eds.) Proceedings of EMNLP (Empirical Methods in Natural Language Processing), pp. 247–254 (2001)

3. Girju, R., Giuglea, A.M., Olteanu, M., et al.: Support vector machines applied to the classification of semantic relations in nominalized noun phrases. In: Proceedings of the HLT-NAACL Workshop on Computational Lexical Semantics, pp. 68–75. Association for Computational Linguistics (2004)
4. Nastase, V., Sayyad-Shirabad, J., Sokolova, M., et al.: Learning noun-modifier semantic relations with corpus-based and WordNet-based features. In: National Conference on Artificial Intelligence, pp. 781–786. AAAI Press (2006)
5. Tratz, S., Hovy, E.: A taxonomy, dataset, and classifier for automatic noun compound interpretation. In: 48th Proceeding of the Annual Meeting of the Association for Computational Linguistics, pp. 678–687 (2010)
6. Dima, C., Hinrichs, E.: Automatic noun compound interpretation using deep neural networks and word embeddings. In: Proceedings of the 11th International Conference on Computational Semantics, pp. 173–183 (2015)
7. Li, Y., Shao, Y.: Annotating Chinese noun phrases based on semantic dependency graph. In: Asian Language Processing (IALP), 2016 International Conference, pp. 18–21. IEEE (2016)
8. Li, Y., Shao, Y., Yang, H.: Semantic dependency labeling of Chinese noun phrases based on semantic Lexicon. In: Sun, M., Wang, X., Chang, B., Xiong, D. (eds.) CCL/NLP-NABD - 2017. LNCS (LNAI), vol. 10565, pp. 237–248. Springer, Cham (2017). https://doi.org/10.1007/978-3-319-69005-6_20
9. Chawla, N.V., Japkowicz, N., Kotcz, A.: Special issue on learning from imbalanced data sets. ACM Sigkdd Explor. Newsl. **6**(1), 1–6 (2004)
10. Chawla, N.V., Bowyer, K.W., Hall, L.O., Kegelmeyer, W.P.: SMOTE: synthetic minority over-sampling technique. J. Artif. Intell. Res. **16**, 321–357 (2002)
11. Mikolov, T., Sutskever, I., Chen, K., Corrado, G.S., Dean, J.: Distributed representations of words and phrases and their compositionality. In: Advances in Neural Information Processing Systems, pp. 3111–3119 (2013)
12. Santos, C.N.D., Xiang, B., Zhou, B.: Classifying relations by ranking with convolutional neural networks. arXiv preprint arXiv:1504.06580 (2015)
13. Srivastava, R.K., Greff, K., Schmidhuber, J.: Training very deep networks. In: Advances in Neural Information Processing Systems, pp. 2377–2385 (2015)

Learning Term Weight with Long Short-Term Memory for Question Retrieval

Xifeng Huang(✉) and Xiang Dai

China Electronics Technology Group Corporation No. 10 Research Institute, Beijing, China
huangsixiao@163.com, dai.xiang@hotmail.com

Abstract. Most of previous methods on question retrieval treat all words as equally important. This paper employs a bidirectional long short-term memory network to predict word salience weight in the question, which is hinted by the word's matching status in the answer. Our method is trained on a large corpus of natural question-answer pairs, and so it requires no human annotation. We conduct experiments on question retrieval in a cQA dataset. The results show that our model outperforms traditional methods by a wide margin.

Keywords: Question answering · Question retrieval · Word salience weight

1 Introduction

The community-based question answering (cQA) attracts considerable attention in recent years, where question retrieval is an important subtask. In the general settings, a bundle of question-answer pairs are collected from cQA services like Baidu Zhidao and Yahoo Answer. Given a new question, the system is required to rank the candidate questions via a question-question relevance model, and return the most relevant questions.

Traditional cQA retrieval methods are based on word matching, which suffer from the severe lexical gap problem. Besides this, most of previous methods tend to treat all terms in a question as independent and of uniform importance. Simple heuristics, such as inverse document frequency (*idf*), are often used as term weight models, but they are very rigid and the performance is quite limited.

Figure 1 shows an example. Given the query question, most of previous methods, such as *tf-idf* weights, return the second similar question, which shares many common words with respect to the original question but is not the expected one. The traditional methods fail to capture the salient word "seafood" in the question, which carries the most important information to convey the user's querying intent.

In this paper, we address the issue of word weighting strategy for question retrieval. The contributions of this paper are in three folds.

J.-F. Hong et al. (Eds.): CLSW 2018, LNAI 11173, pp. 615–622, 2018.
https://doi.org/10.1007/978-3-030-04015-4_53

Table 1. An example of question retrieval. Our dynamic word salience weight in this paper retrieves the relevant question, while the *tf-idf* method retrieves the unexpected one.

Query question:
去(go to) 三亚(Sanya) 买(buy) ***海鲜(seafoods)*** 哪里(where) 比较(more) 便宜(cheap)?
Where can we buy cheaper seafoods in Sanya?
Retrieved question by our method:
三亚(Sanya) ***海鲜(seafoods)*** 价格(price) 怎么样(how about)?
How about the price of seafoods in Sanya?
Retrieved question by the tf-idf weight:
去(go to) 三亚(Sanya) *机票(plane ticket)* 在(at) 哪里(where) 买(buy) 比较(more) 便宜(cheap)?
Where can we buy cheaper plane tickets to Sanya?

- We assume that the matching status in question-answer pairs reflects a word semantic importance, and the experimental results prove our assumption.
- We propose a novel word weighting strategy by employing a bi-directional LSTM network, which is trained on the natural occurring question-answer pairs but applied to question-question retrieval. So our model is unsupervised and needs no human effort for annotation.
- We seamlessly integrate our dynamic word salience weight into the existing retrieval methods, and our model outperforms previous methods significantly.

2 Related Work

Most previous methods in question retrieval were devoted to address the lexical gap problem, but they treated all words as equally important. Only a few researches paid attention to the word salience weight. Bendersky and Croft [5] constructed a set of features and used a supervised machine learning method for key concept identification and weighting. In the work of [13], domain-specific term weight with multiple evidences is utilized to improve the performance of archived question search. Bendersky et al. [6] exploited statistic features to estimate term weight for a concept, including endogenous features and exogenous features, and the exogenous features used external data sources, such as a large sample of query logs.

We can see there are limitations in the previous methods. They employed supervised machine learning methods, so a large corpus with human annotation as well as feature engineering is needed. For the domain-specific term weight, their weight functions only depend on statistical counts and are static within a specific domain, and thus cannot well capture the dynamic contextual information for each sentence.

Another relevant topic with our work is neural network method for modelling sentences, which aim to embed the variable length sentences into fixed-length vectors. The methods include recurrent neural network (RNN) [11], recursive neural network (RNN) [8] and convolutional neural network (CNN) [7]. In recent times, the LSTM network is also widely applied to model sentences in natural language processing tasks [1, 2, 12].

3 Long Short-Term Memory Network

We give a brief introduction to the LSTM network and its bidirectional extension. The LSTM network utilizes memory cells and gates to learn long range dependencies within a sequence [9]. Given an input sentence $S = (x_0, x_1, \ldots x_t)$, where x_t the word embedding at time t, the hidden representation h_t can be calculated as:

$$i_t = \sigma(W_i \cdot [x_t, h_{t-1}] + b_i) \tag{1}$$

$$f_t = \sigma(W_f \cdot [x_t, h_{t-1}] + b_f) \tag{2}$$

$$c_{new} = \tanh(W_c \cdot [x_t, h_{t-1}] + b_c) \tag{3}$$

$$c_t = f_t \cdot c_{t-1} + i_t \cdot c_{new} \tag{4}$$

$$o_t = \sigma(W_o \cdot [x_t, h_{t-1}] + b_o) \tag{5}$$

$$h_t = o_t \cdot \tanh(c_t) \tag{6}$$

where i, f, o denote the input, forget and output gates respectively, c is the cell memory and h is the hidden representation. The Eq. (4) uses the input gate to threshold the information flow into the network memory from a new input.

The bi-directional LSTM processes the input text from both forward and backward directions using two separate LSTM models. The output hidden representation at time t for bi-directional LSTM is composed of two parts, denoted as $h_t = [\vec{h}_t, \overleftarrow{h}_t]$.

4 Model Description

4.1 Intuition

In cQA, the most appropriate answer with respect to a question often explicitly mentions some key points of the question. In other words, if a word in the question also occurs frequently in the answer, it would carry important information for the semantic of the question. See an example in Table 2:

Table 2. An example of a question and its relevant answer

Question: I want to know where is the most delicious *spicy hot pot* in Beijing?
Answer: On a cold winter day, you may like to have something hot with your family. Then the *spicy hot pot* is perhaps the best choice for you. Now let's introduce the most famous *hot pots* in Beijing below…

The question focuses on "hot spicy pot" and the answer also mentions it several times. So the matching status of a question word in the answer can be seen as a hint of this word's semantic importance.

4.2 Dynamic Word Salience Weight

Following this observation, we propose a sequential labelling task to predict each word's semantic saliency. The question-answer pairs are the natural training data for this task. As shown in Fig. 1, we give each word in the question a label TRUE if it also occurs in the answer, and assign other words with the label FALSE that don't occur in the answer. In this matching process, we exclude the functional words, because they are too common to bring more useful information to our model.

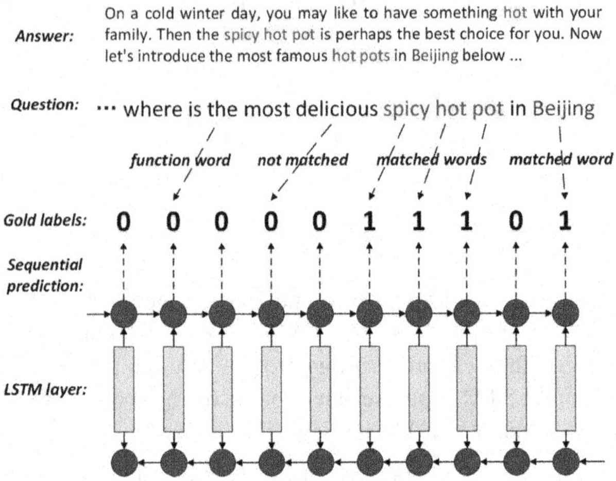

Fig. 1. LSTM based word weighting strategy

Since the word saliency depends not only on the word itself, but also on its forward and backward context of the question, we train a bi-directional LSTM to incorporate the contextual information.

After getting the hidden representation h_t by a bi-LSTM network, we then employ a perception layer at each word's position to predict its hint label:

$$p(label = 1|w_t) = \sigma(W_{predict} \cdot h_t + b_{predict}) \quad (7)$$

where w_t is the word itself, h_t denotes the hidden representation at position t, $W_{predict}$ and $b_{predict}$ are the parameters of the regression layer.

In the question retrieval process, given a new question, we use the trained LSTM network to predict the word saliency in the question. The output probability of each word is treated as its dynamic salience weight within the question.

4.3 Similarity Computing

We adopt Eq. (8) to calculate the relevance scores of the question-question pairs:

$$\cos(q_1, q_2) = \frac{\sum_k w_k^{q_1} \cdot w_k^{q_2}}{(\sum_k w_k^{q_1^2})^{\frac{1}{2}} \cdot (\sum_k w_k^{q_2^2})^{\frac{1}{2}}.} \tag{8}$$

where $w_k^{q_1}$ and $w_k^{q_2}$ denote the kth word's weight in the question q_1 and q_2, respectively.

We integrate our weighting strategy into the traditional methods, by replacing the term weight w_k^q with our dynamic word salience weight $p(label = 1|w_t)$.

4.4 Baseline Methods

We also adopt various kinds of weighting strategies to serve as the baselines.

Tf-idf Score: This is the most popular weighting method in natural language processing. Let f_{ij} denote the term i's frequency in document j, N is the number of documents, n_i is the number of documents occurring the term i. The *tf-idf* score is computed as:

$$idf = \log \frac{N}{n_i} \tag{9}$$

$$w_{ij} = f_{ij} \times idf \tag{10}$$

Okapi Score: Let *dl* denote the abbreviation of document length, it is calculated as:

$$w_{ij} = \frac{f_{ij}}{0.5 + 1.5 \cdot \frac{dl}{avg\_dl} + f_{ij}} \cdot idf(w_{ij}) \tag{11}$$

Term Entropy Score: It is calculated as:

$$w_{ij} = 1 + \sum_{j=1}^{N} \frac{\frac{f_{ij}}{F_j} \cdot \log(\frac{f_{ij}}{F_j})}{\log N} \tag{12}$$

5 Experiment

5.1 Experimental Data

The dataset comes from Baidu Zhidao, which is one of the most popular cQA services in China. We have crawled 180,000 question-answer pairs under the "travelling" topic. The data was preprocessed with Chinese word segmentation and part of speech tagging using *ICTCLAS* [3]. We removed the pairs which have too short answer or question

(<= 5 words) or consist of only URL string. Finally, there are 160,000 pairs remained, which constitute the training data of our model.

For the question retrieval task, we have to manually annotate the testing dataset. We selected other 800 question-answer pairs, which are the real user's queries and not included in our training dataset. For each target question, we first use Lucene to retrieve 100 similar questions from our training data of 160,000 questions, which serve as the candidate questions. From these candidate questions, we manually annotate the questions that have the same meaning with the target. If no such questions are found, the target question is discarded. Finally, there are 500 questions left in the testing dataset. In average, there are 9 similar questions per target question.

5.2 Experiment Setup

In our experiment, the word embeddings are pretrained using word2vec [10] on Baidu Zhidao corpus, including the whole data of 160,000 question-answer pairs. The dimension of word embeddings is set to 200. The h_t length is also set to 200.

We evaluate the model performance using two metrics: Precision@1 (P@1) and Mean Reciprocal Rank (MRR), which are widely used in information retrieval.

5.3 Results and Analysis

Table 3 reports the experimental results. In traditional methods, the *tf-idf* word weighting method preforms the best. Our dynamic word salience weight significantly outperforms other kinds of weights, which gets 6.2% increase on P@1 and 7.1% increase on MRR, compared with the *tf-idf* weight.

To further understand the performance of different weights, see the query question in Table 1 as an example. Figure 2 lists each word's weight assigned by the traditional *tf-idf* method and our LSTM weighting strategy, respectively.

As shown in Table 1, the cosine similarity with the *tf-idf* weight retrieves an irrelevant question, which contains almost the same words with the target except the key point "seafoods". Figure 2 illustrates the reason. The *tf-idf* weight gives the term "seafoods" a very low weight score 0.229, but computes a relatively high score 0.455 to the frequent word "go to". On the contrary, our dynamic word salience weight assigns a high score to "seafood" (0.744), by taking advantage of both the forward and backward context information captured by the bi-LSTM, thus retrieves the correct relevant question.

Table 3. Experimental results on question retrieval

Method	p@1	MRR
Tf-idf	40.2	53.9
Okapi	25.7	38.6
Term entropy	39.8	53.5
Our method	46.4	61.0

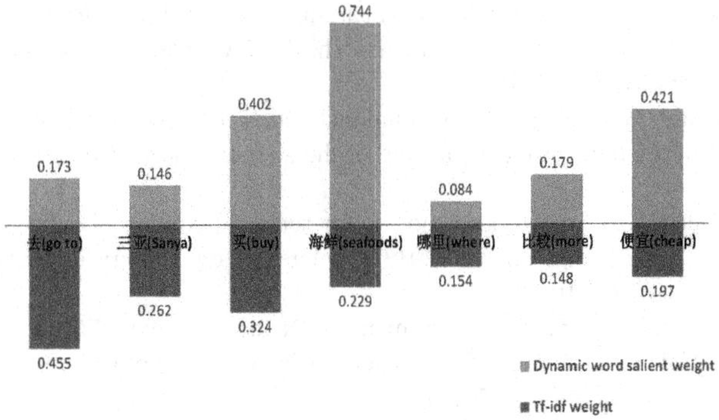

Fig. 2. Weight strategies comparison between our dynamic word salient weight and the traditional tf-idf weight

6 Conclusion

In this paper, we propose a novel weighting strategy for question retrieval. We employ a bi-directional LSTM network to dynamically predict the word salience weight in the query question, by using the question word's matching status in the answer as a hint for its semantic importance. The experimental results show that our dynamic word salience weight significantly outperforms the traditional word weighting strategies.

Our method is unsupervised that needs no human annotation; our method is language independent that needs no language-specific knowledge. So our method can be easily adapted to other tasks (such as textual entailment) and other languages (such as English).

References

1. Chris, D., Miguel, B., Wang, L., Austin, M., Noah, A.: Transition based dependency parsing with stack long short-term memory. In: Proceedings of the 53rd Annual Meeting of the Association for Computational Linguistics and the 7th International Joint Conference on Natural Language Processing (2015)
2. Di, W., Eric, N.: A long short-term memory model for answer sentence selection in question answering. In: Proceedings of the 53rd Annual Meeting of the Association for Computational Linguistics and the 7th International Joint Conference on Natural Language Processing (2015)
3. Hua-Ping, Z., Hong-Kui, Y., De-Yi, X., Qun, L.: Hhmm-based chinese lexical analyzer ictclas. In: SIGHAN 2003 Proceedings of the Second SIGHAN Workshop on Chinese Language Processing (2003)
4. John, C., Elad, H., Yoram, S.: Adaptive sub gradient methods for online learning and stochastic optimization. J. Mach. Learn. Res. **12**(7), 257–269 (2011)
5. Michael, B., Bruce Croft, W.: Discovering key concepts in verbose queries. In: Proceedings of the 31st Annual International ACM SIGIR Conference on Research and Development in Information Retrieval (2008)

6. Michael, B., Metzler, D., Croft, B.: Learning concept importance using a weighted dependence model. In: Proceedings of the Third ACM International Conference on Web Search and Data Mining (2010)
7. Nal, K., Edward, G., Phil, B.: A convolutional neural network for modelling sentences. In: Proceedings of the 52nd Annual Meeting of the Association for Computational Linguistics (2014)
8. Richard, S., et al.: Recursive deep models for semantic compositionality over a sentiment treebank. In: Proceedings of the 2013 Conference on Empirical Methods in Natural Language Processing (2013)
9. Sepp, H., Jurgen, S.: Long-short term memory. Neural Compute **9**(8), 1735–1780 (1997)
10. Tomas, M., Kai, G.C., Jeffrey, D.: Efficient estimation of word representations in vector space. In: Workshop at ICLR (2013)
11. Tomas, M., Martin, K., Lukas, B., Jan, C., Sanjeev, K.: Recurrent neural network based language model. In: INTERSPEECH (2010)
12. Xin, W., Yuanchao, L., Chengjie, S., Baoxun, W., Xiaolong, W.: Predicting polarities of tweets by composing word embeddings with long short-term memory. In: Proceedings of the 53rd Annual Meeting of the Association for Computational Linguistics and the 7th International Joint Conference on Natural Language Processing (2015)
13. Ming, Z.-Y., Chua, T., Cong, G.: Discovering key concepts in verbose queries exploring domain-specific term weight in archived question search. In: Proceedings of the 19th ACM International Conference on Information and Knowledge Management (2010)

Improved Implementation of Expectation Maximization Algorithm on Graphic Processing Unit

Si-Yuan Jing(✉), Rui Sun, Chun-Ming Xie, Peng Jin, Yi Liu, and Cai-Ming Liu

School of Computer Science, Leshan Normal University, Leshan 614000, China
siyuan-jing@qq.com, 30452466@qq.com, dram_218@163.com, jandp@pku.edu.cn, 1965liuyi@163.com, caiming_liu@163.com

Abstract. In our previous work, an efficient implementation of Expectation-Maximization (EM) algorithm using CUDA has been proposed for high-speed word alignment. The proposed algorithm can gain a 16.8-fold speedup compared to a multi-thread algorithm and a 234.7-fold speedup compared to a sequential algorithm on a modern graphic processing unit (GPU). In this paper, we try to improve the algorithm to achieve better performance. Through analysis of the previous algorithm, we find that two places in "E" step (expectation calculation) are unreasonably designed. An improved CUDA implementation of the EM algorithm is proposed in this paper. Experimental results show that the new algorithm can improve the speed of expectation calculation by 29.4%.

Keywords: Word alignment · GPU · Parallel computation
Expectation-maximization algorithm · CUDA

1 Introduction

Given a training corpus which contains a set of aligned parallel sentence pairs, the aim of word alignment is to identify translation relationships among the words in each bi-text. This task has been regarded as the starting point when building a modern statistical machine translation system. A well-known technique for word alignment is IBM model 1-5 [1] in which an EM algorithm is used to compute alignment probability among the words in each parallel sentence. On the basis of IBM model 1-5, Och et al. [2] developed GIZA++ which is the most popular word alignment tool in last decade. However, GIZA++ has a large time overhead that makes the task become unbearable. Gao et al. [4] developed MGIZA++ in which the EM algorithm is implemented by multi-thread technique. However, we think that the performance is also unsatisfactory.

In our previous work [3], we proposed an efficient implementation of EM algorithm for word alignment using CUDA. The best experimental results show a 16.8-fold speedup compared to the multi-thread algorithm (i.e. MGIZA++) and a 234.7-fold speedup compared to the sequential algorithm (i.e. GIZA++). In this paper, we try to improve the previous algorithm to achieve better performance.

J.-F. Hong et al. (Eds.): CLSW 2018, LNAI 11173, pp. 623–629, 2018.
https://doi.org/10.1007/978-3-030-04015-4_54

The rest of the paper is organized as follow. Section 2 briefly recalls some knowledge about CUDA programming. Section 3 firstly introduces the data structure which plays an important role in our algorithm. Then, we explain the shortcomings of the previous algorithm and present an improved implementation of EM algorithm on GPU. Section 4 shows experimental results. Finally, Sect. 5 gives conclusions.

2 Preliminaries of CUDA Programming

CUDA is the most popular GPU programming model proposed by Nvidia. A typical CUDA program can be divided into two parts, i.e. a sequential host program and one or more parallel device program (called ***kernels***). The former is executed on CPU and the latter is parallel executed on GPU. A kernel will be parallel executed on GPU according to user-defined parameters, including number of thread and number of thread block [6]. Therefore, design and optimization of kernels are key to high performance programming on GPU. Next, we will briefly introduce some keynotes in CUDA programming.

A kernel executes a scalar sequential program across a set of parallel threads. For CUDA, thread is the basic unit for program execution. Furthermore, all the threads are hierarchically organized. A number of threads constitute a thread block, and a number of thread blocks form a grid. A kernel thus consists of a grid of one or more thread blocks. The threads in a thread block are concurrent and they can cooperate amongst themselves through barrier synchronization and a per-block shared memory space private to that block. This is a key feature of CUDA [9].

Single Instruction Multiple Threads (SIMT) is another important feature of CUDA [7]. SIMT means that threads are executed in bundles (called ***warps***). The threads in a warp share a single multithreaded instruction unit. This design allows the programs to achieve substantial efficiencies when executing data-parallel program. To achieve the best efficiency, kernels should avoid execution divergence, since different execution path will lead to performance penalty. However, difference among warps will introduce no performance loss. In modern GPUs, a warp consists of 32 threads. In another words, the number of threads in a thread block must be a multiple of 32. This ensures that the resource would not be wasted.

Finally, it is necessary to indicate that the CUDA relies on multi-thread switch to hide the latency of transactions with external memory. Different from CPU, there is no cache in current GPUs. Thus, we should launch enough threads to keep the machine fully utilized. For current GPUs, a minimum of round 5,000 threads must be live simultaneously to efficiently utilize the entire resource.

3 Parallelization of Expectation-Maximization Algorithm Using CUDA

3.1 Expectation Maximization Algorithm for Word Alignment

Given a parallel bilingual corpus, denoted by (**E**, **F**), where **E** represents a set of source language sentences and **F** represents a set of target language sentences. Let ($\boldsymbol{e}, \boldsymbol{f}$) denote the s-th sentence pair in the corpus, where $\boldsymbol{e} = \{e_1, e_2, \ldots, e_l\}$ contains l source language words, and $\boldsymbol{f} = \{f_1, f_2, \ldots, f_m\}$ contains m target language words. The aim of word alignment task is to find a set of binary relation $<e_i, f_j>$, where e_i and f_j are translations of each other in the sentence pair. Generally, we model the problem as an aligning function $a : j \rightarrow i$, which represents that a source language word e_i is aligned to a target language word f_j. The aim is to get this function [5].

In IBM model 1-5, word alignment is obtained by training a lexical translation model. Brown [1] uses a generative modeling method and an EM algorithm to get the lexical translation model. The core idea of the algorithm includes two steps:

(1) Based on current translation model, we can calculate the aligning probability of arbitrary word pairs in a sentence pair, denoted as $P(a \mid e, f)$. The formula is shown below. The meaning of this step is that we apply a known translation model to data, and then obtain an unknown aligning probability. This is the "E" step of the EM algorithm.

$$P(a|\boldsymbol{e},\boldsymbol{f}) = \prod_{j=1}^{m} \frac{t(f_j|e_{a(j)})}{\sum_{i=0}^{l} t(f_j|e_i)}$$

(2) With the new word alignment probability, we can re-estimate the translation probability of all source - target language word pairs in corpus. The formula is shown below. This is the "M" step of the EM algorithm.

$$t(f|e) = \frac{\sum_{(\boldsymbol{e},\boldsymbol{f})} c(f|e;\, \boldsymbol{e},\boldsymbol{f})}{\sum_{f} \sum_{(\boldsymbol{e},\boldsymbol{f})} c(f|e;\, \boldsymbol{e},\boldsymbol{f})}$$

Here, $c(f \mid e;\, e, f)$ is a function which counts how many times a specific source language word e is translated to a target language word f in a sentence. $\delta(x, y)$ is the Kronecker function, $\delta(x, y) = 1$ if $x = y$, otherwise $\delta(x, y) = 0$.

$$c(f|e;\, \boldsymbol{e},\boldsymbol{f}) = \frac{t(f|e)}{\sum_{j=1}^{l} t(f|e_i)} \sum_{i=1}^{l} \delta(e, e_i) \sum_{j=1}^{m} \delta(f, f_j)$$

Two steps will be repeated several iterations and the algorithm finally converge to a stable point.

3.2 Data Structure

In our previous work, a specific hash table is designed for accessing data of word alignment on GPU. In this section, this data structure will be simply recalled.

The hash table is shown in Fig. 1. In the hash table, "Pool" variable is used to store entries of translation model. Each entry has four member variables which are "Key", "Prob", "Count" and "next", and they store word pair $<e_i, f_j>$, translation probability of the word pair, the number of times that the word pair appears in a sentence, a pointer to the next entry with same hash value, respectively. Another variable 'Buckets' is used to store pointers of entries. The word pairs which have the same hash value are organized into a linked list and the pointer in "Buckets" points to the last one (For linked list, it is the first one). For example, when a new word pair is prepared to be inserted into the hash table, we create a new entry whose "Key" value is set to the word pair, and insert it to the end of the "Pool". Meanwhile we compute its hash value. We set the "next" variable of the new entry to be the location of the first entry in the linked list (with same hash value), and finally let the pointer (in 'Buckets') point to the new entry.

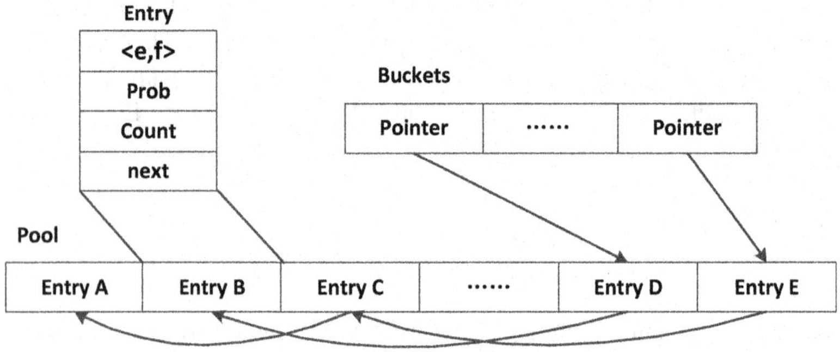

Fig. 1. A specific hash table

3.3 Improved Implementation of Expectation Maximization Algorithm

Our previous algorithm is based on [5], which consists of two subroutines. One is responsible for expectation calculation (i.e. "E" step) and the other is responsible for re-estimating the probabilistic model (i.e. "M" step). Time cost of the algorithm is composed of three parts, including execution time of "E" step, "M" step, and time of data transfer between GPU and the host.

We try to improve the previous algorithm to achieve better performance. From experimental results, we can see that time cost of "E" step is far more than that of "M" step. For instance, when data set has 100 thousands sentence pairs, "E" step will take 810.7 ms and "M" step will take 5.25 ms. It is obvious that improving "M" step would gain little performance. We focus on improvement of "E" step in this work.

Through analysis, we find that there are two places that will lead to performance decrease in our previous algorithm. The first improvement is that structure of loops is changed. In previous algorithm, when getting a parallel sentence pair, the outer loop traverses the source language sentence and the inner loop traverses the target language sentence. Moreover, an array *sTotal[]* is used to assist calculation. In new algorithm, the order of loops is exchanged. The outer loop traverses the target language sentence and the inner loop traverses the other. This change brings us two advantages. On the one hand, the target language sentence is traversed only once; on the other hand, the array *sTotal[]* is replaced by a variable *demon*, that will reduce memory overhead.

The second improvement is that an array *loc[]* is used to store position of word pair <*e[j], f[k]*> when it is located in hash table for the first time. Obviously, this change can greatly improve efficiency of the algorithm, because it can avoid search word pairs again in the hash table. The reason why the previous algorithm does not store location is that the number of register on GPU is limited (registers were previously occupied by *sTotal[]*) (Table 1).

Table 1. An improved algorithm for expectation calculation

```
Input:
1. tModel:  the translation model represented by the hash table
2. corpus:  a set of parallel sentence pairs
3. fTotal:  an array for counting word-pair
4. sentNum: number of sentences
Output:
The updated tModel and fTotal
---------------------------------------------------------------
tid = threadIdx.x + blockIdx.x * blockDim.x ;
offset = gridDim.x * blockDim.x ;
for( i = tid ; i < sentNum ; i += offset )
    < e, f > = get_sentence_pair ( corpus, i ) ;
    loc[] = {0};
    for( k = 0; k <length( f ) ; k++ )
        demon = 0.0;
        for( j = 0; j < length( e ) ; j++ )
            loc[j] = query_word( tModel, e[j], f[k]) ;
            if( tModel.pool[loc[j]] > DEFAULT_PROB )
              demon += tModel.pool[loc[j]].prob ;
            else
              demon += DEFAULT_PROB ;
            end if
        end for
        for( j = 0; j < length( e ) ; j++ )
            if( tModel.pool[loc[j]] > DEFAULT_PROB )
              val = tModel.pool[loc[j]].prob / demon ;
            else
              val = DEFAULT_PROB / demon ;
            end if
            atomicAdd( tModel.pool[loc[j]].count,val );
            atomicAdd( fTotal[ f[k] ], val );
        end for
    end for
end for
```

4 Experiment

This section evaluates the efficiency of the proposed algorithm. It is natural to use our previous algorithm as a baseline. Experiments were performed on a Dell r720 server which has an Nvidia Tesla K40M card with 2880 cores and 12 GB RAM. Data sets used in the experiment are from [8] that is same with our previous work.

The experimental results are shown in Figs. 2 and 3. Figure 2 shows execution time of two algorithms. We can see that the new algorithm performs much better than the old one. For illustration, Fig. 3 shows results of speedup ratio between two algorithms. The results show that the new algorithm can improve the speed of expectation calculation by 29.4%.

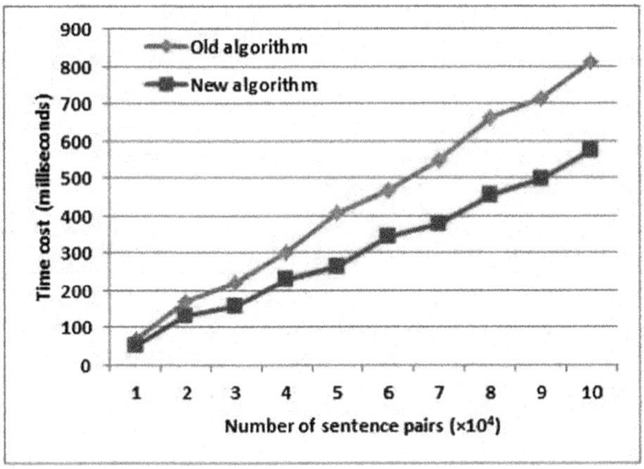

Fig. 2. Comparison of execution time

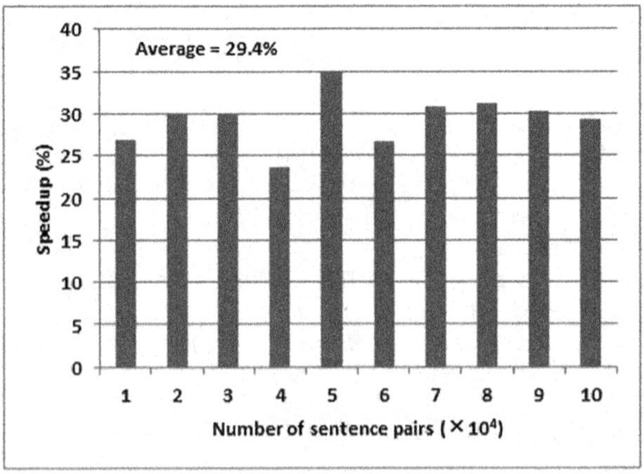

Fig. 3. Speedup

5 Conclusions

This paper proposed an improved implementation of EM algorithm for word alignment on GPU. Since execution time of "M" step is trivial, this work only focuses on the improvement of "E" step. The new algorithm is tested on a modern GPU card, and it is compared with our previous work. The results show that the new algorithm can improve the speed of expectation calculation by 29.4%. This proves the efficiency of the improvement.

Acknowledgement. This work is supported by the Fund of National Nature Science (Grand No. 61373056); the Scientific Research Fund of Sichuan Provincial Department (Grand No. 17ZA0201); the Scientific Research Fund of Leshan Normal University (Grand No. Z1325, XJR17001); the Project of Science and Technology Bureau of Leshan (Grand No. 17GZD032).

References

1. Brown, P.F., Pietra, S.A.D., Pietra, V.J.D., et al.: The mathematics of statistical machine translation: parameter estimation. Comput. Linguist. **19**, 263–311 (1993)
2. Och, F.J., Ney, H.: Improved statistical alignment models. In: Proceedings of the ACL 2000, pp. 440–447 (2000)
3. Jing, S.Y., Yan, G.R., Chen, X.Y., et al.: CUDA-based parallel implementation of IBM word alignment algorithm for statistical machine translation. In: Proceedings of the PDCAT 2016, pp. 189–194 (2016)
4. Gao, Q., Vogel, S.: Parallel implementations of word alignment tool. In: Proceedings of the SETQA-NLP 2008, pp. 49–59 (2008)
5. Koehn, P.: Statistical Machine Translation. Cambridge University Press, London (2010)
6. David, K., Hwu, W.M.: Programming Massively Parallel Processors: A Hand-On Approach. Morgan Kaufmann Publishers Inc., San Francisco (2010)
7. Ryoo, S., Rodrigues, C.I., Baghsorkhi, S.S., et al.: Optimization principles and application performance evaluation of a multi-threaded GPU using CUDA. In: Proceedings of the PPoPP 2008, pp. 73–82 (2008)
8. Xiao, T., Zhu, J.B., Zhang, H., et al.: NiuTrans: an open source toolkit for phrase-based and syntax-based machine translation. In: Proceedings of the ACL 2012, pp. 19–24 (2012)
9. Satish, N., Harris, M., Garland, M.: Designing efficient sorting algorithms for manycore GPUs. In: Proceedings of the IPDPS 2009, pp. 1–10 (2009)

A Deep Learning Baseline for the Classification of Chinese Word Semantic Relations

Yuning Deng, Mengyi Lu, Huayong Li, and Pengyuan Liu(✉)

School of Information Science, Beijing Language and Cultural University, No.15 Xueyuan Road, Beijing 100083, China
13552940428@163.com, lmy0722@foxmail.com, liangsli.mail@gmail.com, liupengyuan@pku.edu.cn

Abstract. The classification of Chinese word semantic relations is a significant research topic in the field of natural language processing. Compared with studies which identify the relation of word-pairs in given texts, the task of context-free lexical relational classification is more challenging due to the lack of context. A common way of solving this problem is to use word embeddings and lexical features to train a classifier. In this paper, we design various combinations of deep learning models and features and propose a joint model based on convolutional neural network and highway network. The joint model has reached a f1 value of 0.58 and outperform all the other deep learning models now available. Furthermore, we design extensive experiments to analyze how the magnitude of the training data influences the model's performance and whether the distribution of data influences model's performance.

Keywords: Classification of word semantic relations
Convolutional neural network · Highway network · Baseline model

1 Introduction

The calculation of lexical relationship means that given a piece of text and a pair of words, the computer needs to identify the relation of the marked words. The number of relation categories varies according to the specific application scenario. The automatic recognition of lexical relationship is an important research topic in the field of natural language processing. There is considerable interest in automatic relation classification, both as an end in itself and as an intermediate step in a variety of NLP applications [1, 2].

The task of lexical relationship classification is a subtask of the lexical relationship. Lexical semantics relationship looks at how the meaning of the lexical units correlates with the structure of the language or syntax. Words with different semantic relations are often mixed together when doing lexical sematic computation, but we need distinguish between them in real-world applications.

In this task, a pair of words are given and the computer needs to automatically divide it into one of the four categories which include synonym, antonym, hyponym as well as meronym. There are many researches on context-based task which shares a great deal of contextual knowledge and is strongly connected with the previous one in terms of lexical semantics. However, in this paper, the most prominent feature of this

J.-F. Hong et al. (Eds.): CLSW 2018, LNAI 11173, pp. 630–642, 2018.
https://doi.org/10.1007/978-3-030-04015-4_55

task is context-independent, that is, when judging the relationship between word pairs, the only information that can be utilized is the words themselves. There is no contextual information. This is harder and more challenging than the lexical relationship calculation task mentioned above.

Traditionally, there are two ways of solving the problem of context-independent lexical relationship classification. One is to use existing semantic resources, such as TongYiCi CiLin and HowNet. The other is to manually design some features and then adopt traditional machine learning algorithms to train a classifier. Generally, hand-crafted features include the character overlap between word pairs, suffix features, part of speech and so on. The disadvantage of the first method is that it is impossible to judge the relation of word pairs which are not in the dictionary. While the second method has two defects. Firstly, it usually takes a lot of time and efforts to exploit the data and design the features. Secondly, the diversity of Chinese vocabulary leads to the fact that hand-crafted features cannot be applied to all samples.

Motivated by the great success of deep neural networks in natural language processing, researchers have started to combine the distributed representation of words with artificially constructed features as inputs to feed the neural network and train a classifier. Deep learning algorithms with strong learning ability are better at mining high-dimensional features of data and capturing semantic differences between words than traditional machine learning algorithms.

Considering the above challenges and inspired by the wide success of leveraging deep neural networks, in this paper, we propose a novel framework that takes advantage of deep learning model which combines convolution neural network with highway network. Under the framework of deep learning, we have performed a series of feature and model selection experiments. The performance of the model is further analyzed and discussed. Our main contributions are two-fold:

1. A classification model combines the convolution neural network with the highway network is proposed. The model outperforms exsiting deep learning models on this task and can be used as a baseline model for subsequent research.
2. Through detailed analyses and discussions, we find that: (a) It is quite difficult to distinguish between synonyms and antonyms. Distributed representation of words only carries the information of the context, but the antonyms and the synonyms usually share similar contexts which make it difficult to distinguish them in vector space; (b) This task is also influenced by the distribution of data.

The following part is arranged as follows: the second section introduces the related work; in the third section, the general models and features used on this task are given; the fourth section is the experimental part; the fifth section spreads out analysis and research; the sixth section concludes this work.

2 Related Work

In the task of lexical relationship calculation in English language, Vylomova [3] proposed to cluster vector offset (the displacement difference between two word vectors) into several categories. Considering that the word vectors can only be used to measure whether the context of two words is similar, Hashimoto [4] proposed a method to train task-specific word vectors to improve the representation ability of word vectors.

Before deep learning is widely used, researchers tended to use traditional machine learning algorithms to deal with the task of relation classification. Deep learning algorithms make it possible to dig deeper and more abstract semantic features of words. Fully connected neural network, convolutional neural network, recurrent neural network and highway network are all basic neural network models. The existing deep learning based models are generally based on fully connected neural network and convolutional neural network [5, 6].

In the Chinese lexical relationship evaluation task of NLPCC2017, Zhou [7] used the word vectors, character vectors, co-occurrence characters between words, prefix and suffix, common substrings as well as the length of each word in word pair as input. Then Logistic Regression algorithm was adopted to train a classifier. Shijia [5] proposed a classifier based on the fully-connected neural network which uses the word vectors, part-of-speech feature and cosine similarity as the input features. Li [6] designed a model based on convolutional neural network using word vectors as input features.

3 Fundamental Models

The existing models of lexical relation classification generally adopt the framework which is illustrated in Fig. 1.

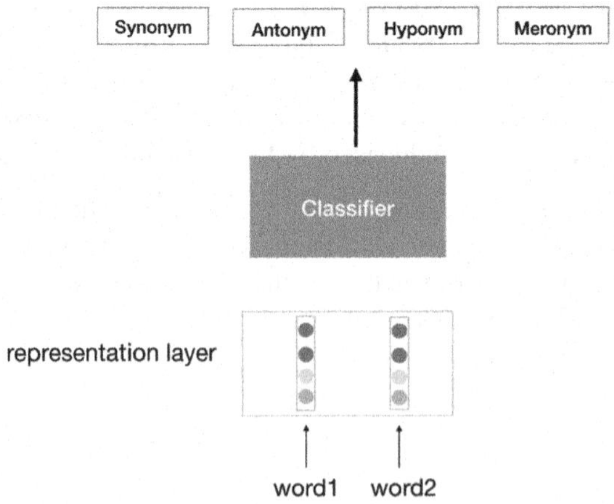

Fig. 1. General model framework.

In the classifier section, traditional machine learning methods that can be used include Support Vector Machine, Logistic Regression, Random Forest and so on. In the field of deep learning, the neural networks that have already been tried include fully connected neural network and convolutional neural network [5, 6].

In this paper, We introduce the architecture of convolutional neural network and highway network. We will detail the process of the module in Sects. 3.2 and 3.3 respectively.

3.1 Fully Connected Network

Fully connected neural network is the most primitive and basic neural network. It is used to perform a linear or nonlinear transformation of the input features. The transformation process can be formulized as follows:

$$Y = \alpha(WX + b) \tag{1}$$

Here Y denotes the transformed feature, X denotes the input feature, α represents the activation function, W and b are trainable parameters of the network.

3.2 Convolutional Neural Network

The convolutional neural network is a network model proposed by Lecun in 2014 [8], which was initially applied to the task of handwritten digits recognition. The convolutional neural network has three distinguishing features: 3D volumes of neurons, local connectivity and shared weights. Convolution and pooling operations of convolutional neural networks also enable it to extract high level characteristics of the input data, so it is widely used in both the field of image processing and the field of natural language processing.

A convolution operation involves a filter $w \in R^{hk}$, which is applied to a window of h words to produce a new feature. For example, a feature c_i is generated from a window of words $x_{i:i+h-1}$ by

$$c_i = F(x_{i:i+h-1}) \tag{2}$$

This filter is applied to each possible window of words in the sentence $\{x_{1:h}, x_{2:h-1}, x_{n-h+1:n}\}$ to produce a feature map $c = [c_1, c_2, c_{n-h+1}]$, with $c \in R^{n-h+1}$. A pooling operation is applied to the feature map:

$$\tilde{c} = \alpha\{c\} \tag{3}$$

Here α denotes the mean function or max function, F represents the general fully connected neural network.

3.3 Highway Network

Highway network [9] is a network model that emerged in 2015. This model can solve the problem of gradient vanishing problem when used to train very deep networks. Under the same structure (same network parameters), the performance of the Highway Network is better than that of the general models.

$$Y = H(X, W_H) \cdot T(X) + X \cdot (1 - T(X)) \tag{4}$$

$$T(x) = \sigma(W_T x + b_T) \tag{5}$$

Here σ denotes the sigmoid function that project the value into a numerical between 0 and 1, $H(X, W_H)$ denotes a general fully connected neural network.

4 Experiments

In this section, we have performed a series of feature and model selection experiment and then have conducted some qualitative analyses.

4.1 Dataset

The training set is the sample data which consists of 200 word pairs provided by the evaluation task (for the convenience of presentation, the NLPCC-2017 evaluation task is referred to as the evaluation task in the next chapter). The test set is also provided by the evaluation task and consists of 2000 word pairs. See Table 1 for details.

Table 1. Statistics of data

Dataset	Synonym	Antonym	Hyponym	Meronym	Total
Train	50	50	50	50	200
Test	500	500	500	500	2000

4.2 Features

In addition to using the commonly used word embedding as the input to the representation layer, we have introduced a series of features, i.e., vector offset, prefix and suffix, cosine similarity and length of the word pairs, to explore which one of the combinations of features works best.

Vector Offset. Vector offset is a algebraic operation performed on two word vectors. For example, "*King – Man + Woman* results in a vector very close to *Queen*", showing that word vectors are surprisingly good at capturing the syntactic regularities in language and that each relation is characterized by a relation-specific vector offset. This allows vector-oriented reasoning based on the offsets between words. Some studies have used clustering of vector offsets to determine the relation category [3]. Vector offset is a commonly used feature in the task of lexical relationship classification [7, 10, 11].

In this way, we have introduced the feature into our model. Given a pair of word vectors $(V_{s_1,} V_{s_2})$, the vector offset V_{info} is defined as follows:

$$V_{info} = V_{s1} - V_{s2} \tag{6}$$

Prefix and Suffix. We have found that the prefix and suffix which word pairs share is a relatively obvious feature in this task. In general, word pairs which share the same suffixes have a higher probability to be the hyponyms, such as "学生" and "大学生", "房间" and "卫生间". For word pairs which share same prefixes, they tend to be meronyms, such as "西瓜" and "西瓜皮", 花" and "花蕾". Therefore, we can use the word structural feature to improve the accuracy of our model. Given two words A and B, we have designed the features in detail and divide them into the following four cases: (1) whether the prefix of A is the same as that of B, (2) whether the suffix of A is the same as that of B, (3) whether the prefix of A is the same as the suffix of B, (4) whether the suffix of A is the same as the prefix of B. Considering the word pairs with variant length, we set the length of prefix and suffix as 1 to 4. The feature p_w is defined as follows:

$$p_w = \begin{cases} 1, & case1. \\ 2, & case2. \\ 3, & case3. \\ 4, & case4. \\ 0, & otherwise. \end{cases} \tag{7}$$

Cosine Similarity. Cosine similarity is a metric of similarity between two non-zero vectors of an inner product space that measures the cosine of the angle between them. We have taken the word embedding as vectors to calculate the cosine similarity of word pairs. Given a pair of words $(V_{s_1} V_{s_2})$, We use c^* to represent the cosine similarity.

$$c^* = \frac{V_{s_1} \cdot V_{s_2}}{\|V_{s1}\| \|V_{s2}\|} \tag{8}$$

Word Length. For Chinese words, the length of the words may contain some specific information. Generally, the longer words contain more specific information than shorter words. Moreover, the length of the words pair may imply the semantic relation of hyponym. Such as "鱼" and "金鱼", "诗" and "古诗". In addition, word pairs of which length for both words are 1 will tend to have a relation of antonym, such as "大" and "小", "美" and "丑". Therefore, in this experiment, we designed 6 metric schemes as the word length feature, $|A|, |B|, |A| + |B|, |A| - |B|, |A \cup B|, |A \cap B|$ where $|A|$ is the length of the word A and $|B|$ is the length of the word B. We have converted the corresponding word length to one-hot vector, and the length is the length of the longest word in the data.

4.3 Experimental Results

In order to find the most effective feature and model, we have conducted a series of comparative experiments. We have used three basic models: fully connected neural

Table 2. Meaning of symbols

Symbol	Meaning
fc	Fully connected neural network
highway	Highway neural network
cnn	Convolutional neural network
a, b	Word embedding for a pair of words
sim	Cosine similarity between two word vectors
len	Length of words
fix	Prefix and suffix
pos	Part of speech
Fs	F1 value for synonym
Fa	F1 value for antonym
Fh	F1 value for hyponym
Fm	F1 value for meronym

Table 3. Performance of all models

ID	Model	Features	Fs	Fa	Fh	Fm	F1-score
1	fc	a, b	0.41	0.46	0.53	0.56	0.49
2	fc	a, b, a−b	0.40	0.53	0.51	0.61	0.52
3	fc	a, b, fix	0.43	0.55	0.49	0.55	0.50
4	fc	a, b, sim	0.42	0.53	0.51	0.59	0.52
5	fc	a, b, len	0.44	0.49	0.49	0.60	0.50
6	fc	a, b, a−b, fix	0.43	0.55	0.49	0.55	0.50
7	fc	a, b, a−b, sim	0.42	0.52	0.51	0.62	0.52
8	fc	a, b, a−b, sim, fix	0.48	0.53	0.56	0.64	0.55
9	fc	a, b, sim, len	0.44	0.53	0.49	0.60	0.52
10	highway	a, b	0.54	0.51	0.52	0.65	0.56
11	highway	a, b, len	0.41	0.51	0.42	0.60	0.49
12	highway	a, b, fix	0.42	0.51	0.42	0.66	0.50
13	highway	a, b, a−b	0.49	0.47	0.41	0.66	0.51
14	highway	a, b, sim	0.34	0.32	0.45	0.39	0.38
15	cnn	a, b	0.39	0.55	0.50	0.59	0.51
16	cnn	a, b, fix	0.51	0.45	0.56	0.61	0.53

(*continued*)

Table 3. (*continued*)

ID	Model	Features	Fs	Fa	Fh	Fm	F1-score
17	cnn	a, b, len	0.42	0.52	0.51	0.58	0.51
18	cnn	a, b, a−b	0.42	0.51	0.51	0.6	0.51
19	cnn	a, b, sim	0.43	0.58	0.57	0.66	0.56
20	cnn+highway	a, b	0.39	0.50	0.50	0.56	0.49
21	cnn+highway	a, b, fix	0.46	0.6	0.58	0.67	**0.58**
22	cnn+highway	a, b, a−b	0.40	0.50	0.51	0.56	0.49
23	cnn+highway	a, b, sim	0.39	0.51	0.45	0.58	0.48
24	cnn+highway	a, b, len	0.43	0.49	0.50	0.57	0.50
25	baseline1	a−b, sim, pos	–	–	–	–	0.527
26	baseline2	a, b	0.39	0.54	0.59	0.52	0.51

network, convolutional neural network and highway network and four type of features mentioned above: vector offset, suffix and prefix, cosine similarity, the length of word.

In this subsection, we show the results of our experiment and analyze the results. The meanings of the various symbols in Table 3 are shown in Table 2:

As described in Table 3, we have designed 24 models with IDs 1 through 24. In order to compare with the existing neural network based classification models, we have reproduced two models which respectively ranked first and second in the evaluation task. The model with ID 25 represents the first-placed model that we reproduced. It is a classifier based on fully connected network. The input features consist of the word vectors, part of speech and cosine similarity of word pairs. The model with ID 26 represents the second-placed model which is based on convolutional neural networks.

As shown in the Table 3, we can see that there does not exist a certain type of feature that can improve the performance of all models. Comparing models with ID 2 to 9 with the model with ID 1, the experimental results address that for a single fully connected neural network, the model performance is improved after adding the features of vector offset, suffix, cosine similarity and length. However, the comparison between models with IDs from 11 to 14 with the model with an ID of 10 indicates that for the highway network, the introduction of any types of features will lead to a decline in model performance. By observing the comparison results of the models with IDs of 6, 7, 8, and 9, we find that the combination of features does not necessarily lead to an improvement in model performance.

In addition, we find that the experimental results with model IDs of 1, 15 indicate that the method based on convolutional neural network achieves better performance than methods based on fully connected network. But after introducing the feature of vector offset (models with IDs 2 or 18), the performance of the fully connected neural network is better than that of convolutional neural network. The performance of the

Table 4. Average performance of all models with ID 1 to 24

Synonym	Antonym	Hyponym	Meronym	F1
0.411	0.491	0.484	0.567	0.510

joint model based on convolutional neural network and the highway network is worse than that of each separate model. However, after introducing the feature of the suffix, the performance of the model is greatly improved (+9%). In summary, we believe that the effectiveness of the features varies according to the model itself.

The performance of all 24 models (IDs from 1 to 24) in the combinational experiment is averaged and the results are reported in Table 4. The most difficult relationship category to identify has been proved to be synonym, with the merely F1 value of 0.411. Through a thorough statistical analysis we found that 50% of the synonyms are predicted as the antonyms, and 30% of the antonyms are predicted to be the synonyms. As for hyponyms and meronyms, the F1 value are slightly higher, indicating that the feature of prefix and suffix is helpful in recognizing the hyponyms and the meronyms. However, synonyms do not have such regularity. On the other hand, vector offsets for synonyms and antonyms are quite close in semantic vector space and hand-crafted features rarely help distinguish these two types of relation category. In addition, our training set is not big enough for the model to achive best performance.

In Table 3, our experiment shows the model with ID 21 has the best performance, not only surpassing the other models designed in this paper, but also surpassing the two baseline systems. Under the framework of deep learning, the above series of experiments have basically considered various methods and features currently available. Therefore, we believe that the model with ID21 (cnn+highway, a, b, fix) can be used as a deep learning based baseline model for this task.

5 Analysis and Discussion

In this section, we perform additional analyses and provide further insights into our strong baseline model. We analyze how the magnitude of the training data influences the model's performance and whether the distribution of data influences model's performance. In addition, we compare the traditional methods with our strong baseline model.

5.1 Data Scale

We have conducted a number of test study on our strong baseline model to examine the effectiveness of the number of training data. Although the result in Table 3 shows our baseline model with ID 21 has the best performance among all others, the performance

Table 5. Statistics for newly collected data

Synonym	Antonym	Hyponym	Meronym	Total
889	889	919	777	3479

is still not ideal with the F1 score 0.58. The main reason may be that deep learning methods need more training data to be fully exploited. To verify this idea, we have extracted a total of 3,479 word pairs from TongYiCi CiLin and online antonym dictionary as well as Baidu Chinese website, as shown in Table 5.

We took 200 word pairs as the unit, which was gradually extracted from the 3479 training data and added to the training set (the original training set has 200 pairs). The results are shown in Fig. 2(a). It can be seen that the performance of the model gradually increases as the amount of data increases. When the number of training data reaches 1200, the performance reaches a F1 value of 0.67. The preliminary results verifies our thoughts.

However, when the amount of data in the training set exceeds 1200, the performance of the model decreases. Through careful observation of the training data, we believe that this phenomenon may be due to the inconsistent distribution of new train samples and test samples. At the same time, the F1 score of 0.67 is also unsatisfactory.

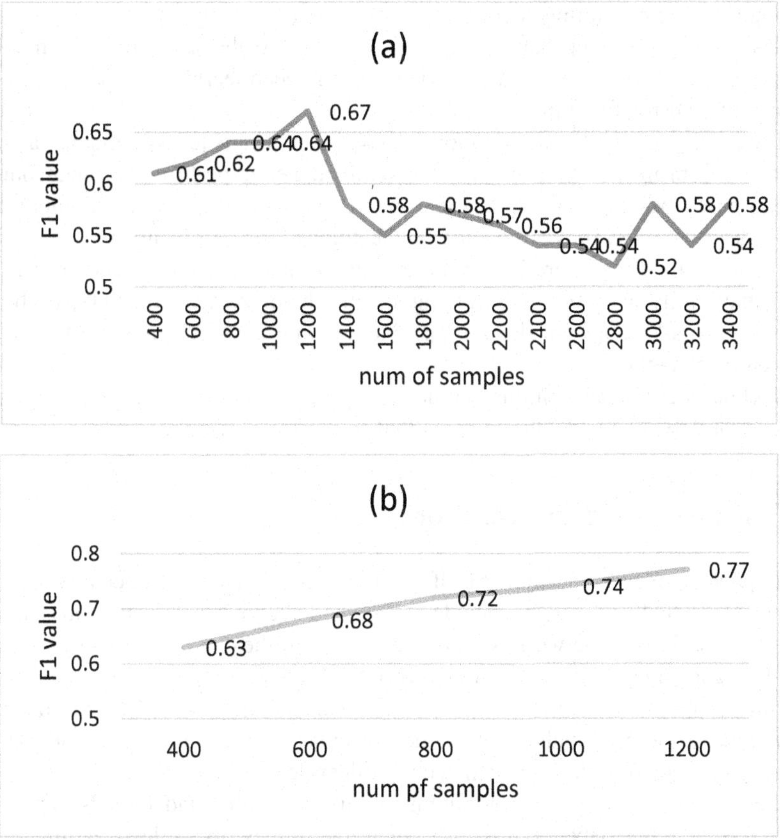

Fig. 2. Data augmentation. (a) shows adding extra data into train set while (b) shows adding part of test data into train set.

In order to verify the effect of the distribution of data on the model performance, we have done another set of comparative experiments.

The experiment still took 200 word pairs as the unit, but it was gradually extracted from the test data and added to the training set, and then the performance of the model was tested in the remaining test data (the final test data is half of the entire test data). This experimental setting can basically guarantees the data consistency of the training data and the test data. The experimental results are shown in Fig. 2(b). As we expected, the performance of model has been improved at a faster rate.

Combining (a) and (b), we can conclude that under the condition of equal number of training samples, the model performs better when the training set and the test set are more consistently distributed.

5.2 Baseline Model and Traditional Model

In many tasks of natural language processing, such as sentence similarity calculation, relation extraction, machine translation [12–14], etc., researchers have abandoned the traditional machine learning algorithms. These tasks are difficult and complex. Although machine learning algorithms also have the ability to mine features, their abilities are much weaker than that of deep learning. At the same time, the number of training data for these tasks is large enough for the deep learning model to learn high-dimensional, abstract features.

However, for this task, a model based on Logistic Regression algorithm (F1 = 0.647) proposed by Zhou [7] has achived better performance than our deep learning based baseline model. The reasons behind this are two-fold. Compared with other tasks mentioned above, there are few features of the word pairs we can use in this task. At the same time, there is very little training data. In this case, the deep learning model may easily overfits to the training set and therefore generalize poorly. It shows that with a small amount of data, a machine learning approach may work better than deep learning method.

Machine learning algorithms should be prioritized in tasks where the amount of data is relatively small and the features that the model can utilize are few.

6 Conclusion and Future Work

In this paper, under the framework of deep learning, a large number of experiments have been carried out and a deep learning model combining convolutional neural network with highway network is proposed in view of the classification task of Chinese lexical relationship. The model outperforms all other models in the combination experiment and scores the F1 value of 0.58, which is higher than all the other deep learning models now available. Due to the particularity of the task, this model can serve as a baseline model under the framework of deep learning.

There are many ways of combining linguistic features and models. The experimental results in this paper address that, under the framework of deep learning, there is not one specific kind of feature that can generally improve the performance of all models.

We averaged the performance of all 24 models (ID from 1 to 24) in the combination experiment and found that the most difficult relation to identify is synonym with the mere F1 value of 0.411. Some of the word pairs can be identified by their prefixes. However, synonyms do not have such patterns and the distribution representation of words is the only information that can be used in learning process. For a pair of words, whether they are synonyms or antonyms, their word vectors are so close in vector space that the model is difficult to predict the relation.

Future work will be carried out in the following two aspects: first, to enhance the ability of the model to distinguish between synonyms and antonyms; second, to introduce the idea of Generative Adversarial Networks into our model.

Ackowledgement. This work is supported by the MOE (Ministry of Education in China) Project of Humanities and Social Sciences (Project No. 18YJA740030), and the Fundamental Research Funds for the Central Universities, and the Research Funds of Beijing Language and Culture University (Project No. 18YCX009).

References

1. Girju, R., Nakov, P., Nastase, V., Szpakowicz, S., Turney, P., Yuret, D.: Classification of semantic relations between nominals. Lang. Resour. Eval. **43**, 105–121 (2009)
2. Iris, H., Su, N.K., Zornitsa, K., Preslav, N., Diarmuid, Ó.S., Sebastian, P., Marco, P., Lorenza, R., Stan, S.: SemEval-2010 task 8: multi-way classification of semantic relations between pairs of nominals. In: Eneko, A., Lluis, M, Richard, W. (eds) Workshop on Semantic Evaluations: Recent Achievements and Future Directions, pp. 94–99. Association for Computational Linguistics, Stroudsburg, PA, USA (2009)
3. Vylomova, E., Rimell, L., Cohn, T., Baldwin, T.: Take and Took, Gaggle and Goose, Book and Read: Evaluating the Utility of Vector Differences for Lexical Relation Learning. Computer Science (2015)
4. Hashimoto, K., Stenetorp, P., Miwa, M., Tsuruoka, Y.: Task-oriented learning of word embeddings for semantic relation classification. Computer Science (2015)
5. Shi, J.E., Jia, S., Xiang, Y.: Study on the Chinese word semantic relation classification with word embedding. In: Huang, X., Jiang, J., Zhao, D., Feng, Y., Hong, Y. (eds.) Natural Language Processing and Chinese Computing. Lecture Notes in Computer Science, vol. 10619, pp. 849–855. Springer, Cham (2017)
6. Li, C., Ma, T.: Classification of Chinese word semantic relations. In: Huang, X., Jiang, J., Zhao, D., Feng, Y., Hong, Y. (eds.) Natural Language Processing and Chinese Computing. Lecture Notes in Computer Science, vol. 10619, pp. 465–473. Springer, Cham (2017)
7. Zhou, Y., Lan, M., Wu, Y.: Effective semantic relationship classification of context-free Chinese words with simple surface and embedding features. In: Huang, X., Jiang, J., Zhao, D., Feng, Y., Hong, Y. (eds) Natural Language Processing and Chinese Computing. Lecture Notes in Computer Science, vol. 10619, pp. 456–464. Springer, Cham (2017)
8. Krizhevsky, A., Sutskever, I., Hinton, G.E.: ImageNet classification with deep convolutional neural networks. In: Pereira, F., Burges, C.J.C., Bottou, L., Weinberger, K.Q. (eds.) Neural Information Processing Systems, vol. 1, pp. 1097–1105. Curran Associates Inc., USA (2012)
9. Srivastava, R.K., Greff, K., Schmidhuber, J.: Training very deep networks. In: Cortes, C., Lee, D. D., Sugiyama, M., Garnett, R. (eds.) Neural Information Processing Systems, vol. 2, pp. 2377–2385. MIT Press, Cambridge (2012)

10. Sanchez, I., Riedel, S.: How well can we predict hypernyms from word embeddings? A dataset-centric analysis. EACL **2**, 401–407 (2017)
11. Mikolov, T., Yih, W., Zweig, G.: Linguistic regularities in continuous space word representations. HLT-NAACL **13**, 746–751 (2013)
12. He, H., Gimpel, K., Lin, J.J.: Multi-perspective sentence similarity modeling with convolutional neural networks. In: EMNLP, pp. 1576–1586 (2015)
13. Zeng, D., Liu, K., Chen, Y., Zhao, J.: Distant supervision for relation extraction via piecewise convolutional neural networks. In: EMNLP, pp. 1753–1762 (2015)
14. Bahdanau, D., Cho, K., Bengio, Y.: Neural machine translation by jointly learning to align and translate. Computer Science (2014)

Attention-Based Bi-LSTM for Chinese Named Entity Recognition

Kai Zhang[1], Weiping Ren[2(✉)], and Yangsen Zhang[1]

[1] Institute of Intelligent Information Processing,
Beijing Information Science & Technology University, Beijing, China
[2] School of Foreign Studies,
Beijing Information Science & Technology University, Beijing, China
renweiping@bistu.edu.cn

Abstract. As an integral part of deep learning, attention mechanism and bi-directional long short-term memory (Bi-LSTM) are widely used in the field of NLP (natural language processing) and their effectiveness has been well recognized. This paper adopts an attention-based Bi-LSTM approach to the question of Chinese NER (named entity recognition). With the use of word2vec, we compile vectorized dictionaries and employ Bi-LSTM models to train text vectors, with which the output eigenvectors of the attention model are multiplied. Finally, softmax is used to classify vectors in order to achieve Chinese NER. In four different configurations, our experiments describe the impact of the domain relevance of Chinese character vectors, phrase vectors, and vectorized datasets on the effectiveness of Chinese NER. The experimental results show that the standard precision (P), recall (R), and F1-score (F1) are 97.51%, 95.33%, and 96.41% respectively.

Keywords: Attention mechanism · Bi-LSTM · Named entity recognition Word2vec

1 Introduction

As the fundamental task of an intelligent answer system, NER also deals with a highly technical aspect of NLP and plays a significant part in accurately identifying nouns with special meanings in a text, such as names of people, places, organizations, etc. The purpose of NER is to provide useful information of this kind for automatic question answering systems, intelligent customer service solutions, automatic summarization, and other similar NLP tasks. Initially, NER depended on expert rules, namely rules formulated by subject-matter (domain) experts and scholars, for recognition tasks. This method required averting conflicts between different rules and consequently necessitated expending considerable time and effort establishing rules. Coupled with the difficulty in transfer learning in different fields, the conventional approach did not work well for complicated tasks. To solve this problem, researchers had begun to use machine learning techniques – in place of "human" rules – to perform NER tasks.

The machine learning methods used for sequence labeling range from conditional random fields (CRF), transfer learning (TL) to hidden Markov model (HMM).

J.-F. Hong et al. (Eds.): CLSW 2018, LNAI 11173, pp. 643–652, 2018.
https://doi.org/10.1007/978-3-030-04015-4_56

Researchers have recently regarded NER as a sequence labeling task to determine the category of each input word or phrase. At present, they are able to identify entities through feature extraction. Xu and Zhu et al. [1] for example, downloaded news articles from NASA's official website and extracted 36 dimensional features, including lexical, morphological, and contextual features. Xu and Zhu also adopted the BIO scheme to tag the beginning, inside, and outside of an entity besides using the CRF model for entity recognition. Li and Wei et al. [2] based on the features of Word, Part of Speech (POS), Left bound + Right bound (LB + RB), Radical (Rad), and Numeral (Num), employed a CRF approach for the recognition of crops, diseases and pesticides named entities. They compared three schemes involving single features, non-contextual feature combinations, and contextual feature combinations and concluded that the scheme of contextual feature combinations produce the best result and have an advantage in some specific research areas.

Nevertheless, in light of the diverse and complex nature of research work, collecting samples for novel fields may not be a cost-effective process. Wang and Shen et al. [3] applied TrAdaBoost to their study and further improved the transferability of algorithms, thus using a non-political news corpus for the entity recognition of political news texts. Traditionally, tagging is mainly about manually selecting a set of task-oriented feature templates, whose quality determines the result of a labeling task. Researchers need to have an intimate knowledge of both relevant fields and linguistics, which makes a lot of demands in terms of time and effort. Zhang and Wu et al. [4] with the SBEIO scheme, used the character-phrase vector combination as the input of a three-layer neural network. Then they applied the Viterbi algorithm to the neural network output for the best labeling result. However, Zhang and Wu did not differentiate the effects of character vectors and phrase vectors on NER.

Recent years have witnessed a wide range of applications of attention mechanisms [5], especially in machine translation, image captioning, and speech recognition [5]. Wang et al. [6] presented an LSTM model and vectorized extracted features. On the basis of the model, they carried out a semantic relation extraction according to the attention-induced local phrase vectors.

Using word2vec to vectorize words and phrases, this paper integrates an attention mechanism with Bi-LSTM for Chinese NER. This approach focuses on both local and global features and therefore can substantially improve the effectiveness of Chinese NER.

2 Bi-LSTM Model Construction Based on an Attention Mechanism

Named entity recognition can be abstracted as a label prediction problem, and can be classified into word label prediction and word label prediction according to the different units of sentence segmentation. Word label prediction is the process of labeling the word "SBMEO" [7] as the basic unit of sentence segmentation. "S" means that the single word is a named entity, B is the first word of the named entity, "M" is the middle word of the named entity, and the "E" table is the last word of the named entity, "O" indicates that the word does not belong to any part of the named entity. The label prediction of words is the basic unit of sentence segmentation and the corresponding entity tagging after the segmentation. For example, the non-named entity is labeled as "O", the name of the person is "PERSON", and the organization is labeled as "ORGANIZATION". The words and words obtained from the two segmentation modes are vectorized to form the character vector matrix $\mathbf{A}_c$ and the phrase vector matrix $\mathbf{A}_w$ of the input text. The two annotation patterns are vectored to get the word marking matrix $\mathbf{P}_c$ and the word tagging matrix $\mathbf{P}_w$.

2.1 Word Vector

The word vector model is divided into one-hot representation and distributed representation. The One-hot vector is a vector length with a dictionary size. Only one of the vectors is 1 and the rest is 0. The word vector dimension is too large and too sparse, and it cannot represent the similarity between words. The distribution is presented in 1985 by Hinton. The idea is to abstract a dictionary into a vector space, and all words are a point in the space, expressed by a fixed length vector, and each dimension of the vector represents a potential feature of the word, which captures the grammatical and semantic features [8].

Word2vec is a software tool used by Google to train word vectors in 2013. The framework includes CBOW and Skip-gram. CBOW uses a number of words in the context to predict the current word, and the size of the corpus is better at the hundred megabytes; and the Skip-gram is just the opposite. The words pretest the context from the current word, suitable for the small size of the corpus [9].

We used word2vec to train and get dictionary DC and dictionary DW. Given a Chinese sentence S, S is composed of n words and can be expressed as C [1:n]. S is made up of M words and can be represented as W[1:m]. The vector $\mathrm{S}_{\mathrm{A}_c}$ and the word vector matrix $\mathrm{S}_{\mathrm{A}_w}$ of S are shown in the formula (1) and the formula (2).

$$\mathrm{S}_{\mathrm{A}_c} = [DC_{C_1}^T, \cdots, DC_{C_n}^T] \tag{1}$$

$$\mathrm{S}_{\mathrm{A}_w} = [DW_{W_1}^T, \cdots, DW_{W_m}^T] \tag{2}$$

Word tagging has i labels, and word tagging has J labels. The word tagging matrix $S_{\mathbf{P}_c}$ and word tagging matrix $S_{\mathbf{P}_w}$ of S can be obtained by one-hot, and their dimensions are $\mathbf{i} \times \mathbf{n}$ and $\mathbf{j} \times \mathbf{m}$.

2.2 Bi-LSTM Model

Recurrent neural network (RNN) is a neural network model for sequential annotation. By adding the self-connected hidden layer across time points, the model has certain memory ability. However, RNN cannot effectively deal with the long-distance dependency problem, and there are gradient disappearance and gradient explosion cases. The LSTM model is an improved method for the traditional recurrent neural network. It uses the memory unit to replace the implicit function of the traditional recurrent neural network. This improvement allows the LSTM model to memorize contexts whose range is longer than that of traditional recurrent neural networks.

Traditional recurrent neural networks read the input data from one end of the sequence to the other, so the data stored in the recurrent neural network at any time has only the information of the current and past time to solve the problem of gradient disappearance and gradient explosion. It has been widely used in all aspects of the Natural Language Processing [10–12]. In the LSTM model, long and short memory functions are realized through Input Gate, Output Gate and Forget Gate. Its structure is shown in Fig. 1.

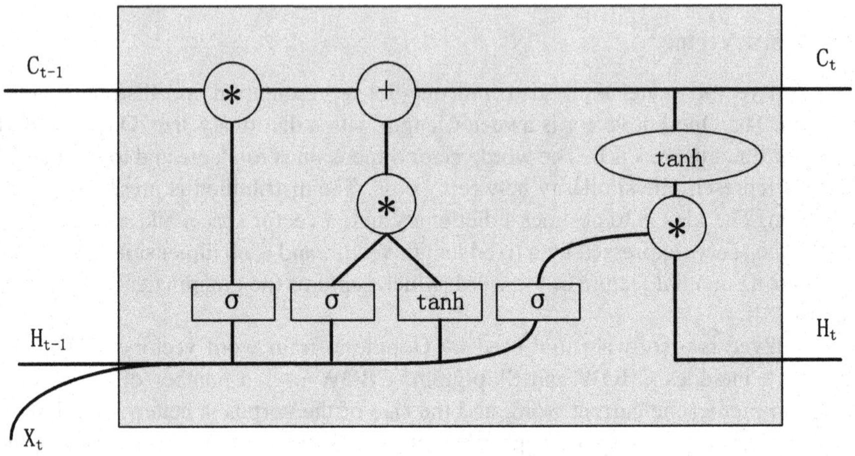

Fig. 1. LSTM single node structure

The following formulas show how a storage unit *t* is updated at each time step:

$$i_t = \sigma(W_i x_t + U_i h_{t-1} + b_i) \tag{3}$$

$$\tilde{C}_t = tanh(W_c x_t + U_c h_{t-1} + b_c) \tag{4}$$

$$f_t = \sigma(W_f x_t + U_f h_{t-1} + b_f) \tag{5}$$

$$C_t = i_t * \tilde{C}_t + f_t * C_{t-1} \tag{6}$$

$$o_t = \sigma(W_o x_t + U_o h_{t-1} + b_o) \tag{7}$$

$$h_t = o_t * \tanh(C_t) \tag{8}$$

Among them, x_t is the input of unit t, $W_i, W_c, W_f, W_o, U_i, U_c, U_f, U_o$ are weight matrix, b_i, b_c, b_f, b_o and W_f are bias vectors.

2.3 Attention Mechanism

Soft Attention Model [12] is a probability distribution of the attention probability of each input calculation, which can highlight the importance of a particular word to the whole sentence and consider more contextual semantic association [6]. The attention mechanism is based on the input character vector or the phrase vector, and outputs one dimensional vector $\mathrm{SAM}_c = [\mathrm{k}_1 \cdots \mathrm{k}_n]$ and $\mathrm{SAM}_w = [\mathrm{k}_1 \cdots \mathrm{k}_m]$ in which k_x represents the attention probability of position x. Using the attention probability to update the phrase vector output of the Bi-LSTM model, we get $\mathrm{S}_{\mathrm{A}_c}$, such as formula (9).

$$\mathrm{S}_{\mathrm{A}_c} = \tilde{S}^T_{\mathrm{A}_c} \times \mathrm{SAM}_c \tag{9}$$

$\tilde{S}^T_{\mathrm{A}_c}$ represents the transpose matrix of the output of the Bi-LSTM model, and the updated phrase vector $\mathrm{S}_{\mathrm{A}_w}$ can be obtained similarly.

2.4 An Attention-Based Bi-LSTM Model

In this paper, we first use word2vec to vectorize the text, after which the vectorized numerical matrix is input into an attention-based model and a Bi-LSTM model for parallel computing. Then we multiply the results of the two models. Finally, we use softmax to classify vector types for Chinese NER.

The Bi-LSTM model is a three-layer neural network, which consists of two recurrent neural networks and a fully connected layer. Of the two recurrent neural networks, one computes the vector from front to back, and the other from back to front. Then a fully connected layer is used to integrate the results for local feature extraction. An attention mechanism is used to extract global features through the output attention probability matrix. The model's network structure is shown in Fig. 2.

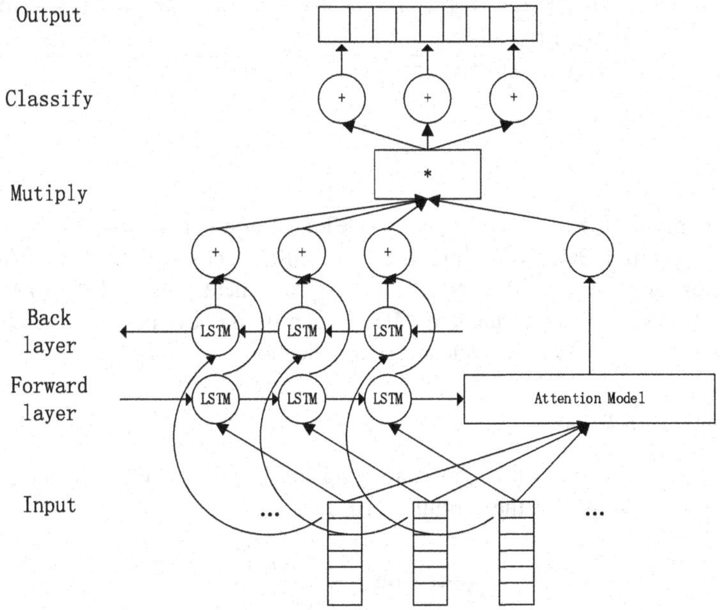

Fig. 2. Network structure

3 Development Experiments

3.1 Corpus

This paper selects the January 1998 (RMRB-98-1) corpus as the development set. On the basis of Stanford NER's named entity markup to RMRB-98-1, two postgraduates are used to proofread the results respectively, and the error marks existing in the tagging tool are modified, and the error instances are listed as follows.

The vectorized model in this paper uses a corpus of about 398 MB in data size and the January 1998 issues of the People's Daily (RMRB-98-1), which are about 6.38 MB in data size. The character vectors and phrase vectors are trained by CBOW and Skip-gram models respectively. The above two corpuses are manually proofread, so this paper ignores the errors that may be caused by quality of segmentation.

In this paper, we use a corpus of the January 1998 issues the People's Daily (RMRB-98-1) as the development set. After the Stanford NER is adopted for it, two postgraduate students are respectively assigned to the tasks of double-checking the recognition results, and the error mark and missing mark in the annotation tool are modified. The error examples are shown in the following Table 1.

Table 1. Labeling error instances

Missed labeling	以/O 江/O 泽民/O 同志/O 为/O 核心/O 本报/O 记者/O 王/PERSON 楚/O
Mistaken Labeling	高举/O **邓小平理论/PERSON** 的/O 伟大/O 旗帜/O 香港/GPE 特区/GPE 行政/O 长官/O 董/O 建华/GPE 等/O **特区/LOCATION** 政府 /ORGANIZATION
Redundant labeling	``/O 插图/O 本/O 中国/MISC 通史/MISC **''/MISC**

The Stanford NER can be divided into 8 types: non entity standard O; coordinate azimuth standard LOCATION; province etc. GPE; factory and others FACILITY; organization and others ORGANIZATION; government, etc. DEMONYM; person name PERSON; and other standard MISC, such as money, number, serial number, percentage, time, continuous sequence, and collection.

3.2 Evaluation Index

The evaluation indexes of this paper are precision, recall and F-score, and the calculation method is shown in the formulae (10–12).

$$\textbf{precision} = \frac{correct_{out}}{all_{out}} \tag{10}$$

$$\mathbf{recall} = \frac{correct_{out}}{all_{test}} \tag{11}$$

$$\mathbf{F_{score}} = \frac{2 \times precision \times recall}{precision + recall} \tag{12}$$

In which $correct_{out}$ is the correct number of non "O" tags, all_{out} is the total number of non "O" tags, and all_{test} is the total number of non "O" tags in the test set.

3.3 Experiment Planning

We used RMRB-98-1 as a data set to analyze the parameter output dimensions in the Bi-LSTM model and compared the changes of the evaluation indexes under different dimensions. The experimental results are shown in Fig. 3.

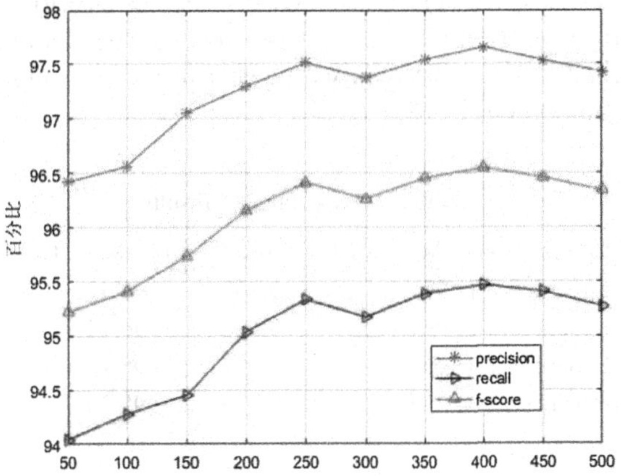

Fig. 3. Output dimension settings

The two local maxims of the output dimension are 250 and 400, and the more the number of dimensions is, the slower the system runs, and the effect of the experimental results is not significantly improved. Therefore, the output dimension is set to 250.

3.4 Experimental Results

We carried out four groups of experiments, the main purpose of which was to compare the effects of character vectors and phrase vectors as input vectors and phrase vector training corpus size on model recognition. In the first group of experiments, RMRB-98-1 was used as the training vector of basic corpus, the character vector as the input of attention model, and the phrase vector as the input of Bi-LSTM model. In the second group of the experiments, the corpus of character segmentation was used as the basic training vector, the phrase vector was the input of the attention model and the character vector was the input of the Bi-LSTM model. In the third group of the experiments, the corpus of character segmentation was used as the basic training vector, the character vector was input of the Bi-LSTM model and the character vector was input of the attention model. In the fourth experiment, RMRB-98-1 was used as the basic training vector, the character vector as the input of the Bi-LSTM model and the character vector as the input of the attention model. A total of 13,633 pieces, approximately 70% of the data, were selected as the training set while 5844 pieces, approximately 30% of the data, were used as the cross-validation set to prevent the over-fitting of training. Word2vec was used for unsupervised training of the data to generate character vectors and phrase vectors.

By comparing the results of Experiments 1–2 and Experiments 3–4 in Table 2, it can be concluded that the results of the experiment using RMRB-98-1 as the vectorized data set are slightly higher than that using the corpus with the laboratory word segmentation as the vectorized data set. This is due to the fact that a decrease in the relevance of the vectorized corpus has decreased while the relevance of the phrases, leading to the lower accuracy of the training. By comparing the results of Experiments 1–4 and Experiments 2–3, it can be concluded that character vectors are more effective than phrase vectors in terms of NER. This is because, as a result of the incompleteness of the dictionary, many unlisted words will appear in the recognition process, which will result in recognition errors.

Table 2. Experimental results

Experiments	Accuracy (%)	Recall (%)	F-score (%)
Experiment 1	97.51	95.33	96.41
Experiment 2	97.13	95.06	96.08
Experiment 3	96.37	95.12	95.74
Experiment 4	95.97	94.74	95.35

We compared the named entity recognition algorithm with the CRF algorithm used in the literature [1], and used the plate corpus and the English data set MUC-6 as the basic corpus to train. This model directly quantifies the input in the MUC-6 corpus and inputs the model.

From Table 3, we can find that the use of the Att-BLSTM model in the Chinese language has achieved a better result. The main reason is that the character vectors and phrase vectors in this paper are handled separately, whereas word vectors, which are typical of the English language, do not apply to the system in question. This model is

Table 3. Experiment result comparisons

Experiments	Corpus	Accuracy (%)	Recall (%)	F-score (%)
Att-BLSTM	Plate corpus	90.51	88.33	89.41
CRF algorithm	Plate corpus	84.58	79.63	82.03
Att-BLSTM	MUC-6	86.34	81.17	83.68
CRF algorithm	MUC-6	85.92	81.31	83.55

better than the traditional CRF algorithm, although the Recall rate is lower than that of the CRF algorithm in the English domain, but the F-score is higher in general.

4 Conclusion

This paper proposes an attention-based Bi-LSTM approach to Chinese NER, which helps to effectively extract local and global features. By experiment we compared the effects of character vectors, phrase vectors, and vectorized foundation datasets on Chinese NER. The result empirically demonstrates that phrase vectors integrated with a highly domain-relevant corpus produces consistently better performance. At present, not much research has been carried out in the field of vector corpus and whether data can be realized in domain transfer. We consider adding data in the field of Finance in the next step to further observe the mobility of the system. Furthermore, it is predicted that our model has a distinctive advantage over traditional CRF algorithms in analyzing the stock market.

References

1. Xu, J.Z., Zhu, J., Zhao, R., Zhang, L., Li, J.J.: Astronautics named entity recognition based on CRF algorithm. J. Electronic Design Engineering. **25**, 42–46 (2017). 1674-6236(2017) 20-0042-05
2. Li, X., Wei, X.H., Jia, L., Chen, X., Liu, L., Zhang, Y.E.: Recognition of crops, diseases and pesticides named entities in Chinese based in conditional random fields. Trans. Chin. Soc. Agric. Mach. **48** (2017). https://doi.org/10.6041/j.issn.1000-1298.2017.S0.029
3. Wang, H.B., Shen, Q., Xian, Y.T.: Research on Chinese named entity recognition fusing transfer learning. J. Chin. Mini-Micro Comput. Syst. **38**, 346–351 (2017). 1000-1220(2017) 02-0346-06
4. Zhang, H.N., Wu, D.Y., Liu, Y., Cheng, X.Q.: Chinese named entity recognition based on deep neural network. J. Chin. Inf. Process. **31**, 8–35 (2017). 1003-0077(2017)04-0028-08
5. Rocktäschel, T., Grefenstette, E., Hermann, K.M., et al.: Reasoning about entailment with neural attention. ICLR (2016). https://www.researchgate.net/publication/282181875
6. Wang, H., Shi, J.Z., Zhang, Z.W.: Text semantic relation of LSTM based on attention. Appl. Res. Comput. **35**, 1417–1440 (2018). https://doi.org/10.3969/j.issn.1001-3695.2018.05.029
7. Liu, B.Y., Wu, D.Y., Liu, X.R., Cheng, X.Q.: Chinese named entity recognition incorporating global word boundary features. J. Chin. Inf. Process. **31**, 86–91 (2017). 1003-0077(2017)02-0086-06
8. Feng, Y.H., Yu, H., Sun, G., Sun, J.J.: Named entity recognition method based on BLSTM. Comput. Sci. **45**, 261–268 (2018). https://doi.org/10.11896/j.issn.1002-137X.2018.02.045
9. Hu, J., Zhang, J.C.: Bidirectional recurrent networks for Chinese word segmentation. J. Chin. Comput. Syst. **03**, 522–526 (2017). http://xwxt.sict.ac.cn/EN/abstract/abstract3837.shtml
10. Guo, M.S., Zhang, Y., Liu, T.: Research advances and prospect of recognizing textual entailment and knowledge acquisition. Chin. J. Comput. **40**, 889–910 (2017). https://doi.org/10.11897/SP.J.1016.2017.00889

11. Cao, C.Y., Lv, Q.: Using bidirectional LSTM deep neural network for protein residue contact prediction. J. Chin. Comput. Syst. **03**, 531–535 (2017). http://xwxt.sict.ac.cn/EN/Y2017/V38/I3/531
12. Bahdanau, D., Cho, K., Bengio, Y.: Neural machine translation by jointly learning to align and translate. J. Comput. Sci. (2014). https://www.researchgate.net/publication/265252627_Neural_Machine_Translation_by_Jointly_Learning_to_Align_and_Translate

Lexical Resources

Emotional Knowledge Corpus Construction for Deep Understanding of Text

Xin Chen[1], Yang Li[1], Suge Wang[1,2](✉), Deyu Li[1,2], and Wanqing Mu[1]

[1] School of Computer and Information Technology, Shanxi University, Taiyuan 030006, China
wsg@sxu.edu.cn
[2] Key Laboratory of Computational Intelligence and Chinese Information Processing of Ministry of Education, Shanxi University, Taiyuan 030006, China

Abstract. Emotional knowledge corpus will provide data support for deep understanding of text. However, the problems of incomplete coverage and lacking of emotional skeleton are found from semantics, and from the perspective of pragmatic, the scarcity problem is more serious. To adapt literary works, we expand the existing emotional lexicon, and construct sentimental phrase knowledge corpus and discourse-based sentimental collocation networks from the perspective of semantics. In addition, the rhetoric is an important component of pragmatics, so the emotional knowledge corpus based on the rhetoric is constructed. Finally, with the emotional knowledge corpus, a comprehensive and accurate answer for the reading and appreciating question is obtained.

Keywords: Deep understanding of text · Emotional knowledge corpus Semantics · Pragmatics · Rhetoric

1 Introduction

The development of natural language understanding can be divided into four levels, which include morphology, syntax, semantics and pragmatics. And with the order of the four levels, the difficulty of analysis has gradually increased. At present, morphology and syntax have achieved gratifying performances, and semantics is becoming a hot research [1], however, pragmatics is recently studied as language understanding and application [2]. From the perspective of semantics and pragmatics, according to Psychology Dictionary, the emotion is defined as people's attitude towards whether or not things satisfy their needs. The emotion is complex and changeable, which exists in the daily life. In social media, people express their emotions for products by comment texts; during the creation of literary works, the author develops a unique emotional context based on the development of the story; and in the dialog between people and machines, participants are constantly updating their emotions with the change of chat content.

In order to understand the emotions deeply, not only the related technologies for analyzing emotion are needed, but also a knowledge corpus. From semantics point of view, the knowledge corpus has been constructed. For the word level, the English

J.-F. Hong et al. (Eds.): CLSW 2018, LNAI 11173, pp. 655–666, 2018.
https://doi.org/10.1007/978-3-030-04015-4_57

sentiment lexicons include SentiWordNet [3], General Inquirer [4], Opinion Lexicon [5] and HowNet [6], and the Chinese lexicons are represented by NTUSD [7] and DUTIR [8]. But the lexicons are constructed orienting to the social media, not the literary work which contains a large number of emotional idioms and phrases. For sentence and discourse level, English corpus DSRC [9] is constituted by four kinds of emotional information, which includes holders, objects, modifiers and opinion words. And the Chinese emotional corpus [10–13] is annotated with the object, sentiment orientation and others information for the fields of electronics, entertainment, finance, literary works and others. However, the corpus doesn't reveal the emotional transfer. From the pragmatics point of view, there is a few of knowledge corpus, which contains incomplete tagging information of corpus [13, 14]. Therefore, from the perspective of semantics, focusing on literary works, the lexicon DUTIR [8] is expanded, the sentimental phrase knowledge corpus and the discourse-based sentimental collocation networks are constructed.

As an important part of pragmatics, rhetoric is a manifestation of the ability to use language comprehensively. If we make analogies by medicine, grammar is like anatomy, logic is like hygiene, and rhetoric is like cosmetology [1]. Therefore, people often express their emotion using rhetoric, and the specific examples are as follows:

Sentence 1: 妈妈像参天的大树，让我感受凉快。
(My mother is like a towering tree, making me feel cool.)

Sentence 2: 生命是母爱的慈祥；生命是父爱的严厉；生命是爱人的柔情；生命是朋友的关切；生命是感情的组合体。
(Life is the kindness of maternal love, life is the sternness of fatherly love, life is the tenderness of lover, life is the concern of friends, and life is a combination of emotions.)

"Metaphor" and "parallelism" are made use of by *Sentence 1* and *Sentence 2* respectively. *Sentence 1* illustrates the greatness of "mother love" by analogy with the tall image of "towering tree", expressing vividly the ease emotion. *Sentence 2* describes life by "parallelism", enhancing the effectiveness in communication and expressing praise for life.

The extensive application of rhetoric presents a huge challenge to analyze emotion in machine reading, so a large amount of corpus is constructed to promote the research. Among them, the cloze type corpus [15–17] mainly pays attention to the named entities and nouns in the articles, the selection type corpus [18] is annotated by logic reasoning, and the question-answer type corpus [19, 20] is structured that the answer based on extraction technology. They cannot help with a deep understanding from appreciating language. Therefore, an emotional knowledge corpus based on rhetoric is constructed from the perspective of pragmatics, which provides data support for the study of deep understanding.

2 Construction of Semantic Emotional Knowledge Corpus

From the perspective of semantics, there are numbers of related resources [3–14], such as emotional lexicon and sentimental knowledge corpus, while there are some problems. In order to help the machine automatically recognize the emotions hidden in the text expression, the emotional lexicon, the sentimental phrase knowledge corpus, and discourse-based sentimental collocation networks are constructed.

2.1 Collection of Raw Corpus

Taking into account richness and diversity of the emotional expression in literary works, more than 80,000 literary works are collected as the raw corpus from high school textbooks and a number of related networks (http://www.cnprose.com, http://www.sanwen.net, http://www.sanwen8.cn, http://zw.liuxue86.com/sanwen, http://www.duanwenxue.com). In addition, the word segmentation is made by the LTP platform [21], which helps to construct an emotional knowledge corpus.

2.2 Annotation Form of Sematic Emotional Knowledge Corpus

Annotation Form of Emotional Lexicon. Aword possesses sentiment polarity and emotion information. Therefore, a four-tuple formation is defined to expand emotional lexicon, and the specific form is as follows:

$$word = (w, e, i, pol)$$

Where, w denotes an emotional word, and e, i, pol denote the emotional category, intensity, sentiment polarity respectively, whose value are referenced by Xu et al. [8].

Annotation Form of Sentimental Phrase Corpus. Asentimental phrase is defined in the form of two-tuple as follows:

$$phrase = (p, pol)$$

Where, p denotes a sentimental phrase, pol denotes the sentiment polarity(0: neutral, 1: positive, 2: negative, 3: positive and negative).

Annotation Form of Discourse-Based Sentimental Collocation Networks. When authors are creating literary works, they change sentiment constantly with the transition of objects and the plot's ups and downs. In order to facilitate the sentiment analysis, sentiment and position information in the article are noted in the annotating process. A sentiment pair is defined as follows:

$$sentiment - pair = (pair, pol, Sens, LocofSens)$$

Where, *pair* denotes the sentiment collocation, which is represented by "<opinion object, [degree word/negative word], opinion word>", *pol* denotes sentiment polarity (0: neutral, 1: positive, 2: negative, 3: positive and negative), *Sens* denotes the set of sentence that *pair* exists in it, that is [sen_1, sen_2,..., sen_n], *LocofSens* denotes the position set corresponding to *Sens*, that is [$locofSen_1$, $locofSen_2$,..., $locofSen_n$], and $locofSen_i$ is represented by "<*idofArt-idofPara-idofSen*>", where *idofArt*, *idofPara*, and *idofSen* denote the index of article, paragraph, and sentence corresponding to Sen_i.

2.3 Analysis of Sematic Emotional Knowledge Corpus

With data set (Sect. 2.1) and annotation form (Sect. 2.2), emotional lexicon, sentimental phrase corpus, and sentimental collocation networks based on discourse have been constructed. Some examples are shown in Tables 1, 2, and 3.

Table 1. The examples of emotional lexicon

Word	Emotion	Intensity	Polarity
幸福 (happiness)	PA	7	1
美丽 (beauty)	PH	5	1
笔墨官司 (battle of words)	NN	7	2
名声鹊起 (reputation in)	PH	7	1
...	...	...	...

Table 2. The examples of sentimental phrase corpus

Phrase	Polarity
稀巴烂 (smashed to pieces)	2
健健康康 (healthy)	1
一日夫妻百日恩 (A day together as husband and wife means endless devotion the rest of your life.)	1
...	...

From Tables 1 and 2, it is found that the emotional lexicon includes general emotional words, such as "happiness" and "beauty", and also contains the words usually appearing in literary works, for example "battle of words" and "reputation in". In addition, the spoken word "smashed to pieces" is contained in the sentimental phrase corpus, which provides more rounded information for sentiment analysis. And from Table 3, we can find:

(1) Each sentiment collocation exists in multiple sentences, and some collocations also include degree words, such as "more" in "flowers more beautiful".
(2) A sentence containing multiple collocations is collected in the corresponding sentimental collocations. Such as the sentence (*locofSen* = "78410.txt-3-0") contains three collocations, that is "relationship harmony", "neighbors harmony" and "humans harmony", so the sentence is added to the corresponding sentence set.
(3) Each sentence contains location information of the corpus, providing comprehensive information for the analysis of sentimental skeleton.

Table 3. The examples of sentimental collocation networks based on discourse

Pair	Polarity	Sentences	LocofSens
花儿 更 娇艳 (flowers more beautiful)	1	花儿开得更娇艳了…… (The flowers are more beautiful……)	57849.txt-2-2
		女人如花，唯有爱情雨露滋润的花儿开得更娇艳。(A woman is like a flower, and only the flowers moistened by rain and dew are more beautiful.)	49755.txt-14-0
关系 和睦 (relationship harmony)	1	那时的邻里之间关系和睦，彼此照应，真正是"远亲不如近邻"。(At that time, the relationship between the neighbors were in harmony and mutual care, which was really" a far-off relative is not as helpful as a near neighbor")	46057.txt-9-3
		在这栋楼里我们邻里间的关系非常和睦，大家互帮互助，和谐友爱。(In this building, neighbors help each other, and the relationship between them is in harmony and friendship.)	55087.txt-2-0
		换位思考是一种人世间最好的思维方式，……，就会人际关系融洽，邻里关系和睦，社会关系就会和谐。(Empathy is the best way of thinking in the world, ……, the relationship of humans, neighbors, and socials will be in harmony.)	78410.txt-3-0
邻里 和睦 (neighbors harmony)	1	同上	78410.txt-3-0
		…	……
人际关系 融洽 (humans harmony)	1	同上	78410.txt-3-0
		…	……

3 Construction of the Emotional Knowledge Corpus Based on Rhetoric

In order to help the machine to understand emotion of texts deeply from appreciating language, an emotional knowledge corpus based on rhetoric is constructed.

3.1 Formulation of Rhetoric System

Rhetoric makes the language more accurate and vivid, which has great influence at all time. And with the passage of time, rhetoric system has dynamic evolution [22], which was classified from different angles. From the composition of rhetoric, Wu [23] divided the rhetoric into four categories and thirty-eight sub-categories; from the function of rhetoric, Song et al. [24] divided it into four categories and thirty-nine sub-categories; from the frequency, Liang [22] divided it into two categories.

In view of the differences of the classification, all above categories are collected as a pre annotation system to ensure the comprehensiveness of the annotation system. Besides, the textbook is designed to education, so the linguistic in it is norm and rich. Therefore, we annotate rhetoric of literary works in the five high school textbooks, and the specific results are shown in Table 4.

Table 4. The results of rhetorical annotation for five high school textbooks under the pre annotation system

Category	Numbers	Proportion
Contrast	271	23.32%
Simile/Metaphor	256	22.03%
Quote	111	9.55%
Repetition	97	8.35%
Personification	74	6.37%
Parallelism	53	4.56%
Hyperbole	49	4.22%
Rhetorical question with answer	36	3.10%
Hypallage	36	3.10%
Set off	24	2.07%
Rhetorical question	24	2.07%
Metonymy	23	1.98%
Zoosemy	23	1.98%
Nonce words	22	1.89%
Irony	18	1.55%
Description	13	1.12%
Antithesis	8	0.69%
Interlace	7	0.60%
Anadiplosis	7	0.60%
Allegory	4	0.34%
Periphrasis	4	0.34%
Climax	1	0.09%
Antimetabole	1	0.09%

According to the annotated results in Table 4, the proportion of each category in the total category is calculated from 0.09% to 23.32%. In order to relieve the data imbalance among the rhetorical categories, the rhetoric is selected with a proportion greater than 1% as the final rhetorical annotating category.

3.2 Annotation of the Emotional Knowledge Corpus Based on Rhetoric

Data Sources. The high school texts and the background articles of the 2005–2016 college entrance examination are selected as the raw corpus. And considering the limited number, we also collect rhetorical data from the relevant website (https://www.chazidian.com/) in order to ensure the scale of the knowledge croups.

Annotation Formation. Based on the sixteen categories (Sect. 3.1), the three-tuple form is used to construct the emotional knowledge corpus, and the form is as follows:

$$r = (sen, label, e)$$

Where, *sen* denotes the sentence expressed by rhetoric, *label* denotes a rhetorical label, which is included in the sixteen categories (Sect. 3.1), *e* denotes the emotional category of the *sen*, and the classification reference to Xu et al. [8].

Quality Control. Compared to textbooks and background articles of college entrance examination, there are errors and redundancies in the web data. In order to ensure the quality of corpus, we remove duplicates and proofread error data. For example:

(1) 爱心是风，吹遍每个角落。
(Love is the wind, blowing all over the corner.)
(2) 爱心是风，吹遍了每个角落。
(Love is the wind, blowing all over the corner.)
(3) 一般绝望的情绪像狂潮一般涌上我的心头，使我感到浑身冰凉。
(The desperate mood pouring into my heart is like a torrent, making me cold.)

Observing sentence (1)–(3), sentence (1) and sentence (2) have the same meaning, but sentence (2) has one more word ("了") than sentence (1), the sentence (2) is reserved in the corpus to eliminate redundancy. In addition, there exist typos in the sentence (3), the false word (一般, general) is amended to true word (一股, one stream) to guarantee the quality of corpus.

Knowledge Corpus Analysis. Under the quality control, according to the annotation system and specification, an emotional knowledge corpus based on rhetoric is constructed. Some examples are shown in Table 5. Observed from Table 5, it is found that:

(1) The types of "simile/metaphor" in the knowledge corpus include: simple simile sentence (id = 1), simile sentence (id = 2) that the tensor (flower) is far away from the vehicle (little trumpet), a single sentence (id = 3) contains multiple tensor (study hard, do big things) and vehicle (build a house, lay a good foundation).
(2) The parallelism sentences in the knowledge corpus are illustrated by various types, which include: the clause-parallelism sentence (id = 4) that each clause of a complex sentence constitutes a parallelism; the composition-parallelism sentence (id = 5) that the different components in a sentence constitute a parallelism. The types make the corpus more comprehensive.

Table 5. The examples of the emotional knowledge base based on rhetoric

ID	Sentence	Label	Emotion
1	妈妈像参天的大树, 让我感受凉快。(My mother is like a towering tree, making me cool.)	Simile/Metaphor	Be relieved
2	花越开越密, 越开越盛, 不久便挂满了枝头, 走近看, 似乎是一个个生动的小喇叭, 正鼓着劲儿在吹呢。(The flowers open more and more densely, the sooner they will cover branches. Looking closer, they seemed to be little vivid trumpets, trumpeting on the branches.)	Simile/Metaphor	Happiness
3	少壮不努力老大徒伤悲, 告诉我们读好书才能做大事, 就像建房子要打好地基一样。(The proverb, "a young idler, an old beggar", tells us only when we study hard can we do big things, just like building a house need to lay a good foundation.)	Simile/Metaphor	Be relieved
4	生命是母爱的慈祥; 生命是父爱的严厉; 生命是爱人的柔情; 生命是朋友的关切; 生命是感情的组合体。(Life is the kindness of maternal love; life is the sternness of fatherly love; life is the tenderness of lover, life is the concern of friends; and life is a combination of emotions.)	Parallelism	Praise
5	让我随风舞, 随花零, 随雨淋, 随雪飘, 随日出, 随月落, 静静的雕琢, 深深的铭刻, 孤傲的活着。(Let me dance with the wind, withered with flowers, fall with rain, drift with the snow, rise with the sunrise, fall with the moon, carve quietly, impress deeply, proud and aloof alive.)	Parallelism	Sorrow
6	红熟红熟的夕阳害羞了。(The red sunset is shy.)	Personification	Favor
7	然而, 我不能想象人没有思想, 那就成了一块顽石或者一头畜牲了。(However, I can't imagine that people have no thoughts, and that is a stone or a beast.)	Zoosemy	Rage

(3) The "analogy" in knowledge corpus is divided into "personification" and "zoosemy", which can provide more detailed information for the recognition of rhetoric.

4 Application of Emotional Knowledge Corpus

The semantic emotional knowledge corpus (Sects. 2) and emotional knowledge corpus based on rhetoric (Sects. 3) can help to get an answer for the reading and appreciating question. The specific question is as follows:

请赏析语句 "长长的灯河, 红光跳, 绿光闪, 蓝光摇曳, 黄光变幻, 而其余的粉光, 紫光, 桔光呢, 也全都不甘落后, 一齐笑着, 闹着, 挤着, 抢着, 追逐着, 上上下下, 左左右右, 前前后后, 欢畅地闪烁着, 一边唱着关于爱情的古老歌谣。"(4分)

(Please appreciate the sentence "in the long light river, red light jump, green light flash, blue light sway, yellow light change, and the rest of the pink, purple and orange light laugh, squeeze, rush, and chase, they flash cheerfully, up and down, left and right, front and back, singing old songs about love." (4 points))

The reading and appreciating question investigates the ability of appreciating language and analyzing sentiment, so the technologies of recognizing rhetoric and analyzing the article's emotions are executed in order to get the final answer.

4.1 Answers Generation of Reading and Appreciating Questions for Literary

Through analyzing the reading and appreciating questions, it is found that in the process of answering the questions, the answers should be generated from two aspects: the recognition of rhetoric and article's sentiment analysis. The specific answer process is shown in Fig. 1. For the sake of simplicity, EL and EKCBOR denote emotion lexicon and emotional knowledge corpus based on rhetoric respectively in Fig. 1. Observing Fig. 1, in the process of answering questions, firstly we analyze the question and extract the relevant paragraphs, and then according to the results of the question analysis, the rhetorical recognition and article's sentiment analysis are carried out on the relevant paragraphs. Finally, the final answer is generated by the answer templates.

Rhetoric recognition. The method of parallel recognition [25] is executed to distinguish the parallel sentence.

Sentiment analysis. The process is divided into two parts, which include the extraction for description objects and the analysis of article's emotions. Article's title contains core information of entire article, so the noun in the title is used as the description object. During analyzing the article's emotions, based on the emotional lexicon, we get vectors of the given article and labeled article by emotion utilizing bag of words, and the cosine distances between them are obtained. Finally, the given article's emotions are given by labeled article with the closest distance.

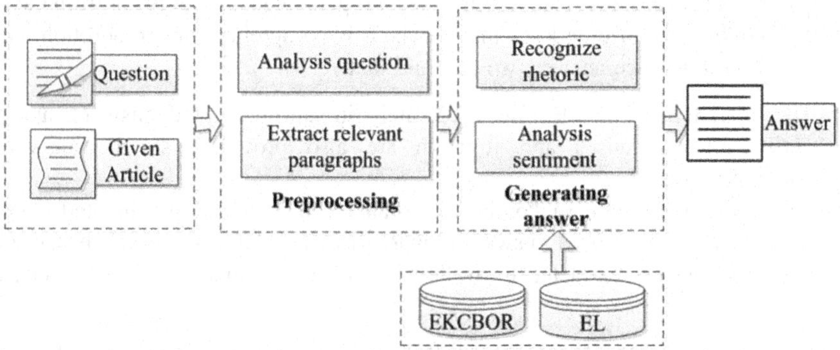

Fig. 1. Answering generation process of reading and appreciating question

Answer generation. In order to generate readable answers, some templates for rhetoric and emotion are constructed, and which are as follows:

Rhetorical template: [sentence fragment] is expressed by the [rhetorical category]. [rhetorical category] [corresponding rhetorical function].

Sentiment analysis template: It illustrates the author's [emotional labels] towards [article's description object].

Combined with the results of rhetorical recognition and sentiment analysis, the final answer is generated by the answer templates.

4.2 Answers Analysis

By the solution (Sect. 4.1), an answer for reading and appreciating question is obtained focusing on literary works, which is shown in Table 6.

Table 6. The question, reference answer and auto-generated answer for reading and appreciating question

Question: Please appreciate the sentence "in the long light river, red light jump, green light flash, blue light sway, yellow light change, and the rest of the pink, purple and orange light laugh, squeeze, rush, and chase, they flash cheerfully, up and down, left and right, front and back, singing old songs about love." (4 points)
Reference Answer: The sentence, using the "simile/metaphor" and "parallelism" (1 points), describes the change of light's color lively, and illustrates the author's excitement and admiration (2 points). The sentence is expressed vividly, and has a strong artistic appeal (1 points) **Auto-generated Answer:** **(1) Rhetoric:** "They flash cheerfully, up and down, left and right, front and back, singing old songs about love. " is expressed by "parallelism". And "parallelism" makes the article have the rhythm, enhances the expressive effect, and deepens the center **(2) Sentiment:** It illustrates the author's cherished and praiseful emotion towards "Tianhe"

By observing Table 6, it is found that the auto-generated answer is got from the two aspects including rhetoric and sentiment, which is comprehensive. In addition, compared with the reference answer, we can find that:

(1) The "parallelism" is identified accurately in auto-generated answers, and the corresponding clauses and function are also provided, so the answer is comprehensive.
(2) The author's emotion of "praiseful" is analyzed in the auto-generated answer. Besides, it is more exact answer compared by the reference answer, because the describe object is extracted from the title "Tianhe Xinhua" of given article, not from the question.

By comparison, it is proved that the emotional knowledge corpus for deep understanding of text can provide an important support to answer the reading and appreciating questions.

5 Conclusion

The emotional knowledge is designed and constructed from semantic and pragmatics in this paper. And with the help of it, a comprehensive and accurate answer for reading and appreciating question is generated. However, in the process of building knowledge corpus, manual annotation is time-consuming and labor-intensive, and the scale is limited. Therefore, in the future work, the active learning method will be adopted to realize the "automatic labeling-manual checking", which will ensure the corpus quality and expand the scale of knowledge corpus.

Acknowledgments. The authors would like to thank all the students' hard work who participate the corpus's labelling including Cheng Qi, Luo Feng, Wang Yanjie, Wen Xin, Xing Ying, Wen Zhi, Lu Xin. Also thank all anonymous reviewers for their valuable comments and suggestions which have significantly improved the quality and presentation of this paper. This work was supported by the National Natural Science Foundation of China (61672331, 61573231, 61672331); the National High-Tech Research and Development Program (863 Program) (2015AA011808).

References

1. Li, D., Liu, G.: Study on the formalization of information processing-oriented context. J. Chin. Inf. Process. **18**(3), 32–38 (2004)
2. Jiang, W.: Contemporary Pragmatics. Peking University Press, Beijing (2003)
3. Baccianella, S., Esuli, A., Sebastiani, F.: Sentiwordnet3.0: an enhanced lexical resource for sentiment analysis and opinion mining. In: Proceeding of International Conference on Language Resources and Evaluation, pp. 2200–2204 (2010)
4. Stone, P.J., Dunphy, D.C., Smith, M.S.: The General Inquirer: A Computer Approach to Content Analysis. MIT Press, Cambridge (1996)
5. Hu, M., Liu, B.: Mining and summarizing customer reviews. In: Proceeding of ACM SIGKDD International Conference on Knowledge Discovery and Data Mining, pp. 168–177 (2004)
6. Dong, Z., Dong, Q.: HowNet (2013). http://www.keenage.com
7. Ku, L.W., Chen, H.H.: Mining opinions from the web: beyond relevance retrieval. J. Am. Soc. Inf. Sci. Technol. **58**(12), 1838–1850 (2007)
8. Xu, L., Li, H., Pan, Y., Ren, H., Chen, J.: Constructing the affective lexicon ontology. J. Chin. Inf. Process. **27**(2), 180–185 (2008)
9. Toprak, C., Jakob, N., Gurevych, I.: Sentence and expression level annotation of opinions in user-generated discourse. In: Proceeding of Conference of the Meeting of the Association for Computational Linguistics, pp. 575–584 (2010)
10. Liao, X., Xu, H., Sun, L., Yao, T.: Construction and analysis of the third Chinese analysis evaluation (COAE2011) corpus. J. Chin. Inf. Process. **27**(1), 56–63 (2013)
11. Liu, K., Wang, S., Liao, X., Xu, H.: Overview of the fourth Chinese opinion analysis evaluation. Pro. Chin. Opin. Anal. Eval. **2012**, 1–32 (2012)
12. Tan, S., Wang, S., Liao, X., Li, W.: Overview of the fifth Chinese opinion analysis evaluation. Proc. Chin. Opin. Anal. Eval. **2013**, 5–33 (2013)
13. Xu, L., Lin, H., Zhao, J.: Construction and analysis of emotional corpus. J. Chin. Inf. Process. **2**(1), 116–122 (2008)

14. Yao, Y., Wang, S., Xu, R., Liu, B., Gui, L., Lu, Q., Wang, X.: The construction of an emotion annotated corpus on Microblog text. J. Chin. Inf. Process. **28**(5), 83–91 (2014)
15. Hermann, K.M., Kočiský, T., Grefenstette, E., Espeholt, L., Kay, W., Suleyman, M., Blunsom, P.: Teaching machines to read and comprehend. In: Proceedings of Conference of the 28th International Conference on Neural Information Processing Systems, pp. 1693–1701 (2015)
16. Hill, F., Bordes, A., Chopra, S., Weston, J.: The goldilocks principle: reading children's books with explicit memory representations. arXiv:1511.02301 (2015)
17. Cui, Y., Liu, T., Chen, Z., Wang, S., Hu, G.: Consensus attention-based neural networks for Chinese reading comprehension. In: Proceedings of Conference of the 26th International Conference on Computational Linguistics: Technical Paper, pp. 1777–1786 (2016)
18. Richardson, M., Burges C.J.C., Renshaw, E.: MCTest: a challenge dataset for the open-domain machine comprehension of text. In: Proceedings of Conference of the 2013 Conference on Empirical Methods in Natural Language Processing, pp. 193–203 (2013)
19. Weston, J., Bordes, A., Chopra, S., Mikolov, T., Rush, A.M.: Towards a complete question answering: a set of prerequisite toy tasks. arXiv:1502.05698 (2015)
20. Rajpurkar, P., Zhang, J., Lopyrev, K., Liang, P.: SQuAD: 100,000 + questions for machine comprehension of text. In: Proceedings of Conference of the 2016 Conference on Empirical Methods in Natural Language Processing, pp. 2383–2392 (2016)
21. Che, W., Li, Z., Liu, T.: LTP: a Chinese language technology platform. In: Proceedings of the International Conference on Computational Linguistics: Demonstrations, pp. 13–16 (2010)
22. Liang, R.: Definition and classification of rhetoric. J. Chin. Inf. Process. **1986**(5), 60–61 (1986)
23. Wu, S.: A preliminary study of the structure of the rhetoric. J. Chin. Inf. Process. **1979**(4), 49–56 (1979)
24. Song, Z., Wu, S., Zhang, G., Wang, X.: Modern Rhetoric. Jilin People's Press, Changchun (1984)
25. Mu, W., Liao, J., Wang, S.: A combination of CNN and structure similarity for parallelism recognition. J. Chin. Inf. Process. **32**(2), 139–146 (2018)

Construction and Application of Chinese Generation Lexicon for Chinese Irregular Collocation Between Verbs and Nouns

Mengxiang Wang[1,2(✉)], Qi Rao[2], and Houfeng Wang[2]

[1] Teachers' College of Beijing Union University, Beijing 100011, China
wmxl984@pku.edu.cn
[2] Institute of Computational Linguistics, Peking University, Beijing 100871, China
{wmxl984, raoqi, wanghf}@pku.edu.cn

Abstract. With the expanding scope of current research, irregular collocation processing began to attract scholars' attention. Based on the Generation Lexicon theory, we build a special word-description system. This knowledge representation system can restore the irregular collocation caused by omitting or metaphor in a clear manner, and then interpret their internal grouping mechanism and general process. The whole process will provide an effective way to deal with the irregular collocation processing problems.

Keywords: Irregular collocation · Generation Lexicon theory
Knowledge base

1 Introduction

In the past when processing on the problems of the collocation between verbs and nouns, the educational circles basically followed the idea of "large lexicon and small grammar", which is that we dealt with the collocation conforming to the rules through the utility of the most prevalent and simple grammar rules, while we applied the approach of constructing a lexicon in term of the collocations deviating from the rules. All those irregular collocations were solidified into a vocabulary for inclusion. Over a long time, the field of information disposal has accordingly established rules for the collocations that complies to the grammar rules, while for the collocations failing to conform to the routine grammar, the general response is to record them into the lexicon. In this way, on the one hand, we have to be forced to construct a larger and more diverse lexicon with the increase of the irregular collocation; On the other hand, the generation mechanism and description rules within the collocation structure will never receive a solution, which may result in a stagnation in the analysis technique for syntax and semantics. Thus, simply assigning the unconventional collocation to a vocabulary reservoir is just a circumvention for the specific questions. It is not compliant with the current processing trend and requirements of the natural language. Yet, this processing is not in accordance with the current trend and requirement for the natural language processing.

J.-F. Hong et al. (Eds.): CLSW 2018, LNAI 11173, pp. 667–678, 2018.
https://doi.org/10.1007/978-3-030-04015-4_58

We have found the following rules of the emergence of these irregular collocations despite that they are freeing off the rules. Usually, these unconventional collocations are accompanied with omitting (such as “rushing the paper” < “cranking out the paper” > and “writing a brush” < “writing with a brush” >) or metaphors (like “read the hard disk” < “read the data from the hard disk” > and “expose the mind sounds” < “expose the minds” >). On the basis made by the predecessor, a lexicon relied on a new knowledge-description system is under the desire to be constructed in this paper, able to restore the omitting and metaphor buried in the unconventional collocations in to their original form and disclose the generation procedures of them, so as to demonstrate or replay the original structures of these irregular collocation. Computers are enabled to recognize these matches, learn these combination rules, understand these semantic features, and perform a deeper processing and analysis. In the construction of this project, it drew on the partial characteristics of *Grammar Information Dictionary*, *Peking University Chinese Concept Dictionary*, and Chinese *Verb Library published by the Peking University*. Therefore, it can be said that it is an extension for the achievements realized by the predecessors.

2 Construction of Chinese Generation Lexicon

2.1 Frame Construction of the Chinese Generation Lexicon

For that it is the combination of verbs and nouns that we mainly face, the generation lexicon formulated by us is majorly under a collocation focusing on the verbs and nouns [4, 5]. The specific description framework is shown as follows (Fig. 1):

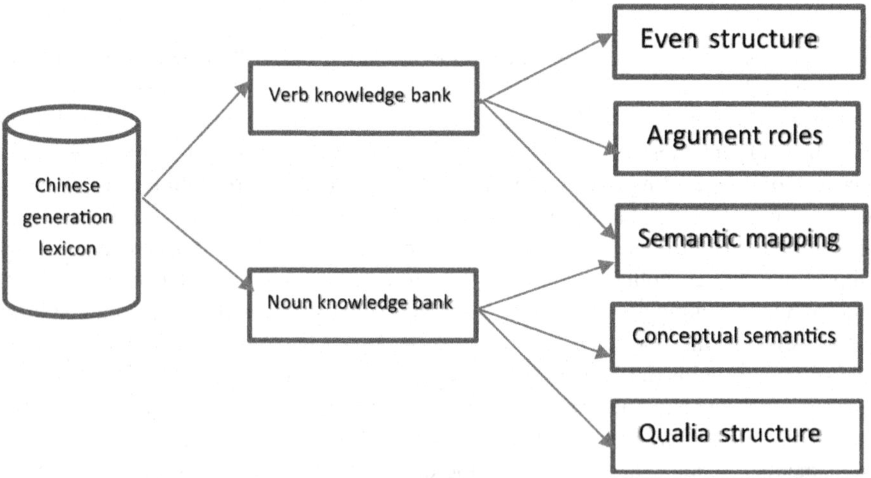

Fig. 1. Frame construction of Chinese generation lexicon

Where, the characteristics of the event structure and the argument role are the primary sculptured features of the verb knowledge bank. Both of the characteristics have been undertaken a related description and study in the Chinese Verb Resource Museum [10], from which we directly drew on the relevant trait knowledge. Similarly, the characteristics of the conceptual semantics and the qualia structure are mainly depicted by the noun knowledge bank, and the features of the semantic mapping are shared by the verbs and nouns.

2.2 Argument Role and Event Structure of the Verbs

The argument role of the verbs refers to the semantic role of the noun following the verb. The combo of the argument role feature of a verb and the conceptual semantic feature of a noun can generate the selectional restriction (SR) for the verb semantics. And the selectional restriction is a necessary condition for the judgement where a collocation of a verb and a noun is an irregular match; within the SR rule, it is a regular collocation, while it can be determined as an irregular collocation when it is beyond the SR rule.

The event structure is set for the determination on the presence of predicate omission in the verb-noun collocation, and the time-measured traits are often showed within the pointed action, representing the beginning and termination, as well as conversion of the action. In the event structure description of the verb, we concentrate on the description about whether the event structure of the verb and the verb itself are the two features of the event verb. Since that the event structure feature of the verb is able to be used to judge the combination order of the verb, and whether it can serve as an event verb determines if it is available to have the ability to connect a predicate behind it. In other words, if a verb is not an event verb and does not have the ability to arouse an occurrence of an event, then it is natured with the implied possibility of a predicate even if the verb is followed by a noun.

When it comes to whether the predicate is implicit or not, we mainly rely on the verb event structure to perform the judgement. Take an example of the two verbs, "like" and "learn"; there are only "like learning" rather than the linked collocation of "learn liking", which is related to whether they are event verbs and the different types of their belonged event structures. Mengxiang Wang (2013)[1] figured out that the event verbs are able to determine whether the verbs can be followed by the VP, and the traits of the event structure can determine the sort of VP following the verbs and illustrate the possibility of predicate omission. In regarded to the extraction of the event verbs, we depend on the Grammar Information Dictionary development by the Peking University on the characteristics of the following components (such as whether to be followed by VP and clauses). For that the event structure is related to the temporal characteristics expressed by the verbs, we take an advantage of the Grammar Information Dictionary (DKB) developed by the Peking University as a reference for the description about the

---

[1] Mengxiang Wang (2013) pointed out that the linkage and collocation of verbs shared a relationship with the type of the verb event structure; Among the three event structures (state, process, and transformation), the VP following each sort of verbs is selective. For example, the possibility that the process verbs are followed by a state verb is large.

event structure; we extract some traits from the grammar dictionary as the combo screening premises, such as through the utility of whether the Chinese character of "Zhe(着), Liao(了), or Guo(过)" is added behind, or whether the Chinese phrase of "zheng zai(正在), or jin xing(进行)" is added in front, or whether the VP is allowed to be attached behind, as well as other premises. At last, 213 event verbs are extracted from the 3000 commonly used words, and the verbs are dealt with a re-division according to the different types of the event structures at the same time. The purpose of this is to determine whether the verb can be followed by a VP and followed by what kind and range of VPs.

2.3 Conceptual Semantics and Qualia Role of the Nouns

Essentially, the conceptual semantics of a noun is the classification of the noun; we basically drew on the conceptual semantic categorization involved by the Chinese Concepts Dictionary (CCD) of the Peking University. For the description of the Qualia Role, we used the description model of Pustejovsky as a reference to represent its form role, constitutive role, telic role and agentive role [4, 5], and added an extra description for the evaluation role of the verb. The basic connotation can be shown in the table below (Table 1):

Table 1. The connotation of each qualia role described by this paper

Qualia role	Form role	Describe the nature of the word item that differs from other objects	Generally described by a noun
	Constitutive role	Describe the constitute of the object referred by the word item	Generally described by a noun
	Telic role	Describe the function and purpose generated by the word item	Generally described by a verb
	Agentive role	Describe the origin of the word item	Generally described by a verb
	Evaluation role	Describe the evaluation on the word item	Generally described by an adjective

With regard to the extraction of qualia roles, we intend to adopt a crowdsourcing format to describe the five qualia roles of the term through group wisdom. This is mainly because the qualia role of the noun is that the thinking dimension is more diversified, but the computer is still unable to achieve it at present. For example, the telic role of "knife" can be "to shred (dish), to cut (wood), and etcetera," or "to kill (person), to rob," or even to be used to "flap cucumber"; and of course, the computer can perform the description on the telic role through obtaining the verbs related to the noun of "knife", but this also involves the classification of verbs. On the other hand, the computer automatic acquisition is likely to be limited by corpus. However, in order to solve the problem on the thoughts confine of the human, we also used the corpora (mainly the Peking University CCL Corpus) as a support. Consequently, the feature acquisition in terms of the qualia role of this project is a crowdsourcing based on the automatic knowledge obtaining by the computer, which is also a new way to solve intelligent problems through "human-machine collaboration." [7–9] Examples are as follows:

Book, belonged level: Object/Specific substance/Artificial substance

Qualia roles:

Formal (FOR): Tangible matter, and artificial substance;

Constitutes (CON): White paper, fossils, stones, bamboo, bamboo piece, bamboo slips, paper piece, paper, cloth, silk, electronics…

Agentive (AGE): Write, write as, edit, publish, engrave, carve…;

Telic (TEL): Read, read aloud, learn, know, cover, use, earn money, propaganda, be an officer, educate, associate, pave, coat the wall, matt, recommend…;

Evaluate (EVA): Big, small, good, bad, hard, ordinary, strange, abnormal, literate, erudite, cultural, cheap, expensive…;

2.4 Features of Semantic Mapping

The feature of semantic mapping refers to the associated features of a verb or a noun. This kind of features on the one hand derived from the synonym of verbs or nouns, and are associated by the metaphorical features contained each word on the other hand. If it is a semantic association based on a synonym set, where its semantic distance is generally a unit, then these words are not featured with metaphorical features, commonly. For example, among the three categories of "pronounce", "read" and "acquire", the "pronounce" and "reading" are at the synonymous level whose semantic distance is a unit and has no metaphorical features; the "read" and "acquire" are at the synonym level, with the semantic distance as a unit, and not natured with metaphorical features. However, between the "pronounce" and "acquire", they can be associated through "read", and the semantic distance are two units; thus, "pronounce" and "acquire" can constitute a semantic mapping with metaphorical features. For example, in the sentence that "the computer is reading the disk data", where the "read" can map the word "acquire." If the mapping is established by the features contained in the term, this requires us to sort out and analyze the features described above, find the association, and then establish the priority between the two concepts in the source and target domains in the metaphor process. level. For example, for the two concepts of "woman" and "tiger", there is "woman" > "tiger" in terms of the selection on superior level of the source domains and target domains; in other words, the word "woman" is inclined to the ontology, while the "tiger" is more inclined to the metaphor. This is also in line with the fact as we state that "the woman is like a tiger" but rarely state "the tiger is like a woman." Based on this, we can determine that the "tiger" is the knowledge of the semantic mapping of "woman", but the reverse process is not available.

In addition, we also can help to complete the metaphorical relationship between terms through some specific words and frameworks. These words include "be, like, symbolize, metaphor," and so on and the framework contains "be like with, similar to…" and others. For this end, the association for each word item is constructed based on these marks, and their internal natures are described through the diverse roles of the qualia structure. In this way, a metaphorical association containing multiple traits is formed.

3 Application of Chinese Generation Lexicon in the Process with Predicate Ellipsis Collocation

The alleged predicate ellipsis collocation refers to the irregular collocation, which contents verb and object collocation in the form, such as "rushing the paper" and "learn a brush", but the verb and the noun share no relationship in the semantics and cannot constitute a semantic collocation, either, and the verb and noun are associated through the implied predicates. For instance, both "rush the paper" and "learn a brush" have imply the predicate "write." If in hope to enable the computer to determine whether a predicated is omitted in a verb-object irregular collocation, an effort should be put on the knowledge expression between the verb and the noun.

First of all, the verb must have the qualification to be followed by a VP, so that an omission can take place. In this regard, we can judge whether the verb is an event verb through the verb knowledge base. If the event verb has the ability to be added a VP behind and obtains the knowledge of the VP which is connected behind to the verb, then a potential VP collocation set is formed. The next step is started at the noun. A pair is performed for the VP set of the central verb through the description to the correlated verb in the noun qualia roles. The specific ideas are illustrated as follows (Fig. 2):

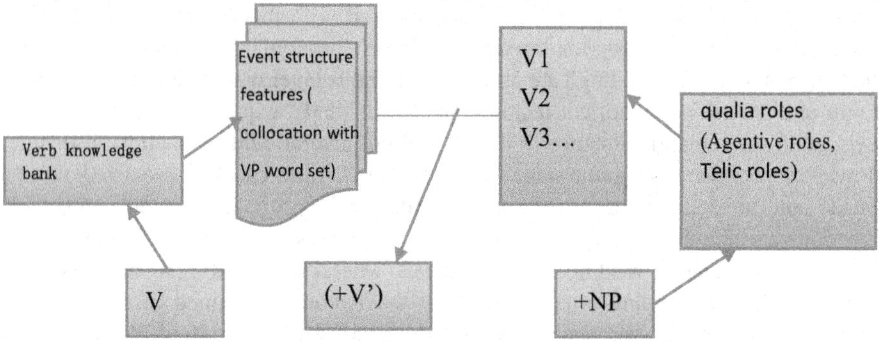

Fig. 2. Thought diagram of the recognition and processing on the predicate ellipsis

We can take the collocations of "play a piano" and "learn the piano" as the examples, and the analysis pattern of "play a piano" is shown as the diagram below (Fig. 3):

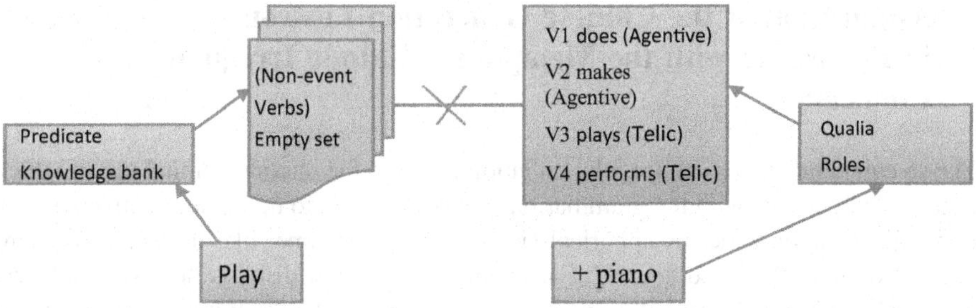

Fig. 3. Analysis flow chart of "play the piano"

Here, the word "play" is not equipped with ability of being followed by VP, and thus it is not an event verb recognized by the verb knowledge base; thus, the predicate ellipsis is not involved. And the analysis mode of "playing a piano" is shown as follows (Fig. 4):

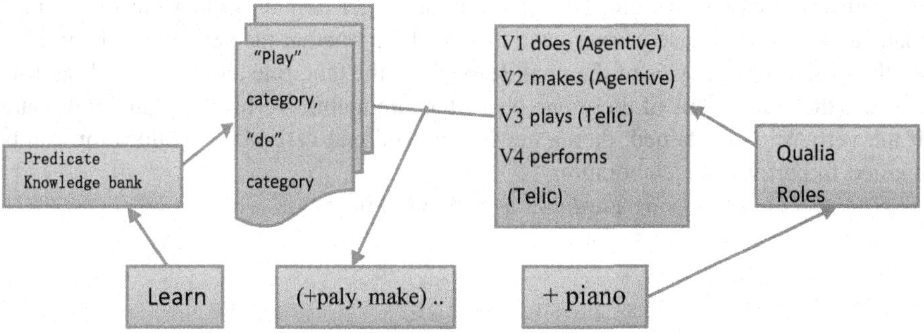

Fig. 4. Analysis flow chart of "Learn the piano"

Here, the word "learn" is an event verb recognized through the verb knowledge base. Based on the followed knowledge of a VP word set, two categories of verb ellipsis can be harvested through the pairing between the agentive role in the qualia roles of "playing piano" and the description on the telic roles (The agentive role refers to how this object is generated, and the telic role implies to what this object is used for).

For the determination on the event verb and selectional restriction of the followed VP, what we have adopted is not the basis of the statistics but the basis of principle. We extracted some grammar information traits related to verbs through the Grammar Information Dictionary by the Peking University, in order to determine the event verbs; while for the VP selectional restriction, we complied with the chronological features sequence of verbs for the screening.

4 Application of the Chinese Generation Lexicon in Processing with the Metaphorical-Mode Irregular Collocation

The so called metaphorical irregular collation refers to the unconventional match which is completely in line with the grammar but not conforming to the logical semantics, and implicitly contain some metaphorical signs at the same time, like the "read the hard disk" and "read the mind sound." For example, the "hard disk" is not assessable via "reading", and thus, the "read" here is actually mapping the "acquire"; And the "mind sound" is not available to "read", either, and thus, the "read" here is practically mapping a category meaning of "listen to, and understand." Our Chinese Generation Lexicon can explain the formation of these irregular collocation and find out the mapping metaphorical association between them through describing the related features of the verbs and nouns, respectively.

For a "V+NP" collocation, we start with the semantic mapping features of the verbs, and find out the mapping features V′ corresponding to the verbs in the naming of the verbs (the main grammatical form is the verb). Then we start from the noun, find the semantic mapping feature NP′ of the noun target domain (when the main grammatical expression is also a noun), and then analyze whether the verb V′ can be implied by the qualia role analysis of the noun (especially the telic role and the role of the role, because the expressions of these two characters are mainly verbs) in the target domain. If the verb 'V' is contained, then a newly conventional verb-object collocation can be applied to perform the elaboration.

The specific processing ideas are as follows (Fig. 5):

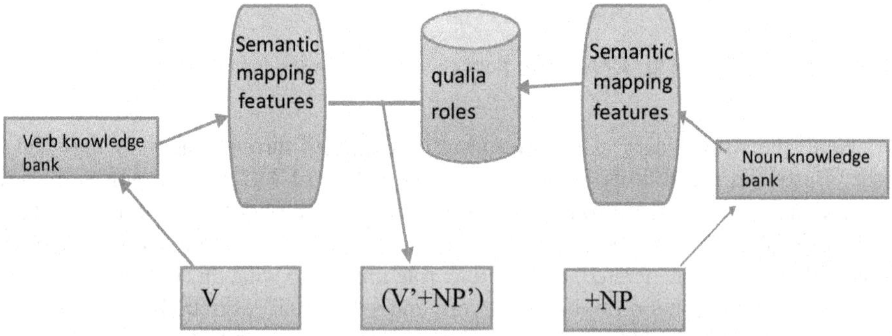

Fig. 5. Analysis flow chart of implied metaphorical irregular collocation

We take the "read the hard disk" as the example (Fig. 6):

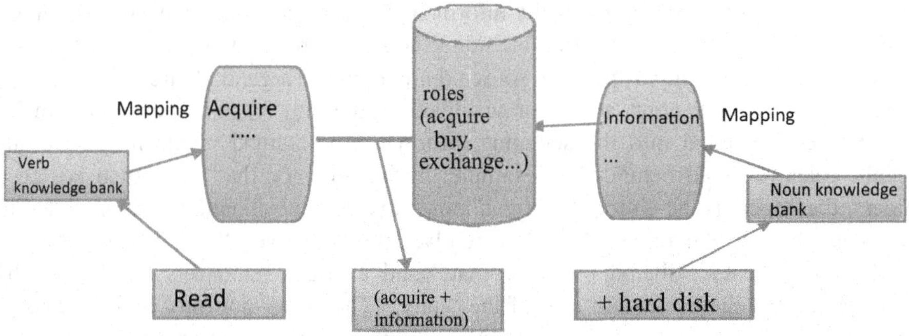

Fig. 6. Analysis flow chart of "reading the hard disk"

Here, the verbs "read" and "acquire" can be directly associated through semantics, and accordingly a semantic mapping is established; but for the semantic mapping between nouns, it is mainly through telic roles. As the example of the association between "hard disk" and "information," it depends on the telic roles. The function of the "hard disk" is to store, while "store" can activate the noun "information" or "data" in turn. Such a type of noun activation feature has received the verification by psychological experiments. Similar with the indication by the experiment conducted by Warren and McConel, Altmann [1, 2], some verbs themselves are born with certain specific noun information; when they activate a verb, they also naturally activate its corresponding noun. For instance, "mourn" is to naturally activate its object "a dead person." For this end, the process of the "hard disk" activating the "information" or "data" and the mapping set up by the people is obeying the psychological thoughts. In other description on the "read a hard disk," we can perceive it as "reading the information stored in the hard disk," and for the "read", we have mapped it as "acquire" through the semantic association. Hence, "reading the hard disk" is interpreted as "acquiring the information" in the form of conventional collocation.

5 Application of the Chinese Generation Lexicon in the Analysis of Metaphorical Text

Let us expound it with two sentences:

(1) A woman is like a tiger (Metaphorical meaning: A woman is as ferocious as a tiger.)
(2) A child is like a tiger (Metaphorical meaning: A child is as vigorous as a tiger.)

These two sentences share an identical structure, which is a quite difficult for the computer to understand them in that the characteristics respectively implied by the "woman," "child," and "tiger." To tackle with this problem, we have to apply the semantic mapping features and qualia roles of words. In fact, the semantic mapping is able to form a feature association with the qualia roles [6], and the specific thoughts are demonstrated as the chart below (Fig. 7):

The black dots here represent the information contained in the concept, which are expressed through grammar forms including nouns, verbs, and adjectives. Nevertheless, the information input from the source domain, under a general circumstance, will be no longer a simple noun, a verb, or an adjective after they reach to the target domain, but be de-constituted into the semantic information contained in the relied various qualia roles reflected behind. For example, in the sentence that "a woman is like a tiger", the "tiger" is the entity of a "tiger" but is one of the evaluation roles included in a tiger, that is, "fierceness." Concurrently, the adjective "fierce" becomes the metaphorical feature shared by a "woman" and a "tiger," and this feature can be represented via the evaluation role of the "tiger." Therefore, not only is the semantic mapping a simple association between two word items, but also an internally semantic feature mapping, which can be explained through the qualia roles.

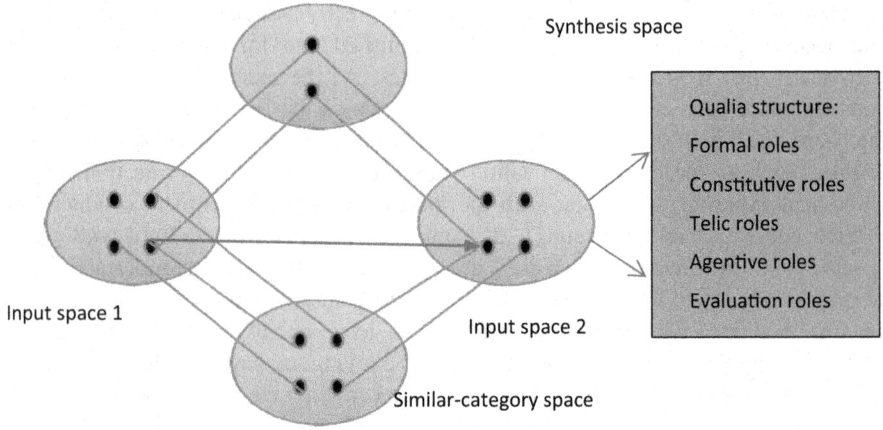

Fig. 7. Thoughts' map of the implied figuration connotation of word items based on the qualia roles.

On the basis of this idea, we can establish an evaluation role level for each noun and rank the evaluation roles of nouns into a sequence. For example, the evaluation roles of a "woman" can be divided into "gentle, virtuous, well-behaved, fierce, cute, lively, and so on," respectively, according to the priority; the evaluation roles of a "tiger" are sequenced respectively into "fierce, mighty, cruel, powerful, vigorous, vicious, and so on;" and the evaluation roles of a "child" have "lively, adorable, childish, innocent, naughty, and so on," in order based on the priority. Then, the feature matching from the nouns in source domain to the nouns in the target domain must be the feature matching with a priority on the front. For instance, the "woman" in the sentence that "a woman is like a tiger" is collocated with "gentle" preferentially, which is however not presented in the nature of a "tiger," and thus only the evaluation role of "fierce" is available for selection which is relatively prior and also relatively prior among the nouns in the target domain. The feature of "fierce" ranks at the top in both of evaluation roles of the "tiger" of the target domain and the "woman" in the source domain; accordingly, after the noun "woman" from the source domain enters the target domain, it is easier to inherit the evaluation role "fierce" of a "tiger" and the essence of the sentence that "a woman is like a tiger" is that "a woman is as ferocious as a tiger." In the same way, the prior evaluation role feature of the "child" in the "a child is like a tiger" is "adorable," which is also relatively prior in evaluation roles of a "tiger" in the target domain; hence, the sentence that "a child is like a tiger" is interpreted as "a child is as vigorous as a tiger." (Figs. 8 and 9)

We can express it with the following diagram:

(1) A woman is like a tiger → A woman is as ferocious as a tiger.
(2) A child is like a tiger → A child is as vigorous as a tiger.

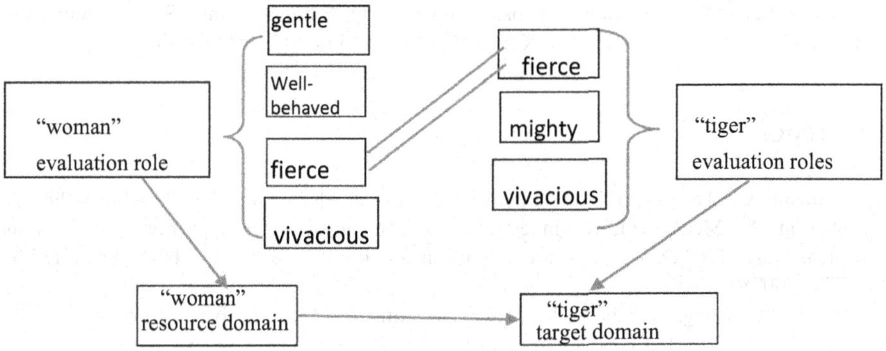

Fig. 8. Analysis flow chart of "a woman is like a tiger."

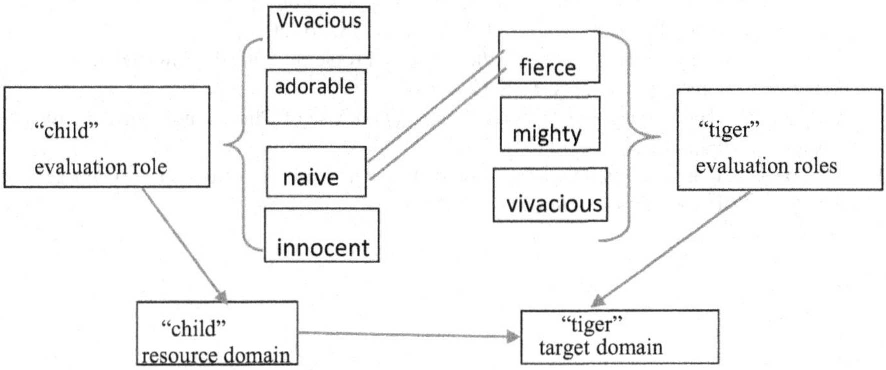

Fig. 9. Analysis flow chart of "a child is like a tiger."

6 Conclusion

The Chinese Generation Lexicon for irregular collocations includes the verb knowledge bank and the noun knowledge bank. At the same time, we make a word-description system. This knowledge representation system can restore the irregular collocation caused by omitting or metaphor in a clear manner. We can use it to interpret internal grouping mechanism of V-N collocations. However, a substantial of problems have been involved in how to apply it in an effective way. For example, how to judge and identify which collocations are unconventional collocations, which requires a study through coupling with the corresponding knowledge about the selectional restriction. As well as the problem of the determination on the metaphor which is also regarded as a key subject of the future research.

Acknowledgment. This research was partly supported by National Natural Science Foundation of China (61602040, 61433015), and China Postdoctoral Fund (2015M580905).

References

1. Altmann, G.: Thematic role assignment in context. J. Mem. Lang. **41**, 124–145 (1999)
2. Warren, T., McConnell, K.: Investigating effects of sectional restriction violations and plausibility violation severity on eye-movements in reading. Psychon. Bull. Rev. **14**, 770–775 (2007)
3. Wang, M., Wang, H., Zhang, L.: Judgment, extraction and selective restriction of chinese eventive verb. In: IALP2013, Urumqi (2013)
4. Pustejovsky, J.: Generative Lexicon. MIT Press, Cambridge (1995)
5. Pustejovsky, J.: Type theory and lexical decomposition. J. Cogn. Sci. **6**, 39–76 (2006)
6. Qiang, Li: On the combination of verb "Read" and nouns from generative lexicon theory. J. Yunnan Norm. Univ. (Ed. Teach. Res. Chin. Foreign Lang.) **2**, 69–80 (2015)
7. Yulin, Yuan: Study on semantic knowledge system based on generative lexicon theory and argument structure theory. J. Chin. Inf. Process. **6**, 23–30 (2013)
8. Yulin, Y., Qiang, L.: How to solve the "Tennis Problem" with the knowledge of qualia Structure? J. Chin. Inf. Process. **5**, 1–12 (2014)
9. Yulin, Yuan: The description system and application case of Chinese noun qualia structure. Contemp. Linguist. **1**, 31–48 (2014)
10. Mengxiang, Wang, Houfeng, Wang, Yang, Liu, Qi, Rao: Construction of Chinese verb library. J. Chin. Inf. Process. **6**, 85–94 (2014)

Construction of Word Sense Tagging Corpus

Hongying Zan(✉), JunYi Chen, XiaoYu Cheng, and Lingling Mu

School of Information Engineering, Zhengzhou University, Zhengzhou 450001, Henan, China
{iehyzan,iellmu}@zzu.edu.cn, junyichen_ch@sina.com

Abstract. The key problem of supervising word sense disambiguation is the lack of a large-scale and high-quality corpus of word sense tagging. Based on the Contemporary Chinese Semantic Dictionary, the Modern Chinese Dictionary (5th Edition) and the Chinese Lexical Semantic Knowledge Base, this paper analyzes the adjectives, nouns and verbs with polysemic in the dictionaries and fuses them together to construct the Zhengzhou University Contemporary Chinese Semantic Dictionary. People's Daily corpus is selected for annotation, and the word sense tagging corpus with 1.87 million words is constructed. It is expected to provide better data support for natural language processing tasks such as semantic automatic analysis and word sense disambiguation. This paper presents a detailed and rigorous specification of word sense tagging in the process of annotation. In addition, in the new domain corpus, the automatic annotation method achieved excellent performance, which can be used for subsequent reference.

Keywords: Word sense tagging · Semantic dictionary
Word sense disambiguation · Corpus · Natural language processing

1 Introduction

The ambiguity of words is one of the basic characteristics and inherent problems of natural language. To realize computer understanding natural language automatically, we must eliminate ambiguity. Therefore, Word Sense Disambiguation (WSD) is a hot topic in Natural Language Processing (NLP). It has important application value in machine translation, information retrieval and other fields. The construction of word sense tagging corpus is of great significance to WSD. Ng et al. [1] point out that the central task of WSD is to build a large-scale word sense tagging corpus and to guide training machine learning model. Veronis [2] believes that there is no substantial advancement in WSD research without a large-scale word sense tagging corpus.

Corpus of linguistics is a linguistic study based on corpus [3]. Corpus is a language database for storing language materials, which occupies an important position in natural language processing. Corpus tasks of rule-based require strong support from corpus, and computational linguistics of statistical-based also needs information from corpus. Word sense tagging corpus refers to mark the correct sense of the polysemic words on the real corpus according to the definition of each sense of the polysemic words in a dictionary [4]. The ideal word sense tagging corpus should have some features such as large scale, wide coverage and high accuracy. The scale of the corpus

J.-F. Hong et al. (Eds.): CLSW 2018, LNAI 11173, pp. 679–690, 2018.
https://doi.org/10.1007/978-3-030-04015-4_59

refers to the total number of tokens that have been marked, and itself has a certain reference value. Corpus coverage is the number of tagged word types, that is, the proportion or number of the polysemic words listed in the dictionary. The accuracy of the corpus is that the sense of the polysemic words tagged in corpus should be accurate, and it is often expressed by the consensus rate of multiple people.

The word sense tagging corpus has been built for several decades. Both English and Chinese have their own word sense tagging corpus. Corpora that have been constructed so far are mainly based on the word sense knowledge base WordNet [5]. The famous corpora have SemCor Corpus [6], SenseVal Corpus and DSO corpus [7]. A tree bank that uses semantic dependency relations for sentence semantic sense [8]. It is small that the scale of corpus for word sense tagging using traditional language dictionaries. Therefore, this paper adopts traditional language dictionaries. Based on the "Contemporary Chinese Semantic Dictionary" (CSD) [9] of Peking University, the "Modern Chinese Dictionary" (5th Edition) (XH5) of Chinese Academy of Social Sciences [10] and "the large-scale Chinese Lexical Semantic Knowledge Base" (CLSKB) [11] jointly established by Zhengzhou University and Peking University, this paper analyzes all the adjectives, nouns and verbs with polysemic in dictionaries and fuses them together to construct the "Zhengzhou University Contemporary Chinese Semantic Dictionary" (ZCSD). Based on the basic processing specifications of corpus in Peking University [12], People's Daily in January 2000 and the first 3 days of January 1998 are selected to make words tagged. This paper introduces the process of word sense tagging and formulates a complete standard of word sense division. In addition, it makes statistics and analysis of the completed corpus. Meanwhile, it also discusses the problems in the tagging process and points out the solution to the problem.

2 Dictionary and Corpus

2.1 Semantic Dictionary

Semantic dictionary is the basis for constructing word sense tagging corpus. It statically describes the sense distinction of words, and helps people to learn or guides computers to disambiguate word sense. The semantic dictionary used for annotation in this paper is ZCSD which is based on CSD, and incorporates Nouns, Verbs, and Adjectives with polysemic in XH5 and CLSKB. In addition, we further improve the semantic dictionary in the process of corpus annotation. Since the entries from XH5 and CLSKB cannot be distinguished by "义项[*yixiang*](*sense*)" and "同形[*tongxing*](*homomorphic*)" fields of the original CSD. Therefore, "新义项编码[*xinyixiangbianma*](*new sense code*)" field is added to the nouns, verbs and adjectives database respectively, and the senses of the polysemic words are recoded to distinguish different word senses.

"新义项编码[*xinyixiangbianma*](*new sense code*)" field corresponding to each polysemic word in ZCSD starts from 1 and the different senses of polysemic word are represented by a unique "新义项编码[*xinyixiangbianma*](*new sense code*)" value. In the word sense tagging corpus, the senses of the polysemic words in different contexts are also denoted by the "新义项编码[*xinyixiangbianma*](*new sense code*)". Samples of noun, verb, and adjective in the ZCSD dictionary are shown in Fig. 1. The attribute fields inherited from the CSD in the dictionary are described in reference [13].

1	词语	词类	拼音	同形	义项	新义项	释义	备注	直接上位	对象	ECAT	兼类	配价数	WORD	语义类	子类	参照体
2	车	n	che1	A		1	交通工具的一种	马˜/˜轮子			N	vq		vehicle	交通工具	null	
3	车	n	ju1	B		2	棋子的一种				N			chariot			
4	车	n	che1	5	5	3	姓				N			che	姓名		
5	车	n	che1		C1	4	指机器。	开˜|˜间									

(a) noun

1	词语	词类	拼音	同形	义项	新义项	释义	备注	主体	CCD	ECAT	兼类	客体	WORD	配价数	特殊句法位置	语义类	子类框架	与事
2	挨	v	ai1	A		1	触，碰，倚；	手˜手/˜了一下	具体事物		V		具体事物	delay	2		接触		
3	挨	v	ai2	B		2	遭受，忍受	˜批评/˜皮鞭/˜	生物		V			suffer	1		其他行为		
4	挨	v	ai1		C1	3	靠近；紧挨	他家˜着工厂。											
5	挨	v	ai2		C2	4	拖延。	他舍不得走，˜											
6	挨	v	ai2		C3	5	困难度过(	苦日子好不容易											

(b) verb

1	词语	词类	拼音	同形	义项	新义项	释义	备注	主体	对象	ECAT	兼类	配价数	WORD	语义类	子类
2	矮	a	ai3	null	1	1	身材短<c>	显得比他妹妹的个头˜/个子˜	人		A		1	short	样貌	null
3	矮	a	ai3		2	2	高度小的<c>	石桥˜˜地伏在水面上	具体事物		A		1	low	高度	
4	矮	a	ai3		C2	3	(级别、地位)低	他在学校里比我˜一级。								

(c) adjective

Fig. 1. Examples of ZCSD dictionary

2.2 Corpus

The annotated corpus includes the People's Daily in January 2000 and part of the corpus in January 1998. The corpus has been segmented with part-of-speech tag, and has been manually proofread. It has a total of 22,000 paragraphs and 1.87 million words. Paragraph (1) is the example of the corpus to be annotated. In this paper only labels nouns, verbs and adjectives with polysemic in the corpus. Each paragraph begins with its number, which represents the information of the year and month and is unique. The senses of word label are consistent with the basic processing specification of Peking University [12].

(1) 20000101-01-001-011/m 进步/vn 终究/d 要/vu 战胜/v 落后/a ,/wd 科学/n 终究/d 要/vu 战胜/v 愚昧/a ,/wd 正义/n 终究/d 要/vu 战胜/v 邪恶/a, /wd 这/rz 是/vl 历史/n 不断/d 昭示/v 人们/n 的/ud 科学/a 真理/n 。/wj 世界/n 和平/n 与/c 发展/vn 的/ud 崇高/a 事业/n 是/vl 不可/vu 阻挡/v 的/ud 。/wj 面对/v 新/a 的/ud 世纪之交/l 和/c 千年/t 之/u 交/Ng, /wd 每个/r 国家/n 有/vx 远见/n 的/ud 政治家/n 都/d 应{ying1}/vu 从/p 历史/n 的/ud 高度/n 思考/v :/wm 未来/t 的/ud 世界/n 应该/vu 是/vl 一个/mq 什么样/rz 的/ud 世界/n, /wd 应该/vu 为{wei4}/p 实现/v 这样/rz 一个/mq 世界/n 作出/v 什么样/rz 的/ud 贡献/n 。 /wj (*20000101-01-001-011 Progress After all, to overcome backwardness, science must defeat ignorance in the end, and justice must defeat evil in the end. This is the scientific truth that history has constantly revealed people. The lofty cause of world peace and development is unstoppable. In the face of the new century turn and the turn of the millennium, each country's visionary politicians should think from the height of history: what kind of world should the future world be and what contribution it should make to realize such a world.*)

3 Word Sense Tagging

3.1 Specification

The word sense distinction is an important issue of word sense tagging. With the dictionary as the semantic system, the word sense tagging must face the problem of the division of senses in the dictionary. This is a major difficulty in the processing of word sense tagging [14]. In the new semantic dictionary constructed in this paper, there are enough clues to distinguish word senses, such as interpretation, example and subject, which can clearly distinguish the sense of words. However, the new dictionary is a combination of three dictionaries, so the senses of polysemic words are inevitably covered and crossed. In addition, there will be words segmentation errors and part-of-speech tag errors in the corpus. To ensure the annotated quality, this paper summarizes the questions that appear in the trial stage and formulates a detailed word sense tagging specification which covers almost all special situations and provides clear reference for tagging personnel. Meanwhile, it also analyzes words that are more difficult to distinguish, and organizes tagging personnel to learn so as to ensure that they can divide the senses. The detailed specification of the word sense tagging is as follows.

a. The basic principle. Firstly, try to mark the original CSD entry, that is, "义项[*yixiang*](*sense*)" field is a numeric or "同形[*tongxing*](*homomorphic*)" field is not empty. Only when the CSD entry does not have an appropriate sense, the supplementary sense is marked.
b. Supplementary the interpretation of CSD. If the "释义[*shiyi*](*interpretation*)" of the CSD entry is empty, we should refer to "ECAT", "WORD", "语义类[*yuyilei*](*semantic class*)" and other fields of the entry for labeling. Meanwhile, the "释义[*shiyi*](*interpretation*)" field is added according to the others fields.
c. Addition of new senses in the dictionary.
   (1) Addition of "X+numeric" senses. If the semantic dictionary does not have an appropriate sense and the interpretation of the entry can be found in the "Modern Chinese Dictionary" (7th Edition)(XH7), we should fill it to the dictionary. The "义项[*yixiang*](*sense*)" field is named "X+numeric" (the numeric is the label of the interpretation in the XH7, the default for no label is 1).
   (2) Addition of "X0+numeric" senses. If there is no appropriate interpretation in the XH7, we should add senses other than the XH7. The "义项[*yixiang*] (*sense*)" field is named "X0+numeric". For example, if a word needs to add multiple senses, the sense items are marked as X01 and X02, which are added in order. In addition to the "释义[*shiyi*](*interpretation*)", we also need to fill in the source of the interpretation in <>, such as, <Baidu Encyclopedia>, <Wikipedia>, <Sogou Encyclopedia>, and write examples in the "备注[*beizhu*](*remark*)" field.
   (3) Addition of "X0" senses. The monosemic words should be marked as X0. For the judgment of the monosemic words, the contents of the "释义[*shiyi*](*interpretation*)" and the "WORD" fields are the same.

(4) Addition of "Y" senses. If there has the original sense of the metaphor in the dictionary, the corresponding original sense item should be written in the "备注[*beizhu*](*remark*)". If there is no original sense in the dictionary, the original sense is added to the "释义[*shiyi*](*interpretation*)", then the source of the "释义[*shiyi*] (*interpretation*)" and the example are added, the addition method is as shown in (Add "X0+numeric" senses).
(5) Addition of "X" senses. If the word segmentation has error, we should add "X" senses to the dictionary. In addition, the error should be recorded in EXCEL. The record format is paragraph label, word, original format, modified format. If the words separated is still the original sense, it is not the word segmentation error. On the contrary, if the sense changes, it belongs to segmentation error. For example, "首席执行官[*shouxizhixingguan*](*CEO*)", it must be merged.
(6) Addition of "X+correct part-of-speech" senses. If the part-of-speech is wrong, we should add "X+correct part-of-speech" senses. Meanwhile, the error should be recorded in EXCEL, the record format is paragraph label, word, original label, correct label.

d. Errors in dictionary. It should be recorded by yourself and modified by the administrator if there have errors in the dictionary.
e. Other cases. If the corpus with special context or it is too short that we don't know how to choose its sense, the best choose is to mark the most commonly used senses. When we don't know how to mark it, mark the paragraph to dis-cuss. The results of the discussion should be documented and sent collectively to the administrator for future reference. The record document includes words to be labeled, semantic analysis, and example. Such as, "全国[*quanguo*](*National*) /全村[*quancun*](*whole village*) /全场[*quanchang*](*full audience*)", when the analysis is unclear, the general default is marked as the interpretation of the "location", when the collocation is "全国上下一致同意(*Unanimous agreement across the country*)/对全国发表讲话(*Speaking to the whole country*)", these mean "people".

3.2 Manual Tagging

Drawing on the construction methods of the same type of corpus, such as the construction process of CFKB [15]. This paper uses the method of manual double-blind annotation to build a corpus, that is, each person in the same group does not know the partner labeling, they first complete the labeling work respectively and then proofread the labeling results of themselves together. After the proofreading is done, the corpus will be post-processed, and the marked senses are replaced with the corresponding "新义项编码[*xinyixiangbianma*](*new sense code*)" in the dictionary.

Manual Tagging Method. In order to facilitate manual tagging and improve the accuracy of labeling results, this paper developed a Web-based auxiliary manual tagging platform using the B/S architecture. It is safety and convenience for administrator to maintain the server deployed on the Linux system. In addition, the platform supports online tagging simultaneously of multiple users and also provides corpus and dictionary download. The other features are as follows.

a. The same corpus can be sent to two tagging personnel respectively as the first annotation corpus and the second annotation corpus. Meanwhile, the tagging results do not affect each other.
b. Each tagging personnel has a user name and password. After logging in, they can only view the paragraphs they need to annotate, and they have no right to view other user annotation results.
c. The platform provides proofreading function after double-blind tagging. After the first and the second annotation of the corpus completed, proofreading can be performed directly on the platform.
d. In order to facilitate the analysis of the corpus, the platform has a statistical analysis function which can automatically calculate the labeling consistency rate, and filter labels with inconsistent words.

These features not only ensure double-blind annotation, but also support the proofreading work, and promote the word sense tagging work.

In the tagging process, the tagging personnel only needs to select the appropriate sense according to the context and the dictionary of the word to be marked, which can effectively avoid manual input errors and shorten the tagging time. The interface of the auxiliary manual tagging platform is shown in Fig. 2. After the annotation completed, the words and corpus with inconsistent labels can be directly screened and proofread in the platform.

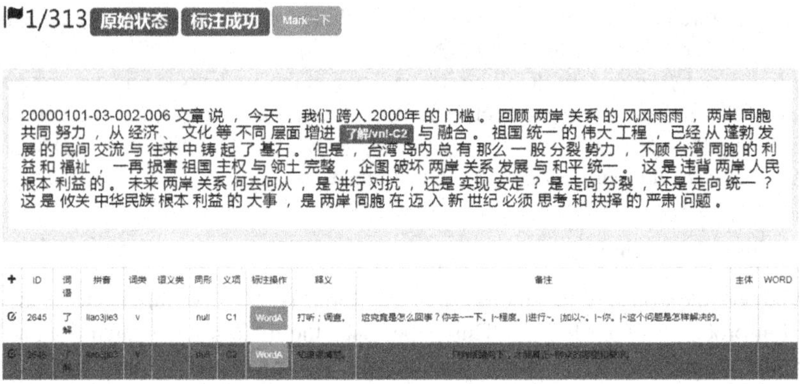

Fig. 2. Interface of auxiliary manual tagging platform

Manual Tagging Result. In the process of manual double-blind annotation, the verbs with higher consistency rate are "解决[*jiejue*](*solve*)", "可以[*keyi*](*can*)", "能[*neng*](*can*)", and the consistency rates respectively are as high as 99.89%, 99.87%, 99.83%. The verbs with poorer consistency rate are "到[*dao*](*reach*)", "运行[*yunxing*](*run*)", "统计[*tongji*](*count*)", and the consistency rates correspondingly are 55.01%, 54.97%, 54.35%. The details are shown in Tables 1 and 2.

The reason for the low consistency rate is attributed to the fact that the sense of the word is not clearly divided. For example, "到[*dao*](reach)" has 3 senses, as shown in

Table 1. Words with higher consistency rate

Word form	Senses no.	Frequency	Consistency rate (%)
解决[*jiejue*](*solve*)	2	939	99.89
可以[*keyi*](*can*)	2	754	99.87
能[*neng*](*can*)	3	1,729	99.83

Table 2. Words with poorer consistency rate

Word form	Senses no.	Frequency	Consistency rate (%)
到[*dao*](*reach*)	3	2,494	55.01
运行[*yunxing*](*run*)	3	171	54.97
统计[*tongji*](*count*)	5	230	54.35

Table 3. Comparing the results of tagging, the interpretations of C2 and C3 are easily confused, making it difficult to distinguish them. On the basis of full investigation and discussion of these senses, the principle of distinguishing the sense of words can be formulated and be recorded in document.

Table 3. Interpretation and examples of "到[*dao*](*reach*)"

Senses	Interpretation	Examples
C1	用作动词的补语，表示动作有结果。(*Used as the complement to verb, indicating that the action has result.*)	看～。(*see*)|办得～。(*do it*)|说～一定要做～。(*Speaking of it must be done*)
C2	达于某一点。做动词的补语。(*Reach at a certain point. Do the complement of the verb.*)	火车～站了。(*The train arrived at the station.*)|从星期三～星期五。(*From Wednesday to Friday*)
C3	往。(*go in a direction.*)	～郊外去。(*Go to the suburbs*)|～群众中去。(*Go to the crowd*)

3.3 Automatic Tagging

This paper proposes a model of automatic machine annotation. It is hoped that the introduction of this model can effectively reduce the input of manpower and material resources in the same type of work in the future under the premise of ensuring the quality of the annotated corpus. The working mode of automatic word sense tagging is man-machine double-blind annotation, that is, people and computer mark their own corpus without knowing the other's label, then proofread the results of the man-machine annotation, and perform post-processing on the corpus.

Automatic Tagging Model. We choose the model is based on the support vector machine (SVM), due to which has the superior performance in text classification tasks [16]. SVM is a binary model whose basic model is a linear classifier with the largest interval defined in the feature space. Its learning strategy is the maximization of interval, which can be formalized as a solution to the convex quadratic programming problem. It is also equivalent to the minimization of the loss function of the hinge, and its learning algorithm is the optimization algorithm for solving the convex quadratic programming [17].

In the mode of automatic tagging, the labeled corpus is used as the training corpus to build the model. After the model is generated, the unlabeled corpus is automatically labeled by the model.

This paper uses word2vec to convert corpus into vector. The context word vector is set to 50 dimensions, and the part of speech vector is set to 3 dimensions, where the noun correspondence vector is (1 1 0), the verb is (0 1 0), the adjective is (0 0 1), and the other part of speech is (0 0 0). The context window is set to 2, and the context vector is a new vector V formed by splicing the context words and the part of speech corresponding vectors. First, based on the manual annotated corpus, the word context vector V and its label are trained by the LIBSVM toolkit [18] to obtain the word model. Then the word model is used to mark unlabeled corpus.

Auxiliary Proofreading Tool. In order to complete the man-machine proofreading work successfully, this paper has developed an auxiliary proofreading tool. In the tool, the manual annotation and the automatic annotation corpus are input respectively, and the inconsistent words in the corpus will be highlighted, then manually select the appropriate senses based on the context of the word and the dictionary. The interface of auxiliary proofreading tool is shown in Fig. 3.

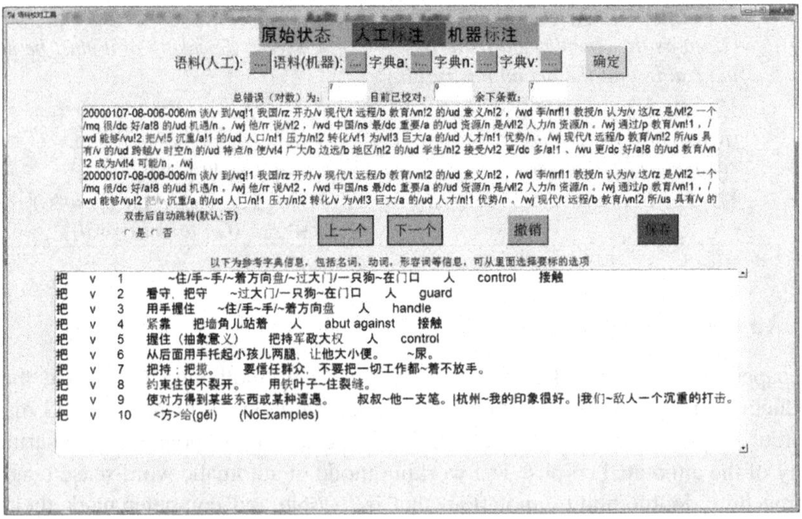

Fig. 3. Interface of auxiliary proofreading tool

Automatic Tagging Results. In order to evaluate the effectiveness of the automatic tagging model, this paper has trained the model based on the January 2000 corpus. The model is used to mark a partial corpus of January 1998. The results are compared with the standard answer (a partial corpus of January 1998 after manual proofreading) and the consistency rate is as high as 83.18%. Based on the corpus in January 1998 and the January 2000 corpus, a closed test is conducted and the consistency rate is as high as 91.32%.

Since the model has achieved excellent performance in the People's Daily corpus, this paper also tries to use this model in other domain corpus for man-machine double-blind labeling, such as military corpus. In the military corpus, the consistency rate of manual labeling and automatic labeling results is 71.25%. At the same time, it is found that the manual tagging method of 1000 paragraphs requires 10–20 h/person, while the automatic tagging model requires 5–10 h/person, saving half the time. It fully demonstrates that the automatic tagging model can effectively improve the tagging efficiency, and save manpower and material resources. So it is worthwhile to continue research.

4 Results and Analysis

4.1 Quality Evaluation Standard

Usually, the Inter Annotator Agreement (IAA) and KAPPA value [19] are used to measure the tagging quality of the word sense tagging corpus. IAA is calculated as shown in Eq. 1.

$$IAA = A/N. \tag{1}$$

Where N is the total number of times the word has been marked, A is the number of times that each tagging personnel (usually two tagging personnel) is consistent. The k value is calculated according to the Kappa value as follows.

$$k = \frac{p_a - p_e}{1 - p_e}. \tag{2}$$

$$p_e = \sum\nolimits_{j=1}^{M} \left(\frac{C_j/2}{N}\right)^2. \tag{3}$$

$$p_a = IAA. \tag{4}$$

Where M is the number of senses of the target word w. C_j is the sum of the number of times that two tagging personnel mark sense j. Generally, k value over 80% is considered to be high quality labeling [20].

4.2 Result Statistics and Analysis

This paper has tagged 3287 polysemic words so far, as shown in Table 4, a total of 64,851 times, covering 27.13% polysemic words in the semantic dictionary, the IAA of result is 93.04%, kappa value is 76.68%, the data shows that the quality of the corpus constructed in this paper is excellent. The IAA of adjective is 83.71%, but the kappa value is only 50.48%. It is because there are 78 adjectives with kappa values less than 0, of which 32 have a kappa value of −1, among the 341 labeled adjectives. Further analysis of the reasons, the 32 words which pa value is 0 and pe value is 0.5 are only marked once, and the two labels are inconsistent. As shown in sentence (2) and (3). "俗[*su*](*vulgar*)" is only marked once in the corpus, the first tagging personnel marked as sense 1 and the second tagging personnel marked as sense 2, which causes the "俗[*su*](*vulgar*)" kappa value to be −1. In the adjectives of dictionary, 9% of the words are this case, causing the kappa value of the adjective being only 50.48%. Combined with the interpretation of the "俗[*su*](*vulgar*)" in dictionary, as shown in Table 5, the corpus is indeed difficult to distinguish, and both senses can be explained, indicating that the sense of the word is still to be further studied.

Table 4. The statistics of result

Part-of-speech	Frequency	Dictionary words no.	Proportion (%)	IAA (%)	Kappa (%)
adjective	7,127	1,318	25.87	83.71	50.48
verb	32,644	4,003	36.37	91.37	71.78
noun	25,080	6,795	21.93	97.87	90.53
Mean			27.13	93.04	76.68

(2) 是/vl!B1$ 题解/n!-C2 , /wd 更/dc 是/vl!B1$ 自我/rr 不/df 避/v!-C2 俗/a!1 怨/v!-C2 的/ud 揶揄/vn 。(*It is a solution, and it is a slogan that the self does not avoid vulgar resentment.*)
(3) 是/vl!B1$ 题解/n!-C2 , /wd 更/dc 是/vl!B1$ 自我/rr 不/df 避/v!-C2 俗/a!2 怨/v!-C2 的/ud 揶揄/vn 。(*It is a solution, and it is a slogan that the self does not avoid common resentment.*)

Table 5. Interpretation and Examples of "俗[*su*](*vulgar*)"

Senses	Interpretation	Examples	WORD
1	庸俗(*vulgar*)<xh7>	～气(*vulgarity*)/这个人很～(*This person is very vulgar*)	vulgar
2	大众的, 普遍的, 流行的. (*common, popular*)<xh7>	～名(*Common name*)/～话 (*Slang*)	common

5 Conclusion

Word sense tagging corpus is an important resource for natural language processing. Its scale and quality largely determine the success or failure of natural language processing tasks. The completion of the construction of a large-scale word sense tagging corpus is of great significance for the current research areas in natural language processing such as automatic semantic analysis, word elimination, and machine translation. The natural language processing laboratory of Zhengzhou University took 1 year to complete the construction of word sense corpus. The consistency rate of the corpus reaches 93.04%, and the kappa value is 76.68%. The marked noun kappa value is as high as 90.53%.

With this corpus, the current accuracy rate of WSD has reached 80%, which is quite significant. The problem of the corpus is the polysemic words that contain only nouns, adjectives and verbs, and the coverage of polysemic words is still not high enough. So it still needs to be improved. The automatic tagging model proposed in this paper has achieved good results. The consistency rates of closed and open tests in People's Daily corpus are 91.32% and 81.38% respectively. It proves that the mode of man-machine annotation is effective and can be used as reference for relevant research, especially in the construction of future corpus.

The future work includes (1) To complement and improve the word sense tagging corpus in conjunction with multi-faceted and multi-angled resources. (2) To use the corpus to conduct research on WSD, and promote the application of word sense tagging corpus in multiple research directions in natural language processing, hoping to promote the development of various research fields. (3) To further improve the automatic tagging model, and expect its accuracy to be comparable to the manual tagging level. Especially with the in-depth study of semi-supervised learning methods, the demand for corpus is more urgent, and the automatic tagging model with high accuracy will be able to promote further development of this research area.

References

1. Ng, H.T., Wang, B., Chan, Y.S.: Exploiting parallel texts for word sense disambiguation: an empirical study. In: Meeting on Association for Computational Linguistics, pp. 455–462 (2003)
2. Vronis, J.: Sense Tagging: Does It Make Sense? (2003)
3. Zan, H.Y., Xu, H.F., Zhang, K.L., et al.: The construction of internet slang dictionary and its analysis. J. Chin. Inf. Process. **30**(6), 133–139 (2016). (in Chinese)
4. Jin, P., Wu, Y.F., Yu, S.W.: Survey of word sense annotated corpus construction. J. Chin. Inf. Process. **22**(3), 16–23 (2008). (in Chinese)
5. Fellbaum, C., Miller, G.: WordNet: an electronic lexical database. Libr. Q. Inf. Community Policy **25**(2), 292–296 (1998)
6. Miller, G.A., Leacock, C., Tengi, R., et al.: A semantic concordance. In: The Workshop on Human Language Technology, pp. 303–308 (1993)
7. Wang, J., Yang, L.J., Jiang, H.F., et al.: A word sense annotated corpus for teaching Chinese as second language. J. Chin. Inf. Process. **31**(1), 221–229 (2017). (in Chinese)
8. You, F., Li, J.Z., Wang, Z.Y.: On construction of a Chinese corpus based on semantic dependency relations. J. Chin. Inf. Process. **17**(1), 46–53 (2003). (in Chinese)
9. Wu, Y., Jin, P., Zhang, Y., Yu, S.: A Chinese corpus with word sense annotation. In: Matsumoto, Y., Sproat, Richard W., Wong, K.-F., Zhang, M. (eds.) ICCPOL 2006. LNCS (LNAI), vol. 4285, pp. 414–421. Springer, Heidelberg (2006). https://doi.org/10.1007/11940098_43
10. Chinese Academy of Social Sciences.: Modern Chinese Dictionary. The Commercial Press, Beijing (2012). (in Chinese)
11. Shi, J.M., Zan, H.Y., Han, Y.J.: Specification of the large-scale Chinese lexical semantic knowledge base building. Learn. Period. Soc. Shanxi Univ. (Nat. Sci. Ed.) **38**(4), 581–587 (2015). (in Chinese)

12. Yu, S.W., Duan, H.M., Zhu, X.F., et al.: The basic processing of contemporary Chinese corpus at peking university specification. J. Chin. Inf. Process. **16**(5), 58–65 (2002). (in Chinese)
13. Wang, H., Zhan, W.D., Yu, S.W.: Structure and application of the semantic knowledge-base of modern Chinese. Appl. Linguist. **1**, 134–141 (2006). (in Chinese)
14. Xiao, H.: The sense relations and sense distinction of polysemes in the dictionary. J. Yunnan Norm. Univ. (Humlties Soc. Sci.) **42**(1), 41–46 (2010). (in Chinese)
15. Zhang, K.L., Zan, H.Y., Chai, Y.M., et al.: Survey of the Chinese function word usage knowledge base. J. Chin. Inf. Process. **29**(3), 1–8 (2015). (in Chinese)
16. Zhou, Z.H.: Machine Learning. Tsinghua University Press, Beijing (2016). (in Chinese)
17. Li, H.: Statistical Learning Method. Tsinghua University Press, Beijing (2012). (in Chinese)
18. Cui, M., Zhang, C.L.: The comparison study of LIBSVM, LIBLINEAR, $SVM^{multiclass}$. Electron. Technol. (6), (2015). (in Chinese)
19. Ng, H.T., Lim, C.Y., Shou, K.F.: A case study on inter-annotator agreement for. (2007)
20. Carletta, J.: Assessing agreement on classification tasks: the kappa statistic. Comput. Linguist. **22**(2), 249–254 (1996)

Construction of Chinese Semantic Annotation Resource of Connective Structures

Bo Chen[1], Chen Lyu[1](✉), and Ziqing Ji[2]

[1] Collaborative Innovation Center for Language Research & Services, Guangdong University of Foreign Studies, Guangzhou 510420, China
cb9928@gmail.com, lvchen1989@gmail.com
[2] College of Computer Science, University of Maryland, College Park 20742, USA
1163539719@qq.com

Abstract. This paper aims to study Chinese connective structures for semantic parsing based on the semantic dependency graph we proposed. The resources we built include three parts: first, Chinese connectives ontology that contains 1291 words; second, a large-scale Chinese connective structure semantic annotation resource with 20,000 sentences; third, a pattern-set of Chinese connective structure that facilitates the next step—automatic analysis. We use manually annotation to ensure the accuracy of the resources. We also make an annotation criteria handbook.

Keywords: Connective structure · Semantic dependency graph
Semantic annotation · Resource construction

1 Introduction

In recent years, the research trend of natural language processing (NLP) has been developing towards the direction of deep semantic parsing, which requires discourse knowledge representation for internal logical and semantic relations. The logical and semantic relations between events can often be marked by the connectives in the discourse. Therefore, the study of connectives has attracted more and more attention in NLP [1–4].

This paper focuses on Chinese connective structures which contain 1 to 4 connectives. In NLP, semantic parsing is always a key issue, and sentence understanding, especially the complex sentences and discourses, has always been one of the most difficult tasks [5]. Connectives are one of the explicit grammatical marks of logical and semantic relations among sentences. Connectives mainly include conjunctions, prepositions, adverbs, fixed phrases, etc., and they are usually used to connect two or more sentences, reflecting the complex logical and semantic relations between sentences. As shown in Examples (1)–(3):

(1) 停电了，李四**就**走了。（A,就B）

J.-F. Hong et al. (Eds.): CLSW 2018, LNAI 11173, pp. 691–697, 2018.
https://doi.org/10.1007/978-3-030-04015-4_60

After the power outage, Li Si left.

(2) **尽管**亚洲一些国家的金融动荡会使这些国家的经济增长受到严重影响，**但**就整个世界经济而言，其他国家的强劲增长势头会弥补这一损失。（尽管A,但B）

Although the financial turmoil in some Asian countries will seriously affect the economic growth of these countries, in terms of the entire world economy, the strong growth momentum of other countries will make up for this loss.

(3) **不管**是意大利的皮鞋、荷兰的花卉，**只要**能增加知识的含量、善用资讯科技来作管理，再加上创新与品质提升，**都**算是知识产业。（不管A,，只要B,都C）

Whether it is Italian leather shoes or Dutch flowers, as long as it can increase the content of knowledge, make good use of information technology for management, plus innovation and quality improvement, it is considered a knowledge industry.

In (1–3), the connective structures respectively compose of single, two, and three connectives, which respectively represent the logical and semantic relations of inheritance, concession, and conditional miscellaneous. The connectives composed of two or more words are called "*paired connectives*", as a relatively fixed collocation. The research object in this paper includes the annotation of not only single connectives, but also paired connectives.

This paper introduces *recursive directed dependency graph* model to represent semantic relations in Chinese discourse using annotating connective structures, and to build a large-scale Chinese semantic annotation resource of connective structures.

2 Semantic Dependency Graph

This paper proposed a complex semantic representation mechanism for Chinese complex sentences. The semantic relations between sentences and between words can be represented as a semantic dependence graph by recursive directed graphs.

The minimum representation unit of a semantic dependency graph is the description of the semantic relation and the type of this relation of sentence [6, 7]. In general, a phrase or sentence can be represented as a set of feature structure triples consisting of an entity, a features, and its value. With These triples, we can represent the semantic relations by multiple-edged nodes [8]. The formal representation of these triples is a recursive directed Dependency graph.

The semantic dependency graph can more comprehensively represent the semantic relations between words in the sentence and between the clauses in the discourse. The semantic dependency graph model is characterized by:

- allowing multiple correlations;
- allowing recursion and nesting;
- formal representations as recursive directed graph.

3 Construction of Chinese Semantic Annotation Resource of Connective Structures

The construction of Chinese semantic annotation corpus, which contains nearly 17,000 sentences (including 58,800 clauses), took three years with the utilization of the manual annotation method.

The annotation process has three major stages, the preparation period, the annotation period and the evaluation period.

The preparation period includes developing the annotation criterion, selecting and collating annotation data, writing annotation software, and selecting and training the annotators. We completed the construction of the connective ontology in the first stage. This phase takes about half a year.

The annotation period consists of two stages: pre-annotation and post-annotation. The data are from CTB 6.1 [9]. The pre-annotation period had annotated 8,000 sentences, while the post-annotation annotated 9,000 sentences. The annotation software will continuously be modified and refined according to the annotation needs. The annotation criterion is supplemented when new exceptions are encountered.

The third phase includes cross-calibration and evaluation of the annotation results.

3.1 Construction of Connective Structure Ontology Resource

We have established an ontology with 1,291 connectives, from the Chinese textbooks of primary and secondary schools, linguistics books, connective dictionaries, and the raw sentences in CTB 6.1, domestic Chinese News data for nearly three years. There are fifteen semantic relations.

3.2 Polysemous Phenomenon of Connectives

There are many polysemous connectives, such as: "而(*and, then, but, if*) ", "才(*only,, just, then, so*)"etc. One of the difficulties of connectives annotation is that there are many polysemous phenomenon during annotation. A connective may have multiple POS (parts-of-speech) and multiple semantic relations. The context, deep semantics, and syntactic structure will be the constraints of determinants of the connectives. According to the connective structure ontology, the typical polysemous connectives are shown in Table 1.

Table 1. Polysemous phenomenon of connectives

Semantic relations	Typical connectives	Description
5	而,则	而:*Coordinate, progressive, hypothetical, inheritance, disjunctive*
4	就, 便, 还, 要不然, 又	就: *hypothesis, inheritance, conditional, cause-effect,* 还:*Coordinate, progressive, inheritance, disjunctive*
3	才, 倒不如, 还不如, 即, 就是, 要不, 也, 以, 再	才: *inheritance, conditional, cause-effect* 也:*Coordinate, hypothetical, disjunctive*

3.3 Construction of Chinese Semantic Annotation Resource of Connective Structure

3.3.1 Corpus Data Source

Considering the representativeness, diversity, homogeneity, timeliness and versatility, we choose data in CTB6.1, which is a universal annotation corpus for NLP. In terms of corpus coverage, the data is from Mainland, Taiwan, Hong Kong, and Singapore; the data content includes political news, economic news, and life news. Regardless of the length of the sentence and the size of the paragraph, we select a complete article as an unit in order to obtain the semantic complete information. The corpus has a total of 16,893 sentences, more than 500,000 words.

3.3.2 Annotation Methods and Annotator Training

We use manual annotation. Annotators are linguistic graduates who can determine the semantic types of connectives. Every week, we exchange the annotation results of all the annotators, modify the wrong and missing places, and focus on specific annotation difficulties.

3.3.3 Annotation Criterion

3.3.3.1 Overview

(1) Defined fifteen Chinese semantic relations: 并列 (*coordinate*), 递进 (*progressive*), 对比 (*contrastive*), 假设 (*hypothetical*), 解说 (*interpretation*), 目的 (*purposive*), 凭借 (*by virtue of*), 顺承 (*inheritance*), 条件 (*conditional*), 选择 (*alternative*), 因果 (*cause-effect*), 转折 (*disjunctive*), 补充 (*complementary*), 包含 (*inclusive*), 和其他 (*others*).

(2) Defined explicit and implicit connective structures. The explicit connective structure includes the fifteen relations, such as: "他一(*just*)来我就(*then*)走。". The implicit connective structures can only be represented by punctuation in the sentence, such as: "他来了，我很高兴。(*he came, I was so happy.*)"

(3) Defined punctuation mark: comma "，", slight-pause mark "、", semicolon "；", colon "：" period "。", exclamation mark "!", and question mark "?".

(4) The connective structures include a single word, such as: 可是(*but*); a pair of words, such as: 因为...所以... (*because... so...*); regular collocations, such as: 原本…却…只因为…因此…(*have done…but…just because... so...*).

(5) The position of connectives: the beginning of the sentence (intra-sentence), the middle of the sentence (intra-sentence), and independent elements (extra-sentence).

(6) Connectives can represent the semantic relations inside a single sentence, between several clauses in a complex sentence, and sometimes among multiple complex sentences.

(7) The annotation with connectives are hierarchical.

(8) Annotation of explicit connectives: the semantic relation and position of the connective.

(9) Annotation of implicit connective structure: annotating the punctuation marks with semantic relations.

3.3.3.2 Annotation Principle

(1) The minimum unit principle: the minimum semantic unit is "word".
(2) The semantic relatedness principle: we focus on the semantic relations between clauses, words in the complex sentence, regardless of the word order and the distance of the words in the sentence.
(3) The recursion principle: the hierarchical semantic relations can be represented in the annotation software.

3.3.4 Annotation Examples

(4) 这项工程的建成投产（S1），不仅将缓解国内尼龙六六盐原料供应的紧张状况（S2），而且将对河南省乃至全国的橡胶、轮胎、化工、化纤行业产生重大影响（S3）。

The completion and commissioning of this project will not only ease the tension of domestic nylon six or six salt raw materials supply, but also have a major impact on the rubber, tire, chemical and chemical fiber industries in Henan Province and even the whole country.

In (4), the single connective "乃至(*even*)" represents progressive relations; the paired connectives "不仅…而且…(*not only...but also...*)" represents progressive relations; the marks of implicit connectives-three consecutive slight-pause mark "、、、" connects four parallel words. The semantic dependency graph of (4) is shown in Fig. 1.

(5) 同时（S1），"八五"时期的对外开放在深度上也创下了历史之最（S2），过去中国的对外开放主要是以商品贸易、技术引进及合资合作为主（S3），如今已开始向引进服务、引进现代资本运作方式等高层次迈进（S4），并开始向海外输出资本（S5），甚至开始参与国际金融运作（S6）。

At the same time, the opening up of the "Eighth Five-Year Plan" period has also reached the highest level in history. In the past, China's opening up to the outside world was mainly based on commodity trade, technology introduction and joint venture cooperation. Now it has begun to introduce services and introduce modern capital operations. The way to move at the same level and began to export capital overseas, and even began to participate in international financial operations.

In (5), "也(*also*)", "、及(*and, regular collocation*)", "、等(*etc., regular collocation*)", represent the semantic relations between words in the clause. "同时(*meantime*)"、"并(*and*)"、"甚至(*even*)"、" 过去……如今……(*past...now...*, *regular collocation*)" represent the semantic relations between clauses. Their positional characteristics are *independence, the beginning of sentence, the beginning of sentence, the beginning of sentence and the beginning of sentence*. Their semantic relations respectively are *coordination, coordination, progression, and inheritance*. The semantic dependency graph of (5) is shown in Fig. 2.

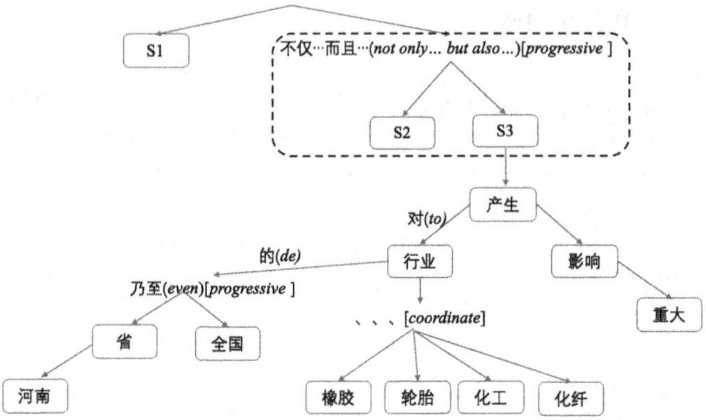

Fig. 1. The annotation example of (4)

In (5), S1 is a connective, as an independent element, represents the semantic relations between the previous discourse and this one. There is no connective between S2 and the following four clauses. Only the comma ",", as an implicit mark, represents the commentary relation. In " 过去……如今……(*past...now... , regular collocation*)", the two words are time nouns, each word is not a connective, however, when two time nouns are used continuously in the discourse, there are recessive relations. Continuous time nouns, or recessive relations, is a frequent phenomenon in real corpus.

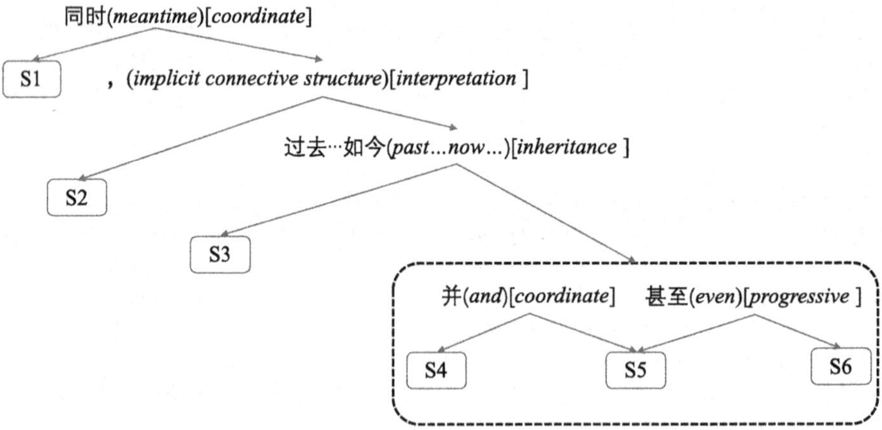

Fig. 2. The annotation example of (5)

4 Conclusion

Using the semantic dependence graph is an attempt to construct Chinese discourse-level connectives semantic annotation resources. We constructed a Chinese connective ontology, a set of templates of connective structure, and a large-scale connective structure annotation resource based on semantic dependency graph. We mainly use the news data from CTB 6.1 to ensure the representativeness, timeliness and versatility of the corpus. We explored the criteria for the determination of semantic dependence graphs and developed specific annotation criteria based on the principles of minimum unit, semantic relatedness and recursion. The resource will help to deepen the understanding of Chinese discourse, the textual entailment, information extraction, discourse coherence, and machine translation.

Acknowledgment. The work is funded by the following projects: National Natural Science Foundation of China No. 61772378, 61702121, Humanities & Social Science Foundation of Ministry of Education of China No. 16YJCZH004, and Science & Technology Project of Guangzhou No. 201704030002.

References

1. Liu, H.J., Che, W.X., Liu, T.: Feature engineering for Chinese semantic role labeling. J. Chin. Inf. Process. **21**(1), 79–84 (2007). (in Chinese)
2. Prasad, R., Dinesh, N., Lee, A., Miltsakaki, E., Robaldo, L., Joshi, A.K., et al.: The penn discourse TreeBank 2.0. In: International Conference on Language Resources and Evaluation, LREC 2008, 26 May–1 June 2008, Marrakech, Morocco, DBLP, pp. 2961–2968 (2008)
3. Xue, N.: Annotating discourse connectives in the Chinese treebank. In: The Workshop on Frontiers in Corpus Annotations Ii: Pie in the Sky. Association for Computational Linguistics, 84–91 (2005)
4. Zhang, W.X., Qiu, L.K.: Study on connectives collocation based on corpus. Chin. Teach. World **82**(4), 64–74 (2007). (in Chinese)
5. Feng, W.H.: The dependency-based analysis of Chinese conjunctions and the related constructions. Wuhan University (2011). (in Chinese)
6. Chen, B., Lyu, C., Wei, X.M., Ji, D.H.: Chinese semantic parsing based on feature structure with recursive directed graph. Wuhan Univ. J. Nat. Sci. **20**(4), 318–322 (2015)
7. Chen, B., Ji, D.H., Chen, L.: Semantic labeling of Chinese subject-predicate predicate sentence based on feature structure. J. Chin. Inf. Process. **26**(3), 22–26 (2012). (in Chinese)
8. Chen, B., Lyu, C., Wei, X., Ji, D.: Semantic labeling of Chinese verb-complement structure based on feature structure. In: Su, X., He, T. (eds.) CLSW 2014. LNCS (LNAI), vol. 8922, pp. 341–348. Springer, Cham (2014). https://doi.org/10.1007/978-3-319-14331-6_34
9. Xue, N., Xia, F., Chiou, F.D., Palmer, M.: The Penn Chinese treebank: phrase structure annotation of a large corpus. Nat. Lang. Eng. **11**(2), 207–238 (2005)

A Research on Construction of Knowledge Fusion Network in Chinese and English Languages

Odmaa Byambasuren[1,2(✉)], Zhifang Sui[1,2], and Baobao Chang[1,2]

[1] Key Laboratory of Computational Linguistics, Ministry of Education, Beijing, China
[2] School of Electronics Engineering and Computer Science, Peking University, Beijing, China
{odmaa_b, szf, chbb}@pku.edu.cn

Abstract. In this paper, we created a prototype of Chinese-English lexical and encyclopedic knowledge fusion network CELK-Net. We integrated Chinese Concept Dictionary (CCD) and Chinese-English knowledge graph XLore by an automatic mapping algorithm inspired by Babelnet. The result is a localized bilingual semantic network with large coverage in Chinese language.

Keywords: Semantic networks · Bilingual semantic networks
Knowledge fusion network

1 Introduction

In the research and applications of Natural Language Processing, lexical knowledge and general human knowledge are essential to achieving the true understanding of the context. Currently, the most popular resource with lexical knowledge is the Princeton WordNet [1], which is the basis of other lexical knowledge resources, such as EuroWordNet [2] and Multilingual Central Repository [3]. In the Chinese language, the pioneering computational lexicon is HowNet [4], created by Chinese Academy of Science, which has designed based upon cognitive knowledge of Chinese concepts. Other lexicons include, Chinese Semantic Dictionary (CSD) [5], WordNet-based Chinese concept dictionary (CCD) [6], Chinese Open WordNet (COW) [7], and Chinese WordNet (CWN) [8].

Even though lexical knowledge resources have covered the majority of the concepts, there is still a lack of human cognitive knowledge. One solution to this issue is integrating the knowledge from Wikipedia, a collaborative resource with human interaction, into the lexical knowledge resources. This solution is applied in YAGO [9] and Babelnet [10, 11]. Although these knowledge bases have the multilingual feature, they still have scarce knowledge in languages other than English. Reflection of this problem is Chinese Wikipedia, which has 15 to 17 times fewer data entries compared to major Chinese encyclopedias, particularly Baidu Baike and Hudong Baike. These two encyclopedias are used in XLore [12], a large-scale knowledge resource with balanced Chinese-English coverage, which has 14.9 million instances and 1.3 million concepts.

J.-F. Hong et al. (Eds.): CLSW 2018, LNAI 11173, pp. 698–704, 2018.
https://doi.org/10.1007/978-3-030-04015-4_61

However, XLore only consists of encyclopedias and does not contain lexical knowledge.

In this paper, we created a prototype of Chinese-English lexical and encyclopedic knowledge fusion semantic network CELK-Net by integrating WordNet-based Chinese concept dictionary (CCD) with XLore. We used existing multilingual semantic network Babelnet as a construction model, considering that Babelnet has integrated WordNet and Wikipedia. Since every instance in XLore belongs to at least one concept, by establishing a mapping between XLore concept and CCD Sense, we obtained an ancestral connection from CCD Sense to XLore instance. We conducted a manual evaluation of 1000 random mappings in CELK-Net.

This paper is organized as follows. Section 2 introduces CELK-Net's structure and its' knowledge resources. Section 3 introduces CELK-Net's mapping methodology and algorithm. Section 4 describes our experiment and result. Finally, Sect. 5 presents our conclusions.

2 CELK-Net: Chinese-English Language and Knowledge Fusion Network

We used state-of-the-art multilingual semantic network Babelnet as our structure model. The knowledge in CELK-Net is labeled as a directed graph $G = (V, E)$, where V is set of vertices (i.e. concepts) and, E is set of edges connecting a pair of vertices (Fig. 1).

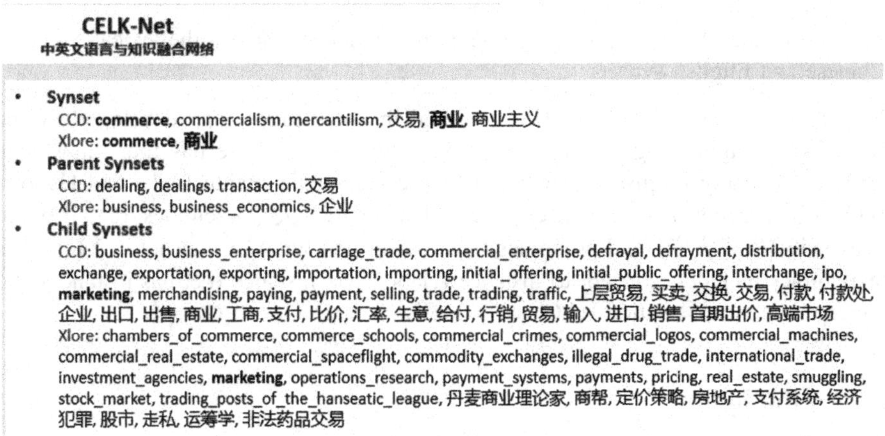

Fig. 1. Mapping result of XLore concept "Commerce|商业" and CCD Sense {commerce, commercialism, mercantilism, 交易, 商业, 商业主义} in CELK-Net. The result shows that the CCD has mostly lexical abstract concept, while XLore has more general human knowledge related realistic concept.

Each vertex is a set of Chinese and English lexicalization of a concept, e.g. {commerce, commercialism, mercantilism, 交易, 商业, 商业主义} and each edge is a semantic relation of a pair of vertices, e.g. $\{\text{is} - \text{a}, \text{part} - \text{of}\}$.

The key difference between CELK-Net and Babelnet is that Babelnet uses a single language to establish a mapping between lexical and encyclopedic resources, and then translates the mapped knowledge into different languages. CELK-Net, on the other hand, takes advantage of the bilingual feature of CCD and XLore, and thus only needs to establish a mapping between the two resources, eliminating the additional translation phase.

2.1 Knowledge Resources

CCD. Chinese Concept Dictionary (CCD) is a WordNet 1.6 based Chinese-English lexical dictionary developed by the Institute of Computational Linguistics of Peking University. Each concept (i.e. Sense) in CCD is expressed as a set of synonyms (called Synset). The total number of Synset in the dictionary is close to 100,000, including 66,025 nouns. Every Sense in CCD has an English Synset and a Chinese CSynset. For example, Synset and CSynset of Sense $S_n^{00706993}$ are,

$$Synset\left(S_n^{00706993}\right) = \{\text{commerce}, \text{commercialism}, \text{mercantilism}\},$$

$$CSynset(S_n^{00706993}) = \{\text{交易}, \text{商业}, \text{商业主义}\},$$

please note that there are no one-to-one correspondence between the lexicalization of Chinese and English synsets.

XLore. XLore is a large-scale Chinese-English knowledge graph developed by the Knowledge Engineering Group at Tsinghua University. XLore has four knowledge resources, namely English Wikipedia, Chinese Wikipedia, Baidu Baike and Hudong Baike. XLore consists of concepts (e.g. University |大学), entities (e.g. Oxford University |牛津大学), and properties (e.g. established time). A concept in XLore has taxonomies includes, concept to instance relation has Instance (i.e. has-instance) and concept to concept relation subClassOf (i.e. is-a).

3 Methodology

Our mapping methodology consists of three parts. Firstly, for each XLore concept, we extract Chinese and English lemmas. Lemma is a dictionary form of a set of words, for example, English lemma of the XLore concept "Commerce|商业" is “Commerce”. Secondly, we acquire candidate CCD Senses for each of the Chinese and English lemmas, and establish probable links between CCD and XLore.

$$\mu(x_{en}, x_{zh}) = \begin{cases} s \in (Senses_{ccd}(x_{zh}) \cap Senses_{ccd}(x_{en})) & \text{If an intersection can be found,} \\ s \in (Senses_{ccd}(x_{zh}) \cup Senses_{ccd}(x_{en})) & \text{else, if the concept is monosemous} \\ & \text{in one of the languages} \\ none & \text{otherwise,} \end{cases} \quad (1)$$

Lastly, we check the ambiguity of the links and establish a mapping for unambiguous links. Unambiguous link in our mapping method is defined in Sect. 3.2. If Chinese and English lemmas of a XLore concept link to a same candidate CCD Sense, we treat the link between the candidate CCD Sense and the XLore concept as unambiguous link; or, if Chinese or English lemmas of a XLore concept is monosemous in both CCD and XLore, we also treat the link as unambiguous. For ambiguous links, we use Babelnet's mapping algorithm, which defines the disambiguation context for the resources, and establish a mapping between the resources (Sect. 3.3). Details of above steps are as follows.

3.1 Mapping Preparation

Given a XLore concept x, its Chinese and English lemmas are defined as x_{zh} and x_{en}. For example, $\boldsymbol{x}$ = **Commerce|商业**, its lemmas are x_{en} = Commerce and $\boldsymbol{x_{zh}}$ = 商业.

Having the lemmas, we acquire candidate CCD Senses $Senses_{ccd}(x_{zh})$ and $Senses_{ccd}(x_{en})$ in each languages, Chinese and English. For example, candidate CCD Senses of $\boldsymbol{x}$ = **Commerce|商业** are,

$$Senses_{ccd}(\text{Commerce}) = \{S_n^{00706993}, S_n^{05340125}\},$$

$$\boldsymbol{Senses_{ccd}(\text{商业}) = \{S_n^{00706993}, S_n^{00709093}, S_n^{06008236}, S_n^{05973804}\}}$$

3.2 Unambiguous Link Mapping

We establish XLore to CCD mapping $\mu(x_{en}, x_{zh})$ by finding the common CCD Senses in the candidates. From the example in Sect. 3.1, we can see that there is only one intersection, and that is $S_n^{00706993}$ in candidate CCD Senses in two languages, so that we establish mapping **μ(Commerce, 商业) =** $\boldsymbol{S_n^{00706993}}$, where

$$Synset(S_n^{00706993}) = \{\textbf{commerce}, \text{commercialism}, \text{mercantilism}\},$$

$$\boldsymbol{CSynset(S_n^{00706993}) = \{\text{交易}, \text{商业}, \text{商业主义}\}}.$$

In some cases, the candidate CCD Senses in two languages do not have any intersection in between, or the candidate CCD Senses have more than one intersection. For these cases, we use Babelnet's mapping algorithm, which is, "for each Wikipage w

whose lemma is monosemous both in Wikipedia and WordNet, map *w* to its only WordNet sense." In CELK-Net, we check whether XLore concept *x*'s lemma is monosemous in both XLore and CCD, and map *x* to its only CCD Sense.

3.3 Ambiguous Link Mapping

In order to establish a mapping between ambiguous resources, we first define disambiguation context for XLore concepts and CCD Senses, as in Babelnet and use the intersection in the hierarchal structure. For this step, we do not separate disambiguation context by Chinese and English languages.

XLore Concept's Disambiguation Context.
For a given XLore concept *x*, the disambiguation context includes, concept label, parent concept (i.e. Category) and child concept (i.e. Sub-concept and related-concept). A Concept in XLore has four types of labels, synonym set label, (e.g. "Universities colleges"), categorized label ("University (teaching institutions)"), monolingual label (e.g. "University"), and bilingual label (e.g. "University (大学)"). For each type of label, we extract lemma and disambiguation context, such as, synonyms of the synonym set label, category of the categorized label, lemma of the monolingual label, and Chinese and English lemmas of the bilingual label.

CCD Sense's Disambiguation Context.
For a given CCD Sense *s*, the disambiguation context includes, synonym sets of Chinese and English CSynset and Synsets, e.g. "university,大学,高校,综合大学,高等学校,高等院校". Hypernym (i.e. generalization) and Hyponym (i.e. specialization) [1] relation of the CCD Sense.

3.4 Mapping Algorithm

Following Babelnet's mapping method, we designed a mapping method for our bilingual resources. Pseudocode of our mapping algorithm is shown below:

```
for each x ∈ Senses_xlore
     μ(x) := ε
for each x ∈ Senses_xlore
     if |Senses_ccd(x_zh) ∩ Senses_ccd(x_en)| = 1 then
         μ(x) := s_n^k
   else then
         if |Senses_xlore(x_zh)| = |Senses_ccd(x_zh)| = 1 then
             μ(x) := s_n^k
         if |Senses_xlore(x_en)| = |Senses_ccd(x_en)| = 1 then
             μ(x) := μ(x) + s_n^m
for each x ∈ Senses_xlore
     if μ(x) = ε then
         if no tie occurs then
             μ(x) := argmax p(s, x)
return μ
```

- lines 1–2: set initial null value for mapping, $\mu(x)$.
- lines 4–5: for candidate CCD Senses of the Chinese and English lemmas, if only one intersection found, map x to the corresponding s, i.e. the Chinese and English lemmas are mutually translatable.
- lines 6–10: if one of x's Chinese lemma or English lemma is monosemous in both XLore and CCD, map x to its only Chinese or English CCD Sense.
- lines 11–14: if no mapping has previously found, we assign most probable Sense s to x, using Babelnet's joint probability method $p(s,x)$.

In the mapping method, sense s which maximizes this probability is determined as:

$$\begin{aligned}\mu(x) &= \underset{s \in Senses_{ccd}(x)}{\operatorname{argmax}} \; p(s,x) \\ &= \underset{s \in Senses_{ccd}(x)}{\operatorname{argmax}} \frac{\text{score(s,x)}}{\sum_{\substack{s' \in Senses_{ccd}(x), \\ x' \in Senses_{xlore}(x)}} score(s',x')}\end{aligned} \tag{2}$$

where $\text{score}(s,x) = |Ctx(s) + Ctx(x)| + 1$. Here $Ctx(s)$ and Ctx(x) represents disambiguation context of CCD Sense and XLore concept x respectively.

4 Experiment and Result

We conducted a mapping experiment on 1000 randomly selected XLore concepts, to see the efficiency of the unambiguous and ambiguous link mapping methods. The experiment result is 37.4% of the XLore concept's Chinese and English lemmas are linked to a same candidate CCD Sense; 18% of the XLore concept's Chinese and English lemmas are both monosemous in each resources (i.e. most of which is medical term of plant name); 20.2% of the XLore concepts are monosemous only in Chinese, while 10.2% of the XLore concepts are monosemous only in English. And the 30.4% of the XLore concepts are ambiguous, i.e. the concept has more than one candidate CCD Sense and not monosemous in XLore, therefore we used the joint probability algorithm to maximize the probability.

Currently, there is no baseline for Chinese-English knowledge base mapping, therefore we conducted a manual evaluation on our mapping results using Babelnet's Chinese knowledge as baseline. By default, we treat unambiguous link mappings in our network as correct, because no other corresponding XLore concept or CCD Sense can found. During our evaluation, we found that 15.38% of the mapping in CELK-Net is new to Babelnet. For example, CELK-Net Synset {line, 物流, 物流公司, 货运公司, 运输公司}, whose XLore concept is "Logistics companies |物流公司", could not be found in Babelnet 3.1 as keyword "Logistics companies" or "物流公司".

5 Conclusion

In this paper, we created a prototype of the Chinese-English semantic network CELK-Net by integrating Chinese Concept dictionary (CCD) with large-scale Chinese-English knowledge base XLore. We used Babelnet as a construction model, and implemented an automatic mapping algorithm designed for our bilingual resources, CCD and XLore respectively. By using the bilingual mapping method, we eliminated the translation phase after the mapping, and discovered more monosemous links between lexical dictionary and encyclopedia.

The XLore knowledge base used in this work has covered major Chinese encyclopedias. Our next step is to apply the mapping method in other bilingual knowledge resources, and validate the bilingual mapping method's effectiveness.

Acknowledgment. This research is supported by the National Basic Research Program of China 2014CB340504 and the National Natural Science Foundation of China 61751201 and M1752013. We would also like to show our gratitude to Professor Liu Yang's team from the Institute of Computational Linguistics of Peking University for providing the CCD database, and Professor Li Juanzi's team from the Knowledge Engineering Group of Tsinghua University for providing the XLore database. We also thank 2 "anonymous" reviewers for their insights.

References

1. Miller, G.A.: WordNet: a lexical database for english. Commun ACM **38**(11), 39–41 (1995). https://doi.org/10.1145/219717.219748
2. Vossen, P. (ed.): EuroWordNet: A Multilingual Database with Lexical Semantic Networks. Springer Netherlands, Dordrecht (1998). https://doi.org/10.1007/978-94-017-1491-4
3. Gonzalez-Agirre, A., Laparra, E., Rigau, G.: Multilingual central repository version 3.0. In: LREC, pp. 2525–2529 (2012)
4. Dong, Z.D., Dong, Q.: Hownet (1999). http://www.keenage.com
5. Wang, H., Zhan, W.D., Yu, S.W.: The specification of the semantic knowledge-base of contemporary Chinese. J. Chin. Lang. Comput. **13**(2), 159–176 (2003). (in Chinese)
6. Yu, J.S., Yu, S.W.: The structure of Chinese concept dictionary. J. Chinese Inform. Process. **16**(4), 13–21 (2002). (in Chinese)
7. Wang, S., Bond, F.: Building the chinese open wordnet (COW): starting from core synsets. In: Proceedings of the 11th Workshop on Asian Language Resources, pp. 10–18 (2013)
8. Huang, C.R., et al.: Chinese wordnet: Design, implementation, and application of an infrastructure for cross-lingual knowledge processing. J. Chin. Inform. Process. **24**(2), 14–23 (2010)
9. Suchanek, F.M., Kasneci, G., Weikum, G.: Yago: a core of semantic knowledge. In: Proceedings of the 16th International Conference on World Wide Web, pp. 697–706. ACM (2007)
10. Navigli, R., Ponzetto, S.P.: Babelnet: building a very large multilingual semantic network. In: Proceedings of the 48th Annual Meeting of the Association for Computational Linguistics, pp. 216–225. Association for Computational Linguistics (2010)
11. Navigli, R., Ponzetto, S.P.: Babelnet: the automatic construction, evaluation and application of a wide-coverage multilingual semantic network. Artif. Intell. **193**, 217–250 (2012)
12. Wang, Z., et al.: Xlore: a large-scale english-chinese bilingual knowledge graph. In: International Semantic Web Conference (Posters & Demos), vol. 1035, pp. 121–124 (2013)

Corpus Linguistics

Research on Verb Reduplication Based on the Corpus of International Chinese Textbooks

Dongdong Guo, Jihua Song(✉), Weiming Peng, and Yinbing Zhang

College of Information Science and Technology, Beijing Normal University, Beijing 100875, China
{dongdongguo, zhangyinbing}@mail.bnu.edu.cn,
{songjh, pengweiming}@bnu.edu.cn

Abstract. Verb reduplication is one of the most common and most important ways of reduplication. It occupies a very important position in the field of international Chinese teaching. Using Chinese information processing technology to study vocabulary reduplication in international Chinese teaching, on the one hand, can improve the efficiency of research and make the research of reduplication more systematic and accurate; on the other hand, trying to transform the existing achievements of Chinese information processing into the field of international Chinese teaching is conducive to promoting deep integration in the two fields. This paper first constructs a knowledge base of verb reduplication structural mode by tagging the verb reduplication in the corpus of a certain scale of international Chinese textbooks. Then the characteristics of the verb reduplication in the field of international Chinese teaching are analyzed through the knowledge base. Finally, the automatic recognition of the verb reduplication in the corpus of international Chinese textbooks is studied.

Keywords: Verb reduplication · Structural mode
International Chinese textbooks · Automatic recognition
Chinese information processing

1 Introduction

Compared with the Indo-European language family, Chinese is short of strict morphological changes. For example, student and students in English are the same words, which are expressed in different forms. Eat, eats, eating, ate and eaten are the same words that appear in different contexts. In Chinese, only "学生[xuesheng]" and "吃[chi]" are expressed, and they do not change in form with the differences in quantity, person, and tense. The composition of the Chinese character is syllable in the form of phonetics, which determines that the Chinese language lacks morphological changes as rich as Indo-European languages. However, the Chinese language has a narrow sense of morphological change—reduplication. In Chinese, the reduplication of verbs, adjectives, quantifiers and so on in a certain extent can be regarded as the morphological changes, such as 看[kan]-看看[kan kan], 漂亮[piaoliang]-漂漂亮亮[piao piao liang liang] and 个[ge]-个个[ge ge]. In Chinese the vocabulary reduplication

J.-F. Hong et al. (Eds.): CLSW 2018, LNAI 11173, pp. 707–719, 2018.
https://doi.org/10.1007/978-3-030-04015-4_62

does not produce new vocabularies, but just adds new grammatical meaning and grammatical function on the basis of its original lexical meaning [1]. Verb reduplication means that the time is short, the momentum is small or the meaning of "having a try"; adjective reduplication generally indicates the degree of aggravation; quantifier reduplication represents the meaning of "every and many".

Vocabulary reduplication is a common language phenomenon in international Chinese teaching, and it is also the key content of international Chinese teaching. There are several places in the Hanyu Shuiping Kaoshi (HSK) syllabus that focus on the vocabulary reduplication [2–7]. The linguistic circle and the field of international Chinese teaching have made a lot of research on the vocabulary reduplication, and have made many achievements [8, 9]. However, there is a lack of related research on vocabulary reduplication by using Chinese information processing technology in international Chinese teaching. Using Chinese information processing technology [10, 11] to study vocabulary reduplication in international Chinese teaching, on the one hand, can improve the efficiency of vocabulary reduplication research and make the research of reduplication more systematic and accurate; on the other hand, trying to transform the existing achievements of Chinese information processing into the field of international Chinese teaching is conducive to promoting deep integration in the two fields.

Verb reduplication is one of the most common and most important ways of reduplication. It has a very important position in the field of international Chinese teaching. In many international Chinese textbooks, the content of verb reduplication has been emphasized in the grammar explanation after the text. This paper first constructs a knowledge base of verb reduplication structural mode by tagging the verb reduplication in the corpus of a certain scale of international Chinese textbooks. Then the characteristics of the verb reduplication in the field of international Chinese teaching are analyzed through the knowledge base. Finally, the automatic recognition of the verb reduplication in the corpus of international Chinese textbooks is studied.

2 Construction of the Verb Reduplication Structural Mode Knowledge Base

2.1 Representation of Structural Mode

The main forms of verb reduplication are: AA, AAB, ABAB, A一A, A了A, A了一A, A了又A and so on, showing that the meaning is holistic, the structure is stable, the syllable rhythm is obvious, and the pattern is strong. In the field of Chinese information processing, verb reduplication is suitable to be treated as a whole, that is, as a dynamic word [12–14]. Therefore, when describing the structural mode of the verb reduplication, we first determine a whole part of speech for verb reduplication, that is, the verb "v". In order to effectively reflect and describe the structural features of verb reduplication from the two levels of the whole and the internal structure, the following four types of information are used to express knowledge of its structural mode: the whole part of speech of verb reduplication, the part of speech of each internal component, the syllable number of each internal component and

现在机票打折吗？
很抱歉，最近哪家航空公司都不打折。
那正常票价是多少？
单程票一千八百一十元，往返票三千五百元。
好的，谢谢你。
不客气。您订吗？现在机票比较紧张。
我再【想[001]一[006]想[001]】【v: v-m-v】，一会儿给你们打电话。

Fig. 1. The annotating result of the verb reduplication "想一想[xiang yi xiang]"

structural relationship between the internal components (it is mainly reduplication relationship, which is represented by the symbol "·").

The knowledge of the verb reduplication structural mode is expressed as follows:

- <structural mode> ::= <the whole part of speech of verb reduplication>: <the part of speech of the internal component><the syllable number of the internal component> [<structural relationship symbol><the part of speech of the internal component><the syllable number of the internal component>]+
- <the whole part of speech of verb reduplication> ::= v
- <the part of speech of the internal component> ::= n | t | f | m | q | r | v | a | d | p | c | u | e | o | Ug

(The "Ug" represents the category of affix morphemes, such as the category of the suffix "儿[er]" in "玩儿[wan er]". The meaning of other letters can refer to the literature [14].)

- <the syllable number of the internal component> ::= <NULL> | 2 | 3 | 4

(The syllable number is the default value 1 when it is NULL. More than four syllables verbs and verb reduplication with more syllables are rare.)

- <structural relationship symbol> ::= · | - | …

(The "·" means reduplication relationship; the "-" indicates affixes/auxiliary structure, other function word structures, and atypical relations between fixed components and other components in a specific structure; the "…" represents a parallel relationship, including a compressed juxtaposition.)

Examples of verb reduplication structural modes are shown in Table 1. The structural mode of "看看[kan kan]" is "v: v·v". In "v: v·v", the "v" before the colon indicates the whole part of speech is a verb; the "v" after the colon indicates the part of speech of the internal component "看[kan]" is a verb and its syllable number is 1 (The syllable number is the default value 1 when it is NULL); the "·" means the relationship between the internal component "看[kan]" (the former) and the "看[kan]" (the latter) is the reduplication relationship. "散散步[san sanbu]" is a AAB type verb reduplication. The AB—"散步[sanbu]" is its basis, and the reduplication part is the morpheme "散[san]" of the "散步[sanbu]". In order to embody the reduplication of the morpheme "散[san]" and the reduplication basis "散步[sanbu]", the structural mode is expressed as the "v: v·v2".

Table 1. Examples of verb reduplication structural modes

reduplication	mode	reduplication	mode
看看	v: v·v	尝尝	v: v·v
散散步	v: v·v2	帮帮忙	v: v·v2
想一想	v: v-m-v	猜一猜	v: v-m-v
指了指	v: v-u-v	谈了谈	v: v-u-v
放松放松	v: v2·v2	熟悉熟悉	v: v2·v2
上上下下	v: v·v…v·v	来来回回	v: v·v…v·v

2.2 Annotating of Corpus

The vocabularies included in the Modern Chinese Dictionary (Sixth Edition) are relatively stable [15]. In order to get the information about verb reduplication structural mode in the corpus of international Chinese textbooks, we use the vocabularies and parts of speech in the Modern Chinese Dictionary as the basis to annotate the internal components of verb reduplication. To analyze the structural mode of verb reduplication, we need to separate its internal components first. The criterion of segmentation is based on the unity of structure and meaning, until each component can find the corresponding sense and part of speech information in the Modern Chinese Dictionary. For example, for the verb reduplication "想一想[xiang yi xiang]", as the Modern Chinese Dictionary contains "想[xiang]" and "一[yi]", the correct segmentation results should be "想[xiang]", "一[yi]" and "想[xiang]".

Six undergraduates and twelve postgraduates with the background of linguistics are organized to annotate the verb reduplication structural mode in the corpus of international Chinese textbooks (include *New Practical Chinese Textbook*, *Happy Chinese*, *Great Wall Chinese*, *Chinese with Me*, *Mandarin Teaching Toolbox*, *Contemporary Chinese*, *Chinese Paradise* and other international Chinese textbooks) manually, and the contents of annotating include the sense of the internal components of verb reduplication in the Modern Chinese Dictionary and the structural mode information of verb reduplication. The annotating results are shown in Fig. 1. Each sense of a vocabulary in the Modern Chinese Dictionary is uniquely identified by the sense code (three digits).

In order to ensure the accuracy and consistency of the annotating results, the text of the same paragraph is annotated by two students at least, and the annotating result is audited by experts. The annotated data which are consistent and approved will be regarded as valid data. If the annotating results are inconsistent or not approved, the annotators and the auditors will be required to discuss about and determine the results.

2.3 Construction of the Knowledge Base

In this paper, 29465 sentences (498965 words) with the annotation information of verb reduplication structural mode are obtained in the corpus of international Chinese textbooks. Regular expressions are used to match and extract the verb reduplication and its structural mode information in the annotated corpus. A regular expression is a formula to match a class of strings in a certain pattern, consisting of a number of

Table 2. The structure of the structural mode knowledge base

Field	Illustration
Id	The serial number of the verb reduplication structural mode
Mode	The name of the verb reduplication structural mode
POS	The whole part of speech of the verb reduplication
Syllable	The syllable number of the verb reduplication
Rule	The regular expression rule for the verb reduplication
Frequency	The frequency of verb reduplication corresponding the structural mode in the corpus
Class	The number of the types of verb reduplication corresponding the structural mode in the corpus
Detail	Every verb reduplication corresponding the structural mode, its internal component sense code and its frequency

ordinary characters and special characters (meta characters). Ordinary characters include small and medium letters, numbers, and Chinese characters, and meta characters refer to special characters with special meanings. The rule of the verb reduplication and its structural mode information in the annotated corpus is clear. Using the regular expression "【.+?】 【.+?】", all the information to be extracted can be accurately matched. According to the statistical analysis of the extracted information, a verb reduplication structural mode knowledge base with 12 structural modes is established. The structure of the verb reduplication structural mode knowledge base is shown in Table 2, and the 12 structural modes are shown in Table 3 by the order of the frequency of verb reduplication corresponding the structural mode in the corpus from high to low.

The specific content of the structural mode "v: v-u-v" in the knowledge base is shown in Table 4. The "(.)了\1" in the "rule" field is a regular expression rule the reduplication satisfies. The "(.)" and "\1" indicate that the first character is the same as the third character. The middle "了" means the middle character of the reduplication is a fixed component—the auxiliary word "了". The "rule" field defines the information of syllable number, the position of the reduplication characters and fixed component of verb reduplication corresponding to the specific structural mode. A combination can generally be judged to be a verb reduplication if it satisfies the regular expression rule and part of speech information, and the specific type of structural mode can also be determined. Thus, the "rule" field is the key information to recognize the verb reduplication and its structural mode.

Table 3. 12 Verb reduplication structural modes

id	mode	example	rule	class	frequency
1	v: v·v	看看	(.)\1	70	548
2	v: v-m-v	看一看	(.)一\1	38	96
3	v: v2·v2	休息休息	(..)\1	32	65
4	v: v·v2	聊聊天	(.)\1.	17	47
5	v: v-u-v	看了看	(.)了\1	10	27
6	v: v-u·v-u	玩儿玩儿	(.)儿\1儿	2	7
7	v: v·v3	聊聊天儿	(.)\1..	2	5
8	v: v-u-m-v-u	玩儿一玩儿	(.)儿一\1儿	1	4
9	v: v-u-v2	号了号脉	(.)了\1.	3	3
10	v: v-m-v2	握一握手	(.)一\1.	2	2
11	v: v·v…v·v	上上下下	(.)\1(.)\2	1	1
12	v: v-u-d-v	想了又想	(.)了又\1	1	1

Table 4. The structural mode "v: v-u-v" in the knowledge base

id	mode	POS	syllable	rule	frequency	class	detail
5	v: v-u-v	v	3	(.)了\1	27	10	【看[101]了[001]看[101]】 14 【笑[001]了[001]笑[001]】 4 【指[003]了[001]指[003]】 2 【皱[002]了[001]皱[002]】 1 【听[001]了[001]听[001]】 1 【想[003]了[001]想[003]】 1 【拍[001]了[001]拍[001]】 1 【逛[001]了[001]逛[001]】 1 【拉[001]了[001]拉[001]】 1 【谈[001]了[001]谈[001]】 1

3 Analysis of Verb Reduplication

The total number of verb reduplication corresponding to 12 structural modes in the verb reduplication structural mode knowledge base is 806, and the total number of verb reduplication classes reaches 179. The structural modes of the verb reduplication whose frequencies are in the top five are shown in Table 5. The number of verb reduplication corresponding to the five structural modes accounts for 97.15% of the total number of verb reduplication, and the number of the verb reduplication classes accounts for 93.30% of the total number of classes. As shown in Table 5, the monosyllabic verb reduplication corresponding to the structural mode "v: v·v" is the most common verb reduplication in the international Chinese textbooks, with a frequency of up to 67.99%, which exceeds the sum of all other types of verb reduplication frequencies. The double syllable verb reduplication corresponding to the structural mode "v: v2·v2" has a relatively high frequency, reaching 8.06%, which is ranked third in all structural modes.

Table 5. The structural modes whose frequencies are in the top five

Id	Mode	Frequency	Frequency/total	Class	Class/total
1	v: v·v	548	67.99%	70	39.11%
2	v: v-m-v	96	11.91%	38	21.23%
3	v: v2·v2	65	8.06%	32	17.88%
4	v: v·v2	47	5.83%	17	9.50%
5	v: v-u-v	27	3.35%	10	5.59%

The number of basic verbs corresponding to the 806 verb reduplication (179 classes) in the international Chinese textbooks is 141. Through analysis of 141 basic verbs and their corresponding senses in the Modern Chinese Dictionary (The senses information of the 10 basic verbs with the highest frequency is shown in Table 6), it is found that all 141 verbs are action verbs indicating action behavior, but no psychological verbs, force-border verbs, judgment verbs, directional verbs, optative verbs or other verbs. It can be seen that whether verbs can overlap or not is closely related to the semantic meaning of verbs. Generally speaking, action verbs can be overlapped, and the reduplication of non-action verbs is rare.

The verb reduplication obtained from the corpus of international Chinese textbooks generally expresses the grammatical meaning of short time, small momentum or having a try. The "听听[ting ting]" and "看看[kan kan]", "问问[wen wen]", "沟通沟通[goutong goutong]" in the following examples (1), (2) and (3) respectively indicate the grammatical meaning of short time, small momentum and having a try. In fact, there is no strict distinction between the short time and the small momentum, and many verb reduplications often show the grammatical meaning of short time and small momentum at the same time. For example, the "洗洗[xi xi]" in the following example (4) not only indicates "洗一会儿[xi yihuier]" of the short time, but also "洗一下儿[xi yixia er]" of the small momentum. Some verb reduplications don't indicate the above grammatical

Table 6. the senses information of the 10 basic verbs with the highest frequency

id	basic verb	frequency	sense code	sense	type
1	看	251	101	使视线接触人或物	动作动词
2	试	58	001	试验；尝试	动作动词
3	想	39	001	开动脑筋；思索	动作动词
4	说	25	101	用话来表达意思	动作动词
5	谈	24	001	说话或讨论	动作动词
6	听	23	001	用耳朵接受声音	动作动词
7	问	22	001	有不知道或不明白的事情或道理请人解答	动作动词
8	尝	21	001	吃一点儿试试；辨别滋味	动作动词
9	等	13	101	等候；等待	动作动词
10	玩	13	001	玩耍	动作动词

meanings, such as “想了又想[xiang le you xiang]” and “上上下下[shang shang xia xia]” in the following examples (5) and (6), and they express the grammatical meaning of long time and repeated actions.

（1）别着急，你看，这是你要的书和音乐光盘，没事儿的时候，你可以听听音乐，看看书。

（2）如果你想吃得又营养又健康，就去问问公共营养师吧，他们会给你一些好建议。

（3）孩子现在虽然小，但是他也会要求平等，我觉得你们应该多沟通沟通。

（4）哎呀，老婆，不就洗洗什么锅碗瓢盆嘛，你就洗洗呗。

（5）回到家，他想了又想，终于想到在红灯和绿灯中间再加一个黄灯，提醒人们注意危险。

（6）香港是一座山城，每天天刚蒙蒙亮，山间小路上就已经出现上上下下的人流。

The verb reduplication will result in the changes in the pragmatic function of the sentence. Take the following sentences from the international Chinese textbooks as examples. In the following example (7), the verb reduplication "打打[da da]" and "唱唱[chang chang]" show a relaxed and casual meaning; the expressive function of the "皱了皱[zhou le zhou]" in the example (8) protrudes the sense of description; in the example (9) the reduplication "看看[kan kan]" is used in the imperative sentence to play the function of easing the mood and expressing the desire euphemism.

（7）晚上去学校的学生活动中心去打打台球，唱唱卡拉OK。

（8）记得刚开学的时候，新老师头一天点名，可刚念到一半，就见他皱了皱眉头，轻声地问了一句："朱，朱什么？"

（9）你过一会儿再来看看吧。

Based on the verb reduplication structural mode knowledge base, combined with the corpus of international Chinese textbooks, this chapter preliminarily analyzes the main forms, scope, grammatical meaning and pragmatic function of the verb reduplication in international Chinese teaching. The verb reduplication structural mode knowledge base contains a lot of valuable information. By further mining, we can have a more comprehensive and deeper understanding of the verb reduplication in international Chinese teaching.

4 Automatic Recognition of Verb Reduplication

The realization of automatic recognition of verb reduplication is of great importance to the research and teaching of verb reduplication in international Chinese teaching, and it is also an important part of realizing automatic segmentation and POS tagging for international Chinese teaching. This chapter explores automatic recognition of the verb reduplication in the raw corpus of international Chinese textbooks on the basis of the previous work. In the process of recognition, we need to use the "rule" field, the "syllable" field in the knowledge base, and the Modern Chinese Dictionary (including frequency information about every item from a large Chinese Treebank). In order to objectively reflect the automatic recognition effect of verb reduplication, 3 groups of raw corpus of international Chinese textbooks (hundreds of thousands of Chinese characters in each group) were selected randomly for the experiment.

4.1 Recognition Process

The automatic recognition process of the verb reduplication is as follows. In the process of automatic recognition, the recognition sequence of verb reduplication in different structural modes is different.

1. First, the "rule" field "(.)\1(.)\2" of the structural mode "v: v·v…v·v" is used to match the combinations in the raw corpus which satisfy the regular expression rule, and the verb reduplication candidates with the structural mode "v: v·v…v·v" will be obtained. Then the candidate items are filtered through using the Modern Chinese Dictionary and the vocabularies are deleted which have been included in the Modern Chinese Dictionary. Finally, the first character (use "A" to represent) and the third character (use "B" to represent) are extracted in the candidate item. By looking up the Modern Chinese Dictionary to determine whether "AB" exists and whether it is a verb, if it exists and is a verb, the candidate item would be defined as verb reduplication of the structural mode "v: v·v…v·v". If "AB" doesn't exist, then the parts of speech of "A" and "B" will be searched separately. If they are all verbs, the candidate item will be defined as verb reduplication of the structural mode "v: v·v…v·v". The recognition content that has been identified as verb reduplication is no longer involved in the subsequent recognition operations.
   The part of speech of the "AB", "A" or "B" would be determined according to the frequency of the parts of speech in the Modern Chinese Dictionary when it is a multi-category word. It will be identified as a verb if the verb frequency is the highest.
2. First, the "rule" field of the structural mode "v: v·v3" is used to match the combinations in the raw corpus which satisfy the regular expression rule, and the verb reduplication candidates with the structural mode "v: v·v3" will be obtained. Then the candidate items are filtered through using the Modern Chinese Dictionary and the vocabularies are deleted which have been included in the Modern Chinese Dictionary. Finally, the last three characters are extracted in the candidate item. By looking up the Modern Chinese Dictionary to determine whether it exists and whether it is a verb, if it exists and is a verb, the candidate item would be defined as verb reduplication of the structural mode "v: v·v3". If it exists and is a multi-category word, the method of determining the part of speech is the same as 1 above. Once again according to this method verb reduplications of the structural modes "v: v·v2", "v: v-u-v2" and "v: v-m-v2" are recognized in turn.
3. First, the "rule" field of the structural mode "v: v2·v2" is used to match the combinations in the raw corpus which satisfy the regular expression rule, and the verb reduplication candidates with the structural mode "v: v2·v2" will be obtained. Then the candidate items are filtered through using the Modern Chinese Dictionary and the vocabularies are deleted which have been included in the Modern Chinese Dictionary. Finally, the first two characters are extracted in the candidate item. By looking up the Modern Chinese Dictionary to determine whether it exists and whether it is a verb, if it exists and is a verb, the candidate item would be defined as verb reduplication of the structural mode "v: v2·v2". If it exists and is a multi-category word, the method of determining the part of speech is the same as 1 above. Once again according to this method the verb reduplication of the structural mode "v: v·v" is recognized.

4. For the rest of structural modes (add the structural mode “v: v-u-m-v” of the verb reduplication type “A了一A”, and the “rule” field is “(.)了一\1”), the combinations in the raw corpus which satisfy the regular expression rules are matched separately, and the verb reduplication candidates with various types of structural modes will be obtained. Then the candidate items are filtered through using the Modern Chinese Dictionary and the vocabularies are deleted which have been included in the Modern Chinese Dictionary. The remaining candidates can be defined as the verb reduplication corresponding to various structural modes.

4.2 Experimental Result

According to the above recognition process, the automatic recognition experiment is carried out on 3 groups of randomly selected raw corpus, and the result is shown in Table 7.

Table 7. Verb reduplication recognition result

Raw corpus	Precision rate	Recall rate	F-measure
Group 1	86.42%	97.15%	91.47%
Group 2	84.78%	94.96%	89.58%
Group 3	82.35%	95.06%	88.25%

According to the experimental result, it can be concluded that the verb reduplication structural mode knowledge base has a significant effect on automatic recognition of verb reduplication. The precision rate of automatic recognition is lower than the recall rate. Both the recognition precision rate and recall rate of verb reduplication are high, and the experimental results are ideal. Through analysis of the experimental data, it is found that the reasons for reducing the precision rate and recall rate of automatic recognition are mainly the following aspects:

1. For the multi-category word which has verb and adjective two parts of speech at the same time, it is not rigorous enough to determine its specific part of speech only based on the part of speech frequency. The recognition error occurs during the specific recognition process.
2. It’s difficult to avoid some ambiguities in the process of recognition. This will cause some recognition errors. For example, for the “好好说说[hao hao shuo shuo]” from the sentence “你和他好好说说这件事[ni he ta haohao shuo shuo zhe jian shi]”, because there is the verb “好说[haoshuo]” in the Modern Chinese Dictionary, it is easy to be included in the verb reduplication of the structural mode “v: v·v…v·v”. The ambiguities need to be further eliminated by improving the recognition process.
3. Regular expression rules can only reflect the partial external characteristics of verb reduplication, and can’t fully reflect the characteristics of verb overlapping. It is necessary to dig out more effective and quantifiable feature information with the in-depth study of verb reduplication.

4. In the process of recognizing verb reduplication, restrictions and screening conditions are limited. The research resources and achievements in the field of linguistics, language teaching and Chinese information processing are needed to further enrich the recognition conditions of verb reduplication.

5 Conclusion

In this paper, we use the method of knowledge engineering to analyze the verb reduplication in the corpus of international Chinese textbooks, and preliminarily build a knowledge base of verb reduplication structural mode for international Chinese teaching. Then based on the structural mode knowledge base and the corpus of international Chinese textbooks, the related features of the verb reduplication in the field of international Chinese teaching are analyzed. Finally, on the basis of the structural mode knowledge base, the verb reduplication in the corpus of international Chinese textbooks is automatically recognized. This research method can be further extended to the study of other parts of speech reduplication in the international Chinese textbooks, so as to better serve international Chinese teaching and information processing for international Chinese teaching.

References

1. Bin, Z.: The Modern Chinese Grammar. Commercial Press, Beijing (2010)
2. Confucius Institute Headquarters (Hanban). HSK Test Syllabus Level 1. People's Education Press, Beijing (2015)
3. Confucius Institute Headquarters (Hanban). HSK Test Syllabus Level 2. People's Education Press, Beijing (2015)
4. Confucius Institute Headquarters (Hanban). HSK Test Syllabus Level 3. People's Education Press, Beijing (2015)
5. Confucius Institute Headquarters (Hanban). HSK Test Syllabus Level 4. People's Education Press, Beijing (2015)
6. Confucius Institute Headquarters (Hanban). HSK Test Syllabus Level 5. People's Education Press, Beijing (2015)
7. Confucius Institute Headquarters (Hanban). HSK Test Syllabus Level 6. People's Education Press, Beijing (2015)
8. Cheng, Z.: The Change of Verb Reduplication on Realis-Irrealis Distinction. J. Tsinghua Univ. (Philos. Soc. Sci.) **31**(03), 135–144+194 (2010)
9. Hongbing, X.: Statistical analysis of the reduplication structure of Chinese words. Lang. Teach. Linguist. Stud. **01**, 32–37 (2000)
10. Shiwen, Y.: An Introduction to Computational Linguistics. Commercial Press, Beijing (2003)
11. Jihua, S., Erhong, Y., Qiangjun, W.: Chinese Information Processing Tutorial. Higher Education Press, Beijing (2011)
12. Peng, W., Song, J., Sui, Z., Guo, D.: Formal schema of diagrammatic chinese syntactic analysis. In: Lu, Q., Gao, H.H. (eds.) CLSW 2015. LNAI, vol. 9332, pp. 701–710. Springer, Heidelberg (2015)

13. Guo, D., Zhu, S., Peng, W., Song, J., Zhang, Y.: Construction of the dynamic word structural mode knowledge base for the international chinese teaching. In: Dong, M., Lin, J., Tang, X. (eds.) CLSW 2016. LNAI, vol. 10085, pp. 251–260. Springer, Heidelberg (2016)
14. Dongdong, G.: Analyzing on Dynamic Words and Their Structural Modes in Building the Sentence-based Treebank. Beijing Normal University, Beijing (2016)
15. The Dictionary Editing Room in the Linguistics Institute of Chinese Academy of Social Sciences. Modern Chinese Dictionary. Commercial Press, Beijing (2012)

The Annotation Scheme of Sematic Structure Relations Based on Semantic Dependency Graph Bank

Xinghui Cheng and Yanqiu Shao(✉)

Information Science School, Beijing Language and Culture University, Beijing 10083, China
mulin17@163.com, Yqshao163@163.com

Abstract. Semantic Dependency Graph is a kind of deep semantic analysis method. In order to annotate every component of a sentence, we proposed an annotation scheme including three different types of semantic relations. They are semantic roles, semantic structure relations and semantic marks. Specifically semantic structure relations deal with the situations in which a sentence contains more than one verbal concepts. This paper will focuses on the three sub-structures of semantic structure relations—Reverse Relations, Nested Relations and Event Relations.

Keywords: Semantic Dependency Graph · Annotation scheme
Structure relations · Statistics

1 Introduction

Semantic Dependency Graph (SDG) is a theory which analyses the deep meaning of human languages. SDG aims to find all the word pairs with real semantic relations and link up each word pair with a dependency arc with a semantic label on it [1]. And based on this theory we have founded a corpus containing 30000 sentences. In order to describe every tiny meaning, we tried to set semantic labels as detailed as possible. And then considering the multiplicity of semantic labels, we set two levels in label hierarchy to make distinctions when coping with different applications. So finally we got an annotation scheme of two layers and three types. The two layers are coarse-grained labels and fine-grained labels. The three types are semantic roles, semantic structure relations and semantic marks. In paper [2], we have introduced the knowledge of semantic roles. In this paper, semantic structure relations will be interpreted clearly.

Specifically, semantic structure relations are made to deal with the complex semantic events, which means there are several predicates in one complete semantic event. As we know, there can be one and only one core predicate named ROOT in the SDG. And the relationships between ROOT and the rest predicates are complicated. According to the different semantic connections among them, we defined three sub-structures: they are Reverse Relations, Nested Relations and Event Relations. And they will be described separately in Sects. 3, 4 and 5 as follows. In each section we will introduce the related researches, make comparisons of our scheme and present some basic statistics.

J.-F. Hong et al. (Eds.): CLSW 2018, LNAI 11173, pp. 720–732, 2018.
https://doi.org/10.1007/978-3-030-04015-4_63

2 Reverse Relations

When it comes to Reverse Relations, which means in Chinese there can be some verbs that they transform their functions from a verbal concept to a nominal concept and usually show in the attributive central constructions. Here is an example: *出席的贵宾 (the present VIP)* In this phrase, *"出席"* is a verb while here it serves a role as a modifier. Because of the non-inflectional feature of Chinese, we cannot differentiate a transitional verb from a predicate verb. This is a specific type of complicated semantic structures. So it is necessary to make targeted annotation guidelines.

2.1 Related Researches

There are some researches had done on this issue:

From a domestic perspective, we did survey on two annotation systems. Luchuan did a profound research on the transposition of verbal semonode [3]. He divided the transposition into two types: (1) the additional section is the 'verbal semonode' of transposition; (2) the additional section is the 'nominal semonode' of transposition. Corresponding examples are below and the three lines are Chinese, English translation and the annotation of Lu Chuan respectively:

*(1)*出席的贵宾	*(2)*贵宾的出席
(The present VIP)	*(VIP's attendance)*
[Action-agent]	*[Agent-action]*

Also, He Baorong (2017) built a Chinese Semantic Labeling Corpus [4] and its annotation scheme is on the basis of the argument-predicate annotation guidelines of modern Chinese of Peking University [5]. Because the annotated objects are mainly the relations between verbal components and nominal components (seldom relations between two verbal components). So in her thesis, she gave up tagging the Reverse Relations.

We did not find similar studies in English. That is easy to understand. Because English is an inflectional language. The components that can appear in the attributive positon have clear case tag or they are some certain parts of speech.

2.2 Our Annotation Scheme

Combined with the features of Chinese as well as the results of automatic segmentation, we proposed our annotation scheme only corresponding to the first situation of Luchuan's. That is to say, the verbal concept changes its function as a modifier. The second case is excluded from this type because of the result of POS. In Chinese, the part of speech is not fixed. And there are not very clear boundaries among some words, such as *"发展 (develop/development)" "出版 (publish/publishment)"*. These kind of words can be a NOUN or a VERB freely. Some linguists call this phenomenon 'the nominalization of verbs' [6]. And here are two annotation results in SDG to illustrate the examples in Sect. 2.1 (Fig. 1).

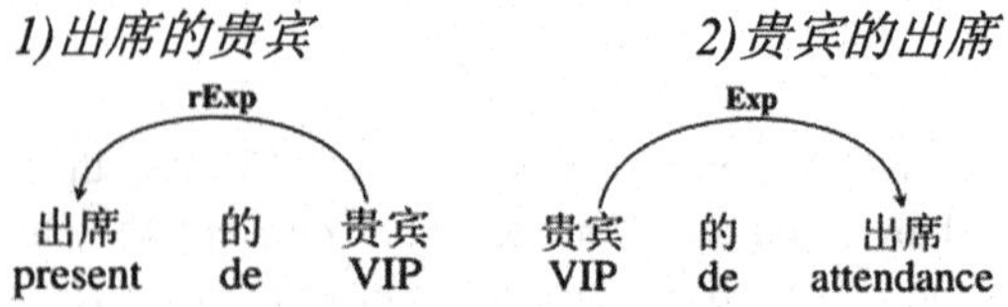

Fig. 1. Example of Reverse Relations

The labels of Reverse Relations are based on semantic roles. And they begin the labels with an English character 'r' to show its category. So the total number of Reverse Relations is the same with the semantic roles. And the number of fine-grained labels is 45 and the number of coarse-grained labels is 17. Also it has the same subtypes corresponding to semantic roles. They are reverse subjective relations, reverse objective relations and reverse circumstanced relations.

2.3 Statistics

Based on the SDG corpus, we did some basic statistics of Reverse Relations.

The frequency of each reverse relation is easy to calculate. But limited to paper length, only the highest frequency relations of the top five are shown here. In order to better understand the meaning of each number, the counterparts of the frequency of semantic roles are also illustrated in the box below (Table 1).

Table 1. The top 5 frequency of Reverse Relations

Reverse roles	Freq.	Semantic roles	Freq.
r-Experiencer	1780	Experiencer	24697
r-Agent	1146	Agent	23582
r-Content	941	Content	11222
r-Patient	730	Patient	8907
r-Product	358	Product	2173

The total number of Reverse Relations is far less than that of semantic roles. For example, the Agent role appears almost 20 times more than r-Agent role in the corpus within 30000 sentences. And the Experiencer role, Content role and Product role is 13.8,11,12 times more than their counterparts of Reverse Relations respectively. That is to say, the transposition of verbal concepts is a type of specific phenomenon in Chinese. Actually the total amount of labels that occurs in the corpus is 471,039 and that number of Reverse Relations is only 6661(taken up 1.4% only).

Although the 45 kinds of semantic roles should have all counterparts form the theoretical level, but in fact, from the annotation experience, they don't. There are 9 kinds of Reverse Relations never show up. They are r-Compare, r-initial Time, r-various Number, r-initial Number, r-Frequency, r-Sequence, r-Host, r-Name modifier, etc. And there are also some Reverse Relations in very low frequency. So we can conclude that only a part of verbal concepts with certain meanings can be used as modifier.

As we know, subjective roles and objective roles are the core roles in a semantic event while circumstanced roles are non-core roles. Figure 2 is a pie chart to show the proportions of subtypes of Reverse Relations.

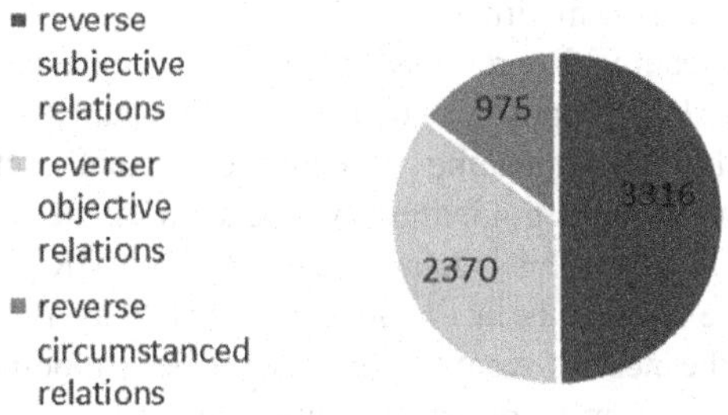

Fig. 2. Proportions of subtypes of Reverse Relations

Mainly the core Reverse Relations can change their functions in a sentence. These two types take up more than 85% of all Reverse Relations. It is because that circumstanced roles are already the descriptive components in sentences. So almost all the verbs that dominated core roles need to transform their functions.

3 Nested Relations

Another special semantic structure is called Nested Relations. Usually one verbal concept evokes one semantic event. When a single sentence contains more than one verbal concepts, there can be more than one single event in this sentence. Apart from the ROOT node, other verbal concepts are downgraded as an argument of the ROOT node. This phenomenon is different from Reverse Relations, in which the non-ROOT verbal concepts transform to be nominal concepts acted as a modifier. And also it is also different from the Event Relations that will be introduced in Sect. 4, in which the different verbal concepts have some semantic connections. Here is an example of Nested Relation:

鲁迅在一篇文章里,主张打落水狗。
(Lu Xun suggested to hit the drowning dogs in one of his articles.)

There are two verbs in this sentence—*"主张 (suggest)"* and *"打 (hit)"*. And these two verbs point to two events, one is *"鲁迅主张做……(Lu Xun suggested to do sth. in his article)"*,the other one is *"打落水狗 (hit the drowning dogs)"*. But the second semantic event isn't a complete one. It downgrades to be argument (Content role) of the ROOT *"主张 (suggest)"*.

3.1 Related Researches

There are some annotation schemes mentioning this specific language structure clearly. However there are also some annotation schemes that don't make implicit annotation guidelines but they deal with this language phenomenon in an explicit way.

In the system of Lu Chuan's semantic parataxis networks, nested relation is a kind of connectional relations. He also separated the Nested Relations into two main sections. One is the downgraded event used as an argument and the other one is that the downgraded event used as a modifier.

AMR (Abstract Meaning Representation) is a new representation of the abstract meaning of sentences. It is proposed to describe the meanings of English. However it can also represent the deep meaning of Chinese. Actually in AMR's annotation guidelines there are no obvious guidelines to cope with the nested events. But we can find some clues how they treat this language structure. In AMR-guidelines [7], they pay attention to the relative clauses. In fact relative clause such as *'the boy <who believes>'* is the situation that the nested event downgrade to be a modifier. By extension the nested event also can exist in many subordinate clauses.

Due to the differences between English and Chinese, when the annotation methods were introduced into Chinese, it should make some changes. Li Bin [8] has transferred the AMR guidelines to annotate Chinese. Even though there is no clear scheme focusing on nested event but they noticed this specific phenomenon. For example (Fig. 3):

男孩想去学校。
(The boy wants to go to school)

```
男孩想去学校
x/想-01
    :arg0 x1/男孩
    :arg1 x2/去-01
        :arg0 x1
        :arg1 x3/学校
```

Fig. 3. An example of AMR

They emphasized that AMR is good at dealing with the co-arguments. So the Chinese AMR specification annotated that verb *"想(want)"* and *"去(go)"* share the same subjective role *"男孩(the boy)"*.

However, we hold a different view of this type of sentence. We agreed that there can be multi-father nodes in dependency analysis [9]. But for the concrete annotation details, we disagree with Chinese AMR.

3.2 Our Annotation Scheme

Based on Lu Chuan's system and the semantic roles, our annotation scheme of Nested Relations is similar to Reverse Relations. They share the same system of semantic roles. The number of coarse-grained nested roles is 17 and the number of fine-grained nested roles is 45. Also it has the same subtypes corresponding to semantic roles. They are nested subjective relations, nested objective relations and nested circumstanced relations.

The labels begin with 'd' to show its category, which it is the first character of 'downgrade'. We still take the example above.

男孩想去学校。
(The boy wants to go to school)

In our scheme, *"去(go)"* and *"想(want)"* don't share the same subjective role *"男孩(the boy)"*, because no matter the meaning is *"男孩想学校(the boy wants school)"* or *"男孩去学校(the boy go to school)"*, both of them are different from the meaning of the original sentence. The original sentence is talking about an idea of the boy's. So the event *"去学校 (go to school)"* downgrade as an argument of the ROOT *"想(root)"*. The annotation result shown in the form of SDG is below (Fig. 4):

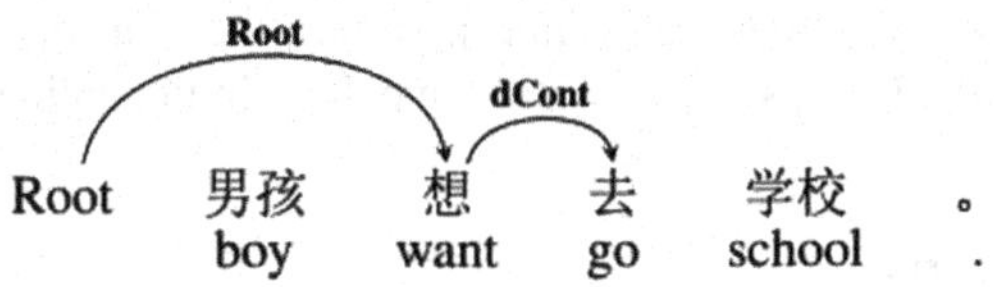

Fig. 4. Example of Nested Relations

3.3 Statistics

Based on the SDG corpus, we did some basic statistics of Nested Relations.

The total number of Nested Relations is 15,443 and it takes up only 3.3% of all the annotated labels. Unlike the Reverse Relations, the distribution of the Nested Relations labels is very unbalanced. That is to say which kinds of semantic roles are often downgraded doesn't depend on whether they are core roles or non-core roles. Table 2 is the results of the top 4 Nested Relations labels which the frequency is over 1000. And the frequency of their counterparts of semantic roles is on the right 2 columns.

Table 2. The top 4 frequency of Nested Relations

Nested roles	Freq.	Semantic roles	Freq.
d-Content	7922	Content	11222
d-Description	2526	Description	29069
d-Experiencer	1356	Experiencer	24697
d-Time	1301	Time	7407

As we can see from the table above, d-Content is the highest frequency label. Its frequency is higher than the total amount of the next three labels. Considering the total amount of this category is 15443, the d-Content label takes up almost half. And the second highest frequency label is d-Description. Actually the statistics are in high agreement with the definition that we made for Nested Relations. That is to say, the events that downgraded are used as two main functions, one is the argument of ROOT, and the other one is the description of some certain grammatical item in the sentence.

As for d-Experience, it mainly shows in the sentence pattern that subject-predicate phrases act as a subject. As for d-Time, it mainly shows up in the sentence pattern named adverbial clause of time. Here are two examples below:

(1) *客人提前半小时到达是一件讨厌的事。(The arrival of a guest half an hour early is a nuisance.)*
(2) *当她刚要擦窗户时,门铃响了。*
(The doorbell rang as she wiped the window.)

The sentence 1 is an example of dExp. ROOT is *"是 (is)"*, and *"客人提前到达 (guest arrives half an hour early)"*is the d-Experiencer label. The sentence 2 is an example dTime. ROOT is *"响 (ring)"*, while the *"当她刚要擦窗户时 (when she wiped the windows)"* is an event to show the time that 'bell rang'.

Also there are some theoretical nested labels that never show up. For example, d-initial Location label, d-Sequence, d-Time modifier, etc. But the labels are not cancelled for that once the label is used we still have them in the online annotation system.

4 Event Relations

Event Relations deal with the situation where there are more than one verbal concepts in one semantic event, while the verbal concepts doesn't transform or downgrade. They correspond to compound sentences from the syntactic level. Here we can make comparisons among these three different semantic structures.

(1) *吃饭的孩子们*
(Eating children)
(2) *当孩子们吃饭的时候, 爸爸回来了。*
(Daddy came home when the children was eating)
(3) *只要孩子们好好吃饭, 爸爸就很开心。*
(Father will be very happy only if his children have good meals)

In sentence 1, *"吃饭 (eating)"* is the reverse Agent role(rAgt) of *"孩子们 (children)"*. In sentence 2, *"吃饭 (eating)"* is the nested time role(dTime) of *"回来 (come home)"* while in sentence 2 *"吃饭 (eating)"* is a condition of *"爸爸就很开心 (Daddy is happy)"*.

From these sentences above, it is easy to understand that the different situations that verbal concepts made in natural language.

4.1 Related Researches

When it comes to Event Relations, there are two points of penetration. From one perspective, Event Relations can be the largest units to analyze the sentences. And from the other perspective, Event Relations can be the smallest units to deal with the research of discourses. From these two different views, there are many related researches on this issue.

In the system of Lu Chuan's connectional relations, he defined 16 types of relations between events, such as antecedent, succedent, cause, result etc. And he also points out that there are some basic combinatorial pattern such as cause-result, abandonment-preference and so on. For example:

与其跪着生，不如站着死。
(It is better to die than to kneel.)
[Abandonment-preference]

Lu Chuan's system is based on the view that complex semantic event is the highest unit. Also there are some researches in the realm of discourse. Li Yancui [10] proposed a system of Chinese discourse structure that contains four categories and 17 subtypes. The four categories are causality relationship, coordinate relationship, and adversative relationship and commentary relations. Based on this system, she built a Chinese discourse corpus and did some statistics.

Apart from these two, there are also researches on this issue. There are some domestic studies on this issue. For example, Fuyi [11] divided Chinese compound sentences into three types and 12 subtypes. And based on this theory a corpus of Chinese compound sentences was built by Huazhong Normal University [12]. Zhou-qiang [13] proposed a new annotation scheme for Chinese treebank and they made a set of relative labels including 27 types. The 27 labels are composed of simple sentences and compound sentences, such as 'ZW' is designed to annotate the subject-predicate structure and 'YG' is designed to annotate the cause-effect structure.

Also there are some very important foreign researches. RST (Rhetorical Structure Theory) [14] contains more than 20 kinds of Event Relations, such as Circumstance, Solutionhood and so on. What worth mentioning here is that these 20 kinds relations can be aggregated into two classes—mononuclear relations and ploy-nuclear relations. The annotation manual of Prague Dependency Treebank (PDT) [15] mentions almost 11 kinds of functors to deal with Event Relations. Such as 'CSQ' to annotate the consequential relations. And the system of PDTB [16] organized by three layers—4 kinds of categories, 16 kinds of types and 23 subtypes. The annotation specification of AMR also involves parts of discourse information. For example, they use ': op' to distinguish the parallel or alternative relations. And there exists several rough labels to annotate the relationships of purpose, cause, concession and condition. However, the related annotations of AMR are not very systematic.

4.2 Our Annotation Scheme

Our annotation scheme is based on previous studies. It contains two annotation layers. The coarse-grained labels include 6 types and the fine labels contains 19 subtypes. All the labels begin with an English character 'e' (the first character of 'event') to show its category. Table 3 is the Event Relations:

Table 3. The layers of Event Relations

Coarse-grained labels	Fine-grained labels
1. eCOO	1. eCoo; 2. eEqu; 3. eRect
2. eSELT	4.eSelt; 5. eAban; 6. ePref
3. ePREC	7. ePerc; 8. eCau; 9. eCond; 10. eSupp; 11. eMetd; 12. eConc
4. eSUCC	13. eSucc; 14. eProg
5. eEFFT	15. ePurp; 16. eRes; 17. eInf
6. eSUM	18. eSum

For the table above, there are several points to be announced:

- eCOO: e-coordinate relation contains three subtypes—e-coordinate relation, e-quivalent relation and e-Recount.relation. Coordinate relation is a simple but universal event relation.
- eSELT: e-selective relation contains three subtypes, too—selective relation, abandonment relation and preference relation.
- ePREC vs eSUCC: Precedent relation with succedent relation is usually a pair of concepts that is based on timeline. Since the theoretical base is Dependency Graph, so there is only ONE ROOT node in a sentence. And the root node usually is the first core predicate concept. Moreover, Chinese is a language with a very flexible word order. If the clause of succedent event is on the front, the following predicate concept can be annotated as an ePrec label. And the converse is also true. As Zhou [17] (2012) said, these two arguments (he named the clauses as Arg1 and Arg2) are defined based on the physical location. Here are two sentences of same meaning with opposite order:

(1) *只要坚持治疗，这个病是会痊愈的。*
(2) *这个病是会痊愈的，只要坚持治疗。*

Translation: As long as the treatment is persisted, the disease will heal.

No matter what the order is, *"坚持治疗 (persist treatment)"* is always the condition of *"痊愈 (heal)"*, and *"痊愈 (heal)"* is the result of *"坚持治疗 (persist treatment)"*. Once the ROOT node is annotated, the relationship of the following predicate nodes are also determined. The annotation results are shown in the graph of SDG below and the labels in brackets are in fine-grained (Figs. 5 and 6).

(1) *只要坚持治疗，这个病是会痊愈的。*

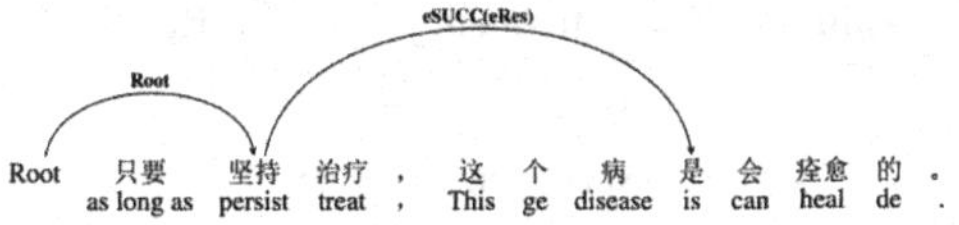

Fig. 5. An example of Event Relation

(2) *这个病是会痊愈的，只要坚持治疗。*

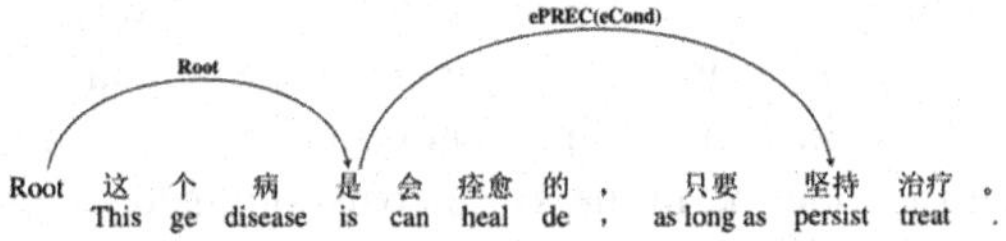

Fig. 6. An example of Event Relation

And no matter what it is—a cause or a method or a condition—it can be seen as a precedent event. Because they are the prerequisites of a semantic event.

- eSUCC vs eEFFT: succedent event contains two subtypes—succedent event and progressive event. Effect event includes three subtypes—purpose event, result event and inference event. In fact these two types of events both happened latter on the timeline. But succedent events happen by simply time connection while effect events happen by some implicative relationship such as a result of a certain cause or a method and so on.
- eAdvb: actually in the table above, there are only 18 kinds of fine-grained labels. The last one is adversative event. In modern Chinese [18], there are three kinds of adversative classified by mood. When it comes to the specific sentences, annotators can tag the labels as 'eSucc' or 'eEFFT' by the seriousness of the tone.

4.3 Statistics

Based on the SDG corpus, we did some basic researches on Reverse Relations.

The frequency of each reverse relation is easily to calculate. But limited for paper length, only the highest frequency relations of the top five will be shown here. In order to better understand the meaning of each number, the counterparts of the frequency of semantic roles are also illustrated in the box below. Based on the SDG corpus, we did some basic statistics of Event Relations.

The total amount of Nested Relations is 43,951 and it takes up only 9.3% of all the annotated labels. The top 5 highest frequency of Event Relations are presented in the Table 4 below:

Table 4. Top 5 frequency of Event Relations

Labels	Freq.
e-Succedent	15208
e-Coordinate	13110
e-Equivalent	2732
e-Result	2683
e-Purpose	2198

As we can see from the box, succedent events and coordinate events are the most common events in Chinese. And there are 4 fine-grained relations appearing in the corpus less than 100 times, they are e-Precedent (96), e-Summary (73), e-Abandonment (41), and e-Method (13). In fact the frequency that occurs in the corpus is another important factor that they can be in the same coarse-grained category.

As mentioned above, Li Yancui built a Chinese discourse corpus that did some basic statistics. We made a mapping relation between her annotation results and ours. She has 17 subtypes and 4 types while we have 19 kinds of subtypes. Fine–grained labels are not in the relation of one-to-one correspondence. So we classified the subtypes to the 4 categories and then made comparisons of the results. Table 5 is the results of two annotation schemes on this issue.

Table 5. The results of two annotation schemes

Categories	Result of Li.		Result of SDG	
	Freq.	Ratio	Freq.	Ratio
Casualty	1331	18.2%	7322	16.7%
Coordinate	4151	56.8%	33938	77.2%
Adversative	212	2.9%	2364	5.4%
Commentary	1616	22.1%	327	0.7%
Total	7310	100%	43951	100%

With regard to this result, the following points should be paid attention to:

- The cause and effect event are almost the same proportion in different corpora.
- The coordinate events take the great mass of proportion both in the two corpora. However, the result of ours is much larger. The inner reason behind the statistics is that our 'eCoo' label sometimes is used to annotate the parallel relations of arguments.
- As for adversative relations, they take up the minimum proportion of the total. In fact, adversative relation can be very confusing when annotating the sentence, especially in Chinese. Because there can be no conjunctions in Chinese compound sentences. So sometimes it is hard to capture the implicit deep meanings. For example:

事情到了后头，他倒不干了。

(At the end of this matter, he gave up.)

Some book regards it as adversative sentence in a light mood. But it is also acceptable to be regard as a succedent event.

- The proportion of commentary event of Li's is much larger than ours. That can be explained by two reasons. First the containing contents of each scheme is different. Li counted the example event and comment event in. Second, the corpora are different. Her corpus is all from news while our corpus is from news and textbooks as well as some oral materials.

So we can make a simple conclusion that from the macro point of view, the two results are in some extent of consistency.

5 Conclusions

This paper mainly introduces the semantic structure relations of SDG annotation scheme. There are many complicated semantic events in natural languages. There are three sub-structures when there are more than one verbal concepts. Relatively speaking, Reverse Relations and Nested Relations are still the internal relationship in a single sentence. While the Event Relations can not only be the highest level to deal with a sentence, but also can be the basic level to do discourse researches. From this perspective the Event Relations are external relations among sentences or even discourses.

Meanwhile all the relations have two annotation hierarchies. In this paper, we don't introduce too many details about the layers of Reverse Relations and Nested Relations because they share the layers with semantic roles which have been introduced in the previous studies. As for Event Relations, since the annotation labels and relationships are more complicated, we make some mappings with other researches and present the annotation layers in details as well as their inner logic.

Doing some basic annotation works of complicated sentences is very important. It can construct corpora to support higher researches and applications of natural language processing. Also it can help linguists to better understand the human language.

Acknowledgement. Thanks for the National Natural Science Foundation of China (No. 61872402) and Ministry of Education Humanities and Social Science Planning Fund (No. 17YJAZH068).

References

1. Yanqiu, S., Lijuan, Z.: Deep semantic analysis: from dependency tree to dependency graph. Int. J. Adv. Intell. **8**(1), 22–30 (2016)
2. Xinghui, C., Yaqui, S.: The evaluation standards of semantic roles: based on semantic dependency graph ban. In: International Conference on Asia Language Processing, pp. 214–217 (2017)
3. Chuan, L.: The Parataxis Networks of Chinese Grammar. Commercial Press, Beijing (2001)

4. Baorong, H.: Statistical Analysis of Self-built Chinese Semantic Role Labeling Corpus. Ludong University (2017)
5. Weidong, Z. et al.: The Annotation of Argument – Predicate in Modern Chinese (Internal Reference)
6. Dexi, Z., Jiawen, L., Zhen, M.: The issues on the nominalization of verbs and adjectives. J. Peking Univ. (Philos. Soc. Sci.) **4**, 53–66 (1961)
7. https://github.com/amrisi/amrguidelines/blob/master/amr.md
8. Bin, L., Yuan, W., et al.: A comparative analysis of the AMR graphs between english and Chinese Corpus of the little Prince. J. Chin. Inf. Process. **31**(1), 50–57 (2017)
9. Lijuan, Z., Yanqiu, S., Erhong, Y.: Analysis of the non-projective phenomenon in Chinese semantic dependency graph. J. Chin. Inf. Process. **28**(06), 41–47 (2014)
10. Yancui, L.: Research of Chinese discourse structure representation and resource construction. Soochow University (2015)
11. Fuyi, X.: A Study of Chinese Compound Sentences. Commercial Press, Beijing (2001)
12. Jinzhu, H., Wei, S., Chaohua, D.: Preliminary investigation on the relative of the complex sentences based on rules. In: Third Symposium on Student Computational Linguistics (2006)
13. Qiang, Z.: Annotation scheme for Chiense treebank. J. Chin. Inf. Process. **18**(4), 1–8 (2004)
14. Mann, W.C., Thompson, S.A.: Rhetorical structure theory: a theory of text organization. University of Southern California, Information Sciences Institute (1987)
15. Mikulová, et al.: Annotation on the tectogrammatical level in the Prague Dependency Treebank. Annotation manual. TR-2006-30, ÚFAL MFF, Prague, UK (2006)
16. Prasad R.,Dinesh N. et al: The Penn Discourse Treebank2.0. In: Proceedings of LREC2961-2968(2008)
17. Yuping, Z., Nianwen, X.: PDTB-style Discourse Annotation of Chinese text. ACL (2012)
18. Borong, H., Xudong, L.: Modern Chinese. Commercial Press, Beijing (2004)

Study on Chinese Discourse Semantic Annotation Based on Semantic Dependency Graph

Bo Chen[1], Chen Lyu[1(✉)], and Ziqing Ji[2]

[1] Collaborative Innovation Center for Language Research & Services, Guangdong University of Foreign Studies, Guangzhou 510420, China
cb9928@gmail.com, lvchen1989@gmail.com
[2] College of Computer Science, University of Maryland, College Park 20742, USA
1163539719@qq.com

Abstract. Semantic annotation of discourse is always one of most important tasks in natural language processing (NLP). We proposed a complex semantic representation mechanism for Chinese complex sentences. The semantic relations between sentences and between words can be represented as a semantic dependency graph by recursive directed graph. We studied the basic definition, the types of relations, and dependency direction of semantic dependence, and discussed the formal representation mechanism of semantic dependency from phrase-level, sentence-level and discourse-level. The semantic dependency graph model is characterized by allowing multiple correlations, allowing recursion and nesting, and formal representations are shown in recursive directed graph. The semantic dependency graph can more comprehensively represent the semantic relations between words and between the clauses in the discourse.

Keywords: Semantic dependency graph · Discourse
Semantic annotation · Recursion

1 Introduction

In recent years, the research trend of natural language processing (NLP) has been developing towards the direction of deep semantic parsing. This paper proposed a complex semantic representation mechanism for Chinese complex sentences. The semantic relations between words and between sentences can be represented as a semantic dependency graph by recursive directed graph.

There are four parts of the semantic dependency graph research:

Semantic dependence: including the basic definition; the types of relations; determination of dependency direction by syntax or semantics; the annotation of Chinese special sentence structures, such as *double-subjects structure, pivotal structure, verb-complement structure, coordinate structure, and anaphoric reference* [1–3].

J.-F. Hong et al. (Eds.): CLSW 2018, LNAI 11173, pp. 733–742, 2018.
https://doi.org/10.1007/978-3-030-04015-4_64

The representation mechanism of semantic dependence: how to represent semantics; the principle of determining the relations, dependency direction, and the dependency head [4–6].
The node of semantic dependency graph: the language unit represented by the node. Each node in the dependency graph can be a phrase, a clause, or even a complex sentence composed of multiple clauses, or a non-continuous paired connectives [7, 8].
Connective structures: how to determine the semantic dependence roles of connectives [9–11].

2 Basic Representation of Semantic Dependency Graph

The minimum representation unit of a semantic dependency graph is the description of the semantic relation and the type of this relation of sentence [12, 13]. In general, a phrase or sentence can be represented as a set of feature structure triples consisting of an entity, a feature, and its value. With these triples we can represent the semantic relations by multiple-edged nodes [1]. The formal representation of these triples is a recursive directed dependency graph. As shown in Fig. 1.

Feature Structure Triple: [Entity, Feature, Value]

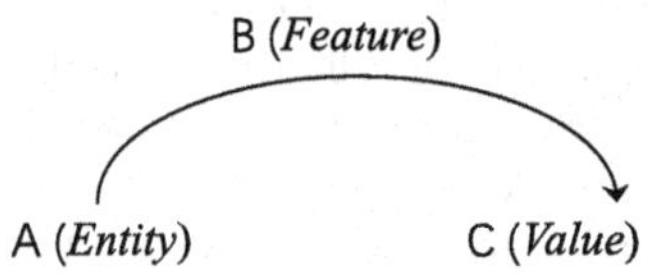

Fig. 1. The basic of semantic dependency graph: the formal representation of a feature structure triple

In Fig. 1, A is the entity, B is the feature, C is its value. Semantic dependency graph consists of nodes and directed edges. While nodes represent entities, edges represent the semantic relations between entities. It is feasible to use *directed graph* to represent semantic dependency structure. First, the nodes of graph can correspond to semantic concepts (such as *words, phrases, single sentences, complex sentences,* or *discourse*). Second, the nodes of graph allow recursive and multiple correlations. Third, directionality of the edge indicates the direction of dependence.

3 Formalization of Semantic Dependency Graph

In this paper, according to the language units, we discussed the formal representation of semantic dependency graph from phrase, sentence and discourse.

3.1 Formalization of Chinese Phrases of Semantic Dependency Graph

(1) 头发很长 (*long hair*)

In (1), there are semantic correlations between "头发 (*hair*)" and "长 (*long*)", "很 (*very*)" and "长 (*long*)". The triples can be analyzed as (Fig. 2):

Triple 1. [长(*long*) , , 头发(*hair*)]

Triple 2. [长(*long*) , , 很(*very*)]

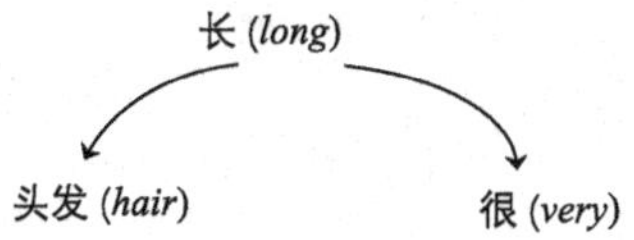

Fig. 2. The semantic dependency graph of (1)

(2) 一张纸 (*a piece of paper*)

In (2), the feature of "纸 (*paper*)" is "张 (*piece*)", "一 (*one*)" is the value of "张 (*piece*)". Its triple is:

Triple 1. [纸 (*paper*) , 张 (*piece*) , 一 (*one*)]

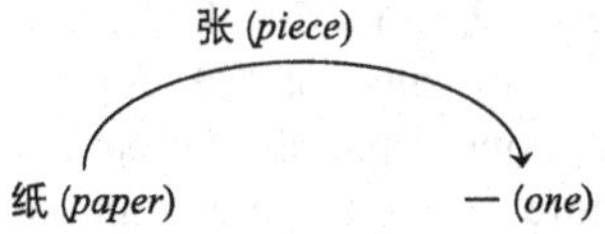

Fig. 3. The semantic dependency graph of (2)

Entity, feature, and its value are three elements in a model. They are not fixed. They describe the semantic relations between words. Therefore, in different triples, the role of a word changes as the specific conceptual correlations and the types of correlations change. Both feature and its values can appear as entities in the feature structure. As Example 3 (Figs. 3 and 4):

(3) 中高级职称研究人员

the researchers with medium and senior professional titles

Triple 1. [研究 (*to research*), , 人员 (*personnel*)]
Triple 2. [人员 (*personnel*), 职称 (*title*),]
Triple 3. [职称 (*title*), 级 (*level*), 中高 (*medium and high*)]
Triple 4. [中 (*medium*), ,高 (*high*)]

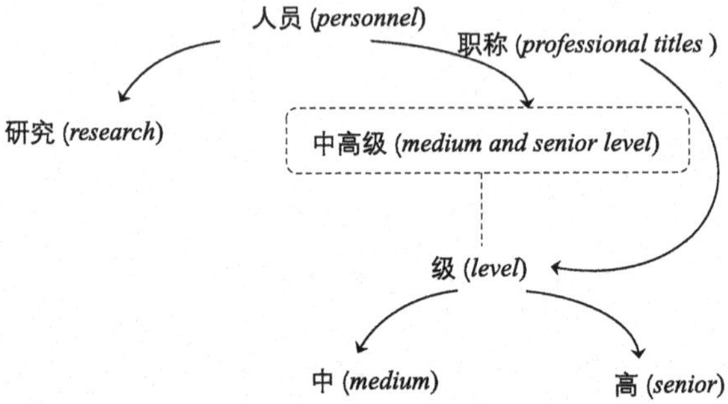

Fig. 4. The semantic dependency graph of (3)

Intuitively, “人员 (*personnel*)” is the agent of “研究 (*to research*)”. “职称 (*professional title*)” is the feature of “人员 (*personnel*)”, but the value (*such as Associate Professor, etc.*) does not appear. “级 (*level*)” is the feature of “职称 (*professional title*)”. “中高 (*medium and high*)” is the value of “级 (*level*)”. It can be found that “人员 (*personnel*)” acts as a value in one triple and an entity in another triple. “职称 (*professional title*)” acts as a feature in one triple and an entity in another triple.

3.2 Formalization of Chinese Sentences of Semantic Dependency Graph

3.2.1 Single Node

Each node in the semantic dependency graph is a word or a phrase. This is the most frequent type. As shown in (4) (Fig. 5).

(4) 他饿了。

He is hungry.
Triple 1. [饿 (*hungry*) , , 了 (*le*)]
Triple 2. [饿 (*hungry*) , , 他 (*he*)]

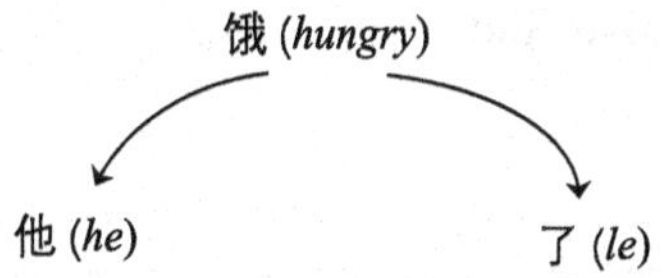

Fig. 5. The semantic dependency graph of (4)

3.2.2 Multi-dependency Node

The traditional dependency grammar is a one-to-one single node. The semantic dependency graph we discussed can represent the complex semantic relations of one-to-many and many-to-many. As shown in Fig. 6.

(5) 杯子摔破了。

The cup is broken.

Triple 1. [摔 (*to fall*) , , 杯子 (*cup*)]

Triple 2. [破 (*broken*) , , 杯子 (*cup*)]

Triple 3. [摔 (*to fall*) , , 破 (*broken*)]

Triple 4. [破 (*broken*) , , 了 (*le*)]

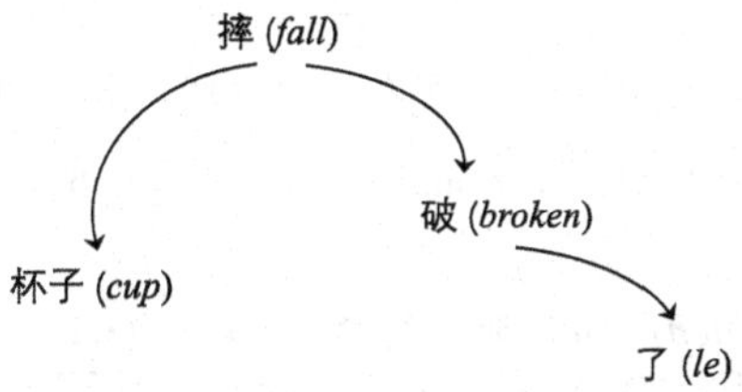

Fig. 6. The semantic dependency graph of (5)

(5) is an example of multi-dependency. One node is semantically associated with two and more nodes at the same time. "杯子 (*cup*)" - "摔 (*fall*)", "杯子 (*cup*)" - "破 (*broken*)" have simultaneously semantic relations; "摔 (*broken*)" - "摔 (*fall*)", "破 (*broken*)" - "杯子 (*cup*)", "破 (*broken*)" - "了 (*le*)" have simultaneously semantic relations.

3.2.3 Multi-layer Recursive Node

(6) 老陈说明天很冷。

Lao Chen said that the weather is very cold.

Triple 1. [说， ，老陈]

[说， ，[[冷， ，明天] [冷， ，很]]]

Triple 2. [说， ，明天很冷]

Triple 3. [冷， ，明天]

Triple 4. [冷， ，很]

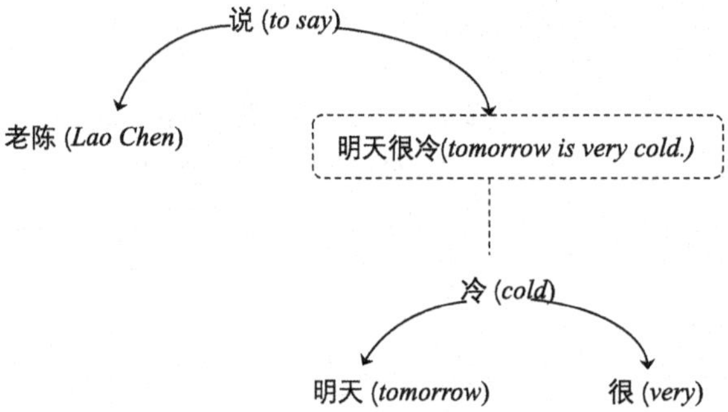

Fig. 7. The semantic dependency graph of (6)

In (6), "老陈 (*Lao Chen*)" and "明天很冷 (*Tomorrow is cold*)" are respectively the values of "说 (*to say*)". For "明天很冷 (*Tomorrow is cold*)", the structure as a whole is correlated to "说 (*to say*)", in which any word in the structure cannot be correlated to "说 (*to say*)" alone. Therefore, a node itself can be a graph, in this way, we allow nesting and multiple correlations.

3.3 Formalization of Chinese Discourses of Semantic Dependency Graph

The representation of Chinese discourse texts by semantic dependency graph is more complicated. This paper focus on the discourse annotation of connective structures, including four aspects, such as the determination of connectives, the status of connectives, the determination of semantic dependency relations, and the processing of implicit connective structures.

First, the determination of connectives. We can rely on the construction of connective ontology, and we can use disambiguation method to determinate the homographs with different functions.

Second, the determination of semantic dependency relations. We judge the semantic relations between sentences and between words in the form of Question & Answering.

This kind of mechanism is feasible, if there are semantic relations between two clauses, one of them can usually ask questions in terms of the original text context.

(7) 我一来李四就走了。
When I came, Li Si left.

For (7), we can ask the following questions:

(a) Who is coming?
(b) What happened after I came here?
(c) Who is leaving?
(d) Why is Li Si gone?

The semantic correlations between the clauses can be determined from the responses to these questions (Fig. 7).

Third, the status of connectives. In discourses with multiple clauses, we treat connectives as the head. Other clauses depend on connectives. If there are paired connectives, such as: "一边...一边... *(one side... another side)*","不仅...而且... *(not only... but also)*", "如果......那么... *(if...so)*", etc., we act the paired connectives together as the head. The semantic dependency graph of (7) is shown in Fig. 8:

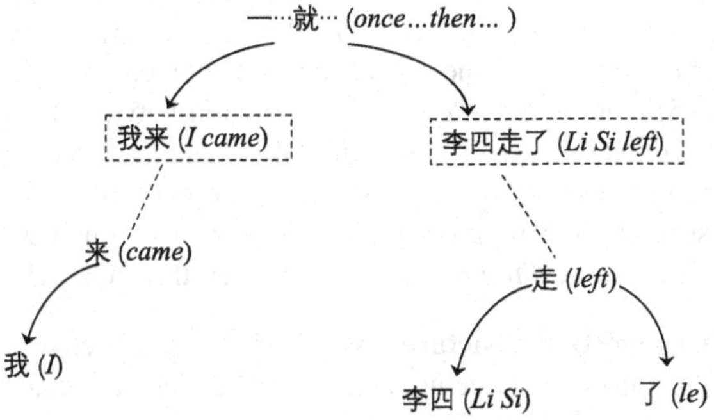

Fig. 8. The semantic dependency graph of (7)

In (7), the paired connectives, "一...就... (*once...then...*)" connect two clauses "我来 (*I came*)" and "李四走了 (*Li Si left*)". The two events of these two clauses are continuous. We try to adopt a new strategy to regard the paired connectives as a whole, such as: "一...就... (*once...then...*)" is a fixed collocation. The previous research often treat it as two separate words [10]. Similar to the study of English discourse coherence [9], we treat the paired connectives as the semantic head in complex sentences, in order to completely describe the semantic relations between sentences.

(8) is a more complicated example. Some connectives with multiple relation categories appear in the discourse to respectively connect multiple clauses.

(8) 国代本属无给职 (S1)，根本没有薪资 (S2)，所领各项费用为助理与工作津贴 (S3)，需以书面提出自何时起至何时止 (S4)，拒领哪项费用 (S5)，才有实质意义 (S6)。

The nationality is unemployed (S1), there is no salary at all (S2), and the expenses are the assistant and work allowance (S3), so it is necessary to submit in writing from when to when (S4), which cost (S5) is rejected, has substantial meaning (S6).

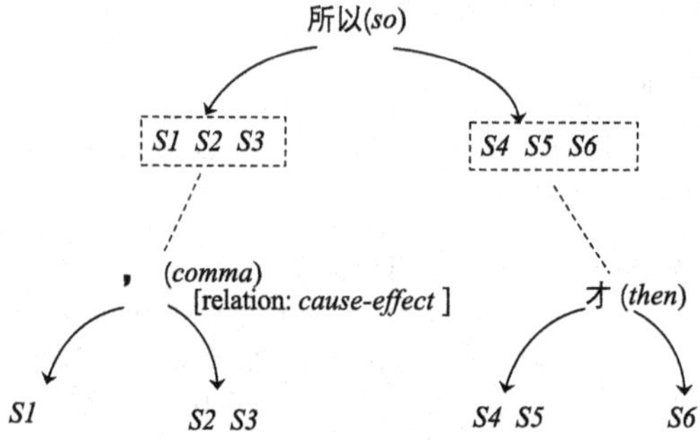

Fig. 9. The semantic dependency graph of (8)

There are six clauses in (8). It is represented by s1, s2, s3, s4, s5, and s6 in Fig. 9. the connective "所以 (*so*)" is connected to the first segment (s1, s2, s3). The second segment (s4, s5, s5) represents the *cause-effect* relation between the two segments. In the first segment, s1 has *cause-effect* relation with s2 and s3. There are no connectives but only a comma in the segment, which works as the mark of the implicit connective structure. In the second segment, the connective "才 (*then*)" connects the clauses s4, s5 and s6, representing the *conditional* relations between three clauses.

Fourth, implicit connective structure. We divide the connective structure into two categories, explicit connective structure and implicit connective structure, according to the presence or absence of connectives in the discourse. When connectives occur, there is an explicit connective structure; when connectives are absent, there is an implicit connective structure. The next step of our research will focus on studying implicit connective structure. Currently, we have annotated 6,000 sentences with implicit connective structure, and will expand to 10,000.

3.4 Formalization of Chinese Special Sentences of Semantic Dependency Graph

There are plenty of special sentence patterns and special language phenomena in Chinese, including *serial-verbs sentence, subject-predicate predicate sentence, double-subjects structure, pivotal structure, verb-complement structure, coordinate structure, and anaphoric reference*, etc. It is difficult to formalize in order to represent their semantic relations. We have explored the semantic parsing of *Chinese subject-predicate predicate sentence, serial-verbs sentence,* and *verb-complement structure* by semantic dependency graph [1–3].

4 Conclusion

Using semantic dependency graph is an attempt to construct Chinese discourse-level connectives semantic annotation resources. Deep semantic parsing is always one of the difficulties in NLP, especially Chinese discourse. The theoretical research we proposed has universal theoretical significance for solving the problems of semantic parsing in different languages. We discussed a complex semantic representation mechanism from phrase-level, sentence-level and discourse-level in terms of language unit. The semantic dependency graph model is characterized by allowing multiple correlations, allowing recursion and nesting and formal representations as recursive directed graph. The semantic dependency graph can more comprehensively represent the semantic relations between words in the sentence and between the clauses in the discourse.

Acknowledgment. The work is funded by the following projects: National Natural Science Foundation of China No. 61772378, 61702121, Humanities & Social Science Foundation of Ministry of Education of China No. 16YJCZH004, and Science & Technology Project of Guangzhou No. 201704030002.

References

1. Chen, B., Ji, D.H., Chen, L.: Semantic labeling of Chinese subject-predicate predicate sentence based on feature structure. J. Chin. Inf. Process. **26**(3), 22–26 (2012). (in Chinese)
2. Chen, B., Ji, D.H., Chen, L.: Semantic labeling of Chinese serial-verbs sentence based on feature structure. J. Chin. Inf. Process. **27**(5), 60–66 (2013). (in Chinese)
3. Chen, B., Lyu, C., Wei, X., Ji, D.: Semantic labeling of Chinese verb-complement structure based on feature structure. In: Su, X., He, T. (eds.) CLSW 2014. LNCS (LNAI), vol. 8922, pp. 341–348. Springer, Cham (2014). https://doi.org/10.1007/978-3-319-14331-6_34
4. Zwicky, A.M.: Heads. J. Linguist. **21**(1), 1–29 (1985)
5. Eisner, J., Smith, N.A.: Parsing with soft and hard constraints on dependency length. In: International Workshop on Parsing Technology, pp. 30–41. Association for Computational Linguistics (2005)
6. Mel'cuk, I.: Dependency Syntax: Theory and Practice. State University of New York Press, Albany (1988)
7. Feng, W.H.: The Dependency-Based Analysis of Chinese Conjunctions and the Related Constructions. Wuhan University (2011). (in Chinese)

8. Qiu, L.K., Jin, P., Wang, H.F.: A multi-view Chinese treebank based on dependency grammar. J. Chin. Inf. Process. **29**(3), 9–15 (2005). (in Chinese)
9. Prasad, R., et al.: The penn discourse TreeBank 2.0. In: International Conference on Language Resources and Evaluation, LREC 2008, 26 May–1 June 2008, Marrakech, DBLP, pp. 2961–2968 (2008)
10. Xue, N.: Annotating discourse connectives in the Chinese Treebank. In: The Workshop on Frontiers in Corpus Annotations II: Pie in the Sky, pp. 84–91. Association for Computational Linguistics (2005)
11. Zhang, W.X., Qiu, L.K.: Study on connectives collocation based on corpus. Chin. Teach. World **82**(4), 64–74 (2007). (in Chinese)
12. Chen, B., Lyu, C., Wei, X.M., Ji, D.H.: Chinese semantic parsing based on feature structure with recursive directed graph. Wuhan Univ. J. Nat. Sci. **20**(4), 318–322 (2015)
13. Chen, B.: Building a Chinese Semantic Resource Based on Feature Structure. Wuhan University Press (2014). (in Chinese)

A Corpus-Based Approach to Studying Chinese Literal and Fictive Motion Sentences in Fiction

Shu-Ping Gong(✉) and Zhao-Ying Huang

Department of Foreign Languages, National Chiayi University, No. 85, Wunlong Village, Minsyong Township, Chiayi County 621, Taiwan
spgong@mail.ncyu.edu.tw, yasminetree@gmail.com

Abstract. This study aims to determine the distribution of three senses of motion verbs in Mandarin Chinese. A fiction corpus was thus constructed to search for 32 motion verb phrases and collect sentences with these motion verbs. These were classified into three senses: (1) literal meanings; (2) fictive motion involving no actual movement in space; and (3) fictive motion involving metaphorical meanings. The corpus data showed that literal meanings had the highest frequency among the three sense categories, followed by metaphorical meanings and, finally, fictive motions. In addition, it was found that literal and fictive motions functioned as intransitive verbs, often expressing location information. However, metaphorical motions functioned as transitive verbs, often expressing themes. Finally, it was found that the preferential use for some verbs was metaphorical in meaning, while others appear to be used as fictive in meaning. The current study has implications for word sense disambiguation in dealing with multiple meanings of motion verbs in Mandarin Chinese.

Keywords: Fictive motion · Metaphorical meanings · Word frequency
Collocation · Lexical analysis

1 Introduction

Motion verbs, which are often high-frequency polysemous words, are pervasive in language. Motion verbs exist in all languages and show similar cross-linguistic patterns of semantic extension [1–8]. For example, the motion verb "go", in English, has 30 senses in WordNet. Some of the senses of "go" have literal meanings and others have metaphorical/fictive meanings.

In the sentence, "The policemen went from door to door looking for the suspect", the verb "went" refers to changing places, representing an actual movement in space, therefore, "went", in this case, can be categorized as a literal meaning. In the sentence, "The money was gone after a few days", the motion verb "gone" indicates the meaning of "to be spent or finished", which does not involve any literal meaning of movement, and thus belongs to the metaphorical meaning category. A third meaning for "go" indicates "changing places" but does not involve an actual movement in space. For instance, in the sentence, "The road goes up to the top of the mountain", the verb "goes", used with the subject, "the road", does not represent movement in the physical

J.-F. Hong et al. (Eds.): CLSW 2018, LNAI 11173, pp. 743–757, 2018.
https://doi.org/10.1007/978-3-030-04015-4_65

sense since, "the road", is not able to perform this act. Instead, it describes the state of the scenery, as in the road can be seen on the mountain up to the top.

Fictive motion does not occur frequently in discourse. However, this kind of motion verbs is often used in fictional works to describe scenery in stories. This study aims to find the distribution of the three senses of motion verbs that occur in Mandarin Chinese. Therefore, a corpus was constructed to collect data from novels to see how often fictive motions occur in Mandarin fiction, as well as their preferred motions.

2 Background

This section will introduce the theoretical background of motion verbs. First and foremost, it will introduce the event structure of motion verbs from the cognitive linguistic perspective. Second, this section will discuss the background of fictive motion and present empirical evidence of the fictive motion sentences found in the corpus. Finally, the rationale of this study will be stated at the end of this section.

2.1 Motion Verbs and Motion Events

Talmy [7, 8] proposed that motion can form an event with four basic semantic components: *motion*, *figure*, *ground*, and *path*. *Motion* involves movements that change places; *figure* conducts the movement; *ground* is the target place to which an entity moves; and *path* is the direction or trajectory of the movement. For example, sentence (1) below demonstrates the four components in the motion event of "go":

(1)	張三	走	回	家
	zhāng sān	zǒu	huí	jiā
	【figure】	【motion】	【path】	【ground】

Another element—*manner*—indicates the way a figure moves. For example, sentence (2) shows an expression involving the motion verb "fly", where "fly" is the *manner* component, conflated with the *motion* component and shows the manner of movement:

(2) 鳥飛到樹上
niǎo fēi dào shù shàng
"The bird flies to the top of the tree."
【motion + manner】

In addition, in Mandarin Chinese, *path* can either be encoded with motion verbs or exist as a satellite after the motion. Sentences (3) and (4) below demonstrate that *path* is conflated with a motion verb and exists as an independent component as a preposition, respectively:

(3) 爸爸進房間了
bà bà jìn fáng jiān le
"Father went into the room."
【motion + path】

(4) 小孩掉到洞裡
xiǎo hái diào dào dòng lǐ
"A child fell into the hole."
【path】

Talmy's study [7] found that languages around the world can be divided into verb-framed language and satellite-framed language. in the former, *path* is conflated with motion verbs while in the latter *manner* is encoded with motion verbs. Therefore, English is a satellite-framed language whereas Spanish and French are classified as verb-framed languages.

However, Mandarin Chinese is an equipollently-framed language, which is similar to both verb-framed and satellite-framed languages [9]. Mandarin has two principles to express the *path* component. The first one is the use of directional verbs occurring after motion verbs (e.g., 上 *shàng* "up", 下 *xià* "down", 進 *jìn* "in", 出 *chū* "out", 回 *huí* "back", 過 *guò* "pass", etc.), as shown in sentence (4). The other is the use of directional verbs as motion verbs encoded with the *path* meaning, as shown in sentence (3).

2.2 Fictive Motion

As mentioned earlier, fictive motion is the metaphorical motion of an object or abstraction through space [7, 8]. Fictive motion sentences involve a motion verb that co-occurs with a figure. However, the figure is often an inanimate object that is not capable of acting out the movement in the physical sense. For example, sentences (5) and (6) below are fictive motion sentences in English and Chinese, respectively:

(5) The highway runs through the city.

(6) 小徑走進森林
xiǎo jīng zǒu jìn sēn lín
"The path goes into the forest."

In sentence (5), the figure "highway" is not capable of performing the motion act of "runs". However, this sentence is syntactically grammatical and semantically acceptable. Similarly, in sentence (6), the figure 小徑 *xiǎo jīng* "the path" is not able to execute the movement 走 *zǒu* "goes", but this sentence is not problematic. The purpose of fictive motion is to emphasize the dynamic imagery of things, like roads moving from one place to another. Therefore, these sentences do not involve any actual movement in the physical sense but instead implicitly indicate the dynamic condition of the motion.

The empirical evidence of dynamic imagery in processing fictive motion has been supported by psycholinguistic experiments [2–4, 10–12], such as Matlock's [11] study, which found that fictive motion sentences seem to have longer trajectories than non-fictive motion sentences, even though these two types of sentences were judged to have similar meanings. For example, sentences (7a) and (7b) below are semantically similar:

(7) a. A sidewalk goes along a canal.
b. A sidewalk is next to a canal.

In Matlock's [11] drawing task, fictive motion sentences and non-fictive motion sentences were read, and the participants had to draw the meanings of the two sentences. The results showed that the trajectory for fictive motion (7a) was longer than that for non-fictive motion (7b). It was concluded that fictive motion expressions can evoke dynamic imagery of inanimate figures that allows one to activate the motions mentally.

2.3 Goal of the Study

Even though cognitive linguists have classified three senses of motion verbs that occur in language, few studies have investigated the distribution of the three senses of motion verbs. Nevertheless, motion verbs are particularly high-frequency words in language. Therefore, it is necessary to understand how motion behaves in discourse, which is beneficial to word sense disambiguation in dealing with these types of verbs in natural language processing.

This study aims to identify the distribution of the three senses of motion verbs in Mandarin Chinese via the corpus-based approach. In addition, the study focuses on fiction data because narrative stories encourage authors to use fictive motions more often than other types of texts.

3 Method

This study investigated the usage preference of motion verbs in expressions. Motion verb expressions were classified into three senses: literal, fictive, and metaphorical meanings. A corpus containing various types of fiction sentences was constructed to analyze the distribution of Chinese motion verbs in fiction.

3.1 Data Collection

First, electronic text files of Chinese novels were collected from the network resource 小說頻道 *xiǎo shuō pín dào* "fiction channel" (ww.nch.com.tw/index.php), which is a free platform of web fiction. This website collected fiction uploaded by authors.

The network platform includes a wide variety of fiction, including romance novels, horror fiction, detective fiction, and science and fantasy novels. Fiction from four categories were collected: literature and romance stories, horror stories, detective stories, and science and fantasy stories. Thirteen novels were selected randomly for the corpus, which contained 371,378 words. The details of the corpus are shown in Table 1 below:

Table 1. Types of novels and the number of words in the fiction corpus

Categories of Novel Types	No. of Novels	Word Freq.
Literature and romance stories	3	99,491
Horror stories	3	91,140
Detective stories	4	92,217
Science and fantasy stories	3	88,530
Total	13	371,378

3.2 Data Analysis

To analyze the motion verbs used in this corpus, a list of motion verbs was generated. According to the definition of the motion event frame [7, 8], nine motion verbs in Chinese expressing *manner* were selected, including 走 *zǒu* "go", 跑 *pǎo* "run", 跳 *tiào* "jump", 爬 *pá* "climb", 逃 *táo* "escape, run away", 跨 *kuà* "cross", 溜 *liū* "slip", 奔 *bēn* "rush", and 轉 *zhuǎn* "turn". These nine motion verbs were selected because they are high-frequency motion verbs in Mandarin and are often composed of other elements as motion compound verbs (e.g., 爬上 *pá shàng* "climb up", 跑出 *pǎo chū* "run out"), which are composed of a motion verb occurring with a *path* verb [13]. Therefore, two types of motion verbs in Mandarin Chinese were included in the list. The first type is one-character motion verbs that express *manner*, and the second type is compound motion verbs, which are two-character verbs that contain one *manner* motion verb (e.g., 走 *zǒu* "go") that occurs with eight kinds of *path* verbs (e.g., 進 *jìn* "in", 出 *chū* "out", 上 *shàng* "up", 下 *xià* "down", 入 *rù* "enter", 過 *guò* "pass", 回 *huí* "back", and 越 *yuè* "through"). The 32 motion verbs are shown in Table 2 below.

The lexical analysis tool Wordsmith was used to analyze the 32 motion verbs. Wordsmith (http://www.lexically.net/wordsmith/) was launched in 1996 and has since been ungraded to the current version 7.0. This tool helps researchers to find patterns in texts via concordance, word list, and keyword functions.

Table 2. Two types of motion verbs used in the study

Categories of Novels	Words
One-character Motion Verbs: Nine Types of One-Character Motions	走 zǒu "go/walk", 跑 pǎo "run" 跳 tiào "jump" 爬 pá "climb" 逃 táo "escape, run away" 跨 kuà "cross" 溜 liū "slip", 奔 bēn "rush" 轉 zhuǎn "turn"
Two-character Motion Verbs: Twenty-three Types of two-character Motions	走進 *zǒu jìn* "go/walk enter" 走出 *zǒu chū* "walk away from" 走入 *zǒu rù* "go/walk into" 走下 *zǒu xià* "go/walk down" 走回 *zǒu huí* "go back" 跑出 *pǎo chū* "run out" 跑回 *pǎo huí* "run back to" 跑上 *pǎo shàng* "run up" 跳出 *tiào chū* "jump out" 跳入 *tiào rù* "jump into" 跳過 *tiào guò* "jump through/cross", 跳上 *tiào shàng* "jump up" 跳下 *tiào xià* "jump down" 爬過 *pá guò* "climb through/cross", 爬上 *pá shàng* "climb up" 爬下 *pá xià* "climb down" 逃出 *táo chū* "escape from" 跨出 *kuà chū* "cross out of" 跨入 *kuà rù* "cross enter" 跨越 *kuà yuè* "cross through" 溜出 *liū chū* "slip out" 進入 *jìn rù* "enter" 通過 *tōng guò* "through/pass".

There were 460 sentences with the 32 motion verbs in the corpus, which were analyzed and placed into three categories: (1) motion verbs with literal meanings that expressed actual movement in space; (2) fictive motion verbs with fictive meanings that did not involve actual movement in space; and (3) motion verbs with fictive meanings that were abstract and metaphorically extended from motion. For example, sentence (8) below belongs to the literal meaning category:

(8) 我走進臥房
wǒ zǒu jìn wò fáng
"I went into the bedroom."

Sentence (8) is classified as having a literal meaning since it contains a human subject, 我 *wǒ* "I", doing the motion, 走進 *zǒu jìn* "went into". This sentence expresses that there is a figure/person moving into a room, which involves actual movement from one place to another place in space.

An example of the second category, fictive motion without actual motion, is shown in sentence (9) below:

(9) 爬了些許黴味的黃燈
pá le xiē xǔ méi wèi de huáng dēng
"Some musty smells crept up from the yellow lamp."

Sentence (9) is classified as fictive motion since the subject, 黴味 méi wèi "musty smells", is not capable of actual movement on the lamp. Sentence (10) below demonstrates the third category, which is fictive motion with metaphorically extended meanings:

(10) 說不定人家對你有不好的印象，之後你轉部門會比較容易
shuō bù dìng rén jiā duì nǐ yǒu bù hǎo de yìn xiàng，zhī hòu nǐ zhuǎn bù mén huì bǐ jiào róng yì
"People may have a bad impression of you. If you want to transfer to another department, it will be easier."

In sentence (10), the motion verb, 轉 *zhuǎn* "transfer", is not the literal meaning of "turn around"; instead, it is metaphorically extended to the meaning of "transferring from one department to another department". Therefore, this kind of sentence is classified as fictive motion with metaphorically extended meaning.

4 Results and Discussion

After categorizing the sentences, the corpus results returned the frequency of the three senses of motion verbs, as shown in Table 3 below:

Table 3. Distribution of the three senses of motion verbs

Categories of motion meanings	Frequency (percentage)
Literal meaning	379 (82%)
Fictive: No actual motion	30 (7%)
Fictive: metaphorical meaning	51 (11%)
Total	460 (100%)

The literal meaning had the highest frequency among the three senses (82%), while the second highest frequency was fictive motion with metaphorical meaning (11%), and the lowest frequency was fictive motion with no actual motion (7%).

Table 4 shows the tokens among the three senses for each motion verb. The results showed that six motion verbs were found in all three sense categories, including 走 zǒu "go/walk", 跳 *tiào* "jump", 逃 *táo* "escape, run away", 進入 *jìn rù* "enter into", 轉 *zhuǎn* "turn", and 通過 *tōng guò* "through/pass". Of these six verbs, four verbs were *manner* motions.

Table 4. The frequency of the three senses of motion verbs

Motion	Literal	Fictive	Metaphorical
走 *zǒu* "go/walk"	142	5	5
走進 *zǒu jìn* "walk into"	18	0	1
走出 *zǒu chū* "walk out"	24	0	0
走入 *zǒu rù* "walk into"	1	0	2
走下 *zǒu xià* "walk down"	5	0	0
走回 *zǒu huí* "go back"	9	0	0
跑 *pǎo* "run"	49	0	1
跑出 *pǎo chū* "run out"	1	0	0
跑回 *pǎo huí* "run back to"	2	0	0
跑上 *pǎo shàng* "run up"	1	0	0
跳 *tiào* "jump"	18	2	7
跳出 *tiào chū* "jump out"	0	0	1
跳入 *tiào rù* "jump into"	2	0	0
跳過 *tiào guò* "jump through/cross"	0	0	3
跳上 *tiào shàng* "jump up"	1	0	0
跳下 *tiào xià* "jump down"	3	0	0
爬 *pá* "climb"	8	3	0
爬過 *pá guò* "climb through/cross"	0	3	0
爬上 *pá shàng* "climb up"	5	1	0
爬下 *pá xià* "climb down"	2	0	0
逃 *táo* "run away"	15	2	1
逃出 *táo chū* "escape from"	1	1	0
跨 *kuà* "cross"	2	0	1
跨出 *kuà chū* "cross out of"	1	1	0
跨入 *kuà rù* "cross enter"	0	0	1
跨越 *kuà yuè* "cross through"	4	3	0
溜 *liū* "slip"	6	0	0
溜出 *liū chū* "slip out"	4	0	0
奔 *bēn* "rush"	1	0	0
進入 *jìn rù* "enter into"	33	3	12
轉 *zhuǎn* "turn"	16	5	15
通過 *tōng guò* "pass"	5	1	1
Total	380 (82%)	30 (6%)	54 (12%)

In addition, it was found that thirteen motion verbs had literal meanings, including 走進 *zǒu jìn* "go/walk into", 走回 *zǒu huí* "go back", 跳上 *tiào shàng* "jump up", 溜出 *liū chū* "slip out", etc. Furthermore, four motion verbs had both literal and metaphorical meanings, including 跑 *pǎo* "run", 跨 *kuà* "cross", 走入 *zǒu rù* "go/walk into", and走進 *zǒu jìn* "walk into". Four motion verbs had literal and fictive meanings: 爬上 *pá shàng* "climb up", 逃出 *táo chū* "escape from", 跨出 *kuà chū* "cross out of", and 跨越 *kuà yuè* "cross through". Finally, one motion verb—爬過 *pá guò* "climb through/cross"—had a fictive meaning, and two motion verbs—跨入 *kuà rù* "cross enter" and 跳過 *tiào guò* "jump through/cross"—had metaphorical meanings.

In addition to the distribution of motion in three meanings, there are three interesting findings in the corpus analysis. First, it is found that one-character motion verbs appear to co-occur with another one-character abstract concept to be metaphorical compounds. As Table 5 shows, there are some metaphorical compounds involving motion verbs. For example, the compound of 走味 *zǒu wèi* is composed of the word 走 *zǒu* "go away" and the word 味 *wèi* "taste", which refers to something losing flavor. The first word is the motion verb 走 *zǒu* "go away" and the second word 味 *wèi* "taste" is the abstract concept "taste". Such expressions can be defined as the idiomatical expressions, extended to the metaphorical meaning of "lose flavour" from the literal meanings "go to somewhere".

Table 5. One-character motions frequently co-occurring with abstract concepts to be metpahoriecla compounds

Motions	Examples
走 *zǒu* "go"	走險 *zǒu xiǎn* "take risks", 走味 *zǒu wèi* "lose flavour"
跑 *pǎo* "run"	跑關 *pǎo guān* "run barriers"
跳 *tiào* "jump"	跳題 *tiào tí* "jump questions"
跨 *kuà* "cross"	跨年 *kuà nián* "cross New Year"
轉 *zhuǎn* "turn"	轉醒 *zhuǎn xǐng* "wake up", 轉小 *zhuǎn xiǎo* "turn small/decrease"

Second, our corpus data shows that fictive motions keep the same syntactic functions, acting as intransitive verbs, while metaphorical motions tend to change to transitive verb and to co-occur with themes. As Tables 6 and 7 show, within the noun phrases occurring with literal motions, there were 19 noun phrases in our corpus data acting like agents (e.g., 員警 *yuán jǐng* "police"), 39 noun phrases as locations (e.g., 警局 *jǐng jú* "police station") and only one noun phrase as themes (e.g., -芭蕾 *bā lěi* "ballet"). In comparison, within the noun phrases occurring with fictive motions, there were 5 noun phrases acting agents (e.g., 字眼 *zì yǎn* "words"), four as locations (e.g., 日記 *rì jì* "diary") and none as themes. In contrast, within the noun phrases occurring with metaphorical meanings, there were 7 noun phrases as agents (e.g., 夏天 *xià tiān* "summer"), 3 as locations (e.g., 話題 *huà tí*, "topics") and 17 as themes (e.g., 世界 *shì jiè* "world"). All the noun phrases occur with 32 motion verbs are listed in Appendix.

In other words, the distribution of type frequency of noun phrases occurring with three types of motions demonstrates that literal and fictive motions were more associated in their meanings and usages. Both kinds of motions were used as intransitive verbs which explicitly expressed locations in motion expressions. This suggests that the location information is important in literal and fictive motion expressions. Metaphorical motions, on the other hand, did not need to express locations in motion expressions. Instead, literal motions were transformed to be transitive verbs, co-occurring with

Table 6. Type frequency of the noun phrases (NP) occurring with 32 motion verbs

Motion / NP	NP as agents	NP as themes	NP as locations
Literal motions	19	1	39
Fictive motions	5	0	4
Metaphorical motions	7	16	3

Table 7. Samples of the noun phrases (NP) occuring with 32 motion verbs

Motion / NP	NP as agents	NP as themes	NP as locations
Literal motions	-員警 *yuán jǐng* "police" -李大冷 *lǐ dà lěng* "Man's name" -車子 *chē zǐ* "car", 風 *fēng* "wind"	-芭蕾 *bā lěi* "ballet"	–警局 *jǐng jú* "police station", –教室 *jiāo shì* "classroom" -腳踏車 *jiǎo tà chē*, "bicycle" –被子 *bèi zǐ* "quilt"
Fictive motions	-黴味 *méi wèi* "musty" -風景 *fēng jǐng* "landscape" -字眼 *zì yǎn* "words" -油花 *yóu huā* "oil flower"	N/A	–黃燈 *huáng dēng* "yellow light" –窗外 *chuāng wài* "window" –日記 *rì jì* "diary", –肉片 *ròu piàn* "sliced meat"
Metaphorical motions	-他 *tā* "he", -夏天 *xià* tiān "summer", -腦袋 *nǎo dài* "head" -力量 *lì liàng* "strength"	–話題 *huà tí*, "topics" –短訊 *duǎn xùn* "short messages" –未知 *wèi zhī* "unknown" –今天 *jīn tiān* "today"	–區間 *qū jiān* "interval" -世界 *shì jiè* "world" -海拔 *hǎi bá* "elevation"

themes. This kind of transformation suggests that the "theme" information is significant in the metaphorical usages.

Third, as mentioned earlier, all motion verbs are frequently used as literal meanings. However, the preferential use of some verbs had metaphorical meanings while other verbs appeared to be used as fictive meanings. For example, we found that two motion verbs with metaphorical meanings were frequently used—進入 *jìn rù* "enter into" and 轉 *zhuǎn* "turn". Specifically, the motion verb 進入 *jìn rù* "enter into" often occurred with abstract concepts, such as 夢鄉 *mèng xiāng* "sleep", 沉睡 *chén shuì* "heavy sleep", 程序 *chéng xù* "procedure", 秋天 *qiū tiān* "autumn", etc., and the motion verb 轉 *zhuǎn* "turn", similarly, was likely to occur with abstract concepts, such as 醒 *xǐng* "awake", 話題 *huà tí* "conversation topics", etc. On the other hand, we found that the word 爬 *pá* "crawl" or "scatter" tends to serve as fictive motion expressions. For example, the word 爬 *pá* "crawl" or "scatter" is expressed as fictive motion in examples (11) and (12). In the two fictive sentences, the structure of inverted sentences is used. The issue of the relationship between the inverted structure and fictive motions needs to be further explored in the future study.

(11) 肉片上爬過油花
ròu piàn shàng pá guò yóu huā
"The oil drops crawled across the sliced meat"

(12) 日記上爬了些許字眼
rì jì shàng pá le xiē xǔ zì yǎn
"A few words were scattered in the diary"

To conclude, it was found that most of the motion verbs had literal meanings from the distribution of tokens of the three senses of motion verbs. In addition, some motion verbs tended to have metaphorical meanings and some preferred fictive motion expressions. Furthermore, we found that one-character motions tended to co-occur with one-character abstract concept to be metaphorical compounds. Moreover, literal and fictive motion behaved as intransitive verbs, often taking the post-verb noun phrases after the motion as location. However, the metaphorical motions behaved as transitive verbs, often taking the post-verb noun phrases as themes, instead of locations. Finally, it was found that fictive motions appeared to occur in the inverted structure, in which noun phrases as agents occurred after the motions.

5 Conclusion and Future Work

This study investigated the distribution of literal, fictive, and metaphorical senses of motion verbs in Mandarin Chinese via a corpus-based approach. Fiction data collected from the Internet and Wordsmith was used to search for 32 motion verbs. A total of 460 motion expressions were collected, analyzed, and categorized into three senses. The corpus results show that the highest frequency of senses of motion verbs is literal usages, followed by metaphorical usages, and, finally, fictive usages. This distribution pattern suggests that fictive motion verbs do not occur frequently in fiction.

Previous studies also discovered that fictive motion expressions did not occur very frequently in daily conversation. Blomberg & Zlatev [7, 8] proposed that fictive motion tended to occur in particular linguistic contexts. Particularly, when a motion sentence was produced from the speaker's point of view, i.e., the first-person perspective, a fictive motion tended to be produced.

Subsequently, Blomberg & Zlatev [7, 8] conducted a picture-based elicitation task to examine whether people would like to produce fictive motion sentences in the first-person perspective context as compared to the third-person perspective ones. They gave participants two kinds of pictures to review. One was the first-person perspective and the other was the third-person perspective. Participants had to write down a sentence to describe each picture. After the picture elicitation task, the resulting sentences were analyzed as to whether fictive motion verbs were used. Blomberg & Zlatev [7, 8] found that the pictures taken from the first-person perspective produced more fictive motion sentences than the ones from the third-person perspective. It was proved that the person-perspective taking affects the use of fictive motion.

In addition to the distribution of three senses of motion, our corpus results show three linguistic behaviors among motion sentences. First, it was found that one-character motion verbs appear to co-occur with other one-character abstract concepts to produce metaphorical compounds, such as 走味 *zǒu wèi* "lose flavor". Second, we found that the literal and fictive motions function as intransitive verbs, often expressing location information. However, the metaphorical motions function as transitive verbs, often expressing the theme information which is linguistically realized in a post-verb NP. Finally, it was found that some verbs tend to be used as metaphorical meanings while the other verbs appear to be used as fictive meanings, e.g., the motion 進入 *jìn rù* "enter" frequently acting as the metaphorical meaning and the motion 爬 *pá* "climb" as the fictive meaning.

This study collected fiction data from romance and literature, horror, detective, and fantasy novels. However, the corpus did not produce as many fictive motion verbs as originally predicted. It is possible that fictive motion verbs have a very low frequency in the four types of fiction categories in our corpus. The fiction collected was written by anonymous writers who mainly focused on storytelling to attract readership, and these stories did not focus on metaphorical descriptions of emotion, scenery, and other abstract concepts. According to this limitation in the corpus, a future study will replicate Blomberg & Zlatev's [7, 8] study via conducting a picture elicitation task. As Blomberg & Zlatev's [7, 8] suggested, the picture elicitation task allows people to produce more fictive motion sentences than the ones produced in the daily conversation. Therefore, it is hoped that more fictive motion sentences can be collected in the future study.

In addition, our corpus data show that fictive motion sentences prefer to use invented structures. For example, in the sentence of 肉片上爬過油花 *ròu piàn shàng pá guò yóu huā* "The oil drops crawled across the sliced meat", the noun phrase 肉片 *ròu piàn* "the sliced meat" functions as the location while the noun phrase 油花 *yóu huā* "the oil drops" functions as the theme. The verb phrase 爬過 *pá guò* "crawled across" is a fictive motion. This kind of sentence order, i.e., location-verb-theme, is the inverted structure, in which fictive motions come before noun phrases as agents. We wonder whether fictive motion expressions are likely to occur in invented structures, which needs to be further explored in the future.

This study has practical implications for word sense disambiguation in dealing with multiple meanings of motion verbs in Mandarin Chinese. Particularly, fictive motion has rarely been studied in most studies. This study also sheds light on understanding how fictive motion verbs behave in fiction.

Acknowledgments. This research was supported by grants from the Ministry of Science and Technology (MOST 105-2410-H-415-025) to the first author. We would like to thank the anonymous reviewers for their comments on this work. Remaining errors are our sole responsibility.

Appendix: Examples of the Noun Phrases Occurring with 32 Motion Verbs

Literal Motions

Noun phrases as agents

我 *wǒ* "I", 他 *tā* "he", 你 *nǐ* "you", 員警 *yuán jǐng* "policeman",
小灰 *xiǎo huī* " Little Gray/dog's name", 李大冷 *lǐ dà lěng* "man's name",
雷利 *léi lì* "man's name", 婼妮 *chuò nī* "woman's name",
潔莉 *jié lì* "woman's name", 海恩 *hǎi ēn* "woman's name",
人影 rén yǐng "silhouette ", 活螞蟻 *huó mǎ yǐ* "ants",
偵防車 *zhēn fáng chē* "detective car", 車子 *chē zǐ* "car", 公車 *gōng chē* "bus",
風 *fēng* "wind", 雨 yǔ "rain", 氣體 *qì tǐ* "gas", 光球 *guāng qiú* "light ball"

Noun phrases as themes

芭蕾 *bā lěi* "ballet"

Noun phrases as locations

剪票口 *jiăn piào kŏu* "ticket gate", 收費站 *shōu fèi zhàn* "toll booth",
屋子 *wū zĭ* "house", 院長室 *yuàn zhăng shì* "dean's room",
病房 *bìng fáng* "ward", 警局 *jĭng jú* "police station",
王宮 *wáng gōng* "royal palace", 房間 *fáng jiān* "room",
狗窩 *gŏu wō* "kennel", 7-11 "convenience stores", 右邊 *yòu biān* "right side",
扶梯 *fú tī* "escalator", 窗台 *chuāng tái* "window sill",
二樓 *èr lóu* "second floor", 樓梯 *lóu tī* "stairs",
逃生門 *táo shēng mén* "escape door", 電梯 *diàn tī* "elevator",
缺口處 *quē kŏu chù* "gap", 教室 *jiāo shì* "classroom",
教堂 *jiāo táng* "church", 家 jiā "home", 會議室 *huì yì shì* "conference room",
超級市場 *chāo jí shì chăng* "supermarket", 警局 *jĭng jú* "police office",
浴室 *yù shì* "bathroom", 大街 *dà jiē* "highway", 山洞 *shān dòng* "cave",
台階 tái jiē "steps", 車架 *chē jià* "car frames", 腳踏車 *jiăo tà chē* "bicycles",
車 *chē* "car", BMW "a kind of car", 後座 *hòu zuò* "back seat",
被子 *bèi zĭ* "quilt", 活死人 *huó sĭ rén* "living dead", 魔陣 *mó zhèn* "magic array",
屍城 *shī chéng* "corpse city", 身體 *shēn tĭ* "body", 胸腔 *xiōng qiāng* "chess" ,
大霧 *dà wù* "heavy fog"

Fictive Motions

Noun phrases as agents

黴味 *méi wèi* "musty", 風景 *fēng jĭng* "landscape", 字眼 *zì yăn* "words",
油花 *yóu huā* "oil drops", 疹子 zhĕn zĭ "rash"

Noun phrases as themes

N/A

Noun phrases as locations

黃燈 *huáng dēng* "yellow light", 窗外 *chuāng wài* "window", 日記 *rì jì* "diary",
肉片 *ròu piàn* "sliced meat"

Metaphorical Motions

Noun phrases as agents

我 wŏ "I", 你 nĭ "you", 他 *tā* "he", 夏天 *xià* tiān "summer", 腦袋 *năo dài* "head",
內心 nèi xīn "heart", 力量 *lì liàng* "strength"

Noun phrases as themes

話題 *huà tí* "topics", 短訊 *duǎn xùn* "short messages", 視野 *shì yě* "vision", 雙眼 *shuāng yǎn* "eyes", 監視 *jiān shì* "surveillance", 4 號 *si hào* "number 4", 你 *nǐ* "you", 電腦 *diàn nǎo* "computer", 未知 *wèi zhī* "unknown", 今天 *jīn tiān* "today", 平靜 *píng jìng* "calm", 夢鄉 *mèng xiāng* "dream", 程序 *chéng xù* "program", 沉睡 *chén shuì* "sleep", 生活 *shēng huó* "life", 遊戲視窗 *yóu xì shì chuāng* "game window"

Noun phrases as locations

區間 *qū jiān* "interval", 世界 *shì jiè* "world", 海拔 *hǎi bá* "elevation"

References

1. Blomberg, J.: Motion in language and experience: actual and non-actual motion in Swedish, French and Thai. Ph.D. thesis. Lund University (2014)
2. Blomberg, J., Zlatev, J.: Actual and non-actual motion: Why experientialist semantics needs phenomenology (and vice versa). Phenomenol. Cogn. Sci. **13**(3), 395–418 (2014)
3. Blomberg, J., Zlatev, J.: Non-actual motion: phenomenological analysis and linguistic evidence. Cogn. Process. **16**, 153–157 (2015)
4. Blomberg, J., Zlatev, J.: The expression of non-actual motion in Swedish. Fr. Thai. Cogn. Linguist. **26**(4), 657–696 (2015)
5. Lakoff, G.: Women, Fire and Dangerous Things. What Categories Reveal About the Mind. University of Chicago Press, Chicago and London (1987)
6. Langacker, R.W.: Foundations of Cognitive Grammar. Theoretical prerequisites, vol. 1. Stanford University Press, Stanford (1987)
7. Talmy, L.: Fictive motion in language and "ception". In: Bloom, P., Peterson, M.A., Lynn Nadel, M.F. (eds.) Language and Space, pp. 211–276. MIT Press, Cambridge (1996)
8. Talmy, L.: Toward a Cognitive Semantics. Conceptual Structuring Systems, vol. I. MIT Press, Cambridge (2000)
9. Chen, L., Guo, J.: Motion events in Chinese novels: evidence for an equipollently-framed language. J. Pragmat. **41**(9), 1749–1766 (2009)
10. Matlock, T.: Fictive motion as cognitive simulation. Mem. Cogn. **32**, 1389–1400 (2004)
11. Matlock, T.: Depicting fictive motion in drawings. In: Luchenbroers, J. (ed.) Cognitive linguistics: investigations across languages, fields, and philosophical boundaries. John H. Benjamins, Amsterdam (2006)
12. Matlock, T., Richardson, D.C.: Do eye movements go with fictive motion? In: (Proceedings) Conference of the Cognitive Science Society. Erlbaum, Mahwah (2004)
13. Li, C.N., Thompson, S.A.: Mandarin Chinese: A functional reference grammar. University of California Press, Berkeley (1981)

A Comparative Study on the Coordinate Relation of Chinese Official Documents in Mainland, Hong Kong and Macau

Wenhe Feng[1,2,3], Haifang Guo[1,3], Dengxia Cao[2,3], and Han Ren[1,3](✉)

[1] Laboratory of Language Engineering and Computing, Guangdong University of Foreign Studies, Guangzhou 510006, China
wenhefeng@gmail.com, hanren@gdufs.edu.cn

[2] National Experimental Teaching Center of Simultaneous Interpreting, Guangdong University of Foreign Studies, Guangzhou 510006, Guangdong, China

[3] School of Foreign Languages, Henan University, Kaifeng 475001, China

Abstract. This paper investigates the coordinate relation in Mainland Chinese, Hong Kong Chinese and Macau Chinese, including explicit relations, implicit relations and their parallel items. In order to conduct the comparative study, a corpus including official documents of Mainland China, Hong Kong and Macau has been built. The study shows that the frequency of the explicit coordinate relation appearing in Hong Kong (53.5%) and Macao texts (23.1%) is much higher than that in Mainland China texts (1.5%), and the explicit coordinate relation occurs most frequently in Hong Kong texts. The study also shows that the connective types in Hong Kong (59 types) and Macao texts (21 types) are much more than that in Mainland China texts (11 types). Such differences are probably derived from the English influence on Hong Kong and Macau Chinese, according to the comparative results of the coordinate relation in English and Chinese texts of Hong Kong and Macau.

Keywords: Coordinate relation · Connective · Chinese of Hong Kong Chinese of Macau

1 Introduction

The previous study of language in Mainland, Hong Kong and Macau mainly focused on morphology [1–4], syntax [5], language forms [6, 7] etc. and less involved with the comparison on the discourse level in official documents. In order to make up the gap, this paper is devoted to the comparison of these three areas in the view of discourse analysis. To avoid the stylistic factors, the comparative corpus in this paper is extracted from official documents. Considering the complexity and diversity of discourse relation, this paper concentrates on the coordinate relation in official documents. According to the previous relevant research [8], the coordinate relation is frequently used in the logical relations of discourses. Through the comparison of the coordinate relation, to some extent, the expression difference of the discourse relations in the three areas will be revealed.

J.-F. Hong et al. (Eds.): CLSW 2018, LNAI 11173, pp. 758–771, 2018.
https://doi.org/10.1007/978-3-030-04015-4_66

Discourse is a linguistic unit, which is larger than a sentence. It contains groups of sentences and complex sentences, the components of which are sentences and clauses respectively. There is no fundamental difference in the expression of logical relations, therefore in this study put them into a unified framework.

A coordinate relation usually means a few parallel events, situations, or several aspects of one object [9]. The connectives of coordinate relation can be explicit (explicit relation), such as "bing(并)" in example (1), or be implicit (implicit relation), which is shown in example (2). Connectives joint two relation items, as in example (1), or more than two relation items, as in example (2), which is distinct from the general logical relation. This paper focuses on the study of coordinate relation, especially explicit, implicit and its parallel items.

（1）建议明年继续向有困难家庭发放经济援助金, /并对现有援助金受益家庭发放多一次的全数援助金。(双项并列)

Jianyi Mingnian Jixu Xiang You Kunnan Jiating Fafang Jingji Yuanzhu Jin, /Bing Dui Xianyou Yuanzhu Jin Shouyi Jiating Fafang Duo Yici De Quanshu Yuanzhu Jin. (Shuangxiang Binglie)

"It is recommended that financial assistance payments should keep going to poverty families next year, / and the aid recipients will receive an additional full amount of assistance." (double-item of coordinate relation)

（2）国内生产总值 47．2 万亿元，比上年增长 92．2%；/公共财政收入 10．37 万亿元，增长 24．8%；/粮食产量 57121 万吨，再创历史新高。(多项并列)

Guonei Shengchan Zongzhi 47.2Wan Yi Yuan, Bi Shangnian Zengzhang 9.2%;/Gonggong Caizheng Shouru 10.37Wan Yi Yuan, Zengzhang 24.8%;/Liangshi Chanliang 57121Wan Dun, Zai Chuang Lishi Xin Gao.(Duoxiang Binglie)

"The GDP was 47.2 trillion yuan increased 9.2% compared with last year; / public revenue was 10.37 trillion yuan, up 24.8%; / grain output was 57.21 million tons, a record high." (multi-item of coordinate relation)

2 Comparable Corpus

2.1 Corpus Selection

The following texts were selected for annotation: Mainland Chinese: Reports on the work of the Chinese government in 2012 and 2014, the report of the 18th National Congress of the Communist Party of China, and the report of the Third Plenary Session of the 18th Central Committee. Chinese of Hong Kong: 2009–2012 Government Policy Address. Chinese of Macau: 2010–2013 Government Policy Address.

Coordinate relation in the corpus is the research subject of this paper. Considering the influence of English, we study the coordinate relation in the English versions of Chinese corpus in Hong Kong and Macao, and the corpus is served as a reference corpus to explain the differences in the Mainland, Hong Kong and Macao.

2.2 Corpus Labeling

The study of the coordinate relation requires the combination of whole structure of the text. We annotated the research corpus of this paper based on a theoretical framework and an annotation platform on the discourse structure and alignment of Chinese and English textual parallel corpora. Example (3) shows a labeling case (in this paper we only provide the relevant annotation information about this article.).

（3） [A]现在，我代表国务院，//[条件] [B]向大会作政府工作报告，/// [目的][C]请予审议，/[并列] [D]并请全国政协各位委员提出意见。

[A]Xianzai, Wo Daibiao Guowuyuan, //[Tiaojian][B]Xiang Dahui Zuo Zhengfu Gongzuo Baogao, ///[Mudi][C]Qing Yu Shenyi, /[Binglie][D]Bing Qing Quanguo Zhengxie Gewei Weiyuan Tichu Yijian. (Zhongguo Zhengfu Gongzuo Baogao, 2014 Nian)

"[1]On behalf of the State Council, //[CONDITION][2] I now present to you the report on the work of the government /// [PURPOSE][3]for your deliberation, /[COORINATION] [4]and I welcome comments on my report from the members of the National Committee of the Chinese People's Political Consultative Conference."

The letters and numbers in the example refer to the clauses and its order respectively. The slash "/" indicates the level of the discourse structure,[1] the square brackets ("[]") show the discourse relationship types, and the underlines indicate the connectives. With special attention paid to coordinate relation, which in (3) is the first divided level, furthermore, both Chinese and English are explicit relation with their explicit markers "并 /and", therefore, there are two parallel items in this coordinate relation. This paper mainly extracts the relevant information of the coordinate relation for research. For example, a coordinate relation is on the first layer in (3), and Chinese and the corresponding English are both explicit. The connectives are "并 /and", the coordinate relation has two parallel items.

2.3 Basic Data

The Table 1 shows the statistics of coordinate relation and all the annotated relations, from which the coordinate relation takes the largest amount. As the Table 1 shows Mainland Chinese ranks the first place (67.6%), followed by Macau (48.4%) and Hong Kong (28.8%). It reveals three distinct government report styles, generally speaking, coordinate relation for description, therefore with more connectives for description, then the report may lack of logical reasoning. In this paper more attention is paid to the different usages of coordinate relation in discourse rather than their language styles. In the following study, annotated connectives are extracted for analysis.

---

[1] According to Li et al. (2014), there are 4 categories and 17 small class relationships in a total amount.

Table 1. The coordinate relation of Chinese in three places.

Relation type	Mainland Chinese		Chinese of Hong Kong		Chinese of Macau	
	Frequency	Percentage	Frequency	Percentage	Frequency	Percentage
Coordinate relation	1710	67.6	826	28.8	906	48.4
All relations	2528	100	2869	100	1873	100.0

3 Explicit and Implicit Expression of the Coordinate Relation

The following Table 2 shows that: First, in terms of the coordinate relation, the explicit relations in Hong Kong and Macao Chinese are significantly larger than that of Mainland Chinese (53.5%, 23.1% > 1.5%). Second, Chinese of Hong Kong and Macao are quite different. The proportion of explicit relation in Hong Kong is distinctively higher than that of Macao.

Table 2. The explicit and implicit expression of the coordinate relation of Chinese in three places.

Explicit and implicit	Mainland Chinese		Chinese of Hong Kong		Chinese of Macau	
	Frequency	Percentage	Frequency	Percentage	Frequency	Percentage
Explicit relation	25	1.5	442	53.5	209	23.1
Implicit relation	1685	98.5	384	46.5	697	76.9
Total	1710	100.0	826	100	906	100.0

Because of the stylistic reason (official documents), the distinct showed in table (2) have nothing to do with register. Considering the degree of the influence of English, the conclusions are as following: firstly, compared with Mainland Chinese, the Chinese of Hong Kong and Macao is more involved with English; secondly, Chinese of Hong Kong is deeply influenced by English compared with Macao's.

The predictions above can be further verified by Table 3, which shows that Hong Kong Chinese displays the highest with its English version in explicit relation (53.5% → 57.5%);while Macao Chinese fails to reach even half amount of its English version (23.1% vs. 51.9%), but which is much higher than Mainland Chinese (23.1% > 1.5%). The difference above manifested in the two main aspects: the language environment and the language policy. On the one hand, with a high level of internationalization in Hong Kong and Macao, especially international finance and tourism attracted people from all over the world, thus both work and life cannot go on without the international language—English, therefore English in the two places booms sharply. The influence of English in Mainland is slighter, though it is a compulsory curriculum in Mainland. On the other hand, the language of Hong Kong can be generalized into four words "liang wen san yu", "liang wen" refers to Chinese and English, while "san yu" is Cantonese, Mandarin and English. "liang wen", Chinese and English play different roles in the society, while English is the official language, only when released to the public the documents will be translated into English-Chinese translation versions. Equally, "san yu", Cantonese, Mandarin and English play their individual roles. In terms of frequency, English ranks first in official condition, followed by Cantonese and Mandarin, while on informal event the order is Cantonese, English and Mandarin. In Macau, Chinese, English and Portuguese are prevail, but they play different roles, among which Chinese and Portuguese are the official languages; but Chinese is the most widely used one for its universal functions. English is highly spoken in finance, technology, education and other fields; though English in Macau is prosperous, it does not catch enough official attention.

According to the above analysis, the conclusion is that English enjoys a higher status in Hong Kong and Macao compared with Mainland, while takes the first place in Hong Kong. Correspondingly, English exerts the largest influence on Hong Kong Chinese, followed by Macao and Mainland respectively. Thus, it explains the explicit difference about coordinate relation.

Table 3. The explicit and implicit expression of the coordinate relation in Hong Kong and Macao English (Official document translation).

Explicit and implicit	Hong Kong English		Macau English	
	Frequency	Percentage	Frequency	Percentage
Explicit relation	473	57.5	498	51.9
Implicit relation	349	42.5	461	48.1
Total	822	100.0	959	100.0

4 The Comparison of Explicit Connectives

4.1 Statistical Comparison

The choices of explicit connectives are various, as are shown in Table 4.

Firstly, the full types of statistics of explicit connectives are different as showing: the number of connectives in Hong Kong is the highest (59), the second in Macao (21), and the least in Mainland (11).

Secondly, some connectives are only applicable in Hong Kong or Macao, instead of Mainland, such as "yiji(以及)"; Chinese in Hong Kong and Macao are different. For example, in Hong Kong, "yi(亦)" ranks second in discourse connectives, which doesn't appear in Macau. Thirdly, though the connectives mentioned above are available in Hong Kong, Macau and Mainland, their usage proportions are various. For example, "bing (并)" occupies the largest part of 35.9%, followed by Hong Kong (22.2%) and the Mainland (12.0%); and "ye (也)" in Mainland is 32.0%, Hong Kong (7.5%) and Macau (6.2%).

Table 4. Connectives of Chinese in three places (section).

connectives	Mainland Chinese		Chinese of Hong Kong		Chinese of Macau	
	Frequency	Percentage	Frequency	Percentage	Frequency	Percentage
bing(并)	3	12.0	98	22.2	75	35.9
yi(亦)	0	0	95	21.4	0	0
Tongshi (同时)	2	8.0	34	7.7	44	21.1
ye(也)	8	32.0	33	7.5	13	6.2
ciwai(此外)	0	0	33	7.5	13	6.2
yiji(以及)	0	0	33	7.5	24	11.5
……	……	……	……	……	……	……
Total	25	100	442	100	209	100.0

4.2 Case Comparison

4.2.1 "yi(亦)"

"yi(亦)" frequently occurs in Hong Kong as a discourse connective, taking the second place among the connectives; however, it is not used in Macau and Mainland.

(4)因应两岸关系发展新形势，我们将按照《基本法》和「钱七条」，积极开展香港与台湾在经济、文化、民生等各方面的合作，中央政府亦鼓励及支持特区在这方面的工作。(香港)

Women Jiang Anzhao JIBENFA He QIAN QITIAO, Jiji Kaizhan Xianggang Yu Taiwan Zai Jingji, Wenhua, Minsheng Deng Fangmian De Hezuo, Zhongyang Zhengfu Yi Guli Ji Zhichi Tequ Zai Zhe Fangmian De Gongzuo.

"In response to the latest development in cross-Strait relations, we will actively pursue economic, cultural, social and other exchanges with Taiwan in accordance with the Basic Law and Qian Qichen's Seven Principles. The Central Government encourages and supports the Hong Kong Special Administrative Region's efforts." (Hong Kong)

(5)建立合作的框架 — 除推动双边商贸合作委员会开展工作外，我们会成立「港台经济文化合作协进会」，以推动与台方多范畴和多层次的交流；我们亦会考虑在适当时候及以适当形式在台湾设立综合性办事机构，加强两地高层次交流。(香港)

Jianli Hezuo De Kuangjia—Chu Tuidong Shuangbian Shangmao Hezuo Weiyuanhui Kaizhan Gongzuo Wai, Women Hui Chengli GANGTAI JINGJI WENHUA HE ZUO XIE JIN HUI, Yi Tuidong Yu Taifang Duo Fanchou He Duo Cengci De Jiaoliu; Women Yi Hui Kaolv Zai Shidang Shihou Ji Yi Shidang Xingshi Zai Taiwan Sheli Zonghexing Banshi Jigou, Jiaqiang Liangdi Gaocengci Jiaoliu.

"Establishing a co-operation framework – Apart from initiating the work of the bilateral business co-operation committees, we will establish a Hong Kong-Taiwan Economic and Cultural Co-operation and Promotion Council to promote multi-faceted, multi-level exchanges with Taiwan. We will consider setting up a multi-functional office in Taiwan at an appropriate time and in an appropriate format to enhance high-level exchanges between the two places." (Hong Kong)

Generally, "yi (亦)" is a discourse connective in classical Chinese, which is replaced by "ye (也)" in modern Chinese. Therefore, we can conclude that classical Chinese still exerts certain influence in Hong Kong.

4.2.2 "yiji(以及)"

"yiji(以及)" as a discourse connective accounts for 7.5% in Hong Kong, 11.5% in Macau, but it is not used in Mainland. For examples:

(6)对台展开经济范畴的双边合作 — 包括以服务业为主调，加强与台湾方面的经济合作，以及在避免双重征税安排方面与台湾开展磋商，务求取得进展和成果。(香港)

Duitai Kaizhan Jingji Fanchou De Shuangbian Hezuo—Baokuo Yi Fuwuye Wei Zhudiao, Jiaqiang Yu Taiwan Fangmian De Jingji Hezuo, Yiji Zai Bimian Shuangchong Zhengshui Anpai Fangmian Yu Taiwan Kaizhan Cuoshang, Wuqiu Qude Jinzhan He Chengguo.

"Fostering bilateral economic co-operation with Taiwan – We will foster economic co-operation with Taiwan, focusing particularly on trade in services, and will commence discussions with Taiwan on arrangements for avoidance of double taxation, with a view to achieving progress and results." (Hong Kong)

(7)我们会积极研究如何进一步发展目前地方行政的模式，提升区议会的职能，发挥区议员的积极性，以及让民政事务专员更有效地统筹政府部门在地区的服务。(香港)

Women Hui Jiji Yanjiu Ruhe Jinyibu Fazhan Muqian Difang Xingzheng De Moshi, Tisheng Quyihui De Zhineng, Fahui Quyiyuan De Jiji Xing, Yiji Rang Minzheng Shiwu Zhuanyuan Geng Youxian De Tongchou Zhengfu Bumen Zai Diqu De Fuwu. (Xianggang)

"We will actively study how to take forward the present mode of district administration to enhance the functions of DCs, enable DC Members to play a more active role in district affairs, and facilitate the co-ordination of government departments in service delivery at district level by the District Officers." (Hong Kong)

(8)通过修订《市区房屋税规章》和《印花税规章》两项法律，以及通过《取消使用登船和离船设施的费用》行政法规，扩大税费减免措施的範围。(澳门)

Tongguo Xiuding SHIQU WANGWUSHUI GUIZHANG He YINHUASHUI GUIZHANG Liangxiang Falv, Yiji Tongguo QUXIAO SHIYONG DENGCHUAN HE LICHUAN SHESHI DE FEIYONG Xingzheng Fagui, Kuoda Shuifei Jianmian Cuoshi De Fanwei.

"Expand the scope of tax relief measures by amending the two regulations of the Urban Housing Tax Regulations and the Stamp Duty Regulations and the Administrative Regulations on the Cancellation of the Use of Boarding and Disembarkation Facilities." (Macao)

(9)特区政府今年首次公布了施政年度的立法计划，以及加强行政与立法之间的沟通，重视立法质量的提升。(澳门)

Tequ Zhengfu Jinnian Shouci Gongbu Le Shizheng Niandu De Lifa Jihua, Yiji Jiaqiang Xingzheng Yu Lifa Zhijian De Goutong, Zhongshi Lifa Zhiliang De Tisheng.

"The SAR Government announced for the first time this year the legislative plan for the administration year, as well as strengthening the communication between the executive and the legislature, and attaching importance to the improvement of the quality of legislation." (Macao)

In the Mainland Chinese, "yiji(以及)" is an intra-sentence connective placed in the end of a phrase, working as a complement for the sentence, as shown in (10).

(10)桌上放着画笔、水盂、调色盘以及两盆初开的菊花。(内地网络语料)

Zhuoshang Fangzhe Huabi, Shuiyv, Tiaosepan Yiji Liangpen Chukai De Jvhua.

"On the table were a brush, a water bottle, a palette, and two pots of chrysanthemums." (Web corpus of Web corpus Mainland)

(11)活化后的中环街市将会成为上班人士在日间的「城市绿洲」，以及市民和游客在晚上和周末的新休闲去处。(香港)

Huohua Hou De Zhonghuan Jieshi Jianghui Chengwei Shangban Renshi Zai Rijian De CHENGSHI LVZHOU, Yiji Shimin He Youke Zai Wanshang He Zhoumo De Xin Xiuxian Quchu.

"The revitalised Central Market will become an "urban oasis" for white collar workers in the daytime and a new hang-out area for locals and tourists in the evenings and on the weekends." (Hong Kong)

However, in Hong Kong and Macao Chinese, "yiji(以及)" is also an intra-sentence connectives in (11), which shows that "yiji" own more usages in Mainland Chinese.

4.2.3 "bing (并)"

The connective "bing" takes up 22.2% in Hong Kong, 35.9% in Macau, and only accounting for 12.0% in Mainland Chinese. For examples:

(12)我们会继续加强与中小企的沟通，并适时提供更多支持。(香港)

Women Hui Jixu Jiaqiang Yu Zhongxiaoqi De Goutong, Bing Shishi Tigong Gengduo Zhichi.(Xianggang)

"We will continue to strengthen our communication with SMEs and render them more support in a timely manner." (Hong Kong)

(13)为确保公私营医疗均衡持续发展，我们应强化公营医疗系统，并提升服务水平和效益，同时协助私营医疗服务发展，并改善监管制度。(香港)

Wei Quebao Gongsiying Yiliao Junheng Chixu Fazhan, Women Ying Qianghua Gongying Yiliao Xitong, Bing Tisheng Fuwu Shuiping he Xiaoyi, Tongshi Xiezhu Siying Yiliao Fuwu Fazhan, Bing Gaishan Jianguan Zhidu.

"To achieve this, we should reinforce the public healthcare system by enhancing its services and effectiveness, while facilitating the development of the private healthcare sector and improving the regulatory mechanism." (Hong Kong)

(14)在新的一年，我们将持续关注及优化各项民生福利政策，并适时采取惠民措施。(澳门)

Zai Xin De Yinian, Women Jiang Chixu Guanzhu Ji Youhua Gexiang Minsheng Fuli Zhengce, Bing Shishi Caiqu Huimin Cuoshi.

"In the coming year, we will continue to focus on and improve policies to augment various aspects of daily life, and will take timely measures for the benefit of the people." (Macao)

(15)保障居民完成非高等教育，并提供修读高等教育或以上课程的机会。(澳门)

Baozhang Jvmin Wancheng Fei Gaodeng Jiaoyu, Bing Tigong Xiudu Gaodeng Jiaoyu Huo Yishang Kecheng De Jihui.

"We will ensure that local residents can complete non-tertiary education, and provide them with opportunities to pursue tertiary education or even further studies." (Macao)

(16)各位代表：现在，我代表国务院，向大会作政府工作报告，请予审议，并请全国政协各位委员提出意见。(内地)

Gewei Daibiao:Xianzai, Wo Daibiao Guowuyuan, Xiang Dahui Zuo Zhengfu Gongzuo Baogao, Qing Yv Shenyi, Bing Qing Quanguo Zheng-xie Gewei Weiyuan Tichu Yijian.

"On behalf of the State Council, I now present to you the report on the work of the government for your deliberation, and I welcome comments on my report from the members of the National Committee of the Chinese People's Political Consultative Conference." (Mainland)

(17)建设好、管理好中国上海自由贸易试验区，形成可复制可推广的体制机制，并开展若干新的试点。(内地)

Jianshe Hao, Guanli Hao Zhongguo Shanghai Ziyou Maoyi Shiyanqu, Xingcheng Ke Fuzhi Ke Tuiguang De Tizhi Jizhi, Bing Kaizhan Ruogan Xin De Shidian.(Neidi)

"We will ensure the successful building and management of the China (Shanghai) Pilot Free Trade Zone so that this model can be copied and extended, and we will launch a number of new trials." (Mainland)

The examples taken from Hong Kong and Macao documents show that "bing" is more widely used in these official documents, which can be omitted without semantic obscureness; while in Mainland the lack of connective "bing" will result in semantic obscureness. Meanwhile, the English translation also adopts other connectives to take the place of "bing", examples (12)–(15) All these indicate that, the adaptation of Chinese connectives is concerned with English.

5 The Parallel Items in the Coordinate Relation

As shown in Table 5: the parallel items of the coordinate relation can be two or more.

Firstly, Hong Kong, Macau and Mainland rarely compose parallel items more than five, and two items are the most frequently used. Secondly, Table 5 shows a significant distinction for the multi-parallel items in the three areas: Mainland embraces the maximum number of parallel items, the 3 parallel items or more items take 41.3%, while in Hong Kong and Macau are 16.2% and 10.8%. Besides, the maximum number of parallel items that they can contain are also various: Mainland Chinese (18 items) > Macau Chinese (11 items) > Hong Kong Chinese (5 items). It dues to the different working style of the three areas, which brought the different volumes of the parallel items. It can be concluded that imperative mood is frequently used in Mainland documents; work plans and tasks report are listed with more multi-parallel items. In comparison, the government's work report in Hong Kong and Macau is more explanatory, which means that the related reasons should be given; therefore, the number of parallel items is reduced. The following examples in (18–20) are extracted from the government work report of the three places, meanwhile, the distinct working styles are revealed.

(18)加快产业结构优化升级。大力培育战略性新兴产业，新能源、新材料、生物医药、高端装备制造、新能源汽车快速发展，三网融合、云计算、物联网试点示范工作步伐加快。企业兼并重组取得新进展。支持重点产业振兴和技术改造，中央预算投资安排150亿元，支持4000多个项目，带动总投资3000亿元。加快发展信息咨询、电子商务等现代服务业，新兴服务领域不断拓宽。交通运输产业快速发展，经济社会发展的基础进一步夯实。(内地)

Table 5. Parallel items in the coordinate relation of Chinese in Mainland, Hong Kong and Macao

Parallel item	Mainland Chinese		Chinese of Hong Kong		Chinese of Macau	
	Frequency	Percentage	Frequency	Frequency	Percentage	Frequency
2	1005	58.7	692	83.8	808	89.2
3	386	22.5	105	12.7	55	6.1
4	158	9.2	24	2.9	26	2.9
5	77	4.5	5	0.6	6	0.7
6	42	2.5	0	0	4	0.4
7	17	1.0	0	0	4	0.4
8	14	0.8	0	0	0	0
9	4	0.2	0	0	0	0
10	1	0.1	0	0	2	0.2
11	1	0.1	0	0	1	0.1
12	2	0.1	0	0	0	0
13	1	0.1	0	0	0	0
15	1	0.1	0	0	0	0
18	1	0.1	0	0	0	0
Total	1710	100.0	826	100.0	906	100.0

Jiakuai Chanye Jiegou Youhua Shengji. Dali Peiyu Zhanlvexing Xinxing Chanye, Xin Nengyuan, Xin Cailiao, Shengwu Yiyao, Gaoduan Zhuangbei Zhizao, Xin Nengyuan Qiche Kuaisu Fazhan, San Wang Ronghe, Yun Jisuan, Wulianwang Shidian Shifan Gongzuo Bufa Jiakuai.Qiye Jianbing Chongzu Qude Xin Jinzhan.Zhichi Zhongdian Chanye Zhenxing He Jishu Gaizao, Zhongyang Yusuan Touzi Anpai 150Yi Yuan, Zhichi 4000Duo Ge Xiangmu, Daidong Zong Touzi 3000Yi Yuan.Jiakuai Fazhan Xinxi Zixun, Dianzi Shangwu Deng Xiandai Fuwuye, Xin Xing Fuwu Lingyu Buduan Tuokuan.Jiaotong Yunshu Chanye Kuaisu Fazhan, Jingji Shehui Fazhan De Jichu Jin Yibu Hangshi.

"We accelerated the optimization and upgrading of the industrial structure. We energetically fostered strategic emerging industries and accelerated development of new energy, new materials, biomedicines, high-end equipment manufacturing and new-energy vehicles, and we sped up pilot projects and demonstrations for integrating the telecommunications network, the radio and television broadcasting network, and the Internet, along with the development of cloud computing and the Internet of Things. We made progress in enterprise mergers and reorganizations. We allocated 15billion yuan from the central government budget to support more than 4, 000 projects to boost key industries and upgrade their technologies. This seed capital attracted a total investment of 300 billion yuan. We accelerated the development of information consulting, e-commerce and other modern service industries, and expanded new service areas. The transportation industry developed quickly, thereby further strengthening the foundation for china's economic and social development." (Mainland)

(19)香港在“一国两制”的宪制安排下回归，“港人治港”，“高度自治”。香港作为国家的特别行政区，一直得到国家的关怀和支持，充分发挥“一国两制”的优势，不仅在内地拓展了经济发展所需的广阔腹地，而且作为国际金融、贸易和航运中心的地位，在世界上亦日益巩固和提高。此外，在香港民主发展的道路上，我们按照《基本法》的规定和全国人大常委会的有关决定，循序渐进推动民主发展。因此，维护国家的主权和《基本法》的权威，符合香港社会的整体和长远利益，亦同时是我们每一个香港市民的责任。(香港)

Xianggang Zai YIGUO LIANGZHI De Xianzhi Anpai Xia Huigui, GUANGREN ZHIGANG, GAODU ZIZHI.Xianggang Zuowei Guojia De Tebie Xingzhengqu, Yizhi Dedao Guojia De guanhuai He Zhichi, Chongfen Fahui YIGUO LIANGZHI De Youshi, Bujin Zai Neidi Tuozhan Le Jingji Fazhan Suo Xu De Guangkuo Fudi, Erqie Zuowei Guoji Jinrong, Maoyi He Hangyun Zhongxin De Diwei, Zai Shijie Shang Yi Riyi Gonggu He Tigao.Ciwai, Zai Xianggang Minzhu Fazhan De Daolu Shang, Women Anzhao JIBEN FA De Guiding He Quanguo Renda Changwu Weiyuanhui De Youguan Jueding, Xunxu-jianjin Tuidong Minzhu Fazhan.Yinci, Weihu Guojia De Zhuquan He JIBEN FA De Quanwei, Fuhe Xianggang Shehui De Zhengti He Changyuan Liyi, Yi Tongshi Shi Women Mei Yige Xianggang Shimin De Zeren.

“Hong Kong has reunified with our motherland. Under the principle of “One Country, Two Systems”, Hong Kong people administer Hong Kong with a high degree of autonomy. As a Special Administrative Region of our country, we receive strong and steadfast support from our country. Capitalizing on the advantages of “One Country, Two Systems”, we have not only opened up the vast Mainland market as our economic hinterland, but also enhanced Hong Kong’s status as an international hub of financial services, trade and shipping. We have made gradual and orderly progress in our democratic development in accordance with the Basic Law and relevant decisions of the Standing Committee of the National People’s Congress (NPC). Therefore, upholding the sovereignty of our country and the authority of the Basic Law is in the overall and long-term interests of Hong Kong. It is also the responsibility of every Hong Kong citizen.” (Hong Kong)

(20)近年本地经济快速发展，通胀结构已发生变化，除输入性因素外，内需带动的因素逐渐突显。政府加强监察食品进口及零售价格，并对有关消费者权益法规进行检讨和修订。基于由内需带动的通胀对民生带来的影响，特区政府采取了多项适切的安排，加强扶助弱势社群，纾缓居民的生活压力。在新的一年，我们将持续关注及优化各项民生福利政策，并适时采取惠民措施，让社会各阶层都能分享经济发展的成果，提升居民的生活素质。(澳门)

Jinnian Bendi Jingji Kuaisu Fazhan, Tongzhang Jiegou Yi Fasheng Bianhua, Chu Shuruxing Yinsu Wai, Neixu Daidong De Yinsu Zhujian Tuxian.Zhengfu Jiaqiang Jiancha Shipin Jinkou Ji Lingshou Jiage, Bing Dui Youguan Xiaofei Zhe Quanyi Fagui Jinxing Jiantao He Xiuding.Jiyu You Neixu Daidong De Tongzhang Dui Minsheng Dailai De Yingxiang, Tequ Zhengfu Caiqu Le Duoxiang Shiqie De Anpai, Jiaqiang

Fuzhu Ruoshi Shequn, Shuhuan Jvmin De Shenghuo Yali.Zai Xin De Yinian, Women Jiang Chixu Guanzhu Ji Youhua Gexiang Minsheng Fuli Zhengce, Bing Shishi Caiqu Huimin Cuoshi, Rang Shehui Ge Jieceng Dou Neng Fenxiang Jingji Fazhan De Chengguo, Tisheng Jvmin De Shenghuo Suzhi.(Aomen)

"In recent years, the local economy has grown rapidly, leading to structural changes in inflation. In addition to imports, domestic demand has become increasingly prominent as a driving factor. The Government has strengthened the monitoring of food imports and retail prices, and has reviewed and amended laws and regulations concerning consumer rights. In light of the impact of domestic-demand-driven inflation on people's well-being, the Government has implemented a string of responsive measures, increasing support for the underprivileged and alleviating the quotidian burden. In the coming year, we will continue to focus on and improve policies to augment various aspects of daily life, and will take timely measures for the benefit of the people, allowing all social sectors to share the fruits of economic development, and ultimately raising people's standard of living." (Macao)

6 Conclusion

Based on the annotated corpus extracted from official documents of Mainland China, Hong Kong and Macao, this paper focuses on the study of coordinate relation, especially including explicit, implicit relations and their parallel items. The frequency of explicit relation in Hong Kong and Macao is much higher than that in Mainland, the highest one is in Hong Kong (53.5% > 23.1% > 1.5%). The types of connectives in Hong Kong and Macao are more variously than those in Mainland. In addition, those in Hong Kong Chinese is used more frequently than Macao's. (59 > 21 > 11). There are differences in the application of connectives in the three varieties of Chinese. For example, "yi(亦)" as a discourse connective is only used in Hong Kong Chinese. Some connectives shared by the three places also have differences in usage and its number, such as "bing (并)" and "ye(也)". "bing (并)" is frequently used in Hong Kong and Macao Chinese, while it is less used in Mainland Chinese. And "ye(也)" is common in Mainland Chinese but not in Hong Kong and Macao Chinese. Thirdly, Chinese tend to use a few of parallel items, but the number of parallel items in Mainland Chinese is higher than that in Hong Kong and Macao Chinese.

The above differences are related to the degree of influence of English, classical Chinese, official document styles, the remains of ancient Chinese and the working style of official documents and other factors have on the three varieties of Chinese:

Firstly, Hong Kong and Macao Chinese are much influenced by English than Mainland Chinese. Therefore, there are more explicit relations in Hong Kong and Macao Chinese than in Mainland Chinese. Hong Kong Chinese is affected by English than Macao Chinese. Therefore, the explicit relation in Hong Kong Chinese is more frequently than that in Macao Chinese.

Secondly, in terms of connectives, there are some classical Chinese discourse connectives still used in Hong Kong and Macao Chinese, such as "yi(亦)" in Hong Kong; more connectives are adopted with the influence of English, for example, "bing (并)" in Hong Kong and Macao Chinese is used more frequently that in Mainland.

Thirdly, the working styles of the official documents in Mainland are shown in examples, therefore more parallel items can be contained. While the official documents in Hong Kong and Macao are more explanatory, therefore few simple parallel items.

Acknowledgments. This paper was supported by Ministry of Education Humanities and Social Sciences Project (15YJC740021), Major Projects of Basic Research in Philosophy of Henan Province (2015-JCZD-022), China Postdoctoral Fund (2013M540594), Special innovation project of Guangdong Education Department (17TS07), Key Laboratory of Language Engineering and Computing Laboratory, Guangdong University of Foreign Studies 2016 (LEC2016Z BKT001, LEC2016ZBKT002).

References

1. Yao, S., Huang, Y.: A quantitative study of the lexical differences in news discourses between Macau and Mainland. Appl. Linguist. **2**, 27–37 (2014)
2. Ma, M.: Hong Kong-style Chinese connective survey report. Chin. Linguist. **4**, 64–72 + 96 (2012)
3. Su, X.: A comparative analysis of the compulsory verbs in the legislative language of Hong Kong and Macao. In: Proceedings of the 7th National Symposium on Language and Literature Applications, pp. 120–126 (2011)
4. Deng, J.: Hong Kong and Macao new words construction 8 methods. J. Jinan Univ. **4**, 124–129 (1996)
5. Zhao, C., Shi, D.: A Comparative Study of "Jing" between Hong Kong and Macao Chinese and Standard Chinese. J. Yunnan Normal Univ. (Humanit. Soc. Sci.) **1**, 25–33 (2015)
6. Sheng, Y.: Talking about the language problems in Chinese official documents in Hong Kong and Macao. Fangyan (Dialect) **2**, 166–170 (2001)
7. Sheng, Y.: A brief talk on Hong Kong and Macao Chinese official document language and form. Secretary **3**, 27–28 (2000)
8. Li, Y., Feng, W., Sun, J., Kong, F., Zhou, G.: Building Chinese discourse corpus with connective-driven dependency tree structure. In: Proceedings of EMNLP, pp. 2105–2114 (2014)
9. Huang, B., Liao, X.: Modern Chinese, 5th edn. Beijing Higher Education Press, Beijing (2011)
10. Feng, W.: Alignment and annotation of Chinese-English discourse structure parallel corpus. J. Chin. Inf. Process. **6**, 158–164 (2013)
11. Yang, C.: Language Problems and Language Policy in Hong Kong – on the Influence of Hong Kong Language Policy of the Language Group (2005). http://web.ntnu.edu.tw/~edwiny/pdf/02-hk-langu-policy.pdf
12. Zeng, W., Liu, S.: The multi-language phenomenon and language policy in Macao. Around Southeast Asia **1**, 103–107 (2010)
13. Zhang, G.: Language status and language policy in Macau: 1991–2006. Appl. Linguist. **3**, 43–51 (2010)
14. Su, J.: The impact of English on the use of Hong Kong language. Stud. Chin. Lang. **3**, 219–226 (1997)

Word Sense Comparison Between DCC and GKB

Lingling Mu(✉), Xiaoyu Cheng, Yingjie Han, and Hongying Zan

School of Information Engineering, Zhengzhou University,
Zhengzhou 450001, Henan, China
{iellmu, ieyjhan}@zzu.edu.cn

Abstract. *Dictionary of Contemporary Chinese* (DCC) is an authoritative, human-oriented dictionary that defines word senses in natural language. *The Contemporary Chinese Grammatical Knowledge Base* (GKB) uses detailed syntactic information to describe word senses. The combination of DCC and GKB will be helpful for studying the problem of word sense distinction and word sense disambiguation (WSD). In this paper, we defined the types of alignment of the individual word sense and the types of word sense granularity correspondence. We also designed semi-auto algorithm that used the similarity of definitions and example sentences to compute words sense alignment. The algorithm turned definitions and example sentences into word sequences, and then used sememes of HowNet to compute the similarity of word sequences. The individual word sense alignment and word sense granularity correspondence are constructed based on the similarity. This algorithm was used to construct the individual word sense alignment table and word sense granularity correspondence relation of intersection words of the two dictionaries. The results of word sense granularity correspondence relation analyzing showed that the word sense alignment between DCC and GKB are quite complicated. The completely "equal" sense mainly exists in the monosemy. Generally speaking, the word sense granularity of GKB is larger than that of DCC. There are "no correspondence" word senses in both dictionaries. The integration of semantic meaning and syntactic information of the two dictionaries can be achieved based on sense alignment and will be helpful for solving natural language processing problems such as WSD.

Keywords: Dictionary of Contemporary Chinese
Contemporary Chinese Grammatical Knowledge Base · Word sense
Similarity · Word sense alignment · Word sense granularity correspondence

1 Introduction

Word sense distinction has always been a hot issue in lexical semantics research, which has important influence on word sense tagging and word sense disambiguation [1]. There are two methods for word sense description: static description and dynamic description. Static description uses natural language, attribute values and frame structure to describe word senses, such as *Dictionary of Contemporary Chinese* (DCC) [2], *Contemporary Chinese Grammatical Knowledge Base* (GKB) [3], *Synonym*

J.-F. Hong et al. (Eds.): CLSW 2018, LNAI 11173, pp. 772–788, 2018.
https://doi.org/10.1007/978-3-030-04015-4_67

Word Forest [4] and *HowNet* [5]. Dynamic description uses instances to describe word senses [6], such as *the Semor corpora* [7], *the DSO corpora* [8] and *the Peking University Word Sense Tagging Corpus* [9]. Static and dynamic word sense are combined according to word sense tagging corpus that are annotated based on knowledge bases [9, 10], which is more conducive to word sense disambiguation and word sense distinction.

DCC is an authoritative, human-oriented dictionary. It uses natural language to define word senses. People use DCC to understand the word senses through introspection and that is not suitable for automatic disambiguation. GKB contains detailed syntactic and semantic information and mainly uses attribute values to describe word senses, which is suitable for computers to understand word senses. The combination of the two dictionaries will be better for people and computers to understand word senses. GKB distinguishes word senses according to grammar information. It doesn't distinguish word senses that have the same meaning without significant difference in grammar usage. Therefore, GKB-based word sense distinction is coarse-grained. The criterion for word sense division of DCC is different from that of GKB.

In this paper, we propose a semi-automatic method that uses the static word sense description of DCC and GKB to establish the individual word sense alignment and word sense granularity correspondence of these two dictionaries. The establishment of word sense alignment will be helpful for integrating word senses of DCC and GKB, and that will better solve natural language processing tasks such as WSD.

The rest of the paper is divided into four parts. The second part describes the word sense representation and distribution in DCC and GKB and defines the classification criterion of word sense alignment and correspondence. In the third part, a word sense alignment algorithm based on glosses and usage examples is designed. This algorithm is used to construct the individual word sense alignment table between DCC and GKB. In the fourth part, we discuss the word sense alignment situations between DCC and GKB. The last part is the conclusion.

2 The Alignment of Static Word Senses Between DCC and GKB

2.1 Word Sense Representation of DCC and GKB

DCC and GKB are two representative dictionaries. DCC uses natural language to describe word sense. This paper uses the electronic version of DCC (Fifth Edition), which consists of structured information that are extracted from plain texts. Word sense is described by fields such as "ID", "词语(*word*)", "义项编码(*s*ense *code*)", "拼音(*pinyin*)", "词性(*part–of-speech*)","释义(*definition*)" and "例句(*example sentence*)". The different word senses of the same word are denoted by "义项编码(*sense codes*)". Each word sense in the dictionary has a unique "ID". The field of "释义(*definition*)" uses natural language to describe the word sense. The field of "例句(*example sentence*)" gives usage samples of the word sense.

GKB is an electronic dictionary and is stored in the form of an Access database. It is divided into a overall table and several sub-tables of part-of-speech. The fields of “词语(*word*)”, “词类(*part-of-speech*)”, and “同形(*homomorphism*)” are used to describe the word sense in the total table. The fields of “义项(*sense*)”, “备注(*remark*)”, “体宾(*substantive-object*)” and “时态(*tense*)” also provide semantic information. The fields of “义项(*sense*)” and “备注(*remark*)” are common attributes of GKB’s different parts-of-speech. The field of “义项(*sense*)” is similar to DCC’s “释义(*definition*)” field. It uses natural language phrases or sentences to explain word sense. The value of the “备注(*remark*)” attribute is usage samples of the word sense.

Definitions (ie. “释义(*definition*)” in DCC and “义项(*sense*)” in GKB) and example sentences (ie “例句(*example sentence*)” in DCC and “备注(*remark*)” in GKB) are the common attributes to express word senses in DCC and GKB, so we can make use of the comparison of their attribute values to automatically align the word senses. For convenience, the fields of DCC’s “释义(*definition*)” and GKB’s “义项(*sense*)” are named as “definition”, and the fields of DCC’s “例句(*example sentence*)” and the GKB’s “备注(*remark*)” are named as “example sentence”.

DCC’s parts-of-speech is divided into 14 categories, they are “名(*noun*), 动(*verb*), 形(*adjective*), 副(*adverb*), 量(*quantifier*), 连(*conjunction*), 代(*pronoun*), 拟(*onomatopoeia*), 助(*particle*), 介(*preposition*), 数(*numeral*), 叹(*interjection*), “未(*undefine*)” and “缀(*affix*)”. GKB has a total of 18 basic parts-of-speech and three other categories, including “noun, verb, adjective, adverb, quantifier, conjunction, pronoun, onomatopoeia, particle, preposition, numeral, interjection, 时间词(*time word*), 方位词(*position word*), 处所词(*location word*), 区别词(*distinguishing word*), 状态词(*status word*), 语气(*modal word*), 成语(*idiom*), 习用语(*idiom*) and 缩略语(*acronym*)”. The first 12 parts-of-speech in DCC and GKB are one-to-one matched. DCC takes “时间词(*time words*)” and “方位词(position word)” as the noun’s attachment, and takes “区别词(*distinguishing word*)” and “状态词(*status word*)” as the adjective’s attachment [2]. Literature [11] pointed out that about 83.5% of the part-of-speech annotation results is identical between DCC and GKB. Therefore, this paper assumes that the part-of-speech is identical between DCC and GKB when the word senses in DCC and GKB are compared. This paper takes “时间词(*time word*), 处所词(*place word*)” and “方位词(*position word*)” as noun; take “区别词(*distinguishing word*)” and “状态词(*status word*)” as adjective; take “语气词(*modal word*)” as particle and take “成语(*idiom*), 习用语(*idiom*), and 缩略语(*acronym*)” as “未(*undefine*)”.This paper only compares word senses that have the same word form and the same part-of-speech.

2.2 The Word Sense Distribution of DCC and GKB

The statistics of words and word senses of DCC and GKB are shown in Table 1. 84.8% of words in DCC are monosemy, 97% of words in GKB are monosemy. The number of GKB’s monosemy is one-third more than that of DCC, while its number of polysemy is only one quarter of that of DCC.

Table 1. Words and word senses statistics of DCC and GKB

Dictionary	Number of words			Number of senses	Average number of senses
	Total	Monosemy	Polysemy		
DCC	62,983	53,403	9,580	75,780	2.3
GKB	77,484	75,185	2,272	80,244	2.2

The words correspondence in DCC and GKB can be divided into the following four situations: (1) words only appear in DCC or GKB; (2) words are monosemy in both dictionaries; (3) words are monosemy in a dictionary but are polysemy in the other dictionary; (4) words are polysemy in both dictionaries.

There are 57,236 words that belong to the situation (1); 33.9% of the words (21,381) in the DCC are not included in the GKB, while 46% of the words (35,855) in GKB are not included in DCC.

The total of 41,602 intersection words of DCC and GKB belong to the situations (2)–(4), which accounting for more than half of the words in DCC and GKB respectively. The sense distribution of intersection words of DCC and GKB is shown in Table 2. Most of intersection words of DCC and GKB are monosemy. The number of monosemy of the intersection words in GKB is 16.6%, which is more than that of DCC. The number polysemy of intersection words and their word senses in DCC is about 10 times that of GKB. It can be seen that there are significant differences in the word sense distinction granularity between DCC and GKB.

Table 2. Word sense statistics of intersection words of DCC and GKB

Part-of-speech	W = DCC ∩ GKB	W ∈ DCC			W ∈ GKB		
		Monosemy	Polysemy		Monosemy	Polysemy	
			Word	Word sense		Word	Word sense
名词(noun)	20,806	17,038	3,768	8,579	20,579	227	457
动词(verb)	11,709	9,113	2,596	6,549	11,292	417	962
形容词(adjective)	3,512	2,757	755	1,786	3,488	24	48
副词(adverb)	793	676	117	297	791	2	4
介词(preposition)	74	52	22	57	72	2	5
量词(quantifier)	335	297	38	86	294	41	92
拟声词(onomatopoeia)	113	107	6	14	111	2	4
助词(particle)	54	29	25	78	43	11	25
代词(pronoun)	110	74	36	99	105	5	11
数词(numeral)	53	43	10	46	52	1	2
连词(conjunction)	155	143	12	26	147	8	18
叹词(interjection)	36	25	11	31	31	5	16
未(undefine)	3,829	3,700	129	271	3,829	0	0
缀(affix)	23	16	7	14	11	12	35
Total	41,602	34,070	7,532	17,933	40,845	757	1,679

The third situation of word correspondence can be further divided into the situation that words are monosemy in DCC and are polysemy in GKB, or vice versa. The corresponding amount of word senses of the intersection words of DCC and GKB is shown in Table 3. The meaning of "1–1, 1–m, m–1, m–m" in the table is described in Table 4. 81.6% of the intersection words are monosemy in both dictionaries. The number of words that are monosemy in DCC and polysemy in GKB is less than 100. More words are monosemy in GKB and polysemy in DCC. It can be seen that the granularity of the DCC word sense distinction is finer.

Table 3. The alignment between the word senses of DCC and GKB intersection words (DCC-GKB)

	W = DCC ∩ GKB	1-1	1-m	m-1	m-n
名词(noun)	20,806	16,995	41	3,487	157
动词(verb)	11,709	9,095	18	2,197	399
形容词(adjective)	3,512	2,755	2	634	16
副词(adverb)	793	676	0	115	2
介词(preposition)	74	52	0	20	2
量词(quantifier)	335	274	23	20	18
拟声词(onomatopoeia)	113	107	0	4	2
助词(particle)	54	28	1	15	10
代词(pronoun)	110	74	0	31	5
数词(numeral)	53	42	1	10	0
连词(conjunction)	155	140	3	7	5
叹词(interjection)	36	25	0	6	5
未(undefine)	3,829	3,700	0	129	0
缀(affix)	23	9	7	2	5
Total	41,602	33,972	96	6,677	626

Table 4. The explanation of word sense alignment

Alignment	1-1	1-m	m-1	m-m
Explain	Word in Both DCC and GKB is monosemy	Word in DCC is monosemy, and in GKB is polysemy	Word in DCC is polysemy, and in GKB is monosemy	Word in Both DCC and GKB is polysemy

2.3 Classification of Individual Word Sense Alignment

Individual word sense alignment refers to the alignment relation between each word sense of a word in *A* dictionary and that of the same word in *B* dictionary. Assuming that the word sense set of word *w* in *A* dictionary is $S_A(w)| = \{S_{Ai}|i = 1, 2, 3, \ldots m\}$, and in *B* dictionary is $S_B(w)| = \{S_{Bj}|i = 1, 2, 3, \ldots m\}$, then the set of individual word sense alignment of *w* in *A* and *B* dictionary is:

$$S_{AB}(w) = S_A(w) \times S_B(w) = \{(S_{Ai}, S_{Bj})|S_{Ai} \in S_A(w) \wedge S_{Bj} \in S_B(w)\} \quad (1)$$

The element (S_{Ai}, S_{Bj}) is the individual word sense alignment between the word sense S_{Ai} and S_{Bj}. The number of individual word sense alignment of the word w in $S_{AB}(w)$ is N:

$$N = m \times n \quad (2)$$

In this paper, individual word sense alignment are defined as five types: "equality", "inequality", "belonging", "inclusion" and "uncertainty".

Definition 1: equality. If the word sense w_{Ai} of word w in A dictionary is exactly the same as the semantic meaning of the word sense w_{Bj} in B dictionary, the alignment between w_{Ai} and w_{Bj} is defined as "equality" relation and can be written as $w_{Ai} = w_{Bj}$.

For example, the noun "单位(*danwei*)" in DCC has a word sense *d1* described as: "*计量事物的标准量的名称。如米为计量长度的单位，千克为计量质量的单位，升为计量容积的单位等 (The name of the standard quantity that measures things. For example, meter is the unit of measurement length, kilogram is the unit of measurement quality, and litre is the unit of measurement volume, etc.)*" The word sense *g2* of "单位(*danwei*)" in GKB is described as: "*计量名称(Measurement name)*". The semantics meaning described with *d1* and *g2* are the same, so the sense alignment between *d1* and *g2* is "equality", denoted as *d1* = *g2*.

Definition 2: inequality. If the word sense w_{Ai} of word w in A dictionary is completely different from the semantic meaning of the word sense w_{Bj} in B dictionary, the individual word sense alignment between w_{Ai} and w_{Bj} is defined as "inequality" and can be denoted as $w_{Ai} \neq w_{Bj}$.

For example, the noun "单位(*danwei*)" in the DCC has a word sense *d2* described as: "*机关、团体 (Organs, groups)*" The semantics descriptions of *d2* and *g2* are completely different. Therefore, the individual word sense alignment between *d2* and *g2* is $d2 \neq g2$.

Definition 3: belonging. If the word sense w_{Ai} of the word w in A dictionary is part of the semantic of the word sense w_{Bj} in B dictionary, the individual word sense alignment between the w_{Ai} and the w_{Bj} is defined as "belonging" relation and can be written as $w_{Ai} \subset w_{Bj}$.

For example, the noun "机关(*jiguan*)" in DCC has the word sense *d3* described as "*周密而巧妙的计谋 (Careful and ingenious strategy.)*" In GKB, the word sense *g1* of "机关(*jiguan*)" is described as: "*控制部件；计谋等 (Control unit; Strategy)*". The sense of *d3* is part of the sense *g1*. Therefore, the individual word sense alignment between *d3* and *g1* is $d3 \subset g1$.

Definition 4: inclusion. If the word sense w_{Ai} of word w in A dictionary includes the word sense w_{Bj} in B dictionary, the individual word sense alignment between w_{Ai} and w_{Bj} is an inclusion relation, denoted as $w_{Ai} \supset w_{Bj}$. For example, the adjective "稳固(*wengu*)" in the DCC has the word sense *d1* described as: "*稳固安定；没有变动 (Stable; no change.)*" The word sense *g1* of "稳固(*wengu*)" in GKB is described as: "*稳固安定(Stable)*". The semantic of the word sense *d1* contains the word sense *g1*. Therefore, the individual word sense alignment between *d1* and *g1* is inclusion relation, and is denoted as $d1 \supset g1$.

Inclusion relationships and belonging relationships are reciprocal, $w_{Ai} \subset w_{Bj} == w_{Bj} \supset w_{Ai}$. In the above example, the word sense alignment $d3 \subset g1$ of "机关(*jiguan*)" may also be represented as $g1 \supset d3$, the word sense alignment $d1 \supset g1$ of "稳固(*wengu*)" may also be expressed as $g1 \subset d1$.

Definition 5: Uncertainty. If the word sense w_{Ai} of word *w* in *A* dictionary and the sense w_{Bj} in *B* dictionary do not belong to the four relations above, the individual word sense alignment between w_{Ai} and w_{Bj} is uncertain relation and is denoted as "uncertainty".

For example, the adjective "左(*zuo*)" in DCC has word sense *d1*: "*偏; 邪; 不正常(partial; evil; abnormal)*" In GKB, the word sense *g1* of "左(*zuo*)" only has the example sentence "*很～(very～)*" without definition. According to the definition and example sentence alone, the individual word sense alignment between *d1* and *g1* cannot be classified into the four types above. Therefore, the individual word sense alignment between *d1* and *g1* is "uncertainty".

2.4 Classification of Word Sense Granularity Correspondence Situation

Word sense distinction has always been a research hotspot for linguists. Different dictionaries use different word sense definition standards based on different design goals. It is convenient to compare the word sense granularity between two dictionaries by using the alignment between individual word senses. Because of the authoritativeness of DCC and GKB, this paper assumes that word sense of DCC and GKB are mutually independent. We define the word sense granularity correspondence between two dictionaries as four types of "equality, greater, less and no correspondence".

Definition 6: Equal granularity. Equal granularity is defined as the granularity of word sense *ds* in *A* dictionary is equal to that of *B* dictionary if the individual word sense alignment is "equality" between the word sense *ds* of word *w* in *A* dictionary and one word sense in *B* dictionary.

Definition 7: Greater granularity. Greater granularity is defined as the granularity of word sense *ds* in *A* dictionary is greater than that of *B* dictionary if the individual word sense alignment is "inclusion" between the word sense *ds* of word *w* in *A* dictionary and at least one word sense of *B* dictionary.

Definition 8: Less granularity. Less granularity is defined as the granularity of word sense *ds* in *A* dictionary is less than that of *B* dictionary if the individual word sense alignment is "belonging" between the word sense *ds* of word *w* in *A* dictionary and at least one word sense of *B* dictionary.

Definition 9: No correspondence. If the semantic cannotation of word sense *ds* in the *A* dictionary is not included in any word sense of *B* dictionary, *ds* has no corresponding word senses in *B* dictionary. If one individual word sense alignment of sense *ds* between *A* dictionary and *B* dictionary is "inequality" and there will be no individual word sense alignments of "equality", "belonging" or "inclusion", and the word sense granularity of *ds* is categorized as "no correspondence" in both dictionary *A* and *B*.

Table 5 summarizes the connection between individual word sense alignment and word sense granularity correspondence.

Table 5. the connection between individual word sense alignment and word sense granularity correspondence

Individual word sense alignment		Word sense granularity correspondence	Remark
Equality	$w_{Ai} = w_{Bj}$	Equal granularity	w_{Ai} has an equal granularity word sense in the *B* dictionary
Inequality	$w_{Ai} \neq w_{Bj}$	Equal granularity | less granularity | greater granularity | no correspondence	when w_{Ai} does not have equality, belonging and inclusion word sense in *B* dictionary, w_{Ai} has no corresponding word sense in *B* dictionary.
Belonging	$w_{Ai} \subset w_{Bj}$	Less granularity	w_{Ai} granularity less than w_{Bj}
Inclusion	$w_{Ai} \supset w_{Bj}$	Great granularity	w_{Ai} granularity greater than w_{Bj}

3 Algorithm of Word Sense Alignment

Definition and example sentence are the common attributes of word sense descriptions in DCC and GKB, which use natural language sentences or phrases and word sense usage examples to describe the semantic meaning of words. 99% of word senses in DCC have definitions, 50% of word senses have example sentences. 97% of "义项(*sense*)" or "备注(*remark*)" fields of the word sense in GKB are not empty. The words of intersection words of DCC and GKB have 40,936 word senses in GKB. Therefore, it can be considered that the word sense distinction of the two dictionaries can be expressed through definitions and example sentences. In this paper, word senses are automatically matched by calculating the similarity of the definitions and the example sentences of DCC and GKB.

The algorithm framework of word sense automatic alignment is described as Algorithm 1. Firstly, we get words set *DCC_words_pos* and *GKB_words_pos* from DCC and GKB according to part-of-speech respectively, and then get intersection and difference sets on *DCC_words_pos* and *GKB_words_pos*. Secondly, the individual word senses alignment table of the intersection words is constructed according to Eq. (1), and the individual words alignment is calculated based on the similarity of definitions and the example sentences. Finally, according to the individual word sense alignment, the word sense granularity correspondence is calculated.

Algorithm 1. Word sense automatic alignment algorithm

Input:
DCC and GKB
Output:
individual word sense alignment, word sense granularity correspondence
Process:
Get words set DCC_words_pos and GKB_words_pos
Get $DCC - GKB$, $GKB - DCC$, $DCC \cap GKB$
Construct $DCC \cap GKB$ individual word sense alignment table
Calculate the individual word sense alignment
Calculate the word sense granularity correspondence

3.1 Individual Word Sense Alignment Calculation

Let the current word be $w \in DCC \cap GKB$. The pseudocode for calculating the individual word sense alignment is shown in Algorithm 2. The algorithm firstly calculates similarity of word senses based on definitions and example sentences, and then automatically judges the alignment "equality", "inequality" and "uncertainty" according to the similarity of word senses. The individual word sense alignment "inclusion" and "belonging" are judged by human based on the similarity.

Algorithm 2. Calculating individual word senses alignment of *w* in DCC and GKB

Input:
word *w*, DCC and GKB
Output:
individual word sense alignment table for *w*
Process:

```
Find all word senses sets S_DCC(w) and S_GKB(w) for w in DCC and GKB;
for ds in S_DCC(w):
   for gs in S_GKB(w):
     sim=Similary(ds, gs)
        if sim==1: Mark the alignment between ds and gs as "equality"
              else if sim==0: Mark the alignment between ds and gs as "inequali-ty"
        else: Mark the alignment between ds and gs as "uncertainty"
   end for
end for
```

The core of the individual word senses alignment algorithm is calculation of word senses similarity based on the definitions and the example sentences. Assume that the word senses of the word *w* in DCC and GKB are *ds* and *gs*, the similarity of *ds* and *gs* is the maximum value of the definition similarity and the example sentences similarity, as Eq. (3) described:

$$Similary(ds, gs) = max(Sim_{def}(ds, gs), Sim_{example}(ds, gs)) \tag{3}$$

Where Sim_{def} is the similarity of definitions, and $Sim_{example}$ is the similarity of example sentences.

Assuming that the definitions' words sequence sets of ds and gs are named as $Def(ds)$ and $Def(gs)$ respectively, the number of words in $Def(ds)$ is n, and the number of words in $Def(gs)$ is d, then $Sim_{def}(ds, gs)$ is defined as Eqs. (4–6):

$$Sim_{def}(ds, gs) = Sim_{sentence}(Def(ds), Def(gs)) \tag{4}$$

$$Sim_{sentence}(x, y) = \begin{cases} max(sim(x^{(i)}, y)), n > d, i \in [1, n-d+1] \\ \frac{\sum_{k=1}^{n} max_m\, sim_w(x_k, y_m)}{n}, n \leq d \\ -1, n = 0 || d = 0 \end{cases} \tag{5}$$

$$\mathrm{sim}\left(x^{(i)}, \mathrm{y}\right) = \frac{\sum_{j=1}^{d} \max_{m} sim_w\left(x_j^{(i)}, y_m\right)}{d} \tag{6}$$

Where the superscript i represents a local word sequence of length d that starts from the i-th word of sequence x, the subscript j represents the j-th word in a local word sequence and the subscript k is the k-th word in x. The subscript m represents the m-th word in y. sim_w is the word similarity that is calculated based on the semems of HowNet [12]:

$$sim_w(w_1, w_2) = max(sim_c(c_{1i}, c_{2j})) \tag{7}$$

$$sim_c(s_1, s_2) = \sum_{i=1}^{4} \beta_i \prod_{k=1}^{i} sim_{set}(s_1, s_2)^k \tag{8}$$

$$sim_{set}(X, Y) = \frac{\frac{\sum_{i=1}^{l_X} max(sim_p(X_i, Y_j))}{l_X} + \frac{\sum_{i=1}^{l_Y} max(sim_p(Y_i, X_j))}{l_Y}}{2} \tag{9}$$

$$sim_p(x, y) = \frac{dis(x, y)}{\alpha + dis(x, y)} \tag{10}$$

$$dis(x, y) = \cos(\theta(\overrightarrow{p_x}, \overrightarrow{p_y})) = \frac{\overrightarrow{p_x} \cdot \overrightarrow{p_y}}{||\overrightarrow{p_x}||||\overrightarrow{p_y}||} \tag{11}$$

$$\vec{p} = cM\vec{p} + (1 - c)\vec{v} \tag{12}$$

$$M_{yx} = \begin{cases} \frac{IC_y}{\sum_{k \in Out(x)} IC_k}, & There\ is\ a\ connection\ between\ sememe\ x\ and\ y \\ 0, & There\ is\ no\ connection\ between\ sememe\ x\ and\ y \end{cases} \tag{13}$$

Each word in HowNet is represented by one or more sense items, and each sense item is described by four types of sememes. The sense items set of w_1 and w_2 are c_1, c_2

respectively, where $c_{1i} \in c_1$, $c_{2j} \in c_2$; β_i are adjustable parameters, and $\beta1 + \beta2 + \beta3 + \beta4 = 1$, $\beta1 \geq \beta2 \geq \beta3 \geq \beta4$; $sim_{set}(X, Y)$ is the similarity of the sememes collection X and Y, sim_p is the sememe similarity, $\vec{p}$ is the sememe vector, and M_{yx} is the transfer matrix. *SIC* is the sememe information capacity descried as Eq. (14):

$$SIC_s = \frac{\log(deep(s)) + 1}{\log(deep_{max} + 1)} \times \left(1 - \frac{\log\left(\sum_{a \in hypo(s)} \frac{1}{deep(a)} + 1\right)}{\log(node_{max})}\right) \tag{14}$$

Where $deep(s)$ represents layer number where the sememe node s is located in the sememe structure graph whose root node is the first layer; $deep_{max}$ is the layer number of the last layer, and $hypo(s)$ is the set consisting of all the descendant sememes of the sememe s; $node_{max}$ is the total number of sememe nodes.

In DCC and GKB, an example sentence usually consists of multiple clauses. For example, the example sentence of the adjective "实在(*shizai*)" in DCC is "*~的本事|心眼儿~(the skill of the ~ |heart ~)*" includes two clauses "*~的本事(the skill of the ~)*" and "*心眼儿~(heart ~)*". Example sentence of "实在(*shizai*)" in GKB is "*她工作做得很~/他干活~(She works very ~ / He works ~)*" that also includes two clauses "*她工作做得很~(She works very ~)*" and "*他干活~(He works ~)*". Therefore, the example sentence similarity should consider the similarity of each clause. Assuming that the clause word sequence sets of example sentence *ds* and example sentence *gs* are $Examples(ds)$ and $Examples(gs)$ respectively. The example sentence similarity $Sim_{example}(ds, gs)$ is defined as Eq. (15), where *en* and *ed* are the number of clauses in $Examples(ds)$ and $Examples(gs)$, $i \in [1, en], j \in [1, ed]$.

$$Sim_{example}(ds, gs) = \begin{cases} -1, & en = 0 \ or \ ed = 0 \\ \frac{\sum_{j=1}^{ed} \max_{i \in en}\left(sim_{sentence}\left(Examples(ds)^{(i)}, Examples(gs)^{(j)}\right)\right)}{\text{ed}}, & else \end{cases} \tag{15}$$

3.2 Word Sense Granularity Correspondence Calculation

According to the individual word sense alignment, we can further analyze the word sense granularity correspondence of *w* in the dictionary. The algorithm pseudo code is shown in Algorithm 3. Algorithm 3 constructs sets to store senses with a variety of word sense granularity correspondence. The elements in set *sameSet* have the equal granularity in DCC and GKB; the word sense granularity of elements in *DCCASet* in DCC is larger than that in GKB; the word sense granularity of elements in *DCCBSet* in DCC is less than that in GKB; the word senses in *DCCNullSet* have no correspond word sense in GKB; the word senses in *GKBNullSet* have no correspond word sense in DCC.

Algorithm 3. Calculating the word sense granularity alignment

Input:
word w, individual word sense alignment table
Output:
word sense granularity for words w in DCC and GKB
Process:
Find out the relevant record set S in the individual word sense alignment table in w;
for $record$ in S:
  if the alignment of $record$ is "equality":
    put $record.ds.id$ into $DCCsameSet$
    put $record.gs.id$ into $GKBsameSet$
  else if the alignment of $record$ is "inclusion":
    put $record.ds.id$ into $DCCASet$
    put $record.gs.id$ into $GKBBSet$
  else if the alignment of $record$ is "belonging":
    put $record.ds.id$ into $DCCBSet$
    put $record.gs.id$ into $GKBASet$
  else if alignment of $record$ is "inequality":
    if $record.ds.id \notin DCCsameSet, DCCASet, DCCBSet$:
      put $record.ds.id$ into $DCCNullSet$
    if $record.gs.id \notin GKBsameSet, GKBASet, GKBBSet$:
      put $record.gs.id$ into $GKBNullSet$
end for

3.3 Individual Word Sense Alignment Table

In this paper, the word sense alignment algorithm and the manual proofreading are used to construct the table of individual word sense alignment of intersection words of DCC and GKB, as shown in Fig. 1.

词语	义项编码	拼音	词性	义项释义	示例	gkb_词语	gkb_词类	gkb_拼音	gkb_同形	gkb_释义	gkb_例句	映射关系	相似度
实在	XH5@0103	shízài	形	诚实；不虚	~的本	实在	a	shi2zai5	B	工作扎实,!	她工作做得	不等于	0.52
实在	XH5@0103	shízài	形	诚实；不虚	~的本	实在	a	shi2zai4	A	诚实;不虚	他是个~人	等于	0.75
实在	XH5@0201	shízài	形	<口>(工作	工作做	实在	a	shi2zai5	B	工作扎实,!	她工作做得	等于	0.71
实在	XH5@0201	shízài	形	<口>(工作	工作做	实在	a	shi2zai4	A	诚实;不虚	他是个~人	不等于	0.70
平易	XH5@0102	píngyì	形	(性情或态度	~近人	平易	a	ping2yi4	1	谦虚和蔼	~可亲	等于	1.00
平易	XH5@0102	píngyì	形	(性情或态度	~近人	平易	a	ping2yi4	2	(文章)浅近	写得很~	不等于	0.63
平易	XH5@0102	píngyì	形	(文章)浅近	语言简	平易	a	ping2yi4	1	谦虚和蔼	~可亲	不等于	0.57
平易	XH5@0102	píngyì	形	(文章)浅近	语言简	平易	a	ping2yi4	2	(文章)浅近	写得很~	等于	1.00

Fig. 1. Examples of individual word sense alignment

There are 14 attributes in the individual word sense alignment table, including six attributes("词语(*words*), 义项编码(*sense codes*), 拼音(*pinyin*), 词性(*part of speech*), 义项释义(*definition*), and 示例(*example sentence*)") from DCC and six attributes ("gkb_词语(*words*), gkb_词类(*parts of speech*), gkb_拼音(*pinyin*), gkb_同形(*homomorphism*), gkb_释义(*definition*), gkb_例句(*example sentences*)") from GKB. The other two attributes are word sense alignment attributes, which are "映射关系(*alignment*)" and "相似度(*similarity*)". They record the individual word sense alignment and similarity respectively.

The individual word sense alignment table includes 55,144 individual word sense alignment relations, including 5,878 "等于(*equality*)" or "不等于(*inequality*)" relations and 49,266 "不确定(*uncertainty*)" relationships. There are 19,412 word sense with similarities between (0,1) in the "uncertainty" relationship, and their alignment may be "inequality, belonging, inclusion and uncertainty". We fail to calculate the similarity of 29,954 word senses due to the lack of definitions or example sentences. Individual word sense alignment labeled "不确定(*uncertainty*)" requires manual proofreading. In this research, we manually proofread the individual word senses alignment of noun, verb and adjective, the total of 40,526 items.

4 Word Sense Alignment Analysis

This paper uses the word sense alignment algorithm to automatically construct the table of construct the individual word sense alignment. The individual word sense alignments of nouns, verbs and adjectives are manually proofread. The statistical results of the individual word sense alignment and word sense granularity correspondence are shown in Table 6 and Table 7 (the meaning of columns "1-1, 1-m, m-1, m-m" in Table 7 is described in Table 4).

56.2% of the words in DCC and GKB with the same word granularity are monosemic words in both dictionaries. In addition to the word sense with equality granularity, there are also "no correspondence", "greater" and "less" word sense granularity correspondence between DCC and GKB.

"No correspondence" means that the word sense appears only in DCC or GKB. At present, the word sense with "no correspondence" granularity includes 57,236 difference word senses and 3,864 intersection word senses. For example, the word senses "下岗(*xiagang*)*XH5@010201*", "不屑(*buxie*)*XH5@010202*" and "再说(*zaishuo*) *XH5@010201*" in DCC and the word senses "而且(*erqie*)" and "倾(*qing*)2" in GKB's have no equivalent sense in another dictionary.

DCC's word sense granularity is basically less than GKB's, but there are also some word senses granularity in DCC larger than that in GKB. For example, the granularity of word sense "套票(*taopiao*)*XH5@010101*" in DCC is larger than word sense "套票(*taopiao*)1" and "套票(*taopiao*)2" in GKB.

Table 6. Statistical of word sense alignment (statistics by POS)

Individual word sense alignment	Equality	Inequality			Inclusion	Belonging	Uncertainty
Word sense granularity correspondance	Word sense equal		GKB has no correspondence	DCC has no correspondence	Greater	Less	
名词(noun)	1,884	1,263	118	898	76	1,641	18,211
动词(verb)	2,408	3,778	267	2,113	92	2,489	5,055
形容词(adjective)	638	352	8	309	4	834	922
副词(adverb)	177	19	15	18			7
介词(preposition)	15	5	2	5			0
量词(quantifier)	120	32	28	26			49
拟声词(onomatopoeia)	52	0	0	0			6
助词(particle)	15	6	0	6			5
代词(pronoun)	33	1	1	1			4
数词(numeral)	8	0	0	0			19
连词(conjunction)	31	17	16	15			33
叹词(interjection)	33	1	1	1			0
未(undefine)	34	0	0	0			3,489
缀(affix)	3	8	8	8			3
Total	5,451	5,483	464	3,400	172	4,964	27,803

Table 7. Statistics of word sense alignment of intersection words of DCC and GKB (according to the number of word senses alignment)

Individual word sense alignment	Equality	Inequality			Inclusion	Belonging	Uncertainty
Word sense granularity correspondence	Equality		GKB has no correspondence	DCC has no correspondence	Greater	Less	
1-1	3,100	34	34	34	1	0	21,800
1-m	45	49	49	16	56	0	1
m-1	1,328	2,118	69	2,118	29	4,544	5,974
m-m	978	3,170	312	1,232	86	420	28
Total	5,451	5,371	464	3,400	171	4,964	27,803

There are 49,266 individual word sense alignment with "uncertainty". There are two reasons cause "uncertainty" individual word sense alignment. (1) The definitions or example sentences in DCC and GKB are blank; (2) some example sentences' semantic meaning in GKB are ambiguous.

The word sense alignment algorithm proposed in this paper is based on the similarity of definitions or example sentences. However, there are no definitions or example sentences for some of the word senses in DCC and GKB. Therefore, the similarity cannot be calculated, and the word sense alignment cannot be confirmed. For example, the definition and example sentence of verb "圈(*quan*)" in GKB are both empty (Fig. 2), so its word sense similarity between DCC and GKB is meaningless, and the individual word sense correspondence is "不确定(*uncertainty*)".

词语	义项编码	拼音	词性	义项释义	示例	gkb_词语	gkb_词类	gkb_拼音	gkb_同形	gkb_释义	gkb_例句	映射关系
圈	XH5@0102	juān	动	用栅栏把	把鸡–起来	圈	v	quan1	B			不确定
圈	XH5@0304	quān	动	在四周加上	–地|用篱笆	圈	v	quan1	B			不确定

Fig. 2. Examples of word senses with blank definitions and example sentences

Some word senses in GKB don't have definitions but have example sentences, but the word sense cannot be distinguished according to the example sentences, as shown in Fig. 3. The example sentences of "乔迁(*qiaoqian*)" and "侨居(*qiaoju*)" in GKB are usage descriptions that cannot explain their word senses. The example sentence of "车(*che*)" contains the example sentence of the verb, and the sense alignment between noun "车(*che*)" in DCC and GKB cannot be determined.

词语	义项编码	拼音	词性	义项释义	示例	gkb_词语	gkb_词类	gkb_拼音	gkb_同形	gkb_释义	gkb_例句	映射关系
乔迁	XH5@0101	qiáoqiān	动	《诗经小	–之喜	乔迁	v	qiao2qiar			只带处所宾语	不等于
侨居	XH5@0101	qiáojū	动	在外国居	–海外	侨居	v	qiao2ju1			只带处所的语	不等于
车	XH5@0101	chē	名	陆地上有	火–|汽	车	n	che1	A		马–/–轮子/––个螺丝钉(v)	不确定

Fig. 3. Examples of GKB example sentences that are not easy to discriminate

5 Conclusion

In this paper, the individual word sense alignment is divided into five types: equality, inequality, belonging, inclusion and uncertain. The word granularity correspondence is divided into four classes: equality, greater, less and no correspondence. We designed an automatic algorithm for word senses alignment based on definitions and example sentences. We used this algorithm to construct individual word sense alignment table of intersection words of DCC and GKB, manually corrected the word sense alignment of nouns, verbs, and adjectives, and analyzed the correspondence of word sense granularity. The results showed that 84.8% and 97% of words in DCC and GKB are monosemy. 33.9% and 46% of words appeared in DCC and GKB respectively. The intersection words of DCC or GKB accounted for 66% of DCC and 53.7% of GKB respectively, 81.6% of intersection words are monosemy in both dictionaries. There are more than 50,000 individual word sense alignments between DCC and GKB. Because of the shortage of the algorithm and the lack of definitions and example sentences, at least half of word senses correspondence cannot automatically determined, but require manual proofreading. Through the preliminary analysis, it has been found that the alignment between DCC and GKB is complex, and little of word sense granularity is completely "equal". The word sense granularity of GKB is generally larger than that of DCC. There are word senses with "no correspondence" in DCC and GKB. The description granularity of word sense in DCC is finer, but GKB is more abundant in the usage description of words. The integration of DCC and GKB with word sense alignment is more conducive for the computer to accomplish natural language processing tasks such as WSD.

References

1. Xiao, H.: The sense relations and sense distinction of polysemy in the dictionary. J. Yunnan Normal Univ. **42**(1), 41–46 (2016). (Philosophy and Social Science Edition), (in Chinese)
2. Chinese Academy of Social Sciences Language Institute Dictionary Room: Dictionary of Contemporary Chinese, 5th edn. The Commercial Press, Beijing (2005). (in Chinese)
3. Yu, S.W.: Detailed explanation of Contemporary Chinese Grammatical Knowledge Base. Tsinghua University Press, Beijing (2003). (in Chinese)
4. Mei, J.J., Zhu, Y.M., Gao, Y.Q.: Synonym word forest, 2nd edn. Shanghai Lexicographical Publishing House, Shanghai (1996). (In Chinese)
5. Dong, Z.D., Dong, Q.: The study of the Hownet and Chinese. Contemp. Linguist. **3**(1), 33–44 (2016). (in Chinese)
6. Jing, P., Wu, Y.F., Yu, S.W.: Survey of word sense annotated corpus construction. J. Chin. Inf. Process. **22**(3), 16–23 (2008). (in Chinese)
7. Miller, G.A., Leacock, C., Tengi, R., et al.: A semantic concordance. In: The Workshop on Human Language Technology, pp. 303–308 (2018)
8. Ng, H.T., Lee, H.B.: Integrating multiple knowledge sources to disambiguate word sense: an exemplar-based approach. In: Proceedings of the 34th Annual Meeting on Association for Computational Linguistics, pp. 40–47. Association for Computational Linguistics (1996)
9. Wu, Y., Jin, P., Zhang, Y., Yu, S.: A Chinese corpus with word sense annotation. In: Matsumoto, Y., Sproat, Richard W., Wong, K.-F., Zhang, M. (eds.) ICCPOL 2006. LNCS (LNAI), vol. 4285, pp. 414–421. Springer, Heidelberg (2006). https://doi.org/10.1007/11940098_43
10. Xiao, H., Yang, L.J.: Dictionary informed corpus word sense annotation. Appl. Linguist. **2**, 135–141 (2010). (in Chinese)

11. Qiu, L.K., Zhao, H., Yu, S.W., et al.: Analysis of parts-of-speech correspondence between DCC an GKB. J. Chin. Inf. Process. **31**(5), 1–7 (2017). (in Chinese)
12. Li, H., Mu, L., Zan, H.: Computation of word similarity based on the information content of Sememes and PageRank algorithm. Chinese Lexical Semantics. LNCS (LNAI), vol. 10085, pp. 416–425. Springer, Cham (2016). https://doi.org/10.1007/978-3-319-49508-8_39

The Study of the Homoatomic Quasi Fixed Phrase

Chengyu Du and Pengyuan Liu(✉)

School of Information Science, Beijing Language and Cultural University, No. 5 Xueyuan Road 15, 100083 Beijing, China
2550611409@qq.com, liupengyuan@pku.edu.cn

Abstract. The quasi fixed phrase is situated between the fixed phrase and the free phrase. The research on the quasi fixed phrases mainly focused on a common format of the quasi fixed phrases to explore the use of law and historical evolution. However, there is little research on categories of the quasi fixed phrase, so this paper is based on large corpus and studies the homoatomic quasi fixed phrase, which is a special category of the quasi fixed phrases. The homoatomic quasi fixed phrase is a phrase that has the same fixed components. Through this study, we found that the fixed components of the homoatomic quasi fixed phrases will limit the POS of the replaceable components and the semantic relations between two replaceable components prefer to be similar or opposite. In addition, the frequency of the fixed components is related to the frequency of the phrase itself.

Keywords: Homoatomic quasi fixed phrase · Choice of POS
Semantic relation

1 Introduction

The quasi fixed phrase is a linguistic unit between fixed phrase and free phrase. In form, the quasi fixed phrase is similar to the idiom, but quasi fixed phrase are not more stable than idioms, and some components can be temporarily replaced according to the needs of communication; in the meaning, the fixed components of quasi fixed phrases stipulates the meaning of format and relation of the whole phrase, and the replaceable components of quasi fixed phrases express the concrete and practical meaning of the whole phrase. On the syllable, the quasi fixed phrase is compact and mainly four syllables. The research object of this paper is a special category of the quasi fixed phrase: the homoatomic quasi fixed phrase. The homoatomic quasi fixed phrase is a phrase that has the same fixed components, such as "半人半兽/half man and half best", "半真半假/half true half fake".

Predecessors have done many researches on quasi fixed phrases:

First, the raising of quasi fixed phrases. In the analysis of the language phenomenon of Chinese, Zhiwei Lu [1] discovered the Chinese character of the internal organization of the four word phrase, that is, there is not only a phrase like "能工巧匠/skilled craftsmen", but also a pair of two words, such as "不三不四/indecent", "东说西说/keep talking" in Chinese. Lu called these phrases

J.-F. Hong et al. (Eds.): CLSW 2018, LNAI 11173, pp. 789–800, 2018.
https://doi.org/10.1007/978-3-030-04015-4_68

"并立四字格/four words phrase" which is related to the quasi fixed phrases, but the scope of the study of the quasi fixed phrases is not limited to this; Liu [2] puts forward the "fixed phrase-to-be" that refers to those phrases that are not fixed phrases but have most of the characteristics of a fixed phrase, the structure pattern of these phrases is relatively fixed, and the meaning of the phrase is relatively simple; Wen [3] first proposed the name of the quasi fixed phrases, which are similar to idioms and have specific formats and functions.

Since the concept of "quasi fixed phrase" was put forward, many scholars began to notice and study this kind of language unit between fixed phrase and free phrase. Qi [4] studied the fixed components of quasi fixed phrases and divided them into two components and three components. Chen and Li [5] counted 300 kinds of formats of quasi fixed phrases in modern Chinese and divided them into five basic types, such as even-position embedded type, odd-position embedded type and so on. They also establish a corpus of more than 6,000 quasi fixed phrases.

In addition, there is research on some common formats of quasi fixed phrases. Shao [6, 7] studied the semantics and order of "半A半B/half A half B", "一A一B/one A one B" and "没A没B/no A no B". Wang [8] studied the "一A就C/A as soon as B", Li [9] studied the "V来V去/V all the time". In addition to the above academic papers, a large number of books on specific formats have appeared.

The above research on quasi fixed phrases and common formats of quasi fixed phrases has reached a certain level in terms of scope and depth. However, the study of quasi fixed phrases should not be limited to the comparative analysis of a certain format, but should be from the whole system of quasi fixed phrases and study the categories of quasi fixed phrases to mine the generality between categories and the general rules of the quasi fixed phrase. In this paper, we study the homoatomic quasi fixed phrase which is a special category of quasi fixed phrases and find out the characteristics of these phrases.

The following chapters are arranged as follows: the second chapter is the research object, data and method; the third chapter is an overall analysis of 11 formats; the fourth chapter reveals the relation between the POS of replaceable components and fixed components; the fifth chapter reveals the semantic relation between the two replaceable components; the sixth chapter reveals the relation between fixed components and the frequency and generation ability of the format; the seventh chapter summarizes the full paper and proposes the prospect.

2 Research Objects, Data and Methods

2.1 Research Objects

According to the statistics, it is found that the homoatomic quasi fixed phrase is even-position embedded type, that is, the first and the third positions of the four word phrase are the same fixed components, and the second and the fourth positions are the replaceable components. For the sake of argument, this paper uses the letter XAXB to represent the homoatomic quasi fixed phrase.

The research object of this paper is 11 formats of homoatomic quasi fixed phrase in the Modern Chinese Dictionary [10], which are: "半 A 半 B/half A half B", "不 A不 B/neither A nor B", "大 A 大 B/A and B hardly", "非 A 非 B/not A not B", "没 A 没 B/no A no B", "且 A 且 B/A and B", "随 A 随 B/A as soon as B", "无 A 无 B/noA no B", "现 A 现 B/A as soon as B", "一A一B/one A one B", "有 A 有 B/have A and B".

2.2 Data

Peking University Chinese Linguistics Research Center (CCL) Corpus.

2.3 Methods

According to Lv [11], the phenomenon of modern Chinese double syllables and four syllables is dominant. This article focuses on the analysis of four syllable phrases. In the CCL corpus, 2482 phrases are selected, then these phrases are analyzed and interpreted by a combination of descriptive and explanatory methods to find the characteristics of the homoatomic quasi fixed phrases.

3 Overall Analysis of 11 Formats

The POS of the replaceable components of 11 formats maybe verbs, adjectives, nouns, distinguishing words, quantifiers, pronouns, and numerals. Most of the replaceable components are verbs, adjectives and verbs. Only a few replacement parts can be numeral, pronoun and quantifier. The specific situation is shown in Fig. 1.

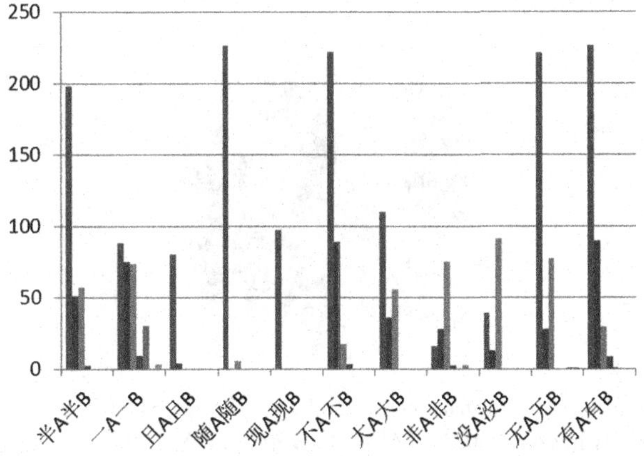

Fig. 1. The POS of the replaceable components of 11 formats. The 7 columns in turn are the number of verbs, adjectives, nouns, distinguishing words, quantifiers, pronouns and numerals.

There are two main semantic relations between two replaceable components in the 11 formats: the opposite relation and the similar relation, but the semantic relation between two replaceable components of "随 A 随 B/A as soon as B" and "现 A 现 B/A as soon as B" is special and the A is carried out first, and then B is carried on; In most formats, the semantic relation between A and B is similar rather than opposite, as shown in Fig. 2.

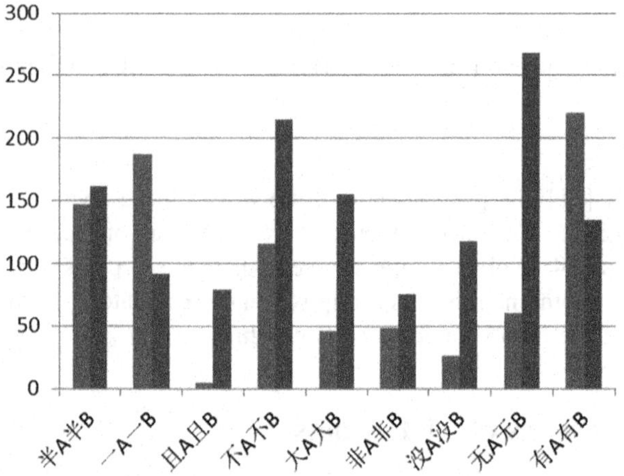

Fig. 2. The semantic relations between two replaceable components in the 11 formats. The first column is the phrase number of similar relation, the second column is the phrase number of opposite relation.

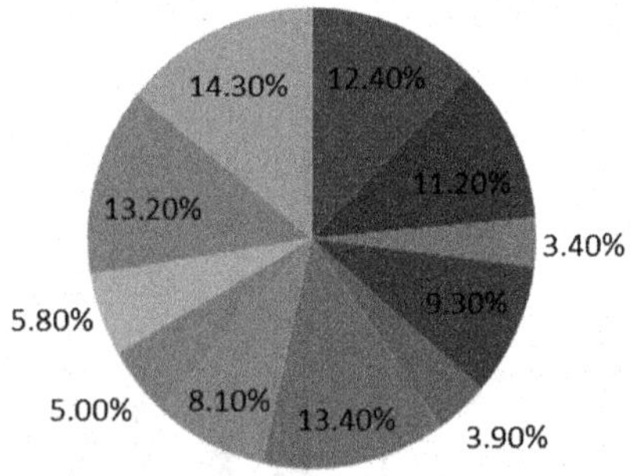

Fig. 3. The proportion of 11 formats on the number of phrases. The number ranges from large to small as "有 A 有 B/have A and B", "不 A 不 B/neither A nor B", "无 A 无 B/no A no B", "半 A 半 B/half A half B", "一A一B/one A one B", "随 A 随 B/A soon as B", "大 A 大 B/A and B hardly", "没 A 没 B/no A no B", "非 A 非 B/not A not B", "现 A 现 B/A as soon as B", "且 A 且 B/A and B".

The proportion of 11 formats on the number of phrases is shown in Fig. 3. Among them, the examples of "半A半B/half A half B" and "不A不B/neither nor B" account for a large proportion, while the examples of "且A且B/A and B" and "非A非B/not A not B A not B" account for a small proportion. What's more, we find that the number of phrases is large if the fixed components of a format are the adverb.

4 The POS of the Replaceable Components

The fixed components of 11 formats are "半/half", "一/one", "且/and", "随/when", "现/when", "不/not", "大/hardly", "非/not", "没/no", "无/no", "有/have". Most of these words are basic words in modern Chinese and they are widely and frequently used. Therefore, the formats made by these words are highly productive and the replaceable components are affected by these words, so the replaceable component shows a strong regularity. Table 1 shows the POS of replacement components.

Table 1. The POS of replacement components.

POS	Format	Phrase number	Proportion
Verb	半A半B、不A不B、大A大B、非A非B、没A没B、且A且B、随A随B、无A无B、现A现B、一A一B、有A有B	1523	61.5%
Adjective	半A半B、不A不B、大A大B、非A非B、没A没B、且A且B、无A无B、一A一B、有A有B	414	16.7%
Noun	半A半B、不A不B、大A大B、非A非B、没A没B、无A无B、一A一B、有A有B	479	19.3%
Distinction word	半A半B、不A不B、非A非B、且A且B、随A随B、现A现B、一A一B、有A有B	24	1.0%
Classifier	有A有B、一A一B	31	1.2%
Pronoun	无A无B、非A非B	3	0.1%
Numeral	无A无B、一A一B	4	0.2%

We can see that the fixed components of 11 formats are mainly adverbs and adverbs often follow verbs, so we can find that the replaceable components are more likely to be verbs in the Fig. 1. In addition, monosyllabic verbs occupy a large proportion in monosyllabic words and the homoatomic quasi fixed phrase are mostly four syllables, so the replaceable components are mainly monosyllabic verbs.

The POS of replaceable components depends on the fixed components of the phrase. The fixed components "且/and", "现/when", "不/not", "没/no", "非/not" are adverbs; "半/half" is an adverb when it means "incomplete" and "大" is an adverb when it means "the degree of something is deep", what's more, "一" can be used before verbs and momentum words to indicate that some action occurs. The POS of these fixed components determines that the replaceable components are verbs or adjectives. However, the "现 A 现 B/A as soon as B" is an exception, the replaceable components can only be a verb. This is because "现/when" is an adverb when it means "temporary", so this meaning restricts it to be followed by adjectives and the replacement components cannot be an adjective. The usage of "随" is the same as "现/when" here. The verbs "无/no" and "有/have" cannot generally be directly followed by adjectives or verbs, so verbs or adjectives that enter the formats of "无 A 无 B/no A no B" and "有 A 有 B/have A and B" are rare, and verbs and adjectives entering this phrases are nominalized, for example,

(1) 我们的人民在法律面前*无贵无贱*、一律平等。
Our people are *no honor and no mean* in law.

(2) 市场形成了一定规模，幕名而来的摊贩和居民越来越多，*有买有卖*，生意日渐红火。

The market has formed a certain scale, so more and more vendors and residents come to the market. *There are buying and selling*, and the business is getting better and better.

In (1), "贵/honorable" and "贱/poor" are not adjectives, but nouns, meaning "honorable people" and "poor people"; in (2), "买/buy" and "卖/sell" represent "people who buy things" and "people who sell things".

"无/no", "非/not", "有/have", "没/no" are verbs and "大/hardly" is an adjective, so they can be used to match nouns themselves; "一" can match nouns when it means "just one" and "whole"; "半/half" can match nouns when it means "in the middle of". Negative adverb "不/no" generally cannot directly match nouns, so there are not many nouns in the "不 A 不 B/neither A nor B". if nouns would enter this phrase, nouns have been used as adjectives or verbs, for example,

(3) 在我们这座*不南不北*的城市里，冬天并没有你想象的那么冷。
In our city, which is *not south or north*, winter is not as cold as you think.

(4) 首长的打扮*不军不民*，首长的头发*不男不女*，首长的表情*不人不鬼*。

The dress of the chief is *neither like soldiers nor people*, and his hair is *neither male nor female*.

In (3) "南/south" and "北/north" are temporarily used as verbs and it means "a place is neither close to the south nor close to the north". in (4), "不军不民" means "a person is neither like the soldier nor like common people", so "军/soldier" means "look like a soldier" and "民/common people" means "look like a common people", they are used as verbs. "不军不民" is the same as "不人不鬼/a person is neither like the people nor like ghost".

The distinguishing words and adjectives are similar. If the fixed components A and B can be adjectives, they can basically be distinguishing words except for the "大A大B/A and B hardly" format. In this format, A and B can be adjectives, but they cannot be distinguishing words. This is because "大/hardly" can only match the adjective when it means "deep", and the distinguishing word cannot match the degree adverb, so the distinguishing word cannot enter the format.

The quantifiers mainly enter the "一A一B/A and B hardly" phrase, because "一/one" is a numeral word, which can be followed by the quantifier. In addition, in the phrase "有分有寸/be in a suitable position", "分" and "寸" are quantifiers, but they have been used as a noun in practical applications. The POS of the replaceable components are few pronouns and numerals, so it is not representative and we will not go into details.

5 Structural Symmetry of the Homoatomic Quasi Fixed Phrase

The semantic relation between two replaceable components in one phrase is opposite relation or similar relation. Ex(5) and ex(6) are opposite relation, ex(7) and ex(8) are similar relation. However, the semantic relation between two replaceable components of "随A随B/A as soon as B" and "现A现B/A as soon as B" is an exception and the A is carried out first, and then B is carried on, such as ex(9) and ex(10).

(5) 即使在文章中存在跑题的现象，在结尾也要尽量把内容往论点上集中，使得这*一头一尾*构成文章的核心。

Even if there is a problem in the article, try to concentrate the content on the argument at the end and make *the beginning and the ending* the core of the article.

(6) 母亲做医生经常*没日没夜*，父亲承担了很多家务事。
My mother often worked as a doctor *day and night*, and my father did a lot of housework.

(7) 我不过是赚了点钱，我并*没偷没抢*!
I just made a bit of money, and I *didn't steal and rob it.*

(8) 经过一场*大劫大难*，孙悟空终于大彻大悟，最终重振雄风，歼灭群妖，喜登灵山，完成取经大业。

After a big catastrophe, Sun Wukong finally *realized the great glory*, and finally revived the glory, annihilated the group of demon, hid the Lingshan, and completed the great cause.

(9) 宰杀日期更是至关重要，要*现杀现卖*，立即上市。
The date of slaughter is even more important. It is necessary to *kill and sell now*, and to go public immediately.

(10) 加强列车卫生工作，做到*随脏随扫*，及时清理。
Strengthen the train health work, so that it can *be cleaned with the dirt* and cleaned up in time.

According to Table 2, we can see that the opposite relation and the similar relation are the majority, accounting for 87%, which is largely related to the principle of "iconicity" in language [12].

Table 2. The semantic relation between two replacement components.

	Opposite relation	Similar relation	Others	Total
Phrase number	855	1300	323	2478
Proportion	34.5%	52.5%	13%	100%

The principle of iconicity is an important principle in cognitive linguistics [13]. Haiman (1985) defined the function of iconicity as follows: "when a language expression is parallel to the concept, experience or communication strategy encoded by this expression in terms of appearance, length, complexity and various interrelations between components, we say that the language expression has similar properties." Symmetric iconicity means that the concept of symmetry is corresponding to the symmetrical language form, and there are many symmetrical concepts in language, such as mutual relations, simultaneous events, interdependent events, alternating events, etc. However because of the linear principle of language, symmetry seems to be one of the most difficult concepts to be expressed in a language. In this regard, Haiman puts forward different opinions. He thought the concept of symmetry is still the easiest in human language and is one of the most often expressed in image in spite of the limitation of linear features. The fixed components of phrases are the same, and the semantic relations between the replaceable components are similar or opposite, which are related to the iconicity principle of the language.

6 The Relation Between Fixed Components and Frequency and Generation Capacity of Format

In this paper, the fixed components and formats are put into the CCL corpus for retrieval. The frequency of the fixed components and formats are shown in the following Table 3:

Column C represents the number of phrases produced by the format, Column D represents the total frequency of a format, and Column E represents the frequency of fixed component.

Statistical significance test was conducted to obtain Table 4:

Table 3. The frequency of the fixed components and formats

Format	C	D	E	Format	C	D	E
半A半B	308	2192	183096	大A大B	201	11644	2003727
一A一B	278	39820	3199401	非A非B	123	533	313327
且A且B	84	212	199702	没A没B	143	2619	576666
随A随B	231	1796	182073	无A无B	328	10084	475056
现A现B	97	1287	917488	有A有B	354	21773	2320898
不A不B	331	57374	2195655				

Table 4. The result of the statistical significance test

		C	D	E
C	Pearson	1	0.599	0.449
	Sig	278	0.052	0.166
	N	11	11	11
D	Pearson	0.599	1	0.806
	Sig	0.052		0.003
	N	11	11	11
E	Pearson	0.449	0.806	1
	Sig	0.166	0.003	
	N	11	11	11

It can be seen from the above table that the frequency of fixed components is significantly correlated with the frequency of format, that is, the higher the frequency of fixed components is, the higher the frequency of format. In addition, the number of phrase produced by format represent the generating ability of the format and it is not related to the frequency of fixed components and the frequency of format, that is because some phrases are temporarily replaced by some components according to the needs of communication. Some phrases are no longer used after the task of communication, or the frequency of use is very low, but they are also treated as homoatomic quasi fixed phrases, such as "有贬有升/some go up or down", "一滞一俏/One is slow to sell and one is hot", "不盈不亏/no profit and no loss". They are used in special occasions and are not used after one use, but they are still the homoatomic quasi fixed phrases. Their presence causes that the generating ability of the format is not related to the frequency of fixed components and the frequency of format.

7 Summary

This paper uses a large scale corpus as a tool and a combination of descriptive and explanatory as methods to study the homoatomic quasi fixed phrases. Through this study, we find that the homoatomic quasi fixed phrases have their own unique characteristics. Different fixed components of the format not only cause different frequency of the format, but also limit the POS of the replaceable components. Most of the fixed components are adverbs or verbs, so most of the replaceable components are verbs, adjectives and nouns, among which the verbs account for the largest proportion. In terms of semantics, there are two main semantic relations between the replaceable components A and B, which are similar relation and opposite relation, but "随 A 随 B/A as soon as B", "现 A 现 B/A as soon as B" are special. The replaceable components of "随 A 随 B/A as soon as B" and "现 A 现 B/A as soon as B" are two verbs with sequential order. In these three kinds of situations, the number of phrases whose semantic relations are close and opposite is the majority, which is related to the iconicity principle in cognition.

Compared with fixed phrases, the current study about the homoatomic quasi fixed phrases needs to be strengthened. In the future, the study of the homoatomic quasi fixed phrases can focus on the five categories to mine the generality between categories and find the general rules of the quasi fixed phrases.

Acknowledgments. This work is supported by the MOE (Ministry of Education in China) Project of Humanities and Social Sciences (Project No. 18YJA740030) and the Fundamental Research Funds for the Central Universities, and the Research Funds of Beijing Language and Culture University (Project No. 18YCX005).

Appendix: The POS and Semantic Relation of 11 Formats

Format	POS	Opposite relation	Similar relation	Phrase number	Proportion
半A半B	Verb	89	109	198	64.3%
	Adjective	36	15	51	16.6%
	Noun	20	37	57	18.5%
	Distinction word	2	0	2	0.6%
	Total	147	161	308	100%
一A一B	Verb	69	19	88	31.7%
	Adjective	75	0	75	27.0%
	Noun	34	39	73	26.3%
	Distinction word	9	0	9	3.2%
	Classifier	0	30	30	10.8%
	Numeral	0	3	3	1.0%
	Total	187	91	278	100%
且A且B	Adjective	0	4	4	4.8%
	Verb	5	75	80	95.2%
	Total	5	79	84	100%
随A随B	Noun	0	5	5	2.2%
	Verb			226	97.8%
	Total			231	100%
现A现B	Verb			97	100%
	Total			97	100%
不A不B	Verb	40	182	222	67.1%
	Adjective	63	26	89	26.9%
	Noun	10	7	17	5.1%
	Distinction word	3	0	3	0.9%
	Total	116	215	331	100%
大A大B	Verb	32	78	110	54.7%
	Adjective	11	25	36	17.9%
	Noun	3	52	55	27.4%
	Total	46	155	201	100%
非A非B	Verb	11	5	16	13%
	Adjective	21	7	28	22.8%
	Noun	14	61	75	61%
	Distinction word	2	0	2	1.6%
	Pronoun	0	2	2	1.6%
	Total	48	75	123	100%
没A没B	Verb	5	34	39	27.3%
	Adjective	13	0	13	9.1%
	Noun	8	83	91	63.6%
	Total	26	117	143	100%
无A无B	Verb	21	200	221	67.4%
	Adjective	20	8	28	8.5%
	Noun	19	58	77	23.5%
	Pronoun	0	1	1	0.3%
	Numeral	0	1	1	0.3%
	Total	60	268	328	100%
有A有B	Verb	105	121	226	63.8%
	Adjective	87	3	90	25.4%
	Noun	20	9	29	8.2%
	Classifier	0	1	1	0.3%
	Distinction word	8	0	8	2.3%
	Total	220	134	354	100%

References

1. Lu, Z.: Chinese four words. Chinese Research (1956). (in Chinese)
2. Liu, S.: Fixed Phrases and Their Categories. Linguistic Theory (1982). (in Chinese)
3. Wen, L.: Fixed phrases and quasi fixed phrases. Teaching Chinese in the World, 65–67 (1988). (in Chinese)
4. Qi, H.: Questions about Quasi fixed phrases. Rhetoric Study, 2–8 (2001). (in Chinese)
5. Chen, C., Li, C.: A study of quasi fixed phrases in Modern Chinese. Xue Lin Publishing House (2012). (in Chinese)
6. Shao, J., Cui, S.: The order and semantics of the "One A One B" Frame Structure. Contemporary Rhetoric, 74–79 (2010). (in Chinese)
7. Shao, J., Yuan, Z.: The semantic increment and derogatory tendency of "No A No B" frame structure. Chinese Research, pp. 7–10 (2010). (in Chinese)
8. Wang, H.: The study of "Once A Then C". Chin. Lang., 134–140 + 191–192 (2001). (in Chinese)
9. Li, J.: "V Comes to V" Format and Its Grammaticalization. Language Research, 63–69 (2002). (in Chinese)
10. Chinese Academy Of Social, I.O.L.S.: Modern Chinese Dictionary, 7th edn. Commercial Press (2016). (in Chinese)
11. Liu, S.: The Problem of Monosyllabic Syllables in Modern Chinese. Chinese Language (1963). (in Chinese)
12. Chinese Academy Of Social, I.O.L.S.: Modern Chinese Dictionary, 7th edn. Commercial Press (2016). (in Chinese)
13. You, S.: A Cognitive Analysis of "Half A Half B" Format. Jinan University (2010). (in Chinese)

The Attention to Safety Issues from Mainland China and Taiwan

Shan Wang[1(✉)] and Xinyan Wang[2]

[1] Department of Chinese Language and Literature, University of Macau, Taipa, Macau
shanwang@umac.mo

[2] Department of Chinese Language Studies, The Education University of Hong Kong, Tai Po, Hong Kong

Abstract. Language safety is an important part of national security and it concerns the development of countries and regions. With the increasingly close exchanges between Mainland China and Taiwan, there is more and more in-depth research on the integration and differences of Chinese between them. However, the existing research seldom systematically analyzes the safety issues across the Taiwan Strait. Focusing on the global issue of "safety", this paper uses Tagged Chinese Gigaword (second edition) to explore the safety issues of common and respective concerns of the two sides and analyze the characteristics of similarities and differences based on the data of Xinhua News Agency (xin) and Central News Agency (cna) from the 1990s to the beginning of the 21st century. This study can help us better understand the Chinese language use and social phenomenon on both sides of the Taiwan Straits.

Keywords: Safety · Mainland China · Taiwan · Lexicon
Xinhua News Agency (xin) · Central News Agency (cna)

1 Introduction

An international big country must take responsibility and bear international obligations. International obligations not only manifest in general international affairs, but also in international cultural affairs and language business [1]. The issue of language safety is not only an integral part of the language industry, but also an important part of national security. It concerns the development of the country and the region. With the increasingly close economic and cultural exchanges between the two sides of the Taiwan Strait, the study of the integration and differences of the Chinese language in Mainland and Taiwan has aroused more and more attention among experts and scholars in the field of linguistics. As an important factor in language, vocabulary has become the fastest and most prominent aspect in the process of development. However, the existing research does not systematically analyze the safety issues of common concerns between the two sides of the Taiwan Strait. Focusing on the global issue of safety, this paper uses the Tagged Chinese Gigaword (second edition), which has more than 800 million POS tagged words, to explore the safety and security phenomena of common

J.-F. Hong et al. (Eds.): CLSW 2018, LNAI 11173, pp. 801–818, 2018.
https://doi.org/10.1007/978-3-030-04015-4_69

and respective concerns and the characteristics for their similarities and differences between the two sides of Taiwan Straits from 1990s to early 21st Century.

2 Related Research

2.1 Research on Language Safety Issues

The existing research on language safety mainly focused on three aspects: first, starting with the introduction of the US language strategy, the language safety issue in China is deeply studied. Wang [2] introduced the background, the strategic content and the goal of the American language strategy and the achieved level in the four years of implementation. Based on this, he put forward what our language strategy can learn from: (1) establishing an early warning management mechanism of national safe language strategy; (2) establishing a special institution responsible for the national safe language strategy; (3) the country must determine the key languages of our country as soon as possible and reserve foreign language talents for future economic competitiveness of the country. Huang [3] started with the linguistic strategy of the United States. By analyzing the role of language strategy in national security, mother tongue and foreign language education, he pointed out many problems in the promotion of language and writing work in China and put forward suggestions for them. He believes that strengthening the planning and construction of language work has far-reaching significance for national security. Second, from the perspective of national security, the issue of language safety in the construction of the "One Belt and One Road" was studied. It is believed that the exchange of language and culture is a basic project, a pilot project, and a public-minded project for the construction of the "One Belt and One Road" [4]. Language security is a problem that cannot be ignored in the service and promotion of the "Belt and Road" construction [5]. The exchange of language and culture is the premise of the construction of the "Belt and Road" and the Chinese language should be promoted to the world [6]. Third, the relationship between language and national security from the perspective of language planning is investigated. Dai [7] pointed out that the problems that may exist in the country's current language planning should be solved through further research in order to improve the national language ability. Chen [8] gave a multi-angle and multi-level interpretation of the relationship between language planning and national security in the context of globalization.

2.2 Differences in Vocabulary Across the Taiwan Straits

The study of cross-strait vocabulary differences mainly focuses on patterns of cross-strait vocabulary differences, the reasons for the differences, and the vocabulary differences in specific areas.

Patterns of Cross-Strait Vocabulary Differences. The study of vocabulary differences between the two sides begins with exploring the types of differences. Zheng [9] first proposed four main differences between the Chinese language in Taiwan and Mainland China: new word differences, old word differences, translation differences, and dialect differences. Since then, scholars have basically the same classification of difference patterns, mainly focusing on three aspects: homomorphisms, synonyms, words in Taiwan but not in mainland China, or words in Mainland China but not in Taiwan [10–13]. From the 21st century, with the deepening of research, scholars have placed research perspectives on certain specific words. For example, Jiang [14] explored the different patterns between appellations and foreign words of the two sides in addition to exploring the different patterns between general words.

From existing research, it is not difficult to find that scholars divided the cross-strait words into different patterns mentioned above, and then explained them through some examples, so that people can have an intuitive understanding of the differences between the two sides of the strait, providing reference for the future research.

Reasons of Cross-Strait Vocabulary Differences. The exploration of the causes of cross-strait vocabulary differences is a long-term concern. The causes of differences involve many factors, such as political and economic changes [11, 13–17], the influence of dialects and loan words [11, 12, 14–17], different social and cultural backgrounds [12, 14–17], and different perspectives on word formation [11, 17].

The Vocabulary Differences in Specific Areas. With the deepening of the research, researchers began to focus on the micro-contrast study of the vocabulary differences between the two sides of the strait in a specific field. It includes three aspects. (1) Comparison of lexical differences between news media. Ma [18] used the newsletter of the "Reading Today" column in Awakening News Networks, summing up four different aspects on both sides. (2) Contrasting the vocabulary differences in teaching Chinese as a foreign language. For example, Fan [19] selected two primary Chinese textbooks from both sides of the strait, analyzed the differences in word selection, and explored factors that lead to the differences. (3) Compilation of cross-strait vocabulary reference books. For example, Sun [20] made a comparative study of the loanwords from two dictionaries of Mainland China and Taiwan.

2.3 The Integration of Vocabulary Across the Taiwan Straits

Under the influence of many factors such as politics and history, Mainland China and Taiwan have been in isolation before 1980s, and later the opportunity for exchange and contact has gradually increased. Diao [21] explored the two-way linguistic phenomenon of two-way integration between the two regions of mainland China and Taiwan and summarized several cases of two-way integration with a large number of examples.

Existing research shows that scholars have made multi-angle analysis on language safety issues, the patterns of vocabulary differences, the reasons for differences, the vocabulary of specific fields, and the integration of vocabulary, but there is no research on the "safety" issues in the two sides between 1990s to the early 21st Century. The study of vocabulary itself is a key part of the study of language differences and the issue of "safety" is also the focus of attention in various regions and countries. Therefore, an in-depth exploration of the "safety" issue across the straights highlights its unique significance.

3 Research Methods

3.1 Corpus Selection

This study selected Chinese Gigaword (second edition), which is a corpus created by David Graff, Ke Chen, Junbo Kong, and Kazuaki Maeda[1] in 2005. The first edition was published by David Graff and Ke Chen in 2003[2] and the second edition was released in 2005. Tagged Chinese Gigaword (second edition) was form through making word segmentation and part-of-speech tagging [22].

The texts used in this article are from two parts of this corpus: xin and cna, where xin refers to the Xinhua News Agency, providing data from 1990 to December 2004; cna refers Central News Agency, providing data from 1991 to December 2004. The corpus includes the following four types of texts[3]:

Story	This type of DOC represents a coherent report on a particular topic or event, consisting of paragraphs and full sentences
Multi	This type of DOC contains a series of unrelated "blurbs," each of which briefly describes a particular topic or event: "summaries of today's news," "news briefs in…" (some general area like finance or sports), and so on
Advis	These are DOCs which the news service addresses to news editors, they are not intended for publication to the "end users"
Other	These DOCs clearly do not fall into any of the above types; these are things like lists of sports scores, stock prices, temperatures around the world, and so on

3.2 Chinese Word Sketch Engine

Chinese Word Sketch Engine is a grammar knowledge generation system that combines large-scale corpora. It can not only search keywords and its context, but also provide the sketch of grammatical relations and synonymy comparisons. It is combined with the LDC Chinese Gigaword (second edition) of 1.4 billion characters and provides a description of the actual usage rules for a large number of Chinese words. This study extracted the words with a minimum word frequency of 2 in the grammatical relationship of 安全 *ānquán* 'safe; safety' in this corpus, as shown in Fig. 1. Then it compared the common words and unique words that collocates with 安全 *ānquán* 'safe; safety' from Xinhua News Agency and Central News Agency, and further analyzes the reasons for similarities and differences according to the frequency and significance.

There are two kinds of grammatical relations in both Xinhua News Agency and Central News Agency: *subject* and *modifies*, which respectively mean "XX *ānquán*" (XX stands for *Subject*) and "*ānquán* XX" (XX stands for the modified word, head). The word types are shown in Table 1. In the data of xin, there are 415 word types of

[1] https://catalog.ldc.upenn.edu/LDC2005T14.

[2] https://catalog.ldc.upenn.edu/LDC2003T09.

[3] https://catalog.ldc.upenn.edu/LDC2003T09.

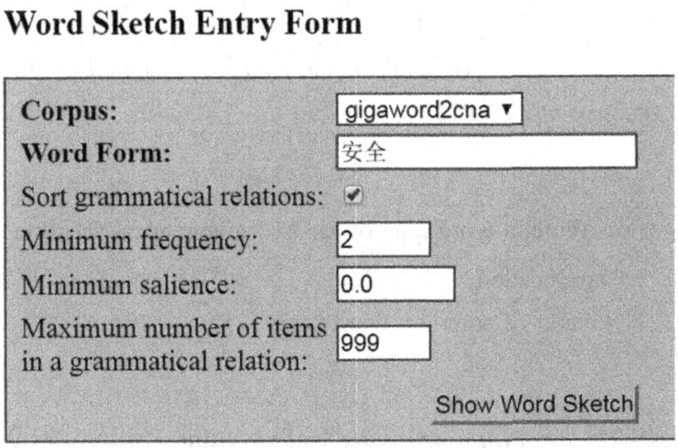

Fig. 1. Word sketch entry form

"XX" in "XX *ānquán*" and 450 word types of "XX" in the "*ānquán* XX". In the data of cna, there are 449 word types of "XX" in "XX *ānquán*" and 724 word types of "XX" in "*ānquán* XX". In total, cna has 308 more word types than xin, of which 34 are *subjects* and 274 are being modified.

4 The Common Words Collocated with 安全 *ānquán* 'Safe; Safety' in Xinhua News Agency and Central News Agency

"Common words" refers to the words used in both Xinhua News Agency and Central News Agency that are collocated with 安全 *ānquán* 'safe; safety' during the period from the 1990s to the early 21st century. Research on common words can help us understand the overlap of vocabulary in the actual language use between Mainland China and Taiwan and can gain a deeper understanding of the common concerns of the people on both sides of the strait on the safety issue.

On the basis of the word types listed in Table 1, we separately counted the common word types of Xinhua News Agency and the Central News Agency appearing in the relations of "XX *ānquán*" and "*ānquán* XX". There are 155 common word types as *subject* and 251 ones as *modifies*, as shown in Table 2.

"XX *ānquán*" with XX embodying the *subject* function are mostly noun phrases and only a number of them are verb phrases, such as 威脅安全 *wēixié ānquán* 'threaten safety', 保證安全 *bǎozhèng ānquán* 'assure safety' and 影響安全 *yǐngxiǎng ānquán* 'affect safety'.

Semantically, most of them are more specific topics of "safety", such as 食物安全 *shíwù ānquán* 'food safety', 網絡安全 *wǎngluò ānquán* 'cyber safety', 能源安全 *néngyuán ānquán* 'energy safety', and 日美安全 *rìměi ānquán* 'Japan-US safety'. "安全XX" with XX embodying the *modifies* function are also mostly noun phrases, which can be roughly divided into two categories. One is to emphasize the safety of certain things such as安全產品 *ānquán chǎnpǐn* 'safe products', 安全飲用水 *ānquán yǐnyòngshuǐ* 'safe drinking water', 安全言論 *ānquán yánlùn* 'safe speeches', the other is to emphasize the safety characteristics such as 安全必要性 *ānquán bìyàoxìng* 'safety

Table 1. The number of words in the two grammatical relations between xin and cna

Classification	xin *subject*	xin *modifies*	cna *subject*	cna *modifies*
Number of types of words	415	450	449	724

Table 2. Number of common word type of the two grammatical functions of xin and cna

Classification	*subject*	*modifies*
Number of common word types	155	251

necessity', 安全脆弱性 *ānquán cuìruòxìng* 'safety vulnerability', 安全多發性 *ānquán duōfāxìng* 'safety multiplicity'.

4.1 Characteristics of the Common Words in the *Subject* Position

The common words that function as *subjects* in the corpora of Xinhua News Agency and Central News Agency mainly have the following features. (1) Regarding the aspect of number of syllables, the common words are dominated by disyllabic words, accounting for 88.4%, which fully demonstrates that double-syllabicization is the mainstream way of word formation on both sides of the Taiwan Strait. It is followed by trisyllabic words, accounting for only 5.2% (Table 3).

(2) This study uses the eight first-level semantic categories of the dictionary *A Thesaurus of Modern Chinese* [23] to classify common words of the two sides, so as to find out the major semantic categories of common concerns on safety issues. The most important feature of this dictionary is to classify words according to their meaning. The annotation and statistical results are shown in Table 4. Among the common words of the *subject* function on both sides, the top semantic categories they belong to are abstract things, concrete objects and living thing. The semantic category of all words is dominated by abstract things, accounting for 31.6%. This indicates that the words which reflect the function as *subject* are mostly nouns, and the proportion of adjectives and verbs is very small. This proves that both sides of the strait are more concerned about the safety status of some things, such as 人身安全 *rénshēn ānquán* 'personal safety', 財産安全 *cáichǎn ānquán* 'property safety' and 國家安全 *guójiā ānquán* 'national safety'.

Although the interests of both sides of the strait are similar, the degree of attention is very different evidenced from the saliency different in Tables 5 and 6, which list the words that the saliency difference is higher than 6 in the *subject* relationship between Xinhua News Agency and Central News Agency.

By comparing the saliency differences of common words, we can see the different levels of attention to the same thing between the two sides. For example, Mainland China's attentions to 網絡安全 *wǎngluò ānquán* 'network safety', 傳統安全 *chuántǒng ānquán* 'traditional safety', 日美安全 *rìměi ānquán* 'Japan and the United States safety' and 生態安全 *shēngtài ānquán* 'ecological safety' are much higher than Taiwan, while Taiwan is not very concerned about them; Taiwan is much more concerned about its own safety, regional safety, social safety and defense safety than Mainland

Table 3. The number of syllables of the common words with the *subject* function

Number of syllables	Number of common words	Percentage
1	6	3.9%
2	137	88.4%
3	8	5.2%
4	2	1.3%
5	2	1.3%
Total	155	100.0%

Table 4. The semantic category distribution of common words with the *subject* function

First level semantic category	Number	Percentage
抽象事物 *chōuxiàng shìwù* 'abstract things'	49	31.60%
具體物 *jùtǐ wù* 'concrete things'	40	25.80%
生物 *shēngwù* 'living things'	38	24.50%
社會活動 *shèhuì huódòng* 'social activities'	9	5.80%
時空 *shíkōng* 'time and space'	9	5.80%
運動與變化 *yùndòng yǔ biànhuà* 'movement and changes'	3	1.90%
生物活動 *shēngwù huódòng* 'biological activities'	3	1.90%
性質與狀態 *xìngzhì yǔ zhuàngtài* 'nature and state'	3	1.90%
社會活動、抽象事物 *shèhuì huódòng, chōuxiàng shìwù* 'social activities, abstract things'	1	0.60%
Total	155	100.00%

China, while Mainland China is less concerned with them. This shows that during the period from 1990s to early 21st Century, Taiwan was concerned about its own stability and safety. In addition, both sides have paid great attention to national political issues. The word 國家 *guójiā* "country" has a high saliency both in Taiwan and Mainland China, 48.14 and 33.71 respectively. In social democracy, Mainland China pays more attention to the safety of food and transportation, such as 航運安全 *hángyùn ānquán* 'shipping safety' and 糧食安全 *liángshi ānquán* 'food safety', while Taiwan pays more attention to the safety of the masses, such as 民眾 *mínzhòng* "people", 學生 *xuéshēng* "students", 乘客 *chéngkè* "passengers", 行人 *xíngrén* "pedestrians", 兒童 *értóng* "children", 師生 *shīshēng* "teachers and students", 居民 *jūmín* "residents", 市民 *shìmín* "citizens" and so on.

4.2 Characteristics of Common Words in the *Modifies* Position

The common words of the *modifies* function have the following characteristics. (1) They are dominated by disyllabic words, with a proportion as high as 91.6%, followed by the trisyllabic words, accounting for 6%. The data is shown in Table 7. It is in accordance with the syllable distribution of the *subject* function.

Table 5. The *subject* function words that have higher saliency in xin than that of cna

Word	cna-*subject.* frequency	*cna-subject. saliency*	xin-*subject.* frequency	*xin-subject. saliency*	Saliency difference
網絡 *wǎngluò* 'the internet'	2	3.48	73	22.56	19.08
傳統 *chuántǒng* 'traditional'	2	2.02	32	20.47	18.45
日美 *rì měi* 'Japanese and American'	7	14.42	29	30.32	15.9
生態 *shēngtài* 'ecology'	2	0.81	26	15.54	14.73
航運 *hángyùn* 'shipping'	2	2.45	16	16.59	14.14
保證 *bǎozhèng* 'guarantee'	3	3.36	29	17.42	14.06
糧食 *liángshí* 'food'	15	12.89	115	26.28	13.39
能源 *néngyuán* 'energy'	10	7.81	44	19.79	11.98
鐵路 *tiělù* 'railway'	3	1.71	32	13	11.29
航空 *hángkōng* 'aviation'	19	6.04	43	16.42	10.38
食物 *shíwù* 'food'	3	3.32	9	12.47	9.15
大堤 *dàdī* 'embankment'	2	6.96	12	15.49	8.53
船舶 *chuánbó* 'ship'	6	8.48	18	16.41	7.93
內閣 *nèigé* 'cabinet'	5	2.96	12	10.7	7.74
電網 *diànwǎng* 'power grid'	3	8.94	16	16.37	7.43
北京市 *běijīng shì* 'Beijing city'	4	6.55	23	13.42	6.87

(2) The common words of the *modifies* relationship are also classified according to the eight first-level semantic categories of *A Thesaurus of Modern Chinese* [23]. The data is shown in Table 8. It can be seen that the words that collocate with 安全 *ānquán* 'safe; safety' are mainly abstract things, accounting for 71.7%, such as 因素 *yīnsù* 'factors', 說法 *shuōfǎ* 'statements', and 氣氛 *qìfēn* 'atmosphere', which shows that people of the two sides have the most attention to "abstract things" related to safety. Second, there are some specific nouns and space-time nouns, which account for 11.2% and 6% respectively. In contrast, the proportion of the two categories of "nature and state" and "living things' activity" is very small, 1.6% and 0.8% respectively, such as 多發性 *duōfā xìng* 'multiplicity', 重要性 *zhòngyào xìng* 'importance', and 首要 *shǒuyào* 'foremost'.

Table 6. The *subject* function words that have higher saliency in cna than that of xin

Word	cna-subject. frequency	*cna-subject. saliency*	xin-subject. frequency	*xin-subject. saliency*	Saliency difference
自身 *zìshēn* 'oneself'	80	38.28	28	18.01	20.27
區域 *qūyù* 'area'	63	21.01	5	3.61	17.4
社會 *shèhuì* 'society'	177	21.58	31	5.28	16.3
國防 *guófáng* 'national defense'	76	23.9	10	8.48	15.42
輻射 *fúshè* 'radiation'	23	18.14	2	3	15.14
國家 *guójiā* 'country'	1740	48.14	748	33.71	14.43
民眾 *mínzhòng* 'people'	109	14.85	2	2.27	12.58
學生 *xuéshēng* 'student'	62	13.47	5	1.64	11.83
乘客 *chéngkè* 'passenger'	38	21.47	8	9.99	11.48
行人 *xíngrén* 'pedestrian'	13	16.08	2	4.79	11.29
場所 *chǎngsuǒ* 'place'	30	17.24	6	6.1	11.14
水庫 *shuǐkù* 'reservoir'	32	17.16	6	7.14	10.02
影響 *yǐngxiǎng* 'influence'	44	8.96	4	0.14	8.82
兒童 *értóng* 'child'	33	13.36	9	4.57	8.79
師生 *shīshēng* 'teacher and student'	15	13.87	3	5.39	8.48
水上 *shuǐshàng* 'water'	36	27.25	17	18.93	8.32
車 *chē* 'car'	15	11.38	3	3.08	8.3
飲用水 *yǐnyòng shuǐ* 'drinking water'	13	16.88	4	8.6	8.28
衛生 *wèishēng* 'health'	67	19.89	28	11.79	8.1
設施 *shèshī* 'facility'	30	12.65	12	4.77	7.88
整體 *zhěngtǐ* 'overall'	19	9.86	3	2.07	7.79
海防 *hǎifáng* 'coast defense'	7	14.12	2	6.52	7.6

(*continued*)

Table 6. (*continued*)

Word	cna-*subject.* frequency	*cna-subject. saliency*	xin-*subject.* frequency	*xin-subject. saliency*	Saliency difference
南非 *Nánfēi* 'South Africa'	22	12.07	6	5.21	6.86
生活 *shēnghuó* 'life'	24	8.14	8	1.46	6.68
居民 *jūmín* 'resident'	39	14.52	17	7.95	6.57
環境 *huánjìng* 'surroundings'	27	7.39	8	0.9	6.49
交易 *jiāoyì* 'transaction'	28	10.53	7	4.09	6.44
農藥 *nóngyào* 'pesticide'	6	9.61	2	3.39	6.22
市民 *shìmín* 'citizen'	16	8.35	4	2.23	6.12

Table 7. The number of syllables of the common words with the *modifies* function

Number of syllables	Number of common words	Percentage
1	4	1.6%
2	230	91.6%
3	15	6.0%
4	2	0.8%
Total	251	100.0%

In order to reflect the differences of the concern about safety issues of common things between the two sides of the strait in the *modifies* function, we summarized the words with the saliency difference larger than 6, shown in Tables 9 and 10. It is found that the saliency in the safety of events, situation and social life of Mainland China is much higher than Taiwan, while the saliency in the safety of doubt, guarantee, determination and contribution is much higher than Mainland China. This may indicate that Taiwan has doubts about security issues and is eager to seek protection. Perhaps it is partially due to the events of Taiwan's main island and Penghu lifting the ban in 1987, followed by Jinmen and Mazu in 1991.

In short, there are many similarities in the safety issues that are concerned by the two sides of the strait. However, the significant difference in saliency also shows the difference in the focus of their respective concerns. It needs to be comprehensively examined in light of the social and historical background of that period.

Table 8. The semantic category distribution of common words with the *modifies* function

First level semantic category	Number	Percentage
抽象事物 *chōuxiàng shìwù* 'abstract things'	180	71.7%
具體物 *jùtǐ wù* 'concrete things'	28	11.2%
時空 *shíkōng* 'time and space'	15	6.0%
生物 *shēngwù* 'living things'	10	4.0%
社會活動 *shèhuì huódòng* 'social activities'	8	3.2%
性質與狀態 *xìngzhì yǔ zhuàngtài* 'nature and state'	4	1.6%
生物活動 *shēngwù huódòng* 'biological activities'	2	0.8%
輔助詞 *fǔzhù cí* 'auxiliary words'	1	0.4%
抽象事物、社會活動 *chōuxiàng shìwù, shèhuì huódòng* 'abstract things, social activities'	1	0.4%
抽象事物、生物活動 *chōuxiàng shìwù, shēngwù huódòng* 'abstract things, biological activities'	1	0.4%
抽象事物、具體物 *chōuxiàng shìwù, jùtǐ wù* 'abstract things, concrete things'	1	0.4%
Total	251	100.0%

5 The Unique Words Collocated with 安全 *ānquán* 'Safe; Safety' in Xinhua News Agency and Central News Agency

"Unique words" refer to the words that appear in only one of the two regions of Mainland China and Taiwan. These words can reflect the distinctive characteristics of the times and geographical features, and can help us more effectively and intuitively understand the differences in the perspectives of the safety in politics, customs, and living habits between the two sides of the strait.

With respect to the unique words collocated with 安全 *ānquán* 'safe; safety', in Xinhua News Agency, there are 260 word types functioning as *subject* and 199 word types functioning as *modifies*; while in Central News Agency, there are 294 word types functioning as *subject* and 473 word types functioning as *modifies*, as shown in Table 11. In the following, we will analyze the syllables and characteristics of unique words in Mainland China and Taiwan.

5.1 Comparison of the Number of Syllables of the Unique Words

The statistics of the syllable number of unique words that are collocated with 安全 *ānquán* 'safe; safety' functioning as *subject* and *modifies* are detailed in Table 12. First of all, both Mainland China and Taiwanese words are dominated by disyllable words, accounting for 63.83% and 74.58% respectively, indicating that the development trend of disyllablization in Chinese is common to both sides of the strait. Out of all the unique words, when functioning as *subject*, disyllabic words account for 59.23% and 70.41% respectively in Mainland China and Taiwan; when functioning as *modifies*, disyllabic words take up 69.85% and 77.17% respectively. Secondly, in the 3–6 syllable polysyllabic words, out of all the unique words, Mainland China accounts for

Table 9. The words of the *modifies* function words that have higher saliency in xin than that of cna

Word	cna-modifies. frequency	*cna-modifies. saliency*	xin-modifies. frequency	*xin-modifies. saliency*	Saliency
多發性 *duōfā xìng* 'multiplicity'	3	9.75	15	28.42	18.67
同時 *tóngshí* 'simultaneously'	22	6.67	76	18.9	12.23
大事 *dàshì* 'event'	3	3.37	17	15.19	11.82
氣氛 *qìfēn* 'atmosphere'	3	1.08	16	12.56	11.48
性生活 *xìng shēnghuó* 'sexual life'	2	6.09	5	17.19	11.1
飲用水 *yǐnyòng shuǐ* 'drinking water'	19	18.73	34	29.2	10.47
地帶 *dìdài* 'zone'	3	4.44	14	14.17	9.73
大局 *dàjú* 'overall situation'	3	5.85	17	14.95	9.1
產品 *chǎnpǐn* 'product'	22	4.89	75	13.51	8.62
高度 *gāodù* 'height'	16	6.68	30	14.85	8.17
言論 *yánlùn* 'speech'	2	1.2	6	8.78	7.58
毒瘤 *dúliú* 'malignant tumor'	2	7.54	5	15.02	7.48
條款 *tiáokuǎn* 'terms'	2	1.06	6	8.19	7.13
暴力 *bàolì* 'violence'	9	5.19	14	11.92	6.73
未來 *wèilái* 'future'	11	0.53	11	7.17	6.64
行爲 *xíngwéi* 'behavior'	91	19.53	115	26.03	6.5
核心 *héxīn* 'core'	3	2.44	12	8.75	6.31
主導權 *zhǔdǎo quán* 'dominance'	2	4.38	3	10.5	6.12
必要性 *bìyào xìng* 'necessity'	4	6.47	7	12.47	6

31.59% and Taiwan accounts for 23.08%. The former is 8.51% higher than the latter. This is because there are a lot of proper nouns in the unique words of Mainland China and the trend of polysyllabic is more obvious, such as 八塘火車站 *Bātáng huǒchēzhàn*

Table 10. The words of the *modifies* function words that have higher saliency in cna than that of xin

Word	cna-*modifies*. frequency	*cna-modifies. saliency*	xin-*modifies*. frequency	*xin-modifies. saliency*	Saliency
疑慮 *yílǜ* 'doubt'	126	34.26	3	7.28	26.98
保障 *bǎozhàng* 'protection'	336	39.49	40	15.19	24.3
決心 *juéxīn* 'determination'	121	28.48	10	8.79	19.69
貢獻 *gòngxiàn* 'contribution'	54	19.23	6	2.13	17.1
觀點 *guāndiǎn* 'view'	38	19.92	3	3.99	15.93
性行爲 *xìng xíngwéi* 'sexual behavior'	68	37.13	10	22.09	15.04
空間 *kōngjiān* 'space'	90	21.38	10	8.25	13.13
屏障 *píngzhàng* 'barrier'	22	27.37	9	15.02	12.35
漏洞 *lòudòng* 'loophole'	15	16.47	2	4.16	12.31
承諾 *chéngnuò* 'promise'	165	32.54	37	20.87	11.67
重要性 *zhòngyào xìng* 'importance'	201	39.55	58	27.95	11.6
信心 *xìnxīn* 'confidence'	54	17.5	9	6.63	10.87
方法 *fāngfǎ* 'method'	58	19.43	15	8.7	10.73
場所 *chǎngsuǒ* 'site'	44	18.59	10	8.75	9.84
原則 *yuánzé* 'principle'	137	24.44	41	14.64	9.8
生活 *shēnghuó* 'life'	56	12.38	12	2.64	9.74
看法 *kànfǎ* 'view'	36	12.66	3	3.31	9.35
家園 *jiāyuán* 'homeland'	15	13.11	3	3.85	9.26
工作 *gōngzuò* 'job'	119	10.89	35	1.7	9.19
立場 *lìchǎng* 'position'	83	16.77	13	7.84	8.93
行徑 *xíngjìng* 'misdeed'	11	13.59	3	4.7	8.89

(*continued*)

Table 10. (*continued*)

Word	cna-*modifies.* frequency	*cna-modifies. saliency*	xin-*modifies.* frequency	*xin-modifies. saliency*	Saliency
環境 *huánjìng* 'environment'	550	37.08	246	28.28	8.8
狀況 *zhuàngkuàng* 'situation'	31	9.91	4	1.31	8.6
範圍 *fànwéi* 'range'	33	11.33	6	2.82	8.51
觀念 *guānniàn* 'concept'	38	15.38	9	6.89	8.49
避風港 *bìfēnggǎng* 'haven'	20	28.97	7	20.79	8.18
問題 *wèntí* 'problem'	470	22.55	152	14.64	7.91
行列 *hángliè* 'rank'	13	10.52	2	2.61	7.91
知識 *zhīshì* 'knowledge'	10	7.6	2	0.11	7.49
危機 *wéijī* 'crisis'	25	8.24	3	0.76	7.48
做法 *zuòfǎ* 'practice'	45	18.71	15	11.62	7.09
物品 *wùpǐn* 'goods'	15	11.12	3	4.16	6.96
作法 *zuòfǎ* 'practice'	49	17.35	6	10.41	6.94
當務之急 *dāngwùzhījí* 'urgent matter'	7	11.47	2	5.02	6.45
時候 *shíhòu* 'time'	18	10.96	6	4.57	6.39
地點 *dìdiǎn* 'location'	47	16.19	9	9.83	6.36
整體 *zhěngtǐ* 'overall'	17	7.06	2	0.76	6.3

Table 11. The number of unique words in xin and cna respectively

Classification	Unique words of xin with the *subject* function	Unique words of cna with the *subject* function	Unique words of xin with the *modifies* function	Unique words of cna with the *modifies* function
Number of unique words	260	294	199	473

'Batang train station', 陽江河輪 *Yángjiāng hélún* 'the Yangjiang River wheel', 荆江大堤 *Jīngjiāng dàdī* 'the Jingjiang dyke'. Although the proportion of the polysyllabic words in Taiwan is not as high as that of Mainland China, it also presents its own characteristics in the process of development. For example, the abbreviated form 台澎金馬 *Táipēngjīnmǎ* refers to Taiwan, Penghu, Jinmen and Mazu. Third, the proportion of monosyllabic words in the two sides is not high, but the frequency is high. Just as pointed out by Tang [24], the use of very high frequency monosyllabic words is the basis of the Chinese language system, especially the foundation of the vocabulary system, which is very persistent and rarely changed.

Table 12. The distribution of syllables with unique words in Mainland China and Taiwan

Number of syllables	*Subject* function				*Modifies* function				Total			
	Mainland China		Taiwan		Mainland China		Taiwan		Mainland China		Taiwan	
	Number	Percent	Number	Percent	Number	Percent	Number	Percent	Number	Percent	Number	Percent
1	17	6.54%	10	3.40%	4	2.01%	8	1.69%	21	4.58%	18	2.35%
2	154	59.23%	207	70.41%	139	69.85%	365	77.17%	293	63.83%	572	74.58%
3	68	26.15%	65	22.11%	43	21.61%	86	18.18%	111	24.18%	151	19.69%
4	14	5.38%	12	4.08%	10	5.03%	12	2.54%	24	5.23%	24	3.13%
5	5	1.92%	0	0.00%	1	0.50%	1	0.21%	6	1.31%	1	0.13%
6	2	0.77%	0	0.00%	2	1.01%	1	0.21%	4	0.87%	1	0.13%
Total	260	100.00%	294	100.00%	199	100.00%	473	100.00%	459	100.00%	767	100.00%

5.2 Characteristics of the Unique Words of Mainland China

First of all, many unique words of mainland China are related to international relations of other countries or regions. For example, the security of 沙特 *Shātè* 'Saudi', 蘇丹國家 *Sūdān guójiā* 'Sudan country', 俄國家 *É guójiā* 'Russia country', 巴勒斯坦國家 *Bālèsītǎn guójiā* 'Palestine country' in "XX *ānquán*"; 第三國 *dì sānguó* 'third country', 中美洲 *Zhōng měizhōu* 'Central America', 難民營 *nànmín yíng* 'refugee camps', 北約 *Běiyuē* 'NATO' in "*ānquán* XX". This shows that Mainland China paid much attention to international political issues between the 1990s and the early 21st century. In addition, the Palestine-Israel conflict was resolved peacefully during this period. In 1993, the two parties signed a peace agreement and announced the Palestinian self-government plan; in 1994, Alfarat returned to Gaza. As a result, some words collocated with 安全 *ānquán* 'safe; safety' were related to these events, such as 巴勒斯坦國家 *Bālèsītǎn guójiā* 'Palestine', 巴方 Bā fāng 'Pakistan side', 巴以 *Bā yǐ* 'Palestine and Israel'.

Secondly, many unique words of Mainland China involve the names of the provinces and cities of mainland China. For example, 白銀市 *Báiyín shì* 'Baiyin City', 海南省 *Hǎinán shěng* 'Hainan Province', 天津市 *Tiānjīn shì* 'Tianjin City', 武漢市 *Wǔhàn shì* 'Wuhan City' in the *subject* function and 永定河 *Yǒngdìng hé* 'Yongding River' in the *modifies* relation. It shows that Mainland China is more concerned about the security and stability of various district and counties. There are also many regional related words in Taiwan's unique words, such as 高雄廠 *Gāoxióng chǎng* 'Kaohsiung factory'.

In addition, there are many words related to holidays in Mainland China's unique words. For example, words in the *subject* relation, 春運 *chūnyùn* 'the spring festival',

黃金周 *huángjīn zhōu* 'golden week', 節日 *jiérì* 'festival' and words in the *modifies* relation, 黃金周 *huángjīn zhōu* 'the golden week', 佳節 *jiājié* 'holiday', 節日 *jiérì* 'festival' and 春節 *chūnjié* 'Spring Festival'. It shows that Mainland China attaches great importance to the safety of traditional holidays, especially the Spring Festival. Taiwan also has holiday-related words, such as 年貨 *niánhuò* 'the annual goods' and 月餅 *yuèbǐng* 'moon cakes' in the *modifies* relation. It indicates that both sides of the Taiwan Straits have paid attention to the safety of holidays, especially traditional festivals, but Mainland China has a higher degree of attention. In addition, the focus of both sides is also different. Taiwan is more concerned about the representatives of some festivals, while Mainland China pays more attention to holidays and festivals.

Finally, some unique words of Mainland China and Taiwan express the same or similar meanings, which is named as heteronyms. For example, 航天飛機(陸)—航空器(台) *hángtiān fēijī (lù)—hángkōngqì (tái)* 'aerospaceplane (Mainland China) – aircraft (Taiwan)', 信息(陸)—資訊(台) *xìnxī (lù)—zīxùn (tái)* 'information (Mainland China) - information (Taiwan)', 科索沃(陸)—柯索伏(台) Kēsuǒwò (lù)—*Kē suǒ fú (tái)* 'Kosovo (Land) - Kosovo (Taiwan)'.

5.3 Characteristics of Taiwan's Unique Words

First of all, the safety issues that Taiwan and Mainland China focused on are different. In the unique words with the *subject* function, the most frequent and salient words in Taiwan and Mainland China are 勞工 *láogōng* 'labor' and 巴*bā* 'Palestine' respectively. Thus, the most concerned event in Taiwan is the social security issue of 勞工安全 *láogōng ānquán* 'labor safety', while the most concerned event in Mainland China is 巴安全 *Bā ānquán* 'Palestine safety' in the Palestinian Israeli conflict. In the unique words of the *modifies* function in Taiwan, the top 3 words according to frequency are 顧慮 *gùlǜ* 'concerns'', 理由 *lǐyóu* 'reasons'' and 情形 *qíngxíng* 'situation'; in the unique words of the *modifies* function, the top 3 words in Mainland China according to frequency are 國際 *guójì* 'international', 刑事 *xíngshì* 'criminal', and 會議 *huìyì* 'conference'. Second, Taiwan paid more attention to the issues of the people's livelihood, such as 勞動 *láodòng* 'labor', 居家 *jūjiā* 'home', 建築物 *jiànzhúwù* 'building', and 婦幼 *fùyòu* 'maternity and child care' in the *subject* function, and 違建*wéijiàn* 'illegal construction, 社會 *shèhuì* 'society', 反應爐 *fǎnyìnglú* 'reactor', 防護網 *fánghù wǎng* 'protective net', 消防局 *xiāofángjú* 'fire station', 猪肉 *zhūròu* 'pork', 校園 *xiàoyuán* 'campus', and 蔬果 *shūguǒ* 'fruits and vegetables' in the *modifies* function. In addition, in Taiwan's unique words, there are many regional vocabulary related to Taiwan, such as 高雄廠 *Gāoxióng chǎng* 'Kaohsiung factory', 豪廷省 *Háotíng shěng* 'Haoting Province', and 捷運局 *Jiéyùn jú* 'Department of Rapid Transit Systems' in the *subject* function; 美國在台協會 *Měiguó zài Tái xiéhuì* 'the United States Association for Taiwan' in the *modifies* function.

6 Conclusion

Based on a large-scale corpus, this paper examines the words collocated with 安全*ānquán* 'safe; safety' in Xinhua News Agency of Mainland China and Central News Agency of Taiwan from the 1990s to the beginning of the 21st century. It analyzes the characteristics of common words and unique words in each region, including syllables, semantic categories, and saliency. The results can help us deepen the understanding of the integration and differences of words between the two sides.

Although the core of the Chinese language used by Mainland China and Taiwan is relatively stable, there are certain differences in the phenomena concerned by the two sides. Even for a same phenomenon, the attention it received can be very different in Mainland China and Taiwan. Some differences are reflected in the language, which eventually lead to the differences in the use of vocabulary across the strait. With the increasingly close exchanges between the two sides of the Strait, the language interaction of different Chinese communities will be further enriched and developed, which will help deepen exchanges and cooperation between the two sides.

Acknowledgement. This research is partially supported by the Start-up Research Grant of University of Macau (SRG2018-00126-FAH).

References

1. Li, Y.: Some thoughts on foreign language planning in China. J. Foreign Lang. **33**, 1 (2010)
2. Wang, J.: US "Critical Languages" strategy and China's national security language strategy (美國"關鍵語言"戰略與我國國家安全語言戰略). J. Yunnan Normal Univ. **42**, 2 (2010)
3. Huang, D.: Language affairs from the perspective of national security (國家安全視域下的語言文字工作). Linguist. Sci. **13**, 1 (2014)
4. Zhao, S.: Languages needs for the construction of "The Belt and Road Initiative" ("一帶一路"建設的語言需求及服務對策). J. Yunnan Normal Univ. **47**, 4 (2015)
5. Shen, Q.: Strategy for linguistic security on "the belt and road initiatives" ("一帶一路"建設中的語言安全戰略). Chin. J. Lang. Policy Plan. **2**, 6 (2016)
6. Wang, M.: The Belt and Road Initiative and language strategy construction ("一帶一路"建設與語言戰略構建). Foreign Lang. Educ. China (Q.) **10**, 1 (2017)
7. Dai, M.: National language capabilities, language planning and national security (國家語言能力、語言規劃與國家安全). Appl. Linguist. **4** (2011)
8. Chen, X.: Language planning and language security under the new situation (新形勢下的語言規劃與語言安全). J. Lang. Policy Lang. Plan. **2**, 1 (2015)
9. Zheng, Q.: A preliminary study of the vocabulary differences between the two sides of the Taiwan Strait (海峽兩岸用語差异初探). Taiwan Res. J. **1** (1989)
10. Zhu, J., Zhou, W.: The main differences of vocabulary between Taiwan Mandarin and Putonghua (臺灣國語詞匯與普通話的主要差异). J. Anhui Normal Univ. **1** (1990)
11. Yan, F.: A comparison between the words of Taiwan and the Mainland (臺灣國語詞匯與大陸普通話詞匯的比較). Jinan J. **2** (1992)
12. Su, J.: The reasons, patterns and countermeasures of the differences between Taiwan and Mainland China's vocabulary (臺灣和大陸詞語差异的原因、模式及其對策). Appl. Linguist. **4** (1994)

13. Diao, Y.: The differences between Chinese and Taiwanese words and the reasons (大陸臺灣詞語的差別及造成原因). J. Lit. Hist. (1994)
14. Jiang, Y.: Reasons of differences in the Chinese vocabulary across Taiwan Straits (海峽兩岸漢語詞匯的差异及其原因). J. Jimei Univ. **9**, 3 (2006)
15. Hu, S.: A brief discussion on the differences of words between Mainland, Hong Kong and Taiwan (略論大陸與港臺的詞語差异). Linguist. Res. **3** (1989)
16. Yu, X., Gu, X.: The politico-cultural factors contributing to vocabulary differences between both sides along the Taiwan Straits (海峽兩岸詞語差异的政治文化因素). Shantou Univ. J. (Hum. Q.) **16**, 4 (2008)
17. Li, H.: Viewing the heteronyms from the Common Word Dictionary of Modern Chinese on both sides of the Taiwan Strait (從《兩岸現代漢語常用詞典》看兩岸的同實异名詞語). Rhetoric Learn. **2** (2005)
18. Ma, J.: The Research and Analysis of the Vocabulary of Taiwan "Awaking News" (臺灣《醒報》詞匯考察與分析). Hebei University, Baoding (2011)
19. Fan, G.: Comparative Study on Cross-Strait Elementary Chinese Textbooks About Words ——Based on Far East Chinese and Experiencing Chinese Basic Course (兩岸初級對外漢語教材詞匯對比–以《遠東生活華語》和《體驗漢語基礎教程》爲例). Beijing Foreign Language University, Beijing (2016)
20. Sun, X.: A comparative analysis of the loanwords of Chinese in Mainland China and Taiwan (基于辭書整理的大陸與臺灣漢語外來詞對比分析). J. Univ. South China **14**, 4 (2013)
21. Diao, Y.: Difference and Harmony——Comparison of Language Application Across the Taiwan Straits (差异與融洽——海峽兩岸語言應用對比). Jiangxi Education Publishing House, Jiangxi (2000)
22. Huang, C.-R.: Tagged Chinese Gigaword (version 2.0) (2009). http://www.ldc.upenn.edu/Catalog/catalogEntry.jsp?catalogId=LDC2009T14. Tagged from Chinese Gigaword version 2.0. https://catalog.ldc.upenn.edu/LDC2005T14
23. Su, X.: A Thesaurus of Modern Chinese (現代漢語分類詞典). The Commercial Press, Beijing (2013)
24. Tang, Z.: The synchronic status of contemporary Chinese vocabulary and its evolution: a study of the status quo of Chinese vocabulary in Mainland China, Hong Kong and Taiwan in the 1990s (當代漢語詞語的共時狀況及其嬗變——九十年代中國大陸、香港、臺灣漢語詞現狀研究). Fudan University Press, Shanghai (2001)

Author Index

Printed in the United States
By Bookmasters